W9-DDP-050

THE RECORD OF AMERICAN DIPLOMACY

THE RECORD OF
American Diplomacy

Documents and Readings in the History of American Foreign Relations

Edited by RUHL J. BARTLETT

Professor of History in Tufts College and Professor of Diplomatic History in the Fletcher School of Law and Diplomacy

THIRD EDITION, REVISED AND ENLARGED

NEW YORK : ALFRED A. KNOPF

1959

L.C. catalog card number: 54–2821

THIS IS A BORZOI BOOK,
PUBLISHED BY ALFRED A. KNOPF, INC.

Manufactured in the United States of America. Published in Canada by McClelland & Stewart Limited.

Published September 22, 1947
Second Edition, Enlarged, August 1950
Third Edition, Revised and Enlarged, May 1954
Reprinted, August 1956
Reprinted, April 1959

NOTE FOR THE THIRD EDITION

THE GLOBAL character of American diplomacy since the Second World War makes its record voluminous and increases the difficulty of presenting its main features in brief documentary form. The difficulty has been augmented by the tendency of those most responsible for foreign policy to avoid clear policy statements. This is notably true with regard to American policy concerning Germany and Japan. Indications of foreign policy must frequently be sought in legislative acts of the federal government, in policies advocated or opposed in the United Nations, in reports of the administrators of agencies connected with foreign affairs, and in the findings of Congressional committees. For these reasons policy during the postwar era is often more clearly seen in key documents showing what was done than in extensive and elaborate statements purporting to explain policy.

In preparing this new edition some temptation existed to make drastic reductions in the earlier chapters of the work in order to make room for materials on recent American policies which lie for the most part on the periphery of American diplomacy. This temptation was resisted for two reasons. First, essential new materials could be added without increasing the size of the volume to unreasonable proportions. Second, amidst the increasing flux of ideas about American foreign policies, it seemed especially inappropriate to stress the fleeting present rather than the deeper roots of American experience.

R. J. B.

Tufts College, Medford, Mass.
1954

PREFACE

THE ideals most persistent in the minds of the American people, regarding both domestic and foreign policy, have probably been best expressed by their first Secretary of State, Thomas Jefferson. He believed, to paraphrase his statements freely, that the objectives of the new American nation should not be to amass wealth, become large, or wield power. Other nations had devoted themselves to these ends always at the expense of human values. He wanted this nation to devote itself to the freedom and happiness of its people. This objective could be realized, he thought, if the government were not allowed to waste the substance of the people under the pretense of taking care of them, or their energy in the preparation for wars they knew not of, and might not come, if such preparation had not been made. In foreign affairs he advocated the cultivation of friendship with all nations, entangling alliances with none, and believed that the American people should be free to produce whatever goods their genius and resources afforded, to carry them undisturbed across the free seas – the broad highway of nations – and exchange them without discrimination in the markets of the world. If other nations, through their improvidence and folly, engaged in wars, the American people should pursue their peaceful ways and their commerce as if for them such wars did not exist.

Jefferson knew, however, the difference between the statement of an ideal and its realization. The United States did not exist separate from the world but was one of the family of nations. What its people could do depended not only upon their own acts but also upon the acts of others. When, therefore, American commerce abroad was discriminated against, he thought that something should be done about it. When it appeared that the Mississippi River would be closed to American use he was willing, if necessary, to make an entangling alliance and to acquire more territory. And when predatory European power threatened American independence and security through intervention in Latin America, he advised making common cause with another nation against this danger. Never for a moment did he contemplate the final abandonment of American rights on the high seas. Thus the first Secretary of State represented in his own statements and acts the grand theme of American diplomacy: the application of practical policies best designed under existing circumstances to achieve ultimately the greatest possible freedom and happiness of the American people.

It is a fascinating subject, American diplomacy. Sometimes it has been carried on by men of narrow outlook who lost from sight or never saw the true goal of American policy. Sometimes they sought empire and dominion without considering the price of their success. At other times they abandoned duty in the vain belief that security and prosperity could be attained in seclusion and without responsibility. But for the most part it has been conducted by men of character and vision, many of whom have adorned the human race and deserve its homage.

The complete record of this diplomacy is far beyond the scope of a single volume. Only a small part of the record is included here, and then, with a few exceptions, in edited form. The difficulty in editing documents and readings is obvious. Laws, whether they are treaties, legislative acts, or constitutions, are adopted in their entirety. Few if any of them would have been approved if even one article or section had been omitted. The same principle applies to declarations of policy, instructions to ministers, and to almost any statement. This difficulty, however, is inherent in all selective works, and cannot be avoided.

I am under no illusion concerning the prospect that probably every teacher of American diplomacy will look in vain for some particular item that he thinks is indispensable and should have been included at the expense of something, in his opinion, less important. It seems desirable, nevertheless, to provide an opportunity, particularly for college students, to read some of the important treaties, pronouncements of statesmen, instructions to ministers, debates, speeches, editorials, and other materials that constitute or illustrate the most substantial threads in the great fabric of American foreign relations. Through the use of this collection students should be able to compare policies adopted at different times regarding the same area or subject, trace the evolution of major policies, and examine the reasoning used to defend or advance American foreign interests.

A small part of the materials have been taken from unpublished sources. By far the largest part, however, may be found in printed works. Some of these materials are not available in many college libraries. In others, where they are available, it seldom if ever happens that sufficient copies exist to warrant an assignment to a large group. The principal object of this collection is to make a limited amount of significant material accessible to an entire class for comparison and discussion.

Introductions to chapters and editorial notes have been reduced to the barest minimum. This policy was adopted partly to conserve space, but mostly in the belief that students would need to seek elsewhere a general account of American diplomacy, and that needless duplication should be avoided.

My most pleasant duty in presenting this volume is to recognize gratefully the kindness and assistance that I have received from Professor Samuel Flagg Bemis of Yale University, who carefully examined the entire collection. Some selections would have been left out had he not indicated their particular merits, and his comments and suggestions were of great value. Since, however, all decisions were necessarily mine, he should not be charged in the least with omissions or defects of the work.

R. J. B.

Tufts College
January 2, 1947

ACKNOWLEDGMENTS

The editor gratefully acknowledges the kindness of societies, publishers, and individuals in permitting the reproduction of copyright and other material in this book as follows:

The Carnegie Institution of Washington: for the "Treaty of Whitehall" from *European Treaties Bearing on the History of the United States,* edited by Francis G. Davenport.

The Macmillan Company: for a letter from the Earl of Hardwicke to the Duke of Newcastle, from *England in the Age of the American Revolution,* by L. B. Namier.

Princeton University Press: for the document dated January 13, 1778 on Franco-American relations, from *French Policy and the American Alliance of 1778,* by Edward S. Corwin.

Charles Scribner's Sons: for a quotation from Volume IV of the *History of the United States during the Administration of Thomas Jefferson,* by Henry Adams.

Carnegie Endowment for International Peace: for quotations from Volumes I, II, and III, of the *Diplomatic Correspondence of the United States Concerning the Independence of the Latin American Nations,* edited by William R. Manning.

Carnegie Endowment for International Peace: for quotations from *Treaties and Agreements With and Concerning China,* edited by John V. A. MacMurray.

J. B. Lippincott Company: for a quotation from Volume IV of *The Memoirs of John Quincy Adams,* edited by Charles Francis Adams.

J. B. Lippincott Company: for quotations from the *Works of James Buchanan,* edited by John Bassett Moore.

Houghton Mifflin Company: for quotation from Volume V of the *Works of William H. Seward,* edited by George E. Baker.

The World Peace Foundation: for quotations from Vol. III of *Documents of American Foreign Relations,* edited by S. Shepard Jones and Denys P. Myres, and from Volume IV, edited by Leland M. Goodrich and Marie J. Carroll.

American Society of International Law: for quotation from *Proceedings of the American Society of International Law* for 1922.

CONTENTS

Contents

Contents

THE RECORD OF AMERICAN DIPLOMACY

CHAPTER I

THE COLONIAL ERA

◇◇◇◇◇◇◇◇◇◇◇◇◇

FOR MORE than two and three-quarters centuries prior to the American Revolution, the maritime nations of Europe struggled among themselves for trade and empire in America. As a result of this strife the "Iberian monopoly" was broken, the French and Dutch colonies were reduced, save in Guiana, to insular possessions, and the Swedish settlements were absorbed by the British. The Danes, who came to America late, secured only a few small islands.

War in Europe generally spread to the colonies, and conflicts in the colonies tended to disturb Europe. Attempts were frequently made, however, to establish the principle that war might exist "beyond the line" of Europe without disturbing the peace at home, and the complementary principle that peace might exist on American frontiers regardless of events in Europe. Thus the doctrine of the two spheres so important in the later foreign policy of the United States was well embedded in pre-Revolutionary European thought. An example of this doctrine, and one of the most interesting documents of the Colonial era, is the Treaty of Whitehall of November 6/16, 1686, between France and Great Britain (1). The attempt, however, to establish neutrality in America was unsuccessful. France, Britain, and Spain continued their intercolonial struggle.

The settlement of 1763, which closed the last of the pre-Revolutionary wars, clarified the situation in America and placed the colonial boundaries on a more substantial basis than they had ever been before. In this settlement it was agreed, among other things, to restore Cuba to Spain, to make the Mississippi River the eastern boundary of Louisiana, and to leave the British in possession of Canada. Some French statesmen urged that Britain be offered other areas rather than Canada, and that the eastern boundary of Louisiana be the Appalachian watershed. A group of British statesmen counseled against the expansion of the British Empire, or favored the acquisition of West Indian areas rather than Canada. The case against the retention of Canada is presented here, in the letter of the Earl of Hardwicke to the Duke of Newcastle (2A), and the opposite view is illustrated in the pamphlet, written earlier, by Benjamin Franklin and Richard Jackson (2B). In the end, however, the British secured both Canada and the eastern bank of the Mississippi River (3). It was entirely logical, therefore, that at the close of the Revolutionary War, the thirteen American states should desire the territories they had claimed as colonies of Great Britain. They had a reasonable claim to the territory northwest of the Ohio River, based not only on the conquest of that area during the

Revolutionary War, but also on colonial grants, and on their part in the long struggle against the French (4). In a similar way they had a reasonable historical basis for claiming the territory north of Florida and east of the Mississippi River, as well as the free navigation of the river itself (5).

◇◇◇◇◇◇◇◇◇◇◇◇◇

1. TREATY OF WHITEHALL: 1686[1]

. . . WHEREAS to the Most Serene and Most Potent prince Louis XIV . . . and to the Most Serene and Most Potent prince James the Second, King of Great Britain, nothing is more dear than to establish more and more, day by day, mutual friendship between themselves, and a sincere concord and correspondence between their kingdoms, dominions, and subjects, and whereas toward that end it has seemed good to them to enter into a treaty of peace, good correspondence, and neutrality in America, whereby, so far as is possible, all controversies and differences may be prevented which might arise between the subjects of both crowns in those more remote regions, the Most Serene kings have commissioned plenipotentiaries on both sides to treat and agree respecting this matter. . . .

1. It is concluded and agreed that from this day on there shall be firm peace, union, concord, and good correspondence, both on land and on sea, between the French and British nations in both North America and South America, and throughout those islands, colonies, fortresses, states, and governments, without distinction of place, which lie in America under the jurisdiction of the Most Serene Most Christian King and of the Most Serene King of Great Britain, and are governed by the officers of those kings respectively.

2. That no ships or vessels, larger or smaller, belonging to the subjects of the Most Serene Most Christian King in the aforesaid islands, colonies, fortresses, states, and governments under French jurisdiction, shall be prepared or sent forth for aggression upon the subjects of the Most Serene King of Great Britain in his islands, colonies, fortresses, states, and governments or for the bringing of any injury or damage to them. Similarly, that no ships or vessels, greater or smaller, belonging to subjects of the Most Serene King of Great Britain in the aforesaid islands, colonies, fortresses, states, and governments under English jurisdiction shall be prepared or sent out for aggression upon subjects of the Most Serene Most Christian King in his islands, colonies, fortresses, states, and governments or for the bringing of any injury or damage upon them. . . .

---

[1] Concluded between France and Great Britain, November 6/16, 1686. Ratification by France, November 29, 1686, and by Great Britain, November 30/December 10, 1686. Frances Gardiner Davenport, ed.: *European Treaties Bearing on the History of the United States and its Dependencies* (Washington, D.C.: Carnegie Institution of Washington, 1917–1937), Vol. 11, pp. 309–23.

12. And out of more abundant caution for the security of the subjects of the Most Serene Most Christian King and the Most Serene King of Great Britain, in order that no harm may be inflicted upon them by war-ships of the other party or other ships prepared at private expense for warfare, all ship-captains, both of the Most Serene Most Christian King and of the Most Serene King of Great Britain, and all their subjects who fit out ships at their own expense, and all privileged communities on both sides, shall be prohibited from all injury and harm toward the other party, but shall give security and be restrained from damage on any account and satisfy the interested party by reparation and restitution, under obligation of person and goods. . . .

18. It is furthermore declared and agreed that if ever any rupture shall occur in Europe between the said crowns (which God forbid), no act of hostility, whether by sea or by land, shall be committed by any garrisons or soldiers of the Most Serene Most Christian King or any subjects of islands, colonies, fortresses, states, and governments which now are or hereafter shall be under French rule in America against subjects of the Most Serene King of Great Britain dwelling or sojourning in any colonies of America, and reciprocally that in the aforesaid case of rupture in Europe no act of hostility, either by sea or by land, shall be committed by any garrisons or soldiers of the Most Serene King of Great Britain or by any subjects of islands, colonies, fortresses, states, and governments which now are or hereafter shall be under English rule in America against subjects of the Most Serene Most Christian King dwelling or sojourning in any colonies of America. But true and firm peace and neutrality shall continue in America between the aforesaid French and British nations, in the same manner as if no such rupture had occurred in Europe. . . .

◇◇◇◇◇◇◇◇◇◇◇◇◇◇

2. THE BRITISH ACQUISITION OF CANADA

(A) HARDWICKE'S CASE AGAINST THE RETENTION OF CANADA [2]

[*Hardwicke to Newcastle, April 2, 1762*]

. . . AS TO the retention of conquests, Mr. Pitt made North-America entirely his object. Some of his enemies objected to him that he did this out of partiality to his friend Beckford, and out of condescension to the particular interests of our Sugar Colonies; but in that I suppose they did him wrong; tho' I allways suspected that one reason why he contended so much for the totality of the Fishery, impracticable to be obtain'd, was

[2] The Earl of Hardwicke was a famous lawyer, a friend, adviser of the Prime Minister, the Duke of Newcastle. The letter given here is quoted in L. B. Namier: *England in the Age of the American Revolution* (London: Macmillan and Co., Ltd., 1930), pp. 323–5.

that he saw the country of Canada was not greatly worth keeping. Your Grace knows what has been debated in pamphlets, whether we should keep Canada or Guadaloupe. It will come now to be a more grave question whether you should restore to France all her Sugar-Colonies, or great part of Canada. The most material argument for retaining Canada has been the delivering your Northern Colonies from such bad neighbours, and from the danger of French encroachments for the future; but some persons have thought that could never be securely attain'd without conquering Louisiana also; and that for this purpose some parts of Canada might serve as well as the whole. The question now may come between Canada, or a great part of Canada, and all the French Sugar Colonies, except St. Domingo.

Canada is a cold northern climate, unfruitful; furnishes no trade to Europe that I know of, but the fur trade, the most inconsiderable of all trades; and therefore never compensated to France the expense of maintaining and defending it. It's products are mostly or nearly of the same kind with those of Great Britain, and consequently will take off not much of our's. Besides, if you remove the French inhabitants, this Kingdom and Ireland cannot furnish, or procure, people enough to settle and inhabit it in centuries to come; and, if you don't remove the French inhabitants, they will never become half subjects, and this country must maintain an army there to keep them in subjection.

It will be said that none of these objections occur against the *French Sugar-Colonies.* They are fertile countries; may be easily peopled, and, being islands, be easily defended, particularly by your squadrons now in use to be sent annually. They must take all the necessaries of life from the Mother Country, as your own islands now do. The sugar-trade is a most profitable one, and you may engross almost the whole of it, and serve all the European markets. To defend them you will not want troops, or, at the most, a very few.

A great deal of this reasoning has been already retail'd in the pamphlets; but, when it was confin'd to Guadaloupe only, it did not carry so great weight, for France still remain'd in possession of the greater part. But it will come with redoubled force, now you have acquired the possession of *all* the Caribbee Islands, especially if what is said be true *that they are the key of the whole West-Indies.* I am very glad that Rodney did not put this into his public letter.

I have seen no body but my horse all this day, so have not talked to, or heard, any body upon the subject. Nor will I raise one word about it to morrow, nor at all without communication with your Grace and our friends; for I see the delays and difficulties that may arise from your being to form in some measure, a new plan of peace. And yet the national interest must be attended to in so important and decisive a conjuncture, in which new circumstances will give rise to new ways of thinking. I have scribbled this very hastily, that your Grace may turn it in your serious thoughts, and perhaps you may get some lights by talking, *at a proper time,* to your friend Sir William Baker upon the subject. If these Caribbee Islands could be kept it might possibly be worth the while of this country to restore almost any thing, except a greater proportion of the Fishery than was yielded in our last ultimatum. . . .

(B) FRANKLIN'S ARGUMENT FOR RETAINING CANADA [3]

Very good

. . . CANADA, in the hands of Britain, will endanger the kingdom of France as little as any other cession; and from its situation and circumstances cannot be hurtful to any other state. Rather, if peace be an advantage, this cession may be such to all Europe. The present war teaches us, that disputes arising in America may be an occasion of embroiling nations, who have no concerns there. If the French remain in Canada and Louisiana, fix the boundaries as you will between us and them, we must border on each other for more than fifteen hundred miles. The people that inhabit the frontiers are generally the refuse of both nations, often of the worst morals and the least discretion; remote from the eye, the prudence, and the restraint of government. Injuries are therefore frequently, in some part or other of so long a frontier, committed on both sides, resentment provoked, the colonies are first engaged, and then the mother countries. And two great nations can scarce be at war in Europe, but some other prince or state thinks it a convenient opportunity to revive some ancient claim, seize some advantage, obtain some territory, or enlarge some power at the expense of a neighbour. The flames of war, once kindled, often spread far and wide, and the mischief is infinite. . . .

. . . The security desirable in America may be considered as of three kinds. 1. A security of possession, that the French shall not drive us out of the country. 2. A security of our planters from the inroads of savages, and the murders committed by them. 3. A security that the British nation shall not be obliged, on every new war, to repeat the immense expense occasioned by this, to defend its possessions in America. . . .

Now all the kinds of security we have mentioned are obtained by subduing and *retaining* Canada. Our present possessions in America are secured; our planters will no longer be massacred by the Indians, who, depending absolutely on us for what are now become the necessaries of life to them (guns, powder, hatchets, knives, and clothing), and having no other Europeans near, that can either supply them, or instigate them against us; there is no doubt of their being always disposed, if we treat them with common justice, to live in perpetual peace with us. And, with regard to France, she cannot, in case of another war, put us to the immense

[3] Portions of a pamphlet entitled *The Interest of Great Britain Considered, with Regard to Her Colonies and the Acquisition of Canada and Guadaloupe*, printed in London, April or May, 1760. Richard Jackson assisted Franklin in writing the pamphlet and may have written the larger part. The text here is taken from Jared Sparks: *The Works of Benjamin Franklin* (Boston: Hilliard, Gray, and Co., 1840), Vol. IV, pp. 1–54. For a good bibliography of the pamphlet warfare over Canada see Clarence Walworth Alvord: *The Mississippi Valley in British Politics* (Cleveland: Arthur H. Clark Co., 1917), Vol. II, pp. 253–64.

expense of defending that long-extended frontier; we shall then, as it were, have our backs against a wall in America; the sea-coast will be easily protected by our superior naval power; and here "our own watchfulness and our own strength" will be properly, and cannot but be successfully, employed. In this situation, the force now employed in that part of the world may be spared for any other service here or elsewhere; so that both the offensive and defensive strength of the British empire, on the whole, will be greatly increased. . . .

Our North American colonies are to be considered as the *frontier of the British empire* on that side. The frontier of any dominion being attacked, it becomes not merely "the cause" of the people immediately attacked, the inhabitants of that frontier, but properly "the cause" of the whole body. Where the frontier people owe and pay obedience, there they have a right to look for protection. No political proposition is better established than this. It is therefore invidious to represent the "blood and treasure," spent in this war, as spent in "the cause of the colonies" only; and that they are "absurd and ungrateful," if they think we have done nothing, unless we "make conquests for them," and reduce Canada to gratify their "vain ambition," &c. It will not be a conquest for *them,* nor gratify any vain ambition of theirs. It will be a conquest for the *whole;* and all our people will, in the increase of trade, and the ease of taxes, find the advantage of it. . . .

I am far from entertaining . . . any fears of their [the American Colonies] becoming either useless or dangerous to us; and I look on those fears to be merely imaginary, and without any probable foundation. . . .

Our trade to the West India Islands is undoubtedly a valuable one; but, whatever is the amount of it, it has long been at a stand. Limited as our sugar planters are by the scantiness of territory, they cannot increase much beyond their present number; and this is an evil, as I shall show hereafter, that will be little helped by our keeping Guadaloupe.

The trade to our northern colonies is not only greater, but yearly increasing with the increase of the people; and even in a greater proportion, as the people increase in wealth and the ability of spending, as well as in numbers. . . .

. . . In fact, the occasion for English goods in North America, and the inclination to have and use them, is, and must be for ages to come, much greater than the ability of the people to pay for them; they must therefore, as they now do, deny themselves many things they would otherwise choose to have, or increase their industry to obtain them. And thus, if they should at any time manufacture some coarse article, which, on account of its bulk or some other circumstance, cannot so well be brought to them from Britain; it only enables them the better to pay for finer goods, that otherwise they could not indulge themselves in; so that the exports thither are not diminished by such manufacture, but rather increased. . . .

. . . Thus much as to the apprehension of our colonies becoming useless to us. I shall next consider the other supposition, that their growth may render them *dangerous*. Of this, I own, I have not the least conception, when I consider that we have already *fourteen separate governments* on the maritime coast of the continent; and, if we extend our settlements, shall probably have as many more behind them on the inland side. Those we now have are not only under different governors, but have different forms of government, different laws, different interests, and some of them different religious persuasions, and different manners.

Their jealousy of each other is so great, that, however necessary a union of the colonies has long been, for their common defence and security against their enemies, and how sensible soever each colony has been of that necessity; yet they have never been able to effect such a union among themselves, nor even to agree in requesting the mother country to establish it for them. Nothing but the immediate command of the crown has been able to produce even the imperfect union, but lately seen there, of the forces of some colonies. If they could not agree to unite for their defence against the French and Indians, who were perpetually harassing their settlements, burning their villages, and murdering their people; can it reasonably be supposed there is any danger of their uniting against their own nation, which protects and encourages them, with which they have so many connexions and ties of blood, interest, and affection, and which, it is well known, they all love much more than they love one another?

In short, there are so many causes that must operate to prevent it, that I will venture to say, a union amongst them for such a purpose is not merely improbable, it is impossible. And if the union of the whole is impossible, the attempt of a part must be madness; as those colonies, that did not join the rebellion, would join the mother country in suppressing it. When I say such a union is impossible, I mean, without the most grievous tyranny and oppression. People, who have property in a country which they may lose, and privileges which they may endanger, are generally disposed to be quiet, and even to bear much, rather than hazard all. While the government is mild and just, while important civil and religious rights are secure, such subjects will be dutiful and obedient. *The waves do not rise but when the winds blow.*

. . . If the visionary danger of independence in our colonies is to be feared, nothing is more likely to render it substantial, than the neighbourhood of foreigners at enmity with the sovereign governments, capable of giving either aid, or an asylum, as the event shall require. . . .

. . . But, if Canada is restored on this principle, [to discourage disaffections in the British Colonies] will not Britain be guilty of all the blood to be shed, all the murders to be committed, in order to check this dreaded growth of our own people? Will not this be telling the French in plain terms, that the horrid barbarities they perpetrate with Indians on our colonists are agreeable to us; and that they need not apprehend the resentment of a government, with whose views they so happily concur? Will not the colonies view it in this light? Will they have reason to consider themselves any longer as subjects and children, when they find their cruel enemies hallooed upon them by the country from whence they sprung; the government that owes them protection, as it requires their obedience? Is not this the most likely means of driving them into the arms of the French, who can invite them by an offer of security, their own government chooses not to afford them? . . .

. . . I have before said, I do not deny the utility of the conquest, or even of our future possession of Guadaloupe, if not bought too dear. The trade of the West Indies is one of our most valuable trades. Our possessions there deserve our greatest care and attention. So do those of North America. I shall not enter into the invidious task of comparing their due estimation. It would be a very long and a very disagreeable one, to run through every thing material on this head. It is enough to our present point, if I have shown, that the value of North America is capable of an immense increase, by an acquisition and measures, that must necessarily have an effect the direct contrary of what we have been industriously taught to fear; and that Guadaloupe is, in point of advantage, but a very small addition to our West India possessions; rendered many ways less valuable to us, than it is to the French, who will probably set more value upon it, than upon a country [Canada] that is much more valuable to us than to them. . . .

◇◇◇◇◇◇◇◇◇◇◇◇◇◇

3. THE TREATY OF PARIS: 1763[4]

. . . IV. HIS MOST Christian Majesty renounces all pretensions, which he has heretofore formed, or might form, to Nova Scotia or Acadia, in all its parts, and guaranties the whole of it, with all its dependencies, to the King of Great Britain: moreover, his most Christian Majesty cedes and and guaranties to his said Britannic Majesty, in full right, Canada, with all its dependencies, as well as the Island of Cape Breton, and all the other islands and coasts in the gulph and river St. Laurence, and, in general, every thing that depends on the said countries, lands, islands, and coasts, with the sovereignty, property, possession, and all rights, acquired by treaty or otherwise, which the most Christian King, and the crown of France, have had till now over the said countries, islands, lands, places, coasts, and their inhabitants, so that the most Christian King cedes and makes over the whole to the said King, and to the crown of Great Britain, and that in the most ample manner and form, without restriction, and without any liberty to depart from the said session and guaranty, under any pretence, or to disturb Great Britain in the possessions above-men-

[4] Signed by Great Britain, Spain, and France, and acceded to by Portugal, on February 10, 1763. Ratification by Great Britain February 21, 1763, and by France, February 23, 1763. George Chalmers: *A Collection of Treaties Between Great Britain and Other Powers* (London, 1790, 2 Vols.). Vol. I, pp. 467–94.

tioned. His Britannic Majesty, on his side, agrees to grant the liberty of the Catholic religion to the inhabitants of Canada: he will consequently give the most precise and most effectual orders, that his new Roman Catholic subjects may profess the worship of their religion, according to the rites of the Romish church, as far as the laws of Great Britain permit. His Britannic Majesty further agrees, that the French inhabitants, or others who had been subjects of the most Christian King in Canada, may retire, with all safety and freedom, wherever they shall think proper, and may sell their estates, provided it be to subjects of his Britannic Majesty, and bring away their effects, as well as their persons, without being restrained in their emigration, under any pretence whatsoever, except that of debts, or of criminal prosecutions: the term limited for this emigration shall be fixed to the space of eighteen months, to be computed from the day of the exchange of the ratifications of the present treaty. . . .

VII. In order to re-establish peace on solid and durable foundations, and to remove for ever all subject of dispute with regard to the limits of the British and French territories on the continent of America; it is agreed, that, for the future, the confines between the dominions of his Britannic Majesty, and those of his most Christian Majesty, in that part of the world, shall be fixed irrevocably by a line drawn along the middle of the river Mississippi, from its source to the river Iberville, and from thence, by a line drawn along the middle of this river, and the lakes Maurepas and Pontchartrain, to the sea; and for this purpose, the most Christian King cedes in full right, and guaranties to his Britannic Majesty, the river and port of the Mobile, and every thing which he possesses, or ought to possess, on the left side of the river Mississippi, except the town of New Orleans, and the island in which it is situated, which shall remain to France; provided that the navigation of the river Mississippi shall be equally free, as well to the subjects of Great Britain as to those of France, in its whole breadth and length, from its source to the sea, and expresly that part which is between the said island of New Orleans and the right bank of that river, as well as the passage both in and out of its mouth. It is further stipulated, that the vessels belonging to the subjects of either nation shall not be stopped, visited, or subjected to the payment of any duty whatsoever. The stipulations, inserted in the IVth article, in favour of the inhabitants of Canada, shall also take place with regard to the inhabitants of the countries ceded by this article. . . .

XX. In consequence of the restitution stipulated in the preceding article,[5] his Catholic Majesty cedes and guaranties, in full right, to his Britannic Majesty, Florida, with Fort St. Augustin, and the Bay of Pensacola, as well as all that Spain possesses on the continent of North America, to the east, or to the south-east, of the river Mississippi; and, in general, every thing that depends on the said countries, and lands, with the sovereignity, property, possession, and all rights, acquired by treaties or otherwise, which the Catholic King, and the crown of Spain, have had,

[5] This article referred to Cuba.

till now, over the said countries, lands, places, and their inhabitants; so that the Catholic King cedes and makes over the whole to the said King, and to the crown of Great Britain, and that in the most ample manner and form. . . .

◇◇◇◇◇◇◇◇◇◇◇◇◇

4. ROYAL PROCLAMATION CONCERNING THE BRITISH POSSESSIONS IN AMERICA: OCTOBER 7, 1763 [6]

WHEREAS we have taken into our royal consideration the extensive and valuable acquisitions in America, secured to our crown by the late definitive treaty of peace concluded at Paris the 10th day of February last; and being desirous that all our loving subjects, as well of our kingdoms as of our colonies in America, may avail themselves, with all convenient speed, of the great benefits and advantages which must accrue therefrom to their commerce, manufactures, and navigation; we have thought fit, with the advice of our privy council, to issue this our royal proclamation, hereby to publish and declare to all our loving subjects, that we have, with the advice of our said privy council, granted our letters patent under our great seal of Great Britain, to erect, within the countries and islands ceded and confirmed to us by the said treaty, four distinct and separate governments, stiled and called by the names of Quebec, East Florida, West Florida, and Grenada, and limited and bounded as follows, viz.

First, the government of Quebec, bounded on the Labrador coast by the river St. John, and from thence by a line drawn from the head of that river, through the lake St. John, to the South end of the lake Nipissim; from whence the said line, crossing the river St. Lawrence and the lake Champlain in 45 degrees of North latitude, passes along the High Lands, which divide the rivers that empty themselves into the said river St. Lawrence, from those which fall into the sea; and also along the North coast of the Baye de Chaleurs, and the coast of the Gulph of St. Lawrence to Cape Rosieres, and from thence crossing the mouth of the river St. Lawrence by the West end of the island of Anticosti, terminates at the aforesaid river St. John.

Secondly, The government of East Florida, bounded to the Westward by the Gulph of Mexico and the Apalachicola river; to the Northward by a line drawn from that part of the said river where the Catahouchee and Flint rivers meet, to the source of St. Mary's river, and by the course of the said river to the Atlantic Ocean; and to the East and South by the Atlantic Ocean, and the Gulph of Florida, including all islands within six leagues of the sea coast.

Thirdly, The government of West Florida, bounded to the Southward by the Gulph of Mexico, including all islands within six leagues of the

[6] *The Annual Register, 1763,* Sixth edition (London, 1810), pp. 208–13.

coast from the river Apalachicola to lake Pontchartrain; to the Westward by the said lake, the lake Maurepas, and the river Missisippi; to the Northward, by a line drawn due East from that part of the river Missisippi which lies in thirty-one degrees North latitude, to the river Apalachicola, or Catahouchee; and to the Eastward by the said river. . . .

We have also, with the advice of our privy council, thought fit to annex the islands of St. John and Cape Breton, or Isle Royale, with the lesser islands adjacent thereto, to our government of Nova Scotia.

We have also, with the advice of our privy council aforesaid, annexed to our province of Georgia, all the lands lying between the rivers Attamaha and St. Mary's. . . .

◇◇◇◇◇◇◇◇◇◇◇◇◇◇

5. PROCLAMATION CONCERNING THE BOUNDARY OF FLORIDA: MAY 9, 1764[7]

(THE Council approve an instrument submitted on 1 May by the law officers on an order of 26 March approving a Board of Trade representation of 23 March, viz:-) By Your Majesty's Royal Proclamation of the 7th of October last, and Your Majesty's Commission to your governor of West Florida, it is declared that the said Province shall be bounded to the North by a line drawn due East from that part of the River Mississippi which lyes in Thirty one Degrees North Latitude to the River Apalachicola; but, it is our duty to Represent to your Majesty, that We are Informed by your Majesty's Governor, that it appears, from Observations and Surveys made since the said Province has been in your Majesty's Possession, that there are not only very considerable Settlements upon the East Bank of the Mississippi above the Line, but also that the Town and Settlement of Mobile[8] itself is some Miles to the North of it; and therefore We humbly beg leave to propose, that an Instrument may pass under the Great Seal (in like manner as was directed in the Case of the extension of the South boundary of Georgia) declaring that the Province of West Florida shall be bounded to the North by a Line drawn from the Mouth of the River Yasons, where it unites with the Mississippi due East to the River Apalachicola, by which we humbly conceive every material Settlement depending upon West Florida will be comprehended within the Limits of that Government.

---

[7] James Munro, ed.: *Acts of the Privy Council, Colonial Series, 1745–1766* (London, 1911), Vol. IV, p. 668.

[8] This was an error; the settlement of Mobile was clearly within the limits of Florida.

Chapter II

DIPLOMACY OF THE REVOLUTION

THE ROOTS of American Revolutionary diplomacy are deeply imbedded in the foreign relations of France and in the domestic relations of Great Britain with her American colonies. France, particularly since 1763, had kept a watchful eye upon the British colonial controversy, and for a part of the time had maintained a secret agent in America. The Continental Congress, on November 29, 1775, appointed a committee to correspond with certain nations friendly to the colonial cause, and eventually decided to send an agent, Silas Deane, to France. The instructions given by the Congress to Deane afford, therefore, a good beginning for the diplomacy of the Revolution (1).

After American independence had been formally declared, Benjamin Franklin, Silas Deane, and Arthur Lee were elected special commissioners to France, and the Continental Congress formulated a broad policy regarding treaties in its Treaty Plan of 1776 (2). The considerations that influenced France to make an alliance with the United States are well set forth in the statement of January 13, 1778 (3), while the attitude of the American envoys toward British attempts at conciliation which did not include the recognition of the independence of the United States, is shown in Franklin's letter to David Hartley, a friend and member of Parliament (4). The Franco-American treaties of commerce and alliance were finally signed on February 6, 1778 (5 and 6).

The instructions given by the Count de Vergennes, the French Foreign Minister, to Conrad Alexandre Gérard, the first Minister Plenipotentiary of France to the United States, provide an example of the attitude of France toward her new American ally (7). The announcement of the Empress of Russia with respect to the commercial rights of neutrals and the resultant Armed Neutrality of 1780 (8), together with the outbreak of war between Great Britain and Holland in December of the same year, further complicated the international situation.

The Continental Congress, in the meantime, had considered what the terms of peace should be at the conclusion of hostilities. As a result of their deliberations, John Adams was chosen as Minister Plenipotentiary for negotiating a treaty of peace and commerce with Great Britain and was furnished with instructions dated August 14, 1779 (9). Subsequent instructions were written October 18, 1780 (10), and the following June a commission was elected to replace the single commissioner (11). When the treaties of Alliance and of Amity and Commerce between the United States and France were concluded, a separate and secret act was signed reserving the right of the King of Spain to agree to the treaties. Spain, however, did not avail herself of the opportunity. The desire of the United States for an alliance with Spain is clearly demonstrated by a comparison of the instructions to John Jay of September 29, 1779 (12), October 4, 1780 (13), and February 15, 1781 (14).

Although the final treaty of peace was not signed until September 3, 1783, a provisional treaty was concluded between Great Britain and the United States on November 30, 1782. The memorandum presented by Franklin to the special agent of Lord Shelburne, Richard Oswald, on April 18, 1782 (15), sets forth on what terms the negotiations for peace were commenced, and the treaty itself shows the degree of success achieved by American diplomacy (16).

◇◇◇◇◇◇◇◇◇◇◇◇◇

1. INSTRUCTIONS TO SILAS DEANE FROM THE COMMITTEE OF SECRET CORRESPONDENCE OF THE CONTINENTAL CONGRESS [1]

Philadelphia, March 3, 1776.

ON YOUR arrival in France you will, for some time, be engaged in the business of providing goods for the Indian trade. This will give good countenance to your appearing in the character of a merchant, which we wish you continually to retain among the French in general, it being probable that the court of France may not like it should [it] be known publicly that any agent from the Colonies is in that country. When you come to Paris, by delivering Dr. Franklin's letter to Monsieur Le Roy,[2] at the Louvre, and M. Dubourg,[3] you will be introduced to a set of acquaintance, all friends to the Americans. By conversing with them you will have a good opportunity of acquiring Parisian French, and you will find in M. Dubourg a man prudent, faithful, secret, intelligent in affairs, and capable of giving you very sage advice.

It is scarce necessary to pretend any other business at Paris than the gratifying of that curiosity, which draws numbers thither yearly, merely to see so famous a city. With the assistance of Monsieur Dubourg, who understands English, you will be able to make immediate application to Monsieur de Vergennes, *ministre des affaires étrangères,* either personally or by letter, if M. Dubourg adopts that method, acquainting him that you

---

[1] Francis Wharton, ed.: *The Revolutionary Diplomatic Correspondence of the United States* (Washington, 1889), Vol. II, pp. 78–80. The committee consisted of Benjamin Franklin, Benjamin Harrison, John Dickinson, Robert Morris, and John Jay. The instructions were drafted by Franklin.

[2] Julien David Le Roy, architect and scholar, with whom Franklin maintained regular correspondence.

[3] Dr. Barbeu Dubourg, who published in 1773 his *Oeuvres Completes de Franklin* and later, 1777, published a popular edition in French of *Poor Richard's Almanac.*

are in France upon business of the American Congress, in the character of a merchant, having something to communicate to him that may be mutually beneficial to France and the North American Colonies; that you request an audience of him, and that he would be pleased to appoint the time and place. At this audience, if agreed to, it may be well to show him first your letter of credence, and then acquaint him that the Congress, finding that in the common course of commerce, it was not practicable to furnish the continent of America with the quantity of arms and ammunition necessary for its defense (the ministry of Great Britain having been extremely industrious to prevent it), you have been dispatched by their authority to apply to some European power for a supply. That France had been pitched on for the first application, from an opinion that if we should, as there is a great appearance we shall, come to a total separation from Great Britain, France would be looked upon as the power whose friendship it would be fittest for us to obtain and cultivate. That the commercial advantages Britain had enjoyed with the Colonies had contributed greatly to her late wealth and importance. That it is likely great part of our commerce will naturally fall to the share of France, especially if she favors us in this application, as that will be a means of gaining and securing the friendship of the Colonies; and that as our trade was rapidly increasing with our increase of people, and, in a greater proportion, her part of it will be extremely valuable. That the supply we at present want is clothing and arms for twenty-five thousand men, with a suitable quantity of ammunition, and one hundred field pieces. That we mean to pay for the same by remittances to France, or through Spain, Portugal, or the French Islands, as soon as our navigation can be protected by ourselves or friends; and that we, besides, want great quantities of linens and woolens, with other articles for the Indian trade, which you are now actually purchasing, and for which you ask no credit, and that the whole, if France should grant the other supplies, would make a cargo which it might be well to secure by a convoy of two or three ships of war.

If you should find M. de Vergennes reserved, and not inclined to enter into free conversation with you, it may be well to shorten your visit, request him to consider what you have proposed, acquaint him with your place of lodging, that you may yet stay sometime at Paris, and that, knowing how precious his time is, you do not presume to ask another audience; but that, if he should have any commands for you, you will, upon the least notice, immediately wait upon him. If, at a future conference, he should be more free, and you find a disposition to favor the Colonies, it may be proper to acquaint him that they must necessarily be anxious to know the disposition of France on certain points, which, with his permission, you would mention, such as whether, if the Colonies should be forced to form themselves into an independent State, France would probably acknowledge them as such, receive their ambassadors, enter into any treaty or alliance with them, for commerce or defense, or both? If so, on what principal conditions? Intimating that you shall speedily have an opportunity of sending to America, if you do not immediately return, and that he may be assured of your fidelity and secrecy in transmitting carefully anything he would wish to convey to the Congress on that subject. In subsequent conversations you may as you find it convenient, enlarge on these topics that have been the subjects of our conferences with you, to which you may occasionally add the well-known substantial answers we usually give to the several calumnies thrown out against us. If these supplies on the credit of the Congress should be refused, you are to endeavor the obtaining a permission of purchasing those articles, or so much of them as you can find credit for. You will keep a daily journal of all your material transactions, and particularly of what passes in your conversation with great personages; and you will, by every safe opportunity, furnish us with such information as may be important. When your business in France admits of it, it may be well to go into Holland, and visit our agent there, M. Dumas, conferring with him on subjects that may promote our interest, and on the means of communication. . . .

◇◇◇◇◇◇◇◇◇◇◇◇◇

2. TREATY PLAN OF 1776[4]

CONGRESS took into consideration the plan of treaties to be proposed to foreign nations. . . .

Resolved, That the following plan of a treaty be proposed to His Most Christian Majesty. . . .

Art. XV. The Merchant Ship of either of the Parties, which shall be making into a Port belonging to the Enemy of the other Ally, and concerning whose Voyage, and the Species of Goods on board her, there shall be just Grounds of Suspicion, shall be obliged to exhibit, as well upon the high Seas as in the Ports and Havens, not only her Passports, but like wise Certificates, expressly shewing that her Goods are not of the Number of those which have been prohibited, as Contraband.

Art. XVI. If by the exhibiting of the above Certificates, the other Party discover there are any of those Sorts of Goods, which are prohibited and declared Contraband, and consigned for a Port under the obedience of his Enemies, it shall not be lawfull to break up the Hatches of such Ship, or to open any chest, coffers, packs, casks, or any other Vessells found therein or to remove the smallest Parcells of her Goods, whether such Ship belong to the Subjects of France, or the Inhabitants of the said United States, unless the lading be brought on Shore in the Presence of the officers of the Court of Admiralty, and an Inventory thereof made; but there shall be no allowance to sell, exchange, or alienate the same in any manner, untill after that due and lawfull Process shall have been had

[4] Adopted by the Continental Congress, September 17, 1776. Carlton Savage, ed.: *Policy of the United States Toward Maritime Commerce in War* (Washington, D.C.: Government Printing Office, 1934), Vol. 1, pp. 132–4.

against such prohibited Goods, and the Courts of Admiralty shall, by a Sentence pronounced, have confiscated the same, saving always as well the Ship itself, as any other Goods found therein, which by this Treaty, are to be esteemed free, neither may they be detained on Pretence of their being as it were infected by the prohibited Goods, much less shall they be confiscated as lawfull Prize: But if not the whole Cargo, but only Part thereof shall consist of prohibited or contraband Goods, and the Commander of the Ship shall be ready and willing to deliver them to the Captor who has discovered them, in such Case the Captor having received those Goods, shall forthwith discharge the Ship, and not hinder her by any Means freely to prosecute the Voyage on which she was bound.

Art. XVII. On the Contrary, it is agreed, that whatever shall be found to be laden by the Subjects and Inhabitants of either Party, on any Ship belonging to the Enemy of the other, or to his Subjects, although it be not of the Sort of prohibited Goods, may be confiscated in the same Manner as if it belonged to the Enemy himself, except such Goods and Merchandise as were put on board such Ship before the Declaration of War, or even after such Declaration, if so be it were done without the Knowledge of such Declaration. So that the Goods of the Subjects or People of either Party, whether they be of the Nature of such as are prohibited, or otherwise which, as is aforesaid, were put on board any Ship belonging to an Enemy before the War, or after the Declaration of it, without the Knowledge of it, shall no wise be liable to Confiscation, but shall well and truly be restored without delay to the Proprietors demanding the same; but so as that if the said Merchandises be contraband, it shall not be any Ways lawfull to carry them afterwards to any Ports belonging to the Enemy. . . .

Art. XXVI. It shall be lawfull for all and Singular the Subjects of the most Christian King, and the Citizens, People, and Inhabitants of the said States, to Sail with their Ships, with all manner of Liberty and Security; no distinction being made, who are the Proprietors of the Merchandizes laden thereon from any Port, to the Places of those who now are, or hereafter shall be at Enmity with the most Christian King, or the United States. It shall likewise be lawfull for the Subjects and Inhabitants aforesaid, to sail with the Ships and Merchandizes aforementioned; and to trade with the same Liberty, and Security, from the Places, Ports, and Havens of those who are Enemies of both or either Party, without any opposition or Disturbance whatsoever, not only directly from the Places of the Enemy aforementioned to neutral Places; but also from one Place belonging to an Enemy, to another Place belonging to an Enemy, whether they be under the Jurisdiction of the same Prince or under Several: And it is hereby Stipulated that free Ships shall also give a Freedom to Goods, and that every Thing shall be deemed to be free and exempt, which shall be found on board the Ships, belonging to the Subjects of either of the Confederates; although the whole Lading or any Part thereof, should appertain to the Enemies of Either, Contraband Goods being always excepted. It is also agreed in like manner, that the same Liberty, be extended to Persons, who are on board a free Ship with this Effect, that although they be Enemies to both or either Party, they are not to be taken out of that free Ship, unless they are Soldiers, and in actual Service of the Enemies.

Art. XXVII. This Liberty of Navigation and Commerce shall extend to all Kinds of Merchandizes, excepting those only which are distinguished by the Name of Contraband: and under this Name of Contraband, or prohibited Goods, shall be comprehended Arms, Great Guns, Bombs with their Fuzees, and other Things belonging to them; Fire Balls, Gunpowder, Match, Cannon Ball, Pikes, Swords, Lances, Spears, Halberds, Mortars, Petards, Granadoes, Saltpetre, Musketts, Muskett Balls, Helmets, Head Pieces, Breast Plates, Coats of Mail, and the like Kind of Arms proper for arming Soldiers, Muskett rests, Belts, Horses with their Furniture, and all other war like Instruments whatsoever. These Merchandizes which follow, shall not be reckoned among Contraband or prohibited Goods; that is to Say, all Sorts of Cloths, and all other Manufactures woven of any Wool, Flax, Silk, Cotton, or any other Material whatever; all Kinds of Wearing apparell, together with the Species whereof they are used to be made; Gold and Silver, as well coined as uncoined, Tin, Iron, Lead, Copper, Brass, Coals; as also Wheat and Barley, and any other Kind of Corn and Pulse; Tobacco, and likewise all manner of Spices; Salted and Smoked Flesh, Salted Fish, Cheese and Butter, Beer, Oils, Wines, Sugars, and all Sorts of Salt; and in General, all Provisions which Serve for the Nourishment of Mankind, and the Sustenance of Life: Furthermore, all Kinds of Cotton, Hemp, Flax, Tar, Pitch, Ropes, Cables, Sails, Sail Cloth, Anchors, and any Parts of Anchors; also Ships' Masts, Planks, Boards, and Beams, of what Tree Soever; and all other Things proper either for building or repairing Ships, and all other Goods whatsoever which have not been worked into the Form of any Instrument or Thing prepared for War, by Land or by Sea, shall not be reputed Contraband, much less such as have been already wrought and made up for any other use; all which shall wholly be reckoned among free Goods; as likewise all other Merchandizes and Things which are not comprehended, and particularly mentioned in the foregoing Enumeration of Contraband Goods; So that they may be transported and carried in the freest Manner by the Subjects of both Confederates, even to Places belonging to an Enemy, such Towns and Places being only excepted as are at that time beseiged, blocked up, or invested.

◇◇◇◇◇◇◇◇◇◇◇◇◇

3. FRENCH REASONS FOR THE FRANCO-AMERICAN ALLIANCE

[THE FRENCH minister of foreign affairs, Count de Vergennes, advocated a declaration of war by France against Great Britain as soon as the news of the Declaration of Independence reached Paris. Later he pursued a vacillating policy. By December 1777, however, he was ready to renew his advocacy of war. Although the statement of January 13, 1778 is unsigned, it contains phrases employed earlier by Vergennes, and includes the principal arguments for the Franco-American alliance.[5]]

13 January 1778.

The quarrel which exists between England and the Colonies of North America is as important to France as to Great Britain, and its issue will have equal influence on the reputation and power of those two Crowns. It is, therefore, essential that France should decide upon and fix the policy it is advisable she should adopt in such a conjuncture.

The Americans have been struggling for the last three years against the efforts of Great Britain, and they have up to the present maintained a sort of superiority; but the war which they wage fatigues and exhausts them, and must necessarily weary the people and awaken in them a desire for repose.

England, for her part, crushed by the expenditure occasioned by this same war, and convinced of the impossibility of reducing the Colonies, is occupied with the means of re-establishing peace. With this view she is taking the most urgent and animated steps with the Deputies from Congress, and it is natural that the United States should at last decide to listen to their proposals.

In this state of affairs it is desirable to examine what course it is proper for France to take.

There exist two courses only, – that of abandoning the Colonies, and that of supporting them.

If we abandon them, England will take advantage of it by making a reconciliation, and in that case she will either preserve her supremacy wholly or partially, or she will gain an ally. Now it is known that she is disposed to sacrifice that supremacy and to propose simply a sort of family compact, that is to say, a league against the House of Bourbon.

The result of this will be that the Americans will become our perpetual enemies, and we must expect to see them turn all their efforts against our possessions, and against those of Spain. This is all the more probable as the Colonies, require a direct trade with the sugar islands. England will offer them that of our islands after having conquered them, which will be easy for her.

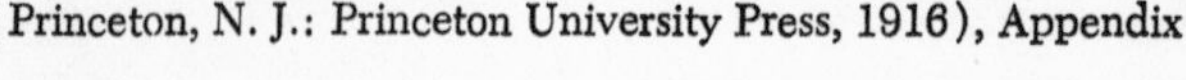

[5] Quoted in Edward S. Corwin: *French Policy and the American Alliance of 1778* (Princeton, N. J.: Princeton University Press, 1916), Appendix III, pp. 398–403.

Thus the coalition of the English and the Americans will draw after it our expulsion, and probably that of the Spaniards, from the whole of America; it will limit our shipping and our commerce to the European seas only, and even this trade will be at the mercy of English insolence and greed.

It would be a mistake to suppose that the United States will not lend themselves to the proposals of the Court of St. James's. Those States took up arms only in order to establish and defend their independence and the freedom of their commerce; if, therefore, England offers them both, what reason will they have for refusing? Their treaty with that Power will give them more safety than the engagements which they might make with other Powers, or than all the guarantees which we might offer them. Indeed, what opinion can they have of our means, and even of our good-will, since we have not dared to co-operate in securing an independence of which we would afterwards propose the empty guarantee? Their surest guarantee will be in the community of interests and views which will be established between them and their former mother-country; we have nothing to offer which can counterbalance that.

Such will be the effects of the independence of the United States of America, if it is established without our concurrence.

It follows from this that the glory, the dignity and the essential interest of France demand that she should stretch out her hand to those States, and that their independence should be her work.

The advantages which will result are innumerable; we shall humiliate our natural enemy, a perfidious enemy who never knows how to respect either treaties or the right of nations; we shall divert to our profit one of the principal sources of her opulence; we shall shake her power, and reduce her to her real value; we shall extend our commerce, our shipping, our fisheries; we shall ensure the possession of our islands, and finally, we shall re-establish our reputation, and shall resume amongst the Powers of Europe the place which belongs to us. There would be no end if we wished to detail all these points; it is sufficient to indicate them in order to make their importance felt.

In presupposing that the independence of the Americans is to be the work of France, it is necessary to examine what line of conduct it is desirable for us to observe in order to attain that end; there is but one,—to assist the Colonies.

But in order to determine the sort of assistance to be given, it is essential not to deviate from the two following truths: 1st, that whatever sort of assistance we give the Americans, it will be equivalent to a declaration of war against Great Britain: 2nd that when war is inevitable, it is better to be beforehand with one's enemy than to be anticipated by him.

Starting with these two principles, it appears that France cannot be too quick in making with the Americans a treaty of which recognised independence will be the basis, and that she should take her measures for acting before England can anticipate her.

It is all the more urgent to hasten the arrangements to be made with the Americans, as the Deputies are hard pressed by emissaries of the English Ministry, and as, if we are not the first to bind them, they will give the Court of London a foundation for proposing a plan of reconciliation at the re-assembly of Parliament, which will take place on the 20th instant, and then all will be over with us, and it will only remain for us to prepare to undertake war against the English and against the insurgents, whereas we could and ought to have begun it in concert with the latter.

In all that has just been said, the co-operation of Spain has been presupposed.

But in the event of that Power not adopting the principles and plan of France, or of her judging the moment of putting it into execution not yet arrived, what course will France, thus isolated, have to follow?

The independence of the Colonies is so important a matter for France, that no other should weaken it, and France must do her utmost to establish it, even if it should cost her some sacrifices; I mean that France must undertake the war for the maintenance of American independence, even if that war should be in other respects disadvantageous. In order to be convinced of this truth, it is only necessary to picture to ourselves what England will be, when she no longer has America.

Thus France must espouse the American cause, and use for that purpose all her power, even if Spain should refuse to join her. From this one of two things will happen; either that Power will still remain neutral, or she will decide to join France. In the first case, although she will be passive, she will nevertheless favour our operations, because she will be armed, and England will see her constantly placed behind us, and ready, if need be, to assist us: but in order to maintain this opinion, we must also maintain that of a good understanding between the two Courts. The second case has no need of development.

But Spain is awaiting a rich fleet from Vera Cruz, and that fleet will not arrive until about next spring. Its arrival must unquestionably be ensured, and that may be done in two ways; 1st by prolonging the period of our operations, or else, 2nd, by sending a squadron to meet the fleet. Spain has vessels at Cadiz and Ferrol; they are armed and ready to put to sea. A cruise might be given as a pretext in order to mask their real destination.

If the King adopts the course of going forward without the participation of Spain, he will take away from that Power all just reason for complaint, by stipulating for her eventually all the advantages which she would have claimed, had she been a contracting party. These advantages will be the same as those which His Majesty will ask for himself.

◇◇◇◇◇◇◇◇◇◇◇◇◇

4. ATTITUDE OF BENJAMIN FRANKLIN TOWARD CONCILIATION WITH ENGLAND[6]

[*Benjamin Franklin to David Hartley*]

Passy, February 26, 1778

I RECEIVED yours of the 18th and 20th of this month, with Lord North's proposed bills.[7] The more I see of the ideas and projects of your ministry, and their little arts and schemes of amusing and dividing us, the more I admire the prudent, manly, and magnanimous propositions contained in your intended motion for an address to the king. What reliance can we have on an act expressing itself to be only a declaration of the *intention* of Parliament concerning the *exercise* of the right of imposing taxes in America, when in the bill itself, as well as in the title, a right is supposed and claimed which never existed; and a *present intention* only is declared not to use it, which may be changed by another act next session, with a preamble that, this *intention* being found expedient, it is thought proper to repeal this act, and resume the exercise of *the right* in its full extent. If any solid permanent benefit was intended by this, why is it confined to the Colonies of North America, and not extended to the loyal ones in the sugar islands? But it is now needless to criticise, as all acts that suppose your future government of the Colonies can be no longer significant.

In the act for appointing commissioners, instead of full powers to agree upon terms of peace and friendship, with a promise of ratifying such treaty as they shall make in pursuance of those powers, it is declared that their agreements shall have no force nor effect, nor be carried into execution, till approved of by Parliament; so that everything of importance will be uncertain. But they are allowed to proclaim a cessation of arms, and revoke their proclamation as soon as, in consequence of it, our militia have been allowed to go home; they may suspend the operation of acts prohibiting trade, and take off that suspension when our merchants, in consequence of it, have been induced to send their ships to sea; in short, they may do everything that can have a tendency to divide and distract us, but nothing that can afford us security. Indeed, sir, your ministers do not know us. We may not be quite so cunning as they, but we have really more sense, as well as more courage, than they have ever been willing to give us credit for; and I am persuaded these acts will rather obstruct peace than promote it, and that they will not answer in America the mischievous and malevolent ends for which they were intended. In England they may indeed amuse the public creditors, give hopes and expectations that shall be of

[6] Wharton, *Revolutionary Diplomatic Correspondence of the United States,* II, pp. 504–6.

[7] In December 1777, Lord North announced he would offer measures designed to conciliate the former colonies of Great Britain.

some present use, and continue the mismanagers a little longer in their places. *Voila tout!*

In return for your repeated advice to us not to conclude any treaty with the house of Bourbon, permit me to give (through you) a little advice to the whigs in England. Let nothing induce them to join with the tories in supporting and continuing this wicked war against the whigs of America, whose assistance they may hereafter want to secure their own liberties, or whose country they may be glad to retire to for the enjoyment of them.

If peace, by a treaty with America upon equal terms, were really desired, your commissioners need not go there for it; supposing, as by the bill they are empowered "to treat with such person or persons as in their wisdom and discretion they shall think meet," they should happen to conceive that the commissioners of the Congress at Paris might be included in that description.

I am ever, dear sir, etc.,

B. Franklin

P.S.-Seriously, on further thoughts, I am of opinion, that if wise and honest men, such as Sir George Saville, the Bishop of St. Asaph, and yourself, were to come over here immediately with powers to treat, you might not only obtain peace with America, but prevent a war with France.

◇◇◇◇◇◇◇◇◇◇◇◇◇

5. TREATY OF AMITY AND COMMERCE BETWEEN THE UNITED STATES AND FRANCE[8]

[*Concluded at Paris, February 6, 1778; ratified by Congress, May 4, 1778; ratifications exchanged at Paris, July 17, 1778.*]

. . . *ARTICLE* 2. The most Christian King, and the United States engage mutually not to grant any particular Favour to other Nations in respect of Commerce and Navigation, which shall not immediately become common to the other Party, who shall enjoy the same Favour, freely, if the Concession was freely made, or on allowing the same Compensation, if the Concession was Conditional. . . .

Article 19.[9] It shall be lawful for the Ships of War of either Party & Privateers freely to carry whithersoever they please the Ships and Goods taken from their Enemies, without being obliged to pay any Duty to the Officers of the Admiralty or any other Judges; nor shall such Prizes be arrested or seized, when they come to and enter the Ports of either Party;

[8] Hunter Miller, ed.: *Treaties and Other International Acts of the United States of America* (Washington, 1931), Vol. II, pp. 3–27. The Treaty was signed by Conrad Alexandre Gérard, Benjamin Franklin, Silas Deane, and Arthur Lee.

[9] The treaty as it was signed and later ratified by Congress, May 4, 1778, contained two Articles, numbers 11 and 12, which were later revoked under an agreement with France.

nor shall the Searchers or other Officers of those Places search the same or make examination concerning the Lawfulness of such Prizes, but they may hoist Sail at any time and depart and carry their Prizes to the Places express'd in their Commissions, which the Commanders of such Ships of War shall be obliged to shew: On the contrary no Shelter or Refuge shall be given in their Ports to such as shall have made Prize of the Subjects, People or Property of either of the Parties; but if such shall come in, being forced by Stress of Weather or the Danger of the Sea, all proper means shall be vigorously used that they go out and retire from thence as soon as possible. . . .

Article 24. It shall not be lawful for any foreign Privateers, not belonging to Subjects of the most Christian King nor Citizens of the said United States, who have Commissions from any other Prince or State in enmity with either Nation to fit their Ships in the Ports of either the one or the other of the aforesaid Parties, to sell what they have taken or in any other manner whatsoever to exchange their Ships, Merchandizes or any other lading; neither shall they be allowed even to purchase victuals except such as shall be necessary for their going to the next port of that Prince or State from which they have commissions.

Article 25. . . . And it is hereby stipulated that free Ships shall also give a freedom to Goods, and that every thing shall be deemed to be free and exempt, which shall be found on board the Ships belonging to the Subjects of either of the Confederates, although the whole lading or any Part thereof should appertain to the Enemies of either, contraband Goods being always excepted. It is also agreed in like manner that the same Liberty be extended to Persons, who are on board a free Ship, with this Effect, that although they be Enemies to both or either Party, they are not to be taken out of that free Ship, unless they are Soldiers and in actual Service of the Enemies.

Article 26. This Liberty of Navigation and Commerce shall extend to all kinds of Merchandizes, excepting those only which are distinguished by the name of contraband; And under this Name of Contraband or prohibited Goods shall be comprehended, Arms, great Guns, Bombs with the fuzes, and other things belonging to them, Cannon Ball, Gun powder, Match, Pikes, Swords, Lances, Spears, halberds, Mortars, Petards, Granades Salt Petre, Muskets, Musket Ball, Bucklers, Helmets, breast Plates, Coats of Mail and the like kinds of Arms proper for arming Soldiers, Musket rests, belts, Horses with their Furniture, and all other Warlike Instruments whatever. These Merchandizes which follow shall not be reckoned among Contraband or prohibited Goods, that is to say, all sorts of Cloths, and all other Manufactures woven of any wool, Flax, Silk, Cotton or any other Materials whatever; all kinds of wearing Apparel together with the Species, whereof they are used to be made; gold & Silver as well coined as uncoin'd, Tin, Iron, Latten, Copper, Brass Coals, as also Wheat and Barley and any other kind of Corn and pulse; Tobacco and likewise all manner of Spices; salted and smoked Flesh, salted Fish, Cheese and Butter,

Beer, Oils, Wines, Sugars and all sorts of Salts; & in general all Provisions, which serve for the nourishment of Mankind and the sustenence of Life; furthermore all kinds of Cotton, hemp, Flax, Tar, Pitch, Ropes, Cables, Sails, Sail Cloths, Anchors and any Parts of Anchors; also Ships Masts, Planks, Boards and Beams of what Trees soever; and all other Things proper either for building or repairing Ships, and all other Goods whatever, which have not been worked into the form of any Instrument or thing prepared for War by Land or by Sea, shall not be reputed Contraband, much less such as have been already wrought and made up for any other Use; all which shall be wholly reckoned among free Goods: as likewise all other Merchandizes and things, which are not comprehended and particularly mentioned in the foregoing enumeration of contraband Goods: so that they may be transported and carried in the freest manner by the Subjects of both Confederates even to Places belonging to an Enemy such Towns or Places being only excepted as are at that time beseiged, blocked up or invested. . . .

◇◇◇◇◇◇◇◇◇◇◇◇◇

6. TREATY OF ALLIANCE BETWEEN FRANCE AND THE UNITED STATES[10]

[*Concluded February 6, 1778; ratified by the Continental Congress May 4, 1778; ratifications exchanged at Paris, July 17, 1778*]

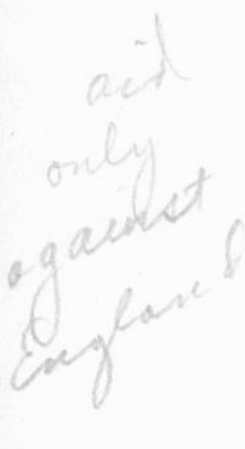

. . . *ARTICLE 1.* If War should break out betwan france and Great Britain, during the continuence of the present War betwan the United States and England, his Majesty and the said united States, shall make it a common cause, and aid each other mutually with their good Offices, their Counsels, and their forces, according to the exigence of Conjunctures as becomes good & faithful Allies.

Article 2. The essential and direct End of the present defensive alliance is to maintain effectually the liberty, Sovereignty, and independance absolute and unlimited of the said united States, as well in Matters of Gouvernement as of commerce. . . .

Article 5. If the united States should think fit to attempt the Reduction of the British Power remaining in the Northern Parts of America, or the Islands of Bermudas, those Contries or Islands in case of Success, shall be confederated with or dependant upon the said united States.

Article 6. The Most Christian King renounces for ever the possession of the Islands of Bermudas as well as of any part of the continent of North america which before the treaty of Paris in 1763. or in virtue of that Treaty, were acknowledged to belong to the Crown of Great Britain, or to the

[10] Hunter Miller: *Treaties and Other International Acts of the United States of America*, Vol. II, pp. 35–47. The Treaty was signed by Conrad Alexandre Gérard, Benjamin Franklin, Silas Deane, and Arthur Lee.

united States heretofore called British Colonies, or which are at this Time or have lately been under the Power of The King and Crown of Great Britain.

Article 7. If his Most Christian Majesty shall think proper to attack any of the Islands situated in the Gulph of Mexico, or near that Gulph, which are at present under the power of Great Britain, all the said Isles, in case of success, shall appertain to the Crown of france.

Article 8. Neither of the two Parties shall conclude either Truce or Peace with Great Britain, without the formal consent of the other first obtain'd; and they mutually engage not to lay down their arms, until the Independence of the united states shall have been formally or tacitly assured by the Treaty or Treaties that shall terminate the War. . . .

Article 11. The two Parties guarantee mutually from the present time and forever, against all other powers, to wit, the united states to his most Christain Majesty the present Possessions of the Crown of france in America as well as those which it may acquire by the future Treaty of peace: and his most Christian Majesty guarantees on his part to the united states, their liberty, Sovereignty, and Independence absolute, and unlimited, as well in Matters of Government as commerce and also thair Possessions, and the additions or conquests that their Confedération may obtain during the war, from any of the Dominions now or heretofore possessed by Great Britain in North America, conformable to the 5th & 6th articles above written, the whole as their Possessions shall be fixed and assured to the said States at the moment of the cessation of their present War with England. . . .

◇◇◇◇◇◇◇◇◇◇◇◇◇

7. INSTRUCTIONS FROM COUNT DE VERGENNES TO CONRAD ALEXANDER GERARD [11]

Paris, March 29, 1778

. . . THE independence of North America, and her permanent alliance with France have been the principal aim of the king; and it was to secure both of these that his majesty approved the conditional stipulations contained in the treaty of alliance, and that he did not secure for himself any exclusive advantages in the treaty of commerce. . . .

The first and most essential of all is that neither of the two parties shall make either peace or truce without the consent of the other. The faithful execution of this clause guaranties the advantages that the parties procure for themselves during the war, and it is essential that Mr. Gerard should impress Congress with that truth, and forewarn it in that way against the suggestions which the English may make to induce a separate peace. He

[11] Wharton: *Revolutionary Diplomatic Correspondence of the United States,* Vol. II, pp. 523–6.

will assure Congress at the same time in the most emphatic manner that the king, on his part, will reject all propositions of that nature that may be made to him by the common enemy, and that he will only lay down his arms when the full and absolute independence of the thirteen United States shall have been recognized by Great Britain. . . .

There is one point of great consequence to the king, and which will demand all the dexterity of Mr. Gerard — the stipulations to be undertaken in favor of Spain. He knows that that power has taken no part in the two treaties, though she has not opposed them, and that up to the present time she has said nothing of the conditions on which she may accede to them in the future. However, we have reason to think that she would desire to acquire the Floridas, a share in the fisheries of the banks of Newfoundland, and Jamaica. The last object is in the hands of the king, since it is secured contingently by the last treaty of alliance. The second will depend equally on him, at least in a great measure, so there will be nothing left to negotiate with Congress about that.

The Floridas enter into the plans of conquest of the Americans. It will therefore be necessary to prepare them for the contingency of a surrender of their claims. The king charges Mr. Gerard with this in a particular manner, and his majesty leaves entirely to his prudence the means to be employed to attain that object.

It is only necessary to remind him that he must carefully avoid speaking in the name of Spain; for his catholic majesty has as yet said nothing relative to his intentions and views. Moreover, Mr. Gerard knows the principal motives that make Spain desire the Floridas. He will give such efficacy to them as is in his power, but if he can not succeed in securing the whole territory, he will strive at least to obtain Pensacola and such parts of the coasts as are considered to be the most suited to the interests of the court of Madrid. . . .

The envoys of Congress (in Paris) have proposed to the king to enter into an engagement to favor the conquest by the Americans of Canada, Nova Scotia, and the Floridas, and he has reason to think that Congress has taken this project to heart. But the king has considered that the possession of those three countries, or at least of Canada, by England, will be an element of disquiet and anxiety to the Americans, which will make them feel the more the need they have of the alliance and the friendship of the king, and which it is not his interest to remove.

In this view, his majesty thinks that he had better make no engagement relating to the conquest in question. If Congress propose it, however, as is probable, Mr. Gerard will answer that the king will always lend himself with eagerness to everything that may suit the United States, and that he will unite willingly in carrying out their plan of conquest, as far as circumstances will permit, but that the uncertainty and the variety of his engagements do not permit him to enter into any formal agreement to that effect. This is his majesty's position in respect to that question, and his intention is that Mr. Gerard should be guided by it in his remarks and suggestions. If, however, Congress should become too pressing and Mr. Gerard should judge that the king could not refuse to co-operate in their views without having his goodwill and the rectitude of his intentions suspected, he can then acquiesce in their wishes, but give them to understand that the conquest which it is proposed to make is not to be an essential condition of the future peace. Mr. Gerard will himself perceive that the last suggestion should be made with such delicacy as not to offend Congress. . . .

8. DECLARATION OF HER MAJESTY THE EMPRESS OF RUSSIA RELATING TO THE COMMERCIAL RIGHTS OF NEUTRALS: FEBRUARY 28, 1780[12]

THE EMPRESS of all the Russias has manifested so visibly the sentiments of justice, equity, and moderation which animate her, and has given, during the whole course of the war maintained against the Ottoman Porte, such convincing proofs of her attention to the rights of neutrality and the freedom of commerce in general, that in this respect she may appeal to the testimony of all Europe. This conduct, as well as the scrupulous exactness with which she has observed the rules of neutrality during the course of this war, has given her room to hope that her subjects would peaceably enjoy the fruits of their industry and the advantages which belong to all neutral nations. Experience has, however, taught her the contrary, since neither these considerations nor the regard due to what the law of nations in general prescribes have been able to hinder the subjects of her majesty from being oftentimes troubled in their navigation or interrupted or retarded in their commerce by the subjects of the belligerent powers. These interruptions having come upon business in general, and that of Russia in particular, are of a nature to awaken the attention of all the neutral nations, and oblige her majesty the empress to seek to deliver herself from them by all means suitable to her dignity and the well-being of her subjects.

But before she shall put them in execution, being filled with a sincere desire to prevent all subsequent acts of violence, she has thought that it was consistent with her equity to lay open to all Europe the principles which will govern her, and which are indispensable to prevent all misunderstanding, as well as all which might give occasion to it. . . .

Article I. That all neutral vessels ought to navigate freely from one port to another, as well as upon the coasts of the powers now at war.

[12] Wharton, *Revolutionary Diplomatic Correspondence of the United States,* Vol. III, pp. 607–8. For a variant translation of the French text, the French text itself, and many other documents connected with the Armed Neutralities of 1780 and 1800, see James Brown Scott, ed., *The Armed Neutralities of 1780 and 1800* (New York: Oxford University Press, 1918), a publication of the Carnegie Endowment for International Peace.

Article II. That the effects belonging to the subjects of the belligerent powers shall be free in neutral ships, excepting always contraband goods.

Article III.[13] That her imperial majesty, in consequence of the limits above fixed, will adhere strictly to that which is stipulated by the tenth and eleventh articles of her treaty of commerce with Great Britain, concerning the manner in which she ought to conduct towards all the belligerent powers.

Article IV. That as to what concerns a port blocked up, we ought not, in truth, to consider as such any but those which are found so well shut up by a fixed and sufficient number of vessels belonging to the power which attacks it that one can not attempt to enter into such port without evident danger.

Article V. That these principles above laid down ought to serve as a rule in all proceedings, whenever there is a question concerning the legality of prizes.

From these considerations her Imperial majesty makes no difficulty to declare that, wishing to insure the execution of that which is herein before declared, to maintain at the same time the honor of her flag, as well as the safety of the commerce of her states, and also to protect the navigation of her subjects against all those whom it may concern, she has given orders that a considerable portion of her maritime forces shall be put to sea, with no other intention than to insure the observation of the most exact and the most strict neutrality, which her majesty proposes to keep as long as she shall not see herself absolutely forced to depart from that system of moderation and of perfect neutrality which she has adopted, in such sort that it will not be but in the last extremity that her fleet will exercise her final orders to go wherever the necessity and the circumstances may require. . . .

[13] Articles 10 and 11 of the treaty between Great Britain and Russia of June 20, 1766, here referred to, were the following:

Article 10. The subjects of the two high contracting Parties shall be at liberty to go, come, and trade freely with the States, with which one or other of the parties shall at this or any future period be engaged in war, provided they do not carry warlike stores to the enemy.

This liberty, however, not to extend to places actually blocked up, or besieged, either by sea or land. At all other times, and with the single exception of warlike stores, the aforesaid subjects may transport to these places all sorts of merchandise, as well as passengers, without the least impediment. In the searching of merchant ships, men of war and privateers shall behave as favorably, as a state of actual war can possibly permit towards the most friendly neutral Powers, observing, as far as may be, the principles and maxims of the law of nations, that are generally acknowledged.

Article 11. All cannon, mortars, firearms, pistols, bombs, grenades, bullets, balls, fuses, flint, stones, matches, powder, salt-peter, sulphur, breastplates, pikes, swords, belts, cartouch-bags, saddles and bridles, beyond the quantity that may be necessary for the use of the ship, or beyond what every man serving on board the ship, and every passenger ought to have, shall be accounted ammunition or warlike stores, and if found shall be confiscated according to law, as contraband goods, or prohibited effects, but neither the ships nor passengers, nor the other merchandises found at the same time, shall be detained or hindered from prosecuting their voyage.

◇◇◇◇◇◇◇◇◇◇◇◇◇

9. FIRST INSTRUCTIONS OF CONGRESS RELATIVE TO A TREATY OF PEACE WITH GREAT BRITAIN[14]

YOU WILL herewith receive a commission, giving you full power to negotiate a treaty of peace with Great Britain; in doing which you will conform to the following information and instructions:

1. The United States are sincerely desirous of peace, and wish by every means consistent with their dignity and safety to spare the further effusion of blood. They have, therefore, by your commission and these instructions, labored to remove the obstacles to that event before the enemy have evidenced their disposition for it. But as the great object of the present defensive war on the part of the allies is to establish the independence of the United States, and as any treaty whereby this end can not be obtained must be only ostensible and illusory, you are therefore to make it a preliminary article to any negotiation that Great Britain shall agree to treat with the United States as sovereign, free, and independent.

2. You shall take especial care also that the independence of the said States be effectually assured and confirmed by the treaty or treaties of peace according to the form and effect of the treaty of alliance with his most Christian majesty; and you shall not agree to such treaty or treaties unless the same be thereby so assured and confirmed.

3. The boundaries of these States are as follows, viz: These States are bounded north by a line to be drawn from the north west angle of Nova Scotia along the highlands which divide those rivers which empty themselves into the river St. Lawrence from those which fall into the Atlantic Ocean to the northwesternmost head of Connecticut River; thence down along the middle of that river to the forty-fifth degree of north latitude; thence due west in the latitude of forty-five degrees north from the equator to the north westernmost side of the river St. Lawrence or Cadaraqui; thence straight to the south and of Nepissing; and thence straight to the source of the river Mississippi. West by a line to be drawn along the middle of the river Mississippi from its source to where the said line shall intersect the thirty-first degree of north latitude. South by a line to be drawn due east from the termination of the line last mentioned in the latitude of thirty-one degrees north from the equator to the middle of the river Appalachicola, or Catahouchi; thence along the middle thereof to its junction with the Flint River; thence straight to the head of St. Mary's River; and thence down along the middle of the St. Mary's River to the Atlantic Ocean. And east by a line to be drawn along the middle of the St. John's River from its source to its mouth in the Bay of Fundy; comprehending all islands within twenty leagues of any part of the shores of the United States and lying between lines to be drawn due east from the points where

[14] Wharton: *Revolutionary Diplomatic Correspondence of the United States,* Vol. III, pp. 300–2. These instructions were passed by Congress on August 14, 1779, nearly six weeks before John Adams was chosen as minister.

the aforesaid boundaries between Nova Scotia on the one part and East Florida on the other part shall respectively touch the Bay of Fundy on the Atlantic Ocean. You are therefore strongly to contend that the whole of the said countries and islands lying within the boundaries aforesaid, and every citadel, fort, post, place harbor, and road to them belonging be absolutely evacuated by the land and sea forces of his Britannic majesty and yielded to the powers of the States to which they respectively belong in such situation as they may be at the termination of the war. But notwithstanding the clear right of these states and the importance of the object, yet they are so much influenced by the dictates of religion and humanity, and so desirous of complying with the earnest request of their allies, that if the line to be drawn from the mouth of the lake Nepissing to the head of the Mississippi can not be obtained without continuing the war for that purpose, you are hereby empowered to agree to some other line between that point and the river Mississippi, provided the same shall in no part thereof be to the southward of latitude forty-five degrees north. And in like manner, if the eastern boundary above described cannot be obtained, you are hereby empowered to agree that the same shall be afterwards adjusted by commissioners to be duly appointed for that purpose according to such line as shall be by them settled and agreed on as the boundary between that part of the State of Massachusetts Bay, formerly called the Province of Maine, and the colony of Nova Scotia, agreeably to their respective rights; and you may also consent that the enemy shall destroy such fortifications as they may have erected.

4. Although it is of the utmost importance to the peace and commerce of the United States that Canada and Nova Scotia should be ceded, and more particularly that their equal common right to the fisheries should be guarantied to them, yet a desire of terminating the war has induced us not to make the acquisition of these objects an ultimatum on the present occasion.

5. You are empowered to agree to a cessation of hostilities during the negotiation, provided our ally shall consent to the same, and provided it shall be stipulated that all the forces of the enemy shall be immediately withdrawn from the United States.

6. In all other matters not above mentioned you are to govern yourself by the alliance between his most Christian majesty and these States, by the advice of our allies, by your knowledge of our interests, and by your own discretion, in which we repose the fullest confidence.

10. INSTRUCTIONS OF CONGRESS TO JOHN ADAMS: OCTOBER 18, 1780[15]

ON THE report of a committee to whom were referred the letters of 23d and 24th March last from the honorable John Adams, minister plenipotentiary of the United States for negotiating a treaty of peace and a treaty of commerce with Great Britain,

Resolved, That the said minister be informed it is clearly the opinion of Congress that a short truce would be highly dangerous to these United States.

That if a truce be proposed for so long a period or for an indefinite period requiring so long notice previous to a renewal of hostilities as to evince that it is on the part of Great Britain a virtual relinquishment of the object of the war and an expedient only to avoid the mortification of an express acknowledgment of the independence and sovereignty of these United States, the said minister be at liberty, with the concurrence of our ally, to accede thereto, provided the removal of the British land and naval armaments from the United States be a condition of it.

That in case a truce shall be agreed on by the belligerent parties, Congress rely on his attention and prudence to hold up the United States to the world in a style and title not derogatory to the character of an independent and sovereign people.

That with respect to those persons who have either abandoned or been banished from any of the United States since the commencement of the war, he is to make no stipulations whatsoever for their readmittance; and as to an equivalent for their property, he may attend to propositions on that subject only on reciprocal stipulation that Great Britain will make full compensation for all the wanton destruction which the subjects of that nation have committed on the property of the citizens of the United States.

That in a treaty of peace it is the wish of Congress not to be bound by any public engagements to admit British subjects to any of the rights or privileges of citizens of the United States, but at all times to be at liberty to grant or refuse such favors according as the public interest and honor may dictate, and that it is their determination not to admit them to a full equality in this respect with the subjects of his most Christian majesty unless such a concession should be deemed by the said minister preferable to a continuance of the war on that account.

---

15 Wharton: *Revolutionary Diplomatic Correspondence of the United States,* Vol. IV, pp. 100–1.

11. INSTRUCTIONS OF CONGRESS OF JUNE 15, 1781 TO PEACE COMMISSION[16]

TO THE Hon. John Adams, Benjamin Franklin, John Jay, Henry Laurens, and Thomas Jefferson, ministers plenipotentiary in behalf of the United States to negotiate a treaty of peace:

Gentlemen: You are hereby authorized and instructed to concur, in behalf of these United States, with his most Christian majesty in accepting the mediation proposed by the Empress of Russia and the Emperor of Germany.

You are to accede to no treaty of peace which shall not be such as may, *1st,* effectually secure the independence and sovereignty of the thirteen United States, according to the form and effect of the treaties subsisting between the said United States and his most Christian majesty; and, *2dly,* in which the said treaties shall not be left in their full force and validity.

As to disputed boundaries and other particulars, we refer you to the instructions given to Mr. John Adams, dated 14th of August, 1779, and 18th of October, 1780, from which you will easily perceive the desires and expectations of Congress. But we think it unsafe, at this distance, to tie you up by absolute and peremptory directions upon any other subject than the two essential articles above mentioned. You are, therefore, at liberty to secure the interest of the United States in such a manner as circumstances may direct, and as the state of the belligerent and the disposition of the mediating powers may require. For this purpose you are to make the most candid and confidential communications upon all subjects to the ministers of our generous ally, the King of France; to undertake nothing in the negociations for peace or truce without their knowledge and concurrence; and ultimately to govern yourselves by their advice and opinion, endeavoring in your whole conduct to make them sensible how much we rely upon his majesty's influence for effectual aid in everything that may be necessary to the peace, security, and future prosperity of the United States of America.

If a difficulty should arise in the course of the negociations for peace from the backwardness of Great Britain to acknowledge our independence, you are at liberty to agree to a truce, or to make such other concessions as may not affect the substance of what we contend for, and provided that Great Britain be not left in possession of any part of the United States.

[16] Wharton: *Revolutionary Diplomatic Correspondence of the United States,* Vol. IV, pp. 504–5.

◇◇◇◇◇◇◇◇◇◇◇◇◇

12. INSTRUCTIONS OF CONGRESS TO JOHN JAY: SEPTEMBER 29, 1779[17]

BY THE treaties subsisting between his most Christian majesty and the United States of America a power is reserved to his Catholic majesty to accede to the said treaties, and to participate in their stipulations at such time as he shall judge proper, it being well understood, nevertheless, that if any of the stipulations of the said treaties are not agreeable to the court of Spain, his Catholic majesty may propose other conditions analogous to the principal aim of the alliance, and conformable to the rules of equality, reciprocity, and friendship. Congress is sensible of the friendly regard to these States manifested by his most Christian majesty in reserving a power to his Catholic majesty of acceding to the alliance entered into between his most Christian majesty and these United States; and therefore, that nothing may be wanting on their part to facilitate the views of his most Christian majesty, and to obtain a treaty of alliance and of amity and commerce with his Catholic majesty, have thought proper to anticipate any propositions which his Catholic majesty might make on that subject by yielding up to him those objects which they conclude he may have principally in view; and for that purpose have come to the following resolution:

"That if his Catholic majesty shall accede to the said treaties, and, in concurrence with France and the United States of America, continue the present war with Great Britain for the purpose expressed in the treaties aforesaid, he shall not thereby be precluded from securing to himself the Floridas; on the contrary, if he shall obtain the Floridas from Great Britain, these United States will guaranty the same to his Catholic majesty; provided always, that the United States shall enjoy the free navigation of the river Mississippi into and from the sea."

You are therefore to communicate to his most Christian majesty the desire of Congress to enter into a treaty of alliance and of amity and commerce with his Catholic majesty. . . .

You are particularly to endeavor to obtain some convenient port or ports below the thirty-first degree of north latitude on the river Mississippi for all merchant vessels, goods, wares, and merchandises belonging to the inhabitants of these States.

The distressed state of our finances and the great depreciation of our paper money inclined Congress to hope that his Catholic majesty, if he shall conclude a treaty with these States, will be induced to lend them money; you are therefore to represent to him the great distress of these States on that account, and to solicit a loan of five millions of dollars upon the best terms in your power, not exceeding six per cent. per annum, effectually to enable them to co-operate with the allies against the common

[17] Ibid., Vol. III, pp. 352–3.

enemy. But before you make any propositions to his Catholic majesty for a loan you are to endeavor to obtain a subsidy in consideration of the guaranty aforesaid.

◇◇◇◇◇◇◇◇◇◇◇◇

13. INSTRUCTIONS OF CONGRESS TO JOHN JAY: OCTOBER 4, 1780[18]

[ON THE report of a committee to whom were referred certain instructions to the delegates of Virginia by their constituents, and a letter of the 26th of May from the honorable John Jay, Congress unanimously agreed to the following instructions to the honorable John Jay, minister plenipotentiary of the United States of America at the Court of Madrid:]

That the said minister adhere to his former instructions respecting the right of the United States of America to the free navigation of the river Mississippi into and from the sea; which right, if an express acknowledgment of it can not be obtained from Spain, is not by any stipulation on the part of America to be relinquished. To render the treaty to be concluded between the two nations permanent, nothing can more effectually contribute than a proper attention not only to the present but the future reciprocal interests of the contracting powers.

The river Mississippi being the boundary of several States in the Union,[19] and their citizens, while connected with Great Britain, and since the Revolution, having been accustomed to the free use thereof, in common with the subjects of Spain, and no instance of complaint or dispute having resulted from it, there is no reason to fear that the future mutual use of the river by the subjects of the two nations, actuated by friendly dispositions, will occasion any interruption of that harmony which it is the desire of America, as well as of Spain, should be perpetual. That if the unlimited freedom of the navigation of the river Mississippi, with a free port or ports below the thirty-first degree of north latitude, accessible to merchant ships, can not be obtained from Spain, the said minister in that case be at liberty to enter into such equitable regulations as may appear a necessary security against contraband; provided the right of the United States to the free navigation of the river be not relinquished, and a free port or ports as above described be stipulated to them.

That with respect to the boundary alluded to in his letter of the 26th of May last, the said minister be, and hereby is, instructed to adhere strictly to the boundaries of the United States as already fixed by Congress.

---

[18] Wharton: *Revolutionary Diplomatic Correspondence of the United States*, Vol. IV, pp. 78–9.

[19] Mr. Wharton believed it was noteworthy that by this wording "the national idea was subordinated to that of the States," and that Mr. Madison in his report of January 8, 1782, took the same position.

Spain having by the treaty of Paris ceded to Great Britain all the country to the northeastward of the Mississippi, the people inhabiting these States, while connected with Great Britain, and also since the Revolution, have settled themselves at divers places to the westward near the Mississippi, are friendly to the Revolution, and being citizens of these United States, and subject to the laws of those to which they respectively belong, Congress can not assign them over as subjects to any other power.

That the said minister be further informed that in case Spain shall eventually be in possession of East and West Florida at the termination of the war, it is of the greatest importance to these United States to have the use of the waters running out of Georgia through West Florida into the Bay of Mexico for the purpose of navigation; and that he be instructed to endeavor to obtain the same, subject to such regulations as may be agreed on between the contracting parties; and that, as a compensation for this, he be, and hereby is, empowered to guaranty the possession of the said Floridas to the crown of Spain.

◇◇◇◇◇◇◇◇◇◇◇◇◇

14. INSTRUCTIONS OF CONGRESS TO JOHN JAY: FEBRUARY 15, 1781[20]

CONGRESS having since their instructions to you of the 29th September, 1779, and the 4th October, 1780, relative to the claim of the United States to the free navigation of the river Mississippi, and to a free port or ports below the 31st degree of north latitude, resumed the consideration of that subject; and being desirous to manifest to all the world, and particularly to his Catholic majesty, the moderation of their views, the high value they place on the friendship of his Catholic majesty, and their disposition to remove every reasonable obstacle to his accession to the alliance subsisting between his most Christian majesty and these United States, in order to unite the more closely in their measures and operations three powers who have so great a unity of interests, and thereby to compel the common enemy to a speedy, just, and honorable peace, have resolved, and you are hereby instructed, to recede from the instructions above referred to, so far as they insist on the free navigation of that part of the river Mississippi which lies below the 31st degree of north latitude and on a free port or ports below the same, provided such cession shall be unalterably insisted on by Spain, and provided the free navigation of the said river above the said degree of north latitude shall be acknowledged and guaranteed by his Catholic majesty to the citizens of the United States in common with his own subjects. It is the order of Congress at the same time that you exert every possible effort to obtain from his Catholic majesty

[20] Wharton: *Revolutionary Diplomatic Correspondence of the United States,* Vol. IV, p. 257.

the use of the river aforesaid with a free port or ports below the said 31st degree of north latitude for the citizens of the United States under such regulations and restrictions only as may be a necessary safeguard against illicit commerce.

◇◇◇◇◇◇◇◇◇◇◇◇◇◇

15. FRANKLIN'S SUGGESTIONS TO RICHARD OSWALD, APRIL 18, 1782, REGARDING TERMS OF PEACE [21]

[*Notes for Conversation*]

TO MAKE a peace durable, what may give occasion for future wars should, if practicable, be removed.

The territory of the United States and that of Canada, by long extended frontiers, touch each other.

The settlers on the frontiers of the American provinces are generally the most disorderly of the people, who, being far removed from the eye and control of their respective governments, are more bold in committing offences against neighbors, and are forever occasioning complaints and furnishing matter for fresh differences between their States.

By the late debates in Parliament and public writings it appears that Britain desires a *reconciliation* with the Americans. It is a sweet word. It means much more than a mere peace and what is heartily to be wished for. Nations make a peace whenever they are both weary of making war. But if one of them has made war upon the other unjustly, and has wantonly and unnecessarily done it great injuries and refuses reparation, there may, for the present, be peace; the resentment of those injuries will remain, and will break out again in vengeance when occasions offer. These occasions will be watched for by one side, feared by the other, and peace will never be secure; nor can any cordiality subsist between them.

Many houses and villages have been burnt in America by the English and their allies, the Indians. I do not know that the Americans will insist on reparation; perhaps they may. But would it not be better for England to offer it? Nothing would have a greater tendency to conciliate, and much of the future commerce and returning intercourse between the two countries may depend on the reconciliation. Would not the advantage of reconciliation by such means be greater than the expense?

If, then, a way can be proposed which may tend to efface the memory of injuries, at the same time that it takes away the occasions of fresh quarrels and mischief, will it not be worth considering, especially if it can be done, not only without expense, but be a means of saving?

[21] Wharton: *Revolutionary Diplomatic Correspondence of the United States,* Vol. V, pp. 541–2. Franklin had prepared a memorandum that he had intended to use as a basis of his talk with Oswald. Oswald noticed that Franklin referred to the memorandum and asked for a copy.

Britain possesses Canada. Her chief advantage from that possession consists in the trade for peltry. Her expenses in governing and defending that settlement must be considerable. It might be humiliating to her to give it up on the demand of America. Perhaps America will not demand it; some of her political rulers may consider the fear of such a neighbor as the means of keeping the thirteen States more united among themselves, and more attentive to military discipline. But on the mind of the people in general, would it not have an excellent effect if Britain should voluntarily offer to give up this province; though on these conditions that she shall, in all times coming, have and enjoy the right of free trade thither, unincumbered with any duties whatsoever; that so much of the vacant lands there shall be sold as will raise a sum sufficient to pay for the houses burnt by the British troops and their Indians; and also to indemnify the royalists for the confiscation of their estates?

This is mere conversation matter between Mr. Oswald and Mr. Franklin, as the former is not empowered to make propositions, and the latter can not make any without the concurrence of his colleagues.

◇◇◇◇◇◇◇◇◇◇◇◇◇◇

16. TREATY OF PEACE BETWEEN THE UNITED STATES AND GREAT BRITAIN: SEPTEMBER 3, 1783[22]

[*Concluded at Paris, September 3, 1783; ratified by Congress January 14, 1784; proclaimed January 14, 1784*]

ARTICLE 1st. His Britannic Majesty acknowledges the sd United States, viz. New-Hampshire, Massachusetts Bay, Rhode-Island, & Providence Plantations, Connecticut, New York, New Jersey, Pennsylvania, Delaware, Maryland, Virginia, North Carolina, South Carolina & Georgia, to be free sovereign & Independent States; that he treats with them as such, and for himself his Heirs & Successors, relinquishes all Claims to the Government Propriety & Territorial Rights of the same & every Part thereof.

Article 2d. And that all Disputes which might arise in future on the Subject of the Boundaries of the said United States, may be prevented, it is hereby agreed and declared, that the following are and shall be their Boundaries, Viz. From the NorthWest Angle of Nova Scotia, viz. That Angle which is formed by a Line drawn due North from the Source of Saint Croix River to the Highlands along the said Highlands which divide those Rivers that empty themselves into the River St. Lawrence, from those which fall into the Atlantic Ocean, to the Northwestern-most Head of Connecticut River: Thence down along the middle of that River to the

[22] Hunter Miller: *Treaties and Other International Acts of the United States,* Vol. II, pp. 151–7. The treaty was signed by David Hartley, John Adams, Benjamin Franklin, and John Jay.

forty fifth Degree of North Latitude; From thence by a Line due West on said Latitude until it strikes the River Iroquois or Cataraquy; Thence along the middle of said River into Lake Ontario; through the Middle of said Lake until it strikes the Communication by Water between that Lake & Lake Erie; Thence along the middle of said Communication into Lake Erie; through the middle of said Lake, until it arrives at the Water Communication between that Lake & Lake Huron; Thence along the middle of said Water-Communication into the Lake Huron, thence through the middle of said Lake to the Water Communication between that Lake and Lake Superior, thence through Lake Superior Northward of the Isles Royal & Phelipeauz to the Long Lake; Thence through the Middle of said Long-Lake, and the Water Communication between it & the Lake of the Woods, to the said Lake of the Woods; Thence through the said Lake to the most Northwestern Point thereof, and from thence on a due West Course to the River Mississippi, Thence by a Line to be drawn along the Middle of the said River Mississippi until it shall intersect the Northernmost Part of the thirty first Degree of North Latitude. South, by a Line to be drawn due East from the Determination of the Line last mentioned, in the Latitude of thirty one Degrees North of the Equator to the middle of the River Apalachicola or Catahouche. Thence along the middle thereof to its Junction with the Flint River; Thence strait to the Head of St. Mary's River, and thence down along the middle of St Mary's River to the Atlantic Ocean. East, by a Line to be drawn along the Middle of the River St Croix, from its Mouth in the Bay of Fundy to its Source; and from its Source directly North to the aforesaid Highlands, which divide the Rivers that fall into the Atlantic Ocean, from those which fall into the River St. Lawrence; comprehending all Islands within twenty Leagues of any Part of the Shores of the United States, & lying between Lines to be drawn due East from the Points where the aforesaid Boundaries between Nova Scotia on the one Part and East Florida on the other, shall respectively touch the Bay of Fundy and the Atlantic Ocean, excepting such Islands as now are or heretofore have been within the Limits of the said Province of Nova Scotia.

Article 3d. It is agreed that the people of the United States shall continue to enjoy unmolested the Right to take Fish of every kind on the Grand Bank and on all the other Banks of New-foundland, also in the Gulph of St Lawrence, and at all other Places in the Sea where the Inhabitants of both Countries used at any time heretofore to fish. And also that the Inhabitants of the United States shall have Liberty to take Fish of every Kind on such Part of the Coast of New-foundland as British Fishermen shall use, (but not to dry or cure the same on that Island) And also on the Coasts Bays & Creeks of all other of His Britannic Majesty's Dominions in America, and that the American Fishermen shall have Liberty to dry and cure Fish in any of the unsettled Bays Harbours and Creeks of Nova Scotia, Magdalen Islands, and Labrador, so long as the same shall remain unsettled but so soon as the same or either of them shall be settled, it shall not be lawful for the said Fishermen to dry or cure Fish at such Settlements, without a previous Agreement for that purpose with the Inhabitants, Proprietors or Possessors of the Ground.

Article 4th. It is agreed that Creditors on either Side shall meet with no lawful Impediment to the Recovery of the full Value in Sterling Money of all bona fide Debts heretofore contracted.

Article 5th. It is agreed that the Congress shall earnestly recommend it to the Legislatures of the respective States to provide for the Restitution of all Estates, Rights and Properties which have been confiscated belonging to real British Subjects; and also of the Estates Rights and Properties of Persons resident in Districts in the Possession of his Majesty's Arms, and who have not borne Arms against the said United States. And that Persons of any other Description shall have free Liberty to go to any Part or Parts of any of the thirteen United States and therein to remain twelve Months unmolested in their Endeavours to obtain the Restitution of such of their Estates Rights & Properties as may have been confiscated, And that Congress shall also earnestly recommend to the several States, a Reconsideration and Revision of all Acts or Laws regarding the Premises, so as to render the said Laws or Acts perfectly consistent, not only with Justice and Equity, but with that Spirit of Conciliation which, on the Return of the Blessings of Peace should universally prevail. And that Congress shall also earnestly recommend to the several States, that the Estates, Rights and Properties of such last mentioned Persons shall be restored to them, they refunding to any Persons who may be now in Possession, the Bonâ fide Price (where any has been given) which such Persons may have paid on purchasing any of the said Lands, Rights or Properties, since the Confiscation.

And it is agreed that all Persons who have any Interest in confiscated Lands, either by Debts, Marriage Settlements, or otherwise, shall meet with no lawful Impediment in the Prosecution of their just Rights.

Article 6th. That there shall be no future Confiscations made nor any Prosecutions commenc'd against any Person or Persons for or by Reason of the Part, which he or they may have taken in the present War, and that no Person shall on that Account suffer any future Loss or Damage, either in his Person Liberty or Property; and that those who may be in Confinement on such Charges at the Time of the Ratification of the Treaty in America shall be immediately set at Liberty, and the Prosecutions so commenced be discontinued.

Article 7th. There shall be a firm and perpetual Peace between his Britannic Majesty and said States and between the Subjects of the one, and the Citizens of the other, wherefore all Hostilities both by Sea and Land shall from henceforth cease: All Prisoners on both Sides shall be set at Liberty, and his Britannic Majesty shall with all convenient speed, and without causing any Destruction, or carrying away any Negroes of other Property of the American Inhabitants, withdraw all his Armies, Garrisons & Fleets from the said United States, and from every Port, Place and Harbour within the same; leaving in all Fortifications the American Artillery that may be therein: And shall also Order & cause all Archives, Records, Deeds & Papers belonging to any of the said States, or their Citizens, which in the Course of the War may have fallen into the Hands of his Officers, to be forthwith restored and deliver'd to the proper States and Persons to whom they belong.

Article 8th. The Navigation of the River Mississippi, from its source to the Ocean shall for ever remain free and open to the Subjects of Great Britain and the Citizens of the United States. . . .

Chapter III

THE DIPLOMACY OF THE CONFEDERATION

ONE OF the most important initial tasks of American diplomacy was the negotiation of commercial treaties. Congress considered this subject and adopted as basic policy the treaty plan of 1784 (1). By 1786 favorable commercial arrangements had been concluded with France, the Netherlands, Sweden, and Prussia (2). It was particularly desirable to establish similar agreements with Great Britain, Spain, and the Barbary States. For a brief period during the progress of the peace negotiations it seemed probable that Great Britain would adopt a conciliatory commercial policy toward the United States as a counterbalance to the Franco-American alliance. Vigorous opposition arose, however, on the part of British merchants and shipowners to any relaxation of the navigation acts. Canadian merchants and loyalists who desired a monopoly of trade with the West Indies supported the British merchants. One of the most effective statements of the mercantilist's point of view was a treatise by Lord Sheffield entitled *Observations on the Commerce of the United States,* which first appeared in 1783 and rapidly passed through several editions (3). When John Adams arrived at London as the first minister of the United States to the Court of St. James, he immediately discovered that a change in official opinion regarding American commerce had occurred, and that the British government not only opposed any deviation from its commercial policy but also was unwilling to fulfill certain of its obligations under the treaty of peace. It had secretly ordered the governor-general of Canada to retain the frontier posts, and had issued the order the day before George III proclaimed the ratification of the treaty. Adams did not know this but he explained the situation as he observed it in his letter of August 6, 1785 (4), and suggested what methods the United States should employ in order to secure a more favorable consideration of their commercial needs. Since these remedies were not feasible Adams was unable to negotiate a commercial treaty. The policy of Great Britain regarding the treaty of peace was defined by Lord Carmarthen in 1786 (5) and remained in that status at the end of the Confederation period.

During this time, diplomatic negotiations between the United States and Spain centered about three particular points: commercial arrangements, the navigation of the Mississippi River, and the southern boundary of the United States. The Spanish government sent a capable envoy, Don Diego de Gardoqui, to the United States to discuss these controversial matters. The envoy arrived at New York in 1785 and immediately entered into discussions with John Jay, whom Congress had appointed to negotiate with him. The instructions given to Jay by Congress were explicit as far as the Mississippi River and boundary questions were concerned. They stipulated the boundaries stated in the treaty of 1783, and the right of the United States to the free navigation of the Mississippi River. Jay and Gardoqui were able to agree upon commercial matters, but not upon the free navigation of the Mississippi. Jay decided, therefore, to propose that the United States should suspend the assertion of the right to free navigation for thirty years, the term of the proposed treaty, and thus make a commercial treaty possible. He made this proposal to Congress on August 3, 1786 (6). One of the most able arguments against Jay's position was made by Charles Pinckney of South Carolina (7). Pinckney had been a member of the Constitutional Convention, and later he was governor of South Carolina, Senator, and minister to Spain. Although Jay's proposals won a majority in Congress, they did not receive the two-thirds majority necessary for the ratification of a treaty. Pinckney's ideas won increasing approval, but the Spanish controversy remained unsettled at the end of the Confederation.

◇◇◇◇◇◇◇◇◇◇◇◇◇

1. TREATY PLAN OF 1784[1]

. . . *RESOLVED,* That in the formation of these treaties the following points be carefully stipulated:

. . . 4. That it be proposed, though not indispensably required, that if war should hereafter arise between the two contracting parties, the merchants of either country, then residing in the other, shall be allowed to remain nine months to collect their debts and settle their affairs, and may depart freely, carrying off all their effects without molestation or hindrance; and all fishermen, all cultivators of the earth, and all artisans or manufacturers, unarmed and inhabiting unfortified towns, villages or places, who labour for the common subsistence and benefit of mankind, and peaceably following their respective employments, shall be allowed to continue the same, and shall not be molested by the armed force of the enemy, in whose power, by the events of war, they may happen to fall; but if any thing is necessary to be taken from them for the use of such armed force, the same shall be paid for at a reasonable price; and all merchants and traders exchanging the products of different places, and thereby rendering the necessaries, conveniences and comforts of human life more easy to obtain and more general, shall be allowed to pass free

[1] Adopted by Congress, May 7, 1784. Carlton Savage, ed.: *Policy of the United States Toward Maritime Commerce in War* (Washington, D.C.: Government Printing Office, 1934), Vol. 1, pp. 157–60.

and unmolested; and neither of the contracting powers shall grant or issue any commission to any private armed vessels empowering them to take or destroy such trading ships, or interrupt such commerce.

5. And in case either of the contracting parties shall happen to be engaged in war with any other nation, it be farther agreed, in order to prevent all the difficulties and misunderstandings that usually arise respecting the merchandize heretofore called contraband, such as arms, ammunition and military stores of all kinds, that no such articles carrying by the ships or subjects of one of the parties to the enemies of the other, shall on any account, be deemed contraband, so as to induce confiscation and a loss of property to Individuals. Nevertheless, it shall be lawful to stop such ships, and detain them for such length of time as the Captors may think necessary to prevent the inconvenience or damage that might ensue from their proceeding on their voyage, paying, however, a reasonable compensation for the loss such arrest shall occasion to the proprietors; and it shall further be allowed to use, in the service of the Captors, the whole or any part of the Military Stores so detained, paying the owners the full value of the same to be ascertained by the current price at the place of its destination. But if the other contracting party will not consent to discontinue the confiscation of contraband goods, then that it be stipulated, that if the master of the vessel stopped will deliver out the goods charged to be contraband, he shall be admitted to do it, and the vessel shall not in that case be carried into any port, but shall be allowed to proceed on her voyage.

6. That in the same case, where either of the contracting parties shall happen to be engaged in war with any other power, all goods not contraband belonging to the Subjects of that other power, and shipped in the bottoms of the party hereto, who is not engaged in the war, shall be entirely free. And that to ascertain what shall constitute the blockade of any place or port, it shall be understood to be in such predicament, when the assailing power shall have taken such a station as to expose to imminent danger any ship or ships that would attempt to sail in or out of the said port; and that no vessel of the party who is not engaged in the said war shall be stopped without a material and well-grounded cause; and in such cases justice shall be done, and an indemnification given, without loss of time to the persons aggrieved and thus stopped without sufficient cause.

7. That no rights be stipulated for aliens to hold real property within these States, this being utterly inadmissible by their several laws and policy; but where on the death of any person holding real estate within the territories of one of the contracting parties, such real estate would by their laws descend on a Subject or Citizen of the other, were he not disqualified by alienage, there he shall be allowed a reasonable time to dispose of the same, and withdraw the proceeds without molestation.

8. That such treaties be made for a term not exceeding ten years from the exchange of ratifications. . . .

◇◇◇◇◇◇◇◇◇◇◇◇◇

2. TREATY BETWEEN THE UNITED STATES AND PRUSSIA: 1785 [2]

. . . *ARTICLE 12.* If one of the contracting parties should be engaged in war with any other power the free intercourse & commerce of the Subjects or Citizens of the party remaining neuter with the belligerent powers shall not be interrupted. On the contrary in that case as in full peace, the Vessels of the neutral party may navigate freely to & from the ports and on the coasts of the belligerent parties, free Vessels making free goods insomuch that all things shall be adjudged free which shall be on board any Vessel belonging to the neutral party, although such things belong to an enemy of the other: and the same freedom shall be extended to persons who shall be on bourd a free Vessel, although they should be enemies to the other party unless they be Soldiers in actual Service of such enemy.

Article 13. And in the same case of one of the contracting parties being engaged in war with any other power, to prevent all the difficulties & misunderstandings that usually arise respecting the merchandize heretofore called contraband, such as arms ammunition & military stores of every Kind, no such articles carried in the Vessels or by the Subjects or Citizens of one of the parties to the enemies of the other shall be deemed contraband so as to induce confiscation or condemnation & a loss of property to individuals. Nevertheless it shall be lawful to stop such Vessels & articles and to detain them for such length of time as the captors may think necessary to prevent the inconvenience or damage that might ensue from their proceeding, paying however a reasonable compensation for the loss such arrest shall occasion to the proprietors: And it shall further be allowed to use in the Service of the captors the whole or any part of the military stores so detained paying the owners the full value of the same to be ascertained by the current price at the place of its destination. . . .

Article 15. . . . And to prevent entirely all disorder & violence in such cases, it is stipulated that when the Vessels of the neutral party sailing without Convoy, shall be met by any Vessel of war public or private of the other party, such Vessel of war shall not approach within cannonshot of the said neutral Vessel, nor send more than two or three men in their boat on board the same to examine her sealetters or passports. And all persons belonging to any Vessel of war public or private who shall molest

[2] This treaty is of special interest because of its liberal provisions regarding maritime commerce, and because Article 12 was revived in the Treaty of 1828 which, as far as it was binding, remained in force until Congress declared war on Germany on April 6, 1917.

The Treaty of 1785 was concluded September 10, 1785, ratified by Congress May 17, 1786, and proclaimed the same day. Miller: *Treaties and Other International Acts of the United States,* Vol. II, pp. 162–84. For further study of this treaty and relevant treaties and documents see James Brown Scott, ed.: *The Treaties of 1785, 1799 and 1828 Between the United States and Prussia* (New York: Oxford University Press, 1918).

or injure in any manner whatever the people, Vessels or effects of the other party shall be responsible in their persons & property for damages & interest sufficient security for which shall be given by all Commanders of private armed Vessels before they are commissioned. . . .

Article 23. If war should arise between the two contracting parties, the merchants of either country then residing in the other shall be allowed to remain nine months to collect their debts & settle their affairs, and may depart freely carrying off all their effects, without molestation or hindrance: and all women & children, scholars of every faculty, Cultivators of the earth, artizans, manufacturers, and fishermen unarmed, and inhabiting, unfortified towns, villages or places & in general all others whose occupations are for the common subsistance & benefit of mankind shall be allowed to continue their respective employments, & shall not be molested in their persons, nor shall their houses or goods be burnt or otherwise destroyed nor their fields wasted by the armed force of the enemy into whose power by the events of war they may happen to fall: but if any thing is necessary to be taken from them for the use of such armed force, the same shall be paid for at a reasonable price. . . .

Article 26. . . . If either party shall hereafter grant to any other nation any particular favour in navigation or commerce, it shall immediately become common to the other party, freely where it is freely granted to such other nation, or on yeilding the compensation where such nation does the same. . . .

◇◇◇◇◇◇◇◇◇◇◇◇◇

3. VIEWS OF LORD SHEFFIELD REGARDING AMERICAN COMMERCE[3]

AS A sudden revolution — an unprecedented case — the independence of America, has encouraged the wildest sallies of imagination; Systems have been preferred to experience, Rash theory to successful practice, and the Navigation Act itself, the guardian of the prosperity of Britain, has been almost abandoned by the levity or ignorance of those, who have never seriously examined the spirit or the happy consequences of it. Our calmer reflections will soon discover, that so great a sacrifice is neither requisite nor expedient; truth and fact are against it; and the knowledge only and consideration of the exports and imports of the American States will afford us just principles, whereby we may ascertain the real value of their trade, foresee and judge of their true interest and probable conduct, and choose the wisest measures (the wisest are always the most simple) for securing and improving the benefits of a commercial intercourse with this now foreign and independent nation. For it is in the light of a foreign

[3] John Lord Sheffield: *Observations on the Commerce of the United States,* new edition (London, 1784), pp. 1–5, 198–202, 214–18.

country that America must henceforward be viewed—it is the situation she herself has chosen by asserting her independence, and the whimsical definition of a people *sui generis*, is either a figure of rhetoric which conveys no distinct idea, or the effort of cunning, to unite at the same time the advantages of two inconsistent characters. By asserting their independence, the Americans have at once renounced the privileges, as well as the duties, of British subjects—they are become foreign states; and if in some instances, as in the loss of the carrying-trade, they should feel the inconvenience of their choice, they could not, nor ought they to complain; but should they on the other hand be placed on the footing of the most favored nation, they must surely applaud our liberality and friendship, without going so far as to expect that for their emolument, we should sacrifice the navigation and of course the naval power of Great Britain. By the simple expedient of permitting the acts of navigation to operate in respect to the American States, as they operate in respect to the most favored foreign nation, we shall escape the unknown mischiefs of crude and precipitate systems, we shall avoid the rashness of hasty and pernicious concessions; concessions which could never be resumed without provoking their jealousy, and perhaps not without an entire commercial breach with the American States.

In the youthful ardor for grasping the advantages of the American trade, a bill, still depending, was first introduced into parliament. Had it passed into a law, it would have affected our most essential interests in every branch of commerce, and in every part of the world; it would have deprived of their efficacy our navigation laws, and undermined the whole naval power of Britain; it would have endangered the repose of Ireland, and excited the just indignation of Russia and other countries: the West India planters would have been the only subjects of Britain who could have derived any benefit, however partial and transient, from their open intercourse directly with the American States, and indirectly through them with the rest of the world. Fortunately some delays have intervened, and if we diligently use the opportunity of inquiry and reflection, which these delays have afforded us, the future welfare of our country may depend on this salutary pause.

Our impatience to preoccupy the American market, should perhaps be rather checked than encouraged. The same eagerness has been indulged by our rival nations: they have vied with each other in pouring their manufactures into America. . . . It is experience alone that can demonstrate to the French, or Dutch trader, the fallacy of his eager hopes, and *that* experience will operate every day in favor of the British merchant. He alone is able and willing to grant that liberal credit, which must be extorted from his competitors by the rashness of their early ventures; they will soon discover that America had neither money nor sufficient produce to send in return, and cannot have for some time; and not intending or being able to give credit, their funds will be exhausted, their agents will never return, and the ruin of the first creditors will serve as a lasting warning to their countrymen. . . .

It will not be an easy matter to bring the American states to act as a nation; they are not to be feared as such by us. It must be a long time before they can engage, or will concur, in any material expense. A Stamp act, a Tea act, or such act, that can never again occur, could alone unite them; their climate, their staples, their manners, are different; their interests opposite; and that which is beneficial to one, is destructive to the other. We might as reasonably dread the effects of combinations among the German as among the American States, and depricate the resolves of the Diet, as those of Congress. In short, every circumstance proves, that it will be extreme folly to enter into any engagements, *by which we may not wish to be bound hereafter.* It is impossible to name any material advantage the American States will, or can give us in return, more than what we of course shall have. No treaty can be made with the American States that can be binding on the whole of them. . . . No Treaty that could be made, would suit the different interests. . . .

At least four-fifths of the importations from Europe into the American States, were at all times made upon credit; and undoubtedly the States are in greater want of credit at this time than at former periods. It can be had only in Great Britain. . . . It is therefore obvious, from this and the foregoing state of imports and exports, into what channels the commerce of the American States must inevitably flow, and that nearly four-fifths of their importations will be from Great Britain directly. . . .

These observations have been thrown out as they occurred, in a hurry, and without a nice attention to method or to ornament. The purpose, however, will be answered, if they should lead men, to see the necessity of maintaining the spirit of our navigation laws, which we seemed almost to have forgot, although to them we owe our consequence, our power, and almost every great national advantage. The Navigation act, the basis of our great power at sea, gave us the trade of the world: if we alter that act, by permitting any state to trade with our islands, or by suffering any state to bring into this country any produce but its own, we desert the Navigation act, and sacrifice the marine of England. . . . This country has not found itself in a more interesting and critical situation than it is at present. It is now to be decided whether we are to be ruined by the independence of America, or not. The peace, in comparison, was a trifling object; and, if the neglect of any one interest more than another deserves impeachment, surely it will be the neglect of this, which involves in it, not merely the greatness, but even the very existence of our country. . . .

◇◇◇◇◇◇◇◇◇◇◇◇◇◇

4. VIEWS OF JOHN ADAMS RELATIVE TO AMERICAN RELATIONS WITH GREAT BRITAIN[4]

[*John Adams to John Jay*]

Grosvenor Square, Westminster, August 6, 1785

I FIND the spirit of the times very different from that which you and I saw, when we were here together, in the months of November and December, 1783.

Then, the commerce of the United States had not fully returned to these kingdoms; then the nation had not digested its system nor determined to adhere so closely to its navigation acts, relatively to the United States; then it was common in conversation to hear a respect and regard for America, professed and even boasted of.

Now, the boast is that our commerce has returned to its old channels and that it can follow in no other, now the utmost contempt of our commerce is freely expressed in pamphlets, gazettes, coffee-houses, and in common street talk. I wish I could not add to this the discourses of Cabinet Counsellors, and Ministers of State, as well as members of both Houses of Parliament.

The national judgment and popular voice, is so decided in favor of the navigation acts, that neither administration nor opposition, dare avow a thought of relaxing them farther than has been already done.

This decided cast has been given to the public opinion and the national councils, by two facts, or rather presumptions. The first is, that in all events this country is sure of the American commerce. Even in case of war, they think that British manufactures will find their way to the United States, through France, Holland, the Austrian low countries, Spain, Portugal, Sweden, the French and Dutch West Indies, and even through Canada and Nova Scotia. The second is, that the American States are not, and cannot be united. The landed interest will never join with the commercial interest, nor the southern States with the northern in any measures of retaliation, or expressions of resentment. These things have been so often affirmed to this people by the refugees, and they have so often repeated them to one another, that they now fully believe them, and I am firmly persuaded they will try the experiment as long as they can maintain the credit of their stocks. It is our part then to try our strength. You know better than I do whether the States will give Congress the power, and whether Congress, when they have the power, will judge it necessary or expedient to exert it in its plentitude.

You were present in Congress, Sir, in 1774, when many members discussed in detail the commercial relations between the United States, then United Colonies, and Great Britain, Ireland, the British West Indies, and

[4] Francis Preston Blair, ed.: *Diplomatic Correspondence of the United States of America, September 10, 1783 to March 4, 1789* (Washington, 1833), Vol. IV, pp. 277–9.

all other parts of the British Empire, and showed to what a vast amount, the wealth, power, and revenue of Great Britain would be affected by a total cessation of exports and imports. The British revenue is now in so critical a situation, that it might be much sooner and more essentially affected, than it could be then. You remember, however, Sir, that although the theory was demonstrated the practice was found very difficult.

Britain has ventured to begin commercial hostilities. I call them hostilities, because their direct object is not so much the increase of their own wealth, ships, or sailors, as the diminution of ours. A jealousy of our naval power, is the true motive, the real passion which actuates them; they consider the United States as their rival, and the most dangerous rival they have in the world. I see clearly they are less afraid of an augmentation of French ships and sailors than American.

They think they foresee, that if the United States had the same fisheries, the same carrying trade, and the same market for ready built ships, which they had ten years ago, they would be in so respectable a posture and so happy in their circumstances, that their own seamen, manufacturers and merchants too, would hurry over to them.

If Congress should enter in earnest into this commercial war, it must necessarily be a long one before it can fully obtain the victory, and it may excite passions on both sides which may break out into a military war. It is to be hoped, therefore, that the people and their councils will proceed with all the temperance and circumspection which such a state of things requires. I would not advise to this commercial struggle if I could see a prospect of justice without it, but I do not; every appearance is on the contrary.

I have not indeed obtained any direct evidence of the intentions of the Ministry, because I have received no answer to any of my letters to Lord Carmarthen; [5] and it seems to me, to press them, at his juncture, with any great appearance of anxiety, would not be good policy. Let them hear a little more news from Ireland, France, and perhaps, Spain, as well as America, which I think will operate in our favor.

5. POSITION OF THE BRITISH GOVERNMENT REGARDING THE REMOVAL OF TROOPS FROM THE NORTHWEST POSTS [6]

[*Lord Carmarthen to John Adams*]

St. James, February 28, 1786

. . . THE SEVENTH article both of the provisional and of the definitive treaties, between his Majesty and the United States, clearly stipulates the

[5] Lord Carmarthen was the British Foreign Minister.

[6] Blair: *Diplomatic Correspondence, 1783–1789,* Vol. V, pp. 7–8.

withdrawing with all convenient speed, his Majesty's armies, garrisons and fleets from the said United States, and from every port, place, and harbor, within the same, and no doubt, can possibly arise respecting either the letter or spirit of such an engagement.

The fourth article of the same treaties as clearly stipulates that creditors, on either side shall meet with no lawful impediment to the recovery of the full value in sterling money of all *bona fide* debts, heretofore contracted.

The little attention paid to the fulfilling this engagement on the part of the subjects of the United States in general, and the direct breach of it, in many particular instances, have already reduced many of the King's subjects to the utmost degree of difficulty and distress; nor have their applications for redress, to those whose situations in America naturally pointed them out as the guardians of public faith, been as yet successful in obtaining them that justice, to which, on every principle of law, as well as of humanity, they were clearly and indisputably entitled.

The engagements entered into by treaty, ought to be mutual, and equally binding on the respective contracting parties. It would, therefore, be the height of folly, as well as injustice, to suppose one party alone obliged to a strict observance of the public faith, while the other might remain free to deviate from its own engagements, as often as convenience might render such deviation necessary, though, at the expense of its own national credit and importance.

I flatter myself, however, sir, that justice will speedily be done to British creditors; and I can assure you, sir, that, whenever America shall manifest a real determination to fulfil her part of the treaty, Great Britain will not hesitate to prove her sincerity, to co-operate in whatever points depend upon her, for carrying every article of it into real and complete effect. . . .

6. JOHN JAY'S ADDRESS BEFORE CONGRESS ON SPANISH-AMERICAN DIPLOMACY: AUGUST 3, 1786[7]

. . . IT APPEARS to me, that a proper commercial treaty with Spain, would be of more importance to the United States, than any they have formed or can form with any other nation. I am led to entertain this opinion from the influence which Spain may and will have, both on our politics and our commerce.

France, whom we consider as our ally, and to whom we shall naturally

[7] Blair: *Diplomatic Correspondence, 1783–1789,* Vol. VI, pp. 165–77. It was customary for the Secretary of Foreign Affairs to address Congress on matters relating to his department.

turn our eyes for aid, in case of war, etc., is strongly bound to Spain by the family compact; and the advantages she derives from it are so various and so great, that it is questionable whether she could even remain neuter, in case of a rupture between us and his Catholic Majesty. Besides, we are well apprized of the sentiments of France relative to our western claims, in which I include that of freely navigating the river Mississippi. I take it for granted, that while the compact in question exists, France will invariably think it her interest to prefer the good will of Spain to the good will of America, and although she would very reluctantly give umbrage to either, yet if driven to take part with one or the other, it would not be in our favor.

Unless we are friends with Spain, her influence, whether more or less, on the councils of Versailles, will always be against us. . . .

Recent transactions tell us that the influence of Spain, in Barbary, is not contemptible. When time shall have cast a thicker veil over the memory of past and long continued hostilities; when the convenience of Spanish money and Spanish favors shall become better known, and more felt at Fez, Algiers, etc., it is more than probable that those powers will be little inclined to disoblige a nation, whose arms have given them much trouble, and from whose gratuities they derive more wealth and advantages than they have ever been able to reap from depredations, and from plunder, often hardly gained.

The influence which the Catholic King will and must have, in greater or less degrees, in Italy, with several of whose Sovereigns he is allied by blood as well as by treaties, merits some consideration. The trade of the Mediterranean deserves our notice, and Spain has convenient ports in that sea. . . .

It is well known that they consume more than they export, and consequently that the balance of trade is and must be against them: hence it is that the millions they yearly bring from the mines of America, so soon disappear, flying out of Spain by every road and port in it.

Details would be tedious, and considering where I am, unnecessary; it is sufficient to observe, that there is scarcely a single production of this country but what may be advantageously exchanged in the Spanish European ports for gold and silver. . . .

The conclusion I draw from what has been said is, that on general principles of policy and commerce, it is the interest of the United States to be on the best terms with Spain. This conclusion would be greatly strengthened by a review of our present local and other circumstances; but they are well known, and their language is strong and intelligible. . . .

It appears to me that the independence, situation, temper, resources and other circumstances of the United States, lead the court of Spain to regard them with much attention, and I may add, with jealousy and apprehension.

Their conduct induces me to think that their present policy and design is to cultivate our friendship, and to insure the continuance of it by such advantages in a treaty, as may prevent its becoming our interest to break with them.

To this cause I ascribe the civilities shewn to the United States, by the release of their citizens at the Havana, and by the interposition of his Catholic Majesty in their favor, at Morocco, &c.

To the same cause I ascribe the very liberal and beneficial articles, which their Plenipotentiary here is willing to have inserted in the treaty. I am now negotiating with him, and which are specified in the following notes of them, viz:

1. That all commercial regulations affecting each other shall be founded in perfect reciprocity. Spanish merchants shall enjoy all the commercial privileges of native merchants in the United States, and American merchants shall enjoy all the commercial privileges of native merchants in the kingdom of Spain, and in the Canaries and other Islands belonging and adjacent thereto. The same privilege shall extend to their respective vessels and merchandize, consisting of the manufacture and productions of their respective countries. . . .

3. That the *bona fide* manufactures and productions of the United States (tobacco only excepted, which shall continue under its present regulations) may be imported in American or Spanish vessels, into any parts of his Majesty's European dominions and Islands aforesaid, in like manner as if they were the productions of Spain: And on the other hand, that the *bona fide* manufactures and productions of his Majesty's dominions may be imported into the United States in Spanish or American vessels, in like manner as if they were the manufactures and productions of the said States. And further, that all such duties and imposts, as may mutually be thought necessary to lay on them by either party, shall be ascertained and regulated on principles of exact reciprocity, by a tariff, to be formed by a convention for that purpose, to be negotiated and made within *one* year after the exchange of ratifications of this treaty; and in the mean time, that no other duties or imposts shall be exacted from each other's merchants and ships, than such as may be payable by natives in like cases.

4. That inasmuch as the United States, from not having mines of gold and silver, may often want supplies of specie for a circulating medium, his Catholic Majesty as a proof of his good will, agrees to order the masts and timber which may from time to time be wanted for his royal army, to be purchased and paid for in specie, in the United States; provided the said masts and timber shall be of equal quality, and when brought to Spain shall not cost more than the like may there be paid for from other countries. . . .

My attention is chiefly fixed on two obstacles, which at present divide us, viz: the navigation of the Mississippi, and the territorial limits between them and us.

My letters written from Spain, when our affairs were the least promising, evince my opinion respecting the Mississippi, and oppose every idea of our relinquishing our right to navigate it. I entertain the same sentiments of that right and of the importance of retaining it, which I then did.

Mr. Gardoqui strongly insists on our relinquishing it. We have had many conferences and much reasoning on the subject, not necessary now to detail. His concluding answer to all my arguments has steadily been, that the King will never yield that point, nor consent to any compromise about it, for that it always has been, and continues to be one of their maxims of policy, to exclude all mankind from their American shores. . . .

Circumstanced as we are, I think it would be expedient to agree that the treaty should be limited to 25 or 30 years, and that one of the articles should stipulate that the United States would forbear to use the navigation of that river below their territories to the ocean. Thus the duration of the treaty, and of the forbearance in question, would be limited to the same period.

Whether Mr. Gardoqui would be content with such an article, I cannot determine; my instructions restraining me from even sounding him respecting it. I nevertheless think the experiment worth trying for several reasons:

1st. Because, unless that matter can in some way or other, be settled, the treaty however advantageous, will not be concluded.

2d. As that navigation is not *at present* important, nor will probably become much so in less than twenty-five or thirty years, a forbearance to use it while we do not *want* it is no great sacrifice.

3d. Spain now excludes us from that navigation, and with a strong hand holds it against us; she will not yield it peaceably, and therefore we can only acquire it by war. Now, as we are not prepared for a war with any power, as many of the States would be little inclined to a war with Spain for that object, at this day; and as such a war would for those and a variety of obvious reasons, be inexpedient, it follows that Spain will, for a long space of time yet to come, exclude us from that navigation. Why, therefore, should we not (for a valuable consideration too) consent to forbear to use, what we know is not in our power to use. . . .

With respect to territorial limits, it is clear to me that Spain can justly claim nothing east of the Mississippi, but what may be comprehended within the bounds of the Floridas.

How far those bounds extend, or ought to extend, may prove a question of more difficulty to negotiate than to decide. Pains I think should be taken to conciliate and settle all such matters amicably, and it would be better even to yield a few acres than to part in ill humor. If their demands, when ascertained, should prove too extravagant, and too pertinaciously adhered to, one mode of avoiding a rupture will still be left, viz: referring that dispute to impartial commissioners. I do not mean by this, that any third Sovereign should be called in to mediate or arbitrate about the matter. They make troublesome arbitrators, and not always the most impartial. I mean private men for commissioners; and to me there appears little difficulty in finding proper ones: for not being prepared for war, I think it much our interest to avoid placing ourselves in such a situation, as that our forbearing hostilities may expose us to indignities. . . .

Permit me, Sir, to make one or two observations more. If the system of Spain respecting us, really is what I suppose it to be, then it follows that this is the best season for making a treaty with her that can be expected. . . .

At a time when other nations are shewing us no extraordinary marks of respect, the court of Spain is even courting our friendship, by strong marks, not only of polite and friendly attention, but by offering us favors not common for her to hold out or bestow; for I consider the terms she proposes as far more advantageous, than any to be found in her commercial treaties with other nations. . . .

The Mississippi would continue shut; France would tell us our claim to it was ill-founded; the Spanish posts on its banks, and even those out of Florida in our country, would be strengthened, and that nation would there bid us defiance with impunity, at least until the American nation shall become more really and truly a nation than it at present is; for, unblessed with an efficient government, destitute of funds, and without public credit, either at home or abroad, we should be obliged to wait in patience for better days, or plunge into an unpopular and dangerous war, with very little prospect of terminating it by a peace, either advantageous or glorious. Supposing the Spanish business out of question, yet the situation of the United States appears to me to be seriously delicate, and to call for great circumspection in our conduct, both at home and abroad; nor, in my opinion, will this cease to be the case, until a vigorous national government be formed, and public credit and confidence established. . . .

◇◇◇◇◇◇◇◇◇◇◇◇◇◇

7. ADDRESS OF CHARLES PINCKNEY AGAINST JAY'S PROPOSED TREATY WITH SPAIN[8]

. . . I WILL agree that an equal commercial treaty would be of more advantage to this country, with Spain, than with any other in Europe, except Portugal; but I am not convinced that the relative situation of Spain and the United States is such as ought to render us, at this time, particularly anxious to conclude a treaty upon the principles proposed.

It is thought, if a difference should exist between us, that France will probably be the friend of Spain; as her close connection by compact, and the benefits she derives from her alliance with Spain, are greater than any she can expect from America. If I understand the politics of France, or if we are to depend upon our communications from thence, we are to suppose that her present system, is a system of perfect peace. . . .

[8] Delivered in Congress, August 16, 1786. John C. Fitzpatrick, ed.: *Journals of the Continental Congress, 1774–1789* (Washington, D.C.: Government Printing Office, 1934), Vol. XXXI, pp. 935–48.

Though the animosities of Great Britain are still warm, yet there is sufficient wisdom in her councils to make them yield to her interest. Though she loves us not, she hates France and Spain, and would avail herself of any opportunity, even upon less than equal terms, to strike a blow. With them she never can be in any other than a rival situation; with us, when the present differences shall have terminated, it will ever be her interest to be closely connected. Our language, governments, religion and policy, point to this, as an alliance that will hereafter be formed, as most likely to be permanent and productive of good consequences. In a war with France and Spain, the contiguity of the United States, and the convenience of their ports and supplies, would render the aid of this country peculiarly important in any enterprise against their islands.

We also know, if any respect is to be paid to the intelligence and communications of Mr. Adams, your Minister at the Court of London, that the cabinet of Great Britain are at this time turning a serious eye to South America. The divesting, he says, Spain of that country, and opening to it a free trade, is considered by them as of the first importance, and if any event should take place in which even a distant hope of accomplishing this object should offer, there can be no doubt of her availing herself of it.

So far therefore from fearing the additional weight of Great Britain, we are to presume if she suffers her interest and her wishes to prevail, that she will importantly interfere in our favour. . . .

Upon investigating the situation of Spain, it will be found she has strong reasons to be particularly anxious to treat with you at this time.

Independent of the knowledge she must have of the intentions of Great Britain, she views with a jealous eye the emancipation of these States, and dreads their neighbourhood to her rich and extensive, tho' feeble colonies of South America. She is desirous to prevent an intimacy between them, well knowing the danger of such an intercourse. Hence we find she holds the deserts of Florida as a barrier, and wishes to deprive our citizens of the use of the Mississippi, hoping by these means to postpone an event which she dreads, and fears is at no considerable distance. Being acquainted with your situation, the deranged state of your finances, and the inefficacy of your government, she thinks that this is the time to push her demands, and supposes your distress will force you into a compliance; but I still trust our inconveniencies when compared to her's, are but temporary. A little firmness and perseverance on the part of Congress, and of recollection on the part of the States, may yet subdue all our difficulties; whereas the Spanish Monarchy carries in its bosom the seeds of its dissolution. Our situation, though unpleasant, is not yet sufficiently desperate to force us into measures derogatory to our national honor. Spain has more to risque, and more to dread from a rupture than we can fear, and though it is undoubtedly her interest to treat at present, it can be only ours on very advantageous terms. . . .

The articles with which Spain is now supplied from this country, she receives upon terms equally beneficial with those proposed by the treaty, and so advantageous is this trade to her, that there cannot be the most distant danger of her ever shutting her ports against us; she does not produce them, and they are necessary and essential to her, it is therefore her policy to open her ports to all that do; this creates a competition, and she is always sure of being well and cheaply supplied. The object of the treaty is therefore unimportant, because it is only to secure that partial intercourse with Spain which now exists, and which it will always be her interest to promote. . . .

I trust that upon a candid and disinterested view of the proposed arrangement the partial, not to say ungenerous, manner in which it is offered, and the few advantages to be derived from its operation, which we do not at present enjoy, that Congress will be induced to suppose it is not an offer of that liberal and extensive kind, which promises a lasting or mutually beneficial intercourse, nor does it hold out such privileges as we might have expected from a power who wishes to tempt us to even the temporary surrender of an important national right. In my judgment she proposes nothing more than she will always be willing to grant you without a treaty, and nothing which can be termed an equivalent for the forbearance she demands.

The true mode to determine this, is to examine the nature and consequences of the demand she makes, on our compliance with which alone a treaty may be formed with her.

It is to forbear the assertion of the right of the United States to navigate the river Mississippi, for the terms of 25 or 30 years. It is said the treaty will not be concluded without this stipulation: That the navigation is unimportant, and that a forbearance will be no sacrifice, as Spain excludes us by force, and will continue to do so; that it would be disgraceful to continue the claim without asserting it; that war is inexpedient, and that the best way would be to enter into a treaty with them, and consent to suspend the claim for a certain time.

The right of the United States to navigate the Mississippi has been so often asserted, and so fully stated by Congress, that it is unnecessary to say any thing upon this subject, particularly as the Secretary in his Report appears to be in sentiment with Congress. But if the treaty proposed was of the most advantageous nature in other respects, while it insisted upon the forbearance, I should think the impolicy of consenting to it, must be obvious for the following reasons:

Because the sale and disposal of the lands ceded in the western territory, has ever been considered by Congress as a sufficient fund, under proper management, for the discharge of the domestic debt. Large sums of efficient money have already been expended in quieting the Indians, purchasing their rights of soil, and in sending out persons to survey it. The offers which are to be made the purchasers, and already established by your resolutions, are the protection and support of the Union; the establishment of republican governments, and the equal enjoyment of all the privileges of citizens of the United States. To those in the least acquainted with that country, it is known that the value of their lands must altogether depend upon the right to navigate the Mississippi. This is the great outlet with which, and with the rivers running into it, nature washes their shores, points to them the mode of exporting their productions, and of establishing a commercial intercourse with the rest of the world. Inform them you have consented to relinquish it even for a time, you check, perhaps destroy, the spirit of emigration, and prevent the accomplishment of the object proposed by the sale. But, it is said, the Spaniards already oppose us in the navigation, and that this will as effectually prevent emigration, as our consenting to suspend it. To this it may be shortly replied, that while the purchasers know that the United States claim and insist upon the right, and are negotiating for it, that if the Spaniards refuse to admit us to a participation, the occlusion will be founded in injury, must be supported by force, and will be resisted whenever circumstances shall authorise; a reliance on the support and protection of their parent state, will operate as a spur to emigration.

To me it appears most extraordinary that a doctrine should be attempted to prove, that because we have not at present a government sufficiently energetic to assert a national right, it would be more honorable to relinquish it.

The British government, in violation of the late treaty, hold by force and garrison posts within the territory of the United States. . . .

Another object more important than the sale and disposal of the Western territory, presents itself in objection to the suspension of the right.

Nature has so placed this country, that they must either be the future friends or enemies of the Atlantic states, and this will altogether depend upon the policy they shall observe towards them.

If they assist them in rearing their infant governments to maturity, and by extending the gentle influence of their laws gradually, cement their union with us upon equal principles, it is fair to suppose they may be an acquisition, rather than a disadvantage.

In their first settlement, exports cannot be much attended to, but if these states increase in the same proportion the United States did, and we are to presume they will exceed them, in the course of a few years, they will turn their views to the best mode of exporting and disposing of their productions. The large navigable rivers which all terminate in the Mississippi, point to them, as has been mentioned, this mode of export; should the right remain unceded by Congress, the consideration of the future force of the inhabitants, and a number of eventual circumstances in our favor, which it is impossible at present to foresee, but which are probable, may induce, perhaps compel, Spain to yield us a share in the navigation.

But should it be surrendered, you at once deprive the citizens of the Atlantic states from navigating it, or from having any intercourse with the settlements on its banks, and within your territory. You immediately destroy all connections between them and the inhabitants of the western country: for, after you have rendered them thus dependent on Spain, by using the first opportunity in your power to sacrifice their interests to those of the Atlantic States, can they be blamed for immediately throwing themselves into her arms for that protection and support which you have denied them — for the enjoyment of that right which you have placed it out of your power to grant. Is it not to be clearly seen by those who will see, that the policy of Spain, in thus inducing us to consent to a surrender of the navigation for a time, is, that by having a clear and unincumbered right, she may use it for the purpose of separating the interests of the inhabitants of the western country entirely from us, and making it subservient to her own purposes? Will it not produce this? It will. Will it not give her influence the entire command of the numerous and extensive Indian tribes within this country? It will certainly have this effect. When once this right is ceded, no longer can the United States be viewed as the friend or parent of the new States, nor ought they to be considered in any other light, than in that of their oppressors.

There is one consideration, and of some consequence, which ought to be recollected; that is, the impropriety of the United States ever acting under the influence of that kind of policy which is calculated to acquire benefits for one part of the confederacy at the expence of the other.

It is confessed our government is so feeble and unoperative, that unless a new portion of strength is infused, it must in all probability soon dissolve. Congress have it in contemplation to apply to the States on this subject. The concurrence of the whole will be necessary to effect it. Is it to be supposed, that if it is discovered a treaty is formed upon principles calculated to promote the interests of one part of the union at the expence of the other, that the part conceiving itself injured will ever consent to invest additional powers? Will they not urge, and with great reason, the impropriety of vesting that body with farther powers, which has so recently abused those they already possess? I have no doubt they will. . . .

Upon the whole, as the present treaty proposes no real advantage that we do not at present enjoy, and it will always be the interest and policy of Spain to allow; as our situation by no means presses us to the formation of new connections; and as the suspension demanded, may involve us in uneasinesses with each other at a time when harmony is so essential to our true interests — as it may be the means of souring the states, and indispose them to grant us those additional powers of government, without which we cannot exist as a nation, and without which all the treaties you may form must be ineffectual; let me hope that upon this occasion the general welfare of the United States will be suffered to prevail, and that the house will on no account consent to alter Mr. Jay's instructions, or permit him to treat upon any other terms than those he has already proposed.

Chapter IV

DIPLOMATIC RELATIONS WITH ENGLAND AND SPAIN 1789—1795

JOHN ADAMS closed the American legation in London and returned to the United States in 1788 without having accomplished much in the way of promoting British-American amity: British troops still possessed the northwest posts of the United States, and British navigation acts, inimical to American commerce, remained in force. There was a growing sentiment in the United States that more vigorous measures should replace diplomatic protests, but the American government, under the Articles of Confederation, was virtually powerless. The new Constitution, however, provided greater opportunity for national action in foreign affairs (1). President Washington sent Gouverneur Morris to London on a special mission, and although Mr. Morris accomplished nothing of importance, the British government, aroused at last over the danger of aggressive measures on the part of the United States, dispatched a minister, George Hammond, to Philadelphia. The Secretary of State welcomed the renewal of diplomatic discussion and accordingly drew up a brief statement of American grievances against the British government (2). Mr. Hammond, in reply, presented a lengthy and detailed account of British grievances against the United States (3). Thus diplomatic negotiations were fairly opened and the next move rested with the Secretary of State. Mr. Jefferson was quick to avail himself of the opportunity, and his dispatch of May 29, 1792 presented a complete analysis of the American position (4). The British minister, being at a loss for an answer, made no attempt at more than a perfunctory reply. This course of action by Mr. Hammond was encouraged by the extraordinary conduct of Alexander Hamilton, Secretary of the Treasury. Hamilton discussed Jefferson's note with Hammond and declared that he did not approve it, and that it did not fully represent the attitude of the administration. There the discussion rested for the time being.

A few days prior to Mr. Jefferson's retirement from the Department of State he submitted a report to the House of Representatives on the subject of American commerce (5), and recommended some form of economic retaliation against nations who would not agree to reciprocal commercial arrangements. In consequence of a growing anti-British sentiment, President Washington decided to send John Jay on a special mission to London in an attempt to effect a settlement (6). The resultant Jay's

Treaty (7) was sharply criticized in the United States, but it was accepted by the President and the Senate, and it postponed, at least, more serious difficulties until a later time.

Meanwhile the controversy between the United States and Spain over boundaries and the navigation of the Mississippi River remained unsettled. In an attempt to settle these difficulties the American minister at London, Thomas Pinckney, was sent to Madrid as a special envoy. A series of fortuitous circumstances enabled Pinckney to conclude a treaty of commerce and amity with the Spanish government (8). The bitter controversies over foreign policies that characterized Washington's administration were reflected in his Farewell Address (9). Placed here in order to indicate its connection with Anglo-American difficulties, the Address might have been placed with equal propriety in the next chapter to show its connection with Franco-American problems. Chronologically it belongs in both places.

◇◇◇◇◇◇◇◇◇◇◇◇◇

1. THE CONTROL OF FOREIGN RELATIONS UNDER THE CONSTITUTION[1]

The Constitution of the United States

Article I

. . . *SECTION 7.* All Bills for raising Revenue shall originate in the House of Representatives; but the Senate may propose or concur with Amendments as on other Bills.

Every Bill which shall have passed the House of Representatives and the Senate, shall, before it become a Law, be presented to the President of the United States; If he approve he shall sign it, but if not he shall return it, with his Objections to that House in which it shall have originated, who shall enter the Objections at large on their Journal, and proceed to reconsider it. If after such Reconsideration two thirds of that House shall agree to pass the Bill, it shall be sent, together with the Objections, to the other House, by which it shall likewise be reconsidered, and if approved by two thirds of that House, it shall become a Law. But in all such Cases the Votes of both Houses shall be determined by Yeas and Nays, and the Names of the Persons voting for and against the Bill shall be entered on the Journal of each House respectively. If any Bill shall not be returned by the President within ten Days (Sundays excepted) after it shall have been presented to him, the Same shall be a Law, in like Manner as if he

[1] The famous two-thirds provision in Article I, Section 2, of the Constitution regarding the advice and consent of the Senate in making treaties, has elicited a large literature. The relationship of this provision to the Jay-Gardoqui negotiations of 1786, and to other contemporary circumstances, and the important subject of treaty making and enforcement had to be omitted here.

had signed it, unless the Congress by their Adjournment prevent its Return, in which Case it shall not be a Law.

Every Order, Resolution, or Vote to which the Concurrence of the Senate and House of Representatives may be necessary (except on a question of Adjournment) shall be presented to the President of the United States; and before the Same shall take Effect, shall be approved by him, or being disapproved by him, shall be repassed by two thirds of the Senate and House of Representatives, according to the Rules and Limitations prescribed in the Case of a Bill.

Section 8. The Congress shall have Power To lay and collect Taxes, Duties, Imposts and Excises. . . .

To regulate Commerce with foreign Nations, and among the several States, and with the Indian Tribes;

To establish an uniform Rule of Naturalization, and uniform Laws on the subject of Bankruptcies throughout the United States. . . .

To define and punish Piracies and Felonies committed on the high Seas, and Offences against the Law of Nations;

To declare War, grant Letters of Marque and Reprisal, and make Rules concerning Captures on Land and Water. . . .

Section 10. No State shall enter into any Treaty, Alliance, or Confederation; grant Letters of Marque and Reprisal. . . .

No State shall, without the Consent of the Congress, lay any Imposts or Duties on Imports or Exports, except what may be absolutely necessary for executing it's inspection Laws: and the net Produce of all Duties and Imposts, laid by any State on Imports or Exports, shall be for the Use of the Treasury of the United States; and all such Laws shall be subject to the Revision and Controul of the Congress.

No State shall, without the Consent of Congress, lay any Duty of Tonnage, keep Troops, or Ships of War in time of Peace, enter into any Agreement or Compact with another State, or with a foreign Power, or engage in War, unless actually invaded, or in such imminent Danger as will not admit of delay. . . .

Article II

. . . *Section 2.* The President shall be Commander in Chief of the Army and Navy of the United States, and of the Militia of the several States, when called into the actual Service of the United States. . . .

He shall have Power, by and with the Advice and Consent of the Senate, to make Treaties, provided two thirds of the Senators present concur; and he shall nominate, and by and with the Advice and Consent of the Senate, shall appoint Ambassadors, other public Ministers . . .

Article III

Section 1. The judicial Power of the United States, shall be vested in one supreme Court, and in such inferior Courts as the Congress may from time to time ordain and establish.

Section 2. The judicial Power shall extend to all Cases, in Law and Equity, arising under this Constitution, the Laws of the United States, and Treaties made, or which shall be made, under their Authority; to all Cases affecting Ambassadors, other public Ministers and Consuls; to all Cases of admiralty and maritime Jurisdiction; to Controversies to which the United States shall be a Party. . . .

ARTICLE IV

Section 3. . . . The Congress shall have Power to dispose of and make all needful Rules and Regulations respecting the Territory or other Property belonging to the United States; and nothing in this Constitution shall be so construed as to Prejudice any Claims of the United States, or of any particular State. . . .

ARTICLE VI

All Debts contracted and Engagements entered into, before the Adoption of this Constitution, shall be as valid against the United States under this Constitution, as under the Confederation.

This Constitution, and the Laws of the United States which shall be made in Pursuance thereof; and all Treaties made, or which shall be made, under the Authority of the United States, shall be the supreme Law of the Land; and the Judges in every State shall be bound thereby, any Thing in the Constitution or Laws of any State to the Contrary notwithstanding. . . .

◇◇◇◇◇◇◇◇◇◇◇◇◇◇

2. THE AMERICAN VIEW OF BRITISH OBLIGATIONS UNDER THE TREATY OF PEACE[2]

[*Thomas Jefferson to George Hammond*]

Philadelphia, December 15, 1791

I AM to acknowledge the honor of your letter of November 30th, and to express the satisfaction with which we learn, that you are instructed to discuss with us the measures, which reason and practicability may dictate, for giving effect to the stipulations of our treaty, yet remaining to be executed. . . . I have the honor to propose that we shall begin by specifying, on each side, the particular acts which each considers to have been done by the other, in contravention of the treaty. I shall set the example.

The provisional and definitive treaties, in their 7th article, stipulated that his "Britannic Majesty should, with all convenient speed, and without causing any destruction, or *carrying away any negroes, or other property,* of the American inhabitants, *withdraw all his armies, garrisons, and fleets,*

[2] Walter Lowrie and Mathew St. Clair Clarke: *American State Papers, Foreign Relations* (Washington, D.C., 1832), Vol. I, p. 190.

from the said United States, and from every port, place, and harbor, within the same."

But the Britsh garrisons were not withdrawn with all convenient speed, nor have ever yet been withdrawn from Michillimackinac, on Lake Michigan; Detroit, on the strait of Lakes Erie and Huron; Fort Erie, on Lake Erie; Niagara, Oswego, on Lake Ontario; Oswegatchie, on the river St. Lawrence; Point Au-fer, and Dutchman's Point, on Lake Champlain.

2d. The British officers have undertaken to exercise a jurisdiction over the country and inhabitants in the vicinities of those forts; and

3d. They have excluded the citizens of the United States from navigating, even on our side of the middle line of the rivers and lakes established as a boundary between the two nations.

By these proceedings, we have been intercepted entirely from the commerce of furs with the Indian nations to the northward — a commerce which had ever been of great importance to the United States, not only for its intrinsic value, but as it was the means of cherishing peace with those Indians, and of superseding the necessity of that expensive warfare we have been obliged to carry on with them, during the time that these posts have been in other hands.

On withdrawing the troops from New York, 1st. A large embarkation of negroes, of the property of the inhabitants of the United States, took place before the commissioners on our part, for inspecting and superintending embarkations, had arrived there, and without any account ever rendered thereof. 2d. Near three thousand others were publicly carried away by the avowed order of the British commanding officer, and under the view, and against the remonstrances of our commissioners. 3d. A very great number were carried off in private vessels, if not by the express permission, yet certainly without opposition on the part of the commanding officer, who alone had the means of preventing it, and without admitting the inspection of the American commissioners; and 4th. Of other species of property carried away, the commanding officer permitted no examination at all. . . .

A difference of opinion too having arisen as to the river intended by the plenipotentiaries to be the boundary between us and the dominions of Great Britain, and by them called the St. Croix, which name, it seems, is given to two different rivers, the ascertaining of this point becomes a matter of present urgency: it has heretofore been the subject of application from us to the Government of Great Britain. . . .

3. THE BRITISH VIEW OF AMERICAN OBLIGATIONS UNDER THE TREATY OF PEACE[3]

[*George Hammond to Thomas Jefferson*]

Philadelphia, March 5, 1792

IN CONFORMITY to the mode which you have pursued and suggested, I have now the honor of submitting to you an abstract of such particular acts of the United States as appear to me infractions, on their part, of the definitive treaty of peace, concluded between the King, my master, and the United States. . . .

Immediately after the ratification of the definitive treaty of peace, the Congress of the United States, by a proclamation, announcing that event, and by a resolve, dated 14 January, 1784, required and enjoined all bodies of magistracy, legislative, executive, and judiciary, to carry into effect the definitive articles, and every clause and sentence thereof, sincerely, strictly, and completely; and earnestly recommended to the Legislatures of the respective States, to provide for the restitution of all estates, rights, and properties, confiscated, belonging to real British subjects, and of estates, rights, and properties of persons resident in districts in possession of his Majesty's arms, between the 30th Nov. 1782, and 14th Jan. 1784, who had not borne arms against the United States; and that persons of any other description should have liberty to go to any part of the United States, to remain twelve months, unmolested in their endeavors to obtain the restitution of their estates, rights, and properties, confiscated. It was also recommended to the several States to reconsider and revise all laws regarding the premises, so as to render them perfectly consistent with justice and that spirit of conciliation, which, on the return of the blessings of peace, should universally prevail; and it was farther recommended, that the estates, rights, and properties of such last mentioned persons should be restored to them, they refunding the bona fide price, paid on purchasing any of the said lands, rights, and properties, since the confiscation. . . .

It is observable that Congress, neither in this proclamation or recommendation, take any notice of the fourth article of the treaty of peace, by which it was *agreed* that creditors on either side should meet with no lawful impediment to the recovery of the full value, in sterling money, of all bona fide debts, theretofore contracted; nor does either the proclamation or recommendation extend to the stipulations in the close of the fifth article, whereby it was *agreed* that all persons who have any interests in confiscated lands, either by debts, marriage settlements, or otherwise, should meet with no lawful impediment in the prosecution of their just rights. . . .

Having thus stated the measures pursued by Congress to give validity and effect to the engagements contained in the treaty of peace, it is now

[3] Lowrie and Clarke: *American State Papers, Foreign Relations*, Vol. I, pp. 193–7.

expedient to specify in detail the particular acts which Great Britain considers as infractions of the treaty on the part of the United States; and it will tend to simplify the discussion to make the following arrangement:

I. To define what Congress has enforced or omitted.

II. To advert to the conduct observed by the individual States generally, in respect to the Treaty of Peace –

In not repealing laws that existed antecedently to the pacification;

In enacting laws, subsequent to the peace, in contravention of the treaty,

And in the decisions of the State courts upon questions affecting the rights of British subjects.

As to the first of these points, it cannot be presumed that the commissioners, who negotiated the treaty of peace, would engage in behalf of Congress to make recommendations to the Legislatures of the respective States, which they did not expect to be effectual, or enter into direct stipulations, which they had not the power to enforce. And yet the laws were not repealed which Congress recommended to be repealed, nor were the stipulations enforced which Congress was absolutely pledged to fulfil. It does not appear that any of the State Legislatures repealed their confiscation laws, or provided for the restitution of all estates, rights, and properties, of real British Subjects, which had been confiscated, and of persons resident in districts in the possession of his Majesty's arms, who had not borne arms against the United States; that persons of other descriptions were at liberty to remain twelve months in the United States, unmolested in their endeavors to obtain the restoration of their confiscated estates, rights, and properties; that the acts of the several States which respected confiscations, were in many of the States reconsidered or revised; nor, finally, have British creditors been countenanced or supported, either by the respective Legislatures, or by the State courts, in their endeavors to recover the full value of debts, contracted antecedently to the treaty of peace. . . .

During the war, the respective legislatures of the United States passed laws to confiscate and sell, to sequester, take possession of, and lease, the estates of the loyalists, and to apply the proceeds thereof towards the redemption of certificates and bills of credit, or towards defraying the expenses of the war; to enable debtors to pay into the State treasuries, or loan offices, paper money, then exceedingly depreciated, in discharge of their debts. Under some of the laws, many individuals were attainted by name, others were banished forever from the country, and, if found within the State, declared felons, without benefit of clergy. In some States, the estates and rights of married women, of widows, and of minors, and of persons who had died within the territories possessed by the British arms, were forfeited. Authority also was given to the Executive department, to require persons who adhered to the crown to surrender themselves, by a given day, and to abide their trials for high treason; in failure of which, the parties so required were attainted, were subject to, and suffered, all the pains, penalties, and forfeitures, awarded against persons attainted of high treason. In one State, (New York) a power was vested in the courts to prefer bills of indictment against persons alive or dead, who had adhered to the King, or joined his fleets or armies, if in full life, and generally reputed to hold or claim, or, if dead, to have held or claimed, at the time of their decease, real or personal estate. And upon notice or neglect to appear and traverse the indictment, or, upon trial and conviction, the persons charged in the indictment, whether *in full life or deceased,* were respectively declared guilty of the offences charged, and their estates were forfeited, whether in possession, reversion, or remainder. In some of the States, confiscated property was applied to the purposes of public buildings and improvements; in others, was appropriated as rewards to individuals for military services rendered during the war; and, in one instance, property mortgaged to a British creditor was liberated from the incumbance by a special act of the Legislature, as a provision for the representatives of the mortgager, who had fallen in battle.

A general repeal of these laws, under the stipulated exceptions, would have been a compliance with the terms of the treaty of peace. . . .

Such is the nature of the specific facts which the King, my master, has considered as infractions of the treaty on the part of the United States, and, in consequence of which, his Majesty has deemed it expedient to suspend the full execution, on his part, of the 7th article of that treaty. On this head, also, it is necessary to premise the following evident distinction: that the King has contented himself with a mere suspension of that article of the treaty; whereas, the United States have not only withheld from subjects of the crown that redress to which they were entitled, under the terms of the treaty, but, also, many of the States have, subsequent to the peace, passed new legislative regulations, in violation of the treaty, and imposing additional hardships on individuals, whom the national faith of the United States was pledged, under precise and solemn stipulations, to ensure and protect from future injury. . . .

◇◇◇◇◇◇◇◇◇◇◇◇◇

4. JEFFERSON'S REPLY TO HAMMOND'S NOTE OF MARCH 5, 1792[4]

Philadelphia, May 29, 1792

YOUR FAVOR of March 5th has been longer unanswered than consisted with my wishes, to forward as much as possible explanations of the several matters it contained. But these matters were very various, and the evidence of them not easily to be obtained, even where it could be obtained at all. It has been a work of time and trouble, to collect from the different States all the acts themselves, of which you had cited the titles, and to investigate the judiciary decisions which were classed with those acts as infractions

[4] Lowrie and Clarke: *American State Papers, Foreign Relations,* Vol. I, pp. 201–16.

of the treaty of peace. To these causes of delay may be added the daily duties of my office, necessarily multiplied during the sessions of the Legislature.

Section 1. I can assure you with truth, that we meet you on this occasion, with the sincerest dispositions to remove from between the two countries those obstacles to a cordial friendship, which have arisen from an inexecution of some articles of the treaty of peace. The desire entertained by this country, to be on the best terms with yours, has been constant, and has manifested itself through its different forms of administration, by repeated overtures to enter into such explanations and arrangements as should be right and necessary to bring about a complete execution of the treaty. The same dispositions lead us to wish, that the occasion now presented should not be defeated by useless recapitulations of what had taken place anterior to that instrument. It was with concern, therefore, I observed that you had thought it necessary to go back to the very commencement of the war, and in several parts of your letter to enumerate and comment on all the acts of our different Legislatures, passed during the whole course of it, in order to deduce from thence, imputations which your justice would have suppressed, had the whole truth been presented to your view, instead of particular traits, detached from the ground on which they stood. However easy it would be to justify our country, by bringing into view the whole ground, on both sides, to show that Legislative warfare began with the British Parliament; that when they levelled at persons or property, it was against entire towns or countries, without discrimination of cause or conduct, while we touched individuals only; naming them man by man, after due consideration of each case, and careful attention not to confound the innocent with the guilty; however advantageously we might compare the distant and tranquil situation of their Legislature with the scenes in the midst of which ours were obliged to legislate; and might then ask, whether the difference of circumstance and situation would not have justified a contrary difference of conduct, and whether the wonder ought to be, that our Legislatures had done so much, or so little? We will waive all this, because it would lead to recollections, as unprofitable as unconciliating. . . .

Section 2. We now come together to consider that instrument which was to heal our wounds, and begin a new chapter in our history. The state in which that found things, is to be considered as rightful: so says the law of nations. . . . It was stipulated, indeed, by the ninth article, that "if, before its arrival in America," any place or territory, belonging to either party, should be conquered by the arms of the other, it should be restored. This was the only case in which transactions, intervening between the signature and publication, were to be nullified.

Congress, on the 24th of March, 1783, received informal intelligence from the Marquis de la Fayette, that provisional articles were concluded; and, on the same day, they received a copy of the articles, in a letter of March 19th, from General Carleton and Admiral Digby. They immediately gave orders for recalling all armed vessels, and communicated the orders to those officers, who answered, on the 26th and 27th, that they were not authorized to concur in the recall of armed vessels, on their part. On the 11th of April, Congress receive an official copy of these articles from Doctor Franklin, with notice that a preliminary treaty was now signed between France, Spain, and England. The event having now taken place on which the provisional articles were to come into effect, on the usual footing of preliminaries, Congress immediately proclaim them, and, on the 19th of April, a cessation of hostilities is published by the commander-in-chief. These particulars place all acts preceding the 11th of April out of the present discussion, and confine it to the treaty itself, and the circumstances attending its execution. I have therefore taken the liberty of extracting from your list of American acts all of those preceding that epoch, and of throwing them together in the paper No. 6, as things out of question. The subsequent acts shall be distributed, according to their several subjects, of I. Exile and confiscation: II. Debts: and III. Interest on those debts:

Beginning, I. with those of exile and confiscation, which will be considered together, because blended together in most of the acts, and blended also in the same article of the treaty.

Sect. 3. It cannot be denied that the state of war strictly permits a nation to seize the property of its enemies found within its own limits, or taken in war, and in whatever form it exists, whether in action or possession. . . . Yet the confiscations of property [5] were by no means universal, and that of debts still less so. What effect was to be produced on them by the treaty, will be seen by the words of the fifth article. . . .[6]

Sect. 5. Observe, that in every other article, the parties agree expressly, that such and such things *shall be done;* in this, they only agree to *recommend* that they shall be done. You are pleased to say, (page 7) "It cannot be presumed, that the Commissioners, who negotiated the treaty of peace, would engage, in behalf of Congress, to make *recommendations* to the Legislatures of the respective States, which they did not expect to be effectual, or enter into direct stipulations which they had not the power to enforce." On the contrary, we may fairly presume, that, if they had had the power to *enforce,* they would not merely have *recommended.* When, in every other article, they agree expressly *to do,* why in this do they change the style suddenly, and agree only to *recommend*? Because the things here proposed to be done were retrospective in their nature — would tear up the laws of the several States, and the contracts and transactions, private and public, which had taken place under them; and retrospective laws were forbidden by the constitutions of several of the States. Between persons whose native language is that of this treaty, it is unnecessary to explain the difference between *enacting* a thing to be done, and *recommending* it to be done; the words themselves being as well under-

5 Confiscations of the property of British subjects and Loyalists.

6 Article V of the Treaty of 1783, see page 41.

stood as any by which they could be explained. But it may not be unnecessary to observe, that *recommendations* to the people, instead of *laws*, had been introduced among us, and were rendered familiar in the interval between discontinuing the old, and establishing the new governments. The conventions and committees who then assembled, to guide the conduct of the People, having no authority to oblige them by law, took up the practice of simply recommending measures to them. These recommendations they either complied with or not, at their pleasure. If they refused, there was complaint, but no compulsion. So, after organizing the Governments, if at any time it became expedient that a thing should be done, which Congress, or any other of the organized bodies, were not authorized to ordain, they simply recommended, and left to the People, or their Legislatures, to comply, or not, as they pleased. It was impossible that the negotiators, on either side, should have been ignorant of the difference between agreeing *to do* a thing, and agreeing only to *recommend* it to be done. The import of the terms is so different, that no deception or surprise could be supposed, even if there were no evidence that the difference was attended to, explained, and understood.

Sect. 6. But the evidence on this occasion removes all question. It is well known, that the British court had it extremely at heart, to procure a restitution of the estates of the refugees who had gone over to their side; that they proposed it in the first conferences, and insisted on it to the last; that our commissioners, on the other hand, refused it from first to last, urging, 1st. That it was unreasonable to restore the confiscated property of the refugees, unless they would reimburse the destruction of the property of our citizens, committed on their part; and 2ndly, That it was beyond the powers of the commissioners to stipulate, or of Congress to enforce. On this point, the treaty hung long. It was the subject of a special mission of a confidential agent of the British negotiator from Paris to London. It was still insisted on, on his return, and still protested against, by our commissioners; and when they were urged to agree only, that Congress should *recommend* to the State Legislatures to restore the estates, etc. of the refugees, they were expressly told that the Legislatures would not regard the recommendation. In proof of this, I subjoin extracts from the letters and journals of Mr. Adams and Dr. Franklin, two of our commissioners, the originals of which are among the records of the Department of State, and shall be open to you for a verification of the copies. These prove, beyond all question, that the difference between an express agreement to do a thing, and to recommend it to be done, was well understood by both parties, and that the British negotiators were put on their guard by those on our part, not only that the Legislatures would be free to refuse, but that they probably would refuse. And it is evident, from all circumstances, that Mr. Oswald accepted the *recommendation* merely to have something to oppose to the clamors of the refugees — to keep alive a hope in them, that they might yet get their property from the State Legislatures; and that, if they should fail in this, they would have ground to demand indemnification from their own Government; and he might think it a circumstance of present relief at least, that the question of indemnification by them should be kept out of sight, till time and events should open it upon the nation insensibly. . . .

Sect. 9. The British negotiators had been told by ours, that all the States would refuse to comply with this recommendation; one only, however, refused altogether. The others complied in a greater or less degree . . . but, had all of them refused, it would have been no violation of the 5th article. . . .

[*In the following 13 sections of his note Mr. Jefferson considered the acts passed by each of the thirteen states in order to prove that the recommendations of Congress to the states in accordance with the Treaty of Peace, had been fulfilled.*]

Sec. 23. And we may further observe, with respect to the same acts, that they have been considered as infractions not only of the 5th article, which recommended the restoration of the confiscations which *had taken place during the war*, but also of that part of the 6th article which forbade *future* confiscations. But not one of them touched an estate which had not been before confiscated: for you will observe, that an act of the Legislature, confiscating lands, stands in place of *an office found* in ordinary cases; and that, *on the passage of the act,* as *on the finding of the office,* the States stands, ipso facto, possessed of the lands, without a formal entry. The confiscation then is complete by the passage of the act. Both the title and possession being divested out of the former proprietor, and vested in the State, no subsequent proceedings relative to the lands are acts of confiscation, but are mere exercises of ownership, whether by levying profits, conveying for a time, by lease, or in perpetuo, by an absolute deed. I believe, therefore, it may be said with truth, that there was not a single confiscation made in any one of the United States, after notification of the treaty. . . .

Sect. 26. II. The article of debts is next in order; but to place in their true grounds our proceedings relative to them, it will be necessary to take a view of the British proceedings, which are the subject of complaint in my letter of December 15. . . .

[*Mr. Jefferson proceeded to analyze the British infractions of the treaty. He also noted the promise made by the British minister of foreign affairs that the British government would fulfill its obligations as soon as the United States fulfilled theirs. This promise was made February 28, 1786.*]

Sect. 38. . . . The Secretary for Foreign Affairs of the United States, by order of Congress, immediately wrote circular letters to the Governors of the several States, dated May 3, 1786, No. 31, to obtain information how far they had complied with the proclamation of January 14, 1784. . . .

Sect. 39. In consequence of these letters, New Hampshire, Massachusetts, Rhode Island, Connecticut, New York, Delaware, Maryland, Virginia and North Carolina, passed the acts No. 32, 33, 34, 35, 36, 37, 38, 39, 40.[7] New Jersey and Pennsylvania declared that no law existed with them repugnant to the treaty. . . . Georgia had no law existing against the treaty. South Carolina, indeed, had a law existing. . . . But the liberality of her conduct on the other points is proof that she would have conformed in this also, had it appeared that the fullest conformity would have moved Great Britain to compliance, and had an express repeal been really necessary. . . .

Sect. 57. I have now, sir, gone through the several acts and proceedings enumerated in your appendix, as infractions of the treaty, omitting, I believe, not a single one, as may be seen by a table hereto subjoined, wherein every one of them, as marked and numbered in your appendix, is referred to the section of this letter in which it is brought into view; and the result has been, as you have seen –

1. That there was no absolute stipulation to restore *antecedent* confiscations, and that none *subsequent* took place;

2. That the recovery of the debts was obstructed *validly* in none of our States, *invalidly* only in a few, and that not till long after the infractions committed on the other side; and

3. That the decisions of courts and juries against the claims of interest are too probably founded to give cause for questioning their integrity. These things being evident, I cannot but flatter myself, after the assurances received from you of his Britannic Majesty's desire to remove every occasion of misunderstanding from between us, that an end will now be put to the disquieting situation of the two countries, by as complete execution of the treaty as circumstances render practicable at this late day: that it is to be done so late has been the source of heavy losses, of blood, and treasure, to the United States. Still our desire of friendly accommodation is, and has been, constant. No *"lawful impediment* has been opposed to the prosecution of the just rights of your citizens." And if any instances of *unlawful* impediment have existed in any of the inferior tribunals, they would, like other unlawful proceedings, have been overruled on appeal to the higher courts. If not overruled there, a complaint to the Government would have been regular, and their interference probably effectual. If your citizens would not prosecute their rights, it was impossible they should recover them, or be denied recovery; and till a denial of right through all the tribunals, there is no ground for complaint, much less for a refusal to comply with solemn stipulations, the execution of which is too important to us ever to be dispensed with. These difficulties being removed from between the two nations, I am persuaded the interests of both will be found in the strictest friendship. The considerations which lead to it are too numerous and forcible to fail of their effect; and that they may be permitted to have their full effect, no one wishes more sincerely than he, who has the honor to be, &c.

[7] These numbers refer to documents appended to Jefferson's note which quote the laws of the several states.

◇◇◇◇◇◇◇◇◇◇◇◇◇

5. REPORT OF THE SECRETARY OF STATE ON THE PRIVILEGES AND RESTRICTIONS ON THE COMMERCE OF THE UNITED STATES IN FOREIGN COUNTRIES[8]

Philadelphia, Dec. 16, 1793

THE SECRETARY of State, to whom was referred, by the House of Representatives, the report of a committee on the written message of the President of the United States, of the 14th of February, 1791, with instruction to report to Congress the nature and extent of the privileges and restrictions of the commercial intercourse of the United States with Foreign nations, and the measures which he should think proper to be adopted for the improvement of the commerce and navigation of the same, has had the same under consideration, and thereupon makes the following report: [9]

. . . Such being the restrictions on the commerce and navigation of the United States, the question is, in what way they may best be removed, modified, or counteracted?

As to commerce, two methods occur. 1. By friendly arrangements with the several nations with whom these restrictions exist; or, 2. By the separate act of our own Legislatures for countervailing their effects.

There can be no doubt but that, of these two, friendly arrangement is the most eligible. Instead of embarrassing commerce under piles of regulating laws, duties, and prohibitions, could it be relieved from all its shackles in all parts of the world; could every country be employed in producing that which nature has best fitted it to produce, and each be free to exchange with others mutual surplusses for mutual wants, the greatest mass possible would then be produced of those things which contribute to human life and human happiness; the numbers of mankind would be increased, and their condition bettered. . . .

But should any nation, contrary to our wishes, suppose it may better find its advantage by continuing its system of prohibitions, duties, and regulations, it behooves us to protect our citizens, their commerce, and navigation, by counter prohibitions, duties, and regulations, also. Free commerce and navigation are not to be given in exchange for restrictions and vexations, nor are they likely to produce a relaxation of them.

Our navigation involves still higher considerations. As a branch of industry, it is valuable, but as a resource of defence, essential.

Its value, as a branch of industry, is enhanced by the dependence of so many other branches on it. In times of general peace, it multiplies competitors for employment in transportation, and so keeps that at its proper

[8] Lowrie and Clarke: *American State Papers, Foreign Relations,* Vol. I, pp. 300–4.

[9] The first part of the report is a summary of American foreign commerce.

level; and in times of war, that is to say, when those nations who may be our principal carriers, shall be at war with each other, if we have not within ourselves the means of transportation, our produce must be exported in belligerent vessels, at the increased expense of war-freight and insurance, and the articles which will not bear that, must perish on our hands.

But it is as a resource of defence, that our navigation will admit neither neglect nor forbearance. The position and circumstances of the United States leave them nothing to fear on their land-board, and nothing to desire beyond their present rights. But on their sea-board, they are open to injury, and they have there, too, a commerce, which must be protected. This can only be done by possessing a respectable body of citizen-seamen, and of artists and establishments in readiness for ship-building.

Were the ocean, which is the common property of all, open to the industry of all, so that every person and vessel should be free to take employment wherever it could be found, the United States would certainly not set the example of appropriating to themselves, exclusively, any portion of the common stock of occupation. They would rely on the enterprise and activity of their citizens, for a due participation of the benefits of the seafaring business, and for keeping the marine class of citizens equal to their object. But if particular nations grasp at undue shares, and, more especially, if they seize on the means of the United States, to convert them into aliment for their own strength, and withdraw them entirely from the support of those to whom they belong, defensive and protecting measures become necessary on the part of the nation whose marine resources are thus invaded; or it will be disarmed of its defence, its productions will lie at the mercy of the nation which has possessed itself exclusively of the means of carrying them, and its politics may be influenced by those who command its commerce. The carriage of our own commodities, if once established in another channel, cannot be resumed in the moment we may desire. If we lose the seamen and artists whom it now occupies, we lose the present means of marine defence, and time will be requisite to raise up others, when disgrace or losses shall bring to our feelings, the error of having abandoned them. The materials for maintaining our due share of navigation, are ours in abundance. And, as to the mode of using them, we have only to adopt the principles of those who thus put us on the defensive, or others equivalent and better fitted to our circumstances. . . .

2. Where a nation refuses permission to our merchants and factors to reside within certain parts of their dominions, we may, if it should be thought expedient, refuse residence to theirs in any and every part of ours, or modify their transactions.

3. Where a nation refuses to receive, in our vessels, any productions but our own, we may refuse to receive, in theirs, any but their own productions. The first and second clauses of the bill reported by the committee, are well formed to effect this object.

4. Where a nation refuses to consider any vessel as ours, which has not been built within our territories, we should refuse to consider as theirs, any vessel not built within their territories.

5. Where a nation refuses to our vessels, the carriage even of our own productions, to certain countries under their domination, we might refuse to theirs of every description, the carriage of the same productions to the same countries. But, as justice and good neighborhood would dictate that those who have no part in imposing the restriction on us, should not be the victims of measures adopted to defeat its effect, it may be proper to confine the restriction to vessels owned or navigated by any subjects of the same dominant power, other than the inhabitants of the country to which the said productions are to be carried. And to prevent all inconvenience to the said inhabitants, and to our own, by too sudden a check on the means of transportation, we may continue to admit the vessels marked for future exclusion, on an advanced tonnage, and for such length of time only, as may be supposed necessary to provide against that inconvenience.

The establishment of some of these principles by Great Britain, alone, has already lost us in our commerce with that country and its possessions, between eight and nine hundred vessels of near 40,000 tons burden, according to statements from official materials, in which they have confidence. This involves a proportional loss of seamen, shipwrights, and ship-building, and is too serious a loss to admit forbearance of some effectual remedy.

It is true, we must expect some inconvenience in practice from the establishment of discriminating duties. But in this, as in so many other cases, we are left to choose between two evils. These inconveniences are nothing, when weighed against the loss of wealth and loss of force, which will follow our perseverance in the plan of indiscrimination. When once it shall be perceived that we are either in the system or in the habit of giving equal advantages to those who extinguish our commerce and navigation by duties and prohibitions, as to those who treat both with liberality and justice, liberality and justice will be converted by all, into duties and prohibitions. It is not to the moderation and justice of others we are to trust for fair and equal access to market with our productions, or for our due share in the transportation of them; but to our own means of independence, and the firm will to use them. Nor do the inconveniences of discrimination merit consideration. Not one of the nations before mentioned, perhaps not a commercial nation on earth, is without them. In our case, one distinction alone will suffice: that is to say, between nations who favor our productions and navigation, and those who do not favor them. One set of moderate duties, say the present duties, for the first, and a fixed advance on these as to some articles, and prohibitions as to others, for the last.

Still, it must be repeated, that friendly arrangements are preferable with all who will come into them; and, that we should carry into such arrangements, all the liberality and spirit of accommodation which the nature of the case will admit.

◇◇◇◇◇◇◇◇◇◇◇◇

6. INSTRUCTIONS TO JOHN JAY[10]

Philadelphia, May 6, 1794

THE MISSION upon which you are about to enter, as envoy extraordinary to the court of London, has been dictated by considerations of an interesting and pressing nature. . . .

A full persuasion is entertained that, throughout the whole negotiation, you will make the following its general objects: To keep alive in the mind of the British minister that opinion which the solemnity of a special mission must naturally inspire, of the strong agitations excited in the people of the United States, by the disturbed condition of things between them and Great Britain; to repel war, for which we are not disposed, and into which the necessity of vindicating our honor and our property may, but can alone, drive us; to prevent the British ministry, should they be resolved on war, from carrying with them the British nation; and, at the same time, to assert, with dignity and firmness, our rights, and our title to reparation for past injuries. . . .

You will perceive that one of the principles, upon which compensation is demanded for the injuries under the instructons of the 8th of June, 1793, is, that provisions, except in the instance of a seige, blockade, or investment, are not to be ranked among contraband. To a country remote as the United States are from Europe and its troubles, it will be of infinite advantage to obtain the establishment of this doctrine. . . .

Compensation for all the injuries sustained, and captures, will be strenuously pressed by you. The documents which the agent in the West Indies is directed to transmit to London will place these matters in the proper legal train, to be heard on appeal. It cannot be doubted that the British ministry will insist that, before we complain to them, their tribunals, in the last resort, must have refused justice. This is true in general; but peculiarities distinguish the present from past cases. Where the error complained of consists solely in the misapplication of the law, it may be corrected by a superior court; but where the error consists in the law itself, it can be corrected only by the law maker, who, in this instance, was the King, or it must be compensated by the Government. The principle, therefore, may be discussed and settled without delay; and, even if you should be told to wait until the result of the appeals shall appear, it may be safely said to be almost certain that some one judgment in the West

[10] Lowrie and Clarke: *American State Papers, Foreign Relations*, Vol. I, pp. 472–4.

Indies will be confirmed; and this will be sufficient to bring the principle in question with the British ministry. . . .

If the British ministry should hint at any supposed predilection in the United States for the French nation, as warranting the whole or any part of these instructions, you will stop the progress of this subject, as being irrelative to the question in hand. It is a circumstance which the British nation have no right to object to us; because we are free in our affections and independent in our government. But it may be safely answered, upon the authority of the correspondence between the Secretary of State and Mr. Hammond, that our neutrality has been scrupulously observed.

II. A second cause of your mission, but not inferior in dignity to the preceding, though subsequent in order, is to draw to a conclusion all points of difference between the United States and Great Britain, concerning the treaty of peace. . . .

In this negotiation as to the treaty of peace, we have been amused by transferring the discussions concerning its inexecution and infractions from one side of the Atlantic to the other. In the mean time, one of the consequences of holding the posts has been much bloodshed on our frontiers by the Indians, and much expense. The British Government having denied their abetting of the Indians, we must of course acquit them. But we have satisfactory proofs, (some of which, however, cannot, as you will discover, be well used in public) that British agents are guilty of stirring up, and assisting with arms, ammunition, and warlike implements, the different tribes of Indians against us. It is incumbent upon that Government to restrain those agents; or the forbearance to restrain them cannot be interpreted otherwise than as a determination to countenance them. It is a principle from which the United States will not easily depart, either in their conduct towards other nations, or what they expect from them, that the Indians dwelling within the territories of one shall not be interfered with by the other.

It may be observed here, as comprehending both of the foregoing points, that the United States testify their sincere love of peace, by being nearly in a state of war, and yet anxious to obviate absolute war by friendly advances; and if the desire of Great Britain to be in harmony with the United States be equally sincere, she will readily discover what kind of sensations will at length arise, when their trade is plundered; their resources wasted in an Indian war; many of their citizens exposed to the cruelties of the savages; their rights by treaty denied; and those of Great Britain enforced in our courts. But you will consider the inexecution and infraction of the treaty as standing on distinct grounds from the vexations and spoliations: so that no adjustment of the former is to be influenced by the latter.

III. It is referred to your discretion whether, in case the two preceding points should be so accommodated as to promise the continuance of tranquillity between the United States and Great Britain, the subject of a commercial treaty may not be listened to by you, or even broken to the British ministry. If it should, let these be the general objects:

1st. Reciprocity in navigation, particularly to the West Indies and even to the East Indies.

2d. The admission of wheat, fish, salt meat, and other great staples, upon the same footing with the admission of the great British staples in our ports.

3d. Free ships to make free goods.

4th. Proper security for the safety of neutral commerce in other respects; and particularly,

By declaring provisions never to be contraband, except in the strongest possible case, as the blockade of a port; or, if attainable, by abolishing contraband altogether:

By defining a blockade, if contraband must continue in some degree, as it is defined in the armed neutrality:

By restricting the opportunities of vexation in visiting vessels: and

By bringing under stricter management privateers; and expediting recoveries against them for misconduct.

5th. Exemption of emigrants, and particularly manufacturers, from restraint.

6th. Free exports of arms and military stores.

7th. The exclusion of the terms "the most favored nation," as being productive of embarrassment.

8th. The convoy of merchant ships by the public ships of war, where it shall be necessary, and they be holding the same course.

9th. It is anxiously to be desired, that the fishing grounds now engrossed by the British should be opened to the citizens of the United States.

10th. The intercourse with England makes it necessary that the disabilities, arising from alienage in cases of inheritance, should be put upon a liberal footing, or rather abolished.

11th. You may discuss the sale of prizes in our ports while we are neutral; and this perhaps may be added to the considerations which we have to give, besides those of reciprocity.

12th. Proper shelter, defence, and succor, against pirates, shipwreck, etc.

13th. Full security for the retiring of the citizens of the United States from the British dominions, in case a war should break out.

14th. No privateering commissions to be taken out by the subjects of the one, or citizens of the other party, against each other.

15th. Consuls, etc., to be admitted in Europe, the West and East Indies.

16th. In case of an Indian war, none but the usual supplies in peace shall be furnished.

17th. In peace, no troops to be kept within a limited distance from the Lakes.

18th. No stipulation whatsoever is to interfere with our obligations to France.

19th. A treaty is not to continue beyond fifteen years. . . .

But if a treaty of commerce cannot be formed upon a basis as advantageous as this, you are not to conclude or sign any such; it being conceived that it would not be expedient to do any thing more than to digest with the British ministry the articles of such a treaty as they appear willing to accede to; referring them here for consideration and further instruction previous to a formal conclusion. . . .

V. You will have no difficulty in gaining access to the ministers of Russia, Denmark, and Sweden, at the court of London. The principles of the armed neutrality would abundantly cover our neutral rights. If, therefore, the situation of things with respect to Great Britain should dictate the necessity of taking the precaution of foreign co-operation upon this head; if no prospect of accommodation should be thwarted by the danger of such a measure being known to the British court; and if an entire view of all our political relations shall, in your judgment, permit the step, you will sound those ministers upon the probability of an alliance with their nations to support those principles. . . .

VI. Such are the outlines of the conduct which the President wishes you to pursue. He is aware that, at this distance, and during the present instability of public events, he cannot undertake to prescribe rules, which shall be irrevocable. You will therefore consider the ideas, herein expressed, as amounting to recommendations only, which in your discretion you may modify, as seems most beneficial to the United States, except in the two following cases, which are immutable. 1st. That, as the British ministry will doubtless be solicitous to detach us from France, and may probably make some overture of this kind, you will inform them that the Government of the United States will not derogate from our treaties and engagements with France, and that experience has shown, that we can be honest in our duties to the British nation, without laying ourselves under any particular restraints as to other nations; and 2d. That no treaty of commerce be concluded or signed contrary to the foregoing prohibition.

◇◇◇◇◇◇◇◇◇◇◇◇◇◇

7. TREATY OF COMMERCE AND NAVIGATION BETWEEN THE UNITED STATES AND GREAT BRITAIN: 1794[11]

[*Concluded November 19, 1794; ratifications exchanged October 28, 1795; proclaimed February 29, 1796*]

. . . *ARTICLE II.* His Majesty will withdraw all His Troops and Garrisons from all Posts and Places within the Boundary Lines assigned by the Treaty of Peace to the United States. This Evacuation shall take place on or before the first Day of June One thousand seven hundred and ninety six. . . .

Article III. It is agreed that it shall at all Times be free to His Majesty's

[11] Hunter Miller: *Treaties and Other International Acts of the United States of America,* Vol. II, pp. 245–67.

Subjects, and to the Citizens of the United States, and also to the Indians dwelling on either side of the said Boundary Line freely to pass and repass by Land, or Inland Navigation, into the respective Territories and Countries of the Two Parties on the Continent of America (the Country within the Limits of the Hudson's Bay Company only excepted) and to navigate all the Lakes, Rivers, and waters thereof, and freely to carry on trade and commerce with each other. But it is understood, that this Article does not extend to the admission of Vessels of the United States into the Sea Ports, Harbours, Bays, or Creeks of His Majesty's said Territories; nor into such parts of the Rivers in His Majesty's said Territories as are between the mouth thereof, and the highest Port of Entry from the Sea, except in small vessels trading bona fide between Montreal and Quebec, under such regulations as shall be established to prevent the possibility of any Frauds in this respect. Nor to the admission of British vessels from the Sea into the Rivers of the United States, beyond the highest Ports of Entry for Foreign Vessels from the Sea. The River Mississippi, shall however, according to the Treaty of Peace be entirely open to both Parties; And it is further agreed, That all the ports and places on its Eastern side, to whichsoever of the parties belonging, may freely be resorted to, and used by both parties, in as ample a manner as any of the Atlantic Ports or Places of the United States, or any of the Ports or Places of His Majesty in Great Britain. . . .

Article VI. Whereas it is alledged by divers British Merchants and others His Majesty's Subjects, that Debts to a considerable amount which were bónâ fide contracted before the Peace, still remain owing to them by Citizens or Inhabitants of the United States. . . . It is agreed that in all such Cases where full Compensation for such losses and damages cannot, for whatever reason, be actually obtained had and received by the said Creditors in the ordinary course of Justice, The United States will make full and complete Compensation for the same to the said Creditors. . . .

Article X. Neither the Debts due from Individuals of the one Nation, to Individuals of the other, nor shares, nor monies, which they may have in the public funds, or in the public or private Banks shall ever, in any Event of war, or national differences be sequestered, or confiscated, it being unjust and impolitick that Debts and Engagements contracted and made by Individuals having confidence in each other, and in their respective Governments, should ever be destroyed or impaired by national authority, on account of national Differences and Discontents. . . .

Article XII. His Majesty Consents that it shall and may be lawful, during the time hereinafter Limited, for the Citizens of the United States, to carry to any of His Majesty's Islands and Ports in the West Indies from the United States in their own Vessels, not being above the burthen of Seventy Tons, any Goods or Merchandizes, being of the Growth, Manufacture, or Produce of the said States, which it is, or may be lawful to carry to the said Islands or Ports from the said States in British Vessels, and that the said American Vessels shall be subject there to no other or higher Tonnage Duties or Charges, than shall be payable by British vessels, in the Ports of the United States; and that the Cargoes of the said American Vessels shall, be subject there to no other or higher Duties or Charges, than shall be payable on the like Articles, if imported there from the said States in British vessels.

And His Majesty also consents that it shall be lawful for the said American Citizens to purchase, load and carry away, in their said vessels to the United States from the said Islands and Ports, all such articles being of the Growth, Manufacture or Produce of the said Islands, as may now by Law be carried from thence to the said States in British Vessels, and subject only to the same Duties and Charges on Exportation to which British Vessels and their Cargoes are or shall be subject in similar circumstances.

Provided always that the said American vessels do carry and land their Cargoes in the United States only, it being expressly agreed and declared that during the Continuance of this article, the United States will prohibit and restrain the carrying any Meolasses, Sugar, Coffee, Cocoa or Cotton in American vessels, either from His Majesty's Islands or from the United States, to any part of the World, except the United States, reasonable Sea Stores excepted. Provided, also, that it shall and may be lawful during the same period for British vessels to import from the said Islands into the United States, and to export from the United States to the said Islands, all Articles whatever being of the Growth, Produce or Manufacture of the said Islands, or of the United States respectively, which now may, by the Laws of the said States, be so imported and exported. And that the Cargoes of the said British vessels, shall be subject to no other or higher Duties or Charges, than shall be payable on the same articles if so imported or exported in American Vessels.

It is agreed that this Article, and every Matter and Thing therein contained, shall continue to be in Force, during the Continuance of the war in which His Majesty is now engaged; and also for Two years from and after the Day of the signature of the Preliminary or other Articles of Peace by which the same may be terminated. . . .

Article XVIII. In order to regulate what is in future to be esteemed Contraband of war, it is agreed that under the said Denomination shall be comprized all Arms and Implements serving for the purposes of war . . . as also Timber for Shipbuilding, Tar or Rosin, Copper in Sheets, Sails, Hemp, and Cordage, and generally whatever may serve directly to the equipment of Vessels, unwrought Iron and Fir planks only excepted, and all the above articles are hereby declared to be just objects of Confiscation, whenever they are attempted to be carried to an Enemy.

And Whereas the difficulty of agreeing on the precise Cases in which alone Provisions and other articles not generally contraband may be regarded as such, renders it expedient to provide against the inconveniences and misunderstandings which might thence arise: It is further agreed that whenever any such articles so becoming Contraband according to the existing Laws of Nations, shall for that reason be seized, the same shall not be confiscated, but the owners thereof shall be speedily and completely indemnified; and the Captors, or in their default the Government under whose authority they act, shall pay to the Masters or Owners of such Vessels the full value of all such Articles, with a reasonable mercantile Profit thereon, together with the Freight, and also the Demurrage incident to such Detension. . . .

Article XXIV. It shall not be lawful for any Foreign Privateers (not being Subjects or Citizens of either of the said Parties) who have Commissions from any other Prince or State in enmity with either Nation, to arm their Ships in the Ports of either of the said Parties, nor to sell what they have taken, nor in any other manner to exchange the same, nor shall they be allowed to purchase more provisions than shall be necessary for their going to the nearest Port of that Prince or State from whom they obtained their Commissions.

Article XXV. It shall be lawful for the Ships of war and Privateers belonging to the said Parties respectively to carry whithersoever they please the Ships and Goods taken from their Enemies without being obliged to pay any Fee to the Officers of the Admiralty, or to any Judges whatever; nor shall the said Prizes when they arrive at, and enter the Ports of the said Parties be detained or seized, neither shall the Searchers or other Officers of those Places visit such Prizes (except for the purpose of preventing the Carrying of any of the Cargo thereof on Shore in any manner contrary to the established Laws of Revenue, Navigation or Commerce) nor shall such Officers take Cognizance of the Validity of such Prizes; but they shall be at liberty to hoist Sail, and depart as speedily as may be, and carry their said Prizes to the place mentioned in their Commissions or Patents, which the Commanders of the said Ships of war or Privateers shall be obliged to shew. No Shelter or Refuge shall be given in their Ports to such as have made a Prize upon the Subjects or Citizens of either of the said Parties; but if forced by stress of weather or the Dangers of the Sea, to enter therein, particular care shall be taken to hasten their departure, and to cause them to retire as soon as possible. Nothing in this Treaty contained shall however be construed or operate contrary to former and existing Public Treaties with other Sovereigns or States. But the Two parties agree, that while they continue in amity neither of them will in future make any Treaty that shall be inconsistent with this or the preceding article. . . .

Article XXVIII. It is agreed that the first Ten Articles of this Treaty shall be permanent and that the subsequent Articles except the Twelfth shall be limited in their duration to Twelve years. . . .

Additional Article.[12] It is further agreed between the said contracting parties, that the operation of so much of the twelfth Article of the said Treaty as respects the trade which his said Majesty thereby consents may

[12] Amendment of the Senate by its resolution advising ratification, June 24, 1795, accepted by Great Britain.

be carried on between the United States and his Islands in the West Indies, in the manner and on the terms and conditions therein specified, shall be suspended.

◇◇◇◇◇◇◇◇◇◇◇◇◇

8. TREATY OF FRIENDSHIP, BOUNDARIES, COMMERCE, AND NAVIGATION BETWEEN THE UNITED STATES AND SPAIN: 1795[13]

[*Concluded October 27, 1795; ratifications exchanged April 25, 1796*]

. . . *ARTICLE II.* To prevent all disputes on the subject of the boundaries which separate the territories of the two High contracting Parties, it is hereby declared and agreed as follows: to wit: The Southern boundary of the United States which divides their territory from the Spanish Colonies of East and West Florida, shall be designated by a line beginning on the River Mississippi at the Northernmost part of the thirtyfirst degree of latitude North of the Equator, which from thence shall be drawn due East to the middle of the River Apalachicola or Catahouche, thence along the middle thereof to its junction with the Flint, thence straight to the head of St. Mary's River, and thence down the middle there of to the Atlantic Ocean. And it is agreed that if there should be any troops, Garrisons or settlements of either Party in the territory of the other according to the abovementioned boundaries, they shall be withdrawn from the said territory within the term of six months after the ratification of this treaty or sooner if it be possible and that they shall be permitted to take with them all the goods and effects which they possess. . . .

Article IV. It is likewise agreed that the Western boundary of the United States which separates them from the Spanish colony of Louissiana, is in the middle of the channel or bed of the River Mississippi from the Northern boundary of the said States to the completion of the thirtyfirst degree of latitude North of the Equator; and his Catholic Majesty has likewise agreed that the navigation of the said River in its whole breadth from its source to the Occean shall be free only to his Subjects, and the Citizens of the United States, unless he should extend this privilege to the Subjects of other Powers by special convention.

Article V. The two High contracting Parties shall by all the means in their power maintain peace and harmony among the several Indian Nations who inhabit the country adjacent to the lines and Rivers which by the preceeding Articles form the boundaries of the two Floridas; and the beter to obtain this effect both Parties oblige themselves expressly to restrain by force all hostilities on the part of the Indian Nations living within their boundaries: so that Spain will not suffer her Indians to attack the

[13] Hunter Miller: *Treaties and Other International Acts of the United States of America,* Vol. II, pp. 318–38.

Citizens of the United States, nor the Indians inhabiting their territory; nor will the United States permit these last-mentioned Indians to commence hostilities against the Subjects of His Catholic Majesty, or his Indians, in any manner whatever. . . .

Article XV. It shall be lawful for all and singular the Subjects of his Catholic Mayesty, and the Citizens People, and inhabitants of the said United States to sail with their Ships with all manner of liberty and security, no distinction being made who are the propietors of the merchandizes laden thereon from any Port to the Places of those who now are or hereafter shall be at enmity with His Catholic Majesty or the United States. It shall be likewise lawful for the Subjects and inhabitants aforesaid to sail with the Ships and merchandizes aforementioned, and to trade with the same liberty and security from the Places, Ports, and Havens of those who are Enemies of both or either Party without any opposition or disturbance whatsoever, not only directly from the Places of the Enemy aforementioned to neutral Places but also from one Place belonging to an Enemy to another Place belonging to an Enemy, whether they be under the jurisdiction of the same Prince or under several, and it is hereby stipulated that Free Ships shall also give freedom to goods, and that every thing shall be deemed free and exempt which shall be found on board the Ships belonging to the Subjects of either of the contracting Parties although the whole lading or any part thereof should appartain to the Enemies of either; contraband goods being always excepted. It is also agreed that the same liberty be extended to persons who are on board a free Ship, so that, although they be Enemies to either Party they shall not be made Prisoners or taken out of that free Ship unless they are Soldiers and in actual service of the Enemies.

Article XVI. This liberty of navigation and commerce shall extend to all kinds of merchandizes excepting those only which are distinguished by the name of contraband; and under this name of contraband or prohibited goods shall be comprehended arms . . . horses with their furniture and all other warlike instruments whatever. . . .

Article XIX. Consuls shall be reciprocally established with the privileges and powers which those of the most favoured Nations enjoy in the Ports where their consuls reside, or are permitted to be. . . .

Article XXII. . . . And in consequence of the stipulations contained in the IV article his Catholic Majesty will permit the Citizens of the United States for the space of three years from this time to deposit their merchandize and effects in the Port of New Orleans, and to export them from thence without paying any other duty than a fair price for the hire of the stores, and his Majesty promises either to continue this permission if he finds during that time that it is not prejudicial to the interests of Spain, or if he should not agree to continue it there, he will assign to them on another part of the banks of the Mississippi an equivalent establishment. . . .

◇◇◇◇◇◇◇◇◇◇◇◇◇

9. WASHINGTON'S FAREWELL ADDRESS[14]

. . . OBSERVE good faith and justice toward all nations. Cultivate peace and harmony with all. Religion and morality enjoin this conduct. And can it be that good policy does not equally enjoin it? It will be worthy of a free, enlightened, and at no distant period a great nation to give to mankind the magnanimous and too novel example of a people always guided by an exalted justice and benevolence. Who can doubt that in the course of time and things the fruits of such a plan would richly repay any temporary advantages which might be lost by a steady adherence to it? Can it be that Providence has not connected the permanent felicity of a nation with its virtue? The experiment, at least, is recommended by every sentiment which ennobles human nature. Alas! is it rendered impossible by its vices?

In the execution of such a plan nothing is more essential than that permanent, inveterate antipathies against particular nations and passionate attachments for others should be excluded, and that in place of them just and amicable feelings toward all should be cultivated. The nation which indulges toward another an habitual hatred or an habitual fondness is in some degree a slave. It is a slave to its animosity or to its affection, either of which is sufficient to lead it astray from its duty and its interest. Antipathy in one nation against another disposes each more readily to offer insult and injury, to lay hold of slight causes of umbrage, and to be haughty and intractable when accidental or trifling occasions of dispute occur.

Hence frequent collisions, obstinate, envenomed, and bloody contests. The nation prompted by ill will and resentment sometimes impels to war the government contrary to the best calculations of policy. The government sometimes participates in the national propensity, and adopts through passion what reason would reject. At other times it makes the animosity of the nation subservient to projects of hostility, instigated by pride, ambition, and other sinister and pernicious motives. The peace often, sometimes perhaps the liberty, of nations has been the victim.

So, likewise, a passionate attachment of one nation for another produces a variety of evils. Sympathy for the favorite nation, facilitating the illusion of an imaginary common interest in cases where no real common interest exists, and infusing into one the enmities of the other, betrays the former into a participation in the quarrels and wars of the latter without

[14] This famous address was printed in the *American Daily Advertiser,* Sept. 17, 1796. It has been more frequently referred to than read, and should always be considered in connection with the circumstances of its inception. A good treatise on it is: Samuel Flagg Bemis, "Washington's Farewell Address," *American Historical Review,* Vol. XXXIX, pp. 250–68. The text of the address may be found in many places, perhaps most conveniently in: James D. Richardson: *A Compilation of the Messages and Papers of the Presidents* (Washington, D.C.: Government Printing Office, 1896), Vol. I, pp. 213–24.

adequate inducement or justification. It leads also to concessions to the favorite nation of privileges denied to others, which is apt doubly to injure the nation making the concessions by unnecessarily parting with what ought to have been retained, and by exciting jealousy, ill will, and a disposition to retaliate in the parties from whom equal privileges are withheld; and it gives to ambitious, corrupted, or deluded citizens (who devote themselves to the favorite nation) facility to betray or sacrifice the interests of their own country without odium, sometimes even with popularity, gilding with the appearances of a virtuous sense of obligation, a commendable deference for public opinion, or a laudable zeal for public good the base or foolish compliances of ambition, corruption, or infatuation.

As avenues to foreign influence in innumerable ways, such attachments are particularly alarming to the truly enlightened and independent patriot. How many opportunities do they afford to tamper with domestic factions, to practice the arts of seduction, to mislead public opinion, to influence or awe the public councils! Such an attachment of a small or weak toward a great and powerful nation dooms the former to be the satellite of the latter. Against the insidious wiles of foreign influence (I conjure you to believe me, fellow-citizens) the jealousy of a free people ought to be *constantly* awake, since history and experience prove that foreign influence is one of the most baneful foes of republican government. But that jealousy, to be useful, must be impartial, else it becomes the instrument of the very influence to be avoided, instead of a defense against it. Excessive partiality for one foreign nation and excessive dislike of another cause those whom they actuate to see danger only on one side, and serve to veil and even second the arts of influence on the other. Real patriots who may resist the intrigues of the favorite are liable to become suspected and odious, while its tools and dupes usurp the applause and confidence of the people to surrender their interests.

The great rule of conduct for us in regard to foreign nations is, in extending our commercial relations to have with them as little *political* connection as possible. So far as we have already formed engagements let them be fulfilled with perfect good faith. Here let us stop.

Europe has a set of primary interests which to us have none or a very remote relation. Hence she must be engaged in frequent controversies, the causes of which are essentially foreign to our concerns. Hence, therefore, it must be unwise in us to implicate ourselves by artificial ties in the ordinary vicissitudes of her politics or the ordinary combinations and collisions of her friendships or enmities.

Our detached and distant situation invites and enables us to pursue a different course. If we remain one people, under an efficient government, the period is not far off when we may defy material injury from external annoyance; when we may take such an attitude as will cause the neutrality we may at any time resolve upon to be scrupulously respected; when belligerent nations, under the impossibility of making acquisitions upon us, will not lightly hazard the giving us provocation; when we may choose peace or war, as our interest, guided by justice, shall counsel.

Why forego the advantages of so peculiar a situation? Why quit our own to stand upon foreign ground? Why, by interweaving our destiny with that of any part of Europe, entangle our peace and prosperity in the toils of European ambition, rivalship, interest, humor, or caprice?

It is our true policy to steer clear of permanent alliances with any portion of the foreign world, so far, I mean, as we are now at liberty to do it. . . .

Taking care always to keep ourselves by suitable establishments on a respectable defensive posture, we may safely trust to temporary alliances for extraordinary emergencies. . . .

Chapter V

RELATIONS WITH FRANCE

1789–1800

THE DIPLOMATIC relations between the United States and France from 1789 to 1800 were marked by a singular lack of statesmanship on the part of the French government, and at least a tortuous policy on the part of the American government. After the beginning of the war between France and England it became the unpleasant task of President Washington to determine and fulfill the obligations of the United States under the treaties with France and at the same time to maintain the position of a neutral toward England (1). It was necessary for the Secretary of State to inform the French minister, Edmond C. Genêt, that the arming of French privateers could not be permitted within American ports (2). A continuance of undiplomatic conduct on the part of Genêt, together with a total disregard for the policy of the United States, led to a request for his recall (3). France, in turn, requested the recall of the American minister in Paris, Gouverneur Morris. Friendly relations between the two nations were quickly restored by the appointment of James Monroe as minister to France and the arrival of a new French minister, Jean Fauchet, to replace the irascible Genêt. It was but a short time, however, until a new source of controversy arose between the two nations. The French government objected to the treaty between the United States and England, negotiated by John Jay, on the ground that it circumvented the Franco-American Treaty of Amity and Commerce of 1778. James Monroe, who was inclined to agree with the French point of view, was recalled by his government. France in turn refused to receive his successor, Charles Cotesworth Pinckney, and recalled the French minister to the United States, Pierre Adet, who had replaced Jean Fauchet. France initiated a policy of reprisals against American commerce, and the United States began to prepare for war with France. In the midst of this difficulty John Adams became President of the United States and decided to send a diplomatic commission to France. The commission, consisting of Charles Cotesworth Pinckney, John Marshall, and Elbridge Gerry, reached Paris in October 1797. They were not received officially by the French government, and the publication of their diplomatic correspondence, known as the X Y Z dispatches (4), still further aroused anti-French sentiment in the United States. Congress, on July 7, 1798, abrogated the existing treaties with France, and warlike preparations continued. Neither the French nor the American governments, however, desired war. The Minister of Foreign Relations, Talleyrand, on August 28, 1798, let it be known through the secretary of the French Legation at The Hague that France would properly receive a minister from the United States if one were sent. President Adams welcomed the opportunity to avoid further difficulties with France, and a new commission, consisting of Oliver Ellsworth, William R. Davie, and William Vans Murray was sent to Paris (5). When the commission assembled in Paris, March 2, 1800, Napoleon was in control of the French government. Although negotiations were considerably prolonged, they were conducted in a straightforward manner, and a convention was signed, September 30, 1800 (6).

1. PROCLAMATION OF NEUTRALITY: 1793[1]

WHEREAS it appears that a state of war exists between Austria, Prussia, Sardinia, Great Britain, and the United Netherlands, of the one part, and France on the other; and the duty and interest of the United States require, that they should with sincerity and good faith adopt and pursue a conduct friendly and impartial toward the belligerent Powers:

I have therefore thought fit by these presents to declare the disposition of the United States to observe the conduct aforesaid towards those Powers respectively; and to exhort and warn the citizens of the United States carefully to avoid all acts and proceedings whatsoever, which may in any manner tend to contravene such disposition.

And I do hereby also make known, that whosoever of the citizens of the United States shall render himself liable to punishment or forfeiture under the law of nations, by committing, aiding, or abetting hostilities against any of the said Powers, or by carrying to any of them those articles which are deemed contraband by the *modern* usage of nations, will not receive the protection of the United States, against such punishment or forfeiture; and further, that I have given instructions to those officers, to whom it belongs, to cause prosecutions to be instituted against all persons, who shall, within the cognizance of the courts of the United States, violate the law of nations, with respect to the Powers at war, or any of them.

In testimony whereof, I have caused the seal of the United States of America to be affixed to these presents. . . .

[1] Lowrie and Clarke: *American State Papers, Foreign Relations,* Vol. I, p. 140. President Washington issued a second proclamation of neutrality, March 24, 1794, and Congress enacted a neutrality law June 5, 1794.

2. PRIVATEERS AND AMERICAN NEUTRALITY[2]

[*Thomas Jefferson to Edmond C. Genêt*]

Philadelphia, June 5, 1793

IN MY LETTER of May 15th, to M. de Ternant, your predecessor . . . it was observed that a part remained still unanswered, of that which respected the fitting out armed vessels in Charleston, to cruise against nations with whom we were at peace.

In a conversation which I had afterwards the honor of holding with you, I observed that one of those armed vessels, the Citizen Genet, had come into this port with a prize; that the President had thereupon taken the case into further consideration; and, after mature consultation and deliberation, was of opinion, that the arming and equipping vessels in the ports of the United States, to cruise against nations with whom we are at peace, was incompatible with the territorial sovereignty of the United States; that it made them instrumental to the annoyance of those nations, and thereby tended to compromit their peace; and that he thought it necessary, as an evidence of good faith to them, as well as a proper reparation to the sovereignty of the country, that the armed vessels of this description should depart from the ports of the United States. . . .

The respect due to whatever comes from you, friendship for the French nation, and justice to all, have induced him to re-examine the subject, and particularly to give to your representations thereon the consideration they deservedly claim. After fully weighing again, however, all the principles and circumstances of the case, the result appears still to be, that it is the *right* of every nation to prohibit acts of sovereignty from being exercised by any other within its limits, and the *duty* of a neutral nation to prohibit such as would injure one of the warring Powers; that the granting military commissions, within the United States, by any other authority than their own, is an infringement on their sovereignty, and particularly so when granted to their own citizens, to lead them to commit acts contrary to the duties they owe their own country; that the departure of vessels, thus illegally equipped, from the ports of the United States, will be but an acknowledgment of respect, analagous to the breach of it, while it is necessary on their part, as an evidence of their faithful neutrality. On these considerations, sir, the President thinks that the United States owe it to themselves, and to the nations in their friendship, to expect this act of reparation on the part of vessels, marked in their very equipment with offence to the laws of the land, of which the law of nations makes an integral part. . . .

---

[2] Ibid., p. 150.

3. REQUEST FOR THE RECALL OF GENÊT[3]

[*Thomas Jefferson to Gouverneur Morris*]

Philadelphia, August 16, 1793

. . . ON THE declaration of war between France and England, the United States being at peace with both, their situation was so new and unexperienced by themselves, that their citizens were not, in the first instant, sensible of the new duties resulting therefrom, and of the restraints it would impose even *on their dispositions* towards the belligerent Powers. . . . In this state of the public mind . . . the President thought it expedient, through the channel of a proclamation, to remind our fellow-citizens, that we were in a state of peace with all the belligerent Powers. . . . This proclamation, ordered on the 19th, and signed the 22d day of April, was sent to you in my letter of the 26th of the same month.

On the day of its publication, we received, through the channel of the newspapers, the first intimation that Mr. Genet had arrived on the 8th of the month at Charleston, in the character of minister plenipotentiary from his nation to the United States, and soon after, that he had sent on to Philadelphia the vessel in which he came, and would himself perform the journey by land. His landing at one of the most distant ports of the Union from his points both of departure and destination, was calculated to excite attention; and very soon afterwards we learnt that he was undertaking to authorize the fitting and arming of vessels in that port, enlisting men, foreigners and citizens, and giving them commissions to cruise and commit hostilities on nations at peace with us; that these vessels were taking and bringing prizes into our ports; that the consuls of France were assuming to hold courts of admiralty on them; to try, condemn, and authorize their sale as legal prize; and all this before Mr. Genet had presented himself or his credentials to the President, before he was received by him, without his consent or consultation, and directly in contravention of the state of peace existing, and declared to exist, in the President's proclamation, and incumbent on him to preserve, till the constitutional authority should otherwise declare. These proceedings became immediately, as was naturally to be expected, the subject of complaint by the representative here of that Power against whom they would chiefly operate. The British minister presented several memorials thereon, to which we gave the answer of May 15, heretofore enclosed to you, corresponding in substance with a letter of the same date, written to Mr. Ternant, the minister of France, then residing here, a copy of which I send herewith. On the next day Mr. Genet reached this place, about five or six weeks after he had arrived at Charleston, and might have been at Philadelphia, if he had steered for it directly. He was immediately presented to the President, and received by him as the minister of the republic; and as the conduct

[3] Lowrie and Clarke: *American State Papers, Foreign Relations,* Vol. I, pp. 167–72.

before stated seemed to bespeak a design of forcing us into the war, without allowing us the exercise of any free will in the case, nothing could be more assuaging than his assurances to the President at his reception . . . that, on account of our remote situation, and other circumstances, France did not expect that we should become a party to the war, but wished to see us pursue our prosperity and happiness in peace. In a conversation a few days after, Mr. Genet told me that M. de Ternant had delivered him my letter of May 15; he spoke something of the case of the Grange, and then of the armament at Charleston; explained the circumstances which had led him to it before he had been received by the Government and consulted its will; expressed a hope that the President had not so absolutely decided against the measure but that he would hear what was to be said in support of it; that he would write me a letter on the subject, in which he thought he could justify it under our treaty; but that, if the President should finally determine otherwise, he must submit: for that assuredly his instructions were to do what would be agreeable to us. He accordingly wrote the letter of May 27. The President took the case again into consideration, and found nothing in that letter which could shake the grounds of his former decision. My letter of June 5th, notifying this to him, his of June 8 and 14, mine of the 17th, and his again of the 22d, will show what further passed on this subject, and that he was far from retaining his disposition to acquiesce in the ultimate will of the President. . . .

That friendship, which dictates to us to bear with his conduct yet awhile, lest the interests of his nation here should suffer injury, will hasten them to replace an agent, whose dispositions are such a misrepresentation of theirs, and whose continuance here is inconsistent with order, peace, respect, and that friendly correspondence which we hope will ever subsist between the two nations. . . . Lay the case, then, immediately before his Government; accompany it with assurances, which cannot be stronger than true, that our friendship for the nation is constant and unabating . . . that, in opposing the extravagances of an agent whose character they seem not sufficiently to have known, we have been urged by motives of duty to ourselves, and justice to others, which cannot but be approved by those who are just themselves. . . .

◇◇◇◇◇◇◇◇◇◇◇◇◇

4. THE X Y Z REPORT[4]

[*United States Envoys*[5] *to France to Timothy Pickering*]

October 22, 1797

ALL OF US having arrived at Paris on the evening of the 4th instant, on the next day we verbally, and unofficially, informed the Minister of For-

[4] Ibid., Vol. II, pp. 157–60.
[5] The envoys were Charles Cotesworth Pinckney, John Marshall, and Elbridge Gerry.

eign Affairs [6] therewith, and desired to know when he would be at leisure to receive one of our secretaries with the official notification. . . .

On Saturday, the 14th Major Mountflorence informed General Pinckney that he had had a conversation with Mr. Osmond, the private and confidential secretary of the Minister of Foreign Affairs, who told him that the Directory were greatly exasperated at some parts of the President's speech, at the opening of the last session of Congress, and would require an explanation of them from us. The particular parts were not mentioned. In another conversation, on the same day, the secretary informed the major that the minister had told him it was probable we should not have a public audience of the Directory till such time as our negotiation was finished; that probably persons might be appointed to treat with us, but they would report to him, and he would have the direction of the negotiation. The major did not conceal from Mr. Osmond his intention to communicate these conversations to us.

In the morning of October the 18th, Mr. W. . . called on General Pickney and informed him that a Mr. X., who was in Paris . . . was a gentleman of considerable credit and reputation . . . and that we might place great reliance on him.

In the evening of the same day, Mr. X. called on General Pinckney, and after having sat some time . . . whispered him that he had a message from M. Talleyrand to communicate when he was at leisure. General Pinckney immediately withdrew with him into another room; and, when they were alone, Mr. X. said that he was charged with a business in which he was a novice; that he had been acquainted with M. Talleyrand . . . and that he . . . was very desirous that a reconciliation should be brought about with France; that, to effectuate that end, he was ready, if it was thought proper, to suggest a plan, confidentially, that M. Talleyrand expected would answer the purpose. General Pinckney said he should be glad to hear it. M. X. replied that the Directory, and particularly two of the members of it, were exceedingly irritated at some passages of the President's speech, and desired that they should be softened; and that this step would be necessary previous to our reception. That, besides this, a sum of money was required for the pocket of the Directory and ministers, which would be at the disposal of M. Talleyrand; and that a loan would also be insisted on. M. X. said if we acceded to these measures, M. Talleyrand had no doubt that all our differences with France might be accommodated. On inquiry, M. X. could not point out the particular passages of the speech that had given offence, nor the quantum of the loan, but mentioned that the douceur for the pocket was twelve hundred thousand livres, about fifty thousand pounds sterling. General Pinckney told him . . . that, with regard to the propositions made, he could not even consider of them before he had communicated them to his colleagues; that, after he had done so, he should hear from him. After a communication and consultation had, it was agreed that General Pinckney should call on

[6] This was C. M. de Talleyrand-Périgord.

M. X. and request him to make his propositions to us all; and, for fear of mistake of misapprehension, that he should be requested to reduce the heads into writing. Accordingly, on the morning of October 19, General Pinckney called on M. X., who consented to see his colleagues in the evening, and to reduce his propositions to writing. He said his communication was not immediately with M. Talleyrand, but through another gentleman in whom M. Talleyrand had great confidence. This proved afterwards to be M. Y.

At six in the evening, M. X. came and left with us the first set of propositions, which, translated from the French, are as follows: "A person who possesses the confidence of the Directory, on what relates to the affairs of America, convinced of the mutual advantages which would result from the re-establishment of the good understanding between the two nations, proposes to employ all of his influence to obtain this object. He will assist the commissioners of the United States in all the demands which they may have to make from the Government of France, inasmuch as they may not be contradictory to those which he proposes himself to make, and of which the principal will be communicated confidentially. It is desired that in the official communications there should be given a softening turn to a part of the President's speech to Congress, which has caused much irritation. It is feared that, in not satisfying certain individuals in this respect, they may give way to all their resentment. The nomination of commissioners will be consented to on the same footing as they have been named in the treaty with England, to decide on the reclamations which individuals of America may make on the Government of France, or on French individuals. The payment which, agreeably to the decisions of the commissioners, shall fall to the share of the French Government, are to be advanced by the American Government itself. It is desired that the funds which, by this means, shall enter again into the American trade, should be employed in new supplies for the French colonies. Engagements of this nature, on the part of individuals reclaiming, will always hasten, in all probability, the decisions of the French commissioners; and perhaps it may be desired that this clause should make a part of the instructions which the Government of the United States should give to the commissioners they may choose. The French Government desires, besides, to obtain a loan from the United States; but so that that should not give any jealousy to the English Government, nor hurt the neutrality of the United States. This loan shall be masked by stipulating, that the Government of the United States consents to make the advances for the payment of the debts contracted by the agents of the French Government with the citizens of the United States, and which are already acknowledged, and the payment ordered by the Directory, but without having been yet effectuated. . . . The amount of the loan he could not ascertain precisely, but understood it would be according to our ability to pay. The sum which would be considered as proper, according to diplomatic usage, was about twelve hundred thousand livres. He could not state to us what parts of the President's speech were excepted to, but said he would inquire and inform us. He agreed to breakfast with Mr. Gerry the morning of the 21st, in order to make such explanations as we had then requested, or should think proper to request; but, on the morning of the 20th, M. X. called, and said that M. Y., the confidential friend of M. Talleyrand, instead of communicating with us through M. X. would see us himself and make the necessary explanations. We appointed to meet him the evening of the 20th at seven o'clock, in General Marshall's room. At seven, M. Y. and M. X. entered; and the first mentioned gentleman, being introduced to us as the confidential friend of M. Talleyrand. . . . Then he made us the second set of propositions, which were dictated by him and written by Mr. X. in our presence, and delivered to us, and which, translated from the French, are as follows: "There is demanded a formal disavowal in writing, declaring that the speech of the citizen president, Barras, did not contain anything offensive to the Government of the United States, nor any thing which deserved the epithets contained in the whole paragraph. Secondly, reparation is demanded for the article by which it shall be declared, that the decree of the Directory there mentioned did not contain any thing contrary to the treaty of 1778, and had none of those fatal consequences that the paragraph reproaches to it. Thirdly, it is demanded that there should be an acknowledgement, in writing, of the depredations exercised on our trade by the English and French privateers. Fourthly, the Government of France, faithful to the profession of public faith, which it has made not to intermeddle in the internal affairs of foreign Governments with which it is at peace, would look upon this paragraph as an attack upon its loyalty, if this was intended by the President. It demands, in consequence, a formal declaration that it is not the Government of France, not its agents, that this paragraph meant to designate. In consideration of these reparations, the French republic is disposed to renew with the United States of America a treaty which shall place them reciprocally in the same state that they were in 1778. By this new treaty, France shall be placed, with respect to the United States, exactly on the same footing as they stand with England, in virtue of the last treaty which has been concluded between them. A secret article of this new treaty would be a loan to be made by the United States to the French republic; and, once agreed upon the amount of the loan, it would be endeavored to consult the convenience of the United States with respect to the best method of preventing its publicity."

On reading the speech M. Y. dilated very much upon the keenness of the resentment it had produced, and expatiated largely on the satisfaction he said was indispensably necessary as a preliminary to negotiation. "But, said he, gentlemen, I will not disguise from you, that this satisfaction being made, the essential part of the treaty remains to be adjusted; il faut de l'argent – il faut beaucoup d'argent;" *you must pay money, you must pay a great deal of money.* He spoke much of the force, the honor, and the jealous republican pride of France; and represented to us strongly the advantages which we should derive from the neutrality thus to be purchased. He said that the receipt of the money might be so disguised as to prevent its being considered as a breach of neutrality by England; and thus save us from being embroiled with that power. Concerning the twelve hundred thousand livres little was said; that being completely understood, on all sides, to be required for the officers of Government, and, therefore, needing no further explanation. These propositions, he said, being considered as the admitted basis of the proposed treaty, M. Talleyrand trusted that, by his influence with the Directory, he could prevail on the Government to receive us. We asked whether we were to consider it as certain, that, without a previous stipulation to the effect required, we were not to be received. He answered that M. Talleyrand himself was not authorized to speak to us the will of the Directory, and consequently could not authorize him. The conversation continued until half after nine, when they left us; having engaged to breakfast with Mr. Gerry the next morning. . . .

We required an explanation of that part of the conversation, in which M. Y. had hinted at our finding means to avert the demand concerning the President's speech. He answered, that he was not authorized to state those means, but that we must search for them and propose them ourselves. If, however, we asked his opinion as a private individual, and would receive it as coming from him, he would suggest to us the means which, in his opinion, would succeed. On being asked to suggest the means, he answered, money; that the Directory were jealous of its own honor and of the honor of the nation; that it insisted on receiving from us the same respect with which we had treated the King; that this honor must be maintained in the manner before required, unless we substituted, in the place of those reparations, something, perhaps, more valuable, that was money. He said further, that if we desired him to point out the sum which he believed would be satisfactory, he would do so. We requested him to proceed; and he said that there were thirty-two millions of florins, of Dutch inscriptions, worth ten shillings in the pound, which might be assigned to us at twenty shillings in the pound; and he proceeded to state to us the certainty that, after a peace, the Dutch Government would repay us the money; so that we should ultimately lose nothing, and the only operation of the measure would be, an advance from us to France of thirty-two millions, on the credit of the Government of Holland. We asked him whether the fifty thousand pounds sterling, as a douceur to the Directory, must be in addition to this sum. He answered in the affirmative. We told him that, on the subject of the treaty, we had no hesitation in saying that our powers were ample; that, on the other points proposed to us, we would retire into another room, and return in a few minutes with our answer.

We committed immediately to writing the answer we proposed, in the following words: "Our powers respecting a treaty are ample; but the proposition of a loan, in the form of Dutch inscriptions, or in any other form, is not within the limits of our instructions; upon this point, therefore, the Government must be consulted; one of the American ministers will, for the purpose, forthwith embark for America; provided the Directory will suspend all further captures on American vessels, and will suspend proceedings on those already captured, as well where they have been already condemned, as where the decisions have not yet been rendered; and that where sales have been made, but the money not yet received by the captors, it shall not be paid until the preliminary questions, proposed to the ministers of the United States, be discussed and decided;" which was read as a verbal answer; and we told them they might copy it if they pleased. M. Y. refused to do so; his disappointment was apparent; he said we treated the money part of the proposition as if it had proceeded from the Directory; whereas, in fact, it did not proceed even from the minister, but was only a suggestion from himself, as a substitute to be proposed by us in order to avoid the painful acknowledgment that the Directory had determined to demand of us. It was told him that we understood that matter perfectly; that we knew the proposition was in form to be ours; but that it came substantially from the minister. . . .

He said that we should certainly not be received; and seemed to shudder at the consequences. We told him, that America had made every possible effort to remain on friendly terms with France; that she was still making them: that if France would not hear us, but would make war on the United States, nothing remained for us but to regret the unavoidable necessity of defending ourselves. . . .

◇◇◇◇◇◇◇◇◇◇◇◇◇

5. INSTRUCTIONS TO OLIVER ELLSWORTH, WILLIAM RICHARDSON DAVIE, AND WILLIAM VANS MURRAY[7]

October 22, 1799

. . . THE TREATMENT experienced by the former envoys of the United States to the French republic, having determined the President not to send thither other ministers, without direct and unequivocal assurances previously signified by its Minister of Foreign Relations, that they would be received in character to an audience of the Directory, and that they should enjoy all the prerogatives attached to that character by the law of nations, and that a minister or ministers of equal powers should be appointed and commissioned to treat with them: the French Government, by Mr. Talleyrand, its Minister of Foreign Relations, has declared, *that it will receive the envoys of the United States in the official character with which they are invested; that they shall enjoy all the prerogatives attached to it by the law of nations; and that one or more ministers shall*

[7] Lowrie and Clarke: *American State Papers, Foreign Relations,* Vol. II, pp. 301–6.

be duly authorized to treat with them. This the President deems to be substantially the assurance which he required as the previous condition of the envoys entering on their mission. . . . If, however, your passports to Paris should be unreasonably withheld; if an audience of the Directory should be denied or procrastinated; if the appointment of a minister or ministers, with equal powers, to treat with you, should be delayed; or, if when appointed, they postpone the intended negotiation; you are to relinquish your mission, demand your passports, and leave France; and, having once resolved to terminate the mission, you are not to resume it, whatever fresh overtures or assurances may be tendered to you by the French Government. . . .

I. At the opening of the negotiation you will inform the French ministers, that the United States expect from France, as an indispensable condition of the treaty, a stipulation to make to the citizens of the United States full compensation for all losses and damages which they shall have sustained, by reason of irregular or illegal captures or condemnations of their vessels and other property, under color of authority or commissions from the French republic or its agents. And all captures and condemnations are deemed irregular or illegal, when contrary to the law of nations generally received and acknowledged in Europe, and to the stipulations in the treaty of amity and commerce, of the 6th of February, 1778, fairly and ingeneously interpreted, while that treaty remained in force. . . .

III. If the preceding claims shall be duly attended to, and adequate arrangements made for adjusting and satisfying them, you will then turn your thoughts to the regulation of navigation and commerce, and to some other points interesting to the two nations.

IV. It may be stipulated that there shall be a reciprocal and entirely perfect liberty of commerce and navigation between France and the United States, and their territories and dominions, in every part of the world; but without admitting the vessels of either country into the rivers of the other beyond the highest ports of entry from the sea.

With the usual policy of European nations, France may object to the free admission of American vessels into the ports of her colonies. But the singular injuries our commerce has sustained from France, during the present war, which no payments to be made by her, under the preceding stipulations, can ever fully compensate, plead for an entire liberty of trade with her colonies, at least during the term of the proposed treaty, and until the stipulated compensations shall actually have been made. Another reason will naturally operate in favor of this claim; the inability of France immediately to furnish the requisite navigation and supplies for the commerce of her distant possessions. . . .

XXI. The seventeenth and twenty-second articles of the commercial treaty between the United States and France, of February 6th, 1778, have been the source of much altercation between the two nations during the present war. The dissolution of that and our other treaties with France leaves us at liberty with respect to future arrangements; with the exception of the now preferable right secured to Great Britain, by the twenty-fifth article of the treaty of amity and commerce. In that article we promise mutually that, while we continue in amity, neither party will in future make any treaty that shall be inconsistent with that article or the one preceding it. We cannot, therefore, renew with France the seventeenth and twenty-second articles of the treaty of 1778. . . .

The following points are to be considered as ultimated:

1. That an article be inserted for establishing a board, with suitable powers, to hear and determine the claims of our citizens, for the causes herein before expressed, and binding France to pay or secure payment of the sums which shall be awarded.

2. That the treaties and consular convention, declared to be no longer obligatory by act of Congress, be not in whole or in part revived by the new treaty; but that all the engagements, to which the United States are to become parties, be specified in the new treaty.

3. That no guaranty of the whole or any part of the dominions of France be stipulated, nor any engagement made, in the nature of an alliance.

4. That no aid or loan be promised in any form whatever.

5. That no engagement be made inconsistent with the obligations of any prior treaty; and, as it may respect our treaty with Great Britain, the instruction herein marked XXI is to be particularly observed.

6. That no stipulation be made granting powers to consuls or others, under color of which tribunals can be established within our jurisdiction, or personal privileges be claimed by Frenchmen, incompatible with the complete sovereignty of the United States in matters of policy, commerce, and government.

7. That the duration of the proposed treaty be limited to twelve years, at furthest, from the day of the exchange of the ratifications, with the exceptions respecting its permanence in certain cases, specified under the instruction marked XXX.

◇◇◇◇◇◇◇◇◇◇◇◇◇

6. CONVENTION OF PEACE, COMMERCE, AND NAVIGATION BETWEEN THE UNITED STATES AND FRANCE[8]

[*Concluded September 30, 1800; ratifications exchanged at Paris, July 31, 1801*]

. . . *ARTICLE II.* The Ministers Plenipotentiary of the two Parties, not being able to agree at present, respecting the Treaty of Alliance of 6th February 1778, the Treaty of Amity and Commerce of the same date, and

[8] Hunter Miller: *Treaties and Other International Acts of the United States of America,* Vol. II, pp. 457–82.

the . . . Convention of 14th November 1788, nor upon the indemnities mutually due, or claimed, the Parties will negotiate further on these subjects at a convenient time, and untill they may have agreed upon these points, the said Treaties, and . . . Convention shall have no operation, and the relations of the two Countries shall be regulated as follows.

Article III. The Public Ships, which have been taken on one part, and the other, or which may be taken before the exchange of ratifications shall be restored. . . .

Article VI. Commerce between the Parties shall be free. The vessels of the two nations, and their Privateers, as well as their prizes, shall be treated in the respective ports, as those of the nation the most favoured; and in general the two parties shall enjoy in the ports of each other, in regard to commerce, and navigation, the privileges of the most favoured nation. . . .

Article XIII. In order to regulate what shall be deemed contraband of war, there shall be comprised under that denomination, Gun-powder, salt-petre Petards, match, ball, bombs, grenades, carcasses, Pikes, Halberts, swords, belts, Pistols, holsters, cavalry saddles, and furniture, Cannon, Mortars, their carriages, and beds, and generally all kinds of arms, ammunition of war, and instruments fit for the use of Troops, all the above articles whenever they are destined to the port of an enemy, are hereby declared to be contraband, and just objects of confiscation: but the vessel in which they are laden, and the residue of the cargo shall be considered free, and not in any manner infected by the prohibited goods, whether belonging to the same or a different Owner.

Article XIV. It is hereby stipulated that free ships shall give a freedom to goods, and that everything shall be deemed to be free, and exempt which shall be found on board the ships belonging to the citizens of either of the contracting parties, altho' the whole lading, or any part thereof should appertain to the enemies of either, contraband goods being always excepted. It is also agreed in like manner, that the same liberty be extended to persons, who are on board a free ship, with this effect, that altho' they be enemies to either party, they are not to be taken out of that free ship, unless they are soldiers and in actual service of the enemy. . . .

Article XVI. The Merchant ships belonging to the citizens of either of the contracting parties, which shall be bound to a port of the enemy of one of the parties, and concerning whose voyage, and the articles of their cargo, there shall be just grounds of suspicion, shall be obliged to exhibit, as well upon the high seas, as in the ports or roads, not only their passports, but likewise their certificates, showing that their goods are not of the quality of those which are specified to be contraband in the thirteenth Article of the present Convention. . . .

Article XX. In all cases where vessels shall be captured, or detained, under pretence of carrying to the enemy contraband goods, the Captor shall give a receipt for such of the papers of the Vessel as he shall retain, which receipt shall be annexed to a descriptive list of the said papers: and it shall be unlawful to break up, or open the hatches, chests, trunks, casks, bales, or vessels found on board, or remove the smallest part of the goods, unless the lading be brought on shore, in presence of the competent officers, and an inventory be made by them of the said goods. Nor shall it be lawful to sell, exchange or alienate the same, in any manner, unless there shall have been lawful process, and the competent judge or judges shall have pronounced against such goods sentence of confiscation, saving always the ship and the other goods which it contains. . . .

Article XXV. It shall not be lawful for any foreign Privateers who have commissions from any Prince, or State, in enmity with either nation, to fit their ships in the ports of either nation, to sell their prizes, or in any manner to exchange them; neither shall they be allowed to purchase provisions, except such as shall be necessary for their going to the next port of that Prince, or State, from which they have received their commissions. . . .

[*Note:* The Senate of the United States voted, February 3, 1801, to consent to and advise the ratification of the Convention providing the second article be expunged and another article be added limiting the duration of the treaty to eight years from the time of the exchange of ratifications. The French government agreed to the Senate's reservations but added a stipulation of its own as follows: "*Provided,* that by this retrenchment [Art. II] the two states renounce the respective pretentions which are the object of said article." The Senate approved the French reservation, December 19, 1801, and the treaty was proclaimed December 21, 1801.]

Chapter VI

THE LOUISIANA PURCHASE

◇◇◇◇◇◇◇◇◇◇◇◇◇

THE CONVENTION of Peace, Commerce, and Navigation between the United States and France was signed on September 30, 1800. The following day the representatives of Spain and France reached an agreement, which, if carried into effect, would certainly have nullified the Franco-American amity so recently concluded, and would have deprived the United States of whatever benefits it had received from the Treaty of 1795 with Spain. This Franco-Spanish agreement was the Treaty of St. Ildefonso, under which Spain agreed to recede to France the Province of Louisiana. It was a secret treaty, but the minister of the United States in London, Rufus King, heard rumors concerning it and informed his government of that fact in March 1801. The American government could not discover immediately whether such a treaty had been concluded, but it was greatly aroused over the danger of losing the free navigation of the Mississippi River, and inaugurated a movement that would afford greater security to the United States. The new policy was to purchase the territory in the vicinity of New Orleans from Spain, if that country still possessed it, and from France, if the Treaty of St. Ildefonso had been signed. President Jefferson's letter on this subject of April 18, 1802, to Robert R. Livingston, American minister in Paris, is one of the notable dispatches of American diplomacy (1). Public sentiment in the United States, already hostile to the acquisition of Louisiana by France, was greatly aroused over a proclamation of the Spanish Intendant at New Orleans, suspending the right of Americans to deposit their goods at that place. President Jefferson decided to send a special minister to France and to Spain in order to accelerate negotiations regarding the purchase of New Orleans. The President explained the situation to Livingston in a letter of February 3, 1803 (2). Ten days later Livingston wrote to the Secretary of State that France had offered to sell not only New Orleans but all of Louisiana (3). After some discussion the offer was accepted by the United States. Livingston hastened to explain to the Secretary of State his opinions regarding the boundary limits of the newly acquired territory (4).

There remained a long controversy with Spain over the boundaries of Louisiana and a short controversy over the American right to purchase it from France, since France had agreed not to alienate that area. The dispatch of the Secretary of State to the Spanish minister, the Marquis d'Yrujo, of October 4, 1803 (5), practically ended the second of these controversies, but the former was not settled until 1819. The discussion in the United

States over the Louisiana purchase is illustrated by speeches in Congress of Timothy Pickering (6) of Massachusetts and John Breckenridge of Kentucky (7).

◇◇◇◇◇◇◇◇◇◇◇◇◇

1. AMERICAN FOREIGN POLICY AND THE FRENCH ACQUISITION OF LOUISIANA[1]

[*Thomas Jefferson to Robert R. Livingston*]

Washington, April 18, 1802

THE CESSION of Louisiana and the Floridas by Spain to France, works most sorely on the United States. On this subject the Secretary of State has written to you fully, yet I cannot forbear recurring to it personally, so deep is the impression it makes on my mind. It completely reverses all the political relations of the United States, and will form a new epoch in our political course. Of all nations of any consideration, France is the one which, hitherto, has offered the fewest points on which we could have any conflict of right, and the most points of a communion of interests. From these causes, we have ever looked to her as our *natural friend*, as one with which we never could have an occasion of difference. Her growth, therefore, we viewed as our own, her misfortunes ours. There is on the globe one single spot, the possessor of which is our natural and habitual enemy. It is New Orleans, through which the produce of three-eighths of our territory must pass to market, and from its fertility it will ere long yield more than half of our whole produce, and contain more than half of our inhabitants. France, placing herself in that door, assumes to us the attitude of defiance. Spain might have retained it quietly for years. Her pacific dispositions, her feeble state, would induce her to increase our facilities there, so that her possession of the place would be hardly felt by us, and it would not, perhaps, be very long before some circumstance might arise, which might make the cession of it to us the price of something of more worth to her. Not so can it ever be in the hands of France: the impetuosity of her temper, the energy and restlessness of her character, placed in a point of eternal friction with us, and our character, which, though quiet and loving peace and the pursuit of wealth, is high-minded, despising wealth in competition with insult or injury, enterprising and energetic as any nation on earth; these circumstances render

it impossible that France and the United States can continue long friends, when they meet in so irritable a position. They, as well as we, must be blind if they do not see this; and we must be very improvident if we do not begin to make arrangements on that hypothesis. The day that France takes possession of New Orleans, fixes the sentence which is to

[1] *House Ex. Docs.* (4531) 57th Congress, 2nd Session, no. 431, pp. 15–18.

restrain her forever within her low-water mark. It seals the union of two nations, who, in conjunction, can maintain exclusive possession of the ocean. From that moment, we must marry ourselves to the British fleet and nation. We must turn all our attention to a maritime force, for which our resources place us on very high ground; and having formed and connected together a power which may render reinforcement of her settlements here impossible to France, make the first cannon which shall be fired in Europe the signal for the tearing up any settlement she may have made, and for holding the two continents of America in sequestration for the common purposes of the United British and American nations. This is not a state of things we seek or desire. It is one which this measure, if adopted by France, forces on us as necessarily, as any other cause, by the laws of nature, brings on its necessary effect. It is not from a fear of France that we deprecate this measure proposed by her. For however greater her force is than ours, compared in the abstract, it is nothing in comparison of ours, when to be exerted on our soil. But it is from a sincere love of peace, and a firm persuasion, that bound to France by the interests and the strong sympathies still existing in the minds of our citizens, and holding relative positions which insure their continuance, we are secure of a long course of peace. Whereas, the change of friends, which will be rendered necessary if France changes that position, embarks us necessarily as a belligerent power in the first war of Europe. In that case, France will have held possession of New Orleans during the interval of a peace, long or short, at the end of which it will be wrested from her. Will this short-lived possession have been an equivalent to her for the transfer of such a weight into the scale of her enemy? Will not the amalgamation of a young, thriving nation, continue to that enemy the health and force which are at present so evidently on the decline? And will a few years' possession of New Orleans add equally to the strength of France? She may say she needs Louisiana for the supply of her West Indies. She does not need it in time of peace, and in war she could not depend on them, because they would be so easily intercepted. I should suppose that all these considerations might, in some proper form, be brought into view of the Government of France. Though stated by us, it ought not to give offence; because we do not bring them forward as a menace, but as consequences not controllable by us, but inevitable from the course of things. We mention them, not as things which we desire by any means, but as things we deprecate; and we beseech a friend to look forward and to prevent them for our common interest.

If France considers Louisiana, however, as indispensable for her views, she might perhaps be willing to look about for arrangements which might reconcile to it our interests. If anything could do this, it would be the ceding to us the island of New Orleans and the Floridas. This would certainly, in a great degree, remove the causes of jarring and irritation between us, and perhaps for such a length of time, as might produce other means of making the measure permanently conciliatory to our interests and friendships. It would, at any rate, relieve us from the necessity of taking immediate measures for countervailing such an operation by arrangements in another quarter. But still we should consider New Orleans and the Floridas as no equivalent for the risk of a quarrel with France, produced by her vicinage. . . .

◇◇◇◇◇◇◇◇◇◇◇◇◇

2. REASONS FOR SENDING JAMES MONROE AS MINISTER EXTRAORDINARY TO FRANCE AND SPAIN[2]

[*Thomas Jefferson to Robert R. Livingston*]

Washington, February 3, 1803

MY LAST to you was by Mr. Dupont. Since that I received yours of May 22d. Mr. Madison supposes you have written a subsequent one which has never come to hand. A late suspension by the Intendant of New Orleans of our right of deposit there, without which the right of navigation is impractical, has thrown this country into such a flame of hostile disposition as can scarcely be described. The western country was peculiarly sensible to it as you may suppose. Our business was to take the most effectual pacific measures in our power to remove the suspension, and at the same time to persuade our countrymen that pacific measures would be the most effectual and the most speedily so. The opposition caught it as a plank in a shipwreck, hoping it would enable them to tack the Western people to them. They raised the cry of war, were intriguing in all quarters to exasperate the Western inhabitants to arm and go down on their own authority and possess themselves of New Orleans, and in the meantime were daily reiterating, in new shapes, inflammatory resolutions for the adoption of the House. As a remedy to all this we determined to name a minister extraordinary to go immediately to Paris and Madrid to settle this matter. This measure being a visible one, and the person named peculiarly proper with the Western country, crushed at once and put an end to all further attempts on the Legislature. From that moment all has become quiet; and the more readily in the Western country, as the sudden alliance of these new federal friends had of itself already began to make them suspect the wisdom of their own course. The measure was moreover proposed from another cause. We must know at once whether we can acquire New Orleans or not. We are satisfied nothing else will secure us against a war at no distant period; and we cannot press this reason without beginning those arrangements which will be necessary if war is hereafter to result. For this purpose it was necessary that the negotiators should be fully possessed of every idea we have on the subject, so as to meet the

[2] Ibid., pp. 96–7.

propositions of the opposite party, in what ever form they may be offered; and give them a shape admissible by us without being obliged to await new instructions hence. With this view, we have joined Mr. Monroe with yourself at Paris, and to Mr. Pinckney at Madrid, although we believe it will be hardly necessary for him to go to this last place. Should we fail in this object of the mission, a further one will be superadded for the other side of the channel. . . . The future destinies of our country hang on the event of this negotiation, and I am sure they could not be placed in more able or more zealous hands. On our parts we shall be satisfied that what you do not effect, cannot be effected. Accept therefore assurances of my sincere and constant affection and high respect.

◇◇◇◇◇◇◇◇◇◇◇◇◇◇

3. FRENCH PROPOSAL FOR THE SALE OF LOUISIANA[3]

[*Robert R. Livingston to James Madison*]

Paris, April 13, 1803, midnight

I HAVE just come from the Minister of the Treasury.[4] Our conversation was so important, that I think it necessary to write it, while the impressions are strong upon my mind; and the rather, as I fear I shall not have time to copy and send this letter, if I defer it till morning.

By my letter of yesterday, you learned that the Minister [5] has asked me whether I would agree to purchase Louisiana, etc. On the 12th, I called upon him to press this matter further. He then thought proper to declare that his proposition was only personal, but still requested me to make an offer; and, upon my declining to so do, as I expected Mr. Monroe the next day, he shrugged up his shoulders, and changed the conversation. Not willing, however, to lose sight of it, I told him I had been long endeavoring to bring him to some point; but, unfortunately, without effect; that I wished merely to have the negotiation opened by any proposition on his part; and, with that view, had written him a note which contained that request, grounded upon my apprehension of the consequence of sending General Bernadotte without enabling him to say a treaty was begun. He told me he would answer my note, but that he must do it evasively, because Louisiana was not theirs. I smiled at this assertion, and told him I had seen the treaty recognizing it; that I knew the Consul had appointed officers to govern the country, and that he had himself told me that General Victor was to take possession; that, in a note written by the express order of the First Consul, he had told me that General Bernadotte was to treat relative to it in the United States, etc. He still persisted that they had it in comtemplation to obtain it, but had it not. I told him that I was

[3] Ibid., pp. 159–63.
[4] Barbé Marbois.
[5] The Minister of Foreign Affairs, Talleyrand.

very well pleased to understand this from him, because, if so, we should not commit ourselves with them in taking it from Spain, to whom, by his account, it still belonged; and that, as we had just cause of complaint against her, if Mr. Monroe concurred in opinion with me, we should negotiate no further on the subject, but advise our Government to take possession. He seemed alarmed at the boldness of the measure, and told me he would answer my note, but that it would be evasively. I told him I should receive with pleasure any communication from him, but that we were not disposed to trifle; that the times were critical, and though I did know what instructions Mr. Monroe might bring, I was perfectly satisfied that they would require a precise and prompt notice; that I was very fearful, from the little progress I had made, that my Government would consider me as a very indolent negotiator. He laughed, and told me that he would give me a certificate that I was the most importunate he had met with. . . .

This day Mr. Monroe passed with me in examining my papers; and while he and several other gentlemen were at dinner with me, I observed the Minister of the Treasury walking in my garden. I sent out Colonel Livingston to him; he told him he would return when we had dined. While we were taking coffee he came in; and, after being some time in the room, we strolled into the next room, when he told me he heard I had been at his house two days before, when he was at St. Cloud; that he thought I might have something particular to say to him, and had taken the first opportunity to call on me. I saw that this was meant as an opening to one of those free conversations which I had frequently had with him. I accordingly began on the subject of the debt, and related to him the extraordinary conduct of the Minister, etc. He told me that this led to something important, that had been cursorily mentioned to him at St. Cloud; but as my house was full of company, he thought I had better call on him any time before 11 that night. He went away, and, a little after, when Mr. Monroe took leave, I followed him. He told me that he wished me to repeat what I had said relative to M. Talleyrand's requesting a proposition from me as to the purchase of Louisiana. I did so; and concluded with the extreme absurdity of his evasions of that day, and stated the consequence of any delay on this subject, as it would enable Britain to take possession, who would readily relinquish it to us. He said that this proceeded upon a supposition of her making so successful a war as to be enabled to retain her conquests. I told him that it was probable that the same idea might suggest itself to the United States; in which case, it would be their interest to contribute to render her successful, and I asked whether it was prudent to throw us into her scale? This led to long discussions of no moment to repeat. We returned to the point: he said, that what I had told him led him to think that what the Consul had said to him on Sunday, at St. Cloud, (the day on which, as I told you, the determination had been taken to sell,) had more of earnest than he thought at the time; that the Consul had asked him what news from England? . . .

He (Marbois) then took occasion to mention his sorrow that any cause of difference should exist between our countries. The Consul told him, in reply, "Well, you have the charge of the treasury; let them give you one hundred millions of francs, and pay their own claims, and take the whole country." Seeing, by my looks, that I was surprised at so extravagant a demand, he added that he considered the demand as exorbitant, and had told the First Consul that the thing was impossible; that we had not the means of raising that. The Consul told him that we might borrow it. I now plainly saw the whole business: first, the Consul was disposed to sell; next, he distrusted Talleyrand, . . . and meant to put the negotiation into the hands of Marbois, whose character for integrity is established. I told him that the United States were anxious to preserve peace with France; that, for that reason, they wished to remove them to the west side of the Mississippi; that we would be perfectly satisfied with New Orleans and the Floridas, and had no disposition to extend across the river; that, of course, we would not give any great sum for the purchase; that he was right in his idea of the extreme exorbitancy of the demand, which would not fall short of one hundred and twenty-five millions; that, however, we would be ready to purchase, provided the sum was reduced to reasonable limits. He then pressed me to name the sum. I told him that this was not worth while, because, as he only treated the inquiry as a matter of curiosity, any declaration of mine would have no effect. If a negotiation was to be opened, we should (Mr. Monroe and myself) make the offer after mature reflection. This compelled him to declare, that, though he was not authorized expressly to make the inquiry from me, yet, that, if I could mention any sum that came near the mark, that could be accepted, he would communicate it to the First Consul. I told him that we had no sort of authority to go to a sum that bore any proportion to what he mentioned; but that, as he himself considered the demand as too high, he would oblige me by telling me what he thought would be reasonable. He replied that, if we would name sixty millions, and take upon us the American claims, to the amount of twenty more, he would try how far this would be accepted. I told him that it was vain to ask anything that was so greatly beyond our means; that true policy would dictate to the First Consul not to press such a demand; that he must know that it would render the present Government unpopular, and have a tendency, at the next election, to throw the power into the hands of men who were most hostile to a connection with France; and that this would probably happen in the midst of a war. I asked him whether the few millions acquired at this expense would not be too dearly bought?

He frankly confessed that he was of my sentiments; but that he feared the Consul would not relax. I asked him to press this argument upon him, together with the danger of seeing the country pass into the hands of Britain. I told him that he had seen the ardor of the Americans to take it by force, and the difficulty with which they were restrained by the prudence of the President; that he must easily see how much the hands of the war party would be strengthened, when they learned that France was upon the eve of a rupture with England. He admitted the weight of all this: "But," says he, "you know the temper of a youthful conqueror; everything he does is rapid as lightning; we have only to speak to him as an opportunity presents itself, perhaps in a crowd, when he bears no contradiction. When I am alone with him, I can speak more freely, and he attends; but this opportunity seldom happens, and is always accidental. Try, then, if you can not come up to my mark. Consider the extent of the country, the exclusive navigation of the river, and the importance of having no neighbors to dispute you, no war to dread." I told him that I considered all these as important considerations, but there was a point beyond which we could not go, and that fell far short of the sum he mentioned. . . .

Mr. Monroe will be presented to the Minister to-morrow, when we shall press for as early an audience as possible from the First Consul. I think it will be necessary to put in some proposition to-morrow: the Consul goes in a few days to Brussels, and every moment is precious.

◇◇◇◇◇◇◇◇◇◇◇◇◇

4. THE BOUNDARIES OF LOUISIANA[6]

[*Robert R. Livingston to James Madison*]

Paris, May 20, 1803

THE SUBJECT of this letter is too important to admit of delay, in case the treaties should have been any time in your hands; but, as it has not yet been fully considered by Mr. Monroe, he thinks he can not make it that of a joint letter till we have more fully discussed it, which we propose to do to-morrow or the next day. . . .

I informed you long since, that, on inquiring whether the Floridas were within the cession of Spain, I was told by M. Marbois he was sure that Mobile was, but could not answer further. I believed his information incorrect, because I understood that Louisiana, as it then was, made the object of the cession; and that since the possession of the Floridas by Britain, they had changed their names. But the moment I saw the words of the Treaty of Madrid I had no doubt but it included all the country that France possessed by the name of Louisiana, previous to their cession to Spain, except what had been conveyed by subsequent treaties. I accordingly insisted, with M. Marbois, at the time we negotiated, that this would be considered as within our purchase. He neither assented nor denied, but said that all they received from Spain was intended to be conveyed to us. That my construction was right, is fairly to be inferred from the words of the treaties, and from a comment upon them contained in the

[6] Ibid., pp. 199–201.

Spanish Minister's letter to Mr. Pinckney, in which he expressly says that France had recovered Louisiana as it formerly belonged to her, saving the rights of other Powers. This leaves no doubt upon the subject of the intention of the contracting parties. Now, it is well known that Louisiana, as possessed by France, was bounded by the river Perdido, and that Mobile was the metropolis. For the facts relative to this I refer you to Reynal and to his maps. I have also seen maps here which put the matter out of dispute.

I called this morning upon M. Marbois for a further explanation on this subject, and to remind him of his having told me that Mobile made a part of the cession. He told me that he had no precise idea on the subject, but that he knew it to be an historical fact, and that on that only he had formed his opinion. I asked him what orders had been given to the prefect, who was to take possession, or what orders had been given by Spain as to the boundary, in ceding it? He assured me that he did not know; but that he would make the inquiry, and let me know. At 4 o'clock I called for Mr. Monroe to take him to the Minister of Foreign Affairs; but he was prevented from accompanying me. I asked the Minister what were the east bounds of the territory ceded to us? He said he did not know; we must take it as they had received it. I asked him how Spain meant to give them possession? He said, according to the words of the treaty. But what did you mean to take? I do not know. Then you mean that we shall construe it our own way? I can give you no direction; you have made a noble bargain for yourselves, and I suppose you will make the most of it.

Now, sir, the sum of this business is, to recommend to you, in the strongest terms, after having obtained the possession, that the French Commissary will give you, to insist upon this as a part of your right; and to take possession, at all events, to the river Perdido. I pledge myself that your right is good; and, after the explanations that have been given here, you need apprehend nothing from a decisive measure. Your Ministers here and at Madrid, can support your claim; and the time is peculiarly favorable to enable you to do it without the smallest risk at home. It may also be important to anticipate any designs that Britain may have upon that country. Should she possess herself of it, and the war terminate favorably for her, she will not readily relinquish it. With this in your hand, East Florida will be of little moment, and may be yours whenever you please. At all events, proclaim your rights and take possession.

◇◇◇◇◇◇◇◇◇◇◇◇◇◇

5. THE RIGHT OF THE UNITED STATES TO BUY LOUISIANA FROM FRANCE[7]

[*James Madison to the Marquis d'Yrujo*]

October 4, 1803

I HAVE duly received your two letters of the 4th and 27th ultimo, and have laid them before the President.

The repugnance manifested in these communications, on the part of His Catholic Majesty, to the cession of Louisiana lately made by the French Republic to the United States, was as little expected as the objections to the transaction can avail against its solidity.

The United States have given unquestionable proofs to the Spanish Government and nation of their justice, their friendship, and their desire to maintain the best neighborhood; and the President confides too much in the reciprocity of these sentiments, so repeatedly and so recently declared on the part of His Catholic Majesty, to have supposed that he would see with dissatisfaction a convenient acquisition by the United States of territories which were no longer to remain with Spain. With respect to the transaction itself, by which the United States have acquired Louisiana, it would be superfluous to say more in justification of its perfect validity than to refer to the official communication made by Mr. Cevallos to the Minister Plenipotentiary of the United States at Madrid, in a note dated on the 4th of May last. His words are: "Por la retrocesion hecha a la Francia de la Luisiana, recobro esta Potencia dicha provincia con los limites con que lon tubo, y salvos los derechos adquiridos por otras Potencias. *La de los Estados Unidos podra dirigirse al Gobierno Frances para negociar la adquisician de territorios que convengan a su interes.*"[8] Here is an explicit and positive recognition of the right of the United States and France to enter into the transaction which has taken place.

To these observations, which I have been charged by the President to make to you, I have only to add, sir, that his high respect for His Catholic Majesty, and his desire to cherish and strengthen the friendly sentiments happily subsisting between the two nations, will induce him to cause such explanations and representations to be made through the Minister Plenipotentiary of the United States at Madrid as can not fail to reconcile His Catholic Majesty to an event so essentially connected with the respect which the United States owe to their character and their interest.

---

[7] Ibid., p. 244.

[8] "By the retrocession of Louisiana to France, this power recovers the said province with the boundaries that it had, excepting rights acquired by other powers. The United States can address themselves to the Government of France in order to negotiate for the acquisition of territories which may suit their interest."

◇◇◇◇◇◇◇◇◇◇◇◇◇

6. OPPOSITION TO THE PURCHASE OF LOUISIANA[9]

. . . THE TREATY between the United States and the French Republic, professing to cede Louisiana to the United States, appeared to him (Mr. Pickering) to contain such an exceptionable stipulation -- a stipulation which cannot be executed by any authority now existing. It is declared in the third article, that "the inhabitants of the ceded territory shall be incorporated in the Union of the United States." But neither the President and Senate, nor the President and Congress, are competent to such an act of incorporation. He believed that our Administration admitted that this incorporation could not be effected without an amendment of the Constitution; and he conceived that this necessary amendment could not be made in the ordinary mode by the concurrence of two-thirds of both Houses of Congress, and the ratification by the Legislatures of three-fourths of the several States. He believed the assent of each individual State to be necessary for the admission of a foreign country as an associate in the Union: in like manner as in a commercial house, the consent of each member would be necessary to admit a new partner into the company; and whether the assent of every State to such an indispensable amendment were attainable, was uncertain. But the articles of a treaty were necessarily related to each other; the stipulation in one article being the consideration for another. If, therefore, in respect to the Louisiana Treaty, the United States fail to execute, and within a reasonable time, the engagement in the third article, (to incorporate that Territory into the Union,) the French Government will have a right to declare the whole treaty void. We must then abandon the country, or go to war to maintain our possession. But it was to prevent war that the pacific measures of the last winter were adopted – they were to "lay the foundation for future peace."

. . . There was another serious objection to this treaty. It purported to contain a cession of Louisiana to the United States. The first article had often been read and commented upon; yet he begged leave to refer to it once more. It was therein stated, by the third article of the Treaty of St. Ildefonso, made the first of October, 1800, that the King of Spain promised and engaged, on certain conditions, "to cede to the French Republic the 'colony or province of Louisiana.' . . ." That is, by that treaty, France acquired a right to demand an actual cession of the territory, provided she fulfilled all the conditions on which Spain promised to cede. But we know Spain declares that those conditions have not been fully performed; and, by her remonstrances, warns the United States not to touch Louisiana. Now we, standing (as some gentlemen have expressed themselves) in the shoes of France, can have only the same right relative to the subject in question. We can ask of Spain an actual cession, or a confirmation of the

[9] Speech by Timothy Pickering in the Senate November 3, 1803. The subject of debate was an appropriation bill for the purchase of Louisiana. *Annals of the Congress of the United States,* 8th Congress, 1st Session, pp. 43–7.

claim we have purchased of the French Republic, provided we will and can fulfil the conditions of the Treaty of St. Ildefonso; and what are these conditions? We cannot tell. Mr. P. believed that our Executive knew not what they were; and he believed, too, that even our Envoys, who negotiated the treaty for Louisiana, were alike uninformed. He believed that they never saw (for they had not intimated that they had ever seen) any other part of the Treaty of St. Ildefonso, than what is recited in the first article of our treaty with France; and this defect has not been supplied by any guaranty of the territory on the part of France. She has not stipulated, nor is under any obligation, to procure the assent of Spain, as a confirmation of the cession to the United States. . . .

Mr. P. said, that whatever way he turned his eyes, war was in prospect, as the final result of our pacific measures – measures deemed so wise as to have been ascribed to divine inspiration! He wished they might merit that high character; but feared, in the end, they would bear the stamp of indiscretion, perhaps of folly. . . .

◊◊◊◊◊◊◊◊◊◊◊◊◊◊

7. DEFENSE OF THE PURCHASE OF LOUISIANA[10]

PERMIT ME to examine some of the principal reasons which are deemed so powerful by gentlemen as to induce them to vote for the destruction of this treaty. Unfortunately for the gentlemen, no two of them can agree on the same set of objections; and what is still more unfortunate, I believe there is no two of them concure in any one objection. In one thing only they seem to agree, and that is to vote against the bill. An honorable gentleman from Delaware (Mr. White) considers the price to be enormous. An honorable gentleman from Connecticut, who has just sat down, (Mr. Tracy,) says he has no objection whatever to the price; it is, he supposes, not too much. An honorable gentleman from Massachusetts (Mr. Pickering) says that France acquired no title from Spain, and therefore our title is bad. The same gentleman from Connecticut (Mr. Tracy) says, he has no objection to the title of France; he thinks it a good one. The gentleman from Massachusetts (Mr. Pickering) contends that the United States cannot under the Constitution acquire foreign territory. The gentleman from Connecticut is of a different opinion, and has no doubt but that the United States can acquire and hold foreign territory; but that Congress alone have the power of incorporating that territory into the Union. Of what weight, therefore, ought all their lesser objections be entitled to, when they are at war among themselves on the greater one?

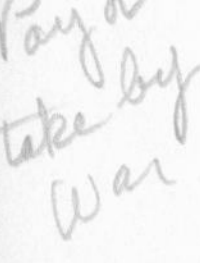

As to the enormity of price, I would ask that gentleman, would his mode of acquiring it through fifty thousand men have cost nothing? Is he so confident of this as to be able to pronounce positively that the price is

[10] Speech of John Breckenridge in the Senate, November 3, 1803. Ibid., pp. 58–67.

enormous? Does he make no calculation on the hazard attending this conflict? Is he sure the God of battles was enlisted on his side? Were France and Spain, under the auspices of Bonaparte, contemptible adversaries? Good as the cause was, and great as my confidence is in the courage of my countrymen, sure I am, that I shall never regret, as the gentleman seems to do, that the experiment was not made. I am not in the habit Mr. President, on this floor, of panegyrizing those who administer the Government of this country. Their good works are their best panegyrists, and of these my fellow-citizens are as competent to judge as I am; but if my opinion were of any consequence, I should be free to declare, that this transaction from its commencement to its close, not only as to the mode in which it was pursued, but as to the object achieved, is one of the most splendid which the annals of any nation can produce. To acquire an empire of perhaps half the extent of the one we possessed, from the most powerful and warlike nation on earth, without bloodshed, without the oppression of a single individual, without in the least embarrassing the ordinary operations of your finances, and all this through the peaceful forms of negotiation, and in despite too of the opposition of a considerable portion of the community, is an achievement of which the archives of the predecessors, at least, of those now in office, cannot furnish a parallel.

The same gentleman has told us, that this acquisition will, from its extent, soon prove destructive to the Confederacy.

This, continued Mr. B., is an old and hackneyed doctrine; that a Republic ought not to be too extensive. But the gentleman has assumed two facts, and then reasoned from them. First, that the extent is too great; and secondly, that the country will be soon populated. I would ask, sir, what is his standard extent for a Republic? How does he come at that standard? Our boundary is already extensive. Would his standard extent be violated by including the island of Orleans and the Floridas? I presume not, as all parties seem to think their acquisition, in part or in whole, essential. Why not then acquire territory on the west, as well as on the east side of the Mississippi? Is the Goddess of Liberty restrained by water courses? Is she governed by geographical limits? Is her dominion on this continent confined to the east side of the Mississippi? So far from believing in the doctrine that a Republic ought to be confined within narrow limits, I believe, on the contrary, that the more extensive its dominion the more safe and more durable it will be. In proportion to the number of hands you intrust the precious blessings of a free government too, in the same proportion do you multiply the chances for their preservation. I entertain, therefore, no fears for the Confederacy on account of its extent. . . .

Suppose, continues the same gentleman, we should discover before the end of the session that France had acquired from Spain no title to Louisiana; would you not put it out of your power to withhold the stock, by passing this bill? If such a discovery had any possibility of existence, there would be some force in the objection; but with the information before us, such discovery is impossible. By the treaty, France declares and covenants that she has an "incontestable title." Spain has sanctioned that covenant by a similar declaration that the right is in France, and has parted, so far as is in her power, with the possession, by the delivery to France of the royal order for its surrender. It would, therefore, be a strange discovery now to make, that France had no title, nevertheless the declarations and the acts of Spain to the contrary. But how could we reconcile such conduct to ourselves and to the world, after what has passed? A purchase has been made from France, and no exception taken during the negotiation to her title. The treaty has been ratified and proclaimed by the President; Congress have passed an act authorizing him to take possession. He has no doubt made the arrangements, and is at this moment carrying into execution the injunction of that act; but when we are about to fulfil the only stipulation which is important to France we are called on to hold our hands, and examine if we cannot discover some flaw in the title we have purchased. Is this a candid, a becoming, an honorable course of proceeding? . . .

◇◇◇◇◇◇◇◇◇◇◇◇◇◇

8. TREATY BETWEEN THE UNITED STATES AND FRANCE FOR THE CESSION OF LOUISIANA[11]

[*Concluded April 30, 1803; ratifications exchanged October 21, 1803*]

. . . *ARTICLE I.* Whereas by the Article the third of the Treaty concluded at St. Ildefonso the 9th Vendémiaire and 9/1st October 1800 between the First Consul of the French Republic and his Catholic Majesty it was agreed as follows.

"His Catholic Majesty promises and engages on his part to cede to the French Republic six months after the full and entire execution of the conditions and Stipulations herein relative to his Royal Highness the Duke of Parma, the Colony or Province of Louisiana with the Same extent that it now has in the hands of Spain, & that it had when France possessed it; and Such as it Should be after the Treaties subsequently entered into between Spain and other States."

And whereas in pursuance of the Treaty and particularly of the third article the French Republic has an incontestible title to the domain and to the possession of the said Territory — The First Consul of the French Republic desiring to give to the United States a strong proof of his friendship doth hereby cede to the said United States in the name of the French Republic for ever and in full Sovereignty the said Territory with all its rights and appurtenances as fully and in the Same manner as they have

[11] Hunter Miller: *Treaties and Other International Acts of the United States,* Vol. II, pp. 498–505. The treaty was signed by Robert R. Livingston, James Monroe, and Barbé Marbois.

been acquired by the French Republic in virtue of the above mentioned Treaty concluded with his Catholic Majesty. . . .

Article III. The inhabitants of the ceded territory shall be incorporated in the Union of the United States and admitted as soon as possible acording to the principles of the federal Constitution to the enjoyment of all the rights, advantages and immunities of citizens of the United States, and in the mean time they shall be maintained and protected in the free enjoyment of their liberty, property and the Religion which they profess. . . .

Article VII. As it is reciprocally advantageous to the commerce of France and the United States to encourage the communication of both nations for a limited time in the country ceded by the present treaty until general arrangements relative to the commerce of both nations may be agreed on; it has been agreed between the contracting parties that the French Ships coming directly from France or any of her colonies loaded only with the produce and manufactures of France or her Said Colonies; and the Ships of Spain coming directly from Spain or any of her colonies loaded only with the produce or manufactures of Spain or her Colonies Shall be admitted during the Space of twelve years in the Port of New-Orleans and in all other legal ports-of-entry within the ceded territory in the Same manner as the Ships of the United States coming directly from France or Spain or any of their Colonies without being Subject to any other or greater duty on merchandize or other or greater tonnage than that paid by the citizens of the United States. . . .

Article IX. The particular Convention Signed this day by the respective Ministers having for its object to provide for the payment of debts due to the Citizens of the United States by the French Republic prior to the 30th September 1800 (8th Vendémiaire and 9) is approved and to have its execution in the Same manner as if it had been inserted in this present treaty and it Shall be ratified in the Same form and in the Same time So that the one Shall not be ratified distinct from the other.

Another particular Convention Signed at the Same date as the present treaty relative to a definitive rule between the contracting parties is in the like manner approved and will be ratified in the Same form, and in the Same time and jointly. . . .

Chapter VII

NEUTRAL RIGHTS AND IMPRESSMENT: 1806–1812

◇◇◇◇◇◇◇◇◇◇◇◇◇◇

CONTROVERSIES, long drawn out, between the United States and Great Britain over maritime rights included the impressment of seamen, the definition of contraband, colonial trade, the search of vessels on the high seas, and the enforcement of blockades. Although the American government wavered now and then in the insistence it placed upon its rights regarding impressment, its position on that subject was fundamentally sound, and in the end impressment was the most important cause of the War of 1812. The policy of the United States regarding its maritime rights is clearly stated in the instructions of January 5, 1804, of Jefferson's Secretary of State, James Madison, to the American minister in London, James Monroe (1). Monroe, departing from his instructions on impressment, signed a treaty with Great Britain in 1806, but it was promptly rejected by President Jefferson.

After war was renewed in Europe following the Peace of Amiens, American commerce was increasingly menaced by the British Orders in Council of May 16, 1806, of January 7 (2), and November 11, 1807 (3), and by the Berlin (4) and Milan Decrees (5) of the French government. The answer of the United States to these measures was the Embargo Act of December 22, 1807 (7), and later the Non-Intercourse Act of March 1, 1809 (8). The account by Henry Adams of the reasons for the British Orders in Council of November 11, 1807, provides a brief commentary on British policy (6).

The nearest approach to a settlement of the difficulties between Great Britain and the United States was the so-called Erskine Agreement (9, 10). At no time subsequent to this agreement, which was rejected by Great Britain, was the American government willing to concede so much.

On May 1, 1810 the United States replaced its Non-Intercourse Act with Macon's Bill No. 2 (11). This afforded France the opportunity to issue the Cadore letter (12) purporting to repeal the Berlin and Milan Decrees. A discussion over the practical application of the Cadore letter (13) led to the Bassano letter (14) which, in effect, terminated the period of American neutrality prior to the War of 1812. Clay's speech in Congress of December 31, 1811 (15), illustrates the ardor of those who thought that the rights of the United States were being frittered away and that the time for stronger action had come.

◇◇◇◇◇◇◇◇◇◇◇◇◇◇

Neutral Rights and Impressment: 1806–1812

1. INSTRUCTIONS TO JAMES MONROE[1]

January 5, 1804

. . . ALTHOUGH there are many important objects which may be thought to invite conventional regulations between the United States and Great Britain, it is evidently proper to leave, for subsequent consideration, such as are less urgent in their nature, or more difficult in their adjustment, and thereby to render the way plainer and shorter to an agreement with respect to objects which cannot be much longer delayed without danger to the good understanding between the two nations. With this view, the plan of a convention contemplated by the President is limited to the cases of impressments of our seamen, of blockades, of visiting and searching our vessels, of contraband of war, and of the trade with hostile colonies, with a few other cases affecting our maritime rights; embracing, however, as inducements to Great Britain to do us justice therein, a provision for the surrender of deserting seamen and soldiers, and for the prevention of contraband supplies to her enemies.

The plan digested for your use is subjoined. The first column contains the articles which are to be proposed in the first instance, and which are considered as within our just expectations; the second modifies the articles into the concessions which the British Government may possibly require, and which it may be expedient for us ultimately to admit.[2]

SECOND AND ULTIMATUM

Article I. No seaman, seafaring, or other person shall, upon the high seas and without the jurisdiction of either party, be demanded or taken out of any ship or vessel belonging to the citizens or subjects of one of the parties, by the public or private armed ships belonging to, or in the service of, the other party; and strict and effectual orders shall be given for the due observance of this engagement; but it is to be understood that this article shall not exempt any person on board the ships of either of the parties from being taken therefrom by the other party, in cases where they may be liable to be so taken according to the laws of nations, which liability, however, shall not be construed to extend in any case to seamen, or seafaring persons being actually part of the crew of the vessel in which they may be, nor to persons of any description passing from one port to another port of either of the parties. . . .

Article IV. Contraband of war shall consist of the following articles only: salt petre, sulphur, cuirasses, pikes, swords, sword belts, knapsacks, saddles and bridles, cannons, mortars, fire arms, pistols, bombs, granades, bullets, firelocks, flints, matches, and gunpowder, excepting, however, the quantity of the said articles which may be necessary for the defence or

[1] Lowrie and Clarke: *American State Papers, Foreign Relations,* Vol. III, pp. 81–91.

[2] Since the second column indicated what the United States was willing to accept, the articles included in the first column are omitted.

use of the ship, and those who comprise the crew; and no other articles whatever, not here enumerated, shall be reputed contraband, or liable to confiscation, but shall pass freely, without being subjected to the smallest difficulty, unless they be enemy's property; and it is to be particularly understood, that under the denomination of enemy's property is not to be comprised the merchandise of the growth, produce, or manufactures of the countries or dominions at war, which shall have been acquired by the citizens or subjects of the neutral Power, and shall be transported for their account; which merchandise cannot, in any case, or on any pretext, be excepted from the freedom of the neutral flag. . . .

Article VI. In order to determine what characterizes a blockaded port, that denomination is given only to a port where there is, by the disposition of the Power which attacks it with ships stationary or sufficiently near, an evident danger in entering. . . .

OBSERVATIONS ON THE PRECEDING PLAN

[On Article I] . . . Although Great Britain has not yet adopted in the same latitude with most other nations the immunities of a neutral flag, she will not deny the general freedom of the high seas, and of neutral vessels navigating them, with such exceptions only as are annexed to it by the law of nations. She must produce, then, such an exception in the law of nations in favor of the right she contends for. . . . But nowhere will she find an exception to this freedom of the seas, and of neutral flags, which justifies the taking away of any person, not an enemy in military service, found on board a neutral vessel.

If treaties, British as well as others, are to be consulted on this subject, it will equally appear that no countenance to the practice can be found in them. . . .

It is not, then, from the law or the usage of nations, nor from the tenor of treaties, that any sanction can be derived for the practice in question. And surely it will not be pretended that the sovereignty of any nation extends, in any case whatever, beyond its own dominions, and its own vessels on the high seas; such a doctrine would give just alarm to all nations, and, more than any thing, would countenance the imputation of aspiring to a universal empire of the seas. It would be the less admissible, too, as it would be applicable to times of peace as well as to times of war, and to property as well as to persons. If the law of allegiance, which is a municipal law, be in force at all on the high seas on board foreign vessels, it must be so at all times there, as it is within its acknowledged sphere. If the reason alleged for it be good in time of war, namely, that the sovereign has then a right to the service of all his subjects, it must be good at all times, because at all times he has the same right to their service. War is not the only occasion for which he may want their services, nor is external danger the only danger against which their services may be required for his security. Again: if the authority of a municipal law can operate on persons in foreign vessels on the high seas, because, within the dominion of their sovereign, they would be subject to that law, and are violating that law by being in that situation, how reject the inference that the authority of a municipal law may equally be enforced on board foreign vessels on the high seas, against articles of property exported in violation of such a law, or belonging to the country from which it was exported? And thus every commercial regulation, in time of peace, too, as well as of war, would be made obligatory on foreigners and their vessels, not only whilst within the dominion of the sovereign making the regulation, but in every sea, and at every distance, where an armed vessel might meet with them. Another inference deserves attention: if the subjects of one sovereign may be taken by force from the vessels of another on the high seas, the right of taking them when found, implies the right of searching for them; a vexation of commerce, especially in time of peace, which has not yet been attempted, and which, for that as well as other reasons, may be regarded as contradicting the principle from which it would flow.

Taking reason and justice for the tests of this practice, it is peculiarly indefensible, because it deprives the dearest rights of persons of a regular trial, to which the most inconsiderable article of property captured on the high seas is entitled, and leaves their destiny to the will of an officer, sometimes cruel, often ignorant, and generally interested, by his want of mariners, in his own decisions. Whenever property found in a neutral vessel is supposed to be liable on any grounds to capture and condemnation, the rule in all cases is, that the question shall not be decided by the captor, but be carried before a legal tribunal, where a regular trial may be had, and where the captor himself is liable to damages for an abuse of his power. Can it be reasonable, then, or just, that a belligerent commander, who is thus restricted and thus responsible in a case of mere property of trivial amount, should be permitted, without recurring to any tribunal whatever, to examine the crew of a neutral vessel to decide the important question of their respective allegiances, and to carry that decision into instant execution, by forcing every individual he may choose into a service abhorrent to his feelings, cutting him off from his most tender connexions, exposing his mind and his person to the most humiliating discipline, and his life itself to the greatest dangers? Reason, justice, and humanity unite in protesting against so extravagant a proceeding. And what is the pretext for it? It is, that the similarity of language and of features between American citizens and British subjects are such as not easily to be distinguished; and that, without this arbitrary and summary authority to make the distinction, British subjects would escape, under the name of American citizens, from the duty which they owe to their sovereign. Is, then, the difficulty of distinguishing a mariner of one country from the mariner of the other, and the importance of his services, a good plea for referring the question, whether he belongs to the one or to the other, to an arbitrary decision on the spot, by an interested and irresponsible officer? In all other cases, the difficulty and the importance of questions are considered as reasons for requiring greater care and formality in investigating them, and greater security for a right decision on them. To say that precautions of this sort are incompatible with the object, is to admit that the object is unjustifiable; since the only means by which it can be pursued are such as cannot be justified. . . .

[On Article IV.] This enumeration of contraband articles is copied from the treaty of 1781 between Great Britain and Russia. . . . The sequel of the article . . . is taken from the same model, with the addition of the terms, "in any case or on any pretext." This addition is meant to embrace more explicitly our right to trade freely with the colonies at war with Great Britain, and between them and all parts of the world, in colonial productions, being at the time not enemy's, but neutral property. . . .

[On Article VI.] The fictitious blockades proclaimed by Great Britain, and made the pretext for violating the commerce of neutral nations, has been one of the greatest abuses ever committed on the high seas. During the late war they were carried to an extravagance, which would have been ridiculous, if in their effects they had not inflicted such serious and extensive injuries on neutral nations. Ports were proclaimed in a state of blockade, previous to the arrival of any force at them, were considered in that state without regard to intermissions in the presence of the blockading force, and the proclamations left in operation after its final departure, the British cruisers during the whole time seizing every vessel bound to such ports, at whatever distance from them, and the British prize courts pronouncing condemnations wherever a knowledge of the proclamation at the time of sailing could be presumed, although it might afterwards be known that no real blockade existed. The whole scene was a perfect mockery, in which fact was sacrificed to form, and right to power and plunder. The United States were among the greatest sufferers; and would have been still more so, if redress for some of the spoliations proceeding from this source had not fallen within the provisions of an article in the treaty of 1794.

From the effect of this and other arbitrary practices of Great Britain on the temper and policy of neutral nations toward her; from the spirit of her treaty made near the close of the late war with Russia; from the general disposition manifested at the beginning of the present towards the United States, and the comparative moderation observed in Europe with respect to blockades, (if indeed the two cases of the Weser and Elbe are not to be excepted), it was hoped that the mockeries and mischiefs practised under the name of the blockades would no where be repeated. It is found, however, that the West Indies are again the theatre of them. The three entire and extensive islands of Martinique, Guadaloupe, and St. Domingo have been published as in a state of blockade, although the whole naval force applied to the purpose is inconsiderable; although it appears that a part of this inconsiderable force is occasionally seen at the distance of many leagues at sea; although it does not appear that more than one or two ports at the most have at any time been actually blockaded; and although complaints are heard, that the British ships of war do not protect their own trade against the numerous cruisers from the islands under this pretended blockade. . . .

◇◇◇◇◇◇◇◇◇◇◇◇◇

2. BRITISH ORDERS IN COUNCIL: JANUARY 7, 1807[3]

At a court at the Queen's Palace, the 7th of January, 1807: Present the King's Most Excellent Majesty in Council.

WHEREAS the French Government has issued certain orders. . . . His Majesty is thereupon pleased, by and with the advice of his Privy Council, to order, and it is hereby ordered, that no vessels shall be permitted to trade from one port to another, both which ports shall belong to or be in the possession of France or her allies, or shall be so far under their control as that British vessels may not trade freely thereat; and the commanders of His Majesty's ships of war and privateers shall be, and are hereby, instructed to warn every neutral vessel coming from any such port, and destined to another such port, to discontinue her voyage, and not to proceed to any such port; and any vessel, after being so warned, or any vessel coming from any such port, after a reasonable time shall have been afforded for receiving information of this His Majesty's order, which shall be found proceeding to another such port, shall be captured and brought in, and together with her cargo shall be condemned as lawful prize; and His Majesty's principal Secretaries of State, the Lords Commissioners of the Admiralty, and the Judges of the High Court of Admiralty, and the Courts of Vice Admiralty, are to take the necessary measures herein as to them shall respectively appertain.

◇◇◇◇◇◇◇◇◇◇◇◇◇

3. BRITISH ORDERS IN COUNCIL: NOVEMBER 11, 1807[4]

At the Court at the Queen's Palace, the 11th of November 1807: Present, the King's Most Excellent Majesty in Council.

WHEREAS certain orders, establishing an unprecedented system of warfare against this Kingdom, and aimed especially at the destruction of its commerce and resources, were . . . issued by the Government of France. . . .

His Majesty is therefore pleased, by and with the advice of his Privy

[3] *Annals of the Congress of the United States*, 10th Congress, 2nd Session (Washington, 1853), p. 1695.
[4] Ibid., pp. 1698–1701.

Council, to order, and it is hereby ordered, that all the ports and places of France and her allies, or of any other country at war with His Majesty, and all other ports or places in Europe, from which, although not at war with His Majesty, the British flag is excluded, and all ports or places in the colonies belonging to His Majesty's enemies, shall, from henceforth, be subject to the same restrictions in point of trade and navigation, with the exceptions herein after mentioned, as if the same were actually blockaded by His Majesty's naval forces, in the most strict and rigorous manner: And it is hereby further ordered and declared, that all trade in articles, which are of the produce or manufacture of the said countries or colonies, shall be deemed and considered to be unlawful; and that every vessel trading from or to the said countries or colonies, together with all goods and merchandise on board, and all articles of the produce or manufacture of the said countries or colonies, shall be captured and condemned as prize to the captors. . . .

◇◇◇◇◇◇◇◇◇◇◇◇◇

4. BERLIN DECREE: NOVEMBER 21, 1806[5]

Imperial Camp, Berlin

. . . WE HAVE resolved to enforce against England the usages which she has consecrated in her maritime code.

The present decree shall be considered as the fundamental law of the Empire, until England has acknowledged that the rights of war are the same on the land as at sea; that it cannot be extended to any private property whatever, nor to persons who are not military, and until the right of blockade be restrained to fortified places, actually invested by competent forces. . . .

Art. 1. The British islands are declared in a state of blockade.

Art. 2. All Commerce and correspondence with the British islands are prohibited. In consequence, letters or packets addressed either to England, to an Englishman, or in the English language, shall not pass through the post office, and shall be seized.

Art. 3. Every subject of England, of what rank and condition soever, who shall be found in the countries occupied by our troops, or by those of our allies, shall be made a prisoner of war.

Art. 4. All magazines, merchandise, or property whatsoever belonging to a subject of England, shall be declared lawful prize.

Art. 5. The trade in English merchandise is forbidden. All merchandise belonging to England, or coming from its manufactories and colonies, is declared lawful prize.

Art. 6. One-half of the proceeds of the confiscation of the merchandise, and property declared good prize by the preceding articles, shall be ap-

[5] Ibid., pp. 1749–51.

plied to indemnify the merchants for the losses which they have suffered by the capture of merchant vessels by English cruisers.

Art. 7. No vessel coming directly from England, or from the English colonies, or having been there since the publication of the present decree, shall be received in any port.

Art. 8. Every vessel contravening the above clause, by means of a false declaration, shall be seized, and the vessel and cargo confiscated as if they were English property.

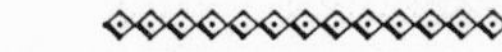

5. MILAN DECREE: DECEMBER 17, 1807[6]

Napoleon, Emperor of the French, King of Italy and Protector of the Rhenish Confederation:

At Our Royal Palace at Milan

OBSERVING the measures adopted by the British Government, on the 11th November last. . . .

Observing that . . . the English . . . have availed themselves of the tolerance of Government to establish the infamous principle that the flag of a nation does not cover goods and to have to their right of blockade an arbitrary extension . . . we have decreed and do decree as follows:

Art. 1. Every ship, to whatever nation it may belong, that shall have submitted to be searched by an English ship, or to a voyage to England, or shall have paid any tax whatsoever to the English Government, is thereby, and for that alone, declared to be denationalized, to have forfeited the protection of its king, and to have become English property.

Art. 2. Whether the ships thus denationalized by the arbitrary measures of the English Government enter into our ports, or those of our allies, or whether they fall into the hands of our ships of war, or of our privateers, they are declared to be good and lawful prize.

Art. 3. The British islands are declared to be in a state of blockade, both by land and sea. Every ship, of whatever nation, or whatsoever the nature of its cargo may so be, that sails from the ports of England, or those of the English colonies, and of the countries occupied by English troops, and proceeding to England, or to the English colonies, or to countries occupied by English troops, is good and lawful prize, as contrary to the present decree, and may be captured by our ships of war, or our privateers, and adjudged to the captor.

Art. 4. These measures, which are resorted to only in just retaliation of the barbarous system adopted by England, which assimilates its legislation to that of Algiers, shall cease to have any effect with respect to all nations who shall have the firmness to compel the English Government to respect their flag. They shall continue to be rigorously in force as long

[6] Ibid., pp. 1751–2.

as that Government does not return to the principle of the law of nations, which regulates the relations of civilized States in a state of war. The provisions of the present decree shall be abrogated and null, in fact, as soon as the English abide again by the principles of the law of nations, which are also the principles of justice and of honor.

All our ministers are charged with the execution of the present decree, which shall be inserted in the bulletin of the laws.

◇◇◇◇◇◇◇◇◇◇◇◇◇

6. BRITISH REASONS FOR THE ORDERS IN COUNCIL[7]

. . . MANY MEMBERS of the British government and nearly the whole British navy were growing rich on the plunder of American commerce. From King George downward, mighty influences were involved in maintaining a system which corrupted law officers, judges, admirals, and even the King himself. Spencer Perceval's proposed Order in Council extended these abuses over whatever branches of commerce had hitherto been exempt; turned a new torrent of corruption into the government; and polluted the sources of British honor. In the light of Lord Bathurst's protest, and his significant avowal that the object of the proposed order, though general in form, was in fact nothing but the colonial trade carried on through America, Canning might well wish to *publish* nothing that would draw attention to what he called the "commercial" side of the affair. Jefferson's measures of peaceful coercion bore unexpected results, reacting upon foreign nations by stimulating every mean and sordid motive. No possible war could have so degraded England.

As the Cabinet came closer to the point, the political, or retaliatory, object of the new order disappeared, and its commercial character was exclusively set forth. In a letter written about November 30, by Spencer Perceval to Charles Abbot, Speaker of the House of Commons, not a word was said of retaliation, or of any political motive in this process of "recasting the law of trade and navigation, as far as belligerent principles are concerned, for the whole world."

"The short principle is," said Perceval,[8] "that trade in British produce and manufactures, and trade either from a British port or with a British destination, is to be protected as much as possible. For this purpose all the countries where French influence prevails to exclude the British flag shall have no trade but to or from this country, or from its allies. All other countries, the few that remain strictly neutral (with the exception of the

---

[7] Henry Adams: *History of the United States of America During the Administration of Thomas Jefferson*, 4 vols. (New York: Charles Scribner's Sons, 1890); reprinted by Albert and Charles Boni (New York, 1930), Vol. IV, pp. 97–9. Spencer Perceval was Chancellor of the Exchequer, and George Canning was Foreign Minister.

[8] Spencer Perceval to Speaker Abbot: *Diary and Correspondence of Lord Colchester*, ii, p. 134.

colonial trade, which backward and forward direct they may carry on), cannot trade but through this being done as an ally with any of the countries connected with France. If therefore we can accomplish our purpose, it will come to this, – that either those countries will have no trade, or they must be content to accept it through us. This is a formidable and tremendous state of the world; but all the part of it which is particularly harassing to English interests was existing through the new severity with which Bonaparte's decrees of exclusion against our trade were called into action. Our proceeding does not aggravate our distress from it. If he can keep out our trade he will; and he would do so if he could, independent of our orders. Our orders only add this circumstance: they say to the enemy, 'If you will not have *our* trade, as far as we can help it you shall have *none;* and as to so much of any trade as you can carry on yourselves, or others carry on with you through us, if you admit it you shall pay for it. The only trade, cheap and untaxed, which you shall have shall be either direct from us, in our own produce and manufactures, or from our allies, whose increased prosperity will be an advantage to us.' "

These private expressions implied that retaliation upon France for her offence against international law was a pretence on the part of Perceval and Canning, under the cover of which they intended to force British commerce upon France contrary to French wishes. The act of Napoleon in excluding British produce from French dominions violated no rule of international law, and warranted no retaliation except an exclusion of French produce from British dominions. The rejoinder, "If you will not have *our* trade you shall have *none,*" was not good law, if law could be disputed when affirmed by men like Lord Eldon and Lord Stowell, echoed by courts, parliaments, and press, – not only in private, but in public; not only in 1807, but for long years afterward; and not only at moments, but without interruption. . . .

◇◇◇◇◇◇◇◇◇◇◇◇◇

7. THE EMBARGO ACT: DECEMBER 22, 1807[9]

An Act laying an Embargo on all ships and vessels in the ports and harbors of the United States.

BE IT enacted by the Senate and House of Representatives of the United States of America in Congress assembled, That an embargo be, and hereby is laid on all ships and vessels in the ports and places within the limits or jurisdiction of the United States, cleared or not cleared, bound to any foreign port or place; and that no clearance be furnished to any ship or vessel bound to such foreign port or place, except vessels under the immediate direction of the President of the United States: and that the Presi-

[9] *Public Statutes at Large of the United States,* Vol. II, pp. 451–3.

dent be authorized to give such instructions to the officers of the revenue, and of the navy and revenue cutters of the United States, as shall appear best adapted for carrying the same into full effect: *Provided,* that nothing herein contained shall be construed to prevent the departure of any foreign ship or vessel, either in ballast, or with the goods, wares and merchandise on board of such foreign ship or vessel, when notified of this act.

Sec. 2. And be it further enacted, That during the continuance of this act, no registered, or sea letter vessel, having on board goods, wares and merchandise, shall be allowed to depart from one port of the United States to any other within the same, unless the master, owner, consignee or factor of such vessel shall first give bond, with one or more sureties to the collector of the district from which she is bound to depart, in a sum of double the value of the vessel and cargo, that the said goods, wares, or merchandise shall be relanded in some port of the United States, dangers of the seas excepted, which bond, and also a certificate from the collector where the same may be relanded, shall by the collector respectively be transmitted to the Secretary of the Treasury. All armed vessels possessing public commissions from any foreign power, are not to be considered as liable to the embargo laid by this act.

◇◇◇◇◇◇◇◇◇◇◇◇◇

8. NON-INTERCOURSE ACT: MARCH 1, 1809[10]

BE IT enacted by the Senate and House of Representatives of the United States of America in Congress assembled, That from and after the passing of this act, the entrance of the harbors and waters of the United States and of the territories thereof, be, and the same is hereby interdicted to all public ships and vessels belonging to Great Britain or France, excepting vessels only which may be forced in by distress, or which are charged with despatches or business from the government to which they belong, and also packets having no cargo nor merchandise on board. . . .

Sec. 3. And be it further enacted, That from and after the twentieth day of May next, the entrance of the harbors and waters of the United States and the territories thereof be, and the same is hereby interdicted to all ships or vessels sailing under the flag of Great Britain or France, or owned in whole or in part by any citizen or subject of either. . . .

Sec. 4. And be it further enacted, That from and after the twentieth day of May next, it shall not be lawful to import into the United States or the territories thereof, any goods, wares or merchandise whatever, from any port or place situated in Great Britain or Ireland, or in any of the colonies or dependencies of Great Britain, nor from any port or place situated in France, or in any of her colonies or dependencies, nor from any port or place in the actual possession of either Great Britain or France. . . .

---

10 *Public Statutes at Large of the United States,* Vol. II, pp. 528–33.

Sec. 11. And be it further enacted, That the President of the United States, be and he hereby is authorized, in case either France or Great Britain shall so revoke or modify her edicts, as that they shall cease to violate the neutral commerce of the United States, to declare the same by proclamation; after which the trade of the United States, suspended by this act, and by the act laying an embargo on all ships and vessels in the ports and harbors of the United States, and the several acts supplementary thereto, may be renewed with the nation so doing: *Provided,* that all penalties and forfeitures which shall have been previously incurred, by virtue of this or of any other act, the operation of which shall so cease and determine, shall be recovered and distributed, in like manner as if the same had continued in full force and virtue. . . .

Sec. 17. And be it further enacted, That the act to prohibit the importation of certain goods, wares and merchandise, passed the eighteenth of April, one thousand eight hundred and six, and the act supplementary thereto, be, and the same are hereby repealed, from and after the said twentieth day of May next: . . .

Sec. 19. And be it further enacted, That this act shall continue and be in force until the end of the next session of Congress, and no longer. . . .

9. CANNING'S INSTRUCTIONS TO DAVID M. ERSKINE OF JANUARY 23, 1809[11]

IF THERE really exist in those individuals who are to have a leading share in the new administration of the United States that disposition to come to a complete and cordial understanding with Great Britain, of which you have received from them such positive assurances in meeting that disposition, it would be useless and unprofitable to recur to a recapitulation of the causes from which the differences between the two Governments have arisen, or of the arguments already so often repeated in support of that system of retaliation to which His Majesty has unwillingly had recourse.

That system His Majesty must unquestionably continue to maintain, unless the object of it can be otherwise accomplished.

But after the profession, on the part of so many of the leading members of the Government of the United States, of a sincere desire to contribute to that object in a manner which should render the continuance of the system adopted by the British Government unnecessary, it is thought right that a fair opportunity should be afforded to the American Government to explain its meaning, and to give proof of its sincerity.

The extension of the interdiction of the American harbors to the ships of war of France as well as of Great Britain, is, as stated in my former

[11] Lowrie and Clarke: *American State Papers, Foreign Relations,* Vol. III, pp. 300–1.

despatch, an acceptable symptom of a system of impartiality towards both belligerents; the first that has been publicly manifested by the American Government.

The like extension of the non-importation act to other belligerents is equally proper in this view. These measures remove those preliminary objections, which must otherwise have precluded any useful or amicable discussion.

In this state of things, it is possible for Great Britain to entertain propositions which, while such manifest partiality was shown to her enemies, were not consistent either with her dignity or her interest.

From the report of your conversations with Mr. Madison, Mr. Gallatin, and Mr. Smith, it appears:

1. That the American Government is prepared, in the event of His Majesty's consenting to withdraw the orders in council of January and November, 1807, to withdraw contemporaneously on its part the interdiction of its harbours to ships of war, and all non-intercourse and non-importation acts, so far as respects Great Britain; leaving them in force with respect to France, and the Powers which adopt or act under her decrees.

2. (What is of the utmost importance, as precluding a new source of misunderstanding, which might arise after the adjustment of the other questions,) that America is willing to renounce, during the present war, the pretension of carrying on in time of war all trade with the enemy's colonies, from which she was excluded during peace.

3. Great Britain, for the purpose of securing the operation of the embargo, and of the *bona fide* intention of America to prevent her citizens from trading with France and the Powers adopting and acting under the French decrees, is to be considered as being at liberty to capture all such American vessels as may be found attempting to trade with the ports of any of these Powers; without which security for the observance of the embargo, the raising of it nominally with respect to Great Britain alone, would, in fact, raise it with respect to all the world.

On these conditions His Majesty would consent to withdraw the orders in council of January and November, 1807, so far as respects America.

As the first and second of these conditions are the suggestions of the persons in authority in America to you, and as Mr. Pinckney has recently (but for the first time) expressed to me his opinion that there will be no indisposition on the part of his Government to the enforcement, by the naval power of Great Britain, of the regulations of America with respect to France and the countries to which these regulations continue to apply, but that his Government was itself aware that without such enforcement those regulations must be altogether nugatory, I flatter myself that there will be no difficulty in obtaining a distinct and official recognition of these conditions from the American Government.

For this purpose, you are at liberty to communicate this despatch *in extenso* to the American Government.

Upon receiving through you, on the part of the American Government, a distinct and official recognition of the three above-mentioned conditions, His Majesty will lose no time in sending to America a minister fully empowered to consign them to a formal and regular treaty.

As, however, it is possible that the delay which must intervene before the actual conclusion of a treaty may appear to the American Government to deprive this arrangement of part of its benefits, I am to authorize you, if the American Government should be desirous of acting upon the agreement before it is reduced into a regular form, (either by the immediate repeal of the embargo and the other acts in question, or by engaging to repeal them on a particular day,) to assure the American Government of His Majesty's readiness to meet such a disposition in the manner best calculated to give it immediate effect.

Upon the receipt here of an official note containing an engagement for the adoption by the American Government of the three conditions above specified, His Majesty will be prepared, on the faith of such engagement, either immediately (if the repeal shall have been immediate in America) or on any day specified by the American Government for that repeal, reciprocally to recall the orders in council, without waiting for the conclusion of the treaty; and you are authorized, in the circumstances herein described, to make such reciprocal engagement on his majesty's behalf.

◇◇◇◇◇◇◇◇◇◇◇◇◇

10. THE FAILURE OF THE ERSKINE AGREEMENT[12]

[*David M. Erskine to Robert Smith*]

Washington, August 14, 1809

. . . THE EXPLANATIONS which you request from me. . . shall be given with candor. . . .

After some other observations, Mr. Madison . . . [referring to a statement of Madison when he was Secretary of State] stated . . . that, as the world must be convinced that America had in vain taken all the means in her power to obtain from Great Britain and France a just attention to her rights, as a neutral Power, by representations and remonstrances, she would be fully justified in having recourse to hostilities with either belligerent, and that she only hesitated to do so from the difficulty of contending with both; but that she must be driven even to endeavor to maintain her rights against the two greatest Powers in the world, unless either of them should relax their restrictions upon neutral commerce; in which case, the United States would at once side with that Power against the other which might continue its aggressions. . . .

I understood, very distinctly, that the observations of the Secretary of

[12] Lowrie and Clarke: *American State Papers, Foreign Relations,* Vol. III, pp. 305–6.

State were intended to convey an opinion, as to what ought and would be the course pursued by the United States, in the event of His Majesty's orders in council being withdrawn.

In these sentiments and opinions you concurred, as I collected from the tenor of several conversations which I held with you at that period. . . .

In the course of a private interview I had with Mr. Gallatin, the Secretary of the Treasury, he intimated that the non-intercourse law which was then likely to be passed by the Congress, might be considered as removing two very important grounds of difference with Great Britain, viz: the non-importation act, as applicable to her alone, and also the President's proclamation, whereby the ships of Great Britain were excluded from the ports of the United States, while those of France were permitted to enter; but that, by the non-intercourse law, both Powers were placed on the same footing. He did not pretend to say that this measure had been taken from any motives of concession to Great Britain; but as, in fact, those consequences followed, he conceived they might be considered as removing the two great obstacles to a conciliation.

He adverted also to the probability of an adjustment of another important point in dispute between the two countries, as he said he knew that it was intended by the United States to abandon the attempt to carry on a trade with the colonies of the belligerents in time of war, which was not allowed in time of peace, and to trust to their being permitted by the French to carry on such trade in peace, so as to entitle them to a continuance of it in time of war. . . .

Such was the substance, sir, of the unofficial conversations which I had held with Mr. Madison, Mr. Gallatin, and yourself, which I did not consider, or represent to His Majesty's Government, as intended with any other view than to endeavor to bring about the repeal of the orders in council, by showing that many of the obstacles which had stood in the way of an amicable adjustment of the differences between the two countries were already removed, and that a fair prospect existed of settling what remained; since the United States exhibited a determination to resist the unjust aggressions upon her neutral rights, which was all that Great Britain had ever required; but I certainly never received any assurances from the American Government that they would pledge themselves to adopt the conditions specified in Mr. Canning's instructions as preliminaries; nor did I ever hold out such an expectation to His Majesty's Government; having always stated to them that, in the event of His Majesty's thinking it just or expedient, to cause his orders in council to be withdrawn the President would take off the embargo as respected England, leaving it in operation against France, and the Powers which adopted or acted under her decrees, according to the authority which was vested in him at that time by the Congress of the United States; and that there was every reason to expect that a satisfactory arrangement might be made upon the points of the colonial trade, which had been so long in dispute between the two countries. . . .

It would be unavailing at the present moment to enter upon an examination of the "pretensions set forth in Mr. Canning's letter of instructions," which you are pleased to term "extraordinary."

I consider it, however, to be my duty to declare that, during my negotiation with you, which led to the conclusion of the provisional agreement, I found no reason to believe that any difficulties would occur in the accomplishment of the two former conditions, as far as it was in the power of the President of the United States to accede to the first, and consistently with the explanation which I have before given of the second point; on the contrary, I received assurances, through you, that the President would comply (as far as it was in his power) with the first condition, and that there could be no doubt that the Congress would think it incumbent upon them to assert the rights of the United States against such Powers as should adopt or act under the decrees of France, as soon as their actual conduct or determination upon that subject could be ascertained; but that, in the mean time, that the President had not the power, and could not undertake the pledge himself in the formal manner required to that effect.

I received also assurances from you that no doubt could be reasonably entertained that a satisfactory arrangement might be made in a treaty upon the subject of the second condition mentioned in Mr. Canning's instructions, according to my explanation of it in the foregoing part of this letter, but that it necessarily would form an article of a treaty, in which the various pretensions of the two countries should be settled.

The third condition you certainly very distinctly informed me could not be recognised by the President, but you added, what had great weight in my mind, that you did not see why any great importance should be attached to such a recognition; because it would be impossible that a citizen of the United States could prefer a complaint to his Government, on account of the capture of his vessel, while engaged in a trade absolutely interdicted by the laws of his country.

Under these circumstances, therefore, finding that I could not obtain the recognitions specified in Mr. Canning's despatch of the 23d of January, (which formed but *one part* of his instructions to me,) in the formal manner required, I considered that it would be in vain to lay before the Government of the United States the despatch in question, which I was at *liberty* to have done *in extenso*, had I thought proper. But as I had such strong grounds for believing that the object of His Majesty's Government could be attained, though in a different manner, and the spirit, at least, of my several letters of instructions be fully complied with, I felt a thorough conviction upon my mind that I should be acting in conformity with His Majesty's wishes; and, accordingly, concluded the late provisional agreement, on His Majesty's behalf, with the Government of the United States.

The disavowal, by His Majesty, is a painful proof to me that I had formed an erroneous judgment of His Majesty's views and the intention of my instructions; and I have most severely to lament that an act of mine (though unintentionally) should produce any embarrassment in the relations between the two countries. . . .

◇◇◇◇◇◇◇◇◇◇◇◇◇

11. MACON'S BILL, NO. 2: MAY 1, 1810[13]

BE IT enacted by the Senate and House of Representatives of the United States of America in Congress assembled, That from and after the passage of this act, no British or French armed vessel shall be permitted to enter the harbors or waters under the jurisdiction of the United States . . . except when they shall be forced in by distress, by the dangers of the sea, or when charged with despatches or business from their government, or coming as a public packet for the conveyance of letters. . . .

Sec. 2. And be it further enacted, That all pacific intercourse with any interdicted foreign armed vessels, the officers or crew thereof, is hereby forbidden. . . .

Sec. 4. And be it further enacted, That in case either Great Britain or France shall, before the third Day of March next, so revoke or modify her edicts as that they shall cease to violate the neutral commerce of the United States, which fact the President of the United States shall declare by proclamation, and if the other nation shall not within three months thereafter so revoke or modify her edicts in like manner, then the third, fourth, fifth, sixth, seventh, eight, ninth, tenth and eighteenth sections of the act, entitled "An act to interdict the commercial intercourse between the United States and Great Britain and France and their dependencies, and for other purposes,"[14] shall, from and after the expiration of three months from the date of the proclamation aforesaid, be revived and have full force and effect, so far as relates to the dominions, colonies and dependencies, and to the articles the growth, produce or manufacture of the dominions, colonies and dependencies of the nation thus refusing or neglecting to revoke or modify her edicts in the manner aforesaid. And the restrictions imposed by this act shall, from the date of such proclamation, cease and be discontinued in relation to the nation revoking or modifying her decrees in the manner aforesaid.

---

13 *Public Statutes at Large of the United States,* Vol. II, pp. 605–6.
14 This was the act of March 1, 1809. See Ibid., pp. 528–33.

◇◇◇◇◇◇◇◇◇◇◇◇◇

12. THE CADORE LETTER[15]

[*The Duc de Cadore to General John Armstrong*]

August 5, 1810

I HAVE laid before His Majesty, the Emperor and King, the act of Congress of the 1st of May,[16] taken from the Gazette of the United States, which you have sent to me. . . .

The act of the 1st March[17] has raised the embargo, and substituted for it a measure the most injurious to the interests of France.

This act, of which the Emperor knew nothing until very lately, interdicted to American vessels the commerce of France, at the time it authorized that to Spain, Naples, and Holland, that is to say, to the countries under French influence, and denounced confiscation against all French vessels which should enter the ports of America. Reprisal was a right, and commanded by the dignity of France, a circumstance on which it was impossible to make a compromise (de transiger). The sequestration of all the American vessels in France has been the necessary consequence of the measure taken by Congress.

Now Congress retrace their steps, (revient sur sespas;) they revoke the act of the 1st of March; the ports of America are open to French commerce, and France is no longer interdicted to the Americans; In short, Congress engages to oppose itself to that one of the belligerent Powers which should refuse to acknowledge the rights of neutrals.

In this new state of things, I am authorized to declare to you, sir, that the decrees of Berlin and Milan are revoked, and that after the first of November they will cease to have effect; it being understood that, in consequence of this declaration, the English shall revoke their orders in council, and renounce the new principles of blockade, which they have wished to establish; or that the United States, conformably to the act you have just communicated, shall cause their rights to be respected by the English. . . .

◇◇◇◇◇◇◇◇◇◇◇◇◇

13. REVOCATION OF THE FRENCH DECREES[18]

[*James Monroe to A. J. Foster*]

July 23, 1811

I HAVE submitted to the President your several letters of the 3d and 16th of this month, relative to the British orders in council, and the block-

[15] Lowrie and Clarke: *American State Papers, Foreign Relations,* Vol. III, pp. 386–7.
[16] Macon's Bill No. 2 of May 1, 1810.
[17] Non-Intercourse Act: March 1, 1809.
[18] Lowrie and Clarke: *American State Papers, Foreign Relations,* Vol. III, pp. 439–42.

ade of May, 1806, and I have now the honor to communicate to you his sentiments on the view which you have presented of those measures of your Government. . . .

The United States are as little disposed now as heretofore to enter into the question concerning the priority of aggression by the two belligerents, which could not be justified by either, by the priority of those of the other. But as you bring forward that plea in support of the orders in council, I must be permitted to remark that you have yourself furnished a conclusive answer to it, by admitting that the blockade of May, 1806, which was prior to the first of the French decrees, would not be legal unless supported through the whole extent of the coast, from the Elbe to Brest, by an adequate naval force. That such a naval force was actually applied, and continued, in the requisite strictness, until that blockade was comprised in and superseded by the orders of November of the following year, or even until the French decree of the same year, will not, I presume, be alleged.

But waiving this question of priority, can it be seen, without both surprise and regret, that it is still contended that the orders in council are justified by the principle of retaliation, and that this principle is strengthened by the inability of France to enforce her decrees? A retaliation is, in its name, and its essential character, a returning a like for like. Is the deadly blow of the orders in council against one-half of our commerce a return of like for like to an empty threat in the French decrees against the other half? It may be a vindictive hostility as far as its effect falls on the enemy. But when falling on a neutral, who, on no pretext, can be liable for more than the measure of injury received through such neutral, it would not be a retaliation, but a positive wrong, by the plea on which it is founded. . . .

Heretofore it has been the usage of belligerent nations to carry on their trade through the intervention of neutrals, and this had the beneficial effect of extending to the former the advantages of peace while suffering under the calamities of war. To reverse the rule, and to extend to nations at peace the calamities of war, is a change as novel and extraordinary as it is at variance with justice and public law. . . .

In the discussions which have taken place on the subject of the orders in council and blockade of May, 1806, the British Government, in conformity to the principle on which the orders in council are said to be founded, declared that they should cease to operate as soon as France revoked her edicts. It was stated also that the British Government would proceed *pari passu* with the Government of France in the revocation of her edicts. I will proceed to show that the obligation on Great Britain to revoke her orders is complete, according to her own engagement, and that the revocation ought not to be longer delayed. . . .

On the 5th August, 1810, the French Minister of Foreign Affairs addressed a note to the minister plenipotentiary of the United States at Paris, informing him that the decrees of Berlin and Milan were revoked, the revocation to take effect on the 1st November following; that the measure had been taken by his Government, in confidence that the British Government would revoke its orders, and renounce its new principle of blockade, or that the United States would cause their rights to be respected, conformably to the act of May 1, 1810. . . .

The letter of the 5th August, which announced the revocation of the French decrees, was communicated to this Government, in consequence of which the President issued a proclamation on the 2d November, the day after that on which the repeal of the French decrees was to take effect, in which he declared that all the restrictions imposed by the act of May 1, 1810, should cease and be discontinued in relation to France and her dependencies. It was a necessary consequence of this proclamation, also, that, if Great Britain did not revoke her edicts, the non-importation law would operate against her at the end of three months. This actually took place. She declined the revocation, and, on the 2d of February last, that law took effect. In confirmation of the proclamation, an act of Congress was passed on the 2d March following.

Great Britain still declines to revoke her edicts, on the pretension that France has not revoked hers. Under that impression, she infers that the United States have done her injustice by carrying into effect the non-importation law against her.

The United States maintain that France has revoked her edicts, so far as they violated their neutral rights and were contemplated by the law of May 1, 1810, and have, on that ground, particularly claimed and do expect of Great Britain a similar revocation. . . .

In denying the revocation of the decrees, so far as it is a proper subject of discussion between us, it might reasonably be expected that you would produce some examples of vessels taken at sea in voyages to British ports or on their return home, and condemned under them by a French tribunal. None such have been afforded by you; none such are known to this Government. . . .

14. THE BASSANO LETTER[19]

[*The Duke of Bassano to Mr. Barlow*]

Paris, May 10, 1812

IN CONVERSING with you about the note which you did me the honor to address to me on the 1st May, I could not conceal from you my surprise at the doubt which you had expressed in that note respecting the revoca-

[19] When the French government was pressed for proof of the revocation of the Berlin and Milan decrees with regard to the United States, the French Foreign Minister, the Duc de Bassano, sent to the American Minister in Paris, Joel Barlow, a letter dated May 10, 1812, inclosing a decree allegedly dated April 28, 1811. Lowrie and Clarke: *American State Papers, Foreign Relations,* Vol. III, p. 603.

tion of the decrees of Berlin and Milan. That revocation was proven by many official acts, by all my correspondence with your predecessors and with you, by the decisions in favor of American vessels. You have done me the honor to ask a copy of the letters which the Grand Judge and the Minister of Finance wrote on the 25th of December, 1810, to secure the first effects of that measure; and you have said, sir, that the decree of the 28th April, 1811, which proves definitively the revocation of the decrees of Berlin and Milan in regard to the Americans, was not known to you.

I have the honor to send you, as you have desired, a copy of these three acts: you will consider them, without doubt, sir, as the plainest answer which I could give to this part of your note. . . .

[*NAPOLEON, Emperor of the French, &c. &c.*]

Palace of St. Cloud, April 28, 1811

On the report of our Minister of Foreign Relations:
Seeing, by a law passed on the 2d of March, 1811, the Congress of the United States has ordered the execution of the provisions of the act of non-intercourse which prohibits the vessels and merchandise of Great Britain, her colonies, and dependencies, from entering into the ports of the United States:

Considering that the said law is an act of resistance to the arbitrary pretensions consecrated by the British orders in council, and a formal refusal to adhere to a system invading the independence of neutral Powers, and of their flag, we have decreed, and do decree, as follows:

The decrees of Berlin and Milan are definitively, and to date from the 1st day of November last, considered as not having existed [*non avenus*] in regard to American vessels.

Napoleon.

15. REASONS FOR WAR WITH GREAT BRITAIN [20]

. . . MR. C. [CLAY] proceeded more particularly to inquire into the object of the force. That object, he understood, to be war, and war with Great Britain. . . .

What are we to gain by war, has been emphatically asked? In reply, he would ask, what are we not to lose by peace? – commerce, character, a nation's best treasure, honor! If pecuniary considerations alone are to govern, there is sufficient motive for the war. Our revenue is reduced, by the operation of the belligerent edicts, to about six million of dollars, according to the Secretary of the Treasury's report. The year preceding the embargo, it was sixteen. . . .

[20] Speech of Henry Clay in Congress, December 31, 1811. *Annals of the Congress of the United States,* 12th Congress, 1st Session, pp. 600 ff. The subject under discussion was a bill to increase the size of the Army.

He had no disposition to swell, or dwell upon the catalogue of injuries from England. He could not, however, overlook the impressment of our seamen; an aggression upon which he never reflected without feelings of indignation, which would not allow him appropriate language to describe its enormity. Not content with seizing upon all our property, which falls within her rapacious grasp, the personal rights of our countrymen – rights which forever ought to be sacred, are trampled upon and violated. The Orders in Council were pretended to have been reluctantly adopted as a measure of retaliation. The French decrees, their alleged basis, are revoked. England resorts to the expedient of denying the fact of the revocation, and Sir William Scott, in the celebrated case of the Fox and others, suspends judgment that proof may be adduced of it. And, at the moment when the British Ministry through that judge, is thus affecting to controvert that fact, and to place the release of our property upon its establishment, instructions are prepared for Mr. Foster to meet at Washington the very revocation which they were contesting. And how does he meet it? By fulfilling the engagement solemnly made to rescind the orders? No, sir, but by demanding that we shall secure the introduction into the Continent of British manufactures. England is said to be fighting for the world, and shall we, it is asked, attempt to weaken her exertions? If, indeed, the aim of the French Emperor be universal dominion (and he was willing to allow it to the argument,) what a noble cause is presented to British valor. But, how is her philanthropic purpose to be achieved? By scrupulous observance of the rights of others; by respecting that code of public law, which she professes to vindicate, and by abstaining from self-aggrandizement. Then would she command the sympathies of the world. What are we required to do by those who would engage our feelings and wishes in her behalf? To bear the actual cuffs of her arrogance, that we may escape a chimerical French subjugation! We are invited, conjured to drink the potion of British poison actually presented to our lips, that we may avoid the imperial dose prepared by perturbed imaginations. We are called upon to submit to debasement, dishonor, and disgrace – to bow the neck to royal insolence, as a course of preparation for manly resistance to Gallic invasion! What nation, what individual was ever taught, in the schools of ignominious submission, the patriotic lessons of freedom and independence? Let those who contend for this humiliating doctrine, read its refutation in the history of the very man against whose insatiable thirst of dominion we are warned. . . .

He contended that the real cause of British aggression, was not to distress an enemy but to destroy a rival. A comparative view of our commerce with England and the continent, would satisfy any one of the truth of this remark. . . . It is apparent that this trade, the balance of which was in favor, not of France, but of the United States, was not of very vital consequence to the enemy of England. Would she, therefore, for the sole purpose of depriving her adversary of this commerce, relinquish her valuable trade with this country, exhibiting the essential balance in her favor

— nay, more; hazard the peace of the country? No, sir, you must look for an explanation of her conduct in the jealousies of a rival. She sickens at your prosperity, and beholds in your growth — your sails spread on every ocean, and your numerous seamen — the foundations of a Power which, at no very distant day, is to make her tremble for naval superiority. . . .

Chapter VIII

THE DIPLOMACY OF THE WAR of 1812

NOTWITHSTANDING the cordial relations that existed between the British minister, A. J. Foster, and the Secretary of State, James Monroe, it became increasingly evident during the year 1811 that the United States and Great Britain were drifting toward war. No common ground for conciliation appeared to exist as long as President Madison persisted in his contention that the Berlin and Milan decrees were revoked, and Great Britain persisted in disregarding American neutral rights on the seas, demanding at the same time and under threat of retaliation, that the American government abandon its non-intercourse policy. The President's war message to Congress (1) of June 1 produced a declaration of war which was formally announced on June 18, 1812. A little over two months later, August 24, the American government held out an olive branch to Great Britain in the form of an armistice proposal, while the British government, which, on June 16, had announced the repeal of the Orders in Council in so far as America was concerned, held out to the United States an olive branch on September 30, also in the form of an armistice proposal.

The armistice proposals failed to avert the war (2), but it was scarcely begun before an offer was made by the Russian government to mediate the controversy between the United States and Great Britain. President Madison accepted the Russian offer, immediately appointed peace commissioners to represent the United States, and formal instructions (3), dated April 13, 1813, were prepared for their guidance. The failure of the British government to accept Russian mediation occasioned a long delay in the formal opening of peace negotiations. It was not until August 8, 1812, that a reconstructed American peace commission was able to discuss plans for peace with British commissioners at Ghent. Very little progress was made toward peace during August as the document dated August 12 demonstrates (4). The virtual abandonment on the part of the United States of its demands concerning impressment, and the proposals of the British of October 8 (5) and 21 (6) regarding the problem of the Indians, tended to eliminate some of the more troublesome questions. But as late as October 25 the American commissioners were inclined to think there was no immediate prospect for peace. On the last day of October, however, the British commissioners began to display a more conciliatory attitude, and from that time on progress toward peace was made until a treaty was signed on December 24, 1814 (7).

The treaty was unanimously ratified by the United States Senate and was favorably received by the American people. In Great Britain, however, considerable disappointment over the treaty was reflected in the press and in Parliament (8).

◇◇◇◇◇◇◇◇◇◇◇◇◇

1. THE WAR MESSAGE OF PRESIDENT MADISON[1]

June 1, 1812

. . . BRITISH cruisers have been in the continued practice of violating the American flag on the great highway of nations, and of seizing and carrying off persons sailing under it, not in the exercise of a belligerent right, founded on the law of nations against an enemy, but of a municipal prerogative over British subjects. . . .

The practice, hence, is so far from affecting British subjects alone, that, under the pretext of searching for these, thousands of American citizens, under the safeguard of public law and of their national flag, have been torn from their country, and from everything dear to them; have been dragged on board ships of war of a foreign nation; and exposed, under the severities of their discipline, to be exiled to the most distant and deadly climes, to risk their lives in the battles of their oppressors, and to be the melancholy instruments of taking away those of their own brethren. . . .

British cruisers have been in the practice also of violating the rights and the peace of our coasts. They hover over and harass our entering and departing commerce. To the most insulting pretensions they have added the most lawless proceedings in our very harbors, and have wantonly spilt American blood within the sanctuary of our territorial jurisdiction. The principles and rules enforced by that nation, when a neutral nation, against armed vessels of belligerents hovering near her coasts, and disturbing her commerce, are well known. When called on, nevertheless, by the United States, to punish the greater offences committed by her own vessels, her government has bestowed on their commanders additional marks of honour and confidence.

Under pretended blockades, without the presence of an adequate force, and sometimes without the practicability of applying one, our commerce has been plundered in every sea; the great staples of our country have been cut off from their legitimate markets; and a destructive blow aimed at our agricultural and maritime interests. . .

Not content with the occasional expedients for laying waste our neutral trade, the Cabinet of Great Britain resorted, at length, to the sweeping

[1] *Annals of the Congress of the United States,* 12th Congress, 1st Session (Washington, 1853), pp. 1714–19.

system of blockades, under the name of Orders in Council, which has been moulded and managed as might best suit its political views, its commercial jealousies, or the avidity of British cruisers. . . .

There was a period when a favorable change in the policy of the British Cabinet was justly considered as established. The Minister Plenipotentiary of His Britannic Majesty here proposed an adjustment of the differences more immediately endangering the harmony of the two countries. The proposition was accepted with the promptitude and cordiality corresponding with the invariable professions of this Government. A foundation appeared to be laid for a sincere and lasting reconciliation. The prospect, however, quickly vanished. The whole proceeding was disavowed by the British Government, without any explanations which could, at that time, repress the belief that the disavowal proceeded from a spirit of hostility to the commercial rights and prosperity of the United States. . . .

In reviewing the conduct of Great Britain towards the United States, our attention is necessarily drawn to the warfare just renewed by the savages, on one of our extensive frontiers; a warfare which is known to spare neither age nor sex, and to be distinguished by features peculiarly shocking to humanity. It is difficult to account for the activity and combinations which have for some time been developing themselves among tribes in constant intercourse with British traders and garrisons, without connecting their hostility with that influence, and without recollecting the authenticated examples of such interpositions heretofore furnished by the officers and agents of that Government. . . .

We behold, in fine, on the side of Great Britain, a state of war against the United States; and on the side of the United States, a state of peace towards Great Britain.

Whether the United States shall continue passive under these progressive usurpations . . . or, opposing force to force in defence of their national rights, shall commit a just cause into the hands of the Almighty Disposer of events . . . is a solemn question, which the Constitution wisely confides to the Legislative Department of the Government. . . .

Having presented this view of the relations of the United States with Great Britain, and of the solemn alternative growing out of them, I proceed to remark, that the communication last made to Congress, on the subject of our relations with France, will have shown, that since the revocation of her decrees, as they violated the neutral rights of the United States, her Government has authorized illegal captures by its privateers and public ships; and that other outrages have been practised on our vessels and our citizens. It will have been seen, also, that no indemnity had been provided, or satisfactorily pledged, for the extensive spoliations committed under the violent and retrospective orders of the French Government against the property of our citizens seized within the jurisdiction of France. I abstain, at this time, from recommending to the consideration of Congress definitive measures with respect to that nation, in the expectation that the result of unclosed discussions between our Minister Plenipotentiary at Paris and the French Government will speedily enable Congress to decide, with greater advantage, on the course due to the rights, the interests, and the honor of our country.

◇◇◇◇◇◇◇◇◇◇◇◇◇

2. REJECTION OF BRITISH ARMISTICE PROPOSALS[2]

[*James Monroe to Admiral Warren*]

October 27, 1812

. . . IT APPEARS that you are authorized to propose a cessation of hostilities between the United States and Great Britain. . . .

Without further discussing questions of right, the President is desirous to provide a remedy for the evils complained of on both sides. The claim of the British Government is to take from the merchant vessels of other countries British subjects. In the practice, the commanders of British ships of war often take from the merchant vessels of the United States American citizens. If the United States prohibit the employment of British subjects in their service, and enforce the prohibition by suitable regulations and penalties, the motive for the practice is taken away. It is in this mode that the President is willing to accommodate this important controversy with the British Government, and it cannot be conceived on what ground the arrangement can be refused.

A suspension of the practice of impressment, pending the armistice, seems to be a necessary consequence. . . . If the British Government is willing to suspend the practice of impressment from American vessels, on consideration that the United States will exclude British seamen from their service, the regulations by which this compromise should be carried into effect would be solely the object of negotiation. The armistice would be of short duration: if the parties agreed, peace would be the result; if the negotiation failed, each would be restored to its former state and to all its pretensions by recurring to war. . . .

I abstain from entering, in this communication, into other grounds of difference. The orders in council having been repealed, with a reservation not impairing a corresponding right on the part of the United States, and no illegal blockades revived or instituted in their stead, and an understanding being obtained on the subject of impressment in the mode herein proposed, the President is willing to agree to a cessation of hostilities, with a view to arrange by treaty, in a more distinct and ample manner, and to the satisfaction of both parties, every other subject of controversy.

I will only add that, if there be no objection to an accommodation of the difference relating to impressment in the mode proposed other than

[2] Lowrie and Clarke: *American State Papers, Foreign Relations*, Vol. III, pp. 596–7.

the suspension of the British claim to impressment during the armistice, there can be none to proceeding without the armistice to an immediate discussion and arrangement of an article on that subject. This great question being satisfactorily adjusted, the way will be open for an armistice, or any other course leading most conveniently and expeditiously to a general pacification.

◇◇◇◇◇◇◇◇◇◇◇◇

3. INSTRUCTIONS TO THE PLENIPOTENTIARIES OF THE UNITED STATES FOR TREATING OF PEACE WITH GREAT BRITAIN[3]

April 15, 1813

THE IMPRESSMENT of our seamen and illegal blockades, as exemplified more particularly in the orders in council, were the principal causes of the war. Had not Great Britain persevered obstinately in the violation of these important rights, the war would not have been declared. It will cease as soon as these rights are respected. The proposition made by Mr. Russell to the British Government immediately after the war, and the answer given by this Department to Admiral Warren's letter since, show the ground on which the United States were willing to adjust the controversy relative to impressment.

This has been further evinced by a report of the Committee of Foreign Relations of the House of Representatives, and an act of Congress passed in consequence of that report. By these documents you will see that, to accommodate this important difference, the United States are disposed to exclude British seamen altogether from the American service. This being effectually done, the British Government can have no pretext for the practice. How shall it be done? By restraints to be imposed by each nation on the naturalization of the seamen of the other, excluding, at the same time, all others not naturalized? Or shall the right of each nation to naturalize the seamen of the other be prohibited, and each exclude from its service the natives of the other? Whatever the rule is, it ought to be reciprocal. If Great Britain is allowed to naturalize American seamen, the United States should enjoy the same privilege. If it is demanded that the United States shall exclude from their service all native British subjects, a like exclusion of American citizens from British service ought to be reciprocated. The mode also should be common to both countries. Each should be at liberty to give the same facilities, or be bound to impose the same restraints that the other does. The President is willing to agree to either alternative, and to carry it into effect by the most eligible regulations that can be devised. . . .

[3] Ibid., pp. 695–700.

As a necessary incident to an adjustment on the principle of either alternative, it is expected that all American seamen, who have been impressed, will be discharged, and that those who have been naturalized, under the British laws, by compulsive service, will be permitted to withdraw. . . .

Of the right of the United States to be exempted from the degrading practice of impressment, so much has been already said, and with such ability, that it would be useless, especially to you, who are otherwise so well acquainted with it, to dilate on its merits. I must observe, however, that the practice is utterly repugnant to the law of nations; that it is supported by no treaty with any nation; that it was never acquiesced in by any; and that a submission to it by the United States would be the abandonment, in favor of Great Britain, of all claim to neutral rights, and of all other rights on the ocean. . . .

The British Government has recently, in two formal acts, given definitions of blockade, either of which would be satisfactory. The first is to be seen in a communication from Mr. Merry to this Department, bearing date on the 12th of April, 1804. The following are the circumstances attending it. Commodore Hood, the commander of a British squadron in the West Indies, in 1803, having declared the islands of Martinique and Guadaloupe in a state of blockade, without applying an adequate force to maintain it, the Secretary of State remonstrated against the illegality of the measure, which remonstrance was laid before the Lords Commissioners of the Admiralty, in England, who replied that they had sent "orders not to consider any blockade of those islands as existing unless in respect to particular ports, which might be actually invested, and then not to capture vessels, bound to such ports, unless they shall previously have been warned not to enter them." The second definition is to be found in a convention between Great Britain and Russia, in June, 1801, 4th section, 3d article, which declares, "that, in order to determine what characterizes a blockaded port, that denomination is given only to a port where there is, by the disposition of the Power which attacks it, with ships stationary or sufficiently near, an evident danger in entering." The President is willing for you to adopt either of these definitions; but prefers the first as much more precise and determinate; and when it is considered that it was made the criterion by so formal an act, between the two Governments, it cannot be presumed that the British Government will object to the renewal of it. . . .

Upon the whole subject I have to observe, that your first duty will be to conclude a peace with Great Britain, and that you are authorized to do it, in case you obtain a satisfactory stipulation against impressments, one which shall secure, under our flag, protection to the crew. The manner in which it may be done has been already stated, with the reciprocal stipulations which you may enter into to secure Great Britain against the injury of which she complains. If this encroachment of Great Britain is not provided against, the United States have appealed to arms in vain. If your efforts to accomplish it should fail, all further negotiations will cease, and you will return home without delay. It is possible that some difficulty may occur in arranging this article respecting its duration. To obviate this, the President is willing that it be limited to the present war in Europe. Resting, as the United States do, on the solid ground of right, it is not presumable that Great Britain, especially after the advantage she may derive from the arrangement proposed, would ever revive her pretension. In forming any stipulation on this subject, you will be careful not to impair by it the right of the United States, or to sanction the principle of the British claim.

It is deemed highly important, also, to obtain a definition of the neutral rights which I have brought to your view, especially of blockade, and in the manner suggested; but it is not to be made an indispensable condition of peace. . . .

◇◇◇◇◇◇◇◇◇◇◇◇◇

4. REPORT OF THE AMERICAN PEACE COMMISSIONERS TO THE SECRETARY OF STATE[4]

Ghent, August 12, 1814

WE HAVE the honor to inform you that the British commissioners, Lord Gambier, Henry Goulburn, Esq. and William Adams, Esq. arrived in this city on Saturday evening, the sixth instant. The day after their arrival, Mr. Baker, their secretary, called upon us to give us notice of the fact, and to propose a meeting at a certain hour on the ensuing day. The place having been agreed upon, we accordingly met at one o'clock on Monday, the 8th instant. . . .

The British commissioners then stated the following subjects as those upon which it appeared to them that the discussions would be likely to turn, and on which they were instructed.

1st. The forcible seizure of mariners on board of merchant vessels, and, in connexion with it, the claim of His Britannic Majesty to the allegiance of all the native subjects of Great Britain.

We understood them to intimate that the British Government did not propose this point as one which they were particularly desirous of discussing; but that, as if it had occupied so prominent a place in the disputes between the two countries, it necessarily attracted notice, and was considered as a subject which would come under discussion.

2d. The Indian allies of Great Britain to be included in the pacification, and a definite boundary to be settled for their territory.

The British commissioners stated that an arrangement upon this point was a *sine qua non;* that they were not authorized to conclude a treaty of peace which did not embrace the Indians as allies of His Britannic Majesty;

[4] Ibid., pp. 705–6. The report was signed by John Quincy Adams, James A. Bayard, Henry Clay, and Jonathan Russell.

and that the establishment of a definite boundary of the Indian territory was necessary to secure a permanent peace, not only with the Indians, but also between the United States and Great Britain.

3[d]. A revision of the boundary line between the United States and the adjacent British colonies.

With respect to this point, they expressly disclaimed any intention on the part of their Government, to acquire an increase of territory, and represented the proposed revision as intended merely for the purpose of preventing uncertainty and dispute.

After having stated these three points as subjects of discussion, the British commissioners added, that before they desired any answer from us, they felt it incumbent upon them to declare, that the British Government did not deny the right of the Americans to the fisheries generally, or in the open seas; but that the privileges formerly granted by treaty to the United States, of fishing within the limits of the British jurisdiction, and of landing and drying fish on the shores of the British territories, would not be renewed without an equivalent. . . .

There could be no hesitation on our part in informing the British commissioners that we were not instructed on the subjects of Indian pacification or boundary, and of fisheries; nor did it seem probable, although neither of these points had been stated with sufficient precision in the first verbal conference, that they could be admitted in any shape. We did not wish, however, to prejudge the result, or, by any hasty proceeding, abruptly to break off the negotiation. It was not impossible that, on the subject of the Indians, the British Government had received erroneous impressions from the Indian traders in Canada, which our representations might remove. And it appeared, at all events, important to ascertain distinctly the precise intentions of Great Britain on both points. We, therefore, thought it advisable to invite the British commissioners to a general conversation on all the points; stating to them, at the same time, our want of instructions on two of them, and holding out no expectation of the probability of our agreeing to any article respecting these.

At our meeting on the ensuing day, we informed the British commissioners that, upon the first and third points proposed by them, we were provided with instructions; and we presented as further subjects considered by our Government as suitable for discussion:

1st. A definition of blockade, and, as far as might be mutually agreed, of other neutral and belligerent rights.

2[d]. Claims of indemnity in certain cases of capture and seizure.

We then stated that the two subjects, 1st, of Indian pacification and boundary, 2d, of fisheries, were not embraced by our instructions. . . . No such provision had been inserted in the treaty of peace in 1783, nor in any other treaty between the two countries. No such provision had, to our knowledge, ever been inserted in any treaty made by Great Britain, or any other European Power, in relation to the same description of people, existing under like circumstances. We would say, however, that it could not be doubted that peace with the Indians would certainly follow a peace with Great Britain; that we had information that commissioners had already been appointed to treat with them; that a treaty to that effect might, perhaps, have been already concluded; and that the United States, having no interest nor any motive to continue a separate war against the Indians, there could never be a moment when our Government would not be disposed to make peace with them. . . .

The British commissioners, after having repeated that their instructions on the subject of the Indians were peremptory, stated that, unless we could give some assurance that our powers would allow us to make at least a provisional arrangement on the subject, any farther discussion would be fruitless, and that they must consult their own Government on this state of things. They proposed, accordingly, a suspension of the conferences, until they should have received an answer, it being understood that each party might call a meeting whenever they had any proposition to submit. They despatched a special messenger the same evening, and we are now waiting for the result. . . .

◇◇◇◇◇◇◇◇◇◇◇◇◇◇

5. BRITISH DEMANDS ON THE SUBJECT OF AMERICAN INDIANS [5]

[*British Commissioners to the American Commissioners*]

Ghent, October 8, 1814

. . . AS THE continuance of the negotiation exclusively depends upon the question relating to the pacification and rights of the Indian nations, the undersigned are unwilling to extend their observations to the other subjects brought forward in the note of the American plenipotentiaries further than may be required for necessary explanation. . . .

It remains only to notice two objections, which the American plenipotentiaries have urged against the proposal of Indian pacification, advanced by the undersigned; first, that it is not reciprocal; secondly, that, as the United States could have no security that the Indian nations would conclude a peace on the terms proposed, the objection would be, in effect, unilateral.

The article now proposed by the undersigned, and herewith enclosed, is free from both objections, and appears to them so characterized by a spirit of moderation and peace, that they earnestly anticipate the concurrence of the American plenipotentiaries.

In making a last effort in this stage of the war, the undersigned are not apprehensive that the motives which have influenced His Royal Highness

[5] Ibid., pp. 721–3. The British Commissioners were Lord Gambier, Henry Goulburn, and William Adams.

the Prince Regent to direct a renewal of the proposition, with its present modifications, can be misunderstood or misrepresented.

Whatever may be the result of the proposition thus offered, the undersigned deliver it as their ultimatum, and now await with anxiety the answer of the American plenipotentiaries, on which their continuance in this place will depend. . . .

The United States of America engage to put an end, immediately after the ratification of the present treaty, to hostilities with all the tribes or nations of Indians with whom they may be at war at the time of such ratification, and forthwith to restore to such tribes or nations respectively, all the possessions, rights, and privileges, which they may have enjoyed, or been entitled to, in 1811, previous to such hostilities.

Provided, always, That such tribes or nations shall agree to desist from all hostilities against the United States of America, their citizens and subjects, upon the ratification of the present treaty being notified to such tribes or nations, and shall so desist accordingly.

And His Britannic Majesty engages, on his part, to put an end, immediately after the ratification of the present treaty, to hostilities with all the tribes or nations of Indians with whom he may be at war at the time of such ratification, and forthwith to restore to such tribes or nations respectively, all the possessions, rights, and privileges, which they may have enjoyed, or been entitled to, in 1811, previous to such hostilities.

Provided, always, That such tribes or nations shall agree to desist from all hostilities against His Britannic Majesty and his subjects, upon the ratification of the present treaty being notified to such tribes or nations, and shall so desist accordingly.

6. FURTHER PROPOSALS FROM THE BRITISH COMMISSIONERS [6]

Ghent, October 21, 1814

THE UNDERSIGNED have had the honor of receiving the note of the American plenipotentiaries of the 13th instant, communicating their acceptance of the article which the undersigned had proposed on the subject of the pacification and rights of the Indian nations. . . .

The undersigned having stated, at the first conference, the points upon which His Majesty's Government considered the discussions between the two countries as likely to turn, cannot better satisfy the request of the American plenipotentiaries than by referring them to that conference for a statement of the points which, in the opinion of His Majesty's Government, yet remain to be adjusted.

With respect to the forcible seizure of mariners from on board merchant

[6] Ibid., pp. 724–5.

vessels on the high seas, and the right of the King of Great Britain to the allegiance of all his native subjects and with respect to the maritime rights of the British empire, the undersigned conceive that, after the pretensions asserted by the Government of the United States, a more satisfactory proof of the conciliatory spirit of His Majesty's Government cannot be given than by not requiring any stipulation on those subjects, which, though most important in themselves, no longer, in consequence of the maritime pacification of Europe, produce the same practical results. . . .

On the question of the boundary between the dominions of His Majesty and those of the United States, the undersigned are led to expect, from the discussion which this subject has already undergone, that the northwestern boundary, from the Lake of the Woods to the Mississippi, (the intended arrangement of 1803,) will be admitted without objection.

In regard to other boundaries, the American plenipotentiaries, in their note of August 24th, appeared in some measure to object to the propositions then made by the undersigned, as not being on the basis of *uti possidetis.* The undersigned are willing to treat on that basis, subject to such modifications as mutual convenience may be found to require; and they trust that the American plenipotentiaries will show, by their ready acceptance of this basis, that they duly appreciate the moderation of His Majesty's Government in so far consulting the honor and fair pretensions of the United States as, in the relative situation of the two countries, to authorize such a proposition.

◇◇◇◇◇◇◇◇◇◇◇◇◇

7. TREATY OF PEACE AND AMITY BETWEEN THE UNITED STATES AND GREAT BRITAIN[7]

[*Concluded at Ghent December 24, 1814, proclaimed February 18, 1815*]

ARTICLE the First. There shall be a firm and universal Peace between His Britannic Majesty and the United States, and between their respective Countries, Territories, Cities, Towns, and People of every degree without exception of places or persons. All hostilities both by sea and land shall cease as soon as this Treaty shall have been ratified by both parties as hereinafter mentioned. All territory, places, and possessions whatsoever taken by either party from the other during the war, or which may be taken after the signing of this Treaty, excepting only the Islands hereinafter mentioned, shall be restored without delay and without causing any destruction or carrying away any of the Artillery or other public property originally captured in the said forts or places, and which shall remain

[7] Hunter Miller: *Treaties and Other International Acts of the United States,* Vol. II, pp. 574–84. The treaty was signed by Lord Gambier, Henry Goulburn, William Adams, John Quincy Adams, James A. Bayard, Henry Clay, Jonathan Russell, and Albert Gallatin.

therein upon the Exchange of the Ratifications of this Treaty, or any Slaves or other private property; And all Archives, Records, Deeds, and Papers, of a public nature or belonging to private persons, which in the course of the war may have fallen into the hands of the Officers of either party, shall be, as far as may be practicable, forthwith restored and delivered to the proper authorities and persons to whom they respectively belong. Such of the Islands in the Bay of Passamaquoddy as are claimed by both parties shall remain in the possession of the party in whose occupation they may be at the time of the Exchange of the Ratifications of this Treaty until the decision respecting the title to the said Islands shall have been made in conformity with the fourth Article of this Treaty. No disposition made by this Treaty as to such possession of the Islands and territories claimed by both parties shall in any manner whatever be construed to affect the right of either. . . .

Article the Ninth.[8] The United States of America engage to put an end immediately after the Ratification of the present Treaty to hostilities with all the Tribes or Nations of Indians with whom they may be at war at the time of such Ratification, and forthwith to restore to such Tribes or Nations respectively all the possessions, rights, and privileges which they may have enjoyed or been entitled to in one thousand eight hundred and eleven previous to such hostilities. Provided always that such Tribes or Nations shall agree to desist from all hostilities against the United States of America, their Citizens, and Subjects upon the Ratification of the present Treaty being notified to such Tribes or Nations, and shall so desist accordingly. And His Britannic Majesty engages on his part to put an end immediately after the Ratification of the present Treaty to hostilities with all the Tribes or Nations of Indians with whom He may be at war at the time of such Ratification, and forthwith to restore to such Tribes or Nations respectively all the possessions, rights, and privileges, which they may have enjoyed or been entitled to in one thousand eight hundred and eleven previous to such hostilities. Provided always that such Tribes or Nations shall agree to desist from all hostilities against His Britannic Majesty and His Subjects upon the Ratification of the present Treaty being notified to such Tribes or Nations, and shall so desist accordingly.

Article the Tenth. Whereas the Traffic in Slaves is irreconcilable with the principles of humanity and Justice, and whereas both His Majesty and the United States are desirous of continuing their efforts to promote its entire abolition, it is hereby agreed that both the contracting parties shall use their best endeavors to accomplish so desirable an object. . . .

8 Articles 4–8 provided for the settlement of boundary disputes.

8. RECEPTION OF THE TREATY IN GREAT BRITAIN[9]

. . . ON APRIL 11, *Mr. Hart Davis* rose to move an address of thanks to the Prince Regent for the treaty of peace entered into with the United States of America. He said, he believed there were few men in this country who did not agree that the war declared by America was unprovoked on our part, at the same time, that person must have singular views of the policy of Great Britain, who should think that it ought to be continued by us for the purpose of territorial aggrandizement, or from vindictive feelings. Our sole object was to resist aggression, and to support our maritime rights. We had gloriously defended Canada, had surrendered no rights, and had made a peace in the spirit of peace, which would open again a wide field for the commerce and manufactures of this country. . . .

Mr. Ponsonby declared that . . . he could not agree to the address, as he thought it their duty to inform his Royal Highness of what he conceived the gross misconduct and mismanagement of ministers in the progress of the negociations. In this treaty no one subject of dispute between the two countries that existed before its signature, does not still exist; and all the pretensions advanced by his Majesty's ministers in the course of the negociations were, one by one, abandoned by them. The right hon. gentleman then dwelt upon the circumstance of the long, and as it appeared, the unnecessary delay of the signature of this treaty. . . . The first conference between the commissioners of the two countries did not take place till August 8th, when terms were laid before the Americans as a *sine-qua-non,* which were, pacification with the Indians, and defining the boundaries of their territories; the military occupation of the lakes in Canada, and the cession of certain islands which the Americans had occupied since 1783. These terms were absolutely rejected by the American commissioners; and being transmitted to the president, and presented to the congress, were unanimously refused by that body, and by the people of all parties. By the delay arising from these demands, which were all subsequently given up, except the simple pacification with the Indians, and the possession of the islands, which was referred to a future decision, the signature of the treaty did not take place till December 24th; and in the meantime military operations had gone on, occasioning a great waste of treasure, and the shedding of the best blood of the country. Mr. P. concluded with proposing a long amendment to the address, which contained all the points of inculpation of the measures pursued in negociating the treaty that had been dwelt on in his speech.

Mr. Goulburn then rose in defence of himself and his brother commissioners. With regard to the delay of the treaty, he said that the American

[9] Extracts from an account of the debate over the treaty in the House of Commons, April 11, 1815. *The Annual Register . . . For the Year 1815* (Baldwin, Cradock, and Joy: London, 1816), pp. 15–17. The speakers were Hart Davis and Henry Goulburn for the government, and George Ponsonby and Alexander Baring for the opposition.

commissioners had been instructed to make no peace without our relinquishment of the right of impressment, and our admission that the American flag covered all who sailed under it; and the 25th of June was the first day on which they were authorised to allow these matters to remain undecided, and to sign a treaty exclusive of their consideration, on which day the first conference was held at Ghent. . . .

Mr. Baring warmly condemned the whole conduct of the negociation on the part of this country. He said that the American Commissioners seemed willing to have entered into the question relative to the impressment of our seamen, but that ours refused to listen to the proposal, and had left the matter upon the worst possible footing. It was doubtless a point of much difficulty, but for his own part he was convinced of the practicability of an arrangement. . . .

After several other speakers had taken part in the discussion, in which the delay of the treaty appeared to be more forcibly attacked than satisfactorily defended, the House divided upon the amendment, which was negatived by 128 to 37, and the address was then agreed to. . . .

CHAPTER IX

FLORIDA AND THE LOUISIANA BOUNDARY

◇◇◇◇◇◇◇◇◇◇◇◇◇

THE BOUNDARIES of Louisiana were not clearly defined in the treaty by which the United States acquired that territory from France. Very soon after the treaty was signed, the American minister in Paris, Robert R. Livingston, adopted the idea that the boundary between Florida and Louisiana was the Perdido River. President Jefferson, after a thorough study of the situation, arrived at the same conclusion, and Congress, in conformity with this idea, authorized the President to establish a customs district for Mobile. In consequence of vigorous protests on the part of Spain against the American claims to West Florida, President Jefferson sent James Monroe to Madrid as envoy-extraordinary to assist the regular minister, Charles Pinckney, to adjust the Louisiana boundary and to press for the settlement of certain claims of American citizens against Spain. Negotiations between the two American envoys and the Spanish Foreign Minister, Pedro de Cevallos, began in January 1805 and continued for nearly five months without appreciable result. Monroe returned to London, and in October, 1805, Pinckney returned to the United States, leaving George W. Erving as chargé d'affaires. During the following five years the diplomacy of the United States regarding Florida was complicated by the rising power of Napoleon in Spanish affairs and an inept and circuitous American policy. In the meantime, West Florida remained in the possession of Spain. In 1810, however, a revolution was organized, the Spanish authority at Baton Rouge was overthrown, and the revolutionary government requested the annexation of West Florida by the United States. On October 27, 1810, President Madison proclaimed the acquisition of West Florida, and three years later Mobile was occupied. During the years from 1810 to 1815 territorial adjustments between Spain and the United States were delayed by the Napoleonic invasion of Spain and the Anglo-American War. Negotiations were resumed at Madrid in 1816, but the whole Florida controversy was transferred to Washington where it was taken up by the Spanish minister, Don Luis de Onis (1, 2), and the Secretary of State, John Quincy Adams (3). In the midst of an exchange of notes between these two consummate diplomats, General Jackson invaded Florida. Secretary Adams vigorously defended the invasion and the American position in general in a notable dispatch of November 28, 1818 (4). With the trump cards all in the possession of the United States, diplomacy was somewhat accelerated and a treaty was signed in February 1819 dealing with the problem of Florida and with the boundaries of Louisiana in so far as they related to Spain (5).

◇◇◇◇◇◇◇◇◇◇◇◇◇◇

1. SPANISH CLAIMS TO WEST FLORIDA RESTATED [1]

[*Don Luis de Onis to John Quincy Adams*]

December 29, 1817

. . . I HOPE you will have no objection to agree to a succinct examination of the question of boundaries, and to a rational and fair inquiry into the titles and grounds on which each Government rests its rights and pretensions, the natural order seems to require that we should begin this examination and inquiry with what relates to the eastern boundaries of Louisiana; that, after establishing them as they ought to be, we may proceed to examine and establish, in like manner, those which regard the western; it being, nevertheless, well understood that neither by this act, nor any one whatever of those which contribute to produce the present negotiation, it shall be inferred that His Catholic Majesty renounces, in any manner, the right he has, or may have, to reclaim against the nonfulfilment of the treaty of St. Ildefonso, concluded between Spain and France in the year 1800, and against the solemn stipulations contained in the additional articles of the same treaty, forming an essential part of the contract between the two nations.

The boundaries of Louisiana, on that side, join those of West Florida, and are so precisely established and fixed by public treaties, that I do not think your Government can still persist in the opinion that Louisiana ought to be extended by this Spanish province, to the river Perdido. If, however, the imagination, resorting to specious subtleties and abstractions, carries us back to the period when France formed settlements on the left of the Mississippi, and possessed what are now two distinct provinces, namely, Louisiana and West Florida, still the certain and incontestable fact will follow, that Spain acquired neither of the Floridas from France. That Power, while in possession of those territories, as she was until 1763, might name them, and point out their respective limits as she thought fit. That is quite unimportant to the present question. It is certain that, by the treaty of 1763, France ceded to England all the territory possessed by her to the eastward of the Mississippi, with the exception of the island of Orleans; and it is also certain that England united, as her own, from that year, the same territory to Florida, which, by the same treaty, Spain had ceded to her; and that, having added thereto the district and port of Pensacola, she called it West Florida, by which name, and no other, it

[1] Lowrie and Clarke: *American State Papers, Foreign Relations,* Vol. IV, pp. 452–5.

has ever since been known. In the war of 1779, Spain conquered the said territory of West Florida from England; and this right of conquest was afterwards secured by a solemn treaty, between England and Spain, in September, 1783. It is by this title that West Florida belongs, until the present day, to Spain, in addition to East Florida, which was also ceded by the said treaty. It is evident, then, that Spain neither acquired or received from France either of the Floridas, but that she acquired them both of England in 1783, classed as two distinct provinces, and universally known by the names of West Florida and East Florida. She has, from that period, possessed them separate and distinct, without having ever confounded either of them with Louisiana, either in whole or in part. They are laid down distinct and separate in the maps, charts, and geographies of all nations, from the year 1763, to the present day. In all the public acts and instruments which speak of them, they appear distinct and separate, as they do in the different treaties in which they are mentioned.

This being the case, how can your government still maintain its opinion? The United States acquired Louisiana from France such as *she* had acquired it from Spain by the treaty of St. Ildefonso. In this treaty nothing is stipulated but the retrocession of Louisiana; nor is there a single word in the whole treaty that bears the most distant allusion to West Florida, which is the object to which the dispute is reduced in that quarter. The clauses of the treaty are clear, precise, and conclusive; they fix the sense of the stipulation invariably, and leave no room for vague or specious constructions. The very title given to that treaty by the contracting parties at once pointed out the territory restored by Spain to France, in exchange for the kingdom of Etruria. The title says, "Retrocession of Louisiana"; and the word "retrocession" has not, nor ever had, any other signification, in the Spanish or French language, than the act of restoring to an individual, or a nation, that which had before been received from him, or from it; so that a different signification cannot be given to this word (adopted by the contracting parties to express the nature of their stipulation) without changing the proper and genuine acceptation, in both languages, of the definite term they have respectively employed, and without substantially changing the intentions which serve as the basis of the contract.

The three clauses by which they afterwards go on to fulfil this convention agree perfectly with the said title, and, by supporting and explaining each other, they fix it in a clear and precise manner. The first clause says: "That His Catholic Majesty restores Louisiana to France, with the same extent it had when possessed by Spain." It is well known that no part of the Floridas, or other Spanish possessions, was then included in Louisiana, or annexed to it. At that time Louisiana was, in the hands of Spain, precisely what it was when ceded by France, in virtue of the treaty of 1764. In the same treaty its eastern boundaries are marked by a line running eastward from Manchac point, thence following the course of the river Iberville, and dividing the lakes Borgne, Pontchartrain, and Maurepas, and finally terminating at the gulf of Mexico, without leaving the smallest doubt as to the true points of the frontier. This is the territory which Spain retroceded to France, because it is the only one which she possessed under the name of Louisiana. The second clause agrees with the first, and opportunely declares and fixes its import. — It says: "and with the same extent it had when possessed by France," expressions which necessarily refer to the period of time which intervened between the cession by France to England of the territory possessed by her on the left bank of the Mississippi, and the cession made by the same Power to Spain of Louisiana. As the first of these two cessions took place in the year 1763, and the second in 1764, it is evident that, during that interval, France possessed Louisiana in the manner stated. And with the same extent did she cede it to Spain; nor could she cede it with more, as she then possessed nothing more in that part of the American continent. . . .

You cannot but be fully convinced, sir, of this truth; and on proceeding to the examination of the third clause, you will find what I have just stated still more comprehensively and clearly demonstrated. This clause says: "and as it ought to be after the treaties concluded between Spain and other Powers." The only treaties to which this clause could refer, were the following:

1. That of 1764, by which France ceded Louisiana to Spain. In this treaty the eastern boundaries of Louisiana are marked by the course of the Mississippi, and next by the river Iberville, the lakes Borgne, Pontchartrain, and Maurepas. It was consequently proper here to recall what was set forth in this treaty. 2. That of 1783 between Spain and England, by which the latter confirmed to Spain the possession and property of West Florida, which she had conquered during the war, and ceded to her East Florida. It is a very fit moment to recall the inviolability of this treaty, since it is evident, from it, that the Floridas are two provinces independent of Louisiana, absolutely unconnected with and distinct from it; and that they came into the possession of Spain by very different titles, in consideration of which, one thing cannot be confounded with another. And the 3d is that of 1795, concluded between Spain and the United States. As in this treaty the frontiers between the United States and the Spanish possessions are described, and the Floridas are named as provinces notoriously unconnected with and distinct from Louisiana; as by it the dismemberment of Natchez, Nogales, etc. was effected; and as it is therein stipulated, that the navigation of the Mississippi shall be free to the Americans and the Spaniards, and a place granted in favour of the former for their commodities on the banks of the Mississippi, for which purpose New Orleans was designated for the term of three years; it was consequently thought proper to refer to this treaty, and show that it, as well as those of 1764 and 1783, is, and ought to be, in full force and effect. . . .

◇◇◇◇◇◇◇◇◇◇◇◇◇

2. SPANISH CLAIMS TO TEXAS [2]

[*Don Luis de Onis to John Quincy Adams*]

January 5, 1818

. . . IN MY NOTE of the 29th of last month, I proved to you . . . what are and ought to be the eastern boundaries of Louisiana. . . . As I have not yet received your answer to the said note . . . I anticipate the examination of the western boundaries of Louisiana. . . .

It is unquestionable, from the historical series of facts and the most unexceptionable documents, that the province of Texas extended to the river Mississippi, and that the French never crossed the river into that district but through the sufferance or permission of the Spanish Governors; and that, in consequence of the former abusing the generosity with which they were permitted to trade with the Indians of that territory, and to hold, for that purpose only, the posts of Natchez and Natchitoches, positive orders were issued to drive the French from the whole district, and destroy the said posts. The Spanish commandant advanced with a sufficient force to execute those orders; but he acceded to the proposals of the French at Natchitoches, which were confined to this: *that Arroyo Hondo, which is midway between Natchitoches and Adaes, should be considered as the dividing line, until the determination of the two courts.* In this state things remained without further change, and so continued until the cession of Louisiana to Spain relieved those provinces of Spanish America from all embarrassment and trouble from the French. But it always was an undeniable fact, established by the irresistible titles and documents, that the French neither held nor had held, to the westward of the Mississippi, in 1719, any other post than Natchitoches, which they held merely by the condescension of Spain; and that the Spanish settlement of Adaes, only five leagues distant from the Rio Roxo, (Red River,) existed much earlier, and did so exist until Louisiana was transferred to Spain. The parochial records of Nacogdochez and Adaes, with the registers of births, baptisms, and deaths, attest it still more circumstantially, as well as the proceedings of the pastoral visit made in 1805, by don Primo Feliciano Marin, bishop of the new kingdom of Leon, who visited the district of Adaes and the whole province of Texas.

The right which Spain always had to all the territories to the north and east of New Mexico, as far as the right bank of the Mississippi and the Missouri, is proved with equal certainty. All these territories, and the different branches, falls, and waters of the Mississippi, were always comprehended within the line of the Spanish dominion in that part of America from the earliest periods of its discovery and conquest. Although the French penetrated several times from Mobile and Biloxi to different parts of that line, they never acquired any right to them. Their excursions were

[2] Ibid., IV, pp. 455–60.

confined to trading, or smuggling, or exploring the country. The huts or posts which they had in some Indian nations were trifling establishments, clandestine and precarious, which they were unable to preserve. The Spaniards had traded much earlier than the French with all these Indian nations; with the Missouris, extending along the river of that name; the Padorcas, beyond the river La Platte; and, still farther to the northwest, with the Latanes; and, finally, with several others, as being within the dominions of the Crown of Spain. . . .

As these boundaries, to the westward of the Mississippi . . . have not been marked out with the formality necessary to avoid doubts . . . and as it is only evident that they undoubtedly proceed from the Mexican Gulf, by the river Mermento or Mermentao, and Arroyo Hondo, by drawing a line between Nachitoches and Adaes, which crosses the Red river, and extends towards the Missouri, I have done no more than point out the basis for a line of demarkation. . . .

◇◇◇◇◇◇◇◇◇◇◇◇◇

3. WEST FLORIDA AND TEXAS: THE AMERICAN VIEW[3]

[*John Quincy Adams to Don Luis de Onis*]

March 12, 1818

. . . I AM directed by the President to confine the observations upon your late notes to those parts of them which have relation to the essential subjects of controversy between the two nations.

To give a single instance of that argument which you represent as equivalent to mathematical demonstration in favor of Spain, it will be sufficient to refer to your assertions in relation to the question of the eastern boundaries of Louisiana, as retroceded to France by the treaty of St. Ildefonso in 1800, and ceded by France to the United States in 1803. The claim of the United States, under that cession, to the territory east of the Mississippi, as far as the river Perdido, rests, as you well know, upon the words in the two treaties describing the colony or province of Louisiana ceded by them as having the same extent not only that it had at the time of the retrocession in the *hands of Spain but also that it had when France possessed it*, and such as it should be, after the treaties subsequently entered into between Spain and other states. You know, also, with what force it was urged by the ministers of the United States at Aranjuez, in 1805, that those words, (referring to the primitive possession of the province by France), could have had no other meaning than that of extending the retrocession to the Perdido, because the province had always had that extent when in the possession of France. And what is your reply to this argument, which you are pleased to include under the general censure of

[3] Ibid., IV, pp. 468–78.

vague and groundless positions? It is no other than the supposition of a treaty of 1764, by virtue of which, you say, France ceded the western remnant of Louisiana to Spain, a year after having ceded the eastern part of it, from the Mississippi to the Perdido, to England. With the aid of this treaty, you are enabled, first, to discover an interval of time between the two cessions, and during which France possessed Louisiana, bounded eastward by the Mississippi; and secondly, to include this treaty between *Spain* and *France* among those described in the article of the treaty of St. Ildefonso, as "the treaties subsequently entered into between Spain and *other states.*"

There is reason to believe that no such treaty of 1764 ever existed; that the cessions of Louisiana, westward of the Mississippi, to Spain, and eastward of that river to the Perdido to England, were made by France both on the 3d of November, 1762, is certain, and that the acceptance by the King of Spain of the cession made to him, took place on the 13th of the same November, 1762; the proof of which is in the very order from the king of France to L'Abbadie, for the delivery of the province to the officers of the king of Spain. The province had never belonged to France a single day, without extending to the Perdido. Nor can it be necessary to remind you that the very treaty of cession, by which France surrendered her possession of Louisiana to Spain, cannot be comprehended in the description of treaties *subsequently* entered into between Spain and *other states.*

As this simple reference to a notorious and unquestionable fact annihilates all that course of reasoning upon which your understanding rejects all doubt, so a recurrence to another fact, equally notorious, replies as decisively to your appeal to the treaty of 6th February, 1778, between the United States and France. You say that in the year 1800, France could not have acquired any territory east of the Mississippi, without a *monstrous violation* of that treaty, forgetting that that treaty, and all its obligations upon France, had, before the year 1800, ceased to exist.

The fact that the cessions of the two parts of Louisiana to Spain and England were made on the same day may serve no less as a reply to all the verbal criticisms, so gravely urged by Mr. Cevallos, and now repeated by you, on the force of the terms *retrocede* and *retrocession,* used in the treaty of St. Ildefonso. The plain import of the words is neither more nor less than *giving back, restoring.* It does not, and cannot be made to imply, that both the parties to the restoration must, of necessity, be the same as both the parties to the grant. They only imply that the object and the party granting, and the party receiving it, as restored, are the same. . . .

There would then be nothing in the terms *retrocede* and *retrocession,* which could limit the territories restored by Spain to the boundaries under which she had first received part of them from France; even if the original cessions of the two parts had been made at different times; and even if those words, "*with the same extent it had when in the hands of France,*" had not been inserted in the treaty of St. Ildefonso. But when it is considered that the cessions by France, of the two parts of Louisiana were made to Spain and to England on the same day, when we know that the cession of the part ceded to England, had been made for the benefit of Spain, as it was an equivalent for the restoration by England of the island of Cuba to Spain, and when we seek for any possible meaning to the words referring to the extent of Louisiana when before owned by France, to our minds, sir, the conclusion is irresistible, that the terms *retrocede* and *retrocession* can have, in this case, no other meaning than that for which we contend, and that they include the giving back to France the whole of Louisiana which had ever belonged to France, and which it was, at the time of the signature of the treaty of St. Ildefonso, in the power of Spain to restore. . . .

Let us pass to the consideration of the western boundary of Louisiana. . . .

It is remarkable, that in imitation of Mr. Cevallos, you also, after repeatedly insisting that the boundaries of Louisiana were well known, and always acknowledged by France, finally conclude by admitting that they never were fixed or agreed upon. You repeat, time after time, that the French *never disputed* the right of Spain to all the territory westward of the Mississippi, while you cannot deny the settlement of La Salle at the bay of St. Bernard, in 1684; nor that the French settlements of Natchez and Natchitoches were made and maintained in spite of all the military expeditions, rigorous executions, and exterminating orders, which the Viceroys of Mexico could send against them.

We may admit that, so long as the Spanish viceroys could exterminate every foreigner who dared to penetrate into the gulf of Mexico, they had the royal order of Philip the second for so doing. The bull of Pope Alexander the sixth is a document of still earlier date, and at least of less disgusting import, upon which Spain once rested her claims to yet more extensive dominion in this western world. With equal show of reason, and with less outrage upon the rights of humanity, might you have alleged that bull as the incontrovertible proof of the Spanish claims, as to bring forth at this day, for its only substitute, that royal order of Philip the second.

You know, sir, and your own notes furnish, themselves, the most decisive proofs, that France, while she held the colony of Louisiana, never did acknowledge the Mississippi as the western boundary of that province. The claim of France always did extend westward to the Rio Bravo, and the only boundaries ever acknowledged by her, before the cession to Spain of 3d November, 1762, were those marked out in the grant from Louis fourteenth to Crozat. She always claimed the territory, which you call Texas, as being within the limits, and forming part of Louisiana; which, in that grant, is declared to be bounded westward by New Mexico, eastward by Carolina, and extending inward to the Illinois and to the sources of the Mississippi, and of its principal branches.

Mr. Cevallos says that these claims of France were never admitted nor recognised by Spain. Be it so. Neither were the claims of Spain ever acknowledged or admitted by France: the boundary was disputed and never settled; it still remains to be settled. . . .

The negotiation of the special mission of the United States at Aranjuez, in 1805, occupied a period of nearly five months, from the beginning of January, when Mr. Monroe arrived at Madrid, to the 22d of May, when he took leave of the King, to return to London. In his address to the King on that occasion, he said: "On my arrival here, I had the honour to assure your Majesty, of the high consideration of my Government for your Majesty's person and Government. I then hoped to have had the honour to conclude the special mission with which I was charged in conjunction with the minister plenipotentiary near your Majesty, to the advantage and satisfaction of both parties; but being disappointed in this respect, *all our propositions having been rejected, and none others ever offered on the part of your Majesty's Government, though often invited,* it becomes my duty to return to my station at London."

This assertion, made to the king of Spain in person, at the close of that mission, was fully warranted by the transactions under it. Every one of the topics, now included in your four notes, as embracing all the subjects of difference between the two countries, were discussed at great length, much in the same manner which you have now insisted upon repeating. The questions of indemnities for spoliations, Spanish and French, and for the suppression of the deposite at New Orleans; of the eastern and of the western boundary of Louisiana, were descanted upon with pertinacity as indefatigably by Don Pedro Cevallos as by yourself. He bestowed as many pages upon the terms *retrocede* and *retrocession* as you have done. He appealed with equal confidence and alacrity to the opinions, and cited with equal complacency the testimonials of the ministers of Napoleon, and reminded Messrs. Monroe and Pinckney, with a satisfaction not inferior to your own, of the "very pointed" manner in which the French minister of foreign relations, Mr. Talleyrand, announcing the sentiments of His Imperial Majesty, observed, that "to *make known* the rights which France had acquired, was to indicate the *extent* and the *limits* of those which she transmitted to the federal government." To everything that had the semblance of reason and argument, adduced in the successive notes of Mr. Cevallos, the American ministers temperately and patiently replied; they unfolded, with a clearness and precision to which nothing can now be added, the claims of the United States, and the facts and principles by which they were supported. They proposed, at the commencement of the negotiation, a project of a convention for the adjustment of all the interests in dispute. After all the subjects had been thoroughly discussed, they presented a second project, modified in the most conciliatory spirit of accommodation to Spain. They invited, and reiterated, almost to importunity, the invitation, to a counter project, or proposals on the the part of the Spanish

Government. These unwearied efforts were met by a constant, invariable, inflexible refusal either to accept their proposals, or to make to them any whatsoever in return. . . .

You perceive, sir, that the Government of the United States is not prepared either to renounce any of the claims which it has been so long urging upon the justice of Spain, or to acquiesce in any of those arguments which appear to you so luminous and irresistible. . . .

◇◇◇◇◇◇◇◇◇◇◇◇

4. THE INVASION OF FLORIDA[4]

[*John Quincy Adams to George W. Erving*]

Department of State, Washington, November 28, 1818

YOUR despatches to No. 92, inclusive, with their enclosures, have been received at this Department. Among these enclosures are the several notes addressed to you by Mr. Pizarro. . . .

In the fourth and last of those notes Mr. Pizarro has given formal notice that the King, his master, has issued orders for the suspension of the negotiation between the United States and Spain until satisfaction shall have been made by the American Government to him for these proceedings of General Jackson. . . .

Within a very few days after this notification, Mr. Pizarro must have received . . . the determination which had been taken by the President to restore the places of Pensacola, with the fort of Barrancas, to any person properly authorized on the part of Spain to receive them, and the fort of St. Mark to any Spanish force adequate to its protection against the Indians, by whom its forcible occupation had been threatened for purposes of hostility against the United States. The officer commanding at the post has been directed to consider two hundred and fifty men as such adequate force. . . .

It may be . . . proper to remind the Government of His Catholic Majesty of the incidents in which this Seminole war originated. . . .

In the month of August, 1814, while war existed between the United States and Great Britain, to which Spain had formally declared herself neutral, a British force . . . landed in Florida, took possession of Pensacola and the fort of Barrancas, and invited . . . all the runaway negroes, all savage Indians, all the pirates . . . to join their standard . . . and thus violated territory of Spain. The land commander of the British force was a certain Colonel Nicholls. . . . A part of this force consisted of a corps of colonial marines . . . and Robert Christie Ambrister was a lieutenant.

As between the United States and Great Britain, we should be willing

[4] Ibid., IV, pp. 539–45.

to bury this transaction . . . had the hostilities of Colonel Nicholls terminated with the war; but he did not consider the peace which ensued . . . as having put an end . . . to his negotiations with the Indians against the United States. . . .

The negro fort, however, abandoned by Colonel Nicholls, remained on the Spanish territory, occupied by the banditti to whom he had left it. . . .

In the year 1817, Alexander Arbuthnot . . . a British subject, first appeared as an English trader in Spanish Florida, and as the successor of Colonel Nicholls in the employment of instigating the Seminole and outlawed Red Stick Indians to hostilities against the United States. . . . No sooner did he make his appearance among the Indians . . . than the peaceful inhabitants on the borders of the United States were visited with all the horrors of savage war – the robbery of their property, and the barbarous and indiscriminate murder of woman, infancy and age.

After the repeated expostulations, warnings and offers of peace . . . orders were given to General Jackson, and an adequate force was placed at his disposal to terminate the war. . . . The necessity of crossing the line was indispensable; for it was from beyond the line that the Indians made their murderous incursions within that of the United States. . . .

In the course of his pursuit, as he approached St. Mark's, he was informed direct from the Governor of Pensacola that a party of the hostile Indians had threatened to seize that fort. . . . By all the laws of neutrality and of war . . . he was warranted in anticipating his enemy by the amicable, and, that being refused, by the forcible occupation of the fort. . . .

The conduct of the Governor of Pensacola was not less marked by a disposition of enmity to the United States, and by an utter disregard to the obligations of the treaty by which he was bound to restrain, by force, the Indians from hostilities against them. . . . He had permitted free ingress and agress at Pensacola to the avowed savage enemies of the United States. . . .

He [General Jackson] took possession, therefore, of Pensacola and the fort of Barrancas . . . not in a spirit of hostility to Spain, but as a necessary measure of self defence; giving notice that they should be restored whenever Spain should place commanders and a force there able and willing to fulfil the engagements of Spain toward the United States. . . .

This exposition of the origin, the causes, and the character of the war with the Seminole Indians . . . will, it is hoped, enable you to present other and sounder views of the subject to His Catholic Majesty's Government.

It will enable you to show that the occupation of Pensacola and St. Mark's was occasioned neither by a spirit of hostility to Spain, nor with a view to extort prematurely the province from her possession; that it was rendered necessary by the neglect of Spain to perform her engagements . . . and by the culpable countenance, encouragement, and assistance given to those Indians, in their hostilities, by the Spanish Governor and commandant at those places; that the United States have a right to demand, as the President does demand, of Spain the punishment of those officers for their misconduct; and he further demands of Spain a just and reasonable indemnity to the United States for the heavy and necessary expenses which they have been compelled to incur by the failure of Spain to perform her engagements to restrain the Indians. . . . And if . . . the necessities of self defense should again compel the United States to take possession of the Spanish forts and places in Florida, [we] declare, with the frankness and candor that become us, that another unconditional restoration of them must not be expected. . . .

◇◇◇◇◇◇◇◇◇◇◇◇◇◇

5. TREATY OF AMITY, SETTLEMENT AND LIMITS, BETWEEN SPAIN AND THE UNITED STATES[5]

[*Concluded February 22, 1819; ratifications exchanged February 22, 1821*]

. . . *ARTICLE II.* His Catholic Majesty cedes to the United-States, in full property and sovereignty, all the territories which belong to him, situated to the Eastward of the Mississippi, known by the name of East and West Florida. . . .

Article III. The Boundary Line between the two Countries, West of the Mississippi, shall begin on the Gulph of Mexico, at the mouth of the River Sabine in the Sea, continuing North, along the Western Bank of that River, to the 32d degree of Latitude; thence by a Line due North to the degree of Latitude, where it strikes the Rio Roxo of Nachitoches, or Red-River, then following the course of the Rio-Roxo Westward to the degree of Longitude, 100 West from London and 23 from Washington, then crossing the said Red-River, and running thence by a Line due North to the River Arkansas, thence, following the Course of the Southern bank of the Arkansas to its source in Latitude 42. North, and thence by that parallel of Latitude to the South-Sea. . . .

The Two High Contracting Parties agree to cede and renounce all their rights, claims and pretensions to the Territories described by the said Line: that is to say. — The United States hereby cede to His Catholic Majesty, and renounce forever, all their rights, claims, and pretensions to the Territories lying West and South of the above described Line; and, in like manner, His Catholic Majesty cedes to the said United-States all his rights, claims, and pretensions to any Territories, East and North of the said Line, and, for himself, his heirs and successors, renounces all claim to the said Territories forever. . . .

Article VI. The Inhabitants of the Territories which His Catholic Maj-

[5] Hunter Miller: *Treaties and Other International Acts of the United States,* Vol. III, pp. 3–18.

esty cedes to the United-States by this Treaty, shall be incorporated in the Union of the United-States, as soon as may be consistent with the principles of the Federal Constitution, and admitted to the enjoyment of all the privileges, rights and immunities of the Citizens of the United-States. . . .

Article VIII. All the grants of land made before the 24th of January 1818, by His Catholic Majesty or by his lawful authorities in the said Territories ceded by His Majesty to the United-States, shall be ratified and confirmed to the persons in possession of the lands, to the same extent that the same grants would be valid if the Territories had remained under the Dominion of His Catholic Majesty. But the owners in possession of such lands, who by reason of the recent circumstances of the Spanish Nation and the Revolutions in Europe, have been prevented from fulfilling all the conditions of their grants, shall complete them within the terms limited in the same respectively, from the date of this Treaty; in default of which the said grants shall be null and void. All grants made since the said 24th of January 1818, when the first proposal on the part of His Catholic Majesty, for the cession of the Floridas was made, are hereby declared and agreed to be null and void. . . .

Article XI. The United-States, exonerating Spain from all demands in future, on account of the claims of their Citizens, to which the renunciations herein contained extend, and considering them entirely cancelled, undertake to make satisfaction for the same, to an amount not exceeding Five Millions of Dollars. To ascertain the full amount and validity of those claims, a Commission, to consist of three Commissioners, Citizens of the United-States, shall be appointed by the President, by and with the advice and consent of the Senate; which Commission shall meet at the City of Washington, and within the space of three years, from the time of their first meeting, shall receive, examine and decide upon the amount and validity of all the claims included within the descriptions above mentioned. . . .

CHAPTER X

THE MONROE DOCTRINE

THE Monroe Doctrine grew out of two particular circumstances. One was the attempt of Russia to extend her control along the northwest coast of America, and the other was the possibility that the Quadruple Alliance would assist Spain to recover her American colonies. That part of the Monroe Doctrine which related to Russia was clear and direct, not specifically connected with other foreign problems, and was foreshadowed by the dispatch of the Secretary of State, of July 22, 1823 (2), to the American minister to Russia, in protest against the Russian Ukase of September 4, 1821 (1). The other part of the Doctrine had its immediate origin in a conference between the American minister in London, Richard Rush, and the British Foreign Minister, George Canning. Although the United States, unlike Great Britain, had already recognized the independence of some Latin American states (3), the British minister suggested the issuance of a joint declaration on the part of their respective governments in opposition to interference of any foreign power in Spanish America. On the day following this conference, August 20, 1823, Canning made a formal proposition to Rush (4), who immediately transmitted it to his government. President Monroe not only submitted the question to his Cabinet but also requested the opinion of other influential men. The reply of Thomas Jefferson is of special interest (5).

Failing to receive the immediate acceptance of his plan by the United States (6), Canning entered into a series of discussions on the Spanish colonial question with the French Ambassador in London, the Prince de Polignac (7). These discussions rendered the proposed joint declaration unnecessary as far as Great Britain was concerned. The United States, however, had important reasons (8) for issuing a separate declaration (9). The limited scope of the Monroe Doctrine, at the time of its promulgation, is indicated in the Adams–Salazar correspondence of July and August 1824 (10, 11). The comments of Adams to Rush of November 29, 1823, and the ideas expressed earlier in his memoirs, provide an interesting contrast and show the scope and development of his thought on American foreign policy (12).

1. RUSSIAN UKASE OF SEPTEMBER 4, 1821[1]

Rules Established for the Limits of Navigation and Order of Communication Along the Coast of the Eastern Siberia, the North-west Coast of America, and the Aleutian, Kurile, and other Islands.

1. The pursuits of commerce, whaling, and fishery, and of all other industry on all islands, posts, and gulfs, including the whole of the northwest coast of America, beginning from Behring Straits to the 51° of northern latitude, also from the Aleutian Islands to the eastern coast of Siberia, as well as along the Kurile Islands from Behring Straits to the south cape of the Island of Urup, viz., to the 45° 50′ north latitude, is exclusively granted to Russian subjects.

2. It is therefore prohibited to all foreign vessels not only to land on the coasts and islands belonging to Russia as stated above, but also, to approach them within less than 100 Italian miles. The transgressor's vessel is subject to confiscation along with the whole cargo.

3. An exception to this rule is to be made in favour of vessels carried thither by heavy gales, or real want of provisions, and unable to make any other shore but such as belongs to Russia; in these cases they are obliged to produce convincing proofs of actual reason for such an exception. Ships of friendly Governments, merely on discoveries, are likewise exempt from the foregoing Rule 2. In this case, however, they must be previously provided with passports from the Russian Minister of the Navy.

4. Foreign merchant-ships which, for reasons stated in the foregoing rule, touch at any of the above-mentioned coasts, are obliged to endeavour to choose a place where Russians are settled, and to act as hereafter stated. . . .

12. It is prohibited to these foreign ships to receive on board, without special permission of the Commanders, any of the people in the service of the Company, or of the foreigners living in the Company's Settlements. Ships proved to have the intention of carrying off any person belonging to the Colony shall be seized. . . .

14. It is likewise interdicted to foreign ships to carry on any traffic or barter with the natives of the islands, and of the north-west coast of America, in the whole extent here above mentioned. A ship convicted of this trade shall be confiscated.

---

[1] *Sen. Ex. Doc.* (4600) 58th Congress, 2nd Session, No. 162, pp. 25–6. The document was signed by Count D. Gurief, Minister of Finance.

2. AMERICAN PROTEST AGAINST THE RUSSIAN UKASE OF SEPTEMBER 4, 1821[2]

[*John Quincy Adams to Henry Middleton*]

Washington, July 22, 1823

. . . FROM THE tenor of the ukase, the pretensions of the Imperial Government extend to an exclusive territorial jurisdiction from the forty-fifth degree of north latitude on the Asiatic coast to the latitude of fifty-one north on the western coast of the American continent; and they assume the right of interdicting the *navigation* and the fishery of all other nations to the extent of one hundred miles from the whole of that coast.

The United States can admit no part of these claims. Their right of navigation and of fishing is perfect, and has been in constant exercise from the earliest times, after the peace of 1783, throughout the whole extent of the Southern Ocean, subject only to the ordinary exceptions and exclusions of the territorial jurisdictions, which, so far as Russian rights are concerned, are confined to certain *islands* north of the fifty-fifth degree of latitude, and have no existence on the continent of America. . . .

It does not appear that there ever has been a permanent Russian settlement on this continent south of latitude 59; that of New Archangel, cited by Mr. Poletica, in latitude 57° 30′, being upon an island. So far as prior *discovery* can constitute a foundation of right, the papers which I have referred to prove that it belongs to the United States as far as 59° north, by the transfer to them of the rights of Spain. There is, however, no part of the globe where the mere fact of discovery could be held to give weaker claims than on the North-west coast. "The great sinuosity," says Humboldt, "formed by the coast between the 55th and 60th parallels of latitude embraces discoveries made by Gali, Behring and Tchivikoff, Quadra, Cook, La Perouse, Malespier, and Vancouver. No European nation has yet formed an establishment upon the immense extent of coast from Cape Mendosino to the 59th degree of latitude. Beyond that limit the Russian factories commence, most of which are scattered and distant from each other, like the factories established by the European nations for the last three centuries on the coast of Africa. Most of these little Russian colonies communicate with each other only by sea, and the new denominations of Russian America, or Russian possessions in the new continent, must not lead us to believe that the coast of Behrings Bay, the peninsula of Alaska, or the country of Ischugatschi, have become Russian *provinces* in the same sense given to the word when speaking of the Spanish provinces of Sonora or New Biscay." – (Humboldt's New Spain, vol. 2d, book 3d, ch. 8, p. 496). . . .

The right of the United States from the forty-second to the forty-ninth parallel of latitude on the Pacific Ocean we consider as unquestionable.

[2] Ibid., pp. 47–51.

being founded, first, on the acquisition by the treaty of February 22, 1819, of all the rights of Spain; second, by the discovery of the Columbia River, first from sea at its mouth, and then by land by Lewis and Clarke; and third, by the settlement at its mouth in 1811. This territory is to the United States of an importance which no possession in North America can be of to any European nation, not only as it is but the continuity of their possessions from the Atlantic to the Pacific Ocean, but as it offers their inhabitants the means of establishing hereafter water communications from the one to the other.

It is not conceivable that any possession upon the continent of North America should be of use or importance to Russia for any other purpose than that of traffic with the natives. This was in fact the inducement to the formation of the Russian American Company and to the charter granted them by the Emperor Paul. It was the inducement to the ukase of the Emperor Alexander. By offering free and equal access for a term of years to navigation and intercourse with the natives to Russia, within the limits to which our claims are indisputable, we concede much more than we obtain. It is not to be doubted that, long before the expiration of that time, our settlement at the mouth of the Columbia River will become so considerable as to offer means of useful commercial intercourse with the Russian settlements on the islands of the northwest coast.

With regard to the territorial claim, separate from the right of traffic with the natives and from any system of colonial exclusions, we are willing to agree to the boundary line within which the Emperor Paul had granted exclusive privileges to the Russian American Company, that is to say, latitude 55°. . . .

◇◇◇◇◇◇◇◇◇◇◇◇◇◇

3. THE RECOGNITION OF LATIN-AMERICAN STATES[3]

. . . THE revolutionary movement in the Spanish Provinces in this hemisphere attracted the attention and excited the sympathy of our fellow-citizens from its commencement. This feeling was natural and honorable to them, from causes which need not be communicated to you. It has been gratifying to all to see the general acquiescence which has been manifested in the policy which the constituted authorities have deemed it proper to pursue in regard to this contest. As soon as the movement assumed such a steady and consistent form as to make the success of the Provinces probable, the rights to which they were entitled by the law of nations as equal parties to a civil war were extended to them. Each party was permitted to enter our ports with its public and private ships, and to take from them every article which was the subject of commerce with other nations. Our

[3] The Message of President Monroe to Congress, March 8, 1822. Richardson: *Messages and Papers of the Presidents,* Vol. II, pp. 116–18,

citizens, also, have carried on commerce with both parties, and the Government has protected it with each in articles not contraband of war. Through the whole of this contest the United States have remained neutral, and have fulfilled with the utmost impartiality all the obligations incident to that character.

This contest has now reached such a stage and been attended with such decisive success on the part of the Provinces that it merits the most profound consideration whether their right to the rank of independent nations, with all the advantages incident to it in their intercourse with the United States, is not complete. Buenos Ayres assumed that rank by a formal declaration in 1816, and has enjoyed it since 1810 free from invasion by the parent country. The Provinces composing the Republic of Colombia, after having separately declared their independence, were united by a fundamental law of the 17th of December, 1819. A strong Spanish force occupied at that time certain parts of the territory within their limits and waged a destructive war. That force has since been repeatedly defeated, and the whole of it either made prisoners or destroyed or expelled from the country, with the exception of an inconsiderable portion only, which is blockaded in two fortresses. The Provinces on the Pacific have likewise been very successful. Chili declared independence in 1818, and has since enjoyed it undisturbed; and of late, by the assistance of Chili and Buenos Ayres, the revolution has extended to Peru. Of the movement in Mexico our information is less authentic, but it is, nevertheless, distinctly understood that the new Government has declared its independence, and that there is now no opposition to it there nor a force to make any. For the last three years the Government of Spain has not sent a single corps of troops to any part of that country, nor is there any reason to believe it will send any in future. Thus it is manifest that all those Provinces are not only in the full enjoyment of their independence, but, considering the state of the war and other circumstances, that there is not the most remote prospect of their being deprived of it. . . .

The Provinces belonging to this hemisphere are our neighbors, and have successively, as each portion of the country acquired its independence, pressed their recognition by an appeal to facts not to be contested, and which they thought gave them a just title to it. To motives of interest this Government has invariably disclaimed all pretension, being resolved to take no part in the controversy or other measure in regard to it which should not merit the sanction of the civilized world. . . .

Of the views of the Spanish Government on this subject no particular information has been recently received. . . . Nor has any authentic information been recently received of the disposition of other powers respecting it. A sincere desire has been cherished to act in concert with them in the proposed recognition, of which several were some time past duly apprised; but it was understood that they were not prepared for it. The immense space between those powers, even those which border on the Atlantic, and these Provinces makes the movement an affair of less interest and excitement to them than to us. It is probable, therefore, that they have been less attentive to its progress than we have been. It may be presumed, however, that the late events will dispel all doubt of the result. . . .

◇◇◇◇◇◇◇◇◇◇◇◇

4. BRITISH PROPOSAL REGARDING THE SPANISH-AMERICAN COLONIES [4]

[*George Canning to Richard Rush*]

Foreign office [*London*], *August 20, 1823*

PRIVATE AND CONFIDENTIAL

MY Dear Sir: Before leaving Town, I am desirous of bringing before you in a more distinct, but still in an unofficial and confidential, shape, the question which we shortly discussed the last time that I had the pleasure of seeing you.

Is not the moment come when our Governments might understand each other as to the Spanish American Colonies? And if we can arrive at such an understanding, would it not be expedient for ourselves, and beneficial for all the world, that the principles of it should be clearly settled and plainly avowed?

For ourselves we have no disguise.

1. We conceive the recovery of the Colonies by Spain to be hopeless.
2. We conceive the question of the recognition of them, as Independent States, to be one of time and circumstances.
3. We are, however, by no means disposed to throw any impediment in the way of an arrangement between them, and the mother country by amicable negotiation.
4. We aim not at the possession of any portion of them ourselves.
5. We could not see any portion of them transferred to any other Power, with indifference.

If these opinions and feelings are as I firmly believe them to be, common to your Government with ours, why should we hesitate mutually to confide them to each other; and to declare them in the face of the world?

If there be any European Power which cherishes other projects, which looks to a forcible enterprize for reducing the Colonies to subjugation, on the behalf or in the name of Spain; or which meditates the acquisition of any part of them to itself, by cession or by conquest; such a declaration on the part of your government and ours would be at once the most effectual and the least offensive mode of intimating our joint disapprobation of such projects.

[4] William R. Manning, ed.: *Diplomatic Correspondence of the United States Concerning the Independence of the Latin-American Nations* (New York: Oxford University Press, 1925), Vol. III, pp. 1478–9.

It would at the same time put an end to all the jealousies of Spain with respect to her remaining Colonies – and to the agitation which prevails in those Colonies, an agitation which it would be but humane to allay; being determined (as we are) not to profit by encouraging it.

Do you conceive that under the power which you have recently received, you are authorized to enter into negotiation, and to sign any Convention upon this subject? Do you conceive, if that be not within your competence, you could exchange with me ministerial notes upon it?

Nothing could be more gratifying to me than to join with you in such a work, and, I am persuaded, there has seldom, in the history of the world, occurred an opportunity when so small an effort, of two friendly Governments, might produce so unequivocal a good and prevent such extensive calamities.

I shall be absent from London but three weeks at the utmost: but never so far distant but that I can receive and reply to any communication, within three or four days.

◇◇◇◇◇◇◇◇◇◇◇◇◇

5. JEFFERSON'S SUPPORT OF CO-OPERATION WITH ENGLAND[5]

[*Thomas Jefferson to President Monroe*]

October 24, 1823

THE QUESTION presented by the letters you have sent me, is the most momentous which has ever been offered to my contemplation since that of Independence. That made us a nation, this sets our compass and points the course which we are to steer through the ocean of time opening on us. And never could we embark on it under circumstances more auspicious. Our first and fundamental maxim should be, never to entangle ourselves in the broils of Europe. Our second, never to suffer Europe to intermeddle with cis-Atlantic affairs. America, North and South, has a set of interests distinct from those of Europe, and peculiarly her own. She should therefore have a system of her own, separate and apart from that of Europe. While the last is laboring to become the domicile of despotism, our endeavor should surely be, to make our hemisphere that of freedom.

One nation, most of all, could disturb us in this pursuit; she now offers to lead, aid, and accompany us in it. By acceding to her proposition, we detach her from the bands, bring her mighty weight into the scale of free government, and emancipate a continent at one stroke, which might otherwise linger long in doubt and difficulty. Great Britain is the nation which can do us the most harm of any one, or all on earth; and with her on our side we need not fear the whole world. With her then, we should most sedulously cherish a cordial friendship; and nothing would tend more to

[5] H. A. Washington, ed.: *The Writings of Thomas Jefferson,* Vol. VII, pp. 315–17.

knit our affections than to be fighting once more, side by side, in the same cause. Not that I would purchase even her amity at the price of taking part in her wars. But the war in which the present proposition might engage us, should that be its consequence, is not her war, but ours. Its object is to introduce and establish the American system, of keeping out of our land all foreign powers, of never permitting those of Europe to intermeddle with the affairs of our nations. It is to maintain our own principle, not to depart from it. And if, to facilitate this, we can effect a division in the body of the European powers, and draw over to our side its most powerful member, surely we should do it. But I am clearly of Mr. Canning's opinion, that it will prevent instead of provoking war. With Great Britain withdrawn from their scale and shifted into that of our two continents, all Europe combined would not undertake such a war. For how would they propose to get at either enemy without superior fleets? Nor is the occasion to be slighted which this proposition offers, of declaring our protest against the atrocious violations of the rights of nations, by the interference of any one in the internal affairs of another, so flagitiously begun by Bonaparte, and now continued by the equally lawless Alliance, calling itself Holy. . . .

I could honestly, therefore, join in the declaration proposed, that we aim not at the acquisition of any of those possessions, that we will not stand in the way of any amicable arrangement between them and the mother country; but that we will oppose, with all our means, the forcible interposition of any other power, as auxiliary, stipendiary, or under any other form or pretext, and most especially, their transfer to any power by conquest, cession, or acquisition in any other way. I should think it, therefore, advisable, that the Executive should encourage the British government to a continuance in the dispositions expressed in these letters, by an assurance of his concurrence with them as far as his authority goes; and that as it may lead to war, the declaration of which requires an act of Congress, the case shall be laid before them for consideration at their first meeting, and under the reasonable aspect in which it is seen by himself. . . .

◇◇◇◇◇◇◇◇◇◇◇◇◇◇

6. THE STUMBLING BLOCK OF ANGLO-AMERICAN CO-OPERATION[6]

[*Richard Rush to John Quincy Adams*]

London, August 28, 1823

SINCE my last despatch, I have received a second confidential note from Mr. Canning. . . .

Mr. Canning having now distinctly informed me, that he has received

[6] Manning: *Diplomatic Correspondence of the United States Concerning the Independence of the Latin-American Nations*, Vol. III, pp. 1483–85.

notice of measures being in projection by the powers of Europe relative to the affairs of Spanish America, as soon as the French succeed in their military movements in Spain, — which it would seem they expect soon to do, — I cannot avoid seeing this subject under the complications to which Mr. Canning alludes.

My first object will be to urge upon this government the obvious expediency of an immediate and unreserved recognition of the independence of the South American states.

It will be seen by my note to Mr. Canning of yesterday, that I have made a beginning in this work, and, should the opportunity be afforded me, it is my intention to follow it up zealously.

Should I be asked by Mr. Canning, whether, *if the recognition be made by Great Britain without more delay*, I am, on my part, prepared to make a declaration in the name of my government that it will not remain inactive under an attack upon the independence of those states by the Holy Alliance, the present determination of my judgment is, that I will make this declaration, explicitly, and avow it before the world.

I am not unaware of the responsibility which I should, by such a measure, assume upon myself. My reasons for assuming it, I have not, at present, the leisure to recount with the requisite fulness. The leading ones would be, in brief, as follow:

1. I may thereby aid in achieving an immediate and positive good to those rising states in our hemisphere; for such I should conceive their recognition at this juncture by Great Britain, in itself, to be.

2. Such recognition, cooperating with the declaration which this government has already in effect made, that it will not look quietly on if Spanish America is attacked, and followed up by a similar (though not joint) declaration from me that neither will the United States, would prove at least a probable means of warding off the attack. The minister of foreign affairs of this government, it appears, is under a strong persuasion that it would forestall it, and this without the recognition by England being, as yet, a part of his case.

3. Should the issue of things be different, and events notwithstanding arise threatening the peace of the United States, or otherwise seriously to commit them, under such a declaration from me, it would still remain with the wisdom of my government to disavow my conduct, as I should manifestly have acted without its previous warrant, though hoping for its subsequent sanction. I would take to myself all the reproach, consoled if not justified under the desire that had animated me to render benefits of great magnitude to the cause of South American independence and freedom at a point of time, which, if lost, was not to be regained; and believing that, at all events, I should have rendered some benefits to it, in being instrumental towards accelerating the recognition by Great Britain. . . .

7. THE POLIGNAC MEMORANDUM[7]

[*Memorandum of a Conference between The Prince de Polignac and Mr. Canning, begun October 9, and Concluded October 12, 1823*]

THE PRINCE de Polignac having announced to Mr. Canning, that His Excellency was now prepared to enter with Mr. Canning into a frank explanation of the views of his Government respecting the question of Spanish America, in return for a similar communication which Mr. Canning had previously offered to make to The Prince de Polignac on the part of the British Cabinet, Mr. Canning stated. . . .

That the near approach of a crisis, in which the affairs of Spanish America must naturally occupy a great share of the attention of both Powers, made it desirable that there should be no misunderstanding between them on any part of a subject so important:

That the British Government were of opinion, that any attempt to bring Spanish America again under its ancient submission to Spain, must be utterly hopeless: that all negotiation for that purpose would be unsuccessful; and that the prolongation or renewal of War for the same object would be only a waste of human life, and an infliction of calamity on both Parties, to no end:

That the British Government would, however, not only abstain from interposing any obstacle, on their part, to any attempt at negotiation, which Spain might think proper to make, but would aid and countenance such negotiation, provided it were founded upon a basis which appeared to them to be practicable; and that they would, in any case, remain strictly neutral in a War between Spain and the Colonies, if War should be unhappily prolonged:

But that the junction of any Foreign Power, in an Enterprize of Spain against the Colonies, would be viewed by them as constituting an entirely new question; and one upon which they must take such decision as the interests of Great Britain might require:

That the British Government absolutely disclaimed, not only any desire of appropriating to itself any portion of the Spanish Colonies, but any intention of forming any political connexion with them, beyond that of amity and commercial intercourse:

That in those respects, so far from seeking an exclusive preference for British Subjects over those of Foreign States, England was prepared, and would be contented, to see the Mother Country (by virtue of an amicable arrangement) in possession of that preference; and to be ranked, after Her, equally with Others, on the footing of the most favoured Nation:

That, completely convinced that the ancient system of the Colonies could not be restored, the British Government could not enter into any

[7] *British and Foreign State Papers,* Vol. XI, pp. 49–53.

stipulation binding itself either to refuse or to delay it's recognition of their Independence:

That the British Government had no desire to precipitate that recognition, so long as there was any reasonable chance of an accommodation with the Mother Country, by which such a recognition might come first from Spain:

But that It could not wait indefinitely for that result; that it could not consent to make it's recognition of the New States *dependent* upon that of Spain; and that it would consider any Foreign interference, by force or by menace, in the dispute between Spain and the Colonies, as a motive for recognizing the latter without delay. . . .

That permission to trade with the Spanish Colonies had been conceded to Great Britain in the year 1810, when the mediation of Great Britain between Spain and her Colonies was asked by Spain, and granted by Great Britain: – that this mediation, indeed, was not afterwards employed, because Spain changed her counsel; but that it was not, therefore, practicable for Great Britain to withdraw commercial capital once embarked in Spanish America, and to desist from commercial intercourse once established. . . .

That, with these general opinions, and with these peculiar claims, England could not go into a joint deliberation upon the subject of Spanish America, upon an equal footing with other Powers, whose opinions were less formed upon that question, and whose interests were less implicated in the decision of it:

That She thought it fair, therefore, to explain beforehand, to what degree Her mind was made up, and Her determination taken.

The Prince de Polignac declared,

That his Government believed it to be utterly hopeless to reduce Spanish America to the state of its former relation to Spain;

That France disclaimed, on Her part, any intention or desire to avail Herself of the present State of the Colonies, or of the present situation of France towards Spain, to appropriate to Herself any part of the Spanish Possessions in America, or to obtain for Herself any exclusive advantages:

And that, like England, She would willingly see the Mother Country in possession of superior commercial advantages, by amicable arrangements; and would be contented, like Her, to rank, after the Mother Country, among the most favoured Nations:

Lastly, that She abjured, in any case, any design of acting against the Colonies by force of arms. . . .

The Monroe Doctrine

8. INSTRUCTIONS TO RICHARD RUSH[8]

[*John Quincy Adams to Richard Rush*]

Washington, November 29, 1823

YOUR despatches numbered 323–325–326–330–331–332–334 and 336 have been received; containing the reports of your conferences, and copies of your confidential correspondence, with Mr. Secretary Canning, in relation to certain proposals made by him, tending to a concert of principles, with reference to the affairs of South America, between the United States and Great Britain, and a combined manifestation of them to the world.

The whole subject has received the deliberate consideration of the President, under a deep impression of its genial importance, a full conviction of the high interests and sacred principles involved in it, and an anxious solicitude for the cultivation of that harmony of opinions and unity of object, between the British and American Nations, upon which so much of the peace and happiness and liberty of the world obviously depend.

I am directed to express to you the President's entire approbation of the course which you have pursued in referring to your Government the proposals contained in Mr. Canning's private and confidential letter to you, of 20 August; and I am now to signify the determination of the President concerning them: — a determination which he wishes to be at once candid, explicit and conciliatory; and which being formed by refering each of the proposals to the single and unvarying standard of right and wrong, as understood and maintained by us, will present to the British Government the whole system of opinions and of purposes of the American Government with regard to South America.

The first of the *principles* of the British Government, as set forth by Mr. Canning, is —

1. We conceive the recovery of the colonies by Spain, to be hopeless.

In this we concur.

The second is —

2. We conceive the question of the recognition of them, as independent States, to be one of time and circumstances.

We *did* so conceive it, until with a due regard to all the rights of Spain, and with a due sense of our responsibility to the judgment of mankind, and of posterity, we had come to the conclusion that the recovery of them by Spain *was hopeless.* Having arrived at that conclusion, we considered that the people of these emancipated Colonies, were, *of right* independent of all other nations, and that it was our duty so to acknowledge them. We did so acknowledge them, in March, 1822; from which time the recognition has no longer been a question *to us.* We are aware of considerations, just and proper in themselves, which might deter Great Britain from fixing

[8] Manning: *Diplomatic Correspondence,* op. cit., Vol. I, pp. 210–12.

upon the same *time* for this recognition, with us; but we wish to press it earnestly upon her consideration, whether, after having settled the point that the recovery of the colonies by Spain was *hopeless,* and after maintaining, at the cannon's mouth, commercial relations with them, incompatible with their colonial condition, while subject to Spain, the *moral* obligation does not necessarily result of recognizing them as independent States.

"3. We are however, by no means disposed to throw any impediment in the way of an arrangement between them and the mother country by *amiable negociation.*"

Nor are we — Recognizing them as independent States, we acknowledge them as possessing full power to levy war, conclude peace, contract alliances, establish commerce, and do all other acts and things which independent States may of right do. Among these, an arrangement between them and Spain, by amicable negociation is one which far from being disposed to impede, we would earnestly desire, and, by every proper means in our power, endeavour to promote, provided it should be founded on the basis of independence. But recognizing them as independent States, we do, and shall justly and necessarily, claim in our relations political and commercial, to be placed upon a footing of equal favour, with the most favoured nation.

"4. We aim not at the possession of any portion of them ourselves."

"5. We would not see any portion of them transferred to any other Power, with indifference."

In both these positions we concur, — and we add —

That we could not see with indifference, any attempt by one or more powers of Europe to restore those new states to the crown of Spain, or to deprive them, in any manner, whatever of the freedom and independence which they have acquired.

With a view to this object, it is indispensable that the British Government take like ground with that which is now held by the United States, and that it recognize the independence of the new Governments. That measure being taken, we may then harmonize in all the arrangements and acts which may be necessary for its accomplishment. It is upon this ground alone, as we conceive that a firm and determined stand could now be jointly taken by Great-Britain and the United States, in behalf of the *Independence of Nations:* and never, in the history of mankind, was there a period when a stand so taken and maintained, would exhibit to present and future ages, a more glorious example of power, animated by justice, and devoted to the ends of beneficence. On this basis this Government is willing to move in concert with Great-Britain for the purposes specified.

We believe, however, that for the most effectual accomplishment of the object, common to both Governments, a perfect understanding with regard to it being established between them, it will be most advisable that they should act separately, each making such representations to the Continental European Allies, or either of them, as circumstances may render proper, and mutually communicating to each other, the purport of such representations, and all information respecting the measures and purposes of the Allies, the knowledge of which may enlighten the councils of Great Britain and of the United States, in the course of policy, and towards the honourable end, which will be common to them both. Should an emergency occur, in which a *joint* manifestation of opinion, by the two Governments may tend to influence the Councils of the European Allies, either in the aspect of persuasion or of admonition, you will make it known to us without delay, and we shall according to the principles of our Government, and in the forms prescribed by our Constitution, cheerfully join in any act by which we may contribute to support the cause of human freedom, and the Independence of the South American Nations.

◇◇◇◇◇◇◇◇◇◇◇◇◇◇

9. THE MONROE DOCTRINE[9]

[*Message of President Monroe to Congress, December 2, 1823*]

AT THE proposal of the Russian Imperial Government, made through the minister of the Emperor residing here, a full power and instructions have been transmitted to the minister of the United States at St. Petersburg to arrange by amicable negotiation the respective rights and interests of the two nations on the northwest coast of this continent. A similar proposal has been made by his Imperial Majesty to the Government of Great Britain, which has likewise been acceded to. The Government of the United States has been desirous by this friendly proceeding of manifesting the great value which they have invariably attached to the friendship of the Emperor and their solicitude to cultivate the best understanding with his Government. In the discussions to which this interest has given rise and in the arrangements by which they may terminate the occasion has been judged proper for asserting, as a principle in which the rights and interests of the United States are involved, that the American continents, by the free and independent condition which they have assumed and maintain, are henceforth not to be considered as subjects for future colonization by any European powers. . . .

It was stated at the commencement of the last session that a great effort was then making in Spain and Portugal to improve the condition of the people of those countries, and that it appeared to be conducted with extraordinary moderation. It need scarcely be remarked that the result has been so far very different from what was then anticipated. Of events in that quarter of the globe, with which we have so much intercourse and from which we derive our origin, we have always been anxious and interested spectators. The citizens of the United States cherish sentiments

9 J. D. Richardson, ed.: *Messages and Papers of the Presidents*, Vol. II, pp. 209 ff.

the most friendly in favor of the liberty and happiness of their fellow-men on that side of the Atlantic. In the wars of the European powers in matters relating to themselves we have never taken any part, nor does it comport with our policy so to do. It is only when our rights are invaded or seriously menaced that we resent injuries or make preparation for our defense. With the movements in this hemisphere we are of necessity more immediately connected, and by causes which must be obvious to all enlightened and impartial observers. The political system of the allied powers is essentially different in this respect from that of America. This difference proceeds from that which exists in their respective Governments; and to the defense of our own, which has been achieved by the loss of so much blood and treasure, and matured by the wisdom of their most enlightened citizens, and under which we have enjoyed unexampled felicity, this whole nation is devoted. We owe it, therefore, to candor and to the amicable relations existing between the United States and those powers to declare that we should consider any attempt on their part to extend their system to any portion of this hemisphere as dangerous to our peace and safety. With the existing colonies or dependencies of any European power we have not interfered and shall not interfere. But with the Governments who have declared their independence and maintained it, and whose independence we have, on great consideration and on just principles, acknowledged, we could not view any interposition for the purpose of oppressing them, or controlling in any other manner their destiny, by any European power in any other light than as the manifestation of an unfriendly disposition toward the United States. In the war between those new Governments and Spain we declared our neutrality at the time of their recognition, and to this we have adhered, and shall continue to adhere, provided no change shall occur which, in the judgment of the competent authorities of this Government, shall make a corresponding change on the part of the United States indispensable to their security.

The late events in Spain and Portugal shew that Europe is still unsettled. Of this important fact no stronger proof can be adduced than that the allied powers should have thought it proper, on any principle satisfactory to themselves, to have interposed by force in the internal concerns of Spain. To what extent such interposition may be carried, on the same principle, is a question in which all independent powers whose governments differ from theirs are interested, even those most remote, and surely none more so than the United States. Our policy in regard to Europe, which was adopted at an early stage of the wars which have so long agitated that quarter of the globe, nevertheless remains the same, which is, not to interfere in the internal concerns of any of its powers; to consider the government *de facto* as the legitimate government for us; to cultivate friendly relations with it, and to preserve those relations by a frank, firm, and manly policy, meeting in all instances the just claims of every power, submitting to injuries from none. But in regard to those continents circumstances are eminently and conspicuously different. It is impossible that the allied powers should extend their political system to any portion of either continent without endangering our peace and happiness; nor can anyone believe that our southern brethren, if left to themselves, would adopt it of their own accord. It is equally impossible, therefore, that we should behold such interposition in any form with indifference. If we look to the comparative strength and resources of Spain and those new Governments, and their distance from each other, it must be obvious that she can never subdue them. It is still the true policy of the United States to leave the parties to themselves, in the hope that other powers will pursue the same course. . . .

◇◇◇◇◇◇◇◇◇◇◇◇◇◇

10. REQUEST FOR EXPLANATION OF THE MONROE DOCTRINE[10]

[*Don José Maria Salazar to John Quincy Adams*]

Washington, July 2, 1824

AFTER having had the honour of giving you an informal verbal account of the present political state of the Republic of Colombia, I am about to lay before you agreeably to your desire, in this confidential Note, the explanations which my Government wishes to be given to that of the United States.

I said in our conference that the Republic has gone on ameliorating in all the branches of its administration, and for this I refer to the Message of the Executive of which I enclose you a copy: everything has revived under the influence of free institutions, and if peace shall perfect the benefit which they produce, the progress of the public prosperity would be very rapid.

Colombia, however, does not flatter herself with this hope, in the present state of affairs of the Governments of Europe, and her fears are founded on the obstinacy of Spain in not recognizing her independence, on the language of the Ministerial papers of France, particularly the Journal of Debates of Paris of the months of October and November last in which the antient Colonial system is warmly advocated, or to substitute another in a different form; and on the well known views of the Holy Alliance: nothing induces the opinion that she has renounced the direful principle of interference in the domestic concerns of other states, a principle derogatory to its Sovereignty, and contrary to international law.

There does not appear to be so great an objection on the part of the Holy Alliance to the independence of the new American states as to the principles which they profess, and to the republican form; the attempt to place a Bourbon Prince over Buenos Ayres is well known: French em-

[10] Manning: *Diplomatic Correspondence*, op. cit., Vol. II, pp. 1281–2.

missaries made a similar suggestion in Mexico, and ultimately a gentleman named Chaserieux is just arrived at Caraccas who calls himself the envoy of His Christian Majesty near the Government of Colombia, who has used the same language as I have read in the public papers of that City; he says that his Government is disposed to recognize Colombia but on rational terms, and by them he understands, leaving it a Republic.

Colombia is resolved to defend at every hazard its independence and liberty against every foreign influence and power; for this purpose it augments its army and its marine, it puts in a good state its forts and internal fortifications, and reposes on the devotion of its sons and on the justice of its cause. It has likewise concluded Treaties of Alliance with the other States of America formerly Spanish to ensure the issue of their present contest, and the Government is striving to convene an assembly of Plenipotentiaries to represent it and to agree upon its defence.

My Government has seen with the greatest pleasure the Message of the President of the United States, a work very worthy of its author, and which expresses the public sentiments of the people over whom he presides: it cannot be doubted, in virtue of this document, that the Government of the United-States endeavours to oppose the policy and ultimate views of the Holy Alliance, and such appears to be the decision of Great Britain from the sense of the Nation, some acts of the Ministry, and the language of her Commissioners in Bogota.

In such circumstances the Government of Colombia is desirous to know in what manner the Government of the United-States intends to resist on its part any interference of the Holy Alliance for the purpose of subjugating the new Republics or interfering in their political forms: if it will enter into a Treaty of Alliance with the Republic of Colombia to save America in general from the calamities of a despotic system; and finally if the Government of Washington understands by foreign interference the employment of Spanish forces against America at the time when Spain is occupied by a French Army, and its Government under the influence of France and her Allies.

It appears that it is already in the situation intended by this declaration, since it [is] generally asserted that an expedition has sailed from Cadiz destined for the coasts of Peru composed of the Ship Asia and of some frigates and brigs; there is no doubt that Spain does not furnish this force by herself alone in her present state of despotism and anarchy, without an army, without a marine and without money. This Nation notwithstanding its spirit of domination would have ere now decided for peace had it not been assisted for war.

In the name of my Government therefore, and reposing on the sympathy of the United States, I request the said explanations which may serve for its government in its policy and its system of defence.

I pray you, Sir, to accept [etc.].

◇◇◇◇◇◇◇◇◇◇◇◇◇◇

11. THE SCOPE OF THE MONROE DOCTRINE[11]

[*John Quincy Adams to Don José Maria Salazar*]

Department of State, Washington, 6 August, 1824

I HAVE laid before the President of the United States, your confidential Note of the 2nd. ultimo, and it has received his deliberate and full consideration.

He is disposed to hope, that some misunderstanding may have been occasioned by the language attributed to Mr. Chasserieux at Caraccas — Being unwilling to believe that France or any other European Power, will make its acknowledgment of the political Independence of the Republic of Colombia, dependent in any manner upon the form of Government, which the People of Colombia, are alone competent to determine for themselves, and which they have accordingly determined — Were it possible to believe that France should found upon such a principle her conduct towards the Republic of Colombia, the President learns with satisfaction from your Note, that which his respect for your Nation would not otherwise permit him to doubt, that they will maintain at every hazard their real Independence and accept no recognition of it upon conditions incompatible with it — Such a recognition, carrying self contradiction and absurdity upon its face.

From various recent Acts and Declarations of the French Government, and of Officers acting under it, France appears explicitly to disclaim any design of aiding Spain by any application of Force, for the recovery of her antient dominion in this Hemisphere. — The absurdity of such an attempt becoming from day to day more manifest, leads to the conclusion that France having already assumed this principle, will by the course of time and events be constantly more confirmed in her adhesion to it — Should even the proposals of her Agents, in the first instance present the establishment of a Monarchical or Aristocratic Government, as the price of her recognition, and should such proposals be met, by a firm and unequivocal refusal, the only consequence to be expected will be the postponement of the recognition, and that, as may be readily foreseen only for a short time — With regard to the language of certain political journals, at Paris in the months of October and November last, it has been since amply ascertained, that the sentiments avowed by them were not such as the French Government has since been willing to support.

With respect to the question "in what manner the Government of the United States intends to resist on its part any interference of the Holy Alliance for the purpose of subjugating the new Republic or interfering in their political forms" you understand that by the constitution of the United States, the ultimate decision of this question belongs to the Legislative Department of the Government. The probability of such interfer-

[11] Ibid., Vol. I, pp. 224–6.

ence of the Holy alliance, having in a great measure disappeared, the occasion for recurring to the dispositions of the Legislature did not occur during the late Session of Congress.

The sentiments of the President remain as they were expressed in his last annual message to Congress – Should the crisis which appeared then to be approaching, and which gave rise to the remarks then made, hereafter recur, he will be ready to give them effect by recommending to the Legislature the adoption of the measures exclusively of their resort, and by which the principles asserted by him, would with the concurrence if given, be on the part of the United States, efficaciously maintained.

As however the occasion for this resort could arise only by a deliberate and concerted system of the allied Powers to exercise force against the freedom and Independence of your Republic; so it is obvious that the United States could not undertake resistance to them by force of Arms, without a previous understanding with those European Powers, whose Interests and whose principles would secure from them an active and efficient cooperation in the cause – This there is no reason to doubt could be obtained but it could only be effected by a negotiation preliminary to that of any alliance between the United States and the Colombian Republic, or in any event coeval with it.

The employment of Spanish force in America, while Spain is occupied by a French army and its Government under the influence of France and her allies, does not constitute a case upon which the United States would feel themselves justified in departing from the neutrality which they have hitherto observed – The force itself being necessarily small; and in no wise changing the nature of the contest in the American Hemisphere. . . .

◇◇◇◇◇◇◇◇◇◇◇◇◇

12. CO-OPERATION VS. DOMINATION

[*The Future of the United States*] [12]

. . . HE [Mr. Crawford] said he had been conversing with Mr. Lowndes, who told him that, both in England and France, everybody with whom he had conversed appeared to be profoundly impressed with the idea that we were an ambitious and encroaching people, and he thought we ought to be very guarded and moderate in our policy, to remove this impression.

I said I doubted whether we ought to give ourselves any concern about it. Great Britain, after vilifying us twenty years as a mean, low-minded, peddling nation, having no generous ambitions and no God but gold, had

[12] Charles Francis Adams, ed.: *Memoirs of John Quincy Adams,* 4 Vols. (Philadelphia: J. B. Lippincott & Co., 1875), Vol. IV, pp. 438–9. This excerpt from diary of Mr. Adams covers a part of a discussion between President Monroe and several members of his cabinet. The date is November 16, 1819. William H. Crawford was Secretary of the Treasury.

now changed her tone, and was endeavoring to alarm the world at the gigantic grasp of our ambition. Spain was doing the same; and Europe, who, even since the commencement of our Government under the present Constitution, had seen those nations intriguing with the Indians and negotiating to bound us by the Ohio, had first been startled by our acquisition of Louisiana, and now by our pretension to extend to the South Sea, and readily gave credit to the envious and jealous clamor of Spain and England against our ambition. Nothing that we could say or do would remove this impression until the world shall be familiarized with the idea of considering our proper dominion to be the continent of North America. From the time when we became an independent people it was as much a law of nature that this should become our pretension as that the Mississippi should flow to the sea. Spain had possessions upon our southern and Great Britain upon our northern border. It was impossible that centuries should elapse without finding them annexed to the United States; not that any spirit of encroachment or ambition on our part renders it necessary, but because it is a physical, moral, and political absurdity that such fragments of territory, with sovereigns at fifteen hundred miles beyond sea, worthless and burdensome to their owners, should exist permanently contiguous to a great, powerful, enterprising, and rapidly-growing nation. Most of the Spanish territory which had been in our neighborhood had already become our own by the most unexceptionable of all acquisitions — fair purchase for a valuable consideration. This rendered it still more unavoidable that the remainder of the continent should ultimately be ours. But it is very lately that we have distinctly seen this ourselves; very lately that we have avowed the pretension of extending to the South Sea; and until Europe shall find it a settled geographical element that the United States and North America are identical, any effort on our part to reason the world out of a belief that we are ambitious will have no other effect than to convince them that we add to our ambition hypocrisy. . . .

Chapter XI

THE ANNEXATION OF TEXAS

AS SECRETARY of State in 1819 when the western boundary of Louisiana was established, John Quincy Adams had been reluctant to relinquish American claims to Texas. He continued to desire the acquisition of Texas and was able as President of the United States in 1827 to initiate negotiations for its purchase (1). This attempt to acquire all or a part of Texas failed and a later attempt made by President Jackson met with a similar fate. After Texas had acquired its independence from Mexico as the result of a successful revolution, it was eager to join the American Union. President Van Buren promptly declined the offer (2) and the question of annexation became a major political controversy intimately connected with sectionalism and party politics (3).

The letter from John C. Calhoun to Duff Green illustrates the fears and beliefs of the ultra pro-slavery people (4), while the letters of Lord Aberdeen (5) and Ashbel Smith (6) indicate the extent of British intrigue. Spurred to action by the reports of British activities in Texas (7), the American government concluded a treaty of annexation with Texas on April 12, 1844. The treaty was rejected by the Senate of the United States and the whole Texan question became an issue in the political campaign of 1844. In his annual message to Congress of December 3, 1844, President Tyler explained the reasons why Texas should be annexed to the United States (8), and annexation was finally accomplished through a joint resolution of Congress (9). President Polk, in his first annual message, December 2, 1845, made a notable statement of the Monroe Doctrine as he interpreted it in relation to the territorial problems of the time (10).

1. OFFER OF THE UNITED STATES TO PURCHASE TEXAS[1]

[Henry Clay to Joel R. Poinsett]

Washington, March 15, 1827

THE GREAT extent and the facility which appears to have attended the procurement of grants from the Government of the United Mexican States,

[1] *House Ex. Doc.* (311) 25th Congress, 1st Session, No. 42, pp. 8–10.

for large tracts of country to citizens of the United States, in the province of Texas, authorize the belief that but little value is placed upon the possession of the province by that Government. These grants seem to have been made without any sort of equivalent, judging according to our opinions of the value of land. They have been made to, and apparently in contemplation of being settled by, citizens from the United States. These emigrants will carry with them our principles of law, liberty, and religion; and however much it might be hoped that they might be disposed to amalgamate with the ancient inhabitants of Mexico, so far as political freedom is concerned, it would be almost too much to expect that all collisions would be avoided on other subjects. Already some of these collisions have manifested themselves, and others, in the progress of time, may be anticipated with confidence. These collisions may insensibly enlist the sympathies and feelings of the two republics and lead to misunderstandings.

The fixation of a line of boundary of the United States on the side of Mexico, should be such as to secure, not merely certainty and apparent safety in the respective limits of the two countries, but the consciousness of freedom from all danger of attack on either side, and the removal of all motives for such attack. That of the Sabine brings Mexico nearer our great Western commercial capital than is desirable; and although we now are, and for a long time may remain, perfectly satisfied with the justice and moderation of our neighbor, still it would be better for both parties that neither should feel that he is in any condition of exposure on the remote contingency of an alteration in existing friendly sentiments.

Impressed with these views, the President has thought the present might be an auspicious period for urging a negotiation, at Mexico, to settle the boundary between the territories of the two republics. The success of the negotiation will probably be promoted by throwing into it other motives than those which strictly belong to the subject itself. If we could obtain such a boundary as we desire, the Government of the United States might be disposed to pay a reasonable pecuniary consideration. The boundary which we prefer is that which, beginning at the mouth of the Rio del Norte in the sea, shall ascend that river to the mouth of the Rio Puerco, thence ascending this river to its source, and from its source, by a line due north, to strike the Arkansas, thence following the course of the southern bank of the Arkansas to its source, in latitude 42° north, and thence by that parallel of latitude to the South sea. The boundary thus described would, according to the United States Tanner's map, published in the United States, leave Santa Fé within the limits of Mexico and the whole of Red River or Rio Roxo and the Arkansas, as far up as it is probably navigable, within the limits assigned to the United States. If that boundary be unattainable, we would, as the next most desirable, agree to that of the Colorado, beginning at its mouth, in the bay of Bernardo, and ascending the river to its source, and thence by a line due north to the Arkansas, and thence, as above traced, to the South sea. This latter boundary would probably also give us the whole of the Red River, would throw us somewhat farther from Santa Fé, but it would strike Arkansas possibly at a navigable point. To obtain the first-described boundary, the President authorizes you to offer to the Government of Mexico a sum not exceeding one million of dollars. If you find it impracticable to procure that line, you are then authorized to offer, for the above line of the Colorado, the sum of five hundred thousand dollars. If either of the above offers should be accepted, you may stipulate for the payment of the sum of money, as you may happen to agree, within any period not less than three months after the exchange at the city of Washington of the ratification of the treaty. . . .

◇◇◇◇◇◇◇◇◇◇◇◇◇◇

2. REFUSAL OF ANNEXATION[2]

[*John Forsyth to Memucan Hunt*]

August 25, 1837

. . . THE QUESTION of the *annexation* of a foreign independent State to the United States has never before been presented to this Government. Since the adoption of their Constitution, two large additions have been made to the domain originally claimed by the United States. In acquiring them, this Government was not actuated by a mere thirst for sway over a broader space. Paramount interests of many members of the Confederacy, and the permanent well-being of all, imperatively urged upon this Government the necessity of an extension of its jurisdiction over Louisiana and Florida. As peace, however, was our cherished policy, never to be departed from unless honor should be perilled by adhering to it, we patiently endured for a time serious inconveniences and privations, and sought a transfer of those regions by negotiations and not by conquest. . . .

So long as Texas shall remain at war, while the United States are at peace with her adversary, the proposition of the Texan minister plenipotentiary necessarily involves the question of war with that adversary. The United States are bound to Mexico by a treaty of amity and commerce, which will be scrupulously observed on their part, so long as it can be reasonably hoped that Mexico will perform her duties and respect our rights under it. The United States might justly be suspected of a disregard of the friendly purposes of the compact, if the overture of General Hunt were to be even reserved for future consideration, as this would imply a disposition on our part to espouse the quarrel of Texas with Mexico — a disposition wholly at variance with the spirit of the treaty, with the uniform policy and the obvious welfare of the United States.

The inducements mentioned by General Hunt, for the United States to

[2] *Sen. Ex Doc.* (435) 28th Congress, 1st Session, No. 341, pp. 112–14. Memucan Hunt was the Texan minister at Washington.

annex Texas to their territory, are duly appreciated; but powerful and weighty as certainly they are, they are light when opposed in the scale of reason to treaty obligations and respect for that integrity of character by which the United States have sought to distinguish themselves since the establishment of their right to claim a place in the great family of nations. . . . If the answer which the undersigned has been directed to give to the proposition of General Hunt should unfortunately work such a change in the sentiments of that Government (Texas) as to induce an attempt to extend commercial relations elsewhere, upon terms prejudicial to the United States, this Government will be consoled by a consciousness of the rectitude of its intentions, and a certainty that although the hazard of transient losses may be incurred by a rigid adherence to just principles, no lasting prosperity can be secured when they are disregarded. . . .

◇◇◇◇◇◇◇◇◇◇◇◇◇

3. OPPOSITION TO ANNEXATION[3]

[*Public statement of prominent men*]

Washington, March 3, 1843

. . . WE HESITATE not to say that *annexation*, effected by any act or proceeding of the federal government, or any of its departments, WOULD BE IDENTICAL WITH DISSOLUTION. It would be a violation of our national compact, its objects, designs, and the great elementary principles which entered into its formation, of a character so deep and fundamental, and would be an attempt to eternize an institution and a power of nature so unjust in themselves, so injurious to the interests and abhorrent to the feelings of the people of the free states, as, in our opinion, not only inevitably to result in a dissolution of the union, but fully to justify it; and we not only assert that the people of the free states "ought not to submit to it," but we say, with confidence, THEY WOULD NOT SUBMIT TO IT. We know their present temper and spirit on this subject too well to believe for a moment that they would become *particeps criminis* in any such subtle contrivance for the *irremediable perpetuation* OF AN INSTITUTION which the wisest and best men who formed our federal constitution, as well from the slave as the free states, *regarded as an evil and a curse,* soon to become extinct under the operation of laws to be passed prohibiting the slave trade, and the progressive influence of the principles of the revolution.

To prevent the success of this nefarious project – to preserve from such gross violation the constitution of our country, adopted expressly *"to secure the blessings of liberty"* and not the perpetuation of slavery – and to

[3] *Niles' Register* (May 13, 1843), Vol. LXIV, p. 175.

prevent the speedy and violent dissolution of the union, we invite you to unite, without distinction of party, in an immediate expression of your views on this subject, in such manner as you may deem best calculated to answer the end proposed.

John Quincy Adams,	*Nathaniel B. Borden,*
Seth M. Gates,	*Thos. C. Chittenden,*
William Slade,	*John Mattocks,*
William B. Calhoun,	*Christopher Morgan,*
Joshua R. Giddings,	*Joshua M. Howard,*
Sherlock J. Andrews,	*Victory Birdseye,*
	Hiland Hall.

◇◇◇◇◇◇◇◇◇◇◇◇◇◇

4. OPPOSITION TO BRITISH ACTIVITY IN TEXAS[4]

[*John C. Calhoun to Duff Green*]

September 8, 1843

I HAVE read with interest your letter. It gives me much important information, which confirms my previous impressions. I have, in the present remarkable state of things, not been inattentive to the course of events in England, and have come to the conclusion, that it would take the turn you anticipate. England has but one alternative; to harmonize her interests with that of the other portions of the civilized world, or resort to force to maintain her pre-eminence. If she adopts the former, freedom of commerce and non interference with the institutions of other nations must be the basis of her policy; but if the latter, she must prepare for universal conflict with the civilized world. The danger is, that she will select the latter. If so, it will present a scene of struggle and violence unparalleled in the history of the world, which will end in her downfall; but if the former, it will open a new page of prosperity and civilization never before known on the Globe.

Strange as it may seem, the discussion of the corn law question and the sugar duties, will go far to decide this great issue. In the advanced state of commerce and the arts, the great point of policy for the older and more advanced nations is to command the trade of the newer and less advanced; and that cannot be done, but by opening a free trade in provisions and raw materials with them. The effect of the contrary policy is not only to cripple their commerce and manufactures, by curtailing exchanges; but to force the newer and less advanced portion to become prematurely their competitors. This England now sees and feels, and that to remedy the evil, the corn laws and sugar duties in favor of her colonies, must be repealed, or

[4] J. Franklin Jameson, ed.: "Correspondence of John C. Calhoun," *Annual Report* of the American Historical Association, 1899, Vol. II, pp. 545–6.

that she must resort to force to maintain her commercial and manufacturing superiority. But, if force is resorted to, the blow will first be struck at the U. States, Brazil and other slave holding countries. The reason is obvious. It is indispensible to give her a monopoly of the great staples they produce, and through them, a monopoly of the trade of the world. The abolition of slavery would transfer the production of cotton, rice, and sugar etc. to her colonial possessions, and would consummate the system of commercial monopoly, which she has been so long and systematically pursuing. Hence the movements in Texas and elsewhere on the abolition subject at this time. . . .

◇◇◇◇◇◇◇◇◇◇◇◇◇◇

5. BRITISH POLICY REGARDING TEXAS[5]

[*Lord Aberdeen to Sir Richard Pakenham*]

Foreign Office, [*London*] *December 26, 1843*

AS MUCH agitation appears to have prevailed of late in the United States relative to the designs which Great Britain is supposed to entertain with regard to the Republic of Texas, Her Majesty's Government deem it expedient to take measures for stopping at once the misrepresentations which have been circulated, and the errors into which the Government of the United States seems to have fallen, on the subject of the policy of Great Britain with respect to Texas. That policy is clear and simple, and may be stated in a few words.

Great Britain has recognized the independence of Texas; and, having done so, she is desirous of seeing that independence finally and formally established, and generally recognized, especially by Mexico. But this desire does not arise from any motive of ambition or self-interest, beyond that interest, at least, which attaches to the general extension of our commercial dealings with other countries.

We are convinced that the recognition of Texas by Mexico must conduce to the benefit of both these countries, and as we take an interest in the well-being of both, and in their steady advance in power and wealth, we have put ourselves forward in pressing the Government of Mexico to acknowledge Texas as independent. But in thus acting, we have no occult design, either in reference to any peculiar influence which we might seek to establish in Mexico or in Texas, or even in reference to the slavery which now exists, and which we desire to see abolished in Texas.

With regard to the latter point, it must be and is well-known both to The United States and to the whole world that Great Briain desires and is constantly exerting herself to procure the general abolition of slavery throughout the world; but the means which she has adopted, and will con-

[5] *British and Foreign State Papers,* Vol. XXXIII, pp. 232–3.

tinue to adopt, for this humane and virtuous purpose, are open and undisguised. She will do nothing secretly or underhand. She desires that her motives may be generally understood, and her acts seen by all.

With regard to Texas, we avow that we wish to see slavery abolished there, as elsewhere, and we should rejoice if the recognition of that country by the Mexican Government should be accompanied by an engagement on the part of Texas to abolish slavery eventually, and under proper conditions, throughout the Republic. But although we earnestly desire and feel it to be our duty to promote such a consummation, we shall not interfere unduly, or with an improper assumption of authority, with either party, in order to insure the adoption of such a course. We shall counsel, but we shall not seek to compel or unduly control either party. So far as Great Britain is concerned, provided other States act with equal forbearance, those Governments will be fully at liberty to make their own unfettered arrangements with each other, both in regard to the abolition of slavery and to all other points.

Great Britain, moreover, does not desire to establish in Texas, whether partially dependent on Mexico, or entirely independent, (which latter alternative we consider in every respect preferable,) any dominant influence. She only desires to share her influence equally with all other nations. Her objects are purely commercial, and she has no thought or intention of seeking to act, directly or indirectly, in a political sense, on The United States through Texas.

The British Government, as the United States well know, have never sought in any way to stir up disaffection or excitement of any kind in the slave-holding States of the American Union. Much as we should wish to see those States placed on the firm and solid footing which we conscientiously believe is to be obtained by general freedom alone, we have never in our treatment of them made any difference between the slaveholding and the free States of the Union. All are in our eyes entitled, as component members of the Union, to equal political respect, favour, and forbearance on our part. To that wise and just policy we shall continue to adhere; and the Governments of the slaveholding States may be assured that, although we shall not desist from those open and honest efforts which we have constantly made for procuring the abolition of slavery throughout the world, we shall neither openly nor secretly resort to any measures which can tend to disturb their internal tranquillity, or thereby to affect the prosperity of the American Union.

You will communicate this despatch to the United States' Secretary of State, and if he should desire it, you will leave a copy of it with him.

◇◇◇◇◇◇◇◇◇◇◇◇◇

6. BRITISH INTRIGUE IN TEXAS[6]

[Ashbel Smith to Anson Jones]

London, June 24, 1844

I HAVE HAD an interview to day with Lord Aberdeen at his request concerning the relations of Texas and chiefly in reference to the negotiations at Washington in the United States for 'annexation'. . . .

Lord Aberdeen observed that Her British Majesty's Government and that of France had communicated with each other touching the "annexation"; — that, entire harmony of opinion subsists and that they will act in concert in relation to it: — that, though the rejection of the Annexation Treaty by the American Senate was regarded as nearly or quite certain, nothing would be done by these Governments until the American Congress shall have finally disposed of the subject for the present session. He stated that then the British and French Governments would be willing, if Texas desired to remain independent, to settle the whole matter by a "Diplomatic Act:" — this diplomatic act in which Texas would of course participate would ensure peace and settle boundaries between Texas and Mexico, guarantee the separate independence of Texas, etc., etc.; — the American Government would be invited to participate in the "Act" as one of the parties guaranteeing etc., equally with the European Governments; — that Mexico, as I think I clearly understood his Lordship, would be invited to become a party to the Diplomatic Act, and in case of her refusal, would be forced to submit to its decisions: — and lastly, in case of the infringement of the terms of settlement by either of the parties, to wit, Texas or Mexico, the other parties would be authorized under the Diplomatic Act, to compel the infringing party to a compliance with the terms.

Lord Aberdeen did not as I remember use the word Treaty, but employed the phraze Diplomatic Act. It would however have all the obligations of a treaty, and the rights of all the parties under it would of course be *perpetual.* I say, of course; for the other parties could not be expected to make a treaty of this nature limited for such a period as would suit the convenience of Texas. Such act would too, as you will have already remarked give to the European Governments, parties to it, a perfect right to forbid for all time to come the annexation of Texas to the United States, as also even the peaceful incorporation of any portion of Mexico beyond the boundary to be settled, which might hereafter wish to unite itself with Texas.

Lord Aberdeen observed that France will be guided in this matter by

[6] George P. Garrison, ed.: "Diplomatic Correspondence of The Republic of Texas," *Annual Report* of the American Historical Association, 1908, Vol. II, Part III, pp. 1153–6. Ashbel Smith was the Texan minister to England and Anson Jones was the Secretary of State of Texas.

the counsels of England he suggested therefore that if such diplomatic act shall be passed, it shall be done at London. . . .

The permanent perpetual character of a diplomatic act of the nature spoken of by Lord Aberdeen, appears to me as it will doubtless to you, worthy of our gravest consideration before acceding to it; and the inviting of European Governments to make compulsory settlement of dissensions between the countries of America and the conferring on them of the right to interfere in our affairs may lead to the greatest inconveniences on our side of the Atlantic; as such interference and settlements have been the pretexts for inflicting atrocious wrongs and oppressions on the smaller states of Europe. I have believed that the objections to a Diplomatic Act as mentioned above will be deemed by our Government greater perhaps than the inconveniences of our unsettled relations with Mexico.

I am clearly of opinion that these Govts. will not urge on Mexico to make peace, except in some such manner as I have stated above or on such conditions and guarantees as shall insure the permanent independence of Texas. Further, I should not be surprised were they to counsel Mexico not to make peace under present circumstances except with such conditions and guarantees, lest by so doing annexation should be facilitated by removing one of the obstacles to its accomplishment on the part of the United States.

Lord Aberdeen more than once made observations to the effect that he regretted the agitation of the abolition of Slavery in Texas, as it had created so much feeling and dissatisfaction on our side of the Atlantic; and that hereafter he would have nothing to say or do in relation to this subject. . . .

7. OPPOSITION TO BRITISH ANTI-SLAVERY ACTIVITY[7]

[*John C. Calhoun to Sir Richard Pakenham*]

Washington, April 18, 1844

THE Undersigned, Secretary of State of The United States, has laid before the President the note of the Right Honourable Mr. Pakenham, Envoy Extraordinary and Minister Plenipotentiary of Her Britannic Majesty, addressed to this department on the 26th of February last, together with the accompanying copy of a despatch of Her Majesty's Principal Secretary of State for Foreign Affairs to Mr. Pakenham. In reply, the Undersigned is directed by the President to inform the Right Honourable Mr. Pakenham, that while he regards with pleasure the disavowal of Lord Aberdeen of any intention on the part of Her Majesty's Government "to resort to any measures, either openly or secretly, which can tend to disturb the internal

[7] *Sen. Ex. Doc.* (435) 28th Congress, 1st Session, No. 341, pp. 50–3.

tranquillity of the slaveholding States, and thereby affect the tranquillity of this Union," he at the same time regards with deep concern the avowal, for the first time, made to this Government, "that Great Britain desires and is constantly exerting herself to procure, the general abolition of slavery throughout the world."

So long as Great Britain confined her policy to the abolition of slavery in her own possessions and colonies, no other country had a right to complain. It belonged to her exclusively to determine, according to her own views of policy, whether it should be done or not. But when she goes beyond, and avows it as her settled policy, and the object of her constant exertions, to abolish it throughout the world, she makes it the duty of all other countries, whose safety or prosperity may be endangered by her policy, to adopt such measures as they may deem necessary for their protection.

It is with still deeper concern that the President regards the avowal of Lord Aberdeen of the desire of Great Britain to see slavery abolished in Texas; and as he infers, is endeavoring through her diplomacy to accomplish it, by making the abolition of slavery one of the conditions on which Mexico should acknowledge her independence. It has confirmed his previous impressions as to the policy of Great Britain in reference to Texas, and made it his duty to examine with much care and solicitude what would be its effects on the prosperity and safety of The United States, should she succeed in her endeavours. The investigation has resulted in the settled conviction that it would be difficult for Texas, in her actual condition, to resist what she desires, without supposing the influence and exertions of Great Britain would be extended beyond the limits assigned by Lord Aberdeen; and that, if Texas could not resist the consummation of the object of her desire, would endanger both the safety and prosperity of the Union. Under this conviction, it is felt to be the imperious duty of the Federal Government, the common representative and protector of the States of the Union, to adopt in self-defence the most effectual measures to defeat it. . . .

Acting in obedience to this obligation, on which our federal system of government rests, the President directs me to inform you that a Treaty has been concluded between The United States and Texas, for the annexation of the latter to the former, as a part of its territory, which will be submitted without delay to the Senate for its approval. This step has been taken as the most effectual, if not the only means of guarding against the threatened danger, and securing their permanent peace and welfare. . . .

It is well known that Texas has long desired to be annexed to this Union. . . . The United States have heretofore declined to meet her wishes; but the time has now arrived when they can no longer refuse. . . . They had no agency in bringing about the state of things which has terminated in the separation of Texas from Mexico. . . .

They are equally without responsibility for that state of things, already, adverted to as the immediate cause of imposing on them, in self-defense, the obligation of adopting the measure they have. They remained passive, so long as the policy on the part of Great Britain, which has led to its adoption, had no immediate bearing on their peace and safety. While they conceded to Great Britain the right of accepting whatever policy she might deem best, in reference to the African race, within her own possessions, they on their part claim the same right for themselves. The policy she has adopted in reference to the portion of that race in her dominions may be humane and wise; but it does not follow, if it prove so, that it would be so in reference to the United States and other countries, whose situation differs from ours. . . .

Without, then, controverting the wisdom and humanity of the policy of Great Britain, so far as her own possessions are concerned, it may be safely affirmed, without reference to the means by which it would be effected, that, could she succeed in accomplishing, in The United States, what she avows it to be her desire and the object of her constant exertions to effect throughout the world, so far from being wise or humane, she would involve in the greatest calamity the whole country, and especially the race which it is the avowed object of her exertions to benefit. . . .

◇◇◇◇◇◇◇◇◇◇◇◇◇

8. PRESIDENT TYLER'S SUPPORT OF ANNEXATION[8]

[*Message to Congress*]

December 3, 1844

. . . IN MY LAST annual message I felt it to be my duty to make known to Congress, in terms both plain and emphatic, my opinion in regard to the war which has so long existed between Mexico and Texas, which since the battle of San Jacinto has consisted altogether of predatory incursions, attended by circumstances revolting to humanity. I repeat now what I then said, that after eight years of feeble and ineffectual efforts to reconquer Texas it was time that the war should have ceased. The United States have a direct interest in the question. The contiguity of the two nations to our territory was but too well calculated to involve our peace. Unjust suspicions were engendered in the mind of one or the other of the belligerents against us, and as a necessary consequence American interests were made to suffer and our peace became daily endangered; in addition to which it must have been obvious to all that the exhaustion produced by the war subjected both Mexico and Texas to the interference of other powers, which, without the interposition of this Government, might eventuate in the most serious injury to the United States. This Government from time to time exerted its friendly offices to bring about a termination of hostilities upon terms honorable alike to both the belligerents. Its ef-

[8] *Sen. Ex. Doc.* (449) 28th Congress, 2nd Session, No. 1, pp. 1–18.

forts in this behalf proved unavailing. Mexico seemed almost without an object to persevere in the war, and no other alternative was left the Executive but to take advantage of the well-known dispositions of Texas and to invite her to enter into a treaty for annexing her territory to that of the United States. . . .

The treaty which had thus been negotiated had failed to receive the ratification of the Senate. One of the chief objections which was urged against it was found to consist in the fact that the question of annexation had not been submitted to the ordeal of public opinion in the United States. However untenable such an objection was esteemed to be, in view of the unquestionable power of the Executive to negotiate the treaty and the great and lasting interests involved in the question, I felt it to be my duty to submit the whole subject to Congress as the best expounders of popular sentiment. No definitive action having been taken on the subject by Congress, the question referred itself directly to the decision of the States and people. The great popular election which has just terminated afforded the best opportunity of ascertaining the will of the States and the people upon it. Pending that issue it became the imperative duty of the Executive to inform Mexico that the question of annexation was still before the American people, and that until their decision was announced any serious invasion of Texas would be regarded as an attempt to forestall their judgment and could not be looked upon with indifference. I am most happy to inform you that no such invasion has taken place; and I trust that whatever your action may be upon it Mexico will see the importance of deciding the matter by a resort to peaceful expedients in preference to those of arms. The decision of the people and the States on this great and interesting subject has been decidedly manifested. . . . It is the will of both the people and the States that Texas shall be annexed to the Union promptly and immediately. . . .

Nothing has occurred since your last session to induce a doubt that the dispositions of Texas remain unaltered. No intimation of an altered determination on the part of her Government and people has been furnished to the Executive. She still desires to throw herself under the protection of our laws and to partake of the blessings of our federative system, while every American interest would seem to require it. The extension of our coastwise and foreign trade to an amount almost incalculable, the enlargement of the market for our manufactures, a constantly growing market for our agricultural productions, safety to our frontiers, and additional strength and stability to the Union – these are the results which would rapidly develop themselves upon the consummation of the measure of annexation. In such event I will not doubt but that Mexico would find her true interest to consist in meeting the advances of the Government in a spirit of amity.

Nor do I apprehend any serious complaint from any other quarter; no sufficient ground exists for such complaint. We should interfere in no respect with the rights of any other nation. There cannot be gathered from the act any design on our part to do so with their possessions on this continent. We have imposed no impediments in the way of such acquisitions of territory, large and extensive as many of them are, as the leading powers of Europe have made from time to time in every part of the world. We seek no conquest made by war. No intrigue will have been resorted to or acts of diplomacy essayed to accomplish the annexation of Texas. Free and independent herself, she asks to be received into our Union. It is a question for our own decision whether she shall be received or not.

The two Governments having already agreed through their respective organs on the terms of annexation, I would recommend their adoption by Congress in the form of a joint resolution or act to be perfected and made binding on the two countries when adopted in like manner by the Government of Texas. . . .

9. JOINT RESOLUTION OF ANNEXATION[9]

[*Joint Resolution of Both Houses of Congress, February 27, 1845 and Approved by President Tyler, March 1, 1845*]

BE IT resolved by the Senate and House of Representatives of the United States of America in Congress assembled, That Congress doth consent that the territory properly included within, and rightfully belonging to the republic of Texas, may be erected into a new State, to be called the *State of Texas,* with a republican form of government, to be adopted by the people of said republic, by deputies in convention assembled, with the consent of the existing government, in order that the same may be admitted as one of the States of this Union.

Sec. 2. And be further resolved, That the foregoing consent of Congress is given upon the following conditions, and with the following guaranties, to wit:

First. Said State to be formed, subject to the adjustment by this government of all questions of boundary that may arise with other governments; and the constitution thereof, with the proper evidence of its adoption by the people of said republic of Texas, shall be transmitted to the President of the United States, to be laid before Congress for its final action, on or before the first day of January, one thousand eight hundred and forty-six.

Second. Said State, when admitted into the Union, after ceding to the United States all public edifices, fortifications, barracks, ports and harbors, navy and navy yards, docks, magazines, arms, armaments, and all other property and means pertaining to the public defence, belonging to said republic of Texas, shall retain all the public funds, debts, taxes, and dues of every kind, which may belong to or be due or owing said republic; and

[9] *Congressional Globe,* Vol. XIV, 28th Congress, 2nd Session, pp. 362–3.

shall also retain all the vacant and unappropriated lands lying within its limits, to be applied to the payment of the debts and liabilities of said republic of Texas; and the residue of said lands, after discharging said debts and liabilities, to be disposed of as said State may direct; but in no event are said debts and liabilities to become a charge upon the government of the United States.

Third. New States, of convenient size, not exceeding four in number, in addition to said State of Texas, and having sufficient population, may hereafter, by the consent of said State, be formed out of the territory thereof, which shall be entitled to admission under the provisions of the federal constitution. And such States as may be formed out of that portion of said territory lying south of thirty-six degrees thirty minutes north latitude, commonly known as the Missouri compromise line, shall be admitted into the Union, with or without slavery, as the people of each State asking admission may desire. And in such State or States as shall be formed out of said territory north of said Missouri compromise line, slavery or involuntary servitude (except for crimes) shall be prohibited.

Sec. 3. And be it further resolved, That if the President of the United States shall, in his judgment and discretion, deem it most advisable, instead of proceeding to submit the foregoing resolution to the republic of Texas, as an overture on the part of the United States for admission, to negotiate with that republic, then

Be it resolved, That a State, to be formed out of the present republic of Texas, with suitable extent and boundaries, and with two representatives in Congress until the next apportionment of representation, shall be admitted into the Union by virtue of this act, on an equal footing with the existing States, as soon as the terms and conditions of such admission, and the cession of the remaining Texian territory to the United States shall be agreed upon by the governments of Texas and the United States; and the sum of $100,000 is hereby appropriated to defray the expenses of missions and negotiations, to agree upon the terms of said admission and cession, either by treaty to be submitted to the Senate, or by articles to be submitted to the two Houses of Congress, as the President may direct.

10. POLK'S DEFINITION OF THE MONROE DOCTRINE [10]

[*Message of James K. Polk to Congress, December 2, 1845*]

. . . THE RAPID extension of our settlements over our territories heretofore unoccupied, the addition of new States to our Confederacy, the expansion of free principles, and our rising greatness as a nation are attracting the attention of the powers of Europe, and lately the doctrine has been

[10] James D. Richardson: *Messages and Papers of the Presidents,* Vol. IV, pp. 398–9.

broached in some of them of a "balance of power" on this continent to check our advancement. The United States, sincerely desirous of preserving relations of good understanding with all nations, can not in silence permit any European interference on the North American continent, and should any such interference be attempted will be ready to resist it at any and all hazards.

It is well known to the American people and to all nations that this Government has never interfered with the relations subsisting between other governments. We have never made ourselves parties to their wars or their alliances; we have not sought their territories by conquest; we have not mingled with parties in their domestic struggles; and believing our own form of government to be the best, we have never attempted to propagate it by intrigues, by diplomacy, or by force. We may claim on this continent a like exemption from European interference. The nations of America are equally sovereign and independent with those of Europe. They possess the same rights, independent of all foreign interposition, to make war, to conclude peace, and to regulate their internal affairs. The people of the United States can not, therefore, view with indifference attempts of European powers to interfere with the independent action of the nations on this continent. The American system of government is entirely different from that of Europe. Jealousy among the different sovereigns of Europe, lest any one of them might become too powerful for the rest, has caused them anxiously to desire the establishment of what they term the "balance of power." It can not be permitted to have any application on the North American continent, and especially to the United States. We must ever maintain the principle that the people of this continent alone have the right to decide their own destiny. Should any portion of them, constituting an independent state, propose to unite themselves with our Confederacy, this will be a question for them and us to determine without any foreign interposition. We can never consent that European powers shall interfere to prevent such a union because it might disturb the "balance of power" which they may desire to maintain upon this continent. Near a quarter of a century ago the principle was distinctly announced to the world, in the annual message of one of my predecessors, that—

> The American continents, by the free and independent condition which they have assumed and maintain, are henceforth not to be considered as subjects for future colonization by any European powers.

This principle will apply with greatly increased force should any European power attempt to establish any new colony in North America. In the existing circumstances of the world the present is deemed a proper occasion to reiterate and reaffirm the principle avowed by Mr. Monroe and to state my cordial concurrence in its wisdom and sound policy. The reassertion of this principle, especially in reference to North America, is at this day but the promulgation of a policy which no European power should cherish the disposition to resist. Existing rights of every European nation should be respected, but it is due alike to our safety and our interests that the efficient protection of our laws should be extended over our whole territorial limits, and that it should be distinctly announced to the world as our settled policy that no future European colony or dominion shall with our consent be planted or established on any part of the North American continent. . . .

Chapter XII

DIPLOMATIC RELATIONS WITH MEXICO: 1845—1860

◇◇◇◇◇◇◇◇◇◇◇◇◇

THE ANNEXATION of Texas materially increased the difficulties that had arisen between the United States and Mexico. Since Mexico regarded Texas as a part of her national domain, and had already warned the United States, November 3, 1843, that the annexation of that area would be followed by a declaration of war, her Minister at Washington, General Juan Almonte, demanded his passports as soon as annexation was accomplished. The American government, still hoping to settle the existing difficulties through the medium of diplomacy, inquired through the American consul at Mexico City whether the Mexican government would receive a special envoy from the United States. The consul, John Black, was able to secure a written statement from the Mexican Minister of Foreign Relations, Manuel de la Peña y Peña, that such an envoy would be received. John Slidell was immediately sent to Mexico with full instructions, dated November 10, 1845 (1). The Mexican foreign minister, despite his promise to the contrary, refused to receive Slidell (2), who was recalled by his government. The letter of the Secretary of State, James Buchanan, to the American consul at Monterey, Thomas O. Larkin, is a precise statement of the American government's attitude toward California (3).

In order that the war might be terminated at the earliest possible moment, President Polk sent Nicholas P. Trist as a special commissioner to reside at the headquarters of the American army in Mexico, with full powers to negotiate for peace whenever the opportunity should arise (4). The Mexican government chose to prolong the war until it was evident that complete conquest of Mexico would be necessary, and accordingly Trist was recalled. Disregarding his recall, Trist remained in Mexico, explaining his conduct to the Secretary of State in a letter dated December 6, 1847 (5), and eventually signed the treaty of Guadalupe-Hidalgo (6). Almost immediately a dispute arose over a portion of the boundary established by the treaty. That controversy, together with the desire of the United States for a practicable southern route for a Pacific railway, led to the negotiation of the Gadsden Treaty in 1853 (8).

◇◇◇◇◇◇◇◇◇◇◇◇◇

Diplomatic Relations with Mexico: 1845–1860

1. INSTRUCTIONS TO JOHN SLIDELL[1]

[*James Buchanan to John Slidell*]

Washington, November 10, 1845

. . . IN THE present crisis of the relations between the two countries, the office for which you have been selected is one of vast importance. To counteract the influence of foreign powers exerted against the United States in Mexico, and to restore those ancient relations of peace and good will which formerly existed between the governments and the citizens of the sister republics, will be principal objects of your mission. . . .

The nations on the continent of America have interests peculiar to themselves. Their free forms of government are altogether different from the monarchical institutions of Europe. The interests and the independence of these sister nations require that they should establish and maintain an American system of policy for their own protection and security, entirely distinct from that which has so long prevailed in Europe. To tolerate any interference on the part of European sovereigns with controversies in America – to permit them to apply the worn-out dogma of the balance of power to the free States on this continent – and, above all, to suffer them to establish new colonies of their own, intermingled with our free republics, would be to make to the same extent a voluntary sacrifice of our independence. . . .

The first subject which will demand your attention is the claims of our citizens on Mexico. It would be useless here to trace the history of these claims, and the outrages from which they spring. The archives of your legation will furnish all the necessary information on this subject. The history of no civilized nation presents, in so short a period of time, so many wanton attacks upon the rights of persons and property as have been endured by citizens of the United States from the Mexican authorities. These never would have been tolerated by the United States from any nation on the face of the earth, except a neighboring and sister republic. . . .

But in what manner can this duty [settlement of claims] be performed consistently with the amicable spirit of your mission? The fact is but too well known to the world, that the Mexican government are not now in a condition to satisfy these claims by the payment of money. Unless the debt should be assumed by the government of the United States, the claimants cannot receive what is justly their due. Fortunately, the joint resolution of Congress, approved 1st March, 1845, "for annexing Texas to the United States," presents the means of satisfying these claims, in perfect consistency with the interests, as well as the honor, of both republics. It has reserved to this government the adjustment "of all questions of boundary that may arise with other governments." This question of boundary may, therefore, be adjusted in such a manner between the two republics as to cast the

[1] *Sen. Ex. Doc.* (509) 30th Congress, 1st Session, No. 52, pp. 71–81.

burden of the debt due to American claimants upon their own government, whilst it will do no injury to Mexico. . . .

Besides, it is greatly to be desired that our boundary with Mexico should now be established in such a manner as to preclude all future difficulties and disputes between the two republics. A great portion of New Mexico being on this side of the Rio Grande, and included within the limits already claimed by Texas, it may hereafter, should it remain a Mexican province, become a subject of dispute and a source of bad feeling between those who, I trust, are destined in future to be always friends.

On the other hand, if, in adjusting the boundary, the province of New Mexico should be included within the limits of the United States, this would obviate the danger of future collisions. Mexico would part with a remote and detached province, the possession of which can never be advantageous to her; and she would be relieved from the trouble and expense of defending its inhabitants against the Indians. Besides, she would thus purchase security against their attacks for her other provinces west of the del Norte, as it would at once become the duty of the United States to restrain the savage tribes within their limits, and prevent them from making hostile incursions into Mexico. From these considerations, and others which will readily suggest themselves to your mind, it would seem to be equally the interest of both powers that New Mexico should belong to the United States.

But the President desires to deal liberally by Mexico. You are, therefore, authorized to offer to assume the payment of all the just claims of our citizens against Mexico; and, in addition, to pay five millions of dollars in case the Mexican government shall agree to establish the boundary between the two countries from the mouth of the Rio Grande, up the principal stream to the point where it touches the line of New Mexico; thence west of the river along the exterior line of that province, and so as to include the whole within the United States, until it again intersects the river; thence up the principal stream of the same to its source; and thence due north until it intersects the forty-second degree of north latitude.

A boundary still preferable to this would be an extension of the line from the northwest corner of New Mexico, along the range of mountains until it would intersect the forty-second parallel.

Should the Mexican authorities prove unwilling to extend our boundary beyond the del Norte, you are, in that event, instructed to offer to assume the payment of all the just claims of citizens of the United States against Mexico, should she agree that the line shall be established along the boundary defined by the act of Congress of Texas, approved December 19, 1836, to wit: beginning at "the mouth of the Rio Grande; thence up the principal stream of said river to its source; thence due north to the forty-second degree of north latitude.". . .

There is another subject of vast importance to the United States, which will demand your particular attention. From information possessed by this department, it is to be seriously apprehended that both Great Britain and France have designs upon California. . . .

The possession of the bay and harbor of San Francisco is all important to the United States. The advantages to us of its acquisition are so striking, that it would be a waste of time to enumerate them here. If all these should be turned against our country by the cession of California to Great Britain, our principal commercial rivals, the consequences would be most disastrous.

The government of California is now but nominally dependent upon Mexico; and it is more than doubtful whether her authority will ever be reinstated. Under these circumstances, it is the desire of the President that you shall use your best efforts to obtain a cession of that province from Mexico to the United States. Could you accomplish this object, you would render immense service to your country, and establish an enviable reputation for yourself. Money would be no object, when compared with the value of the acquisition. Still, the attempt must be made with great prudence and caution, and in such a manner as not to alarm the jealousy of the Mexican government. Should you, after sounding the Mexican authorities on the subject, discover a prospect of success, the President would not hesitate to give, in addition to the assumption of the just claims of our citizens on Mexico, twenty-five millions of dollars for the cession. Should you deem it expedient, you are authorized to offer this sum for a boundary running due west from the southern extremity of New Mexico to the Pacific Ocean, or from any other point on its western boundary which would embrace Monterey within our limits. If Monterey cannot be obtained, you may, if necessary, in addition to the assumption of these claims, offer twenty millions of dollars for any boundary commencing at any point on the western line of New Mexico and running due west to the Pacific, so as to include the bay and harbor of San Francisco. The larger the territory south of this bay, the better. Of course, when I speak of any point on the western boundary of New Mexico, it is understood that from the del Norte to that point our boundary shall run according to the first offer which you have been authorized to make. I need scarcely add, that in authorizing the offer of five millions, or twenty-five millions, or twenty millions of dollars, these are to be considered as maximum sums. If you can accomplish either of the objects contemplated for a less amount, so much more satisfactory will it prove to the President. . . .

◇◇◇◇◇◇◇◇◇◇◇◇◇

2. MEXICAN REFUSAL TO RECEIVE THE AMERICAN ENVOY[2]

[*Manuel de la Peña y Peña to John Slidell*]

Mexico, December 20, 1845

THE UNDERSIGNED, minister of foreign relations and government of the Mexican republic, had the honor to receive the note which Mr. John Slidell was pleased to address to him on the 8th instant, making known his arrival at the capital, in the character of envoy extraordinary and minister plenipotentiary of the United States of America, near the government of the undersigned, and requesting that a time and a place should be appointed for his admission to present his credentials, of which he was pleased to send copies enclosed.

The undersigned, having submitted the whole to his excellency the President of the republic, and having also considered attentively the note addressed to him by the Secretary of State of the United States, relative to the mission of Mr. Slidell, regrets to inform him that, although the supreme government of the republics animated by the pacific and conciliatory intentions which the undersigned manifested to the consul of the United States in his confidential note of the 14th of October last, it does not conceive that, in order to fulfill the object proposed by the said consul, in the name of the American government, and accepted by the undersigned, it should admit his excellency Mr. Slidell in the character with which he is invested, of envoy extraordinary and minister plenipotentiary residing in the republic.

In order to place this refusal upon its proper grounds, the undersigned will briefly communicate to Mr. Slidell the reasons by which his excellency the President is guided.

The proposition in question emanated spontaneously from the government of the United States, and the Mexican government accepted it, in order to give a new proof, that in the midst of grievances, and its firm decision to exact adequate reparation, it did not repel or contemn the measure of reason and peace to which it was invited; so that this proposition, as well as its acceptance, rested upon the precise and definite understanding that the commissioner should be *ad hoc* – that is to say, commissioned to settle, in a peaceful and honorable manner, the questions relative to Texas. This has not been done, as Mr. Slidell does not come invested with that character, but with the absolute and general functions of an envoy extraordinary and minister plenipotentiary, to reside in this quality near the Mexican government.

If his excellency Mr. Slidell be admitted in this character, which differs substantially from that proposed for his mission on the part of the United States, and accepted by the government of the undersigned, there would

[2] *House Ex. Doc.*, 30th Congress, 1st Session, No. 60, pp. 37–9.

be reason to believe that thenceforth the relations between the two republics were open and frank, which could not be the case until the questions which have led to the present interruption of those relations should have been settled in a manner peaceful, but at the same time honorable to Mexico.

Although it be true that, in the credential letter brought by his excellency Mr. Slidell, it is stated that he is informed of the desire of the President of the United States to *restore,* cultivate, and strengthen friendship and good correspondence between the two countries, it is also no less true that in this clause the single word *restore* is by no mean sufficient to give to Mr. Slidell the special character of commissioner, or plenipotentiary *ad hoc;* to make propositions as to the affairs of Texas, calculated to establish peace firmly, and to arrest the evils of war by means of an adequate agreement. Mr. Slidell is too enlightened not himself to see that the powers of such a plenipotentiary ought to refer, and be adequate, and directed definitely to the business for which he is appointed; and that he is very far from possessing these requisites, in virtue of the character in which he appears, of an absolute and general minister, of an ordinary plenipotentiary, to reside near the Mexican government. . . .

The supreme government of Mexico, therefore, cannot admit his excellency Mr. Slidell to the exercise of the functions of the mission conferred on him by the United States government. . . .

◇◇◇◇◇◇◇◇◇◇◇◇◇

3. AMERICAN POLICY REGARDING CALIFORNIA[3]

[*James Buchanan to Thomas O. Larkin*]

Washington, October 17, 1845

I FEEL much indebted to you for the information which you have communicated to the Department from time to time in relation to California. The future destiny of that country is a subject of anxious solicitude for the Government and people of the United States. The interests of our commerce and our whale fisheries on the Pacific ocean demand that you should exert the greatest vigilance in discovering and defeating any attempts which may be made by foreign governments to acquire a control over that country. In the contest between Mexico and California we can take no part, unless the former should commence hostilities against the United States; but should California assert and maintain her independence, we shall render her all the kind offices in our power, as a sister Republic. This Government has no ambitious aspirations to gratify and no desire to extend our federal system over more territory than we already possess, unless by the free and spontaneous wish of the independent people of adjoining

[3] John Bassett Moore, ed.: *The Works of James Buchanan,* Philadelphia, 1908–11, 12 vols., VI, pp. 275–8.

territories. The exercise of compulsion or improper influence to accomplish such a result, would be repugnant both to the policy and principles of this Government. But whilst these are the sentiments of the President, he could not view with indifference the transfer of California to Great Britain or any other European Power. The system of colonization by foreign monarchies on the North American continent must and will be resisted by the United States. It could result in nothing but evil to the colonists under their dominion who would naturally desire to secure for themselves the blessings of liberty by means of republican institutions; whilst it must prove highly prejudicial to the best interests of the United States. Nor would it in the end benefit such foreign monarchies. On the contrary, even Great Britain, by the acquisition of California, would sow the seeds of future war and disaster for herself; because there is no political truth more certain than that this fine Province could not long be held in vassalage by any European Power. The emigration to it of people from the United States would soon render this impossible.

I am induced to make these remarks in consequence of the information communicated to this Department in your despatch of the 10th July, last. From this it appears that Mr. Rea, the Agent of the British Hudson Bay Company, furnished the Californians with arms and money in October and November, last, to enable them to expel the Mexicans from the country; and you state that this policy has been reversed, and now no doubt exists there, but that the Mexican troops about to invade the province have been sent for this purpose at the instigation of the British Government; and that "it is rumored that two English houses in Mexico have become bound to the new General to accept his drafts for funds to pay his troops for eighteen months." Connected with these circumstances, the appearance of a British Vice Consul and a French Consul in California at the present crisis, without any apparent commercial business, is well calculated to produce the impression, that their respective governments entertain designs on that country which must necessarily be hostile to its interests. . . . Whilst I repeat that this Government does not, under existing circumstances, intend to interfere between Mexico and California, it would vigorously interpose to prevent the latter from becoming a British or French Colony. In this they might surely expect the aid of the Californians themselves.

Whilst the President will make no effort and use no influence to induce California to become one of the free and independent States of this Union, yet if the people should desire to unite their destiny with ours, they would be received as brethren, whenever this can be done without affording Mexico just cause of complaint. Their true policy for the present in regard to this question, is to let events take their course, unless an attempt should be made to transfer them without their consent either to Great Britain or France. This they ought to resist by all the means in their power, as ruinous to their best interests and destructive of their freedom and independence. . . .

◇◇◇◇◇◇◇◇◇◇◇◇◇

4. INSTRUCTIONS TO NICHOLAS P. TRIST[4]

[*James Buchanan to Nicholas P. Trist*]

Washington, April 15, 1847

YOU ARE herewith furnished with a projét of a treaty, (marked A,) embraced in eleven articles, and founded upon just and liberal principles towards Mexico; which, together with your instructions, you may communicate confidentially to Major General Scott and Commodore Perry.

Should a Mexican plenipotentiary meet you, duly authorized by his government to conclude a treaty of peace, you will, after a mutual exchange of your full powers, deliver him a copy of this projét, with the sum in blank contained in the fifth article as a consideration for the extension of our boundaries, and inform him that you are prepared to sign it, on behalf of the government of the United States, as soon as the sum with which the blank is to be filled shall be agreed upon by the parties. This sum ought to be as much below the fifteen millions contained in the article as you can accomplish. Considering the heavy expenses and sacrifices of the war on our part, and the brilliant success of our arms, as well as the large amount which, under the projét, this government has assumed to pay our own citizens for claims due to them by Mexico, justice would seem to require that the treaty should not stipulate for the payment of a very large sum.

You may, in conversation with him, ascertain what change in the terms of the projét the Mexican government would require; and if this should become indispensable to attain the object, you may modify these terms, including the amount to be paid to Mexico, in the following particulars:

1. Instead of fifteen millions of dollars stipulated to be paid by the fifth article for the extension of our boundary over New Mexico and Upper and Lower California, you may increase the amount to any sum not exceeding thirty millions of dollars, payable by instalments of three millions per annum, provided the right of passage and transit across the isthmus of Tehuantepec, secured to the United States by the eighth article of the projét, shall form a part of the treaty.

2. Whilst it is of the greatest importance to the United States to extend their boundaries over Lower California, as well as New Mexico and Upper California, you are not to consider this as a *sine qua non* to the conclusion of a treaty. You will, therefore, not break off the negotiation if New Mexico and Upper California can alone be acquired. In that event, however, you will not stipulate to pay more than twenty millions of dollars for these two provinces without the right of passage and transit across the isthmus of Tehuantepec.

3. You are authorized to stipulate for the payment of any sum not exceeding twenty-five millions of dollars for New Mexico and Upper Cali-

[4] *Sen. Ex. Doc.*, 30th Congress, 1st Session, No. 52, pp. 81–4.

fornia, without Lower California, provided the stipulation securing the right of passage and transit across the isthmus of Tehuantepec shall be retained in the treaty; or, if this should be stricken out, you are authorized to stipulate for the payment of the like sum of twenty-five millions of dollars for Lower California, in addition to New Mexico and Upper California. . . .

The extension of our boundaries over New Mexico and Upper California, for a sum not exceeding twenty millions of dollars, is to be considered a *sine qua non* of any treaty. You may modify, change, or omit the other terms of the projét if needful, but not so as to interfere with this ultimatum. . . .

◇◇◇◇◇◇◇◇◇◇◇◇◇◇

5. TRIST'S REASONS FOR DISREGARDING HIS INSTRUCTIONS[5]

[*Nicholas P. Trist to James Buchanan*]

Headquarters of the U. S. Army, Mexico, December 6, 1847

REFERRING to my previous despatches. . . I will here enter at greater length into the considerations by which I have been brought to a resolve[6] so fraught with responsibility to myself; whilst, on the other hand, the circumstances under which it is taken are such as to leave the Government at perfect liberty to disavow my proceeding, should it be deemed disadvantageous to our country. . . .

I place my determination on the ground of my conviction, "*first,* that peace is still the desire of my government; *secondly,* that if the present opportunity be not seized *at once,* all chance for making a treaty *at all* will be lost for an indefinite period—probably forever; *thirdly,* that this (the boundary proposed by me) is the utmost point to which the Mexican government can, by any possibility, venture." I also state, that the determination of my government to withdraw the offer to negotiate, of which I was made the organ, has been "taken with reference to a supposed state of things in this country *entirely the reverse of that which actually exists.*" These four points constitute the heads under which the development of the subject naturally arranges itself.

1. "*First,* that peace is still the desire of my government." Upon this point the words of the President, as I took leave of him, are still fresh in my memory: "Mr. Trist, if you succeed in making a treaty, you will render a great service to your country". . . .

Such having been the state of the President's mind at the time of my

[5] Department of State, *Despatches from Mexico,* XIV, pp. 1–53.

[6] This "resolve" was the determination to conclude a treaty with Mexico after he had been recalled.

departure, and such the spirit in which I was sent here, I have carefully examined the despatches last received by me, (those by which I am recalled,) with special reference to the point now under consideration; that is to say, taking those despatches as the latest expression of the wish and intention of our government as to the restoration or non-restoration of peace, I have examined them with a view to discover whether any change has occurred in the President's mind, in other words the recognised mind of our government, on this particular subject. I have found there no intimation or indication of any such change; nothing whatever which would at all warrant the supposition that he has ceased to believe, or believes any the less strongly now than he did then, that the restoration of peace is highly desirable to the country whom he is charged with the grave responsibility of thinking for, and judging for, and determining for, at this fearful turning point of her destinies. On the contrary, the determination of the President to put an end to the mission committed to me, is expressly placed on the ground of his belief "that your (my) continued presence with the army *can be productive of no good,* but *may do much harm.*" How? The conclusion of the sentence gives the answer: "by encouraging the delusive hopes and false impressions of the Mexicans." The delusive hopes and false impressions here referred to are those to which, in the sentences immediately preceding, the pertinacity of the Mexicans in continuing the war is ascribed: "They must attribute our liberality to fear, or they must take courage from our supposed political divisions. Some such cause is necessary to account for their strange infatuation." It is, therefore, *because* of its supposed tendency to *prolong the war,* that the President apprehends that the continuance of this mission *"may do much harm."* Here, then, is a conclusive proof, that, upon the point now before us, the President is still of the same mind as when I left Washington; that now, as then, he considers the protraction of the war a great evil; that now, as then, he believes that to restore peace would be to render a great service to our country; in a word, *"that peace is still the desire of my government."*. . .

2. *Secondly,* that if the present opportunity be not seized *at once,* all chance for making a treaty *at all* will be lost for an indefinite period—probably forever. . . .

The efforts made by the friends of peace . . . have been crowned with success far exceeding their most sanguine expectations. They first built up the "provisional government" of Pena y Pena, a government pledged to the cause of peace, and *known* to be sincerely devoted to it. This government they defended and upheld against the ceaseless machinations of the puros, acting in concert with the Santanistas and all the other personal factions who could be brought into the alliance. . . . And, finally, they have succeeded in bringing together at the seat of government the governors of the respective States; and, after full conference, in obtaining their concurrence (with one single exception—the governor of Potosi) in the peace policy, and the pledge of their support.

Such is the character and the condition, actual and prospective, of the peace party: . . . But this party cannot possibly stand, *unless the object for which alone it has formed itself be speedily accomplished.* Without this its destitution of pecuniary resources must become aggravated every day; and this cannot continue much longer without sealing its fate: a catastrophe which would involve a total dissolution of the federal government and of the Union. . . .

3. "*Thirdly,* that this (the boundary proposed by me) is the utmost point to which the Mexican government can, by any possibility venture."

Under this head, I can do but little else than state my perfect conviction, resulting from the best use I am capable of making of the opportunities afforded by my position, that such is the fact. The nature of the subject scarcely admits of my doing more. I will, however, call attention to the fact, that, independently of Texas, this boundary takes from Mexico about *one half of her whole territory;* and upon this fact remark, that, however helpless a nation may feel, there is necessarily a point beyond which she cannot be expected to go, under any circumstances, in surrendering her territory as the price of peace. . . .

4. "That the determination of my government to withdraw the offer to negotiate, of which I was made the organ, has been taken with reference to a supposed state of things in this country *entirely the reverse of that which actually exists.*"

Under this head nothing more is requisite than a general reference to what has been stated under the three preceding. . . .

---

6. TREATY OF PEACE, FRIENDSHIP, LIMITS, AND SETTLEMENT BETWEEN THE UNITED STATES AND MEXICO[7]

[*Concluded February 2, 1848; ratifications exchanged May 30, 1848*]

. . . *ARTICLE V.* The Boundary line between the two Republics shall commence in the Gulf of Mexico, three leagues from land, opposite the mouth of the Rio Grande, otherwise called Rio Bravo del Norte, or opposite the mouth of it's deepest branch, if it should have more than one branch emptying directly into the sea; from thence, up the middle of that river, following the deepest channel, where it has more than one, to the point where it strikes the southern boundary of New Mexico; thence, westwardly, along the whole southern boundary of New Mexico (which runs north of the town called Paso) to it's western termination; thence,

[7] Hunter Miller: *Treaties and Other International Acts of the United States,* Vol. V, pp. 207–36. The treaty was signed by N. P. Trist, Luis G. Cuevas, Bernardo Couto, and Mig. Atristain.

northward, along the western line of New Mexico, until it intersects the first branch of the river Gila; (or if it should not intersect any branch of that river, then, to the point on the said line nearest to such branch, and thence in a direct line to the same;) thence down the middle of the said branch and of the said river, until it empties into the Rio Colorado; thence, across the Rio Colorado, following the division line between Upper and Lower California, to the Pacific Ocean. . . .

Article XI. Considering that a great part of the territories which, by the present Treaty, are to be comprehended for the future within the limits of the United States, is now occupied by savage tribes, who will hereafter be under the exclusive controul of the Government of the United States, and whose incursions within the territory of Mexico would be prejudicial in the extreme; it is solemnly agreed that all such incursions shall be forcibly restrained by the Government of the United States, whensoever this may be necessary; and that when they cannot be prevented, they shall be punished by the said Government, and satisfaction for the same shall be exacted: all in the same way, and with equal diligence and energy, as if the same incursions were meditated or committed within it's own territory against it's own citizens. . . .

Article XII. In consideration of the extension acquired by the boundaries of the United States, as defined in the fifth Article of the present Treaty, the Government of the United States engages to pay to that of the Mexican Republic the sum of fifteen Millions of Dollars. . . .

Article XIII. The United States engage moreover, to assume and pay to the claimants all the amounts now due them, and those hereafter to become due, by reason of the claims already liquidated and decided against the Mexican Republic, under the conventions between the two Republics severally concluded on the eleventh day of April eighteen hundred and thirty-nine, and on the thirtieth day of January eighteen hundred and forty-three: so that the Mexican Republic shall be absolutely exempt, for the future, from all expense whatever on account of the said claims. . . .

Article XXI. If unhappily any disagreement should hereafter arise between the Governments of the two Republics, whether with respect to the interpretation of any stipulation in this treaty, or with respect to any other particular concerning the political or commercial relations of the two Nations, the said Governments, in the name of those Nations, do promise to each other, that they will endeavour in the most sincere and earnest manner, to settle the differences so arising, and to preserve the state of peace and friendship, in which the two countries are now placing themselves: using, for this end, mutual representations and pacific negotiations. And, if by these means, they should not be enabled to come to an agreement, a resort shall not, on this account, be had to reprisals, aggression or hostility of any kind, by the one Republic against the other, until the Government of that which deems itself aggrieved, shall have maturely considered, in the spirit of peace and good neighbourship, whether it would not be better that such difference should be settled by the arbitration of Commissioners appointed on each side, or by that of a friendly nation. And should such course be proposed by either party, it shall be acceded to by the other, unless deemed by it altogether incompatible with the nature of the difference, or the circumstances of the case. . . .

◇◇◇◇◇◇◇◇◇◇◇◇◇

7. THE GADSDEN TREATY[8]

[*Treaty of Boundary and Cession of Territory between the United States and Mexico, Concluded December 30, 1853; ratifications exchanged June 30, 1854*]

. . . *ARTICLE I.* The Mexican Republic agrees to designate the following as her true limits with the United States for the future: Retaining the same dividing line between the two Californias as already defined and established, according to the 5th article of the treaty of Guadalupe Hidalgo, the limits between the two republics shall be as follows: Beginning in the Gulf of Mexico, three leagues from land, opposite the mouth of the Rio Grande, as provided in the fifth article of the treaty of Guadalupe Hidalgo; thence, as defined in the said article, up the middle of that river to the point where the parallel of 31° 47′ north latitude crosses the same; thence due west one hundred miles; thence south to the parallel of 31° 20′ north latitude; thence along the said parallel of 31° 20′ to the 111th meridian of longitude west of Greenwich; thence in a straight line to a point on the Colorado River twenty English miles below the junction of the Gila and Colorado Rivers; thence up the middle of the said river Colorado until it intersects the present line between the United States and Mexico. . . .

Article II. The government of Mexico hereby releases the United States from all liability on account of the obligations contained in the eleventh article of the treaty of Guadalupe Hidalgo; and the said article and the thirty-third article of the treaty of amity, commerce, and navigation between the United States of America and the United Mexican States concluded at Mexico, on the fifth day of April, 1831, are hereby abrogated.

Article III. In consideration of the foregoing stipulations, the Government of the United States agrees to pay to the government of Mexico, in the city of New York, the sum of ten millions of dollars, of which seven millions shall be paid immediately upon the exchange of the ratifications of this treaty, and the remaining three millions as soon as the boundary line shall be surveyed, marked, and established. . . .

[8] *Public Statutes at Large of the United States,* Vol. X, pp. 1032–7. The treaty was signed by James Gadsden, Manuel Diez De Bonilla, José Salazar Ylarrequi, and J. Mariano Monterde.

Chapter XIII

BOUNDARIES, FISHERIES, AND THE SLAVE TRADE

◇◇◇◇◇◇◇◇◇◇◇◇◇◇

THE DIPLOMATIC relations between the United States and Great Britain from 1814 to 1860 touched upon many points of controversy. The question of armaments on the Great Lakes was settled by the Rush-Bagot agreement of 1817 (1), but the problems of the boundaries and the fisheries were more difficult of solution. With respect to the fisheries, the problem was whether the United States enjoyed, after the War of 1812, the rights which they had acquired by the Treaty of 1783. President Monroe sent Albert Gallatin from Paris to London to assist Richard Rush in negotiating on this and other subjects, with the result that the Convention of 1818 was concluded (2). This convention did not settle the northeastern boundary difficulty, and made only a temporary arrangement concerning Oregon. By 1840 the Oregon and northeastern boundary questions were of growing importance, and in addition other problems had arisen, notably over the *Caroline* incident (3) and the right of search (5), on the part of Great Britain, of suspected slavers carrying the American flag. The *Caroline* difficulty was settled in a satisfactory manner through an exchange of notes between the Secretary of State, Daniel Webster, and the British minister to the United States, Lord Ashburton (4). The northeastern boundary was finally established by the Treaty of 1842 (6), and an arrangement was made in the same treaty for the suppression of the slave trade. As early as 1818 the United States had offered to settle the Oregon question by dividing the territory in dispute at 49° north latitude. This suggestion was unsatisfactory to Great Britain at the time, but an agreement was reached whereby the citizens of both nations could settle in the disputed area. In 1844 the Secretary of State presented again the claims of the United States to Oregon (7), and in the following year suggested a compromise arrangement (8). This being rejected by Great Britain, President Polk asked Congress to terminate the so-called joint occupation agreement (9). Great Britain was willing to settle the Oregon question, however, for political and economic reasons, and the result was the Oregon Treaty of 1846 (10).

◇◇◇◇◇◇◇◇◇◇◇◇◇◇

1. THE RUSH-BAGOT AGREEMENT[1]

[*An Arrangement between the United States and Great Britain, concluded at Washington, April 28–29, 1817; proclaimed by President Monroe, April 28, 1818*]

HIS ROYAL Highness, acting in the name and on the behalf of His Majesty, agrees, that the Naval Force to be maintained upon the American Lakes by His Majesty and the Government of the United States shall henceforth be confined to the following Vessels on each side – that is

On Lake Ontario to one Vessel not exceeding one hundred Tons burthen and armed with one eighteen pound cannon.

On the Upper Lakes, to two Vessels not exceeding like burthen each and armed with like force.

On the Waters of Lake Champlain to one Vessel not exceeding like burthen and armed with like force.

And His Royal Highness agrees, that all other armed Vessels on these Lakes shall be forthwith dismantled, and that no other Vessels of War shall be there built or armed.

His Royal Highness further agrees that if either Party should hereafter be desirous of annulling this Stipulation, and should give notice to that effect to the other Party, it shall cease to be binding after the expiration of six months from the date of such notice. . . .

His Royal Highness has issued Orders to His Majestys Officers on the Lakes directing, that the Naval Force so to be limited shall be restricted to such Services as will in no respect interfere with the proper duties of the armed Vessels of the other party.

◇◇◇◇◇◇◇◇◇◇◇◇◇

2. CONVENTION OF 1818 BETWEEN THE UNITED STATES AND GREAT BRITAIN[2]

[*Concluded October 20, 1818; ratifications exchanged January 30, 1819*]

. . . *ARTICLE I.* Whereas differences have arisen respecting the Liberty claimed by the United States for the Inhabitants thereof, to take, dry, and cure Fish on certain Coasts, Bays, Harbours, and Creeks of His Britannic Majesty's Dominions in America, it is agreed between the High Contract-

---

[1] Hunter Miller: *Treaties and Other International Acts of the United States,* Vol. II, pp. 645–6. This was signed by Charles Bagot. The agreement was in the form of an exchange of notes.

[2] Ibid., pp. 658–61. The treaty was signed by Albert Gallatin, Richard Rush, Frederick John Robinson, and Henry Goulburn.

ing Parties, that the Inhabitants of the said United States shall have forever, in common with the Subjects of His Britannic Majesty, the Liberty to take Fish of every kind on that part of the Southern Coast of Newfoundland which extends from Cape Ray to the Rameau Islands, on the Western and Northern Coast of Newfoundland, from the said Cape Ray to the Quirpon Islands on the Shores of the Magdalen Islands, and also on the Coasts, Bays, Harbours, and Creeks from Mount Joly on the Southern Coast of Labrador, to and through the Streights of Belleisle and thence Northwardly indefinitely along the Coast, without prejudice however, to any of the exclusive Rights of the Hudson Bay Company: And that the American Fishermen shall also have liberty forever, to dry and cure Fish in any of the unsettled Bays, Harbours, and Creeks of the Southern part of the Coast of Newfoundland hereabove described, and of the Coast of Labrador; but so soon as the same, or any Portion thereof, shall be settled, it shall not be lawful for the said Fishermen to dry or cure Fish at such Portion so settled, without previous Agreement for such purpose with the Inhabitants, Proprietors, or Possessors of the Ground. And the United States hereby renounce forever, any Liberty heretofore enjoyed or claimed by the Inhabitants thereof, to take, dry, or cure Fish on, or within three marine Miles of any of the Coasts, Bays, Creeks, or Harbours of His Britannic Majesty's Dominions in America not included within the above mentioned Limits; provided however, that the American Fishermen shall be admitted to enter such Bays or harbours for the purpose of Shelter and of repairing Damages therein, of purchasing Wood, and of obtaining Water, and for no other purpose whatever. But they shall be under such Restrictions as may be necessary to prevent their taking, drying or curing Fish therein, or in any other manner whatever abusing the Privileges hereby reserved to them.

Article II. It is agreed that a Line drawn from the most North Western Point of the Lake of the Woods, along the forty Ninth Parallel of North Latitude, or, if the said Point shall not be in the Forty Ninth Parallel of North Latitude, then that a Line drawn from the said Point due North or South as the Case may be, until the said Line shall intersect the said Parallel of North Latitude, and from the Point of such Intersection due West along with the said Parallel shall be the Line of Demarcation between the Territories of the United States, and those of His Britannic Majesty, and that the said Line shall form the Northern Boundary of the said Territories of the United States, and the Southern Boundary of the Territories of His Britannic Majesty, from the Lake of the Woods to the Stony Mountains.

Article III. It is agreed, that any Country that may be claimed by either Party on the NorthWest Coast of America, Westward of the Stony Mountains, shall, together with its Harbours, Bays, and Creeks, and the Navigation of all Rivers within the same, be free and open, for the term of ten Years from the date of the Signature of the present Convention, to the Vessels, Citizens, and Subjects of the Two Powers: it being well understood, that this Agreement is not to be construed to the Prejudice of any Claim, which either of the Two High Contracting Parties may have to any part of the said Country, nor shall it be taken to affect the Claims of any other Power or State to any part of the said Country; the only Object of The High Contracting Parties, in that respect, being to prevent disputes and differences amongst Themselves. . . .

◇◇◇◇◇◇◇◇◇◇◇◇◇

3. THE *CAROLINE* INCIDENT[3]

[*Daniel Webster to Henry S. Fox*]

Washington, April 24, 1842

. . . THE UNDERSIGNED has now to signify to Mr. Fox that the Government of the United States has not changed the opinion which it has heretofore expressed to Her Majesty's Government, of the character of the act of destroying the "Caroline."

It does not think that that transaction can be justified by any reasonable application or construction of the right of self defence, under the laws of nations. It is admitted that a just right of self-defence attaches always to nations as well as to individuals, and is equally necessary for the preservation of both. But the extent of this right is a question to be judged of by the circumstances of each particular case; and when its alleged exercise has led to the commission of hostile acts within the territory of a Power at peace, nothing less than a clear and absolute necessity can afford ground of justification. . . .

The Government of the United States has not considered it as sufficient to confine the duties of neutrality and non-interference to the case of Governments whose territories lie adjacent to each other. The application of the principle may be more necessary in such cases, but the principle itself they regard as being the same, if those territories be divided by half the globe. The rule is founded in the impropriety and danger of allowing individuals to make war on their own authority, or, by mingling themselves in the belligerent operations of other nations, to run the hazard of counteracting the policy or embroiling the relations of their own Government. And the United States have been the first among civilized nations to enforce the observance of this just rule of neutrality and peace by special and adequate legal enactments. . . .

Under these circumstances, and under those immediately connected with the transaction itself, it will be for Her Majesty's Government to show upon what state of facts, and what rules of national law, the destruction of the "Caroline" is to be defended. It will be for that Government to show a necessity of self defence, instant, overwhelming, leaving no choice

[3] *House Ex. Doc.* (418) 27th Congress, 3rd Session, No. 2, pp. 124–9. Henry S. Fox was the British minister at Washington.

of means, and no moment for deliberation. It will be for it to show, also, that the local authorities of Canada, even supposing the necessity of the moment authorized them to enter the territories of the United States at all, did nothing unreasonable or excessive, since the act, justified by the necessity of self-defence, must be limited by that necessity, and kept clearly within it. It must be shown that admonition or remonstrance to the persons on board the "Caroline" was impracticable, or would have been unavailing. It must be shown that daylight could not be waited for; that there could be no attempt at discrimination between the innocent and the guilty; that it would not have been enough to seize and detain the vessel; but that there was a necessity, present and inevitable, for attacking her in the darkness of the night, while moored to the shore, and while unarmed men were asleep on board, killing some and wounding others, and then drawing her into the current, above the cataract, setting her on fire, and, careless to know whether there might not be in her the innocent with the guilty, or the living with the dead, committing her to a fate which fills the imagination with horror. A necessity for all this the Government of the United States cannot believe to have existed. . . .

This republic does not wish to disturb the tranquillity of the world; its object is peace, its policy peace. . . . But it cannot admit that its Government has not both the will and the power to preserve its own neutrality, and to enforce the observance of its own law upon its own citizens. It is jealous of its rights, and among others, and most especially, of the right of the absolute immunity of its territory against agression from abroad; and these rights it is the duty and determination of this Government fully and at all times to maintain, while it will, at the same time, as scrupulously refrain from infringing on the rights of others. . . .

4. BRITISH EXPLANATION OF THE *CAROLINE* INCIDENT[4]

[*Lord Ashburton to Daniel Webster*]

Washington, July 28, 1842

IN THE COURSE of our conferences on the several subjects of difference which it was the object of my mission to endeavor to settle, the unfortunate case of the "Caroline," with its attendant consequences, could not escape our attention; for, although it is not of a description to be susceptible of any settlement by a convention or treaty, yet, being connected with the highest considerations of national honor and dignity, it has given rise, at times, to deep excitements, so as more than once to endanger the maintenance of peace. . . .

[4] Ibid., pp. 130–5.

After some tumultuous proceedings in Upper Canada, which were of short duration, and were suppressed by the militia of the country, the persons criminally concerned in them took refuge in the neighboring State of New York, and, with a very large addition to their numbers, openly collected, invaded the Canadian territory, taking possession of Navy island.

This invasion took place the 16th of December, 1837; a gradual accession of numbers and of military ammunition continued openly, and though under the sanction of no public authority, at least with no public hinderance, until the 29th of the same month, when several hundred men were collected; and twelve pieces of ordnance, which could only have been procured from some public store or arsenal, were actually mounted on Navy island, and were used to fire within easy range upon the unoffending inhabitants of the opposite shore. . . .

It appears, from every account, that the expedition was sent to capture the Caroline when she was expected to be found on the British ground of Navy island, and that it was only owing to the orders of the rebel leader being disobeyed, that she was not so found. When the British officer came round the point of the island in the night, he first discovered that the vessel was moored to the other shore. He was not by this deterred from making the capture, and his conduct was approved. . . .

Although it is believed that a candid and impartial consideration of the whole history of this unfortunate event will lead to the conclusion that there were grounds of justification as strong as were ever presented in such cases, and, above all, that no slight of the authority of the United States was intended, yet it must be admitted that there was in the hurried execution of this necessary service a violation of territory; and I am instructed to assure you that Her Majesty's Government consider this as a most serious fact; and that, far from thinking that an event of this kind should be lightly risked, they would unfeignedly deprecate its recurrence. Looking back to what passed at this distance of time, what is perhaps most to be regretted is, that some explanation and apology for this occurrence was not immediately made; this, with a frank explanation of the necessity of the case, might and probably would have prevented much of the exasperation, and of the subsequent complaints and recriminations to which it gave rise. . . .

I trust, sir, I may now be permitted to hope that all feelings of resentment and ill will, resulting from these truly unfortunate events, may be buried in oblivion, and that they may be succeeded by those of harmony and friendship, which it is certainly the interest, and, I also believe, the inclination of all to promote.

◇◇◇◇◇◇◇◇◇◇◇◇◇◇

5. THE SLAVE TRADE AND THE RIGHT OF SEARCH[5]

[*Andrew Stevenson to Viscount Palmerston*]

London, April 16, 1841

IT IS with unfeigned regret that I have the honour of acquainting your Lordship, that it has been made my duty again to invite the attention of Her Majesty's Government to the subject of the continued seizure and detention of American vessels by British cruizers on the high seas, and to express the painful surprise with which the Government of the United States have learned that the repeated representations which have heretofore been made on the subject have not only remained without effect in obtaining a favourable decision, but have failed to receive the attention which their importance merited. That a series of such open and unprovoked aggressions as those which have been practised for the last 2 or 3 years, by Her Majesty's cruizers, on the vessels and commerce of The United States, and which were made the subject of complaint, would have been permitted to have remained so long undecided, was not to have been anticipated. On the contrary, my Government had confidently expected that the justice of the demands which had been made would either have been acknowledged or denied, or satisfactory reasons for the delay adduced. This was to have been expected, not less from the justice of Her Majesty's Government than the respect which was due to that of The United States. Her Majesty's Government, however, have not seen fit to adopt this course, but have permitted a delay to take place of so marked a character as not only to add greatly to the individual injuries which have been sustained, but to become itself a fit subject of complaint. . . .

It becomes my duty therefore again distinctly to express to your Lordship the fixed determination of my Government, that their flag is to be the safeguard and protection to the persons and property of its citizens, and all under it, and that these continued aggressions upon the vessels and commerce of The United States cannot longer be permitted. Nor is there in this course anything which can justly be considered as at all in conflict with the laws and policy of The United States on the subject of the African Slave Trade. In prohibiting, under the severest penalties, the participation of their citizens and vessels in that trade, there is no pretence for the exercise of a right of search on the part of foreign nations. The violation of the laws of The United States is a matter exclusively for their own authorities, and however sincere the desire of their Government may be, as in truth it is, to punish those of their citizens who participate in the trade, it cannot permit foreign nations to interfere in the enforcement of their penal laws. Yielding, as The United States, readily do, to other nations the undoubted and full exercise of their sovereign rights, their

[5] *British and Foreign State Papers,* Vol. XXX, pp. 1141–4. Andrew Stevenson was the American minister to England.

own dignity and security require the vindication of their own. For the abolition of the Slave Trade, The United States have adopted such measures as were deemed most efficacious and proper. If they have not been such as Her Majesty's Government wished to have seen adopted, it may be cause for regret, but not for intervention. Each nation must be led to judge for itself; each be the arbiter of its own justice. This, it is needless to remind your Lordship, is an essential right of sovereignty, which no independent nation will consent to yield to another. It should also be borne in mind that in making the Slave Trade piracy, the Government of The United States have not thereby made it an offence against the law of nations, inasmuch as one nation cannot increase or limit offences against the public law. Reluctant then as The United States must always be to take any course which, in the opinion of Her Majesty's Government, might have the effect of throwing obstacles in the way of the total abolition of this inhuman and detestable traffic, it can never consent, even for such a purpose, to allow foreign vessels the right of entering or searching those of The United States, or violating the freedom of her flag.

I have accordingly been instructed to bring this subject again under your Lordship's notice, and to express the confident expectation of my Government that these outrages upon the vessels and property of its citizens, by Her Majesty's naval officers, will not only be disavowed by Her Majesty's Government, and the individuals concerned in their perpetration punished, but that ample redress for the injuries sustained will be made with as little delay as possible. . . .

6. WEBSTER-ASHBURTON TREATY [6]

[*Concluded August 9, 1842; ratifications exchanged October 13, 1842*]

. . . *ARTICLE I.* It is hereby agreed and declared that the line of boundary shall be as follows: Beginning at the monument at the source of the river St. Croix, as designated and agreed to by the Commissioners under the fifth article of the Treaty of 1794, between the Governments of the United States and Great Britain; thence, north, following the exploring line run and marked by the Surveyors of the two Governments in the years 1817 and 1818, under the fifth article of the Treaty of Ghent, to its intersection with the river St. John, and to the middle of the channel thereof: thence, up the middle of the main channel of the said river St. John, to the mouth of the river St. Francis; thence, up the middle of the channel of the said river St. Francis, and of the lakes through which it flows, to the outlet of the Lake Pohenagamook; thence, southwesterly, in a straight

[6] Hunter Miller: *Treaties and Other International Acts of the United States,* Vol. IV, pp. 363–72. The treaty was signed by Daniel Webster and Lord Ashburton.

line to a point on the northwest branch of the river St. John, which point shall be ten miles distant from the mainbranch of the St. John, in a straight line, and in the nearest direction; but if the said point shall be found to be less than seven miles from the nearest point of the summit or crest of the highlands that divide those rivers which empty themselves into the river Saint Lawrence from those which fall into the river Saint John, then the said point shall be made to recede down the said northwest branch of the river St. John, to a point seven miles in a straight line from the said summit or crest; thence, in a straight line, in a course about south eight degrees west, to the point where the parallel of latitude of 46° 25′ north, intersects the southwest branch of the St. John's; thence, southerly, by the said branch, to the source thereof in the highlands at the Metjarmette Portage; thence, down along the said highlands which divide the waters which empty themselves into the river Saint Lawrence from those which fall into the Atlantic Ocean, to the head of Hall's Stream; thence, down the middle of said Stream, till the line thus run intersects the old line of boundary surveyed and marked by Valentine and Collins, previously to the year 1774, as the 45th degree of north latitude, and which has been known and understood to be the line of actual division between the States of New York and Vermont on one side, and the British Province of Canada on the other; and, from said point of intersection, west, along the said dividing line as heretofore known and understood, to the Iroquois or St. Lawrence river. . . .

Article III. In order to promote the interests and encourage the industry of all the inhabitants of the countries watered by the river St. John and its tributaries, whether living within the State of Maine or the Province of New Brunswick, it is agreed that, where, by the provisions of the present treaty, the river St. John is declared to be the line of boundary, the navigation of the said river shall be free and open to both Parties, and shall in no way be obstructed by either. . . .

Article VII. It is further agreed, that the channels in the river St. Lawrence, on both sides of the Long Sault Islands, and of Barnhart Island; the channels in the river Detroit, on both sides of the Island Bois Blanc, and between that Island and both the American and Canadian shores; and all the several channels and passages between the various Islands lying near the junction of the river St. Clair with the lake of that name, shall be equally free and open to the ships, vessels, and boats of both Parties.

Article VIII. The parties mutually stipulate that each shall prepare, equip, and maintain in service, on the coast of Africa, a sufficient and adequate squadron, or naval force of vessels, of suitable numbers and descriptions, to carry in all not less than eighty guns, to enforce, separately and respectively, the laws, rights, and obligations, of each of the two countries, for the suppression of the Slave Trade, the said squadrons to be independent of each other, but the two Governments stipulating, nevertheless, to give such orders to the officers commanding their respective forces as shall enable them most effectually to act in concert and cöoperation, upon mutual consultation, as exigencies may arise, for the attainment of the true object of this article; copies of all such orders to be communicated by each Government to the other, respectively. . . .

◇◇◇◇◇◇◇◇◇◇◇◇◇

7. AMERICAN CLAIMS TO OREGON[7]

[*John C. Calhoun to Richard Pakenham*]

Washington, September 3, 1844

. . . OUR CLAIMS to the portion of the territory drained by the Columbia River may be divided into those we have in our own proper right and those we have derived from France and Spain. We ground the former, as against Great Britain, on priority of discovery and priority of exploration and settlement. We rest our claim to discovery, as against her, on that of Captain Gray, a citizen of the United States, who, in the ship Columbia, of Boston, passed its bar and anchored in the river, ten miles above its mouth, on the 11th of May, 1792; and who, afterwards, sailed up the river 12 or 15 miles, and left it on the 20th of the same month, calling it "*Columbia,*" after his ship; which name it still retains. . . .

Nor is the evidence of the priority of our discovery of the head branches of the river and its exploration less conclusive. Before the treaty was ratified by which we acquired Louisiana, in 1803, an expedition was planned, at the head of which were placed Meriwether Lewis and William Clarke, to explore the river Missouri and its principal branches to their sources, and then to seek and trace to its termination in the Pacific some stream, "*whether the Columbia, the Oregon, the Colorado, or any other which might offer the most direct and practicable water communication across the continent for the purpose of commerce.*" The party began to ascend the Missouri in May, 1804, and in the summer of 1805 reached the head waters of the Columbia river. . . .

It took place many years before it was visited and explored by any subject of Great Britain, or of any other civilized nation, so far as we are informed. It as clearly entitles us to the claim of priority of discovery as to its head branches and the exploration of the river and region through which it passes, as the voyages of Captain Gray and the Spanish navigator, Heceta, entitle us to priority in reference to its mouth and the entrance into its channel.

Nor is our priority of settlement less certain. Establishments were formed by American citizens on the Columbia as early as 1809 and 1810. . . .

Such are the facts on which we rest our claims to priority of discovery and priority of exploration and settlement, as against Great Britain, to the

[7] *House Ex. Doc.* (480) 29th Congress, 1st Session, No. 2, pp. 146–53.

region drained by the Columbia river. So much for the claims we have in our own proper right to that region.

To these we have added the claims of France and Spain. The former, we obtained by the treaty of Louisiana, ratified in 1803; and the latter by the treaty of Florida, ratified in 1819. By the former, we acquired all the rights which France had to Louisiana *"to the extent it now has* (1803) *in the hands of Spain, and that it had when France possessed it, and as it should be after the treaties subsequently entered into by Spain and other States."* By the latter, his Catholic majesty *"ceded to the United States all his rights, claims, and pretensions"* to the country lying west of the Rocky mountains and north of a line drawn on the 42nd parallel of latitude, from a point on the south bank of the Arkansas, in that parallel, to the South Sea; that is, to the whole region claimed by Spain west of those mountains, and north of that line. . . .

When the first convention was concluded, in 1818, our whole population did not exceed nine millions of people. . . . Now, our population may be safely estimated at not less than nineteen millions, of which at least eight millions inhabit the States and territories in the valley of the Mississippi. . . .

To this great increase of population. . . may be added the increased facility of reaching the Oregon territory. . . . These joint causes have had the effect of turning the current of our population towards the territory. . . . There can, then, be no doubt now that the operation of the same causes which impelled our population westward from the shores of the Atlantic. . . to the valley of the Mississippi, will impel them onward. . . into the valley of the Columbia, and that the whole region drained by it is destined to be peopled by us. . . .

◇◇◇◇◇◇◇◇◇◇◇◇◇

8. OREGON BOUNDARY-COMPROMISE OFFER OF THE UNITED STATES[8]

[*James Buchanan to Richard Pakenham*]

Washington, July 12, 1845

. . . OUR OWN American title to the extent of the valley of the Columbia, resting as it does on discovery, exploration, and possession, (a possession acknowledged by a most solemn act of the British government itself) is a sufficient assurance against all mankind, whilst our superadded title from Spain extends our exclusive rights over the whole territory in dispute as against Great Britain.

Such being the opinion of the President in regard to the title of the United States, he would not have consented to yield any portion of the

[8] Ibid., pp. 163–9.

Oregon territory, had he not found himself embarrassed, if not committed, by the acts of his predecessors. They had uniformly proceeded upon the principle of compromise in all their negotiations. Indeed, the first question presented to him after entering upon the duties of his office, was, whether he should abruptly terminate the negotiation which had been commenced and conducted between Mr. Calhoun and Mr. Pakenham on the principle avowed in the first protocol, not of contending for the whole territory in dispute, but of treating of the respective claims of the parties, "with the view to establish a permanent boundary between the two countries westward of the Rocky mountains."

In view of these facts, the President has determined to pursue the present negotiation to its conclusion upon the principle of compromise in which it commenced, and to make one more effort to adjust this long pending controversy. In this determination he trusts that the British government will recognize his sincere and anxious desire to cultivate the most friendly relations between the two countries, and to manifest to the world that he is actuated by a spirit of moderation. He has, therefore, instructed the undesigned again to propose to the government of Great Britain that the Oregon territory shall be divided between the two countries by the forty-ninth parallel of north latitude from the Rocky mountains to the Pacific ocean; offering at the same time to make free to Great Britain any port or ports on Vancouver's island, south of this parallel, which the British government may desire. He trusts, that Great Britain may receive this proposition in the friendly spirit by which it was dictated, and that it may prove the stable foundation of lasting peace and harmony between the two countries. The line proposed will carry out the principle of continuity equally for both parties, by extending the limits both of ancient Louisiana and Canada to the Pacific along the same parallel of latitude which divides them east of the Rocky mountains; and it will secure to each a sufficient number of commodious harbors on the northwest coast of America. . . .

◇◇◇◇◇◇◇◇◇◇◇◇◇

9. THE TERMINATION OF THE BRITISH-AMERICAN OREGON AGREEMENT[9]

[*Extract from the Annual Message of President Polk, December 2, 1845*]

. . . MY ATTENTION was early directed to the negotiation which on the 4th of March last I found pending at Washington between the United States and Great Britain on the subject of the Oregon Territory. Three several attempts had been previously made to settle the questions in dispute between the two countries by negotiation upon the principle of compromise, but each had proved unsuccessful. . . .

[9] James D. Richardson, *Messages and Papers of the Presidents,* op. cit., Vol. IV, pp. 392–416.

All attempts at compromise having failed, it becomes the duty of Congress to consider what measures it may be proper to adopt for the security and protection of our citizens now inhabiting or who may hereafter inhabit Oregon, and for the maintenance of our just title to that Territory. In adopting measures for this purpose care should be taken that nothing be done to violate the stipulations of the convention of 1827, which is still in force. . . . Under that convention a year's notice is required to be given by either party to the other before the joint occupancy shall terminate and before either can rightfully assert or exercise exclusive jurisdiction over any portion of the territory. This notice it would, in my judgment, be proper to give, and I recommend that provision be made by law for giving it accordingly, and terminating in this manner the convention of the 6th of August, 1827.

It will become proper for Congress to determine what legislation they can in the meantime adopt without violating this convention. Beyond all question the protection of our laws and our jurisdiction, civil and criminal, ought to be immediately extended over our citizens in Oregon. They have had just cause to complain of our long neglect in this particular, and have in consequence been compelled for their own security and protection to establish a provisional government for themselves. . . . They are anxious that our laws should be extended over them, and I recommend that this be done by Congress with as little delay as possible in the full extent to which the British Parliament have proceeded in regard to British subjects in that Territory by their act of July 2, 1821, "for regulating the fur trade and establishing a criminal and civil jurisdiction within certain parts of North America.". . .

At the end of the year's notice, should Congress think it proper to make provision for giving that notice, we shall have reached a period when the national rights in Oregon must either be abandoned or firmly maintained. That they can not now be abandoned without a sacrifice of both national honor and interest is too clear to admit of doubt. . . .[10]

◇◇◇◇◇◇◇◇◇◇◇◇◇◇

10. OREGON TREATY OF 1846[11]

[*Concluded June 15, 1846; ratifications exchanged July 17, 1846*]

. . . *ARTICLE I.* From the point on the forty-ninth parallel of north latitude where the boundary laid down in existing treaties and conventions between the United States and Great Britain terminates, the line of

---

10 President Polk continued at this point in his message with a statement of the Monroe Doctrine (see above page 201) which was applicable to the Oregon as much as it was to Texas.

11 Hunter Miller: *Treaties and Other International Acts of the United States,* Vol. V, pp. 3–5. This treaty was signed by James Buchanan and Richard Pakenham.

boundary between the territories of the United States and those of Her Britannic Majesty shall be continued westward along the said forty-ninth parallel of north latitude to the middle of the channel which separates the continent from Vancouver's Island; and thence southerly through the middle of the said channel, and of Fuca's Straits to the Pacific Ocean; provided, however, that the navigation of the whole of the said channel and Straits south of the forty ninth parallel of north latitude, remain free and open to both Parties.

Article II. From the point at which the forty-ninth parallel of north latitude shall be found to intersect the great northern branch of the Columbia River, the navigation of the said branch shall be free and open to the Hudson's Bay Company and to all British subjects trading with the same, to the point where the said branch meets the main stream of the Columbia, and thence down the said main stream to the Ocean, with free access into and through the said River or Rivers, it being understood that all the usual portages along the line thus described shall in like manner be free and open. . . .

Article III. In the future appropriation of the territory, south of the forty-ninth parallel of north latitude, as provided in the first article of this Treaty, the possessory rights of the Hudson's Bay Company and of all British subjects who may be already in the occupation of land or other property, lawfully acquired within the said Territory, shall be respected.

Article IV. The farms, lands, and other property of every description belonging to the Puget's Sound Agricultural Company on the north side of the Columbia River, shall be confirmed to the said Company. . . .

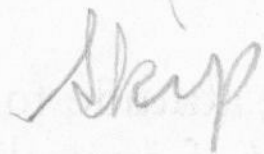

CHAPTER XIV

CUBA AND THE UNITED STATES to 1860

◇◇◇◇◇◇◇◇◇◇◇◇◇

THE CUBAN policy of the United States was for a long time one of the major problems of American foreign relations. In 1823 the situation in Cuba was precarious: Spanish power in Cuba was at a low ebb due to the invasion of Spain by France; Cuban patriots were contemplating a movement for independence; and rumors were current concerning British designs on the island. It was under the urge of these circumstances that the Secretary of State, John Quincy Adams, formulated the first important statement of American policy regarding Cuba (1). The offer of the United States in 1848 to purchase Cuba from Spain (2), for reasons stated by the Secretary of State, was not a departure from the earlier policy but an attempt to hasten the annexation of the island, an eventuality which Adams had anticipated. The attempt on the part of France and England, in 1852, to establish a joint protectorate over Cuba afforded another opportunity for a statement of American policy (3). The reasons presented by Secretary Marcy for the purchase of Cuba in 1854 (4) and the Ostend Manifesto (5) of the same year should be compared carefully with the earlier offer of purchase and former statements of policy.

◇◇◇◇◇◇◇◇◇◇◇◇◇

1. CUBAN POLICY OF THE UNITED STATES IN 1823[1]

[*John Quincy Adams to Hugh Nelson*]

Washington, April 28, 1823

THE PERIOD at which you enter upon the Mission[2] with which you are charged is of no common interest; and the relations of the United States with the country to which you are destined, at all times important, are now of the deepest moment. . . .

It has been a maxim in the policy in these United States from the time when their independence was achieved to keep themselves aloof from the political questions and contentions of Europe. To this principle it is yet the purpose of the President to adhere; and in the war about to commence,

[1] Department of State: *Instructions to United States Ministers,* Vol. IX, pp. 183–243.
[2] Minister to Spain.

the attitude to be assumed and maintained by the United States will be that of neutrality.

But the experience of our National history has already shown that however sincerely this policy was adopted and however earnestly and perseveringly it was maintained, it yielded ultimately to a course of events by which the violence and injustice of European powers involved the immediate interests, and brought in conflict the essential rights of our own country. . . .

In the *maritime* Wars of Europe we have indeed a direct and important interest of our own; as they are waged upon an element which is the common property of all, and as our participation in the possession of that property is perhaps greater than that of any other nation. The existence of maritime war itself enlarges and deepens the importance of this interest; and it introduces a state of things in which the conflict of neutral and belligerent rights becomes itself a continual and formidable instigation to war. To all martime wars Great Britain can scarcely fail of becoming a party; and from that moment arises a collision between her and the United States, peculiar to the situation, interests and rights of the two countries and which can scarcely form a subject of discussion between other nations, or between any other nation, and either of them. . . .

But in the war between France and Spain, now commencing, other interests, peculiarly ours, will, in all probability, be deeply involved. Whatever may be the issue of this war, as between those two European powers, it may be taken for granted that the dominion of Spain upon the American continent, north and south, is irrecoverably gone. But the islands of Cuba and Porto Rico still remain nominally, and so far really, dependent upon her, that she yet possesses the power of transferring her own dominion over them, together with the possession of them, to others. These islands from their local position and natural appendages to the North American continent, and one of them, Cuba, almost in sight of our shores, from a multitude of considerations, has become an object of transcendent importance to the commercial and political interests of our Union. Its commanding position with reference to the Gulf of Mexico and the West India seas; the character of its population, its situation midway between our southern coast and the island of St. Domingo; its safe and capacious harbor of Havanna, fronting a long line of shores destitute of the same advantage; the nature of its productions and of its wants, furnishing the supplies and needing the returns of a commerce immensely profitable and mutually beneficial, – give it an importance in the sum of our national interests with which that of no other foreign territory can be compared, and little inferior to that which binds the different members of this Union together.

Such, indeed, are, between the interests of that island and of this country, the geographical, commercial, moral, and political relations, formed by nature, gathering in the process of time, and even now verging to maturity, that, in looking forward to the probable course of events, for the short period of half a century, it is scarcely possible to resist the conviction that the annexation of Cuba to our federal republic will be indispensable to the continuance and integrity of the Union itself. It is obvious, however, that for this event we are not yet prepared. Numerous and formidable objections to the extension of our territorial domains beyond the sea, present themselves to the first contemplation of the subject; obstacles to the system of policy by which alone that result can be compassed and maintained, are to be foreseen and surmounted, both from at home and abroad; but there are laws of political, as well as of physical gravitation, and if an apple, severed by a tempest from its native tree, cannot choose but fall to the ground, Cuba, forcibly disjoined from its own unnatural connection with Spain, and incapable of self-support, can gravitate only toward the North American Union, which, by the same law of nature, cannot cast her off from its bosom.

In any other state of things than that which springs from this incipient war between France and Spain, these considerations would be premature. They are now merely touched upon to illustrate the position that, in the war opening upon Europe, the United States have deep and important interests involved, perculiarly their own. The condition of Cuba cannot but depend upon the issue of this war. . . .

Great Britain has formally withdrawn from the councils of the European alliance in regard to Spain; she disapproves the war which they have sanctioned, and which is undertaken by France, and she avows her determination to defend Portugal against the application of the principles upon which the invasion of Spain raises its only pretense of right. To the war, as it commences, she has declared her intention of remaining neutral; but the spirit of the British nation is so strongly and with so much unamity pronounced against France, their interests are so deeply involved in the issue, their national resentments and jealousies will be so forcibly stimulated by the progress of the war, whatever it may be, that, unless the conflict should be as short and the issue as decisive as that of which Italy was recently the scene, it is scarcely possible that the neutrality of Great Britain should be long maintained. The prospect is that she will be soon engaged on the side of Spain; but in making common cause with her, it is not to be supposed that she will yield her assistance upon principles altogether disinterested and gratuitous. As the price of her alliance, the two remaining islands of Spain in the West Indies present objects no longer of much possible value or benefit to Spain, but of such importance to Great Britain that it is impossible to suppose her indifferent to the acquisition of them. . . .

The transfer of Cuba to Great Britain would be an event unpropitious to the interests of this Union. This opinion is so generally entertained, that even the groundless rumors that it was about to be accomplished, which have spread abroad, and are still teeming, may be traced to the deep and almost universal feeling of aversion to it, and to the alarm which the mere probability of its occurrence has stimulated. The question both of our right and of our power to prevent it, if necessary, by force, already obtrudes itself upon our councils, and the administration is called upon, in the performance of its duties to the nation, at least to use all of the means within its competency to guard against and forfend it. . . .

◇◇◇◇◇◇◇◇◇◇◇◇◇

2. OFFER TO PURCHASE CUBA[3]

[*James Buchanan to Romulus M. Saunders*]

Washington, June 17, 1848

BY DIRECTION of the President, I now call your attention to the present condition and future prospects of Cuba. The fate of this island must ever be deeply interesting to the people of the United States. We are content that it shall continue to be a colony of Spain. Whilst in her possession we have nothing to apprehend. Besides, we are bound to her by the ties of ancient friendship, and we sincerely desire to render these perpetual.

But we can never consent that this island shall become a colony of any other European power. In the possession of Great Britain, or any strong naval power, it might prove ruinous both to our domestic and foreign commerce, and even endanger the union of the States. The highest and first duty of every independent nation is to provide for its own safety; and, acting upon this principle, we should be compelled to resist the acquisition of Cuba by any powerful maritime State, with all the means which Providence has placed at our command.

Cuba is almost within sight of the coast of Florida, situated between that State and the peninsula of Yúcatan, and possessing the deep, capacious and impregnably fortified harbor of the Havana. If this island were under the dominion of Great Britain, she could command both the inlets to the Gulf of Mexico. She would thus be enabled, in time of war, effectively to blockade the mouth of the Mississippi, and to deprive all the western States of this Union, as well as those within the gulf, teeming as they are with an industrious and enterprising population, of a foreign market for their immense productions. But this is not the worst: she could also destroy the commerce by sea between our ports on the gulf and our Atlantic ports, a commerce of nearly as great a value as the whole of our foreign trade. Is there any reason to believe that Great Britain desires to acquire the island of Cuba? We know that it has been her uniform policy, throughout her past history, to seize upon every valuable commercial point throughout the world, whenever circumstances have placed this in her power. And what point so valuable as the island of Cuba?

The United States are the chief commercial rival of Great Britain; our tonnage at the present moment is nearly equal to hers, and it will be

[3] *House Ex. Doc.* (648) 32nd Congress, 1st Session, No. 121, pp. 42–9.

greater, within a brief period, if nothing should occur to arrest our progress. Of what vast importance would it, then, be to her to obtain the possession of an island from which she could at any time destroy a very large portion both of our foreign and coasting trade? Besides, she well knows that if Cuba were in our possession her West India islands would be rendered comparatively valueless. From the extent and fertility of this island, and from the energy and industry of our people, we should soon be able to supply the markets of the world with tropical productions, at a cheaper rate than these could be raised in any of her possessions. . . .

This can never become a local question. With suitable fortifications at the Tortugas, and in possession of the strongly fortified harbor of Havana as a naval station on the opposite coast of Cuba, we could command the outlet of the Gulf of Mexico, between the peninsula of Florida and that island. This would afford ample security both to the foreign and coasting trade of the western and southern States, which seek a market for their surplus productions through the ports on the gulf. . . .

Desirable, however, as the possession of this island may be to the United States, we would not acquire it except by the free will of Spain. Any acquisition not sanctioned by justice and honor, would be too dearly purchased. . . .

Should the government of Spain feel disposed to part with the island of Cuba, the question, what should we offer for it? would then arise. In deciding this question, it will be important to ascertain, 1st. What net revenue it yields at the present moment to the royal treasury, after deducting all the expenditure incurred on its account; and, 2d. What net revenue would it yield to the government of the United States in its present condition?

The first inquiry I have no means of answering with accuracy. McCulloch, in his Gazetteer, states "that the whole revenues of the island, at an average of the five years ending with 1837, amounted to $8,945,581 per year," and it is stated in Hunt's Merchants' Magazine for October, 1845, that the revenue for the year 1844 amounted to $10,490,252.87½. Since 1844 we have no information on the subject in the department, upon which reliance can be placed. Mr. Calderon informs me that the Spanish treasury at Madrid have never received from Cuba in any one year a sum exceeding $2,000,000. In answer to an inquiry, how the remainder of the revenue was expended, he stated that it was appropriated to defray the expense of its colonial government, and to pay and support the troops and maintain the vessels of war necessary for its defence and security.

It will occur to you that if Spain should cede Cuba to the United States, she would at once relieve herself from a great part, if not the whole of this civil, military and naval expenditure. In this view of the subject, it would seem that the sum of $50,000,000 would be an ample pecuniary indemnity to Spain for the loss of the island. . . .

The apprehensions which existed for many years after the origin of this government, that the extension of our federal system would endanger the

Union, seem to have passed away. Experience has proved that this system of confederated republics, under which the federal government has charge of interests common to the whole, whilst local governments watch over the concerns of the respective States, is capable of almost indefinite extension, with increasing strength. This, however, is always subject to the qualification that the mass of the population must be of our own race, or must have been educated in the school of civil and religious liberty. With this qualification, the more we increase the number of confederated States, the greater will be the strength and security of the Union, because the more dependent for their mutual interests will the several parts be upon the whole, and the whole upon the several parts. It is true that of the 418,291 white inhabitants which Cuba contained in 1841, a very large proportion is of the Spanish race: still, many of our citizens have settled on the island, and some of them are large holders of property. Under our government it would speedily be *Americanized,* as Louisiana has been. Within the boundaries of such a federal system alone can a trade exempt from duties and absolutely free be enjoyed. With the possession of Cuba we should have throughout the Union a free trade on a more extended scale than any which the world has ever witnessed, arousing an energy and activity of competition which would result in a most rapid improvement in all that contributes to the wellfare and happiness of the human race. . . . Cuba, justly appreciating the advantages of annexation, is now ready to rush into our arms. Once admitted, she would be entirely dependent for her prosperity, and even existence, upon her connexion with the Union, whilst the rapidly increasing trade between her and the other States would shed its blessings and its benefits over the whole. Such a state of mutual dependence, resulting from the very nature of things, the world has never witnessed. This is what will insure the perpetuity of our Union.

With all these considerations in view, the President believes that the crisis has arrived when an effort should be made to purchase the island of Cuba from Spain, and he has determined to intrust you with the performance of this most delicate and important duty. . . .

At your interview with the Minister for Foreign Affairs you might introduce the subject by referring to the present distracted condition of Cuba, and the danger which exists that the population will make an attempt to accomplish a revolution. This must be well known to the Spanish government. . . .

The President would be willing to stipulate for the payment of one hundred millions of dollars. This, however, is the maximum price; and if Spain should be willing to sell, you will use your best efforts to purchase it at a rate as much below that sum as practicable. In case you should be able to conclude a treaty, you may adopt as your model, so far as the same may be applicable, the two conventions of April 30, 1803, between France and the United States, for the sale and purchase of Louisiana. The seventh and eighth articles of the first of these conventions ought, if possible, to be omitted; still, if this should be indispensable to the accomplishment of the object, articles similar to them may be retained.

I transmit you a full power to conclude such a treaty.

You will be careful to make a full and faithful report to this department of all the conversations and proceedings on this subject between yourself and the Spanish Minister for Foreign Affairs. Should you succeed in accomplishing the object, you will associate your name with a most important and beneficial measure for the glory and prosperity of your country.

◇◇◇◇◇◇◇◇◇◇◇◇◇

3. AMERICAN OBJECTION TO JOINT DECLARATION CONCERNING CUBA[4]

[*Edward Everett to the Comte de Sartiges*]

Washington, December 1, 1852

YOU ARE well acquainted with the melancholy circumstances which have hitherto prevented a reply to the note which you addressed to my predecessor on the 8th of July.[5]

That note, and the instruction of M. de Turgot of the 31st March, with a similar communication from the English minister, and the *projet* of a convention between the three powers relative to Cuba, have been among the first subjects to which my attention has been called by the President.

The substantial portion of the proposed convention is expressed in a single article in the following terms: "The high contracting parties hereby severally and collectively disclaim, now and for hereafter, all intention to obtain possession of the island of Cuba, and they respectively bind themselves to discountenance all attempt to that effect on the part of any power or individuals whatever."

"The high contracting parties declare, severally and collectively, that they will not obtain or maintain for themselves, or for any one of themselves, any exclusive control over the said island, nor assume nor exercise any dominion over the same."

The President has given the most serious attention to this proposal, to the notes of the French and British ministers accompanying it, and to the instructions of M. de Turgot and the Earl of Malmesbury, transmitted with the project of the convention; and he directs me to make known to you the view which he takes of this important and delicate subject. . . .

M. de Turgot states that France could never see with indifference the possession of Cuba by *any* power but Spain, and explicitly declares that she has no wish or intention of appropriating the island to herself; and the

---

4 *Sen. Ex. Doc.* (660) 32nd Congress, 2nd Session, No. 13, pp. 15–23.

5 This refers to the death of Daniel Webster. The Comte de Sartiges was the French minister at Washington.

English minister makes the same avowal on behalf of his government. M. de Turgot and Lord Malmesbury do the government of the United States no more than justice in remarking that they have often pronounced themselves substantially in the same sense. The President does not covet the acquisition of Cuba for the United States; at the same time, he considers the condition of Cuba as mainly an American question. The proposed convention proceeds on a different principle. It assumes that the United States have no other or greater interest in the question than France or England; whereas it is necessary only to cast one's eye on the map to see how remote are the relations of Europe, and how intimate those of the United States, with this island. . . .

But the President has a graver objection to entering into the proposed convention. He has no wish to disguise the feeling that the compact, although equal in its terms, would be very unequal in substance. France and England, by entering into it, would disable themselves from obtaining possession of an island remote from their seats of government, belonging to another European power, whose natural right to possess it must always be as good as their own – a distant island in another hemisphere, and one which by no ordinary or peaceful course of things could ever belong to either of them. If the present balance of power in Europe should be broken up, if Spain should become unable to maintain the island in her possession, and France and England should be engaged in a death struggle with each other, Cuba might then be the prize of the victor. Till these events all take place, the President does not see how Cuba can belong to any European power but Spain.

The United States, on the other hand, would, by the proposed convention, disable themselves from making an acquisition which might take place without any disturbance of existing foreign relations, and in the natural order of things. The island of Cuba lies at our doors. It commands the approach to the Gulf of Mexico, which washes the shores of five of our States. It bars the entrance of that great river which drains half the North American continent, and with its tributaries forms the largest system of internal water-communication in the world. It keeps watch at the door-way of our intercourse with California by the Isthmus route. If an island like Cuba, belonging to the Spanish crown, guarded the entrance of the Thames and the Seine, and the United States should propose a convention like this to France and England, those powers would assuredly feel that the disability assumed by ourselves was far less serious than that which we asked them to assume. . . .

Spain, meantime, has retained of her extensive dominions in this hemisphere but the two islands of Cuba and Porto Rico. A respectful sympathy with the fortunes of an ancient ally and a gallant people, with whom the United States have ever maintained the most friendly relations, would, if no other reason existed, make it our duty to leave her in the undisturbed possession of this little remnant of her mighty trans-Atlantic empire. The President desires to do so; no word or deed of his will ever question her title or shake her possession. But can it be expected to last very long? Can it resist this mighty current in the fortunes of the world? Is it desirable that it should do so? Can it be for the interest of Spain to cling to a possession that can only be maintained by a garrison of twenty-five or thirty-thousand troops, a powerful naval force, and an annual expenditure for both arms of the service of at least twelve millions of dollars? Cuba, at this moment, costs more to Spain than the entire naval and military establishment of the United States costs the federal government. So far from being really injured by the loss of this island, there is no doubt that, were it peacefully transferred to the United States, a prosperous commerce between Cuba and Spain, resulting from ancient associations and common language and tastes, would be far more productive than the best contrived system of colonial taxation. . . .

◇◇◇◇◇◇◇◇◇◇◇◇◇◇

4. OFFER TO PURCHASE CUBA RENEWED[6]

[*William L. Marcy to Pierre Soulé*]

Washington, April 3, 1854

THE UNSETTLED condition of political affairs in Spain, and the troubles which may arise in the island of Cuba, from the experiment now making to introduce a new system for supplying the demand for agricultural labor, are here regarded as circumstances which may open the way to the accomplishment of the object so much desired by the United States.

In view of the contingencies which may arise, the President has deemed it proper that you should be furnished with full power to enter into a convention or treaty for the purchase of Cuba. . . .

Should circumstances present a favorable opportunity, you are directed by the President to renew the attempt to purchase that island. He is aware that this will be a delicate and difficult negotiation, and the manner of conducting it is left wholly to your discretion.

The maximum sum which our minister Mr. Saunders was authorized to offer on a former occasion was $100,000,000. This is regarded by the President as a liberal price, yet the acquisition of that Island is so very desirable that he would not have the negotiation fail if an additional amount of 20 or 30 millions were required to effect the object.

The difficulties of a direct purchase were discussed in our interviews before you left the United States; they may have been diminished, if not removed, by the events which have since taken place in the internal condition of Spain. The change of policy in Cuba, particularly in regard to supplying the demand for agricultural labor, has increased discontent and created alarm among the people of that island, and made them more

[6] Department of State, *Instructions to Spain,* Vol. XV, pp. 45–9.

averse to the continuance of Spanish rule, and more willing to come under the protection of the United States. . . .

Though the pride of Spain might revolt at the proposition to sell the island of Cuba to a foreign power, it has been suggested that she might be induced to consent to its independence, and that the United States might essentially contribute to such a result. In any conceivable arrangement of this kind the people of Cuba must necessarily be a party to it. There is now no political organization in the island which can act for the people, nor is it possible there can be under its present system of government. No body of men are permitted to associate for the purpose of accepting or offering terms. Should the despotic rule now established be so far relaxed as to allow of any such association, the United States would readily countenance and aid its efforts to release the island from dependence on Spain. Any assistance this country might give to the people of Cuba, to enable them to induce Spain to consent to their independence might be fully compensated by advantages which they would be able to secure to the United States.

This government would look with favor upon such an arrangement, and aid in any useful way to bring it about; but, without knowing whether anything can be done to effect that object, or what part the United States could properly take in furtherance of it, it is not possible to give you any special instructions for your action in such a contingency. . . .

5. THE OSTEND MANIFESTO[7]

[*James Buchanan, John Y. Mason, and Pierre Soulé, to William L. Marcy*]

Aix La Chapelle, October 18, 1854

THE UNDERSIGNED, in compliance with the wish expressed by the President in the several confidential despatches you have addressed to us, respectively, to that effect, have met in conference, first at Ostend, in Belgium, on the 9th, 10th, and 11th instant, and then at Aix la Chapelle, in Prussia, on the days next following, up to the date hereof.

There has been a full and unreserved interchange of views and sentiments between us, which we are most happy to inform you has resulted in a cordial coincidence of opinion on the grave and important subjects submitted to our consideration.

We have arrived at the conclusion, and are thoroughly convinced, that an immediate and earnest effort ought to be made by the government of the United States to purchase Cuba from Spain. . . .

It can scarcely be apprehended that foreign powers, in violation of international law, would interpose their influence with Spain to prevent

[7] *House Ex. Doc.* (790) 33rd Congress, 2nd Session., No. 93, pp. 127–32.

our acquisition of the island. Its inhabitants are now suffering under the worst of all possible governments, that of absolute despotism, delegated by a distant power to irresponsible agents, who are changed at short intervals, and who are tempted to improve the brief opportunity thus afforded to accumulate fortunes by the basest means.

As long as this system shall endure, humanity may in vain demand the suppression of the African slave trade in the island. This is rendered impossible whilst that infamous traffic remains an irresistible temptation and a source of immense profit to needy and avaricious officials, who, to attain their ends, scruple not to trample the most sacred principles under foot. . . .

Under no probable circumstances can Cuba ever yield to Spain one per cent. on the large amount[8] which the United States are willing to pay for its acquisition. But Spain is in imminent danger of losing Cuba, without remuneration.

Extreme oppression, it is now universally admitted, justifies any people in endeavoring to relieve themselves from the yoke of their oppressors. The sufferings which the corrupt, arbitrary, and unrelenting local administration necessarily entails upon the inhabitants of Cuba, cannot fail to stimulate and keep alive that spirit of resistance and revolution against Spain, which has, of late years, been so often manifested. In this condition of affairs it is vain to expect that the sympathies of the people of the United States will not be warmly enlisted in favor of their oppressed neighbors.

But if Spain, dead to the voice of her own interest, and actuated by stubborn pride and a false sense of honor, should refuse to sell Cuba to the United States, then the question will arise, What ought to be the course of the American government under such circumstances?

Self-preservation is the first law of nature, with States as well as with individuals. All nations have, at different periods, acted upon this maxim. Although it has been made the pretext for committing flagrant injustice, as in the partition of Poland and other similar cases which history records, yet the principle itself, though often abused, has always been recognized. . . .

After we shall have offered Spain a price for Cuba far beyond its present value, and this shall have been refused, it will then be time to consider the question, does Cuba, in the possession of Spain, seriously endanger our internal peace and the existence of our cherished Union?

Should this question be answered in the affirmative, then, by every law, human and divine, we shall be justified in wresting it from Spain if we possess the power; and this upon the very same principle that would justify an individual in tearing down the burning house of his neighbor if there were no other means of preventing the flames from destroying his own home.

---

[8] $120,000,000.00

Under such circumstances we ought neither to count the cost nor regard the odds which Spain might enlist against us. We forbear to enter into the question, whether the present condition of the island would justify such a measure? We should, however, be recreant to our duty, be unworthy of our gallant forefathers, and commit base treason against our posterity, should we permit Cuba to be Africanized and become a second St. Domingo, with all its attendant horrors to the white race, and suffer the flames to extend to our own neighboring shores, seriously to endanger or actually to consume the fair fabric of our Union. . . .

CHAPTER XV

CENTRAL AMERICAN DIPLOMACY 1846–1860

◇◇◇◇◇◇◇◇◇◇◇◇◇

AMERICAN relations with New Granada (Colombia), Mexico, and the Central American states regarding a possible trans-Isthmian canal are complicated and not easily illustrated by a small group of readings. Prior to the Civil War, however, the most important items of American Isthmian diplomacy, concerned the treaty with New Granada in 1846 (1), and the Clayton-Bulwer Treaty. By 1848 it had become clear to the American government that Great Britain was extending her influence in Central America over areas that would control important canal routes. During 1848 an American diplomatic agent in Central America, Elijah Hise, negotiated a treaty with Nicaragua which would have caused a serious controversy with Great Britain (2). John M. Clayton, who became Secretary of State on March 7, 1849, in the midst of the Central American controversy, was anxious to prevent an open break with Great Britain and at the same time to prevent further British expansion in the Caribbean. Clayton's anxiety to settle the difficulty led him to conclude a treaty with Great Britain rather hastily and apparently without due consideration of the weakness of the British position (3), although information on that subject had been supplied by the American minister to Great Britain. After the treaty (4) was ratified by the American Senate and some of the diplomatic correspondence regarding it was published, there appeared in the United States not only a considerable amount of dissatisfaction with its terms but also a difference of opinion between the British (6) and American (5) governments over its interpretation. After a prolonged negotiation President Buchanan was able to announce in 1860 that the difficulty had been settled in a satisfactory manner (7).

◇◇◇◇◇◇◇◇◇◇◇◇◇

1. TREATY BETWEEN THE UNITED STATES AND NEW GRANADA[1]

[*Concluded December 12, 1846; ratifications exchanged June 10, 1848*]

. . . *ARTICLE XXXV.* The United States of America and the Republic of New Granada desiring to make as durable as possible, the relations which are to be established between the two parties by virtue of this treaty, have declared solemnly, and do agree to the following points

1st For the better understanding of the preceding articles, it is, and has been stipulated, between the high contracting parties, that the citizens, vessels and merchandise of the United States shall enjoy in the ports of New Granada, including those of the part of the granadian territory generally denominated *Isthmus of Panamá* from its southermost extremity until the boundary of Costa Rica, all the exemptions, privileges and immunities, concerning commerce and navigation, which are now, or may hereafter be enjoyed by Granadian citizens, their vessels and merchandise; and that this equality of favours shall be made to extend to the passengers, correspondence and merchandise of the United States in their transit across the said territory, from one sea to the other. The Government of New Granada guarantees to the Government of the United States, that the right of way or transit across the *Isthmus of Panamá,* upon any modes of communication that now exist, or that may be, hereafter, constructed, shall be open and free to the Government and citizens of the United States, and for the transportation of any articles of produce, manufactures or merchandise, of lawful commerce, belonging to the citizens of the United States; that no other tolls or charges shall be levied or collected upon the citizens of the United States, or their said merchandise thus passing over any road or canal that may be made by the Government of New Granada, or by the authority of the same, than is under like circumstances levied upon and collected from the granadian citizens: that any lawful produce, manufactures or merchandise belonging to citizens of the United States thus passing from one sea to the other, in either direction, for the purpose of exportation to any other foreign country, shall not be liable to any import duties whatever; or having paid such duties, they shall be entitled to drawback, upon their exportation: nor shall the citizens of the United States be liable to any duties, tolls, or charges of any kind to which native citizens are not subjected for thus passing the said Isthmus. And, in order to secure to themselves the tranquil and constant enjoyment of these advantages, and as an especial compensation for the said advantages and for the favours they have acquired by the 4th, 5th, and 6th articles of this Treaty, the United States guarantee positively and efficaciously to New Granada, by the present stipulation, the perfect

[1] Hunter Miller: *Treaties and Other International Acts of the United States,* Vol. V, pp. 115–43. The treaty was signed by B. A. Bidlack and M. M. Mallarino.

neutrality of the before mentioned Isthmus, with the view that the free transit from the one to the other sea, may not be interrupted or embarrassed in any future time while this treaty exists; and in consequence, the United States also guarantee, in the same manner, the rights of sovereignty and property which New Granada has and possesses over the said territory. . . .

◇◇◇◇◇◇◇◇◇◇◇◇◇

2. AN EXPLANATION OF THE CENTRAL AMERICAN NEGOTIATIONS OF ELIJAH HISE[2]

[*John M. Clayton to President Fillmore*]

Washington, July 19, 1850

. . . THE SECRETARY of State, to whom was referred by the President the resolution of the House of Representatives of the 24th of January last, in regard to Central America, has the honor to report the facts disclosed by the accompanying correspondence, which is respectfully submitted in response to the resolution.

The Secretary of State of the State of Nicaragua, Senor Buitrago, in a letter to the Hon. James Buchanan, late Secretary of State of the United States, dated the 12th day of November, 1847, solicited the friendly offices of this government to prevent an attack upon the town of San Juan de Nicaragua, then contemplated by the British authorities as allies of the Mosquito King. This letter, a translation of which is herewith sent, distinctly charges that "the object of the British government in taking this key of the continent is, not to protect the small tribe of Mosquitos, but to establish their own empire over the Atlantic extremity of the line by which a canal connecting the two oceans is most practicable, insuring to them the preponderance on the American continent as well as their direct relations with Asia, the East Indies, and other important countries in the world." No answer appears to have been returned to this letter. . . .

On the 8th day of February, 1848, (six days after the negotiations, by Mr. Trist, of the treaty of Guadalupe Hidalgo,) the British ships of war "Alarm" and "Vixen" arrived at San Juan de Nicaragua, and took possession of that town, the name of which was changed to "Greytown." On the 12th of that month the British forces attacked and, after a sharp action, captured the port of Serapaqui, then garrisoned by the troops of Nicaragua. The war was ended on the 7th of March, 1848, by articles of agreement concluded by Captain Granvill Gower Loch, the commander of the expedition, on the part of Great Britain, with the commissioner of the State of Nicaragua, a copy of which accompanies the note of the Minister of Foreign Affairs of Nicaragua to the Secretary of State of the United States, under date of the 17th of March, 1848. . . .

[2] *House Ex. Doc.* (579) 31st Congress, 1st Session, No. 75, pp. 3–11.

Elijah Hise, having been appointed chargé d'affaires of the United States to Guatemala, received his instructions on the 3d day of June, 1848, (a copy of which is herewith transmitted,) in which it is declared that "the independence, as well as the interests of the nations on this continent, require that they should maintain the American system of policy entirely distinct from that which prevails in Europe. . . .

These instructions . . . authorize Mr. Hise to conclude treaties of commerce and navigation with the States of Guatemala and San Salvador; but conclude by saying that it was not deemed advisable to empower him to negotiate with the States of Nicaragua, Costa Rica or Honduras, "until he should have communicated to the Department of State more full and statistical information than that which it then possessed.". . .

The maps accompanying the correspondence exhibit the extent to which the limits of the Mosquito kingdom have been carried in Central America. One of these maps has been supplied by our present chargé d'affaires at Guatemala; the other is a British map recently published by authority of the British government, and transmitted to the Department of State by our present minister in London. From these and other maps, it appears that the limits of the Mosquito kingdom have been changed from time to time, until they embraced more than half of Central America, and have even been pushed beyond the boundaries of New Grenada, as far as Boca del Toro. . . .

On the 26th day of May, 1848, in a letter addressed to the Secretary of State, Mr. Hempstead represented that the Indians in Yucatan had "applied to her Majesty's superintendent at Belize for protection, and had desired him to take possession of the territory which they occupied, and take them under his protection, as British subjects;" and he further added, that, in the event of the success of their application, "the British government would then have possession of the entire coast from Cape Conte to San Juan de Nicaragua." Again, on the 29th of July, 1848, he wrote: "I have no doubt but the designs of her Majesty's officers, here and on the Mosquito shore, are to obtain territory on this continent." The receipt of this letter was regularly acknowledged on the 29th of August, 1848. . . .

The island of Tigre, in the State Honduras, was occupied by British forces on the 16th day of October, 1849, by order of Mr. Chatfield, her Britannic Majesty's chargé d'affaires in Central America. No instructions appear to have been given to him for that purpose by the British government, nor were any given to the American chargé d'affaires in that country to negotiate for the cession of this or any other territory to the United States. As soon as it was known to me that Mr. Squier had commenced such negotiations, he was instructed that the capitalists who proposed to construct the ship navigation between the Atlantic and Pacific oceans through the lakes Nicaragua and Managua had never applied to this government for any treaty with Honduras on that subject, and that his instructions from the Department of State, by which he should be governed, did not warrant the negotiation of a treaty acquiring more territory for the United States. . . .

With regard to the special convention negotiated by Mr. Hise with the State of Nicaragua, it is proper to remark that, inasmuch as he had been positively instructed to make no treaty – not even a treaty of commerce – with Nicaragua, Costa Rica, or Honduras, it was not imagined that he would act in opposition to his instructions; and in September last the Executive was for the first time informed that he had negotiated two treaties with the State of Nicaragua – the one a treaty of commerce, the other a treaty for the proposed ship canal – both of which he brought with him on his return home. . . .

The twelfth article of the treaty negotiated by Mr. Hise in effect guaranties the independence of the State of Nicaragua, and her sovereignty over her alleged limits, from the Caribbean sea to the Pacific ocean, pledging the naval and military power of the United States to support it. This treaty authorizes the chartering of a corporation by this government to cut a canal outside of the limits of the United States, and gives to us the exclusive right to fortify and command it. The late President did not approve it, nor did he submit it to the Senate for ratification – not merely because of the facts already mentioned, but because, on the 31st of December last; Señor Eduardo Carcache, on being accredited to this government as chargé d'affaires from the State of Nicaragua, in a note to the Secretary of State (a translation of which is herewith transmitted) declared that "the special convention concluded at Guatemala, by Mr. Hise, the chargé d'affaires of the United States, and Señor Selva, the Commissioner of Nicaragua, had (as was publicly and universally known) been disapproved by his government.". . .

◇◇◇◇◇◇◇◇◇◇◇◇◇

3. BRITISH CLAIMS IN CENTRAL AMERICA[3]

[*Abbott Lawrence to John M. Clayton*]

London, April 19, 1850

NOT LONG after my arrival in this country, I became satisfied that there was a very serious difference of opinion between Great Britain and the United States relative to the protectorate claimed by the former over the Mosquito Indians; and, thinking it most probable that I should be called upon officially to defend this difference upon our part, I early commenced, and have steadily pursued, the investigation of that question, using the great means which my locality has placed in my power. . . .

You are aware that the British argument for the independence of Mosquito rests on the following grounds: first, a denial that Spain ever ac-

[3] *Sen. Ex. Doc.* (660) 32nd Congress, 2nd Session, No. 27, pp. 73–98.

quired a title in the territory in question; second, the assertion that whatever show of title she had was abandoned by the treaty of 1670, in view of a long-previous and then-existing "possession" of that country by England, which possession, it is said, was subsequently maintained and further fortified by the submission of several Mosquito kings in succession, and was in existence at the time of concluding the treaties of 1783 and 1786; and, third, the claim that, whatever might have been the former legal condition of these Indians, or whatever might have been the just construction of the treaties of 1783 and 1786, yet, when the States of Central America threw off allegiance to Spain and worked out their independence, those treaties became, by that very act, nullities as to those States, at least until their political recognition by Spain, which Lord Palmerston asserts has never been diplomatically done, and that, in consequence of the want of such recognition, those States are incapable of inheriting *any* Spanish rights in Mosquito, whether acquired by discovery, conquest, occupation, treaty, or in any other way, but must show, to avail, a title acquired by themselves, independently of the mother country. . . .

With these preliminary statements, I now arrive at an examination of the positions taken by her Majesty's government.

The first is a denial that Spain ever acquired any right in Mosquito. . . .

Columbus, in his fourth voyage, first made land on the North American continent at Cape Honduras, near the present town of Truxillo, on the 17th of August, 1502; and thence, proceeding easterly, shortly afterwards entered the mouth of Black river, and, in accordance with his instructions, landed and took formal possession of the country, in the presence of the unresisting natives, in the name of the crown of Castile. In the early Spanish maps this river is called the Rio del Possession, a name given it by Columbus himself, in commemoration of this event. He next touched and took possession at Cape Gracias a Dios, where he remained a short time, holding friendly intercourse with the natives, whom he described more favorably than he did their country. Thence he coasted leisurely southward toward Veragua, communicating often with the inhabitants, and touching particularly at the Bluefields river, and at the mouth of the San Juan. . . .

As early as 1524, Cortez wrote to the Emperor Charles V that only two of the many tribes of Honduras remained unconquered. Shortly after, these yielded to the power of Alverado. Some fled to the mountains and the country now known as Mosquito, where they remained unmolested, protected by their own weakness and by the want of mineral wealth in the soil on which they had taken refuge. They were shielded, too, by a still stronger arm. Spain, ever jealous of the interference of other European powers in her traffic, left this region unsettled, to be a barrier between the Atlantic and the golden regions of the west. But, though she neglected to cultivate, she never neglected to protect and defend. *Guardas costa* were early established to protect the coast, and watch over the argosies as they set sail for the old world.

The natives of Mosquito were thenceforward constantly under the influence both of the Franciscan and Dominican orders of missionaries. From 1575 to a very late period, Spanish missionaries have almost always resided, by order of government, among the numerous tribes of Mosquito. Sometimes as many as twenty at a time were there, exerting a great influence in softening the barbarity of those savage tribes. It is true that many of them were subjected to the most revolting cruelties, and suffered death itself; yet, in almost every instance, these were caused by the hostilities and treacheries of those warlike tribes among themselves, and not, as the English writers assert, by their hatred of the Spanish yoke. The missionary was destroyed, not by the tribe with which he lived, but by its enemies. Fortunately, the histories of the Franciscan and Dominican orders give ample details of these extraordinary missions.

I think I have now established all I promised with reference to the discovery, conquest, and settlement of this country by Spain. . . .

This brings me to the second position of the British government.

By the 7th article of the treaty of Madrid, "it is agreed that the most serene King of Great Britain, his heirs and successors, shall have, hold, keep, and enjoy forever, with plenary right of sovereignty, dominion, possession, and propriety, all those lands, regions, islands, colonies, and places, whatsoever, being or situated in the West Indies, or any part of America, which the said King of Great Britain or his subjects *do at present hold and possess.*" It is plainly of great importance to the present inquiry to determine what lands, regions, islands, colonies, or places, King Charles or his subjects held or possessed in America on the conclusion of that treaty. . . .

The contemporaneous construction of the treaty of Madrid shows that the right of Spain to the whole of Central America was not questioned. Sir William Godolphin, the ambassador to Spain who negotiated and signed the treaty on the part of Great Britain on the 10–20th May, 1672, wrote to Lord Arlington from Madrid as follows: "Your lordship hath required my opinion touching the cutting of logwood in the West Indies by some English on pretence that the parts where they take the same are not inhabited or possessed by the Spaniards. . . . In answer . . . the said wood is brought from Jucatan, a large province of New Spain extending into the North sea like to a peninsula, about a hundred leagues in length, sufficiently peopled in respect of other places of those Indies, having several good towns, as Merida, Valladolid, San Francisco de Campeche, etc., the government thereof being likewise esteemed one of the most considerable there – next to the two vice-royalties of Peru and Mexico." . . .

I shall now assume it to be clearly proved that, in 1670, while the English had no right, either directly or indirectly, in Mosquito, Spain held undoubted sovereignty over it; and shall travel forward to the year 1739, when hostilities commenced between Great Britain and Spain, during which a permanent occupation of this country by the former power was for the first time attempted. Most of the acts of occupation or protection, (for they sometimes take the one form and sometimes the other,) on the part of England, took place between this date and the peace of Paris in 1763, and were either done during a time of hostilities or were themselves causes of a subsequent war. It is plain, therefore, that, being aggressive, they cannot now be used by Great Britain to set up the alleged title in the Indians. . . .

The treaty of Paris assumes to define the respective rights of the parties in Central America. By article 17, it is provided that "his Britannic Majesty shall cause to be demolished all fortifications which his subjects shall have erected in the Bay of Honduras *and other places of the territory of Spain in that part of the world,*" etc.; and then the right is given to the English to cut logwood on the "Spanish coasts and territories." . . .

It is now claimed by Great Britain that, before the conclusion of this treaty, Mosquito had become an independent nation, and therefore was not embraced within its provisions. The argument upon which this is founded involves the consideration of the English title.

Starting from the position that the Indians have never been conquered, and therefore were not within Spanish jurisdiction, (the fallacy of which I have already shown,) all English writers rely on these, and only these, circumstances to establish the Mosquito protectorate—all of which are stated by Lord Palmerston in his note to Mr. Castellon of July 16, 1849: *1st.* A submission by the Mosquito King to the governor of Jamaica, on behalf of the King of England, in 1687, founded on an alleged prior submission between 1645 and 1660; *2d.* A convention between the governor of Jamaica and the King of the Mosquitoes, concluded June 25, 1720; *3d.* Certain reports and resolutions made in 1774 in the House of Assembly of Jamaica.

To all this I might reply, that the Mosquitoes could not of themselves change their political connexion; that, not being an independent nation, all acts done by them as such are void; that the demolition of fortifications shows England's construction of the treaty of Paris; and that the treaty of Versailles uses the broad language of the "Spanish continent," and affirms Spanish sovereignty. . . .

If I have demonstrated that the sovereignty in Mosquito was clearly and unequivocally in Spain, independently of treaties; that it was, therefore, unaffected by treaties, (except so far as acknowledged by them, or so far as the promise not to oppress the Indians;) that it grew out of the relation between the European and the Indian, and followed the jurisdiction of the former; that it vested in the sovereign only through his connexion with the colonist; and, therefore, when the European in the new world threw off his allegiance in the old, it passed into him as perfect as it had existed before in his ancient monarch, resting in the respective States as they had before been bounded under the crown,—if I have demonstrated this, I have no need to go further and touch upon any rights existing by virtue of the treaties of 1783 and 1786. And, indeed, I have used language to very little purpose if I have failed to convey my belief that no new rights were created by those instruments. They only exhibit a solemn abandonment by England of a fictitious claim. . . .

◇◇◇◇◇◇◇◇◇◇◇◇◇◇

4. THE CLAYTON-BULWER TREATY AND MEMORANDA[4]

[*Concluded April 19, 1850; ratifications exchanged July 4, 1850*]

. . . *ARTICLE I.* The Governments of the United States and Great Britain hereby declare, that neither the one nor the other will ever obtain or maintain for itself any exclusive control over the said Ship Canal; agreeing, that neither will ever erect or maintain any fortifications commanding the same, or in the vicinity thereof, or occupy, or fortify, or colonize, or assume, or exercise any dominion over Nicaragua, Costa Rica, the Mosquito Coast, or any part of Central America; nor will either make use of any protection which either affords or may afford, or any alliance which either has or may have, to or with any State or People for the purpose of erecting or maintaining any such fortifications, or of occupying, fortifying, or colonizing Nicaragua, Costa Rica, the Mosquito Coast or any part of Central America, or of assuming or exercising dominion over the same; nor will the United States or Great Britain take advantage of any intimacy, or use any alliance, connection or influence that either may possess with any State or Government through whose territory the said Canal may pass, for the purpose of acquiring or holding, directly or indirectly, for the citizens or subjects of the one, any rights or advantages in regard to commerce or navigation through the said Canal, which shall not be offered on the same terms to the citizens or subjects of the other. . . .

Article IV. The contracting parties will use whatever influence they respectively exercise, with any State, States or Governments possessing, or claiming to possess, any jurisdiction or right over the territory which the said Canal shall traverse, or which shall be near the waters applicable thereto; in order to induce such States, or Governments, to facilitate the construction of the said Canal by every means in their Power: and furthermore, the United States and Great Britain agree to use their good offices, wherever or however it may be most expedient, in order to procure the establishment of two free Ports, – one at each end of the said Canal.

Article V. The contracting parties further engage that, when the said Canal shall have been completed, they will protect it from interruption, seizure or unjust confiscation, and that they will guarantee the neutrality

[4] Hunter Miller: *Treaties and Other International Acts of the United States,* Vol. V, pp. 671–82. The treaty was signed by H. L. Bulwer and John M. Clayton.

thereof, so that the said Canal may forever be open and free, and the capital invested therein, secure. Nevertheless, the Governments of the United States and Great Britain, in according their protection to the construction of the said Canal, and guaranteeing its neutrality and security when completed, always understand that, this protection and guarantee are granted conditionally, and may be withdrawn by both Governments, or either Government, if both Governments, or either Government, should deem that the persons, or company, undertaking or managing the same, adopt or establish such regulations concerning the traffic thereupon, as are contrary to the spirit and intention of this Convention, – either by making unfair discriminations in favor of the commerce of one of the contracting parties over the commerce of the other, or by imposing oppressive exactions or unreasonable tolls upon passengers, vessels, goods, wares, merchandise or other articles. Neither party, however, shall withdraw the aforesaid protection and guarantee, without first giving six months notice to the other. . . .

Article VIII. The Governments of the United States and Great Britain having not only desired in entering into this Convention, to accomplish a particular object, but, also, to establish a general principle, they hereby agree to extend their protection, by Treaty stipulations, to any other practicable communications, whether by Canal or rail-way, across the Isthmus which connects North and South America; and, especially, to the interoceanic communications, – should the same prove to be practicable, whether by canal or rail-way, – which are now proposed to be established by the way of Tehuantepec, or Panama. In granting, however, their joint protection to any such Canals, or rail-ways, as are by this Article specified, it is always understood by the United States and Great Britain, that the parties constructing or owning the same, shall impose no other charges or conditions of traffic thereupon, than the aforesaid Governments shall approve of, as just and equitable; and, that the same Canals, or rail-ways, being open to the citizens and subjects of the United States and Great Britain on equal terms, shall, also, be open on like terms to the citizens and subjects of every other State which is willing to grant thereto, such protection as the United States and Great Britain engage to afford. . . .

DECLARATION

In proceeding to the exchange of the Ratifications of the Convention signed at Washington on the 19th of April 1850 between Her Britannick Majesty and the United States of America, relative to the establishment of a communication by ship canal between the Atlantic and Pacific oceans, The undersigned, Her Britannick Majesty's Plenipotentiary, has received Her Majesty's instructions to declare, that Her Majesty does not understand the engagements of that Convention to apply to Her Majesty's settlement at Honduras or to its Dependencies.

Her Majesty's Ratification of the said convention is exchanged under the explicit Declaration above mentioned.

MEMORANDUM

Department of State, Washington, July 5, 1850

THE within declaration of Sir H. L. Bulwer was received by me on the 29th day of June 1850. In reply I wrote him my note of the 4th of July acknowledging that I understood British Honduras was not embraced in the treaty of the 19th day of April last; but at the same time carefully declining to affirm or deny the British title in their settlement or its alleged dependencies. After signing my note last night I delivered it to Sir Henry and we immediately proceeded without any further or other action to exchange ratifications of said treaty. . . . The consent of the Senate to the declaration was not required and the treaty was ratified as it stood when it was made.

N.B. The rights of no Central American state have been compromised by the treaty or by any part of the negotiations.

5. AMERICAN INTERPRETATION OF CLAYTON-BULWER TREATY[5]

[*James Buchanan to Lord Clarendon*]

London, September 11, 1855

THE UNDERSIGNED, envoy extraordinary and minister plenipotentiary of the United States, has been instructed by the President again to call the attention of the Earl of Clarendon, her majesty's principal secretary of state for foreign affairs, to the Central American questions pending between the two governments, under the convention of the 19th April, 1850.

The President has directed the undersigned, before retiring from his mission, to request from the British government a statement of the positions which it has determined to maintain in regard to the Bay Islands, the territory between the Sibun and the Sarstoon, as well as the Belize settlement, and to the Mosquito protectorate. . . .

After having carefully reviewed and reconsidered all the questions involved, with the light cast upon them by the Earl of Clarendon's statement of the 2d May, 1854, the President has expressed his unwillingness to believe that the positions which he conceives to be rather indicated therein than finally adopted will be adhered to by the British government.

It was, in his opinion, the manifest intention of the convention to exclude both the contracting parties from holding or occupying, as well as from acquiring territorial possessions in Central America; and that this intention is not clothed in ambiguous language, but is set forth in explicit terms. The United States have bound themselves not to acquire any such possessions, and Great Britain has stipulated not to "assume or exercise any

[5] *Sen. Ex. Doc.* (810) 34th Congress, 1st Session, No. 1, pp. 73–5.

dominion over any part of Central America." Indeed, without such a reciprocal engagement, no mutuality whatever would have existed between the covenants of the contracting parties. Whilst the United States are excluded from occupying, colonizing, or exercising dominion over any part of Central America, it cannot be admitted that the same restriction, imposed in the very same language, is not equally applicable to Great Britain.

The President, therefore, confidently believes that Great Britain is bound by the first article of the convention of 1850 to withdraw from the possession she now holds of Ruatan and the other Central American islands on the coast of the State of Honduras, as well as from the territory in Central America between the Sibun and the Sarstoon, which has been encroached upon by her majesty's subjects. He is also of opinion that the possession of the British government at the Belize should be restricted to the limits and objects specified in the treaties between Great Britain and Spain of 1783 and 1786.

In regard to the alleged protectorate over the so-called Mosquito kingdom, the President has instructed the undersigned to say it was his confident belief that this protectorate had been finally disposed of by the convention. It is therefore much to his regret that he finds it is still continued as the basis of British dominion over an extensive region in Central America. . . .

The declaration of the British government, that this protectorate is only employed for the security of the rights of the Mosquito Indians, and that it is ready to abstain from further interference in that country whenever these rights can, in a proper manner, be guaranteed to them, cannot be recognized by the United States as having any foundation in the convention. The President considers this to be a question between Nicaragua and the Indians within its territory, with which neither Great Britain nor the United States has any right to interfere, except in friendly conference with the authorities of that State. . . .

◇◇◇◇◇◇◇◇◇◇◇◇◇◇

6. BRITISH INTERPRETATION OF CLAYTON-BULWER TREATY[6]

[*The Earl of Clarendon to James Buchanan*]

Foreign Office, September 28, 1855

THE UNDERSIGNED . . . has the honor to acknowledge the receipt of the note which Mr. Buchanan . . . addressed to him on the 11th instant. . . .

In answer, therefore, to the questions put by Mr. Buchanan, the undersigned has the honor to state to him, that her majesty's government adhere to the opinion which they have uniformly held, that the convention

[6] Ibid., pp. 76–8.

of April 19, 1850, was merely prospective in its operation, and did not in any way interfere with the state of things existing at the time of its conclusion. If it had been intended to do so, there can be no question but that, in conformity with what the undersigned believes to be the universal rule in regard to instruments of this nature, it would have contained, in specific terms, a renunciation, on the part of Great Britain, of the possessions and rights which, up to the conclusion of the convention, she had claimed to maintain, and such renunciation would not have been left as a mere matter of inference. . . .

But looking to the object which the contracting parties had in view at the conclusion of the convention, namely, the security of the proposed ship canal, the British government consider that the design of the contracting parties was not to disturb any state of things then existing, but to guard against the future creation of a state of things which might by possibility interfere with the security of the proposed canal. That such was the true design of the convention is obvious from the provision in the sixth article, by which the contracting parties engaged to invite every State to enter into stipulations with them similar to those contained in the convention. But if the position of the United States government were sound, and the convention was intended to interfere with the state of things existing at the time of its conclusion, and to impose upon Great Britain to withdraw from portions of territory occupied by it, a similar obligation would be contracted by other States acceding to the convention, and the governments of the Central American States would, by the mere act of accession, sign away their rights to the territories in which they are situated. . . .

The British government neither have the wish to extend the limits of their possessions or the sphere of their influence in that quarter, nor would any British interest be promoted by doing so; but the British government are not prepared to contract either the one or the other, in pursuance of the interpretation of a convention, to which interpretation they cannot subscribe.

The undersigned requests Mr. Buchanan to accept the assurance of his highest consideration.

◇◇◇◇◇◇◇◇◇◇◇◇◇

7. SETTLEMENT OF CENTRAL AMERICAN CONTROVERSY[7]

[*Fourth Annual Message of President Buchanan to Congress, December 3, 1860*]

. . . OUR RELATIONS with Great Britain are of the most friendly character. Since the commencement of my Administration the two dangerous questions arising from the Clayton and Bulwer treaty and from the right

[7] James D. Richardson, *Messages and Papers of the Presidents,* Vol. V, p. 639.

of search claimed by the British Government have been amicably and honorably adjusted.

The discordant constructions of the Clayton and Bulwer treaty between the two Governments, which at different periods of the discussion bore a threatening aspect, have resulted in a final settlement entirely satisfactory to this Government. In my last annual message I informed Congress that the British Government had not then "completed treaty arrangements with the Republics of Honduras and Nicaragua in pursuance of the understanding between the two Governments. It is, nevertheless, confidently expected that this good work will ere long be accomplished." This confident expectation has since been fulfilled. Her Britannic Majesty concluded a treaty with Honduras on the 28th November, 1859, and with Nicaragua on the 28th August, 1860, relinquishing the Mosquito protectorate. Besides, by the former the Bay Islands are recognized as a part of the Republic of Honduras. It may be observed that the stipulations of these treaties conform in every important particular to the amendments adopted by the Senate of the United States to the treaty concluded at London on the 17th October, 1856, between the two Governments. . . .

CHAPTER XVI

THE FAR EAST TO 1868

◇◇◇◇◇◇◇◇◇◇◇◇◇

ALTHOUGH the United States appointed a consular agent to China in 1786, the first official diplomatic mission to the Far East was that of Edmund Roberts in 1832 (1). Mr. Roberts negotiated treaties with the governments of Siam and Muscat but did not attempt to treat with the government of China. Spurred to action, however, by the Opium War and the British success in China, the American government sent Caleb Cushing to China in 1843 with instructions (2) to demand commercial arrangements equal to those which China accorded to the most favored nation. The mission resulted in the Treaty of 1844 (3).

Since it was soon discovered that the treaty with China was difficult to enforce, due partly to the Taiping Rebellion, the American Minister, Robert M. McLane, recommended, in 1854, that the United States should unite with France and Great Britain in an aggressive policy. This recommendation was rejected (4), and the advice of a later Minister, Peter Parker, that the United States should seize Formosa was also rejected. In the instructions, however, written by Secretary of State Lewis Cass to William B. Reed (5), the latter was authorized to exert "peaceful cooperation" with France and Great Britain. The treaty negotiated by Mr. Reed in 1858 (6), and elaborately explained to the Secretary of State in a letter dated June 30 of the same year (7), remained as the basis of American policy in China for ten years.

On several occasions following the mission of Edmund Roberts to the Far East, the American government attempted to enter into diplomatic and commercial arrangements with Japan. It was not until 1852 that Commodore Matthew C. Perry was provided with a strong naval force and instructed to negotiate a treaty. The objects of the expedition and the methods which were to be employed for their accomplishment were outlined in a dispatch from the Acting Secretary of State, C. M. Conrad, to the Secretary of the Navy, John P. Kennedy (8). Commodore Perry concluded a Treaty with Japan March 31, 1854 (10), and the policy pursued by him in its negotiation may be followed in the notes which he transmitted to the Secretary of the Navy on August 3, 1853 and March 20, 1854 (9). Four years later Townsend Harris negotiated a new treaty (11) with Japan which remained the basis of American relations with that country until 1894. It may be instructive to compare the instructions given by the Secretary of State to the Minister to China, Robert M. McLane, in 1855, with the instructions given by a later Secretary of State to the Minister to Japan, Robert H. Pruyn, in 1864 (12).

◇◇◇◇◇◇◇◇◇◇◇◇◇

1. FIRST AMERICAN DIPLOMATIC MISSION TO THE FAR EAST[1]

[*Edward Livingston to Edmund Roberts*]

Washington, 27 Jany., 1832

THE PRESIDENT having named you as his agent for the purpose of examining, in the Indian Ocean, the means of extending the commerce of the United States by commercial arrangement with the powers whose dominions border on those seas, you will embark on board the United States Sloop of War, the Peacock, in which vessel (for the purpose of concealing your mission from powers whose interest it might be to thwart the objects the President has in view) you will be rated as Captain's Clerk. Your real character is known to Captain Geisenger, and need not be to any other person on board, unless you find it necessary, for the purpose of your mission, to communicate it to others.

As you will enter the Indian Ocean from the eastward the first place at which your duties will begin will be Cochin China. Here you will proceed to the capital of the country, Hué, sometimes called Huefoo, or such other of the Royal cities as the King may reside at. . . .

On your arrival you will present yourself to the King, with your power, and the letter addressed to him. You will state that the President having heard of his fame for justice, and the desire to improve the advantages of commerce for the good of his people, has sent you to inquire whether he is willing to admit our ships into his harbors with such articles of merchandise as will be useful to him and his people, and to receive, in return, the products of their industry or of their soil. – That we manufacture, or can bring, arms, ammunition, – cloths of cotton and wool, glass etc. ennumerating all the articles that you find they usually import, – that we can furnish them cheaper than any other nation because it is against the principles of our nation to build forts, or make expensive establishments in foreign countries – that we never make conquests, or ask any nation to let us establish ourselves in their countries as the English, the French, and the Dutch have done, in the East Indies. . . .

You will be furnished with a power to conclude a treaty, if one can be obtained on the terms above specified, and such others as shall hereafter be mentioned, – and to promise, which you may do verbally or in writing, that the usual present shall be made on the exchange of the ratification – of which you may settle a list of such things as may be most agreeable not exceeding ten thousand dollars in value for each Power. . . .

[1] Department of State: *Special Missions*, Vol. I, pp. 73–5.

◇◇◇◇◇◇◇◇◇◇◇◇◇

2. INSTRUCTIONS TO CALEB CUSHING[2]

[*Daniel Webster to Caleb Cushing*]

Washington, May 8, 1843

. . . OCCURRENCES happening in China within the last two years have resulted in events which are likely to be of much importance, as well to the United States as to the rest of the civilized world. . . . The hostilities which have been carried on between that empire and England have resulted, among other consequences, in opening four important ports to English commerce, viz: Amoy, Ning-po, Shang-hai, and Fu-chow. . . .

A leading object of the mission in which you are now to be engaged is, to secure the entry of American ships and cargoes into these ports in terms as favorable as those which are enjoyed by English merchants. . . .

As your mission has in view only friendly and commercial objects—objects, it is supposed, equally useful to both countries—the natural jealousy of the Chinese, and their repulsive feeling toward foreigners, it is hoped, may be in some degree removed or mitigated by prudence and address on your part. Your constant aim must be to produce a full conviction in the minds of the Government and the people, that your mission is entirely pacific; that you come with no purpose of hostility or annoyance; that you are a messenger of peace, sent from the greatest Power in America to the greatest Empire in Asia, to offer respect and good will, and to establish the means of friendly intercourse. . . .

It is of course desirable that you should be able to reach Peking, and the Court and person of the Emperor, if practicable. . . . You will inform the officers of the Government that you have a letter of friendship from the President of the United States to the Emperor, signed by the President's own hand, which you cannot deliver except to the Emperor himself, or some high officer of the Court in his presence. . . . You may expect to encounter, of course, if you get to Peking the old question of the Kotou. In regard to the mode of managing this matter, much must be left to your discretion, as circumstances may occur. All pains should be taken to avoid the giving of offence, or the wounding of the national pride; but, at the same time, you will be careful to do nothing which may seem, even to the Chinese themselves, to imply any inferiority on the part of your Government, or anything less than perfect independence of all nations. . . .

The remoteness of the United States from China, and still more the fact that they have no colonial possessions in her neighborhood, will naturally lead to the indulgence of a less suspicious and more friendly feeling than may have been entertained toward England even before the late war between England and China. It cannot be doubted that the immense power of England in India must be regarded by the Chinese Government with

[2] *Sen. Ex. Doc.* (457) 28th Congress, 2nd Session, No. 138, pp. 1–5.

dissatisfaction, if not with some degree of alarm. You will take care to show strongly how free the Chinese Government may well be from all jealousy arising from such causes toward the United States. Finally, you will signify, in decided terms and a positive manner, that the Government of the United States would find it impossible to remain on terms of friendship and regard with the Emperor, if greater privileges or commercial facilities should be allowed to the subject of any other Government than should be granted to the citizens of the United States. . . .

◇◇◇◇◇◇◇◇◇◇◇◇◇◇

3. TREATY OF PEACE, AMITY, AND COMMERCE BETWEEN THE UNITED STATES AND CHINA: 1844[3]

[*Concluded July 3, 1844; ratifications exchanged December 31, 1845*]

. . . *ARTICLE II.* Citizens of the United States resorting to China for the purposes of commerce will pay the duties of import and export prescribed in the Tariff, which is fixed by and made a part of this Treaty. They shall, in no case, be subject to other or higher duties than are or shall be required of the people of any other nation whatever. . . . If the Chinese Government desire to modify, in any respect, the said Tariff, such modifications shall be made only in consultation with consuls or other functionaries thereto duly authorized in behalf of the United States, and with consent thereof. . . .

Article III. The citizens of the United States are permitted to frequent the five ports of Kwangchow, Amoy, Fuchow, Ningpo and Shanghai, and to reside with their families and trade there, and to proceed at pleasure with their vessels and merchandize to and from any foreign port and either of the said five ports, and from either of the said five ports to any other of them. But said vessels shall not unlawfully enter the other ports of China, nor carry on a clandestine and fraudulent trade along the coasts thereof. And any vessel belonging to a citizen of the United States, which violates this provision, shall, with her cargo, be subject to confiscation to the Chinese government.

Article IV. For the superintendence and regulation of of the concerns of citizens of the United States doing business at the said five ports, the government of the United States may appoint Consuls, or other officers, at the same, who shall be duly recognized as such by the officers of the Chinese government, and shall hold official intercourse and correspondence with the latter, either personal or in writing, as occasions may require, on terms of equality and reciprocal respect. . . .

---

[3] Hunter Miller: *Treaties and Other International Acts of the United States,* Vol. IV, pp. 559–70. The treaty was signed by Tsiyeng and C. Cushing.

Article V. At each of the said five ports, citizens of the United States lawfully engaged in commerce, shall be permitted to import from their own or any other ports into China, and sell there, and purchase therein, and export to their own or any other ports, all manner of merchandize, of which the importation or exportation is not prohibited by this Treaty, paying the duties which are prescribed by the Tariff hereinbefore established, and no other charges whatsoever. . . .

Article XVIII. It shall be lawful for the officers or citizens of the United States to employ scholars and people of any part of China without distinction of persons, to teach any of the languages of the Empire, and to assist in literary labors; and the persons so employed shall not, for that cause, be subject to any injury on the part either of the government or of individuals: and it shall in like manner be lawful for citizens of the United States to purchase all manner of books in China. . . .

Article XXI. Subjects of China who may be guilty of any criminal act towards citizens of the United States, shall be arrested and punished by the Chinese authorities according to the laws of China: and citizens of the United States, who may commit any crime in China, shall be subject to be tried and punished only by the Consul, or other public functionary of the United States, thereto authorized according to the laws of the United States. And in order to the prevention of all controversy and disaffection, justice shall be equitably and impartially administered on both sides. . . .

◇◇◇◇◇◇◇◇◇◇◇◇◇◇

4. NONAGGRESSIVE POLICY OF THE UNITED STATES IN CHINA[4]

[*W. L. Marcy to Robert M. McLane*]

Washington, 26th February, 1855

I HAVE submitted your despatch No. 20 to the President, but he has not yet definitely settled the course which he will instruct you to pursue on several matters therein presented. I think, however, that I can anticipate that he will have serious objections to uniting with Great Britain and France in what you call the aggressive policy – that is the bringing together a united naval force of the three powers in order to obtain the revision of the Treaties with China, securing larger commercial privileges by intimidation, or possibly by force. The powers with which we should cooperate in that case, not to call them allies, would probably have less reluctance to that mode of negotiation than this Government. Such an association would not at all suit the present feeling of this country. It would be hardly worth while to send out the Naval Force for the purpose you suggest without authority to use it in case the mere exhibition of it

[4] Department of State: *Instructions to China*, Vol. I, p. 1056.

did not answer the purpose of intimidation; and it could not properly be used, as you rightly conceive, without the authority of Congress. It is quite certain that a case could not have been presented which would afford any hope that such authority could be obtained from it. . . .

◇◇◇◇◇◇◇◇◇◇◇◇◇

5. AMERICAN POLICY IN CHINA[5]

[*Lewis Cass to William B. Reed*]

Washington, May 10, 1857

I HAVE already announced to you your appointment as envoy extraordinary and minister plenipotentiary from the United States to China, and I am now to furnish you for your guidance with the general views of the President upon the subjects connected with your mission. Many of these views are contained in the communication of April 10 last, from this department, to Lord Napier, the British minister, of which a copy accompanies this letter, and to which your attention is specially directed. You will also receive, herewith, copies of several communications from Lord Napier, and of dispatches from the British government to some of its officers, which disclose the purposes of that government in China, and the measures by which it expects to accomplish them. As to these objects and measures, there seems to be an entire unanimity of sentiment and action between Great Britain and France, extending even to armed cooperation, and you will find from the papers annexed, that the United States have been invited to join the alliance and to participate in its hostile movements. . . .

The objects which it is understood the allies seek to accomplish by treaty stipulations are:

1. To procure from the Chinese government a recognition of the right of other powers to have accredited ministers at the court of Pekin, to be received by the emperor, and to be in communication with the authorities charged with the foreign affairs of the empire.

2. An extension of commercial intercourse with China, which is now restricted to five ports enumerated in the treaty.

3. A reduction of the tariff of duties levied upon domestic produce in its transit from the interior to the coast, as the amount now imposed is said to be a violation of the treaty.

On this subject you will be able to ascertain the true state of the alleged grievance when you reach China, and to act accordingly.

4. A stipulation for religious freedom to all foreigners in China.

5. An arrangement for the suppression of piracy.

---

[5] *Sen. Ex. Doc.* (1032) 36th Congress, 1st Session, No. 30, pp. 6–11.

6. Provision for extending the benefits of the proposed treaty to all the other civilized powers of the earth.

These objects are recognized by the President as just and expedient, and so far as you can do so by peaceful cooperation, he expects that you will aid in their accomplishment. In conformity with this policy, you will communicate frankly with the British and French ministers upon all the points of common interest, so that it may be distinctly understood that the three nations are equally influenced by a determination to obtain justice, and by a desire to procure treaty arrangements for the extension and more adequate protection of their commercial intercourse with China. But on your side these efforts must be confined to firm representations, appealing to the justice and policy of the Chinese authorities, and leaving to your own government to determine upon the course to be adopted, should your representations be fruitless. . . .

This country, you will constantly bear in mind, is not at war with the government of China, nor does it seek to enter that empire for any other purposes than those of lawful commerce, and for the protection of the lives and property of its citizens. The whole nature and policy of our government must necessarily confine our action within these limits, and deprive us of all motives either for territorial aggrandizement or the acquisition of political power in that distant region. . . . You will therefore not fail to let it be known to the Chinese authorities that we are no party to the existing hostilities, and have no intention to interfere in their political concerns, or to gain a foothold in their country. We go there to engage in trade, but under suitable guarantees for its protection. The extension of our commercial intercourse must be the work of individual enterprise, and to this element of our national character we may safely leave it. With the domestic institutions of China we have no political concern, and to attempt a forcible interference with them would not only be unjust in itself, but might defeat the very object desired. Fortunately, however, commerce itself is one of the most powerful means of civilization and national improvement. By coming into peaceful contact with men of other regions and other races, with different habits and greater knowledge, the jealous system of seclusion which has so long separated China from the rest of the world will gradually give way, and with increased intercourse will come those meliorations in the moral and physical condition of its people which the Christian and the philanthropist have so long and so ardently desired. . . .

◇◇◇◇◇◇◇◇◇◇◇◇◇

6. TREATY OF PEACE, AMITY, AND COMMERCE BETWEEN THE UNITED STATES AND CHINA: 1858[6]

[*Concluded June 18, 1858; ratifications exchanged August 16, 1859*]

. . . *ARTICLE V.* The Minister of the United States of America in China, whenever he has business, shall have the right to visit and sojourn at the capital of his Majesty, the Emperor of China, and there confer with a member of the Privy Council, or any other high officer of equal rank deputed for that purpose, on matters of common interest and advantage. His visits shall not exceed one in each year, and he shall complete his business without unnecessary delay. He shall be allowed to go by land or come to the mouth of the Peiho, into which he shall not bring ships of war, and he shall inform the authorities at that place in order that boats may be provided for him to go on his journey. He is not to take advantage of this stipulation to request visits to the capital on trivial occasions. Whenever he means to proceed to the capital he shall communicate, in writing, his intention to the Board of Rites at the capital, and thereupon the said board shall give the necessary directions to facilitate his journey and give him necessary protection and respect on his way. On his arrival at the capital he shall be furnished with a suitable residence prepared for him, and he shall defray his own expenses; and his entire suite shall not exceed twenty persons, exclusive of his Chinese attendants, none of whom shall be engaged in trade.

Article VI. If at any time his Majesty the Emperor of China shall, by treaty voluntarily made, or for any other reason, permit the representative of any friendly nation to reside at his capital for a long or short time, then, without any further consultation or express permission, the representative of the United States in China shall have the same privilege. . . .

Article XI. All citizens of the United States of America in China, peaceably attending to their affairs, being placed on a common footing of amity and good will with subjects of China, shall receive and enjoy for themselves and everything appertaining to them the protection of the local authorities of government, who shall defend them from all insult or injury of any sort. If their dwellings or property be threatened or attacked by mobs, incendiaries, or other violent or lawless persons, the local officers, on requisition of the consul, shall immediately despatch a military force to disperse the rioters, apprehend the guilty individuals, and punish them with the utmost rigor of the law. Subjects of China guilty of any criminal act towards citizens of the United States shall be punished by the Chinese authorities according to the laws of China; and citizens of the United States, either on shore or in any merchant vessel, who may insult,

[6] *Public Statutes at Large of the United States,* Vol. XII, pp. 1023–30. The treaty was signed by William B. Reed, Kweiliang, and Hwashana.

trouble, or wound the persons or injure the property of Chinese, or commit any other improper act in China, shall be punished only by the consul or other public functionary thereto authorized, according to the laws of the United States. Arrests in order to trial may be made by either the Chinese or the United States authorities. . . .

Article XXIX. The principles of the Christian religion, as professed by the Protestant and Roman Catholic churches, are recognized as teaching men to do good, and to do to others as they would have others do to them. Hereafter those who quietly profess and teach these doctrines shall not be harassed or persecuted on account of their faith. Any person whether citizen of the United States or Chinese convert, who, according to these tenets, peaceably teach and practice the principles of Christianity, shall in no case be interfered with or molested. . . .

◇◇◇◇◇◇◇◇◇◇◇◇◇

7. COMMENTS ON TREATY OF 1858[7]

[*William B. Reed to Lewis Cass*]

Tientsin, June 30, 1858

. . . THE 11th article combines the 19th and 21st articles of the treaty of Wanghia, with the additional stipulation that arrests, in order to trial, may be made either by American or Chinese officials.

I may make this article the subject of separate communication, but I cannot allow it to pass now without saying, in the most emphatic terms, that no greater wrong could be done to a weak nation, no clearer violation of the spirit or letter of a treaty, than claiming exemption from local law for our citizens who commit crime, and then failing to punish them ourselves. We extort from China "ex-territoriality" the ammenability of guilty Americans to our law, and then we deny to our judicial officers the means of punishing them. There are consular courts in China to try American thieves and burglars and murderers, but there is not a single jail where the thief or burglar may be confined. Our consuls in this, as in many other particulars, have to appeal to English or French liberality, and it often happens that the penitentiary accommodations of England and France are inadequate to their own necessities, and the American culprit is discharged. Hence it follows that many claim the privilege of American citizenship, in order to have the benefit of this immunity, and every vagabond Englishman, or Irishman, or Scotchman, any one, who, speaking our language, can make out a *prima facie* claim to citizenship, commits crime according to his inclination, secure that if he is tried in the American courts there is no power of punishment. In the case of the murder, the provision of the act of Congress of 1848 is, that before the capital sentence can be

[7] *Sen. Ex. Doc.* (1032) 36th Congress, 1st Session, No. 30, pp. 351–63.

carried into effect, the prisoner must be detained a year in custody. This, so long as the United States refuse or neglect to provide for the erection of prisons, gives to the worst crime the greatest privilege, and the wretch — and I regret to say there are many capable of this crime now haunting the coast — who commits a deliberate murder is sure of escape. I consider the exaction of "ex-territoriality" from the Chinese, so long as the United States refuse or neglect to provide the means of punishment, an approbium of the worst kind. It is as bad as the cooly or the opium trade. Were it not that I have strong confidence that when this matter is fully understood Congress will apply the remedy, I should be ashamed to put my name to a treaty which asserts this boasted privilege of "ex-territoriality." . . .

The 12th article contains a most important modification of the treaty of Wanghia, and one to which my attention was particularly directed by my instructions. The former treaty (article 17) provided for the interposition of the local authorities before the site of any leasehold property could be determined. The effect of this was to create an unnecessary embarrassment; for the officials, knowing that their previous consent was necessary, were always ready to interpose, and forbid the selection of a site which they or any interested or ill-disposed person wished to prevent. No such previous consent is now needed, and perfect freedom of individual contract is secured, and the authorities are only permitted to interfere when there is a direct appeal to them. This change is considered here of great advantage. The concluding provision of the article of the former treaty, which required the local authorities, in concert with the consuls, to define the limits beyond which it would not be lawful for the citizens of the United States to go, is omitted. There is no express prohibition of a citizen of the United States going anywhere in the neighborhood of the open ports, provided he engages in no unlawful trade in fraud of the revenue. . . .

In the treaty of Wanghai, (Article 33), dealing in opium was in terms prohibited to American citizens. In the new treaty I have omitted the word "opium," and left the trade to be dealt with as with that of any other article declared by law to be contraband. My reasons for this were twofold. In the first place, the retention of the word made the open defiance of the treaty more scandalous; and when, at every port, I found Americans dealing in opium freely and unreservedly, and at least one American built, but British owned steamer, with the American flag, plying regularly up and down the coast as a quick carrier of the poison, I felt that it was worse than a mockery to retain the specific prohibition, and much better to class opium in the general list of contraband. Another motive, also, influenced me. In one of the few interviews I have had with Lord Elgin, he expressed a strong wish that the word "opium" should be omitted in the American and Russian treaties. He seemed to think, and I thought with some reason, that it was a reflection on England, who derived a large revenue from the trade, and he assured me that if I would accede to this he would not attempt to legalize the trade by treaty, as he was instructed to do. (Dispatch of the Earl of Clarendon to Lord Elgin, April 20, 1857.) I confess this was an inducement to me, for I could not but believe, from the great indifference the Chinese commissioners at Takoo expressed on the subject, they might be easily persuaded to legalize the trade if the English insisted on it, and I thought Lord Elgin's half-expressed reluctance to comply with his instructions was very creditable to him, believing as I do that he feels a strong repugnance to this infamous traffic, and the connection of his government with it. . . .

The 29th article providing for the toleration of Christianity and the protection of Chinese converts. Though I may have occasion hereafter to address you particularly on this subject so soon as I am informed of the exact stipulations of the other treaties, I beg to say a word or two here in explanation of the form of this article. The recognition of both forms of Christian faith, professed by the Roman Catholic and Protestant churches, is rendered necessary by the fact that in the Chinese language different terms are used to describe them. The sign [Chinese characters] interpreted "the religion of the Lord of Heaven" is generally understood as applying only to the former, while [Chinese characters] or "religion of Jesus Christ" is applied to the latter. In the Chinese text of this treaty both characters are used. . . .

I cannot allow this occasion to pass without an incidental tribute to the missionary cause, as I observe it promoted by my own countrymen in China. Having no enthusiasm on the subject, I am bound to say that I consider the missionary element in China a great conservative and protecting principle. It is the only barrier between the unhesitating advance of commercial adventure and the not incongruous element of Chinese imbecile corruption. The missionary, according to my observation, is content to live under the treaty and the law it creates, or if, in his zeal, he chooses to go beyond it, he is content to take the risk without troubling his government to protect him in his exorbitance. But taking a lower and more practical view of the matter, I am bound to say further that the studies of the missionary and those connected with the missionary cause are essential to the interests of our country. Without them as interpreters, the public business could not be transacted. . . . There is not an American merchant in China (and I have heard of but one English) who can write or read a single sentence of Chinese. . . .

◇◇◇◇◇◇◇◇◇◇◇◇◇◇

8. INSTRUCTIONS TO COMMODORE PERRY[8]

[*C. M. Conrad to M. P. Kennedy*]

Washington, November 5, 1852

AS THE squadron destined for Japan will shortly be prepared to sail, I am directed by the President to explain the objects of the expedition, and to give some general directions as to the mode by which those objects are to be accomplished.

Since the islands of Japan were first visited by European nations, efforts have constantly been made by the various maritime powers to establish commercial intercourse with a country whose large population and reputed wealth hold out great temptations to mercantile enterprise. Portugal was the first to make the attempt, and her example was followed by Holland, England, Spain, and Russia; and finally by the United States. All these attempts, however, have thus far been unsuccessful; the permission enjoyed for a short period by the Portuguese to trade with the islands, and that granted to Holland to send annually a single vessel to the port of Nagasaki, hardly deserving to be considered exceptions to this remark.

China is the only country which carries on any considerable trade with these islands.

So rigorously is this system of exclusion carried out, that foreign vessels are not permitted to enter their ports in distress, or even to do an act of kindness to their own people. . . .

When vessels are wrecked or driven ashore on the islands their crews are subjected to the most cruel treatment. Two instances of this have recently occurred. . . .

Every nation has undoubtedly the right to determine for itself the extent to which it will hold intercourse with other nations. The same law of nations, however, which protects a nation in the exercise of this right imposes upon her certain duties which she cannot justly disregard. Among these duties none is more imperative than that which requires her to succor and relieve those persons who are cast by the perils of the ocean upon her shores. This duty is, it is true, among those that are denominated by writers on public law imperfect, and which confer no right on other nations to exact their performance; nevertheless, if a nation not only habitually and systematically disregards it, but treats such unfortunate persons as if they were the most atrocious criminals, such nations may justly be considered as the most common enemy of mankind.

That the civilized nations of the world should for ages have submitted to such treatment by a weak and semi-barbarous people, can only be accounted for on the supposition that, from the remoteness of the country, instances of such treatment were of rare occurrence, and the difficulty of chastising it very great. It can hardly be doubted that if Japan were situ-

[8] *Sen. Ex. Doc.* (751) 33rd Congress, 2nd Session, No. 34, pp. 4–9.

ated as near the continent of Europe or of America as it is to that of Asia, its government would long since have been either treated as barbarians, or been compelled to respect those usages of civilized states of which it receives the protection. . . .

Recent events – the navigation of the ocean by steam, the acquisition and rapid settlement by this country of a vast territory on the Pacific, the discovery of gold in that region, the rapid communication established across the isthmus which separates the two oceans – have practically brought the countries of the east in closer proximity to our own; although the consequences of these events have scarcely begun to be felt, the intercourse between them has already greatly increased, and no limits can be assigned to its future extension. . . .

The object sought by this government are –

1. To effect some permanent arrangement for the protection of American seamen and property wrecked on these islands, or driven into their ports by stress of weather.

2. The permission to American vessels to enter one or more of their ports in order to obtain supplies of provisions, water, fuel, &c., or, in case of disasters, to refit so as to enable them to prosecute their voyage.

It is very desirable to have permission to establish a depot for coal, if not on one of the principal islands, at least on some small uninhabited one, of which, it is said, there are several in their vicinity.

3. The permission to our vessels to enter one or more of their ports for the purpose of disposing of their cargoes by sale or barter. . . .

The next question is, how are the above mentioned objects to be attained?

It is manifest, from past experience, that arguments or persuasion addressed to this people, unless they be seconded by some imposing manifestation of power, will be utterly unavailing.

You will, therefore, be pleased to direct the commander of the squadron to proceed, with his whole force, to such point on the coast of Japan as he may deem most advisable, and there endeavor to open a communication with the government, and, if possible, to see the emperor in person, and deliver to him the letter of introduction from the President with which he is charged. He will state that he has been sent across the ocean by the President to deliver that letter to the emperor, and to communicate with his government on matters of importance to the two countries. That the President entertains the most friendly feeling towards Japan, but has been surprised and grieved to learn, that when any of the people of the United States go, of their own accord, or are thrown by the perils of the sea within the dominions of the emperor, they are treated as if they were his worst enemies. . . .

If, after having exhausted every argument and every means of persuasion, the commodore should fail to obtain from the government any relaxation of their system of exclusion, or even any assurance of humane treatment of our ship-wrecked seamen, he will then change his tone, and inform them in the most unequivocal terms that it is the determination of this government to insist, that hereafter all citizens or vessels of the United States that may be wrecked on their coasts, or driven by stress of weather into their harbors shall, so long as they are compelled to remain there, be treated with humanity; and that if any acts of cruelty should hereafter be practised upon citizens of this country, whether by the government or by the inhabitants of Japan, they will be severely chastised. In case he should succeed in obtaining concessions on any of the points above mentioned, it is desirable that they should be reduced into the form of a treaty, for negotiating which he will be furnished with the requisite powers. . . .

◇◇◇◇◇◇◇◇◇◇◇◇◇

9. VISIT OF COMMODORE PERRY TO JAPAN[9]

[*Commodore Perry to the Secretary of the Navy, August 3, 1853*]

THE SQUADRON, consisting of the steamers Susquehanna and Mississippi, and the sloops of war Plymouth and Saratoga, commanded respectively by Commanders Buchanan, Lee, Kelly, and Walker, left Napa Keang, island of Lew-Chew, on Saturday the 2d, and anchored off the city of Uraga, bay of Yedo, Japan, on the afternoon of Friday the 8th of July.

I had, before reaching the coast, fully considered and determined upon the course I should pertinaciously pursue in conducting the delicate and responsible duties which had been entrusted to my charge.

It was to adopt an entirely contrary plan of proceeding from that of all others who had hitherto visited Japan on the same errand – to demand as a right, and not to solicit as a favor, those acts of courtesy which are due from one civilized nation to another; to allow of none of those petty annoyances which have been unsparingly visited upon those who had preceded me, and to disregard the acts as well as the threats of the authorities, if they in the least conflicted with my own sense of what was due to the dignity of the American flag. . . .

I was well aware that the more exclusive I should make myself, and the more exacting I might be, the more respect these people of forms and ceremonies would be disposed to award me; hence my object, and the sequel will show the correctness of these conclusions. . . .

On the following morning, the 9th, the governor of Uraga, "Kayama Yezaimon," came on board. . . .

The governor, after a long discussion, in which he more than once declared that the Japanese laws made it impossible that the letter should be received at Uraga, that the squadron must go to Nagasaki, and even if the letter of the President were to be received at this place, a reply would be sent to Nagasaki. In answer to this he was told that I would never con-

[9] Ibid., pp. 45–55

sent to such an arrangement, and would persist in delivering it where I then was; that if the Japanese government did not appoint a suitable person to receive the documents addressed to the emperor, I would go on shore with a sufficient force and deliver them, whatever the consequences might be.

On this being communicated to him, he said he would return to the city and send a communication to Yedo asking for further instructions; that it would require four days to obtain a reply; upon which he was told that I would wait until Tuesday, the 12th, three days, when I should certainly expect a definite answer. . . .

Wednesday, July 13. The governor came on board in the afternoon of this day, apologizing for not being earlier, by saying that the high officer from Yedo had only just arrived; he brought with him the original order of the emperor addressed to the functionary who had to receive me, as also a copy and translation of the same in Dutch, and a certificate of his own verifying the authenticity of the appointment; he also said that the person appointed by the emperor had no power to enter into discussion with me, but was empowered merely to receive the papers and carry them to his sovereign. . . .

Thursday, July 14th. – This being the day appointed for my reception on shore, and every preparation having been made for landing a formidable escort, composed of officers, seamen, and marines, from the respective ships, about 400 in number, all well armed and equipped, and being ready for disembarcation, the two steamers moved to a position commanding the proposed landing-place, (the sloops-of-war not being able to move for want of wind,) and shortly after the detachment forming the escort were in the boats, and on their way to the shore, where they landed and formed, and were immediately followed by me.

The whole shore of the bay, extending more than a mile, was crowded with Japanese troops – from five to seven thousand – drawn up under arms. These troops were composed of cavalry, artillery, infantry, and archers; some of the infantry with flint muskets, others with match-locks.

On landing, I proceeded at once to the building erected for the purpose, and was there received by the prince of Idzu, first counsellor of the emperor, and his coadjutor, the prince of Iwami. To the former of these I presented the President's letter, my letter of credence, and three communications from myself, together with transcripts of the same in the English, Dutch and Chinese languages, for which the prince of Idzu gave me a receipt.

The princes were attended by the governor of Uraga, the chief interpreter, and a secretary.

As it was understood that there was to be no discussion at this meeting, I remained but a short time, taking my departure and embarking with the same ceremony with which I had landed. . . .

It is proper that I should add, in conclusion, that the governor, in the several conferences on shipboard, evinced great anxiety to learn how long

I intended to remain upon the coast, remarking repeatedly that it was the custom of the Japanese government to be very slow in deciding upon matters having reference to foreign countries. Upon these representations, and knowing that the propositions contained in the President's letter were of such importance as to require time for deliberation, overturning as they would, if acceded to, many of the fundamental laws of the empire, I deemed it advisable not to wait for a reply, and for the following reasons:

I had not provisions or water sufficient to allow of my remaining on the coast more than a month longer. I well knew that they could easily and very reasonably defer for a long time any satisfactory reply, for reason of the alleged necessity of calling together and consulting the princes of the empire, as also to consult the dairi or ecclesiastical emperor. Thus I should be put off from day to day, and ultimately be obliged to sail without any satisfaction whatever. This would be construed into a triumph by them and cause a serious injury to the success of my mission.

Taking into view, also, the present disturbed state of China, and the need of one or more ships of the squadron in that quarter, and considering that not a single vessel which had been promised by the department should immediately follow me had yet joined my force, and being without the presents sent from the United States, and those expected in the Vermont, I was glad to have a good excuse for consenting to wait until the ensuing spring for the final answer of the Japanese government.

◇◇◇◇◇◇◇◇◇◇◇◇◇

10. TREATY OF PEACE, AMITY, AND COMMERCE BETWEEN THE UNITED STATES AND JAPAN: 1854[10]

Concluded March 31, 1854; ratifications exchanged February 21, 1855.

. . . *ARTICLE II.* The port of Simoda, in the principality of Idzu, and the port of Hakodade, in the principality of Matsmai, are granted by the Japanese as ports for the reception of American ships, where they can be supplied with wood, water, provisions, and coal, and other articles their necessities may require, as far as the Japanese have them. The time for opening the first-named port is immediately on signing this treaty; the last-named port is to be opened immediately after the same day in the ensuing Japanese year.

[Note: – A tariff of prices shall be given by the Japanese officers of the things which they can furnish, payment for which shall be made in gold and silver coin.]

Article III. Whenever ships of the United States are thrown or wrecked

[10] *Public Statutes at Large of the United States,* Vol. XI, pp. 597–8. The treaty was signed by Matthew Calbraith Perry and Hayashi.

on the coast of Japan, the Japanese vessels will assist them, and carry their crews to Simoda, or Hakodade, and hand them over to their countrymen appointed to receive them; whatever articles the shipwrecked men may have preserved shall likewise be restored, and the expenses incurred in the rescue and support of Americans and Japanese who may thus be thrown upon the shores of either nation are not to be refunded. . . .

Article VII. It is agreed that ships of the United States resorting to the ports open to them shall be permitted to exchange gold and silver coin and articles of goods for other articles of goods, under such regulations as shall be temporarily established by the Japanese government for that purpose. It is stipulated, however, that the ships of the United States shall be permitted to carry away whatever articles they are unwilling to exchange. . . .

Article IX. It is agreed that if at any future day the government of Japan shall grant to any other nation or nations privileges and advantages which are not herein granted to the United States and the citizens thereof, that these same privileges and advantages shall be granted likewise to the United States and to the citizens thereof, without any consultation or delay. . . .

◇◇◇◇◇◇◇◇◇◇◇◇◇

11. TREATY BETWEEN THE UNITED STATES AND JAPAN: 1858[11]

Concluded July 29, 1858; ratifications exchanged May 22, 1860.

. . . *ARTICLE III.* In addition to the ports of Simoda and Hakodade, the following ports and towns shall be opened on the dates respectively appended to them, that is to say: Kanagawa, on the (4th of July, 1859) fourth day of July, one thousand eight hundred and fifty-nine; Nagasaki, on the (4th of July, 1859) fourth day of July, one thousand eight hundred and fifty-nine; Nee-e-gata, on the (1st of January, 1860) first day of January, one thousand eight hundred and sixty; Hiogo, on the (1st of January, 1863) first day of January, one thousand eight hundred and sixty-three.

If Nee-e-gata is found to be unsuitable as a harbor, another port on the west coast of Nipon shall be selected by the two governments in lieu thereof. Six months after the opening of Kanagawa the port of Simoda shall be closed as a place of residence and trade for American citizens. In all the foregoing ports and towns American citizens may permanently reside; they shall have the right to lease ground, and purchase the buildings thereon, and may erect dwellings and warehouses. But no fortification or place of military strength shall be erected under pretence of building

[11] Ibid., Vol. XII, pp. 1051–68. The treaty was signed by Townsend Harris.

dwelling or warehouses; and to see that this article is observed, the Japanese authorities shall have the right to inspect, from time to time, any buildings which are being erected, altered, or repaired. The place which the Americans shall occupy for their buildings, and the harbor regulations, shall be arranged by the American consul and the authorities of each place, and if they cannot agree the matter shall be referred to and settled by the American diplomatic agent and the Japanese government.

No wall, fence, or gate shall be erected by the Japanese around the place of residence of the Americans, or anything done which may prevent a free egress and ingress to the same.

From the (1st of January, 1862) first day of January, one thousand eight hundred and sixty-two, Americans shall be allowed to reside in the city of Yedo; and from the (1st of January, 1863) first day of January, one thousand eight hundred and sixty-three, in the city of Osaca, for the purposes of trade only. In each of these two cities a suitable place within which they may hire houses, and the distance they may go, shall be arranged by the American diplomatic agent and the government of Japan. Americans may freely buy from Japanese and sell to them any articles that either may have for sale, without the intervention of any Japanese officers in such purchase or sale, or in making or receiving payment for the same; and all classes of Japanese may purchase, sell, keep, or use any articles sold to them by the Americans.

The Japanese government will cause this clause to be made public in every part of the Empire as soon as the ratifications of this treaty shall be exchanged.

Munitions of war shall only be sold to the Japanese government and foreigners.

No rice or wheat shall be exported from Japan as cargo, but all Americans resident in Japan, and ships, for their crews and passengers, shall be furnished with sufficient supplies of the same. The Japanese government will sell, from time to time at public auction, any surplus quantity of copper that may be produced. Americans residing in Japan shall have the right to employ Japanese as servants or in any other capacity. . . .

Article VI. Americans committing offences against Japanese shall be tried in American consular courts, and when guilty shall be punished according to American law. Japanese committing offences against Americans shall be tried by the Japanese authorities and punished according to Japanese law. The consular courts shall be open to Japanese creditors, to enable them to recover their just claims against American citizens, and the Japanese courts shall in like manner be open to American citizens for the recovery of their just claims against Japanese.

All claims for forfeitures or penalties for violations of this treaty, or of the articles regulating trade which are appended hereunto, shall be sued for in the consular courts, and all recoveries shall be delivered to the Japanese authorities. . . .

Article VIII. Americans in Japan shall be allowed the free exercise of their religion, and for this purpose shall have the right to erect suitable places of worship. No injury shall be done to such buildings, nor any insult be offered to the religious worship of the Americans. American citizens shall not injure any Japanese temple or mia, or offer any insult or injury to Japanese religious ceremonies, or to the objects of their worship.

The Americans and Japanese shall not do anything that may be calculated to excite religious animosity. The government of Japan has already abolished the practice of trampling on religious emblems. . . .

◇◇◇◇◇◇◇◇◇◇◇◇◇◇

12. AMERICAN POLICY IN THE FAR EAST IN 1864[12]

[*William H. Seward to Robert H. Pruyn*]

Washington, August 20, 1864

LORD LYONS, has by direction of Earl Russell, Her Britannic Majesty's principal Secretary of State for Foreign Affairs, submitted to me for my perusal, in confidence, a copy of the Earl's instructions of the 26 of July to Sir Rutherford Alcock, in relation to the course to be pursued by him at the present moment in regard to the existing troubles in Japan. . . .

The sum of Earl Russell's note is that his policy concurs with the views which are expressed in your aforementioned note. It may be stated as follows:

1st. To give every encouragement and support to such of the Tycoons ministers, and to such of the Daimios as are favorable to foreign trade, and thus lead to the ultimate revoking of the feudal system, and of the exclusive theory of Japan.

2d. To make arrangements with the Japanese Government for the protection of the foreign settlements at Yokohama.

3d. To keep for the present a strong squadron in the Japanese seas.

4th. To endeavor to establish an understanding with the Government of France, the Netherlands, and the United States, with a view to our common interest in Japan.

I have now to inform you that the President approves of the policy thus defined.

In the present condition of our affairs we shall probably find it inconvenient to keep constantly a naval force in the Japanese seas, but we shall endeavor to have some one vessel appear there so often as to make a suitable impression upon the Japanese Government.

The substance of this instruction will be made known to Her Britannic Majesty's Government.

---

[12] *Papers Relating to Foreign Affairs,* 1864, Vol. III, p. 594.

Chapter XVII

CIVIL WAR DIPLOMACY

◇◇◇◇◇◇◇◇◇◇◇◇◇◇

THE CIVIL WAR diplomacy of the United States involved the determination of many important problems affecting the rights and duties of neutrals and equally important problems regarding the Monroe Doctrine. The selections in this chapter relate primarily to the first group of questions and are significant not only for the diplomacy of the era but also for later American policy. At the beginning of the war the foreign policy of the Secretary of State was clearly stated in a remarkable document entitled "Some Thoughts for The President's Consideration." (1) Although President Lincoln did not favor Secretary Seward's ideas, and proclaimed a blockade (2) of Southern ports after the Confederate attack on Fort Sumter, the danger of war with Great Britain was not immediately averted (3). The attitude of the Federal Government toward the rights of neutrals involved a consideration of the Declaration of Paris and a possibile change in the policy which had been formulated with great clarity by William M. Marcy in 1856 (4). The decisions of the Supreme Court of the United States in the *Springbok, Bermuda,* and *Peterhoff,* cases established important precedents in American interpretation of maritime law (5).

The initial foreign policy of the Confederacy is indicated in the instructions of March 16, 1861 (6) to Confederate agents abroad, whose optimistic outlook is shown in their report of July 15, 1861 (7).

The most serious difficulty that confronted Secretary Seward during the first year of the war was the Trent Affair. The Secretary's letter of December 26, 1861 (8) to Lord Lyons was a masterful and ingenious handling of a difficult and precarious situation. From 1861 until the end of the war the Federal government was concerned mainly with the task of preventing European intervention in the war, maintaining its position regarding the blockade, and opposing the construction of ships in England intended for the Confederacy. This was accomplished through threats of a servile insurrection in the South, through the rejection of proposals for mediation (9), and through actual threats of war (10). The success of the diplomacy of the United States during the war naturally entailed Confederate diplomatic defeat. The final appeal of the Confederacy for European recognition (11), December 27, 1864, was indicative of its ultimate collapse.

◇◇◇◇◇◇◇◇◇◇◇◇◇◇

Beginning of Civil War

1. THE FOREIGN POLICY OF WILLIAM H. SEWARD[1]

[*Some Thoughts for the President's Consideration, April 1, 1861*]

FIRST. We are at the end of a month's administration, and yet without a policy either domestic or foreign.

Second. This, however, is not culpable, and it has even been unavoidable. The presence of the Senate, with the need to meet applications for patronage, have prevented attention to other and more grave matters.

Third. But further delay to adopt and prosecute our policies for both domestic and foreign affairs would not only bring scandal on the administration, but danger upon the country.

Fourth. To do this we must dismiss the applicants for office. But how? I suggest that we make the local appointments forthwith, leaving foreign or general ones for ulterior and occasional action.

Fifth. The policy at home. I am aware that my views are singular, and perhaps not sufficiently explained. My system is built upon this idea as a ruling one, namely, that we must

CHANGE THE QUESTION BEFORE THE PUBLIC FROM ONE UPON SLAVERY, OR ABOUT SLAVERY, for a question upon UNION OR DISUNION:

In other words, from what would be regarded as a party question, to one of patriotism or union.

The occupation or evacuation of Fort Sumter, although not in fact a slavery or a party question, is so regarded. Witness the temper manifested by the Republicans in the free States, and even by the Union men in the South.

I would therefore terminate it as a safe means for changing the issue. I deem it fortunate that the last administration created the necessity.

For the rest, I would simultaneously defend and reinforce all the ports in the gulf, and have the navy recalled from foreign stations to be prepared for a blockade. Put the island of Key West under martial law.

This will raise distinctly the question of union or disunion. I would maintain every fort and possession in the South.

FOR FOREIGN NATIONS

I would demand explanations from Spain and France, categorically, at once.

I would seek explanations from Great Britain and Russia, and send agents into Canada, Mexico, and Central America to rouse a vigorous continental spirit of independence on this continent against European intervention.

[1] This document was found by Nicolay and Hay in Lincoln's papers and is printed in most collections of his works. John G. Nicolay and John Hay, eds.: *Complete Works of Abraham Lincoln,* Vol. VI, pp. 234–6.

And, if satisfactory explanations are not received from Spain and France,
Would convene Congress and declare war against them.

But whatever policy we adopt, there must be an energetic prosecution of it.

For this purpose it must be somebody's business to pursue and direct it incessantly.

Either the President must do it himself, and be all the while acting in it, or

Devolve it on some member of his cabinet. Once adopted, debates on it must end, and all agree and abide.

It is not in my especial province;

But I neither seek to evade nor assume responsibility.

2. LINCOLN'S PROCLAMATION OF BLOCKADE, APRIL 19, 1861 [2]

WHEREAS an insurrection against the Government of the United States has broken out in the States of South Carolina, Georgia, Alabama, Florida, Mississippi, Louisiana, and Texas, and the laws of the United States for the collection of the revenue cannot be effectually executed therein conformably to that provision of the Constitution which requires duties to be uniform throughout the United States:

And whereas a combination of persons engaged in such insurrection, have threatened to grant pretended letters of marque to authorize the bearers thereof to commit assaults on the lives, vessels, and property of good citizens of the country lawfully engaged in commerce on the high seas and in waters of the United States:

And whereas an Executive Proclamation has been already issued, requiring the persons engaged in these disorderly proceedings to desist therefrom, calling out a militia force for the purpose of repressing the same, and convening Congress in extraordinary session, to deliberate and determine thereon:

Now, therefore, I, Abraham Lincoln, President of the United States, with a view to the same purposes before mentioned, and to the protection of the public peace, and the lives and property of quiet and orderly citizens pursuing their lawful occupations, until Congress shall have assembled and deliberated on the said unlawful proceedings, or until the same shall have ceased, have further deemed it advisable to set on foot a blockade of the ports within the States aforesaid, in pursuance of the laws of the United States, and of the law of Nations in such case provided. For this purpose a competent force will be posted so as to prevent entrance

[2] Savage, *Policy of the United States Toward Maritime Commerce in War*, Vol. 1, pp. 415–16.

and exit of vessels from the ports aforesaid. If, therefore, with a view to violate such blockade, a vessel shall approach, or shall attempt to leave either [sic] of the said ports, she will be duly warned by the Commander of one of the blockading vessels, who will endorse on her register the fact and date of such warning, and if the same vessel shall again attempt to enter or leave the blockaded port, she will be captured and sent to the nearest convenient port, for such proceedings against her and her cargo as prize, as may be deemed advisable.

And I hereby proclaim and declare that if any person, under the pretended authority of the said States, or under any other pretense, shall molest a vessel of the United States, or the persons or cargo on board of her, such person will be held amenable to the laws of the United States for the prevention and punishment of piracy. . . .

◇◇◇◇◇◇◇◇◇◇◇◇◇◇

3. WAR BETWEEN THE UNITED STATES AND EUROPE A POSSIBILITY[3]

[*William H. Seward to Charles F. Adams*]

May 21, 1861

. . . THIS GOVERNMENT considers that our affairs in Europe have reached a crisis, in which it is necessary for it to take a decided stand, on which not only its immediate measures, but its ultimate and permanent policy can be determined and defined. At the same time it neither means to menace Great Britain nor to wound the susceptibilities of that or any other European nation. That policy is developed in this paper. . . .

Mr. Dallas, in a brief dispatch of May 2, tells us that Lord John Russell recently requested an interview with him on account of the solicitude which his lordship felt concerning the effect of certain measures represented as likely to be adopted by the President. In that conversation the British Secretary told Mr. Dallas that the three representatives of the Southern Confederacy were then in London, that Lord John Russell had not yet seen them, but that he was not unwilling to see them unofficially. He further informed Mr. Dallas that an understanding exists between the British and French governments which would lead both to take one and the same course as to recognition. . . .

Intercourse of any kind with the so-called commissioners is liable to be construed as a recognition of the authority which appointed them. Such intercourse would be none the less hurtful to us for being called unofficial, and it might be even more injurious, because we should have no means of knowing what points might be resolved by it. Moreover, unofficial in-

[3] *Papers Relating to Foreign Relations,* (Diplomatic Correspondence), Washington, D.C., 1861, pp. 71–4.

tercourse is useless and meaningless if it is not expected to ripen into official intercourse and direct recognition. . . . You will, in any event, desist from all intercourse whatever, unofficial as well as official, with the British government, so long as it shall continue intercourse of either kind with the domestic enemies of this country. When intercourse shall have been arrested for this cause, you will communicate with this department and receive further directions. . . .

As to the blockade, you will say that by our own laws and the laws of nature, and the laws of nations, this government has a clear right to suppress insurrection. An exclusion of commerce from national ports which have been seized by insurgents, in the equitable form of blockade, is a proper means to that end. You will not insist that our blockade is to be respected, if it be not maintained by a competent force; but passing by that question as not now a practical or at least an urgent one, you will add that the blockade is now, and it will continue to be, so maintained, and therefore we expect it to be respected by Great Britain. You will add that we have already revoked the *exequatur* of a Russian consul who had enlisted in the military service of the insurgents, and we shall dismiss or demand the recall of every foreign agent, consular or diplomatic, who shall either disobey the Federal laws or disown the Federal authority.

As to the recognition of the so-called Southern Confederacy, it is not to be made a subject of technical definition. It is, of course, direct recognition to publish an acknowledgment of the sovereignty and independence of a new power. It is direct recognition to receive its embassadors, ministers, agents or commissioners, officially. A concession of belligerent rights is liable to be construed as a recognition of them. No one of these proceedings will pass unquestioned by the United States in this case.

Hitherto, recognition has been moved only on the assumption that the so-called Confederate States are *de facto* a self-sustaining power. Now, after long forbearance, designed to soothe discontent and avert the need of civil war, the land and naval forces of the United States have been put in force to suppress insurrection. The true character of the pretended new state is at once revealed. It is seen to be a power existing in *pronunciamento* only. It has never won a field. It has obtained no forts that were not virtually betrayed into its hands or seized in breach of trust. It commands not a single port on the coast nor any highway out from its pretended capital by land. Under these circumstances, Great Britain is called upon to intervene and give it body and independence by resisting our measures of suppression. British recognition would be British intervention, to create within our territory a hostile state by overthrowing this Republic itself. . . .

As to the treatment of privateers in the insurgent service, you will say that this is a question exclusively our own. We treat them as pirates. They are our own citizens, or persons employed by our citizens, preying on the commerce of our country. If Great Britain should choose to recognize them as lawful belligerents, and give them shelter from our pursuit and punishment, the laws of nations afford an adequate and proper remedy.

Happily, however, her Britannic Majesty's government can avoid all these difficulties. It invited us in 1856 to accede to the declaration of the Congress of Paris, of which body Great Britain was herself a member, abolishing privateering everywhere in all cases and forever. You already have our authority to propose to her our accession to that declaration. If she refuse it, it can only be because she is willing to become the patron of privateering when aimed at our devastation.

These positions are not elaborately defended now, because to vindicate them would imply a possibility of our waiving them.

We are not insensible of the grave importance of this occasion. We see how, upon the result of the debate in which we are engaged, a war may ensue between the United States and one, two, or even more European nations. War in any case is as exceptional from the habits as it is revolting from the sentiments of the American people. But if it come it will be fully seen that it results from the action of Great Britain, not our own; that Great Britain will have decided to fraternize with our domestic enemy either without waiting to hear from you our remonstrances and our warnings, or after having heard them. War in defence of national life is not immoral, and war in defence of independence is an inevitable part of the discipline of nations. . . .

◇◇◇◇◇◇◇◇◇◇◇◇◇

4. SECRETARY SEWARD AND THE DECLARATION OF PARIS[4]

THE ADVOCATES of benevolence and the believers in human progress, encouraged by the slow though marked meliorations of the barbarities of war which have obtained in modern times, have been, as you are well aware, recently engaged with much assiduity in endeavoring to effect some modifications of the law of nations in regard to the rights of neutrals in maritime war. In the spirit of these movements the President of the United States, in the year 1854, submitted to the several maritime nations two propositions, to which he solicited their assent as permanent principles of international law, which were as follows:

1. Free ships make free goods; that is to say, that the effects or goods belonging to subjects or citizens of a power or State at war are free from capture or confiscation when found on board of neutral vessels, with the exception of articles contraband of war.

2. That the property of neutrals on board an enemy's vessel is not subject to confiscation unless the same be contraband of war.

[4] Seward to the American Minister in Great Britain, C. F. Adams, April 24, 1861. Savage: *Policy of the United States Toward Maritime Commerce in War*, Vol. I, pp. 416–19.

Several of the governments to which these propositions were submitted expressed their willingness to accept them, while some others, which were in a state of war, intimated a desire to defer acting thereon until the return of peace should present what they thought would be a more auspicious season for such interesting negotiations.

On the 16th of April, 1856, a congress was in session at Paris. It consisted of several maritime powers, represented by their plenipotentiaries, namely, Great Britain, Austria, France, Russia, Prussia, Sardinia, and Turkey. That congress having taken up the general subject to which allusion has already been made in this letter, on the day before mentioned, came to an agreement, which they adopted in the form of a declaration, to the effect following, namely:

1. Privateering is and remains abolished.

2. The neutral flag covers enemy's goods, with the exception of contraband of war.

3. Neutral goods, with the exception of contraband of war, are not liable to capture under enemy's flag.

4. Blockades, in order to be binding, must be effective; that is to say, maintained by forces sufficient really to prevent access to the coast of the enemy. . . .

The declaration was, in due time, submitted by the governments represented in the congress at Paris to the government of the United States.

The President, about the 14th [28th?] of July, 1856, made known to the States concerned his unwillingness to accede to the declaration. In making that announcement on behalf of this government, my predecessor, Mr. Marcy, called the attention of those States to the following points, namely:

1st. That the second and third propositions contained in the Paris declaration are substantially the same with the two propositions which had before been submitted to the maritime States by the President.

2d. That the Paris declaration, with the conditions annexed, was inadmissible by the United States in three respects, namely: 1st. That the government of the United States could not give its assent to the first proposition contained in the declaration, namely, that "Privateering is and remains abolished," although it was willing to accept it with an amendment which should exempt the private property of individuals, though belonging to belligerent States, from seizure or confiscation by national vessels in maritime war. 2d. That for this reason the stipulation annexed to the declaration, viz: that the propositions must be taken altogether or rejected altogether, without modification, could not be allowed. 3d. That the fourth condition annexed to the declaration, which provided that the parties acceding to it should enter into no negotiation for any modifications of the law of maritime war with nations which should not contain the four points contained in the Paris declaration, seemed inconsistent with a proper regard to the national sovereignty of the United States. . . .

The President of the United States has now taken the subject into consideration, and he is prepared to communicate his views upon it, with a disposition to bring the negotiation to a speedy and satisfactory conclusion.

For that purpose you are hereby instructed to seek an early opportunity to call the attention of her Majesty's government to the subject, and to ascertain whether it is disposed to enter into negotiations for the accession of the government of the United States to the declaration of the Paris congress, with the conditions annexed by that body to the same; and if you shall find that government so disposed, you will then enter into a convention to that effect, substantially in the form of a project for that purpose herewith transmitted to you; the convention to take effect from the time when the due ratifications of the same shall have been exchanged. . . .

◇◇◇◇◇◇◇◇◇◇◇◇

5. OPINIONS OF THE UNITED STATES SUPREME COURT IN THE *SPRINGBOK* AND *PETERHOFF* CASES [5]

(A) THE CASE OF THE *Springbok*

. . . WE HAVE already held in the case of the Bermuda, where goods, destined ultimately for a belligerent port, are being conveyed between two neutral ports by a neutral ship, under a charter made in good faith for that voyage, and without any fraudulent connection on the part of her owners with the ulterior destination of the goods, that the ship, though liable to seizure in order to the confiscation of the goods, is not liable to condemnation as prize.

We think that the Springbok fairly comes within this rule. Her papers were regular, and they all showed that the voyage on which she was captured was from London to Nassau, both neutral ports within the definitions of neutrality furnished by the international law. The papers, too, were all genuine, and there was no concealment of any of them and no spoliation. Her owners were neutrals, and do not appear to have had any interest in the cargo; and there is no sufficient proof that they had any knowledge of its alleged unlawful destination. . . .

The testimony of the master was that the vessel was destined to and for Nassau to deliver her cargo and return to the United Kingdom, and that her papers were entirely true and fair. And his testimony in this regard is corroborated by that of the other witnesses. . . .

The case of the cargo is quite different from that of the ship. . . .

Looking at the cargo with this view, we find that a part of it was specially fitted for use in the rebel military service, and a larger part, though not so specially fitted, was yet well adapted to such use. Under the first head we include the sixteen dozen swords, and the ten dozen rifle-

5 Ibid., pp. 460–6.

bayonets, and the forty-five thousand navy buttons, and the one hundred and fifty thousand army buttons; and, under the latter, the seven bales of army cloth and the twenty bales of army blankets and other similar goods. We cannot look at such a cargo as this, and doubt that a considerable portion of it was going to the rebel States, where alone it could be used; nor can we doubt that the whole cargo had one destination.

Now if this cargo was not to be carried to its ultimate destination by the Springbok (and the proof does not warrant us in saying that it was), the plan must have been to send it forward by transshipment. And we think it evident that such was the purpose. We have already referred to the bills of lading, the manifest, and the letter of Speyer & Haywood, as indicating this intention; and the same inference must be drawn from the disclosures by the invocation, that Isaac, Campbell & Co., had before supplied military goods to the rebel authorities by indirect shipments, and that Begbie was owner of the Gertrude and engaged in the business of running the blockade.

If these circumstances were insufficient grounds for a satisfactory conclusion, another might be found in the presence of the Gertrude in the harbor of Nassau with undenied intent to run the blockade, about the time when the arrival of the Springbok was expected there. It seems to us extremely probable that she had been sent to Nassau to await the arrival of the Springbok and to convey her cargo to a belligerent and blockaded port, and that she did not so convey it, only because the voyage was intercepted by the capture.

All these condemnatory circumstances must be taken in connection with the fraudulent concealment attempted in the bills of lading and the manifest, and with the very remarkable fact that not only has no application been made by the claimants for leave to take further proof in order to furnish some explanation of these circumstances, but that no claim, sworn to personally, by either of the claimants, has ever been filed.

Upon the whole case we cannot doubt that the cargo was originally shipped with intent to violate the blockade; that the owners of the cargo intended that it should be transshipped at Nassau into some vessel more likely to succeed in reaching safely a blockaded port than the Springbok; that the voyage from London to the blockaded port was, as to cargo, both in law and in the intent of the parties, one voyage; and that the liability to condemnation, if captured during any part of that voyage, attached to the cargo from the time of sailing. . . .

(B) THE CASE OF THE *Peterhoff*[6]

The Peterhoff was captured near the island of St. Thomas, in the West Indies, on the 25th of February, 1863, by the United States Steamship

[6] Opinion of the United States Supreme Court, December, 1866 (5 Wall. 49–62). Savage: *Policy of the United States Toward Maritime Commerce in War,* Vol. I, pp. 466–76. The important case of the *Bermuda* is omitted because its most essential features are covered in the *Peterhoff* decision.

Vanderbilt. She was fully documented as a British merchant steamer, bound from London to Matamoras, in Mexico, but was seized, without question of her neutral nationality, upon suspicion that her real destination was to the blockaded coast of the States in rebellion, and that her cargo consisted, in part, of contraband goods. . . .

We proceed to inquire, . . . whether the mouth of the Rio Grande was, in fact, included in the blockade of the rebel coast? . . .

In determining the question whether this blockade was intended to include the mouth of the Rio Grande, the treaty with Mexico, in relation to that river, must be considered. It was stipulated in the 5th article that the boundary line between the United States and Mexico should commence in the Gulf, three leagues from land opposite the mouth of the Rio Grande, and run northward with the middle of the river. And in the 7th article it was further stipulated that the navigation of the river should be free and common to the citizens of both countries without interruption by either without the consent of the other, even for the purpose of improving the navigation.

The mouth of the Rio Grande was, therefore, for half its width, within Mexican territory, and, for the purposes of navigation, was, altogether, as much Mexican as American. . . .

We have no hesitation, therefore, in holding that the mouth of the Rio Grande was not included in the blockade of the ports of the rebel States, and that neutral commerce with Matamoras, except in contraband, was entirely free. . . .

We come next to the question whether an ulterior destination to the rebel region, which we now assume as proved, affected the cargo of the Peterhoff with liability to condemnation. We mean the neutral cargo; reserving for the present the question of contraband, and questions arising upon citizenship or nationality of shippers.

It is an undoubted general principle, recognized by this court in the case of *The Bermuda,* and in several other cases, that an ulterior destination to a blockaded port will infect the primary voyage to a neutral port with liability for intended violation of blockade.

The question now is whether the same consequence will attend an ulterior destination to a belligerent country by inland conveyance. . . .

The doctrine of *The Bermuda* case, supposed by counsel to have an important application to that before us, has, in reality, no application at all. There is an obvious and broad line of distinction between the cases. The Bermuda and her cargo were condemned because engaged in a voyage ostensibly for a neutral, but in reality either directly or by substitution of another vessel, for a blockaded port. The Peterhoff was destined for a neutral port with no ulterior destination for the ship, or none by sea for the cargo to any blockaded place. In the case of the Bermuda, the cargo destined primarily for Nassau could not reach its ulterior destination without violating the blockade of the rebel ports; in the case before us the cargo, destined primarily for Matamoras, could reach an ulterior destination in Texas without violating any blockade at all.

We must say, therefore, that trade, between London and Matamoras, even with intent to supply, from Matamoras, goods to Texas, violated no blockade, and cannot be declared unlawful. . . .

And this brings us to the question: Was any portion of the cargo of the Peterhoff contraband?

The classification of goods as contraband or not contraband has much perplexed text writers and jurists. A strictly accurate and satisfactory classification is perhaps impracticable; but that which is best supported by American and English decisions may be said to divide all merchandise into three classes. Of these classes, the first consists of articles manufactured and primarily and ordinarily used for military purposes in time of war; the second, of articles which may be and are used for purposes of war or peace, according to circumstances; and the third, of articles exclusively used for peaceful purposes. Merchandise of the first class, destined to a belligerent country or places occupied by the army or navy of a belligerent, is always contraband; merchandise of the second class is contraband only when actually destined to the military or naval use of a belligerent; while merchandise of the third class is not contraband at all, though liable to seizure and condemnation for violation of blockade or siege.

A considerable portion of the cargo of the Peterhoff was of the third class, and need not be further referred to. A large portion, perhaps, was of the second class, but is not proved, as we think, to have been actually destined to belligerent use, and cannot therefore be treated as contraband. Another portion was, in our judgment, of the first class, or, if of the second, destined directly to the rebel military service. . . .

We are obliged to conclude that the portion of the cargo which we have characterized as contraband must be condemned.

◇◇◇◇◇◇◇◇◇◇◇◇◇◇

6. FOREIGN POLICY OF THE CONFEDERACY[7]

[*Instructions from Robert Toombs to William L. Yancey, Pierre A. Rost, and A. Dudley Mann*]

Montgomery, March 16, 1861

YOU HAVE been appointed by the President, by and with the advice and consent of Congress, special commissioners to Europe. . . .

In view of the importance of the mission with which you are charged, it is desirable that you should proceed to London with all dispatch con-

[7] *Official Records of the Union and Confederate Navies in the War of the Rebellion*, Series II, Vol. III (Washington, 1922), pp. 191–5.

sistent with your convenience and enter upon the discharge of your duties. . . .

Although it will not be necessary to enter into a detailed statement of the reasons which compelled the people of the Confederate States to dissolve their union with the United States, it may be well to allude to some of the more prominent of the causes which produced that result. . . .

You can point with force to the efforts which have been persistently made by the manufacturing States of the North to compel the agricultural interests of the South, out of the proceeds of their industry, to pay bounties to Northern manufacturers in the shape of high protective duties on foreign imports. Since the year 1828, whenever they had the power, the manufacturing Northern States, disregarding the obligations of our compact, in violation of the principles of justice and fair dealing, and in contempt of all remonstrance and entreaty, have carried this policy to great extremes, to the serious detriment of the industry and enterprise of the South.

This policy, the injustice of which is strikingly illustrated by the high-protective tariff just adopted by the Government at Washington, furnishes a strong additional vindication of the wisdom of the action of the Confederate States, especially in the estimation of those countries whose commercial interests, like those of Great Britain, are diametrically opposed to protective tariffs. . . .

The Confederate States have a well-organized Government, instituted by the free will of their citizens in their active exercise of all the functions of sovereignty, and are capable of defending themselves. . . .

As soon as you shall be received officially by Great Britain you will propose to negotiate a treaty of friendship, commerce, and navigation, and you are accordingly furnished herewith with full powers for that purpose. The principal aim of the Confederate States in their policy with foreign governments is peace and commerce. It will be their constant care to employ every means consistent with honor to maintain the one and extend the other. In their traffic with foreign countries they intend to act upon that wise maxim of political economy, "Buy where you can buy cheapest and sell where you can sell dearest." Import duties for mere revenue purposes, so moderate as to closely approximate free trade, will render their market peculiarly accessible to the manufactories of Europe, while their liberal navigation system will present valuable attractions to countries largely engaged in that enterprising pursuit. . . .

The Confederate States produce nearly nineteen-twentieths of all the cotton grown in the states which recently constituted the United States. There is no extravagance in the assertion that the gross amount of the annual yield of the manufactories of Great Britain from the cotton from the Confederate States reaches $600,000,000. The British ministry will comprehend fully the condition to which the British return would be reduced if the supply of our staple should suddenly fail or even be considerably diminished. A delicate allusion to the probability of such an occurrence might not be unkindly received by the minister of foreign affairs, an occurrence, I will add, that is inevitable if this country shall be involved in protracted hostilities with the North.

◇◇◇◇◇◇◇◇◇◇◇◇

7. REPORT OF CONFEDERATE AGENTS IN EUROPE[8]

[W. L. Yancey and A. Dudley Mann to Robert Toombs]

July 15, 1861

. . . WE ARE satisfied that our cause is slowly though surely gaining ground in England, although information of movements in both North and South is derived solely from Northern journals. The public mind here seems to be fully impressed with the falsity of Northern journalism, and receives its statements with much allowance. We are satisfied that the Government is sincere in its desire to be strictly neutral in the contest, and will not countenance any violation of its neutrality. The best-informed Englishmen (and we think the opinion is decidedly the prevailing one), while denying the right of secession and being divided on the question of there being sufficient justifying cause for the movement, seem to agree that the great principle underlying the contest, and by which it should be judged, is that of self-government, and that, looking at the contest from this point of view, eleven great United States have the right to throw off the power of a Union which they think is used to their injury and to form a new Confederacy, and that to resist the exercise of their right by arms is to deny the truth of the Declaration of Independence 1776. Public opinion here as to the power of the North to overcome the South has undergone a considerable change. While it may not be considered as unanimous, yet we are satisfied that it is now the decidedly prevailing impression in the governing circle that it is folly to think that the North can subdue the South. The former opinion that there was a considerable party in the Confederate States anxious for a reconstruction of the late Union has given way before the march of events, and has been abandoned. In consequence, there is now a universal desire to see an early peace established between the two sections, and that England, when occasion offers, should tender her mediation.

We are more fully satisfied of the correctness of the opinion advanced in our previous dispatches that the question of the recognition of the independence of the Confederate States is considered both here and on the continent as but a question of time. . . .

As soon as a favorable military event is officially announced to us we expect to demand an official recognition of our presence here as Commissioners, and to press the question of the recognition of our Government to

[8] Richardson, *Messages and Papers of the Confederacy*, Vol. II, pp. 42–6.

a determination. If such an event does not occur, we are satisfied that we cannot expect it before the cotton is picked and the supply of that article here is exhausted, and no other means of replenishing it can be found than through treaties with the Confederate States.

One other cause of delay in our negotiation is to be found, we think, in the position of the two great parties here. They are nearly balanced, and any move of the Cabinet on that question, for or against us, unless in perfect concert, might well be seized upon by the opposition as the means of overthrowing it. Parliament will be prorogued on the 10th proximo to meet again in February next. We consider it fortunate that the British Cabinet will then have to deal with the question without fear of parliamentary inquiry or discussion at the time. . . .

The British and French Governments are kept well informed by their Consuls and Ministers, and it is evident that the Commission must be at much disadvantage in communicating with those Governments, if in ignorance of occurrences at home. We further suggest that the Commission be kept fully informed of every fact connected with the blockade; of the ports blockaded and the force before each; of those not blockaded; of violations of the blockade; and of captures made by the blockading squadrons.

The blockade question we consider to be the greatest lever which will eventually decide the relations between Europe and the South.

We suggest also that the Commission be kept fully informed of military events, successful or otherwise, that will affect the public mind here. The Northern journals, we have no doubt, will conceal as far as possible our successes and their defeats. . . .

◇◇◇◇◇◇◇◇◇◇◇◇◇

8. THE TRENT AFFAIR[9]

[*William H. Seward to Lord Lyons*]

Washington, December 26, 1861

. . . THE BRITISH government has rightly conjectured, what it is now my duty to state, that Captain Wilkes, in conceiving and executing the proceeding in question, acted upon his own suggestions of duty, without any direction or instruction, or even foreknowledge of it, on the part of this government. No direction had been given to him, or any other naval officer, to arrest the four persons named,[10] or any of them, on the Trent or on any other British vessel, or on any other neutral vessel, at the place where it occurred or elsewhere. The British government will justly infer from these facts that the United States not only have had no purpose, but even no thought, of forcing into discussion the question which has arisen,

[9] George E. Baker, ed.: *The Works of William H. Seward,* Boston, 1884, Vol. V, pp. 295–309.

[10] James M. Mason, E. J. McFarland, John Slidell, and George Eustis.

or any other which could affect in any way the sensibilities of the British nation. . . .

The question before us is, whether this proceeding [the acts of Captain Wilkes] was authorized by and conducted according to the law of nations. It involves the following inquiries. . . .

I address myself to the first inquiry, namely, Were the four persons mentioned, and their supposed despatches, contraband?

Maritime law so generally deals, as its professors say, *in rem,* that is with property, and so seldom with persons, that it seems a straining of the term contraband to apply it to them. But persons, as well as property, may become contraband, since the word means broadly "contrary to proclamation, prohibited, illegal, unlawful." . . .

The second inquiry is, whether Captain Wilkes had a right by the law of nations to detain and search the Trent.

The Trent, though she carried mails, was a contract or merchant vessel – a common carrier for hire. Maritime law knows only three classes of vessels – vessels of war, revenue vessels, and merchant vessels. The Trent falls within the latter class. Whatever disputes have existed concerning a right of visitation or search in time of peace, none, it is supposed, has existed in modern times about the right of a belligerent in time of war to capture contraband in neutral and even friendly merchant vessels, and of the right of visitation and search, in order to determine whether they are neutral, and are documented as such according to the law of nations.

I assume in the present case what, as I read British authorities, is regarded by Great Britain herself as true maritime law: That the circumstance that the Trent was proceeding from a neutral port to another neutral port does not modify the right of the belligerent captor.

The third question is whether Captain Wilkes exercised the right of search in a lawful and proper manner.

If any doubt hung over this point, as the case was presented in the statement of it adopted by the British government, I think it must have already passed away before the modifications of that statement which I have already submitted.

I proceed to the fourth inquiry, namely: Having found the suspected contraband of war on board the Trent, had Captain Wilkes a right to capture the same?

Such a capture is the chief, if not the only recognized, object of the permitted visitation and search. The principle of the law is, that the belligerent exposed to danger may prevent the contraband persons or things from applying themselves or being applied to the hostile uses or purposes designed. The law is so very liberal in this respect that when contraband is found on board a neutral vessel, not only is the contraband forfeited, but the vessel which is the vehicle of its passage or transportation, being tainted, also becomes contraband, and is subjected to capture and confiscation.

Only the fifth question remains, namely: Did Captain Wilkes exercise the right of capturing the contraband in conformity with the law of nations?

It is just here that the difficulties of the case begin. What is the manner which the law of nations prescribes for disposing of the contraband when you have found and seized it on board of the neutral vessel? The answer would be easily found if the question were what you shall do with the contraband vessel. You must take or send her into a convenient port, and subject her to a judicial prosecution there in admiralty, which will try and decide the questions of belligerency, neutrality, contraband, and capture. So, again, you would promptly find the same answer if the question were, What is the manner of proceeding prescribed by the law of nations in regard to the contraband, if it be property or things of material or pecuniary value? . . .

In the present case, Captain Wilkes, after capturing the contraband persons and making prize of the Trent in what seems to be a perfectly lawful manner, instead of sending her into port, released her from the capture, and permitted her to proceed with her whole cargo upon her voyage. He thus effectually prevented the judicial examination which might otherwise have occurred. . . .

I have not been unaware that, in examining this question, I have fallen into an argument for what seems to be the British side of it against my own country. But I am relieved from all embarrassment on that subject. I had hardly fallen into that line of argument when I discovered that I was really defending and maintaining, not an exclusively British interest, but an old, honored, and cherished American cause, not upon British authorities, but upon principles that constitute a large portion of the distinctive policy by which the United States have developed the resources of a continent, and, thus becoming a considerable maritime power, have won the respect and confidence of many nations. These principles were laid down for us in 1804, by James Madison, when secretary of state in the administration of Thomas Jefferson, in instructions given to James Monroe, our minister to England. Although the case before him concerned a description of persons different from those who are incidentally the subjects of the present discussion, the ground he assumed then was the same I now occupy, and the arguments by which he sustained himself upon it, have been an inspiration to me in preparing this reply. . . .

If I decide this case in favor of my own government, I must disavow its most cherished principles, and reverse and forever abandon its essential policy. The country cannot afford the sacrifice. If I maintain those principles, and adhere to that policy, I must surrender the case itself. It will be seen, therefore, that this government could not deny the justice of the claim presented to us in this respect upon its merits. We are asked to do to the British nation just what we have always insisted all nations ought to do to us. . . .

The four persons in question are now held in military custody at Fort Warren, in the State of Massachusetts. They will be cheerfully liberated. Your lordship will please indicate a time and place for receiving them.

◇◇◇◇◇◇◇◇◇◇◇◇◇

9. FRENCH PROPOSAL OF MEDIATION REJECTED[11]

[*William H. Seward to W. L. Dayton*]

February 6, 1863

. . . WHAT M. Drouyn de l'Huys suggests is that this government shall appoint commissioners to meet, on neutral ground, commissioners of the insurgents. . . .

The suggestion is not an extraordinary one, and it may well have been thought by the Emperor of the French, in the earnestness of his benevolent desire for the restoration of peace, a feasible one. But when M. Drouyn de l'Huys shall come to review it in the light in which it must necessarily be examined in this country, I think he can hardly fail to perceive that it amounts to nothing less than a proposition that, while this government is engaged in suppressing an armed insurrection, with the purpose of maintaining the constitutional national authority, and preserving the integrity of the country, it shall enter into diplomatic discussion with the insurgents upon the questions whether that authority shall not be renounced, and whether the country shall not be delivered over to disunion, to be quickly followed by ever increasing anarchy.

If it were possible for the government of the United States to compromise the national authority so far as to enter into such debates, it is not easy to perceive what good results could be obtained by them.

The commissioners must agree in recommending either that the Union shall stand or that it shall be voluntarily dissolved; or else they must leave the vital question unsettled, to abide at last the fortunes of the war. The government has not shut out knowledge of the present temper, any more than of the past purposes of the insurgents. There is not the least ground to suppose that the controlling actors would be persuaded at this moment, by any arguments which national commissioners could offer, to forego the ambition that has impelled them to the disloyal position they are occupying. Any commissioners who should be appointed by these actors, or through their dictation or influence, must enter the conference imbued with the spirit and pledged to the personal fortunes of the insurgent chiefs. The loyal people in the insurrectionary states would be unheard, and any offer of peace by this government, on the condition of the maintenance of the Union, must necessarily be rejected.

On the other hand, as I have already intimated, this government has not

[11] Baker: *Works of William H. Seward,* Vol. V, pp. 376–81.

the least thought of relinquishing the trust which has been confided to it by the nation under the most solemn of all political sanctions; and if it had any such thought, it would still have abundant reason to know that peace proposed at the cost of dissolution would be immediately, unreservedly, and indignantly rejected by the American people. It is a great mistake that European statesmen make, if they suppose this people are demoralized.

Whatever, in the case of an insurrection, the people of France, or of Great Britain, or of Switzerland, or of the Netherlands would do to save their national existence, no matter how the strife might be regarded by or might affect foreign nations, just so much, and certainly no less, the people of the United States will do, if necessary, to save for the common benefit the region which is bounded by the Pacific and the Atlantic coasts, and by the shores of the Gulfs of St. Lawrence and Mexico, together with the free and common navigation of the Rio Grande, Missouri, Arkansas, Mississippi, Ohio, St. Lawrence, Hudson, Delaware, Potomac and other natural highways by which this land, which to them is at once a land of inheritance and a land of promise, is opened and watered. Even if the agents of the American people now exercising their power should, through fear or faction, fall below this height of the national virtue, they would be speedily, yet constitutionally, replaced by others of sterner character and patriotism.

I must be allowed to say, also, that M. Drouyn de l'Huys errs in his description of the parties to the present conflict. We have here, in the political sense, no North and South, no Northern and Southern States. We have an insurrectionary party which is located chiefly upon and adjacent to the shore of the Gulf of Mexico; and we have, on the other hand, a loyal people, who constitute not only Northern States but also Eastern, Middle, Western, and Southern States. . . .

It is true, indeed, that peace must come at some time, and that conferences must attend, if they are not allowed to precede the pacification. There is, however, a better form for such conferences than the one which M. Drouyn de l'Huys suggests. The latter would be palpably in derogation of the Constitution of the United States, and would carry no weight, because destitute of the sanction necessary to bind either the disloyal or the loyal portions of the people. On the other hand, the Congress of the United States furnishes a constitutional forum for debates between the alienated parties. Senators and representatives from the loyal portion of the people are there already, freely empowered to confer; and seats also are vacant, and inviting senators and representatives of this discontented party who may be constitutionally sent there from the states involved in the insurrection. Moreover, the conferences which can thus be held in Congress have this great advantage over any that could be organized upon the plan of M. Drouyn de l'Huys, namely, that the Congress, if it were thought wise, could call a national convention to adopt its recommendations, and give them all the solemnity and binding force of organic law. Such conferences between the alienated parties may be said to have already begun. Maryland, Virginia, Kentucky, Tennessee, and Missouri – states which are claimed by the insurgents – are already represented in Congress, and submitting in perfect freedom and in a proper spirit their advice upon the course best calculated to bring about, in the shortest time, a firm, lasting, and honorable peace. Representatives have been sent also from Louisiana, and others are understood to be coming from Arkansas. . . .

◇◇◇◇◇◇◇◇◇◇◇◇

10. THE QUESTION OF THE IRON CLADS [12]

[*Charles Francis Adams to Lord Russell*]

September 5, 1863

AT THIS moment, when one of the iron-clad vessels is on the point of departure from this kingdom, on its hostile errand against the United States, I am honored with the reply of your lordship to my notes of the 11th, 16th and 25th of July, and of the 14th of August. I trust I need not express how profound is my regret at the conclusion to which her Majesty's government have arrived. I can regard it no otherwise than as practically opening to the insurgents free liberty in this kingdom to execute a policy described in one of their late publications in the following language:

"In the present state of the harbor defences of New York, Boston, Portland, and smaller northern cities, such a vessel as the Warrior would have little difficulty in entering any of these ports and inflicting a vital blow upon the enemy. The destruction of Boston alone would be worth a hundred victories in the field. It would bring such a terror to the 'blue-noses,' as to cause them to wish eagerly for peace, despite their overweening love of gain which has been so freely administered to since the opening of this war. Vessels of the Warrior class would promptly raise the blockade of our ports, and would even, in this respect, confer advantages which would soon repay the cost of their construction."

It would be superfluous in me to point out to your lordship that this is war. No matter what may be the theory adopted of neutrality in a struggle, when this process is carried on in the manner indicated, from a territory and with the aid of the subjects of a third party, that third party to all intents and purposes ceases to be neutral. Neither is it necessary to show, that any government which suffers it to be done fails in enforcing the essential conditions of national amity towards the country against whom the hostility is directed. In my belief it is impossible that any nation, retaining a proper degree of self-respect, could tamely submit to a continuance of relations so utterly deficient in reciprocity. I have no idea that Great Britain would do so for a moment.

[12] *Papers Relating to Foreign Affairs,* 1863, Part I, pp. 418–19.

After a careful examination of the full instructions with which I have been furnished, in preparation for such an emergency, I deem it inexpedient for me to attempt any recurrence to arguments for effective interposition in the present case. Under these circumstances, I prefer to desist from communicating to your lordship even such further portions of my existing instructions as are suited to the case, lest I should contribute to aggravate difficulties already far too serious. I therefore content myself with informing your lordship that I transmit, by the present steamer, a copy of your note for the consideration of my government, and shall await the more specific directions that will be contained in the reply.

◇◇◇◇◇◇◇◇◇◇◇◇◇◇

11. THE FINAL APPEAL OF THE SOUTH FOR RECOGNITION [13]

[*J. P. Benjamin to John Slidell*]

Department of State, Richmond, December 27, 1864

. . . WHAT IS the present aspect of the war now waged in these states? Our seacoast is guarded by numerous fleets, against which we have been deprived of all means of defense by the joint action of France and England. On the land we are pressed not only by the superior number of our foes, but by armies of mercenaries, very many of whom come from British soil to New York and Boston under British flags. While engaged in defending our country on terms so unequal, the foes whom we are resisting profess the intention of resorting to the starvation and extermination of our women and children as a means of securing conquest over us. . . .

Whilst unshaken in the determination never again to unite ourselves under a common government with a people by whom we have been so deeply wronged, the enquiry daily becomes more pressing, what is the policy and what are the purposes of the western powers of Europe in relation to this contest? Are they determined never to recognize the Southern Confederacy until the United States assent to such action on their part? . . . If on the other hand there be objections not made known to us, which have for four years prevented the recognition of our independence notwithstanding the demonstration of our right to assert and our ability to maintain it, justice equally demands that an opportunity be afforded us for meeting and overcoming these objections, if in our power to do so. We have given ample evidence that we are not a people to be appalled by danger or to shrink from sacrifice in the attainment of our object. That object, the sole object for which we would ever have consented to commit our all to the hazards of this war, is the vindication of our right to self-

[13] *Official Records of the Union and Confederate Navies,* Series II, Vol. III, pp. 1253–6.

government and independence. For that end no sacrifice is too great, save that of honor.

If then the purpose of France and Great Britain have been, or be now, to exact terms or conditions before conceding the right we claim, a frank exposition of that purpose is due to humanity. It is due now, for it may enable us to save many lives most precious to our country by consenting to such terms in advance of another year's campaign.

This dispatch will be handed to you by the Hon. Duncan F. Kenner. . . . It is proper, however, that I should authorize you officially to consider any communication that he may make to you verbally on the subject embraced in this dispatch as emanating from this Department under the instruction of the President.

CHAPTER XVIII

EUROPEAN INTERVENTION IN MEXICO

THE AMERICAN government had been aware for some time prior to 1861 that a crisis was near in the foreign affairs of Mexico (1). Domestic revolution and disorder had led to foreign dissatisfaction, and some factions in Mexico had encouraged foreign intervention. Soon after the Mexican government, on July 17, 1861, suspended payments on foreign loans, Great Britain, France, and Spain agreed on joint military intervention. Secretary of State William H. Seward and the American minister to Mexico, Thomas Corwin, thought for a time that foreign intervention could be averted through a treaty arrangement between the United States and Mexico (2). This initial policy having failed, the Secretary pursued a course of action toward Mexican affairs designed to avoid a foreign war in defense of the Monroe Doctrine and at the same time to retain friendly relations with the Mexican government (3). He rejected, therefore, the invitation for American participation in the joint intervention enterprise (4), remained neutral during the French war in Mexico (5), but left the way clear for more drastic action at a later time. When the American Civil War was over and no other serious complications were in the way, the Secretary of State calmly but firmly insisted on the withdrawal of French troops from Mexico (6).

1. THE MEXICAN SITUATION[1]

[Thomas Corwin to William H. Seward]

Mexico City, July 29, 1861

IN MY LAST despatch to the department . . . I suggested the probability of an armed European intervention in the affairs of Mexico, or a partition of its territory.

Since that time events here have given greater plausibility to those fears. On the 17th day of this month the Mexican congress passed a decree suspending the payment of all debts of every sort due from the government for the term of two years.

[1] *House Ex. Doc.* (1136) 37th Congress, 2nd Session, No. 100, pp. 15–17.

The English and French ministers immediately sent in their protests respectively. . . .

At the expiration of the time mentioned in these protests, the legations of both these powers took down their flags and signs, and advised the department of foreign affairs here that all diplomatic intercourse with their respective governments and Mexico was at an end. England and France seem to be acting in concert in this movement. They either intend to frighten Mexico into a repeal of the obnoxious decree, or they take this step as the best and quickest means to initiate such movements as will end in possible occupation of the entire maritime frontier of the republic, which would inevitably lead to the possession of the whole of the interior.

I beg the department to consider whether, *if it be possible,* our duty and interest do not require of us to prevent the consummation of this scheme.

If the interest of the debt due to English bondholders could be secured, say for five years, that alone would put a stop to every attempt of the kind suggested above. The bondholders' debt is now about sixty-two millions, bearing an interest of three per cent. per annum. The interest on this debt would amount to less than two millions a year. If Mexico should offer any equivalent acceptable to our government for the guarantee of the payment of this interest for five years, would it not be our interest to close with such a proposition?

England and Spain are now in possession of the best of the West India islands, (for I consider San Domingo is certain to fall into the hands of Spain before our rebellion is quelled,) and Mexico a colony of England, with the British power on the north of our possessions, would leave on the map of this continent a very insignificant part for the United States, especially should the present unnatural rebellion end in the final severance from us of eight or nine, or all of the slave States.

Mexico, I am persuaded, would be willing to pledge all her public lands and mineral rights in Lower California, Chihuahua, Sonora, and Sinaloa, as well as her national faith, for the payment of this guarantee. This would probably end in the cession of the sovereignty to us. It would be certain to end thus if the money were not promptly paid as agreed on. By such an arrangement two consequences would follow: First, all hope of extending the dominion of a *separate* southern republic in this quarter or in Central America would be extinguished, and any further attempt in all time to come to establish European power on this continent would cease to occupy the minds of either England or continental Europe. If the republics of Mexico or Central America could maintain themselves against southern filibusters or European cupidity, I should not desire either to intermeddle in their concerns or add any of their territory to ours, except, perhaps, Lower California, which may become indispensable to the protection of our Pacific possessions.

The reasons, however, for a departure from this rule, arising out of our present apparent weakness, stimulating aggression, as well by filibusters as Europeans seem to demand serious consideration. The United States are the only safe guardians of the independence and true civilization of this continent. It is their mission, and they should fulfil it. This task would have been comparatively easy but for the madness of the south, plunging us into our present difficulties.

Europe is quite willing to see us humbled, and will not fail to take advantage of our embarrassments to execute purposes of which she would not have dreamed had we remained at peace.

I repeat these suggestions as my reasons for desiring instructions on the points stated above, relating to aid to Mexico in some form suitable to her present exigencies. . . .

2. PROPOSAL FOR TREATY BETWEEN THE UNITED STATES AND MEXICO[2]

[*William H. Seward to Thomas Corwin*]

Washington, September 2, 1861

YOUR DESPATCH of the 29th July last, numbered 3, has just now been received. The account of the Mexican complications which it gives is painfully interesting. The President greatly desires that the political *status* of Mexico as an independent nation shall be permanently maintained. The events you communicate alarm him upon this point; and he conceives that the people of the United States would scarcely justify him were he to make no effort for preventing so great a calamity on this continent as would be the extinction of that republic. He has therefore determined to authorize and empower you, and you are hereby authorized and empowered, to negotiate a treaty with the republic of Mexico for the assumption by the government of the United States of the payment of the interest, at three per cent., upon the funded debt of that country due to Mexican bondholders, the principal of which is understood to be about sixty-two millions of dollars, for the term of five years from the date of the decree recently issued by the government of Mexico suspending such payment, provided that that government will pledge to the United States its faith for the reimbursement of the money so to be paid, with six per cent. interest thereon, to be secured by a specific lien upon all the public lands and mineral rights in the several Mexican States of Lower California, Chihuahua, Sonora, and Sinaloa, the property so pledged to become absolute in the United States at the expiration of the term of six years from the time when the treaty shall go into effect, if such reimbursement shall not have been made before that time. This course is rendered necessary by circumstances as new as they are eventful, while the Mexican crisis seems to ad-

[2] Ibid., p. 22.

mit of no delay. The President therefore accepts the responsibility, and will submit his action in the premises to the consideration of the Senate of the United States, so soon as that body shall be convened, for the constitutional sanction, without which the treaty when made would be of no effect.

It must be understood, however, that these instructions are conditional upon the attainment of consent on the part of the British and French governments to forbear from resort to action against Mexico on account of her failure or refusal to pay the interest in question until after the treaty shall have been submitted to the Senate, and, if ratified, then so long thereafter as the interest shall be punctually paid by the government of the United States. I shall immediately instruct our ministers in London and Paris to apply to the British and French governments for their consent to the terms thus indicated. You will see at once the importance of urging the Mexican government to give its best efforts to the support of these applications.

I am to be understood, moreover, as giving you not specific but general instructions, to be modified as to sums, terms, securities, and other points, as you may find necessary, subject to approval when made known to me. . . .

3. REJECTION OF THE PROPOSAL FOR JOINT ACTION IN MEXICO[3]

[*William H. Seward to Spanish, French, and British Ministers in Washington*]

Washington, December 4, 1861

THE UNDERSIGNED, Secretary of State of the United States, has the honor to acknowledge the receipt of a note which was addressed to him on the 30th day of November last, by Mr. Gabriel G. y Tassara, minister plenipotentiary of her Majesty the Queen of Spain; Mr. Henri Mercier, minister plenipotentiary of his Majesty the Emperor of the French; and the Lord Lyons, minister plenipotentiary of her Majesty the Queen of the United Kingdom of Great Britain and Ireland.

With that paper, the aforesaid ministers have submitted the text of a convention which was concluded at London on the 31st of October last, between the sovereigns beforenamed, with a view of obtaining, through a common action, the redress of their grievances against the republic of Mexico. . . .

The plenipotentiaries, in their note to the undersigned, invite the United States to accede to the convention. The undersigned, having submitted the subject to the President, will proceed to communicate his views thereon.

[3] Ibid., pp. 187–90.

First. As the undersigned has heretofore had the honor to inform each of the plenipotentiaries now addressed, the President does not feel himself at liberty to question, and he does not question, that the sovereigns represented have undoubted right to decide for themselves the fact whether they have sustained grievances, and to resort to war against Mexico for the redress thereof, and have a right also to levy the war severally or jointly.

Secondly. The United States have a deep interest which, however, they are happy to believe is an interest held by them in common with the high contracting powers and with all other civilized states, that neither the sovereigns by whom the convention has been concluded shall seek or obtain any acquisition of territory or any advantage peculiar to itself, and not equally left open to the United States and every other civilized state, within the territories of Mexico, and especially that neither one nor all of the contracting parties shall, as a result or consequence of the hostilities to be inaugurated under convention, exercise in the subsequent affairs of Mexico any influence of a character to impair the right of the Mexican people to choose and freely to constitute the form of its own government.

The undersigned renews on this occasion the acknowledgment heretofore given, that each of the high contracting parties had informed the United States substantially, that they recognized this interest, and he is authorized to express the satisfaction of the President with the terms in which that recognition is clearly embodied in the treaty itself.

It is true, as the high contracting parties assume, that the United States have, on their part, claims to urge against Mexico. Upon due consideration, however, the President is of opinion that it would be inexpedient to seek satisfaction of their claims at this time through an act of accession to the convention. Among the reasons for this decision which the undersigned is authorized to assign, are, first, that the United States, so far as it is practicable, prefer to adhere to a traditional policy recommended to them by the father of their country and confirmed by a happy experience, which forbids them from making alliances with foreign nations; second, Mexico being a neighbor of the United States on this continent, and possessing a system of government similar to our own in many of its important features, the United States habitually cherish a decided good will towards that republic, and a lively interest in its security, prosperity, and welfare. . . .

The undersigned is further authorized to state to the plenipotentiaries, for the information of the sovereigns of Spain, France, and Great Britain, that the United States are so earnestly anxious for the safety and welfare of the republic of Mexico, that they have already empowered their minister residing there to enter into a treaty with the Mexican republic, conceding to it some material aid and advantages which it is hoped may enable that republic to satisfy the just claims and demands of the said sovereigns, and so avert the war which these sovereigns have agreed among each other to levy against Mexico. The sovereigns need not be informed that this proposal to Mexico has been made, not in hostility to them, but with a knowledge of the proceeding formally communicated to them, and with the hope that they might find, through the increased ability of Mexico to result from the treaty, and her willingness to treat with them upon just terms, a mode of averting the hostilities which it is the object of the convention now under consideration to inaugurate. What has thus far been done by the American minister at Mexico, under those instructions, has not yet become known to this government, and the information is looked for with deep interest. . . .

◇◇◇◇◇◇◇◇◇◇◇◇◇

4. AMERICAN ATTITUDE TOWARD EUROPEAN INTERVENTION IN MEXICO[4]

[*William H. Seward to Charles Francis Adams*]

Washington, 3 March, 1862

WE OBSERVE indications of a growing opinion in Europe that the demonstrations which are being made by Spanish, French and British forces against Mexico, are likely to be attended by a revolution in that country which will bring in a monarchical government there, in which the crown will be assumed by some foreign Prince. This country is deeply concerned in the peace of nations and aims to be loyal at the same time in all its relations as well to the Allies as to Mexico. The President has therefore instructed me to submit his views on the new aspect of affairs to the parties concerned.

He has relied upon the assurances given to this government by the Allies that they were seeking no political objects, and only a redress of grievances. He does not doubt the sincerity of the Allies, and his confidence in their good faith, if it could be shaken, would be reinspired by explanations apparently made in their behalf, that the governments of Spain, France, and Great Britain are not intending to intervene, and will not intervene to effect a change of the Constitutional form of government now existing in Mexico, or to produce any political change there in opposition to the will of the Mexican people. Indeed, he understands the Allies to be unanimous in declaring that the proposed revolution in Mexico is moved only by Mexican citizens now in Europe.

The President, however, deems it his duty to express to the Allies, in all candor and frankness, the opinion that no monarchical government which could be founded in Mexico, in the presence of foreign navies and armies in the waters, and upon the soil of Mexico, would have any prospect of security or permanence.

Secondly, that the instability of such a monarchy there, would be en-

[4] Department of State: *Instructions to Great Britain,* Vol. XVIII, pp. 138–40.

hanced if the throne should be assigned to any person not of Mexican nativity. That, under such circumstances, the new government must speedily fall, unless it could draw into its support European alliances, which, relating back to the first invasion, would in fact make it the beginning of a permanent policy of armed European monarchical intervention, injurious and practically hostile to the most general system of government on the continent of America, and this would be the beginning rather than the ending of revolution in Mexico.

These views are grounded upon some knowledge of the political sentiments and habits of society in America.

In such a case, it is not to be doubted that the permanent interests and sympathies of this country would be with the other American republics. It is not intended, on this occasion, to predict the course of events which might happen as a consequence of the proceeding contemplated, either on this continent or in Europe. It is sufficient to say that, in the President's opinion, the emancipation of this continent from European control, has been the principal feature in its history during the last century. It is not probable that a revolution in a contrary direction would be successful in an immediately succeeding century, while population in America is so rapidly increasing, resources so rapidly developing, and society so steadily forming itself upon principles of Democratic American government. Nor is it necessary to suggest to the Allies the improbability that European nations could steadily agree upon a policy favorable to such a counter-revolution as one conducive to their own interests, or to suggest that, however studiously, the allies may act to avoid lending the aid of their land and naval forces to domestic revolutions in Mexico, the result would nevertheless be traceable to the presence of those forces there, although for a different purpose, since it may be deemed certain that, but for their presence there, no such revolution could probably have been attempted or even conceived.

The Senate of the United States has not indeed given its official sanction to the precise measures which the President has proposed for lending our aid to the existing government in Mexico, with the approval of the Allies, to relieve it from its present embarrassments. This however, is only a question of domestic administration. It would be very erroneous to regard such a disagreement as indicating any serious difference of opinion in this Government or among the American people, in their cordial good wishes for the safety, welfare and stability of the republican system of government in that country.

◇◇◇◇◇◇◇◇◇◇◇◇◇

5. THE OBJECTIVES OF FRANCE IN MEXICO[5]

[*Napoleon III to General Forey*]

"Fontainebleau," July 3, 1862

AT THE MOMENT when you are about to leave for Mexico, charged with political and military powers, I deem it useful that you should understand my wishes.

"This is the line of conduct which you are expected to pursue: 1. To issue a proclamation on your arrival, the principal ideas of which will be indicated to you. 2. To receive with the greatest kindness all Mexicans who may join you. 3. To expouse the quarrel of no party, but to announce that all is provisional until the Mexican nation shall have declared its wishes; to show a great respect for religion, but to reassure at the same time the holders of national property. 4. To supply, pay, and arm, according to your ability, the auxiliary Mexican troops: to give them the chief part in combats. 5. To maintain among your troops, as well as among the auxiliaries, the most severe discipline; to repress with vigor every act, every design, which might wound the Mexicans, for their pride of character must not be forgotten, and it is of the first importance to the success of the undertaking to conciliate the good will of the people.

"When we shall have reached the city of Mexico, it is desirable that you should have an understanding with the notable persons of every shade of opinion who shall have espoused our cause, in order to organize a provisional government. This government will submit to the Mexican people the question of the form of political rule which shall be definitively established. An assembly will be afterwards elected in accordance with the Mexican laws.

"You will aid the new government to introduce into the administration of affairs, and especially into the finances, that regularity of which France offers the best example. To effect this, persons will be sent thither capable of aiding this new organization.

"The end to be attained is not to impose upon the Mexicans a form of government which will be distasteful to them, but to aid them to establish, in conformity with their wishes, a government which may have some chance of stability, and will assure to France the redress of the wrongs of which she complains.

"It is not to be denied that if they prefer a monarchy it is in the interest of France to aid them in this path.

"Persons will not be wanting who will ask you why we propose to spend men and money to establish a regular government in Mexico.

"In the present state of the world's civilization Europe is not indifferent to the prosperity of America; for it is she which nourishes our industry and gives life to our commerce. It is our interest that the republic of the United

[5] *Sen. Ex. Doc.* (1209) 38th Congress, 2nd Session, No. 11, pp. 272–3.

States shall be powerful and prosperous, but it is not at all to our interest that she should grasp the whole Gulf of Mexico, rule thence the Antilles as well as South America, and be the sole dispenser of the products of the New World. We see to-day, by sad experience, how precarious is the fate of an industry which is forced to seek its raw material in a single market, under all the vicissitudes to which that market is subject.

"If, on the contrary, Mexico preserve its independence, and maintain the integrity of its territory, if a stable government be there established with the aid of France, we shall have restored to the Latin race on the other side of the ocean its force and its prestige; we shall have guaranteed the safety of our own and the Spanish colonies in the Antilles. We shall have established our benign influence in the centre of America, and this influence, while creating immense outlets for our commerce, will procure the raw material which is indispensable to our industry.

"Mexico thus regenerated will always be favorable to us, not only from gratitude, but also because her interests will be identical with our own, and because she will find a support in the good will of European powers.

"To-day, therefore, our military honor involved, the demands of our policy, the interest of our industry and our commerce, all impose upon us the duty of marching upon Mexico, there boldly planting our flag, and establishing perhaps a monarchy, if not incompatible with the national sentiment of the country, but at least a government which will promise some stability.

◇◇◇◇◇◇◇◇◇◇◇◇◇

6. DEMAND FOR THE WITHDRAWAL OF FRENCH TROOPS FROM MEXICO[6]

[*William H. Seward to the Marquis de Montholon*]

Washington, February 12, 1866

. . . FRANCE is entitled, by every consideration of respect and friendship, to interpret for herself the objects of the expedition, and of the whole of her proceedings in Mexico. Her explanation of those motives and objects is, therefore, accepted on our part with the consideration and confidence which we expect for explanations of our own when assigned to France or any other friendly power. Nevertheless, it is my duty to insist that, whatever were the intentions, purposes, and objects of France, the proceedings which were adopted by a class of Mexicans for subverting the republican government there, and for availing themselves of French intervention to establish on its ruins an imperial monarchy, are regarded by the United States as having been taken without the authority, and prosecuted against the will and opinions, of the Mexican people. For these reasons it seems to this government that, in supporting institutions thus established in derogation of the inalienable rights of the people of Mexico,

[6] *House Ex. Doc.* (1261) 39th Congress, 1st Session, No. 93, pp. 589–98.

the original purposes and objects of the French expedition, though they have not been, as a military demand of satisfaction, abandoned, nor lost out of view by the Emperor of the French, were, nevertheless, left to fall into a condition in which they seem to have become subordinate to a political revolution, which certainly would have not occurred if France had not forcibly intervened, and which, judging from the genius and character of the Mexican people, would not now be maintained by them if that armed intervention should cease. The United States have not seen any satisfactory evidence that the people of Mexico have spoken, and have called into being or accepted the so-called empire which it is insisted has been set up in their capital. The United States, as I have remarked on other occasions, are of opinion that such an acceptance could not have been freely procured or lawfully taken at any time in the presence of the French army of invasion. The withdrawal of the French forces is deemed necessary to allow such a proceeding to be taken by Mexico. Of course the Emperor of France is entitled to determine the aspect in which the Mexican situation ought to be regarded by him. Nevertheless, the view which I have thus presented is the one which this nation has accepted. It therefore recognizes, and must continue to recognize, in Mexico only the ancient republic, and it can in no case consent to involve itself, either directly or indirectly, in relation with or recognition of the institution of the Prince Maximilian in Mexico.

This position is held, I believe, without one dissenting voice by our countrymen. I do not presume to say that this opinion of the American people is accepted or will be adopted generally by other foreign powers, or by the public opinion of mankind. The Emperor is quite competent to form a judgment upon this important point for himself. I cannot, however, properly exclude the observation that, while this question affects by its bearings, incidentally, every republican state in the American hemisphere, every one of those states has adopted the judgment which, on the behalf of the United States, is herein expressed. Under these circumstances it has happened, either rightfully or wrongfully, that the presence of European armies in Mexico, maintaining a European prince with imperial attributes, without her consent and against her will, is deemed a source of apprehension and danger, not alone to the United States, but also to all the independent and sovereign republican States founded on the American continent and its adjacent islands. France is acquainted with the relations of the United States towards the other American States to which I have referred, and is aware of the sense that the American people entertain in regard to the obligations and duties due from them to those other States. We are thus brought back to the single question which formed the subject of my communication of the 6th of December last, namely, the desirableness of an adjustment of a question the continuance of which must be necessarily prejudicial to the harmony and friendship which have hitherto always existed between the United States and France. . . .

The United States have not claimed, and they do not claim, to know what arrangements the Emperor may make for the adjustment of claims for indemnity and redress in Mexico. It would be, on our part, an act of intervention to take cognizance of them. We adhere to our position that the war in question has become a political war between France and the republic of Mexico, injurious and dangerous to the United States and to the republican cause, and we ask only that in that aspect and character it may be brought to an end. It would be illiberal on the part of the United States to suppose that, in desiring or pursuing preliminary arrangements, the Emperor contemplates the establishment in Mexico, before withdrawing his forces, of the very institutions which constitute the material ground of the exceptions taken against his intervention by the United States. It would be still more illiberal to suppose for a moment that he expects the United States to bind themselves indirectly to acquiesce in or support the obnoxious institutions.

On the contrary, we understand him as announcing to us his immediate purpose to bring to an end the service of his armies in Mexico, to withdraw them, and in good faith to fall back, without stipulation or condition on our part, upon the principle of non-intervention upon which he is henceforth agreed with the United States. We cannot understand his appeal to us for an assurance that we ourselves will abide by our own principles of non-intervention in any other sense than as the expression, in a friendly way, of his expectation that when the people of Mexico shall have been left absolutely free from the operation, effects, and consequences of his own political and military intervention, we will ourselves respect their self-established sovereignty and independence. . . .

With these explanations I proceed to say that, in the opinion of the President France need not for a moment delay her promised withdrawal of military forces from Mexico, and her putting the principle of non-intervention into full and complete practice in regard to Mexico, through any apprehension that the United States will prove unfaithful to the principles and policy in that respect which, on their behalf, it has been my duty to maintain in this now very lengthened correspondence. The practice of this government, from its beginning, is a guarantee to all nations of the respect of the American people for the free sovereignty of the people in every other state. We received the instruction from Washington. We applied it sternly in our early intercourse even with France. The same principle and practice have been uniformly inculcated by all our statesmen, interpreted by all our jurists, maintained by all our Congresses, and acquiesced in without practical dissent on all occasions by the American people. It is in reality the chief element of foreign intercourse in our history. Looking simply toward the point to which our attention has been steadily confined, the relief of the Mexican embarrassments without disturbing our relations with France, we shall be gratified when the Emperor shall give to us, either through the channel of your esteemed correspondence or otherwise, definitive information of the time when French military operations may be expected to cease in Mexico. . . .

Chapter XIX

ALASKA, SANTO DOMINGO, AND THE DANISH WEST INDIES

DURING the years immediately following the Civil War a good portion of the American people experienced a wave of expansionist enthusiasm not unlike that which had swept over the country during the decade of the "roaring forties." Seward's Mexican policy of 1861 implied the expansion of the United States into northern Mexico, Alaska was annexed in 1867, an attempt was made to acquire Santo Domingo and the Danish West Indies, and a few people, at least, cast covetous eyes toward Canada. The treaty with Mexico which might have resulted in the acquisition of territory by the United States was not ratified by the Senate, but the annexation of Alaska was accomplished quickly and without a great deal of diplomatic correspondence (1). The project for the annexation of Santo Domingo, however, experienced a hectic career and finally ended in a fiasco. In that connection it is profitable to read the instructions given by the Secretary of State authorizing the treaty of annexation (2), the reasons presented by the President to Congress showing why its annexation was desirable (3), and the acrid address of Senator Sumner in opposition to the measure (4). The details of the project to purchase the Danish West Indies are probably most succinctly recorded in a report of the Committee on Foreign Relations of the Senate of the United States, March 31, 1898 (5).

1. THE ACQUISITION OF ALASKA[1]

[*Treaty for the Cession of the Russian Possessions in North America; Concluded March 30, 1867; ratifications exchanged June 20, 1867*]

. . . *ARTICLE I.* His Majesty the Emperor of all the Russias agrees to cede to the United States, by this convention, immediately upon the exchange of the ratifications thereof, all the territory and dominion now possessed by his said Majesty on the continent of America and in the adjacent islands, the same being contained within the geographical limits herein set forth, to wit: The eastern limit is the line of demarcation between the

[1] *United States Statutes at Large,* Vol. XV, pp. 539–44. The treaty was signed by William H. Seward and Edouard de Stoeckl.

Russian and the British possessions in North America, as established by the convention between Russia and Great Britain, of February 28 – 16, 1825, and described in Articles III and IV of said convention, in the following terms:

"Commencing from the southernmost point of the island called Prince of Wales Island, which point lies in the parallel of 54 degrees 40 minutes north latitude, and between the 131st and the 133d degree of west longitude, (meridian of Greenwich,) the said line shall ascend to the north along the channel called Portland channel, as far as the point of the continent where it strikes the 56th degree of north latitude; from this last-mentioned point, the line of demarcation shall follow the summit of the mountains situated parallel to the coast as far as the point of intersection of the 141st degree of west longitude, (of the same meridian;) and finally, from the said point of intersection, the said meridian line of the 141st degree, in its prolongation as far as the Frozen ocean.

"IV. With reference to the line of demarcation laid down in the preceding article, it is understood –

"1st. That the island called Prince of Wales Island shall belong wholly to Russia," (now, by this cession, to the United States.)

"2d. That whenever the summit of the mountains which extend in a direction parallel to the coast from the 56th degree of north latitude to the point of intersection of the 141st degree of west longitude shall prove to be at the distance of more than ten marine leagues from the ocean, the limit between the British possessions and the line of coast which is to belong to Russia as above mentioned (that is to say, the limit to the possessions ceded by this convention) shall be formed by a line parallel to the winding of the coast, and which shall never exceed the distance of ten marine leagues therefrom."

The western limit within which the territories and dominion conveyed, are contained, passes through a point in Behring's straits on the parallel of sixty-five degrees thirty minutes north latitude, at its intersection by the meridian which passes midway between the islands of Krusenstern, or Ignalook, and the island of Ratmanoff, or Noonarbook, and proceeds due north, without limitation, into the same Frozen ocean. The same western limit, beginning at the same initial point, proceeds thence in a course nearly southwest through Behring's straits and Behring's sea, so as to pass midway between the northwest point of the island of St. Lawrence and the southeast point of Cape Choukotski, to the meridian of one hundred and seventy-two west longitude; thence, from the intersection of that meridian, in a southwesterly direction, so as to pass midway between the island of Attou and the Copper island of the Kormandorski couplet or group in the North Pacific ocean, to the meridian of one hundred and ninety-three degrees west longitude, so as to include in the territory conveyed the whole of the Aleutian islands east of that meridian. . . .

Article VI. In consideration of the cession aforesaid, the United States agree to pay at the treasury in Washington, within ten months after the exchange of the ratifications of this convention, to the diplomatic representative or other agent of his Majesty the Emperor of all the Russias, duly authorized to receive the same, seven million two hundred thousand dollars in gold. . . .

◇◇◇◇◇◇◇◇◇◇◇◇◇

2. PROPOSAL FOR THE ANNEXATION OF SANTO DOMINGO [2]

[*Hamilton Fish to Orville E. Babcock*]

Washington, November 6, 1869

THE PRESIDENT having directed you to meet Mr. Raymond H. Perry in San Domingo, and to advise with him, unofficially, as to the execution of the powers with which he is intrusted to conclude a treaty and a convention with the Dominican Republic, and he also having further directed you in case of the execution of such treaty and convention, then, as an officer of the army of the United States, to take steps to carry out the agreement of the United States contained in said treaty, to protect the people of that republic against foreign interference while the nation is expressing its will, and also to protect the interests and rights which the United States may obtain under such convention, I now place in your hands herewith draughts of such a treaty and of such a convention as the United States are prepared to enter into with that republic. And it being contemplated that the United States shall make an advance to that republic, the President has also determined to place the advance in your hands, to be given to Mr. Perry when the negotiations shall have advanced to the proper point for its use; you will accordingly receive herewith, for that purpose, a draft on New York for one hundred thousand dollars, and also a quantity of arms and ammunition, valued at fifty thousand dollars, of which a schedule is annexed. Mr. Perry having been instructed to govern his course by your advice, I will add a few suggestions for your guidance in that respect, in the expectation that the minister for foreign affairs in the Dominican Republic will welcome you to his conferences with Mr. Perry.

No apprehension is felt that any serious objections will be made by the Dominican Republic to the language used in these instruments. They are framed with a view to carry out the understanding which the authorities of that republic came to with you on your late visit. If it should be proposed, however, to vary the form or language, and by doing so the negotiations can be facilitated, Mr. Perry should yield to the wishes of that government in this respect, provided none of the essential features of the draughts are altered, and no new principle introduced. It is, however, possible that the Dominican government may propose that this republic shall

[2] *Sen. Ex. Doc.* (1440) 41st Congress, 3rd Session, No. 17, pp. 80–2.

be admitted into the Union as a State. Should this be the case, you will not fail to advise Mr. Perry to make it clear to them that, in the opinion of the President, that course would conflict with the spirit of the Constitution of the United States. That instrument provides but one way for the admission of new States into the Union; namely, through the agency of Congress. The third section of the fourth article of the Constitution says, explicitly: New States may be admitted *by the Congress* into this Union. . . .

Mr. Perry will further say that the President does not doubt that Congress will be ready, when the proper time shall come, and at no distant day, to admit to the Union as a State the Territory of the Dominican Republic, should the proposed treaty be executed and ratified.

My attention has also been called to what is known as the Hartmont loan, and I am informed that the holders of that loan will claim a lien on Samana, and may even pretend that the lien is independent of the loan and may exist after its payment. I inclose transactions of the contracts under which that loan was effected, which contracts were published in the Bulletin official of September 25, 1869, from which I judge that the first claim is well founded, and that the latter is without foundation. It is understood that the Dominican government has received fifty thousand pounds on account of the loan provided for by this contract, and only fifty thousand pounds. If any more has been received it must be deducted from the sum of one million five hundred thousand dollars, which is to be named in the treaty as the sum to be paid by this Government to that of San Domingo, and the contract or "treaty" with Messrs. Hartmont & Co. must be duly and legally canceled or relinquished by the holders before Mr. Perry signs any convention or treaty with the Dominican government; and he is, in any such event, to provide for the entire release of Samana from any and every lien or claim, in case any money is to be paid by the United States. . . .

Anticipating the probable execution of these instruments, the Navy Department will receive orders from the President to place at your disposal, in the harbor of San Domingo, a force sufficient to enable the United States to comply with their agreement in the proposed treaty to protect the Dominican Republic until the will of its people can be ascertained, and also to receive possession of the territory and waters leased by the proposed convention to the United States.

As to the former object, you will, when the treaty shall be executed, point out to the naval officer in command the obligation which the United States will have assumed, and will leave him to execute it.

As to the latter object, in case of the delivery to the Dominican Republic of the one hundred and fifty thousand dollars, and the execution of the proposed convention, the officer detailed for that purpose will proceed to the Bay of Samana, and will there, under instructions from the Navy Department, take actual possession of the lands, coasts, islands, waters, and property leased, in the name of the United States, whenever it shall appear that the cession of the sovereignty and the dominions of the republic is not to be completed, and will give public notice that the occupation, title, and jurisdiction have changed, and that the United States will not respect any grants or concessions made by the Dominican Republic within the bounds of the territory leased subsequently to the preliminary arrangement made in September last, and that thereafter all titles must be derived from the United States. . . .

The President enjoins that the fact and the object of your visit to San Domingo, as well as the provisions of the proposed instruments, shall be kept a secret as long as practicable. . . .

◇◇◇◇◇◇◇◇◇◇◇◇◇

3. SUPPORT OF THE ANNEXATION OF SANTO DOMINGO[3]

[*Message of President Grant to The Senate of The United States*]

May 31, 1870

I TRANSMIT to the Senate, for consideration with a view to its ratification, an additional article to the treaty of the 29th of November last, for the annexation of the Dominican Republic to the United States, stipulating for an extension of the time for exchanging the ratifications thereof, signed in this city on the 14th instant by the plenipotentiaries of the parties.

It was my intention to have also negotiated with the plenipotentiary of San Domingo amendments to the treaty of annexation to obviate objections which may be urged against the treaty as it is now worded; but on reflection I deem it better to submit to the Senate the propriety of their amending the treaty as follows: First, to specify that the obligations of this Government shall not exceed the $1,500,000 stipulated in the treaty; secondly, to determine the manner of appointing the agents to receive and disburse the same; thirdly, to determine the class of creditors who shall take precedence in the settlement of their claims; and, finally, to insert such amendments as may suggest themselves to the minds of Senators to carry out in good faith the conditions of the treaty submitted to the Senate of the United States in January last, according to the spirit and intent of that treaty. From the most reliable information I can obtain, the sum specified in the treaty will pay every just claim against the Republic of San Domingo and leave a balance sufficient to carry on a Territorial government until such time as new laws for providing a Territorial revenue can be enacted and put in force.

I feel an unusual anxiety for the ratification of this treaty, because I believe it will redound greatly to the glory of the two countries interested, to civilization, and to the extirpation of the institution of slavery.

[3] Richardson, James D., *Messages and Papers of the Presidents*, Vol. VII, pp. 61–3.

The doctrine promulgated by President Monroe has been adhered to by all political parties, and I now deem it proper to assert the equally important principle that hereafter no territory on this continent shall be regarded as subject of transfer to a European power.

The Government of San Domingo has voluntarily sought this annexation. It is a weak power, numbering probably less than 120,000 souls, and yet possessing one of the richest territories under the sun, capable of supporting a population of 10,000,000 people in luxury. The people of San Domingo are not capable of maintaining themselves in their present condition, and must look for outside support.

They yearn for the protection of our free institutions and laws, our progress and civilization. Shall we refuse them?

I have information which I believe reliable that a European power stands ready now to offer $2,000,000 for the possession of Samana Bay alone. If refused by us, with what grace can we prevent a foreign power from attempting to secure the prize?

The acquisition of San Domingo is desirable because of its geographical position. It commands the entrance to the Caribbean Sea and the Isthmus transit of commerce. It possesses the richest soil, best and most capacious harbors, most salubrious climate, and the most valuable products of the forests, mine, and soil of any of the West India Islands. Its possession by us will in a few years build up a coastwise commerce of immense magnitude, which will go far toward restoring to us our lost merchant marine. It will give to us those articles which we consume so largely and do not produce, thus equalizing our exports and imports.

In case of foreign war it will give us command of all the islands referred to, and thus prevent an enemy from ever again possessing himself of rendezvous upon our very coast.

At present our coast trade between the States bordering on the Atlantic and those bordering on the Gulf of Mexico is cut into by the Bahamas and the Antilles. Twice we must, as it were, pass through foreign countries to get by sea from Georgia to the west coast of Florida.

San Domingo, with a stable government, under which her immense resources can be developed, will give remunerative wages to tens of thousands of laborers not now on the island.

This labor will take advantage of every available means of transportation to abandon the adjacent islands and seek the blessings of freedom and its sequence — each inhabitant receiving the reward of his own labor. Porto Rico and Cuba will have to abolish slavery, as a measure of self-preservation to retain their laborers.

San Domingo will become a large consumer of the products of Northern farms and manufactories. The cheap rate at which her citizens can be furnished with food, tools, and machinery will make it necessary that the contiguous islands should have the same advantages in order to compete in the production of sugar, coffee, tobacco, tropical fruits, etc. This will open to us a still wider market for our products.

The production of our own supply of these articles will cut off more than one hundred millions of our annual imports, besides largely increasing our exports. With such a picture it is easy to see how our large debt abroad is ultimately to be extinguished. With a balance of trade against us (including interest on bonds held by foreigners and money spent by our citizens traveling in foreign lands) equal to the entire yield of the precious metals in this country, it is not so easy to see how this result is to be otherwise accomplished.

The acquisition of San Domingo is an adherence to the "Monroe doctrine"; it is a measure of national protection; it is asserting our just claim to a controlling influence over the great commercial traffic soon to flow from east to west by the way of the Isthmus of Darien; it is to build up our merchant marine; it is to furnish new markets for the products of our farms, shops, and manufactories; it is to make slavery insupportable in Cuba and Porto Rico at once and ultimately so in Brazil; it is to settle the unhappy condition of Cuba, and end an exterminating conflict; it is to provide honest means of paying our honest debts, without overtaxing the people; it is to furnish our citizens with the necessaries of everyday life at cheaper rates than ever before; and it is, in fine, a rapid stride toward that greatness which the intelligence, industry, and enterprise of the citizens of the United States entitle this country to assume among nations.

◇◇◇◇◇◇◇◇◇◇◇◇◇

4. "NABOTH'S VINEYARD"[4]

[*Address of Senator Charles Sumner in the Senate of the United States*]

December 21, 1870

THE RESOLUTION before the Senate commits Congress to a dance of blood. It is a new step in a measure of violence. Already several steps have been taken, and Congress is now summoned to another. . . .

The negotiation for annexion began with a person known as Buenaventura Baez. All the evidence, official and unofficial, shows him to be a political jockey. But he could do little alone; he had about him two other political jockeys, Cazneau and Fabens; and these three together, a precious copartnership, seduced into their firm a young officer of ours, who entitled himself "Aide-de-Camp to the President of the United States." Together they got up what was called a protocol, in which the young officer entitling himself "Aide-de-Camp to the President" proceeds to make certain promises for the President. . . .

[4] *The Works of Charles Sumner:* (Lee and Shepard, Boston, Mass., 1883) Vol. XIV, pp. 89–132. See also: *Cong. Globe,* 41st Congress, 3rd Session, Part I, pp. 227–31. December 21, 1870.

"I. His Excellency, General Grant, President of the United States, promises, *privately*, to use all his influence, in order that the idea of annexing the Dominican Republic to the United States may acquire such a degree of popularity among members of Congress as will be necessary for its accomplishment."

. . . This is not all, Sir; I broaden the allegation. Ever since the signature of the treaty, and especially since its rejection, Baez has been sustained in power by the presence of our naval force. Such I aver to be the fact. I state it with all the responsibility of my position, and with full conviction of its truth. I ask you, Sir, to go to the State Department and Navy Department and read the reports there on file, and I feel sure that what I state will be found to be substantially true. I ask you also to confer with any naval officer who has been there, or with any patriot citizen. . . .

Sir, I have presented but half of this case, and perhaps the least painful part. I am now brought to another aspect of it. This naval force to which I have referred has also been directed against the neighboring Republic of Hayti (the only colored Government now existing in the world, a republic seeking to follow our great example,) penetrating its harbors and undertaking to dictate what it should do. If you will read again the reports at the Navy Department, you will find that I do not overstate when I say that they have undertaken to dictate to the Government of Hayti what it should do. Nor is this all. In an unhappy moment, the commodore of an American fleet, going ashore, allowed himself to insult and menace the Government there, saying, that, if it interfered in any way with the territory of Dominica, he would blow the town down. . . .

I have called it an act of war, – war, Sir, made by the Executive without the consent of Congress. If Congress had declared war against this feeble republic, then it would have been the part of the Executive to carry that declaration into effect; but until then what right had our Executive to do this thing? None which can be vindicated by the laws of our country, none except what is found in the law of force. . . .

History is often said to repeat itself. More or less it does. It repeats itself now. This whole measure of annexion, and the spirit with which it is pressed, find a parallel in the Kansas and Nebraska Bill, and in the Lecompton Constitution, by which it was sought to subjugate a distant Territory to Slavery. The Senator from Indiana was not here during those days, although he was acting well his part at home; but he will remember the pressure to which we were then exposed. And now we witness the same things: violence in a distant island, as there was violence in Kansas; also the same Presidential appliances; and shall I add, the same menace of personal assault filling the air? All this naturally flowers in the Presidential proposition that the annexion shall be by joint resolution of the two Houses of Congress; so that we have violence to Dominica, violence to Hayti, violence to Public Law, including violence to the Constitution of Dominica, and also to a Treaty between Dominica and Hayti, crowned by violence to the Constitution of the United States. . . .

There is one other consideration, vast in importance and conclusive in character, to which I allude only. The island of San Domingo, situated in tropical waters, and occupied by another race, of another color, never can become a permanent possession of the United States. You may seize it by force of arms or by diplomacy, where a naval squadron does more than the minister; but the enforced jurisdiction cannot endure. Already by a higher statute is that island set apart to the colored race. It is theirs by right of possession, by their sweat and blood mingling with the soil, by tropical position, by its burning sun, and by unalterable laws of climate. Such is the ordinance of Nature, which I am not the first to recognize. San Domingo is the earliest of that independent group destined to occupy the Caribbean Sea, toward which our duty is plain as the Ten Commandments. Kindness, beneficence, assistance, aid, help, protection, all that is implied in good neighborhood, – these we must give, freely, bountifully; but their independence is as precious to them as is ours to us, and it is placed under the safeguard of natural laws which we cannot violate with impunity.

Long ago it was evident that the Great Republic might fitly extend the shelter of its protection to the governments formed in these tropical islands, dealing with them graciously, generously, and in a Christian spirit, – helping them in their weakness, encouraging them in their trials, and being to them always a friend; but we take counsel of our supposed interests rather than theirs, when we seek to remove them from the sphere in which they have been placed by Providence.

I conclude as I began. I protest against this legislation as another stage in a drama of blood. I protest against it in the name of Justice outraged by violence, in the name of Humanity insulted, in the name of the weak trodden down, in the name of Peace imperilled, and in the name of the African race, whose first effort at Independence is rudely assailed. . . .

5. THE DANISH WEST INDIES [5]

[*Report of the Committee on Foreign Relations of the Senate of the United States, March 31, 1898*]

. . . THE FIRST negotiations of the United States for the purchase of the Danish Islands were begun by Mr. Seward, then Secretary of State, in January, 1865, at least so it is supposed. There is mention in contemporary pamphlets of a dinner party at the French embassy, where Mr. Seward first expressed to General Raaslof, the Danish chargé d'affaires, the desire of the United States to buy the Danish Islands in the Antilles. Afterwards other conferences followed of an unofficial character, Mr. Seward urging

[5] *Sen. Ex. Doc.* (4239) 57th Congress, 1st Session, No. 284, Appendix A, pp. 16–18.

the Danish minister, who replied that Denmark had no desire to sell the islands. Great secrecy was insisted upon and preserved. This was under the Presidency of Lincoln. General Raaslof, who was himself opposed to the sale, reported these interviews to his Government, who replied that it would be advisable to drop the negotiations, as the Danish Government had no desire to part with these colonies. Mr. Seward's carriage accident, consequent illness, and temporary incapacity for public affairs confirmed this attitude on the part of Denmark.

In April came the assassination of the President, the wounding of Mr. Seward, and the accession of Mr. Johnson to the Chief Executive. Mr. Seward's recovery was slow, and it was not until December, 1865, on the eve of his departure for the South, a journey taken to restore his health, that the Secretary of State again mentioned the matter to General Raaslof. The complexion of affairs was now somewhat altered. A new ministry had come into power at Copenhagen, and it was less opposed to the sale than the former one had been. Hence, a note to Mr. Seward, declaring that although the Government had no desire to sell, still it was not unwilling to entertain the Secretary's propositions. A request was made that the United States declare how much it was willing to give.

Mr. Seward departed, and during his absence visited St. Thomas and convinced himself of the necessity of the purchase. On his return he pressed General Raaslof to name a price, and the Danish minister in turn demanded that, as the United States wished to buy and not Denmark to sell, an offer should be made by the American Government. Finally, on July 17, 1866, as General Raaslof was leaving for Copenhagen, Mr. Seward delivered to him a note offering, on behalf of the United States, $5,000,000 for the three Danish islands, St. Thomas, St. John, and Santa Cruz. Mr. Seward personally informed General Raaslof that the representative of the United States in Denmark would, for a time, have charge of the affair; also that the United States was not pressed for an answer. A few days after General Raaslof left America, and soon after his arrival at Copenhagen he was appointed minister of war, and, in the work of reorganizing the Danish army, lost sight of affairs in America.

Count Frijs, the Danish minister for foreign affairs, who consequently now had charge of the negotiations, was in favor of the sale, but still the affair dragged until January 19, 1867, when Mr. Yeaman, United States minister at Copenhagen, received the following telegram from Mr. Seward: "Tell Raaslof haste important." However, nothing was done for two months. Denmark felt a good deal of hesitation, owing to the uncertainty of the treaty being ratified by the Senate, but she became more assured by the absence of opposition in the United States to the purchase scheme and by the speedy ratification of the Alaska purchase treaty. Nevertheless, at the end of two months Mr. Seward telegraphed again to Mr. Yeaman, "Want yea or nay now." Mr. Yeaman at once communicated with General Raaslof, but it was not until the 17th of May, 1867, that Count Frijs made a counter proposition to Mr. Seward's note. Through the medium of Mr.

Yeaman, he declined on behalf of Denmark the offer of $5,000,000 and offered the islands for $15,000,000, or St. Thomas and St. John for $10,000,000, with the option of taking Santa Cruz for $5,000,000 more.

Count Frijs explained that the ratification of the treaty of cession by the Rigsdag would be necessary, and that the Danish Government would require that the consent of the people of the islands should be freely and formally given. In ten days Mr. Yeaman was in receipt of Mr. Seward's answer to this proposition, which was in substance this: "The United States will pay for the three islands $7,500,000 in gold." Mr. Seward objected, however, to the condition that the consent of the inhabitants of the islands was necessary, and thought it sufficient that they should have the free choice of leaving the islands within two years or remaining and becoming American citizens. Mr. Yeaman immediately communicated these instructions to the Danish minister for foreign affairs, who promised an early answer. This answer was given in a month, in an interview between Count Frijs and Mr. Yeaman. Mr. Seward's second offer was refused and a counter proposition made. This was that Denmark would cede the islands for $11,250,000 or 20,000,000 Danish rix dollars, or St. Thomas and St. John for $7,500,000, and Santa Cruz at option for $3,750,000. Count Frijs further declared that taking a vote of the people of the islands before the cession was absolutely indispensable.

Mr. Seward's second offer being thus formally rejected by the Danish Government, Mr. Yeaman now informed Count Frijs that his instructions obliged him to announce that the offer of the United States was withdrawn and the negotiations ended. Nevertheless, on July 6, 1867, Mr. Seward telegraphed to Mr. Adams in London: "Tell Yeaman close with Denmark's offer. St. John, St. Thomas, seven and one-half millions. Report brief by cable. Send treaty ratified immediately." Still the negotiations lagged. Mr. Seward was strongly opposed to the vote by the islanders, but the Danish Government was firm on this point, and he finally cabled to Mr. Yeaman: "Concede question of vote." On the 24th of October, 1867, the treaty was finally signed by the Danish minister and by Mr. Yeaman on behalf of the United States.

There remained the vote of the islanders. Mr. Carstensen was sent as Danish commissioner to take the vote, and Mr. Seward dispatched Dr. Hawley to the islands to attend to American interests. He arrived at St. Thomas on the 12th of November, 1867; on the 18th of November, before the vote was taken, there occurred a terrible earthquake, which did much damage to the island, and affairs came temporarily to a standstill. They were resumed on November 26, and on January 9, 1868, the vote was taken in St. Thomas, and on the following day in St. John. In the larger island there was cast 1,039 votes for the cession and only 22 against it, and in the smaller 205 votes for and none against. There were fears in Denmark that the United States would not ratify even after Denmark was fully committed, but Mr. Seward calmed these fears with renewed assurances of success, and after some hesitation the treaty was ratified by the Rigsdag and signed by the King on January 31, 1868. This ratification occurred in the midst of the fierce political war between President Johnson and Congress. The limit of time named in the treaty for ratification was February 24, 1868, and this went by without action by Congress. The time was then extended to October 14, 1868. All, however, was useless. Denmark made repeated endeavors, in the person of her minister and through the medium of other powers, to conclude the negotiations, but in vain. The treaty fell a victim to the storm of political hatred then raging in this country, and in the session of 1868, after an adverse report, the United States Senate dropped it. . . .

Chapter XX

ARBITRATION AND CONCILIATION 1865—1931

THE CONTROVERSY between the United States and Great Britain with respect to the obligations of the latter as a neutral nation during the American Civil War was serious and extended. An amicable settlement of the difficulty was postponed for several years on account of the exigencies of the domestic politics of each nation concerned, the extreme demands of a few cantankerous American political leaders, and at least a fair amount of obstinacy on the part of British statesmen. The conflicting positions of the two governments were stated in many diplomatic notes. The letter of Charles Francis Adams to Lord John Russell of May 20, 1865 (1), and the answer of Lord Russell of August 30, 1865 (2), present with reasonable accuracy the status of the controversy at the close of the war. Adams and Russell were unable to effect an agreement, but the successor to Adams as minister to Great Britain, Reverdy Johnson, negotiated and signed the Johnson-Clarendon Convention of January 14, 1869 (3). While this convention was acceptable to the President of the United States and to his Secretary of State, it failed to receive the approval of the Senate. It remained for a new Secretary of State, Hamilton Fish, and a new minister to England, Lothrop Motley, to explain to the British government the Senate's objections as best they could and renew negotiations if possible (4). They were unable to accomplish very much through the formal diplomatic channels, but eventually an unofficial agreement (5) was arranged by Secretary Fish and Sir John Rose, Canadian Minister of Finance, who acted under British authorization.

The Rose-Fish memorandum provided the basis for the Treaty of Washington (6), which in turn, created the Geneva Tribunal. The tribunal made its decision and award September 14, 1872 (7).

In the years following the Geneva award many American statesmen were interested in promoting the peaceful settlement of international disputes by arbitration or conciliation. One of the most important efforts in this direction was the Anglo-American arbitration treaty of 1897, which failed to secure the advice and consent of the Senate to its ratification (8). Arbitration treaties with a more limited objective were negotiated during the years 1908–9 (9), but President Taft's attempt to extend the scope of arbitration was not successful. Although the Senate voted to give its advice and consent to the Taft treaties of 1911, it attached amendments to them which the President was unwilling to accept (10). Many conciliation treaties were negotiated during the years 1913–14 (11), and after the first World War, a new series of arbitration treaties, similar to those of 1908–9, were signed by Secretary of State Kellogg (12).

◇◇◇◇◇◇◇◇◇◇◇◇

1. AMERICAN CLAIMS AGAINST GREAT BRITAIN[1]

[*Charles Francis Adams to Earl Russell*]

London, May 20, 1865

MY LORD: I have had the honor to receive your note of the 4th instant, in reply to mine of the 7th of last month. . . .

And here I would beg leave to remark that if I am to judge of the general statement made of my position by the abstract of it presented to me by your lordship, I must have very grievously failed in offering the logical sequence of my propositions as distinctly as I had desired to do.

This will render necessary another effort to place them before you in the following brief recapitulation. It was my wish to maintain,

1. That the act of recognition by her Majesty's government of insurgents as belligerents on the high seas before they had a single vessel afloat was precipitate and unprecedented.
2. That it had the effect of creating these parties belligerents after the recognition, instead of merely acknowledging an existing fact.
3. That this creation has been since effected exclusively from the ports of her Majesty's kingdom and its dependencies with the aid and co-operation of her Majesty's subjects.
4. That during the whole course of the struggle in America, of nearly four years in duration, there has been no appearance of the insurgents as a belligerent on the ocean excepting in the shape of British vessels, constructed, equipped, supplied, manned and armed in British ports.
5. That during the same period it has been the constant and persistent endeavor of my government to remonstrate in every possible form against this abuse of the neutrality of this kingdom, and to call upon her Majesty's government to exercise the necessary powers to put an effective stop to it.
6. That although the desire of her Majesty's ministers to exert themselves in the suppression of these abuses is freely acknowledged, the efforts which they made proved in a great degree powerless, from the inefficiency of the law on which they relied, and from their absolute refusal, when solicited, to procure additional powers to attain the objects.
7. That by reason of the failure to check this flagrant abuse of neutrality, the issue from British ports of a number of British vessels, with the aid of the recognition of their belligerent character in all the ports of her Majesty's dependencies around the globe, has resulted in the burning and de-

[1] *Papers Relating to Foreign Affairs,* 1865, Part I, pp. 375–83.

stroying on the ocean a large number of merchant vessels, and a very large amount of property, belonging to the people of the United States.

8. That in addition to this direct injury, the action of these British built, manned and armed vessels has had the indirect effect of driving from the sea a large portion of the commercial marine of the United States, and to a corresponding extent enlarging that of Great Britain, thus enabling one portion of the British people to derive an unjust advantage from the wrong committed on a friendly nation by another portion.

9. That the injuries thus received by a country which has meanwhile sedulously endeavored to perform all its obligations, owing to the imperfection of the legal means at hand to prevent them, as well as the unwillingness to seek for more stringent powers, are of so grave a nature as in reason and justice to constitute a valid claim for reparation and indemnification. . . .

The insurgents ultimately became a belligerent on the ocean solely by reason of the facilities furnished them in her Majesty's ports. The fact appears to me to be indisputable. For down to the close of the war, with the exception mentioned in my former note, of two passenger steamers stolen from the citizens of New York, not a single effective vessel of theirs has been seen on the ocean, excepting the six or seven which have been wholly supplied in and from this kingdom. Of the preparation of these steamers for the purpose indicated, I have endeavored from time to time to furnish your lordship with such evidence as I had it in my power to obtain. For a considerable time I found myself unable to stem the combined effect of the secret sympathy of her Majesty's officers in the port of Liverpool, and of your lordship's very natural incredulity based on their reports, in procuring more than formal attention to my representations.

Thus it was that the gunboat Oreto got away, and soon after became the armed privateer the Florida.

All the statements I had the honor to submit proved true to the letter, but, nevertheless, the facility with which the evasion had been accomplished furnished the strongest encouragement to the subsequent great extension of the field of operations.

It was at that moment that a deliberate policy was adopted by the insurgents, under which a base was made in this kingdom for all the extensive warlike operations since conducted by them. The officers were then established, and all the ramifications of a bureau regularly organized.

The next example was that of gunboat No. 290, afterwards well known as the cruiser the Alabama. I refer to this case once more only because it has been particularly referred to by your lordship. I do so for the purpose of expressing my dissent from the statement made in your note in regard to certain important particulars.

Your lordship is pleased to state that the papers affording evidence of a design to equip this ship for the confederate service were furnished to you on the 22d and on the 24th of July. This is certainly true. But your lordship will be kind enough to remember that my first note giving information as to the character of that vessel was dated on the 23d of June, that is, one month preceding. On the 4th of July the commissioners of her Majesty's customs, to whom that representation was referred, made a report admitting the fact that the vessel was certainly built for a ship-of-war, but affirming that the evidence presented of her being intended for the so-called confederate government was not sufficient to justify a detention. . . .

It now appears that from the day when, by the flagrant negligence of her Majesty's board of customs, this vessel, admitted to be intended for war purposes, was suffered to depart from the port of Liverpool, down to the hour of her destruction by the United States steamer Kearsarge off the coast of France, she came again and again into ports within her Majesty's jurisdiction, and instead of being treated as her Majesty's government directed if she should go to Nassau, she was everywhere hailed with joy and treated with hospitality as a legitimate cruiser. . . .

It is, then, with undoubting confidence in the justice of the reasoning here presented that I take the liberty to reaffirm the validity of the claims of my government for all the damage done by this vessel during her career, and ask reparation therefor. . . .

Passing from this point to the more general question between the two countries, I proceed to the task of considering an argument of your lordship of a widely different description. This is one drawn entirely from the authority supplied by the previous practice of the government which I have the honor to represent. You cite this as an example to sustain the position taken by her Majesty's government against the present claim. It is urged in at least two instances cited, where similar claims were presented by the representatives of foreign powers to the United States; they were replied to with substantially the same reasoning now repeated by her Majesty's government. These are the cases of Spain and Portugal, the commerce of which countries had suffered from depredations on the ocean, committed by vessels built, armed, manned, and equipped by citizens of the United States and despatched from their ports.

The first remark that I would pray permission to submit in connexion with this view of the subject is this: that even if it were true that the government of the United States had, half a century since, refused to recognize the just claims of other powers for damage done by reason of their omission to prevent the abuse of their neutral ports to the commerce of those powers, it could in no degree change the nature of any subsequent omission or neglect committed by other powers at this day. It is a principle of morals too thoroughly known to your lordship to require my dwelling upon it for a moment, that the wrongdoing of one party cannot be cited in justification of a repetition of the act by another. . . .

Thus it is that whatever may be the line of argument I pursue, I am compelled ever to return to the one conclusion. The nation that recognized a power as a belligerent before it had built a vessel and became itself the sole source of all the belligerent character it has ever possessed on the ocean, must be regarded as responsible for all the damage that has ensued from that cause to the commerce of a power with which it was under the most sacred of obligations to preserve amity and peace. . . .

◇◇◇◇◇◇◇◇◇◇◇◇◇

2. THE POSITION OF GREAT BRITAIN REGARDING AMERICAN CLAIMS [2]

[*Lord Russell to Charles Francis Adams*]

London, August 30, 1865

HAVING purposely delayed an answer to your letter of the 20th of May, I now resume our correspondence at a time when the civil war has entirely ceased – when the whole territory of the United States is subject to the government of the Union, and the United States have not an enemy in the world. . . .

The question, then, as I understand it, is now reduced to these terms: Whether her Majesty's government have judged rightly the state of a friendly nation disturbed by a formidable insurrection, and whether they have correctly applied the law of nations in respect to their duty toward that friendly nation. . . .

Differing, as her Majesty's government do, from your statement of the facts upon which the judgment of the two governments is to be ultimately formed, I lay down with confidence the following proposition:

1. That the history of modern nations affords no example of an insurrection against a central government so widely extended, so immediate in its operation, so well and so long prepared, so soon and so completely furnished with the machinery of civil government; a national representation, generals and officers of high military reputation, armies fully equipped, and fortifications recently in the possession of the established government.

2. That intelligence reached her Majesty's government in the spring of 1861 that seven combined States had declared in favor of this insurrection; that three more States, including the great and powerful State of Virginia, were preparing to join them; that these States commanded upwards of 3,000 miles of sea-coast; that they comprised more than 5,000,000 of people, exclusive of the negro slaves; that the president of the insurgent government had proclaimed his intention of issuing letters of marque and reprisal; that the President of the United States, on the other hand, had proclaimed his intention to establish a blockade of all the ports of the southern States, and that in these circumstances the commander of her Majesty's naval forces on the North American station earnestly solicited instructions for his guidance.

[2] Ibid., pp. 536–45.

3. That in view of these extraordinary events, unexpected and undesired, her Majesty decided to proclaim her neutrality in this contest; to allow the belligerent blockade of more than 3,000 miles of coast, including, of course, the right of search, detention, and capture on the part of the United States, and, on the other hand, as in duty bound, to recognize in the so-called Confederate States the right of a belligerent power.

4. That her Majesty's government put in force with fairness and impartiality the neutrality they had proclaimed.

5. That the foreign enlistment act which is intended in aid of the duties and rights of a neutral nation can only be applied when a ship is armed or fitted out, or begun to be armed or fitted out; and even in that case only when proof can be obtained that the ship so armed or equipped, or begun to be armed or equipped, is intended for the service of a power at war with a friend or ally of her Majesty.

6. That in the instance of the Oreto, the case justifying the detention of the vessel was not complete; and in the case of the Alabama, the proof was declared to be complete only on the very morning when the owners of the Alabama, having by some means obtained information of what was intended, got away on a false pretence.

7. That the Oreto was begun to be built here, was afterwards detained and tried at Nassau, was acquitted, and was afterwards completed at Wilmington, (Mobile?) a port of the confederates.

8. That the iron-clad rams were detained, and afterwards seized at Birkenhead; that the so-called Canton, or Pampero, was prosecuted and convicted in Scotland; that the Victor, afterwards the Rappahannock, was forced to take refuge at Calais, in order to avoid seizure, and till the close of the war never appeared on the seas.

9. That it is not enough to say that the foreign enlistment act might have been amended and made more efficient unless it be shown that the amendments suggested would have been clearly efficient, and would have been consistent with the laws of a free country.

10. That nothing but the most extensive employment of spies, and informers, and the most arbitrary powers of detention and seizure on the most vague and slight suspicions, could have prevented a British or American merchant, in combination with a confederate enemy of the United States, from sending an unarmed ship to distant neutral waters, from sending arms to the same waters, and from combining the ship and the arms in a hostile cruiser against the commerce of the United States.

11. That the Shenandoah was despatched and armed in this manner.

12. That there was no reason or ground whatever to accuse her Majesty's government of failure in the performance of their international obligations during the four years of civil war, and consequently no valid claim can be made for reparation and indemnification.

With respect to your allegation that the concession of belligerent rights to the confederates was "precipitate and unprecedented," I answer both epithets by saying, first, that our declaration followed, and did not precede your own declaration of the intended blockade of six or seven considerable ports, and the declaration of an intention on the part of the confederates to issue letters of marque; and, secondly, that a sudden insurrection of such magnitude being unprecedented, our recognition of its existence was necessarily likewise unprecedented. . . .

What you contend for, I imagine, both as to the commencement of the war and as to its close, is, that the United States of America had a full claim to exercise all the rights of belligerents, but that Great Britain had no just claims to exercise any of the rights of neutrals.

This position, however, Great Britain never can admit. . . .

With respect to the Oreto and the Alabama, I have only again to repeat that, up to the time when the Oreto left these shores, and up to the day when the Alabama escaped on a false pretence, the law officers of the Crown had not, by any legal opinion, enabled her Majesty's government to give any order for the detention of these vessels.

I entirely concur with you that there was no use in giving orders on the 31st of July for detaining a vessel which had made its escape on the 29th. But up to the 29th the law officers had not thought the evidence sufficient to justify detention; and I cannot, by any means, admit, what you seem to insinuate, that the law officers were deficient either in knowledge of the law, or in willingness to apply it.

Her Majesty's government fully accept the responsibility of these opinions. . . .

But there is one essential point on which the United States and Great Britain appear entirely to agree. The United States, when neutral, refused to be responsible for captures at sea not brought within their jurisdiction, or to listen to a proposal to appoint a commission to assess damages; the government of the United Kingdom have taken a similar course. It is true that in applying the principle there has been a divergency of practice. The United States admitted their prizes to their harbors, but restored them, if practicable, when called upon by the decrees of courts of law, to their owners. The government of Great Britain refused admission altogether to such prizes. The principle is the same, and it is hardly worth while to dispute which course was most inconvenient to the insurgent cruisers. It appears to me, I confess, that the course pursued by her Majesty's government tended more effectually to discourage insurgent cruisers than that pursued by the United States.

But as to the principle involved, let me ask you, supposing a merchant or passenger vessel belonging to the United States were to go to the coast of Madagascar, and were there to meet a ship from Boston with cannon and muskets, and the merchant ship, being then armed, were to take part against Brazil in the war between Brazil and Paraguay; let me ask, I say, whether your government would think themselves bound to afford reparation to Brazil for all the captures made by that ship? Yet, such is the case of the Shenandoah.

It seems to her Majesty's government that, if the liability of neutral nations were stretched thus far, this pretension, new to the law of nations, would be most burdensome, and indeed most dangerous.

A maritime nation, whose people occupy themselves in constructing ships, and cannon, and arms, might be made responsible for the whole damages of a war in which that nation had taken no part. . . .

It appears to her Majesty's government that there are but two questions by which the claim of compensation could be tested; the one is, have the British government acted with due diligence, or, in other words, in good faith and honesty, in the maintenance of the neutrality they proclaimed? The other is, have the law officers of the Crown properly understood the foreign enlistment act, when they declined, in June, 1862, to advise the detention and seizure of the Alabama, and on other occasions when they were asked to detain other ships, building or fitting in British ports?

It appears to her Majesty's government that neither of these questions could be put to a foreign government with any regard to the dignity and character of the British Crown and the British nation. Her Majesty's government are the sole guardians of their own honor. They cannot admit that they have acted with bad faith in maintaining the neutrality they professed. The law officers of the Crown must be held to be better interpreters of a British statute than any foreign government can be presumed to be. Her Majesty's government must, therefore, decline either to make reparation and compensation for the captures made by the Alabama, or to refer the question to any foreign state. Her Majesty's government conceive that if they were to act otherwise, they would endanger the position of neutrals in all future wars.

Her Majesty's government, however, are ready to consent to the appointment of a commission, to which shall be referred all claims arising during the late civil war, which the two powers shall agree to refer to the commissioners. . . .

◇◇◇◇◇◇◇◇◇◇◇◇◇

3. THE JOHNSON-CLARENDON CONVENTION[3]

[*Signed January 14, 1869*]

. . . *ARTICLE I.* The high contracting parties agree that all claims on the part of the citizens of the United States upon the government of her Britannic Majesty, including the so-called Alabama claims, and all claims on the part of subjects of her Britannic Majesty upon the government of the United States, which may have been presented to either government for its interposition with the other since the 26th of July, 1853, the day of the exchange of the ratifications of the convention concluded between the United States of America and Great Britain, at London, on the 8th of

[3] Ibid., 1868, Part I, pp. 401–4.

February, 1853, and which yet remain unsettled; as well as any other such claims which may be presented within the time specified in Article III of this convention, whether or not arising out of the late civil war in the United States, shall be referred to four commissioners, to be appointed in the following manner, that is to say: two commissioners shall be named by the President of the United States, by and with the advice and consent of the Senate, and two by her Britannic Majesty. . . .

The Commissioners shall then, and before proceeding to any other business, name some person to act as an arbitrator or umpire, to whose final decision shall be referred any claim upon which they may not be able to come to a decision. If they should not be able to agree upon an arbitrator or umpire, the commissioners on either side shall name a person as arbitrator or umpire; and in each and every case in which the commissioners may not be able to come to a decision, the commissioners shall determine by lot which of the two persons so named shall be the arbitrator or umpire in that particular case. . . .

Article II. The commissioners shall then forthwith proceed to the investigation of the claims which shall be presented to their notice. . . . Should they fail to decide by a majority upon any individual claim, they shall call to their assistance the arbitrator or umpire whom they may have agreed upon, or who may be determined by lot, as the case may be. . . .

Nevertheless, if the commissioners, or any two of them, shall think it desirable that a sovereign or head of a friendly state should be arbitrator or umpire in case of any claim, the commissioners shall report to that effect to their respective governments, who shall thereupon, within six months, agree upon some sovereign or head of a friendly state, who shall be invited to decide upon such claim, and before whom shall be laid the official correspondence which has taken place between the two governments, and the other written documents or statements which may have been presented to the commissioners in respect of such claims.

The decision of the commissioners, and of the arbitrator or umpire, shall be given upon each claim in writing, and shall be signed by them respectively, and dated.

In the event of a decision involving the question of compensation to be paid, being arrived at by a special arbitrator or umpire, the amount of such compensation shall be referred back to the commissioners for adjudication; and in the event of their not being able to come to a decision, it shall then be decided by the arbitrator or umpire appointed by them, or who shall have been determined by lot. . . .

The President of the United States of America, and her Majesty the Queen of the United Kingdom of Great Britain and Ireland, hereby solemnly and sincerely engage to consider the decision of the commissioners, or of the arbitrator or umpire, as the case may be, as absolutely final and conclusive upon each of such claims decided upon by him or them respectively, and to give full effect to such decision, without any objection or delay whatsoever.

It is agreed that no claim arising out of any transaction of a date prior to the 26th of July, 1853, the day of the exchange of the ratifications of the convention of the 8th of February 1853, shall be admissible under this convention. . . .

◇◇◇◇◇◇◇◇◇◇◇◇◇

4. REJECTION OF THE JOHNSON-CLARENDON CONVENTION BY THE UNITED STATES[4]

[*Hamilton Fish to J. Lothrop Motley*]

Washington, May 15, 1869

. . . YOUR PREDECESSOR has already been directed to notify Lord Clarendon that the Senate has refused its advice and consent to the ratification of the convention signed at London on the 14th January last, for the settlement of all outstanding claims. . . .

This adverse judgment, while unanimous, or nearly so, in its conclusion, was not reached by any single train of argument, nor from any one standpoint of policy, nor with any single standard of estimate of the claims either of the nation or of its citizens, nor with the same degree of importance attached to various points that have been discussed in the correspondence referred to in the convention. Various sources furnished currents running through differing and widely separated channels, but meeting to form one common stream of thought.

Both with the people and in the Senate, different minds, viewing it from different standpoints, each measuring by its own standard, and judging in its own way, arrived at the one conclusion.

The time and the circumstances under which the convention was negotiated were very unfavorable to its acceptance either by the people or the Senate.

The nation had just emerged from its periodical choice of a chief magistrate, and having changed the depository of its confidence and its power, looked with no favor on an attempt at the settlement of the great and grave questions depending, by those on the eve of retiring from power, without consulting or considering the views of the ruler recently intrusted with their confidence, and without communication with the Senate, to whose approval the treaty would be constitutionally submitted, or with any of its members. . . .

He [the President] hopes that when the question shall again be considered, it may comport with the views of her Majesty's government to embrace within the scope of the negotiation some agreement by the two governments, defining their respective rights and duties as neutrals in case the other government becomes unfortunately involved in war with a third power.

[4] *Sen. Ex. Doc.* (1440) 41st Congress, 3rd Session, No. 11, pp. 2–4.

The absence of some agreement or definition on this subject was among the causes leading to the rejection of the recent convention, under which, had it been adopted by the two countries, none of the grave questions which have arisen would have been passed upon by a tribunal whose decision either party (much less other nations) would regard as authority, so as to prevent repetition or retaliation. It might, indeed, well have occurred in the event of the selection by lot of the arbitrator or umpire in different cases, involving, however, precisely the same principles, that different awards, resting upon antagonistic principles, might have been made.

If, however, the two great leading maritime commercial nations of the world establish a rule to govern themselves, each with respect to the other, they may reasonably hope that their conclusion will be accepted by the other powers, and will become for the future recognized as a part of the public law of the civilized world.

The President recognizes the right of every power, when a civil conflict has arisen within another state, and has attained a sufficient complexity, magnitude, and completeness, to define its own relations and those of its citizens and subjects toward the parties to the conflict, so far as their rights and interests are necessarily affected by the conflict.

The necessity and the propriety of the original concession of belligerency by Great Britain at the time it was made have been contested and are not admitted. They certainly are questionable, but the President regards that concession as a part of the case only so far as it shows the beginning and the animus of that course of conduct which resulted so disastrously to the United States. It is important, in that it foreshadows subsequent events.

There were other powers that were contemporaneous with England in similar concession, but it was in England only that the concession was supplemented by acts causing direct damage to the United States. The President is careful to make this discrimination, because he is anxious as much as possible to simplify the case, and to bring into view these subsequent acts, which are so important to determining the question between the two countries.

You will, therefore, be pleased, in your social and private intercourse and conversation, as well as when it becomes necessary in your official conversation and intercourse, to adopt this view of the issuance of the declaration of neutrality by Great Britain, and the other powers, and to place the cause of grievance against Great Britain, not so much upon the issuance of her recognition of the insurgents' state of war, but upon her conduct under, and subsequent to, such recognition. And it is desirable that you avail yourself of early and suitable occasion, in your social intercourse with the representatives of other powers which made similar recognition, to let them understand the position of this Government on that question, and that the United States make such recognition by them no ground of complaint.

◇◇◇◇◇◇◇◇◇◇◇◇◇

5. PROPOSAL FOR A JOINT COMMISSION[5]

[*Memorandum of points taken in a conversation between Secretary Fish and Sir John Rose at Mr. Fish's House, January 9, 1871*]

"SIR JOHN ROSE stated that he had been requested by the British Government informally, unofficially, and personally, as one-half American, one-half English, enjoying the confidence of both governments, to ascertain what could be done for settling the pending questions between the two governments; and that he was authorized to say that, if it would be acceptable to the Government of the United States to refer all those subjects to a joint commission framed something upon the model of the commission which made the treaty of Ghent, he could say that the British Government was prepared to send out such a commission on their part, composed of persons of the highest rank in the realm. He dwelt upon the importance of settling these questions now. . . . Mr. Fish replied that before agreeing to go into such a commission there should be a certainty of success – for failure would leave things much worse than they were before – and he asked whether, in going into a commission, the British Government would be prepared to admit a liability for what were known as the *Alabama* claims.

"Sir John said that he would be wanting in frankness if he did not state that such a concession would not be made; that, in his own judgment, the Government of Great Britain would be found to be liable for the damage committed by the *Alabama,* and as to the other vessels it would be doubtful; that the government was prepared to agree to a submission to arbitration, either to continental jurists, or to a mixed court composed of English and American jurists or to any other tribunal that the two governments might agree upon; but that the feeling in England was such that the government would not be supported in Parliament in agreeing to admit the liability for the acts of the *Alabama.*

"Mr. Fish replied that with equal candor he must say that this government would not, in his judgment, be supported by the Senate or by the country in making a treaty which did not recognize that liability; that under our Constitution one third of the Senate and one Senator in addition could defeat a treaty; that most of the present Senators had voted against the Johnson-Clarendon treaty, and were committed as to the liability of England as to the *Alabama;* that the discussion made at that time had left a feeling among the people which would tend to prevent any change in the vote of the Senate; that the changes which were to be made in the Senate on the 4th of March would probably not make much change in this respect; that he thought that the nation might possibly be satisfied with a recognition of liability for the acts of the *Alabama,* and be recon-

[5] John Bassett Moore: *History and Digest of The International Arbitrations to which the United States has been a Party,* 6 vols., (Washington, 1898) Vol. I, pp. 521–2.

ciled to the submission of the liability as to the other vessels; and that therefore unless Great Britain could concede that point it would be useless to go into a commission.

"Sir John Rose endeavored at great length to combat these views, and urged in a forcible way his own conviction that, if the two nations once met in commission, the commissioners would not part without agreeing to a settlement. He also argued, quoting Mr. Lowe, that the people who furnished the money for and superintended the fitting out of the *Alabama*, who were Americans, were now in the full enjoyment of their rights as citizens of the United States, and that the question was a domestic one between this government and its citizens.

"Mr. Fish replied that the British Government was estopped, by the recognition of the South as belligerents, from denying their character as public enemies. He repeated the necessity for a recognition of liability as to the *Alabama* as a preliminary. He said that he did not ask England to humiliate herself – to say that her laws were inefficient, or her government unfaithful to its duties; that it seemed to him that England might very well feel that, owing to the negligence or unfaithfulness of a local officer, this vessel had been allowed to escape against the directions of the government, and that thereby the government had become liable; and should couple this statement with an expression of regret for what had taken place to disturb the relations of the two countries, – that less than this the United States ought not to be and would not be satisfied with.

"Some discussion was also had as to the manner in which the questions should be raised.

"Sir John Rose said that the British Government could not take the initiative in the question of the *Alabama* claims, and suggested that, in case the way for a settlement seemed clear, the British Government should propose a commission for the settlement of the San Juan boundary, the fisheries, and other Canadian questions, and that the United States should accede, provided the claims for the acts of the vessels should be also considered. Mr. Fish assented to this."

◇◇◇◇◇◇◇◇◇◇◇◇◇◇

6. THE TREATY OF WASHINGTON[6]

[*Concluded May 8, 1871; ratifications exchanged June 17, 1871*]

. . . *ARTICLE I.* Whereas differences have arisen between the Government of the United States and the Government of Her Britannic Majesty,

[6] *Public Statutes at Large of The United States,* Vol. XVII, pp. 863–76. The treaty was signed by Hamilton Fish, Samuel Nelson, Geo. H. Williams, Stafford H. Northcote, John A. MacDonald, Robt. C. Schenck, Ebenezer Rockwood Hoar, De Grey & Ripon, Edwd. Thornton, and Montague Bernard.

and still exist, growing out of the acts committed by the several vessels which have given rise to the claims generically known as the "Alabama Claims": . . .

Now, in order to remove and adjust all complaints and claims on the part of the United States, and to provide for the speedy settlement of such claims, which are not admitted by Her Britannic Majesty's Government, the high contracting parties agree that all the said claims, growing out of acts committed by the aforesaid vessels, and generically known as the "Alabama Claims," shall be referred to a tribunal of arbitration to be composed of five Arbitrators, to be appointed in the following manner, that is to say: One shall be named by the President of the United States; one shall be named by Her Britannic Majesty; His Majesty the King of Italy shall be requested to name one; the President of the Swiss Confederation shall be requested to name one; and His Majesty the Emperor of Brazil shall be requested to name one. . . .

Article II. The Arbitrators shall meet at Geneva, in Switzerland, at the earliest convenient day after they shall have been named, and shall proceed impartially and carefully to examine and decide all questions that shall be laid before them on the part of the Governments of the United States and Her Britannic Majesty respectively. All questions considered by the tribunal, including the final award, shall be decided by a majority of all the Arbitrators.

Each of the high contracting parties shall also name one person to attend the tribunal as its Agent to represent it generally in all matters connected with the arbitration. . . .

Article VI. In deciding the matters submitted to the arbitrators, they shall be governed by the following three rules, which are agreed upon by the high contracting parties as rules to be taken as applicable to the case, and by such principles of international law not inconsistent therewith as the Arbitrators shall determine to have been applicable to the case.

Rules

A neutral Government is bound —

First, to use due diligence to prevent the fitting out, arming, or equipping, within its jurisdiction, of any vessel which it has reasonable ground to believe is intended to cruise or to carry on war against a Power with which it is at peace; and also to use like diligence to prevent the departure from its jurisdiction of any vessel intended to cruise or carry on war as above, such vessel having been specially adapted, in whole or in part, within such jurisdiction, to warlike use.

Secondly, not to permit or suffer either belligerent to make use of its ports or waters as the base of naval operations against the other, or for the purpose of the renewal or augmentation of military supplies or arms, or the recruitment of men.

Thirdly, to exercise due diligence in its own ports and waters, and, as to all persons within its jurisdiction, to prevent any violation of the foregoing obligations and duties. . . .

Article VII. The said tribunal shall first determine as to each vessel separately whether Great Britain has, by any act or omission, failed to fulfil any of the duties set forth in the foregoing three rules, or recognized by the principles of international law not inconsistent with such rules, and shall certify such fact as to each of the said vessels. In case the tribunal find that Great Britain has failed to fulfil any duty or duties as aforesaid, it may, if it think proper, proceed to award a sum in gross to be paid by Great Britain to the United States for all the claims referred to it; and in such case the gross sum so awarded shall be paid in coin by the Government of Great Britain to the Government of the United States, at Washington, within twelve months after the date of the award. . . .

Article X. In case the tribunal finds that Great Britain has failed to fulfil any duty or duties as aforesaid, and does not award a sum in gross, the high contracting parties agree that a board of assessors shall be appointed to ascertain and determine what claims are valid, and what amount or amounts shall be paid by Great Britain to the United States on account of the liability arising from such failure, as to each vessel, according to the extent of such liability as decided by the Arbitrators.

The board of assessors shall be constituted as follows: One member thereof shall be named by the President of the United States, one member thereof shall be named by Her Britannic Majesty, and one member thereof shall be named by the Representative at Washington of His Majesty the King of Italy; and in case of a vacancy happening from any cause, it shall be filled in the same manner in which the original appointment was made. . . .

◇◇◇◇◇◇◇◇◇◇◇◇◇◇

7. THE GENEVA DECISION AND AWARD[7]

. . . WHEREAS, having regard to the VIth and VIIth articles of the said treaty [Treaty of Washington], the arbitrators are bound under the terms of the said VIth article, "in deciding the matters submitted to them, to be governed by the three rules therein specified and by such principles of international law, not inconsistent therewith, as the arbitrators shall determine to have been applicable to the case";

AND WHEREAS the "due diligence" referred to in the first and third of

[7] *Papers Relating to the Treaty of Washington.* Vol. IV, pp. 49–54, *Geneva Arbitration* (Washington, Government Printing Office, 1872). The rule concerning "due diligence" in the Geneva decision was not followed in the Convention (XIII) Concerning the Rights and Duties of Neutral Powers in Naval War, signed at The Hague, October 18, 1907. Article 25 of that Convention reads as follows:

> A neutral Power is bound to exercise such surveillance as the means at its disposal allow to prevent any violation of the provisions of the above articles occurring in its ports or roadsteads or in its waters.

the said rules ought to be exercised by neutral governments in exact proportion to the risks to which either of the belligerents may be exposed, from a failure to fulfill the obligations of neutrality on their part; . . .

And Whereas the effects of a violation of neutrality committed by means of the construction, equipment, and armament of a vessel are not done away with by any commission which the government of the belligerent power, benefited by the violation of neutrality, may afterwards have granted to that vessel; and the ultimate step, by which the offense is completed, cannot be admissible as a ground for the absolution of the offender, nor can the consummation of his fraud become the means of establishing this innocence;

And Whereas the privilege of exterritoriality accorded to vessels of war has been admitted into the law of nations, not as an absolute right, but solely as a proceeding founded on the principle of courtesy and mutual deference between different nations, and therefore can never be appealed to for the protection of acts done in violation of neutrality; . . .

And Whereas, with respect to the vessel called the *Alabama,* it clearly results from all the facts relative to the construction of the ship at first designated by the number "290" in the port of Liverpool, and its equipment and armament in the vicinity of Terceira through the agency of the vessels called the *Agrippina* and the *Bahama,* dispatched from Great Britain to that end, that the British government failed to use due diligence in the performance of its neutral obligations; and especially that it omitted, notwithstanding the warnings and official representations made by the diplomatic agents of the United States during the construction of the said number "290," to take in due time any effective measures of prevention, and that those orders which it did give at last, for the detention of the vessel, were issued so late that their execution was not practicable; . . .

And Whereas the government of Her Britannic Majesty cannot justify itself for a failure in due diligence on the plea of insufficiency of the legal means of action which it possessed:

Four of the arbitrators, for the reasons above assigned, and the fifth for reasons separately assigned by him,

Are of opinion—

That Great Britain has in this case failed, by omission, to fulfill the duties prescribed in the first and the third of the rules established by the VIth article of the Treaty of Washington. . . .

The tribunal, making use of the authority conferred upon it by Article VII. of the said treaty, by a majority of four voices to one, awards to the United States a sum of $15,500,000 in gold, as the indemnity to be paid by Great Britain to the United States, for the satisfaction of all the claims referred to the consideration of the tribunal, conformably to the provisions contained in Article VII. of the aforesaid treaty. . . .

◇◇◇◇◇◇◇◇◇◇◇◇◇

8. ANGLO-AMERICAN TREATY OF ARBITRATION OF 1897[8]

ARTICLE I. The High Contracting Parties agree to submit to Arbitration in accordance with the provisions and subject to the limitations of this Treaty all questions in difference between them which they may fail to adjust by diplomatic negotiation.

Article II. All pecuniary claims or groups of pecuniary claims which do not in the aggregate exceed £100,000 in amount, and which do not involve the determination of territorial claims, shall be dealt with and decided by an Arbitral Tribunal constituted as provided in the next following Article. . . .

Article III. Each of the High Contracting Parties shall nominate one arbitrator who shall be a jurist of repute and the two arbitrators so nominated shall within two months of the date of their nomination select an umpire. . . .

The person so selected shall be the President of the Tribunal and the award of the majority of the Members thereof shall be final.

Article IV. All pecuniary claims or groups of pecuniary claims which shall exceed £100,000 in amount and all other matters in difference, in respect of which either of the High Contracting Parties shall have rights against the other under Treaty or otherwise, provided that such matters in difference do not involve the determination of territorial claims, shall be dealt with and decided by an Arbitral Tribunal, constituted as provided in the next following Article.

Article V. Any subject of Arbitration described in Article IV shall be submitted to the Tribunal provided for by Article III, the award of which Tribunal, if unanimous, shall be final. If not unanimous either of the High Contracting Parties may within six months from the date of the award demand a review thereof. In such case the matter in controversy shall be submitted to an Arbitral Tribunal consisting of five jurists of repute, no one of whom shall have been a member of the Tribunal whose award is to be reviewed and who shall be selected as follows, viz: – two by each of the High Contracting Parties and, one to act as umpire, by the four thus nominated and to be chosen within three months after the date of their nomination. . . .

The person so selected shall be the President of the Tribunal and the award of the majority of the members thereof shall be final.

Article VI. Any controversy which shall involve the determination of territorial claims shall be submitted to a Tribunal composed of six members

[8] Signed in Washington January 11, 1897. *Papers Relating to the Foreign Relations of the United States,* 1896, pp. 238–40. The Senate debated the treaty at length, adopted extensive amendments, and then refused to give its advice and consent to the ratification of the treaty as amended. References to documentary sources are given in "Arbitration and the United States," World Peace Foundation *Pamphlets,* Vol. IX, pp. 500–13.

three of whom (subject to the provisions of Article VIII) shall be Judges of the Supreme Court of the United States or Justices of the Circuit Courts to be nominated by the President of the United States, and the other three of whom, (subject to the provisions of Article VIII) shall be Judges of the British Supreme Court of Judicature or Members of the Judicial Committee of the Privy Council to be nominated by Her Britannic Majesty, whose award by a majority of not less than five to one shall be final. In case of an award made by less than the prescribed majority, the award shall also be final unless either Power shall, within three months after the award has been reported protest that the same is erroneous, in which case the award shall be of no validity.

In the event of an award made by less than the prescribed majority and protested as above provided, or if the members of the Arbitral Tribunal shall be equally divided, there shall be no recourse to hostile measures of any description until the mediation of one or more friendly Powers has been invited by one or both of the High Contracting Parties. . . .

Article VIII. In cases where the question involved is one which concerns a particular State or Territory of the United States, it shall be open to the President of the United States to appoint a judicial officer of such State or Territory to be one of the Arbitrators under Article III or Article V or Article VI.

In like manner in cases where the question involved is one which concerns a British Colony or possession, it shall be open to Her Britannic Majesty to appoint a judicial officer of such Colony or possession to be one of the Arbitrators under Article III or Article V or Article VI. . . .

Article XIV. This Treaty shall remain in force for five years from the date at which it shall come into operation, and further until the expiration of twelve months after either of the High Contracting Parties shall have given notice to the other of its wish to terminate the same.

◇◇◇◇◇◇◇◇◇◇◇◇◇

9. ARBITRATION TREATIES OF 1908–9[9]

ARTICLE I. Differences which may arise of a legal nature, or relating to the interpretation of treaties existing between the two contracting parties, and which it may not have been possible to settle by diplomacy, shall be referred to the Permanent Court of Arbitration established at The Hague by the Convention of July 29, 1899, provided, nevertheless, that they do not affect the vital interests, the independence, or the honor of the two contracting states, and do not concern the interests of third parties.

[9] Twenty-five treaties, virtually the same as the one quoted here, signed with France, February 10, 1908, were negotiated during 1908–9. A brief history of these is in "Arbitration and the United States," World Peace Foundation *Pamphlets,* Vol. IX, pp. 521–3. *Treaties . . . and Agreements Between the United States and Other Powers,* Vol. I, p. 549.

Article II. In each individual case the high contracting parties, before appealing to the Permanent Court of Arbitration, shall conclude a special agreement defining clearly the matter in dispute, the scope of the powers of the arbitrators, and the periods to be fixed for the formation of the arbitral tribunal and the several stages of the procedure. It is understood that on the part of the United States such special agreements will be made by the President of the United States, by and with the advice and consent of the Senate, and on the part of France they will be subject to the procedure required by the constitutional laws of France.

Article III. The present convention shall be ratified by the President of the United States of America, by and with the advice and consent of the Senate thereof; it shall become effective on the day of such ratification, and shall remain in force for a period of five years thereafter. . . .

10. ARBITRATION TREATIES OF 1911 [10]

ARTICLE I. All differences hereafter arising between the High Contracting Parties, which it has not been possible to adjust by diplomacy, relating to international matters in which the High Contracting Parties are concerned by virtue of a claim of right made by one against the other under treaty or otherwise, and which are justiciable in their nature by reason of being susceptible of decision by the application of the principles of law or equity, shall be submitted to the Permanent Court of Arbitration established at The Hague by the Convention of October 18, 1907, or to some other arbitral tribunal, as *shall* [may] be decided in each case by special agreement, which special agreement shall provide for the organization of such tribunal if necessary, define the scope of the powers of the arbitrators, the question or questions at issue, and settle the terms of reference and the procedure thereunder. . . .

---

[10] Identic treaties signed with Great Britain and France August 3, 1911. The Senate gave its advice and consent to the ratification of these treaties but with amendments striking out the parts shown in brackets, and with the following proviso:

PROVIDED, That the Senate advises and consents to the ratification of the said treaty with the understanding, to be made part of such ratification, that the treaty does not authorize the submission to arbitration of any question which affects the admission of aliens into the United States, or the admission of aliens to the educational institutions of the several States, or the territorial integrity of the several States or of the United States, or concerning the question of the alleged indebtedness or monied obligation of any State of the United States, or any question which depends upon or involves the maintenance of the traditional attitude of the United States concerning American questions, commonly described as the Monroe doctrine, or other purely governmental policy.

Since the President refused to accept the Senate's amendments, the treaties never came into force.

Senate Document No. 476, 62nd Congress, 2nd Session, (6176) pp. 2–6.

The special agreement in each case shall be made on the part of the United States by the President of the United States, by and with the advice and consent of the Senate thereof. . . .

Article II. The High Contracting Parties further agree to institute as occasion arises, and as hereinafter provided, a Joint High Commission of Inquiry to which, upon the request of either Party, shall be referred for impartial and conscientious investigation any controversy between the Parties within the scope of Article I, before such controversy has been submitted to arbitration, and also any other controversy hereafter arising between them even if they are not agreed that it falls within the scope of Article I. . . .

Article III. . . . (It is further agreed, however, that in cases in which the Parties disagree as to whether or not a difference is subject to arbitration under Article I of this Treaty, that question shall be submitted to the Joint High Commission of Inquiry; and if all or all but one of the members of the Commission agree and report that such difference is within the scope of Article I, it shall be referred to arbitration in accordance with the provisions of this Treaty.)

◇◇◇◇◇◇◇◇◇◇◇◇◇◇

11. THE CONCILIATION TREATIES OF 1913–14[11]

ARTICLE I. The high contracting parties agree that all disputes between them, of every nature whatsoever, which diplomacy shall fail to adjust, shall be submitted for investigation and report to an International Commission, to be constituted in the manner prescribed in the next succeeding Article; and they agree not to declare war or begin hostilities during such investigation and report.

Article II. The International Commission shall be composed of five members, to be appointed as follows: One member shall be chosen from each country, by the Government thereof; one member shall be chosen by each Government from some third country; the fifth member shall be chosen by common agreement between the two Governments. The expenses of the Commission shall be paid by the two Governments in equal proportion.

The International Commission shall be appointed within four months after the exchange of the ratifications of this treaty; and vacancies shall be filled according to the manner of the original appointment.

Article III. In case the high contracting parties shall have failed to adjust a dispute by diplomatic methods, they shall at once refer it to the International Commission for investigation and report. The International Commission may, however, act upon its own initiative, and in such case

[11] Secretary of State, William Jennings Bryan, negotiated thirty treaties essentially the same as the one quoted here, signed with Guatemala, September 20, 1913. Twenty-one of the original treaties came into force. Sen. Doc. No. 348, 64 Cong. 4th Sess., *Treaties . . . and Agreements Between the United States and Other Powers*, 1910–1923, pp. 2666–7.

it shall notify both Governments and request their cooperation in the investigation.

The report of the International Commission shall be completed within one year after the date on which it shall declare its investigation to have begun, unless the high contracting parties shall extend the time by mutual agreement. The report shall be prepared in triplicate; one copy shall be presented to each Government, and the third retained by the Commission for its files.

The high contracting parties reserve the right to act independently on the subject-matter of the dispute after the report of the Commission shall have been submitted.

12. THE KELLOGG ARBITRATION TREATIES[12]

ARTICLE I. All differences relating to international matters in which the High Contracting Parties are concerned by virtue of a claim of right made by one against the other under treaty or otherwise, which it has not been possible to adjust by diplomacy, which have not been adjusted as a result of reference to an appropriate commission of conciliation, and which are justiciable in their nature by reason of being susceptible of decision by the application of the principles of law or equity, shall be submitted to the Permanent Court of Arbitration established at The Hague by the Convention of October 18, 1907, or to some other competent tribunal, as shall be decided in each case by special agreement, which special agreement shall provide for the organization of such tribunal if necessary, define its powers, state the question or questions at issue, and settle the terms of reference.

The special agreement in each case shall be made on the part of the United States of America by the President of the United States of America by and with the advice and consent of the Senate thereof, and on the part of Germany in accordance with its constitutional laws.

Article II. The provisions of this treaty shall not be invoked in respect of any dispute the subject matter of which

(a) is within the domestic jurisdiction of either of the High Contracting Parties,

(b) involves the interests of third Parties,

(c) depends upon or involves the maintenance of the traditional attitude of the United States concerning American questions, commonly described as the Monroe Doctrine,

(d) depends upon or involves the observance of the obligations of Germany in accordance with the Covenant of the League of Nations. . . .

[12] Between 1918 and 1931, eighteen arbitration treaties, similar to the one quoted here, signed with Germany, May 5, 1928, were negotiated with non-American states. Sen. Doc. No. 134, 75 Cong. 3d Sess., *Treaties . . . and Agreements Between the United States and Other Powers,* 1923–1937, pp. 4210–11.

Chapter XXI

THE VENEZUELAN BOUNDARY

IN 1895 the American government precipitated itself into the British-Venezuelan boundary controversy and virtually announced to the world that the Monroe Doctrine was a part of American foreign policy which would be vigorously maintained if not actually extended. The boundary controversy had been the subject of discussions between Great Britain and Venezuela for a long time, but the two nations appeared to get further apart in their positions concerning it. Although the American government on several occasions had taken official notice of the controversy, it was not until about 1899 that the American people began seriously to consider the possibility of British territorial expansion in Latin America under the guise of a boundary settlement. When President Cleveland decided that the time had come for vigorous action, the famous dispatch of his Secretary of State, of July 20, 1895 (1) to the American ambassador in London, left no doubt as to the position of the United States. The British government sent a belated reply in two dispatches, one dealing with the Monroe Doctrine (2) and the other with the boundary question (3). President Cleveland considered that the British position was untenable and with characteristic bluntness sent a message to Congress (4) which was as startling as Secretary Olney's dispatch of July 20. The result was that the British and American governments found themselves in a tense situation which might easily have become much more serious. In the end calm judgments prevailed, Great Britain came forward with a proposal (5) for a peaceful solution of the difficulty, and, in less than a year after the crisis had arisen, a settlement was effected satisfactory to all parties concerned (6).

1. AMERICA'S INTEREST IN THE VENEZUELAN BOUNDARY CONTROVERSY[1]

[*Richard Olney to Thomas F. Bayard*]

Washington, July 20, 1895

I AM directed by the President to communicate to you his views upon a subject to which he has given much anxious thought and respecting which he has not reached a conclusion without a lively sense of its great im-

[1] *House Ex. Doc.* (3368) 54th Congress, 1st Session, No. 1, Pt. I, pp. 545–62.

portance as well as of the serious responsibility involved in any action now to be taken.

It is not proposed, and for present purposes is not necessary, to enter into any detailed account of the controversy between Great Britain and Venezuela respecting the western frontier of the colony of British Guiana. The dispute is of ancient date and began at least as early as the time when Great Britain acquired by the treaty with the Netherlands of 1814 "the establishments of Demerara, Essequibo, and Berbice.". . .

It does not seem to be asserted, for instance, that in 1814 the "establishments" then acquired by Great Britain had any clearly defined western limits which can now be identified and which are either the limits insisted upon today, or, being the original limits, have been the basis of legitimate territorial extensions. On the contrary, having the actual possession of a district called the Pomaron district, she apparently remained indifferent as to the exact area of the colony until 1840, when she commissioned an engineer, Sir Robert Schomburgk, to examine and lay down its boundaries. The result was the Schomburgk line which was fixed by metes and bounds, was delineated on maps, and was at first indicated on the face of the country itself by posts, monograms, and other like symbols. If it was expected that Venezuela would acquiesce in this line, the expectation was doomed to speedy disappointment. Venezuela at once protested and with such vigor and to such purpose that the line was explained to be only tentative – part of a general boundary scheme concerning Brazil and the Netherlands as well as Venezuela – and the monuments of the line set up by Schomburgk were removed by the express order of Lord Aberdeen. . . .

Several other features of the situation remain to be briefly noticed – the continuous growth of the undefined British claim, the fate of the various attempts at arbitration of the controversy, and the part in the matter heretofore taken by the United States. As already seen, the exploitation of the Schomburgk line in 1840 was at once followed by the protest of Venezuela and by proceedings on the part of Great Britain which could fairly be interpreted only as a disavowal of that line. Indeed – in addition to the facts already noticed – Lord Aberdeen himself in 1844 proposed a line beginning at the River Moroco, a distinct abandonment of the Schomburgk line. Notwithstanding this, however, every change in the British claim since that time has moved the frontier of British Guiana farther and farther to the westward of the line thus proposed. The Granville line of 1881 placed the starting point at a distance of twenty-nine miles from the Moroco in the direction of Punta Barima. The Rosebery line of 1886 placed it west of the Guiama River, and about that time, if the British authority known as the Statesman's Year Book is to be relied upon, the area of British Guiana was suddenly enlarged by some 33,000 square miles – being stated as 76,000 square miles in 1885 and 109,000 square miles in 1887. . . .

The important features of the existing situation, as shown by the foregoing recital, may be briefly stated.

The Venezuelan Boundary

1. The title to territory of indefinite but confessedly very large extent is in dispute between Great Britain on the one hand and the South American Republic of Venezuela on the other.

2. The disparity in the strength of the claimants is such that Venezuela can hope to establish her claim only through peaceful methods – through an agreement with her adversary either upon the subject itself or upon an arbitration.

3. The controversy, with varying claims on the part of Great Britain, has existed for more than half a century, during which period many earnest and persistent efforts of Venezuela to establish a boundary by agreement have proved unsuccessful.

4. The futility of the endeavor to obtain a conventional line being recognized, Venezuela for a quarter of a century has asked and striven for arbitration.

5. Great Britain, however, has always and continuously refused to arbitrate, except upon the condition of a renunciation of a large part of the Venezuelan claim and of a concession to herself of a large share of the territory in controversy.

6. By the frequent interposition of its good offices at the instance of Venezuela, by constantly urging and promoting the restoration of diplomatic relations between the two countries, by pressing for arbitration of the disputed boundary, by offering to act as arbitrator, by expressing its grave concern whenever new alleged instances of British aggression upon Venezuelan territory have been brought to its notice, the Government of the United States has made it clear to Great Britain and to the world that the controversy is one in which both its honor and its interests are involved and the continuance of which it can not regard with indifference. . . .

That America is in no part open to colonization, though the proposition was not universally admitted at the time of its first enunciation, has long been universally conceded. We are now concerned, therefore, only with that other practical application of the Monroe doctrine the disregard of which by an European power is to be deemed an act of unfriendliness towards the United States. The precise scope and limitations of this rule cannot be too clearly apprehended. It does not establish any general protectorate by the United States over other American states. It does not relieve any American state from its obligations as fixed by international law nor prevent any European power directly interested from enforcing such obligations or from inflicting merited punishment for the breach of them. It does not contemplate any interference in the internal affairs of any American state or in the relations between it and other American states. It does not justify any attempt on our part to change the established form of government of any American state or to prevent the people of such state from altering that form according to their own will and pleasure. The rule in question has but a single purpose and object. It is that no European power or combination of European powers shall forcibly deprive an American

state of the right and power of self-government and of shaping for itself its own political fortunes and destinies. . . .

Is it true, then, that the safety and welfare of the United States are so concerned with the maintenance of the independence of every American state as against any European power as to justify and require the interposition of the United States whenever that independence is endangered? The question can be candidly answered in but one way. The states of America, South as well as North, by geographical proximity, by natural sympathy, by similarity of governmental constitutions, are friends and allies, commercially and politically, of the United States. To allow the subjugation of any of them by an European power is, of course, to completely reverse that situation and signifies the loss of all the advantages incident to their natural relations to us. But that is not all. The people of the United States have a vital interest in the cause of popular self-government. They have secured the right for themselves and their posterity at the cost of infinite blood and treasure. They have realized and exemplified its beneficient operation by a career unexampled in point of national greatness or individual felicity. They believe it to be for the healing of all nations, and that civilization must either advance or retrograde accordingly as its supremacy is extended or curtailed. Imbued with these sentiments, the people of the United States might not impossibly be wrought up to an active propaganda in favor of a cause so highly valued both for themselves and for mankind. But the age of the Crusades has passed, and they are content with such assertion and defense of the right of popular self-government as their own security and welfare demand. It is in that view more than in any other that they believe it not to be tolerated that the political control of an American state shall be forcibly assumed by an European power.

The mischiefs apprehended from such a source are none the less real because not immediately imminent in any specific case, and are none the less to be guarded against because the combination of circumstances that will bring them upon us cannot be predicted. The civilized states of Christendom deal with each other on substantially the same principles that regulate the conduct of individuals. The greater its enlightenment, the more surely every state perceives that its permanent interests require it to be governed by the immutable principles of right and justice. Each, nevertheless, is only too liable to succumb to the temptations offered by seeming special opportunities for its own aggrandizement, and each would rashly imperil its own safety were it not to remember that for the regard and respect of other states it must be largely dependent upon its own strength and power. Today the United States is practically sovereign on this continent, and its fiat is law upon the subjects to which it confines its interposition. Why? It is not because of the pure friendship or good will felt for it. It is not simply by reason of its high character as a civilized state, nor because wisdom and justice and equity are the invariable characteristics of the dealings of the United States. It is because, in addition to all other grounds, its infinite resources combined with its isolated position render it master of the situation and practically invulnerable as against any or all other powers.

All the advantages of this superiority are at once imperiled if the principle be admitted that European powers may convert American states into colonies or provinces of their own. The principle would be eagerly availed of, and every power doing so would immediately acquire a base of military operations against us. What one power was permitted to do could not be denied to another, and it is not inconceivable that the struggle now going on for the acquisition of Africa might be transferred to South America. If it were, the weaker countries would unquestionably be soon absorbed, while the ultimate result might be the partition of all South America between the various European powers. The disastrous consequences to the United States of such a condition of things are obvious. The loss of prestige, of authority, and of weight in the councils of the family of nations, would be among the least of them. Our only real rivals in peace as well as enemies in war would be found located at our very doors. Thus far in our history we have been spared the burdens and evils of immense standing armies and all the other accessories of huge warlike establishments, and the exemption has largely contributed to our national greatness and wealth as well as to the happiness of every citizen. But, with the powers of Europe permanently encamped on American soil, the ideal conditions we have thus far enjoyed can not be expected to continue. We too must be armed to the teeth, we too must convert the flower of our male population into soldiers and sailors, and by withdrawing them from the various pursuits of peaceful industry we too must practically annihilate a large share of the productive energy of the nation. . . .

Thus, as already intimated, the British demand that her right to a portion of the disputed territory shall be acknowledged before she will consent to an arbitration as to the rest seems to stand upon nothing but her own *ipse dixit*. She says to Venezuela, in substance: "You can get none of the debatable land by force, because you are not strong enough; you can get none by a treaty, because I will not agree; and you can take your chance of getting a portion by arbitration, only if you first agree to abandon to me such other portion as I may designate." It is not perceived how such an attitude can be defended nor how it is reconcilable with that love of justice and fair play so eminently characteristic of the English race. It in effect deprives Venezuela of her free agency and puts her under virtual duress. Territory acquired by reason of it will be as much wrested from her by the strong hand as if occupied by British troops or covered by British fleets. It seems therefore quite impossible that this position of Great Britain should be assented to by the United States, or that, if such position be adhered to with the result of enlarging the bounds of British Guiana, it should not be regarded as amounting, in substance, to an invasion and conquest of Venezuelan territory. . . .

◇◇◇◇◇◇◇◇◇◇◇◇◇◇

2. BRITISH OPINION OF THE MONROE DOCTRINE [2]

[*Lord Salisbury to Sir Julian Pauncefote*]

Foreign Office, [London] November 26, 1895

. . . THE CONTENTIONS set forth by Mr. Olney . . . are represented by him as being an application of the political maxims which are well known in American discussion under the name of the Monroe doctrine. As far as I am aware, this doctrine has never been before advanced on behalf of the United States in any written communication addressed to the Government of another nation; but it has been generally adopted and assumed as true by many eminent writers and politicians in the United States. It is said to have largely influenced the Government of that country in the conduct of its foreign affairs: though Mr. Clayton, who was Secretary of State under President Taylor, expressly stated that that Administration had in no way adopted it. But during the period that has elapsed since the Message of President Monroe was delivered in 1823, the doctrine has undergone a very notable development, and the aspect which it now presents in the hands of Mr. Olney differs widely from its character when it first issued from the pen of its author. The two propositions which in effect President Monroe laid down were, first, that America was no longer to be looked upon as a field for European colonization; and, secondly, that Europe must not attempt to extend its political system to America, or to control the political condition of any of the American communities who had recently declared their independence. . . .

The dangers which were apprehended by President Monroe have no relation to the state of things in which we live at the present day. There is no danger of any Holy Alliance imposing its system upon any portion of the American Continent, and there is no danger of any European State treating any part of the American Continent as a fit object for European colonization. It is intelligible that Mr. Olney should invoke, in defence of the views on which he is now insisting, an authority which enjoys so high a popularity with his own fellow-countrymen. But the circumstances with which President Monroe was dealing, and those to which the present American Government is addressing itself, have very few features in common. Great Britain is imposing no "system" upon Venezuela, and is not concerning herself in any way with the nature of the political institutions under which the Venezuelans may prefer to live. But the British Empire and the Republic of Venezuela are neighbors, and they have differed for some time past, and continue to differ, as to the line by which their dominions are separated. It is a controversy with which the United States have no apparent practical concern. It is difficult, indeed, to see how it can materially affect any State or community outside those primarily interested, except perhaps other parts of Her Majesty's dominions, such as Trinidad.

[2] *House Ex. Doc.* (3368) 54th Congress, 1st Session, No. 1, Pt. I, pp. 563–7.

The disputed frontier of Venezuela has nothing to do with any of the questions dealt with by President Monroe. It is not a question of the colonization by a European Power of any portion of America. It is not a question of the imposition upon the communities of South America of any system of government devised in Europe. It is simply the determination of the frontier of a British possession which belonged to the Throne of England long before the Republic of Venezuela came into existence. But even if the interests of Venezuela were so far linked to those of the United States as to give to the latter a *locus standi* in this controversy, their Government apparently have not formed, and certainly do not express, any opinion upon the actual merits of the dispute. The Government of the United States do not say that Great Britain, or that Venezuela, is in the right in the matters that are in issue. But they lay down that the doctrine of President Monroe, when he opposed the imposition of European systems, or the renewal of European colonization, confers upon them the right of demanding that when a European Power has a frontier difference with a South American community, the European Power shall consent to refer that controversy to arbitration; and Mr. Olney states that unless Her Majesty's Government accede to this demand, it will "greatly embarrass the future relations between Great Britain and the United States. . . ."

In the remarks which I have made, I have argued on the theory that the Monroe doctrine in itself is sound. I must not, however, be understood as expressing any acceptance of it on the part of Her Majesty's Government. It must always be mentioned with respect, on account of the distinguished statesman to whom it is due, and the great nation who have generally adopted it. But international law is founded on the general consent of nations; and no statesmen, however eminent, and no nation, however powerful, are competent to insert into the code of international law a novel principle which was never recognized before, and which has not since been accepted by the Government of any other country. The United States have a right, like any other nation, to interpose in any controversy by which their own interests are affected; and they are the judge whether those interests are touched, and in what measure they should be sustained. But their rights are in no way strengthened or extended by the fact that the controversy affects some territory which is called American. Mr. Olney quotes the case of the recent Chilean war, in which the United States declined to join with France and England in an effort to bring hostilities to a close, on account of the Monroe doctrine. The United States were entirely in their right in declining to join in an attempt at pacification if they thought fit; but Mr. Olney's principle that "American questions are for American decision," even if it receive any countenance from the language of President Monroe (which it does not), can not be sustained by any reasoning drawn from the law of nations. . . .

◇◇◇◇◇◇◇◇◇◇◇◇◇◇

3. BRITISH DEFENSE OF HER VENEZUELAN POLICY[3]

[*Lord Salisbury to Sir Julian Pauncefote*]

Foreign Office, [*London*] *November 26, 1895*

IN MY PRECEDING despatch of today's date I have replied only to the latter portion of Mr. Olney's despatch of the 20th July last, which treats of the application of the Monroe doctrine to the question of the boundary dispute between Venezuela and the colony of British Guiana. But it seems desirable, in order to remove some evident misapprehensions as to the main features of the question, that the statement of it contained in the earlier portion of Mr. Olney's despatch should not be left without reply. . . .

Her Majesty's Government, while they have never avoided or declined argument on the subject with the Government of Venezuela, have always held that the question was one which had no direct bearing on the material interests of any other country, and have consequently refrained hitherto from presenting any detailed statement of their case either to the United States or to other foreign Governments.

It is, perhaps, a natural consequence of this circumstance that Mr. Olney's narration of what has passed bears the impress of being mainly, if not entirely, founded on *ex parte* statements emanating from Venezuela, and gives, in the opinion of Her Majesty's Government, an erroneous view of many material facts. . . .

It is true, as stated by Mr. Olney, that, in the Venezuelan Constitution of 1830, Article 5 lays down that "the territory of Venezuela comprises all that which previously to the political changes of 1810 was denominated the Captaincy-General of Venezuela." Similar declarations had been made in the fundamental laws promulgated in 1819 and 1821.

I need not point out that a declaration of this kind made by a newly self-constituted State can have no valid force as against international arrangements previously concluded by the nation from which it has separated itself.

But the present difficulty would never have arisen if the Government of Venezuela had been content to claim only those territories which could be proved or even reasonably asserted to have been practically in the possession and under the effective jurisdiction of the Captaincy-General of Venezuela. . . .

In submitting the maps of his survey, on which he indicated the line which he would propose to Her Majesty's Government for adoption, Sir R. Schomburgk called attention to the fact that Her Majesty's Government might justly claim the whole basin of the Cuyuni and Yuruari on the ground that the natural boundary of the Colony included any territory

---

3 Ibid., pp. 567–76.

through which flow rivers which fall into the Essequibo. . . . But, on grounds of complaisance towards Venezuela, he proposed that Great Britain should consent to surrender her claim to a more extended frontier inland in return for the formal recognition of her right to Point Barima. It was on this principle that he drew the boundary-line which has since been called by his name.

Undoubtedly, therefore, Mr. Olney is right when he states that "it seems impossible to treat the Schomburgk line as being the boundary claimed by Great Britain as matter of right, or as anything but a line originating in considerations of convenience and expediency." The Schomburgk line was in fact a great reduction of the boundary claimed by Great Britain as matter of right, and its proposal originated in a desire to come to a speedy and friendly arrangement with a weaker Power with whom Great Britain was at the time, and desired to remain, in cordial relations. . . .

As the progress of settlement by British subjects made a decision of some kind absolutely necessary, and as the Venezuelan Government refused to come to any reasonable arrangement, Her Majesty's Government decided not to repeat the offer of concessions which had not been reciprocated, but to assert their undoubted right to the territory within the Schomburgk line, while still consenting to hold open for further negotiation, and even for arbitration, the unsettled lands between that line and what they considered to be the rightful boundary, as stated in the note to Señor Rojaz of the 10th January, 1880. . . .

Although the negotiations in 1890, 1891, and 1893 did not lead to any result, Her Majesty's Government have not abandoned the hope that they may be resumed with better success, and that when the internal politics of Venezuela are settled on a more durable basis than has lately appeared to be the case, her Government may be enabled to adopt a more moderate and conciliatory course in regard to this question than that of their predecessors. Her Majesty's Government are sincerely desirous of being of friendly relations with Venezuela, and certainly have no design to seize territory that properly belongs to her, or forcibly to extend sovereignty over any portion of her population.

They have, on the contrary, repeatedly expressed their readiness to submit to arbitration the conflicting claims of Great Britain and Venezuela to large tracts of territory which from their auriferous nature are known to be of almost untold value. But they can not consent to entertain, or to submit to the arbitration of another Power or of foreign jurists, however eminent, claims based on the extravagant pretensions of Spanish officials in the last century, and involving the transfer of large numbers of British subjects, who have for many years enjoyed the settled rule of a British Colony, to a nation of different race and language, whose political system is subject to frequent disturbance, and whose institutions as yet too often afford very inadequate protection to life and property. No issue of this description has ever been involved in the questions which Great Britain and the United States have consented to submit to arbitration, and Her Majesty's Government are convinced that in similar circumstances the Government of the United States would be equally firm in declining to entertain proposals of such a nature. . . .

◇◇◇◇◇◇◇◇◇◇◇◇◇

4. PROPOSAL FOR A BOUNDARY COMMISSION[4]

[*Message of President Cleveland to the Congress of The United States, December 17, 1895*]

IN MY ANNUAL message addressed to the Congress on the third instant I called attention to the pending boundary controversy between Great Britain and the Republic of Venezuela and recited the substance of a representation made by this Government to Her Britannic Majesty's Government suggesting reasons why such dispute should be submitted to arbitration for settlement, and inquiring whether it would be so submitted. . . .

If a European power, by an extension of its boundaries, takes possession of the territory of one of our neighboring Republics against its will and in derogation of its rights, it is difficult to see why to that extent such European power does not thereby attempt to extend its system of government to that portion of this continent which is thus taken. This is the precise action which President Monroe declared to be "dangerous to our peace and safety," and it can make no difference whether the European system is extended by an advance of frontier or otherwise.

It is also suggested in the British reply that we should not seek to apply the Monroe doctrine to the pending dispute because it does not embody any principle of international law which "is founded on the general consent of nations," and that "no statesman, however eminent, and no nation, however powerful, are competent to insert into the code of international law a novel principle which was never recognized before, and which has not since been accepted by the Government of any other country."

Practically the principle for which we contend has peculiar if not exclusive relation to the United States. It may not have been admitted in so many words to the code of international law, but since in international councils every nation is entitled to the rights belonging to it, if the enforcement of the Monroe doctrine is something we may justly claim it has its place in the code of international law as certainly and as securely as if it were specifically mentioned, and where the United States is a suitor before the high tribunal that administers international law the question to be determined is whether or not we present claims which the justice of that code of law can find to be right and valid. . . .

In the belief that the doctrine for which we contend was clear and

[4] Ibid., pp. 542–5.

definite, that it was founded upon substantial considerations and involved our safety and welfare, that it was fully applicable to our present conditions and to the state of the world's progress and that it was directly related to the pending controversy and without any conviction as to the final merits of the dispute, but anxious to learn in a satisfactory and conclusive manner whether Great Britain sought, under a claim of boundary, to extend her possessions on this continent without right, or whether she merely sought possession of territory fairly included within her lines of ownership, this Government proposed to the Government of Great Britain a resort to arbitration as the proper means of settling the question to the end that a vexatious boundary dispute between the two contestants might be determined and our exact standing and relation in respect to the controversy might be made clear.

It will be seen from the correspondence herewith submitted that this proposition has been declined by the British Government, upon grounds which in the circumstances seem to me to be far from satisfactory. It is deeply disappointing that such an appeal actuated by the most friendly feelings towards both nations directly concerned, addressed to the sense of justice and to the magnanimity of one of the great powers of the world and touching its relations to one comparatively weak and small, should have produced no better results. . . .

Assuming, however, that the attitude of Venezuela will remain unchanged, the dispute has reached such a stage as to make it now incumbent upon the United States to take measures to determine with sufficient certainty for its justification what is the true divisional line between the Republic of Venezuela and British Guiana. The inquiry to that end should of course be conducted carefully and judicially and due weight should be given to all available evidence records and facts in support of the claims of both parties.

In order that such an examination should be prosecuted in a thorough and satisfactory manner I suggest that the Congress make an adequate appropriation for the expenses of a Commission, to be appointed by the Executive, who shall make the necessary investigation and report upon the matter with the least possible delay. When such report is made and accepted it will in my opinion be the duty of the United States to resist by every means in its power as a willful aggression upon its rights and interests the appropriation by Great Britain of any lands or the exercise of governmental jurisdiction over any territory which after investigation we have determined of right belongs to Venezuela.

In making these recommendations I am fully alive to the responsibility incurred, and keenly realize all the consequences that may follow.

I am nevertheless firm in my conviction that while it is a grievous thing to contemplate the two great English-speaking peoples of the world as being otherwise than friendly competitors in the onward march of civilization, and strenuous and worthy rivals in all the arts of peace, there is no calamity which a great nation can invite which equals that which follows a supine submission to wrong and injustice and the consequent loss of national self respect and honor beneath which are shielded and defended a people's safety and greatness.

◇◇◇◇◇◇◇◇◇◇◇◇◇

5. BRITISH PROPOSAL FOR A SETTLEMENT OF THE VENEZUELAN QUESTION[5]

[*Lord Salisbury to Sir Julian Pauncefote*]

Foreign Office, [*London*] *May 22, 1896*

I SENT YOU in a dispatch under date of the 18th instant some observations upon Mr. Olney's communication to you with regard to the subject of general arbitration.

As it is possible, however, that we shall not see our way to surmount the difficulties which still separate the views of the two Governments in regard to the larger and more general question, I propose in this dispatch to convey to you proposals for the settlement of the Venezuelan dispute, which I should be glad if you would submit to the Government of the United States, acting as the friend of Venezuela in this matter. From the first our objection has been to subject to the decision of an arbiter, who, in the last resort, must, of necessity, be a foreigner, the rights of British colonists who have settled in the territory which they had every ground for believing to be British, and whose careers would be broken, and their fortunes possibly ruined, by a decision that the territory on which they have settled was subject to the Venezuelan Republic. At the same time we are very conscious that the dispute between ourselves and the Republic of Venezuela affects a very large portion of land which is not under settlement, and which could be disposed of without any injustice to any portion of the colonial population. We are very willing that the territory which is comprised within this definition should be subjected to the results of an arbitration, even though some portion of it should be found to fall within the Schomburgk line. With that end in view, we propose the following basis of settlement of the Venezuelan boundary dispute:

A commission to be created by agreement between Great Britain and the United States, consisting of four members, namely, two British subjects and two citizens of the United States; the above commission to investigate and to report upon the facts which affect the rights of the United Netherlands and of Spain, respectively, at the date of the acquisition of British Guiana by Great Britain.

This commission will only examine into questions of fact, without reference to the inferences that may be founded on them; but the finding of a majority of the commission upon those questions shall be binding upon both Governments.

[5] *House Ex. Doc.* (3477) 54th Congress, 2nd Session, No. 1, pp. 247–9.

Upon the report of the above commission being issued, the two Governments of Great Britain and Venezuela, respectively, shall endeavor to agree to a boundary line upon the basis of such report. Failing agreement, the report, and every other matter concerning this controversy on which either Government desire to insist, shall be submitted to a tribunal of three, one nominated by Great Britain, the other by Venezuela, and the third by the two so nominated; which tribunal shall fix the boundary line upon the basis of such report, and the line so fixed shall be binding upon Great Britain and Venezuela. Provided, always, that in fixing such line the tribunal shall not have power to include as the territory of Venezuela any territory which was bona fide occupied by subjects of Great Britain on the 1st of January, 1887, or as the territory of Great Britain any territory bona fide occupied by Venezuelans at the same date.

In respect to any territory with which, by this provision, the tribunal is precluded from dealing, the tribunal may submit to the two Powers any recommendations which seem to it calculated to satisfy the equitable rights of the parties, and the two Powers will take such recommendations into their consideration.

It will be evident from this proposal that we are prepared to accept the finding of a commission voting as three to one upon all the facts which are involved in the question of Dutch and Spanish rights at the time of the cession of Guiana to Great Britain. We are also prepared to accept the decision of an arbitral tribunal with regard to the ownership of all portions of the disputed territory which are not under settlement by British subjects or Venezuelan citizens. If the decision of the commission shall affect any territory which is so settled, it will be in the power of either Government to decline to accept the decision so arrived at, so far as it affects the territory alleged to be settled. But I need not point out to you that even upon that question, although the decision of the arbitral tribunal will not have a final effect, it will, unless it be manifestly unfair, offer a presumption, against which the protesting Government will practically find it difficult to contend.

◇◇◇◇◇◇◇◇◇◇◇◇◇

6. AMICABLE SETTLEMENT OF BOUNDARY DISPUTE[6]

[*Heads of proposed treaty between Venezuela and Great Britain for settlement of Venezuela boundary question as agreed upon between Great Britain and the United States*]

[*November 12, 1896*]

I. AN ARBITRAL tribunal shall be immediately appointed to determine the boundary line between the colony of British Guiana and the Republic of Venezuela.

[6] Ibid., pp. 254–5. The agreement was signed by Richard Olney and Sir Julian Pauncefote.

II. The tribunal shall consist of two members nominated by the judges of the Supreme Court of the United States and two members nominated by the judges of the British supreme court of justice and of a fifth juror selected by the four persons so nominated, or, in the event of their failure to agree within three months from the time of their nomination, selected by His Majesty the King of Sweden and Norway.

The person so selected shall be president of the tribunal.

The persons nominated by the judges of the Supreme Court of the United States and of the British supreme court of justice, respectively, may be judges of either of said courts.

III. The tribunal shall investigate and ascertain the extent of the territories belonging to or that might lawfully be claimed by the United Netherlands or by the Kingdom of Spain, respectively, at the time of the acquisition by Great Britain of the colony of British Guiana – and shall determine the boundary line between the colony of British Guiana and the Republic of Venezuela.

IV. In deciding the matters submitted the arbitrators shall ascertain all the facts which they deem necessary to a decision of the controversy and shall be governed by the following rules, which are agreed upon by the high contracting parties as rules to be taken as applicable to the case, and by such principles of international law not inconsistent therewith as the arbitrators shall determine to be applicable to the case.

Rules

(a) Adverse holding or prescription during a period of fifty years shall make a good title. The arbitrators may deem exclusive political control of a district, as well as actual settlement thereof, sufficient to constitute adverse holding or to make title by prescription.

(b) The arbitrators may recognize and give effect to rights and claims resting on any other ground whatever, valid according to international law, and on any principles of international law which the arbitrators may deem to be applicable to the case and which are not in contravention of the foregoing rule.

(c) In determining the boundary line, if territory of one party be found by the tribunal to have been at the date of this treaty in the occupation of the subjects or citizens of the other party, such effect shall be given to such occupation as reason, justice, the principles of international law, and the equities of the case shall, in the opinion of the tribunal, require.

CHAPTER XXII

AMERICAN EXPANSION INTO THE PACIFIC

◇◇◇◇◇◇◇◇◇◇◇◇◇

IT IS PROBABLE that the Hawaiian Islands were visited by an American citizen for the first time in 1789. The increase of interest of the American government in the Hawaiian Islands, and in the Pacific area in general, was reflected in the policy formed by Secretary of State John Quincy Adams with respect to Russian expansion on the continent of North America. Although a consul was designated for the Hawaiian Islands in 1823, the first real Hawaiian policy of the United States was formulated by President Tyler in 1842 (1). In 1855 President Pierce was willing to annex the Islands to the United States (2), but various circumstances prevented the fulfillment of his desire. In 1881 Secretary James G. Blaine formulated a more comprehensive Pacific policy (3) for the American government than it had possessed before, but it was not until 1892 that a movement in Hawaii looking to annexation became imminent (4). President Harrison advocated the annexation of the Islands in 1893 and a treaty providing for annexation was signed. President Cleveland, however, acting upon the advice of his Secretary of State (5), opposed the policy, but failed to take the necessary steps to effect a policy of his own (6). There the matter rested until 1898.

The unique features of the Samoan policy of the United States are illustrated by the quasi-protectorate of 1878 (7), and the Tripartite Treaty of 1889 (8).

◇◇◇◇◇◇◇◇◇◇◇◇◇

1. AMERICAN INTEREST IN THE HAWAIIAN ISLANDS[1]

[*Message of President Tyler to The Congress of The United States, December 30, 1842*]

I COMMUNICATE herewith to Congress copies of a correspondence which has recently taken place between certain agents of the Government of the Hawaiian or Sandwich Islands and the Secretary of State.

The condition of those islands has excited a good deal of interest, which is increasing by every successive proof that their inhabitants are making progress in civilization, and becoming more and more competent to maintain regular and orderly civil government. They lie in the Pacific Ocean, much nearer to this continent than the other, and have become an im-

[1] *Foreign Relations of the United States,* 1894, *Appendix,* II, pp. 39–41.

portant place for the refitment and provisioning of American and European vessels.

Owing to their locality and to the course of the winds which prevail in this quarter of the world, the Sandwich Islands are the stopping-place for almost all vessels passing from continent to continent, across the Pacific Ocean. They are especially resorted to by a great number of vessels of the United States, which are engaged in the whale fishery in those seas. The number of vessels of all sorts, and the amount of property owned by citizens of the United States, which are found in those islands in the course of a year, are stated, probably with sufficient accuracy in the letter of the agents.

Just emerging from a state of barbarism, the Government of the islands is as yet feeble; but its dispositions appear to be just and pacific, and it seems anxious to improve the condition of its people, by the introduction of knowledge, of religious and moral institutions, means of education, and the arts of civilized life.

It cannot but be in conformity with the interest and wishes of the Government and the people of the United States that this community thus existing in the midst of a vast expanse of ocean should be respected, and all its rights strictly and conscientiously regarded. And this must also be the true interest of all other commercial states. Far remote from the dominions of European Powers, its growth and prosperity as an independent state may yet be in a high degree useful to all whose trade is extended to those regions, while its near approach to this continent, and the intercourse which American vessels have with it – such vessels constituting five-sixths of all which annually visit it – could not but create dissatisfaction on the part of the United States at any attempt by another power, should such attempt be threatened or feared, to take possession of the islands, colonize them, and subvert the native Government. Considering, therefore, that the United States possesses so very large a share of the intercourse with those islands, it is deemed not unfit to make the declaration that their Government seeks nevertheless no peculiar advantages, no exclusive control over the Hawaiian Government, but is content with its independent existence, and anxiously wishes for its security and prosperity. Its forbearance in this respect, under the circumstances of the very large intercourse of their citizens with the islands, would justify the Government, should events hereafter arise, to require it, in making a decided remonstrance against the adoption of an opposite policy by any other power. Under the circumstances, I recommend to Congress to provide for a moderate allowance to be made out of the Treasury to the consul residing there, that in a Government so new and a country so remote American citizens may have respectable authority to which to apply for redress, in case of injury to their person and property, and to whom the Government of the country may also make known any acts committed by American citizens of which it may think it has a right to complain. . . .

◇◇◇◇◇◇◇◇◇◇◇◇◇

Pres Pierce wanted annex

2. POSSIBLE ANNEXATION OF THE HAWAIIAN ISLANDS [2]

[*William M. Marcy to David L. Gregg*]

Washington, January 31, 1855

THE POLICY of the United States in relation to the future of the Sandwich Islands is presented in the instructions heretofore given to you. That policy is not to accelerate or urge on any important change in the government of that country, but if it has or should become so far enfeebled that it can not be continued, and the sovereignty of the islands must be transferred to another power, then a state of things will exist in which it will be proper for the United States to have a regard to the future condition of that country.

If the Hawaiian Government and people become convinced of the necessity of such a change, it is probable that they will, if left to their free choice, look to the United States as the country to which they would wish to be united. To a proper arrangement of this kind this Government certainly has no objection.

My dispatch of the 4th of April last has reference to such a contingency which it was then supposed was about to happen. In case a transfer of the islands was proffered to the United States, you were directed to enter into negotiations as to the terms of it and conclude a treaty on that subject. The outlines of such a treaty were contained in that dispatch.

You have apprised the Department that as soon as negotiations were opened you perceived that stipulations different from those indicated in your instructions were insisted on, and you very properly notified the Hawaiian authorities that you could only entertain them as matters to be referred to your Government for its approval or rejection.

The draft of a treaty you have forwarded to the Department has been considered by the President, and he directs me to say that he can not approve of some of the articles. If ratified in its present shape at Honolulu and sent hither, he would not probably submit it to the Senate. There are in his mind strong objections to the immediate incorporation of the islands in their present condition into the Union as an independent State. It was expected that the Hawaiian Government would be willing to offer the islands to the United States as a territory, and to leave the question in relation to their becoming a State to the determination of this Government, unembarrassed by stipulations on that point. The interests of both parties would seem to indicate this as the wisest course. A treaty which would embarrass the United States in their action on this question would therefore be objectionable.

There are other objections to the draft which you have sent to the Department, though less formidable than that which the second article pre-

[2] Ibid., pp. 133–4. David L. Gregg was the American agent in Hawaii.

sents. The amount to be paid as annuities, etc., according to the draft, is much larger than was contemplated.

I think it would be proper that you should inform the Hawaiian Government that the United States would not be likely to approve of a treaty differing in important particulars from the terms contained in the dispatch of the 4th of April.

This Government will receive the transfer of the sovereignty of the Sandwich Islands with all proper provisions relative to the existing rights and interests of the people thereof, such as are usual and appropriate to territorial sovereignty. It will be the object of the United States, if clothed with the sovereignty of that country, to promote its growth and prosperity. This consideration alone ought to be a sufficient assurance to the people that their rights and interests will be duly respected and cherished by this Government.

In presenting objections to the draft of the treaty which you have sent to this Department, the President desires me to assure you that he takes no exception whatever to your course in this difficult and embarrassing negotiation, but, on the contrary, it is highly approved. Your efforts have been properly directed and your ability is appreciated and commended. It gives me pleasure to concur in and communicate the President's approbation of your conduct.

◇◇◇◇◇◇◇◇◇◇◇◇◇◇

3. THE POLICY OF THE UNITED STATES IN THE PACIFIC AREA[3]

[*James G. Blaine to James M. Comly*]

Washington, December 1, 1881

. . . I HAVE HAD recent occasion to set forth the vitally integral importance of our Pacific possessions, in a circular letter addressed on the 24th of June last to our representatives in Europe, touching the necessary guarantees of the proposed Panama Canal as a purely American waterway to be treated as part of our own coast line. The extension of commercial empire westward from those states is no less vitally important to their development than is their communication with the Eastern coast by the Isthmian channel. And when we survey the stupendous progress made by the western coast during the thirty years of its national life as a part of our dominion, its enormous increase of population, its vast resources of agriculture and mines, and its boundless enterprise, it is not easy to set a limit to its commercial activity or foresee a check to its maritime supremacy in the waters of the Orient, so long as those waters afford, as now, a free and neutral scope for our peaceful trade.

[3] *Papers Relating to the Foreign Relations of the United States,* 1881, pp. 635–9. James M. Comly was the American minister in Hawaii.

In thirty years the United States has acquired a legitimately dominant influence in the North Pacific, which it can never consent to see decreased by the intrusion therein of any element of influence hostile to its own. The situation of the Hawaiian Islands, giving them the strategic control of the North Pacific, brings their possession within the range of questions of purely American policy, as much so as that of the Isthmus itself. Hence the necessity, as recognized in our existing treaty relations, of drawing the ties of intimate relationship between us and the Hawaiian Islands so as to make them practically a part of the American system without derogation of their absolute independence. The reciprocity treaty of 1875 has made of Hawaii the sugar-raising field of the Pacific slope and gives to our manufacturers therein the same freedom as in California and Oregon. . . .

The policy of this country with regard to the Pacific is the natural complement to its Atlantic policy. The history of our European relations for fifty years shows the jealous concern with which the United States has guarded its control of the coast from foreign interference, and this without extension of territorial possession beyond the main land. It has always been its aim to preserve the friendly neutrality of the adjacent states and insular possessions. Its attitude toward Cuba is in point. That rich island, the key to the Gulf of Mexico, and the field for our most extended trade in the Western Hemisphere is, though in the hands of Spain, a part of the American commercial system. Our relations, present and prospective, toward Cuba, have never been more ably set forth than in the remarkable note addressed by my predecessor, Mr. Secretary Everett, to the ministers of Great Britain and France in Washington, on the 1st of December, 1852, in rejection of the suggested tripartite alliance to forever determine the neutrality of the Spanish Antilles. In response to the proposal that the United States, Great Britain, and France, should severally and collectively agree to forbid the acquisition of control over Cuba, by any or all of them, Mr. Everett showed that, without forcing or even coveting possession of the island, its condition was essentially an American question; that the renunciation forever by this government of contingent interest therein would be far broader than the like renunciation by Great Britain or France; that if ever ceasing to be Spanish, Cuba must necessarily become American, and not fall under any other European domination, and that the ceaseless movement of segregation of American interests from European control and unification in a broader American sphere of independent life could not and should not be checked by any arbitrary agreement.

Nearly thirty years have demonstrated the wisdom of the attitude then maintained by Mr. Everett and have made indispensable its continuance and its extension to all parts of the American Atlantic system where a disturbance of the existing status might be attempted in the interest of foreign powers. The present attitude of this government toward any European project for the control of an isthmian route is but the logical sequence of the resistance made in 1852 to the attempted pressure of an active foreign influence in the West Indies.

Hawaii, although much farther from the Californian coast than is Cuba from the Floridian peninsula, holds in the western sea much the same position as Cuba in the Atlantic. It is the key to the maritime dominion of the Pacific states, as Cuba is the key to the Gulf trade. The material possession of Hawaii is not desired by the United States any more than was that of Cuba. But under no circumstances can the United States permit any change in the territorial control of either which would cut it adrift from the American system, whereto they both indispensably belong.

In this aspect of the question, it is readily seen with what concern this government must view any tendency toward introducing into Hawaii new social elements, destructive of its necessarily American character. The steady diminution of the native population of the islands, amounting to some ten per cent. between 1872 and 1878, and still continuing, is doubtless a cause of great alarm to the government of the kingdom, and it is no wonder that a solution should be sought with eagerness in any seemingly practicable quarter. The problem, however, is not to be met by a substitution of Mongolian supremacy for native control – as seems at first sight possible through the rapid increase in Chinese immigration to the islands. Neither is a wholesale introduction of the coolie element, professedly Anglo-Indian, likely to afford any more satisfactory outcome to the difficulty. The Hawaiian Islands cannot be joined to the Asiatic system. If they drift from their independent station it must be toward assimilation and identification with the American system, to which they belong by the operation of natural laws, and must belong by the operation of political necessity. . . .

In this line of action the United States does its simple duty both to Hawaii and itself; and it cannot permit such obvious neglect of national interest as would be involved by silent acquiescence in any movement looking to a lessening of those American ties and the substitution of alien and hostile interests. It firmly believes that the position of the Hawaiian Islands as the key to the dominion of the American Pacific demands their neutrality, to which end it will earnestly co-operate with the native government. And if, through any cause, the maintenance of such a position of neutrality should be found by Hawaii to be impracticable, this government would then unhesitatingly meet the altered situation by seeking an avowedly American solution for the grave issues presented. . . .

4. A NEW PROPOSAL FOR HAWAIIAN ANNEXATION[4]

[John L. Stevens to John W. Foster]

Honolulu, November 20, 1892

FIDELITY to the trust imposed on me by the President, the Department of State, and the Senate, requires that I should make a careful and full statement of the financial, agricultural, social, and political condition of these islands. An intelligent and impartial examination of the facts can hardly fail to lead to the conclusion that the relations and policy of the United States toward Hawaii will soon demand some change, if not the adoption of decisive measures, with the aim to secure American interests and future supremacy by encouraging Hawaiian development and aiding to promote responsible government in these islands. . . .

THE EXISTING BUSINESS STATUS

It is well to consider the existing state of things here resulting from the change in the United States sugar tariff. Only personal observation and a careful investigation of the facts can give an adequate idea of the severe blow sugar raised here has received. The production of sugar being the main business of the islands, the great reduction of the market price has effected powerfully the entire affairs and condition of the islands. I think it underestimating the truth to express the opinion that the loss to the owners of the sugar plantations and mills, etc., and the consequent depreciation of other property by the passage of the McKinley bill, wise and beneficial as that measure is proving to be for the vast interests of the United States, has not been less than $12,000,000, a large portion of this loss falling on Americans residing here and in California. Unless some positive measures of relief be granted, the depreciation of sugar property here will continue to go on. Wise, bold action of the United States will rescue the property holders from great loss, give the islands a government which will put an end to a worse than useless expenditure of a large proportion of the revenues of that country, using them for the building of roads and bridges, thus helping to develop the natural resources of the islands, aiding to diversify the industries, and to increase the number of the responsible citizens.

WHAT SHOULD BE DONE?

One of two courses seem to me absolutely necessary to be followed, either bold and vigorous measures for annexation or a "customs union," an ocean cable from the Californian coast to Honolulu, Pearl Harbor perpetually ceded to the United States, with an implied but not necessarily stipulated American protectorate over the islands. I believe the former to be the better, that which will prove much the more advantageous to the islands, and the cheapest and least embarrassing in the end for the United

[4] *Foreign Relations of the United States,* 1894, *Appendix,* II, pp. 188–96. John L. Stevens was American minister to Hawaii.

States. If it was wise for the United States, through Secretary Marcy, thirty-eight years ago, to offer to expend $100,000 to secure a treaty of annexation, it certainly can not be chimerical or unwise to expend $100,000 to secure annexation in the near future. To-day the United States has five times the wealth she possessed in 1854, and the reasons now existing for annexation are much stronger than they were then. I can not refrain from expressing the opinion with emphasis that the golden hour is near at hand. A perpetual customs union and the acquisition of Pearl Harbor, with an implied protectorate, must be regarded as the only allowable alternative. This would require the continual presence in the harbor of Honolulu of a United States vessel of war and the constant watchfulness of the United States minister while the present bungling, unsettled, and expensive political rule would go on, retarding the development of the islands, leaving at the end of twenty-five years more embarrassment to annexation than exists today, the property far less valuable, and the population less American than they would be if annexation were soon realized. . . .

To give Hawaii a highly favorable treaty while she remains outside the American Union would necessarily give the same advantages to hostile foreigners, those who would continue to antagonize our commercial and political interests here, as well as those of American blood and sympathies. It is a well authenticated fact that the American sentiment here in 1890, the last year of the great prosperity under the sugar provisions of the reciprocity treaty, was much less manifest than before the treaty had gone into effect, and less pronounced than when Secretary Marcy authorized the negotiation of the annexation treaty in 1854. It is equally true that the desire here at this time for annexation is much stronger than in 1889. Besides, so long as the islands retain their own independent government there remains the possibility that England or the Canadian Dominion might secure one of the Hawaiian harbors for a coaling station. Annexation excludes all dangers of this kind. . . .

◇◇◇◇◇◇◇◇◇◇◇◇◇

5. REVOLUTION IN HAWAII [5]

[*Walter Q. Gresham to President Cleveland*]

Washington, October 18, 1893

THE FULL and impartial reports submitted by the Hon. James H. Blount, your special commissioner to the Hawaiian Islands, established the following facts:

Queen Liliuokalani announced her intention on Saturday, January 14, 1893, to proclaim a new constitution, but the opposition of her ministers and others induced her to speedily change her purpose and make public announcement of that fact.

[5] Ibid., pp. 459–63.

At a meeting in Honolulu, late on the afternoon of that day, a so-called committee of public safety, consisting of thirteen men, being all or nearly all who were present, was appointed "to consider the situation and devise ways and means for the maintenance of the public peace and the protection of life and property," and at a meeting of this committee on the 15th, or the forenoon of the 16th of January, it was resolved amongst other things that a provisional government be created "to exist until terms of union with the United States of America have been negotiated and agreed upon." At a mass meeting which assembled at 2 p.m. on the last-named day, the Queen and her supporters were condemned and denounced, and the committee was continued and all its acts approved.

Later the same afternoon the committee addressed a letter to John L. Stevens, the American minister at Honolulu, stating that the lives and property of the people were in peril and appealing to him and the United States forces at his command for assistance. This communication concluded "we are unable to protect ourselves without aid, and therefore hope for the protection of the United States forces." On receipt of this letter Mr. Stevens requested Capt. Wiltse, commander of the U.S.S. *Boston,* to land a force "for the protection of the United States legation, the United States consulate, and to secure the safety of American life and property." The well-armed troops, accompanied by two gatling guns, were promptly landed and marched through the quiet streets of Honolulu to a public hall, previously secured by Mr. Stevens for their accommodation. This hall was just across the street from the Government building, and in plain view of the Queen's palace. . . .

The station house was occupied by a well-armed force, under the command of a resolute capable, officer. The same afternoon the Queen, her ministers, representatives of the Provisional Government, and others held a conference at the palace. Refusing to recognize the new authority or surrender to it, she was informed that the Provisional Government had the support of the American minister, and, if necessary, would be maintained by the military force of the United States then present; that any demonstration on her part would precipitate a conflict with that force; that she could not, with hope of success, engage in war with the United States, and that resistance would result in a useless sacrifice of life. Mr. Damon, one of the chief leaders of the movement, and afterwards vice-president of the Provisional Government, informed the Queen that she could surrender under protest and her case would be considered later at Washington. . . .

In his dispatch to Mr. Foster of January 18, describing the so-called revolution, Mr. Stevens says:

> The committee of public safety forthwith took possession of the Government building, archives, and treasury, and installed the Provisional Government at the head of the respective departments. This being an accomplished fact, I promptly recognized the Provisional Government as the *de facto* government of the Hawaiian Islands.

In Secretary Foster's communication of February 15 to the President, laying before him the treaty of annexation, with the view to obtaining the advice and consent of the Senate thereto, he says:

> At the time the Provisional Government took possession of the Government building no troops or officers of the United States were present or took any part whatever in the proceedings. No public recognition was accorded to the Provisional Government by the United States minister until after the Queen's abdication, and when they were in effective possession of the Government building, the archives, the treasury, the barracks, the police station, and all the potential machinery of the Government.

Similar language is found in an official letter addressed to Secretary Foster on February 3 by the special commissioners sent to Washington by the Provisional Government to negotiate a treaty of annexation.

These statements are utterly at variance with the evidence, documentary and oral, contained in Mr. Blount's reports. They are contradicted by declarations and letters of President Dole and other annexationists and by Mr. Stevens's own verbal admissions to Mr. Blount. . . .

The earnest appeals to the American minister for military protection by the officers of that Government, after it had been recognized, show the utter absurdity of the claim that it was established by a successful revolution of the people of the Islands. Those appeals were a confession by the men who made them of their weakness and timidity. Courageous men, conscious of their strength and the justice of their cause, do not thus act. It is not now claimed that a majority of the people, having the right to vote under the constitution of 1887, ever favored the existing authority or annexation to this or any other country. They earnestly desire that the government of their choice shall be restored and its independence respected.

Mr. Blount states that while at Honolulu he did not meet a single annexationist who expressed willingness to submit the question to a vote of the people, nor did he talk with one on that subject who did not insist that if the Islands were annexed suffrage should be so restricted as to give complete control to foreigners or whites. Representative annexationists have repeatedly made similar statements to the undersigned.

The Government of Hawaii surrendered its authority under a threat of war, until such time only as the Government of the United States, upon the facts being presented to it, should reinstate the constitutional sovereign, and the Provisional Government was created "to exist until terms of union with the United States of America have been negotiated and agreed upon." A careful consideration of the facts will, I think, convince you that the treaty which was withdrawn from the Senate for further consideration should not be resubmitted for its action thereon.

Should not the great wrong done to a feeble but independent State by an abuse of the authority of the United States be undone by restoring the legitimate government? Anything short of that will not, I respectfully submit, satisfy the demands of justice. . . .

◇◇◇◇◇◇◇◇◇◇◇◇◇◇

6. CLEVELAND'S DILEMMA[6]

[*Special Message of President Cleveland to Congress, December 18, 1893*]

IN MY RECENT annual message to the Congress I briefly referred to our relations with Hawaii and expressed the intention of transmitting further information on the subject when additional advices permitted.

Though I am not able now to report a definite change in the actual situation, I am convinced that the difficulties lately created both here and in Hawaii and now standing in the way of a solution through Executive action of the problem presented, render it proper, and expedient, that the matter should be referred to the broader authority and discretion of Congress, with a full explanation of the endeavor thus far made to deal with the emergency and a statement of the considerations which have governed my action.

I suppose that right and justice should determine the path to be followed in treating this subject. If national honesty is to be disregarded and a desire for territorial extension, or dissatisfaction with a form of government not own own, ought to regulate our conduct, I have entirely misapprehended the mission and character of our Government and the behavior which the conscience of our people demands of their public servants. . . .

As I apprehend the situation, we are brought face to face with the following conditions:

The lawful Government of Hawaii was overthrown without the drawing of a sword or the firing of a shot by a process every step of which, it may safely be asserted, is directly traceable to and dependent for its success upon the agency of the United States acting through its diplomatic and naval representatives.

But for the notorious predilections of the United States Minister for annexation, the Committee of Safety, which should be called the Committee of Annexation, would never have existed.

But for the landing of the United States forces upon false pretexts respecting the danger to life and property the committee would never have exposed themselves to the pains and penalties of treason by undertaking the subversion of the Queen's Government.

But for the presence of the United States forces in the immediate vicinity and in position to afford all needed protection and support the committee would not have proclaimed the provisional government from the steps of the Government building.

And finally, but for the lawless occupation of Honolulu under false pretexts by the United States forces, and but for Minister Stevens's recognition of the provisional government when the United States forces were its sole support and constituted its only military strength, the Queen and her Government would never have yielded to the provisional government,

[6] Ibid., pp. 445–58.

even for a time and for the sole purpose of submitting her case to the enlightened justice of the United States. . . .

I have not, however, overlooked an incident of this unfortunate affair which remains to be mentioned. The members of the provisional government and their supporters, though not entitled to extreme sympathy, have been led to their present predicament of revolt against the Government of the Queen by the indefensible encouragement and assistance of our diplomatic representative. This fact may entitle them to claim that in our effort to rectify the wrong committed some regard should be had for their safety. . . .

Actuated by these desires and purposes, and not unmindful of the inherent perplexities of the situation nor of the limitations upon my power, I instructed Minister Willis to advise the Queen and her supporters of my desire to aid in the restoration of the status existing before the lawless landing of the United States forces at Honolulu on the 16th of January last, if such restoration could be effected upon terms providing for clemency as well as justice to all parties concerned. The conditions suggested, as the instructions show, contemplate a general amnesty to those concerned in setting up the provisional government and a recognition of all its *bona fide* acts and obligations. In short, they require that the past should be buried, and that the restored Government should reassume its authority as if its continuity had not been interrupted. These conditions have not proved acceptable to the Queen, and though she has been informed that they will be insisted upon, and that, unless acceded to, the efforts of the President to aid in the restoration of her Government will cease, I have not thus far learned that she is willing to yield them her acquiescence. The check which my plans have thus encountered has prevented their presentation to the members of the provisional government, while unfortunate public misrepresentations of the situation and exaggerated statements of the sentiments of our people have obviously injured the prospects of successful Executive mediation. . . .

In commending this subject to the extended powers and wide discretion of the Congress, I desire to add the assurance that I shall be much gratified to coöperate in any legislative plan which may be devised for the solution of the problem before us which is consistent with American honor, integrity, and morality.

◇◇◇◇◇◇◇◇◇◇◇◇◇

7. QUASI-PROTECTORATE OVER SAMOA[7]

[*Treaty between the United States and the Samoan Government, concluded January 17, 1878; ratifications exchanged February 11, 1878*]

ARTICLE I. There shall be perpetual peace and friendship between the Government of the United States and the Government of the Samoan Islands.

Article II. Naval vessels of the United States shall have the privilege of entering and using the port of Pagopago, and establishing therein and on the shores thereof a station for coal and other naval supplies for their naval and commercial marine, and the Samoan Government will hereafter neither exercise nor authorize any jurisdiction within said port adverse to such rights of the United States or restrictive thereof. The same vessels shall also have the privilege of entering other ports of the Samoan Islands. The citizens of the United States shall likewise have free liberty to enter the same ports with their ships and cargoes of whatsoever kind, and to sell the same to any of the inhabitants of those islands, whether natives or foreigners, or to barter them for the products of the Islands. All such traffic in whatever articles of trade or barter shall be free, except that the trade in firearms and munitions of war in the Islands shall be subject to regulations by that government. . . .

Article V. If, unhappily, any differences should have arisen, or shall hereafter arise, between the Samoan Government and any other government in amity with the United States, the government of the latter will employ its good offices for the purpose of adjusting those differences upon a satisfactory and solid foundation. . . .

Article VII. The present treaty shall remain in force for ten years from its date. . . .

◇◇◇◇◇◇◇◇◇◇◇◇◇◇

8. TRIPARTITE SAMOAN TREATY[8]

[*Concluded at Berlin between the United States, Germany, and England, June 14, 1889; ratifications exchanged April 12, 1890; assented to by Samoa April 19, 1890*]

. . . *ARTICLE I.* It is declared that the Islands of Samoa are neutral territory in which the citizens and subjects of the Three Signatory Powers have equal rights of residence, trade and personal protection. The Three Powers recognize the independence of the Samoan Government and the free right of the natives to elect their Chief or King and choose their form

[7] *Statutes at Large of the United States*, Vol. XX, pp. 704–5. The treaty was signed by William Maxwell Evarts and M. K. Le Mamea.

[8] Ibid., Vol. XXVI, pp. 1497–1507. The treaty was signed by John A. Kasson, Wm. Walter Phelps, Geo. H. Bates, H. Bismarck, Holstein, R. Krauel, Edward B. Malet, Charles S. Scott, and J. A. Crowe.

of Government according to their own laws and customs. Neither of the Powers shall exercise any separate control over the Islands or the Government thereof. . . .

Article III. Section 1. A Supreme Court shall be established in Samoa to consist of one Judge, who shall be styled Chief Justice of Samoa, and who shall appoint a Clerk and a Marshal of the Court; and record shall be kept of all orders and decisions made by the Court, or by the Chief Justice in the discharge of any duties imposed on him under this Act. The Clerk and Marshal shall be allowed reasonable fees to be regulated by order of the Court.

Section 2. With a view to secure judicial independence and the equal consideration of the rights of all parties, irrespective of nationality, it is agreed that the Chief Justice shall be named by the Three Signatory Powers in common accord; or, failing their agreement, he may be named by the King of Sweden and Norway. He shall be learned in law and equity, of mature years, and of good repute for his sense of honour, impartiality and justice. . . .

Section 6. In case any question shall hereafter arise in Samoa respecting the rightful election or appointment of King or of any other Chief claiming authority over the Islands; or respecting the validity of the powers which the King or any Chief may claim in the exercise of his office, such question shall not lead to war but shall be presented for decision to the Chief Justice of Samoa, who shall decide it in writing, conformably to the provisions of this Act and to the laws and customs of Samoa not in conflict therewith; and the Signatory Governments will accept and abide by such decision.

Section 7. In case any difference shall arise between either of the Treaty Powers and Samoa which they shall fail to adjust by mutual accord, such difference shall not be held cause for war, but shall be referred for adjustment on the principles of justice and equity to the Chief Justice of Samoa, who shall make his decision thereon in writing.

Section 8. The Chief Justice may recommend to the Government of Samoa the passage of any law which he shall consider just and expedient for the prevention and punishment of crime and for the promotion of good order in Samoa outside the Municipal District and for the collection of taxes without the District.

Section 9. Upon the organization of the Supreme Court there shall be transferred to its exclusive jurisdiction

1. All civil suits concerning real property situated in Samoa and all rights affecting the same.

2. All civil suits of any kind between natives and foreigners or between foreigners of different nationalities.

3. All crimes and offences committed by natives against foreigners or committed by such foreigners as are not subject to any consular jurisdiction; subject however to the provisions of section 4 Article V defining the jurisdiction of the Municipal Magistrate of the District of Apia. . . .

Chapter XXIII

THE SPANISH-AMERICAN WAR AND IMPERIALISM

◇◇◇◇◇◇◇◇◇◇◇◇◇

AT THE TIME of the Ostend Manifesto it was generally supposed that a revolution in Cuba was imminent. When the revolution finally began in 1868 there was even more expansionist sentiment in America than had existed in 1854, and as the revolt continued, a considerable sentiment arose in favor of American intervention. The most important statement of American policy regarding Cuba was made by Secretary Hamilton Fish on November 5, 1875 (1). A short time later President Grant considered the question of Cuban belligerency in a message to Congress (2). The position that had been taken by the United States regarding the duties of neutrals during the American Civil War, the general attitude of European powers toward American intervention, and the growing success of Spain in dealing with the rebellion, all contributed to the decision on the part of America to remain neutral.

When a new revolution broke out in Cuba in 1895, Secretary Olney sent a stern warning to Spain regarding the status of American opinion and the possible consequences of another long period of strife in Cuba (3). As time went on American public opinion sympathetic to the rebellion increased. Although the Spanish government vigorously defended its Cuban policy, notably in an important dispatch of August 4, 1897 (4), in October of the same year it announced a more conciliatory program (5) in an effort to appease American hostility. This new policy failed to avert a crisis (6) in Spanish-American relations and fresh concessions (7) on the part of Spain were without apparent influence. American public sentiment became increasingly aroused against Spain, and President McKinley was impatient with conciliation or compromise. The war message (8) of President McKinley should be compared with President Grant's statement regarding Cuban belligerency (2), with the American notes of March 26 and 27 (6), 1898, and the telegram of April 5, 1898 (7) from the American minister to Spain.

In his instructions (9) to the Peace Commission, the President explained the reasons why the United States should secure the Philippines under the treaty of peace (10).

Well before 1898 a new expansionist and imperialist sentiment had arisen in the United States. Writers such as Josiah Strong and Alfred Thayer Mahan provided the intellectual basis for the imperialism of Henry Cabot Lodge and Theodore Roosevelt. No one, however, expressed the imperialistic sentiment more eloquently than Albert J. Beveridge (11). The anti-imperialistic view is shown in the platform of the American Anti-Imperialist League (12).

◇◇◇◇◇◇◇◇◇◇◇◇◇

1. THREATENED INTERVENTION IN CUBA DURING THE TEN YEARS' WAR[1]

[*Hamilton Fish to Caleb Cushing*]

Washington, November 5, 1875

PURSUANT to the intimation conveyed in my No. 242, I deem it necessary to recur to the general question of our relations with Spain, and to consider the progress which has been made in disposing of the outstanding questions which for some time past have seriously threatened the relations of the two countries. . . .

While remembering and observing the duties which this Government, as one of the family of nations, owes to another member, by public law, treaties, or the particular statutes of the United States, it would be idle to attempt to conceal the interest and sympathy with which Americans in the United States regard any attempt of a numerous people on this continent to be relieved of ties which hold them in the position of colonial subjection to a distant power, and to assume the independence and right of self-control which natural rights and the spirit of the age accord to them.

When, moreover, this struggle, [in Cuba] in progress on our very borders, from its commencement has involved the property and interests of citizens of the United Stateas, has disturbed our tranquillity and commerce, has called upon us not infrequently to witness barbarous violations of the rules of civilized warfare, and compelled us for the sake of humanity to raise our voice by way of protest; and when, more than all, we see in the contest the final struggle in this hemisphere between slavery and freedom, it would be strange indeed if the Government and people of this country failed at any time to take peculiar interest in the termination of such contest. . . .

It will be apparent that such a state of things can not continue. It is absolutely necessary to the maintenance of our relations with Spain, even on their present footing, that our just demands for the return to citizens of the United Stataes of their estates in Cuba, unincumbered, and for securing to them a trial for offenses according to treaty provisions and all other rights guaranteed by treaty and by public law should be complied with. . . .

A disastrous conflict of more than seven years' duration has demonstrated

[1] *Senate Report* (3624), 55th Congress, 2nd Session, No. 885, pp. 44–52.

the inability of Spain to maintain peace and order in an island lying at our door. Desolation and destruction of life and property have been the only results of this conflict. . . .

The Government of the United States has heretofore given expression to no policy in reference to the insurrection in Cuba, because it has honestly and sincerely hoped that no declaration of policy on its part would be required.

The President feels that longer reticence would be inconsistent with the interests of both Governments.

Our relations with Spain are in that critical position that another seizure similar to that of the *Virginius*, other executions of citizens of the United States in Cuba, other wrongs of a less objectionable character even than many which have been already suffered by our citizens with simple remonstrance, or possibly even some new act of exceptional severity in Cuba, may suddenly produce a feeling and excitement which might force events which this Government anxiously desires to avoid.

The President hopes that Spain may spontaneously adopt measures looking to a reconciliation and to the speedy restoration of peace and the organization of a stable and satisfactory system of government in the Island of Cuba.

In the absence of any prospect of a termination of the war, or of any change in the manner in which it has been conducted on either side, he feels that the time is at hand when it may be the duty of other Governments to intervene, solely with a view of bringing to an end a disastrous and destructive conflict, and of restoring peace in the island of Cuba. No Government is more deeply interested in the order and peaceful administration of this island than is that of the United States, and none has suffered as has the United States from the condition which has obtained there during the past six or seven years. He will, therefore, feel it his duty at an early day to submit the subject in this light, and accompanied by an expression of the views above presented, for the consideration of Congress. . . .

◇◇◇◇◇◇◇◇◇◇◇◇◇

2. PRESIDENT GRANT'S CUBAN POLICY[2]

[*Annual Message of President Grant to Congress, December 7, 1875*]

. . . THE PAST YEAR has furnished no evidence of an approaching termination of the ruinous conflict which has been raging for seven years in the neighboring island of Cuba. The same disregard of the laws of civilized warfare and of the just demands of humanity which has heretofore called forth expressions of condemnation from the nations of Christendom has

[2] *Papers Relating to the Foreign Relations of the United States,* 1875, Vol. I, pp. i–xxvii.

continued to blacken the sad scene. Desolation, ruin, and pillage are pervading the rich fields of one of the most fertile and productive regions of the earth, and the incendiaries' torch, firing plantations and valuable factories and buildings, is the agent marking the alternate advance or retreat of contending parties. . . .

While conscious that the insurrection in Cuba has shown a strength and endurance which make it at least doubtful whether it be in the power of Spain to subdue it, it seems unquestionable that no such civil organization exists which may be recognized as an independent government capable of performing its international obligations and entitled to be treated as one of the powers of the earth. A recognition under such circumstances would be inconsistent with the facts, and would compel the power granting it soon to support by force the government to which it had really given its only claim of existence. In my judgment, the United States should adhere to the policy and the principles which have heretofore been its sure and safe guides in like contests between revolted colonies and their mother country, and, acting only upon the clearest evidence, should avoid any possibility of suspicion or of imputation.

A recognition of the independence of Cuba being, in my opinion, impracticable and indefensible, the question which next presents itself is that of the recognition of belligerent rights in the parties to the contest.

In a former message to Congress I had occasion to consider this question, and reached the conclusion that the conflict in Cuba, dreadful and devastating as were its incidents, did not rise to the fearful dignity of war. Regarding it now, after this lapse of time, I am unable to see that any notable success, or any marked or real advance on the part of the insurgents, has essentially changed the character of the contest. It has acquired greater age, but not greater or more formidable proportions. It is possible that the acts of foreign powers, and even acts of Spain herself, of this very nature, might be pointed to in defense of such recognition. But now, as in its past history, the United States should carefully avoid the false lights which might lead it into the mazes of doubtful law and of questionable propriety, and adhere rigidly and sternly to the rule, which has been its guide, of doing only that which is right and honest and of good report. The question of according or of withholding rights of belligerency must be judged, in every case, in view of the particular attending facts. Unless justified by necessity, it is always, and justly, regarded as an unfriendly act, and a gratuitous demonstration of moral support to the rebellion. It is necessary, and it is required, when the interests and rights of another government or of its people are so far affected by a pending civil conflict as to require a definition of its relations to the parties thereto. But this conflict must be one which will be recognized in the sense of international law as war. Belligerence, too, is a fact. The mere existence of contending armed bodies, and their occasional conflicts, do not constitute war in the sense referred to. Applying to the existing condition of affairs in Cuba the tests recognized by publicists and writers on international law, and which have been observed by nations of dignity, honesty, and power, when free from sensitive or selfish and unworthy motives, I fail to find in the insurrection the existence of such a substantial political organization, real, palpable, and manifest to the world, having the forms and capable of the ordinary functions of government toward its own people and to other states, with courts for the administration of justice, with a local habitation, possessing such organization of force, such material, such occupation of territory, as to take the contest out of the category of a mere rebellious insurrection, or occasional skirmishes, and place it on the terrible footing of war, to which a recognition of belligerency would aim to elevate it. The contest, moreover, is solely on land; the insurrection has not possessed itself of a single sea-port whence it may send forth its flag, nor has it any means of communication with foreign powers except through the military lines of its adversaries. No apprehension of any of those sudden and difficult complications which a war upon the ocean is apt to precipitate upon the vessels, both commercial and national, and upon the consular officers of other powers, calls for the definition of their relations to the parties to the contest. Considered as a question of expediency, I regard the accordance of belligerent rights still to be as unwise and premature, as I regard it to be, at present, indefensible as a measure of right. . . . I am satisfied that, while the accordance of belligerent rights to the insurgents in Cuba might give them a hope and an inducement to protract the struggle, it would be but a delusive hope, and would not remove the evils which this Government and its people are experiencing, but would draw the United States into complications which it has waited long and already suffered much to avoid. . . .

◇◇◇◇◇◇◇◇◇◇◇◇◇

3. THE CUBAN POLICY OF THE CLEVELAND ADMINISTRATION[3]

[*Richard Olney to Dupuy de Lôme*]

Washington, April 4, 1896

IT MIGHT well be deemed a dereliction of duty to the government of the United States, as well as a censurable want of candor to that of Spain, if I were longer to defer official expression as well of the anxiety with which the President regards the existing situation in Cuba as of his earnest desire for the prompt and permanent pacification of that island. Any plan giving reasonable assurance of that result and not inconsistent with the just rights and reasonable demands of all concerned would be earnestly promoted by him by all the means which the Constitution and laws of this country place at his disposal. . . .

[3] *Spanish Diplomatic Correspondence and Documents,* 1896–1900, Washington, 1905, pp. 4–8.

That the United States cannot contemplate with complacency another ten years of Cuban insurrection, with all its injurious and distressing incidents, may certainly be taken for granted. The object of the present communication, however, is not to discuss intervention, nor to propose intervention, nor to pave the way for intervention. The purpose is exactly the reverse — to suggest whether a solution of present troubles cannot be found which will prevent all thought of intervention by rendering it unnecessary. What the United States desires to do, if the way can be pointed out, is to co-operate with Spain in the immediate pacification of the island on such a plan as, leaving Spain her rights of sovereignty, shall yet secure to the people of the island all such rights and powers of local self-government as they can reasonably ask. To that end, the United States offers and will use her good offices at such time and in such manner as may be deemed most advisable. Its mediation, it is believed, should not be rejected in any quarter since none could misconceive or mistrust its purpose. Spain could not, because our respect for her sovereignty and our determination to do nothing to impair it have been maintained for many years at great cost, and in spite of many temptations. The insurgents could not, because anything assented to by this government which did not satisfy the reasonable demands and aspirations of Cuba, would arouse the indignation of our whole people. It only remains to suggest that, if anything can be done in the direction indicated, it should be done at once and on the initiative of Spain. The more the contest is prolonged, the more bitter and more irreconcilable is the antagonism created, while there is danger that concessions may be so delayed as to be chargeable to weakness and fear of the issue of the contest, and thus be infinitely less acceptable and persuasive than if made while the result still hangs in balance, and they could be properly credited, in some degree at least, to a sense of right and justice. Thus far Spain has faced the insurrection sword in hand, and has made no sign to show that surrender and submission would be followed by anything but a return to the old order of things. Would it not be wise to modify that policy and to accompany the application of military force with an authentic declaration of the organic changes that are meditated in the administration of the island with a view to remove all just grounds of complaint? It is for Spain to consider and determine what those changes would be. But should they be such that the United States could urge their adoption as substantially removing well-founded grievances, its influence would be exerted for their acceptance, and, it can hardly be doubted, would be most potential for the termination of hostilities and the restoration of peace and order to the island. One result of the course of proceeding outlined, if no other, would be sure to follow, namely, that the rebellion would lose largely, if not altogether, the moral countenance and support it now enjoys from the people of the United States. . . .

◇◇◇◇◇◇◇◇◇◇◇◇◇◇

4. SPANISH DEFENSE OF THE *RECONCENTRADO* POLICY[4]

[*Duke de Tetuán to Dupuy de Lôme*]

August 4, 1897

. . . ALL CIVILIZED countries which, like Spain at present, have found themselves under the harsh necessity of resorting to arms to crush rebellions, not always so evidently unjustifiable as that of Cuba, proceed and have proceeded in the same manner. In the United States itself, during the war of secession, recourse was had to concentrations of peaceable inhabitants, to seizures and confiscation of property, to the destruction of all agricultural and industrial property, particularly of cotton and tobacco, without the safeguard of their foreign flags, in the case of the important factories of Roswell, for instance, sufficing to save them; to the burning of entire cities; to the ruin and devastation of immense and most fertile regions – in short, to the destruction of all the property of the adversary, to the abolition of constitutional rights by the total suspension of the writ of habeas corpus, and to the development of a military and dictatorial system which, in the states opposed to the Union, lasted many years after the termination of the bloody contest. . . .

The invincible General Sherman explained on various occasions the supreme justice of these acts, and in perusing his memoirs and the official reports which he addressed to the directing council of war at Washington are found remarkable statements as to the severity with which it is necessary to proceed against the enemy to make the operations of the military forces efficient and successful. "War is war," said this able general, "and the tremendous responsibility for civil wars rests upon their authors and upon those who are their direct or indirect instruments. . . ."

Moreover, we must bear in mind that this system of the total destruction of Cuban property has always been advocated by the filibustering junta at New York, composed, in great part, of naturalized North Americans, and that this very junta has issued the most cruel orders; so that, by a most amazing coincidence, the authors of the admittedly abominable devastation which, according to the secretary of state, has so greatly aroused the sympathies of the North American people, are citizens of the Union and organizations working without hinderance in its bosom. . . .

---

[4] *Spanish Diplomatic Correspondence and Documents,* op. cit., pp. 29–33. The Duke of Tetuán was the Spanish minister of State.

5. A NEW SPANISH REGIME IN CUBA[5]

[*Duke of Tetuán to Stewart L. Woodford*]

[*Madrid,*] *October 23, 1897*

THE GOVERNMENT of His Majesty. . . is determined to put into immediate practice the political system which the present president of the council of ministers announced to the nation in his manifesto of the 24th of June of this year. . . .

To military operations, uninterrupted for a single day and as energetic and active as circumstances demand, but ever humanitarian and careful to respect all private rights as far as may be possible, must be joined political action honestly leading to the autonomy of the colony in such a manner that upon the full guaranty of the immutable Spanish sovereignty shall arise the new personality which is to govern itself in all affairs peculiar to itself by means of an executive organization and the insular council or chamber. This programme, which constitutes true self-government, will give to the Cubans their own local government, whereby they shall be at one and the same time the initiators and regulators of their own life, but always forming part of the integral nationality of Spain. In this way the island of Cuba will form a personality with its own peculiar functions and powers (atribuciones) and the mother country, moving in the sphere of action which is exclusively its own, will take charge of those matters – such as foreign relations, the army, the navy, and the administration of justice – which involve national requirements or needs.

In order to realize this plan, which it advocates as a solemn political engagement voluntarily assumed while its members were in opposition, the Government of His Majesty proposes to modify existing legislation so far as necessary, doing so in the form of decrees to admit of its more speedy application, and leaving for the Cortes of the Kingdom, with the cooperation of the senators and deputies of the Antillas, the solution of the economical problem and a patriotic and fair apportionment of the payment of the debt. . . .

The Spanish and American Governments agreeing in the same desire to secure immediate peace in Cuba, and both being interested therein, although in different degrees, the Government of his Majesty being interested as a sovereign and the United States in the character of a friend and neighbor, there will doubtless be found suitable bases for a friendly understanding, whereby Spain shall continue to put forth armed efforts, at the same time decreeing the political concessions which she may deem prudent and adequate, while the United States exert within their borders the energy and vigilance necessary to absolutely prevent the procurement of the resources of which from the beginning the Cuban insurrection has availed itself as from an inexhaustible arsenal.

[5] *House Ex. Doc.* (3743) 55th Congress, 3rd Session, No. I, pp. 582–9.

On various occasions the Governments of His Majesty have found themselves obliged to call the attention of the Government of the United States to the manner in which the so-called laws of neutrality are fulfilled in the territory of the Union. Despite the express provisions of those laws and the doctrines maintained by the American Government in the famous Alabama arbitration with regard to the diligence which should be used to avoid whatsoever aggressive act against a friendly nation, it is certain that filibustering expeditions have set forth and unfortunately continue to set forth from the United States, and that, in the sight of all men, there is operating in New York an insurrectionary junta which publicly boasts of organizing and maintaining armed hostility and constant provocation against the Spanish nation.

To effect the disappearance of such a state of things, as is demanded by general international friendship, would be, in the belief of the Government of His Majesty, the most effectual aid in the attainment of peace that the President of the United States could render. . . .

6. AMERICAN PROPOSALS OF MARCH 26 and 27, 1898[6]

[*William R. Day to Stewart L. Woodford*]

Washington, March 26, 1898

THE PRESIDENT'S desire is for peace. He can not look upon the suffering and starvation in Cuba save with horror. The concentration of men, women, and children in the fortified towns and permitting them to starve is unbearable to a Christian nation geographically so close as ours to Cuba. All this has shocked and inflamed the American mind, as it has the civilized world, where its extent and character are known. It was represented to him in November that the Blanco government would at once release the suffering and so modify the Weyler order as to permit those who were able to return to their homes and till the fields from which they had been driven. There has been no relief to the starving except such as the American people have supplied. The reconcentration order has not been practically superseded. There is no hope of peace through Spanish arms. The Spanish Government seems unable to conquer the insurgents. More than half of the island is under control of the insurgents; for more than three years our people have been patient and forbearing; we have patrolled our coast with zeal and at great expense, and have successfully prevented the landing of any armed force on the island. The war has disturbed the peace and tranquillity of our people. We do not want the island. The President has evidenced in every way his desire to preserve and continue friendly relations with Spain. He has kept every international obligation with fidelity.

[6] Ibid., p. 704.

He wants an honorable peace. He has repeatedly urged the Government of Spain to secure such a peace. She still has the opportunity to do it, and the President appeals to her from every consideration of justice and humanity to do it. Will she? Peace is the desired end.

For your own guidance, the President suggests that if Spain will revoke the reconcentration order and maintain the people until they can support themselves and offer to the Cubans full self-government, with reasonable indemnity, the President will gladly assist in its consummation. If Spain should invite the United States to mediate for peace and the insurgents would make like request, the President might undertake such office of friendship.

[*Mr. Day to Mr. Woodford*] [7]

Washington, March 27, 1898

. . . SEE IF the following can be done:

First. Armistice until October 1. Negotiations meantime looking for peace between Spain and insurgents through friendly offices of President United States.

Second. Immediate revocation of reconcentrado order so as to permit people to return to their farms, and the needy to be relieved with provisions and supplies from United States cooperating with authorities so as to afford full relief.

Add, if possible:

Third. If terms of peace not satisfactorily settled by October 1, President of the United States to be final arbiter between Spain and insurgents.

If Spain agrees, President will use friendly offices to get insurgents to accept plan. Prompt action desirable.

7. SPANISH DESIRE FOR AN ARMISTICE IN CUBA [8]

[*Stewart L. Woodford to President McKinley*]

Madrid, April 5, 1898

SHOULD the Queen proclaim the following before 12 o'clock noon of Wednesday, April 6, will you sustain the Queen, and can you prevent hostile action by Congress?

At the request of the Holy Father, in this Passion Week and in the name of Christ, I proclaim immediate and unconditional suspension of hostilities in the island of Cuba.

This suspension is to become immediately effective so soon as accepted

[7] Ibid., pp. 711–12.
[8] Ibid., pp. 734–5.

by the insurgents in that island, and is to continue for the space of six months, to the 5th day of October, eighteen ninety-eight.

I do this to give time for passions to cease, and in the sincere hope and belief that during this suspension permanent and honorable peace may be obtained between the insular government of Cuba and those of my subjects in that island who are now in rebellion against the authority of Spain.

I pray the blessing of Heaven upon this Truce of God, which I now declare in His name and with the sanction of the Holy Father of all Christendom.

April 5, 1898

Please read this in the light of all my previous telegrams and letters. I believe that this means peace, which the sober judgment of our people will approve long before next November, and which must be approved at the bar of final history.

I permit the papal nuncio to read this telegram, upon my own responsibility and without committing you in any manner. I dare not reject this last chance for peace. I will show your reply to the Queen in person, and I believe that you will approve this last conscientious effort for peace.

8. THE WAR MESSAGE OF PRESIDENT McKINLEY[9]

[*Message of the President to the Congress of the United States, April 11, 1898*]

OBEDIENT to that precept of the Constitution which commands the President to give from time to time to the Congress information of the state of the Union and to recommend to their consideration such measures as he shall judge necessary and expedient, it becomes my duty now to address your body with regard to the grave crisis that has arisen in the relations of the United States to Spain by reason of the warfare that for more than three years has raged in the neighboring island of Cuba. . . .

Since the present revolution began, in February, 1895, this country has seen the fertile domain at our threshold ravaged by fire and sword in the course of a struggle unequaled in the history of the island and rarely paralleled as to the numbers of the combatants and the bitterness of the contest by any revolution of modern times where a dependent people striving to be free have been opposed by the power of the sovereign state. . . .

The war in Cuba is of such a nature that short of subjugation or extermination a final military victory for either side seems impracticable. The alternative lies in the physical exhaustion of the one or the other party, or perhaps of both – a condition which in effect ended the ten years' war by the truce of Zanjon. The prospect of such a protraction and conclusion of

[9] Ibid., pp. 750–60.

the present strife is a contingency hardly to be contemplated with equanimity by the civilized world, and least of all by the United States, affected and injured as we are, deeply and intimately, by its very existence.

Realizing this, it appeared to be my duty, in a spirit of true friendliness, no less to Spain than to the Cubans who have so much to lose by the prolongation of the struggle, to seek to bring about an immediate termination of the war. To this end I submitted, on the 27th ultimo, as a result of much representation and correspondence, through the United States minister at Madrid, propositions to the Spanish Government looking to an armistice until October 1 for the negotiation of peace with the good offices of the President.

In addition, I asked the immediate revocation of the order of reconcentration, so as to permit the people to return to their farms and the needy to be relieved with provisions and supplies from the United States, cooperating with the Spanish authorities, so as to afford full relief.

The reply of the Spanish cabinet was received on the night of the 31st ultimo. It offered, as the means to bring about peace in Cuba, to confide the preparation thereof to the insular parliament, inasmuch as the concurrence of that body would be necessary to reach a final result, it being, however, understood that the powers reserved by the constitution to the central Government are not lessened or diminished. As the Cuban parliament does not meet until the 4th of May next, the Spanish Government would not object, for its part, to accept at once a suspension of hostilities if asked for by the insurgents from the general in chief, to whom it would pertain, in such case, to determine the duration and conditions of the armistice. . . .

The forcible intervention of the United States as a neutral to stop the war, according to the large dictates of humanity and following many historical precedents where neighboring States have interfered to check the hopeless sacrifices of life by internecine conflicts beyond their borders, is justifiable on rational grounds. It involves, however, hostile constraint upon both the parties to the contest as well to enforce a truce as to guide the eventual settlement.

The grounds for such intervention may be briefly summarized as follows:

First. In the cause of humanity and to put an end to the barbarities, bloodshed, starvation, and horrible miseries now existing there, and which the parties to the conflict are either unable or unwilling to stop or mitigate. It is no answer to say this is all in another country, belonging to another nation, and is therefore none of our business. It is specially our duty, for it is right at our door.

Second. We owe it to our citizens in Cuba to afford them that protection and indemnity for life and property which no government there can or will afford, and to that end to terminate the conditions that deprive them of legal protection.

Third. The right to intervene may be justified by the very serious injury to the commerce, trade, and business of our people, and by the wanton destruction of property and devastation of the island.

Fourth, and which is of the utmost importance. The present condition of affairs in Cuba is a constant menace to our peace, and entails upon this Government an enormous expense. With such a conflict waged for years in an island so near us and with which our people have such trade and business relations; when the lives and liberty of our citizens are in constant danger and their property destroyed and themselves ruined; where our trading vessels are liable to seizure and are seized at our very door by war ships of a foreign nation, the expeditions of filibustering that we are powerless to prevent altogether, and the irritating questions and entanglements thus arising — all these and others that I need not mention, with the resulting strained relations, are a constant menace to our peace, and compel us to keep on a semi-war footing with a nation with which we are at peace. . . .

The long trial has proved that the object for which Spain has waged the war can not be attained. The fire of insurrection may flame or may smolder with varying seasons, but it has not been and it is plain that it can not be extinguished by present methods. The only hope of relief and repose from a condition which can no longer be endured is the enforced pacification of Cuba. In the name of humanity, in the name of civilization, in behalf of endangered American interests which give us the right and the duty to speak and to act, the war in Cuba must stop.

In view of these facts and of these considerations, I ask the Congress to authorize and empower the President to take measures to secure a full and final termination of hostilities between the Government of Spain and the people of Cuba, and to secure in the island the establishment of a stable government, capable of maintaining order and observing its international obligations, insuring peace and tranquillity and the security of its citizens as well as our own, and to use the military and naval forces of the United States as may be necessary for these purposes. . . .

The issue is now with the Congress. It is a solemn responsibility. I have exhausted every effort to relieve the intolerable condition of affairs which is at our doors. Prepared to execute every obligation imposed upon me by the Constitution and the law, I await your action.

Yesterday, and since the preparation of the foregoing message, official information was received by me that the latest decree of the Queen Regent of Spain directs General Blanco, in order to prepare and facilitate peace, to proclaim a suspension of hostilities, the duration and details of which have not yet been communicated to me.

This fact with every other pertinent consideration will, I am sure, have your just and careful attention in the solemn deliberations upon which you are about to enter. If this measure attains a successful result, then our aspirations as a Christian, peace-loving people will be realized. If it fails, it will be only another justification for our contemplated action.

◇◇◇◇◇◇◇◇◇◇◇◇◇◇

9. INSTRUCTIONS TO THE PEACE COMMISSION[10]

[*President McKinley to the Peace Commission*]

Washington, September 16, 1898

BY A PROTOCOL signed at Washington August 12, 1898, a copy of which is herewith inclosed, it was agreed that the United States and Spain would each appoint not more than five commissioners to treat of peace, and that the Commissioners so appointed should meet a Paris not later than October 1, 1898. . . .

By these instructions you will observe that the evacuation of Cuba, Porto Rico, and other Spanish Islands in the West Indies is treated as a military operation, and will, when carried into effect, leave the evacuated places in the military occupation of the United States. . . .

It will be proper to confirm these transactions by appropriate clauses in the treaty of peace.

Similar clauses will be inserted in respect to the island ceded to the United States in the Ladrones. This Government has selected the Island of Guam, and you are instructed to embody in the treaty of peace a proper stipulation of cession. . . .

In the correspondence leading up to the signature of that instrument you will observe that this Government waived, for the time being, the requirement of a pecuniary indemnity from Spain. This concession was made in the hope that Spain would thereby be enabled promptly to accept our terms. But if the Spanish Commissioners should, contrary to our just expectations, put forward and insist upon a claim for compensation for public property, you are instructed to put forward as a counterclaim a demand for an indemnity for the cost of the war. . . .

It is my earnest wish that the United States in making peace should follow the same high rule of conduct which guided it in facing war. It should be as scrupulous and magnanimous in the concluding settlement as it was just and humane in its original action. The luster and the moral strength attaching to a cause which can be confidently rested upon the considerate judgment of the world should not under any illusion of the hour be dimmed by ulterior designs which might tempt us into excessive demands or into an adventurous departure on untried paths. It is believed that the true glory and the enduring interests of the country will most surely be served if an unselfish duty conscientiously accepted and a signal triumph honorably achieved shall be crowned by such an example of moderation, restraint, and reason in victory as best comports with the traditions and character of our enlightened Republic.

Our aim in the adjustment of peace should be directed to lasting results and to the achievement of the common good under the demands of civilization, rather than to ambitious designs. The terms of the protocol were

[10] Ibid., pp. 904–8.

framed upon this consideration. The abandonment of the Western Hemisphere by Spain was an imperative necessity. In presenting that requirement, we only fulfilled a duty universally acknowledged. It involves no ungenerous reference to our recent foe, but simply a recognition of the plain teachings of history, to say that it was not compatible with the assurance of permanent peace on and near our own territory that the Spanish flag should remain on this side of the sea. This lesson of events and of reason left no alternative as to Cuba, Porto Rico, and the other islands belonging to Spain in this hemisphere.

The Philippines stand upon a different basis. It is none the less true, however, that, without any original thought of complete or even partial acquisition, the presence and success of our arms at Manila imposes upon us obligations which we can not disregard. The march of events rules and overrules human action. Avowing unreservedly the purpose which has animated all our effort, and still solicitous to adhere to it, we can not be unmindful that, without any desire or design on our part, the war has brought us new duties and responsibilities which we must meet and discharge as becomes a great nation on whose growth and career from the beginning the Ruler of Nations has plainly written the high command and pledge of civilization.

Incidental to our tenure in the Philippines is the commercial opportunity to which American statesmanship can not be indifferent. It is just to use every legitimate means for the enlargement of American trade; but we seek no advantages in the Orient which are not common to all. Asking only the open door for ourselves, we are ready to accord the open door to others. The commercial opportunity which is naturally and inevitable associated with this new opening depends less on large territorial possession than upon an adequate commercial basis and upon broad and equal privileges. . . .

In view of what has been stated, the United States can not accept less than the cession in full right and sovereignty of the island of Luzon. It is desirable, however, that the United States shall acquire the right of entry for vessels and merchandise belonging to citizens of the United States into such ports of the Philippines as are not ceded to the United States upon terms of equal favor with Spanish ships and merchandise, both in relation to port and customs charges and rates of trade and commerce, together with other rights of protection and trade accorded to citizens of one country within the territory of another. You are therefore instructed to demand such concession, agreeing on your part that Spain shall have similar rights as to her subjects and vessels in the ports of any territory in the Philippines ceded to the United States. . . .

◇◇◇◇◇◇◇◇◇◇◇◇◇◇

10. TREATY OF PEACE BETWEEN THE UNITED STATES AND SPAIN[11]

[*Concluded at Paris, December 10, 1898; ratifications exchanged April 11, 1899*]

. . . *ARTICLE I.* Spain relinquishes all claim of sovereignty over and title to Cuba.

And as the island is, upon its evacuation by Spain, to be occupied by the United States, the United States will, so long as such occupation shall last, assume and discharge the obligations that may under international law result from the fact of its occupation, for the protection of life and property.

Article II. Spain cedes to the United States the island of Porto Rico and other islands now under Spanish sovereignty in the West Indies, and the island of Guam in the Marianas or Ladrones.

Article III. Spain cedes to the United States the archipelago known as the Philippine Islands. . . .

The United States will pay to Spain the sum of twenty million dollars ($20,000,000) within three months after the exchange of the ratifications of the present treaty.

Article IV. The United States will, for the term of ten years from the date of the exchange of the ratifications of the present treaty, admit Spanish ships and merchandise to the ports of the Philippine Islands on the same terms as ships and merchandise of the United States.

Article V. The United States will, upon the signature of the present treaty, send back to Spain, at its own cost, the Spanish soldiers taken as prisoners of war on the capture of Manila by the American forces. The arms of the soldiers in question shall be restored to them.

Spain will, upon the exchange of the ratifications of the present treaty, proceed to evacuate the Philippines, as well as the island of Guam, on terms similar to those agreed upon by the Commissioners appointed to arrange for the evacuation of Porto Rico and other islands in the West Indies, under the Protocol of August 12, 1898, which is to continue in force till its provisions are completely executed. . . .

Article X. The inhabitants of the territories over which Spain relinquishes or cedes her sovereignty shall be secured in the free exercise of their religion. . . .

---

[11] *Statutes at Large of the United States,* Vol. XXX, pp. 1754–62. The treaty was signed by William R. Day, William P. Frye, Whitelaw Reid, B. De Abarzuza, W. R. De Villa Urrutia, Cushman K. Davis, Geo. Gray, Eugenio Montero Ríos, J. De Garnica, and Rafael Cerero.

◇◇◇◇◇◇◇◇◇◇◇◇◇◇

11. IMPERIALISM AT ITS HEIGHT[12]

MR. PRESIDENT, I address the Senate at this time because Senators and Members of the House on both sides have asked that I give to Congress and the country my observations in the Philippines and the far East, and the conclusions which those observations compel; . . .

Mr. President, the times call for candor. The Philippines are ours forever, "territory belonging to the United States," as the Constitution calls them. And just beyond the Philippines are China's illimitable markets. We will not retreat from either. We will not repudiate our duty in the archipelago. We will not abandon our opportunity in the Orient. We will not renounce our part in the mission of our race, trustee, under God, of the civilization of the world. And we will move forward to our work, not howling out regrets like slaves whipped to their burdens, but with gratitude for a task worthy of our strength, and thanksgiving to Almighty God that He has marked us as His chosen people, henceforth to lead in the regeneration of the world.

This island empire is the last land left in all the oceans. If it should prove a mistake to abandon it, the blunder once made would be irretrievable. If it proves a mistake to hold it, the error can be corrected when we will. Every other progressive nation stands ready to relieve us.

But to hold it will be no mistake. Our largest trade henceforth must be with Asia. The Pacific is our ocean. More and more Europe will manufacture the most it needs, secure from its colonies the most it consumes. Where shall we turn for consumers of our surplus? Geography answers the question. China is our natural customer. She is nearer to us than to England, Germany, or Russia, the commercial powers of the present and the future. They have moved nearer to China by securing permanent bases on her borders. The Philippines give us a base at the door of all the East.

Lines of navigation from our ports to the Orient and Australia; from the Isthmian Canal to Asia; from all Oriental ports to Australia, converge at and separate from the Philippines. They are a self-supporting, dividend-paying fleet, permanently anchored at a spot selected by the strategy of Providence, commanding the Pacific. And the Pacific is the ocean of the commerce of the future. Most future wars will be conflicts for commerce. The power that rules the Pacific, therefore, is the power that rules the world. And, with the Philippines, that power is and will forever be the American Republic. . . .

---

12 Speech of Albert J. Beveridge, Senator for Indiana, in the Senate, January 9, 1900. The Senator spoke on the following resolution:

Be it resolved by the Senate and House of Representatives of the United States of America in Congress assembled, That the Philippine Islands are territory belonging to the United States; that it is the intention of the United States to retain them as such and to establish and maintain such governmental control throughout the archipelago as the situation may demand. *Congressional Globe,* 56 Cong., First Sess., xxxiii, pp. 704–12.

Nothing is so natural as trade with one's neighbors. The Philippines make us the nearest neighbors of all the East. Nothing is more natural than to trade with those you know. This is the philosophy of all advertising. The Philippines bring us permanently face to face with the most sought-for customers of the world. National prestige, national propinquity, these and commercial activity are the elements of commercial success. The Philippines give the first; the character of the American people supply the last. It is a providential conjunction of all the elements of trade, of duty, and of power. If we are willing to go to war rather than let England have a few feet of frozen Alaska, which affords no market and commands none, what should we not do rather than let England, Germany, Russia, or Japan have all the Philippines? And no man on the spot can fail to see that this would be their fate if we retired. . . .

Here, then, Senators, is the situation. Two years ago there was no land in all the world which we could occupy for any purpose. Our commerce was daily turning toward the Orient, and geography and trade developments made necessary our commercial empire over the Pacific. And in that ocean we had no commercial, naval, or military base. To-day we have one of the three great ocean possessions of the globe, located at the most commanding commercial, naval, and military points in the eastern seas, within hail of India, shoulder to shoulder with China, richer in its own resources than any equal body of land on the entire globe, and peopled by a race which civilization demands shall be improved. Shall we abandon it? That man little knows the common people of the Republic, little understands the instincts of our race, who thinks we will not hold it fast and hold it forever, administering just government by simplest methods. We may trick up devices to shift our burden and lessen our opportunity; they will avail us nothing but delay. We may tangle conditions by applying academic arrangements of self-government to a crude situation; their failure will drive us to our duty in the end. . . .

But, Senators, it would be better to abandon this combined garden and Gibraltar of the Pacific, and count our blood and treasure already spent a profitable loss, than to apply any academic arrangement of self-government to these children. They are not capable of self-government. How could they be? They are not of a self-governing race. They are Orientals, Malays, instructed by Spaniards in the latter's worst estate.

They know nothing of practical government except as they have witnessed the weak, corrupt, cruel, and capricious rule of Spain. What magic will anyone employ to dissolve in their minds and characters those impressions of governors and governed which three centuries of misrule has created? What alchemy will change the oriental quality of their blood and set the self-governing currents of the American pouring through their Malay veins? How shall they, in the twinkling of an eye, be exalted to the heights of self-governing peoples which required a thousand years for us to reach, Anglo-Saxon though we are? . . .

Mr. President, self-government and internal development have been the dominant notes of our first century; administration and the development of other lands will be the dominant notes of our second century. And administration is as high and holy a function as self-government, just as the care of a trust estate is as sacred an obligation as the management of our own concerns. Cain was the first to violate the divine law of human society which makes of us our brother's keeper. And administration of good government is the first lesson in self-government, that exalted estate toward which all civilization tends. . . .

The Declaration of Independence does not forbid us to do our part in the regeneration of the world. If it did, the Declaration would be wrong, just as the Articles of Confederation, drafted by the very same men who signed the Declaration, was found to be wrong. The Declaration has no application to the present situation. It was written by self-governing men for self-governing men. . . .

Senators in opposition are estopped from denying our constitutional power to govern the Philippines as circumstances may demand, for such power is admitted in the case of Florida, Louisiana, Alaska. How, then, is it denied in the Philippines? Is there a geographical interpretation to the Constitution? Do degrees of longitude fix constitutional limitations? Does a thousand miles of ocean diminish constitutional power more than a thousand miles of land? . . .

No; the oceans are not limitations of the power which the Constitution expressly gives Congress to govern all territory the nation may acquire. The Constitution declares that "Congress shall have power to dispose of and make all needful rules and regulations respecting the territory belonging to the United States." Not the Northwest Territory only; not Louisiana or Florida only; not territory on this continent only, but any territory anywhere belonging to the nation. The founders of the nation were not provincial. Theirs was the geography of the world. They were soldiers as well as landsmen, and they knew that where our ships should go our flag might follow. They had the logic of progress, and they knew that the Republic they were planting must, in obedience to the laws of our expanding race, necessarily develop into the greater Republic which the world beholds to-day, and into the still mightier Republic which the world will finally acknowledge as the arbiter, under God, of the destinies of mankind. And so our fathers wrote into the Constitution these words of growth, of expansion, of empire, if you will, unlimited by geography or climate or by anything but the vitality and possibilities of the American people: "Congress shall have power to dispose of and make all needful rules and regulations respecting the territory belonging to the United States. . . ."

Mr. President, this question is deeper than any question of party politics; deeper than any question of the isolated policy of our country even; deeper even than any question of constitutional power. It is elemental. It is racial. God has not been preparing the English-speaking and Teutonic peoples for a thousand years for nothing but vain and idle self-contemplation and self-admiration. No! He has made us the master organizers of the world to establish system where chaos reigns. He has given us the spirit of progress to overwhelm the forces of reaction throughout the earth. He has made us adepts in government that we may administer government among savage and senile peoples. Were it not for such a force as this the world would relapse into barbarism and night. And of all our race He has marked the American people as His chosen nation to finally lead in the regeneration of the world. This is the divine mission of America, and it holds for us all the profit, all the glory, all the happiness possible to man. We are trustees of the world's progress, guardians of its righteous peace. The judgment of the Master is upon us: "Ye have been faithful over a few things; I will make you ruler over many things."

What shall history say of us? Shall it say that we renounced that holy trust, left the savage to his base condition, the wilderness to the reign of waste, deserted duty, abandoned glory, forget our sordid profit even, because we feared our strength and read the charter of our powers with the doubter's eye and the quibbler's mind? Shall it say that, called by events to captain and command the proudest, ablest, purest race of history in history's noblest work, we declined that great commission? Our fathers would not have had it so. No! They founded no paralytic government, incapable of the simplest acts of administration. They planted no sluggard people, passive while the world's work calls them. They established no reactionary nation. They unfurled no retreating flag. . . .

Blind indeed is he who sees not the hand of God in events so vast, so harmonious, so benign. Reactionary indeed is the mind that perceives not that this vital people is the strongest of the saving forces of the world; that our place, therefore, is at the head of the constructing and redeeming nations of the earth; and that to stand aside while events march on is a surrender of our interests, a betrayal of our duty as blind as it is base. Craven indeed is the heart that fears to perform a work so golden and so noble; that dares not win a glory so immortal. . . .

Mr. President and Senators, adopt the resolution offered, that peace may quickly come and that we may begin our saving, regenerating, and uplifting work. . . . Reject it, and the world, history, and the American people will know where to forever fix the awful responsibility for the consequences that will surely follow such failure to do our manifest duty. How dare we delay when our soldiers' blood is flowing? [Applause in the galleries]. . . .

12. PLATFORM OF THE AMERICAN ANTI-IMPERIALIST LEAGUE[13]

WE HOLD that the policy known as imperialism is hostile to liberty and tends toward militarism, an evil from which it has been our glory to be free. We regret that it has become necessary in the land of Washington and

[13] Adopted at Chicago, October 18, 1899. *Liberty Tracts,* No. 10, p. 2.

Lincoln to reaffirm that all men, of whatever race or color, are entitled to life, liberty, and the pursuit of happiness. We maintain that governments derive their just powers from the consent of the governed. We insist that the subjugation of any people is "criminal aggression" and open disloyalty to the distinctive principles of our government.

We earnestly condemn the policy of the present National Administration in the Philippines. It seeks to extinguish the spirit of 1776 in those islands. We deplore the sacrifice of our soldiers and sailors, whose bravery deserves admiration even in an unjust war. We denounce the slaughter of the Filipinos as a needless horror. We protest against the extension of American sovereignty by Spanish methods.

We demand the immediate cessation of the war against liberty, begun by Spain and continued by us. We urge that Congress be promptly convened to announce to the Filipinos our purpose to concede to them the independence for which they have so long fought and which of right is theirs.

The United States have always protested against the doctrine of international law which permits the subjugation of the weak by the strong. A self-governing state cannot accept sovereignty over an unwilling people. The United States cannot act upon the ancient heresy that might makes right.

Imperialists assume that with the destruction of self-government in the Philippines by American hands, all opposition here will cease. This is a grievous error. Much as we abhor the war of "criminal aggression" in the Philippines, greatly as we regret the blood of the Filipinos is on American hands, we more deeply resent the betrayal of American institutions at home. The real firing line is not in the suburbs of Manila. The foe is of our own household. The attempt of 1861 was to divide the country. That of 1899 is to destroy its fundamental principles and noblest ideals.

Whether the ruthless slaughter of the Filipinos shall end next month or next year is but an incident in a contest that must go on until the Declaration of Independence and the Constitution of the United States are rescued from the hands of their betrayers. Those who dispute about standards of value while the Republic is undermined will be listened to as little as those who would wrangle about the small economies of the household while the house is on fire. The training of a great people for a century, the aspiration for liberty of a vast immigration are forces that will hurl aside those who in the delirium of conquest seek to destroy the character of our institutions.

We deny that the obligation of all citizens to support their Government in times of grave National peril applies to the present situation. If an Administration may with impunity ignore the issues upon which it was chosen, deliberately create a condition of war anywhere on the face of the globe, debauch the civil service for spoils to promote the adventure, organize a truth-suppressing censorship and demand of all citizens a suspension of judgment and their unanimous support while it chooses to continue the fighting, representative government itself is imperiled.

We propose to contribute to the defeat of any person or party that stands for the forcible subjugation of any people. We shall oppose for reelection all who in the White House or in Congress betray American liberty in pursuit of un-American gains. We still hope that both of our great political parties will support and defend the Declaration of Independence in the closing campaign of the century.

We hold, with Abraham Lincoln, that "no man is good enough to govern another man without that man's consent. When the white man governs himself, that is self-government, but when he governs himself and also governs another man, that is more than self-government – that is despotism." "Our reliance is in the love of liberty which God has planted in us. Our defense is in the spirit which prizes liberty as the heritage of all men in all lands. Those who deny freedom to others deserve it not for themselves, and under a just God cannot long retain it."

We cordially invite the cooperation of all men and women who remain loyal to the Declaration of Independence and the Constitution of the United States.

Chapter XXIV

THE PANAMA CANAL

◇◇◇◇◇◇◇◇◇◇◇◇◇

PRIOR TO 1860 the United States had concluded two treaties of major importance with reference to an Atlantic–Pacific canal. One was the treaty of 1846 with New Granada (Colombia) and the other was the Clayton-Bulwer Treaty with Great Britain. Neither of these treaties gave the United States a right to build a canal, while one of them, the Clayton-Bulwer Treaty, placed certain restrictions upon American ownership and control of a canal. In 1881 Secretary of State James G. Blaine not only re-defined American policy with respect to the Colombian Treaty, but also sought to abrogate the Clayton-Bulwer Treaty (1). Great Britain refused to acquiesce in Blaine's interpretation of the treaty (2) and the American government began to realize that it would be necessary to negotiate a new canal treaty with Great Britain. A new treaty was concluded in 1902 (4). In the meantime an American Isthmian Canal Commission had investigated the possible routes for a canal and had reported its conclusions to the President, December 16, 1901 (3). It remained for Congress to designate which route should be used and for the President to negotiate a canal treaty with the nation through whose territory the route extended. The Hay-Herran Treaty was negotiated forthwith but an obstacle appeared in the refusal of the Colombian government to ratify the treaty. While possible solutions for the difficulty were being considered by the United States the Panama Revolution occurred, and the question of an Isthmian canal was removed from the control of the Colombian government. Colombia vigorously protested (5) against the action of the United States in the Panama affair, and it fell to the lot of Secretary John Hay to make what defense (6) he could of American policy. Although diplomatic relations between Colombia and the United States were not severed, cordial relations were not restored until 1921 (7).

◇◇◇◇◇◇◇◇◇◇◇◇◇

1. AMERICAN DESIRE TO REVISE THE CLAYTON-BULWER TREATY[1]

[*James G. Blaine to James Russell Lowell*]

Washington, November 19, 1881

IN PURSUANCE of the premises laid down in my circular note of June 24 of this year touching the determination of this government with respect to the guarantee of neutrality for the interoceanic canal at Panama, it becomes my duty to call your attention to the convention of April 19, 1850, between Great Britain and the United States, commonly known as the Clayton-Bulwer treaty. . . .

This convention was made more than thirty years ago, under exceptional and extraordinary conditions which have long since ceased to exist – conditions which at best were temporary in their nature, and which can never be reproduced.

The remarkable development of the United States on the Pacific coast since that time has created new duties for this government, and devolved new responsibilities upon it, the full and complete discharge of which requires in the judgment of the President some essential modifications in the Clayton-Bulwer treaty. The interests of Her Majesty's Government involved in this question, in so far as they may be properly judged by the observation of a friendly power, are so inconsiderable in comparison with those of the United States that the President hopes a readjustment of the terms of the treaty may be reached in a spirit of amity and concord.

The respect due to Her Majesty's Government demands that the objections to the perpetuity of the convention of 1850, as it now exists, should be stated with directness and with entire frankness. And among the most salient and palpable of these is the fact that the operation of the treaty practically concedes to Great Britain the control of whatever canal may be constructed.

The insular position of the home government, with its extended colonial possessions, requires the British Empire to maintain a vast naval establishment, which, in our continental solidity, we do not need, and in time of peace shall never create. If the United States binds itself not to fortify on land, it concedes that Great Britain, in the possible case of a struggle for the control of the canal, shall at the outset have an advantage which would prove decisive, and which could not be reversed except by the expenditure of treasure and force. The presumptive intention of the treaty was to place the two powers on a plane of perfect equality, with respect to the canal, but in practice, as I have indicated, this would prove utterly delusive, and would instead surrender it, if not in form, yet in effect, to the control of Great Britain.

The treaty binds the United States not to use its military force in any

[1] *Sen. Ex. Doc.* (3853) 56th Congress, 1st Session, No. 161, pp. 178–84.

precautionary measure, while it leaves the naval power of Great Britain perfectly free and unrestrained, ready at any moment of need to seize both ends of the canal, and render its military occupation on land a matter entirely within the discretion of Her Majesty's Government.

The military power of the United States, as shown by the recent civil war, is without limit, and in any conflict on the American continent altogether irresistible. The Clayton-Bulwer treaty commands this government not to use a single regiment of troops to protect its interests in connection with the interoceanic canal, but to surrender the transit to the guardianship and control of the British navy. If no American soldier is to be quartered on the Isthmus to protect the rights of his country in the interoceanic canal, surely, by the fair logic of neutrality, no war vessel of Great Britain should be permitted to appear in the waters that control either entrance to the canal.

A more comprehensive objection to the treaty is urged by this government. Its provisions embody a misconception of the relative positions of Great Britain and the United States with respect to the interests of each government in questions pertaining to this continent. The Government of the United States has no occasion to disavow an aggressive disposition. Its entire policy establishes its pacific character, and among its chief aims is to cultivate the most friendly and intimate relations with its neighbors, both independent and colonial. At the same time, this government, with respect to European states, will not consent to perpetuate any treaty that impeaches our right and long-established claim to priority on the American continent. . . .

For self-protection to her own interests, therefore, the United States in the first instance asserts her right to control the Isthmus transit. And, secondly, she offers by such control that absolute neutralization of the canal as respects European powers which can in no other way be certainly attained and lastingly assured. . . .

It is earnestly hoped by the President that the considerations now presented will have due weight and influence with Her Majesty's Government, and that the modifications of the treaty desired by the United States will be conceded in the same friendly spirit in which they are asked. . . .

◇◇◇◇◇◇◇◇◇◇◇◇◇

2. REFUSAL OF GREAT BRITAIN TO ALTER THE CLAYTON-BULWER TREATY[2]

[*Lord Granville to Lionel* S. S. *West*]

Foreign Office, London, January 7, 1882

IN MY DISPATCH No. 279*a* of the 13th ultimo I informed you that the United States minister at this court had communicated to me the substance

[2] Ibid., pp. 191–4.

of a dispatch which he had received from Mr. Blaine, then Secretary of State, on the subject of the convention of the 19th April, 1850. . . .

The principles upon which the whole argument of the dispatch is founded are, as far as I am aware, novel in international law. If a discussion of the subject on the abstract grounds of public right were deemed useful or opportune, it would not be difficult to quote passages from publicists of acknowledged authority in both countries in support of this opinion. But for several reasons it will be better to treat the matter from the side of the practical consideration which it involves, without, of course, being precluded from reverting at any future stage, in case of need, to its other aspect.

Her Majesty's Government cannot admit that the analogy which it is sought to draw from the conduct of Great Britain in regard to the Suez Canal is correct or justified by the facts. They have made no attempt to fortify the island of Cyprus, or to establish it as an armed position on an important scale, though they have an undoubted right to do so. The fortress of Gibraltar, the island of Malta, and the military establishment at Aden came into the possession of England at a date long anterior to the time when the Mediterranean and the Red Sea could be regarded as a military route to India. For years afterwards the whole mass of re-enforcements for India was sent by the way of Cape of Good Hope. Nor has any serious addition been made to the strength of these positions since the opening of the canal beyond what has been a natural consequence of the improvements in military science. Although no doubt well adapted by its situation to command the Straits of Bab-el-Mandeb, the Island of Perim has not in any real sense been made a fortified position. The fort and garrison on the island are, in fact, sufficient only to protect the light-house, which has been erected there for the general benefit of navigation, from possible attack by predatory Arabs.

The Navy Department of the United States must be well aware that Her Majesty's Government have never sought to bar or even to restrict the use of the canal by the naval forces of other countries, and that even during the recent war between Russia and Turkey, when the canal itself formed a portion of the territory of one of the belligerents, when the seat of conflict was close at hand, and when British interests might in many other respects have been nearly involved, they contented themselves with obtaining an assurance that the sphere of operations should not be extended to the canal.

Her Majesty's Government cordially concur in what is stated by Mr. Blaine as regards the unexampled development of the United States on the Pacific coast, and the capacity which they possess for further progress. That development has been watched in this country with admiration and interest, and will continue to be so regarded. But though in rapidity it may, and probably has, exceeded the most sanguine calculation, Her Majesty's Government cannot look upon it in the light of an unexpected event, or suppose that it was not within the view of the statesmen who were parties on either side to the Clayton-Bulwer treaty. The declarations of President Monroe and of his cabinet, in 1823 and 1824, whatever may be the view taken of their scope and bearing, and of the admissibility of the principles which they involve, or which it is sought to deduce from them, show at least that at that period – twenty-six years anterior to the treaty now under discussion – there was a clear prevision of the great future reserved to the Pacific coast. It is, in the opinion of Her Majesty's Government, an inadmissible contention that the regular and successful operation of causes so evident at the time, and in their nature so irrepressible, should be held to have completely altered the condition of affairs to the extent of vitiating the foundations of an agreement which cannot be supposed to have been concluded without careful thought and deliberation. . . .

With all deference to the considerations which have prompted the proposals made in Mr. Blaine's dispatch, Her Majesty's Government cannot believe that they would promote this object or be beneficial in themselves. The relations of the United States with the European powers are fortunately of a nature to give rise to no feelings of suspicion or alarm. The general tendency of their foreign policy gives good promise that they will so continue. But if provision is to be made on one side for a different state of affairs, it must be expected that the course thus indicated will find its natural and logical counterpart on the other. Her Majesty's Government can conceive no more melancholy spectacle that a competition among the nations holding West Indian possessions, and others on the Central and South American Continent, in the construction of fortifications to obtain the command over the canal and its approaches, in the event of occasion arising for such a measure. They cannot believe that it would be agreeable or convenient to any South American state through which the canal may pass to find itself called upon to admit a foreign power to construct and garrison on its territory a succession of fortresses of increasing magnitude, designed to oppose such attempts, even though that foreign power be a neighboring one and situated upon the same continent. And when the claim to do this is accompanied by a declaration that the United States will always insist on treating the water-way which shall unite the two oceans "as part of her coast line," it is difficult to imagine that the states to which the territory lying between that water-way and the United States belongs can practically retain as independent a position as that which they now enjoy.

These are the consequences which, in the conviction of Her Majesty's Government, would almost certainly follow from a claim on the part of the United States to assume the supreme authority over the canal and all responsibility for its control. Her Majesty's Government hold, on the contrary, that the principles which guided the negotiators of the convention of 1850 were intrinsically sound, and continue to be applicable to the present state of affairs. Their wish would be that those principles should receive the practical development which was contemplated at the time; and that effect should be given to that portion of the treaty which provides that the contracting parties shall invite all other states with whom they have friendly intercourse to enter into similar stipulations with them. . . .

◇◇◇◇◇◇◇◇◇◇◇◇◇

3. APPROVAL OF THE NICARAGUAN CANAL ROUTE[3]

[*Report of the Isthmian Canal Commission, to the President of the United States, December 16, 1901*]

Conclusions

THE INVESTIGATIONS of this Commission have shown that the selection of "the most feasible and practicable route" for an isthmian canal must be made between the Nicaragua and Panama locations. Furthermore, the complete problem involves both the sea-level plan of canal and that with locks. The Panama route alone is feasible for a sea-level canal, although both are entirely practicable and feasible for a canal with locks. The time required to complete a sea-level canal on the Panama route, probably more than twice that needed to build a canal with locks, excludes it from favorable consideration aside from other serious features of its construction. It is the conclusion of this Commission, therefore, that a plan of canal with locks should be adopted. . . .

The existence of a harbor at each terminus of the Panama route, and a line of railroad across the isthmus, will make it practicable to commence work there, after the concessions are acquired, as soon as the necessary plant can be collected and put in place, and the working force organized. This period of preparation is estimated at one year. In Nicaragua this period is estimated at two years, so as to include also the construction of working harbors and terminal and railroad facilities.

The work of excavation on the Nicaragua route is distributed; it is heaviest near Conchuda, at Tamborcito, and in the divide west of the lake. On the Panama route it is largely concentrated in the Culebra and Emperador cuts, which are practically one. As a rule distributed work affords a greater number of available points of attack, contributing to a quicker completion; but in either of these cases such difficulties as may exist can be successfully met with suitable organization and efficient appliances. . . .

Except for the items of risks and delays, the time required to pass through the canals need be taken into account only as an element in the time required by vessels to make their voyages between terminal ports. Compared on this basis, the Nicaragua route is the more advantageous for all transisthmian commerce except that originating or ending on the west coast of South America. For the commerce in which the United States is most interested, that between our Pacific ports and Atlantic ports, Euro-

[3] *Sen. Ex. Doc.* (4225) 54th Congress, 1st Session, No. 54, pp. 257–63.

pean and American, the Nicaragua route is shorter by about one day. The same advantage exists between our Atlantic ports and the Orient. For our Gulf ports the advantage of the Nicaragua route is nearly two days. For commerce between North Atlantic ports and the west coast of South America the Panama route is shorter by about two days. Between Gulf ports and the west coast of South America the saving is about one day. . . .

The Nicaragua route lies in a region of sparse population and not in a pathway of much trade or movement of people; conditions productive of much sickness do not exist. On the other hand, a considerable population has long existed on the Panama route and it lies on a pathway of comparatively large trade along which currents of moving people from infected places sometimes converge, thus creating conditions favorable to epidemics. Existing conditions indicate hygienic advantages for the Nicaragua route, although it is probable that no less effective sanitary measures must be taken during construction in the one case than in the other. . . .

The Republics of Nicaragua and Costa Rica are untrammeled by any existing concessions or treaty obligations and are free to grant to the United States the rights necessary for the attainment of these ends; and in December, 1900, demonstrated their willingness to have their territory so occupied by the United States by executing protocols by which it was agreed that they would enter into negotiations to settle in detail the plan and agreements necessary to accomplish the construction and provide for the ownership of the proposed canal whenever the President of the United States is authorized by law to acquire the necessary control and authority.

The Government of Colombia, on the contrary, in whose territory the Panama route lies, has granted concessions which belong to or are controlled by the New Panama Canal Company and have many years to run. These concessions, limited in time and defective in other ways, would not be adequate authority for the purposes of the United States, but while they exist Colombia is not free to treat with this Government. If the Panama route is selected these concessions must be removed in order that the two Republics may enter into a treaty to enable the United States to acquire the control upon the isthmus that will be necessary and to fix the consideration. . . .

After considering all the facts developed by the investigations made by the Commission and the actual situation as it now stands, and having in view the terms offered by the new Panama Canal Company, this Commission is of the opinion that "the most practicable and feasible route" for an isthmian canal, to be "under the control, management, and ownership of the United States," is that known as the Nicaragua route.

J. G. Walker,
Rear-Admiral, United States Navy

◇◇◇◇◇◇◇◇◇◇◇◇◇

4. THE HAY-PAUNCEFOTE TREATY[4]

[*Concluded between the United States and Great Britain November 18, 1901; ratifications exchanged February 21, 1902*]

. . . *ARTICLE I.* The High Contracting Parties agree that the present Treaty shall supersede the afore-mentioned Convention of the 19th April, 1850.

Article II. It is agreed that the canal may be constructed under the auspices of the Government of the United States, either directly at its own cost, or by gift or loan of money to individuals or Corporations, or through subscription to or purchase of stock or shares, and that, subject to the provisions of the present Treaty, the said Government shall have and enjoy all the rights incident to such construction, as well as the exclusive right of providing for the regulation and management of the canal.

Article III. The United States adopts, as the basis of the neutralization of such ship canal, the following Rules, substantially as embodied in the Convention of Constantinople, signed the 28th October, 1888, for the free navigation of the Suez Canal, that is to say:

1. The canal shall be free and open to the vessels of commerce and of war of all nations observing these Rules, on terms of entire equality, so that there shall be no discrimination against any such nation, or its citizens or subjects, in respect of the conditions or charges of traffic, or otherwise. Such conditions and charges of traffic shall be just and equitable.

2. The canal shall never be blockaded, nor shall any right of war be exercised nor any act of hostility be committed within it. The United States, however, shall be at liberty to maintain such military police along the canal as may be necessary to protect it against lawlessness and disorder.

3. Vessels of war of a belligerent shall not revictual nor take any stores in the canal except so far as may be strictly necessary; and the transit of such vessels through the canal shall be effected with the least possible delay in accordance with the Regulations in force, and with only such intermission as may result from the necessities of the service.

Prizes shall be in all respects subject to the same Rules as vessels of war of the belligerents.

4. No belligerent shall embark or disembark troops, munitions of war, or warlike materials in the canal, except in case of accidental hindrance of the transit, and in such case the transit shall be resumed with all possible dispatch.

5. The provisions of this Article shall apply to waters adjacent to the canal, within 3 marine miles of either end. Vessels of war of a belligerent shall not remain in such waters longer than twenty-four hours at any one time, except in case of distress, and in such case shall depart as soon as

[4] *Sen. Ex. Doc.* (6582) 63rd Congress, 2nd Session, No. 474, pp. 292–4. The treaty was signed by John Hay and Sir Julian Pauncefote.

possible; but a vessel of war of one belligerent shall not depart within twenty-four hours from the departure of a vessel of war of the other belligerent.

6. The plant, establishments, buildings, and all works necessary to the construction, maintenance, and operation of the canal shall be deemed to be part thereof, for the purposes of this Treaty, and in time of war, as in time of peace, shall enjoy complete immunity from attack or injury by belligerents, and from acts calculated to impair their usefulness as part of the canal. . . .

◇◇◇◇◇◇◇◇◇◇◇◇◇◇

5. COLOMBIAN PROTEST AGAINST AMERICAN ACTION IN PANAMA[5]

[*Rafael Reyes to John Hay*]

Legation of Colombia, Washington, December 23, 1903

THE GOVERNMENT and people of Colombia consider themselves aggrieved by that of the United States in that they are convinced that the course followed by its administration, in relation to the events that have developed and recently been accomplished at Panama, have worked deep injury to their interests. . . .

It is proper to observe that under our constitution the Congress is the principal guardian, defender, and interpreter of our laws. And it can not be denied by anyone, I take it, that the Hay-Herran convention provides for the execution of public works on a vast scale and for the occupancy in perpetuity of a portion of the territory of Colombia, the occupant being not a juridical person whose acts were to be governed by the civil law and the Colombian code, but rather a sovereign political entity, all of which would have given occasion for frequent conflicts, since there would have been a coexistence in Panama of two public powers, the one national, the other foreign.

Hence the earnest efforts evinced by the Senate in ascertaining whether the American Government would agree to accept certain amendments tending especially to avoid as far as practicable any restriction in the treaty of the jurisdiction of the nation within its own territory. There is abundant evidence of the efforts of the Senate in that direction, and I firmly believe that it would have approved the convention with amendments that would probably have been acceptable to the United States had not the American minister at Bogotá repeatedly declared in the most positive manner that his Government would reject any amendment that might be offered. . . .

All governments being, as is well known, bound to respect the rights born of the independence and sovereignty of nations, the premature rec-

[5] Ibid., pp. 481–91.

ognition by the United States of the province of Panama, rising in arms to detach itself from the country of which it is a part, while it is a matter of public knowledge that the mother country commands sufficient forces to subdue it, constitutes, according to the most ancient and modern authorities on international law, not only a grave offense to Colombia, but also a formal attack upon her wealth.

For, as the territory forms the most important part of the national wealth, its dismemberment impairs the revenues applied to the discharge of corporate obligations among which are foreign debts and those enterprises entailed on the insurgent province, from which Colombia derives a considerable income.

If there be an end and eternal and immutable principles in right, that right of Colombia has been injured by the United States by an incredible transgression of the limits set by equity and justice. . . .

It will be well to say that before the news was divulged that a revolution was about to break out on the Isthmus, American cruisers which reached their destination precisely on the eve of the movement were plowing the waters of the Atlantic and Pacific Oceans. Cablegrams that are given public circulation in an official document show that two days before the movement the Secretary of the Navy issued orders to those cruisers not to permit the landing of troops of the Government of Colombia on Panama's territory.

A military officer of the Government of the United States stopped the railway from carrying to Panama, as it was under obligations to do, a battalion that had just arrived at Colon from Bogotá at the very time when its arrival in that city would have impeded or suppressed any revolutionary attempt. A few days thereafter, when my Government intrusted me with the duty of leading the army that was to embark at Puerto Colombia to go and restore order on the Isthmus, being unacquainted except in an imperfect manner with the attitude assumed by the American war ships, I had the honor to address a note on the subject to Vice Admiral Coghlan, and in his reply, which was not delayed, he tells me that—

> his present orders are to prevent the landing of soldiers with hostile intent within the boundary of the State of Panama. . . .

In the note of Mr. Seward, Secretary of State, to Mr. Adams, United States minister, in 1861, this doctrine is found:

> We freely admit that a nation may, and even ought, to recognize a new State which has absolutely and beyond question effected its independence, and permanently established its sovereignty; and that a recognition in such a case affords no just cause of offense to the government of the country from which the new State has so detached itself. On the other hand, we insist that a nation that recognizes a revolutionary State, with a view to aid its effecting its sovereignty and independence, commits a great wrong against the nation whose integrity is thus invaded, and makes itself responsible for a just and ample redress. (Foreign Relations, 1861, pp. 76–7.)

At another point in the same note the Secretary says to the minister:

To recognize the independence of a new State, and so favor, possibly determine, its admission into the family of nations, is the highest possible exercise of sovereign power, because it affects in any case the welfare of two nations, and often the peace of the world. In the European system this power is now seldom attempted to be exercised without invoking a consultation or congress of nations. That system has not been extended to this continent. But there is even a greater necessity for prudence in such cases in regard to American States than in regard to the nations of Europe. (Foreign Relations, 1861, p. 79, Mr. Seward to Mr. Adams, No. 2, April 10, 1861). . . .

If Colombia had not sufficient force to compel Panama to remain a part of the national unit, it would, without doubt, have asked the mediation of some friendly country in order to reach an understanding with the de facto government which has been established there.

But for it to have been able to subdue it by force it was necessary that Your Excellency's Government should remain neutral in the dispute; in not having done so, your Government, itself, violated "the rights of sovereignty and the property which Colombia has and possesses over the said territory," not complying, consequently, with the obligation it contracted to guarantee those rights as set forth in the above-cited part of the thirty-fifth article of the treaty. And it may be observed that the United States continues deriving the advantages granted under the treaty, while we lose those which we gave in order to obtain such guarantees. . . .

Every nation is responsible to other nations for its conduct, whence it follows that all have among themselves rights and obligations, but these rights and obligations are limited by the right of property. The owner of an estate can not oppose the passage through his land – for example, of a railroad which the community needs – but he may demand that he be indemnified for the damage done him. In the same manner a State should certainly not obstruct the passage through its territory of a canal which the progress of the age and the needs of humanity have made necessary, but it has the right to impose conditions which shall save its sovereignty and to demand indemnification for the use thereof. Reasons based on the needs of humanity are undoubtedly very powerful, but they do not convincingly prove that the legitimate owner shall be deprived of a large part of his territory to satisfy such needs. . . .

In this crisis of the life of my country, as unlooked for as it is terrible, Colombia rests its most comforting hopes in the sentiments of justice which animate the Government of your excellency, and confidently trusts that that Government, which has so many times surprised the world by its wisdom, will, on this occasion, astonish it by its example.

In any event, Colombia complies with the duty imposed upon her by the treaty of 1846 in that part of the 35th article which says:

. . . neither of the two contracting parties shall ordain or authorize any acts of reprisal, nor shall declare war against the other on complaints of injuries or damages, until the said party considering itself offended shall have laid before the other a statement of such injuries or damages, verified by competent proofs, demanding justice and satisfaction, and the same shall have been denied, in violation of the laws and of international right.

Since the aforesaid treaty is the law which governs between the two countries, and now that the weakness and ruin of my country, after three years of civil war scarcely at an end, and in which her bravest sons were lost by thousands, place her in the unhappy position of asking justice of the Government of your excellency, I propose that the claims which I make in the present note on account of the violation of the aforesaid treaty, and all other claims which may hereafter be made in connection with the events of Panama, be submitted to the Arbitration Tribunal of The Hague. . . .

◇◇◇◇◇◇◇◇◇◇◇◇◇

6. AN EXPLANATION OF AMERICAN POLICY IN PANAMA[6]

[*John Hay to Rafael Reyes*]

Washington, January 5, 1904

THE GOVERNMENT of the United States has carefully considered the grave complaints so ably set forth in the "statement of grievances" presented on behalf of the Government and people of Colombia, with your note of the 23d ultimo. . . .

On June 28, 1902, the President of the United States gave his approval to the act now commonly referred to as the Spooner Act, to provide for the construction of the interoceanic canal. Following the report of the Isthmian Canal Commission, which confirmed the opinion expressed by the Colombian Government, it embodied the formal decision of the United States in favor of the Panama route. It accordingly authorized the President to acquire, at a cost not exceeding $40,000,000, "the rights, privileges, franchises, concessions," and other property of the New Panama Canal Company, including its interest in the Panama Railroad Company, and to obtain from Colombia on such terms as he might deem reasonable perpetual control for the purposes of the canal of a strip of land not less than six miles wide, such control to include jurisdiction to make and, through such tribunals as might be agreed on, to enforce such police and sanitary rules and regulations as should be necessary to the preservation of order and of the public health.

The act also provided, in a clause to which your statement adverts, that, in case the President should "be unable to obtain for the United States a satisfactory title to the property of the New Panama Canal Company and the control of the necessary territory of the Republic of Colombia," to-

[6] Ibid., pp. 491–504.

gether with the "rights" mentioned in connection therewith, "within a reasonable time and upon reasonable terms," he should turn to Nicaragua. But this provision, while it indicated that the construction of the canal was not wholly to depend upon the success or failure to make reasonable terms with Colombia and the canal company, by no means implied that the question of routes was a matter of indifference.

In the nature of things it could not be so. Not only was the work to endure for all time, but its prompt construction was felt to be of vast importance; and it could not be a matter of less concern to the United States than to Colombia that this Government might possibly be forced to adopt a route which would, as the Colombian minister had observed—

> be longer, more expensive, both in construction and maintenance, and less adapted to the commerce of the world than the short and half-finished canal available at Panama. . . .

After the Spooner Act was approved, negotiations were duly initiated by Colombia. They resulted on January 22, 1903, in the conclusion of the Hay-Herran convention. By this convention every reasonable desire of the Colombian Government was believed to be gratified. . . .

Some time after the convention was signed the Government of the United States learned, to its utter surprise, that the Government of Colombia was taking with the canal company the position that a further permission, in addition to that contained in the convention, was necessary to the transfer of its concessions and those of the Panama Railroad Company, respectively, to the United States, and that, as a preliminary to this permission, the companies must enter into agreements with Colombia for the cancellation of all her obligations to either of them under the concession. This proceeding seemed all the more singular in the light of the negotiations between the two Governments. The terms in which the convention authorized the New Panama Canal Company to sell and transfer its "rights, privileges, properties, and concessions" to the United States were the same as those embodied in the original draft of a treaty presented to this Government by the Colombian minister on March 31, 1902.

No change in this particular was ever suggested by Colombia, in all the discussions that followed, until November 11, 1902. On that day the Colombian minister presented a memorandum in which it was proposed that the authorization should be so modified that "the permission accorded by Colombia to the canal and the railroad companies to transfer their rights to the United States" should "be regulated by a previous special arrangement entered into by Colombia." To this proposal this department answered that "the United States considers this suggestion wholly inadmissible." The proposition was then abandoned by Colombia, and the convention was nearly three months later signed without any modification of the absolute authorization to sell. . . .

The explanations put forward in Colombia's "statement of grievances" merely repeat the pleas devised at the Colombian capital. The sudden discovery that the terms of the convention, as proposed and signed by the Colombian Government, involved a violation of the Colombian constitution, because it required a cession to the United States of the "sovereignty" which is expressly recognized and confirmed, could be received by this Government only with the utmost surprise. Nevertheless, the Colombian Senate unanimously rejected the convention.

This fact was communicated to the department by Doctor Herran on the 22d of August last, by means of a copy of a cablegram from his Government. In that telegram the "impairment" of Colombian "sovereignty" was mentioned as one of the "reasons advanced in debate" for the Senate's action; but joined with it there was another reason, with which the department had long been familiar, namely, the "absence" of a "previous agreement" of the companies with the Colombian Government for the transfer of their privileges. To these reasons there was added a reference to the representations made by Mr. Beaupré; but it was said to be "probable" that the Colombian Congress would "provide bases" for "reopening negotiations. . . ."

Advices came to this Government, not only through the press but also through its own officials, of the existence of dangerous conditions on the Isthmus, as well as in the adjacent States whose interests were menaced. Disorders in that quarter were not new. In the summer of 1902, as well as in that of 1901, this Government had been obliged by its forces to maintain order on the transit route, and it took steps, as it had done on previous occasions, to perform a similar duty should the necessity arise. The form the trouble might take could not be foreseen, but it was important to guard against any destructive effects.

The reasonableness of these precautions soon became evident. The people of Panama rose against an act of the Government at Bogotá that threatened their most vital interests with destruction and the interests of the whole world with grave injury. The movement assumed the form of a declaration of independence. The avowed object of this momentous step was to secure the construction of the interoceanic canal. It was inspired by the desire of the people at once to safeguard their own interests and at the same time to assure the dedication of the Isthmus to the use for which Providence seemed to have designed it. . . .

By the declaration of independence of the Republic of Panama a new situation was created. On the one hand stood the Government of Colombia invoking in the name of the treaty of 1846 the aid of this Government in its efforts to suppress the revolution; on the other hand stood the Republic of Panama that had come into being in order that the great design of that treaty might not be forever frustrated, but might be fulfilled. The Isthmus was threatened with desolation by another civil war, nor were the rights and interests of the United States alone at stake, the interests of the whole civilized world were involved. The Republic of Panama stood for those interests; the Government of Colombia opposed them. Compelled to choose between these two alternatives, the Government of the United States, in no wise responsible for the situation that had arisen, did not hesitate. It recognized the independence of the Republic of Panama, and upon its judgment and action in the emergency the powers of the world have set the seal of their approval.

In recognizing the independence of the Republic of Panama the United States necessarily assumed toward that Republic the obligations of the treaty of 1846. Intended, as the treaty was, to assure the protection of the sovereign of the Isthmus, whether the government of that sovereign ruled from Bogotá or from Panama, the Republic of Panama, as the successor in sovereignty of Colombia, became entitled to the rights and subject to the obligations of the treaty. . . .

Under all the circumstances the department is unable to regard the complaints of Colombia against this Government, set forth in the "Statement of grievances," as having any valid foundation. The responsibility lies at Colombia's own door rather than at that of the United States. This Government, however, recognizes the fact that Colombia has, as she affirms, suffered an appreciable loss. This Government has no desire to increase or accentuate her misfortunes, but is willing to do all that lies in its power to ameliorate her lot. The Government of the United States, in common with the whole civilized world, shares in a sentiment of sorrow over the unfortunate conditions which have long existed in the Republic of Colombia by reason of the factional and fratricidal wars which have desolated her fields, ruined her industries, and impoverished her people.

Entertaining these feelings, the Government of the United States would gladly exercise its good offices with the Republic of Panama, with a view to bring about some arrangement on a fair and equitable basis. For the acceptance of your proposal of a resort to The Hague tribunal, this Government perceives no occasion. . . .

7. THE COLOMBIAN REPARATION TREATY[7]

[*Treaty between the United States and Colombia, signed April 6, 1914; proclaimed, March 30, 1922*]

. . . THE UNITED STATES of America and the Republic of Colombia, being desirous to remove all the misunderstandings growing out of the political events in Panama in November 1903; to restore the cordial friendship that formerly characterized the relations between the two countries, and also to define and regulate their rights and interests in respect of the interoceanic canal which the Government of the United States has constructed across the Isthmus of Panama, have resolved for this purpose to conclude a Treaty. . . .

[7] United States *Treaty Series,* No. 661, Washington, 1922.

Article I. The Republic of Colombia shall enjoy the following rights in respect to the interoceanic Canal and the Panama Railway, the title to which is now vested entirely and absolutely in the United States of America, without any incumbrances or indemnities whatever.

1. The Republic of Colombia shall be at liberty at all times to transport through the interoceanic Canal its troops, materials of war and ships of war, without paying any charges to the United States.

2. The products of the soil and industry of Colombia passing through the Canal, as well as the Colombian mails, shall be exempt from any charge or duty other than those to which the products and mails of the United States may be subject. The products of the soil and industry of Colombia, such as cattle, salt and provisions, shall be admitted to entry in the Canal Zone, and likewise in the islands and mainland occupied or which may be occupied by the United States as auxiliary and accessory thereto, without paying other duties or charges than those payable by similar products of the United States.

3. Colombian citizens crossing the Canal Zone shall, upon production of proper proof of their nationality, be exempt from every toll, tax or duty to which citizens of the United States are not subject.

4. Whenever traffic by the Canal is interrupted or whenever it shall be necessary for any other reason to use the railway, the troops, materials of war, products and mails of the Republic of Colombia, as above mentioned, shall be transported on the Railway between Ancon and Cristobal or on any other Railway substituted therefor, paying only the same charges and duties as are imposed upon the troops, materials of war, products and mails of the United States. The officers, agents and employees of the Government of Colombia shall, upon production of proper proof of their official character or their employment, also be entitled to passage on the said Railway on the same terms as officers, agents and employees of the Government of the United States. . . .

Article II. The Government of the United States of America agrees to pay at the City of Washington to the Republic of Colombia the sum of twenty-five million dollars, gold, United States money, as follows: The sum of five million dollars shall be paid within six months after the exchange of ratifications of the present treaty, and reckoning from the date of that payment, the remaining twenty million dollars shall be paid in four annual installments of five million dollars each. . . .

Chapter XXV

FAR EASTERN POLICY
1898—1918

AMERICAN foreign policy in the Far East had traditionally been characterized by respect for the territorial integrity of China and Japan, the "open door" regarding international trade, and the avoidance of alliances or of co-operation with other powers in Far Eastern affairs. The only exception to this policy was occasional co-operation in specific instances. Near the end of the nineteenth century, however, it became obvious that the partition of China by several of the great powers was imminent, and many people in the United States were alarmed over the influence that partition would have on American interests in China. The dispatch of January 31, 1898, of Edwin Denby (1), American minister to China, is an excellent example of the reasons that were frequently given for a more vigorous Far Eastern policy. Denby's plea was rejected and an inquiry by Great Britain, "whether the British government could count on the co-operation of the United States" in opposing action by foreign powers which might tend to restrict freedom of commerce of all nations in China, received a negative response from Secretary John Sherman.

A change in American policy, which led to the open-door negotiations was soon effected, however, by a notable series of events. Among these was the appointment of John Hay as Secretary of State, the acquisition of the Philippines, the growing influence of imperialistic minded American citizens, and further evidence regarding the imminence of the partition of China. The open-door notes of September 6, 1899 (2 and 3), were sent *mutatis mutandis* to Germany, Great Britain, and Russia, while similar notes were sent to Italy, France, and Japan. These open-door negotiations were scarcely concluded before the outbreak of the Boxer Rebellion and the subsequent intervention in China of the great powers. The policy of the United States at the time of this intervention was stated in the circular note of July 3, 1900 (4).

During the years immediately following 1900 it became increasingly evident that the Hay open-door policy was not accomplishing its purpose and for a number of reasons American relations with Japan became more strained. As a result of this situation the United States revised its Far Eastern policy, first regarding Korea in the Taft-Katsura agreement of 1905 (5), and later regarding China in the Root-Takahira agreement of 1908 (6). Mr. Root's successor in the State Department was not entirely sympathetic with the Root-Takahira policy and sought to return to a more strictly open-door policy through the media of the neutralization of Manchuria (7) and a banking consortium (8). This policy, in turn, was opposed by President Wilson who made a public statement on the subject on March 18, 1913 (9). Secretary Bryan's mild statement of March 13, 1915, and his more incisive statement of May 11, 1915 (10), were made at the time of Japan's famous Twenty-One Demands on China. The Lansing-Ishii agreement (11 and 12) was another attempt on the part of the United States to reach an understanding with Japan concerning China.

The immigration into the United States of Japanese and Chinese nationals presented another problem difficult to solve. With regard to China, the American government was able to conclude a treaty under which the Chinese Exclusion Act of May 6, 1882 was passed (13). The regulation of Japanese immigration was accomplished through the Gentlemen's Agreement of 1907 and the Immigration Act of 1924 (14).

◇◇◇◇◇◇◇◇◇◇◇◇◇

1. AMERICAN INTERESTS IN CHINA[1]

[*Charles Denby to John Sherman*]

January 31, 1898

. . . IN THE MIDST of these events it may not be improper to consider our own position regarding China. I am very thoroughly aware that since Washington's Farewell Address was uttered we have been, what may be called, innately conservative on the question of interfering in the affairs of foreign powers. He would be a bold man who in the United States would advocate political entanglement in the affairs of Europe, Asia, or Africa. That our abnegation tends to weaken our influence and to make us a quantité négligeable is undoubtedly true, but it has its compensations in the enforcement of the Monroe Doctrine.

Still, while preserving all the sanctity of the "Farewell Address," it is worth enquiring whether there is not some middle ground on which we may stand with advantage. We have fifteen hundred missionaries here. Should China be partitioned among the European powers it is quite certain that the work of these missionaries would be impeded. From any country under Russian control they would be excluded. In any country under French control they would be impeded and embarrassed. These missionaries are entitled to our protection just the same as mercantile people are.

Partition would tend to destroy our markets. The Pacific Ocean is destined to bear on its bosom a larger commerce than the Atlantic. As the countries in the Far East and Australia develop their resources the commerce of the United States with them will assume proportions greater in their directness and scope, than our commerce with Europe.

[1] Department of State: *Despatches from China*, Vol. CIII, No. 2858.

In these countries we are destined to find our best customers for manufactured, as well as natural, and agricultural products.

Here are diverse and varied sources of interest in the Far East which directly touch us.

Having such interests in China, is it our duty to remain mute should her autonomy be attacked? Is it exactly right to announce, as was lately done in Reuter's telegrams, that we take no interest in territorial questions? We have a certain moral interest in the affairs of the world, and, in my opinion, that influence should be exacted in all cases in which our interests demand its exercise. We should urge on China the reform of all evils in her government which touch American interests, and the adoption of vigorous measures in the line of material progress. This policy will to her be the surest pathway to independence and prosperity. I have persistently urged this policy. We should not hesitate, also, I think, to announce our disapproval of acts of brazen wrong, and spoliation, perpetrated by other nations towards China, – should any such occur.

In this connection it may not be improper to cite the following extract from the first Article of the Treaty of 1858 between the United States and China: "And if any other nation should act unjustly or oppressively the United States will exert their good offices on being informed of the case, to bring about an amicable arrangement of the question thus showing their friendly feelings. . . ."

2. THE OPEN DOOR IN CHINA[2]

[*John Hay to Andrew D. White*]

Department of State, Washington, September 6, 1899

AT THE TIME when the Government of the United States was informed by that of Germany that it had leased from His Majesty the Emperor of China the port of Kiao-chao and the adjacent territory in the province of Shantung, assurances were given to the ambassador of the United States at Berlin by the Imperial German minister for foreign affairs that the rights and privileges insured by treaties with China to citizens of the United States would not thereby suffer or be in anywise impaired within the area over which Germany had thus obtained control.

More recently, however, the British Government recognized by a formal agreement with Germany the exclusive right of the latter country to enjoy in said leased area and the contiguous "sphere of influence or interest" certain privileges, more especially those relating to railroads and mining en-

[2] *Papers Relating to the Foreign Relations of the United States*, 1899, pp. 129–30. Identical notes, with the necessary changes, were sent on the same day to Germany, Russia, and England. Similar notes were sent later to Japan, Italy, and France.

terprises; but as the exact nature and extent of the rights thus recognized have not been clearly defined, it is possible that serious conflicts of interest may at any time arise not only between British and German subjects within said area, but that the interests of our citizens may also be jeopardized thereby.

Earnestly desirous to remove any cause of irritation and to insure at the same time to the commerce of all nations in China the undoubted benefits which should accrue from a formal recognition by the various powers claiming "spheres of interest" that they shall enjoy perfect equality of treatment for their commerce and navigation within such "spheres," the Government of the United States would be pleased to see His German Majesty's Government give formal assurances, and lend its cooperation in securing like assurances from the other interested powers, that each, within its respective sphere of whatever influence –

First. Will in no way interfere with any treaty port or any vested interest within any so-called "sphere of interest" or leased territory it may have in China.

Second. That the Chinese treaty tariff of the time being shall apply to all merchandise landed or shipped to all such ports as are within said "sphere of interest" (unless they be "free ports"), no matter to what nationality it may belong, and that duties so leviable shall be collected by the Chinese Government.

Third. That it will levy no higher harbor dues on vessels of another nationality frequenting any port in such "sphere" than shall be levied on vessels of its own nationality, and no higher railroad charges over lines built, controlled, or operated within its "sphere" on merchandise belonging to citizens or subjects of other nationalities transported through such "sphere" than shall be levied on similar merchandise belonging to its own nationals transported over equal distances.

The liberal policy pursued by His Imperial German Majesty in declaring Kiao-chao a free port and in aiding the Chinese Government in the establishment there of a customhouse are so clearly in line with the proposition which this Government is anxious to see recognized that it entertains the strongest hope that Germany will give its acceptance and hearty support.

The recent ukase of His Majesty the Emperor of Russia declaring the port of Ta-lien-wan open during the whole of the lease under which it is held from China to the merchant ships of all nations, coupled with the categorical assurances made to this Government by His Imperial Majesty's representative at this captial at the time and since repeated to me by the present Russian ambassador, seem to insure the support of the Emperor to the proposed measure. Our ambassador at the Court of St. Petersburg has in consequence, been instructed to submit it to the Russian Government and to request their early consideration of it. A copy of my instruction on the subject to Mr. Tower is herewith inclosed for your confidential information.

The commercial interests of Great Britain and Japan will be so clearly served by the desired declaration of intentions, and the views of the Governments of these countries as to the desirability of the adoption of measures insuring the benefits of equality of treatment of all foreign trade throughout China are so similar to those entertained by the United States, that their acceptance of the propositions herein outlined and their cooperation in advocating their adoption by the other powers can be confidently expected. I inclose herewith copy of the instruction which I have sent to Mr. Choate on the subject.

In view of the present favorable conditions, you are instructed to submit the above considerations to His Imperial German Majesty's Minister for Foreign Affairs, and to request his early consideration of the subject.

◇◇◇◇◇◇◇◇◇◇◇◇◇◇

3. RECEPTION OF THE OPEN-DOOR POLICY[3]

[*Lord Salisbury to J. H. Choate*]

London, November 30, 1899

WITH REFERENCE to my note of September 29 last, I have the honor to state that I have carefully considered, in communication with my colleagues, the proposal contained in your excellency's note of September 22 that a declaration should be made by foreign powers claiming "spheres of interest" in China as to their intentions in regard to the treatment of foreign trade and interest therein.

I have much pleasure in informing your excellency that Her Majesty's Government will be prepared to make a declaration in the sense desired by your Government in regard to the leased territory of Weihai-Wei and all territory in China which may hereafter be acquired by Great Britain by lease or otherwise, and all spheres of interest now held or that may hereafter be held by her in China, provided that a similar declaration is made by other powers concerned.

[*Count Mouravieff to Charlemagne Tower*]

Ministry of Foreign Affairs, December 18–30, 1899

I HAD the honor to receive your excellency's note dated the 8th–20th of September last, relating to the principles which the Government of the United States would like to see adopted in commercial matters by the powers which have interests in China.

In so far as the territory leased by China to Russia is concerned, the Imperial Government has already demonstrated its firm intention to follow the policy of "the open door" by creating Dalny (Ta-lien-wan) a free port; and if at some future time that port, although remaining free itself, should

[3] Ibid., pp. 136–42.

be separated by a customs limit from other portions of the territory in question, the customs duties would be levied, in the zone subject to the tariff, upon all foreign merchandise without distinction as to nationality.

As to the ports now opened or hereafter to be opened to foreign commerce by the Chinese Government, and which lie beyond the territory leased to Russia, the settlement of the question of customs duties belongs to China herself, and the Imperial Government has no intention whatever of claiming any privileges for its own subjects to the exclusion of other foreigners. It is to be understood, however, that this assurance of the Imperial Government is given upon condition that a similar declaration shall be made by other powers having interests in China. . . .

[*Viscount Aoki to A. E. Buck*]

Department of Foreign Affairs, Tokio,
the 26th day, the 12th month of the 3d year of Meiji.
(December 26, 1899)

I HAVE the honor to acknowledge the receipt of the note No. 176 of the 20th instant, in which, pursuing the instructions of the United States Government, your excellency was so good as to communicate to the Imperial Government the representations of the United States as presented in notes to Russia, Germany, and Great Britain on the subject of commercial interests of the United States in China.

I have the happy duty of assuring your excellency that the Imperial Government will have no hesitation to give their assent to so just and fair a proposal of the United States, provided that all the other powers concerned shall accept the same.

[*Count von Bülow to Andrew D. White*]

Foreign Office, Berlin, February 19, 1900

YOUR EXCELLENCY informed me, in a memorandum presented on the 24th of last month, that the Government of the United States of America had received satisfactory written replies from all the powers to which an inquiry had been addressed similar to that contained in your excellency's note of September 26 last, in regard to the policy of the open door in China. While referring to this, your excellency thereupon expressed the wish that the Imperial Government would now also give its answer in writing.

Gladly complying with this wish, I have the honor to inform your excellency, repeating the statements already made verbally, as follows: As recognized by the Government of the United States of America, according to your excellency's note referred to above, the Imperial Government has, from the beginning, not only asserted, but also practically carried out to the fullest extent, in its Chinese possessions, absolute equality of treatment of all nations with regard to trade, navigation, and commerce. The Imperial Government entertains no thought of departing in the future from this principle, which at once excludes any prejudicial or disadvantageous commercial treatment of the citizens of the United States of America, so long as it is not forced to do so, on account of considerations of reciprocity, by a divergence from it by other governments. If, therefore, the other powers interested in the industrial development of the Chinese Empire are willing to recognize the same principles, this can only be desired by the Imperial Government, which in this case upon being requested will gladly be ready to participate with the United States of America and the other powers in an agreement made upon these lines, by which the same rights are reciprocally secured.

◇◇◇◇◇◇◇◇◇◇◇◇◇

4. AMERICAN POLICY REGARDING CHINA[4]

[*Circular telegram sent by the United States to the powers co-operating in China*]

Washington, July 3, 1900

IN THIS critical posture of affairs in China it is deemed appropriate to define the attitude of the United States as far as present circumstances permit this to be done. We adhere to the policy initiated by us in 1857 of peace with the Chinese nation, of furtherance of lawful commerce, and of protection of lives and property of our citizens by all means guaranteed under extraterritorial treaty rights and by the law of nations. If wrong be done to our citizens we propose to hold the responsible authors to the uttermost accountability. We regard the condition at Pekin as one of virtual anarchy, whereby power and responsibility are practically devolved upon the local provincial authorities. So long as they are not in overt collusion with rebellion and use their power to protect foreign life and property, we regard them as representing the Chinese people, with whom we seek to remain in peace and friendship. The purpose of the President is, as it has been heretofore, to act concurrently with the other powers; first, in opening up communication with Pekin and rescuing the American officials, missionaries, and other Americans who are in danger; secondly, in affording all possible protection everywhere in China to American life and property; thirdly, in guarding and protecting all legitimate American interests; and fourthly, in aiding to prevent a spread of the disorders to the other provinces of the Empire and a recurrence of such disasters. It is of course too early to forecast the means of attaining this last result; but the policy of the Government of the United States is to seek a solution which may bring about permanent safety and peace to China, preserve Chinese territorial and administrative entity, protect all rights guaranteed to friendly powers by treaty and international law, and safeguard for the world the principle of equal and impartial trade with all parts of the Chinese Empire. . . .

[4] Ibid., 1901, *Appendix,* p. 12.

◇◇◇◇◇◇◇◇◇◇◇◇◇

5. THE TAFT-KATSURA AGREEMENT[5]

. . . COUNT KATSURA and Secretary Taft had a long and confidential conversation on the morning of July 27. . . .

First, in speaking of some pro-Russians in America who would have the public believe that the victory of Japan would be a certain prelude to her aggression in the direction of the Philippine Islands, Secretary Taft observed that Japan's only interest in the Philippines would be, in his opinion, to have these islands governed by a strong and friendly nation like the United States, . . . Count Katsura confirmed in the strongest terms the correctness of his views on the point and positively stated that Japan does not harbor any aggressive designs whatever on the Philippines. . . .

Second, Count Katsura observed that the maintenance of general peace in the extreme East forms the fundamental principle of Japan's international policy. Such being the case, . . . the best, and in fact the only, means for accomplishing the above object would be to form good understanding between the three governments of Japan, the United States and Great Britain. . . .

Third, in regard to the Korean question Count Katsura observed that Korea being the direct cause of our war with Russia, it is a matter of absolute importance to Japan that a complete solution of the peninsula question should be made as the logical consequence of the war. If left to herself after the war, Korea will certainly draw back to her habit of improvidently entering into any agreements or treaties with other powers, thus resuscitating the same international complications as existed before the war. In view of the foregoing circumstances, Japan feels absolutely constrained to take some definite step with a view to precluding the possibility of Korea falling back into her former condition and of placing us again under the necessity of entering upon another foreign war. Secretary Taft fully admitted the justness of the Count's observations and remarked to the effect that, in his personal opinion, the establishment by Japanese troops of a suzerainty over Korea to the extent of requiring that Korea enter into no foreign treaties without the consent of Japan was the logical result of the present war and would directly contribute to permanent peace in the East. His judgment was that President Roosevelt would concur in his views in this regard, although he had no authority to give assurance of this. . . .

[5] This document, dated July 29, 1905, was "an agreed memorandum" of a conversation between Count Katsura, Prime Minister of Japan, and William Howard Taft, personal representative in Japan of President Theodore Roosevelt, who later gave his full approval of the agreement. *Miscellaneous Letters of the Department of State*, July, Part III, 1905.

◇◇◇◇◇◇◇◇◇◇◇◇◇◇

6. THE ROOT-TAKAHIRA AGREEMENT[6]

[*K. Takahira to Elihu Root*]

Imperial Japanese Embassy, Washington, November 30, 1908

THE EXCHANGE of views between us, which has taken place at the several interviews which I have recently had the honor of holding with you, has shown that Japan and the United States holding important outlying insular possessions in the region of the Pacific Ocean, the Governments of the two countries are animated by a common aim, policy, and intention in that region.

Believing that a frank avowal of that aim, policy, and intention would not only tend to strengthen the relations of friendship and good neighborhood, which have immemorially existed between Japan and the United States, but would materially contribute to the preservation of the general peace, the Imperial Government have authorized me to present to you an outline of their understanding of that common aim, policy and intention:

1. It is the wish of the two Governments to encourage the free and peaceful development of their commerce on the Pacific Ocean.

2. The policy of both Governments, uninfluenced by any aggressive tendencies, is directed to the maintenance of the existing status quo in the region above mentioned and to the defense of the principle of equal opportunity for commerce and industry in China.

3. They are accordingly firmly resolved reciprocally to respect the territorial possessions belonging to each other in said region.

4. They are also determined to preserve the common interest of all powers in China by supporting by all pacific means at their disposal the independence and integrity of China and the principle of equal opportunity for commerce and industry of all nations in that Empire.

5. Should any event occur threatening the status quo as above described or the principle of equal opportunity as above defined, it remains for the two Governments to communicate with each other in order to arrive at an understanding as to what measures they may consider it useful to take.

If the foregoing outline accords with the view of the Government of the United States, I shall be gratified to receive your confirmation. . . .

[6] *Papers Relating to the Foreign Relations of the United States,* 1908, pp. 510–11.

◇◇◇◇◇◇◇◇◇◇◇◇◇◇

7. THE KNOX PROPOSAL FOR THE NEUTRALIZATION OF MANCHURIA [7]

[*Philander C. Knox to Whitelaw Reid*]

Washington, D. C. November 6, 1909

NOW THAT there has been signed and ratified by an unpublished imperial decree an agreement by which the American and British interests are to cooperate in the financing and construction of the Chinchow-Tsitsihar-Aigun Railroad, the Government of the United States is prepared cordially to cooperate with His Britannic Majesty's Government in diplomatically supporting and facilitating this enterprise, so important alike to the progress and to the commercial development of China. The Government of the United States would be disposed to favor ultimate participation to a proper extent on the part of other interested powers whose inclusion might be agreeable to China and which are known to support the principle of equality of commercial opportunity and the maintenance of the integrity of the Chinese Empire. However, before the further elaboration of the actual arrangement, the Government of the United States asks His Britannic Majesty's Government to give their consideration to the following alternative and more comprehensive projects: First, perhaps the most effective way to preserve the undisturbed enjoyment by China of all political rights in Manchuria and to promote the development of those Provinces under a practical application of the policy of the open door and equal commercial opportunity would be to bring the Manchurian highways, the railroads, under an economic, scientific, and impartial administration by some plan vesting in China the ownership of the railroads through funds furnished for that purpose by the interested powers willing to participate. . . . The Government of the United States has some reason to hope that such a plan might meet favorable consideration on the part of Russia and has reason to believe that American financial participation would be forthcoming. Second, should this suggestion not be found feasible in its entirety, then the desired end would be approximated, if not attained, by Great Britain and the United States diplomatically supporting the Chinchow-Aigun arrangement and inviting the interested powers friendly to complete commercial neutralization of Manchuria to participate in the financing and construction of that line and of such additional lines as future commercial development may demand, and at the same time to supply funds for the purchase by China of such of the existing lines as might be offered for inclusion in this system. The Government of the United States hopes that the principle involved in the foregoing suggestions may commend itself to His Britannic Majesty's Government. . . .

[7] *Papers Relating to the Foreign Relations of the United States,* 1910, pp. 234–5.

8. THE BANKING CONSORTIUM OF 1912[8]

[*Inter-Bank Conference Agreement*]

Paris, June 18, 1912

AN AGREEMENT made the 18th day of June 1912 between the Hong Kong & Shanghai Banking Corporation having its office at 31 Lombard Street in the city of London (hereinafter called "the Hong Kong Bank") of the first part The Deutsch-Asiatische Bank having its office at 31 Unter den Linden Berlin (hereinafter called "the German Bank") of the second part The Banque de l'Indo-Chine having its office at 15 bis Rue Lafitte Paris (hereinafter called "the French Bank") of the third part MESSRS. J. P. MORGAN & CO., Messrs. Kuhn, Loeb & Co., The First National Bank and the National City Bank all of New York (hereinafter called "the American Group") acting as to the United Kingdom by Messrs. Morgan, Grenfell & Co. of 22 Old Broad Street in the city of London as to Germany by Messrs. M. M. Warburg & Co. of Hamburg and as to France by Messrs. Morgan, Harjes & Co. of Paris and Messrs. M. M. Warburg & Co. (all hereinafter collectively called "the American Agents") of the fourth part The Russo-Asiatic Bank having its office at 62 Nevsky Prospect St. Petersburg in Russia (hereinafter called "the Russian Bank") of the fifth part and The Yokohama Specie Bank Limited having its office at Yokohama Japan (hereinafter called "the Japanese Bank") of the sixth part. . . .

2. This agreement relates to the Reorganization Loan [£60,000,000] and to the future business hereinafter in this clause mentioned and is made on the principle of complete equality in every respect between the parties hereto and each of the parties hereto shall take an equal share in all operations and jointly sign all contracts and shall bear in equal shares all charges in connection with any business (except stamp duties and any charges of and in connection with the realization by each of the parties hereto in their respective markets of its share in the operations) and each of the parties hereto shall conclude all contracts with equal rights and obligations as between themselves and each party shall have the same rights privileges prerogatives advantages responsibilities and obligations of every sort and kind. The said preliminary advances shall acccordingly be borne by each of the parties hereto in equal shares and any sums which may have already been paid by the first four parties hereto in respect of preliminary advances or otherwise in connection with the said Reorganization Loan shall as soon as may be after the execution hereof be adjusted on the above-mentioned basis of equality. Until the Reorganization Loan shall have been issued or until a majority of the parties hereto shall have decided not to proceed further with the issue thereof or until a period of five years from the date

[8] John V. A. MacMurray, ed.: *Treaties and Agreements With and Concerning China, 1894–1914*, 2 vols., Carnegie Endowment for International Peace, Washington, 1921, Vol. II, pp. 1021–3.

hereof shall have elapsed whichever event shall first happen each of the parties hereto will offer to the other parties hereto an equal participation with itself in any loan or advance business into which it may after the date of this agreement enter with the Chinese Government with any of the provinces forming part of China with Chinese Government departments or with companies having Chinese Government or Provincial Government guaranties it being understood that there are excepted from this provision (1) current banking business as well as small financial operations coming within the scope of the same and (2) loans or advances to companies having Chinese Government or Provincial Government guaranties provided that such loans or advances do not involve an issue during the currency of this agreement to the public of bonds or other securities. Should one or more of the parties hereto decline a participation in any such future loan or advance business as aforesaid or in the Reorganization Loan or any part thereof the party or parties accepting a participation therein shall be free to undertake the same but shall issue on its or their markets only. Where one or more of the parties who have accepted a participation in any such future loan or advance business notifies the other parties who have also accepted a participation of its intention not to issue its or their participation the party or parties to whom such notice shall be addressed will issue the participation of the party or parties giving such notice upon the same terms and conditions *mutatis mutandis* as are hereinafter contained with regard to the Residuary Participation in the Reorganization Loan.

9. PRESIDENT WILSON'S OPPOSITION TO THE BANKING CONSORTIUM [9]

[*Public Statement of the American Government*]

March 18, 1913

"WE ARE informed that at the request of the last Administration a certain group of American bankers undertook to participate in the loan now desired by the Government of China (approximately one hundred twenty-five million dollars). Our Government wished American bankers to participate along with the bankers of other nations, because it desired that the good-will of the United States towards China should be exhibited in this practical way, that American capital should have access to that great country, and that the United States should be in a position to share with the other powers any political responsibilities that might be associated with the development of the foreign relations of China in connection with her industrial and commercial enterprises. The present Administration has been asked by this group of bankers whether it would also request them

[9] Ibid., p. 1025.

to participate in the loan. The representatives of the bankers through whom the Administration was approached declared that they would continue to seek their share of the loan under the proposed agreements only if expressly requested to do so by the Government. The Administration has declined to make such request, because it did not approve the conditions of the loan or the implications of responsibility on its own part which it was plainly told would be involved in the request.

"The conditions of the loan seem to us to touch very nearly the administrative independence of China itself, and this Administration does not feel that it ought, even by implication, to be a party to those conditions. The responsibility on its part which would be implied in requesting the bankers to undertake the loan might conceivably go the length in some unhappy contingency of forcible interference in the financial, and even the political, affairs of that great Oriental State, just now awakening to a consciousness of its power and of its obligations to its people. The conditions include not only the pledging of particular taxes, some of them antiquated and burdensome, to secure the loan but also the administration of those taxes by foreign agents. The responsibility on the part of our Government implied in the encouragement of a loan thus secured and administered is plain enough and is obnoxious to the principles upon which the Government of our people rests.

"The Government of the United States is not only willing, but earnestly desirous, of aiding the great Chinese people in every way that is consistent with their untrammeled development and its own immemorial principles. The awakening of the people of China to a consciousness of their responsibilities under free government is the most significant, if not the most momentous, event of our generation. With this movement and aspiration the American people are in profound sympathy. They certainly wish to participate and participate very generously in the opening to the Chinese and to the use of the world the almost untouched and perhaps unrivaled resources of China.

"The Government of the United States is earnestly desirous of promoting the most extended and intimate trade relationship between this country and the Chinese Republic. The present Administration will urge and support the legislative measures necessary to give American merchants, manufacturers, contractors, and engineers the banking and other financial facilities which they now lack and without which they are at a serious disadvantage as compared with their industrial and commercial rivals. This is its duty. This is the main material interest of its citizens in the development of China. Our interests are those of the Open Door — a door of friendship and mutual advantage. This is the only door we care to enter."

◇◇◇◇◇◇◇◇◇◇◇◇◇◇

10. STATEMENTS OF BRYAN ON THE OPEN-DOOR POLICY

(A) STATEMENT OF MARCH 13, 1915 [10]

. . . THE UNITED STATES, confident that the principle of mutuality will be preserved by Japan, believes that it may rely upon the often repeated assurances of your excellency's Government relative to the independence, integrity and commerce of China, and that no steps will be taken contrary to the spirit of those assurances.

For two generations American missionaries and teachers have made sacrifices in behalf of religious and educational work in China. American capital has been invested and industries have been established in certain regions. The activity of Americans has never been political, but on the contrary has been primarily commercial with no afterthought as to their effect upon the governmental policy of China. . . . A fourth matter of great moment to the United States is its broad and extensive treaty rights with China. These in general relate to commercial privileges and to the protection of Americans in China. In view of these treaty rights and its increasing economic interests in China, this Government has noted with grave concern certain of the suggestions which Japan has, in the present critical stage of the growth and development of the new Republic, considered it advisable to lay before the Chinese Government. While on principle and under the treaties of 1844, 1858, 1868 and 1903 with China the United States has ground upon which to base objections to the Japanese "demands" relative to Shantung, South Manchuria, and East Mongolia, nevertheless the United States frankly recognizes that territorial contiguity creates special relations between Japan and these districts. . . .

The United States . . . [however] could not regard with indifference the assumption of political, military or economic domination over China by a foreign Power, and hopes that your excellency's Government will find it consonant with their interests to refrain from pressing upon China an acceptance of proposals which would, if accepted, exclude Americans from equal participation in the economic and industrial development of China and would limit the political independence of that country.

The United States is convinced that an attempt to coerce China to submit to these proposals would result in engendering resentment on the part of the Chinese and opposition by other interested Powers, thereby creating a situation which this Government confidently believes the Imperial Government do not desire. . . .

[10] *Papers Relating to the Foreign Relations of the United States,* 1915, pp. 105–11. This statement was made to the Japanese Ambassador in Washington.

(B) STATEMENT OF MAY 11, 1915[11]

"In view of the circumstances of the negotiations which have taken place and which are now pending between the Government of Japan and the Government of China, and of the agreements which have been reached as a result thereof, the Government of the United States has the honor to notify the Imperial Japanese Government that it cannot recognize any agreement or undertaking which has been entered into or which may be entered into between the Governments of Japan and China, impairing the treaty rights of the United States and its citizens in China, the political or territorial integrity of the Republic of China, or the international policy relative to China commonly known as the open door policy.

"An identical note has been transmitted to the Government of the Chinese Republic."

11. THE LANSING-ISHII AGREEMENT[12]

[*Robert Lansing to Viscount Kikujiro Ishii.*]

Department of State, Washington, November 2, 1917

I HAVE the honor to communicate herein my understanding of the agreement reached by us in our recent conversations touching the questions of mutual interest to our Governments relating to the Republic of China.

In order to silence mischievous reports that have from time to time been circulated, it is believed by us that a public announcement once more of the desires and intentions shared by our two Governments with regard to China is advisable.

The Governments of the United States and Japan recognize that territorial propinquity creates special relations between countries, and consequently the Government of the United States recognizes that Japan has special interests in China, particularly in the part to which her possessions are contiguous.

The territorial sovereignty of China, nevertheless, remains unimpaired, and the Government of the United States has every confidence in the repeated assurances of the Imperial Japanese Government that while geographical position gives Japan such special interests they have no desire to discriminate against the trade of other nations or to disregard the commercial rights heretofore granted by China in treaties with other powers.

The Governments of the United States and Japan deny that they have any purpose to infringe in any way the independence or territorial integrity of China, and they declare, furthermore, that they always adhere to the

---

11 Ibid., p. 146. Statement sent to the American Ambassador in Japan for transmission to the Japanese Foreign Minister.

12 *Papers Relating to the Foreign Relations of the United States,* 1917, p. 264.

principle of the so-called "open door" or equal opportunity for commerce and industry in China.

Moreover, they mutually declare that they are opposed to the acquisition by any government of any special rights or privileges that would affect the independence or territorial integrity of China, or that would deny to the subjects or citizens of any country the full enjoyment of equal opportunity in the commerce and industry of China.

I shall be glad to have Your Excellency confirm this understanding of the agreement reached by us.

Protocol to Accompany the Lansing-Ishii Agreement [13]

In the course of the conversations between the Japanese Special Ambassador and the Secretary of State of the United States which have led to the exchange of notes between them dated this day, declaring the policy of the two Governments with regard to China, the question of embodying the following clause in such declaration came up for discussion: "they (the governments of Japan and the United States) will not take advantage of the present conditions to seek special rights or privileges in China which would abridge the rights of the subjects or citizens of other friendly states."

Upon careful examination of the question, it was agreed that the clause above quoted being superfluous in the relations of the two Governments and liable to create erroneous impression in the minds of the public, should be eliminated from the declaration.

It was, however, well understood that the principle enunciated in the clause which was thus suppressed was in perfect accord with the declared policy of the two Governments in regard to China.

◇◇◇◇◇◇◇◇◇◇◇◇◇◇

12. EXPLANATION OF THE LANSING-ISHII NOTES [14]

SIMULTANEOUSLY with the note of November 8, 1917, by which it communicated to the Wai Chiao Pu the text of this exchange of notes, the American Legation in Peking, conveyed under the instructions of its government, to the Chinese Minister for Foreign Affairs the following communication:

"The visit of the Imperial Japanese Mission to the United States afforded an opportunity for free and friendly discussion of interests of the United States and Japan in the Orient by openly proclaiming that the policy of Japan as regards China is not one of aggression and by declaring that there is no intention to take advantage commercially or indirectly of the special relations to China created by geographical position. The representatives of

[13] *Papers Relating to the Foreign Relations of the United States: The Lansing Papers,* Vol. II, p. 450. This protocol was suppressed by its signers, and was not published until the Lansing-Ishii Agreement was replaced by the Washington Treaties.

[14] MacMurray: *Treaties and Agreements With and Concerning China,* 11, 1396–7.

Japan have cleared the diplomatic atmosphere of the suspicions which had been so carefully spread by German propaganda.

"The Governments of the United States and Japan again declare their adherence to the Open Door Policy and recommit themselves, as far as these two Governments are concerned, to the maintenance of equal opportunity for the full enjoyment by the subjects or citizens of any country in the commerce and industry of China. Japanese commercial and industrial enterprises in China manifestly have, on account of the geographical relation of the two countries, a certain advantage over similar enterprises on the part of the citizens or subjects of any other country.

"The Governments of the United States and Japan have taken advantage of a favorable opportunity to make an exchange of expressions with respect to their relations with China. This understanding is formally set forth in the Notes exchanged and now transmitted. The statements in the Notes require no explanation. They not only contain a reaffirmation of the Open Door Policy but introduce a principle of non-interference with the sovereignty and territorial integrity of China which, generally applied, is essential to perpetual international peace, as has been so clearly declared by President Wilson."

On November 9, 1917, the Wai Chiao Pu replied to the following effect:

"The Government of the United States and the Government of Japan have recently, in order to silence mischievous reports, effected an exchange of notes at Washington concerning their desires and intentions with regard to China. A copy of the said notes have been communicated to the Chinese Government by the Japanese Minister at Peking, and the Chinese Government, in order to avoid misunderstanding, hastens to make the following declaration so as to make known the view of the Government:

"The principle adopted by the Chinese Government toward the friendly nations has always been one of justice and equality, and consequently the rights enjoyed by the friendly nations derived from the treaties have been consistently respected, and so even with the special relations between countries created by the fact of territorial contiguity but only in so far as they have already been provided for in her existing treaties. Hereafter the Chinese Government will still adhere to the principle hitherto adopted and hereby it is again declared that the Chinese Government will not allow herself to be bound by any agreement entered into by other nations."

◇◇◇◇◇◇◇◇◇◇◇◇◇

13. THE CHINESE EXCLUSION ACT

[*An Act of the Congress of the United States approved May 6, 1882*] [15]

BE IT enacted by the Senate and House of Representatives of the United States of America in Congress assembled, That from and after the expira-

[15] *The Statutes at Large of the United States of America,* Vol. XXII, pp. 58–61.

tion of ninety days next after the passage of this act, and until the expiration of ten years next after the passage of this act, the coming of Chinese laborers to the United States be, and the same is hereby, suspended; and during such suspension it shall not be lawful for any Chinese laborer to come, or, having so come after the expiration of said ninety days, to remain within the United States.

Sec. 2. That the master of any vessel who shall knowingly bring within the United States on such vessel, and land or permit to be landed, any Chinese laborer, from any foreign port or place, shall be deemed guilty of a misdemeanor, and on conviction thereof shall be punished by a fine of not more than five hundred dollars for each and every such Chinese laborer so brought, and may be also imprisoned for a term not exceeding one year.

Sec. 3. That the two foregoing sections shall not apply to Chinese laborers who were in the United States on the seventeenth day of November, eighteen hundred and eighty, or who shall have come into the same before the expiration of ninety days next after the passage of this act. . . .

Sec. 13. That this act shall not apply to diplomatic and other officers of the Chinese Government traveling upon the business of that government, whose credentials shall be taken as equivalent to the certificate in this act mentioned, and shall exempt them and their body and household servants from the provisions of this act as to other Chinese persons.

Sec. 14. That hereafter no State court or court of the United States shall admit Chinese to citizenship; and all laws in conflict with this act are hereby repealed.

Sec. 15. That the words "Chinese laborers," wherever used in this act, shall be construed to mean both skilled and unskilled laborers and Chinese employed in mining.

◇◇◇◇◇◇◇◇◇◇◇◇◇

14. THE GENTLEMEN'S AGREEMENT AND JAPANESE EXCLUSION

[*Position of the State Department Concerning Japanese Immigration*] [16]

. . . IT IS HARDLY necessary for me to say that I am in favor of suitable restrictions upon immigration. The questions which especially concern the Department of State in relation to the international effects of the proposed measure are these: (1) The question of treaty obligations; (2) the provision excluding Japanese; (3) the establishment of the quotas upon the basis of the census of 1890. . . .

[16] Letter of Secretary Charles E. Hughes to Albert Johnson, chairman of the Committee on Immigration and Naturalization of the House of Representatives, February 8, 1924. The subject of the letter was the proposed Selective Immigration Act of 1924. *House Report,* No. 350, 68 Cong. 1 Sess., pp. 25–31.

Article 1 of the treaty between the United States and Japan, concluded in 1911, provides:

The citizens or subjects of each of the high contracting parties shall have liberty to enter, travel, and reside in the territories of the other to carry on trade, wholesale and retail, to own or lease and occupy houses, manufactories, warehouses and shops, to employ agents of their choice, to lease land for residential and commercial purposes, and generally to do anything incident to or necessary for trade upon the same terms as native citizens or subjects, submitting themselves to the laws and regulations there established. . . .

In my opinion the restrictions of the proposed measure, in view of their application under the definition of "immigrant," are in conflict with treaty provisions. . . . Accordingly, I take the liberty of suggesting that there be included in section 3 of the proposed measure an additional exception to read as follows: "an alien entitled to enter the United States under the provisions of a treaty. . . ."

Section 12 (b) provides as follows:

No alien ineligible to citizenship shall be admitted to the United States unless such alien (1) is admissible as a nonquota immigrant under the provisions of subdivisions (b), (d), or (g) of section 4; or (2) is the wife or unmarried child under eighteen years of age of an immigrant admissible under such subdivision (d), and is accompanying or following to join him; or (3) is not an immigrant as defined in sections 3. . . .

It is apparent that Section 12, sub-division (b) taken in connection with Sections 3 and 4 of the proposed measure, operates to exclude Japanese. This is inconsistent with the provision of the treaty of 1911 abovementioned, and with respect to those defined as immigrants who do not come within the treaty, it establishes a statutory exclusion.

So far as the latter class is concerned, the question presented is one of policy. There can be no question that such a statutory exclusion will be deeply resented by the Japanese people. It would be idle to insist that the provision is not aimed at the Japanese, for the proposed measure (Sec. 25) continues in force the existing legislation regulating Chinese immigration and the barred-zone provisions of our immigration laws which prohibit immigration from certain other portions of Asia. The practical effect of Section 12 (b) is to single out Japanese immigrants for exclusion. The Japanese are a sensitive people, and unquestionably would regard such a legislative enactment as fixing a stigma upon them. I regret to be compelled to say that I believe such legislative action would largely undo the work of the Washington Conference on Limitation of Armament, which so greatly improved our relations with Japan. The manifestation of American interest and generosity in providing relief to the sufferers from the recent earthquake disaster in Japan would not avail to diminish the resentment which would follow the enactment of such a measure, as this enactment would be regarded as an insult not to be palliated by any act of charity. It is useless to argue whether or not such a feeling would be justified; it is quite sufficient to say that it would exist. It has already been manifested in the discussions in Japan with respect to the pendency of this measure, and no amount of argument can avail to remove it.

The question is thus presented whether it is worth while thus to affront a friendly nation with whom we have established most cordial relations and what gain there would be from such action. Permit me to suggest that the legislation would seem to be quite unnecessary even for the purpose for which it is devised. It is to be noted that if the provision of sub-division (b) of Section 12 were eliminated and the quota provided in Section 10 of the proposed measure were to be applied to Japan, there would be a total of only 246 Japanese immigrants entitled to enter under the quota as thus determined. That is to say, this would be the number equal to two per cent. of the number of residents in the United States as determined by the census of 1890 plus 200. There would remain, of course, the non-quota immigrants, but if it could possibly be regarded that the provisions of Section 4 would unduly enlarge the number admitted, these provisions could be modified without involving a statutory discrimination aimed at the Japanese. We now have an understanding with the Japanese Government whereby Japan undertakes to prevent the immigration of laborers from Japan to the United States except the parents, wives, and children of those already resident here. Furthermore, the Japanese Government, incidentally to this undertaking, now regulates immigration to territory contiguous to the United States with the object of preventing the departure from Japan of persons who are likely to obtain surreptitious entry into this country.

If the provision of Section 12 (b) were to be deleted and the provision in regard to certificates for immigrants to this country were to become applicable to Japan, we should with the present understanding with the Japanese Government be in a position to obtain active cooperation by the Japanese authorities in the granting of passports and immigration certificates. We could in addition be assured that the Japanese Government would give its assistance in scrutinizing and regulating immigration from Japan to American territory contiguous to the United States. It is believed that such an arrangement involving a double control over the Japanese quota of less than 250 a year would accomplish a much more effective regulation of unassimilable and undesirable classes of Japanese immigrants than it would be practicable for us, with our long land frontier lines on both north and south, to accomplish by attempting to establish a general bar against Japanese subjects to the loss of cooperation with the Japanese Government in controlling the movement of their people to the United States and adjacent territories.

I am unable to perceive that the exclusion provision is necessary and I must strongly urge upon you the advisability, in the interest of our international relations, of eliminating it. The Japanese Government has already brought the matter to the attention of the Department of State and there is the deepest interest in the attitude of Congress with respect to this subject. . . .

[*Japanese Opposition to the Selective Immigration Act*] [17]

IN VIEW of certain statements in the report of the House Committee on Immigration – "Report No. 350, March 24, 1924" – regarding the so-called "Gentlemen's Agreement," some of which appear to be misleading, I may be allowed to state to you the purpose and substance of that agreement as it is understood and performed by my Government, which understanding and practice are, I believe, in accord with those of your Government on this subject.

The Gentlemen's Agreement is an understanding with the United States Government by which the Japanese Government voluntarily undertook to adopt and enforce certain administrative measures designed to check the emigration to the United States of Japanese laborers. . . .

One object of the Gentlemen's Agreement is, as is pointed out above, to stop the emigration to the United States of all Japanese laborers other than those excepted in the Agreement, which is embodied in a series of long and detailed correspondence between the two Governments, publication of which is not believed to serve any good purpose, but the essential terms and practice of which may be summed up as follows:

(1) The Japanese Government will not issue passports good for the Continental United States to laborers, skilled or unskilled, except those previously domiciled in the United States, or parents, wives, or children under twenty years of age of such persons. The form of the passport is so designed as to omit no safeguard against forgery, and its issuance is governed by various rules of detail in order to prevent fraud.

The Japanese Government accepted the definition of "laborer" as given in the United States Executive Order of April 8, 1907.

(2) Passports are to be issued by a limited number of specially authorized officials only, under close supervision of the Foreign Office, which has the supreme control of the matter and is equipped with the necessary staff for the administration of it. . . .

(3) Issuance of passports to so-called "picture brides" has been stopped by the Japanese Government since March 1, 1920, although it had not been prohibited under the terms of the Gentlemen's Agreement.

(4) Monthly statistics covering incoming and outgoing Japanese are exchanged between the American and Japanese Governments.

(5) Although the Gentlemen's Agreement is not applicable to the Hawaiian Islands, measures restricting issuance of passports for the Islands are being enforced in substantially the same manner as those for the Continental United States.

(6) The Japanese Government are further exercising strict control over emigration of Japanese laborers to foreign territories contiguous to the United States in order to prevent their surreptitious entry into the United States.

[17] Ambassador M. Hanihara to Charles E. Hughes, Apr. 10, 1924. *Papers Relating to the Foreign Relations of the United States,* 1924, Vol. 2, pp. 369–73.

A more condensed substance of these terms is published in the Annual Report of the United States Commissioner-General of Immigration for 1908, 1909 and 1910 on pages 125–6, 121, and 124–5, respectively.

As I stated above, the Japanese Government have been most faithfully observing the Gentlemen's Agreement in every detail of its terms, which fact is, I believe, well known to the United States Government. I may be permitted, in this connection, to call your attention to the official figures published in the Annual Reports of the United States Commissioner-General of Immigration, showing the increase or decrease of Japanese population in the Continental United States by immigration and emigration. According to these reports in the years 1908–1923 the total numbers of Japanese admitted to and departed from the Continental United States were respectively 120,317 and 111,636. In other words the excess of those admitted over those departed was in fifteen years only 8,681, that is to say, the annual average of 578. . . .

Further, if I may speak frankly, at the risk of repeating what, under instructions from my Government, I have represented to you on former occasions, the mere fact that a certain clause, obviously aimed against Japanese as a nation, is introduced in the proposed immigration bill, in apparent disregard of the most sincere and friendly endeavors on the part of the Japanese Government to meet the needs and wishes of the American Government and people, is mortifying enough to the Government and people of Japan. . . .

To Japan the question is not one of expediency, but of principle. To her the mere fact that a few hundreds or thousands of her nationals will or will not be admitted into the domains of other countries is immaterial, so long as no question of national susceptibilities is involved. The important question is whether Japan as a nation is or is not entitled to the proper respect and consideration of other nations. In other words the Japanese Government ask of the United States Government simply that proper consideration ordinarily given by one nation to the self respect of another, which after all forms the basis of amicable international intercourse throughout the civilized world. . . .

It is indeed difficult to believe that it can be the intention of the people of your great country, who always stand for high principles of justice and fair-play in the intercourse of nations, to resort – in order to secure the annual exclusion of 146 Japanese – to a measure which would not only seriously offend the just pride of a friendly nation, that has been always earnest and diligent in its efforts to preserve the friendship of your people, but would also seem to involve the question of the good faith and therefore of the honor of their Government, or at least of its executive branch.

Relying upon the confidence you have been good enough to show me at all times, I have stated or rather repeated all this to you very candidly and in a most friendly spirit, for I realize, as I believe you do, the grave consequences which the enactment of the measure retaining that particular provision would inevitably bring upon the otherwise happy and mutually advantageous relations between our two countries.

[*An Explanation to Japan*] [18]

THE AMBASSADOR called at the Secretary's request.

The Secretary said that he desired to speak of the Immigration Bill which had been passed by both Houses of Congress and was now before the President. The Secretary called attention to the efforts which he had made and which the President had made to secure the elimination or modification of the provision relating to the exclusion of aliens ineligible for citizenship. The Secretary said that despite these efforts the overwhelming opinion of Congress was in favor of the retention of the provision. This was not due to a lack of friendship on the part of the American people toward the Japanese people. That friendship and cordial interest had been abundantly demonstrated. It was due to the strong sentiment in Congress that the question of immigration should not be dealt with by international agreements or understandings but by legislation enacted by Congress. Congress was intent upon asserting its prerogative in this matter and had rejected all overtures of the President and the Secretary for securing opportunity for mutually satisfactory agreements by which the question of admission could be dealt with.

The Secretary said that he wished to call the attention of the Ambassador to the exact situation with which the President was now confronted. The exclusion provision was not before him as a separate matter. If it were, the President would unhesitatingly disapprove it. But this exclusion provision was part of a comprehensive immigration bill. While the Secretary believed that there was strong sentiment throughout the country supporting the position taken by the President and the Secretary as to the exclusion provision, it was also true that there was a very strong sentiment demanding general legislation in restriction of immigration. The Bill was a comprehensive measure dealing in great detail with this subject and providing the necessary administrative machinery. It was necessary that legislation should be passed of this sort before the expiration of the present law on June 30th. It was necessary that such legislation should be passed well in advance of that date so that instructions could be given to consuls. If the President disapproved this measure there would be great confusion and the most serious difficulties might result. On the other hand, the sentiment in Congress was so strong, as the Ambassador had observed from the votes already taken, that there was very little doubt but that if the bill were vetoed, it would be passed over the veto, and no good would have resulted but there would be considerable bitterness and probably acrimonious debate. The President felt in view of all these considerations that he could

---

18 Memorandum by the Secretary of State of a Conversation with the Japanese Ambassador, M. Hanihara, May 23, 1924. Ibid., pp. 393–4.

not properly disapprove the Bill. But he desired that the Japanese Government should know that his approval of the Bill did not imply any change in his sentiment with regard to this provision or any lack of cordial feeling toward Japan. The President had fully endorsed the position the Secretary had taken. . . .

The Ambassador expressed his appreciation of what the Secretary had said. He said that he could understand the Secretary's view and that he would try to make it clear to his Government, but that while the Foreign Office might appreciate the difficulties of the situation, he was quite sure that the Japanese people would not understand it and would be greatly disappointed. . . .

Chapter XXVI

NEUTRALITY: 1914—1917

THE NEUTRALITY of the United States was proclaimed by President Wilson on August 4, 1914, only a few days after the outbreak of the World War. From that time until the United States declared war against Germany the American government endeavored to fulfill its obligations as a neutral and also to maintain vigorously its neutral rights. Although the points of conflict between the United States and the General Powers were numerous, the principal source of controversy was the use by Germany of unrestricted submarine warfare. The American position on that subject was made clear as early as February 10, 1915 (1), but a crisis did not arise until the sinking of the *Lusitania* with the loss of 128 American lives. This event, which occurred on May 7, 1915, followed close upon the torpedoing, May 1, of the American tanker *Gulflight,* with the loss of three American lives, and the sinking, March 28, of the British liner *Falaba,* with the loss of one American life. The so-called *Lusitania* notes covered, therefore, the whole submarine problem and were not confined to the *Lusitania* alone.

The first of the three *Lusitania* notes was sent on May 13, 1915 (2), but the discussion of submarine warfare continued until September 1, when Germany offered what President Wilson was willing to accept as a pledge regarding such warfare in the future. This pledge was flagrantly violated by the sinking of an unarmed French passenger steamer *Sussex* and the injury of several American citizens. The first *Sussex* note of April 18, 1916 (3), marked the second crisis in German-American relations, which was terminated by a second pledge on the part of Germany. Germany's fatal decision to renew submarine warfare led to the entrance of the United States into the war. President Wilson's war message (9), therefore, may be considered as marking the third and final crisis in German-American relations during the period of American neutrality.

The fundamental policy of the United States regarding submarine warfare was not specifically referred to Congress or to the people for approval at the time it was adopted. Popular support for this policy may have been indicated, however, in the presidential and congressional elections of 1916 which were favorable to the government. Perhaps more direct evidence of public thought on the subject is to be gleaned from editorial and other opinion at various critical times when the policy was being announced and applied (4). The President did not fail to warn the nation that the defense of American neutral rights might lead to involvement in war (7).

American difficulties with Great Britain over the rights of neutrals were serious and extensive but they involved property and not the lives of American citizens. The note of October 21, 1915 (5), is an excellent illustration of the character of those difficulties and the extent of British interference with American neutral rights is indicated by later investigation (6).

President Wilson spoke many times during the period of neutrality on the subject of peace. Possibly his most important pronouncement was his address to the Senate of January 22, 1917 (8), in which he stated the essential terms of peace.

◇◇◇◇◇◇◇◇◇◇◇◇◇◇

1. AMERICAN POLICY ON SUBMARINE WARFARE[1]

[*William J. Bryan to J. W. Gerard*]

Washington, February 10, 1915

PLEASE ADDRESS a note immediately to the Imperial German Government to the following effect:

The Government of the United States, having had its attention directed to the proclamation of the German Admiralty issued on the 4th of February, that the waters surrounding Great Britain and Ireland, including the whole of the English Channel, are to be considered as comprised within the seat of war; . . . and that neutral vessels expose themselves to danger within this zone of war because, . . . it may not be possible always to exempt neutral vessels from attacks intended to strike enemy ships, feels it to be its duty to call the attention of the Imperial German Government, . . . to the very serious possibilities of the course of action apparently contemplated under that proclamation.

The Government of the United States views those possibilities with such grave concern that it feels it to be its privilege, and indeed its duty in the circumstances, to request the Imperial German Government to consider before action is taken the critical situation in respect of the relations between this country and Germany which might arise were the German naval forces, in carrying out the policy foreshadowed in the Admiralty's proclamation, to destroy any merchant vessel of the United States or cause the death of American citizens.

It is of course not necessary to remind the German Government that the sole right of a belligerent in dealing with neutral vessels on the high seas is limited to visit and search, unless a blockade is proclaimed and effectively maintained, which this Government does not understand to be proposed in this case. To declare or exercise a right to attack and destroy any vessel entering a prescribed area of the high seas without first certainly determining its belligerent nationality and the contraband character of its cargo would be an act so unprecedented in naval warfare that this Govern-

[1] *Papers Relating to the Foreign Relations of the United States,* 1915, *Supplement,* p. 98.

ment is reluctant to believe that the Imperial Government of Germany in this case contemplates it as possible. The suspicion that enemy ships are using neutral flags improperly can create no just presumption that all ships traversing a prescribed area are subject to the same suspicion. It is to determine exactly such questions that this Government understands the right of visit and search to have been recognized. . . .

If the commanders of German vessels of war should act upon the presumption that the flag of the United States was not being used in good faith and should destroy on the high seas an American vessel or the lives of American citizens, it would be difficult for the Government of the United States to view the act in any other light than as an indefensible violation of neutral rights which it would be very hard indeed to reconcile with the friendly relations now so happily subsisting between the two governments.

If such a deplorable situation should arise, the Imperial German Government can readily appreciate that the Government of the United States would be constrained to hold the Imperial German Government to a strict accountability for such acts of their naval authorities and to take any steps it might be necessary to take to safeguard American lives and property and to secure to American citizens the full enjoyment of their acknowledged rights on the high seas. . . .

◇◇◇◇◇◇◇◇◇◇◇◇◇◇

2. THE FIRST *LUSITANIA* NOTE[2]

[*William J. Bryan to J. W. Gerard*]

Washington, May 13, 1915

PLEASE CALL on the Minister of Foreign Affairs and, after reading to him this communication, leave him with a copy.

In view of the recent acts of the German authorities in violation of American rights on the high seas which culminated in the torpedoing and sinking of the British steamship *Lusitania* on May 7th, 1915, by which over 100 American citizens lost their lives, it is clearly wise and desirable that the Government of the United States and the Imperial German Government should come to a clear and full understanding as to the grave situation which has resulted.

The sinking of the British passenger steamer *Falaba* by a German submarine on March 28, through which Leon C. Thrasher, an American citizen, was drowned; the attack on April 28 on the American vessel *Cushing* by a German aeroplane; the torpedoing on May 1 of the American vessel *Gulflight* by a German submarine, as a result of which two or more American citizens met their death; and, finally, the torpedoing and sinking of the steamship *Lusitania,* constitute a series of events which the Govern-

[2] Ibid., pp. 393–6.

ment of the United States has observed with growing concern, distress, and amazement. . . .

The Government of the United States has been apprised that the Imperial German Government considered themselves to be obliged by the extraordinary circumstances of the present war and the measures adopted by their adversaries in seeking to cut Germany off from all commerce, to adopt methods of retaliation which go much beyond the ordinary methods of warfare at sea, in the proclamation of a war zone from which they have warned neutral ships to keep away. This Government has already taken occasion to inform the Imperial German Government that it cannot admit the adoption of such measures or such a warning of danger to operate as in any degree an abbreviation of the rights of American shipmasters or of American citizens bound on lawful errands as passengers on merchant ships of belligerent nationality; and that it must hold the Imperial German Government to a strict accountability for any infringement of those rights, intentional or incidental. It does not understand the Imperial German Government to question those rights. It assumes, on the contrary, that the Imperial Government accept, as of course, the rule that the lives of noncombatants, whether they be of neutral citizenship or citizens of one of the nations at war, can not lawfully or rightfully be put in jeopardy by the capture or destruction of an unarmed merchantman, and recognize also, as all other nations do, the obligation to take the usual precaution of visit and search to ascertain whether a suspected merchantman is in fact of belligerent nationality or is in fact carrying contraband of war under a neutral flag.

The Government of the United States, therefore, desires to call the attention of the Imperial German Government with the utmost earnestness to the fact that the objection to their present method of attack against the trade of their enemies lies in the practical impossibility of employing submarines in the destruction of commerce without disregarding those rules of fairness, reason, justice, and humanity, which all modern opinion regards as imperative. It is practically impossible for the officers of a submarine to visit a merchantman at sea and examine her papers and cargo. It is practically impossible for them to make a prize of her; and, if they can not put a prize crew on board of her, they can not sink her without leaving her crew and all on board of her to the mercy of the sea in her small boats. These facts it is understood the Imperial German Government frankly admit. We are informed that, in the instances of which we have spoken, time enough for even that poor measure of safety was not given, and in at least two of the cases cited, not so much as a warning was received. Manifestly submaries can not be used against merchantmen, as the last few weeks have shown, without an inevitable violation of many sacred principles of justice and humanity.

American citizens act within their indisputable rights in taking their ships and in traveling wherever their legitimate business calls them upon the high seas, and exercise those rights in what should be the well-justified confidence that their lives will not be endangered by acts done in clear violation of universally acknowledged international obligations, and certainly in the confidence that their own Government will sustain them in the exercise of their rights. . . .

Long acquainted as this Government has been with the character of the Imperial German Government and with the high principles of equity by which they have in the past been actuated and guided, the Government of the United States can not believe that the commanders of the vessels which committed these acts of lawlessness did so except under a misapprehension of the orders issued by the Imperial German naval authorities. It takes it for granted that, at least within the practical possibilities of every such case, the commanders even of submarines were expected to do nothing that would involve the lives of non-combatants or the safety of neutral ships, even at the cost of failing of their object of capture or destruction. It confidently expects, therefore, that the Imperial German Government will disavow the acts of which the Government of the United States complains, that they will make reparation so far as reparation is possible for injuries which are without measure, and that they will take immediate steps to prevent the recurrence of anything so obviously subversive of the principles of warfare for which the Imperial German Government have in the past so wisely and so firmly contended.

The Government and people of the United States look to the Imperial German Government for just, prompt, and enlightened action in this vital matter with the greater confidence because the United States and Germany are bound together not only by special ties of friendship but also by the explicit stipulations of the treaty of 1828 between the United States and the Kingdom of Prussia.

Expressions of regret and offers of reparation in case of the destruction of neutral ships sunk by mistake, while they may satisfy international obligations, if no loss of life results, can not justify or excuse a practice, the natural and necessary effect of which is to subject neutral nations and neutral persons to new and immeasurable risks.

The Imperial German Government will not expect the Government of the United States to omit any word or any act necessary to the performance of its sacred duty of maintaining the rights of the United States and its citizens and of safeguarding their free exercise and enjoyment.

◇◇◇◇◇◇◇◇◇◇◇◇◇◇

3. THE *SUSSEX* NOTE[3]

[*Robert Lansing to J. W. Gerard*]

Washington, April 18, 1916

YOU ARE instructed to deliver to the Secretary of Foreign Affairs a communication reading as follows:

I did not fail to transmit immediately, by telegraph, to my Government your excellency's note of the 10th instant in regard to certain attacks by German submarines, and particularly in regard to the disastrous explosion which, on March 24, last wrecked the French S. S. *Sussex* in the English Channel. I have now the honor to deliver, under instructions from my Government, the following reply to your excellency:

Information now in the possession of the Government of the United States fully established the facts in the case of the *Sussex*, and the inferences which my Government has drawn from that information it regards as confirmed by the circumstances set forth in your excellency's note of the 10th instant. On the 24th of March 1916, at about 2.50 o'clock in the afternoon, the unarmed steamer *Sussex*, with 325 or more passengers on board, among whom were a number of American citizens, was torpedoed while crossing from Folkstone to Dieppe. The *Sussex* had never been armed; was a vessel known to be habitually used only for the conveyance of passengers across the English Channel; and was not following the route taken by troopships or supply ships. About 80 of her passengers, non-combatants of all ages and sexes, including citizens of the United States, were killed or injured. . . .

The Government of the United States, after having given careful consideration to the note of the Imperial Government of the 10th of April, regrets to state that the impression made upon it by the statements and proposals contained in that note is that the Imperial Government has failed to appreciate the gravity of the situation which has resulted, not alone from the attack on the *Sussex*, but from the whole method and character of submarine warfare as disclosed by the unrestrained practice of the commanders of German undersea craft during the past twelvemonth and more in the indiscriminate destruction of merchant vessels of all sorts, nationalities, and destinations. If the sinking of the *Sussex* had been an isolated case, the Government of the United States might find it possible to hope that the officer who was responsible for that act had wilfully violated his orders or had been criminally negligent in taking none of the precautions they prescribed, and that the ends of justice might be satisfied by imposing upon him an adequate punishment, coupled with a formal disavowal of the act and payment of a suitable indemnity by the Imperial Government. But, though the attack upon the *Sussex* was manifestly indefensible and caused a loss of life so tragical as to make it stand forth as one of

[3] Ibid., 1916, *Supplement*, pp. 232–4.

the most terrible examples of the inhumanity of submarine warfare as the commanders of German vessels are conducting it, it unhappily does not stand alone.

On the contrary, the Government of the United States is forced by recent events to conclude that it is only one instance, even though one of the most extreme and most distressing instances, of the deliberate method and spirit of indiscriminate destruction of merchant vessels of all sorts, nationalities, and destinations which have become more and more unmistakable as the activity of German undersea vessels of war has in recent months been quickened and extended.

The Imperial Government will recall that when, in February 1915, it announced its intention of treating the waters surrounding Great Britain and Ireland as embraced within the seat of war and of destroying all merchant ships owned by its enemies that might be found within that zone of danger, and warned all vessels, neutral as well as belligerent, to keep out of the waters thus proscribed or to enter them at their peril, the Government of the United States earnestly protested. . . .

The Imperial Government, notwithstanding, persisted in carrying out the policy announced, expressing the hope that the dangers involved, at any rate to neutral vessels, would be reduced to a minimum by the instructions which it had issued to the commanders of its submarines, and assuring the Government of the United States that it would take every possible precaution both to respect the rights of neutrals and to safeguard the lives of non-combatants.

In pursuance of this policy of submarine warfare against the commerce of its adversaries, thus announced and thus entered upon in despite of the solemn protest of the Government of the United States, the commanders of the Imperial Government's undersea vessels have carried on practices of such ruthless destruction which have made it more and more evident as the months have gone by that the Imperial Government has found it impracticable to put any such restraints upon them as it had hoped and promised to put. . . .

The Government of the United States has been very patient. At every stage of this distressing experience of tragedy after tragedy it has sought to be governed by the most thoughtful consideration of the extraordinary circumstances of an unprecedented war and to be guided by sentiments of very genuine friendship for the people and Government of Germany. It has accepted the successive explanations and assurances of the Imperial Government as, of course, given in entire sincerity and good faith, and has hoped, even against hope, that it would prove to be possible for the Imperial Government so to order and control the acts of its naval commanders as to square its policy with the recognized principles of humanity as embodied in the law of nations. It has made every allowance for unprecedented conditions and has been willing to wait until the facts became unmistakable and were susceptible of only one interpretation.

It now owes it to a just regard for its own rights to say to the Imperial

Government that that time has come. It has become painfully evident to it that the position which it took at the very outset is inevitable, namely, the use of submarines for the destruction of an enemy's commerce is, of necessity, because of the very character of the vessels employed and the very methods of attack which their employment of course involves, utterly incompatible with the principles of humanity, the long-established and incontrovertible rights of neutrals, and the sacred immunities of non-combatants.

If it is still the purpose of the Imperial Government to prosecute relentless and indiscriminate warfare against vessels of commerce by the use of submarines without regard to what the Government of the United States must consider the sacred and indisputable rules of international law and the universally recognized dictates of humanity, the Government of the United States is at last forced to the conclusion that there is but one course it can pursue. Unless the Imperial Government should now immediately declare and effect an abandonment of its present methods of submarine warfare against passenger and freight-carrying vessels, the Government of the United States can have no choice but to sever diplomatic relations with the German Empire altogether. This action the Government of the United States contemplates with the greatest reluctance but feels constrained to take in behalf of humanity and the rights of neutral nations.

◇◇◇◇◇◇◇◇◇◇◇◇◇

4. PUBLIC OPINION ON AMERICAN NEUTRALITY

[*The Outbreak of War*]

THE SUDDEN transformation of Europe from a peaceful continent to a great battlefield is something that so bewilders American public opinion that denunciations of a war so "senseless," so "insane," so "utterly without cause," have been heard on every hand. But more thoughtful consideration by editorial writers of Europe's many political problems, of the events leading to hostilities, and of the explanatory statements issuing from the different European capitals has led to a clearer appreciation of the root causes. . . . Who, ask our papers, are responsible for letting the Austro-Servian crisis precipitate a European war? Many an editorial finger points at William II. of Germany, as he is admitted to be the one overshadowing personality of the opening days of the war. Others divide the blame in varying degrees among the rulers of Berlin, Vienna, and St. Petersburg. In this country little fault is found with the course pursued by the French and British governments. . . .[4]

Much talk is heard about American sympathy in the European War, but thus far it has had no basis except hearsay or very limited personal observation. . . . To approach an answer to this question we have obtained state-

[4] The *Literary Digest*, XLIX, p. 253. August 15, 1914.

ments from between 350 and 400 editors, telling their own attitudes and the feelings of their communities toward the warring nations. . . .

The feeling of the cities and the towns represented is reported as favoring the Allies in 189 cases, for the Germans in 38, and neutral or divided in 140. . . .[5]

[*The Lusitania Notes*]

NO PREVIOUS incident of the war has stirred the American press to such vigorous condemnation as the torpedoing of the British passenger-steamer *Falaba* with its sacrifice of more than a hundred unoffending non-combatants, among them an American citizen. German interpreters of the event agree with Dr. Dernburg [6] that this killing of innocent travelers, while "regrettable," was "perfectly justifiable" in view of the provocation afforded by England and the peculiar difficulties of submarine warfare. . . . But it must be recorded that most of our American papers take a sharply different view of the case. The killing of the *Falaba's* passengers and crew, declares the Philadelphia *Public Ledger,* was "a crime against humanity," and reveals Germany in the attitude of "a frienzied beast at bay." It is "not war, but murder," exclaims the New York *World.* . . . "It is an act of shocking bloodthirstiness," and "a massacre," in the opinion of the Philadelphia *Inquirer,* and the New York *Journal of Commerce* calls it "an atrocity against which the civilized world should protest with one voice." [7]. . .

Technically, remarks the New York *Sun,* the torpedoing of the great British liner *Lusitania* and the sacrifice of hundreds of non-combatants, including American citizens, "possesses neither more nor less significance" than the torpedoing of that other British passenger ship, the *Falaba,* with the loss of one American life. "Technically and logically," it adds, "the concern of our Government with this sensational event is almost incomparably less than in the case of the *Gulflight.*" [8] Yet the fact remains, the same paper goes on to say, that "no episode of the war has startled and aroused public opinion in the country in a greater degree," and "the moral and intellectual effect is bound to be tremendous beyond measurement." "Dastardly," it concludes, "is the word on millions of American lips.". . .

The intensity of feeling aroused in American minds may be gaged by the fact that several leading papers hint at strong measures. . . . "From our Department of State," says the New York *Times,* "there must go to the Imperial Government at Berlin a demand that the Germans shall no longer make war like savages drunk with blood, that they shall cease to seek the attainment of their ends by the assassination of non-combatants and neutrals.". . .[9]

---

[5] Ibid., p. 939. November 14, 1914.

[6] Bernhard Dernburg was a former German Cabinet minister who came to the United States at the beginning of the war to organize German propaganda.

[7] Ibid., L., p. 789. April 10, 1915.

[8] An American tanker, torpedoed May 1, 1915, with the loss of three lives.

[9] Ibid., pp. 1133–4, May 15, 1915.

Drawn suddenly toward the malestrom of this gigantic war by the torpedoing of the *Lusitania* and the killing of more than a hundred American men, women, and children, the native American press meets the crisis with a steadiness and a virtual unity of spirit that must bring comfort, as the Pittsburgh *Dispatch* remarks, to "the clear-eyed statesman in the White House, whose single aim and one prayer in this moment is the welfare of his countrymen." "We can only stand and wait, united in our determination to enforce the will of our government," says the Chicago *Tribune.* "All Americans of undivided allegiance are behind the Government at Washington," declares the New York *Sun*, and this assurance is echoed by the press of all sections. . . .

"Entirely justified" is the verdict that is passed by German-American papers upon the sinking of the *Lusitania.* Germany's right to sink, without immediate notice, a merchant vessel carrying contraband of war, is, to this section of American opinion, so obvious that it hardly merits discussion.[10]. . .

[*The Resignation of Bryan*]

After the exclamations of amazement at the unprecedented and dramatic resignation of the Secretary of State [Mr. Bryan] at a critical state of an important international complication, and after the first flood of denunciation, apology, or praise which filled the press, editors, Washington correspondents, and politicians have settled down to consider the political and diplomatic consequences of the event. . . . Yet, broadly speaking and generally, it appears from their utterances that the press of the nation and such officials and other spokesmen who choose to speak stand with Mr. Wilson, rather than with Mr. Bryan, in so far as the issue is clearly drawn between them. . . . But within twenty-four hours the Democratic press of the country had acknowledged their support of President Wilson in taking those steps which drove Mr. Bryan from the chief place in the Cabinet. . . .

In the Republican press, of course, may be found condemnation of Mr. Bryan on almost every possible ground. Some editors, it is true, congratulate him for leaving the Cabinet when he could no longer honestly remain, but they can find no excuse for his attacks on the policy laid down in the Wilson notes. . . . The New York *Tribune* "can not see how Mr. Bryan's secession from the Cabinet can weaken our diplomatic position." For

> His retirement is not a sign to the world that the Wilson Cabinet is divided. On the contrary, it is a sign that the Wilson Cabinet has ceased to be divided. . . . The German Government may have had reason to think that Mr. Byran's attitude was the attitude which public opinion here would ultimately sustain. It has no excuse for thinking so now.

On the other hand, a number of German-American editors believe with the Cincinnati *Volksblatt* that "public opinion will sustain Mr. Bryan

[10] Ibid., pp. 1197–1200. May 22, 1915.

rather than the President."... No one, says the New York *Evening Post's* Washington correspondent, "ignores the fact that Mr. Bryan may have a considerable following even outside of the German-Americans. . . ."

After his resignation . . . the ex-Secretary gave out a statement "to the American people. . . ." The "real issue," he explained was "not between persons," but "between systems," the system of "force" and "persuasion."

"Force represents the old system, the system that must pass away; persuasion represents the new. . . . In the old system war is the chief cornerstone . . . the new system contemplates a universal brotherhood established through the uplifting power of example. . . .

"As a humble follower of the Prince of Peace . . . I beg to be counted among those who earnestly urge the adoption of a course in this matter which will leave no doubt of our Government's willingness to continue negotiations with Germany until an amicable understanding is reached or at least until, the stress of war over, we can appeal from Philip drunk with carnage to Philip sobered by the memories of a historic friendship and by a recollection of the innumerable ties of kinship that bound the Fatherland to the United States."...

A critical comment on the above Bryan statement is the following from the New York *World:*

Mr. Byran's statement . . . is the lucubration of a religious mystic who is preaching a gospel which he cannot elucidate but which he knows has stirred all his emotions to the depths. It has nothing to do with government or with international law or with neutral rights or with Germany's notion of submarine warfare or with a nation's duties toward its unarmed and defenseless citizens. It has nothing to do with anything except the vague yearnings of Mr. Byran's soul, which is throbbing in response to his conception of the millennium.[11]

The almost unanimous support of the President's position and the nearly as wide-spread criticism of Mr. Bryan's successive utterances . . . mean nothing to the ex-Secretary's staunchest defenders. Thus, for instance, the Mineral City *Pointer* (Ind.), in rural Ohio, answers "some of the big newspapers":

The American nation is a patriotic nation, but not a nation of suppliant fools to be plunged into a spectacular gulf of human blood for the mere honor and glory of their military leaders. There is no question of national honor at stake with the American people in the present bloody crisis, save the honor of keeping out of the bloodiest and most heathenish fight in the history of God's green earth.[12]

[11] Ibid., pp. 1449–52. June 19, 1915.
[12] Ibid., p. 1519. June 26, 1919.

5. BRITISH INTERFERENCE WITH NEUTRAL RIGHTS [13]

[*Robert Lansing to Walter H. Page*]

Washington, October 21, 1915

I DESIRE that you present a note to Sir Edward Grey in the sense of the following:

1. The Government of the United States has given careful consideration to your excellency's notes of January 7, February 10, June 22, July 23, July 31 (2), August 13, and to a *note verbale* of the British Embassy of August 6, relating to restrictions upon American commerce by certain measures adopted by the British Government during the present war. This Government has delayed answering the earlier of these notes in the hope that the . . . "measures taken by the Allied Governments," would in practice not unjustifiably infringe upon the neutral rights of American citizens engaged in trade and commerce. It is, therefore, a matter of regret that this hope has not been realized, but that, on the contrary, interferences with American ships and cargoes destined in good faith to neutral ports and lawfully entitled to proceed have become increasingly vexatious, causing American shipowners and American merchants to complain to this Government of the failure to take steps to prevent an exercise of belligerent power in contravention of their just rights. As the measures complained of proceed directly from orders issued by the British Government, are executed by British authorities, and arouse a reasonable apprehension that, if not resisted, they may be carried to an extent even more injurious to American interests, this Government directs the attention of His Majesty's Government to the following considerations. . . .

3. *First.* The detentions of American vessels and cargoes which have taken place since the opening of hostilities have, it is presumed, been pursuant to the enforcement of the orders in council, which were issued on August 20 and October 29, 1914, and March 11, 1915, and relate to contraband traffic and to the interception of trade to and from Germany and Austria-Hungary. In practice, these detentions have not been uniformly based on proofs obtained at the time of seizure, but many vessels have been detained while search was made for evidence of the contraband character of cargoes or of an intention to evade the non-intercourse measures of Great Britain. The question, consequently, has been one of evidence to support a belief of – in many cases, a bare suspicion of – enemy destination, or occasionally of enemy origin of the goods involved. Whether this evidence should be obtained by search at sea before vessels or cargo is taken into port, and what the character of the evidence should be, which is necessary to justify the detention, are the points to which I direct your excellency's attention.

[13] *Papers Relating to the Foreign Relations of the United States,* 1915, *Supplement,* pp. 578–89.

4. In regard to search at sea, an examination of the instructions issued to naval commanders of the United States, Great Britain, Russia, Japan, Spain, Germany, and France from 1888 to the beginning of the present war shows that search in port was not contemplated by the Government of any of these countries. . . .

7. The British contention that "modern conditions" justify bringing vessels into port for search is based upon the size and seaworthiness of modern carriers of commerce and the difficulty of uncovering the real transaction in the intricate trade operations of the present day. It is believed that commercial transactions of the present time, hampered as they are by censorship of telegraph and postal communications on the part of belligerents, are essentially no more complex and disguised than in the wars of recent years, during which the practice of obtaining evidence in port to determine whether a vessel should be held for prize proceedings was not adopted. The effect of the size and seaworthiness of merchant vessels upon their search at sea has been submitted to a board of naval experts, which reports that:

At no period has it been considered necessary to remove every package of a ship's cargo to establish the character and nature of her trade or the service on which she is bound, nor is such removal necessary. . . .

8. Turning to the character and sufficiency of the evidence of the contraband nature of shipments to warrant the detention of a suspected vessel or cargo for prize proceedings, it will be recalled that when a vessel is brought in for adjudication, courts of prize have heretofore been bound by well-established and long-settled practice to consider at the first hearing only the ship's papers and documents, and the goods found on board, together with the written replies of the officers and seamen to standing interrogatories taken under oath, alone and separately, as soon as possible and without communication with or instruction by counsel, in order to avoid possibility of corruption and fraud.

9. Additional evidence was not allowed to be introduced except upon an order of the court for "further proof," and then only after the cause had been fully heard upon the facts already in evidence or when this evidence furnished a ground for prosecuting the inquiry further. This was the practice of the United States courts during the War of 1812, the American Civil War, and the Spanish-American War, as is evidenced by the reported decisions of those courts, and has been the practice of the British prize courts for over a century. This practice has been changed by the British prize court rules adopted for the present war by the order in council of August 5. Under these new rules there is no longer a "first hearing" on the evidence derived from the ship, and the prize court is no longer precluded from receiving extrinsic evidence for which a suggestion has not been laid in the preparatory evidence. The result is, as pointed out above, that innocent vessels or cargoes are now seized and detained on mere suspicion while efforts are made to obtain evidence from extraneous sources to justify the detention and the commencement of prize proceedings. The effect of this

new procedure is to subject traders to risk of loss, delay, and expense, so great and so burdensome as practically to destroy much of the export trade of the United States to neutral countries of Europe. . . .

14. When goods are clearly intended to become incorporated in the mass of merchandise for sale in a neutral country, it is an unwarranted and inquisitorial proceeding to detain shipments for examination as to whether those goods are ultimately destined for the enemy's country or use. Whatever may be the conjectural conclusions to be drawn from trade statistics, which, when stated by value, are of uncertain evidence as to quantity, the United States maintains the right to sell goods into the general stock of a neutral country, and denounces as illegal and unjustifiable any attempt of a belligerent to interfere with that right on the ground that it suspects that the previous supply of such goods in the neutral country, which the imports renew or replace, has been sold to an enemy. That is a matter with which the neutral vendor has no concern and which can in no way affect his rights of trade. Moreover, even if goods listed as conditional contraband are destined to an enemy country through a neutral country, that fact is not in itself sufficient to justify their seizure.

15. In view of these considerations, the United States, reiterating its position in this matter, has no other course but to contest seizures of vessels at sea upon conjectural suspicion and the practice of bringing them into port for the purpose, by search or otherwise, of obtaining evidence, for the purpose of justifying prize proceedings, of the carriage of contraband or of breaches of the order in council of March 11. Relying upon the regard of the British Government for the principles of justice so frequently and uniformly manifested prior to the present war, this Government anticipates that the British Government will instruct their officers to refrain from these vexatious and illegal practices.

16. *Secondly.* The Government of the United States further desires to direct particular attention to the so-called "blockade" measures imposed by the order in council of March 11. The British note of July 23, 1915, appears to confirm the intention indicated in the note of March 15, 1915, to establish a blockade so extensive as to prohibit trade with Germany or Austria-Hungary, even through the ports of neutral countries adjacent to them. Great Britain, however, admits that it should not, and gives assurances that it will not, interfere with trade with the countries contiguous to the territories of the enemies of Great Britain. Nevertheless, after over six months' application of the "blockade" order, the experience of American citizens has convinced the Government of the United States that Great Britain has been unsuccessful in her efforts to distinguish between enemy and neutral trade. Arrangements have been made to create in these neutral countries special consignees, or consignment corporations, with power to refuse shipments and to determine when the state of the country's resources requires the importation of new commodities. American commercial interests are hampered by the intricacies of these arrangements, and many American citizens justly complain that their *bona-fide* trade with

neutral countries is greatly reduced as a consequence, while others assert that their neutral trade, which amounted annually to a large sum, has been entirely interrupted. . . .

19. The Declaration of Paris in 1856, which has been universally recognized as correctly stating the rule of international law as to blockade, expressly declares that "blockades, in order to be binding, must be effective; that is to say, maintained by force sufficient really to prevent access to the coast of the enemy." The effectiveness of a blockade is manifestly a question of a fact. It is common knowledge that the German coasts are open to trade with the Scandinavian countries and that German naval vessels cruise both in the North Sea and the Baltic and seize and bring into German ports neutral vessels bound for Scandinavian and Danish ports. Furthermore, from the recent placing of cotton on the British list of contraband of war, it appears that the British Government have themselves been forced to the conclusion that the blockade is ineffective to prevent shipments of cotton from reaching their enemies, or else that they are doubtful as to the legality of the form of blockade which they have sought to maintain. . . .

21. Finally, there is no better settled principle of the law of nations than that which forbids the blockade of neutral ports in time of war. The Declaration of London, though not regarded as binding upon the signatories because not ratified by them, has been expressly adopted by the British Government without modification as to blockade in the British order in council of October 29, 1914. Article 18 of the Declaration declares specifically that "the blockading forces must not bar access to neutral ports or coasts." This is, in the opinion of this Government, a correct statement of the universally accepted law as it exists to-day and as it existed prior to the Declaration of London. . . .

32. Before closing this note, in which frequent reference is made to contraband traffic and contraband articles, it is necessary, in order to avoid possible misconstruction, that it should be clearly understood by His Majesty's Government that there is no intention in this discussion to commit the Government of the United States to a policy of waiving any objections which it may entertain as to the propriety and right of the British Government to include in their list of contraband of war certain articles which have been so included. The United States Government reserves the right to make this matter the subject of a communication to His Majesty's Government at a later day.

33. I believe it has been conclusively shown that the methods sought to be employed by Great Britain to obtain and use evidence of enemy destination of cargoes bound for neutral ports, and to impose a contraband character upon such cargoes, are without justification; that the blockade, upon which such methods are partly founded, is ineffective, illegal, and indefensible; that the judicial procedure offered as a means of reparation for an international injury is inherently defective for the purpose; and that in many cases jurisdiction is asserted in violation of the law of nations.

The United States, therefore, can not submit to the curtailment of its neutral rights by these measures, which are admittedly retaliatory, and therefore illegal, in conception and in nature, and intended to punish the enemies of Great Britain for alleged illegalities on their part. The United States might not be in a position to object to them if its interests and the interests of all neutrals were unaffected by them, but, being affected, it can not with complacence suffer further subordination of its rights and interests to the plea that the exceptional geographic position of the enemies of Great Britain require or justify oppressive and illegal practices. . . .

◇◇◇◇◇◇◇◇◇◇◇◇◇◇

6. THE BRITISH BLOCKADE AND AMERICAN COMMERCE [14]

. . . ON JANUARY 28, 1921, the Senate adopted a resolution (No. 438) requesting the President, if not incompatible with the public interest, "to inform the Senate whether any, and if any, what measures have been taken relating to claims and complaints of citizens of the United States against the British Government growing out of restraints on American commerce, and the alleged unlawful seizure and sale of American ships and cargoes by British authorities during the late war. . . .

On April 29, 1926, the Department of State was informed that the British Government was prepared to enter at once upon a preliminary examination of the papers bearing on the claims in question pursuant to the procedure suggested in its *aide memoire* of April, and that J. Joyce Broderick, Esquire, Commercial Counselor of the British Embassy, had been instructed to undertake this examination for the British Government in conjunction with a representative of the Department of State. The British Government's acceptance in principle of the plan outlined by the Department's *aide memoire* of April 7, 1926, marked the first real progress toward a solution of this problem.

In the meantime, the Department of State had undertaken a thorough re-examination of the papers in its claims files. This examination indicated that the volume of correspondence was so great that it would be most confusing were an effort made to deal with it in its existing form. Accordingly a staff of assistant solicitors was instructed to go through all the files and summarize in brief memoranda the significant facts in each individual case. This work required several months time and resulted in the preparation of about 2200 separate memoranda, or synopses, many of which covered more than one complaint since frequently a single complainant would be interested in several different ships or consignments. . . .

[14] The Report of Spencer Phenix to the Secretary of State, Frank B. Kellogg, Nov. 9, 1926. Mr. Phenix was assistant to Assistant Secretary of State, R. E. Olds. *Papers Relating to the Foreign Relations of the United States,* 1926, Vol. II, pp. 251–87.

The duty of representing the Department of State in the joint informal conferences with Mr. Broderick was assigned to me, and, in the light of the facts disclosed by my examination of such memoranda as had then been prepared, I was authorized provisionally to withdraw from consideration during our conferences all cases falling within the following categories, and to state that they would not be presented by the Department if a satisfactory general agreement were reached by the two Governments:

1. Cases involving an actual loss of $500 or less.
2. Cases arising from the inclusion of names in the so-called "black lists" unless special grounds for espousal exist.
3. Cases involving alleged wrongful detention, expulsion or mistreatment of American citizens unless there is clearly evidence of injustice resulting in substantial loss or injury, or of needlessly harsh or arbitrary action.
4. Cases involving claims for purely speculative profits.
5. Cases involving losses due to British export or import or bunker restrictions or maximum price orders unless there has been discrimination against the American interests involved.
6. Cases where without unreasonable delay or expense the subject matter has been released to the interested party in good condition, or its fair cash value paid over to him. . . .

The work of summarizing the cases in the claims file and of preparing memoranda was completed in July, and as soon as these memoranda had been arranged alphabetically and numbered serially, Mr. Broderick and I made a rapid review of them all for the purpose of applying the six rules above mentioned wherever the facts justified. We found that nearly 50 per cent of the cases presented in the summaries could be eliminated by the application of these rules or for equally valid reasons. The remaining 50 per cent consisted principally of cases where the Department's information was inadequate to permit the application of any recognized rules, and it was with respect to this residue that the examination of the records in London was undertaken. . . .

My examination of the British records was completed during the third week of October and Mr. Broderick and I then went over a second time the entire lot of cases for the purpose of reconsidering them in the light of the additional information obtained in London, and of applying the rules of provisional exclusion to which reference has already been made. During this review of the cases the number of the applicable rule was entered by me on the original summary, and when that work was completed I prepared a list of all of the 2658 cases showing with respect to each the rule of exclusion, if any, which had been applied. . . .

It will be noted . . . that of the 2658 cases which have been the subject of my inquiries, 2501 are susceptible of elimination by the application of the above mentioned rules. This leaves a residue of 157 cases for further consideration, included in which are 62 concerning which information has not yet been obtained from the British authorities. . . .

As indicated above, I am of the opinion that 83 of the 95 cases which have been reserved for the Department's further consideration can properly be eliminated for the reasons stated. The remaining 12 cases include 11 which seem to me to possess conspicuous merit. . . .

I should not close this report without recording the fact that I was accorded the most whole-hearted and cordial cooperation by all officials of the British Government with whom I came into contact during my mission. . . . As pointed out, however, in the report which I submitted to Mr. Olds in London last September, there seem to be two fundamental considerations in the minds of the British authorities. The first is that the British Government will not admit that the legality of any of its acts in blockading Germany is open to question by the Government of the United States, and the second is that in view of the political dangers inherent in this entire problem, any settlement requiring an appropriation of funds by Parliament to pay "blockade" claims as such, would, as a matter of practical politics, be impossible. It seems to be generally felt that any British Government which requested an appropriation for this purpose would fall, as would any Government which admitted that the legality of the British Navy's operations during the war was open to question. In these circumstances it seems certain that any proposal by the Government of the United States for the settlement of the claims question which does not take full account of these two elements of the situation will be foredoomed to failure. On the other hand it seems to me that the British Government will accept a formula which does not raise the question of the validity of the blockade, and which permits the settlement of meritorious claims, either through a lump sum adjustment, or through a balancing of accounts between the two Governments.

There is one further aspect of the matter to which the Department should give attention and that is the position of the United States as a belligerent in the next war. We are one of the principal naval forces of the world and should we be involved in another war it would be to our interest to have our naval forces free to operate in any way which would render them most effective against the enemy. We shall undoubtedly find it necessary to restrict neutral maritime commerce with our enemy, and I think it can safely be said that our efforts in that direction might be wholly ineffectual if we limited ourselves to visit and search on the high seas. We shall unquestionably want to pursue very much the same procedure as that followed by the British. In these circumstances we should take no general position in our present discussions which might later hamper our freedom of action in case of emergency.

◇◇◇◇◇◇◇◇◇◇◇◇◇

7. PRESIDENT WILSON'S WARNING ON THE DANGER OF WAR

IN ORDINARY circumstances it has not been necessary for America to think of force, because everybody knows that there is latent in her as much force as resides anywhere in the world. This great body of 100,000,000 people has an average of intelligence and resourcefulness probably unprecedented in the history of the world. Nobody doubts that, given time enough, we can assert any amount of force that may be necessary; but when the world is on fire how much time can you afford to take to be ready? When you know that there are combustible materials in the life of the world and in your own national life, and that the sky is full of floating sparks from a great conflagration, are you going to sit down and say it will be time when the fire begins to do something about it? I do not believe that the fire is going to begin, but I would be surer of it if we were ready for the fire. And I want to come as your responsible servant and tell you this, that we do not control the fire. We are under the influences of it, but we are not at the sources of it. We are where it at any time may affect us, and yet we can not govern its spread and progress. If it once touches us, it may touch the very sources of our life, for it may touch the very things we stand for, and we might for a little while be unable successfully to vindicate and defend them. I am not come here to tell you of any immediate threat of a definite danger, because by very great patience, by making our position perfectly clear, and then steadfastly maintaining the same attitude throughout great controversies, we have so far held difficulty at arm's length; but I want you to realize the task you have imposed upon your Government.

There are two things which practically everybody who comes to the Executive Office in Washington tells me. They tell me, "The people are counting upon you to keep us out of this war." And in the next breath what do they tell, "The people are equally counting upon you to maintain the honor of the United States." Have you reflected that a time might come when I could not do both? And have you made yourselves ready to stand behind your Government for the maintenance of the honor of your country, as well as for the maintenance of the peace of the country? If I am to maintain the honor of the United States and it should be necessary to exert the force of the United States in order to do it, have you made the force ready? You know that you have not, and the very fact that the force is not ready may make the task you have set for me all the more delicate and all the more difficult. I have come away from Washington to remind you of your part in this great business. There is no part that belongs to me that I wish to shirk, but I wish you to bear the part that belongs to you. I want every man and woman of you to stand behind me in pressing a reasonable plan for national defense. . . .[15]

[15] Address at Pittsburgh, Jan. 29, 1916. *House Doc.* No. 803, 64 Cong., 1 Sess., Vol. 144 (7098).

America is not afraid of anybody. I know that I express your feeling and the feeling of all our fellow citizens when I say that the only thing I am afraid of is not being ready to perform my duty. I am afraid of the danger of shame; I am afraid of the danger of inadequacy; I am afraid of the danger of not being able to express the great character of this country with tremendous might and effectiveness whenever we are called upon to act in the field of the world's affairs.

For it is character we are going to express, not power merely. The United States is not in love with the aggressive use of power. It despises the aggressive use of power. There is not a foot of territory belonging to any other Nation which this Nation covets or desires. There is not a privilege which we ourselves enjoy that we would dream of denying any other nation in the world. If there is one thing that the American people love and believe in more than another it is peace and all the handsome things that belong to peace. I hope that you will bear me out in saying that I have proved that I am a partisan of peace. I would be ashamed to be belligerent and impatient when the fortunes of my whole country and the happiness of all my fellow countrymen were involved. But I know that peace is not always within the choice of the Nation, and I want to remind you, and remind you very solemnly, of the double obligation you have laid upon me. I know you have laid it upon me because I am constantly reminded of it in conversation, by letter, in editorial, by means of every voice that comes to me out of the body of the Nation. You have laid upon me this double obligation: "We are relying upon you, Mr. President, to keep us out of this war, but we are relying upon you, Mr. President, to keep the honor of the Nation unstained."

Do you not see that a time may come when it is impossible to do both of these things? Do you not see that if I am to guard the honor of the Nation, I am not protecting it against itself, for we are not going to do anything to stain the honor of our own country. I am protecting it against things that I cannot control, the action of others. And where the action of others may bring us I cannot foretell. You may count upon my heart and resolution to keep you out of the war, but you must be ready if it is necessary that I should maintain your honor. That is the only thing a real man loves about himself. Some men who are not real men love other things about themselves, but the real man believes that his honor is dearer than his life; and a nation is merely all of us put together, and the Nation's honor is dearer than the Nation's comfort and the Nation's peace and the Nation's life itself. So that we must know what we have thrown into the balance; we must know the infinite issues which are impending every day of the year, and when we go to bed at night and when we rise in the morning, and at every interval of the rush of business, we must remind ourselves that we are part of a great body politic in which are vested some of the highest hopes of the human race. . . .[16]

---

[16] Ibid., Address at Cleveland, Jan. 29, 1916.

I dare say you realize, therefore, the solemnity of the feeling with which I come to audiences of my fellow citizens at this time. I can not indulge the reckless pleasure of expressing my own private opinions and prejudices. I speak as the trustee of the Nation, called upon to speak its sober judgments and not its individual opinions; and it is with the feeling of this responsibility upon me that I have come to you to-night and have approached the other audiences that I have had the privilege of addressing upon this journey. Do you realize the peculiar difficulty of the situation in which your Executive is placed? You have laid upon me, not by implication, but explicitly – it has come to me by means of every voice that has been vocal in the Nation – you have laid upon me the double obligation of maintaining the honor of the United States and of maintaining the peace of the United States. Is it not conceivable that the two might become incompatible? Is it not conceivable that, however great our passion for peace, we would have to subordinate it to our passion for what is right? Is it not possible that in maintaining the integrity of the character of the United States it may become necessary to see that no man does that integrity too great violence?

It is a very terrible thing, ladies and gentlemen, to have the honor of the United States intrusted to your keeping. It is a great honor, that honor of the United States! In it runs the blood of generations of men who have built up ideals and institutions on this side of the water intended to regenerate mankind, and any man who does violence to right, any nation that does violence to the principles of just international understandings, is doing violence to the ideals of the United States. We observe the technical limits; we assert these rights only when our own citizens are directly affected, but you know that our feeling is just the same whether the rights of those individual citizens are affected or not, and that we feel all the concern of those who have built up things so great that they dare not let them be torn down or touched with profane hands.

Look at the task that is assigned to the United States, to assert the principles of law in a world in which the principles of law have broken down – not the technical principles of law, but the essential principles of right dealing and humanity as between nation and nation. Law is a very complicated term. It includes a great many things that do not engage our affections, but at the basis of the things that we are now dealing with lie the deepest affections of the human heart, the love of life, the love of righteousness, the love of fair dealing, the love of those things that are just and of good report. The things that are rooted in our very spirit are the stuff of the law that I am talking about now. . . .[17]

[17] Ibid., Address at Chicago, Jan. 31, 1916.

Wilson to Congress

8. ESSENTIAL TERMS OF PEACE[18]

ON THE eighteenth of December last I addressed an identic note to the governments of the nations now at war requesting them to state, more definitely than they had yet been stated by either group of belligerents, the terms upon which they would deem it possible to make peace. I spoke on behalf of humanity and of the rights of all neutral nations like our own, many of whose most vital interests the war puts in constant jeopardy. The Central Powers united in a reply which stated merely that they were ready to meet their antagonists in conference to discuss terms of peace. The Entente Powers have replied much more definitely and have stated, in general terms, indeed, but with sufficient definiteness to imply details, the arrangements, guarantees, and acts of reparation which they deem to be the indispensable conditions of a satisfactory settlement. We are that much nearer a definite discussion of the peace which shall end the present war. We are that much nearer the discussion of the international concert which must thereafter hold the world at peace. In every discussion of the peace that must end this war it is taken for granted that that peace must be followed by some definite concert of power which will make it virtually impossible that any such catastrophe should ever overwhelm us again. Every lover of mankind, every sane and thoughtful man, must take that for granted.

I have sought this opportunity to address you because I thought that I owed it to you, as the counsel associated with me in the final determination of our international obligations, to disclose to you without reserve the thought and purpose that have been taking form in my mind in regard to the duty of our Government in the days to come when it will be necessary to lay afresh and upon a new plan the foundations of peace among the nations.

It is inconceivable that the people of the United States should play no part in that great enterprise. To take part in such a service will be the opportunity for which they have sought to prepare themselves by the very principles and purposes of their polity and the approved practices of their Government ever since the days when they set up a new nation in the high and honourable hope that it might in all that it was and did show mankind the way to liberty. They cannot in honour withhold the service to which they are now about to be challenged. They do not wish to withhold it. But they owe it to themselves and to the other nations of the world to state the conditions under which they will feel free to render it.

That service is nothing less than this, to add their authority and their power to the authority and force of other nations to guarantee peace and justice throughout the world. Such a settlement cannot now be long post-

[18] Address of President Wilson to the Senate, Jan. 22, 1917. *Papers Relating to the Foreign Relations of the United States,* 1917, *Supplement,* Vol. I, pp. 24–9.

poned. It is right that before it comes this Government should frankly formulate the conditions upon which it would feel justified in asking our people to approve its formal and solemn adherence to a League for Peace. I am here to attempt to state those conditions. . . .

I do not mean to say that any American government would throw any obstacle in the way of any terms of peace the governments now at war might agree upon, or seek to upset them when made, whatever they might be. I only take it for granted that mere terms of peace between the belligerents will not satisfy even the belligerents themselves. Mere agreements may not make peace secure. It will be absolutely necessary that a force be created as a guarantor of the permanency of the settlement so much greater than the force of any nation now engaged or any alliance hitherto formed or projected that no nation, no probable combination of nations could face or withstand it. If the peace presently to be made is to endure, it must be a peace made secure by the organized major force of mankind. . . .

The equality of nations upon which peace must be founded if it is to last must be an equality of rights; the guarantees exchanged must neither recognize nor imply a difference between big nations and small, between those that are powerful and those that are weak. Right must be based upon the common strength, not upon the individual strength, of the nations upon whose concert peace will depend. Equality of territory or of resources there of course cannot be; nor any other sort of equality not gained in the ordinary peaceful and legitimate development of the peoples themselves. But no one asks or expects anything more than an equality of rights. Mankind is looking now for freedom of life, not for equipoises of power.

And there is a deeper thing involved than even equality of right among organized nations. No peace can last, or ought to last, which does not recognize and accept the principle that governments derive all their just powers from the consent of the governed, and that no right anywhere exists to hand peoples about from sovereignty to sovereignty as if they were property. . . .

So far as practicable, moreover, every great people now struggling towards a full development of its resources and of its powers should be assured a direct outlet to the great highways of the sea. Where this cannot be done by the cession of territory, it can no doubt be done by the neutralization of direct rights of way under the general guarantee which will assure the peace itself. With a right comity of arrangement no nation need be shut away from free access to the open paths of the world's commerce.

And the paths of the sea must alike in law and in fact be free. The freedom of the seas in the *sine qua non* of peace, equality, and cooperation. No doubt a somewhat radical reconsideration of many of the rules of international practice hitherto thought to be established may be necessary in order to make the seas indeed free and common in practically all circumstances for the use of mankind, but the motive for such changes is convincing and compelling. There can be no trust or intimacy between the peoples of the world without them. The free, constant, unthreatened intercourse of nations is an essential part of the process of peace and of development. It need not be difficult either to define or to secure the freedom of the seas if the governments of the world sincerely desire to come to an agreement concerning it.

It is a problem closely connected with the limitation of naval armaments and the cooperation of the navies of the world in keeping the seas at once free and safe. And the question of limiting naval armaments opens the wider and perhaps more difficult question of the limitation of armies and of all programms of military preparation. Difficult and delicate as these questions are, they must be faced with the utmost candour and decided in a spirit of real accommodation if peace is to come with healing in its wings, and come to stay. Peace cannot be had without concession and sacrifice. There can be no sense of safety and equality among the nations if great preponderating armaments are henceforth to continue here and there to be built up and maintained. The statesmen of the world must plan for peace and nations must adjust and accommodate their policy to it as they have planned for war and made ready for pitiless contest and rivalry. The question of armaments, whether on land or sea, is the most immediately and intensely practical question connected with the future fortunes of nations and of mankind. . . .

And in holding out the expectation that the people and Government of the United States will join the other civilized nations of the world in guaranteeing the permanence of peace upon such terms as I have named I speak with the greater boldness and confidence because it is clear to every man who can think that there is in this promise no breach in either our traditions or our policy as a nation, but a fulfilment, rather, of all that we have professed or striven for.

I am proposing, as it were, that the nations should with one accord adopt the doctrine of President Monroe as the doctrine of the world: that no nation should seek to extend its polity over any other nation or people, but that every people should be left free to determine its own polity, its own way of development, unhindered, unthreatened, unafraid, the little along with the great and powerful.

I am proposing that all nations henceforth avoid entangling alliances which would draw them into competitions of power, catch them in a net of intrigue and selfish rivalry, and disturb their own affairs with influences intruded from without. There is no entangling alliance in a concert of power. When all unite to act in the same sense and with the same purpose all act in the common interest and are free to live their own lives under a common protection.

I am proposing government by the consent of the governed; that freedom of the seas which in international conference after conference representatives of the United States have urged with the eloquence of those who are the convinced disciples of liberty; and that moderation of armaments which makes of armies and navies a power for order merely, not an instrument of aggression or of selfish violence.

These are American principles, American policies. We could stand for no others. And they are also the principles and policies of forward-looking men and women everywhere, of every modern nation, of every enlightened community. They are the principles of mankind and must prevail.

◇◇◇◇◇◇◇◇◇◇◇◇◇

9. PRESIDENT WILSON'S WAR MESSAGE [19]

. . . ON THE THIRD of February last I officially laid before you the extraordinary announcement of the Imperial German Government that on and after the first day of February it was its purpose to put aside all restraints of law or of humanity and use its submarines to sink every vessel that sought to approach either the ports of Great Britain and Ireland or the western coasts of Europe or any of the ports controlled by the enemies of Germany within the Mediterranean. That had seemed to be the object of the German submarine warfare earlier in the war, but since April of last year the Imperial Government had somewhat restrained the commanders of its undersea craft in conformity with its promise then given to us that passenger boats should not be sunk and that due warning would be given to all other vessels which its submarines might seek to destroy, when no resistance was offered or escape attempted, and care taken that their crews were given at least a fair chance to save their lives in their open boats. The precautions taken were meager and haphazard enough, as was proved in distress instance after instance in the progress of the cruel and unmanly business, but a certain degree of restraint was observed. The new policy has swept every restriction aside. Vessels of every kind, whatever their flag, their character, their cargo, their destination, their errand, have been ruthlessly sent to the bottom without warning and without thought of help or mercy for those on board, the vessels of friendly neutrals along with those of belligerents. Even hospital ships and ships carrying relief to the sorely bereaved and stricken people of Belgium, though the latter were provided with safe conduct through the proscribed areas by the German Government itself and were distinguished by unmistakable marks of identity, have been sunk with the same reckless lack of compassion or of principle. . . .

I am not now thinking of the loss of property involved, immense and serious as that is, but only of the wanton and wholesale destruction of the lives of non-combatants, men, women, and children, engaged in pursuits which have always, even in the darkest periods of modern history,

---

[19] Cong. Rec. 65th Congress, 1st Session, Vol. 55, Part I, p. 102.

been deemed innocent and legitimate. Property can be paid for; the lives of peaceful and innocent people cannot be. The present German submarine warfare against commerce is a warfare against mankind.

It is a war against all nations. American ships have been sunk, American lives taken, in ways which it has stirred us very deeply to learn of, but the ships and people of other neutral and friendly nations have been sunk and overwhelmed in the waters in the same way. There has been no discrimination. The challenge is to all mankind. Each nation must decide for itself how it will meet it. The choice we make for ourselves must be made with a moderation of counsel and a temperateness of judgment befitting our character and our motives as a nation. We must put excited feeling away. Our motive will not be revenge or the victorious assertion of the physical might of the nation, but only the vindication of right, of human right, of which we are only a single champion. . . .

There is one choice we cannot make, we are incapable of making: we will not choose the path of submission and suffer the most sacred rights of our Nation and our people to be ignored or violated. The wrongs against which we now array ourselves are no common wrongs; they cut to the very roots of human life.

With a profound sense of the solemn and even tragical character of the step I am taking and of the grave responsibilities which it involves, but in unhesitating obedience to what I deem my constitutional duty, I advise that the Congress declare the recent course of the Imperial German Government to be in fact nothing less than war against the government and people of the United States; that it formally accept the status of belligerent which has thus been thrust upon it; and that it take immediate steps not only to put the country in a more thorough state of defense but also to exert all its power and employ all its resources to bring the Government of the German Empire to terms and end the war. . . .

While we do these things, these deeply momentous things, let us be very clear, and make very clear to all the world what our motives and our objects are. My own thought has not been driven from its habitual and normal course by the unhappy events of the last two months, and I do not believe that the thought of the Nation has been altered or clouded by them. I have exactly the same things in mind now that I had in mind when I addressed the Senate on the twenty-second of January last; the same that I had in mind when I addressed the Congress on the third of February and on the twenty-sixth of February. Our object now, as then, is to vindicate the principles of peace and justice in the life of the world as against selfish and autocratic power and to set up amongst the really free and self-governed peoples of the world such a concert of purpose and of action as will henceforth insure the observance of those principles. Neutrality is no longer feasible or desirable where the peace of the world is involved and the freedom of its peoples, and the menace to that peace and fredom lies in the existence of autocratic governments backed by organized force which is controlled wholly by their will, not by the will of their people. We have seen the last of neutrality in such circumstances. We are at the beginning of an age in which it will be insisted that the same standards of conduct and of responsibility for wrong done shall be observed among nations and their governments that are observed among the individual citizens of civilized states.

We have no quarrel with the German people. We have no feeling towards them but one of sympathy and friendship. It was not upon their impulse that their government acted in entering this war. It was not with their previous knowledge or approval. It was a war determined upon as wars used to be determined upon in the old, unhappy days when peoples were nowhere consulted by their rulers and wars were provoked and waged in the interest of dynasties or of little groups of ambitious men who were accustomed to use their fellow men as pawns and tools. Self-governed nations do not fill their neighbor states with spies or set the course of intrigue to bring about some critical posture of affairs which will give them an opportunity to strike and make conquest. Such designs can be successfully worked out only under cover and where no one has the right to ask questions. Cunningly contrived plans of deception or aggression, carried, it may be, from generation to generation, can be worked out and kept from the light only within the privacy of courts or behind the carefully guarded confidences of a narrow and privileged class. They are happily impossible where public opinion commands and insists upon full information concerning all the nation's affairs. . . .

It is a distressing and oppressive duty, Gentlemen of the Congress, which I have performed in thus addressing you. There are, it may be, many months of fiery trial and sacrifice ahead of us. It is a fearful thing to lead this great peaceful people into war, into the most terrible and disastrous of all wars, civilization itself seeming to be in the balance. But the right is more precious than peace, and we shall fight for the things which we have always carried nearest our hearts, — for democracy, for the right of those who submit to authority to have a voice in their own Governments, for the rights and liberties of small nations, for a universal dominion of right by such a concert of free peoples as shall bring peace and safety to all nations and make the world itself at last free. To such a task we can dedicate our lives and our fortunes, everything that we are and everything that we have, with the pride of those who know that the day has come when America is privileged to spend her blood and her might for the principles that gave her birth and happiness and the peace which she has treasured. God helping her, she can do no other.

Chapter XXVII

THE TREATY OF VERSAILLES AND THE LEAGUE OF NATIONS

◇◇◇◇◇◇◇◇◇◇◇◇◇

IN THE Pre-Armistice Agreement (1) which led to the military capitulation of Germany on November 11, 1918, the United States and the Allies promised to construct peace on the program, with two exceptions, announced by President Wilson in his message to Congress of January 8, 1918 (2), and in subsequent addresses. In the address of January 8, the President stated the "fourteen points" on which world peace should be based. The fourteenth point provided for the creation of an association of nations under which the "political independence and territorial integrity" of all states would be guaranteed. President Wilson believed that the Covenant of the League of Nations (3) fulfilled the broad promise of the fourteenth point, and that Article X of the Covenant fulfilled the specific pledge of collective security.

Opposition arose, however, in the Senate of the United States to some parts of the treaty and of the Covenant, and this opposition was expressed, after much discussion, in reservations, adopted by a majority vote, to the resolution of "advice and consent" which had to pass the Senate by a two-thirds vote, before the treaty would be binding upon the United States. These reservations, although for the most part not written by Senator Henry Cabot Lodge of Massachusetts, have become generally known as the "Lodge Reservations (4)." Of the many speeches in the Senate for or against the reservations, two have been selected as typical, as far as that is possible: the speeches of Senator Harding of Ohio and of Senator Pittman of Nevada (5).

Since the Democratic Party and the Democratic candidate for the Presidency in 1920, James M. Cox, followed so closely the views of President Wilson on the League issue, selections from his discussion of the subject have been chosen for comparison with statements by Senator Harding, the Republican candidate in 1920, and Herbert Hoover, and with a joint statement by thirty-one prominent Republicans (6).

After President Harding assumed office, he declared that he had not favored the establishment of an association of nations for the preservation of world peace, and that the people of the United States in the election of 1920 had voted against the League. He negotiated accordingly, a separate treaty with Germany (7).

◇◇◇◇◇◇◇◇◇◇◇◇◇

The Treaty of Versailles and the League of Nations

1. THE PRE-ARMISTICE AGREEMENT [1]

. . . THE ALLIED Governments have given careful consideration to the correspondence which has passed between the President of the United States and the German Government. Subject to the qualifications which follow they declare their willingness to make peace with the Government of Germany on the terms of peace laid down in the President's address to Congress of January 1918, and the principles of settlement enunciated in his subsequent addresses. They must point out, however, that clause 2, relating to what is usually described as the freedom of the seas, is open to various interpretations, some of which they could not accept. They must, therefore, reserve to themselves complete freedom on this subject when they enter the peace conference.

Further, in the conditions of peace laid down in his address to Congress of January 8, 1918, the President declared that invaded territories must be restored as well as evacuated and freed, the Allied Governments feel that no doubt ought to be allowed to exist as to what this provision implies. By it they understand that compensation will be made by Germany for all damage done to the civilian population of the Allies and their property by the aggression of Germany by land, by sea and from the air. . . .

◇◇◇◇◇◇◇◇◇◇◇◇◇

2. THE FOURTEEN POINTS [2]

[*Address of President Wilson to the Congress of the United States, January 8, 1918*]

. . . WE ENTERED this war because violations of right had occurred which touched us to the quick and made the life of our people impossible unless they were corrected and the world secured once for all against their recurrence. What we demand in this war, therefore, is nothing peculiar to ourselves. It is that the world be made fit and safe to live in; and particularly that it be made safe for every peace-loving nation which, like our own, wishes to live its own life, determine its own institutions, be assured of justice and fair dealing by the other peoples of the world as against force and selfish aggression. All the peoples of the world are in effect partners in this interest, and for our own part we see very clearly that unless justice be done to others it will not be done to us. The programme of the world's peace, therefore, is our programme; and that programme, the only possible programme, as we see it, is this:

[1] *Papers Relating to the Foreign Relations of the United States,* 1918, *Supplement,* Vol. I, pp. 468–9. The text of this agreement was transmitted to the German Government on November 5, 1918.

[2] *Congressional Record,* 65th Congress, 2nd Session, pp. 680–1.

I. Open covenants of peace, openly arrived at, after which there shall be no private international understandings of any kind but diplomacy shall proceed always frankly and in the public view.

II. Absolute freedom of navigation upon the seas, outside territorial waters, alike in peace and in war, except as the seas may be closed in whole or in part by international action for the enforcement of international covenants.

III. The removal, so far as possible, of all economic barriers and the establishment of an equality of trade conditions among all the nations consenting to the peace and associating themselves for its maintenance.

IV. Adequate guarantees given and taken that national armaments will be reduced to the lowest point consistent with domestic safety.

V. A free, open-minded, and absolutely impartial adjustment of all colonial claims, based upon a strict observance of the principle that in determining all such questions of sovereignty the interests of the populations concerned must have equal weight with the equitable claims of the government whose title is to be determined.

VI. The evacuation of all Russian territory and such a settlement of all questions affecting Russia as will secure the best and freest co-operation of the other nations of the world in obtaining for her an unhampered and unembarrassed opportunity for the independent determination of her own political development and national policy and assure her of a sincere welcome into the society of free nations under institutions of her own choosing; and, more than a welcome, assistance also of every kind that she may need and may herself desire. The treatment accorded Russia by her sister nations in the months to come will be the acid test of their good will, of their comprehension of her needs as distinguished from their own interests, and of their intelligent and unselfish sympathy.

VII. Belgium, the whole world will agree, must be evacuated and restored, without any attempt to limit the sovereignty which she enjoys in common with all other free nations. No other single act will serve as this will serve to restore confidence among the nations in the laws which they have themselves set and determined for the government of their relations with one another. Without this healing act the whole structure and validity of international law is forever impaired.

VIII. All French territory should be freed and the invaded portions restored, and the wrong done to France by Prussia in 1871 in the matter of Alsace-Lorraine, which has unsettled the peace of the world for nearly fifty years, should be righted, in order that peace may once more be made secure in the interest of all.

IX. A readjustment of the frontiers of Italy should be effected along clearly recognizable lines of nationality.

X. The peoples of Austria-Hungary, whose place among the nations we wish to see safeguarded and assured, should be accorded the freest opportunity of autonomous development.

XI. Rumania, Serbia, and Montenegro should be evacuated; occupied territories restored; Serbia accorded free and secure access to the sea; and the relations of the several Balkan states to one another determined by friendly counsel along historically established lines of allegiance and nationality; and international guarantees of the political and economic independence and territorial integrity of the several Balkan states should be entered into.

XII. The Turkish portions of the present Ottoman Empire should be assured a secure sovereignty, but the other nationalities which are now under Turkish rule should be assured an undoubted security of life and an absolutely unmolested opportunity of autonomous development, and the Dardanelles should be permanently opened as a free passage to the ships and commerce of all nations under international guarantees.

XIII. An independent Polish state should be erected which should include the territories inhabited by indisputably Polish populations, which should be assured a free and secure access to the sea, and whose political and economic independence and territorial integrity should be guaranteed by international covenant.

XIV. A general association of nations must be formed under specific covenants for the purpose of affording mutual guarantees of political independence and territorial integrity to great and small states alike.

In regard to these essential rectifications of wrong and assertions of right we feel ourselves to be intimate partners of all the governments and peoples associated together against the Imperialists. We cannot be separated in interest or divided in purpose. We stand together until the end. . . .

◇◇◇◇◇◇◇◇◇◇◇◇◇

3. THE COVENANT OF THE LEAGUE OF NATIONS[3]

[*Articles 1 to 26 of the Treaty of Peace between the Allied and Associate Powers and Germany. Signed at Versailles, June 28, 1919*]

THE HIGH Contracting Parties,

In order to promote international co-operation and to achieve international peace and security

by the acceptance of obligations not to resort to war,

by the prescription of open, just and honourable relations between nations,

by the firm establishment of the understandings of international law as the actual rule of conduct among Governments, and

by the maintenance of justice and a scrupulous respect for all treaty obligations in the dealings of organized peoples with one another,

Agree to this Covenant of the League of Nations.

Article 1. The original Members of the League of Nations shall be those

[3] *Sen. Ex. Doc.* (8167) 67th Congress, 4th Session, No. 348, pp. 3336–45.

of the Signatories which are named in the Annex to this Covenant and also such of those other States named in the Annex as shall accede without reservation to this Covenant. Such accession shall be effected by a Declaration deposited with the Secretariat within two months of the coming into force of the Covenant. Notice thereof shall be sent to all other Members of the League.

Any fully self-governing State, Dominion or Colony not named in the Annex may become a Member of the League if its admission is agreed to by two-thirds of the Assembly, provided that it shall give effective guarantees of its sincere intention to observe its international obligations, and shall accept such regulations as may be prescribed by the League in regard to its military, naval and air forces and armaments.

Any Member of the League may, after two years' notice of its intention to do so, withdraw from the League, provided that all its international obligations and all its obligations under this Covenant shall have been fulfilled at the time of its withdrawal.

Article 2. The action of the League under this Covenant shall be effected through the instrumentality of an Assembly and of a Council, with a permanent Secretariat.

Article 3. The Assembly shall consist of Representatives of the Members of the League.

The Assembly shall meet at stated intervals and from time to time as occasion may require at the Seat of the League or at such other place as may be decided upon.

The Assembly may deal at its meetings with any matter within the sphere of action of the League or affecting the peace of the world.

At meetings of the Assembly each Member of the League shall have one vote, and may have not more than three Representatives.

Article 4. The Council shall consist of Representatives of the Principal Allied and Associated Powers, together with Representatives of four other Members of the League. These four Members of the League shall be selected by the Assembly from time to time in its discretion. Until the appointment of the Representatives of the four Members of the League first selected by the Assembly, Representatives of Belgium, Brazil, Spain and Greece shall be members of the Council.

With the approval of the majority of the Assembly, the Council may name additional Members of the League whose Representatives shall always be members of the Council; the Council with like approval may increase the number of the Members of the League to be selected by the Assembly for representation on the Council.[4]

The Council shall meet from time to time as occasion may require, and

---

[4] On July 29, 1926, an amendment came into force to be inserted after this paragraph as follows: "The Assembly shall fix by a two-thirds majority the rules dealing with the election of the non-permanent members of the Council, and particularly such regulations as relate to their term of office and the conditions of re-eligibility."

at least once a year, at the Seat of the League, or at such other place as may be decided upon.

The Council may deal at its meetings with any matter within the sphere of action of the League or affecting the peace of the world.

Any Member of the League not represented on the Council shall be invited to send a Representative to sit as a member at any meeting of the Council during the consideration of matters specially affecting the interests of that Member of the League.

At meetings of the Council, each Member of the League represented on the Council shall have one vote, and may have not more than one Representative.

Article 5. Except where otherwise expressly provided in this Covenant or by the terms of the present Treaty, decisions at any meeting of the Assembly or of the Council shall require the agreement of all the Members of the League represented at the meeting.

All matters of procedure at meetings of the Assembly or of the Council, including the appointment of Committees to investigate particular matters, shall be regulated by the Assembly or by the Council and may be decided by a majority of the Members of the League represented at the meeting.

The first meeting of the Assembly and the first meeting of the Council shall be summoned by the President of the United States of America.

Article 6. The permanent Secretariat shall be established at the Seat of the League. The Secretariat shall comprise a Secretary General and such secretaries and staff as may be required.

The first Secretary General shall be the person named in the Annex; thereafter the Secretary General shall be appointed by the Council with the approval of the majority of the Assembly.

The secretaries and staff of the Secretariat shall be appointed by the Secretary General with the approval of the Council.

The Secretary General shall act in that capacity at all meetings of the Assembly and of the Council.

The expenses of the Secretariat shall be borne by the Members of the League in accordance with the apportionment of the expenses of the International Bureau of the Universal Postal Union.[5]

Article 7. The Seat of the League is established at Geneva.

The Council may at any time decide that the Seat of the League shall be established elsewhere.

All positions under or in connection with the League, including the Secretariat, shall be open equally to men and women.

Representatives of the Members of the League and officials of the League when engaged on the business of the League shall enjoy diplomatic privileges and immunities.

---

[5] By an amendment effective August 13, 1924, this paragraph was replaced by the following: "The expenses of the League shall be borne by Members of the League in the proportion decided by the Assembly."

The buildings and other property occupied by the League or its officials or by Representatives attending its meetings shall be inviolable.

Article 8. The Members of the League recognise that the maintenance of peace requires the reduction of national armaments to the lowest point consistent with national safety and the enforcement by common action of international obligations.

The Council, taking account of the geographical situation and circumstances of each State, shall formulate plans for such reduction for the consideration and action of the several Governments.

Such plans shall be subject to reconsideration and revision at least every ten years.

After these plans shall have been adopted by the several Governments, the limits of armaments therein fixed shall not be exceeded without the concurrence of the Council.

The Members of the League agree that the manufacture by private enterprise of munitions and implements of war is open to grave objections. The Council shall advise how the evil effects attendant upon such manufacture can be prevented, due regard being had to the necessities of those Members of the League which are not able to manufacture the munitions and implements of war necessary for their safety.

The Members of the League undertake to interchange full and frank information as to the scale of their armaments, their military, naval and air programmes and the condition of such of their industries as are adaptable to war-like purposes.

Article 9. A permanent Commission shall be constituted to advise the Council on the execution of the provisions of Articles 1 and 8 and on military, naval and air questions generally.

Article 10. The Members of the League undertake to respect and preserve as against external aggression the territorial integrity and existing political independence of all Members of the League. In case of any such aggression or in case of any threat or danger of such aggression the Council shall advise upon the means by which this obligation shall be fulfilled.

Article 11. Any war or threat of war, whether immediately affecting any of the Members of the League or not, is hereby declared a matter of concern to the whole League, and the League shall take any action that may be deemed wise and effectual to safeguard the peace of nations. In case any such emergency should arise the Secretary General shall on the request of any Member of the League forthwith summon a meeting of the Council.

It is also declared to be the friendly right of each Member of the League to bring to the attention of the Assembly or of the Council any circumstance whatever affecting international relations which threatens to disturb international peace or the good understanding between nations upon which peace depends.

Article 12. The Members of the League agree that if there should arise between them any dispute likely to lead to a rupture, they will submit the matter either to arbitration [6] or to inquiry by the Council, and they agree in no case to resort to war until three months after the award by the arbitrators [7] or the report by the Council.

In any case under this Article the award of the arbitrators [7] shall be made within a reasonable time, and the report of the Council shall be made within six months after the submission of the dispute.

Article 13. The Members of the League agree that whenever any dispute shall arise between them which they recognise to be suitable for submission to arbitration [8] and which cannot be satisfactorily settled by diplomacy, they will submit the whole subject-matter to arbitration.[8]

Disputes as to the interpretation of a treaty, as to any question of international law, as to the existence of any fact which if established would constitute a breach of any international obligation, or as to the extent and nature of the reparation to be made for any such breach, are declared to be among those which are generally suitable for submission to arbitration.[8]

For the consideration of any such dispute the court of arbitration to which the case is referred shall be the Court agreed on by the parties to the dispute or stipulated in any convention existing between them.[9]

The Members of the League agree that they will carry out in full good faith any award [10] that may be rendered, and that they will not resort to war against a Member of the League which complies therewith. In the event of any failure to carry out such an award,[10] the Council shall propose what steps should be taken to give effect thereto.

Article 14. The Council shall formulate and submit to the Members of the League for adoption plans for the establishment of a Permanent Court of International Justice. The Court shall be competent to hear and determine any dispute of an international character which the parties thereto submit to it. The Court may also give an advisory opinion upon any dispute or question referred to it by the Council or by the Assembly.

Article 15. If there should arise between Members of the League any dispute likely to lead to a rupture, which is not submitted to arbitration [11] in accordance with Article 13, the Members of the League agree that they

---

6 The words "or judicial settlement" were added by an amendment effective September 26, 1924.

7 The words "or the judicial decision" were added by an amendment effective September 26, 1924.

8 The words "or judicial settlement" were added by an amendment effective September 26, 1924.

9 This paragraph was changed by an amendment effective September 26, 1924, to read as follows: "For the consideration of any such dispute, the court to which the case is referred shall be the Permanent Court of International Justice, established in accordance with Article 14, or any tribunal agreed on by the parties to the dispute or stipulated in any convention existing between them."

10 The words "or decision" were added by the amendment effective September 26, 1924.

11 The words "or judicial settlement" were added by the amendment effective September 26, 1924.

will submit the matter to the Council. Any party to the dispute may effect such submission by giving notice of the existence of the dispute to the Secretary General, who will make all necessary arrangements for a full investigation and consideration thereof.

For this purpose the parties to the dispute will communicate to the Secretary General, as promptly as possible, statements of their case with all the relevant facts and papers, and the Council may forthwith direct the publication thereof.

The Council shall endeavour to effect a settlement of the dispute, and if such efforts are successful, a statement shall be made public giving such facts and explanations regarding the dispute and the terms of settlement thereof as the Council may deem appropriate.

If the dispute is not thus settled, the Council either unanimously or by a majority vote shall make and publish a report containing a statement of the facts of the dispute and the recommendations which are deemed just and proper in regard thereto.

Any Member of the League represented on the Council may make public a statement of the facts of the dispute and of its conclusions regarding the same.

If a report by the Council is unanimously agreed to by the members thereof other than the Representatives of one or more of the parties to the dispute, the Members of the League agree that they will not go to war with any party to the dispute which complies with the recommendations of the report.

If the Council fails to reach a report which is unanimously agreed to by the members thereof, other than the Representatives of one or more of the parties to the dispute, the Members of the League reserve to themselves the right to take such action as they shall consider necessary for the maintenance of right and justice.

If the dispute between the parties is claimed by one of them, and is found by the Council, to arise out of a matter which by international law is solely within the domestic jurisdiction of that party, the Council shall so report, and shall make no recommendation as to its settlement.

The Council may in any case under this Article refer the dispute to the Assembly. The dispute shall be so referred at the request of either party to the dispute, provided that such request be made within fourteen days after the submission of the dispute to the Council.

In any case referred to the Assembly, all the provisions of this Article and of Article 12 relating to the action and powers of the Council shall apply to the action and powers of the Assembly, provided that a report made by the Assembly, if concurred in by the Representatives of those Members of the League represented on the Council and of a majority of the other Members of the League, exclusive in each case of the Representatives of the parties to the dispute, shall have the same force as a report by the Council concurred in by all the members thereof other than the Representatives of one or more of the parties to the dispute.

Article 16. Should any Member of the League resort to war in disregard of its covenants under Articles 12, 13 or 15, it shall *ipso facto* be deemed to have committed an act of war against all other Members of the League, which hereby undertake immediately to subject it to the severance of all trade or financial relations, the prohibition of all intercourse between their nationals and the nationals of the covenant-breaking State, and the prevention of all financial, commercial or personal intercourse between the nationals of the covenant-breaking State and the nationals of any other State, whether a Member of the League or not.

It shall be the duty of the Council in such case to recommend to the several Governments concerned what effective military, naval or air force the Members of the League shall severally contribute to the armed forces to be used to protect the covenants of the League.

The Members of the League agree, further, that they will mutually support one another in the financial and economic measures which are taken under this Article, in order to minimise the loss and inconvenience resulting from the above measures, and that they will mutually support one another in resisting any special measures aimed at one of their number by the covenant-breaking State, and that they will take the necessary steps to afford passage through their territory to the forces of any of the Members of the League which are co-operating to protect the covenants of the League.

Any Member of the League which has violated any covenant of the League may be declared to be no longer a Member of the League by a vote of the Council concurred in by the Representatives of all the other Members of the League represented thereon.

Article 17. In the event of a dispute between a Member of the League and a State which is not a Member of the League, or between States not Members of the League, the State or States not Members of the League shall be invited to accept the obligations of membership in the League for the purposes of such dispute, upon such conditions as the Council may deem just. If such invitation is accepted, the provisions of Articles 12 to 16 inclusive shall be applied with such modifications as may be deemed necessary by the Council.

Upon such invitation being given the Council shall immediately institute an inquiry into the circumstances of the dispute and recommend such action as may seem best and most effectual in the circumstances.

If a State so invited shall refuse to accept the obligations of membership in the League for the purposes of such dispute, and shall resort to war against a Member of the League, the provisions of Article 16 shall be applicable as against the State taking such action.

If both parties to the dispute when so invited refuse to accept the obligations of membership in the League for the purposes of such dispute, the Council may take such measures and make such recommendations as will prevent hostilities and will result in the settlement of the dispute.

Article 18. Every treaty or international engagement entered into hereafter by any Member of the League shall be forthwith registered with the Secretariat and shall as soon as possible be published by it. No such treaty or international engagement shall be binding until so registered.

Article 19. The Assembly may from time to time advise the reconsideration by Members of the League of treaties which have become inapplicable and the consideration of international conditions whose continuance might endanger the peace of the world.

Article 20. The Members of the League severally agree that this Covenant is accepted as abrogating all obligations or understandings *inter se* which are inconsistent with the terms thereof, and solemnly undertake that they will not hereafter enter into any engagements inconsistent with the terms thereof.

In case any Member of the League shall, before becoming a Member of the League, have undertaken any obligations inconsistent with the terms of this Covenant, it shall be the duty of such Member to take immediate steps to procure its release from such obligations.

Article 21. Nothing in this Covenant shall be deemed to affect the validity of international engagements, such as treaties of arbitration or regional understandings like the Monroe doctrine, for securing the maintenance of peace.

Article 22. To those colonies and territories which as a consequence of the late war have ceased to be under the sovereignty of the States which formerly governed them and which are inhabited by peoples not yet able to stand by themselves under the strenuous conditions of the modern world, there should be applied the principle that the well-being and development of such peoples form a sacred trust of civilization and that securities for the performance of this trust should be embodied in this Covenant.

The best method of giving practical effect to this principle is that the tutelage of such peoples should be entrusted to advanced nations who by reason of their resources, their experience or their geographical position can best undertake this responsibility, and who are willing to accept it, and that this tutelage should be exercised by them as Mandatories on behalf of the League.

The character of the mandate must differ according to the stage of the development of the people, the geographical situation of the territory, its economic conditions and other similar circumstances.

Certain communities formerly belonging to the Turkish Empire have reached a stage of development where their existence as independent nations can be provisionally recognised subject to the rendering of administrative advice and assistance by a Mandatory until such time as they are able to stand alone. The wishes of these communities must be a principal consideration in the selection of the Mandatory.

Other peoples, especially those of Central Africa, are at such a stage that the Mandatory must be responsible for the administration of the territory under conditions which will guarantee freedom of conscience and religion, subject only to the maintenance of public order and morals, the prohibition of abuses such as the slave trade, the arms traffic and the liquor traffic, and the prevention of the establishment of fortifications or military and naval bases and of military training of the natives for other than police purposes and the defence of territory, and will also secure equal opportunities for the trade and commerce of other Members of the League.

There are territories, such as South-West Africa and certain of the South Pacific Islands, which, owing to the sparseness of their population, or their small size, or their remoteness from the centres of civilisation, or their geographical contiguity to the territory of the Mandatory, and other circumstances, can be best administered under the laws of the Mandatory as integral portions of its territory, subject to the safeguards above mentioned in the interests of the indigenous population.

In every case of mandate, the Mandatory shall render to the Council an annual report in reference to the territory committed to its charge.

The degree of authority, control, or administration to be exercised by the Mandatory shall, if not previously agreed upon by the Members of the League, be explicitly defined in each case by the Council.

A permanent Commission shall be constituted to receive and examine the annual reports of the Mandatories and to advise the Council on all matters relating to the observance of the mandates.

Article 23. Subject to and in accordance with the provisions of international conventions existing or hereafter to be agreed upon, the Members of the League:

(*a*) will endeavour to secure and maintain fair and humane conditions of labour for men, women, and children, both in their own countries and in all countries to which their commercial and industrial relations extend, and for that purpose will establish and maintain the necessary international organizations;

(*b*) undertake to secure just treatment of the native inhabitants of territories under their control;

(*c*) will entrust the League with the general supervision over the execution of agreements with regard to the traffic in women and children, and the traffic in opium and other dangerous drugs;

(*d*) will entrust the League with the general supervision of the trade in arms and ammunition with the countries in which the control of this traffic is necessary in the common interest;

(*e*) will make provision to secure and maintain freedom of communications and of transit and equitable treatment for the commerce of all Members of the League. In this connection, the special necessities of the regions devastated during the war of 1914–1918 shall be borne in mind;

(*f*) will endeavour to take steps in matters of international concern for the prevention and control of disease.

Article 24. There shall be placed under the direction of the League all international bureaux already established by general treaties if the parties to such treaties consent. All such international bureaux and all commissions for the regulation of matters of international interest hereafter constituted shall be placed under the direction of the League.

In all matters of international interest which are regulated by general conventions but which are not placed under the control of international bureaux or commissions, the Secretariat of the League shall, subject to the consent of the Council and if desired by the Parties, collect and distribute all relevant information and shall render any other assistance which may be necessary or desirable.

The Council may include as part of the expenses of the Secretariat the expenses of any bureau or commission which is placed under the direction of the League.

Article 25. The Members of the League agree to encourage and promote the establishment and co-operation of duly authorised voluntary national Red Cross organizations having as purposes the improvement of health, the prevention of disease and the mitigation of suffering throughout the world.

Article 26. Amendments to this Covenant will take effect when ratified by the Members of the League whose Representatives compose the Council and by a majority of the Members of the League whose Representatives compose the Assembly.

No such amendment shall bind any Member of the League which signifies its dissent therefrom, but in that case it shall cease to be a Member of the League. . . .

◇◇◇◇◇◇◇◇◇◇◇◇◇◇

4. THE LODGE RESERVATIONS TO THE RATIFICATION BY THE UNITED STATES OF THE TREATY OF VERSAILLES [12]

RESOLVED (*two-thirds of the Senators present concurring therein*), That the Senate advise and consent to the ratification of the treaty of peace with Germany concluded at Versailles on the 28th day of June, 1919, subject to the following reservations and understandings, which are hereby made a part and condition of this resolution of ratification, which ratification is not to take effect or bind the United States until the said reservations and understandings adopted by the Senate have been accepted by an exchange of notes as a part and a condition of this resolution of ratification by at least three of the four principal allied and associated powers, to wit, Great Britain, France, Italy, and Japan:

1. The United States so understands and construes article 1 that in case of notice of withdrawal from the league of nations, as provided in said article, the United States shall be the sole judge as to whether all its international obligations and all its obligations under the said covenant have

[12] *Congressional Record* (Senate) 66th Congress, 1st Session, Vol. 58, pp. 8777–8888.

been fulfilled, and notice of withdrawal by the United States may be given by a concurrent resolution of the Congress of the United States.

2. The United States assumes no obligation to preserve the territorial integrity or political independence of any other country or to interfere in controversies between nations — whether members of the league or not — under the provisions of article 10, or to employ the military or naval forces of the United States under any article of the treaty for any purpose, unless in any particular case the Congress, which, under the Constitution, has the sole power to declare war or authorize the employment of the military or naval forces of the United States, shall by act or joint resolution so provide.

3. No mandate shall be accepted by the United States under article 22, part 1, or any other provision of the treaty of peace with Germany, except by action of the Congress of the United States.

4. The United States reserves to itself exclusively the right to decide what questions are within its domestic jurisdiction and declares that all domestic and political questions relating wholly or in part to its internal affairs, including immigration, labor, coastwise traffic, the tariff, commerce, the suppression of traffic in women and children, and in opium and other dangerous drugs, and all other domestic questions, are solely within the jurisdiction of the United States and are not under this treaty to be submitted in any way either to arbitration or to the consideration of the council or of the assembly of the league of nations, or any agency thereof, or to the decision or recommendation of any other power.

5. The United States will not submit to arbitration or to inquiry by the assembly or by the council of the league of nations, provided for in said treaty of peace, any questions which in the judgment of the United States depend upon or relate to its long-established policy, commonly known as the Monroe doctrine; said doctrine is to be interpreted by the United States alone and is hereby declared to be wholly outside the jurisdiction of said league of nations and entirely unaffected by any provision contained in the said treaty of peace with Germany.

6. The United States withholds its assent to articles 156, 157, and 158, and reserves full liberty of action with respect to any controversy which may arise under said articles between the Republic of China and the Empire of Japan.

7. The Congress of the United States will provide by law for the appointment of the representatives of the United States in the assembly and the council of the league of nations, and may in its discretion provide for the participation of the United States in any commission, committee, tribunal, court, council, or conference, or in the selection of any members thereof and for the appointment of members of said commissions, committees, tribunals, courts, councils, or conferences, or any other representatives under the treaty of peace, or in carrying out its provisions, and until such participation and appointment have been so provided for and the powers and duties of such representatives have been defined by law, no person shall represent the United States under either said league of nations

or the treaty of peace with Germany or be authorized to perform any act for or on behalf of the United States thereunder, and no citizen of the United States shall be selected or appointed as a member of said commissions, committees, tribunals, courts, councils, or conferences except with the approval of the Senate of the United States.

8. The United States understands that the reparation commission will regulate or interfere with exports from the United States to Germany, or from Germany to the United States, only when the United States by act or joint resolution of Congress approves such regulation or interference.

9. The United States shall not be obligated to contribute to any expenses of the league of nations, or of the secretariat, or of any commission, or committee, or conference, or other agency, organized under the league of nations or under the treaty or for the purpose of carrying out the treaty provisions, unless and until an appropriation of funds available for such expenses shall have been made by the Congress of the United States.

10. If the United States shall at any time adopt any plan for the limitation of armaments proposed by the council of the league of nations under the provisions of article 8, it reserves the right to increase such armaments without the consent of the council whenever the United States is threatened with invasion or engaged in war.

11. The United States reserves the right to permit, in its discretion, the nationals of a covenant-breaking State, as defined in article 16 of the covenant of the league of nations, residing within the United States or in countries other than that violating said article 16, to continue their commercial, financial, and personal relations with the nationals of the United States.

12. Nothing in articles 296, 297, or in any of the annexes thereto or in any other article, section, or annex of the treaty of peace with Germany shall, as against citizens of the United States, be taken to mean any confirmation, ratification, or approval of any act otherwise illegal or in contravention of the rights of citizens of the United States.

13. The United States withholds its assent to Part XIII (articles 387 to 427, inclusive) unless Congress by act or joint resolution shall hereafter make provision for representation in the organization established by said Part XIII, and in such event the participation of the United States will be governed and conditioned by the provisions of such act or joint resolution.

14. The United States assumes no obligation to be bound by any election, decision, report, or finding of the council or assembly in which any member of the league and its self-governing dominions, colonies, or parts of empire, in the aggregate have cast more than one vote, and assumes no obligation to be bound by any decision, report, or finding of the council or assembly arising out of any dispute between the United States and any member of the league if such member, or any self-governing dominion, colony, empire, or part of empire united with it politically has voted.

◇◇◇◇◇◇◇◇◇◇◇◇◇

5. THE TREATY AND THE SENATE

[*For the "Lodge" Reservations*] [13]

. . . I HAVE NOT liked this treaty; I think, as originally negotiated, it is the colossal blunder of all time; but, recognizing the aspirations of our own people and the people of the world to do something toward international cooperation for the promotion and preservation of peace and a more intimate and better understanding between nations, I have wished to make it possible to accept this covenant. I could, however, no more vote to ratify this treaty without reservations which make sure America's independence of action, which make sure the preservation of American traditions, which make sure and certain our freedom in choosing our course of action, than I could participate in a knowing betrayal of this Republic. . . .

We are content to give you your league of nations, doubtful as we are about the wisdom of the great experiment. . . .

If this ratification is made with the reservations which have been adopted, there remains the skeleton of a league on which the United States can, if it deems it prudent, proceed in deliberation and calm reflection toward the building of an international relationship which shall be effective in the future.

The trouble with the whole league covenant is that it was hastily negotiated to be made the foundation of a treaty of peace, when there ought to have been a treaty of peace negotiated with a league of nations created in the deliberate aftermath.

Under these circumstances, recognizing conditions, without discussing the partisan phase of it or any political advantage, we have this arrangement, and we must meet it as it exists; and those on the majority side, those against it irreconcilably, and those for the league want these reservations to go to the nations of the Old World to assert and make certain America's freedom of action in the future, and leave a semblance of a league on which to build. . . .

I know, Mr. President, that in this covenant we have originally bartered American independence in order to create a league. We have traded away America's freedom of action in order to establish a supergovernment of the world, and it was never intended to be any less. I speak for one who is old-fashioned enough to believe that the Government of the United States of America is good enough for me. In speaking my reverence for the Government of the United States of America, Senators, I want the preservation of those coordinate branches of government which were conceived and instituted by the fathers; and if there is nothing else significant in the action of this day, you can tell to the people of the United States of Amer-

[13] Speech of Senator Warren G. Harding in the Senate, November 19, 1919. *Cong. Record,* 66th Congress, 1st Session, Vol. 58, Part 9, pp. 8791–2.

ica and to the world that the Senate of the United States has once more reasserted its authority, and representative government abides. . . .

[*Against the "Lodge" Reservations*] [14]

MR. PRESIDENT, while I have always believed that the treaty, particularly that part embracing the covenant of the league, carried with it practically all of the interpretations that were offered by the group referred to by the Senator from Ohio as the mild reservationists, I have never brought myself to the point where I would oppose this treaty, if there were reasonable reservations incorporated in the resolution of ratification. The only question that appeals to my mind to-night is this: Are there reservations included in the resolution of ratification that will not be accepted by those Governments that must accept those reservations to make our participation under the treaty legal?

The Senator from North Dakota [Mr. McCumber] has stated on the floor that in his opinion Great Britain, France, and Italy can not in honor accept the committee reservation with regard to Shantung. Are there other Senators on that side who agree with the Senator from North Dakota? If so, then those Senators can not sincerely vote for this resolution of ratification, if they are in favor of the ratification of the treaty. Surely they do not desire to consummate an act that, while it will not kill the treaty to-night, will result in the death of the treaty two months or three months hence. . . .

But what happened? Why was the Shantung provision put into the resolution? Because a majority of the Republican members of the Foreign Relations Committee, that framed these reservations, were and are now against the treaty. They have always been against the treaty from beginning to end, and they had the power in the committee to frame reservations that in their belief would kill it. They were not able upon the floor of the United States Senate, on a straight vote, to kill the league of nations and the treaty, but they hoped to kill it by subterfuge and they forced these reservations upon the Senate.

On the other side you cast to-night 13 votes against the resolution of ratification. You who on the Republican side favor the treaty have barely more than one-third of the Members of the Senate. You have never had a majority on the other side in favor of this treaty. We have more Members on this side in favor of this treaty; and yet you Republicans on the other side who favor this treaty, who do not constitute as many as we Democrats on this side who favor this treaty, will not stand by us in any amendment or any change that we offer to any one of these abominable reservations that were written by the "treaty killers" on the other side. . . .

All the way through, from the very beginning to the end, there were offered on the other side by the Senator from North Dakota [Mr. McCumber], or there were offered on this side by the Senator from Nebraska

[14] Speech of Senator Key Pittman in the Senate, November 19, 1919. Ibid., pp. 8793–6.

[Mr. Hitchcock] or other Democratic Senators, substitute reservations, for practically every reservation offered by the majority, and in nearly every case those reservations which were offered as substitutes were the reservations that had been prepared by the so-called mild reservationists on the Republican side, and yet the Democrats are said not to have offered any opportunity for compromise. The Democrats voted for them in every case, while the Republicans voted against them in every case.

I contend now, and the *Record* will disclose, that every reservation contained in the Republican resolution of ratification was dictated and framed by the identical men who voted to-night to kill the treaty. There was not a case but what, if those men had not voted against the substitutes for the Republican reservations, the substitutes would have carried. . . .

When you unmask all of the hypocrisy surrounding this whole transaction, when you see the leaders of the great Republican Party, representing the people of this country, pretending that they are doing everything in God's world to ratify a treaty, and at the same time you see them call to their aid to prepare the reservations the men who are killing the treaty, and you see them acting with them for the purpose of defeating amendments of Senators like the Senator from North Dakota [Mr. McCumber], who they admit are honestly for the treaty, their interest and sincerity and consistency at least are open to suspicion on the part of the people of the country.

But they say that we have offered no compromise. I say to you that we have offered compromises on the floor of the Senate which even the Senator from North Dakota would admit would have been accepted two months ago. Why will they not be accepted to-day? Conditions have not changed in the world. The reservations are just the same. The reasons they will not be accepted to-day, and he will admit it, are purely political reasons, and nothing else on earth. Then if he will not accept them on the ground of political reasons he need not appeal to us on the high ground that they are trying to ratify a treaty with those countries for the sake of humanity throughout the world. . . .

I simply want to say this in conclusion, because my time is nearly up, that if Senators on the other side who favor the treaty — and I do not know how many of you there are, and I doubt if there are very many of you — if those of you there who are honest and sincere, if those of you there who hold your country above your party, are willing to join us on this side, I feel assured we can get you enough votes to ratify this treaty with reservations that you yourselves would have accepted two months ago.

If you had adopted the amendment of the Senator from North Dakota with regard to the preamble, if you had adopted his suggestions with regard to article 1, if you had adopted his reservation with regard to the Monroe doctrine, if you had adopted his first suggestion with regard to Shantung, which I offered as a substitute, although there is very little left of the original covenant, and while we are simply standing in the league as advisors, and while we have thrown off the burden of responsibility, there would be something left that possibly when we come into our own senses we could later rectify.

It would be the foundation upon which Republicans and Democrats later on could build a better edifice than the Republican Party have left. Change it in those particulars and I will vote for your reservations, and I will vote for your resolution of ratification, bad and insignificant and destructive as it is.

On the other hand, if you do not cut out of the resolution of ratification those reservations that you know will destroy the treaty, if you persist in that fraud upon the American people and that fraud upon the world, then I tell you there are enough fearless Democrats on this side of the Chamber to prevent its ratification until the American people understand. We may adopt the policy of isolation, and profit; we may decide to remain in an existence of selfishness, greed, and war, but we will not stand for national cowardice, pretense, and dishonesty. . . .

◇◇◇◇◇◇◇◇◇◇◇◇◇

6. THE LEAGUE ISSUE: 1920

[*President Wilson's Views on Article 10 of the Covenant*]

. . . YOU HAVE heard a great deal about Article X of the Covenant of the League of Nations. Article X speaks the conscience of the world. Article X is the article which goes to the heart of this whole bad business, for that article says that the members of this League (that is intended to be all the great nations of the world) engage to respect and to preserve against all external aggression the territorial integrity and political independence of the nations concerned. That promise is necessary in order to prevent this sort of war from recurring, and we are absolutely discredited if we fought this war and then neglect the essential safeguard against it. You have heard it said, my fellow citizens, that we are robbed of some degree of our sovereign, independent choice by articles of that sort. Every man who makes a choice to respect the rights of his neighbors deprives himself of absolute sovereignty, but he does it by promising never to do wrong, and I cannot for one see anything that robs me of any inherent right that I ought to retain when I promise that I will do right, when I promise that I will respect the thing which, being disregarded and violated, brought on a war in which millions of men lost their lives, in which the civilization of mankind was in the balance, in which there was the most outrageous exhibition ever witnessed in the history of mankind of the rapacity and disregard for right of a great armed people.

We engage in the first sentence of Article X to respect and preserve from external aggression the territorial integrity and the existing political independence not only of the other member States, but of all States, and if any member of the League of Nations disregards that promise, then what happens? The council of the League advises what should be done to enforce the respect for that Covenant on the part of the nation attempting to violate it, and there is no compulsion upon us to take that advice except the compulsion of our good conscience and judgment. It is perfectly evident that if, in the judgment of the people of the United States the council adjudged wrong and that this was not a case for the use of force, there would be no necessity on the part of the Congress of the United States to vote the use of force. But there could be no advice of the council on any such subject without a unanimous vote, and the unanimous vote includes our own, and if we accepted the advice we would be accepting our own advice. For I need not tell you that the representatives of the Government of the United States would not vote without instructions from their Government at home, and that what we united in advising we could be certain that the American people would desire to do. There is in that Covenant not only not a surrender of the independent judgment of the Government of the United States, but an expression of it, because that independent judgment would have to join with the judgment of the rest.

But when is that judgment going to be expressed, my fellow citizens? Only after it is evident that every other resource has failed, and I want to call your attention to the central machinery of the League of Nations. If any member of that League, or any nation not a member, refuses to submit the question at issue either to arbitration or to discussion by the council, there ensues automatically by the engagements of this Covenant an absolute economic boycott. There will be no trade with that nation by any member of the League. There will be no interchange of communication by post or telegraph. There will be no travel to or from that nation. Its borders will be closed. No citizen of any other State will be allowed to enter it, and no one of its citizens will be allowed to leave it. It will be hermetically sealed by the united action of the most powerful nations in the world. And if this economic boycott bears with unequal weight, the members of the League agree to support one another and to relieve one another in any exceptional disadvantages that may arise out of it.

I want you to realize that this war was won not only by the armies of the world. It was won by economic means as well. Without the economic means the war would have been much longer continued. What happened was that Germany was shut off from the economic resources of the rest of the globe and she could not stand it. A nation that is boycotted is a nation that is in sight of surrender. Apply this economic, peaceful, silent, deadly remedy and there will be no need for force. It is a terrible remedy. It does not cost a life outside the nation boycotted, but it brings a pressure upon that nation which, in my judgment, no modern nation could resist. . . .

I was pointing out, my fellow citizens, this forenoon, that this Covenant is part of a great document. I wish I had brought a copy with me to show you its bulk. It is an enormous volume, and most of the things you hear talked about in that treaty are not the essential things. This is the first treaty in the history of civilization in which great powers have associated themselves together in order to protect the weak. I need not tell you that I speak with knowledge in this matter, knowledge of the purpose of the men with whom the American delegates were associated at the peace table. They came there, every one that I consulted with, with the same idea, that wars had arisen in the past because the strong took advantage of the weak, and that the only way to stop wars was to bind ourselves together to protect the weak; that the example of this war was the example which gave us the finger to point the way of escape: That as Austria and Germany had tried to put upon Serbia, so we must see to it that Serbia and the Slavic peoples associated with her, and the peoples of Rumania, and the people of Bohemia, and the peoples of Hungary and Austria for that matter, should feel assured in the future that the strength of the great powers was behind their liberty and their independence and was not intended to be used, and never should be used for aggression against them.

So when you read the Covenant, read the treaty with it. I have no doubt that in this audience there are many men which come from that ancient stock of Poland, for example, men in whose blood there is the warmth of old affections connected with that betrayed and ruined country, men whose memories run back to intolerable wrongs suffered by those they love in that country, and I call them to witness that Poland never could have won unity and independence for herself, and those gentlemen sitting at Paris presented Poland with a unity which she could not have won and an independence which she cannot defend unless the world guarantees it to her. There is one of the most noble chapters in the history of the world, that this war was concluded in order to remedy the wrongs which had bitten so deep into the experience of the weaker peoples of that great continent. The object of the war was to see to it that there was no more of that sort of wrong done. Now, when you have that picture in your mind, that this treaty was meant to protect those who could not protect themselves, turn the picture and look at it this way:

Those very weak nations are situated through the very tract of country – between Germany and Persia – which Germany had meant to conquer and dominate, and if the nations of the world do not maintain their concert to sustain the independence and freedom of those peoples, Germany will yet have her will upon them, and we shall witness the very interesting spectacle of having spent millions upon millions of American treasure and, what is much more precious, hundreds of thousands of American lives, to do a futile thing, to do a thing which we will then leave to be undone at the leisure of those who are masters of intrigue, at the leisure of those who are masters in combining wrong influences to overcome right influences, of those who are the masters of the very things that we hate and mean always to fight. For, my fellow citizens, if Germany should ever attempt that again, whether we are in the League of Nations or not, we will join to prevent it. We do not stand off and see murder done. We do not profess to be the champions of liberty and then consent to see liberty destroyed. We are not the friends and advocates of free government and then willing to stand by and see free government die before our eyes. If a power such as Germany was, but thank God no longer is, were to do this thing upon the fields of Europe, then America would have to look to it that she did not do it also upon the fields of the Western Hemisphere, and we should at last be face to face with a power which at the outset we could have crushed, and which now it is within our choice to keep within the harness of civilization. . . .

I want to call your attention, if you will turn to it when you go home, to Article XI, following Article X, of the Covenant of the League of Nations. That article, let me say, is the favorite article in the treaty, so far as I am concerned. It says that every matter which is likely to affect the peace of the world is everybody's business; that it shall be the friendly right of any nation to call attention in the League to anything that is likely to affect the peace of the world or the good understanding between nations, upon which the peace of the world depends, whether that matter immediately concerns the nation drawing attention to it or not. In other words, at present we have to mind our own business. Under the Covenant of the League of Nations we can mind other peoples' business, and anything that affects the peace of the world, whether we are parties to it or not, can by our delegates be brought to the attention of mankind. We can force a nation on the other side of the globe to bring to that bar of mankind any wrong that is afoot in that part of the world which is likely to affect good understanding between nations, and we can oblige them to show cause why it should not be remedied. There is not an oppressed people in the world which cannot henceforth get a hearing at that forum, and you know, my fellow citizens, what a hearing will mean if the cause of those people is just. The one thing that those who are doing injustice have most reason to dread is publicity and discussion, because if you are challenged to give a reason why you are doing a wrong thing it has to be an exceedingly good reason, and if you give a bad reason you confess judgment and the opinion of mankind goes against you. . . .[15]

The solemn thing about Article X is the first sentence, not the second sentence. The first sentence says that we will respect and preserve against external aggression the territorial integrity and existing political independence of other nations; and let me stop a moment on the words "external aggression." Why were they put in? Because every man who sat at that board held that the right of revolution was sacred and must not be interfered with. Any kind of a row can happen inside and it is nobody's right to interfere. The only thing that there is any right to object to or interfere with is external aggression, by some outside power undertaking to take a piece of territory or to interfere with the internal political ar-

[15] Address at Indianapolis, Sept. 4, 1919. *Senate Doc.* No. 120, 66th Congress, 1st Session (7606) pp. 19–28.

rangements of the country which is suffering from the aggression; because territorial integrity does not mean that you cannot invade another country; it means that you cannot invade it and stay there. I have not impaired the territorial integrity of your back yard if I walk into it, but I very much impair it if I insist upon staying there and will not get out, and the impairment of integrity contemplated in this article is the kind of impairment as the seizure of territory, as an attempt at annexation, as an attempt at continuing domination either of the territory itself or of the methods of government inside that territory.

When you read Article X, therefore, you will see that it is nothing but the inevitable, logical center of the whole system of the Covenant of the League of Nations, and I stand for it absolutely. If it should ever in any important respect be impaired, I would feel like asking the Secretary of War to get the boys who went across the water to fight together on some field where I could go and see them, and I would stand up before them and say, "Boys, I told you before you went across the seas that this was a war against wars, and I did my best to fulfill the promise, but I am obliged to come to you in mortification and shame and say I have not been able to fulfill the promise. You are betrayed. You fought for something that you did not get." And the glory of the Armies and the Navies of the United States is gone like a dream in the night, and there ensues upon it, in the suitable darkness of the night, the nightmare of dread which lay upon the nations before this war came; and there will come sometime, in the vengeful Providence of God, another struggle in which, not a few hundred thousand fine men from America will have to die, but as many millions as are necessary to accomplish the final freedom of the peoples of the world. . . .[16]

[*Senator Harding's Position on the League*]

. . . THE ISSUE, which our opponents are endeavoring to bring, is singularly simple and direct. The issue . . . does not present to the American people the question whether they shall favor some form of association among the nations for the purpose of preserving international peace, but whether they favor the particular League proposed by President Wilson.

The (Democratic) Platform, to be sure, approaches its endorsement with winding words . . . but it does, nevertheless, endorse the League as it stands. . . . It goes no further than to suggest that reservations will not be opposed which make clearer or more specific the obligations of the United States and the League.

But there is no need of reservations of this character. The obligations are clear enough and specific enough. I oppose the League not because I fail to understand . . . "what we are being let in for," but because I believe I understand precisely what we are being let in for.

[16] Address at St. Louis, Sept. 5, 1919. Ibid., pp. 29–38.

I do not want to clarify these obligations; I want to turn my back on them. It is not interpretation but rejection, that I am seeking. My position is that the present league strikes a deadly blow at our constitutional integrity and surrenders to a dangerous extent our independence of action. . . .

The issue therefore is clear. I understand the position of the Democratic candidate and he understands mine. . . . It is that he favors going into the Paris League and I favor staying out. . . .

As soon as possible after my election I shall advise with the best minds in the United States. . . . I shall do this to the end that we shall have an association of nations for the promotion of international peace, but one which shall so definitely safeguard our sovereignty and recognise our ultimate and unmortgaged freedom of action . . . that it will have back of it the united support of the American people. . . .[17]

[*Herbert Hoover on the League Issue*]

. . . INASMUCH as forty nations, comprising three-quarters of the people of the globe have embraced the "League of Nations" as a term expressing certain ideas, I prefer that term, but I care little for terminology. . . . The essential thing is that the Republican Party has pledged itself by its platform, by the actions of its majority in the Senate, by the repeated statements of Senator Harding, that they undertake the fundamental mission to put into living being the principle of an organized association of nations for the preservation of peace. The carrying out of this promise is the test of the entire sincerity, integrity, and statesmanship of the Republican Party. . . .

If there be persons supporting the Republican Party today on the belief or hope that this party is the avenue to destruction of this great principle, that the party will not with sincerity and statesmanship carry out their pledges to bring it into effect, then they are counting on the insincerity and infidelity of the Republican Party and its nominee for the Presidency. . . .[18]

[*The "Statement of the 31"*]

THE UNDERSIGNED, who desire that the United States shall do her full part in association with the other civilized nations to prevent war, have earnestly considered how we may contribute most effectively to that end by our votes in the coming election.

The question between the candidates is not whether our country shall join in such an association. It is whether we shall join under an agreement containing the exact provisions negotiated by President Wilson at Paris, or under an agreement which omits or modifies some of those provisions that are very objectionable to great numbers of the American people. . . .

[17] Speech at Des Moines, Oct. 7, 1920. *New York Times*, Oct. 8, 1920.
[18] Speech at Indianapolis, Oct. 9, 1920. *New York Times*, Oct. 10, 1920.

The principal change proposed concerns Article X, of the League Covenant as negotiated at Paris. Mr. Wilson declares this to be "the heart of the League" and the chief controversy is about this.

Article X provides that the nations agreeing to the treaty shall "preserve as against external aggression the territorial integrity and existing political independence of all members of the League."

That is an obligation of the most vital importance and it certainly binds every nation entering into it to go to war whenever war may be necessary to preserve the territorial integrity or political independence of any member of the League against external aggression. . . .

We cannot regard such a provision as necessary or useful for a league to preserve peace.

We have reached the conclusion that the true course to bring America into an effective league to preserve peace is not by insisting with Mr. Cox upon the acceptance of such a provision as Article X, thus prolonging the unfortunate situation created by Mr. Wilson's insistence upon that article, but by frankly calling upon the other nations to agree to changes in the proposed agreement which will obviate this vital objection and other objections less the subject of dispute.

For this course we can look only to the Republican Party and its candidate; the Democratic Party and Mr. Cox are not bound to follow it. The Republican Party is bound by every consideration of good faith to pursue such a course until the declared object is attained. . . .[19]

◇◇◇◇◇◇◇◇◇◇◇◇◇

7. TREATY OF PEACE BETWEEN THE UNITED STATES AND GERMANY

[*Signed at Berlin August 25, 1921; ratifications exchanged at Berlin November 11, 1921*]

. . . *ARTICLE I.* Germany undertakes to accord to the United States, and the United States shall have and enjoy, all the rights, privileges, indemnities, reparations or advantages specified in the aforesaid Joint Resolution of the Congress of the United States of July 2, 1921, including all the rights and advantages stipulated for the benefit of the United States in the Treaty of Versailles which the United States shall fully enjoy notwithstanding the fact that such Treaty has not been ratified by the United States.

Article II. With a view to defining more particularly the obligations of Germany under the foregoing Article with respect to certain provisions in

[19] The "Statement of the 31" was made public Oct. 15, 1920. Among the thirty-one signers of the statement were the following: Herbert Hoover, Charles Evans Hughes, Elihu Root, and Henry L. Stimson. *New York Times,* Oct. 15, 1920.

the Treaty of Versailles, it is understood and agreed between the High Contracting Parties:

(1) That the rights and advantages stipulated in that Treaty for the benefit of the United States, which it is intended the United States shall have and enjoy, are those defined in Section I, of Part IV, and Parts V, VI, VIII, IX, X, XI, XII, XIV, and XV.

The United States in availing itself of the rights and advantages stipulated in the provisions of that Treaty mentioned in this paragraph will do so in a manner consistent with the rights accorded to Germany under such provisions.

(2) That the United States shall not be bound by the provisions of Part I of that Treaty, nor by any provisions of that Treaty including those mentioned in Paragraph (1) of this Article, which relate to the Covenant of the League of Nations, nor shall the United States be bound by any action taken by the League of Nations, or by the Council or by the Assembly thereof, unless the United States shall expressly give its assent to such action.

(3) That the United States assumes no obligations under or with respect to the provisions of Part II, Part III, Sections 2 to 8 inclusive of Part IV, and Part XIII of that Treaty.

(4) That, while the United States is privileged to participate in the Reparation Commission, according to the terms of Part VIII of that Treaty, and in any other Commission established under the Treaty or under any agreement supplemental thereto, the United States is not bound to participate in any such commission unless it shall elect to do so. . . .[20]

---

[20] *The Statutes at Large of the United States,* Vol. 42, Pt. 2, pp. 1939–45. The treaty was signed by Ellis Loring Dresel and Dr. Friedrich Rosen.

Chapter XXVIII

THE LIMITATION OF COMPETITIVE ARMAMENT

FROM THE END of the first World War until well after the second World War had begun in Manchuria and in Ethiopia, some of the principal powers of the world endeavored to reduce the burden of competitive armament. The necessity for arms limitation was one of the cornerstones of President Wilson's program for world peace, and the problem was dealt with in Articles 8 and 9 of the Covenant.

President Wilson believed that, as far as the great powers were concerned, there were only two alternatives with regard to national security. One was for each nation to rely upon its own military strength, and the other was to develop effective international action against aggression. If a nation chose self-help it would be utterly improvident, Wilson thought, if it did not devote its major resources to military preparation, and if it chose collective security, it should join the League of Nations (1).

The people, however, who opposed the League of Nations were unwilling to accept the logic of the Wilsonian alternatives. They held that it was possible to escape the necessity for great military preparation and the burden of arms competition by the reduction of armaments on a parity basis, each nation retaining, after reductions had been effected, the same relative strength that it originally possessed. They believed also that this could be accomplished piecemeal, one category of armament at a time, and that it could be done without reference to political arrangements or to the League. This was the theory underlying the Washington Conference for the Limitation of Naval Armament which met on November 12, 1921.

The conference was successful in drawing up a treaty for the limitation of certain types of naval armament (2A), but political problems were not wholly avoided. The treaty on submarine and chemical warfare (2B), the Nine-Power Treaty (2C), concerning China, and the Four-Power Treaty (2D), concerning the Pacific area, were integral parts of the arrangement effected at the conference.

The Washington treaties received diverse interpretations. President Harding emphasized the negative side of the treaties (3A). Secretary of State Hughes believed that they put an end to naval competition (3B). Elmer Davis, who covered the conference for the *New York Times*, was impressed with the gains secured by Japan (3C). One of the most penetrating analyses of the conference, however, was made by a retired American naval officer, who stressed the weakened position of the United States (3D).

The Washington Conference did not end the attempt to deal with the problem of armament. Continuing the idea of parity reduction established at Washington, a second conference was held at Geneva in 1927, and a third at London in 1930. The Geneva conference was unsuccessful but at London the United States, Great Britain, and Japan agreed, among other matters, to a ratio in cruisers and submarines. Since these conferences did not alter the policy of the United States regarding armament, and the results of the conferences did not change the trends that were noted in the Washington Conference, materials concerning them have been omitted here.

While these several conferences regarding the limitation of naval armament were in progress outside the League of Nations, the League was making plans for a general disarmament conference. The policy of the United States regarding this conference is shown in the proposals of President Hoover of June 22, 1932 (4).

◇◇◇◇◇◇◇◇◇◇◇◇◇◇

1. THE ALTERNATIVE TO INTERNATIONAL NAVAL AND MILITARY COMPETITION

. . . I VENTURE thus again to urge my advice that the action of the Senate with regard to the treaty be taken at the earliest practicable moment because the problems with which we are face to face in the readjustment of our national life are of the most pressing and critical character, will require for their proper solution the most intimate and disinterested cooperation of all parties and all interests, and cannot be postponed without manifest peril to our people and to all the national advantages we hold most dear. May I mention a few of the matters which cannot be handled with intelligence until the country knows the character of the peace it is to have? . . .

Our military plans of course wait upon it. We cannot intelligently or wisely decide how large a naval or military force we shall maintain or what our policy with regard to military training is to be until we have peace not only, but also until we know how peace is to be sustained, whether by the arms of single nations or by the concert of all the great peoples. . . .[1]

Very well, then, if we must stand apart and be the hostile rivals of the rest of the world, then we must do something else. We must be physically ready for anything that comes. We must have a great standing army. We must see to it that every man in America is trained to arms. We must see

[1] Statement of President Wilson to the Committee on Foreign Relations of the United States Senate, Aug. 19, 1919. 66th Congress, 1st Session, Senate Documents, No. 106, p. 499.

to it that there are munitions and guns enough for an army that means a mobilized nation; that they are not only laid up in store, but that they are kept up to date; that they are ready to use tomorrow; that we are a nation in arms; because you cannot be unfriendly to everybody without being ready that everybody shall be unfriendly to you. And what does that mean? Reduction of taxes? No. Not only the continuation of the present taxes but the increase of the present taxes; and it means something very much more serious than that. We can stand that, so far as the expense is concerned, if we care to keep up the high cost of living and enjoy the other luxuries that we have recently enjoyed, but, what is much more serious than that, we have got to have the sort of organization which is the only kind of organization that can handle arms of that sort. We may say what we please of the German Government that has been destroyed, my fellow citizens, but it was the only sort of government that could handle an armed nation. You cannot handle an armed nation by vote. You cannot handle an armed nation if it is democratic, because democracies do not go to war that way. You have got to have a concentrated, militaristic organization of government to run a nation of that sort. You have got to think of the President of the United States, not as the chief counsellor of the Nation, elected for a little while, but as the man meant constantly and every day to be the Commander in Chief of the Army and Navy of the United States, ready to order them to any part of the world where the threat of war is a menace to his own people. And you cannot do that under free debate. You cannot do that under public counsel. Plans must be kept secret. Knowledge must be accumulated by a system which we have condemned, because we have called it a spying system. The more polite call it a system of intelligence. . . .

And you know what the effect of a military government is upon social questions. You know how impossible it is to effect social reform if everybody must be under orders from the Government. You know how impossible it is, in short, to have a free nation, if it is a military nation and under military order.[2] . . .

◇◇◇◇◇◇◇◇◇◇◇◇◇

2. THE WASHINGTON TREATIES

(A). THE LIMITATION OF NAVAL ARMAMENT

. . . *ARTICLE III.* Subject to the provisions of Article II, the Contracting Powers shall abandon their respective capital ship building programs, and no new capital ships shall be constructed or acquired by any of the Contracting Powers except replacement tonnage which may be constructed or acquired as specified in Chapter II, Part 3. . . .

Article IV. The total capital ship replacement tonnage of each of the

[2] Speech of President Wilson at St. Louis, Mo., September 5, 1919. 66th Congress, 1st Session, Senate Documents, No. 120, pp. 42–3.

Contracting Powers shall not exceed in standard displacement, for the United States, 525,000 tons (533,400 metric tons); for the British Empire 525,000 tons (533,400 metric tons); for France 175,000 tons (177,800 metric tons); for Italy 175,000 tons (177,800 metric tons); for Japan 315,000 tons (320,040 metric tons).

Article V. No capital ship exceeding 35,000 tons (35,560 metric tons) standard displacement shall be acquired by, or constructed by, for, or within the jurisdiction of, any of the Contracting Powers.

Article VI. No capital ship of any of the Contracting Powers shall carry a gun with a calibre in excess of 16 inches (406 millimetres).

Article VII. The total tonnage for aircraft carriers of each of the Contracting Powers shall not exceed in standard displacement, for the United States 135,000 tons (137,160 metric tons); for the British Empire 135,000 tons (137,160 metric tons); for France 60,000 tons (60,960 metric tons); for Italy 60,000 tons (60,960 metric tons); for Japan 81,000 tons (82,296 metric tons). . . .

Article XI. No vessel of war exceeding 10,000 tons (10,160 metric tons) standard displacement, other than a capital ship or aircraft carrier, shall be acquired by, or constructed by, for, or within the jurisdiction of, any of the Contracting Powers. Vessels not specifically built as fighting ships nor taken in time of peace under government control for fighting purposes, which are employed on fleet duties or as troop transports or in some other way for the purpose of assisting in the prosecution of hostilities otherwise than as fighting ships, shall not be within the limitations of this Article. . . .

Article IX. The United States, the British Empire and Japan agree that the status quo at the time of the signing of the present Treaty, with regard to fortifications and naval bases, shall be maintained in their respective territories and possessions specified hereunder:

(1) The insular possessions which the United States now holds or may hereafter acquire in the Pacific Ocean, except (a) those adjacent to the coast of the United States, Alaska and the Panama Canal Zone, not including the Aleutian Islands, and (b) the Hawaiian Islands;

(2) Hongkong and the insular possessions which the British Empire now holds or may hereafter acquire in the Pacific Ocean, east of the meridian of 110° east longitude, except (a) those adjacent to the coast of Canada, (b) the Commonwealth of Australia and its Territories, and (c), New Zealand;

(3) The following insular territories and possessions of Japan in the Pacific Ocean, to wit: the Kurile Islands, the Bonin Islands, Anami-Oshima, the Loochoo Islands, Formosa and the Pescadores, and any insular territories or possessions in the Pacific Ocean which Japan may hereafter acquire.

The maintenance of the status quo under the foregoing provisions implies that no new fortifications or naval bases shall be established in the territories and possessions specified that no measures shall be taken to increase the existing naval facilities for the repair and maintenance of naval forces, and that no increase shall be made in the coast defenses of the territories and possessions above specified. This restriction, however, does not preclude such repair and replacement of worn-out weapons and equipment as is customary in naval and military establishments in time of peace. . . .[3]

(B) THE TREATY ON SUBMARINE AND CHEMICAL WARFARE

Article I. The Signatory Powers declare that among the rules adopted by civilized nations for the protection of the lives of neutrals and noncombatants at sea in time of war, the following are to be deemed an established part of international law;

(1) A merchant vessel must be ordered to submit to visit and search to determine its character before it can be seized.

A merchant vessel must not be attacked unless it refuse to submit to visit and search after warning, or to proceed as directed after seizure.

A merchant vessel must not be destroyed unless the crew and passengers have been first placed in safety.

(2) Belligerent submarines are not under any circumstances exempt from the universal rules above stated; and if a submarine can not capture a merchant vessel in conformity with these rules the existing law of nations requires it to desist from attack and from seizure and to permit the merchant vessel to proceed unmolested. . . .

Article IV. The Signatory Powers recognize the practical impossibility of using submarines as commerce destroyers without violating, as they were violated in the recent war of 1914–1918, the requirements universally accepted by civilized nations for the protection of the lives of neutrals and noncombatants, and to the end that the prohibition of the use of submarines as commerce destroyers shall be universally accepted as a part of the law of nations they now accept that prohibition as henceforth binding as between themselves and they invite all other nations to adhere thereto.

Article V. The use in war of asphyxiating, poisonous or other gases, and all analogous liquids, materials or devices, having been justly condemned by the general opinion of the civilized world and a prohibition of such use having been declared in treaties to which a majority of the civilized Powers are parties.

The Signatory Powers, to the end that this prohibition shall be universally accepted as a part of international law binding alike the conscience and practice of nations, declare their assent to such prohibition, agree to be bound thereby as between themselves and invite all other civilized nations to adhere thereto. . . .[4]

[3] Signed by the United States of America, the British Empire, France, Italy, and Japan on February 6, 1922; proclaimed August 21, 1923. United States *Treaty Series*, No. 671, Washington, 1923.

[4] *Treaties . . . Between the United States and Other Powers,* 1910–23, pp. 3117–19.

(C) THE NINE-POWER TREATY.

. . . *Article I.* The Contracting Powers, other than China, agree:

(1) To respect the sovereignty, the independence, and the territorial and administrative integrity of China;

(2) To provide the fullest and most unembarrassed opportunity to China to develop and maintain for herself an effective and stable government;

(3) To use their influence for the purpose of effectually establishing and maintaining the principle of equal opportunity for the commerce and industry of all nations throughout the territory of China;

(4) To refrain from taking advantage of conditions in China in order to seek special rights or privileges which would abridge the rights of subjects or citizens of friendly States, and from countenancing action inimical to the security of such States.

Article II. The Contracting Powers agree not to enter into any treaty, agreement, arrangement or understanding, either with one another, or, individually or collectively, with any Power or Powers, which would infringe or impair the principles stated in Article I.

Article III. With a view to applying more effectually the principles of the Open Door or equality of opportunity in China for the trade and industry of all nations, the Contracting Powers, other than China, agree that they will not seek, nor support their respective nationals in seeking —

(a) any arrangement which might purport to establish in favor of their interests any general superiority of rights with respect to commercial or economic development in any designated region of China;

(b) any such monopoly or preference as would deprive the nationals of any other Power of the right of undertaking any legitimate trade or industry in China, or of participating with the Chinese Government, or with any local authority, in any category of public enterprise, or which by reason of its scope, duration or geographical extent is calculated to frustrate the practical application of the principle of equal opportunity.

It is understood that the foregoing stipulations of this Article are not to be so construed as to prohibit the acquisition of such properties or rights as may be necessary to the conduct of a particular commercial, industrial or financial undertaking or to the encouragement of invention and research.

China undertakes to be guided by the principles stated in the foregoing stipulations of this Article in dealing with applications for economic rights and privileges from Governments and nationals of all foreign countries, whether parties to the present Treaty or not.

Article IV. The Contracting Powers agree not to support any agreements by their respective nationals with each other designed to create Spheres

---

This treaty was signed by the United States, the British Empire, France, Italy, and Japan. France failed to ratify the treaty, however, and it did not come into force.

of Influence or to provide for the enjoyment of mutually exclusive opportunities in designated parts of Chinese territory.

Article V. China agrees that, throughout the whole of the railways in China, she will not exercise or permit unfair discrimination of any kind. In particular there shall be no discrimination whatever, direct or indirect, in respect of charges or of facilities on the ground of the nationality of passengers or the countries from which or to which they are proceeding, or the origin or ownership of goods or the country from which or to which they are consigned, or the nationality or ownership of the ship or other means of conveying such passengers or goods before or after their transport on the Chinese Railways.

The Contracting Powers, other than China, assume a corresponding obligation in respect of any of the aforesaid railways over which they or their nationals are in a position to exercise any control in virtue of any concession, special agreement or otherwise.

Article VI. The Contracting Powers, other than China, agree fully to respect China's rights as a neutral in time of war to which China is not a party; and China declares that when she is a neutral she will observe the obligations of neutrality.

Article VII. The Contracting Powers agree that, whenever a situation arises which in the opinion of any one of them involves the application of the stipulations of the present Treaty, and renders desirable discussion of such application, there shall be full and frank communication between the Contracting Powers concerned. . . .[5]

(D) THE FOUR-POWER TREATY

. . . I. The High Contracting Parties agree as between themselves to respect their rights in relation to their insular possessions and insular dominions in the region of the Pacific Ocean.

If there should develop between any of the High Contracting Parties a controversy arising out of any Pacific question and involving their said rights which is not satisfactorily settled by diplomacy and is likely to affect the harmonious accord now happily subsisting between them, they shall invite the other High Contracting Parties to a joint conference to which the whole subject will be referred for consideration and adjustment.

II. If the said rights are threatened by the aggressive action of any other Power, the High Contracting Parties shall communicate with one another fully and frankly in order to arrive at an understanding as to the most efficient measures to be taken, jointly or separately, to meet the exigencies of the particular situation.

III. This Treaty shall remain in force for 10 years from the time it shall

[5] Signed at Washington, February 6, 1922, by Belgium, the British Empire, China, France, Italy, Japan, the Netherlands, and Portugal; adhered to by Bolivia, Denmark, Mexico, Norway, and Sweden. Ratification advised by the United States Senate, March 30, 1922; in force from August 5, 1925. United States *Treaty Series,* No. 723, Washington, 1925.

take effect, and after the expiration of said period it shall continue to be in force subject to the right of any of the High Contracting Parties to terminate it upon 12 months' notice.

IV. This Treaty shall be ratified as soon as possible in accordance with the constitutional methods of the High Contracting Parties and shall take effect on the deposit of ratifications, which shall take place at Washington, and thereupon the agreement between Great Britain and Japan, which was concluded at London on July 13, 1911, shall terminate. The Government of the United States will transmit to all the signatory Powers a certified copy of the *proces-verbal* of the deposit of ratifications. . . .[6]

3. CONTEMPORARY VIEWS OF THE WASHINGTON TREATIES

(A) PRESIDENT HARDING'S APPEAL TO THE SENATE

I AM NOT unmindful, nor was the conference, of the sentiment in this Chamber against Old World entanglements. Those who made the treaties have left no doubt about their true import. Every expression in the conference has emphasized the purpose to be served and the obligations assumed. Therefore, I can bring you every assurance that nothing in any of these treaties commits the United States, or any other power, to any kind of an alliance, entanglement, or involvement. It does not require us or any power to surrender a worth-while tradition. . . .

The world has been hungering for a better relationship for centuries since it has attained its larger consciousness. The conception of the League of Nations was a response to a manifest world hunger. Whatever its fate, whether it achieves the great things hoped for, or comes to supersedure, or to failure, the American unwillingness to be a part of it has been expressed. That unwillingness has been kept in mind, and the treaties submitted to-day have no semblance or relationship save as the wish to promote peace has been the common inspiration.

The four-power treaty contains no war commitment. It covenants the respect of each nation's rights in relation to its insular possessions. In case of controversy between the covenanting powers it is agreed to confer and seek adjustment, and if said rights are threatened by the aggressive action of any outside power, these friendly powers, respecting one another, are to communicate, perhaps confer, in order to understand what action may be taken, jointly or separately, to meet a menacing situation. There is no commitment to armed force, no alliance, no written or moral obligation to

---

[6] Signed by the United States, the British Empire, France, and Japan, December 13, 1921; in force from August 17, 1923. United States *Treaty Series*, No. 669, Washington, 1923.

join in defence, no expressed or implied commitment to arrive at any agreement except in accordance with our constitutional methods. It is easy to believe, however, that such a conference of the four powers is a moral warning that an aggressive nation, giving affront to the four great powers ready to focus world opinion on a given controversy, would be embarking on a hazardous enterprise.

Frankly, Senators, if nations may not safely agree to respect each other's rights, and may not agree to confer if one to the compact threatens trespass, or may not agree to advise if one party to the pact is threatened by an outside power, then all concerted efforts to tranquilize the world and stabilize peace must be flung to the winds. Either these treaties must have your cordial sanction, or every proclaimed desire to promote peace and prevent war becomes a hollow mockery. . . .[7]

(B) NAVAL COMPETITIONS ENDED

. . . I now have the honor to report on behalf of the committee of the Conference which has been dealing with the subject of armament, that the proposals of the American Government in relation to the limitation of naval armament have been considered and an agreement has been reached which is embodied in a treaty now presented for your adoption. . . .

May I say . . . that with respect to capital ships . . . the integrity of the plan proposed on behalf of the American Government has been maintained, and the spirit, in which that proposal was made, and in which it was received, has dominated the entire negotiations and brought them to a very successful conclusion. . . .

May I say . . . that no more extraordinary or significant treaty has ever been made. It is extraordinary because we no longer merely talk of the desirability of diminishing the burdens of naval armaments, but we actually limit them. It is extraordinary because this limitation is effected in that field in which nations have been most jealous of their power, and in which they have hitherto been disposed to resent any interference with their power.

I shall not enlarge upon the significance of the engagement. Of course, it is obvious that it means an enormous saving of money and the lifting of a very heavy and unnecessary burden from the peoples of the countries who unite in this agreement.

This treaty ends, absolutely ends, the race in competition in naval armament. At the same time it leaves the relative security of the great naval powers unimpaired.

The significance of the treaty is far more than that. In this treaty we are talking of arms in the language of peace. The best thing about the engagement is the spirit which has been manifested throughout our negotiations and to which is due our ability to reach this fortunate conclusion.

---

[7] Address to the Senate, February 10, 1922. 67th Congress, 2nd Session, *Sen. Doc.* No. 126, pp. 7–11.

In other words, we are taking perhaps the greatest forward step in history to establish the reign of peace.[8]

(C) THE SUCCESS OF JAPAN

. . . An estimate of the success or failure of the conference can hardly be made until some decades have passed. . . .

As the score stands at present, it seems hardly too much to say that this conference has been the greatest success in Japanese diplomatic history. Japan has won more at other conferences, but always at the expense of hard feelings left behind. Her triumphs have usually been conditioned by the certainty that the defeated nation was only waiting its chance to start a fight. . . .

The four-power treaty ought to remove much Japanese suspicion of America and much American suspicion of Japan. Japan loses the British Alliance, which would have gone overboard anyway in the case of a war with America, and gains America's promise not to attack her in return for her promise not to attack America.

Japan has given up in Shantung what she had already promised to give up. . . . She has made some concessions with regard to Manchurian finance, but she holds to Port Arthur, and the South Manchurian railroad. She stays in Siberia until she is ready to get out.

In other words, Japan retains her strategic supremacy, military and political, on the continent of Asia, and is reasonably sure that if ever that supremacy should be challenged by Russia or China, Russia or China would have to fight alone. . . . Japan has Asia to herself. . . .

So far, then, everybody wins but Russia. Japan wins most; she wins Eastern Asia, to do with according to her pleasure. And on the wisdom and good sense of future Japanese policy on the continent of Asia must depend the ultimate estimate of the result of the Washington Conference.[9]

(D) AMERICAN NAVAL STRENGTH IMPAIRED

. . . Naval strength is always comparative with that of other naval nations. It is frankly from this restricted viewpoint — the comparative military position in which the Navy of the United States is left — that the limitation of armament by the Washington Conference is considered in this paper. . . .

The ratio of the floating naval strengths to result eventually between the signatories from the acceptance of the American proposal did not appear therein as a definitely stated feature. None the less, the ratio is there, a very important feature, deducible from the tabulations of the proposed allowed strengths in each of the several combatant classes, for each of

[8] Statement of Secretary of State Charles Evans Hughes to the Plenary Session of the Washington Conference of February 1, 1922. Ibid., pp. 140, 151.

[9] Analysis of Elmer Davis, Washington correspondent of the *New York Times. New York Times*, February 6, 1922.

the signatories of the three principal naval Powers. It was accomplished in part, – for capital ships and aircraft carriers only.

Another feature of the proposal that was not definitely stated was the abolition of competition, but the idea lay behind the whole programme. . . . The treaty abolishes competition in two classes only, – battleships and aircraft carriers. These are the most expensive ships to build because of the great tonnage of units; but they are not the most expensive per ton. In the cruiser, flotilla-leader, destroyer and submarine classes, the nations are free to continue competition, untrammeled by the treaty except for the restrictions placed upon the size of individual units (10,000 tons) and the caliber of guns (8 inches). . . .

That the achievements of the treaty are great cannot be denied; it is also undeniable that the American proposal failed of complete success. The most important failure lies in the omission from the treaty of any limitation of the aggregate tonnage of auxiliary combatant ships other than aircraft carriers. This failure carries in its train (a) the partial failure of the principle of the relative ratio of floating strengths, and (b) the failure to put a stop to competition. . . .

It is interesting to note the relative tonnages proposed to be scrapped by the American programme. In the following comparisons the American tonnage scrapped will be used as the basis, reckoned as 100 per cent., and the order of mention will be the United States, Great Britain, and Japan in each instance. Considering total capital ship tonnage scrapped, the percentages are, respectively, 100, 69 and 53. This is the comparison usually stressed in non-technical comment, but it is very misleading because it includes for all three nations a number of superannuated ships due already, or about to become due, for scrapping, Conference or no Conference. The fairest comparison is based upon new tonnage laid down, plus that about to be laid down, and for which expense had been incurred in the preparation of material; on this basis the respective percentages are 100, 28 and 46. The offered sacrifice of the United States was not only the greatest absolutely; it was great out of proportion to the relative ratio of strength proposed to be retained. There is no gainsaying the generosity of the American offer. . . .

Your attention is now invited to one feature of the treaty which . . . cannot be avoided if my professional opinion of the treaty is to be given with honest fulness. . . .

The opening sentence of Article XIX of the treaty reads:

The United States, the British Empire and Japan agree that the *status quo* at the time of the signing of the present Treaty, with regard to fortifications and naval bases, shall be maintained in their respective territories and possessions specified hereunder.

When the specifications are read all the territories and possessions to which they refer are seen to be insular. The agreement includes everything insular that Japan holds now or may acquire outside of the islands of Japan proper; it includes our Aleutian Islands and everything insular, present or future, under our flag west of the Hawaiian Islands; and it includes Hong Kong and present or future insular holdings of the British Empire east of 110 degrees east longitude, excepting the Canadian islands, Australia and its territories and New Zealand. It will be noted that the language of the article is "fortifications *and* naval bases," not "fortifications *of* naval bases," which latter would have been much less sweeping. *Status quo* is defined in the last paragraph as follows:

The maintenance of the *status quo* under the foregoing provisions implies that no new fortifications or naval bases shall be established in the territories and possessions specified, that no measures shall be taken to increase the existing naval facilities for the repair and maintenance of naval forces, and that no increase shall be made in the coast defenses of the territories and possessions above specified.

An examination will now be made of the equities of this remarkable graft upon the proposal of the Government that called the Conference. The proposal made no mention of naval bases, or naval facilities of bases, or fortifications or coast defenses, and it must be presumed that the omission was deliberately intended after the months of preparation for the Conference.

Mahan gives position, strength and resources as subjects for examination in determining the availability of a situation for a naval base. Actual strength and existing naval facilities will first be considered, in doing which it must be remembered that the details of foreign fortifications are rarely known accurately; their general scope is, however, usually known or believed to be known.

The United States has in Guam a location for a naval base that is wonderfully situated strategically. To state that its fortifications and equipment are desirable now is to disclose no secret. This is no fault of the Navy which for years has sought in vain for the appropriations to make Guam a secure base. In the Philippines there is another great site for a naval base in the Manila region. The entrance to Manila Bay is fortified, but the fortifications need modernizing and the naval facilities are far from being what would be necessary to support the operations of a fleet in war. To meet a menace to the territories under our flag in the Western Pacific, we need a secure naval base in the Philippines and another intermediate between them and the Hawaiian Islands. While neither Guam nor Manila is in efficient condition to support a fleet in war, up to February sixth last the United States possessed the sovereign right to make them so. . . .

Japan has fortified Kelung in the northern end of Formosa; and in the Pescadores Islands west of Formosa she is believed to have a strongly fortified and well-equipped base, for light vessels at least, and probably for all classes of ships. And, what is most important, these bases are only about one thousand miles from all the support of the homeland, while, by comparison, Guam is 5500 and Manila 7000 miles from our Pacific Coast.

Reviewing this phase, it is difficult to discover any trace of equity for the United States in Article XIX.

Next, considering resources, those for naval purposes in the islands themselves may be regarded fairly enough as roughly equal for all three nations. Practically all resources must come from the home territories to the existing insular bases. Here distance, a function of position, counts heavily for Japan as compared with either the United States or Great Britain; in time of war this advantage would weigh less heavily against Great Britain than against the United States because Japan flanks our route to the Far East but meets that of Great Britain end on. Regarding the equities in the light of resources the United States again appears to be a loser by Article XIX.

It is, however, in respect of position considered from all sides that the discomfiture of the United States resulting from the *status quo* is completed. In the unfortunate event of hostilities with Japan, our Philippines are 7000 miles from our home coast while only 1500 miles from her home islands; her outlying islands are at farthest about 1000 miles from her home islands while 7500 miles from our continental coast. Japan's possibilities of attack upon our outlying islands, or of defense of her own outlying islands against attack by us, are immeasurably superior to those of similar action by the United States. No fortifications, no provision of naval facilities, can altogether overcome that handicap; and it was precisely for that reason that a disparity of floating force was an essential feature of the proposal. Naval opinion, in accepting the 5–3 ratio of floating strength between the United States and Japan did so on the basis of the *status quo* of sovereign right – not the *status quo* of insular fortifications, naval bases and naval facilities. It had no idea that the latter, if proposed, would be entertained, or the former be yielded. With naval bases in our western islands of the Pacific fully fortified and provided, the 5–3 ratio of floating force would with difficulty enable the United States to maintain parity at sea in those waters; much less would it enable the United States to undertake a policy of aggression, which has never been the aim of the Navy any more than it has been the aim of the general Government. For the defense of our Pacific islands, and with no idea of aggression whatever, secure and well-provided naval bases are necessary. To surrender the right to go beyond the *status quo* is to make the defense of our western possessions – their retention – well-nigh hopeless in case of need. Should they fall, their recapture would only be possible at the cost of great treasure and of very tedious and lengthy operations.

As between Great Britain and the United States no such inequality exists between themselves in respect of distance to the Far East as both countries have with Japan.

Regarded from the viewpoint of position – comparative distances – Article XIX is glaringly inequitable to the United States.

The Japanese doubtless made a sacrifice of national pride in accepting the 5–5–3 ratio of floating strength, which definitely placed them in third position as a naval Power. But whatever they sacrificed in that respect they have more than made up by their success in securing the inclusion of

Article XIX in the treaty. I say their success, because I have never heard of the suggestion coming from any other source, and all the world knows that the Japanese did make it. At practically no cost to themselves they have secured all that they were actually straining, and were prepared still further to strain, their financial resources to obtain by their ambitious building programme, now no longer necessary.

Article XIX fatally impairs for the United States the 5–3 ratio of floating strength with Japan in so far as the Western Pacific is concerned. The United States has yielded the possibility of naval equality in that region; control she has never sought. It is beside the mark to say that we are as well off as we were before the treaty. That is a half-truth – true only in the material sense; in the sense of sovereignty we have given up the right to better our situation, and that without adequate return – certainly without return in kind. Our military prestige has received a blow; and with the waning of military prestige political prestige is likely to wane also. The treaty may very well mark the beginning of a decreased influence in the Far East, with attendant loss to our proper, if selfish, trade interests, and to our altruistic purposes for China and Siberia. . . .[10]

4. THE DISARMAMENT PROPOSAL OF PRESIDENT HOOVER [11]

[*Proposal submitted to the General Disarmament Conference, June 22, 1932*]

THE TIME has come when we should cut through the brush and adopt some broad and definite method of reducing the overwhelming burden of armament which now lies upon the toilers of the world. . . .

I propose that the arms of the world should be reduced by nearly one-third.

LAND FORCES

In order to reduce the offensive character of all land forces as distinguished from their defensive character, I propose the adoption of the presentation already made at the Geneva Conference for the abolition of all tanks, all chemical warfare and all large mobile guns. This would not prevent the establishment or increase of fixed fortifications of any character for the defence of frontiers and sea-coasts. It would give an increased relative strength to such defence as compared with attack.

I propose, furthermore, that there should be a reduction of one-third

[10] Rear Admiral Harry S. Knapp, U.S.N. Ret.: "The Limitation of Armament at the Conference of Washington," *Proceedings of the American Society of International Law*, 1922, pp. 12–19.

[11] Department of State, *Press Release*, June 25, 1932.

in strength of all land armies over and above the so-called police component.

The land armaments of many nations are considered to have two functions. One is the maintenance of internal order in connection with the regular police forces of the country. The strength required for this purpose has been called the "police component." The other function is defence against foreign attack. The additional strength required for this purpose has been called the "defence component." While it is not suggested that these different components should be separated, it is necessary to consider this contention as to functions in proposing a practical plan of reduction in land forces. Under the Treaty of Versailles and the other peace treaties, the armies of Germany, Austria, Hungary and Bulgaria were reduced to a size deemed appropriate for the maintenance of internal order, Germany being assigned one hundred thousand troops for a population of approximately sixty-five million people. I propose that we should accept for all nations a basic police component of soldiers proportionate to the average which was thus allowed Germany and these other States. This formula with necessary corrections for Powers having colonial possessions should be sufficient to provide for the maintenance of internal order by the nations of the world. Having analysed these two components in this fashion, I propose, as stated above, that there should be a reduction of one-third in the strength of all land armies over and above the police component.

Air Forces

All bombing-planes to be abolished. This will do away with the military possession of types of planes capable of attacks upon civil populations and should be coupled with the total prohibition of all bombardment from the air.

Naval Forces

I propose that the treaty number and tonnage of battleships shall be reduced by one-third; that the treaty tonnage of aircraft-carriers, cruisers and destroyers shall be reduced by one-fourth; that the treaty tonnage of submarines shall be reduced by one-third and that no nation shall retain a submarine tonnage greater than 35,000 tons.

The relative strength of naval arms in battleships and aircraft-carriers as between the five leading naval Powers was fixed by the Treaty of Washington.

The relative strength in cruisers, destroyers and submarines was fixed as between the United States, Great Britain and Japan by the Treaty of London. For the purpose of this proposal it is suggested that the French and Italian strength in cruisers and destroyers be calculated as though they had joined in the Treaty of London on a basis approximating the so-called accord of March 1, 1931.

There are various technical considerations connected with these naval reductions which will be presented by the delegation at Geneva.

General

The effect of this plan would be to bring an enormous savings in cost of new construction and replacement of naval vessels. It would also save large amounts in the operating expense in all nations of land, sea and air forces. It would greatly reduce offensive strength compared to defensive strength in all nations.

These proposals are simple and direct. They call upon all nations to contribute something. The contribution here proposed will be relative and mutual. I know of nothing that would give more hope for humanity today than the acceptance of such a programme with such minor changes as might be necessary. It is folly for the world to go on breaking its back over military expenditures, and the United States is willing to take its share of responsibility by making definite proposals that will relieve the world.

Chapter XXIX

ECONOMIC FOREIGN POLICY

1921—1947

◇◇◇◇◇◇◇◇◇◇◇◇◇◇

FOR A LONG TIME prior to the first World War most students of international affairs recognized that one of the fundamental conditions of world peace was the access of all nations, as far as possible on equal terms, to the trade and raw materials of the world. This truism was affirmed in the third of Wilson's Fourteen Points and later was stated in the fourth point of the Atlantic Charter. In the postwar era the United States was especially responsible for leadership in the reduction of trade barriers because of its commanding economic strength in the world and its position as a creditor nation. President Wilson's views on these matters were briefly stated in his veto of the tariff bill of 1921 (1).

President Wilson's ideas did not prevail, however, during the succeeding three administrations. In May 1921, a so-called emergency tariff bill was enacted, and in September 1922, the Fordney-McCumber Bill established rates higher than under any previous tariff in American history. At about the same time the government adopted a change in the fundamental policy of the United States regarding the tariff provisions of treaties; new treaties were to contain, wherever possible, unconditional most-favored-nation provisions (2). In 1930 the tariff rates were further increased under the Hawley-Smoot Act notwithstanding the protest of a distinguished group of American economists (3).

During the first World War and immediately thereafter the United States loaned between ten and eleven billion dollars to the Allies and to the succession states. The American government did not officially recognize any connection between these "war" and "peace" debts, reparations, and tariff policies. Unofficially, however, it recognized some connection between reparations and debt payments through its cooperation in attempts to solve the problem of reparations and through its debt-funding policies which had the effect of reducing the Allied debts to the United States by about fifty per cent. American private investments in European securities, particularly in Germany, tended for a time to bolster reparation payments and to postpone the inevitable effects of the economic maladjustment of the world. When the crisis came, President Hoover proposed a Moratorium (4, A). The State Department expected world-wide benefits from this policy (4, B), but continued to defend American economic isolation (5).

One of the principal objectives of the Roosevelt administration was to reverse the high tariff policies that had prevailed during the preceding twelve years. Under the strong leadership of the Secretary of State, Cordell Hull, Congress passed the Trade Agreements Act of 1934, empowering the President to establish reciprocal tariff treaties under which existing rates could be raised or lowered as much as fifty per cent. Under this act and subsequent extensions of it, Secretary Hull negotiated over twenty trade agreements prior to the attack on Pearl Harbor. Mr. Hull's address of April 30, 1936, is typical of his many statements on the new trade and tariff policies (6).

The Truman Administration continued the economic policies characteristic, in the Roosevelt Administration, of the leadership of Secretary Hull. This was shown particularly in the support given in 1945 to the renewal of the Trade Agreements Act. But the most important statement of American postwar economic policy was in the form of proposals advocating the establishment of an International Trade Organization, and suggesting the principles on which it should be based (7).

◇◇◇◇◇◇◇◇◇◇◇◇

1. TARIFF AND WORLD TRADE: 1921[1]

[*Wilson's Veto of the Emergency Tariff Bill, March 3, 1921*]

I RETURN herewith without my approval H. R. 15,275, an act imposing temporary duties upon certain agricultural products to meet present emergencies to provide revenue and for other purposes. . . .

It is obvious that for the commodities, except sugar and wool, mentioned in the measure, which make up the greater part of our agricultural international trade, the imports can have little or no effect on the prices of the domestic products. This is strikingly true of such commodities as wheat and corn. The imports of wheat have come mainly from Canada and Argentina and have not competed with the domestic crop. Rather they have supplemented it. The domestic demand has been for specific classes and qualities of foreign wheat to meet particular milling and planting needs. They are a small fraction of our total production and of our wheat exports. The price of wheat is a world price; and it is a matter of little moment whether the Canadian wheat goes directly into the markets of the other countries of the world or indirectly through this country. The relatively small quantity of corn imported into this country has a specialized use and does not come into competition with the domestic commodity.

The situation in which many of the farmers of the country find themselves cannot be remedied by a measure of this sort. This is doubtless generally understood. There is no short way out of existing conditions, and measures of this sort can only have the effect of deceiving the farmers and

[1] *Congressional Record,* 66th Congress, 3rd Session, Vol. 60, Part 4, pp. 4498–9.

of raising false hopes among them. Actual relief can come only from the adoption of constructive measures of a broader scope, from the restoration of peace everywhere in the world, the resumption of normal industrial pursuits, the recovery particularly of Europe, and the discovery there of additional credit foundations on the basis of which her people may arrange to take from farmers and other producers of this Nation a greater part of their surplus production. . . .

We have been vigorously building up a great merchant marine and providing for improvement of marketing in foreign countries by the passage of an export trade law and of measures for the promotion of banking agencies in foreign countries. Now it appears that we propose to render these measures abortive in whole or in part. . . .

Changes of a very radical character have taken place. The United States has become a great creditor Nation. She has lent certain Governments of Europe more than $9,000,000,000, and as a result of the enormous excess of our exports there is an additional commercial indebtedness of foreign nations to our own of perhaps not less than $4,000,000,000. There are only three ways in which Europe can meet her part of her indebtedness, namely, by the establishment of private credits, by the shipment of gold, or of commodities. It is difficult for Europe to discover the requisite securities as a basis for the necessary credits. Europe is not in a position at the present time to send us the amount of gold which would be needed, and we could not view further large imports of gold into this country without concern. The result, to say the least, would be a larger disarrangement of international exchange and disturbance of international trade.

If we wish to have Europe settle her debts, governmental or commercial, we must be prepared to buy from her, and if we wish to assist Europe and ourselves by the export either of food, of raw materials, or finished products, we must be prepared to welcome commodities which we need and which Europe will be prepared, with no little pain, to send us.

Clearly, this is no time for the erection here of high trade barriers. It would strike a blow at the large and successful efforts which have been made by many of our great industries to place themselves on an export basis. It would stand in the way of the normal readjustment of business conditions throughout the world, which is as vital to the welfare of this country as to that of all the other nations. The United States has a duty to itself as well as to the world, and it can discharge this duty by widening, not by contracting, its world markets. . . .

◇◇◇◇◇◇◇◇◇◇◇◇◇

2. UNCONDITIONAL MOST-FAVORED-NATION TREATIES[2]

[*Charles E. Hughes to American Diplomatic Officers*]

August 18, 1923

THE DEPARTMENT desires to inform you confidentially and for such comment as you may care to make that the President has authorized the Secretary of State to negotiate commercial treaties with other countries by which the contracting parties will accord to each other unconditional most-favored-nation treatment.

It has long been the view of this Government that it has fulfilled its obligations under its pledges to accord most-favored-nation treatment when it has accorded to a country to which it has guaranteed such treatment the lowest rates of customs duty which it has freely and without special compensation accorded to a third country. In the view heretofore maintained by the American Government, other Governments to which the United States has pledged most-favored-nation treatment have not been entitled to claim the extension to them of tariff concessions accorded by the United States to a third country in return for reciprocal tariff concessions, unless they offer to accord to the United States equivalent concessions. Most of the treaties to which the United States has been or is a party, for example, the Treaty of February 6, 1778, with France and the Treaty of February 21, 1911, with Japan, contain most-favored-nation clauses that are in this respect expressly conditional. Others such as the Treaty of July 3, 1815, with Great Britain, in which the most-favored-nation clause is not expressly conditional, have nevertheless been interpreted as though the condition were specified.

When the conditional most-favored-nation policy was first formulated, discrimination in commercial matters was the general rule among nations, and it was deemed advisable for the United States to adopt a policy of making concessions only to such states as granted in each case some definite and equivalent compensation. Since that time, however, the principle of equality of treatment has made great progress, and it is now considered to be in the interest of the trade of the United States, in competing with the trade of other countries in the markets of the world, to endeavor to extend the acceptance of that principle. The enlarged productive capacity of the United States developed during the World War has increased the need for assured equality of treatment of American commerce in foreign markets.

Today in a large majority of commercial countries most-favored-nation treatment is considered to connote equality of treatment irrespective of concessions that may have been granted by third countries. The convenience of having one uniform practice for the entire commercial world to-

[2] *Papers Relating to the Foreign Relations of the United States*, 1923, Vol. I, pp. 131–2.

gether with the comparatively greater liberality of unconditional most-favored-nation treatment have frequently been urged as reasons for a change of policy on the part of the United States.

A further consideration in favor of the change has been presented by the inclusion of Section 317 in the Tariff Act of 1922. Under this section the President is directed, if he finds such action to be in the public interest, to levy additional import duties upon the products of countries that impose differential customs duties unfavorable in fact to the commerce of the United States. Nothing is said in this section concerning the process by which the discriminations are or shall have been effected, and it may reasonably be assumed that the exception of reductions of duties made in return for reciprocal concessions has not been intended.

In connection with the negotiation of new commercial treaties, therefore, the Department of State has decided to propose a most-favored-nation clause under which the United States will guarantee and expect to be guaranteed unconditional equality of treatment. The United States, in making this proposal, will offer nothing more than a guarantee of the treatment which, in practice, it already accords to the commerce of other countries. . . .

◇◇◇◇◇◇◇◇◇◇◇◇◇◇

3. OPPOSITION TO A HIGH TARIFF POLICY[3]

THE UNDERSIGNED American economists and teachers of economics strongly urge that any measure which provides for a general upward revision of tariff rates be denied passage by Congress, or if passed, be vetoed by the President. . . .

Our export trade, in general, would suffer. Countries cannot permanently buy from us unless they are permitted to sell to us, and the more we restrict the importation of goods from them by means [of] ever higher tariffs, the more we reduce the possibility of our exporting to them.

This applies to such exporting industries as copper, automobiles, agricultural machinery, typewriters and the like fully as much as it does to farming. The difficulties of these industries are likely to be increased still further if we pass a higher tariff.

There are already many evidences that such action would inevitably provoke other countries to pay us back in kind by levying retaliatory duties against our goods. There are few more ironical spectacles than that of the American Government as it seeks, on the one hand, to promote exports through the activity of the Bureau of Foreign and Domestic Commerce, while, on the other hand, by increasing tariffs it makes exportation ever more difficult.

[3] Statement signed by 1,028 economists from 179 American colleges, protesting against the passage of the Smoot-Hawley Tariff Bill. *New York Times*, May 5, 1930.

We do not believe that American manufacturers, in general, need higher tariffs. The report of the President's Committee on Recent Economic Changes has shown that industrial efficiency has increased, that costs have fallen, that profits have grown with amazing rapidity since the end of the World War. Already our factories supply our people with over 96 per cent of the manufactured goods which they consume, and our producers look to foreign markets to absorb the increasing output of their machines.

Further barriers to trade will serve them not well, but ill.

Many of our citizens have invested their money in foreign enterprises. The Department of Commerce has estimated that such investments, entirely aside from the war debts, amounted to between $12,555,000,000 and $14,555,000,000 on Jan. 1, 1929. These investors, too, would suffer if restrictive duties were to be increased, since such action would make it still more difficult for their foreign debtors to pay them the interest due them.

America is now facing the problem of unemployment. The proponents of higher tariffs claim that an increase in rates will give work to the idle. This is not true. We cannot increase employment by restricting trade. American industry, in the present crisis, might well be spared the burden of adjusting itself to higher schedules of duties.

Finally, we would urge our government to consider the bitterness which a policy of higher tariffs would inevitably inject into our international relations. The United States was ably represented at the world economic conference which was held under the auspices of the League of Nations in 1927. This conference adopted a resolution announcing that "the time has come to put an end to the increase in tariffs and to move in the opposite direction."

The higher duties proposed in our pending legislation violate the spirit of this agreement and plainly invite other nations to compete with us in raising further barriers to trade. A tariff war does not furnish good soil for the growth of world peace.

◇◇◇◇◇◇◇◇◇◇◇◇◇

4. PRESIDENT HOOVER'S PROPOSAL FOR THE POSTPONEMENT OF INTERGOVERNMENTAL DEBTS AND REPARATIONS PAYMENTS

(A) THE MORATORIUM

THE AMERICAN Government proposes the postponement during one year of all payments on intergovernmental debts, reparations, and relief debts, both principal and interest, of course, not including obligations of governments held by private parties. Subject to confirmation by Congress, the American Government will postpone all payments upon the debts of foreign governments to the American Government payable during the fiscal year beginning July 1 next, conditional on a like postponement for one year of all payments on intergovernmental debts owing the important creditor powers. . . .

The purpose of this action is to give the forthcoming year to the economic recovery of the world and to help free the recuperative forces already in motion in the United States from retarding influences from abroad.

The world-wide depression has affected the countries of Europe more severely than our own. Some of these countries are feeling to a serious extent the drain of this depression on national economy. The fabric of intergovernmental debts, supportable in normal times, weighs heavily in the midst of this depression.

From a variety of causes arising out of the depression such as the fall in the price of foreign commodities and the lack of confidence in economic and political stability abroad there is an abnormal movement of gold into the United States which is lowering the credit stability of many foreign countries. These and the other difficulties abroad diminish buying power for our exports and in a measure are the cause of our continued unemployment and continued lower prices to our farmers.

Wise and timely action should contribute to relieve the pressure of these adverse forces in foreign countries and should assist in the reestablishment of confidence, thus forwarding political peace and economic stability in the world.

Authority of the President to deal with this problem is limited as this action must be supported by the Congress. It has been assured the cordial support of leading members of both parties in the Senate and the House. The essence of this proposition is to give time to permit debtor governments to recover their national prosperity. I am suggesting to the American people that they be wise creditors in their own interest and be good neighbors.

I wish to take this occasion also to frankly state my views upon our relations to German reparations and the debts owed to us by the allied Governments of Europe. Our Government has not been a party to, or exerted any voice in determination of reparation obligations. We purposely did not participate in either general reparations or the division of colonies or property. The repayment of debts due to us from the Allies for the advance for war and reconstruction were settled upon a basis not contingent upon German reparations or related thereto. Therefore, reparations is necessarily wholly a European problem with which we have no relation.

I do not approve in any remote sense of the cancellation of the debts to us. World confidence would not be enhanced by such action. None of our debtor nations have ever suggested it. But as the basis of the settlement of these debts was the capacity under normal conditions of the debtor to pay, we should be consistent with our own policies and principles if we take into account the abnormal situation now existing in the world. I am sure the American people have no desire to attempt to extract any sum beyond the capacity of any debtor to pay and it is our view that broad vision requires that our Government should recognize the situation as it exists.

This course of action is entirely consistent with the policy which we have hitherto pursued. We are not involved in the discussion of strictly European problems, of which the payment of German reparations is one. It represents our willingness to make a contribution to the early restoration of world prosperity in which our own people have so deep an interest.

I wish further to add that while this action has no bearing on the conference for limitation of land armaments to be held next February, inasmuch as the burden of competitive armaments has contributed to bring about this depression, we trust that by this evidence of our desire to assist we shall have contributed to the good-will which is so necessary in the solution of this major question.[4]

(B) DEFENSE OF THE MORATORIUM

. . . Over two months ago the President felt that some definite step must be taken to break up the despair which was growing out of the world-wide depression. He felt that a strong move was necessary, one which would readjust the minds of men to a more rational outlook. When the President began to consider these things, I do not know, but he began certainly to discuss them early in May. He talked over with Mr. Sackett, our Ambassador to Berlin, the increasingly bad economic situation of Germany and central Europe. He discussed the same matter with the Secretary of State a few days later and asked from the Departments of State and Commerce full reports on economic conditions all over Europe. . . .

In the meantime, however, all reports showed that the situation in Germany and in central Europe was deteriorating so rapidly that a serious crisis might arrive at almost any moment. To prevent this, the President realized that any action which was to be taken must be taken at once, and he directed the Secretary of State to call in immediately as many as possible of the ambassadors and ministers representing the countries which would be affected to explain the proposal to them. He announced this proposal on the 20th of June. Everybody knows the immediate result of that announcement. The world took new hope; everywhere commodity prices went up in value. The farmers and the manufacturers of the United States saw what they believed was the turn of the tide. The price of sugar in Cuba showed the effect of this new hope; the price of silk in far-away Japan was strengthened; in Germany there was instant relief from the grinding fear of disaster which was hanging over the country. The Germany people felt that at last a chance had been given them and that perhaps the world was once more friendly. So, equally, the rest of the world took hope for Germany and the scramble to withdraw foreign money from the country ceased.

---

[4] This proposal was released by President Hoover on June 20, 1931. Dept. of State, *Press Releases*, June 27, 1931.

Instantly Great Britain announced adherence to the plan and promised to extend its benefits to her own dominions. Italy made an immediate and whole-hearted response and has already refused to ask the amounts which fell due on July 1, at the same time depositing in a special account in the Bank of International Settlement in Switzerland the amounts she would herself have paid. Japan, which would have to give up German reparations and had no out-payments to give up in compensation, showed her fine spirit and her solidarity with the rest of the world by announcing wholehearted approval of the plan. France also saw the value of the proposal, but felt that the plan must be worked out in more detail before she could accept. In this connection it must be remembered that France makes greater temporary sacrifices than any other nation except the United States. . . .

I want here to point out that the whole purpose of the President's proposal was to give a year's breathing space in which the recuperative forces of the world could make headway. At no time did he propose or consider any permanent revision of the foreign debt settlements nor of any contract of which we are not a party. He considered the whole subject solely in the aspect of relief to the temporary conditions created by world-wide depression. In fact, all through the discussions the integrity of the agreements already entered into has been constantly upheld.

Possibly not all men have realized just what this bold proposal of the President should do for the world, and I am glad to tell you something of what we in Washington who have been in the thick of the discussions believe that it will accomplish. Its immediate benefits, of course, affect most deeply Germany and the central European countries. As a breathing space of a year is given on all these huge intergovernmental payments, Germany will be given an opportunity to put its house in order and has promised to use the money thus saved for budgetary purposes, that none of it will go into military or naval expenditures.

In the complicated interrelationships between nations to-day, the economic collapse of any one nation must have far-reaching consequences on all other nations. The President, therefore, believed, and rightly, that in giving assistance now where it was most desperately needed, the whole world would participate in the benefits. We are beginning to understand that prosperity depends on the prosperity of our neighbors, not on their misery. . . .

What the President's proposal has so far accomplished is the mobilization of the forces of good-will and good understanding and determination to bring back prosperity. It has opened the gates to a return of prosperity which will affect every citizen of the country. It is up to us to hold the gates open in order that relief may come to the farmers of the nation, in order that the growth of trade which must follow an improvement in conditions abroad may bring employment to all those who are willing to work. I am not making any predictions. All I know is that the world has suddenly been given hope when things looked most hopeless. The courageous leadership of the President has done all this. Now the work of rehabilitation must be taken over by the people in a spirit of courageous optimism. In such a program the American people has never yet failed and it will not fail to-day.[5]

◇◇◇◇◇◇◇◇◇◇◇◇◇

5. DEFENSE OF TARIFF AND OTHER ECONOMIC POLICIES: 1932

. . . WHEN WE SPEAK of foreign debts we generally refer to intergovernmental debts and specifically to the war debts, so-called, owed us by the Allied nations. They are war debts, strictly speaking, only in part, because a major part of the money owing us since the funding of these debts was money advanced after the war for reconstruction purposes. But these debts are small compared to the aggregate amount owed American nationals on loans made privately after the war to European countries, states, municipalities, and private concerns. . . .

When, after the war, the United States changed from the category of a debtor nation to that of a creditor, when our industry was geared high and markets were sought and found in those countries whose industries had been partly or wholly destroyed as a result of the war, when our bankers were searching for new fields in which they might put their surplus capital to work, it was felt that the Department of State ought to be kept closely in touch with the situation, since this outflow of money and goods and service might be made to assist or to interfere with American policy. A part of our work has always been to find new trade outlets. As credit makes trade possible, the Department of State was necessarily interested also in the flow of credit. It was felt that there might well come a time when we might feel it advisable to check this flow of credit in one direction or another as inimical to the best interests of the United States, just as we have always had the right in certain circumstances to object to the export of munitions of war. In March, 1922, therefore, the Department asked bankers considering the flotation of loans on the American market to inform it in writing in advance of such flotation, pointing out at the time that the Government naturally could not undertake to advise on the business risks involved. This business risk it was clearly the duty of the investment houses to investigate in the interest of their clients. . . .

In no letter to the bankers, except that used now when we simply say we are not interested, did we forget to tell the bankers that no reference to the Government was to be made. In some few instances the bankers may have disobeyed this injunction, although I have never happened to hear of any. It is possible, indeed probable, that in some instances bond salesmen, like all drummers on commission eager to sell their wares, may

[5] Radio Address of Acting Secretary of State, William R. Castle, Jr., July 8, 1931, Ibid., July 11, 1931.

have made the false statement that these loans were O.K'd by the Government. But these instances, if they occurred, were certainly few and far between. As a matter of fact, the American public was in the mood for speculating; and when the return from foreign securities looked better than that from domestic securities, the public was perfectly willing to speculate in foreign securities. Eight per cent looked a lot better than 4 per cent, but there were mighty few people with money enough to buy bonds who did not know that the bonds bore 8 per cent interest because they were somewhat speculative and therefore could not have been sold if the rate had been less. Nobody bought foreign bonds because the Department of State said "no question of public policy is involved." If they bought because a callow bond salesman lied about what the Department of State said, they should blame the "prevaricator" – I use the word advisedly as not libelous – not the Government. . . .

It is a tragic thing that hundreds of millions of these foreign securities are now in default, as many of us know to our sorrow. I do not think that in most cases we can blame the investment houses. Even the professional economists failed miserably to forecast the future. Speculation had run mad, and the losses in our own domestic securities are infinitely greater in the aggregate than in foreign securities. These loans constitute one of the many problems of liquidation in a world bent on economic recovery, but this problem can not be dealt with separately from all other financial difficulties. . . .

This brings us face to face with the public debts and, through them, with the tariff. . . .

First then, the tariff in general. There can be no manner of doubt that tariffs restrict the flow of international trade, or at least deflect it in one direction or another. It is possible to imagine a tariff wall so high that it would amount to an embargo. In that case a country would have to depend entirely on its own internal production, and its exports would be practically limited to the amounts its citizens spent abroad and the amount of the services it rendered. This, of course, is not an exact statement, since economic laws are broken all the time in the most irritating manner, so far as the professional economists are concerned. There is also no manner of doubt that tariffs do not interfere with international trade any more or as much as does the quota system on imports recently adopted by so many nations as another means of protection for their own industries. It is impossible to estimate how much, if at all, the latest American tariff has interfered with trade. . . .

If our tariff is a barrier that other nations could not get across, granted normal conditions – and it is fair to say that increased tariffs in the past have never had that effect – and if the difficulty or impossibility of selling to America so depressed conditions in other countries that it was difficult to meet their obligations; then and only then, would it be possible to say that the American tariff prevents other nations from paying what they owe us on the debts. There seem to me to be too many unsolved equations here to make discussion of the matter intelligent. Some people evidently feel, however, that all this is proved and suggest lower tariffs as the remedy. If France can sell large amounts of goods to America, France can, in their opinion, pay the debt. Not as a politician but as a long-time student of this matter I can not follow this argument, and for these reasons. If the duty is to be materially lowered on French products which are made also in the United States, it must result in a serious dislocation of industry in this country. If the tariff is to be materially lowered on purely luxury products, not to any extent made in America, it would bring about a reduction in our revenue which, if the cut were to have any real effect in France, would pretty well balance, through loss in tariff income, the amount we should receive in payment for the debt. If the cut is to be made in products which we ourselves manufacture, then we not only lose the tariff revenue but run the risk of destroying American business.

This brings us inevitably to the broad question, which has to do with tariff but not with tariff rates, of commercial treaties. . . .

For a nation which exports only one or two commodities I can see a possible advantage in bargaining tariff treaties. For a nation which exports everything from wheat to automobiles, from hogs to radios, I can see no opportunity for bargains which will not seriously injure one industry as it opens the doors to another. If every nation treats all other nations alike, there can be no talk of justice or injustice, although, of course, one nation may be able to export where another can not. There are, for example, the questions of propinquity and of labor costs. It is generally not the tariff rate that causes trouble, but the variability of the tariff rate. I am sure that for our own benefit this country should stand by its guns, work unremittingly to bring about a world-wide network of general most-favored-nation treaties. . . .

But as the debts got us into the tariff question, so the tariff question brings us back into the debt question. If it were not so much talked about, this question of debts would not loom as large as it does in the economic world. The sums that various nations are obligated to pay us are small indeed compared to the sums which they spend annually on armament. You and I, if we owe money, try to think of ways of retrenchment so that we can pay, not of ways to avoid payment. But there is no use in looking at this question so simply, because it is not simple. It has been discussed so much that it has become a political issue – not here but abroad – and because of this we have to face it, can not refuse to discuss it. The United States has always been a generous creditor and I hope always will be a generous creditor, within the bounds of fairness to its citizens. You can imagine that we in the Department of State have considered the question long and earnestly because of its international political implications, although it is actually none of our business. The people responsible are Congress, with the Treasury as adviser. The idea recently expressed that, by lowering the tariff through bargaining treaties, European nations might ship us goods in quantities large enough to enable them with ease to pay their debts, was discussed months ago by those of us who have been informally talking over the question. We discarded the idea for the very reasons the President and the Secretary of the Treasury have pointed out. To be of any real effect on the capacity to pay of these nations, the amounts sent to this country would have to be so stupendous that American business would be strangled and the debt payments would not approach the deficit from falling income taxes. It would be quite literally to ask the American people to pay the debts themselves. Far more helpful is the idea, also recently expressed, that we adjust the debts in accord with the increase in European consumption of our own goods. That is a real plan to bring back our long-sought prosperity. . . .

I can say this without any reference to politics. The American tariff does not prevent the payment of the intergovernmental debts. The tariff may be too high or too low – that is a matter for Congress to decide. The rates are far less important than the stability of the rates. To lower rates would not pay the debts because it would not increase the will to pay. To lower tariff rates with this idea in view would only result in an influx of foreign goods to the detriment of our own manufacturers. Some means should rather be found to pay the debts – if this can be done – through increase in our exports. Every machine, every ton of wheat, every bale of cotton sold adds to our own chances of economic recovery, and there is no doubt that as our situation improves it is reflected in better conditions abroad. Let us forget academic discussions and work, each in his own way, to improve conditions in America. My business is to assist in conduct of foreign relations, which is pretty far outside of politics since the bases of foreign relations remain always the same. The only way we can carry on is through scrupulous fairness and courtesy and generosity, because that is the only way that we can get what we must have for ourselves. We in the Department of State have to deal continually with other nations, but we have to think always just one thing – what is the interest of the United States of America.[6]

◇◇◇◇◇◇◇◇◇◇◇◇◇◇

6. RECIPROCAL TRADE TREATIES[7]

[*Address of Cordell Hull before the Chamber of Commerce of the United States*]

Washington, D. C., April 30, 1936

. . . AS TIME goes on, it becomes increasingly clear that no nation can achieve a full measure of stable economic recovery so long as international trade remains in the state of collapse into which it was plunged during the

[6] Address of Under Secretary of State William R. Castle, Jr., Cleveland, Ohio, October 27, 1932. Ibid., No. 391, Oct. 29, 1932.
[7] Ibid., No. 875, 1936

years of the depression. The whole post-war period has been characterized by an ever-increasing drift toward economic nationalism, which has expressed itself in a constant growth of barriers to international trade. This drift has become enormously intensified during the past six years, though responsible statesmen in many countries have never ceased to deplore it. Under its impact the international economic structure of the world has been all but shattered, and individual nations have sought economic improvement more and more by means of purely domestic measures, on the basis of a greater degree of self-containment than was ever before consciously attempted. . . .

A rapid and drastic contraction of international trade of the kind that the world has witnessed during the past few years constitutes a double attack upon the economic well-being of each nation's population. The necessary materials habitually obtained in other parts of the globe become more difficult to secure. The surplus national production habitually shipped to other countries becomes more difficult to sell. Output in the surplus-creating branches of production must be curtailed, or else accumulating surpluses force prices below the level of remunerative return to the producers. In either case, the whole economic structure becomes disrupted. Vast unemployment ensues, not only in the field of production, but also in such lines of activity as transportation, banking, merchandising, and the various avocations and professions. Financial investment and other forms of savings become impaired or are wholly destroyed. Distress spreads throughout the nation in ever-widening circles.

Economic distress quickly translates itself into social instability and political unrest. It opens the way for the demagogue and the agitator, foments internal strife, and frequently leads to the supplanting of orderly democratic government by tyrannical dictatorships. It breeds international friction, fear, envy, and resentment, and destroys the very foundations of world peace. Nations are tempted to seek escape from distress at home in military adventures beyond their frontiers. And as fear of armed conflict spreads, even peace-loving nations are forced to divert their national effort from the creation of wealth and from peaceful well-being to the construction of armaments. Each step in the armament race bristles with new menace of economic disorganization and destruction, multiplies fear for the future, dislocates normal constructive processes of economic life, and leads to greater and greater impoverishment of the world's population. . . .

The foreign-trade program of this Government is based fundamentally upon what to us is an indisputable assumption — namely, that our domestic recovery can be neither complete nor durable unless our surplus-creating branches of production succeed in regaining at least a substantial portion of their lost foreign markets. Our production of cotton, lard, tobacco, fruits, copper, petroleum products, automobiles, machinery, electrical and office appliances, and a host of other specialities is geared to a scale of operation the output of which exceeds domestic consumption by ten to fifty per cent. In his message to Congress recommending the passage of the Trade Agreements Act, the President urged the need of restoring foreign markets in order that our surplus-producing industries may be "spared in part, at least, the heartbreaking readjustments that must be necessary if the shrinkage of American foreign commerce remains permanent. . . ."

Since the end of the World War, we have revised our general tariff structure upward on three different occasions. The third and most drastic of these revisions, embodied in the Smoot-Hawley Tariff Act, occurred at the very outset of the depression, from the devastating effects of which the world is just beginning to recover. Through that ill-starred action, we helped to set into motion a vicious spiral of retaliation and counterretaliation, and to start a race for a forcible contraction of international trade on a stupendous scale. In this race some nations have far outstripped us in the scope and effectiveness of restrictive action. Our export trade has become the victim of the formidable array of economic armament created by other nations, just as the export trade of other nations has likewise become the victim of our thrust into the heights of superprotectionism.

If international trade is to function again on an adequate scale, and if we are to regain our fair share of that trade, the nations of the world must retrace their steps from this supreme folly. As I said at the London Economic Conference in 1933, the nations, in the matter of tariffs, must embark upon a sound middle course between extreme economic internationalism and extreme economic nationalism. All excesses in the matter of trade barriers should be removed, and all unfair trade methods and practices should be abandoned.

When we were formulating our basic policy, there were two ways open to us to make our vital contribution to the process of economic demobilization. We could undertake a downward revision of our tariff by unilateral and autonomous action, in the hope that other nations would, as a result, also begin to move away from their present suicidal policies in the field of foreign trade. Or else we could, by the negotiation of bilateral trade agreements, attempt a mitigation of trade barriers on a reciprocal basis.

We chose the second course as offering by far the better promise of trade improvement. An autonomous reduction of our tariff would provide no assurance that our example would be followed by other nations or, if it would be followed, that the resulting mitigation of trade barriers would, in fact, apply to those commodities which are of the greatest interest to us. On the other hand, the bilateral method, combined with the principle of equality of treatment which I shall presently discuss, contemplates simultaneous action by many countries and, in its effects, operates to drive down excessive trade barriers throughout the world. Moreover, it affords us an opportunity to secure in each country the relaxation of restrictions with respect to those of our export commodities the sale of which in that country's markets is either of special importance to us or else has been particularly hard-hit by recently established restrictions. It was in order to make possible the securing of such concessions for our export trade by negotiation with other countries that Congress empowered the President, for a three-year period, to conclude reciprocal trade agreements and, in connection with such agreements, to modify, within strictly defined limits, customs duties and other import restrictions operative in the United States. . . .

The general aim of our negotiators is to secure concessions for those American exports the marketing of which in the other country offers the best opportunity of development and, at the same time, promises the greatest degree of revival in our export industries; and to grant the other country concessions with respect to commodities the possible increased importation of which would be beneficial to our country. The representatives of the other country are, naturally, actuated by very much the same motives. In the actual experience of negotiation, it has been found possible to reconcile the desires of both sides in sufficient measure for the final agreements to embody worth-while mutual concessions and thus open the way for an increase of mutually profitable trade. . . .

Our trade-agreements program is thus a standing offer to all the nations of the world to deal with each of them in commercial matters on a basis of equal treatment. In carrying out the mandate of Congress in this respect, we have, save only in the case of a few well-recognized exceptions, steadfastly refrained from securing or granting preferential or discriminatory treatment. In generalizing the duty reductions negotiated in the individual trade agreements, we have sought to place on an equal footing those nations which, in turn, extend equality of treatment to our commerce, and to refuse such equality to those nations which refuse equality to us. Thus all phases of our policy are on a reciprocal basis. . . .

Through its trade-agreements program, this country is furnishing its fair share of leadership in the world movement toward a restoration of mutually profitable international trade and, as a consequence, toward an improvement in the employment of labor, a fuller measure of stable domestic prosperity, and the only sound foundation for world peace. . . .

◇◇◇◇◇◇◇◇◇◇◇◇◇

7. PROPOSALS ON WORLD TRADE AND EMPLOYMENT[8]

[*Text of the Proposals*]

A. NEED FOR INTERNATIONAL ECONOMIC COOPERATION

1. COLLECTIVE MEASURES to safeguard the peoples of the world against threats to peace and to reach just settlements of disputes among nations must be based not only on international machinery to deal

[8] Developed by representatives of several agencies of the United States Government, working under the chairmanship of William L. Clayton, Assistant Secretary of State. The proposals were announced, December 6, 1945. Department of State *Bulletin*, Vol. XIII, pp. 912–29.

directly with disputes and to prevent aggression, but also on economic cooperation among nations with the object of preventing and removing economic and social maladjustments, of achieving fairness and equity in economic relations between states, and of raising the level of economic well-being among all peoples.

2. Important contributions have already been made toward the attainment of these objectives. The Food and Agriculture Organization of the United Nations has been established. An International Monetary Fund to maintain reasonable exchange stability and facilitate adjustment in the balance of payments of member countries, and an International Bank for Reconstruction and Development to provide financial resources on a cooperative basis for those purposes are awaiting the action of governments required for their establishment. . . .

B. PROPOSALS CONCERNING EMPLOYMENT

. . . *Effectuation of Aims.* There should be an undertaking that:

1. Each of the signatory nations will take action designed to achieve and maintain full employment within its own jurisdiction, through measures appropriate to its political and economic institutions.

2. No nation will seek to maintain employment through measures which are likely to create unemployment in other countries or which are incompatible with international undertakings designed to promote an expanding volume of international trade and investment in accordance with comparative efficiencies of production. . . .

C. PROPOSALS CONCERNING AN INTERNATIONAL TRADE ORGANIZATION . . .

2. It is accordingly proposed that there be created an International Trade Organization of the United Nations, the members of which would undertake to conduct their international commercial policies and relations in accordance with agreed principles to be set forth in the articles of the Organization. These principles, in order to make possible an effective expansion of world production, employment, exchange, and consumption, should:

a. Provide an equitable basis for dealing with the problems of governmental measures affecting international trade;

b. Provide for the curbing of restrictive trade practices resulting from private international business arrangements; and

c. Govern the institution and operation of intergovernmental commodity arrangements.

[*Proposed International Trade Organization*]

There follows an outline of the principles which it is proposed should be incorporated in the articles of the Organization.

CHAPTER I. *Purposes*

The purposes of the Organization should be:

1. To promote international commercial cooperation by establishing machinery for consultation and collaboration among member govern-

ments regarding the solution of problems in the field of international commercial policies and relations.

2. To enable members to avoid recourse to measures destructive of world commerce by providing, on a reciprocal and mutually advantageous basis, expanding opportunities for their trade and economic development.

3. To facilitate access by all members, on equal terms, to the trade and to the raw materials of the world which are needed for their economic prosperity.

4. In general, to promote national and international action for the expansion of the production, exchange and consumption of goods, for the reduction of tariffs and other trade barriers, and for the elimination of all forms of discriminatory treatment in international commerce; thus contributing to an expanding world economy, to the establishment and maintenance in all countries of high levels of employment and real income, and to the creation of economic conditions conducive to the maintenance of world peace. . . .

CHAPTER III. *General Commercial Policy* . . .

Section B. *Tariffs and Preferences*

1. . . . members should enter into arrangements for the substantial reduction of tariffs and for the elimination of tariff preferences, action for the elimination of tariff preferences being taken in conjunction with adequate measures for the substantial reduction of barriers to world trade, as part of the mutually advantageous arrangements contemplated in this document. . . .

Section C. *Quantitative Trade Restrictions*

1. . . . members should undertake not to maintain any quotas, embargoes, or other quantitative restrictions on their export or import trade with other members. . . .

Section D. *Subsidies*

1. . . . members granting any subsidy which operates to increase exports or reduce imports should undertake to keep the Organization informed as to the extent and nature of the subsidy, as to the reason therefor and as to the probable effects on trade. They should also be prepared, in cases where, under procedures approved by the Organization, it is agreed that serious injury to international trade threatens to result from the operation of the subsidy, to discuss with other members or with the Organization possible limitations on the quantity of the domestic product subsidized. In this paragraph, the term "subsidy" includes any form of internal income or price support. . . .

CHAPTER IV. *Restrictive Business Practices*

1. *Curbing of restrictive business practices.* There should be individual and concerted efforts by members of the Organization to curb those restrictive business practices in international trade (such as combinations or agreements to fix prices and terms of sale, divide markets or territories,

limit production or exports, suppress technology or invention, exclude enterprises from particular fields, or boycott or discriminate against particular firms) which have the effect of frustrating the objectives of the Organization to promote expansion of production and trade, equal access to markets and raw materials, and the maintenance in all countries of high levels of employment and real income. . . .

CHAPTER V. *Intergovernmental Commodity Arrangements*

The production of, and trade in, primary commodities is exposed to certain difficulties different in character from those which generally exist in the case of manufactured goods; and these difficulties, if serious, may have such widespread repercussions as to prejudice the prospect of the general policy of economic expansion. Members should therefore agree upon the procedure which should be adopted to deal with such difficulties. . . .

4. *Principles of intergovernmental commodity agreements.* MEMBERS should undertake to adhere to the following principles governing the institution of intergovernmental commodity agreements. . . .

b. Members should undertake not to enter into intergovernmental commodity agreements involving the limitation of production or exports or the allocation of markets, except after:

1) Investigation by the Study Group of the root causes of the problem which gave rise to the proposal;

2) Determination, in accordance with procedures approved by the Organization; either:

a) that a burdensome surplus of the product concerned has developed or is developing in international trade and is accompanied by widespread distress to small producers accounting for a substantial proportion of the total output and that these conditions cannot be corrected by the normal play of competitive forces because, in the case of the product concerned, a substantial reduction of price leads neither to a significant increase in consumption nor to a significant decrease in production; or

b) that widespread unemployment, unrelated to general business conditions, has developed or is developing in respect of the industry concerned and that such unemployment cannot be corrected by the normal play of competitive forces rapidly enough to prevent widespread and undue hardship to workers because, in the case of the industry concerned, i) a substantial reduction of price does not lead to a significant increase in consumption but leads, instead, to the reduction of employment, and ii) the resulting unemployment cannot be remedied by normal processes of reallocation. . . .

Chapter XXX

AMERICAN INTERNATIONAL CO-OPERATION 1921—1933

◇◇◇◇◇◇◇◇◇◇◇◇◇

FOR A TIME after the beginning of the Administration of President Harding, Secretary of State Charles E. Hughes carried American isolation to the extreme of refusing even to read communications addressed to the United States from the League of Nations. This, however, was a passing phase. Soon the Department of State began to cooperate with various non-political activities of the League and to participate in international conferences. Through the Nine-Power and the Four-Power Treaties the United States indicated its interest in Pacific affairs.

A further indication of American international cooperation was its part in the negotiation of the Kellogg-Briand Pact (1). Although the original sponsors of this treaty were mostly pacifists or isolationists, it was supported also by the so-called internationalists. Contemporary discussion of the Pact centered around its interpretation and its significance for world peace (2).

A more prolonged controversy took place over the adherence of the United States to the Permanent Court of International Justice (The World Court), provided for in Article 14 of the Covenant. After long discussion and after public approval of American adherence to the Court had been amply demonstrated, the Senate gave its advice and consent to the ratification of the protocol of signature, but attached a series of reservations (3A). The American government made every effort to secure the acceptance of the several nations, members of the Court, of the Senate's reservations. How far this effort was successful is indicated in President Hoover's appeal to the Senate to accept a revised statute and protocol of signature (3B). Neither he nor his immediate successor in the White House, however, was successful in coping with the intransigence of the Senate.

Perhaps the greatest opportunity for international cooperation during the era after World War I was afforded the United States by the Japanese invasion of Manchuria on September 18, 1931. Almost immediately after the invasion began, China appealed to the United States to take steps to preserve the peace in the Far East (4A). Secretary of State Stimson notified Japan that the invasion of Manchuria was of concern to the entire world, and that it involved the Nine-Power Treaty and the Kellogg-Briand Pact (4B). A few days later, October 5, 1941, the Secretary communicated a remarkable statement of American policy to the Council of the League (4C). His statement seemed to promise American assistance in case the League decided on forceful action. Mr. Stimson, made no suggestion, however, concerning what appropriate action might be taken, opposed the appointment of a neutral commission of inquiry, and indicated, later, that the United States would have no part in a program of coercion. The League acted slowly and cautiously, but finally decided to appoint a commission of inquiry.

Meanwhile the Japanese military steadily advanced into Manchuria notwithstanding statements and promises of the Japanese government to the contrary. Secretary Stimson decided to take a more vigorous stand. Acting independently of the League, and without consulting the other great powers, he announced on January 7, 1932, his famous non-recognition doctrine (4D). This substantially reaffirmed the policy announced May 11, 1915, by President Wilson concerning Japan's Twenty One Demands on China. After some delay the League of Nations adopted the Stimson doctrine.

The commission of inquiry authorized by the League, the Lytton Commission, made its report on October 1, 1932. The Assembly of the League, basing its policies largely on this report, adopted a series of recommendations concerning the Manchurian affair on February 24, 1933. These recommendations suggested the withdrawal of Japanese troops from Manchuria, proposed an equitable settlement of the Sino-Japanese difficulties, reaffirmed the non-recognition doctrine, and requested the cooperation of non-members of the League who were signatories of the Nine-Power Treaty and the Pact of Paris. The United States complied with the request for cooperation in a communication dated February 25, 1933 (4E). Japan, however, rejected the suggestions of the Assembly and withdrew from the League.

Shortly after the beginning of the Roosevelt administration, the Secretary of State, Cordell Hull, urged the enactment of legislation giving the President authority to establish an arms embargo whenever he found that the foreign sale of arms and ammunitions of war encouraged the employment of force in a dispute between nations. In advocating this legislation, Mr. Hull discussed the Far Eastern situation (4F). Congress failed to act and, instead, moved toward its policy of the so-called "new-neutrality."

◇◇◇◇◇◇◇◇◇◇◇◇◇

1. THE KELLOGG-BRIAND PACT[1]

. . . *ART. 1.* The high contracting parties solemnly declare in the names of their respective peoples that they condemn recourse to war for the solu-

[1] *The General Pact for the Renunciation of War,* United States Government Printing Office, Washington, 1928, pp. 1–3. Concluded at Paris, Aug. 27, 1928; ratification advised by the Senate, Jan. 15, 1929; proclaimed Jan. 24, 1929.

tion of international controversies, and renounce it as an instrument of national policy in their relations with one another.

Art. 2. The high contracting parties agree that the settlement or solution of all disputes or conflicts of whatever nature or of whatever origin they may be, which may arise among them, shall never be sought except by pacific means.

Art. 3. The present treaty shall be ratified by the high contracting parties named in the preamble in accordance with their respective constitutional requirements, and shall take effect as between them as soon as all their several instruments of ratification shall have been deposited at Washington.

This treaty shall, when it has come into effect as prescribed in the preceding paragraph, remain open as long as may be necessary for adherence by all the other powers of the world. Every instrument evidencing the adherence of a power shall be deposited at Washington and the treaty shall immediately upon such deposit become effective as between the power thus adhering and the other powers parties hereto. . . .

2. INTERPRETATIONS OF THE KELLOGG-BRIAND PACT

[*Discussions in the United States Senate*]

[*SENATOR William E. Borah of Idaho*] The question which may be considered first not only in point of time but in some respects in importance is that of the right of self-defense under the treaty. It is conceded upon the part of all now that the right of self-defense is in no wise curtailed or embarrassed by the treaty, the Secretary of State taking the position, and the other governments promptly acceding to it, that the right of self-defense is an inherent right, implicit in every treaty; that it is a right which can not be bartered away, abrogated, or surrendered; and that each nation may under the treaty determine for itself when the right of self-defense arises and the extent to which it may go in defending its rights.

The criticism is at once made that this practically destroys the value of the treaty; that it is a weakness the measure of which can hardly be estimated, it is contended. If, say the critics, a nation may determine for itself what constitutes an attack and what constitutes the right of self-defense, it leaves the entire treaty and its effect within the judgment of any particular nation which may feel disposed to answer to an attack or threatened attack. I frankly concede, Mr. President, there is in that respect a weakness, but it is a weakness which is inherent in human nature and inherent in the conditions which obtain. I presume until we are willing to have a supergovernment, a government of sufficient sovereign power as a supergovernment to execute its decrees, that no nation will ever surrender or undertake to surrender – in my judgment it could not do so – the right of self-defense, and no nation will surrender the right to determine for itself what constitutes an attack or what is justification for defense. This is a right which must be conceded as a part of every treaty.

If the treaty undertook to provide such a surrender, I take it that it would not receive the support of anyone. It never would have been proposed by the President to the Senate, and would not meet with the approval of any Member of the Senate.

In discussing this question of self-defense, the Secretary of State had this to say:

"The Government of the United States believes that the right of self-defense is inherent in every sovereign state, and implicit in every treaty. No specific reference to that inalienable attribute of sovereignty is, therefore, necessary or desirable. . . ."

The only censor – and these things we may understand and frankly admit – the only censor or criticizing power of a nation exercising the right of self-defense, if it does not exercise it upon true principle, is the power of public opinion. There being no supergovernment, no tribunal to which to appeal, and no one willing to create a supergovernment, and no authority otherwise to pass upon the matter, that is the only judge that we can rely upon to censor this part of the treaty. I know of no other tribunal to which we can appeal for the rectitude of nations in the exercise of this right of self-defense.

The second proposition of importance is the question of sanctions. What agreement, express or implied, do the signatories to the treaty make with reference to enforcing the treaty? Is force or punitive measures, express or implied, anywhere provided for in the treaty? If a nation violates the treaty are we under any obligation, express or implied, to apply coercive or punitive measures? I answer emphatically, no!

It will certainly not be contended that the language of the treaty itself makes any such provision. The language of the treaty refutes the proposition. The philosophy of the treaty is not that of preventing war, but that of organizing peace, which is a wholly different thing. The treaty is not founded upon the theory of force or punitive measures at any place or at any time. . . .

We ought to consider the treaty for what it is. It may in the minds of some impair its value when we take away the idea of force being behind the treaty or sanctions existing, express or implied, but nevertheless that is the treaty. There are no sanctions; the treaty rests in a wholly different philosophy. . . .[2]

[*Senator Hiram Johnson of California*] . . . Under the covenant of the League of Nations there was a moral obligation that existed, as the Senator believes?

[2] *Cong. Record,* 70th Congress, 2nd Session, Vol. 70, pp. 1063–6, Jan. 3, 1929.

Mr. Borah. There was an express obligation.

Mr. Johnson. There was an express obligation, and it was an express obligation to enforce a breach of the peace or a violation of the provisions of the league?

Mr. Borah. Yes.

Mr. Johnson. There is no such obligation, express or implied, under the present treaty?

Mr. Borah. No; there is no such obligation. . . .

Mr. Borah. . . . In other words, the covenant of the League of Nations had certain express provisions with reference to maintaining peace. The United States not having joined the league could not be bound by any of the obligations, express or implied, of the league, and, although all members of the league might be bound by reason of certain conditions which should arise, the United States would not be bound.

Mr. Johnson. What I am endeavoring to make plain, if the Senator will permit me, is that the breach was, alike under the covenant of the league and under this treaty, a breach of the peace. All the nations except the United States under the covenant of the league would endeavor to enforce the obligation that rests upon them and against the party that was guilty of the breach. The United States then would stand aloof, the only nation on the face of the earth that was a party to the same breach in a different treaty, doing nothing at all, with no obligation either express or implied.

Mr. Borah. Exactly. In other words, when the treaty is broken the United States is absolutely free. It is just as free to choose its course as if the treaty had never been written. . . .[3]

[*Senator Claude Swanson of Virginia*] . . . The Secretary of State, in his speech of April 28, 1928, which was communicated to all the governments concerned as his interpretation of the pact, stated:

"There is nothing in the American draft of an antiwar treaty which restricts or impairs in any way the right of self-defense. . . ."

This interpretation was concurred in by all signatories of the treaty.

Thus, it is universally acknowledged that all wars of self-defense are excluded from the operation of this treaty, and every nation determines for itself the question of self-defense. It should be noted that this question of self-defense is not limited to territory, but includes anything that any nation may determine is vital for its protection and self-defense. The wars excluded from the operations of this treaty by this interpretation are as limitless as the imagination or the ambition of nations may desire. It practically excludes from the operations of this treaty almost any war that has occurred in the last century. I hardly recall a war that has occurred during this period that the governments engaged did not claim to be a war of self-defense. Every government that engaged in the World War in-

[3] Ibid., p. 1066, Jan. 3, 1929.

sisted it was waged on their part for self-defense. Thus, this treaty would have been wholly ineffective in restraining any of the governments that participated in the World War. This interpretation, given by the Secretary of State and acquiesced in by all the signatories, permits governments desirous of engaging in war to be unrestrained by this treaty, because all they will have to do is to claim it is a war of self-defense, and the interpretations of the treaty make them alone the judge of this question. Its significance as a solemn peace pact by these interpretations is seriously impaired. . . .

Mr. President, although this treaty is a mere gesture, yet it is a gesture of peace, not hostility; of good will and conciliation, not of irritation and defiance. While it may be powerless to prevent war, yet it legalizes no war. It permits but does not approve war. It is a noble gesture or declaration for world peace and as such I shall support it. . . .[4]

[*Senator W. C. Bruce of Maryland*] Mr. President, when I concluded my remarks yesterday I had been saying, among other things, that there were several distinct views that might reasonably be formed as to the practical value of the Kellogg peace pact. I had said that one view that might reasonably be entertained about it was that it was a brutum fulmen, a mere pompous gesture, and that idea I endeavored to expound as effectively as I could. This morning I desire to take up two other views that might reasonably be formed about it.

One view is that it is even worse than a mere parchment futility, because its tendency is to lull our people into a false sense of national security and to lead them to believe that paper professions and promises can take the place of adequate naval and military defenses. In other words, it may be forcibly argued that the tendency of all sanctionless pacts, such as the Kellogg pact, is to create the impression that there is no need for a nation to rely upon the strong hands and stout hearts of its people and adequate preparation in the form of military and naval armaments for its safety at that critical hour involving its welfare, or perhaps even its life, which may at any time come. . . .

But . . . I propose to vote for the ratification of the Kellogg pact because I agree with the statesmen of England and other European statesmen in believing that it at least measurably tends to draw our country into the only two institutions in the world to-day that hold out any real promise of international peace — that is to say, the World Court and the League of Nations.

It is perfectly obvious to my mind that some of the countries that have signed the Kellogg pact would never have done so had they not believed that it sets up a distinct, definite milestone for us on our way to the World Court and the League of Nations. . . .[5]

---

[4] Ibid., pp. 1186–9, Jan. 5, 1929.
[5] Ibid., pp. 1332–3, Jan. 8, 1929.

[*Senator Carter Glass of Virginia*] . . . I may say that I intend to vote for the peace pact; but I am not willing that anybody in Virginia shall think that I am simple enough to suppose that it is worth a postage stamp in the direction of accomplishing permanent international peace.

I think we are about to renounce something as a national policy which no nation on earth for 150 years has ever proclaimed as a national policy. Those who are familiar with the period must know that not even Napoleon was ever willing to concede that war was the national policy of his empire. In fact he rarely ever, if ever – except at Waterloo, when time with him was the deciding factor – went into a great battle without first importuning the adversary monarch against hostilities and begging him to avoid the inevitable sacrifice of life which would be involved in joining battle.

I had purposed speaking on the pact, but when I sat here and reflected that in the 28 years that I have been a Member of one or the other branches of Congress I have never known a speech to change a vote, I decided that I would not encroach upon the time of the Senate or delay the consummation of this great peace pact; yet I am not willing merely to vote and not go into the *Record* as having no confidence whatsoever in the accomplishment of any good by this alleged pact.

I am going to vote for the treaty for the simple reason that I think its defeat will psychologically be a bad thing. I have come to the considered judgment that Mr. Lincoln's most popular aphorism needs amending, wherein he said that "you can not fool all the people all the time." If the word "time" may be applied to an epoch or a period rather than to eternity, I say that all the people all the time for nearly the last 10 years have been fooled. They are going to be fooled now by a so-called peace pact that, in the last analysis, is one of the many devices that have been contrived to solace the awakened conscience of some people who kept the United States out of the League of Nations; and, whether it was so intended or not, it is going to confuse the minds of many good and pious people who think that peace may be secured by polite professions of neighborly and brotherly love. . . .[6]

◇◇◇◇◇◇◇◇◇◇◇◇◇

3. THE WORLD COURT

(A) THE SENATE'S RESERVATIONS [7]

WHEREAS the President, under date of February 24, 1923, transmitted a message to the Senate, accompanied by a letter from the Secretary of State, dated February 17th, 1923, asking the favorable advice and consent of the Senate to the adherence on the part of the United States to the protocol of December 16, 1920, of signature of the statute for the Per-

---

[6] Ibid., p. 1728, Jan. 15, 1929.

[7] Resolution of the Senate of the United States, adopted January 27, 1926. *Cong. Record*, 69th Congress, 1st Session, Vol. 67, pp. 2824–5.

manent Court of International Justice, set out in the said message of the President (without accepting or agreeing to the optional clause for compulsory jurisdiction contained therein), upon the conditions and understandings hereafter stated, to be made a part of the instrument of adherence:

Therefore be it

Resolved (*two-thirds of the Senators present concurring*), That the Senate advise and consent to the adherence on the part of the United States to the said protocol of December 16, 1920, and the adjoined statute for the Permanent Court of International Justice (without accepting or agreeing to the optional clause for compulsory jurisdiction contained in said statute), and that the signature of the United States be affixed to the said protocol, subject to the following reservations and understandings, which are hereby made a part and condition of this resolution, namely:

1. That such adherence shall not be taken to involve any legal relation on the part of the United States to the League of Nations or the assumption of any obligations by the United States under the Treaty of Versailles.
2. That the United States shall be permitted to participate, through representatives designated for the purpose and upon an equality with the other states, members, respectively, of the Council and Assembly of the League of Nations, in any and all proceedings of either the council or the Assembly for the election of judges or deputy judges of the Permanent Court of International Justice or for the filling of vacancies.
3. That the United States will pay a fair share of the expenses of the court as determined and appropriated from time to time by the Congress of the United States.
4. That the United States may at any time withdraw its adherence to the said protocol and that the statute for the Permanent Court of International Justice adjoined to the protocol shall not be amended without the consent of the United States.
5. That the court shall not render any advisory opinion except publicly after due notice to all states adhering to the court and to all interested states and after public hearing or opportunity for hearing given to any state concerned; nor shall it, without the consent of the United States, entertain any request for an advisory opinion touching any dispute or question in which the United States has or claims an interest.

The signature of the United States to the said protocol shall not be affixed until the powers signatory to such protocol shall have indicated, through an exchange of notes, their acceptance of the foregoing reservations and understandings as a part and a condition of adherence by the United States to the said protocol.

Resolved further, as a part of this act of ratification, that the United States approve the protocol and statute hereinabove mentioned, with the understanding that recourse to the Permanent Court of International Justice for the settlement of differences between the United States and any other state or states can be had only by agreement thereto through general or special treaties concluded between the parties in dispute; and

Resolved further, That adherence to the said protocol and statute hereby approved shall not be so construed as to require the United States to depart from its traditional policy of not intruding upon, interfering with, or entangling itself in the political questions of policy or internal administration of any foreign State; nor shall adherence to the said protocol and statute be construed to imply a relinquishment by the United States of its traditional attitude toward purely American questions.

Agreed to, January 16th (Calendar day, January 27th), 1926.

(B) PRESIDENT HOOVER'S MESSAGE TO THE SENATE[8] ON THE REVISED PROTOCOLS

I have the honor to transmit to the Senate for its consideration and action, three documents concerning adherence of the United States to the Court of International Justice. I inclose also a report of November 18, 1929, by the Secretary of State. I trust the protocols may have consideration as soon as possible after the emergency relief and appropriation legislation has been disposed of.

It will be recalled that on January 27, 1926, following extended consideration, the Senate advised and gave consent to adherence to the court with five reservations; and it gave authorization to effect their acceptance by an exchange of notes. Consent to four of these reservations was promptly expressed at a meeting of the nations members of the court, and after negotiations undertaken with the approval of President Coolidge, two protocols were drawn to revise the statutes of the court in order to embody this consent and also to meet the fifth reservation. The protocol of accession of the United States and the protocol of revision have now been signed by practically all the nations which are members of the court and have also already been ratified by a large majority of those nations.

The provisions of the protocols free us from any entanglement in the diplomacy of other nations. We can not be summoned before this court, we can from time to time seek its services by agreement with other nations. These protocols permit our withdrawal from the court at any time without reproach or ill will.

The movement for the establishment of such a court originated with our country. It has been supported by Presidents Wilson, Harding, and Coolidge; by Secretaries of State Hughes, Kellogg, and Stimson; it springs from the earnest seeking of our people for justice in international relations and to strengthen the foundations of peace.

Through the Kellogg-Briand pact we have pledged ourselves to the use of pacific means in settlement of all controversies. Our great Nation, so devoted to peace and justice, should lend its cooperation in this effort of the nations to establish a great agency for such pacific settlements.

8 Message of December 10, 1930. *Cong. Record,* 71st Congress, 3rd Sess, Vol. 74, Part 1, pp. 504–5.

◇◇◇◇◇◇◇◇◇◇◇◇◇

4. THE INVASION OF MANCHURIA

(A) THE APPEAL OF CHINA TO THE UNITED STATES [9]

. . . JAPANESE troops near Shenyang (Mukden), without the slightest provocation, opened an attack on the Chinese barracks on September 18, at 10 p.m., and continued bombarding the Chinese camps and arsenal, killing a large number of Chinese people in spite of the complete non-resistance of the Chinese troops. The whole city of Chenyang and its vicinity were occupied by Japanese troops by September 19, at 6.30 a.m. The occupation of Antung is already confirmed, and possibly other places also are now under Japanese military control.

As the United States, China, and Japan are all signatory powers of the Kellogg pact, and as the United States is the sponsor of the sacred engagements contained in this treaty, the American Government must be deeply interested in this case of unprovoked and unwarranted attack and subsequent occupation of Chinese cities by Japanese troops, which constitutes a deliberate violation of the pact. The Chinese Government urgently appeals to the American Government to take such steps as will insure the preservation of peace in the Far East, and the upholding of the principle of peaceful settlement of international disputes.

(B) DIRECT ACTION OF THE AMERICAN GOVERNMENT [10]

Without going into the background, either as to the immediate provocation or remote causes or motivation, it appears that there has developed within the past four days a situation in Manchuria which I find surprising and view with concern. Japanese military forces, with some opposition at some points by Chinese military forces, have occupied the principal strategic points in south Manchuria, including the principal administrative center, together with some at least of the public utilities. It appears that the highest Chinese authority ordered the Chinese military not to resist, and that, when news of the situation reached Tokyo, but after most of the acts of occupation had been consummated, the Japanese Government ordered cessation of military activities on the part of the Japanese forces. Nevertheless, it appears some military movements have been continuously and are even now in process. The actual situation is that an arm of the Japanese Government is in complete control of south Manchuria.

The League of Nations has given evidence of its concern. The Chinese Government has in various ways invoked action on the part of foreign

---

[9] Note of the Chinese Government to the American Government, Sept. 21, 1931. *Sen. Doc.* No. 55, 72nd Congress, 1st Session, p. 3.

[10] Note of the Secretary of State, Henry L. Stimson, to the Japanese Ambassador, Katsuji Debuchi, Sept. 22, 1931. Ibid., pp. 4–5.

governments, citing its reliance upon treaty obligations and inviting special reference to the Kellogg pact.

This situation is of concern, morally, legally, and politically to a considerable number of nations. It is not exclusively a matter of concern to Japan and China. It brings into question at once the meaning of certain provisions of agreements, such as the nine powers treaty of February 6, 1922, and the Kellogg-Briand pact.

The American Government is confident that it has not been the intention of the Japanese Government to create or to be a party to the creation of a situation which brings the applicability of treaty provisions into consideration. The American Government does not wish to be hasty in formulating its conclusions or in taking a position. However, the American Government feels that a very unfortunate situation exists, which no doubt is embarrassing to the Japanese Government. It would seem that the responsibility for determining the course of events with regard to the liquidating of this situation rests largely upon Japan, for the simple reason that Japanese armed forces have seized and are exercising de facto control in south Manchuria.

It is alleged by the Chinese, and the allegation has the support of circumstantial evidence, that lines of communication outward from Manchuria have been cut or interfered with. If this is true, it is unfortunate.

It is the hope of the American Government that the orders which it understands have been given both by the Japanese and the Chinese Governments to their military forces to refrain from hostilities and further movements will be respected and that there will be no further application of force. It is also the hope of the American Government that the Japanese and the Chinese Governments will find it possible speedily to demonstrate to the world that neither has any intention to take advantage, in furtherance of its own peculiar interests, of the situation which has been brought about in connection with and in consequence of this use of force.

What has occurred has already shaken the confidence of the public with regard to the stability of conditions in Manchuria, and it is believed that the crystallizing of a situation suggesting the necessity for an indefinite continuance of military occupation would further undermine that confidence.

(C) CO-OPERATION WITH THE LEAGUE OF NATIONS [11]

I believe that our cooperation in the future handling of this difficult matter should proceed along the course which has been followed ever since the first outbreak of the trouble fortunately found the Assembly, and Council of the League of Nations in session. The council has deliberated long and earnestly on this matter and the covenant of the League of Nations pro-

11 Memorandum of the Secretary of State of Oct. 5, 1931, communicated to the Council of the League. Ibid., p. 14.

vides permanent and already tested machinery for handling such issues as between States members of the league. Both the Chinese and Japanese have presented and argued their cases before the council and the world has been informed through published accounts with regard to the proceedings there. The council has formulated conclusions and outlined a course of action to be followed by the disputants; and as the said disputants have made commitments to the council, it is most desirable that the league in no way relax its vigilance and in no way fail to assert all the pressure and authority within its competence toward regulating the action of China and Japan in the premises.

On its part the American Government acting independently through its diplomatic representatives will endeavor to reinforce what the league does and will make clear that it has a keen interest in the matter and is not oblivious to the obligations which the disputants have assumed to their fellow signatories in the pact of Paris as well as in the nine-power pact should a time arise when it would seem advisable to bring forward those obligations. By this course we avoid any danger of embarrassing the league in the course to which it is now committed.

(D) NON-RECOGNITION DOCTRINE [12]

With the recent military operations about Chinchow, the last remaining administrative authority of the Government of the Chinese Republic in South Manchuria, as it existed prior to September 18, 1931, has been destroyed. The American Government continues confident that the work of the neutral commission recently authorized by the Council of the League of Nations will facilitate an ultimate solution of the difficulties now existing between China and Japan. But in view of the present situation and of its own rights and obligations therein, the American Government deems it to be its duty to notify both the Governments of the Chinese Republic and the Imperial Japanese Government that it can not admit the legality of any situation de facto nor does it intend to recognize any treaty or agreement entered into between those governments, or agents thereof, which may impair the treaty rights of the United States or its citizens in China, including those which relate to the sovereignty, the independence, or the territorial and administrative integrity of the Republic of China, or to the international policy relative to China, commonly known as the open-door policy; and that it does not intend to recognize any situation, treaty, or agreement which may be brought about by means contrary to the covenants and obligations of the pact of Paris of August 27, 1928, to which treaty both China and Japan, as well as the United States, are parties.

---

[12] Identic note sent by the American Government to the Government of China and Japan, Jan. 7, 1932, Ibid., pp. 53–4.

(E) AMERICAN ENDORSEMENT OF THE LEAGUE'S PROPOSALS [13]

There has been communicated to me the text of your letter of February 24, 1933, transmitting to me a copy of the report of the Committee of Nineteen as adopted by the Assembly of the League of Nations on this day.

I note your request that I communicate to you as soon as possible the reply of the Government of the United States.

In response to that request I have the honor to state the views of the American Government as follows:

In the situation which has developed out of the controversy between China and Japan, the purpose of the United States has coincided in general with that of the League of Nations, the common objective being maintenance of peace and settlement of international disputes by pacific means. In pursuance of that objective, while the League of Nations has been exercising jurisdiction over a controversy between two of its members, the Government of the United States has endeavored to give support, reserving to itself independence of judgment with regard to method and scope, to the efforts of the League on behalf of peace.

The findings of fact arrived at by the League and the understanding of the facts derived by the American Government from reports made to it by its own representatives are in substantial accord. In the light of its findings of fact, the Assembly of the League has formulated a measured statement of conclusions. With those conclusions the American Government is in general accord. In their affirmations respectively of the principle of nonrecognition and their attitude in regard thereto the League and the United States are on common ground. The League has recommended principles of settlement. In so far as appropriate under the treaties to which it is a party, the American Government expresses its general endorsement of the principles thus recommended.

The American Government earnestly hopes that the two nations now engaged in controversy, both of which have long been in friendly relationship with our own and other peoples, may find it possible, in the light of the now clear expression of world opinion, to conform their policies to the need and the desire of the family of nations that disputes between nations shall be settled by none but pacific means. . . .

(F) REQUEST FOR PERMISSION TO ESTABLISH AN ARMS EMBARGO [14]

. . . It has never been the intention and is not now the intention of this Government to use the authority which would be conferred upon the Executive by this Resolution as a means of restoring peace between China

[13] Secretary Stimson to the American Minister in Switzerland, Hugh R. Wilson. *Papers Relating to the Foreign Relations of the United States, Japan,* 1931–1941 (Washington, D.C., 1943), Vol. I, pp. 115–16.

[14] Memorandum by the Secretary of State, Cordell Hull, to the Committee on Foreign Relations of the United States Senate, May 17, 1933. *Peace and War; United States Foreign Policy,* 1931–1941 (Washington, D.C., 1943), pp. 183–6.

and Japan. An embargo on arms and munitions of war would not be an effective means of restoring peace in this case. Japan is an important producer of arms and munitions of war. Her industry is sufficiently developed to supply her present and probable future needs. China is dependent upon her importation of these commodities. An embargo on the exportation of arms and munitions to both China and Japan would, therefore, militate against China and in favor of Japan. An embargo directed against Japan alone would probably result in a Japanese blockade of Chinese ports, in the seizure by the Japanese of arms and munitions intended for China, and thus its ultimate effects would probably be to decrease China's supply of arms and increase, by virtue of seizures, Japan's supply. As this Government concurs in general in the findings of the Lytton Commission which place the major responsibility upon Japan for the international conflict now proceeding in China, this Government would not be disposed to take any action which would favor the military operations of the Japanese. From the information in our possession, it would appear that this view of the situation is shared by the principal powers members of the League of Nations. We do not, therefore, envisage the probability of proposals by the League or by its principal members to this Government to cooperate with them in an embargo on the shipment of arms and munitions to Japan. Should such proposals be made, we would not be disposed to give them favorable consideration, and we would not under any circumstances agree to participate in an international embargo of this kind unless we had secured substantial guarantees from the governments of all of the great powers which would ensure us against the effects of any retaliatory measures which the Japanese might undertake. In brief, this Government does not expect to take any action of this nature in connection with this case; if any action is taken it will certainly be taken with a due and prudent regard for American interests and in particular for our paramount interest of remaining free from any entanglements which would involve this country in a foreign war. One of the most important reasons for the passage of this Resolution at this time is, however, connected with the present situation in the Far East. There is danger that if this legislation is not enacted, certain European governments may find it to their interest to make it appear that this Government is responsible, by virtue of its not being in a position to cooperate, for a failure on their part to proceed with the imposition of sanctions to which they are committed by reason of their membership in the League of Nations. Thus they would make this country appear in the eyes of many of their nationals and of a large section of public opinion in this country to bear the onus of their failure to make effective the peace machinery which they have built up. If the Resolution is passed, it would no longer be possible for them to make the excuse that their failure to come to an agreement among themselves in regard to a course of action was due to the fact that we were not in a position to cooperate with them if requested to do so. Under these circumstances, failure on their part to take action would manifestly be due solely to their own inability to reach an agreement on the basis of which to request our cooperation, and the facts of the situation would be obvious to all the world; they could attribute no responsibility or blame to us.

It is not our policy to have this Government posing before the world as a leader in all the efforts to prevent or put an end to wars but on the other hand it is not our policy to lag behind the other nations of the world in their efforts to promote peace. The passage of this Resolution is necessary in order that this Government may keep pace with other Governments of the world in this movement.

10 thru 16 only

Chapter XXXI

INTER-AMERICAN RELATIONS 1900—1947

FOR SEVERAL YEARS prior to 1900 American influence in the Caribbean area had been increasing both politically and economically. The Olney interpretation of the Monroe Doctrine provided a theoretical basis for political action in Venezuela, while the acquisition of Puerto Rico and the Panama Canal represented positive expansion of American power in the area. American influence was extended over Cuba through the Platt Amendment (1), and over Santo Domingo through a receivership of customs (2). President Theodore Roosevelt's message to Congress of 1904 (3) shows how political theory could keep pace with the progress of events. American economic expansion into Mexico and Central America added to the growing sentiment in Latin America that the United States was the "colossus of the North."

President Wilson was opposed to American imperialism either in Latin America or elsewhere. His Mobile Speech of 1913 (4), and his address to the Pan-American Scientific Congress in 1916 (5) are excellent examples of a new orientation of American policy. The Wilson policy of non-intervention, however, did not mean the abandonment of American hegemony in the Caribbean area as the Bryan-Chamorro Treaty demonstrated (6). The policy of non-intervention was severely criticized, however, by various political and economic groups in the United States who wanted greater protection for their economic interests. The message of President Coolidge to Congress of January 10, 1927, shows the reaction to Wilson's policies (7).

The advent of President Hoover's administration appeared to usher in a new Latin American policy. Actually, however, it brought only an acceleration in the tempo of change which had begun during the latter part of the previous administration. This change was inaugurated very quietly and indirectly through a memorandum on the Monroe Doctrine prepared by J. Reuben Clark and authorized by the Department of State (8). The new policy was really a return to Wilson's policies with the exception of his doctrine of non-recognition (9). Under the guiding hand of Secretary Cordell Hull, the "good neighbor" policy (10) of President Franklin D. Roosevelt led to increasingly cordial Latin American relations. Largely for this reason the inter-American conferences at Montevideo in 1933, and at Buenos Aires in 1936, were unusually productive of treaties for the establishment of inter-American peace and friendship. Among the treaties

and declarations adopted at the latter conference, the Consultative Pact (11), the Treaty of Non-Intervention (12), and a declaration concerning inter-American solidarity were of particular significance (13).

At the Eighth International Conference of American States in 1938, it was agreed that "in case the peace, security, or territorial integrity of any American Republic" was endangered, the several states would consult together, and that, in order to facilitate such consultations, any one of them could call a meeting of their respective foreign ministers. Within a little over a month after the German invasion of Poland the first of a series of meetings of foreign ministers of the American Republics took place in Panama at the invitation of that country. The ministers agreed to a program regarding neutrality (14A), and adopted the Declaration of Panama which proclaimed the establishment of a neutrality zone around the American Republics (14B).

With the rapid success of German aggression in Europe during the first half of 1940, the United States and other American Republics became alarmed over the possible fate of the possessions of Great Britain, France, and the Netherlands in the Western Hemisphere. As a result of this alarm a second meeting of foreign ministers of the American Republics was held in Havana, and the Act of Havana was adopted (14C). A third meeting of foreign ministers, held after the outbreak of war between the United States and the Axis nations, adopted the Act of Rio de Janeiro (14D). Item IV of this Act provided that, prior to the establishment of peace, the American Republics would consult again in order to give their action a "solidary character." The result of this agreement was the Inter-American Conference on Problems of War and Peace, held in Mexico City February 21 to March 8, 1945. The Act of Chapultepec (14E), adopted at this conference, was the culmination of patient and successful effort to promote inter-American solidarity.

The basic policies in the relations between the United States and Canada during the second World War were set forth in the Ogdensburg Agreement (15A), and in the Hyde Park Declaration (15B). A good general analysis of Canadian-American cooperation was made by the Canadian Prime Minister on April 28, 1941 (15C).

1. THE PLATT AMENDMENT[1]

[*Provisions concerning Cuba attached by the Congress of the United States to the Army Appropriation Bill, March 2, 1901*]

. . . *PROVIDED FURTHER*, That in fulfillment of the declaration contained in the joint resolution approved April twentieth, eighteen hundred

1 *The Statutes at Large of the United States*, Vol. XXXI, Part II, pp. 895–8.

and ninety-eight, entitled, "For the recognition of the independence of the people of Cuba, demanding that the Government of Spain relinquish its authority and government in the island of Cuba, and to withdraw its land and naval forces from Cuba and Cuban waters, and directing the President of the United States to use the land and naval forces of the United States to carry these resolutions into effect," the President is hereby authorized to "leave the government and control of the island of Cuba to its people" so soon as a government shall have been established in said island under a constitution which, either as a part thereof or in an ordinance appended thereto, shall define the future relations of the United States with Cuba, substantially as follows:

I. That the government of Cuba shall never enter into any treaty or other compact with any foreign power or powers which will impair or tend to impair the independence of Cuba, nor in any manner authorize or permit any foreign power or powers to obtain by colonization or for military or naval purposes or otherwise, lodgment in or control over any portion of said island.

II. That said government shall not assume or contract any public debt, to pay the interest upon which, and to make reasonable sinking fund provision for the ultimate discharge of which, the ordinary revenues of the island, after defraying the current expenses of government shall be inadequate.

III. That the government of Cuba consents that the United States may exercise the right to intervene for the preservation of Cuban independence, the maintenance of a government adequate for the protection of life, property, and individual liberty, and for discharging the obligations with respect to Cuba imposed by the treaty of Paris on the United States, now to be assumed and undertaken by the government of Cuba.

IV. That all Acts of the United States in Cuba during its military occupancy thereof are ratified and validated, and all lawful rights acquired thereunder shall be maintained and protected.

V. That the government of Cuba will execute, and as far as necessary extend, the plans already devised or other plans to be mutually agreed upon, for the sanitation of the cities of the island, to the end that a recurrence of epidemic and infectious diseases may be prevented, thereby assuring protection to the people and commerce of Cuba, as well as to the commerce of the southern ports of the United States and the people residing therein.

VI. That the Isle of Pines shall be omitted from the proposed constitutional boundaries of Cuba, the title thereto being left to future adjustment by treaty.

VII. That to enable the United States to maintain the independence of Cuba, and to protect the people thereof, as well as for its own defense, the government of Cuba will sell or lease to the United States lands necessary for coaling or naval stations at certain specified points, to be agreed upon with the President of the United States.

VIII. That by way of further assurance the government of Cuba will embody the foregoing provisions in a permanent treaty with the United States.

◇◇◇◇◇◇◇◇◇◇◇◇

2. A RECEIVERSHIP FOR SANTO DOMINGO[2]

[*T. C. Dawson to John Hay*]

Santo Domingo, January 2, 1905

I HAVE the honor to confirm your telegram, as follows:

Washington, December 30, 1904

Confidential. You will sound the President of Santo Domingo, discreetly but earnestly and in a perfectly friendly spirit, touching the disquieting situation which is developing owing to the pressure of other governments having arbitral awards in their favor and who regard our award as conflicting with their rights. Already one European Government strongly intimates that it may resort to occupation of some Dominican customs ports to secure its own payment. There appears to be a concert among them. You will ascertain whether the Government of Santo Domingo would be disposed to request the United States to take charge of the collection of duties and effect an equitable distribution of the assigned quotas among the Dominican Government and the several claimants. We have grounds to think that such arrangement would satisfy the other powers, besides serving as a practical guaranty of the peace of Santo Domingo from external influence or internal disturbance.

and to say that I immediately called upon President Morales.

We entered upon a full and friendly discussion of the international relations and internal politics of this country as affected by its financial obligations, in the course of which I did not disguise from him my conviction that the European creditors would wait no longer for their money. He frankly answered that such was his own conviction and that he was daily expecting a European demand, backed by a war vessel, and a demand from me for the four northern ports under the Improvement award. He clearly realizes that the European creditors will accept no guaranty he can offer, and each would insist on having the full annual amount provided for its own protocol, leaving him nothing, or next to nothing, to run the administration. He said that personally he had long been of the opinion that the best solution was for the United States to take charge of the collection of the revenues, guaranteeing to the Dominican Government enough to live on and arranging with the creditors.

I asked him if he was prepared to make, in the name of his government, a request that my government undertake this task. He answered that he was almost ready; that the opposition to American intervention within his

[2] *Papers Relating to the Foreign Relations of the United States,* 1905, pp. 298–300.

cabinet and among his prominent supporters had much diminished in the last two weeks; Minister Velasquez had despaired of carrying out his own plan; the arrangement at Monte Christi was not working well; it had been proposed in the last cabinet meeting to ask the United States to take charge of that port.

I told him I could not recommend such a proposition to my government; that if we were forced to ask for more ports under the award it would be for Sanchez and Samana, as well as Monte Christi; that I appreciated how great were the political difficulties he was struggling against – difficulties which arose from the deeply grounded prejudice against any sort of American intervention existing among some of his supporters – but that it was for him and not me to say if he had succeeded in removing that prejudice, or if the time had come for him to act in spite of it.

He then asked me to make a written proposition, stating the proportion or amount that I would recommend to be allowed for administrative expenses of the Dominican Government. I begged him to excuse me from doing so, and suggested that the first step had better be a proposition from the Dominican Government, embodying the principle of American collection on a basis that seemed to him just and practicable. He agreed, and said that his own idea was 40 per cent for the creditors and 60 per cent to the Dominican Government.

I expressed some doubts as to whether my government could reach an arrangement with the creditors if limited to such a sum, but agreed to submit it as a tentative proposition as soon as his doubts as to the attitude of his anti-American supporters should be cleared up. Thereupon he asked me to talk with Joubert and Velasquez, with a view to emphasizing the impression already made by the former on the latter's mind. The President said that if Velasquez could be brought to agree, Vasquez and Caceres would follow. Joubert had already half convinced him that the American Government had no selfish or ulterior views in this matter, and an interview with me would tend to convince him further that an American intervention in the custom-houses would be conducted in a manner that would offend Dominican pride as little as possible and not destroy the prerogatives of the office of minister of finance.

Accordingly, in the last three days, I have had several interviews with the President, Joubert, Velasquez, and Sanchez, and this morning I felt justified in sending you the telegram which I hereby confirm:

Santo Domingo, January 2, 1905

Dominican President disposed to request United States take charge of collections all customs on the following conditions: Distribute 40 per cent annual receipts among all creditors – remaining 60 to the Dominican Government.

In the course of these interviews I have been obliged to reject several suggestions which seemed to be inadmissible. The first was that I should commit myself personally in favor of the proposed division of the revenues – 40 per cent and 60 per cent. I remain free to suggest, either personally or officially, if I should be so instructed, either a different percentage or minimum sums for creditors and government, respectively, with a percentage division of the excess. . . .

◇◇◇◇◇◇◇◇◇◇◇◇◇

3. THE THEODORE ROOSEVELT COROLLARY TO THE MONROE DOCTRINE

[*President Roosevelt's Annual Message to Congress, December 6, 1904*] [3]

. . . IT IS NOT TRUE that the United States feels any land hunger or entertains any projects as regards the other nations of the Western Hemisphere save such as are for their welfare. All that this country desires is to see the neighboring countries stable, orderly, and prosperous. Any country whose people conduct themselves well can count upon our hearty friendship. If a nation shows that it knows how to act with reasonable efficiency and decency in social and political matters, if it keeps order and pays its obligations, it need fear no interference from the United States. Chronic wrongdoing, or an impotence which results in a general loosening of the ties of civilized society, may in America, as elsewhere, ultimately require intervention by some civilized nation, and in the Western Hemisphere the adherence of the United States to the Monroe Doctrine may force the United States, however reluctantly, in flagrant cases of such wrongdoing or impotence, to the exercise of an international police power. If every country washed by the Caribbean Sea would show the progress in stable and just civilization which with the aid of the Platt amendment Cuba has shown since our troops left the island, and which so many of the republics in both Americas are constantly and brilliantly showing, all question of interference by this Nation with their affairs would be at an end. Our interests and those of our southern neighbors are in reality identical. They have great natural riches, and if within their borders the reign of law and justice obtains, prosperity is sure to come to them. While they thus obey the primary laws of civilized society they may rest assured that they will be treated by us in a spirit of cordial and helpful sympathy. We would interfere with them only in the last resort, and then only if it became evident that their inability or unwillingness to do justice at home and abroad had violated the rights of the United States or had invited foreign aggression to the detriment of the entire body of American nations. It is a mere truism to say that every nation, whether in America or anywhere else, which desires to maintain its freedom, its independence, must ultimately realize that the right of such independence can not be separated from the responsibility of making good use of it. . . .

[3] *House Documents,* (4780) 58th Congress, 3rd Session, No. 1, pp. XLI–II.

◇◇◇◇◇◇◇◇◇◇◇◇◇

4. A NEW LATIN AMERICAN POLICY[4]

[*Address of President Wilson at Mobile, Alabama, October 27, 1913*]

. . . THE FUTURE, ladies and gentlemen, is going to be very different for this hemisphere from the past. These States lying to the south of us, which have always been our neighbors, will now be drawn closer to us by innumerable ties, and, I hope, chief of all, by the tie of a common understanding of each other. Interest does not tie nations together; it sometimes separates them. But sympathy and understanding does unite them, and I believe that by the new route that is just about to be opened, while we physically cut two continents asunder, we spiritually unite them. It is a spiritual union which we seek. . . .

There is one peculiarity about the history of the Latin American States which I am sure they are keenly aware of. You hear of "concessions" to foreign capitalists in Latin America. You do not hear of concessions to foreign capitalists in the United States. They are not granted concessions. They are invited to make investments. The work is ours, though they are welcome to invest in it. We do not ask them to supply the capital and do the work. It is an invitation, not a privilege; and States that are obliged, because their territory does not lie within the main field of modern enterprise and action, to grant concessions are in this condition, that foreign interests are apt to dominate their domestic affairs, a condition of affairs always dangerous and apt to become intolerable. What these States are going to see, therefore, is an emancipation from the subordination, which has been inevitable, to foreign enterprise and an assertion of the splendid character which, in spite of these difficulties, they have again and again been able to demonstrate. The dignity, the courage, the self-possession, the self-respect of the Latin American States, their achievements in the face of all these adverse circumstances, deserve nothing but the admiration and applause of the world. They have had harder bargains driven with them in the matter of loans than any other peoples in the world. Interest has been exacted of them that was not exacted of anybody else, because the risk was said to be greater; and then securities were taken that destroyed the risk – and admirable arrangement for those who were forcing the terms! I rejoice in nothing so much as in the prospect that they will now be emancipated from these conditions, and we ought to be the first to take part in assisting in that emancipation. I think some of these gentlemen have already had occasion to bear witness that the Department of State in recent months has tried to serve them in that wise. In the future they will draw closer and closer to us because of circumstances of which I wish to speak with moderation and, I hope, without indiscretion.

We must prove ourselves their friends, and champions upon terms of equality and honor. You cannot be friends upon any other terms than upon

[4] *Senate Doc.*, No. 440, 63rd Congress, 2nd Session (6593), pp. 5–8.

the terms of equality. You cannot be friends at all except upon the terms of honor. We must show ourselves friends by comprehending their interest whether it squares with our own interest or not. It is a very perilous thing to determine the foreign policy of a nation in the terms of material interest. It not only is unfair to those with whom you are dealing, but it is degrading as regards your own actions.

Comprehension must be the soil in which shall grow all the fruits of friendship, and there is a reason and a compulsion lying behind all this which is dearer than anything else to the thoughtful men of America. I mean the development of constitutional liberty in the world. Human rights, national integrity, and opportunity as against material interests — that, ladies and gentlemen, is the issue which we now have to face. I want to take this occasion to say that the United States will never again seek one additional foot of territory by conquest. She will devote herself to showing that she knows how to make honorable and fruitful use of the territory she has, and she must regard it as one of the duties of friendship to see that from no quarter are material interests made superior to human liberty and national opportunity. . . .

◇◇◇◇◇◇◇◇◇◇◇◇◇

5. WILSON'S STATEMENT OF THE MONROE DOCTRINE[5]

[*Address to Pan-American Scientific Congress, January 6, 1916*]

. . . THE MONROE DOCTRINE was proclaimed by the United States on her own authority. It always has been maintained and always will be maintained upon her own responsibility. But the Monroe Doctrine demanded merely that European Governments should not attempt to extend their political systems to this side of the Atlantic. It did not disclose the use which the United States intended to make of her power on this side of the Atlantic. It was a hand held up in warning, but there was no promise in it of what America was going to do with the implied and partial protectorate which she apparently was trying to set up on this side of the water; and I believe you will sustain me in the statement that it has been fears and suspicions on this score which have hitherto prevented the greater intimacy and confidence and trust between the Americas. The States of America have not been certain what the United States would do with her power. That doubt must be removed. And latterly there has been a very frank interchange of views between the authorities in Washington and those who represented the other States of this hemisphere, an interchange of views charming and hopeful, because based upon an increasingly sure appreciation of the spirit in which they were undertaken. These gentlemen have seen that if America is to come into her own, into her

[5] The *New York Times*, Jan. 7, 1916.

legitimate own, in a world of peace and order, she must establish the foundations of amity so that no one will hereafter doubt them.

I hope and I believe that this can be accomplished. These conferences have enabled me to foresee how it will be accomplished. It will be accomplished in the first place, by the States of America uniting in guaranteeing to each other absolutely political independence and territorial integrity. In the second place, and as a necessary corollary to that, guaranteeing the agreement to settle all pending boundary disputes as soon as possible and by amicable process; by agreeing that all disputes among themselves, should they unhappily arise, will be handled by patient, impartial investigation, and settled by arbitration; and the agreement necessary to the peace of the Americas, that no State of either continent will permit revolutionary expeditions against another State to be fitted out on its territory, and that they will prohibit the exportation of the munitions of war for the purpose of supplying revolutionists against neighboring Governments.

◇◇◇◇◇◇◇◇◇◇◇◇◇◇

6. THE BRYAN-CHAMORRO TREATY [6]

[*Convention between the United States and Nicaragua; signed August 5, 1914; ratifications exchanged June 22, 1916*]

. . . *ARTICLE I.* The Government of Nicaragua grants in perpetuity to the Government of the United States, forever free from all taxation or other public charge, the exclusive proprietary rights necessary and convenient for the construction, operation and maintenance of an interoceanic canal by way of the San Juan River and the great Lake of Nicaragua or by way of any route over Nicaraguan territory, the details of the terms upon which such canal shall be constructed, operated and maintained to be agreed to by the two governments whenever the Government of the United States shall notify the Government of Nicaragua of its desire or intention to construct such canal.

Article II. To enable the Government of the United States to protect the Panama Canal and the proprietary rights granted to the Government of the United States by the foregoing article, and also to enable the Government of the United States to take any measure necessary to the ends contemplated herein, the Government of Nicaragua hereby leases for a term of ninety-nine years to the Government of the United States the islands in the Caribbean Sea known as Great Corn Island and Little Corn Island; and the Government of Nicaragua further grants to the Government of the United States for a like period of ninety-nine years the right to establish, operate and maintain a naval base at such place on the territory of Nicaragua bordering upon the Gulf of Fonseca as the Government of the United States may select. The Government of the United

[6] *Statutes at Large of the United States,* Vol. XXXIX, pp. 1661–4.

States shall have the option of renewing for a further term of ninety-nine years the above leases and grants upon the expiration of their respective terms, it being expressly agreed that the territory hereby leased and the naval base which may be maintained under the grant aforesaid shall be subject exclusively to the laws and sovereign authority of the United States during the terms of such lease and grant and of any renewal or renewals thereof.

Article III. In consideration of the foregoing stipulations and for the purposes contemplated by this Convention and for the purpose of reducing the present indebtedness of Nicaragua, the Government of the United States shall, upon the date of the exchange of ratifications of this Convention, pay for the benefit of the Republic of Nicaragua the sum of three million dollars United States gold coin. . . .

And whereas, the advice and consent of the Senate of the United States to the ratification of the said Convention was given with the following proviso: "*Provided,* That whereas, Costa Rica, Salvador and Honduras have protested against the ratification of the said Convention in the fear or belief that said Convention might in some respect impair existing rights of said States; therefore, it is declared by the Senate that in advising and consenting to the ratification of the said Convention as amended such advice and consent are given with the understanding, to be expressed as a part of the instrument of ratification, that nothing in said Convention is intended to affect any existing right of any of the said named States;"

And whereas, the said understanding has been accepted by the Government of Nicaragua. . . .

◇◇◇◇◇◇◇◇◇◇◇◇◇

7. AMERICAN POLICY IN NICARAGUA: 1927[7]

[*Message of President Coolidge to the Congress of the United States, January 10, 1927*]

TO THE CONGRESS of the United States:

While conditions in Nicaragua and the action of this Government pertaining thereto have in general been made public, I think the time has arrived for me officially to inform the Congress more in detail of the events leading up to the present disturbances and conditions which seriously threaten American lives and property, endanger the stability of all Central America, and put in jeopardy the rights granted by Nicaragua to the United States for the construction of a canal. It is well known that in 1912 the United States intervened in Nicaragua with a large force and put down a revolution, and that from that time to 1925 a legation guard of

[7] *The Congressional Record,* 69th Congress, 2nd Session, Vol. LXVIII, Pt. II, pp. 1324–6.

American marines was, with the consent of the Nicaraguan Government, kept in Managua to protect American lives and property. In 1923 representatives of the five Central American countries, namely, Costa Rica, Guatemala, Honduras, Nicaragua, and Salvador, at the invitation of the United States, met in Washington and entered into a series of treaties. These treaties dealt with limitation of armament, a Central American tribunal for arbitration, and the general subject of peace and amity. The treaty last referred to specifically provides in Article II that the Governments of the contracting parties will not recognize any other government which may come into power in any of the five Republics through a coup d'état, or revolution, and disqualifies the leaders of such coup d'état, or revolution, from assuming the presidency or vice presidency. . . .

The United States was not a party to this treaty, but it was made in Washington under the auspices of the Secretary of State, and this Government has felt a moral obligation to apply its principles in order to encourage the Central American States in their efforts to prevent revolution and disorder. . . .

The Nicaraguan constitution provides in article 106 that in the absence of the President and Vice President the Congress shall designate one of its members to complete the unexpired term of President. As President Solorzano had resigned and was then residing in California, and as the Vice President, Doctor Sacasa, was in Guatemala, having been out of the country since November, 1925, the action of Congress in designating Señor Diaz was perfectly legal and in accordance with the constitution. Therefore the United States Government on November 17 extended recognition to Señor Diaz. . . .

Immediately following the inauguration of President Diaz and frequently since that date he has appealed to the United States for support, has informed this Government of the aid which Mexico is giving to the revolutionists, and has stated that he is unable solely because of the aid given by Mexico to the revolutionists to protect the lives and property of American citizens and other foreigners. When negotiations leading up to the Corinto conference began, I immediately placed an embargo on the shipment of arms and ammunition to Nicaragua. The Department of State notified the other Central American States, to wit, Costa Rica, Honduras, Salvador, and Guatemala, and they assured the department they would cooperate in this measure. So far as known, they have done so. The State Department also notified the Mexican Government of this embargo and informally suggested to that government like action. The Mexican Government did not adopt the suggestion to put on an embargo, but informed the American ambassador at Mexico City that in the absence of manufacturing plants in Mexico for the making of arms and ammunition the matter had little practical importance.

As a matter of fact, I have the most conclusive evidence that arms and munitions in large quantities have been on several occasions since August, 1926, shipped to the revolutionists in Nicaragua. Boats carrying these munitions have been fitted out in Mexican ports, and some of the munitions bear evidence of having belonged tc the Mexican Government. It also appears that the ships were fitted out with the full knowledge of and, in some cases, with the encouragement of Mexican officials and were in one instance, at least, commanded by a Mexican naval reserve officer. At the end of November, after spending some time in Mexico City, Doctor Sacasa went back to Nicaragua, landing at Puerto Cabezas, near Bragmans Bluff. He immediately placed himself at the head of the insurrection and declared himself President of Nicaragua. He has never been recognized by any of the Central American Republics nor by any other government, with the exception of Mexico, which recognized him immediately. As arms and munitions in large quanties were reaching the revolutionists, I deemed it unfair to prevent the recognized government from purchasing arms abroad, and, accordingly, the Secretary of State has notified the Diaz Government that licenses would be issued for the export of arms and munitions purchased in this country. It would be thoroughly inconsistent for this country not to support the government recognized by it while the revolutionists were receiving arms and munitions from abroad.

During the last two months the Government of the United States has received repeated requests from various American citizens, both directly and through our consuls and legation, for the protection of their lives and property. The Government of the United States has also received requests from the British chargé at Managua and from the Italian ambassador at Washington for the protection of their respective nationals. Pursuant to such requests, Admiral Latimer, in charge of the special service squadron, has not only maintained the neutral zone at Bluefields under the agreement of both parties but has landed forces at Puerto Cabezas and Rio Grande, and established neutral zones at these points where considerable numbers of Americans live and are engaged in carrying on various industries. He has also been authorized to establish such other neutral zones as are necessary for the purposes above mentioned.

For many years numerous Americans have been living in Nicaragua, developing its industries and carrying on business. At the present time there are large investments in lumbering, mining, coffee growing, banana culture, shipping, and also in general mercantile and other collateral business. All these people and these industries have been encouraged by the Nicaraguan Government. That Government has at all times owed them protection, but the United States has occasionally been obliged to send naval forces for their proper protection. In the present crisis such forces are requested by the Nicaraguan Government, which protests to the United States its inability to protect these interests and states that any measures which the United States deems appropriate for their protection will be satisfactory to the Nicaraguan Government.

In addition to these industries now in existence, the Government of Nicaragua, by a treaty entered into on the 5th day of August, 1914, granted in perpetuity to the United States the exclusive proprietary rights necessary and convenient for the construction, operation, and maintenance of an oceanic canal. . . .

There is no question that if the revolution continues American investments and business interests in Nicaragua will be very seriously affected, if not destroyed. The currency, which is now at par, will be inflated. American as well as foreign bond holders will undoubtedly look to the United States for the protection of their interests. . . .

Manifestly the relation of this Government to the Nicaraguan situation, and its policy in the existing emergency, are determined by the facts which I have described. The proprietary rights of the United States in the Nicaraguan canal route, with the necessary implications growing out of it affecting the Panama Canal, together with the obligations flowing from the investments of all classes of our citizens in Nicaragua, place us in a position of peculiar responsibility. I am sure it is not the desire of the United States to intervene in the internal affairs of Nicaragua or of any other Central American Republic. Nevertheless it must be said that we have a very definite and special interest in the maintenance of order and good government in Nicaragua at the present time, and that the stability, prosperity, and independence of all Central American countries can never be a matter of indifference to us. The United States can not, therefore, fail to view with deep concern any serious threat to stability and constitutional government in Nicaragua tending toward anarchy and jeopardizing American interests, especially if such state of affairs is contributed to or brought about by outside influences or by any foreign power. It has always been and remains the policy of the United States in such circumstances to take the steps that may be necessary for the preservation and protection of the lives, the property, and the interests of its citizens and of this Government itself. In this respect I propose to follow the path of my predecessors.

Consequently, I have deemed it my duty to use the powers committed to me to insure the adequate protection of all American interests in Nicaragua, whether they be endangered by internal strife or by outside interference in the affairs of that Republic.

8. THE CLARK MEMORANDUM ON THE MONROE DOCTRINE[8]

[*J. Reuben Clark to Henry L. Stimson*]

Washington, D. C., December 17, 1928

HEREWITH I transmit a Memorandum on the Monroe Doctrine, prepared by your direction, given a little over two months ago. . . .

[8] J. Reuben Clark: *Memorandum on The Monroe Doctrine, Washington,* 1930, pp. IX–XXV.

It is of first importance to have in mind that Monroe's declaration in its terms, relates solely to the relationships between European states on the one side, and, on the other side, the American continents, the Western Hemisphere, and the Latin American Governments which on December 2, 1823, had declared and maintained their independence which we had acknowledged. . . .

In the normal case, the Latin American state against which aggression was aimed by a European power, would be the beneficiary of the Doctrine not its victim. This has been the history of its application. The Doctrine makes the United States a guarantor, in effect, of the independence of Latin American states, though without the obligations of a guarantor to those states, for the United States itself determines by its sovereign will when, where, and concerning what aggressions it will invoke the Doctrine, and by what measures, if any, it will apply a sanction. In none of these things has any other state any voice whatever.

Furthermore while the Monroe Doctrine as declared, has no relation in its terms to an aggression by any other state than a European state, yet the principle "self-preservation" which underlies the Doctrine – which principle, as we shall see, is as fully operative without the Doctrine as with it – would apply to any non-American state in whatever quarter of the globe it lay, or even to an American state, if the aggressions of such state against other Latin American states were "dangerous to our peace and safety," or were a "manifestation of an unfriendly disposition towards the United States," or were "endangering our peace and happiness"; that is, if such aggressions challenged our existence. . . .

In this view, the Monroe Doctrine as such might be wiped out and the United States would lose nothing of its broad, international right; it would still possess, in common with every other member of the family of nations, the internationally recognized right of self-preservation, and this right would fully attach to the matters specified by the Doctrine if and whenever they threatened our existence, just as the right would attach in relation to any other act carrying a like menace. . . .

It is evident from the foregoing that the Monroe Doctrine is not an equivalent for "self-preservation"; and therefore the Monroe Doctrine need not, indeed should not, be invoked in order to cover situations challenging our self-preservation but not within the terms defined by Monroe's declaration. These other situations may be handled, and more wisely so, as matters affecting the national security and self-preservation of the United States as a great power. . . .

The statement of the Doctrine itself that "with the existing colonies or dependencies of any European power we have not interfered and shall not interfere," has been more than once reiterated.

It has also been announced that the Monroe Doctrine is not a pledge by the United States to other American states requiring the United States to protect such states, at their behest, against real or fancied wrongs inflicted by European powers, nor does it create an obligation running from the United States to any American state to intervene for its protection. . . .

The so-called "Roosevelt corollary" was to the effect, as generally understood, that in case of financial or other difficulties in weak Latin American countries, the United States should attempt an adjustment thereof lest European Governments should intervene, and intervening should occupy territory — an act which would be contrary to the principles of the Monroe Doctrine. This view seems to have had its inception in some observations of President Buchanan in his message to Congress of December 3, 1860, and was somewhat amplified by Lord Salisbury in his note to Mr. Olney of November 6, 1895, regarding the Venezuelan boundary dispute.

As has already been indicated above, it is not believed that this corollary is justified by the terms of the Monroe Doctrine, however much it may be justified by the application of the doctrine of self-preservation.

These various expressions and statements, as made in connection with the situations which gave rise to them, detract not a little from the scope popularly attached to the Monroe Doctrine, and they relieve that Doctrine of many of the criticisms which have been aimed against it.

Finally, it should not be overlooked that the United States declined the overtures of Great Britain in 1823 to make a joint declaration regarding the principles covered by the Monroe Doctrine, or to enter into a conventional arrangement regarding them. Instead this Government determined to make the declaration of high national policy on its own responsibility and in its own behalf. The Doctrine is thus purely unilateral. The United States determines when and if the principles of the Doctrine are violated, and when and if violation is threatened. We alone determine what measures if any, shall be taken to vindicate the principles of the Doctrine, and we of necessity determine when the principles have been vindicated. No other power of the world has any relationship to, or voice in, the implementing of the principles which the Doctrine contains. It is our Doctrine, to be by us invoked and sustained, held in abeyance, or abandoned as our high international policy or vital national interests shall seem to us, and to us alone, to demand.

It may, in conclusion, be repeated: The Doctrine does not concern itself with purely inter-American relations; it has nothing to do with the relationship between the United States and other American nations, except where other American nations shall become involved with European governments in arrangements which threaten the security of the United States, and even in such cases, the Doctrine runs against the European country, not the American nation, and the United States would primarily deal thereunder with the European country and not with the American nation concerned. The Doctrine states a case of the United States *vs.* Europe, and not of the United States *vs.* Latin America. Furthermore, the fact should never be lost to view that in applying this Doctrine during the period of one hundred years since it was announced, our Government has over and over again driven it in as a shield between Europe and the Americas to protect Latin America from the political and territorial thrusts of Europe; and this was done at times when the American nations were weak and struggling for the establishment of stable, permanent governments; when the political morality of Europe sanctioned, indeed encouraged, the acquisition of territory by force; and when many of the great powers of Europe looked with eager, covetous eyes to the rich, undeveloped areas of the American hemisphere. Nor should another equally vital fact be lost sight of, that the United States has only been able to give this protection against designing European powers because of its known willingness and determination, if and whenever necessary, to expend its treasure and to sacrifice American life to maintain the principles of the Doctrine. So far as Latin America is concerned, the Doctrine is now, and always has been, not an instrument of violence and oppression, but an unbought, freely bestowed, and wholly effective guaranty of their freedom, independence, and territorial integrity against the imperialistic designs of Europe.

◇◇◇◇◇◇◇◇◇◇◇◇◇

9. THE ABANDONMENT OF WILSON'S NON-RECOGNITION POLICY[9]

[*Address of Henry L. Stimson Before The Council on Foreign Relations*]

New York, Feb. 6, 1931

. . . THE PRACTICE of this country as to the recognition of new governments has been substantially uniform from the days of the administration of Secretary of State Jefferson in 1792 to the days of Secretary of State Bryan in 1913. . . .

The particular considerations upon which our action was regularly based were well stated by Mr. Adee, long the trusted Assistant Secretary of State of this Government, as follows:

> Ever since the American Revolution entrance upon diplomatic intercourse with foreign states has been *de facto,* dependent upon the existence of three conditions of fact: the control of the administrative machinery of the state; the general acquiescence of its people; and the ability and willingness of their government to discharge international and conventional obligations. The form of government has not been a conditional factor in such recognition; in other words, the *de jure* element of legitimacy of title has been left aside. (*Foreign Relations of the United States, 1913,* p. 100.)

With the advent of President Wilson's administration this policy of over a century was radically departed from in respect to the Republic of Mex-

[9] Publication of the State Department, *Latin American Series,* No. 4, Washington, 1931, pp. 6–10.

ico, and, by a public declaration on March 11, 1913, it was announced that –

Cooperation (with our sister republics of Central and South America) is possible only when supported at every turn by the orderly processes of just government based upon law, not upon arbitrary or irregular force. We hold, as I am sure that all thoughtful leaders of republican government everywhere hold, that just government rests always upon the consent of the governed, and that there can be no freedom without order based upon law and upon the public conscience and approval. We shall look to make these principles the basis of mutual intercourse, respect, and helpfulness between our sister republics and ourselves. (*Foreign Relations of the United States*, 1913, p. 7.)

Mr. Wilson's government sought to put this new policy into effect in respect to the recognition of the then Government of Mexico held by President Victoriano Huerta. Although Huerta's government was in *de facto* possession, Mr. Wilson refused to recognize it, and he sought through the influence and pressure of his great office to force it from power. Armed conflict followed with the forces of Mexico, and disturbed relations between us and that republic lasted until a comparatively few years ago. . . .

The present administration has refused to follow the policy of Mr. Wilson and has followed consistently the former practice of this Government since the days of Jefferson. As soon as it was reported to us, through our diplomatic representatives, that the new governments in Bolivia, Peru, Argentina, Brazil, and Panama were in control of the administrative machinery of the state, with the apparent general acquiescence of their people, and that they were willing and apparently able to discharge their international and conventional obligations, they were recognized by our Government. And, in view of the economic depression, with the consequent need for prompt measures of financial stabilization, we did this with as little delay as possible in order to give those sorely pressed countries the quickest possible opportunities for recovering their economic poise.

Such has been our policy in all cases where international practice was not affected or controlled by preëxisting treaty. In the five republics of Central America, Guatemala, Honduras, Salvador, Nicaragua, and Costa Rica, however, we have found an entirely different situation existing from that normally presented under international law and practice. . . . In 1907 a period of strife, involving four of the five republics, had lasted almost without interruption for several years. In that year, on the joint suggestion and mediation of the Governments of the United States and Mexico, the five republics met for the purpose of considering methods intended to mitigate and, if possible, terminate the intolerable situation. By one of the conventions which they then adopted, the five republics agreed with one another as follows:

The Governments of the high contracting parties shall not recognize any other government which may come into power in any of the five republics as a consequence of a *coup d'état,* or of a revolution against the recognized government, so long as the freely elected representatives of the people thereof, have not constitutionally reorganized the country.

Sixteen years later, in 1923, the same five republics, evidently satisfied with the principle they had thus adopted and desiring to reinforce it and prevent any future evasions of that principle, met again, reenacted the same covenant, and further promised each other that even after a revolutionary government had been constitutionally reorganized by the representatives of the people, they would not recognize it if its president should have been a leader in the preceding revolution or related to such a leader by blood or marriage, or if he should have been a cabinet officer or held some high military command during the accomplishment of the revolution. Some four months thereafter, our own Government, on the invitation of these republics, who had conducted their meeting in Washington, announced, through Secretary Hughes, that the United States would in its future dealings with those republics follow out the same principle which they had thus established in their treaty. Since that time we have consistently adhered to this policy in respect to those five republics. . . .

◇◇◇◇◇◇◇◇◇◇◇◇◇

10. THE GOOD NEIGHBOR POLICY[10]

[*Address of Franklin D. Roosevelt at Chautauqua, New York, August 14, 1936*]

. . . LONG BEFORE I returned to Washington as President of the United States, I had made up my mind that, pending what might be called a more opportune moment on other continents, the United States could best serve the cause of peaceful humanity by setting an example. That was why on the 4th of March, 1933, I made the following declaration:

> In the field of world policy I would dedicate this nation to the policy of the good neighbor – the neighbor who resolutely respects himself and because he does so, respects the rights of others – the neighbor who respects his obligations and respects the sanctity of his agreements in and with a world of neighbors.

This declaration represents my purpose; but it represents more than a purpose, for it stands for a practice. To a measurable degree it has succeeded; the whole world now knows that the United States cherishes no predatory ambitions. We are strong; but less powerful nations know that they need not fear our strength. We seek no conquest; we stand for peace.

In the whole of the Western Hemisphere our good neighbor policy has produced results that are especially heartening.

[10] *Peace and War; United States Foreign Policy,* 1931–1941 (U. S. Government Printing Office, Washington, 1943), pp. 323–9.

The noblest monument to peace and to neighborly economic and social friendship in all the world is not a monument in bronze or stone but the boundary which unites the United States and Canada — 3,000 miles of friendship with no barbed wire, no gun or soldier, and no passport on the whole frontier.

Mutual trust made that frontier — to extend the same sort of mutual trust throughout the Americas was our aim.

The American republics to the south of us have been ready always to cooperate with the United States on a basis of equality and mutual respect, but before we inaugurated the good neighbor policy there was among them resentment and fear, because certain administrations in Washington had slighted their national pride and their sovereign rights.

In pursuance of the good neighbor policy, and because in my younger days I had learned many lessons in the hard school of experience, I stated that the United States was opposed definitely to armed intervention.

We have negotiated a Pan-American convention embodying the principle of non-intervention. We have abandoned the Platt amendment which gave us the right to intervene in the internal affairs of the Republic of Cuba. We have withdrawn American marines from Haiti. We have signed a new treaty which places our relations with Panama on a mutually satisfactory basis. We have undertaken a series of trade agreements with other American countries to our mutual commercial profit. At the request of two neighboring republics, I hope to give assistance in the final settlement of the last serious boundary dispute between any of the American nations.

Throughout the Americas the spirit of the good neighbor is a practical and living fact. The twenty-one American republics are not only living together in friendship and in peace; they are united in the determination so to remain. . . .

Of all the nations of the world today we are in many ways most singularly blessed. Our closest neighbors are good neighbors. If there are remoter nations that wish us not good but ill, they know that we are strong; they know that we can and will defend ourselves and defend our neighborhood.

We seek to dominate no other nation. We ask no territorial expansion. We oppose imperialism. We desire reduction in world armaments.

We believe in democracy; we believe in freedom; we believe in peace. We offer to every nation of the world the handclasp of the good neighbor. Let those who wish our friendship look us in the eye and take our hand.

◇◇◇◇◇◇◇◇◇◇◇◇◇

11. THE CONSULTATIVE PACT[11]

[*Convention for the Maintenance, Preservation, and Reestablishment of Peace, signed at Buenos Aires, December 23, 1936, proclaimed September 16, 1937*]

. . . *ARTICLE I.* In the event that the peace of the American Republics is menaced, and in order to coordinate efforts to prevent war, any of the Governments of the American Republics signatory to the Treaty of Paris of 1928 or to the Treaty of Non-Aggression and Conciliation of 1933, or to both, whether or not a member of other peace organizations, shall consult with the other Governments of the American Republics, which, in such event, shall consult together for the purpose of finding and adopting methods of peaceful cooperation.

Article II. In the event of war, or a virtual state of war between American States, the Governments of the American Republics represented at this Conference shall undertake without delay the necessary mutual consultations, in order to exchange views and to seek, within the obligations resulting from the pacts above mentioned and from the standards of international morality, a method of peaceful collaboration; and, in the event of an international war outside America which might menace the peace of the American Republics, such consultation shall also take place to determine the proper time and manner in which the signatory states, if they so desire, may eventually cooperate in some action tending to preserve the peace of the American Continent.

Article III. It is agreed that any question regarding the interpretation of the present Convention, which it has not been possible to settle through diplomatic channels, shall be submitted to the procedure of conciliation provided by existing agreements, or to arbitration or to judicial settlement. . . .

◇◇◇◇◇◇◇◇◇◇◇◇◇

12. NON-INTERVENTION[12]

[*Additional Protocol Relative to Non-Intervention, signed at Buenos Aires, December 23, 1936, proclaimed September 16, 1937*]

. . . *ARTICLE 1.* The High Contracting Parties declare inadmissible the intervention of any one of them, directly or indirectly, and for what-

11 United States *Treaty Series,* No. 922, Washington, 1937. The treaty was signed by the delegates of the United States and of the twenty other American Republics represented at the Convention for the Maintenance, Preservation, and Reestablishment of Peace, Buenos Aires, December 1–23, 1936. The "Non-Intervention Treaty" and "The Convention on Treaty Coordination and Neutrality," items two and three of this chapter, were also signed at the same time and place.

12 United States *Treaty Series,* No. 923, Washington, 1937.

ever reason, in the internal or external affairs of any other of the Parties.

The violation of the provisions of this Article shall give rise to mutual consultation, with the object of exchanging views and seeking methods of peaceful adjustment.

Article 2. It is agreed that every question concerning the interpretation of the present Additional Protocol, which it has not been possible to settle through diplomatic channels, shall be submitted to the procedure of conciliation provided for in the agreements in force, or to arbitration, or to judicial settlement. . . .

◇◇◇◇◇◇◇◇◇◇◇◇◇

13. DECLARATION OF PRINCIPLES OF INTER-AMERICAN SOLIDARITY AND CONFEDERATION[13]

THE GOVERNMENTS of the American Republics, having considered:

That they have a common likeness in their democratic form of government, and their common ideals of peace and justice, manifested in the several Treaties and Conventions which they have signed for the purpose of constituting a purely American system tending towards the preservation of peace, the proscription of war, the harmonious development of their commerce and of their cultural aspirations demonstrated in all of their political, economic, social, scientific and artistic activities;

That the existence of continental interests obliges them to maintain solidarity of principles as the basis of the life of the relations of each to every other American nation;

That Pan-Americanism, as a principle of American International Law, by which is understood a moral union of all of the American Republics in defense of their common interests based upon the most perfect equality and reciprocal respect for their rights of autonomy, independence and free development, requires the proclamation of principles of American International Law; and

That it is necessary to consecrate the principle of American solidarity in all non-continental conflicts, especially since those limited to the American continent should find a peaceful solution by the means established by the Treaties and Conventions now in force or in the instruments hereafter to be executed,

The Inter-American Conference for the Maintenance of Peace declares:

1. That the American nations, true to their republican institutions, proclaim their absolute juridical liberty, their unrestricted respect for their several sovereignty and the existence of a common democracy throughout America;

2. That every act susceptible of disturbing the peace of America affects

[13] Item No. XXVII of the Final Act of the Inter-American Conference for the Maintenance of Peace, 1936. Dept. of State, No. 1088, Washington, 1937.

each and every one of them, and justifies the initiation of the procedure of consultation provided for in the Convention for the Maintenance, Preservation and Reestablishment of Peace, executed at this Conference; and

3. That the following principles are accepted by the international American community:

(a) Proscription of territorial conquest and that, in consequence, no acquisition made through violence shall be recognized;

(b) Intervention by one State in the internal or external affairs of another State is condemned;

(c) Forcible collection of pecuniary debts is illegal; and

(d) Any difference or dispute between the American nations, whatever its nature or origin, shall be settled by the methods of conciliation, or full arbitration, or through operation of international justice.

14. PAN AMERICAN SOLIDARITY

(A) NEUTRALITY [14]

THE MEETING of the Foreign Ministers of the American Republics resolves:

1. To reaffirm the status of general neutrality of the American Republics, it being left to each one of them to regulate in their individual and sovereign capacities the manner in which they are to give it concrete application.

2. To have their rights and status as neutrals fully respected and observed by all belligerents and by all persons who may be acting for or on behalf of or in the interest of the belligerents.

3. To declare that with regard to their status as neutrals, there exist certain standards recognized by the American Republics applicable in these circumstances and that in accordance with them they:

(a) Shall prevent their respective terrestrial, maritime and aerial territories from being utilized as bases of belligerent operations.

(b) Shall prevent, in accordance with their internal legislations, the inhabitants of their territories from engaging in activities capable of affecting the neutral status of the American Republics.

(c) Shall prevent on their respective territories the enlistment of persons to serve in the military, naval, or air forces of the belligerents; the retaining or inducing of persons to go beyond their respective shores for the purpose of taking part in belligerent operations; the setting on foot of any military, naval or aerial expedition in the interests of the belligerents; the fitting out, arming, or augmenting of the forces or armament of any

[14] Resolution of Foreign Ministers of the American Republics, Panama, October 3, 1939. Department of State, *Bulletin,* Vol. I, p. 326.

ship or vessel to be employed in the service of one of the belligerents, to cruise or commit hostilities against another belligerent, or its nationals or property; the establishment by the belligerents or their agents of radio stations in the terrestrial or maritime territory of the American Republics, or the utilization of such stations to communicate with the governments or armed forces of the belligerents. . . .

(e) Shall require all belligerent vessels and aircraft seeking the hospitality of areas under their jurisdiction and control to respect strictly their neutral status and to observe their respective laws and regulations and the rules of international law pertaining to the rights and duties of neutrals and belligerents; and in the event that difficulties are experienced in enforcing the observance of and respect for their rights, the case, if so requested, shall thereupon become a subject of consultation between them.

(f) Shall regard as a contravention of their neutrality any flight by the military aircraft of a belligerent state over their own territory. . . .

(i) Shall consider as lawful the transfer of the flag of a merchant vessel to that of any American Republic provided such transfer is made in good faith, without agreement for resale to the vendor, and that it takes place in the waters of an American Republic. . . .

4. In the spirit of this declaration, the Governments of the American Republics shall maintain close contact with a view to making uniform so far as possible, the enforcement of their neutrality and to safe-guarding it in defense of their fundamental rights. . . .

(B) DECLARATION OF PANAMA [15]

The Governments of the American Republics meeting at Panamá, have solemnly ratified their neutral status in the conflict which is disrupting the peace of Europe, but the present war may lead to unexpected results which may affect the fundamental interests of America and there can be no justification for the interests of the belligerents to prevail over the rights of neutrals causing disturbances and suffering to nations which by their neutrality in the conflict and their distance from the scene of events, should not be burdened with its fatal and painful consequences. . . .

The nature of the present conflagration, in spite of its already lamentable proportions, would not justify any obstruction to inter-American communications which, engendered by important interests, call for adequate protection. This fact requires the demarcation of a zone of security including all the normal maritime routes of communication and trade between the countries of America.

To this end it is essential as a measure of necessity to adopt immediately provisions based on the above-mentioned precedents for the safe-guarding of such interests, in order to avoid a repetition of the damages and suffer-

[15] Meeting of Foreign Ministers of the American Republics, Panama, October 3, 1939, Ibid., p. 331.

ings sustained by the American nations and by their citizens in the war of 1914–1918.

There is no doubt that the Governments of the American Republics must foresee those dangers and as a measure of self-protection insist that the waters to a reasonable distance from their coasts shall remain free from the commission of hostile acts or from the undertaking of belligerent activities by nations engaged in a war in which the said governments are not involved.

For these reasons the Governments of the American Republics *Resolve and hereby declare:*

1. As a measure of continental self-protection, the American Republics, so long as they maintain their neutrality, are as of inherent right entitled to have those waters adjacent to the American continent, which they regard as of primary concern and direct utility in their relations, free from the commission of any hostile act by any non-American belligerent nation, whether such hostile act be attempted or made from land, sea or air.

Such waters shall be defined as follows: All waters comprised within the limits set forth hereafter except the territorial waters of Canada and of the undisputed colonies and possessions of European countries within these limits. . . .

3. The Governments of the American Republics further declare that whenever they consider it necessary they will consult together to determine upon the measures which they may individually or collectively undertake in order to secure the observance of the provisions of this Declaration.

4. The American Republics, during the existence of a state of war in which they themselves are not involved, may undertake, whenever they may determine that the need therefor exists, to patrol, either individually or collectively, as may be agreed upon by common consent, and in so far as the means and resources of each may permit, the waters adjacent to their coasts within the area above defined. . . .

(C) ACT OF HAVANA CONCERNING THE PROVISIONAL ADMINISTRATION OF EUROPEAN COLONIES AND POSSESSIONS IN THE AMERICAS, JULY 30, 1940.[16]

Whereas:

1. The status of regions in this Continent belonging to European powers is a subject of deep concern to all of the Governments of the American Republics;

2. As a result of the present European war there may be attempts at conquest, which has been repudiated in the international relations of the American Republics, thus placing in danger the essence and pattern of the institutions of America;

3. The doctrine of inter-American solidarity agreed upon at the meet-

[16] Second Meeting of Foreign Ministers of The American Republics, Ibid., Vol. III, p. 138.

ings at Lima and at Panama requires the adoption of a policy of vigilance and defense so that systems or regimes in conflict with their institutions shall not upset the peaceful life of the American Republics, the normal functioning of their institutions, or the rule of law and order;

4. The course of military events in Europe and the changes resulting from them may create the grave danger that European territorial possessions in America may be converted into strategic centers of aggression against nations of the American Continent;

The Second Meeting of the Ministers of Foreign Affairs of the American Republics declares:

That when islands or regions in the Americas now under the possession of non-American nations are in danger of becoming the subject of barter of territory or change of sovereignty, the American nations, taking into account the imperative need of continental security and the desires of the inhabitants of the said islands or regions, may set up a regime of provisional administration under the following conditions:

(a) That as soon as the reasons requiring this measure shall cease to exist, and in the event that it would not be prejudicial to the safety of the American Republics, such territories shall, in accordance with the principle reaffirmed by this declaration that peoples of this Continent have the right freely to determine their own destinies, be organized as autonomous states if it shall appear that they are able to constitute and maintain themselves in such condition, or be restored to their previous status, whichever of these alternatives shall appear the more practicable and just;

(b) That the regions to which this declaration refers shall be placed temporarily under the provisional administration of the American Republics and this administration shall be exercised with the two-fold purpose of contributing to the security and defense of the Continent, and to the economic, political and social progress of such regions. . . .

(D) THE ACT OF RIO DE JANIERO [17]

. . . As a result of its deliberations the Third Meeting of Ministers of Foreign Affairs of the American Republics approved the following conclusions:

Breaking of Diplomatic Relations

I. The American Republics reaffirm their declaration to consider any act of aggression on the part of a non-American State against one of them as an act of aggression against all of them, constituting as it does an immediate threat to the liberty and independence of America.

II. The American Republics reaffirm their complete solidarity and their determination to cooperate jointly for their mutual protection until the effects of the present aggression against the Continent have disappeared.

III. The American Republics, in accordance with the procedures estab-

[17] Third Meeting of Foreign Ministers of the American Republics, Rio de Janeiro January 28, 1942. Ibid., VI, pp. 118–19.

lished by their own laws and in conformity with the position and circumstances obtaining in each country in the existing continental conflict, recommend the breaking of their diplomatic relations with Japan, Germany and Italy, since the first-mentioned State attacked and the other two declared war on an American country.

IV. Finally, the American Republics declare that, prior to the reestablishment of the relations referred to in the preceding paragraph, they will consult among themselves in order that their action may have a solidary character.

(E) ACT OF CHAPULTEPEC [18]

Part I. The Governments Represented at the Inter-American Conference on Problems of War and Peace Declare:

1. That all sovereign States are juridically equal among themselves.

2. That every State has the right to the respect of its individuality and independence, on the part of the other members of the international community.

3. That every attack of a State against the integrity or the inviolability of the territory, or against the sovereignty or political independence of an American State, shall, conformably to Part III hereof, be considered as an act of aggression against the other States which sign this Act. In any case invasion by armed forces of one State into the territory of another trespassing boundaries established by treaty and demarcated in accordance therewith shall constitute an act of aggression.

4. That in case acts of aggression occur or there are reasons to believe that an aggression is being prepared by any other State against the integrity or inviolability of the territory, or against the sovereignty or political independence of an American State, the States signatory to this Act will consult among themselves in order to agree upon the measures it may be advisable to take.

5. That during the war, and until the treaty recommended in Part II hereof is concluded, the signatories of this Act recognize that such threats and acts of aggression, as indicated in paragraphs 3 and 4 above, constitute an interference with the war effort of the United Nations, calling for such procedures, within the scope of their constitutional powers of a general nature and for war, as may be found necessary, including: recall of chiefs of diplomatic missions; breaking of diplomatic relations; breaking of consular relations; breaking of postal, telegraphic, telephonic, radio-telephonic relations; interruption of economic, commercial and financial relations; use of armed force to prevent or repel aggression.

6. That the principles and procedure contained in this Declaration shall become effective immediately, inasmuch as any act of aggression or threat of aggression during the present state of war interferes with the war effort

[18] Approved at the plenary session of March 6, 1945, of the Inter-American Conference on Problems of War and Peace, Mexico City, February 21–March 8, 1945. Department of State Publication 2497, *Conference Series* No. 85, pp. 72–5.

of the United Nations to obtain victory. Henceforth, and to the end that the principles and procedures herein stipulated shall conform with the constitutional processes of each Republic, the respective Governments shall take the necessary steps to perfect this instrument in order that it shall be in force at all times.

Part II. The Inter-American Conference on Problems of War and Peace *Recommends:*

That for the purpose of meeting threats or acts of aggression against any American Republic following the establishment of peace, the Governments of the American Republics consider the conclusion, in accordance with their constitutional processes, of a treaty establishing procedures whereby such threats or acts may be met by the use, by all or some of the signatories of said treaty, of any one or more of the following measures: recall of chiefs of diplomatic missions; breaking of diplomatic relations; breaking of consular relations; breaking of postal, telegraphic, telephonic, radio-telephonic relations; interruption of economic, commercial and financial relations; use of armed force to prevent or repel aggression.

Part III. The above Declaration and Recommendation constitute a regional arrangement for dealing with such matters relating to the maintenance of international peace and security as are appropriate for regional action in this Hemisphere. The said arrangement, and the pertinent activities and procedures, shall be consistent with the purposes and principles of the general international organization, when established.

This agreement shall be known as the "*Act of Chapultepec.*"

15. CANADIAN-AMERICAN RELATIONS

(A) THE OGDENSBURG AGREEMENT [19]

THE Prime Minister and the President have discussed the mutual problems of defense in relation to the safety of Canada and the United States.

It has been agreed that a Permanent Joint Board on Defense shall be set up at once by the two countries.

This Permanent Joint Board on Defense shall commence immediate studies relating to sea, land, and air problems including personnel and matériel.

It will consider in the broad sense the defense of the north half of the Western Hemisphere.

The Permanent Joint Board on Defense will consist of four or five members from each country, most of them from the services. It will meet shortly.

[19] Joint Statement of President Roosevelt and Prime Minister Mackenzie King of Canada, Ogdensburg, N. Y., August 18, 1940. Department of State: *Bulletin,* Vol. III, p. 154.

(B) THE HYDE PARK DECLARATION [20]

Among other important matters, the President and the Prime Minister discussed measures by which the most prompt and effective utilization might be made of the productive facilities of North America for the purposes both of local and hemisphere defense and of the assistance which, in addition to their own programs, both Canada and the United States are rendering to Great Britain and the other democracies.

It was agreed as a general principle that in mobilizing the resources of this continent, each country should provide the other with the defense articles which it is best able to produce, and, above all, produce quickly, and that production programs should be coordinated to this end.

While Canada has expanded its productive capacity manyfold since the beginning of the war, there are still numerous defense articles which it must obtain in the United States, and purchases of this character by Canada will be even greater in the coming year than in the past. On the other hand, there is existing and potential capacity in Canada for the speedy production of certain kinds of munitions, strategic materials, aluminum and ships, which are urgently required by the United States, for its own purposes.

While exact estimates cannot yet be made, it is hoped that during the next twelve months Canada can supply the United States with between $200,000,000 and $300,000,000 worth of such defense articles. This sum is a small fraction of the total defense program of the United States, but many of the articles to be provided are of vital importance. In addition, it is of great importance to the economic and financial relations between the two countries that payment by the United States for these supplies will materially assist Canada in meeting part of the cost of Canadian defense purchases in the United States.

Insofar as Canada's defense purchases in the United States consist of component parts to be used in equipment and munitions which Canada is producing for Great Britain, it was also agreed that Great Britain will obtain these parts under the Lease-Lend Act and forward them to Canada for inclusion in the finished article.

The technical and financial details will be worked out as soon as possible in accordance with the general principles which have been agreed upon between the President and the Prime Minister.

(C) ANALYSIS OF AMERICAN-CANADIAN RELATIONS [21]

. . . On March 12, I described the United States Lease-Lend Act as one of the milestones of freedom, pointing the way to ultimate and certain

[20] Joint statement of President Roosevelt and Prime Minister Mackenzie King of Canada, Hyde Park, N. Y., April 20, 1941. Ibid., IV, p. 494.

[21] Statement of Prime Minister Mackenzie King to the Canadian House of Commons, April 28, 1941. S. Shepard Jones and Denys P. Myers: *Documents on American Foreign Relations* (Boston, World Peace Foundation, 1941), Vol. III, pp. 162–8.

victory. The Lease-Lend Act settled the principle of United States assistance to Britain and the other democracies. It did not, however, solve all of the complex economic problems involved in the mobilization of the resources of the United States and Canada in order to render to Britain, in the speediest manner, the most effective assistance and support.

One of the reasons for my recent visit to the United States and my conferences with the President, was the urgent need for Canada to find an immediate solution of some of the problems involved in our wartime economic relations with the United States and with the United Kingdom. Before indicating the extent to which a solution has been found in the Hyde Park Declaration, I shall outline briefly the problems themselves.

It will be readily recognized that we, in Canada, could not possibly have embarked upon our existing program of war production if we had not lived side by side with the greatest industrial nation in the world. Without ready access to the industrial production of the United States, and particularly the machine tools and other specialized equipment so necessary in producing the complex instruments of modern war, Canada's war effort would have been seriously retarded. We would have been forced to embark upon the production of many articles which, because of limited demand, could only have been produced at high cost, and over a considerable period of time. Canada also lacks certain essential raw materials which must be procured from the United States. Since the outbreak of war, we have steadily expanded our purchases in the United States of these essential tools, machines and materials which were required both for our own Canadian war effort, and in the production of war supplies for Britain. . . .

Hon. members will, I am sure, be more interested in the broad significance of the Hyde Park Declaration than in its technical aspects.

Its most immediate significance is that, through the coordination of war production in both countries, it will result in the speeding up of aid to Britain by the United States and Canada. As a result of the better integration of North American industry, the proposed arrangement will, through increasing total production, have the further effect of increasing the total volume of aid to Britain. It will have a corresponding effect upon Canada's war effort. Full utilization of the production facilities we have built up, and specialization on those things which we are best fitted to produce, will increase both our national income and our own armed strength, as well as increasing our capacity to aid Britain. . . .

I have spoken thus far of the immediate significance of the Declaration, of the effect it will have in speeding up aid to Britain in the critical months ahead, and of its importance in assisting us to meet our exchange problem. But beyond its immediate significance the Hyde Park Declaration will have a permanent significance in the relations between Canada and the United States. It involves nothing less than a common plan of the economic defense of the Western Hemisphere. When we pause to reflect upon the consequences, in Europe, of the failure of the peace-loving nations to plan in concert their common defense, while yet there was time, we gain a new appreciation of the significance for the future of both Canada and the United States of the Ogdensburg Agreement and of this new Declaration which might well be called the economic corollary of Ogdensburg.

For Canada, the significance of the Hyde Park Declaration may be summarized briefly as follows: first, it will help both Canada and the United States to provide maximum aid to Britain and to all the defenders of democracy; second, it will increase the effectiveness of Canada's direct war effort; and finally, through the increased industrial efficiency which will result, it will increase our own security and the security of North America.

It is appropriate at this point to emphasize the fact that, while the agreement will increase the effectiveness of our war effort and our assistance to Britain, the self-imposed burden upon the Canadian people will nevertheless remain as great as ever. The sacrifices which we are called upon to make will not be reduced by the Hyde Park Declaration, but the results achieved by our sacrifices will, we believe, be considerably greater. At the same time, the risks of delays and breakdowns will be materially reduced. The utmost effort of the Canadian people is more than ever needed in the present phase of this terrible struggle; but in making that effort we shall have, as the result of the agreement, the added satisfaction of knowing that we are making a greater contribution than otherwise would be possible to the cause of freedom.

In referring to the passage of the Lease-Lend Act, I expressed in this house the view that "Canada's example, as a nation of the new world, actively participating to the utmost limit in the present struggle, has also had its influence in arousing the people of the United States to their present realization that freedom itself is at stake in this war."

Unhesitatingly, to-day, I would go one step farther and would say that the example given by Canada has, I believe, aroused the admiration of our neighbors and made them ready to accept this new partnership.

Last November, I said to hon. members of this house that the link forged by the Ogdensburg Agreement was no temporary axis, formed by nations whose common tie was a mutual desire for the destruction of their neighbors. The Hyde Park Declaration is, I believe, a further convincing demonstration that Canada and the United States are indeed laying the enduring foundations of a new world order, an order based on international understanding, on mutual aid, on friendship and good will.

CHAPTER XXXII

THE NEW NEUTRALITY

◇◇◇◇◇◇◇◇◇◇◇◇◇

THE TERM "New Neutrality" was used to designate a foreign policy, initiated and established by Congress, and based on the assumption that the United States could remain free from foreign wars by the simple expedient of abandoning its neutral rights. President Roosevelt and Secretary of State Cordell Hull never accepted this assumption, although they were obliged to execute the policy, for they believed that a distinction existed between an aggressor and a nonaggressor nation, and that if the United States by the abandonment of its rights assisted the aggressor, it might only postpone a war in self-defense to a time when it would stand alone in a world dominated by an aggressor nation or an alliance of such nations.

The State Department was well informed about the designs of the nations that eventually formed the Axis. It had, for example, the remarkably able analysis by Douglas Miller of the aims of the Germans (1A), and the equally cogent analysis of Japanese aims, written by the American Ambassador to Japan, Joseph C. Grew (1B). Preparations for the Italian invasion of Ethiopia were clearly observed by the American Ambassador in Rome (1C). On many occasions Secretary Hull clearly stated his belief that the United States could not safely and wisely remain aloof from world events. A typical statement of this point of view was his address at New York of January 16, 1935 (2).

As the Italo-Ethiopian crisis drew near, the Emperor of Ethiopia, Haile Selassie, appealed to the United States to consider what measures might be used to effect the observance of the Pact of Paris. Secretary Hull returned an extremely cautious reply offering no hope that the United States would provide any assistance to Ethiopia except moral support. Congress, however, apparently feared that the Administration might involve the United States in the conflict, and hurriedly passed the first so-called Neutrality Act (3). It was a temporary measure, due to expire February 29, 1936, and did not cover the sale of goods other than arms and munitions. President Roosevelt signed the bill but expressed the opinion that an inflexible mandatory measure might do more to drag the country in than to keep it out of war.

The second Neutrality Act (4) gave the President less discretionary power than the first and prohibited loans to belligerents. The third Neutrality Act was still more extensive and contained the "cash and carry" provision (5).

President Roosevelt did not try to prevent the passage of these acts, nor did he veto them. Nevertheless, he did not approve the theories upon which they were based. This was clearly shown in one of the most famous of all his public utterances, the so-called "Quarantine Speech" of October 5, 1937 (6). Many other people besides the President were dissatisfied with the "neutrality" policy. One of the most prominent and influential of these was ex-Secretary of State Henry L. Stimson whose public letter of October 6, 1937 was widely quoted and discussed (7). In no place, however, was the case against the New Neutrality more cogently argued than in an editorial in the *New York Times* (8).

◇◇◇◇◇◇◇◇◇◇◇◇◇

1. THE AIMS OF GERMANY, JAPAN, AND ITALY

(A) THE AIMS OF THE GERMANS [1]

THE fundamental purpose is to secure a greater share of the world's future for the Germans, the expansion of German territory and growth of the German race until it constitutes the largest and most powerful nation in the world, and ultimately, according to some Nazi leaders, until it dominates the entire globe.

The German people suffering from a traditional inferiority complex, smarting from their defeat in the war and the indignities of the post-war period, disillusioned in their hopes of a speedy return to prosperity along traditional lines, inflamed by irresponsible demagogic slogans and flattered by the statement that their German racial inheritance gives them inherent superior rights over other peoples, have to a large measure adopted the National Socialist point of view for the time being.

Economic Aims

There are two other purposes subsidiary to the main purpose. Germany is to be made the economic center of a self-sustaining territorial block whose dependent nations in Central and Eastern Europe will look to Berlin for leadership. This block is to be so constituted that it can defy wartime blockade and be large enough to give the peoples in it the benefits of free trade now enjoyed by the 48 American States. . . .

Social Aims

The second subsidiary purpose is the welding of all individuals in the present and future Greater Germany into a homogeneous racial family, gladly obedient to the will of its leader, with class and cultural differences inside the country eliminated, but a sharp line drawn between Germans

---

1 Memorandum of Douglas Miller, Acting Commercial Attaché in the American Embassy in Berlin, April 17, 1934. *Peace and War: United States Foreign Policy,* 1931–1941 (Washington, 1943), pp. 211–14.

and the foreign world outside. In carrying out this purpose, the Jews are to be entirely eliminated, the Slavic or eastern elements in the population to be minimized and eventually bred out of the race. A national religion is in process of organization; trade unions, political parties and all social, political, cultural, trade or other organizations not affiliated with the National Socialist party, have been abolished, the individual's rights have been largely taken away. In the future the nation is to count for everything, the individual for nothing. Germany is to engage in a gigantic struggle with the rest of the world to grow at the expense of its neighbors. The German population owes the nation the patriotic duty of supporting it and bringing forward all necessary sacrifices to reach the common goal.

Retention of Power

To these long-distance objectives must be added the fourth and most important purpose of all, namely to retain control at all costs. The National Socialist party may compromise on distant objectives, if necessary, but cannot compromise on a question of retaining its absolute hold on the German people. This control had been gained by making most irresponsible and extravagant promises; by the studied use of the press, the radio, public meetings, parades, flags, uniforms, and all methods of working on popular psychology and finally by the use of force. This control once lost, could never be regained. . . .

Danger of War

The Nazis are not satisfied with the existing map of Europe. They are at heart belligerent and aggressive. True, they desire nothing more than a period of peace for several years in which they can gradually re-arm and discipline their people. This period may be 5 years, 10 years, or longer, but the more completely their experiments succeed the more certain is a large-scale war in Europe some day.

Nazis Want to Wipe Out 1918

In estimating the aims and purposes of the National Socialist movement, we must not make the mistake of putting too much reliance on public statements designed for consumption abroad which breathe the spirit of good peace and will and assert the intention of the Government to promote the welfare of the German people and good relations with their neighbors. Nor should we imagine that the present Government leaders will feel and act as we would in their circumstances, namely think only of Germany's welfare. The real emotional drive behind the Nazi program is not so much love of their own country as dislike of other countries. The Nazis will never be content in merely promoting the welfare of the German people. They desire to be feared and envied by foreigners and to wipe out the memory of 1918 by inflicting humiliations in particular upon the French, the Poles, the Czechs and anybody else they can get their hands on.

A careful examination of Hitler's book and his public speeches reveals the fact that he cannot be considered as absolutely sane and normal on this subject. The same is true of many other Nazi leaders. They have capitalized the wounded inferiority complex of the German people, and magnified their own bitter feelings into a cult of dislike against the foreign world which is past the bounds of ordinary good sense and reason. Let us repeat this fact and let it sink in, the National Socialist movement is building a tremendous military machine, physically very poorly armed, but morally aggressive and belligerent. The control of this machine lies in the hands of narrow, ignorant and unscrupulous adventurers who have been slightly touched with madness from brooding over Germany's real or imagined wrongs, as well as the slights and indignities thrown in their own individual way as they attempted to organize the movement. Power of this kind concentrated in hands like these is dangerous. The Nazis are determined to secure more power and more territory in Europe. If this is voluntarily given to them by peaceful means, well and good, but if not, they will certainly use force. That is the only meaning behind the manifold activities of the movement in Germany today.

(B) THE AIMS OF THE JAPANESE [2]

. . . The thought which is uppermost in my mind is that the United States is faced, and will be faced in future, with two main alternatives. One is to be prepared to withdraw from the Far East, gracefully and gradually perhaps, but not the less effectively in the long run, permitting our treaty rights to be nullified, the Open Door to be closed, our vested economic interests to be dissolved and our commerce to operate unprotected. There are those who advocate this course, and who have advocated it to me personally, on the ground that any other policy will entail the risk of eventual war with Japan. . . . In their opinion, "the game is not worth the candle" because the United States can continue to subsist comfortably even after relinquishing its varied interests in the Far East, thereby eliminating the risk of future war.

The other main alternative is to insist, and to continue to insist, not aggressively yet not the less firmly, on the maintenance of our legitimate rights and interests in this part of the world and, so far as practicable, to support the normal development of those interests constructively and progressively.

There has already been abundant indication that the present Administration in Washington proposes to follow the second of these alternatives. For purposes of discussion we may therefore, I assume, discard the hypothesis of withdrawal and examine the future outlook with the assurance that our Government has not the slightest intention of relinquishing the legitimate rights, vested interests, non-discriminatory privileges for equal opportunity and healthful commercial development of the United States in the Far East. . . .

[2] Analysis made by the American Ambassador to Japan, Joseph C. Grew, in a note to the Secretary of State, December 27, 1934. Ibid., pp. 236–44.

It is difficult for those who do not live in Japan to appraise the present temper of the country. An American Senator, according to reports, has recently recommended that we should accord parity to Japan in order to avoid future war. Whatever the Senator's views may be concerning the general policy that we should follow in the Far East, he probably does not realize what harm that sort of public statement does in strengthening the Japanese stand and in reinforcing the aggressive ambitions of the expansionists. The Japanese press of course picks out such statements by prominent Americans and publishes them far and wide, thus confirming the general belief in Japan that the pacifist element in the United States is preponderantly strong and in the last analysis will control the policy and action of our Government. Under such circumstances there is a general tendency to characterize our diplomatic representations as bluff and to believe that they can safely be disregarded without fear of implementation. It would be helpful if those who share the Senator's views could hear and read some of the things that are constantly being said and written in Japan, to the effect that Japan's destiny is to subjugate and rule the world (sic), and could realize the expansionist ambitions which lie not far from the surface in the minds of certain elements in the Army and Navy, the patriotic societies and the intense nationalists throughout the country. Their aim is to obtain trade control and eventually predominant political influence in China, the Philippines, the Straits Settlements, Siam and the Dutch East Indies, the Maritime Provinces and Vladivostok, one step at a time, as in Korea and Manchuria, pausing intermittently to consolidate and then continuing as soon as the intervening obstacles can be overcome by diplomacy or force. With such dreams of empire cherished by many, and with an army and navy capable of taking the bit in their own teeth and running away with it regardless of the restraining influence of the saner heads of the Government in Tokyo (a risk which unquestionably exists and of which we have already had ample evidence in the Manchurian affair), we would be reprehensibly somnolent if we were to trust to the security of treaty restraints or international comity to safeguard our own interests or, indeed, our own property. . . .

I wish that more Americans could come out here and live here and gradually come to sense the real potential risks and dangers of the situation instead of speaking and writing academically on a subject which they know nothing whatever about, thereby contributing ammunition to the Japanese military and extremists who are stronger than they have been for many a day. The idea that a great body of liberal thought lying just beneath the surface since 1931 would be sufficiently strong to emerge and assume control with a little foreign encouragement is thoroughly mistaken. The liberal thought is there, but it is inarticulate and largely impotent, and in all probability will remain so for some time to come.

At this point I should like to make the following observation. From reading this despatch, and perhaps from other reports periodically submitted by the Embassy, one might readily get the impression that we are developing something of an "anti-Japanese" complex. This is not the case. One can dislike and disagree with certain members of a family without necessarily feeling hostility to the family itself. . . .

Having placed the foregoing considerations on record, I have less hesitation in reiterating and emphasizing with all conviction the potential dangers of the situation and the prime importance of American national preparedness to meet it. As a nation we have taken the lead in international efforts toward the restriction and reduction of armaments. We have had hopes that the movement would be progressive, but the condition of world affairs as they have developed during the past twelve years since the Washington Conference has not afforded fruitful ground for such progress. Unless we are prepared to subscribe to a "Pax Japonica" in the Far East, with all that this movement, as conceived and interpreted by Japan, is bound to entail, we should rapidly build up our navy to treaty strength, and if and when the Washington Naval Treaty expires we should continue to maintain the present ratio with Japan regardless of cost, a peace-time insurance both to cover and to reduce the risk of war. In the meantime every proper step should be taken to avoid or to offset the belligerent utterances of jingoes no less than the defeatist statements of pacifists in the United States, many of which find their way into the Japanese press, because the utterances of the former tend to enflame public sentiment against our country, while the statements of the latter convey an impression of American weakness, irresolution and bluff. . . .

Theodore Roosevelt enunciated the policy "Speak softly but carry a big stick." If our diplomacy in the Far East is to achieve favorable results, and if we are to reduce the risk of an eventual war with Japan to a minimum, that is the only way to proceed. Such a war may be unthinkable, and so it is, but the spectre of it is always present and will be present for some time to come. It would be criminally short-sighted to discard it from our calculations, and the best possible way to avoid it is to be adequately prepared, for preparedness is a cold fact which even the chauvinists, the military, the patriots and the ultra-nationalists in Japan, for all their bluster concerning "provocative measures" in the United States, can grasp and understand. The Soviet Ambassador recently told me that a prominent Japanese had said to him that the most important factor in avoiding a Japanese attack on the Maritime Provinces was the intensive Soviet military preparations in Siberia and Vladivostok. I believe this to be true, and again, and yet again, I urge that our own country be adequately prepared to meet all eventualities in the Far East. . . .

(C) AIMS OF THE ITALIANS [3]

. . . All information recently obtained points to a more general preparation for an extensive campaign in Abyssinia than has been indicated by the Italian Government in its various announcements. Supplies and mil-

[3] Report to the Secretary of State of the American Ambassador to Italy, Breckinridge Long, February 14, 1935. Ibid., pp. 247–8.

itary forces are moving clandestinely. Concerted effort is being made to prevent any information getting out as to the size or general nature of shipments. Movements are being made by night and troops called up are kept in barracks and denied freedom.

I have been informed today from sources deemed to be reliable that 30,000 troops have left the port of Naples; that the movement now under way contemplates the use in Ethiopia of some 200,000 or 300,000 troops; and that the troops which are now or have recently been in Tripoli, and thus have had tropical experience, are being moved to Ethiopia and are being replaced by the newly formed forces from Italy.

It is learned from another trustworthy source that the *communiqué* of the Italian Government mentioned in my No. 65, February 11, 5 p.m., was misleading in that the class of 1911, though ostensibly called in sufficient numbers to bring the divisions to war strength, was actually called to form these divisions as the regiments comprising them had already left clandestinely for unknown destinations by the time the *communiqué* had been issued.

Mechanical, motor and air service specialists are being called from the reserves and from the militia of the classes as far back as 1895 and 1893. Factories for the manufacture of trucks, tanks and artillery at and around Milan are working day and night shifts.

Principal movements consist of motor, air and light artillery and, in addition to Naples, embarkation is proceeding from Venice, Messina, Ancona and probably from Leghorn. Supplies are leaving from Genoa, Venice and Trieste, as well as from Naples.

All of these movements are being camouflaged by the use of regular merchant marine without the use of war vessels. The Navy has not participated. If it were to do so, either as carrier or as convoy, it would advertise the movement. Moreover in the absence of an Abyssinian Navy, there is no need for protection and the passage of regular merchant ships through Suez would cause no comment nor evoke criticism, even should the authorities there be disposed to object.

Press stories justifying Italy's action under Paris, London and Geneva date lines, which are reprinted in full or in part in the Italian press, are preparing public opinion, but there has not been a single story under any Italian date line or a single editorial comment on this subject in any Italian newspaper, which constitutes an unusual departure from the established custom.

◇◇◇◇◇◇◇◇◇◇◇◇◇◇

2. AMERICAN INTEREST IN WORLD EVENTS[4]

. . . IT IS often assumed that a nation's foreign policy is or can be altogether determined by the Government of the moment. This is true in fact only within certain very definite limits which greatly restrict the field of choice. I am thinking not merely of historical traditions and conventions which put a brake on the whims of statesmen and insure a certain continuity of foreign policy, or of the obvious fact that each country's policy is affected and to some extent motivated by that of other countries. What I have in mind rather are such external factors as size and resources, geographical location, and technical developments, which constitute the framework within which a nation's foreign policy must evolve and assume its formal characteristics. . . .

Let us consider the effect of some of these elements on American foreign policy. All of them have conspired to force the United States out of its earlier preoccupation with domestic matters into an increasingly active participation in international affairs. The enormous speeding up of trade and communications under the influence of technical discovery and advancement condemns to futility any endeavor to induce this nation again to withdraw into "splendid isolation." Our policies must of necessity be those of a so-called "great power." We cannot, even if we would, fail profoundly to affect international relations; our choice is of the various ways of affecting them which are open to a nation situated as we are. It would be hard to deny that we are so placed that we could, if that were our intention, engage in a policy of imperialistic expansion and aggression to the detriment of others. The alternative course open to us is to make our influence felt through a policy of political, economic, and cultural cooperation to the advantage of all and in an atmosphere of trust and peace. The latter is our policy, a policy so accurately described by the President as that of the "good neighbor.". . .

I realize only too well that neighbors can be estranged even when race and language should make them brothers, and of this the present war in the Chaco is a ghastly reminder. Undoubtedly some of the states to the south in the past viewed the growing proximity of the United States with misgiving, and I cannot but admit that there have been occasions when our words and actions gave some justification to their fears. Today these suspicions are happily vanishing, and I believe the time is at hand when the American republics will be convinced not only that the good-neighbor policy is being carried out in practice, but also that in strictly observing it the President, with magnificent foresight, has adopted a course which the future progress of our two continents makes imperative. The truth is that cooperation is proving itself profitable in every way. The most recent instance is our reciprocity treaty with Cuba, which, in the few months of

[4] Speech of Secretary of State, Cordell Hull, at New York, February 16, 1935. Ibid., pp. 248–55.

its operation, has worked wonders both in the economic and in the political spheres. If the Platt Amendment was symbolical of an early epoch in our inter-American relations, its recent abandonment is an emphatic symbol of a new era in which it becomes our manifest destiny to enter into ever closer relations of free and voluntary collaboration for the furtherance of the prosperity of each and the peace of all.

Thus far I have not dealt with our relations east and west, or what might be called our transoceanic policies. Here again, there is no break in unity but merely an adaptation to the very different geographical and historical situation. The fundamental element is the ocean, the Atlantic on the east, the Pacific on the west. There was a time when the ocean meant, or could mean, a certain degree of isolation. Modern communication has ended this forever; but necessarily a gap remains, and with it the difference in perspective. Seen from the distance of this hemisphere, the manifold boundary lines on the map of Europe become blurred and Europe emerges as an entity. We have no direct concern with the political and economic controversies of the European states. We have time and again expressly disassociated ourselves from these disputes. Nevertheless, we are deeply interested in the peace and stability of Europe as a whole, and have therefore taken part in a number of multilateral efforts to achieve this purpose. . . .

◇◇◇◇◇◇◇◇◇◇◇◇◇

3. THE FIRST NEUTRALITY ACT: 1935[5]

RESOLVED by the Senate and House of Representatives of the United States of America in Congress assembled, That upon the outbreak or during the progress of war between, or among, two or more foreign states, the President shall proclaim such fact, and it shall thereafter be unlawful to export arms, ammunition, or implements of war from any place in the United States, or possessions of the United States, to any port of such belligerent states, or to any neutral port for transshipment to, or for the use of, a belligerent country.

The President, by proclamation, shall definitely enumerate the arms, ammunition, or implements of war, the export of which is prohibited by this Act.

The President may, from time to time, by proclamation, extend such embargo upon the export of arms, ammunition, or implements of war to other states as and when they may become involved in such war. . . .

Except with respect to prosecutions committed or forfeitures incurred prior to March 1, 1936, this section and all proclamations issued thereunder shall not be effective after February 29, 1936. . .

Within ninety days after the effective date of this Act, or upon first engaging in business, every person who engages in the business of manufac-

[5] Act of August 31, 1935. Ibid., pp. 266–71.

turing, exporting, or importing any of the arms, ammunition, and implements of war referred to in this Act, whether as an exporter, importer, manufacturer, or dealer, shall register with the Secretary of State his name, or business name, principal place of business, and places of business in the United States, and a list of the arms, ammunition, and implements of war which he manufactures, imports, or exports.

Every person required to register under this section shall notify the Secretary of State of any change in the arms, ammunition, and implements of war which he exports, imports, or manufactures; and upon such notification the Secretary of State shall issue to such person an amended certificate of registration, free of charge, which shall remain valid until the date of expiration of the original certificate. Every person required to register under the provisions of this section shall pay a registration fee of $500, and upon receipt of such fee the Secretary of State shall issue a registration certificate valid for five years, which shall be renewable for further periods of five years upon the payment of each renewal of a fee of $500.

It shall be unlawful for any person to export, or attempt to export, from the United States any of the arms, ammunition, or implements of war referred to in this Act to any other country or to import, or attempt to import, to the United States from any other country any of the arms, ammunition, or implements of war referred to in this Act without first having obtained a license therefor. . . .

Sec. 3. Whenever the President shall issue the proclamation provided for in section 1 of this Act, thereafter it shall be unlawful for any American vessel to carry any arms, ammunition, or implements of war to any port of the belligerent countries named in such proclamation as being at war, or to any neutral port for transshipment to, or for the use of, a belligerent country. . . .

Sec. 6. Whenever, during any war in which the United States is neutral, the President shall find that the maintenance of peace between the United States and foreign nations, or the protection of the lives of citizens of the United States, or the protection of the commercial interests of the United States and its citizens, or the security of the United States requires that the American citizens should refrain from traveling as passengers on the vessels of any belligerent nation, he shall so proclaim, and thereafter no citizen of the United States shall travel on any vessel of any belligerent nation except at his own risk, unless in accordance with such rules and regulations as the President shall prescribe. . . .

◇◇◇◇◇◇◇◇◇◇◇◇◇◇

4. THE SECOND NEUTRALITY ACT: 1936[6]

RESOLVED by the Senate and House of Representatives of the United States of America in Congress assembled, That section 1 of the joint resolu-

[6] Act of February 29, 1936. Ibid., pp. 313–14.

tion (Public Resolution Numbered 67, Seventy-fourth Congress) approved August 31, 1935, be, and the same hereby is, amended by striking out in the first section, on the second line, after the word "assembled" the following words: "That upon the outbreak or during the progress of war between", and inserting therefor the words: "Whenever the President shall find that there exists a state of war between"; and by striking out the word "may" after the word "President" and before the word "from" in the twelfth line, and inserting in lieu thereof the word "shall"; and by substituting for the last paragraph of said section the following paragraph: "except with respect to offenses committed, or forfeitures incurred prior to May 1, 1937, this section and all proclamations issued thereunder shall not be effective after May 1, 1937."

Sec. 2. There are hereby added to said joint resolution two new sections, to be known as section 1a and 1b, reading as follows:

Sec. 1a. Whenever the President shall have issued his proclamation as provided for in section 1 of this Act, it shall thereafter during the period of the war be unlawful for any person within the United States to purchase, sell, or exchange bonds, securities, or other obligations of the government of any belligerent country, or of any political subdivision thereof, or of any person acting for or on behalf of such government, issued after the date of such proclamation, or to make any loan or extend any credit to any such government or person: *Provided,* That if the President shall find that such action will serve to protect the commercial or other interests of the United States or its nationals, he may, in his discretion, and to such extent and under such regulation as he may prescribe, except from the operation of this section ordinary commercial credits and shorttime obligations in aid of legal transactions and of a character customarily used in normal peace-time commercial transactions. . . .

Sec. 1b. This Act shall not apply to an American republic or republics engaged in war against a non-American state or states, provided the American republic is not cooperating with a non-American state or states in such war.

◇◇◇◇◇◇◇◇◇◇◇◇◇

5. THE THIRD NEUTRALITY ACT: 1937[7]

SECTION 1. (a) Whenever the President shall find that there exists a state of war between, or among, two or more foreign states, the President shall proclaim such fact, and it shall thereafter be unlawful to export, or attempt to export, or cause to be exported, arms, ammunition, or implements of war from any place in the United States to any belligerent state

[7] Act of May 1, 1937. Ibid., 355–65. By joint resolution, January 8, 1937, Congress prohibited the exportation of arms, armaments, ammunition, and implements of war from the United States to Spain.

named in such proclamation, or to any neutral state for transshipment to, or for the use of, any such belligerent state.

(b) The President shall, from time to time, by proclamation, extend such embargo upon the export of arms, ammunition, or implements of war to other states as and when they may become involved in such war.

(c) Whenever the President shall find that a state of civil strife exists in a foreign state and that such civil strife is of a magnitude or is being conducted under such conditions that the export of arms, ammunition, or implements of war from the United States to such foreign state would threaten or endanger the peace of the United States, the President shall proclaim such fact, and it shall thereafter be unlawful to export, or attempt to export, or cause to be exported, arms, ammunition, or implements of war from any place in the United States to such foreign state, or to any neutral state for transshipment to, or for the use of, such foreign state.

(d) The President shall, from time to time by proclamation, definitely enumerate the arms, ammunition, and implements of war, the export of which is prohibited by this section. The arms, ammunition, and implements of war so enumerated shall include those enumerated in the President's proclamation Numbered 2163, of April 10, 1936, but shall not include raw materials or any other articles or materials not of the same general character as those enumerated in the said proclamation, and in the Convention for the Supervision of the International Trade in Arms and Ammunition and in Implements of War, signed at Geneva June 17, 1925. . . .

Section 2. (a) Whenever the President shall have issued a proclamation under the authority of section 1 of this Act and he shall thereafter find that the placing of restrictions on the shipment of certain articles or materials in addition to arms, ammunition, and implements of war from the United States to belligerent states, or to a state wherein civil strife exists, is necessary to promote the security or preserve the peace of the United States or to protect the lives of citizens of the United States, he shall so proclaim, and it shall thereafter be unlawful, except under such limitations and exceptions as the President may prescribe as to lakes, rivers, and inland waters bordering on the United States, and as to transportation on or over lands bordering on the United States, for any American vessel to carry such articles or materials to any belligerent state, or to any state wherein civil strife exists, named in such proclamation issued under the authority of section 1 of this Act, or to any neutral state for transshipment to, or for the use of, any such belligerent state or any such state wherein civil strife exists. The President shall by proclamation from time to time definitely enumerate the articles and materials which it shall be unlawful for American vessels to so transport.

(b) Whenever the President shall have issued a proclamation under the authority of section 1 of this Act and he shall thereafter find that the placing of restrictions on the export of articles or materials from the United States to belligerent states, or to a state wherein civil strife exists, is necessary to promote the security or preserve the peace of the United States or to protect the lives or commerce of citizens of the United States, he shall so proclaim, and it shall thereafter be unlawful, except under such limitations and exceptions as the President may prescribe as to lakes, rivers, and inland waters bordering on the United States, and as to transportation on or over land bordering on the United States, to export or transport, or attempt to export or transport, or cause to be exported or transported, from the United States to any belligerent state, or to any state wherein civil strife exists, named in such proclamation issued under the authority of section 1 of this Act, or to any neutral state for transshipment to, or for the use of, any such belligerent state or any such state wherein civil strife exists, any articles or materials whatever until all right, title, and interest therein shall have been transferred to some foreign government, agency, institution, association, partnership, corporation, or national. . . .

Section 3. (a) Whenever the President shall have issued a proclamation under the authority of section 1 of this Act, it shall thereafter be unlawful for any person within the United States to purchase, sell, or exchange bonds, securities, or other obligations of the government of any belligerent state or of any state wherein civil strife exists, named in such proclamation, or of any political subdivision of any such state, or of any person acting for or on behalf of the government of any such state, or of any faction or asserted government within any such state wherein civil strife exists, or of any person acting for or on behalf of any faction or asserted government within any such state wherein civil strife exists, issued after the date of such proclamation, or to make any loan or extend any credit to any such government, political subdivision, faction, asserted government, or person, or to solicit or receive any contribution for any such government, political subdivision, faction, asserted government, or person: *Provided*, That if the President shall find that such action will serve to protect the commercial or other interests of the United States or its citizens, he may, in his discretion, and to such extent and under such regulations as he may prescribe, except from the operation of this section ordinary commercial credits and shorttime obligations in aid of legal transactions and of a character customarily used in normal peacetime commercial transactions. . . .

Section 4. This Act shall not apply to an American republic or republics engaged in war against a non-American state or states, provided the American republic is not cooperating with a non-American state or states in such war.

Section 5. (a) There is hereby established a National Munitions Control Board (hereinafter referred to as the "Board") to carry out the provisions of this Act. . . .

(d) It shall be unlawful for any person to export, or attempt to export, from the United States to any other state, any of the arms, ammunition, or implements of war referred to in this Act, or to import, or attempt to import, to the United States from any other state, any of the arms, ammunition, or implements of war referred to in this Act, without first having obtained a license therefor. . . .

Section 6. (a) Whenever the President shall have issued a proclamation under the authority of section 1 of this Act, it shall thereafter be unlawful, until such proclamation is revoked, for any American vessel to carry any arms, ammunition, or implements of war to any belligerent state, or to any state wherein civil strife exists, named in such proclamation, or to any neutral state for transshipment to, or for the use of, any such belligerent state or any such state wherein civil strife exists. . . .

Section 9. Whenever the President shall have issued a proclamation under the authority of section 1 of this Act it shall thereafter be unlawful for any citizen of the United States to travel on any vessel of the state or states named in such proclamation, except in accordance with such rules and regulations as the President shall prescribe. . . .

Section 10. Whenever the President shall have issued a proclamation under the authority of section 1, it shall thereafter be unlawful, until such proclamation is revoked, for any American vessel engaged in commerce with any belligerent state, or any state wherein civil strife exists, named in such proclamation, to be armed or to carry any armament, arms, ammunition, or implements of war, except small arms and ammunition therefor which the President may deem necessary and shall publicly designate for the preservation of discipline aboard such vessels. . . .

◇◇◇◇◇◇◇◇◇◇◇◇◇

6. PRESIDENT ROOSEVELT'S QUARANTINE SPEECH[8]

. . . THE POLITICAL situation in the world, which of late has been growing progressively worse, is such as to cause grave concern and anxiety to all the peoples and nations who wish to live in peace and amity with their neighbors.

Some 15 years ago the hopes of mankind for a continuing era of international peace were raised to great heights when more than 60 nations solemnly pledged themselves not to resort to arms in furtherance of their national aims and policies. The high aspirations expressed in the Briand-Kellogg Peace Pact and the hopes for peace thus raised have of late given away to a haunting fear of calamity. The present reign of terror and international lawlessness began a few years ago.

It began through unjustified interference in the internal affairs of other nations or the invasion of alien territory in violation of treaties and has now reached a stage where the very foundations of civilization are seriously threatened. The landmarks and traditions which have marked the progress of civilization toward a condition of law, order, and justice are being wiped away.

[8] Address at Chicago, October 5, 1937. Ibid., pp. 383–7.

Without a declaration of war and without warning or justification of any kind, civilians, including women and children, are being ruthlessly murdered with bombs from the air. In times of so-called peace ships are being attacked and sunk by submarines without cause or notice. Nations are fomenting and taking sides in civil warfare in nations that have never done them any harm. Nations claiming freedom for themselves deny it to others.

Innocent peoples and nations are being cruelly sacrificed to a greed for power and supremacy which is devoid of all sense of justice and humane consideration.

To paraphrase a recent author, "perhaps we foresee a time when men, exultant in the technique of homicide, will rage so hotly over the world that every precious thing will be in danger, every book and picture and harmony, every treasure garnered through two millenniums, the small, the delicate, the defenseless – all will be lost or wrecked or utterly destroyed."

If those things come to pass in other parts of the world let no one imagine that America will escape, that it may expect mercy, that this Western Hemisphere will not be attacked, and that it will continue tranquilly and peacefully to carry on the ethics and the arts of civilization.

If those days come "there will be no safety by arms, no help from authority, no answer in science. The storm will rage till every flower of culture is trampled and all human beings are leveled in a vast chaos."

If those days are not to come to pass – if we are to have a world in which we can breathe freely and live in amity without fear – the peace-loving nations must make a concerted effort to uphold laws and principles on which alone peace can rest secure.

The peace-loving nations must make a concerted effort in opposition to those violations of treaties and those ignorings of humane instincts which today are creating a state of international anarchy and instability from which there is no escape through mere isolation or neutrality.

Those who cherish their freedom and recognize and respect the equal right of their neighbors to be free and live in peace, must work together for the triumph of law and moral principles in order that peace, justice, and confidence may prevail in the world. There must be a return to a belief in the pledged word, in the value of a signed treaty. There must be recognition of the fact that national morality is as vital as private morality. . . .

There is a solidarity and interdependence about the modern world, both technically and morally, which makes it impossible for any nation completely to isolate itself from economic and political upheavals in the rest of the world, especially when such upheavals appear to be spreading and not declining. There can be no stability or peace either within nations or between nations except under laws and moral standards adhered to by all. International anarchy destroys every foundation for peace. It jeopardizes either the immediate or the future security of every nation, large or small. It is, therefore, a matter of vital interest and concern to the people of the United States that the sanctity of international treaties and the maintenance of international morality be restored.

The overwhelming majority of the peoples and nations of the world today want to live in peace. They seek the removal of barriers against trade. They want to exert themselves in industry, in agriculture, and in business, that they may increase their wealth through the production of wealth-producing goods rather than striving to produce military planes and bombs and machine guns and cannon for the destruction of human lives and useful property.

In those nations of the world which seem to be piling armament on armament for purposes of aggression, and those other nations which fear acts of aggression against them and their security, a very high proportion of their national income is being spent directly for armaments. It runs from 30 to as high as 50 percent. . . .

The situation is definitely of universal concern. The questions involved relate not merely to violations of specific provisions of particular treaties; they are questions of war and of peace, of international law, and especially of principles of humanity. It is true that they involve definite violations of agreements, and especially of the Covenant of the League of Nations, the Briand-Kellogg Pact, and the Nine Power Treaty. But they also involve problems of world economy, world security, and world humanity.

It is true that the moral consciousness of the world must recognize the importance of removing injustices and well-founded grievances; but at the same time it must be aroused to the cardinal necessity of honoring sanctity of treaties, of respecting the rights and liberties of others, and of putting an end to acts of international aggression.

It seems to be unfortunately true that the epidemic of world lawlessness is spreading.

When an epidemic of physical disease starts to spread, the community approves and joins in a quarantine of the patients in order to protect the health of the community against the spread of the disease.

It is my determination to pursue a policy of peace and to adopt every practicable measure to avoid involvement in war. It ought to be inconceivable that in this modern era, and in the face of experience, any nation could be so foolish and ruthless as to run the risk of plunging the whole world into war by invading and violating in contravention of solemn treaties the territory of other nations that have done them no real harm and which are too weak to protect themselves adequately. Yet the peace of the world and the welfare and security of every nation is today being threatened by that very thing.

No nation which refuses to exercise forbearance and to respect the freedom and rights of others can long remain strong and retain the confidence and respect of other nations. No nation ever loses its dignity or good standing by conciliating its differences and by exercising great patience with and consideration for the rights of other nations.

War is a contagion, whether it be declared or undeclared. It can engulf states and peoples remote from the original scene of hostilities. We are determined to keep out of war, yet we cannot insure ourselves against the disastrous effects of war and the dangers of involvement. We are adopting such measures as will minimize our risk of involvement, but we cannot have complete protection in a world of disorder in which confidence and security have broken down.

If civilization is to survive the principles of the Prince of Peace must be restored. Shattered trust between nations must be revived.

Most important of all, the will for peace on the part of peace-loving nations must express itself to the end that nations that may be tempted to violate their agreements and the rights of others will desist from such a cause. There must be positive endeavors to preserve peace.

America hates war. America hopes for peace. Therefore, America actively engages in the search for peace.

◇◇◇◇◇◇◇◇◇◇◇◇◇◇

7. VIEWS OF EX-SECRETARY OF STATE HENRY L. STIMSON [9]

AMERICANS are shocked and outraged at what is taking place in the Far East. But to many of them it presents merely a confused picture of distant horrors with which they think we have no necessary connection and to which they can close their eyes and turn their backs in the belief that we owe no duty to the situation except to keep out of it and forget it. It may be useful under such circumstances to try to recall briefly certain broad features inherent in this situation which do relate to us and our ultimate future.

In the first place, many of us do not adequately appraise the size and character of the Chinese nation; the influence of its civilization on Asia in the past and, what is far more important, the influence for good or evil which it may have upon the rest of the entire world, including ourselves, in the years and centuries to come. For four thousand years China has maintained what is far and away the most persistent cultural solidarity which has existed in the world. In all those centuries no foreign conquest and no passage of time has been able permanently to materially change or deflect her development.

In the next place, the dominant characteristic of this culture of these four hundred fifty millions of people, devoted mainly to agriculture, has been for centuries inherently peaceful. . . .

To . . . imperialist leaders in Japan the depression of 1930 brought their opportunity. They had long cherished plans for a military exploita-

[9] Letter to the *New York Times,* October 6, 1937; published by the *Times,* October 7, 1937.

tion of China, and on September 18, 1931, defying the civil leaders of their own government, the Japanese Army seized Manchuria. Within three months they had torn away from China provinces having an aggregate territory as large as Germany and France combined and which were occupied by a population of some thirty millions of Chinese. A few weeks later, in January, 1932, a Japanese expeditionary force attacked Shanghai, aiming a blow at the very center of China's territory and commerce. But meeting an entirely unexpected, courageous, and stubborn resistance by the Chinese Nineteenth Route Army, as well as with vigorous protests from the American Government and the League of Nations, and possibly because the total American fleet was held united at Hawaii on the flank of the Japanese aggression, Japan, in a few months withdrew her forces from Shanghai with her objective unattained.

Since then has ensued a four-year interval, during which significant changes have occurred. In Japan militarism has consolidated its hold upon the Government partly by a campaign of terrorism, which involved the assassination of the more moderate Japanese statesmen, and partly by the appeal which the successful military conquest in Manchuria has made to such an emotional population as the Japanese.

With militarism thus fortified at home, Japan has boldly claimed an economic and political hegemony over China which is in complete disregard of her former promises in the Nine-Power Treaty. Simultaneously she has been pushing forward partly disguised military and political steps to effectuate it. She has instigated attempts to break away some of the northern provinces of China proper and to form in them separate autonomous governments. She has engineered invasions by Manchukuoan troops into Inner Mongolia. . . .

Simultaneously events have been occurring in the outside world which might well make Japan think her opportunity had arrived for a new attack on China. The Fascist dictators of Italy and Germany have boldly and successfully carried through coups involving in Ethiopia, the Rhineland, and Spain acts of treaty violation and indefensible aggression. On the other hand, the peaceful democracies of the world, being absorbed with the work of recuperation from the depression and other consequences of the great war, have yielded to these lawless acts of the dictators with a lack of their customary spirit.

In Britain and America, usually in the van of matters of international morality, the people have seemingly been smitten by a temporary seizure of nervous "jitters." This has been excusable in Britain, faced as she has been and now is with an extremely perilous European condition within range of her home cities. But in America, occupying the most safe and defensible position in the world, there has been no excuse except faulty reasoning for the wave of ostrich-like isolationism which has swept over us and by its erroneous form of neutrality legislation has threatened to bring upon us in the future the very dangers of war which we now are seeking to avoid.

Finally, last winter in Russia, the one nation whose great and growing power lies within reach of Northern China and which is feared by Japan, there occurred domestic incidents which were widely interpreted in the outside world as evidencing grave internal disorders.

Evidently taking advantage of these conditions Japan has struck again, aiming both at Northern China as far as the Yellow River and also at the center of China at Shanghai. No excuse worthy of a moment's consideration has been given for the attack. On the contrary, the statements emanating from Tokyo make abundantly clear that there is no such excuse. The Chinese Government is denounced as infamous for not yielding to Japan's wishes in North China, and the announcement is made in the press that the attack will continue until that government at Nanking is destroyed.

The methods of the attack also indicate that this is the objective. China's coasts are blockaded and her shipping seized and a widespread campaign of bombing the civilian Chinese population, huddled into great defenseless cities and remote from any military movement or objective, is put into effect. These steps make clear a deliberate and systematic attempt by Japan by a general campaign of terrorism practiced upon the civilian population to force the Chinese Government to yield.

Making all allowances for imperfect information, the general scope of what Japan is attempting is abundantly clear. We can also forecast some of the effects which her attempt may have upon the outside world, including ourselves.

In general Japan is trying to take control of the development of modern China and to twist its form and nature to suit her own aims, both political and economic. She is trying to develop China in a way which is the exact opposite of the purpose and policy of the Open Door and the Nine-Power Treaty. Japan makes no secret of this. We do not have to guess. We have a perfectly frank exposition of her plan in what she has already done in Manchukuo and North China.

She does not contemplate "the preservation of China's territorial and administrative integrity." She is actually engaged in carving up China's territory and herself taking over China's administration. She does not propose equality of commercial opportunity among all nations dealing with China. She is seeking to monopolize that opportunity and has already taken effective steps to do so in Manchukuo.

She is thus trying completely to transform China's own business methods and character and culture and to dominate them to her own national ends. Furthermore, she is not seeking to do this by persuasion or education or other peaceful means, but by force and terrorism of the most brutal and barbarous kind. . . .

The lamentable fact is that today the aggression of Japan is being actively assisted by the efforts of men of our own nation and men of the other great democracy in the world – the British Commonwealth of Nations. It is not only being actively assisted, but our assistance is so effective and predominant that without it even today the aggression would in all probability be promptly checked and cease.

Let me explain this and make it absolutely clear. Japan's position as a war-making nation is far from being self-contained. She is peculiarly dependent upon the outside world for her ability to attack China. While she has ample facilities for manufacturing weapons of all kinds, she is extraordinarily lacking in the raw materials with which to carry on such manufactures. In that respect she is extremely vulnerable. She has no supplies of oil worthy of the name. She has no supplies of rubber whatever. She has very little iron ore – about one-seventh of what she uses even in peace times – and she has almost no cotton. . . .

Again, in Japan's present tottering financial condition she is able to make these purchases of raw material for her guns and ammunition only by selling enough of her own products to obtain the requisite foreign exchange to pay for her purchases.

One of these principal Japanese exports is raw silk. This is one of the most generally distributed crops of the Japanese Empire, the production of raw silk taking place in virtually every peasant home and farm. Of that crop the United States in 1935 purchased 85 per cent and in the first six months of 1936, 81 per cent; with Great Britain taking nearly all the rest. With the foreign exchange thus obtained Japan is purchasing from us, as I have said above, the raw materials for her guns. . . .

The second great fact which the present situation brings out is the deep-seated error which has pervaded recent American thinking on international matters. . . .

Our recent neutrality legislation attempts to impose a dead level of neutral conduct on the part of our Government between right and wrong, between an aggressor and its victim, between a breaker of the law of nations and the nations who are endeavoring to uphold the law. It won't work. Such a policy of amoral drift by such a safe and powerful nation as our own will only set back the hands of progress. It will not save us from entanglement. It will even make entanglement more certain. History has already amply shown this last fact.

As if to teach us the folly of our ways, since this legislation was adopted, fate has paraded before our shocked consciences two instances of glaring aggression in Ethiopia and the Far East. Progress is not made in the world by attempting to exclude a consideration of the difference between right and wrong, nor is it wise legislation to attempt to impose upon the President, to whom the Constitution gives the duty of the conduct of our international affairs, shackles of restraint to hold him helpless in all future conditions no matter how complex or unanticipated.

Finally, in this grave crisis in the Far East we not only must not fear to face issues of right and wrong, but we must not fear to cooperate with other nations who are similarly attempting to face those issues. The League of Nations was founded upon a covenant which almost for the first time in human history attempted to base our international civilization upon a reign of law and to make a distinction between a law-breaker and its victim. Five years ago on Japan's first aggression into Manchuria the League, while failing to stop the aggression, did not hesitate to pass judgment upon it in unmistakable language after a full investigation of its facts.

The League did not fail to distinguish between right and wrong in the Far East then, and the then American Government on February 25, 1933, did not hesitate to range itself alongside of the League in that judgment and to declare that its understanding of the facts was in accord with the findings of fact arrived at by the League and that its conclusions were in accord with the conclusions of the League.

Today on China's appeal the League is again engaged in an examination of the present crisis and the formulation of its judgments thereon. Our Government should not hesitate, if the facts are as we believe them, to support the League again by a statement of its concurrence. Such a judgment is not futile. In the process of time law is built up both within and without national boundaries by such decisions and such precedents. Japan is far more friendless today before the tribunal of world opinion than she would have been except for the investigation and judgment which was rendered against her five years ago. We should not fail to take our part in laying such foundations of the structure of international law of the future.

Since the writing of the foregoing letter has come the President's Chicago speech. I am filled with hope that this act of leadership on his part will result in a new birth of American courage in facing and carrying through our responsibilities in this crisis.

◇◇◇◇◇◇◇◇◇◇◇◇◇

8. AN ESTIMATE OF THE NEW NEUTRALITY[10]

THE UNITED STATES has lost its leadership in world affairs and to that fact largely can be attributed the impotence of the Nine-Power Treaty Conference in Brussels. The reason for this loss of influence is plain: treaty-breaking governments and dictators have become convinced that for no cause short of actual invasion will the United States initiate or join in any effective movement to assure world peace.

For this conviction on the part of these treaty-breakers the "isolationists" and "pacifists" in Congress and their vociferous supporters in the country are chiefly responsible. These groups include persons who believe that we can stay out of any world conflict. They attribute our entrance into the last international war to British propaganda and the schemes of bankers to enrich themselves; and they oppose any strong peace measures by this Government, even though to abstain from such might mean the loss of freedom to those who regard it as highly as they themselves, and an impairment of liberty to men and women in this very hemisphere

[10] An editorial in the *New York Times,* November 30, 1937.

It is the assertion of such groups and their Congressional representatives that, because of the gifts of nature and geography, the United States can retain its institutions and live its full life alone in a world where democracy does not elsewhere exist, even though Great Britain and France were shackled by despotisms which turn human beings into machines for conquest and consign liberty to the fallacies of the past.

The power of these groups and their spokesmen has been in the ascendancy, as acts and events plainly indicate. In recent years they have seized upon every occasion when the American Government was seeking to express the scruples of conscience against treaty-breaking and aggression, to proclaim that, in no circumstances, would this people do anything effective to restore moral standards among the nations. Organizing, writing pamphlets, and using the Congressional Record as their gazette, they gave notice as early as when Japan seized Manchukuo that the fixed future policy of the United States would be to keep out of war abroad, and that it would take no steps to prevent it, however clear the threat to our own institutions.

The attitude took form in the so-called Neutrality Act of 1936, with its "declaration of a state of war" and its "cash-and-carry" provisions. By the first named, the President was instructed by Congress, upon discovery of the existence of a state of war abroad, to withhold war material from all concerned, regardless of whether an invaded nation, fighting for its own as in the case of Ethiopia, was left at the mercy of a most ruthless aggressor. By the second named, American vessels were virtually swept from the seas, and only those warring nations which have navies and trade fleets were given access to our markets.

Attempts, in the name of international decency, to distinguish between honest and dishonest governments and to permit aid to nations clearly acting in self-defense against banditry, were beaten down in Congress. The world was put on notice that the United States was out to save its own skin from immediate dangers; and the dictators were informed that the American group controlling policy was prepared to see the world remade on Fascist lines without interference and apparently without understanding that this would mean anything dangerous to us at all.

When the President, recently voicing this people's indignation against the invasion of China by Japan and horror at the butchery at Shanghai, recalled that there still were "quarantines" against governments which did these things, a wholesome fear arose in certain capitals that the Neutrality Act might not represent enduring policy for the United States. And when next day the State Department named Japan as aggressor, the fear spread. But a little inquiry sufficed to prove that the pacifist and isolationist groups would not thus be led. Their Congressional representatives denounced the expressions as violations of the spirit of the Neutrality Act, which in truth they were, and, as soon as Congress met, the press cables carried abroad proposals of war referenda and other evidences that the group which framed the act is unchanged in its attitude. The Japanese Ambassador to

Washington did his duty, and did it accurately and well, when he informed his colleague at Brussels that pacifism was still the American mood. The circulation of this report in the conference capital both tempered the messages to Tokyo and stiffened the rejections therefrom and in its atmosphere the Brussels conference went to its inevitable, inept doom.

Meanwhile, on the pretext that a world alliance against communism is the first essential to peace, Japan, Germany, and Italy have signed a treaty. Outwardly it pledges these governments to stand with force against the encroachment of Soviet teachings and the Soviet form of government. But in some European chancelleries and in Washington the pact is interpreted as a pledge, necessarily not stated in the treaty, that each of these three nations will stand by the two others, defensively and offensively, until each has gained its territorial and other objectives. To illustrate: If Italy further threatens in the Mediterranean and Great Britain steps in to check, Japan will proceed against Hongkong and Singapore. If Germany thrusts southeastward in Europe and Great Britain and France move to check, Italy will extend her Mediterranean spheres and Japan will strike at French and British possessions in the Orient.

The ability of the three Fascist States to carry out the arrangement outlined above is, of course, open to the most serious doubts. Germany's Baltic coast is bare to the attack of the British fleet, and experts are far from convinced that Mussolini could have his way in the Mediterranean, even with Britain greatly preoccupied in Northern European waters. The fact, however, that such a construction by responsible statesmen is placed upon the treaty, which was heretofore largely regarded as a mutual envisioning of bugaboos, now places the alliance where the democracies of the two hemispheres must consider it in stating their policies. And nothing could more effectively give expression to realization of the danger implicit in it than a tangible expression of the determination of this country to stand by the other democracies should the need arise.

This is not a preachment for war measures. The people of the United States are set against military expeditions, and rightly so. But there are effective peace measures, the most recent illustration being the decision of the British and American Governments to negotiate a trade treaty. This should be supplemented by every possible kind of private and public co-operation between Britons and Americans and others who speak, if not the same language, at least the same spiritual tongue. Understandings on trade, money, and credit will serve as certain weapons against treaty-breakers.

Our statesmen and leaders of public thought could aid peace mightily if, losing fear of the blind peace groups and gaining confidence that plain common sense and self-interest can be trusted, they engaged in public exchanges to put the enemies of peace on notice that the great democracies are aware of what is planned and will stand together against it. The sure shadow of economic starvation on spendthrift governments which cannot wage war unless we supply them, and deny supplies to their victims, can be made sufficiently effective as a deterrent without resort to the substance of sanctions or war.

Should such cooperations be publicly and steadily revealed, and such exchanges of thought take place, *The New York Times* believes the American people will awake to the facts which menace this nation; and the world will learn that events are conceivable, that circumstances can arise, outside this hemisphere, which will instantly range American public opinion behind an effective peace policy and make junk overnight of the so-called Neutrality Act. In the face of such exchanges of thought the policy of democratic nations will be stiffened and grooved; and treaty-breakers and dictators will take prudent counsel among themselves.

In such a manner can this nation restore a will for peace in the world and reestablish its lost leadership in international affairs. By such means the ravishers of small or weak neighbors and the enemies of democracy will discover that the United States has not become so timorous and so stupid as to abandon its responsibilities and imperil its greatness and its freedom. It will be wiser to put them on notice at once.

1-20

CHAPTER XXXIII

THE RETREAT FROM ISOLATION

TO THE PEOPLE who did not approve the policy of isolation, the retreat from it seemed interminably slow. The isolationists appeared to hold Congress firmly in their control. But once their lines were breached in September 1939, the retreat was rapid.

Secretary Hull observed events in the Far East, Ethiopia, Spain, and central Europe with ever increasing alarm, and turned to his assault upon the New Neutrality and upon the isolationist philosophy in general, with steady persistence and growing severity. He addressed himself, as did the President, not to Congress particularly but to the people. An excellent example of his efforts is his address of March 17, 1938 (1).

The President continued to exert what moral force he could to stem the growing tide of aggression. He watched the German absorption of Austria without notable comment. When, however, the Germans fomented the Sudeten crisis in September 1938, he appealed to the German Chancellor and to the Italian Premier to avoid war. In March 1939, the Germans violated their pledges made at Munich and invaded Czechoslovakia, and early in April the Italians invaded Albania. The President, fearing the outbreak of a general war in Europe, made another appeal to the German and Italian dictators (2).

By midsummer 1939 the Administration was ready to make a direct attack upon the neutrality legislation. The strategy of the attack was to center upon one feature of it alone, the arms embargo (3). The isolationists still controlled Congress, however, and no change was made. On September 1, 1939 the Germans invaded Poland and brought on the long-dreaded general European war. Almost immediately the President called a special session of Congress and renewed the attack on the arms embargo, this time with success. Congress enacted the fourth Neutrality Act which lifted the embargo (4). Thus the retreat began.

By midsummer 1940 the United States had more serious things to think about than the repeal of the arms embargo. In April of that year Germany invaded Norway and Denmark, in May, Belgium, Holland, and Luxemburg; and in June, France collapsed. Many people in the United States, perhaps the majority of them, believed that the British Isles would be successfully invaded. The President, however, was not idle. Acting under a law of 1917, he increased the supply of arms to the British, and in September, he announced the sensational Destroyer-Bases Agreement (5).

Meanwhile, tension between the United States and Japan continued to increase. Ever since the enactment of the first Neutrality Act the President had the authority to declare that a state of war existed in the Far

East and to embargo the sale of arms and munitions to the belligerents. He had not exercised this power, however, because he believed that such an embargo would be more beneficial to Japan than to China. Some people doubted the validity of this theory and thought that the President's policy toward Japan was one of appeasement. At any rate, Japanese aggression was not stemmed, and in September 1940, Japan seized bases in Indo-China, and signed a treaty of alliance with Germany and Italy. When the Japanese Ambassador in Washington protested to Secretary Hull against the discontinuance of the sale to Japan of American scrap iron, the Secretary replied in terms scarcely ever used in diplomatic conversations (6).

In January 1941 the President appealed to Congress to make the United States the "arsenal of democracy" (7). This initiated a bitter debate over the old problem of isolation, but the lines of the isolationists were no longer invulnerable. The Lend-Lease Bill was passed (8). Although the debate continued (9), the offensive had passed to those who favored aid to the democracies (10). In April 1941, the United States acquired a base in Greenland (11), and in July it assumed the defense of Iceland (12). Political partisanship was slow to give way to the national emergency (13), but no one could doubt that the United States had turned back from the road it had taken when the first Neutrality Act was passed in 1935. If any doubt did exist it should have been dispelled after the announcement of the meeting, in August 1941, of President Roosevelt and Prime Minister Churchill at which the Atlantic Charter was signed (14).

The first American ship to fall victim of a submarine attack was the merchant ship *Robin Moor,* torpedoed May 21, 1941. The President waited, however, until other ships had been attacked before announcing his determination to protect American shipping (15). Meanwhile the Japanese government was making the cabinet decision of July 26, 1940 (16), and the Three Power Pact of September 27, 1940 (17). In view of these developments it is not surprising that Under Secretary of State Sumner Welles, in an Armistice Day Address, November 11, 1941, turned his thoughts to Woodrow Wilson and the principles he advocated (18).

The exact date of the final decision of Japan to attack the possessions of the United States in the Pacific has not been officially determined. It seems probable, however, that the decision was reached at an Imperial Conference, presided over by the Emperor, on July 2, 1941, and that the plans for the attack on Pearl Harbor were dated November 5, 1941, the same day that the Japanese government announced the sending of a special envoy, Saburo Kurusu, to Washington to assist Ambassador Nomura in negotiations for peace. It is doubtful, therefore, that much significance should be attached to the conversations between Secretary Hull and the Japanese envoys during November and December 1941. The United States was not willing to assist Japan in the conquest of the Far East (19), and Japan was unwilling to accept the program for peace suggested by Secretary Hull (20).

◇◇◇◇◇◇◇◇◇◇◇◇◇

1. FUNDAMENTALS OF AMERICAN FOREIGN POLICY[1]

. . . THE PRIMARY objectives of our foreign policy are the maintenance of the peace of our country and the promotion of the economic, the social, and the moral welfare of our people. Unfortunately, the means of attaining these objectives involve today so many factors of great complexity that their real significance is frequently misunderstood and misinterpreted. . . .

On July 16, 1937, I issued a public statement setting forth the fundamental principles to which our Government adheres in the formulation of its foreign policy. On behalf of our Government I transmitted a copy of this statement to every government of the world, requesting such comment as each might see fit to offer. To our profound gratification an overwhelming majority of those governments joined in affirming their faith in these vital principles.

The most important of these principles, which are indispensable to a satisfactory international order, are as follows:

Maintenance of peace should be constantly advocated and practiced. All nations should, through voluntary self-restraint, abstain from use of force in pursuit of policy and from interference in the internal affairs of other nations.

All nations should seek to adjust problems arising in their international relations by processes of peaceful negotiation and agreement.

All nations should uphold the principle of the sanctity of treaties and of faithful observance of international agreements.

Modification of provisions of treaties, when need therefor arises, should be by orderly processes carried out in a spirit of mutual helpfulness and accommodation.

Each nation should respect the rights of others and perform scrupulously its own established obligations; in brief, international law and the spirit which underlies it must be revitalized and strengthened.

Steps should be taken toward promotion of economic security and stability the world over through lowering or removal of barriers to international trade, according of effective equality of commercial opportunity, and application of the principle of equality of commercial treatment.

National armaments should be limited and be progressively reduced; at the same time, realizing the necessity for maintaining armed forces adequate for national security, each nation should to that end be prepared to reduce or increase its own armed forces in proportion as reductions or increases are made by other nations.

Apart from the question of alliances with others, each nation should be prepared to engage in cooperative effort, by peaceful and practicable means, in support of these principles.

---

[1] Address of the Secretary of State, Cordell Hull, at Washington, March 17, 1938. *Peace and War*, op. cit., pp. 407–19.

The peace and progress of every nation are just as dependent on international law and order, based upon the foregoing principles, as the welfare, stability, and progress of a community are dependent upon domestic law and order, based upon legal, moral and other recognized standards of conduct. No government faithful to the sacred trust involved in the task of providing for the safety and well-being of its people can disregard these universal principles. Every nation, whatever its form of government, can support them. Every nation must support them, if civilization is to survive. The longer the nations delay acceptance and observance of these fundamental tenets of constructive statesmanship, the graver will be the jeopardy into which all worth-while international relationships will be plunged, and with them the welfare, the happiness, and the civilized existence of all nations.

The crucial issue today is whether these principles will be vitalized and be firmly established as the foundation of an international order or whether international anarchy based on brute force will inundate the world and ultimately sweep away the very bases of civilization and progress. That issue is universal. No more than a community or a nation, can the world base its existence in part on law and in part on lawlessness, in part on order and in part on chaos, in part on processes of peace and in part on methods of violence. . . .

During the early months of the conflict in the Far East I appealed on several occasions, in the name of our Government, to both Japan and China to desist from using armed force and to resort to the well-recognized processes of peaceful settlement for the adjustment of whatever differences existed between them. I said that we would be glad to be of assistance toward facilitating, in any manner that might be practicable and mutually agreeable, resort by them to such processes.

On August 17, and with frequent reiteration thereafter, I stated that we did not intend to abandon our nationals and our interests in China.

From time immemorial it has been the practice of civilized nations to afford protection, by appropriate means and under the rule of reason, to their nationals and their rights and interests abroad. This policy has been pursued by the Government of the United States throughout the existence of our country. . . .

In announcing our intention to afford appropriate and reasonable protection to our rights and interests in the Far East, I stated clearly that we are fully determined to avoid the extremes either of internationalism or of isolationism. Internationalism would mean undesirable political involvements; isolationism would either compel us to confine all activities of our people within our own frontiers, with incalculable injury to the standard of living and the general welfare of our people, or else expose our nationals and our legitimate interests abroad to injustice or outrage wherever lawless conditions arise. Steering a sound middle course between these two extremes, we are convinced that a policy of affording appropriate protection — under the rule of reason, in such form as may be best suited to the particular circumstances, and in accordance with the principles we advocate – is imperatively needed to serve our national interest.

Our decision in this matter is based not only on what we firmly believe to be a specific and elementary duty of a government toward its citizens, but also on other and broader considerations. Respect by a country for the rights and interests of others is a visible test of the fulfillment of obligations assumed by virtue of acceptance of international law and of undertakings embodied in negotiated international instruments. It is, therefore, a test of the observance of those fundamental principles of civilized relations among nations, which, if firmly established, provide in themselves the best means of protection against violation and abuse of the legitimate rights and interests of every nation.

To waive rights and to permit interests to lapse in the face of their actual or threatened violation – and thereby to abandon obligations – in any important area of the world, can serve only to encourage disregard of law and of the basic principles of international order, and thus contribute to the inevitable spread of international anarchy throughout the world. For this country, as for any country, to act in such manner *anywhere* would be to invite disregard and violation of its rights and interests *everywhere*, by every nation so inclined, large or small. . . .

It is the duty of the Federal Government to insure the safety of our country and to determine what "means of security" are, at any given moment, needed to provide against "the means and the danger of attack." The responsible heads of our naval establishment offer convincing reasons in support of the program, now before the Congress, to render adequate the means of our national defense. No policy would prove more disastrous than for an important nation to fail to arm adequately when international lawlessness is on the rampage. It is my considered judgment that, in the present state of world affairs, to do less than is now proposed would lay our country open to unpredictable hazards. It would, moreover, seriously restrict our Nation's ability to command, without purpose or occasion for resorting to arms, proper respect for its legitimate rights and interests, the surrender of which would constitute abandonment of the fundamental principles of justice and morality and peace among nations.

The maintenance of these principles that are of concern to all nations alike cannot and should not be undertaken by any one nation alone. Prudence and common sense dictate that, where this and other nations have common interests and common objectives, we should not hesitate to exchange information and to confer with the governments of such other nations and, in dealing with the problems confronting each alike, to proceed along parallel lines – this Government retaining at all times its independence of judgment and freedom of action. For nations which seek peace to assume with respect to each other attitudes of complete aloofness would serve only to encourage, and virtually invite, on the part of other nations lawlessly inclined, policies and actions most likely to endanger peace. . . .

In connection with the Far Eastern situation, this Government was confronted with the question of applying the existing neutrality legislation, which was designed primarily to keep our Nation out of war. After mature deliberation the conclusion was reached that in the circumstances attending the controversy in the Far East – a type of circumstances which the authors of the legislation could scarcely have visualized – application of the law would be most likely to endanger the very objectives which the law was designed to promote. Accordingly, exercising the discretion vested in him by the law itself, the President has refrained from putting the provisions of that law into operation. At the same time, in pursuance of our general policy of avoiding unnecessary risks, the President announced, on September 14, 1937, that "Merchant vessels owned by the Government of the United States will not hereafter, until further notice, be permitted to transport to China or Japan any of the arms, ammunition, or implements of war which were listed in the President's proclamation of May 1, 1937," and that "Any other merchant vessels, flying the American flag, which attempt to transport any of the listed articles to China or Japan will, until further notice, do so at their own risk. . . ."

We have affirmed on every possible occasion and have urged upon all nations the supreme need for keeping alive and for practicing sound fundamental principles of relations among civilized nations. We have never entertained and we have not the slightest intention to entertain any such notion as the use of American armed forces for "policing the world." But we equally have not the slightest intention of reversing a tradition of a century and a half by abandoning our deep concern for, and our advocacy of, the establishment everywhere of international order under law, based upon the well-recognized principles to which I have referred. It is our profound conviction that the most effective contribution which we, as a nation sincerely devoted to the cause of peace, can make – in the tragic conditions with which our people, in common with the rest of mankind, are confronted today – is to have this country respected throughout the world for integrity, justice, good will, strength, and unswerving loyalty to principles.

The foregoing is the essence of our foreign policy. The record is an open book. We spare no effort to make known the facts regarding our attitude, our objectives, and our acts. We are always ready to furnish to the members of the Congress essential information. You, gentlemen, have first-hand knowledge of our constant effort to keep the press and the public informed.

There is one thing that we cannot do; and that is, to prepare and to place before every government of the world a detailed chart of the course of policy and action which this country will or will not pursue under any particular set of circumstances. No man, no nation, can possibly foresee all the circumstances that may arise. Moreover, to attempt to make such a detailed chart of future action would merely result in impairing our effectiveness in working for the one objective toward which we constantly strive and on which, I am certain, there is not a vestige of disagreement among the people of our country – the establishment of durable peace.

So strong, indeed, is the desire of this country for peace that many measures have been suggested toward our keeping out of war – some of them in complete disregard of both experience and practicability. It has been urged that we apply the neutrality law automatically in all circumstances, without adequate consideration of the possible consequences of such action for our own peace and for the safety of our citizens. It has been urged that we withdraw precipitately from any part of the world in which violators of international decencies choose to assert themselves. It has even been urged that we change the very basis of our representative form of government in a frantic search for something which the proposers assume would make it more likely that this country avoid war.

I take it for granted that all of us alike are sincere friends of peace. This makes it all the more necessary for every one of us to scrutinize carefully every measure proposed, lest in our attempts to avoid war we imperil the chances of preserving peace.

The problem of the form of government best adapted to this country's needs was one with which the founders of our Republic came to grips in those stirring days when the structure of our independent national existence was being given form and substance. After exhaustive deliberation and discussion they decided upon the system of representative democracy in preference to that of pure democracy as the system through which the people could best safeguard their liberty and promote their national security and welfare. The wisdom of the founders of this Nation in deciding, with conspicuous unanimity, to place the conduct of foreign relations in the hands of the Federal Government has stood the test of generations as providing the most effective means that can be devised for assuring the peace, the security, and the independence of our people.

What warrant is there, in reason or in experience, for the assumption – which underlies such proposals as the plan for a popular referendum on the subject of declaring war – that the Chief Executive and the Congress will be at any time more eager and more likely to embark upon war than would be the general body of citizens to whom they are directly responsible? No President and no Congress have ever carried this country into war against the will of the people. On the other hand, there is not a vestige of doubt that the adoption of a procedure like the referendum plan would hopelessly handicap the Government in the conduct of our foreign relations in general and would thus disastrously impair its ability to safeguard the interests of the Nation, in the forefront among which is that of peace.

Likewise dangerous, from the viewpoint of the preservation of peace, is the proposal that we retire from the Far East, comprising the chief portion of the Pacific area. Unfortunately, many people in this country have wholly misunderstood the position and policy of our Government in relation to that situation. Some have visualized only our trade and investment relationships with China, or our moral and cultural interests there, symbolized by missionary, educational, medical, and similar activities. Some have concentrated their attention solely upon the incidental and exceptional facts of the existence of extraterritoriality and the maintenance of some armed forces to assist in safeguarding our nationals against possible mob violence and similar disorders – special rights which it is our policy to give up and forces which it is our policy to withdraw the moment the unusual conditions disappear.

All these are important. But the interest and concern of the United States – whether in the Far East, in any other part of the Pacific area, in Europe, or anywhere else in the world – are not measured alone by the number of American citizens residing in a particular country, or by the volume of investment and trade, or by exceptional conditions peculiar to the particular area. There is a much broader and more fundamental interest – which is, that orderly processes in international relationships based on the principles to which I have referred be maintained. . . .

The momentous question – let me repeat – is whether the doctrine of force shall become enthroned once more and bring in its wake, inexorably, international anarchy and a relapse into barbarism; or whether this and other peaceful nations, fervently attached to the principles which underlie international order, shall work unceasingly – singly or in cooperation with each other, as circumstances, their traditional policies and practices, and their enlightened self-interest may dictate – to promote and preserve law, order, morality, and justice as the unshakeable bases of civilized international relations.

We might, if we could reconcile ourselves to such an attitude, turn our backs on the whole problem and decline the responsibility and labor of contributing to its solution. But let us have no illusions as to what such a course of action would involve for us as a nation.

It would mean a break with our past, both internationally and domestically. It would mean a voluntary abandonment of some of the most important things that have made us a great nation. It would mean an abject retreat before those forces which we have, throughout our whole natural history, consistently opposed.

It would mean that our security would be menaced in proportion as other nations came to believe that, either through fear or through unwillingness, we did not intend to afford protection to our legitimate national interests abroad, but, on the contrary, intended to abandon them at the first sign of danger. Under such conditions the sphere of our international relationships – economic, cultural, intellectual, and other – would necessarily shrink and shrivel, until we would stand practically alone among the nations, a self-constituted hermit state.

Thrown back upon our own resources, we would find it necessary to reorganize our entire social and economic structure. The process of adaptation to a more or less self-contained existence would mean less production and at higher costs; lower living standards; regimentation in every phase of life; economic distress to wage earners and farmers, and to their families; and the dole, on an ever-increasing scale.

All this we would be doing in pursuit of the notion that by so doing we would avoid war. But would these policies, while entailing such enormous sacrifices and rendering the Nation more and more decadent, really give us any such assurance?

Reason and experience definitely point to the contrary. We may seek to withdraw from participation in world affairs, but we cannot thereby withdraw from the world itself. Isolation is not a means to security; it is a fruitful source of insecurity.

We want to live in a world which is at peace; in which the forces of militarism, of territorial aggression, and of international anarchy in general will become utterly odious, revolting, and intolerable to the conscience of mankind; in which the doctrine or order under law will be firmly established; in which there will no longer be one code of morality, honor, justice, and fair play for the individual in his relations with other individuals, and an entirely different code for governments and nations in their relations with each other. We want to live in a world in which fruitful and constructive international relationships can serve as a medium for disseminating throughout the world the benefits of the material, spiritual, and moral progress of mankind. . . .

◇◇◇◇◇◇◇◇◇◇◇◇

Pres Roosevelt

2. AN APPEAL FOR PEACE[2]

to Germany

YOU REALIZE I am sure that throughout the world hundreds of millions of human beings are living today in constant fear of a new war or even a series of wars.

The existence of this fear – and the possibility of such a conflict – is of definite concern to the people of the United States for whom I speak, as it must also be to the peoples of the other nations of the entire Western Hemisphere. All of them know that any major war, even if it were to be confined to other continents, must bear heavily on them during its continuance and also for generations to come.

Because of the fact that after the acute tension in which the world has been living during the past few weeks there would seem to be at least a momentary relaxation – because no troops are at this moment on the march – this may be an opportune moment for me to send you this message.

On a previous occasion I have addressed you in behalf of the settlement of political, economic, and social problems by peaceful methods and without resort to arms.

But the tide of events seems to have reverted to the threat of arms. If

[2] Note sent by President Roosevelt to Chancellor Hitler and Premier Mussolini, April 14, 1939. Ibid., pp. 455–8.

such threats continue, it seems inevitable that much of the world must become involved in common ruin. All the world, victor nations, vanquished nations, and neutral nations will suffer. I refuse to believe that the world is, of necessity, such a prisoner of destiny. On the contrary, it is clear that the leaders of great nations have it in their power to liberate their peoples from the disaster that impends. It is equally clear that in their own minds and in their own hearts the peoples themselves desire that their fears be ended.

It is, however, unfortunately necessary to take cognizance of recent facts.

Three nations in Europe and one in Africa have seen their independent existence terminated. A vast territory in another independent nation of the Far East has been occupied by a neighboring state. Reports, which we trust are not true, insist that further acts of aggression are contemplated against still other independent nations. Plainly the world is moving toward the moment when this situation must end in catastrophe unless a more rational way of guiding events is found.

You have repeatedly asserted that you and the German people have no desire for war. If this is true there need be no war.

Nothing can persuade the peoples of the earth that any governing power has any right or need to inflict the consequences of war on its own or any other people save in the cause of self-evident home defense.

In making this statement we as Americans speak not through selfishness or fear or weakness. If we speak now it is with the voice of strength and with friendship for mankind. It is still clear to me that international problems can be solved at the council table.

It is therefore no answer to the plea for peaceful discussion for one side to plead that unless they receive assurances beforehand that the verdict will be theirs, they will not lay aside their arms. In conference rooms, as in courts, it is necessary that both sides enter upon the discussion in good faith, assuming that substantial justice will accrue to both; and it is customary and necessary that they leave their arms outside the room where they confer.

I am convinced that the cause of world peace would be greatly advanced if the nations of the world were to obtain a frank statement relating to the present and future policy of governments.

Because the United States, as one of the nations of the Western Hemisphere, is not involved in the immediate controversies which have arisen in Europe, I trust that you may be willing to make such a statement of policy to me as the head of a nation far removed from Europe in order that I, acting only with the responsibility and obligation of a friendly intermediary, may communicate such declaration to other nations now apprehensive as to the course which the policy of your Government may take.

Are you willing to give assurance that your armed forces will not attack or invade the territory or possessions of the following independent nations: Finland, Estonia, Latvia, Lithuania, Sweden, Norway, Denmark, The Netherlands, Belgium, Great Britain and Ireland, France, Portugal,

Spain, Switzerland, Liechtenstein, Luxemburg, Poland, Hungary, Rumania, Yugoslavia, Russia, Bulgaria, Greece, Turkey, Iraq, the Arabias, Syria, Palestine, Egypt and Iran.

Such an assurance clearly must apply not only to the present day but also to a future sufficiently long to give every opportunity to work by peaceful methods for a more permanent peace. I therefore suggest that you construe the word "future" to apply to a minimum period of assured non-aggression – ten years at the least – a quarter of a century, if we dare look that far ahead.

If such assurance is given by your Government, I will immediately transmit it to the governments of the nations I have named and I will simultaneously inquire whether, as I am reasonably sure, each of the nations enumerated above will in turn give like assurance for transmission to you.

Reciprocal assurances such as I have outlined will bring to the world an immediate measure of relief.

I propose that if it is given, two essential problems shall promptly be discussed in the resulting peaceful surroundings, and in those discussions the Government of the United States will gladly take part.

The discussions which I have in mind relate to the most effective and immediate manner through which the peoples of the world can obtain progressive relief from the crushing burden of armament which is each day bringing them more closely to the brink of economic disaster. Simultaneously the Government of the United States would be prepared to take part in discussions looking towards the most practical manner of opening up avenues of international trade to the end that every nation of the earth may be enabled to buy and sell on equal terms in the world market as well as to possess assurance of obtaining the materials and products of peaceful economic life.

At the same time, those governments other than the United States which are directly interested could undertake such political discussions as they may consider necessary or desirable.

We recognize complex world problems which affect all humanity but we know that study and discussion of them must be held in an atmosphere of peace. Such an atmosphere of peace cannot exist if negotiations are overshadowed by the threat of force or by the fear of war.

I think you will not misunderstand the spirit of frankness in which I send you this message. Heads of great governments in this hour are literally responsible for the fate of humanity in the coming years. They cannot fail to hear the prayers of their peoples to be protected from the foreseeable chaos of war. History will hold them accountable for the lives and the happiness of all – even unto the least.

I hope that your answer will make it possible for humanity to lose fear and regain security for many years to come.

A similar message is being addressed to the Chief of the Italian Government.

◇◇◇◇◇◇◇◇◇◇◇◇

3. AN ATTEMPT TO END THE ARMS EMBARGO[3]

. . . THE CONGRESS has pending before it at the present time certain proposals providing for the amendment of the existing so-called neutrality legislation. Some of these proposed changes I regard as necessary to promote the peace and security of the United States.

. . . I shall try to bring out as clearly as I can the important points of agreement and disagreement between those who support the principles contained in the six point peace and neutrality program recommended by the Executive branch of the Government and those who oppose these recommendations.

In substance and in principle both sides of the discussion agree on the following points:

1. Both sides agree that the first concern of the United States must be its own peace and security.

2. Both sides agree that it should be the policy of this Government to avoid being drawn into wars between other nations.

3. Both sides agree that this nation should at all times avoid entangling alliances or involvements with other nations.

4. Both sides agree that in the event of foreign wars this nation should maintain a status of strict neutrality, and that around the structure of neutrality we should so shape our policies as to keep this country from being drawn into war.

On the other hand, the following is the chief essential point of disagreement between those who favor the adoption of the recommendations formulated by the Executive branch of the Government and those who are opposing these recommendations:

The proponents, including the Executive branch of the Government, at the time when the arms embargo was originally adopted called attention to the fact that its enactment constituted a hazardous departure from the principle of international law which recognizes the right of neutrals to trade with belligerents and of belligerents to trade with neutrals. They believe that neutrality means impartiality, and in their view an arms embargo is directly opposed to the idea of neutrality. It is not humanly possible, by enacting an arms embargo, or by refraining from such enactment, to hold the scales exactly even between two belligerents. In either case and due to shifting circumstances one belligerent may find itself in a position of relative advantage or disadvantage. The important difference between the two cases is that when such a condition arises in the absence of an arms embargo on our part, no responsibility attaches to this country, whereas in the presence of an embargo, the responsibility of this country for the creation of the condition is inevitably direct and clear.

There is no theory or practice to be found in international law pertain-

[3] Statement of the Secretary of State, Cordell Hull, transmitted to Congress by President Roosevelt, July 14, 1939. Ibid., pp. 468–74.

ing to neutrality to the effect that the advantages that any particular belligerent might procure through its geographic location, its superiority on land or at sea, or through other circumstances, should be offset by the establishment by neutral nations of embargoes.

The opposition to the present substitute proposal joins issue on this point, and stands for existing rigid embargo as a permanent part of our neutrality policy. And yet by insisting on an arms embargo in time of war they are, to that extent, for the reasons I have stated, urging not neutrality, but what might well result in actual unneutrality, the serious consequences of which no one can predict.

Those who urge the retention of the present embargo continue to advance the view that it will keep this country out of war, — thereby misleading the American people to rely upon a false and illogical delusion as a means of keeping out of war.

I say it is illogical, because while the trade in "arms, ammunition and implements of war" is at present banned, the trade in equally essential war materials, as well as all the essential materials out of which the finished articles are made can continue. For example, in time of war, we can sell cotton for the manufacture of explosives, but not the explosives; we can sell the steel and copper for cannon and for shells but not the cannon nor the shells; we can continue to sell to belligerents the high-powered fuel necessary for the operation of airplanes, but we are not able to sell the airplanes.

I say it is a false delusion because a continuation of the trade in arms is a clearly recognized and traditional right of the nationals of a neutral country in time of war, subject only to effective blockade and to the right of belligerents to treat any such commodities as contraband. The assertion frequently made that this country has ever engaged or may become engaged in serious controversy solely over the fact that its nationals have sold arms to belligerents is misleading and unsupportable. All available evidence is directly to the contrary. Every informed person knows that arms, as absolute contraband, are subject to seizure by a belligerent and that neither the neutral shipper nor his government has the slightest ground for complaint. There is, therefore, no reason to suppose that the sale of arms may lead to serious controversy between a neutral and a belligerent. Furthermore, under the proposals that have been made American nationals would be divested of all right, title and interest in these and other commodities before they leave our shores and American citizens and ships would be kept out of danger zones. As regards possible complications which might arise as a result of the extension of credits to belligerents or of extraordinary profits accruing to any group of producers in this country, it is wholly within the power of Congress at all times to safeguard the national interest in this respect.

Controversies which would involve the United States are far more likely to arise from the entrance of American ships or American citizens in the danger zones or through the sinking on the high seas of American vessels carrying commodities other than those covered by the arms embargo. In the recommendations formulated by the Executive as a substitute for the present legislation it was especially urged that provisions be adopted which would exclude American nationals and American ships from zones where real danger to their safety might exist and which would divest goods of American ownership, thereby minimizing to the fullest extent the danger of American involvement.

Those of us who support the recommendations formulated for the elimination of the embargo are convinced that the arms embargo plays into the hands of those nations which have taken the lead in building up their fighting power. It works directly against the interests of the peace-loving nations, especially those which do not possess their own munitions plants. It means that if any country is disposed toward conquest, and devotes its energy and resources to establish itself as a superior fighting power, that country may be more tempted to try the fortunes of war if it knows that its less well prepared opponents would be shut off from those supplies which, under every rule of international law, they should be able to buy in all neutral countries, including the United States. It means also that some of those countries which have only limited facilities for the production of arms, ammunition and implements of war are put in a position of increased dependence. During peace-time they would feel the compulsion of shaping their political as well as their economic policy to suit the military strength of others; and during wartime their powers of defense would be limited.

For these reasons those who are supporting the recommendations for the amendment of existing legislation recognize definitely that the present embargo encourages a general state of war both in Europe and Asia. Since the present embargo has this effect its results are directly prejudicial to the highest interests and to the peace and to the security of the United States.

In the present grave conditions of international anarchy and of danger to peace, in more than one part of the world, I profoundly believe that the first great step towards safeguarding this nation from being drawn into war is to use whatever influence it can, compatible with the traditional policy of our country of non-involvement, so as to make less likely the outbreak of a major war. This is a duty placed upon our Government which some may fail to perceive or choose to reject. But it must be clear to everyone of us that the outbreak of a general war increases the dangers confronting the United States. This fact cannot be ignored. . . .

As a matter of fact almost all sales of arms and ammunition made in recent years by our nationals have been made to governments whose policies have been dedicated to the maintenance of peace, but who have felt the necessity of creating or of augmenting their means of national self-defense, thereby protecting otherwise helpless men, women and children in the event that other powers resort to war. In the face of the present universal danger all countries, including our own, feel the necessity of increasing armament, and small countries in particular are dependent upon countries like the United States which have the capacity to produce armaments. Our refusal to make it possible for them to obtain such means of necessary self-defense in a time of grave emergency, would contribute solely towards making more helpless the law-abiding and peace-devoted peoples of the world. If such action is moral, and if, on the contrary, sales of the means of self-defense for the protection of peaceful and law-abiding peoples are immoral, then a new definition of morality and immorality must be written. This task might be left to the proponents of the arms embargo.

I must also refer to another impression created by propaganda to the effect that the abandonment of the arms embargo would increase power of action on the part of the Executive branch of the Government and conversely that the maintenance of the embargo would serve as an additional check on the powers of the Executive. It is difficult to see how either of these propositions could possibly hold true. An impartial granting of access to American markets to all countries without distinction gives the Executive no additional power to choose among them and to commit this country to any line of policy or action which may lead it either into a dangerous controversy or into war with any foreign power.

The legislative proposals which were recommended to the Congress through the communications which I transmitted to Senator Pittman and to Congressman Bloom on May 27 providing for the safeguarding of our nation to the fullest possible extent from incurring the risks of involvement in war contemplate the elimination of the existing arms embargo and are as follows:

(1) To prohibit American ships from entering combat areas;
(2) To restrict travel by American citizens in combat areas;
(3) To require that goods exported from the United States to belligerent countries shall be preceded by the transfer of title to the foreign purchasers;
(4) To continue the existing legislation respecting loans and credits to belligerent nations;
(5) To regulate the solicitation and collection in this country of funds for belligerents; and
(6) To continue the National Munitions Control Board and the licensing system with respect to the importation and exportation of arms, ammunition, and implements of war.

This six-point program was the best that could be devised after much painstaking thought and study, and after many conferences with members of the Congress, of how best to keep this country out of a conflict should it arise. It rests primarily on the established rules of international law, plus the curtailment of certain rights of our nationals, the exercise of which is permitted under international law but which might lead to controversies with belligerents and eventual involvement in foreign wars. . . .

◇◇◇◇◇◇◇◇◇◇◇◇◇◇

4. THE FOURTH NEUTRALITY ACT: 1939[4]

. . . *RESOLVED by the Senate and House of Representatives of the United States of America in Congress assembled,*

Section 1. (a) That whenever the President, or the Congress by concurrent resolution, shall find that there exists a state of war between foreign states, and that it is necessary to promote the security or preserve the peace of the United States or to protect the lives of citizens of the United States, the President shall issue a proclamation naming the states involved; and he shall, from time to time, by proclamation, name other states as and when they may become involved in the war. . . .

Section 2. (a) Whenever the President shall have issued a proclamation under the authority of section 1 (a) it shall thereafter be unlawful for any American vessel to carry any passengers or any articles or materials to any state named in such proclamation. . . .

(c) Whenever the President shall have issued a proclamation under the authority of section 1 (a) it shall thereafter be unlawful to export or transport, or attempt to export or transport, or cause to be exported or transported, from the United States to any state named in such proclamation, any articles or materials (except copy-righted articles or materials) until all right, title, and interest therein shall have been transferred to some foreign government, agency, institution, association, partnership, corporation, or national. . . .

Section 3. (a) Whenever the President shall have issued a proclamation under the authority of section 1 (a), and he shall thereafter find that the protection of citizens of the United States so requires, he shall, by proclamation, define combat areas, and thereafter it shall be unlawful, except under such rules and regulations as may be prescribed, for any citizen of the United States or any American vessel to proceed into or through any such combat area. The combat areas so defined may be made to apply to surface vessels or aircraft, or both. . . .

Section 5. (a) Whenever the President shall have issued a proclamation under the authority of section 1 (a) it shall thereafter be unlawful for any citizen of the United States to travel on any vessel of any state named in such proclamation, except in accordance with such rules and regulations as may be prescribed. . . .

Section 6. Whenever the President shall have issued a proclamation under the authority of section 1 (a), it shall thereafter be unlawful, until such proclamation is revoked, for any American vessel, engaged in commerce with any foreign state to be armed, except with small arms and ammunition therefor, which the President may deem necessary and shall publicly designate for the preservation of discipline aboard any such vessel.

[4] Act of November 4, 1939, *Peace and War,* op. cit., pp. 494–506.

Section 7. (a) Whenever the President shall have issued a proclamation under the authority of section 1 (a), it shall thereafter be unlawful for any person within the United States to purchase, sell, or exchange bonds, securities, or other obligations of the government of any state named in such proclamation, or of any political subdivision of any such state, or of any person acting for or on behalf of the government of any such state, or political subdivision thereof, issued after the date of such proclamation, or to make any loan or extend any credit (other than necessary credits accruing in connection with the transmission of telegraph, cable, wireless and telephone services) to any such government, political subdivision, or person. The provisions of this subsection shall also apply to the sale by any person within the United States to any person in a state named in any such proclamation of any articles or materials listed in a proclamation referred to in or issued under the authority of section 12 (i). . . .

Section 9. This joint resolution (except section 12) shall not apply to any American republic engaged in war against a non-American state or states, provided the American republic is not cooperating with a non-American state or states in such war. . . .

Section 12. (a) There is hereby established a National Munitions Control Board (hereinafter referred to as the "Board"). . . .

(b) Every person who engages in the business of manufacturing, exporting, or importing any arms, ammunition, or implements of war listed in a proclamation referred to in or issued under the authority of subsection (i) of this section, whether as an exporter, importer, manufacturer, or dealer, shall register with the Secretary of State his name, or business name, principal place of business, and places of business in the United States, and a list of the arms, ammunition, and implements of war which he manufactures, imports, or exports. . . .

(d) It shall be unlawful for any person to export, or attempt to export, from the United States to any other state, any arms, ammunition, or implements of war listed in a proclamation referred to in or issued under the authority of subsection (i) of this section, or to import, or attempt to import, to the United States from any other state, any of the arms, ammunition, or implements of war listed in any such proclamation, without first having submitted to the Secretary of State the name of the purchaser and the terms of sale and having obtained a license therefor. . . .

5. THE DESTROYER-BASES AGREEMENT[5]

I TRANSMIT herewith for the information of the Congress notes exchanged between the British Ambassador at Washington and the Secretary of State on September 2, 1940, under which this Government has ac-

[5] Message to Congress of President Roosevelt, Sept. 3, 1940. Ibid., pp. 564–5.

quired the right to lease naval and air bases in Newfoundland, and in the islands of Bermuda, the Bahamas, Jamaica, St. Lucia, Trinidad, and Antigua, and in British Guiana; also a copy of an opinion of the Attorney General dated August 27, 1940, regarding my authority to consummate this arrangement.

The right to bases in Newfoundland and Bermuda are gifts – generously given and gladly received. The other bases mentioned have been acquired in exchange for fifty of our over-age destroyers.

This is not inconsistent in any sense with our status of peace. Still less is it a threat against any nation. It is an epochal and far-reaching act of preparation for continental defense in the face of grave danger.

Preparation for defense is an inalienable prerogative of a sovereign state. Under present circumstances this exercise of sovereign right is essential to the maintenance of our peace and safety. This is the most important action in the reinforcement of our national defense that has been taken since the Louisiana Purchase. Then as now, considerations of safety from overseas attack were fundamental.

The value to the Western Hemisphere of these outposts of security is beyond calculation. Their need has long been recognized by our country, and especially by those primarily charged with the duty of charting and organizing our own naval and military defense. They are essential to the protection of the Panama Canal, Central America, the Northern portion of South America, The Antilles, Canada, Mexico, and our own Eastern and Gulf Seaboards. Their consequent importance in hemispheric defense is obvious. For these reasons I have taken advantage of the present opportunity to acquire them.

◇◇◇◇◇◇◇◇◇◇◇◇

6. GROWING TENSION IN THE FAR EAST[6]

THE JAPANESE Ambassador called at his request. He first expressed his regret at the unsatisfactory relations existing between our two countries at this time. . . .

The Ambassador then said that he was instructed by his Government to hand me a note dated October 7, 1940 . . . relative to our scrap iron and steel embargo which was recently proclaimed. . . .

I said that it was really amazing for the Government of Japan, which has been violating in the most aggravating manner valuable American rights and interests throughout most of China, and is doing so in many instances every day, to question the fullest privilege of this Government from every standpoint to impose the proposed scrap iron and steel embargo, and that to go still further and call it an unfriendly act was still more amazing in the light of the conduct of the Japanese Government in disregarding all

[6] Memorandum by the Secretary of State, Cordell Hull, of a conversation with the Japanese Ambassador, Kensuke Horinouchi, October 8, 1940. Ibid., pp. 576–8.

law, treaty obligations and other rights and privileges and the safety of Americans while it proceeded at the same time to seize territory by force to an ever-increasing extent. I stated that of all the countries with which I have had to deal during the past eight years, the Government of Japan has the least occasion or excuse to accuse this Government of an unfriendly act. I concluded with the statement that apparently the theory of the Japanese Government is for all other nations to acquiesce cheerfully in all injuries inflicted upon their citizens by the Japanese policy of force and conquest, accompanied by every sort of violence, unless they are to run the risk of being guilty of an unfriendly act.

The Ambassador again said that he very much regretted the serious differences between our two countries, but that he naturally hoped that trouble may yet be avoided. He added that any Japanese or any American must know that strife between the two countries would be extremely tragic for both alike. To this I replied that, of course, it would be exceedingly unfortunate for such occurrence to take place, but I added that my Government has been patient, extremely patient, and that the Ambassador will bear witness to the long and earnest efforts that he and I have made, and that I have made prior to his coming here, to promote and preserve friendly and satisfactory relations with Japan. I went on to say that we have stood for law and order and treaty observance and justice along with genuine friendliness between our two countries; that it was clear now, however, that those who are dominating the external policies of Japan are, as we here have believed for some years, bent on the conquest by force of all worthwhile territory in the Pacific Ocean area without limit as to extent in the South and in southern continental areas of that part of the world, and that we and all other nations are expected, as stated, to sit perfectly quiet and be cheerful and agreeable, but static, while most of Asia is Manchuria-ized, which would render practically impossible all reasonable or satisfactory relations so far as other nations are concerned; and that corresponding lower levels of existence would be the ultimate lot of the people of most of Asia. The least objection to or taking of issue with Japan with respect to the foregoing matters would be called an unfriendly act, and, as Prime Minister Konoye said recently to the press, it would be the occasion for war so far as Japan was concerned. I added that, of course, if any one country is sufficiently desirous of trouble, it can always find any one of innumerable occasions to start such trouble. In brief, it is not left to the other country to participate in such decision.

The Ambassador undertook to repeat the old line of talk about how fair Japan proposed to be with respect to all rights and privileges of foreign nations within its conquered territory. He agreed that no purpose would be served now to go over the many conversations we have had with respect to these matters. I held up the succession of injuries to American rights and interests in China whenever he referred to the scrap iron embargo.

I reiterated the view that it was unheard of for one country engaged in aggression and seizure of another country, contrary to all law and treaty provisions, to turn to a third peacefully disposed nation and seriously insist that it would be guilty of an unfriendly act if it should not cheerfully provide some of the necessary implements of war to aid the aggressor nation in carrying out its policy of invasion. I made it clear that it is the view of this Government that two nations, one in Europe and one in Asia, are undertaking to subjugate both of their respective areas of the world, and to place them on an international order and on a social basis resembling that of 750 years ago. In the face of this world movement, extending itself from day to day, peaceful and interested nations are to be held up to denunciation and threats if they dare to engage in any lawful acts or utterances in opposition to such wide movements of world conquest.

The Ambassador had little to say. He said virtually nothing in attempted extenuation except that his Government would expect everybody to receive considerate and fair treatment throughout the conquered areas. He emphasized equal treatment, and I replied that when the best interests of other nations in peace and law and order were being destroyed, it was not a matter of any concern as to whether there was discrimination between the nations which were victims of such movements.

◇◇◇◇◇◇◇◇◇◇◇◇◇

7. THE ARSENAL OF DEMOCRACY[7]

I ADDRESS YOU, the Members of the Seventy-seventh Congress, at a moment unprecedented in the history of the Union. I use the word "unprecedented," because at no previous time has American security been as seriously threatened from without as it is today.

Our national policy is this:

First, by an impressive expression of the public will and without regard to partisanship, we are committed to all-inclusive national defense.

Second, by an impressive expression of the public will and without regard to partisanship, we are committed to full support of all those resolute peoples, everywhere, who are resisting aggression and are thereby keeping war away from our hemisphere. By this support, we express our determination that the democratic cause shall prevail; and we strengthen the defense and security of our own Nation.

Third, by an impressive expression of the public will and without regard to partisanship, we are committed to the proposition that principles of morality and considerations for our own security will never permit us to acquiesce in a peace dictated by aggressors and sponsored by appeasers. We know that enduring peace cannot be bought at the cost of other people's freedom.

---

[7] Message to Congress of President Roosevelt, Jan. 6, 1941. Ibid., 608–11. The phrase, "arsenal of democracy" was used by the President in a radio address of December 29, 1940.

In the recent national election there was no substantial difference between the two great parties in respect to that national policy. No issue was fought out on this line before the American electorate. Today, it is abundantly evident that American citizens everywhere are demanding and supporting speedy and complete action in recognition of obvious danger.

Therefore, the immediate need is a swift and driving increase in our armament production.

To change a whole nation from a basis of peacetime production of implements of peace to a basis of wartime production of implements of war is no small task. And the greatest difficulty comes at the beginning of the program, when new tools and plant facilities and new assembly lines and shipways must first be constructed before the actual matériel begins to flow steadily and speedily from them.

The Congress, of course, must rightly keep itself informed at all times of the progress of the program. However, there is certain information, as the Congress itself will readily recognize, which, in the interests of our own security and those of the nations we are supporting, must of needs be kept in confidence.

New circumstances are constantly begetting new needs for our safety. I shall ask this Congress for greatly increased new appropriations and authorizations to carry on what we have begun.

I also ask this Congress for authority and for funds sufficient to manufacture additional munitions and war supplies of many kinds, to be turned over to those nations which are now in actual war with aggressor nations.

Our most useful and immediate role is to act as an arsenal for them as well as for ourselves. They do not need man power. They do need billions of dollars worth of the weapons of defense.

The time is near when they will not be able to pay for them in ready cash. We cannot, and will not, tell them they must surrender, merely because of present inability to pay for the weapons which we know they must have.

I do not recommend that we make them a loan of dollars with which to pay for these weapons — a loan to be repaid in dollars.

I recommend that we make it possible for those nations to continue to obtain war materials in the United States, fitting their orders into our own program. Nearly all of their matériel would, if the time ever came, be useful for our own defense.

Taking counsel of expert military and naval authorities, considering what is best for our own security, we are free to decide how much should be kept here and how much should be sent abroad to our friends who by their determined and heroic resistance are giving us time in which to make ready our own defense.

For what we send abroad, we shall be repaid, within a reasonable time following the close of hostilities, in similar materials, or, at our option, in other goods of many kinds which they can produce and which we need.

Let us say to the democracies: "We Americans are vitally concerned in your defense of freedom. We are putting forth our energies, our resources, and our organizing powers to give you the strength to regain and maintain a free world. We shall send you, in ever-increasing numbers, ships, planes, tanks, guns. This is our purpose and our pledge."

In fulfillment of this purpose we will not be intimidated by the threats of dictators that they will regard as a breach of international law and as an act of war our aid to the democracies which dare to resist their aggression. Such aid is not an act of war, even if a dictator should unilaterally proclaim it so to be.

When the dictators are ready to make war upon us, they will not wait for an act of war on our part. They did not wait for Norway or Belgium or the Netherlands to commit an act of war.

Their only interest is in a new one-way international law, which lacks mutuality in its observance, and, therefore, becomes an instrument of oppression.

The happiness of future generations of Americans may well depend upon how effective and how immediate we can make our aid felt. No one can tell the exact character of the emergency situations that we may be called upon to meet. The Nation's hands must not be tied when the Nation's life is in danger.

We must all prepare to make the sacrifices that the emergency – as serious as war itself – demands. Whatever stands in the way of speed and efficiency in defense preparations must give way to the national need.

A free nation has the right to expect full cooperation from all groups. A free nation has the right to look to the leaders of business, of labor, and of agriculture to take the lead in stimulating effort, not among other groups but within their own groups.

I have called for personal sacrifice. I am assured of the willingness of almost all Americans to respond to that call.

A part of the sacrifice means the payment of more money in taxes. In my Budget message I recommend that a greater portion of this great defense program be paid for from taxation than we are paying today. No person should try, or be allowed, to get rich out of this program; and the principle of tax payments in accordance with ability to pay should be constantly before our eyes to guide our legislation.

If the Congress maintains these principles, the voters, putting patriotism ahead of pocketbooks, will give you their applause.

In the future days, which we seek to make secure, we look forward to a world founded upon four essential human freedoms.

The first is freedom of speech and expression – everywhere in the world.

The second is freedom of every person to worship God in his own way – everywhere in the world.

The third is freedom from want – which, translated into world terms, means economic understandings which will secure to every nation a healthy peacetime life for its inhabitants – everywhere in the world.

The fourth is freedom from fear – which, translated into world terms, means a world-wide reduction of armaments to such a point and in such a thorough fashion that no nation will be in a position to commit an act of physical aggression against any neighbor – anywhere in the world.

That is no vision of a distant millennium. It is a definite basis for a kind of world attainable in our own time and generation. That kind of world is the very antithesis of the so-called new order of tyranny which the dictators seek to create with the crash of a bomb.

To that new order we oppose the greater conception – the moral order. A good society is able to face schemes of world domination and foreign revolutions alike without fear.

Since the beginning of our American history we have been engaged in change – in a perpetual peaceful revolution – a revolution which goes on steadily, quietly adjusting itself to changing conditions – without the concentration camp or the quick-lime in the ditch. The world order which we seek is the cooperation of free countries, working together in a friendly, civilized society.

This Nation has placed its destiny in the hands and heads and hearts of its millions of free men and women; and its faith in freedom under the guidance of God. Freedom means the supremacy of human rights everywhere. Our support goes to those who struggle to gain those rights or keep them. Our strength is in our unity of purpose.

To that high concept there can be no end save victory.

8. LEND-LEASE [8]

BE IT enacted by the Senate and House of Representatives of the United States of America in Congress assembled, That this Act may be cited as "An Act to Promote the Defense of the United States."

Section 2. As used in this Act – (a) The term "defense article" means –

(1) Any weapon, munition, aircraft, vessel, or boat;

(2) Any machinery, facility, tool, material, or supply necessary for the manufacture, production, processing, repair, servicing, or operation of any article described in this subsection;

(3) Any component material or part of or equipment for any article described in this subsection;

(4) Any agricultural, industrial or other commodity or article for defense.

Such term "defense article" includes any article described in this subsection: Manufactured or procured pursuant to section 3, or to which the United States or any foreign government has or hereafter acquires title, possession, or control.

[8] Act of March 11, 1941. Ibid., pp. 627–30.

(b) The term "defense information" means any plan, specification, design, prototype, or information pertaining to any defense article.

Section 3. (a) Notwithstanding the provisions of any other law, the President may, from time to time, when he deems it in the interest of national defense, authorize the Secretary of War, the Secretary of the Navy, or the head of any other department or agency of the Government –

(1) To manufacture in arsenals, factories, and shipyards under their jurisdiction, or otherwise procure, to the extent to which funds are made available therefor, or contracts are authorized from time to time by the Congress, or both, any defense article for the government of any country whose defense the President deems vital to the defense of the United States.

(2) To sell, transfer title to, exchange, lease, lend, or otherwise dispose of, to any such government any defense article, but no defense article not manufactured or procured under paragraph (1) shall in any way be disposed of under this paragraph, except after consultation with the Chief of Staff of the Army or the Chief of Naval Operations of the Navy, or both. The value of defense articles disposed of in any way under authority of this paragraph, and procured from funds heretofore appropriated, shall not exceed $1,300,000,000. The value of such defense articles shall be determined by the head of the department or agency concerned or such other department, agency or officer as shall be designated in the manner provided in the rules and regulations issued hereunder. Defense articles procured from funds hereafter appropriated to any department or agency of the Government other than from funds authorized to be appropriated under this Act, shall not be disposed of in any way under authority of this paragraph except to the extent hereafter authorized by the Congress in the Acts appropriating such funds or otherwise.

(3) To test, inspect, prove, repair, outfit, recondition, or otherwise to place in good working order, to the extent to which funds are made available therefor, or contracts are authorized from time to time by the Congress, or both, any defense article for any such government, or to procure any or all such services by private contract.

(4) To communicate to any such government any defense information, pertaining to any defense article furnished to such government under paragraph (2) of this subsection.

(5) To release for export any defense article disposed of in any way under this subsection to any such government.

(b) The terms and conditions upon which any such foreign government receives any aid authorized under subsection (a) shall be those which the President deems satisfactory, and the benefit to the United States may be payment or repayment in kind or property, or any other direct or indirect benefit which the President deems satisfactory. . . .

(d) Nothing in this Act shall be construed to authorize or to permit the authorization of convoying vessels by naval vessels of the United States.

(e) Nothing in this Act shall be construed to authorize or to permit the authorization of the entry of any American vessel into a combat area in violation of section 3 of the Neutrality Act of 1939. . . .

Section 6. (a) There is hereby authorized to be appropriated from time to time, out of any money in the Treasury not otherwise appropriated, such amounts as may be necessary to carry out the provisions and accomplish the purposes of this Act. . . .

◇◇◇◇◇◇◇◇◇◇◇◇◇

9. AN ISOLATION ARGUMENT[9]

THERE ARE many viewpoints from which the issues of this war can be argued. Some are primarily idealistic. Some are primarily practical. One should, I believe, strive for a balance of both. But, since the subjects that can be covered in a single address are limited, tonight I shall discuss the war from a viewpoint which is primarily practical. It is not that I believe ideals are unimportant, even among the realities of war; but if a nation is to survive in a hostile world, its ideals must be backed by the hard logic of military practicability. If the outcome of war depended upon ideals alone, this would be a different world than it is today.

I know I will be severely criticized by the interventionists in America when I say we should not enter a war unless we have a reasonable chance of winning. That, they will claim, is far too materialistic a viewpoint. They will advance again the same arguments that were used to persuade France to declare war against Germany in 1939. But I do not believe that our American ideals, and our way of life, will gain through an unsuccessful war. And I know that the United States is not prepared to wage war in Europe successfully at this time. We are no better prepared today than France was when the interventionists in Europe persuaded her to attack the Siegfried Line.

I have said before, and I will say again, that I believe it will be a tragedy to the entire world if the British Empire collapses. That is one of the main reasons why I opposed this war before it was declared, and why I have constantly advocated a negotiated peace. I did not feel that England and France had a reasonable chance of winning. France has now been defeated; and, despite the propaganda and confusion of recent months, it is now obvious that England is losing the war. I believe this is realized even by the British Government. But they have one last desperate plan remaining. They hope that they may be able to persuade us to send another American Expeditionary Force to Europe, and to share with England militarily, as well as financially, the fiasco of this war.

I do not blame England for this hope, or for asking for our assistance.

[9] Text of an address as prepared for delivery by Charles A. Lindbergh at a meeting of the America First Committee, New York, April 23, 1941. *New York Times,* April 24, 1941.

But we now know that she declared a war under circumstances which led to the defeat of every nation that sided with her from Poland to Greece. We know that in the desperation of war England promised to all those nations armed assistance that she could not send. We know that she misinformed them, as she has misinformed us, concerning her state of preparation, her military strength, and the progress of the war.

In time of war, truth is always replaced by propaganda. I do not believe we should be too quick to criticize the actions of a belligerent nation. There is always the question whether we, ourselves, would do better under similar circumstances. But we in this country have a right to think of the welfare of America first, just as the people in England thought first of their own country when they encouraged the smaller nations of Europe to fight against hopeless odds. When England asks us to enter this war, she is considering her own future, and that of her empire. In making our reply, I believe we should consider the future of the United States and that of the Western Hemisphere.

It is not only our right, but is our obligation as American citizens to look at this war objectively and to weigh our chances for success if we should enter it. I have attempted to do this, especially from the standpoint of aviation; and I have been forced to the conclusion that we cannot win this war for England, regardless of how much assistance we extend.

I ask you to look at the map of Europe today and see if you can suggest any way in which we could win this war if we entered it. Suppose we had a large army in America, trained and equipped. Where would we send it to fight? The campaigns of the war show only too clearly how difficult it is to force a landing, or to maintain an army, on a hostile coast.

Suppose we took our Navy from the Pacific, and used it to convoy British shipping. That would not win the war for England. It would, at best, permit her to exist under the constant bombing of the German air fleet. Suppose we had an air force that we could send to Europe. Where could it operate? Some of our squadrons might be based in the British Isles; but it is physically impossible to base enough aircraft in the British Isles alone to equal in strength the aircraft that can be based on the Continent of Europe.

I have asked these questions on the supposition that we had in existence an Army and an air force large enough and well enough equipped to send to Europe; and that we would dare to remove our Navy from the Pacific. Even on this basis, I do not see how we could invade the Continent of Europe successfully as long as all of that Continent and most of Asia is under Axis domination. But the fact is that none of these suppositions are correct. We have only a one-ocean Navy. Our Army is still untrained and inadequately equipped for foreign war. Our air force is deplorably lacking in modern fighting planes.

When these facts are cited, the interventionists shout that we are defeatists, that we are undermining the principles of democracy, and that we are giving comfort to Germany by talking about our military weakness. But everything I mention here has been published in our newspapers, and in the reports of congressional hearings in Washington. Our military position is well known to the governments of Europe and Asia. Why, then, should it not be brought to the attention of our own people?

I say it is the interventionist in America, as it was in England and in France, who gives comfort to the enemy. I say it is they who are undermining the principles of democracy when they demand that we take a course to which more than 80 per cent of our citizens are opposed. I charge them with being the real defeatists, for their policy has led to the defeat of every country that followed their advice since this war began. There is no better way to give comfort to an enemy than to divide the people of a nation over the issue of foreign war. There is no shorter road to defeat than by entering a war with inadequate preparation. Every nation that has adopted the interventionist policy of depending on some one else for its own defense has met with nothing but defeat and failure.

When history is written, the responsibility for the downfall of the democracies of Europe will rest squarely upon the shoulders of the interventionists who led their nations into war uninformed and unprepared. With their shouts of defeatism, and their disdain of reality, they have already sent countless thousands of young men to death in Europe. From the campaign of Poland to that of Greece, their prophecies have been false and their policies have failed. Yet these are the people who are calling us defeatists in America today. And they have led this country, too, to the verge of war.

There are many such interventionists in America, but there are more people among us of a different type. That is why you and I are assembled here tonight. There is a policy open to this nation that will lead to success — a policy that leaves us free to follow our own way of life, and to develop our own civilization. It is not a new and untried idea. It was advocated by Washington. It was incorporated in the Monroe Doctrine. Under its guidance, the United States became the greatest nation in the world.

It is based upon the belief that the security of a nation lies in the strength and character of its own people. It recommends the maintenance of armed forces sufficient to defend this hemisphere from attack by any combination of foreign powers. It demands faith in an independent American destiny. This is the policy of the America First Committee today. It is a policy not of isolation, but of independence; not of defeat, but of courage. It is a policy that led this nation to success during the most trying years of our history, and it is a policy that will lead us to success again.

We have weakened ourselves for many months, and still worse, we have divided our own people by this dabbling in Europe's wars. While we should have been concentrating on American defense we have been forced to argue over foreign quarrels. We must turn our eyes and our faith back to our own country before it is too late. And when we do this, a different vista opens before us. Practically every difficulty we would face in invading Europe becomes an asset to us in defending America. Our enemy, and not we, would then have the problem of transporting millions of troops across the ocean and landing them on a hostile shore. They, and not we, would have to furnish the convoys to transport guns and trucks and munitions and fuel across three thousand miles of water. Our battleships and submarines would then be fighting close to their home bases. We would then do the bombing from the air and the torpedoing at sea. And if any part of an enemy convoy should ever pass our navy and our air force, they would still be faced with the guns of our coast artillery and behind them the divisions of our Army.

The United States is better situated from a military standpoint than any other nation in the world. Even in our present condition of unpreparedness no foreign power is in a position to invade us today. If we concentrate on our own defenses and build the strength that this nation should maintain, no foreign army will ever attempt to land on American shores.

War is not inevitable for this country. Such a claim is defeatism in the true sense. No one can make us fight abroad unless we ourselves are willing to do so. No one will attempt to fight us here if we arm ourselves as a great nation should be armed. Over a hundred million people in this nation are opposed to entering the war. If the principles of democracy mean anything at all, that is reason enough for us to stay out. If we are forced into a war against the wishes of an overwhelming majority of our people, we will have proved democracy such a failure at home that there will be little use fighting for it abroad.

The time has come when those of us who believe in an independent American destiny must band together and organize for strength. We have been led toward war by a minority of our people. This minority has power. It has influence. It has a loud voice. But it does not represent the American people. During the last several years I have traveled over this country from one end to the other. I have talked to many hundreds of men and women, and I have letters from tens of thousands more, who feel the same way as you and I.

Most of these people have no influence or power. Most of them have no means of expressing their convictions, except by their vote which has always been against this war. They are the citizens who have had to work too hard at their daily jobs to organize political meetings. Hitherto, they have relied upon their vote to express their feelings; but now they find that it is hardly remembered except in the oratory of a political campaign. These people – the majority of hardworking American citizens, are with us. They are the true strength of our country. And they are beginning to realize, as you and I, that there are times when we must sacrifice our normal interests in life in order to insure the safety and the welfare of our nation.

Such a time has come. Such a crisis is here. That is why the America First Committee has been formed – to give voice to the people who have no newspaper, or newsreel, or radio station at their command; to the people who must do the paying, and the fighting, and the dying if this country enters the war.

Whether or not we do enter the war rests upon the shoulders of you in this audience, upon us here on this platform, upon meetings of this kind that are being held by Americans in every section of the United States today. It depends upon the action we take, and the courage we show at this time. If you believe in an independent destiny for America, if you believe that this country should not enter the war in Europe, we ask you to join the America First Committee in its stand. We ask you to share our faith in the ability of this nation to defend itself, to develop its own civilization, and to contribute to the progress of mankind in a more constructive and intelligent way than has yet been found by the warring nations of Europe. We need your support, and we need it now. The time to act is here.

◇◇◇◇◇◇◇◇◇◇◇◇◇

10. THE CASE AGAINST ISOLATION[10]

IN NEW YORK HARBOR, on an island close to the steamship lanes, stands the most famous statue in the world. It is not the most beautiful statue, but to many millions of passengers coming up the bay it has seemed to be. It stands for one of the dearest dreams in human history – Liberty.

The millions who pursued that dream began to come before there was a statue to greet them. They came first when the shores were lined with solemn woods. They came in sailing ships when the voyage required two months or more. They came in crowded steamship steerage under hardships not much less. They came to Plymouth Rock and to Ellis Island.

They came for one reason, escape: escape from religious or political persecution, from caste systems, from overcrowding and from lack of opportunity. But the hope of leaving all the Old World behind could not be realized. Their hearts and heads forbade it. Their roots in its culture ran too deep. And the sea itself grew ever narrower. Express steamers began to cross it long ago in less than a week. Airplanes can span it now in less than a day. The wireless leaps it in less than a second. Emotion, ideas, even physical force can now move around the world more effectively than they could cross the tiniest country a century and a half ago.

There is no isolation. There are only lines of defense. Distance is vanishing. Strategy is everything. And strategy in this year of grace has become the art and science of survival: survival in the personal sense, survival of ideas, survival of culture and tradition, survival of a way of life.

Those who tell us now that the sea is still our certain bulwark, and that the tremendous forces sweeping the Old World threaten no danger to the New, give the lie to their own words in the precautions they would have us take.

---

[10] An editorial in the *New York Times,* April 30, 1941.

To a man they favor an enormous strengthening of our defenses. Why? Against what danger would they have us arm if none exists? To what purpose would they have us spend these almost incredible billions upon billions for ships and planes, for tanks and guns, if there is no immediate threat to the security of the United States? Why are we training the youth of the country to bear arms? Under pressure of what fear are we racing against time to double and quadruple our industrial production?

No man in his senses will say that we are arming against Canada or our Latin-American neighbors to the south, against Britain or the captive states of Europe. We are arming solely for one reason. We are arming against Hitler's Germany – a great predatory Power in alliance with Japan.

It has been said, times without number, that if Hitler cannot cross the English Channel he cannot cross three thousand miles of sea. But there is only one reason why he has not crossed the English Channel. That is because forty-five million determined Britons in a heroic resistance have converted their island into an armed base from which proceeds a steady stream of sea and air power. As Secretary Hull has said: "It is not the water that bars the way. It is the resolute determination of British arms. Were the control of the seas by Britain lost, the Atlantic would no longer be an obstacle – rather, it would become a broad highway for a conqueror moving westward."

That conqueror does not need to attempt at once an invasion of continental United States in order to place this country in deadly danger. We shall be in deadly danger the moment British sea power fails; the moment the eastern gates of the Atlantic are open to the aggressor; the moment we are compelled to divide our one-ocean Navy between two oceans simultaneously.

The combined Axis fleets outmatch our own: they are superior in numbers to our fleet in every category of vessel, from warships and aircraft-carriers to destroyers and submarines. The combined Axis air strength will be much greater than our own if Hitler strikes in time – and when has he failed to strike in time? The master of Europe will have at his command shipways that can outbuild us, the resources of twenty conquered nations to furnish his materials, the oil of the Middle East to stoke his engines, the slave labor of a continent – bound by no union rules, and not working on a forty-hour week – to turn out his production.

Grant Hitler the gigantic prestige of a victory over Britain, and who can doubt that the first result, on our side of the ocean, would be the prompt appearance of imitation Nazi regimes in a half-dozen Latin-American nations, forced to be on the winning side, begging favors, clamoring for admission to the Axis? What shall we do then? Make war upon these neighbors; send armies to fight in the jungles of Central or South America; run the risk of outraging native sentiment and turning the whole continent against us? Or shall we sit tight while the area of Nazi influence draws ever closer to the Panama Canal and a spreading checkerboard of Nazi airfields provides ports of call for German planes that may choose to bomb our cities?

But even if Hitler gave us time, what kind of "time" would we have at our disposal?

There are moral and spiritual dangers for this country as well as physical dangers in a Hitler victory. There are dangers to the mind and heart as well as to the body and the land.

Victorious in Europe, dominating Africa and Asia through his Axis partners, Hitler could not afford to permit the United States to live an untroubled and successful life, even if he wished to. We are the arch-enemy of all he stands for: the very citadel of that "pluto-democracy" which he hates and scorns. As long as liberty and freedom prevailed in the United States there would be a constant risk for Hitler that our ideas and our example might infect the conquered countries which he was bending to his will. In his own interest he would be forced to harry us at every turn.

Who can doubt that our lives would be poisoned every day by challenges and insults from Nazi politicians; that Nazi agents would stir up anti-American feeling in every country they controlled; that Nazi spies would overrun us here; that Hitler would produce a continual series of lightning diplomatic strokes – alliances and "non-aggression pacts" to break our will; in short, that a continuous war of nerves, if nothing worse, would be waged against us?

And who can doubt that, in response, we should have to turn our own nation into an armed camp, with all our traditional values of culture, education, social reform, democracy and liberty subordinated to the single, all-embracing aim of self-preservation? In this case we should indeed experience "regimentation." Every item of foreign trade, every transaction in domestic commerce, every present prerogative of labor, every civil liberty we cherish, would necessarily be regulated in the interest of defense.

But the most tragic aspect of this attempt to survive, alone on our continent, is that it would amount at best merely to sustaining life in a charnel-house. With Britain gone, with the bright lamp of English liberty extinguished, with all hope of resurrection denied to the little democracies that have contributed so generously to our civilization and our culture, with the hobnailed boots of an ignorant and obscene barbarism echoing in every capital from London to Athens, we should live in a new world, changed beyond all recognition.

In this downfall of democracy outside the United States there would come, for many of our people, a loss of faith in our own democratic system. Our confidence would be undermined, our vision dimmed, our ranks divided. In a dark, uncertain world we should stand alone, deriving from no other country the sustaining strength of a common faith in our democratic institutions.

What would it profit us to achieve, at last, this perfect isolation?

The Statue of Liberty in New York Harbor has looked down across the bay at many men who have crossed the ocean to find freedom. It stands now as a silent witness to the fact that we are already locked in mortal combat with the German system.

American courage and American idealism, together with the sound common sense of the American people, summon us to the defense both of our physical security and of those moral and spiritual values which alone make life worth living. This defense means many things. It means, in the first instance, a clear recognition that the most dangerous of all courses we could follow in this hour of decision is a policy of drift: of do-nothing while there is still time to act effectively; of letting hesitancy ripen into disagreement, and disagreement curdle into factions which will split the country.

It means strong leadership in Washington: a willingness to forego the methods of indirection and surprise and veiled hints and innuendo, and to state the plain facts of the situation boldly. It means leadership which is as generous as it is strong; leadership which is willing to forget old quarrels, ready to bring into positions of high power and into the innermost confidence of the Government the accredited spokesmen of the opposition party; leadership which is at last prepared to delegate all necessary authority to the engineers of American production.

It means a genuinely firm insistence that strikes or lockouts in defense industries will no longer be tolerated by public opinion. It means more immediate aid to the brave people who are now fighting in the front line of our defense. It means encouragement to American aviators who are ready to fly our own planes in the battle over Britain. It means a determination to see that our vital supplies reach England, under the protection of our own guns. Above all else it means a decision to avoid the same mistake that the democracies have made over and over again — the mistake of "too little and too late."

There is no escape in isolation. We have only two alternatives. We can surrender or we can do our part in holding the line. We can defend, with all the means in our power, the rights that are morally and legally ours. If we decide for the American tradition, for the preservation of all that we hold dear in the years that lie ahead, we shall take our place in the line and play our part in the defense of freedom.

◇◇◇◇◇◇◇◇◇◇◇◇◇

11. AMERICAN BASES IN GREENLAND[11]

THE DEPARTMENT of State announced April 10 the signing on April 9, 1941 of an agreement between the Secretary of State, acting on behalf of the Government of the United States of America, and the Danish Min-

[11] Statement by the Department of State, April 10, 1941. *Peace and War*, op. cit., pp. 640–2.

ister, Henrik de Kauffmann, acting on behalf of His Majesty the King of Denmark in his capacity as sovereign of Greenland.

The agreement recognizes that as a result of the present European war there is danger that Greenland may be converted into a point of aggression against nations of the American Continent, and accepts the responsibility on behalf of the United States of assisting Greenland in the maintenance of its present status.

The agreement, after explicitly recognizing the Danish sovereignty over Greenland, proceeds to grant to the United States the right to locate and construct airplane landing fields and facilities for the defense of Greenland and for the defense of the American Continent.

The circumstances leading up to the agreement are as follows.

On April 9, 1940 the German Army invaded and occupied Denmark, and that occupation continues. . . .

This invasion at once raised questions as to the status of Greenland, which has been recognized as being within the area of the Monroe Doctrine. The Government of the United States announces its policy of maintenance of the *status quo* in the Western Hemisphere.

On May 3, 1940 the Greenland Councils, meeting at Godhavn, adopted a resolution in the name of the people of Greenland reaffirming their allegiance to King Christian X of Denmark, and expressed the hope that so long as Greenland remained cut off from the mother country, the Government of the United States would continue to keep in mind the exposed position of the Danish flag in Greenland and of the native and Danish population of Greenland. The Government of the United States expressed its willingness to assure that the needs of the population of Greenland would be taken care of. . . .

During the summer of 1940 German activity on the eastern coast of Greenland became apparent. Three ships proceeding from Norwegian territory under German occupation arrived off the coast of Greenland, ostensibly for commercial or scientific purposes; and at least one of these ships landed parties nominally for scientific purposes, but actually for meteorological assistance to German belligerent operations in the north Atlantic. These parties were eventually cleared out. In the late fall of 1940, air reconnaissance appeared over East Greenland under circumstances making it plain that there had been continued activity in that region.

On March 27, 1941, a German bomber flew over the eastern coast of Greenland and on the following day another German war plane likewise reconnoitered the same territory. Under these circumstances it appeared that further steps for the defense of Greenland were necessary to bring Greenland within the system of hemispheric defense envisaged by the Act of Habana.

The Government of the United States has no thought in mind save that of assuring the safety of Greenland and the rest of the American Continent, and Greenland's continuance under Danish sovereignty. The agreement recognizes explicitly the full Danish sovereignty over Greenland. At the same time it is recognized that so long as Denmark remains under German occupation the Government in Denmark cannot exercise the Danish sovereign powers over Greenland under the Monroe Doctrine, and the agreement therefore was signed between the Secretary of State and the Danish Minister in Washington, acting as representative of the King of Denmark in his capacity as sovereign of Greenland, and with the concurrence of the Governors of Greenland. . . .

◇◇◇◇◇◇◇◇◇◇◇◇◇

12. AN AMERICAN BASE IN ICELAND[12]

I AM transmitting herewith for the information of the Congress a message I received from the Prime Minister of Iceland on July first and the reply I addressed on the same day to the Prime Minister of Iceland in response to this message.

In accordance with the understanding so reached, forces of the United States Navy have today arrived in Iceland in order to supplement, and eventually to replace, the British forces which have until now been stationed in Iceland in order to insure the adequate defense of that country.

As I stated in my message to the Congress of September third last regarding the acquisition of certain naval and air bases from Great Britain in exchange for certain over-age destroyers, considerations of safety from overseas attack are fundamental.

The United States cannot permit the occupation by Germany of strategic outposts in the Atlantic to be used as air or naval bases for eventual attack against the Western Hemisphere. We have no desire to see any change in the present sovereignty of those regions. Assurance that such outposts in our defense-frontier remain in friendly hands is the very foundation of our national security and of the national security of every one of the independent nations of the New World.

For the same reason substantial forces of the United States have now been sent to the bases acquired last year from Great Britain in Trinidad and in British Guiana in the south in order to forestall any pincers movement undertaken by Germany against the Western Hemisphere. It is essential that Germany should not be able successfully to employ such tactics through sudden seizure of strategic points in the south Atlantic and in the north Atlantic.

The occupation of Iceland by Germany would constitute a serious threat in three dimensions:

The threat against Greenland and the northern portion of the North American Continent, including the Islands which lie off it.

The threat against all shipping in the north Atlantic.

[12] Message of President Roosevelt to Congress July 7, 1941. Ibid., pp. 686–7.

The threat against the steady flow of munitions to Britain – which is a matter of broad policy clearly approved by the Congress.

It is, therefore, imperative that the approaches between the Americas and those strategic outposts, the safety of which this country regards as essential to its national security, and which it must therefore defend, shall remain open and free from all hostile activity or threat thereof.

As Commander-in-Chief I have consequently issued orders to the Navy that all necessary steps be taken to insure the safety of communications in the approaches between Iceland and the United States, as well as on the seas between the United States and all other strategic outposts.

This Government will insure the adequate defense of Iceland with full recognition of the independence of Iceland as a sovereign state.

In my message to the Prime Minister of Iceland I have given the people of Iceland the assurance that the American forces sent there would in no way interfere with the internal and domestic affairs of that country, and that immediately upon the termination of the present international emergency all American forces will be at once withdrawn, leaving the people of Iceland and their Government in full and sovereign control of their own territory.

◇◇◇◇◇◇◇◇◇◇◇◇◇◇

13. POLITICAL ASPECTS OF THE STRUGGLE OVER ISOLATION [13]

SINCE the beginning of the war there have been four votes in Congress on questions of critical importance. These votes came on repeal of the arms embargo, on passage of the lease-lend bill, on adoption of the Selective Service Act and on the proposal to extend the period of training under that legislation. Every one of these measures was of vital importance to the defense of the United States. Every one of them was of intense interest to our friends and enemies abroad: to the Latin-American nations which count on our assistance in case of trouble; to the democracies of Europe and Asia which are fighting in defense of their own freedom; to the dictators who believe that democracy is out-of-date – bewildered, disunited and ripe for plucking.

The record shows that every one of these four measures was adopted solely because the President received the support of a large majority of his own party. Not one of them would be law today if the decision had been left to the Republicans in Congress. The tally of Republican votes runs as follows:

On repeal of the arms embargo –
Senate: 8 in favor, 15 against.
House: 21 in favor, 143 against.

[13] An editorial in the *New York Times*, August 14, 1941.

On the passage of the lease-lend bill—
Senate: 10 in favor, 17 against.
House: 24 in favor, 135 against.
On adoption of the Selective Service Act—
Senate: 7 in favor, 10 against.
House: 46 in favor, 88 against.
On extension of the period of training—
Senate: 7 in favor, 13 against.
House: 21 in favor, 133 against.

The Republicans in Congress have achieved, in short, a perfect record of opposition to these measures recommended by the President, by the Secretary of State and by the Army's Chief of Staff.

It is true that the Republicans in Congress have received less cooperation from the President than they were entitled to receive. He has failed to take them into his confidence as fully as he should. He has made the enormous mistake of not consulting their leaders in advance of the submission of such important measures as the lease-lend bill. It is also true that it is the duty of the Republicans to vote according to their convictions and their own best judgment, and no doubt some of them have been sincerely opposed on principle to the adoption of these measures.

But when all this has been said, it is impossible to dismiss the element of plain party politics from votes so heavily one-sided as these. Crisis or no crisis, the Republicans in Congress are still "fighting Roosevelt," still jockeying for position, still trying to write a record which they can turn to profit if and when there occurs that long-delayed "reaction" on which they have built their political hopes.

This may be legitimate strategy in time of peace. But in time of crisis the record they are actually writing is one that will help them only if the Lindbergh-Wheeler version of the war is right and the Lindbergh-Wheeler prophecies come true. This is a fact which a great many rank-and-file Republicans throughout the country must find distasteful.

◇◇◇◇◇◇◇◇◇◇◇◇◇

14. THE ATLANTIC CHARTER [14]

OVER a week ago I held several important conferences at sea with the British Prime Minister. Because of the factor of safety to British, Canadian, and American ships, and their personnel, no prior announcement of these meetings could properly be made.

At the close, a public statement by the Prime Minister and the President was made. I quote it for the information of the Congress and for the record:

The President of the United States and the Prime Minister, Mr. Church-

[14] Message of President Roosevelt to Congress, August 21, 1941. *Peace and War*, op. cit., pp. 717–20.

ill, representing His Majesty's Government in the United Kingdom, have met at sea.

They have been accompanied by officials of their two Governments, including high-ranking officers of their military, naval, and air services.

The whole problem of the supply of munitions of war, as provided by the Lease-Lend Act, for the armed forces of the United States, and for those countries actively engaged in resisting aggression, has been further examined.

Lord Beaverbrook, the Minister of Supply of the British Government, has joined in these conferences. He is going to proceed to Washington to discuss further details with appropriate officials of the United States Government. These conferences will also cover the supply problems of the Soviet Union.

The President and the Prime Minister have had several conferences. They have considered the dangers to world civilization arising from the policies of military domination by conquest upon which the Hitlerite government of Germany and other governments associated therewith have embarked, and have made clear the steps which their countries are respectively taking for their safety in the face of these dangers.

They have agreed upon the following joint declaration:

Joint declaration of the President of the United States of America and the Prime Minister, Mr. Churchill, representing His Majesty's Government in the United Kingdom, being met together, deem it right to make known certain common principles in the national policies of their respective countries on which they base their hopes for a better future for the world.

First, their countries seek no aggrandizement, territorial or other;

Second, they desire to see no territorial changes that do not accord with the freely expressed wishes of the peoples concerned;

Third, they respect the right of all peoples to choose the form of government under which they will live; and they wish to see sovereign rights and self-government restored to those who have been forcibly deprived of them;

Fourth, they will endeavor, with due respect for their existing obligations, to further the enjoyment by all states, great or small, victor or vanquished, of access, on equal terms, to the trade and to the raw materials of the world which are needed for their economic prosperity;

Fifth, they desire to bring about the fullest collaboration between all nations in the economic field with the object of securing, for all, improved labor standards, economic advancement, and social security;

Sixth, after the final destruction of the Nazi tyranny, they hope to see established a peace which will afford to all nations the means of dwelling in safety within their own boundaries, and which will afford assurance that all the men in all the lands may live out their lives in freedom from fear and want;

Seventh, such a peace should enable all men to traverse the high seas and oceans without hindrance;

Eighth, they believe that all of the nations of the world, for realistic as well as spiritual reasons, must come to the abandonment of the use of force. Since no future peace can be maintained if land, sea, or air armaments continue to be employed by nations which threaten, or may threaten, aggression outside of their frontiers, they believe, pending the establishment of a wider and permanent system of general security, that the disarmament of such nations is essential. They will likewise aid and encourage all other practicable measures which will lighten for peace-loving peoples the crushing burden of armaments.

Franklin D. Roosevelt
Winston S. Churchill

The Congress and the President having heretofore determined, through the Lend-Lease Act, on the national policy of American aid to the democracies which East and West are waging war against dictatorships, the military and naval conversations at these meetings made clear gains in furthering the effectiveness of this aid.

Furthermore, the Prime Minister and I are arranging for conferences with the Soviet Union to aid it in its defense against the attack made by the principal aggressor of the modern world – Germany.

Finally, the declaration of principles at this time presents a goal which is worth while for our type of civilization to seek. It is so clearcut that it is difficult to oppose in any major particular without automatically admitting a willingness to accept compromise with nazi-ism; or to agree to a world peace which would give to nazi-ism domination over large numbers of conquered nations. Inevitably such a peace would be a gift to nazi-ism to take breath – armed breath – for a second war to extend the control over Europe and Asia, to the American Hemisphere itself.

It is perhaps unnecessary for me to call attention once more to the utter lack of validity of the spoken or written word of the Nazi government.

It is also unnecessary for me to point out that the declaration of principles includes, of necessity, the world need for freedom of religion and freedom of information. No society of the world organized under the announced principles could survive without these freedoms which are a part of the whole freedom for which we strive.

◇◇◇◇◇◇◇◇◇◇◇◇

15. WAR IN THE ATLANTIC[15]

THE NAVY Department of the United States has reported to me that on the morning of September fourth the United States destroyer *Greer*, proceeding in full daylight towards Iceland, had reached a point southeast of Greenland. She was carrying American mail to Iceland. She was flying the American flag. Her identity as an American ship was unmistakable.

She was then and there attacked by a submarine. Germany admits that it was a German submarine. The submarine deliberately fired a torpedo at the *Greer*, followed later by another torpedo attack. In spite of what Hitler's propaganda bureau has invented, and in spite of what any American obstructionist organization may prefer to believe, I tell you the blunt

[15] Radio address of President Roosevelt, Sept. 11, 1941. Ibid., pp. 737–44.

fact that the German submarine fired first upon this American destroyer without warning, and with deliberate design to sink her.

Our destroyer, at the time, was in waters which the Government of the United States had declared to be waters of self-defense – surrounding outposts of American protection in the Atlantic.

In the north, outposts have been established by us in Iceland, Greenland, Labrador, and Newfoundland. Through these waters there pass many ships of many flags. They bear food and other supplies to civilians; and they bear matériel of war, for which the people of the United States are spending billions of dollars, and which, by congressional action, they have declared to be essential for the defense of their own land.

The United States destroyer, when attacked, was proceeding on a legitimate mission.

If the destroyer was visible to the submarine when the torpedo was fired, then the attack was a deliberate attempt by the Nazis to sink a clearly identified American warship. On the other hand, if the submarine was beneath the surface and, with the aid of its listening devices, fired in the direction of the sound of the American destroyer without even taking the trouble to learn its identity – as the official German communiqué would indicate – then the attack was even more outrageous. For it indicates a policy of indiscriminate violence against any vessel sailing the seas – belligerent or non-belligerent.

This was piracy – legally and morally. It was not the first nor the last act of piracy which the Nazi Government has committed against the American flag in this war. Attack has followed attack.

A few months ago an American-flag merchant ship, the *Robin Moor,* was sunk by a Nazi submarine in the middle of the South Atlantic, under circumstances violating long-established international law and every principle of humanity. The passengers and the crew were forced into open boats hundreds of miles from land, in direct violation of international agreements signed by the Government of Germany. No apology, no allegation of mistake, no offer of reparations has come from the Nazi Government.

In July 1941, an American battleship in North American waters was followed by a submarine which for a long time sought to maneuver itself into a position of attack. The periscope of the submarine was clearly seen. No British or American submarines were within hundreds of miles of this spot at the time, so the nationality of the submarine is clear.

Five days ago a United States Navy ship on patrol picked up three survivors of an American-owned ship operating under the flag of our sister Republic of Panama – the S.S. *Sessa.* On August seventeenth, she had been first torpedoed without warning and then shelled, near Greenland, while carrying civilian supplies to Iceland. It is feared that the other members of her crew have been drowned. In view of the established presence of German submarines in this vicinity, there can be no reasonable doubt as to the identity of the attacker.

Five days ago, another United States merchant ship, the *Steel Seafarer* was sunk by a German aircraft in the Red Sea two hundred and twenty miles south of Suez. She was bound for an Egyptian port.

Four of the vessels sunk or attacked flew the American flag and were clearly identifiable. Two of these ships were warships of the American Navy. In the fifth case, the vessel sunk clearly carried the flag of Panama.

In the face of all this, we Americans are keeping our feet on the ground. Our type of democratic civilization has outgrown the thought of feeling compelled to fight some other nation by reason of any single piratical attack on one of our ships. We are not becoming hysterical or losing our sense of proportion. Therefore, what I am thinking and saying does not relate to any isolated episode.

Instead, we Americans are taking a long-range point of view in regard to certain fundamentals and to a series of events on land and on sea which must be considered as a whole – as a part of a world pattern.

It would be unworthy of a great nation to exaggerate an isolated incident or to become inflamed by some one act of violence. But it would be inexcusable folly to minimize such incidents in the face of evidence which makes it clear that the incident is not isolated but part of a general plan.

The important truth is that these acts of international lawlessness are a manifestation of a design which has been made clear to the American people for a long time. It is the Nazi design to abolish the freedom of the seas and to acquire absolute control and domination of the seas for themselves. . . .

This Nazi attempt to seize control of the oceans is but a counterpart of the Nazi plots now being carried on throughout the Western Hemisphere – all designed toward the same end. For Hitler's advance guards – not only his avowed agents but also his dupes among us – have sought to make ready for him footholds and bridgeheads in the New World, to be used as soon as he has gained control of the oceans. . . .

To be ultimately successful in world-mastery, Hitler knows that he must get control of the seas. He must first destroy the bridge of ships which we are building across the Atlantic, over which we shall continue to roll the implements of war to help destroy him and all his works in the end. He must wipe out our patrol on sea and in the air. He must silence the British Navy.

It must be explained again and again to people who like to think of the United States Navy as an invincible protection, that this can be true only if the British Navy survives. That is simple arithmetic.

For if the world outside the Americas falls under Axis domination, the shipbuilding facilities which the Axis powers would then possess in all of Europe, in the British Isles, and in the Far East would be much greater than all the shipbuilding facilities and potentialities of all the Americas – not only greater but two or three times greater. Even if the United States threw all its resources into such a situation, seeking to double and even redouble the size of our Navy, the Axis powers, in control of the rest of the world, would have the man-power and the physical resources to outbuild us several times over.

It is time for all Americans of all the Americas to stop being deluded by the romantic notion that the Americas can go on living happily and peacefully in a Nazi-dominated world. . . .

The Nazi danger to our Western World has long ceased to be a mere possibility. The danger is here now – not only from a military enemy but from an enemy of all law, all liberty, all morality, all religion.

There has now come a time when you and I must see the cold, inexorable necessity of saying to these inhuman, unrestrained seekers of world-conquest and permanent world-domination by the sword – "You seek to throw our children and our children's children into your form of terrorism and slavery. You have now attacked our own safety. You shall go no further."

Normal practices of diplomacy – note-writing – are of no possible use in dealing with international outlaws who sink our ships and kill our citizens.

One peaceful nation after another has met disaster because each refused to look the Nazi danger squarely in the eye until it actually had them by the throat.

The United States will not make that fatal mistake.

No act of violence or intimidation will keep us from maintaining intact two bulwarks of defense: first, our line of supply of matériel to the enemies of Hitler; and second, the freedom of our shipping on the high seas. . . .

The American people have faced other grave crises in their history – with American courage and American resolution. They will do no less today.

They know the actualities of the attacks upon us. They know the necessities of a bold defense against these attacks. They know that the times call for clear heads and fearless hearts.

And with that inner strength that comes to a free people conscious of their duty and of the righteousness of what they do, they will – with Divine help and guidance – stand their ground against this latest assault upon their democracy, their sovereignty, and their freedom.

◇◇◇◇◇◇◇◇◇◇◇◇◇

16. THE FUNDAMENTAL OBJECTIVES OF JAPAN [16]

(A) JAPANESE CABINET DECISION OF JULY 26, 1940

. . . THE FUNDAMENTAL aim of Japan's national policy . . . is directed toward the construction of a new order of Greater East Asia built upon a firm solidarity of Japan, Manchoukuo and China with this empire as the center.

[16] International Military Tribunal for the Far East. Exhibit No. 541. Doc. No. 2137D.

. . . In the light of the new external and internal circumstances of the empire, we will so amplify armaments as to ensure the execution of national policy on the basis of a state structure for national defense through manifestation of the nation's total strength.

. . . In parallel with the renovation of the educational system in full accord with the fundamental principles of the national policy, we will establish national morality which attaches the first importance to the idea of service to the state. . . .

(B) DECISIONS MADE BY CONFERENCE OF THE PRIME MINISTER AND THE MINISTERS OF WAR, NAVY, AND FOREIGN AFFAIRS, SEPTEMBER 4, 1940, AND BY THE LIAISON CONFERENCE OF SEPTEMBER 19, 1940.

Basic Principles for strengthening the Japanese, German, Italian Axis:

To make fundamental agreement among the three countries, in order that they shall mutually cooperate by all possible means in the establishment of a New Order in Europe and Asia.

. . . Inasmuch as the proposed declaration is to the effect that the three countries will cooperate by all possible means for the construction of the respective New Orders, Japan should be resolved, if need be, to take any action, including recourse to armed force. In so far as Britain is concerned, Germany may not immediately require our armed cooperation. In this event, our main objective will be the United States. . . . Further, in the event of either contracting party entering upon a state of war with the United States, the other contracting party will assist that party by all possible means.

. . . The sphere to be envisaged in the course of negotiations with Germany and Italy as Japan's Sphere of Living for the construction of a Greater East Asia New Order will comprise: The former German Islands under Mandate, French Indo-China and Pacific Islands, Thailand, British Malaya, British Borneo, Dutch East Indies, Burma, Australia, New Zealand, India, etc., with Japan, Manchuria and China as the backbone. . . . Further, Japan will make use of the immigrant and economic foothold, both of importance, which Germany and Italy presently have in South America, in regard to such steps as Japan may in future take with respect to the United States.

◇◇◇◇◇◇◇◇◇◇◇◇

17. THE THREE POWER PACT BETWEEN GERMANY, ITALY, AND JAPAN[17]

. . . *Article 1.* Japan recognizes and respects the leadership of Germany and Italy in the establishment of a new order in Europe.

---

[17] Signed at Berlin, September 27, 1940, and in force as of that date. English translations of the German, Japanese, or Italian texts differ slightly. The text used here is the

Article 2. Germany and Italy recognize and respect the leadership of Japan in the establishment of a new order in Greater East Asia.

Article 3. Germany, Italy and Japan agree to cooperate in their efforts on aforesaid lines. They further undertake to assist one another with all political, economic and military means when one of the three Contracting Powers is attacked by a Power at present not involved in the European War or in the Chinese-Japanese conflict.

Article 4. With the view to implementing the present pact, joint technical commissions, the members of which are to be appointed by the respective Governments of Germany, Italy and Japan, will meet without delay.

Article 5. Germany, Italy and Japan affirm that the aforesaid terms do not in any way affect the political status which exists at present as between each of the three Contracting Parties and Soviet Russia. . . .

◇◇◇◇◇◇◇◇◇◇◇◇◇

18. THE COST OF ISOLATION [18]

TWENTY-THREE years ago today, Woodrow Wilson addressed the Congress of the United States in order to inform the representatives of the American people of the terms of the Armistice which signalized the victorious conclusion of the First World War.

That day marked, as he then said, the attainment of a great objective: the opportunity for the setting up of "such a peace as will satisfy the longing of the whole world for disinterested justice, embodied in settlements which are based upon something much better and much more lasting than the selfish competitive interests of powerful states."

Less than five years later, shrouded in the cerements of apparent defeat, his shattered body was placed in the grave beside which we now are gathered.

He was laid to rest amid the apathy of the many and amid the sneers of those of his opponents who had, through appeal to ignorance, to passion, and to prejudice, temporarily persuaded the people of our country to reject Wilson's plea that the influence, the resources, and the power of the United States be exercised for their own security and for their own advantage, through our participation in an association of the free and self-governed peoples of the world.

And yet, when we reflect upon the course of the years that have since intervened, how rarely in human history has the vision of a statesman been so tragically and so swiftly vindicated.

---

official translation of the British Foreign Office. League of Nations, *Treaty Series,* Vol. CCIV. pp. 386–7.

[18] Address of the Under Secretary of State, Sumner Welles, at Washington, November 11, 1941. *Peace and War,* op. cit., pp. 784–7.

Only a score of years have since elapsed, and today the United States finds itself in far greater peril than it did in 1917. The waves of world-conquest are breaking high both in the East and in the West. They are threatening, more nearly each day that passes, to engulf our own shores.

Beyond the Atlantic a sinister and pitiless conqueror has reduced more than half of Europe to abject serfdom. It is his boast that his system shall prevail even unto the ends of the earth.

In the Far East the same forces of conquest under a different guise are menacing the safety of all nations that border upon the Pacific.

Were these forces to prevail, what place in such a world would there be for the freedoms which we cherish and which we are passionately determined to maintain?

Because of these perils we are arming ourselves to an extent to which we have never armed ourselves before. We are pouring out billions upon billions of dollars in expenditures, not only in order that we may successfully defend ourselves and our sister nations of the Western Hemisphere but also, for the same ends, in order to make available the weapons of defense to Great Britain, to Russia, to China, and to all the other nations that have until now so bravely fought back the hordes of the invaders. And in so doing we are necessarily diverting the greater part of our tremendous productive capacity into channels of destruction, not those of construction, and we are piling up a debt-burden which will inevitably affect the manner of life and diminish the opportunity for progressive advancement of our children and of our children's children.

But far graver than that – for the tides are running fast – our people realize that at any moment war may be forced upon us, and if it is, the lives of all of us will have to be dedicated to preserving the freedom of the United States and to safeguarding the independence of the American people, which are more dear to us than life itself.

The heart-searching question which every American citizen must ask himself on this day of commemoration is whether the world in which we have to live would have come to this desperate pass had the United States been willing in those years which followed 1919 to play its full part in striving to bring about a new world-order based on justice and on "a steadfast concert for peace."

Would the burdens and the dangers which the American people might have had to envisage through that "partnership of democratic nations" which Woodrow Wilson then urged upon them, have represented even an infinitesimal portion of the burdens and the dangers with which they are now confronted?

Solely from the standpoint of the interest of the American people themselves, who saw straight and who thought straight 20 years ago? Was it Woodrow Wilson when he pled with his fellow Americans to insure the safety and the welfare of their country by utilizing the influence and the strength of their great Nation in joining with the other peace-loving powers of the earth in preventing the outgrowth of those conditions which have made possible this new world-upheaval? Or was it that group of self-styled, "practical, hard-headed Americans," who jeered at his idealism, who loudly proclaimed that our very system of government would be destroyed if we raised our voice in the determination of world-affairs, and who refused to admit that our security could be even remotely jeopardized if the whole of the rest of the earth was plunged into the chaos of world-anarchy?

A cycle in human events is about to come to its end.

The American people after full debate, in accordance with their democratic institutions, have determined upon their policy. They are pledged to defend their freedom and their ancient rights against every form of aggression, and to spare no effort and no sacrifice in bringing to pass the final defeat of Hitlerism and all that which that evil term implies.

We have no doubt of the ultimate victory of the forces of liberty and of human decency. But we cannot know, we cannot yet foresee, how long and how hard the road may be which leads to that new day when another armistice will be signed.

And what will come to pass thereafter?

Three months ago the President of the United States and the Prime Minister of the United Kingdom signed and made public a new charter "on which they base their hopes for a better future for the world."

The principles and the objectives set forth in that joint declaration gave new hope and new courage to millions of people throughout the earth. They saw again more clearly the why and the wherefore of this ghastly struggle. They saw once more the gleam of hope on the horizon – hope for liberty; freedom from fear and want; the satisfaction of their craving for security.

These aspirations of human beings everywhere cannot again be defrauded. Those high objectives set forth in the Charter of the Atlantic must be realized. They must be realized, quite apart from every other consideration, because of the fact that the individual interest of every man and woman in the United States will be advanced consonantly with the measure in which the world where they live is governed by right and by justice, and the measure in which peace prevails.

The American people thus have entered the Valley of Decision.

Shall we as the most powerful Nation of the earth once more stand aloof from all effective and practical forms of international concert, wherein our participation could in all human probability insure the maintenance of a peaceful world in which we can safely live?

Can we afford again to refrain from lifting a finger until gigantic forces of destruction threaten all of modern civilization, and the raucous voice of a criminal paranoiac, speaking as the spokesman for these forces from the cellar of a Munich beer hall, proclaims as his set purpose the destruction of our own security, and the annihilation of religious liberty, of political liberty, and of economic liberty throughout the earth?

The decision rests solely with the people of the United States – the power is theirs to determine the kind of world of the future in which they would live. Is it conceivable that, in enlightened self-interest, they could once more spurn that opportunity?

When the time for the making of that great decision is at hand, I believe that they will turn again for light and for inspiration to the ideals of that great seer, statesman, patriot, and lover of his fellow men – Woodrow Wilson – whose memory we here today revere.

Then, again, they will remember that great cause he once held up before their eyes – "A universal dominion of right by such a concert of free peoples as shall bring peace and safety to all nations and make the world itself at last free."

19. JAPAN'S PROPOSAL FOR PEACE IN THE PACIFIC [19]

1. BOTH the Governments of Japan and the United States undertake not to make any armed advancement into any of the regions in the Southeastern Asia and the Southern Pacific area excepting the part of French Indo-China where the Japanese troops are stationed at present.

2. The Japanese Government undertakes to withdraw its troops now stationed in French Indo-China upon either the restoration of peace between Japan and China or the establishment of an equitable peace in the Pacific area.

In the meantime the Government of Japan declares that it is prepared to remove its troops now stationed in the southern part of French Indo-China to the northern part of the said territory upon the conclusion of the present arrangement which shall later be embodied in the final agreement.

3. The Government of Japan and the United States shall cooperate with a view to securing the acquisition of those goods and commodities which the two countries need in Netherlands East Indies.

4. The Governments of Japan and the United States mutually undertake to restore their commercial relations to those prevailing prior to the freezing of the assets.

The Government of the United States shall supply Japan a required quantity of oil.

5. The Government of the United States undertakes to refrain from such measures and actions as will be prejudicial to the endeavors for the restoration of general peace between Japan and China.

[19] Draft Proposal handed to the Secretary of State November 20, 1941, by the Japanese Ambassador, Kichisaburo Nomura, Ibid., 801–2.

20. AMERICAN PROPOSAL FOR PEACE IN THE PACIFIC [20]

Section 1. *Draft Mutual Declaration of Policy*

THE GOVERNMENT of the United States and the Government of Japan both being solicitous for the peace of the Pacific affirm that their national policies are directed toward lasting and extensive peace throughout the Pacific area, that they have no territorial designs in that area, that they have no intention of threatening other countries or of using military force aggressively against any neighboring nation, and that, accordingly, in their national policies they will actively support and give practical application to the following fundamental principles upon which their relations with each other and with all other governments are based:

(1) The principle of inviolability of territorial integrity and sovereignty of each and all nations.

(2) The principle of non-interference in the internal affairs of other countries.

(3) The principle of equality, including equality of commercial opportunity and treatment.

(4) The principle of reliance upon international cooperation and conciliation for the prevention and pacific settlement of controversies and for improvement of international conditions by peaceful methods and processes.

The Government of Japan and the Government of the United States have agreed that toward eliminating chronic political instability, preventing recurrent economic collapse, and providing a basis for peace, they will actively support and practically apply the following principles in their economic relations with each other and with other nations and peoples:

(1) The principle of non-discrimination in international commercial relations.

(2) The principle of international economic cooperation and abolition of extreme nationalism as expressed in excessive trade restrictions.

(3) The principle of non-discriminatory access by all nations to raw material supplies.

(4) The principle of full protection of the interests of consuming countries and populations as regards the operation of international commodity agreements.

(5) The principle of establishment of such institutions and arrangements of international finance as may lend aid to the essential enterprises and the continuous development of all countries and may permit payments through processes of trade consonant with the welfare of all countries.

---

[20] Draft proposals given to the Japanese Ambassador by the Secretary of State, November 26, 1941. Ibid., 810–12.

Section II. *Steps to Be Taken by the Government of the United States and by the Government of Japan*

The Government of the United States and the Government of Japan propose to take steps as follows:

1. The Government of the United States and the Government of Japan will endeavor to conclude a multilateral non-aggression pact among the British Empire, China, Japan, the Netherlands, the Soviet Union, Thailand and the United States.

2. Both Governments will endeavor to conclude among the American, British, Chinese, Japanese, the Netherland and Thai Governments an agreement whereunder each of the Governments would pledge itself to respect the territorial integrity of French Indochina and, in the event that there should develop a threat to the territorial integrity of Indochina, to enter into immediate consultation with a view to taking such measures as may be deemed necessary and advisable to meet the threat in question. Such agreement would provide also that each of the Governments party to the agreement would not seek or accept preferential treatment in its trade or economic relations with Indochina and would use its influence to obtain for each of the signatories equality of treatment in trade and commerce with French Indochina.

3. The Government of Japan will withdraw all military, naval, air and police forces from China and from Indochina.

4. The Government of the United States and the Government of Japan will not support – militarily, politically, economically – any government or regime in China other than the National Government of the Republic of China with capital temporarily at Chungking.

5. Both Governments will give up all extraterritorial rights in China, including rights and interests in and with regard to international settlements and concessions, and rights under the Boxer Protocol of 1901.

Both Governments will endeavor to obtain the agreement of the British and other governments to give up extraterritorial rights in China, including rights in international settlements and in concessions and under the Boxer Protocol of 1901.

6. The Government of the United States and the Government of Japan will enter into negotiations for the conclusion between the United States and Japan of a trade agreement, based upon reciprocal most-favored-nation treatment and reduction of trade barriers by both countries, including an undertaking by the United States to bind raw silk on the free list.

7. The Government of the United States and the Government of Japan will, respectively, remove the freezing restrictions on Japanese funds in the United States and on American funds in Japan.

8. Both Governments will agree upon a plan for the stabilization of the dollar-yen rate, with the allocation of funds adequate for this purpose, half to be supplied by Japan and half by the United States.

9. Both Governments will agree that no agreement which either has concluded with any third power or powers shall be interpreted by it in such a way as to conflict with the fundamental purpose of this agreement, the establishment and preservation of peace throughout the Pacific area.

10. Both Governments will use their influence to cause other governments to adhere to and to give practical application to the basic political and economic principles set forth in this agreement.

1 — 11

CHAPTER XXXIV

WARTIME DIPLOMACY

1941—1945

IN ALMOST all official wartime statements of American foreign policy, emphasis was placed upon the necessity for the complete military defeat of the Axis powers. Popular attention was directed to the term, "unconditional surrender," and responsible statesmen spoke of defeating Fascism and Nazism "once and for all," defeat so complete that they would "never rise again." This emphasis tended to create the impression that the policy of the United Nations in the second World War was sharply different from that of the Allies in the first World War, an assumption which was only partially valid. The policy of the Allied and Associated Powers in the first World War was to achieve the military defeat of the Central Powers, and they were defeated. They capitulated on terms drawn by the Allied High Command, which left them impotent as far as further military action was concerned. The Allies did not occupy all Germany because they did not choose to do so, but they insisted upon the overthrow of the Hohenzollern regime. "Unconditional surrender," moreover, did not mean that the United Nations would be uncommitted at the end of the war to postwar policies. Beginning with the Atlantic Charter, continuing with pronouncements of responsible statesmen, legislative and other acts, agreements drawn up in conferences, and ending with the United Nations Charter, the United Nations were probably as firmly committed regarding the future as were the Allies in 1918.

The selections included in this chapter, together with the United Nations Charter in the following chapter, illustrate the foregoing analysis and are largely self explanatory. Secretary Hull's address of July 23, 1942 (1), one of his many comprehensive wartime statements covers in broad scope the character of American foreign policy. The President's report to Congress of June 11, 1942, includes the text of a basic lend-lease agreement and presents American policy on wartime loans (2). The address of Herbert H. Lehman of June 17, 1943, on relief and rehabilitation, describes American policy on that subject (3).

The dissolution of the Communist International (4) might not be considered, strictly speaking, as a part of the record of American foreign policy. One of the most fundamental assumptions, however, of American wartime diplomacy was that the "Grand Alliance" of Russia, Great Britain, and the United States, created during the war for military purposes, could be continued during the peace. And one of the principal reasons for this hope was the apparent disposition of the Soviet government to discontinue activity abroad designed to overthrow the social and political order of non-Communist nations, or to extend Communism in enemy areas temporarily occupied after the war.

Of the wartime policies of the United States, none produced more bitter controversy within the country than the establishment of diplomatic relations with the French government at Vichy and military arrangements with Admiral Darlan in North Africa. Not until the American invasion of French North Africa had taken place did the Secretary of State explain the character of American policy toward the Vichy government (5A). The President felt called upon to explain the "temporary" character and the "local" scope of the arrangements with the French Admiral (5B). The policy of the United States toward Italy is shown in the Armistice of September 3, and the joint declaration of October 13, 1943 (6).

The Moscow Conference of October 19–30, 1943, was an historic meeting. President Roosevelt and Prime Minister Churchill had met on five previous occasions, but this was the first meeting of the foreign ministers and military officers of the principal nations of the "Grand Alliance." Military agreements effected at the conference were naturally not announced, but political decisions of far-reaching character were made public (7). A little over a month following the Moscow Conference, President Roosevelt met with Prime Minister Churchill and Generalissimo Chiang Kai-shek at Cairo and made plans for the prosecution of the war and for the peace settlement in the Far East (8). These meetings were followed by the Teheran (9) and Crimea Conferences (10). The Potsdam Declaration offered Japan the last opportunity to surrender (11).

◇◇◇◇◇◇◇◇◇◇◇◇◇◇

1. OBJECTIVES OF THE WAR[1]

THE CONFLICT now raging throughout the earth is not a war of nation against nation. It is not a local or regional war or even a series of such wars. On the side of our enemies, led and driven by the most ambitious, depraved, and cruel leaders in history, it is an attempt to conquer and enslave this country and every country. On our side, the side of the United Nations, it is, for each of us, a life-and-death struggle for the preservation of our freedom, our homes, our very existence. We are united in our determination to destroy the world-wide forces of ruthless conquest and brutal enslavement. Their defeat will restore freedom or the opportunity for freedom alike to all countries and all peoples.

From Berlin and Tokyo the assault on human freedom has spread in ever-widening circles. In some cases the victim nations were lulled into in-

[1] Radio address of Secretary of State, Cordell Hull, July 23, 1942. Department of State *Bulletin*, Vol. VII, pp. 639–47.

action by promises or by protestations of peaceful intention. In other cases they were so intimidated that no preparation for resistance was made. In all cases the invaders, before armed attack, set into motion every conceivable device of deceit, subversion, treachery, and corruption within the borders of the intended victim.

As country after country, in Europe and in Asia, was attacked in this way, it became clear that no nation anywhere was immune, that for none was safety to be found in mere desire for peace, in avoidance of provocation, in neutrality, or in distance from the centers of assault. Nation after nation learned – too late – that safety against such an attack lay only in more effective force; in superior will; in concerted action of all free nations directed toward resisting and defeating the common enemies; in applying the law of self-defense and self-preservation rather than in relying upon professions of neutrality, which, in the face of world-wide movement to subjugate all nations and all peoples, are as absurd and as suicidal as are such professions on the part of a citizen of a peaceful community attacked by a band of confessed outlaws.

Today twenty-eight United Nations are fighting against the would-be conquerors and enslavers of the human race. We know what is at stake. By the barbarian invaders of today nothing is spared – neither life, nor morals, nor honor, nor virtue, nor pledges, nor the customs, the national institutions, even the religion of any people. Their aim is to sweep away every vestige of individual and national rights; to substitute, the world over, their unspeakable tyranny for the ways of life developed each for itself by the various nations; to make all mankind subservient to their will; to convert the two billions of the earth's inhabitants into abject victims and tools of their insatiable lust for power and dominion.

We have seen their work in the countries they have invaded – murder of defenseless men, women, and children; rape, torture, and pillage; mass terrorization; the black system of hostages; starvation and deprivations that beggar description; the most thorough-going bondage the world has ever seen.

This is the so-called "New Order" of Hitler and the Japanese war lords – an order as old as slavery – new only in the calculated thoroughness of its cruelty; in the depth of the degradation to which it subjects its victims; in the degree to which it has revived the worst practices of the darkest ages in history.

From time immemorial attempts at conquest and enslavement have checked and harried the great onward march of men and women toward greater freedom and higher levels of civilized existence. The methods employed have been the same as those which we witness today. Ruthless, ambitious men would succeeed in corrupting, coercing, or deceiving into blind obedience enough servile followers to attack or terrify peaceful and law-abiding peoples, too often unprepared to resist. In a few instances whole civilizations collapsed under the impact, and darkness descended on large portions of the world. More often, the attacks were – at great cost

– defeated, and mankind resumed its onward march. Yet throughout the ages two lessons have remained unlearned.

The first is that man's innate striving for freedom cannot be extinguished. Since the world began too many men have fought, suffered, and died for freedom – and not in vain – for doubt to remain on that score. And yet, over and over again would-be conquerors and enslavers of mankind have sought to translate their mad dreams of barbarous domination into reality.

The second lesson is that liberty is truly won only when it is guarded by the same watchfulness, the same courage, the same willingness to fight for it which first secured it. Repeatedly throughout history, free men – having won the fight, having acquired precious rights and privileges which freedom brings – have dropped their guard, relaxed their vigilance, taken their freedom for granted. They have busied themselves with many things and have not noticed the beginnings of new tyrannies, the rise of new threats to liberty. They have become so abhorrent of force and cruelty that they have believed the bully and the gangster could be reformed by reason and justice or be defeated by passive resistance. And so they have been surprised and unprepared when the attacks have come again.

It is perhaps too much to expect that tyrants will ever learn that man's longing for liberty cannot be destroyed. Dreams of conquest have their roots in diseased mentality. And that malady may well be ineradicable.

But it is not too much to expect that free men may learn – and never forget – that lack of vigilance is the greatest danger to liberty; that enjoyment of liberty is the fruit of willingness to fight, suffer, and die for it; that the right to freedom cannot be divorced from the duty of defending it. . . .

We, Americans, are fighting today because we have been attacked. We are fighting, as I have said, to preserve our very existence. We and the other free peoples are forced into a desperate fight because we did not learn the lessons of which I have spoken. We are forced to fight because we ignored the simple but fundamental fact that the price of peace and of the preservation of right and freedom among nations is the acceptance of international responsibilities.

After the last war too many nations, including our own, tolerated, or participated in, attempts to advance their own interests at the expense of any system of collective security and of opportunity for all. Too many of us were blind to the evils which, thus loosed, created growing cancers within and among nations – political suspicions and hatreds; the race of armaments, first stealthy and then the subject of flagrant boasts; economic nationalism and its train of economic depression and misery; and finally the emergence from their dark places of the looters and thugs who found their opportunity in disorder and disaster. The shadow of a new war fell across the world. War began in 1931 when Japan invaded China. . . .

Events have demonstrated beyond question that each of the Axis powers was bent on unlimited conquest. As time went on it became manifest that the United States and the whole Western Hemisphere were ultimate targets. Conclusive proof was given by the international desperadoes themselves through the publication on September 27, 1940 of the Tripartite Pact. By that treaty of alliance Germany, Japan, and Italy in effect agreed that, if any country not then at war with one of them placed obstacles in the way of the program of conquest of any of them, the three would unite in political, military, and economic action against that country. This provision was aimed directly at the United States. One of the highest official spokesmen of the Axis powers openly proclaimed that the objective of the three partners was a new world order to be achieved by force. . . .

In this vast struggle, we, Americans, stand united with those who like ourselves, are fighting for the preservation of their freedom; with those who are fighting to regain the freedom of which they have been brutally deprived; with those who are fighting for the opportunity to achieve freedom. . . .

With victory achieved our first concern must be for those whose sufferings have been almost beyond human endurance. When the armies of our enemies are beaten, the people of many countries will be starving and without means of procuring food; homeless and without means of building shelter; their fields scorched; their cattle slaughtered; their tools gone; their factories and mines destroyed; their roads and transport wrecked. Unknown millions will be far from their homes — prisoners of war, inmates of concentration camps, forced laborers in alien lands, refugees from battle, from cruelty, from starvation. Disease and danger of disease will lurk everywhere. In some countries confusion and chaos will follow the cessation of hostilities. Victory must be followed by swift and effective action to meet these pressing human needs. . . .

During this period of transition the United Nations must continue to act in the spirit of cooperation which now underlies their war effort — to supplement and make more effective the action of countries individually in re-establishing public order, in providing swift relief, in meeting the manifold problems of readjustment.

Beyond these there will lie before all countries the great constructive task of building human freedom and Christian morality on firmer and broader foundations than ever before. This task, too, will of necessity call for both national and international action. . . .

For decades all nations have lived in the shadow of threatened coercion or war. This has imposed heavy burdens of armament, which in the cases of many nations has absorbed so large a part of their production effort as to leave the remainder of their resources inadequate for maintaining, let alone improving, the economic, social, and cultural standards of their people. Closely related to this has been a burden less obvious but of immense weight — the inevitable limitation that fear of war imposes on productive activity. Many men, groups of men, and even nations have dared not plan, create, or increase the means of production, fearing lest war come and their efforts thus be rendered vain.

No nation can make satisfactory progress while its citizens are in the grip of constant fear of external attack or interference. It is plain that some international agency must be created which can – by force, if necessary – keep the peace among nations in the future. There must be international cooperative action to set up the mechanisms which can thus insure peace. This must include eventual adjustment of national armaments in such a manner that the rule of law cannot be successfully challenged and that the burden of armaments may be reduced to a minimum.

In the creation of such mechanisms there would be a practical and purposeful application of sovereign powers through measures of international cooperation for purposes of safeguarding the peace. Participation by all nations in such measures would be for each its contribution toward its own future security and safety from outside attack.

Settlement of disputes by peaceful means, and indeed all processes of international cooperation, presuppose respect for law and obligations. It is plain that one of the institutions which must be established and be given vitality is an international court of justice. It is equally clear that, in the process of re-establishing international order, the United Nations must exercise surveillance over aggressor nations until such time as the latter demonstrate their willingness and ability to live at peace with other nations. How long such surveillance will need to continue must depend upon the rapidity with which the peoples of Germany, Japan, Italy, and their satellites give convincing proof that they have repudiated and abandoned the monstrous philosophy of superior race and conquest by force and have embraced loyally the basic principles of peaceful processes. During the formative period of the world organization, interruption by these aggressors must be rendered impossible.

One of the greatest of all obstacles which in the past have impeded human progress and afforded breeding grounds for dictators has been extreme nationalism. All will agree that nationalism and its spirit are essential to the healthy and normal political and economic life of a people, but when policies of nationalism – political, economic, social, and moral – are carried to such extremes as to exclude and prevent necessary policies of international cooperation, they become dangerous and deadly. Nationalism, run riot between the last war and this war, defeated all attempts to carry out indispensable measures of international economic and political action, encouraged and facilitated the rise of dictators, and drove the world straight toward the present war.

During this period narrow and short-sighted nationalism found its most virulent expression in the economic field. It prevented goods and services from flowing in volume at all adequate from nation to nation and thus severely hampered the work of production, distribution, and consumption and greatly retarded efforts for social betterment.

No nation can make satisfactory progress when it is deprived, by its own action or by the action of others, of the immeasurable benefits of international exchange of goods and services. The Atlantic Charter declares the right of all nations to "access, on equal terms, to the trade and to the raw materials of the world which are needed for their economic prosperity." This is essential if the legitimate and growing demand for the greatest practicable measure of stable employment is to be met, accompanied by rising standards of living. If the actual and potential losses resulting from limitations on economic activity are to be eliminated, a system must be provided by which this can be assured.

In order to accomplish this, and to establish among the nations a circle of mutual benefit, excessive trade barriers of the many different kinds must be reduced, and practices which impose injuries on others and divert trade from its natural economic course must be avoided. Equally plain is the need for making national currencies once more freely exchangeable for each other at stable rates of exchange; for a system of financial relations so devised that materials can be produced and ways may be found of moving them where there are markets created by human need; for machinery through which capital may – for the development of the world's resources and for the stabilization of economic activity – move on equitable terms from financially stronger to financially weaker countries. There may be need for some special trade arrangement and for international agreements to handle difficult surplus problems and to meet situations in special areas. . . .

With peace among nations reasonably assured, with political stability established, with economic shackles removed, a vast fund of resources will be released in each nation to meet the needs of progress, to make possible for all of its citizens an advancement toward higher living standards, to invigorate the constructive forces of initiative and enterprise. The nations of the world will then be able to go forward in the manner of their own choosing in all avenues of human betterment more completely than they ever have been able to do in the past. They will do so through their own efforts and with complete self-respect. Continuous self-development of nations and individuals in a framework of effective cooperation with others is the sound and logical road to the higher standards of life which we all crave and seek. . . .

◇◇◇◇◇◇◇◇◇◇◇◇

2. LEND-LEASE [2]

ON JANUARY 1, 1942, the United States, Great Britain, Russia, China, and 22 other nations united in a declaration that "they are now engaged in a common struggle against savage and brutal forces seeking to subjugate the world." They resolved that "complete victory over their enemies is essential to defend life, liberty, independence, and religious freedom, and to preserve human rights and justice in their own lands as well as in

[2] Report of President Roosevelt to Congress, June 11, 1942. House Doc. No. 779, 77th Congress, 2nd Session, pp. 12–23.

other lands." They subscribed unanimously to the principles and purposes set forth in the Atlantic Charter. They pledged themselves to employ their full military and economic resources in the war, and not to make a separate peace.

The United Nations have thus declared that they are more than a temporary military combination, and that they will wage the war together for a common victory and a common program of peace aims.

To fight a common war which extends around the world, the United Nations need a common plan for the most effective possible use of their resources in men and materials and machines. All the battlefronts are linked together. The United Nations are concentrating their weapons on those battlefronts where pressure is heaviest and where military success is of the greatest strategic importance. They are moving in a coordinated way toward organizing offensives backed by their combined resources.

Our lend-lease program is one means, and a simple one, by which the common economic effort pledged in the Declaration by United Nations may be secured. The lend-lease principle, as it develops, is removing the possibility that considerations of finance can interfere with the full use of material resources. The transfers made under the Lend-Lease Act are not commercial loans to other nations. They are contributions of material to a common pool with which a common war is being waged. In return, other United Nations are contributing their utmost to the common fight – in men, materials and machines – and are furnishing us with the weapons and supplies which we, rather than they, can most effectively use. . . .

Long strides have been made toward achieving the unified direction necessary to put the combined resources of the United Nations to most effective use. Combined agencies have been established by joint action of the United States and Great Britain to coordinate strategy and to map the production and distribution of munitions and raw materials. The members of these combined boards have been instructed to "confer with representatives of the Union of Soviet Socialist Republics, China, and such other of the United Nations as are necessary to attain common purposes and provide for the most effective utilization of the joint resources of the United Nations."

To date, the combined boards which have been created include the Combined Chiefs of Staff, the Munitions Assignments Board, the Combined Raw Materials Board, the Combined Shipping Adjustment Board, the Combined Production and Resources Board, and the Combined Food Board. These expert bodies are welding the American and British war efforts together. As part of their job, they exercise control over all lend-lease transfers. They plan for the production of materials to fill lend-lease needs, determine the quantities of finished and raw materials available for immediate lend-lease transfer, fix their destination, and provide the necessary shipping. By shaping their plans to fit the needs of all United Nations, they are helping us to fight a world-wide war on a world-wide basis. . . .

Lend-Lease and the Peace

The lend-lease program has already become a prime mechanism in the combined efforts the United Nations are making to win the war. The program of lend-lease agreements is also emerging as a factor in the combined effort of the United Nations to weave a pattern for peace. Those agreements are taking shape as key instruments of national policy, the first of our concrete steps in the direction of affirmative post-war reconstruction.

The agreement with Great Britain was signed on February 23, 1942. On June 2, 1942, an agreement was made with the Republic of China embodying the same terms. On June 11, 1942, a similar agreement was signed with the Union of Soviet Socialist Republics. The provisions of these agreements are now being offered to our other allies receiving lend-lease assistance.

These basic lend-lease agreements place the problem of the peacetime settlement in a realistic and appropriate setting. The agreements postpone final determination of the lend-lease account until "the extent of the defense aid is known and until the progress of events makes clearer the final terms and conditions and benefits which will be in the mutual interests" of the signatory nations, and which "will promote the establishment and maintenance of world peace." Final settlement has been postponed since the course of the war may further change the complexion of the issue.

We are now in the war, as we were not in March 1941 when the Lend-Lease Act was passed. We have pledged our resources without limit to win the war, and the peace which will follow it. We look forward to a period of security and liberty, in which men may freely pursue lives of their choice, and governments will achieve policies leading to full and useful production and employment. If the promise of the peace is to be fulfilled, a large volume of production and trade among nations must be restored and sustained. This trade must be solidly founded on stable exchange relationships and liberal principles of commerce. The lend-lease settlement will rest on a specific and detailed program for achieving these ends, which are, as Article VII of the agreements with Great Britain, China and Russia points out, "the material foundations of the liberty and welfare of all peoples."

Cooperative action among the United Nations is contemplated to fulfill this program for economic progress, in the many spheres where action is needed. It is hoped that plans will soon develop for a series of agreements and recommendations for legislation, in the fields of commercial policy, of money and finance, international investment and reconstruction.

Article VII of each of the basic agreements pledges that "the terms and conditions" of the final determination of the benefits to be provided the United States in return for aid furnished under the Act "shall be such as not to burden commerce between the two countries, but to promote mutually advantageous economic relations between them and the betterment of world-wide economic relations." By this provision we have affirmatively declared our intention to avoid the political and economic mistakes of international debt experience during the twenties.

A lend-lease settlement which fulfills this principle will be sound from the economic point of view. But it will have a greater merit. It will represent the only fair way to distribute the financial costs of war among the United Nations.

The real costs of the war cannot be measured, nor compared, nor paid for in money. They must and are being met in blood and toil. But the financial costs of the war can and should be met in a way which will serve the needs of lasting peace and mutual economic well-being.

All the United Nations are seeking maximum conversion to war production, in the light of their special resources. If each country devotes roughly the same fraction of its national production to the war, then the financial burden of war is distributed equally among the United Nations in accordance with their ability to pay. And although the nations richest in resources are able to make larger contributions, the claim of war against each is relatively the same. Such a distribution of the financial costs of war means that no nation will grow rich from the war effort of its allies. The money costs of the war will fall according to the rule of equality in sacrifice, as in effort. . . .

(A) AGREEMENT BETWEEN THE UNITED STATES AND THE UNITED KINGDOM, SIGNED AT WASHINGTON, FEBRUARY 23, 1942. . . .

Article I. The Government of the United States of America will continue to supply the Government of the United Kingdom with such defense articles, defense services, and defense information as the President shall authorize to be transferred or provided.

Article II. The Government of the United Kingdom will continue to contribute to the defense of the United States of America and the strengthening thereof and will provide such articles, services, facilities or information as it may be in a position to supply.

Article III. The Government of the United Kingdom will not without the consent of the President of the United States of America transfer title to, or possession of, any defense article or defense information transferred to it under the Act or permit the use thereof by anyone not an officer, employee, or agent of the Government of the United Kingdom.

Article IV. If, as a result of the transfer to the Government of the United Kingdom of any defense article or defense information, it becomes necessary for that Government to take any action or make any payment in order fully to protect any of the rights of a citizen of the United States of America who has patent rights in and to any such defense article or information, the Government of the United Kingdom will take such action or make such payment when requested to do so by the President of the United States of America.

Article V. The Government of the United Kingdom will return to the

United States of America at the end of the present emergency, as determined by the President, such defense articles transferred under this Agreement as shall not have been destroyed, lost or consumed and as shall be determined by the President to be useful in the defense of the United States of America or of the Western Hemisphere or to be otherwise of use to the United States of America.

Article VI. In the final determination of the benefits to be provided to the United States of America by the Government of the United Kingdom full cognizance shall be taken of all property, services, information, facilities, or other benefits or considerations provided by the Government of the United Kingdom subsequent to March 11, 1941, and accepted or acknowledged by the President on behalf of the United States of America.

Article VII. In the final determination of the benefits to be provided to the United States of America by the Government of the United Kingdom in return for aid furnished under the Act of Congress of March 11, 1941, the terms and conditions thereof shall be such as not to burden commerce between the two countries, but to promote mutually advantageous economic relations between them and the betterment of world-wide economic relations. To that end, they shall include provision for agreed action by the United States of America and the United Kingdom, open to participation by all other countries of like mind, directed to the expansion, by appropriate international and domestic measures, of production, employment, and the exchange and consumption of goods, which are the material foundations of the liberty and welfare of all peoples; to the elimination of all forms of discriminatory treatment in international commerce, and to the reduction of tariffs and other trade barriers; and, in general, to the attainment of all the economic objectives set forth in the Joint Declaration made on August 12, 1941, by the President of the United States of America and the Prime Minister of the United Kingdom.

At an early convenient date, conversations shall be begun between the two Governments with a view to determining, in the light of governing economic conditions, the best means of attaining the above-stated objectives by their own agreed action and of seeking the agreed action of other like-minded Governments.

Article VIII. This Agreement shall take effect as from this day's date. It shall continue in force until a date to be agreed upon by the two Governments.

◇◇◇◇◇◇◇◇◇◇◇◇◇

3. RELIEF AND REHABILITATION [3]

. . . THE PEACE which we all seek must be rooted in the first hurried work of rehabilitation and reconstruction. The dimensions of this task

[3] Address of Herbert H. Lehman, Director of the Office of Foreign Relief and Rehabilitation Operations before the Foreign Policy Association, New York, June 17, 1943. Department of State *Bulletin,* Vol. VIII, pp. 539–43.

can best be measured by the dimensions of the disaster which has overtaken the world. The Axis has extended its despotism over the peoples of some 35 countries and hundreds of islands, the dwelling-places of more than half a billion men, women, and children. Almost all Europe lies under the dark cloud of Nazi rule; Japan has overrun the rich islands of the western Pacific and has penetrated deep toward the heart of heroic China. In occupied Europe and in enslaved Asia the picture is universally the same – starving people, impoverished land, and nations whose whole economies have been wrecked.

Food-condition statistics in the area of Axis occupation are treacherous. But official reports from Europe and Asia leave no doubt that hunger is the general rule, that starvation is commonplace, and that the area enslaved by the Axis is a breeding-place for all the diseases of the body and of the spirit that are born of starvation, suffering, and death.

Agricultural production in Europe has dropped substantially despite the desperate efforts of Germany to make Axis-dominated Europe self-supporting. As the months roll on, the manpower shortage, the wastage and deterioration of machinery, the neglect of the soil, and the increasing disorganization of the economy will cut even deeper into total food-production.

The once matchless flocks and herds of Europe have declined to figures in some cases a third below pre-war levels. Horses are disappearing at a rate that indicates that a shortage of draft animals may be a problem even more acute than the shortage of manpower in the first harvest of peace. The occupied nations have been systematically drained of their resources, raw materials, and commercial goods to serve a vicious new order. Never before has the world witnessed so ruthless a despoliation of so many in so short a time.

A problem so vast and so world embracing, obviously, does not lend itself to piecemeal solution. The problem is to devise means to harness world production, already greatly taxed by war needs, to total world want during the coming months of tremendous human crisis. We must see to it that relief flows smoothly and swiftly into measures to remove the need of relief, and that rehabilitation measures are so devised as to enable the suffering nations to begin their own reconstruction at the earliest possible moment. Our objective is to *help people* to help *themselves* and thereby to help ourselves, by making possible a world in which the four freedoms can have a chance of realization.

We have already made important strides toward meeting these complex problems. Within the last few days the Department of State has placed before the 43 governments of all the United Nations and the other nations associated with us in this war a draft agreement for creation of a United Nations Relief and Rehabilitation Administration through which the productive resources of all the nations of goodwill may shortly be mobilized to bring succor to the victims of war. The Governments of the United States, Great Britain, Russia, and China already have agreed to this plan, indicating their readiness to participate wholeheartedly in an historic effort to see to it that no one shall die for the lack of bread, protection from the elements, or the minimum assistance of modern medicine. . . .

There should be no basic misconception of the idea of relief in the minds of Americans. Relief operations in Europe after the war of 1914–18 by no means entirely took the form of gift. Where governments had cash or assets, they were required in some cases to pay cash and in other cases to pledge assets as security for loans. In other instances, governments which had no assets which could reasonably be regarded as good security, were nevertheless provided with relief and required to pay by means of loans advanced to them under conditions where the commercial soundness of the credit was highly questionable. Most of these loans were subsequently defaulted, and our Government thus was no better off than if the loans had been outright gifts. On the other hand the country receiving relief suffered an impairment of its credit and was less able to borrow for sound projects of reconstruction so long as these loans still complicated its finances. Economic recovery was thus impaired, and one of the forces was put into motion which headed the world toward the tragic cycle which led first to a gigantic depression, then to the rise of Hitler, Mussolini, and the Japanese militarists, and finally to global conflagration.

To avoid the danger of permitting relief to cause fundamental economic derangements which might generate a third world war, a careful balance must be maintained between relief by outright gift and relief by sale or exchange. None of the liberated nations will be seeking the charity of this country. But in some instances it certainly will be the course of prudence and wisdom to advance the goods for relief and rehabilitation as outright gifts. To do otherwise under some conditions would be to impair the credit and economy of the liberated nations and thus make it difficult if not impossible for such nations to procure essential credit and exchange when the initial emergency has passed and the time arrives for sound, long-term reconstruction. In other instances, however, the liberated nations will quickly reestablish governments capable, ready, and willing to purchase the foodstuffs and goods necessary for relief and rehabilitation, and operations of the relief and rehabilitation agency can and should proceed on a commercial basis. In still other instances, the operation undoubtedly must be an admixture of both procedures. But in all situations, the technique of salvage and rehabilitation must constantly be oriented toward the objective of reconstituting the economy of the recipient nation. That is the way to put an end to relief. That is what *we* want. That is what the suffering peoples of the liberated nations will have richly earned.

For these reasons, the President, pending the creation of the United Nations Relief and Rehabilitation Administration, has assigned my office the task not alone of establishing "soup kitchens" and carrying on direct relief, but also of assisting war-stricken peoples in reviving their own production of essential goods and services as rapidly as possible. In each liberated area which the President may designate, the Office of Foreign

Relief and Rehabilitation Operations is to distribute relief goods and goods to facilitate the production of basic civilian necessities, whether these goods be given away, sold, or bartered. In such way we achieve a single supply line to each liberated area and avoid inconsistency and confusion in policy and administration.

The lessons learned in the quarter century during which this war was in the making demonstrate beyond question that the United States and the United Nations have no alternative but to undertake this task. The motives that impel us to this work are readily demonstrable, even without reference to the deep moral motives which of themselves alone would be a justification for assisting those who are suffering and dying. . . .

If we have learned anything from the decades just behind us it is this: That we cannot, even if we would, make ourselves secure in a world in which millions of men, women, and children are dying of want or by epidemic. Let us recognize frankly that freedom from want is a basic component of any enduring peace and that if America is to have any hope of lasting peace and a stable world economy it must help see to it that the liberated peoples of the world are restored as rapidly as possible to a self-sustaining basis.

That is merely enlightened self-interest.

We cannot live with security in a world half rich, half pauperized. International trade cannot flourish or sound economic expansion take place in a world tormented by expectations of the violence that is born of suffering and misery. And the United States, in the period after this war, will need the outlets of a total world market unless our economy is to face a terrific contraction in a shattering post-war depression. We in America must not lose sight of the fact that, once this war has ended, we again will be the greatest producers in the world and will want world markets for our grain, our cotton, our tobacco, and other agricultural staples as well as our steel, our automobiles, and the thousands of products of our mills and factories.

The relief and rehabilitation of war-stricken nations is the necessary first step toward a balanced economy in which a high level of consumption will prevent the piling up of those great stocks of surplus goods which would otherwise be quickly accumulated after this war in all the primary producing countries. Relief and rehabilitation is but the opening phase of the post-war era. The long-range reconstruction which follows this phase must be conducted on the basis of world trade. By emergency relief and rehabilitation measures now we can make it possible for the liberated peoples of Europe and Asia to become in succeeding years the customers for our goods. Thus by restoring the basic economic equilibrium of these peoples we can hope to create demand which will provide jobs for the millions of fighting men who will be streaming home from our victorious armies to take jobs in an industry converting back to production for peace. . . .

The cry of nations and their peoples for assistance in the first hours of liberation will present democracy with a supreme test. The fate of all United Nations' attempt to insure banishment of these global wars may well be determined by the success of the first joint action in relief and rehabilitation administration. This work of binding up the wounds of those who suffer, or preventing and halting death by starvation, exposure, disease, and neglect, transcends the realm of political allegiances and can give full expression to the highest principles and instincts of all peoples. If the nations of the world should fail to work in mutual cooperation for these high principles, what hope could we hold for political cooperation to banish war? If it is true that nations learn to work together by actually working together, then the joint effort of the United Nations to help the liberated peoples of the world may well provide the experience which will make possible the more gigantic enterprises to come.

It is given to us, twice within the span of a lifetime, to attempt to devise a peace in which all men can live in freedom from fear and want. We failed last time. We dare not fail again.

◇◇◇◇◇◇◇◇◇◇◇◇◇◇

4. THE DISSOLUTION OF THE COMMUNIST INTERNATIONAL[4]

THE HISTORIC role of the Communist International, which was founded in 1919 as a result of a political union of the great majority of the old prewar working-class parties, consisted in upholding the principles of the working-class movement, in helping to promote consolidation in a number of countries of the vanguard of the foremost workers in the real working-class parties, and in helping them mobilize workers for the defense of their economic and political interests, and for the struggle against Fascism and the war which the latter was preparing, and for the support of the Soviet Union as the chief bulwark against Fascism.

The Communist International from the first exposed the real meaning of the Anti-Comintern Pact as a weapon for the preparation of war by the Hitlerites. Long before the war it ceaselessly and tirelessly exposed the vicious, subversive work of the Hitlerites, who masked it by their screams about so-called interference of the Communist International in the internal affairs of these states.

But long before the war it became more and more clear that, with increasing complications in internal and international relations of various countries, any sort of international center would encounter insuperable obstacles in solving the problems facing the movement in each separate country.

[4] Resolution of the Presidium of the Communist International, Moscow, May 22, 1943. Leland M. Goodrich and Marie J. Carroll, *Documents on American Foreign Relations,* op. cit., Vol. V, pp. 527–30.

Deep differences of the historic paths of development of various countries, differences in their character and even contradictions in their social orders, differences in the level and the tempo of their economic and political development, differences finally in the degree of consciousness and organization of workers, conditioned different problems affecting the working class of the various countries.

The whole development of events in the last quarter of a century and the experience accumulated by the Communist International convincingly showed that the organizational form of uniting workers, chosen by the First Congress of the Communist International, answered conditions of the first stages of the working-class movement, but it has been outgrown by the growth of this movement and by the complications of its problems in separate countries and has even become a drag on the further strengthening of the national working-class parties.

The World War that the Hitlerites have let loose has still further sharpened the differences in the situation of the separate countries and has placed a deep dividing line between those countries that fell under the Hitlerite tyranny and those freedom-loving peoples who have united in a powerful anti-Hitlerite coalition.

In countries of the Hitlerite bloc the fundamental task of the working class, toilers and all honest people consists in giving all help for the defeat of this bloc by sabotage of the Hitlerite military machine from within and by helping to overthrow the governments guilty of war.

In countries of the anti-Hitlerite coalition the sacred duty of the widest masses of the people, and in the first place of foremost workers, consists in aiding by every means the military efforts of the governments of these countries aimed at the speediest defeat of the Hitlerite bloc and the assurance of the friendship of nations based on their equality.

At the same time the fact must not be lost sight of that the separate countries that are members of the anti-Hitlerite coalition have their own particular problems. For example, in countries occupied by the Hitlerites that have lost their state of independence the basic task of the foremost workers and of the wide masses of people consists in promoting the armed struggle developing into a national war of liberation against Hitlerite Germany.

At the same time the war of liberation of freedom-loving peoples against the Hitlerite tyranny, which has brought into movement the masses of people, uniting them without difference of party or religion in the ranks of the powerful anti-Hitlerite coalition, has demonstrated with still greater clearness that the general national uprising and mobilization of people for the speediest victory over the enemy can be best of all and most fruitfully carried out by the vanguard of the working-class movement of each separate country, working within the framework of its own country.

Already the Seventh Congress of the Communist International meeting in 1935, taking into account the change that had taken place both in the international situation and in working-class movements that demanded great flexibility and independence of its sections in deciding the problems confronting them, emphasized the necessity for the Executive Committee of the Communist International, in deciding all questions of the working-class movement arising from concrete conditions and peculiarities of each country, to make a rule of avoiding interference in the internal organizational affairs of the Communist parties.

These same considerations guided the Communist International in considering the resolution of the Communist party of the United States of America of November 1940, on its withdrawal from the ranks of the Communist International.

Guided by the judgment of the founders of Marxism and Leninism, Communists have never been supporters of the conservation of organizational forms that have outlived themselves. They have always subordinated forms of organization of the working-class movement, and methods of working of such organization, to the fundamental political interest of the working-class movement as a whole, to peculiarities of the concrete historical situation and to problems immediately resulting from this situation.

They remember the example of the great Marx, who united foremost workers in the ranks of the Working Men's International Association, and when the First International had fulfilled its historical task of laying the foundations for the development of working-class parties in the countries of Europe and America, and, as a result of the matured situation creating mass national working-class parties, dissolved first the International, inasmuch as this form of organization already no longer corresponded to the demands confronting it.

In consideration of the above and taking into account the growth and the political maturity of Communist parties and their leading cadres in separate countries, and also having in view the fact that during the present war some sections have raised the question of the dissolution of the Communist International as the directing center of the international working-class movement, the Presidium of the Executive Committee of the Communist International, in the circumstances of the World War, not being able to convene a Congress of the Communist International, puts forward the following proposal for ratification by the sections of the Communist International:

The Communist International, as the directing center of the international working-class movement, is to be dissolved, thus freeing the sections of the Communist International from their obligations arising from the statutes and resolutions of the Congresses of the Communist International.

The Presidium of the Executive Committee of the Communist International calls on all supporters of the Communist International to concentrate their energies on the whole-hearted support of and active participation in the war of liberation of the peoples and the states of the anti-Hitlerite coalition for the speediest defeat of the deadly enemy of the working class and toilers — German Fascism and its associates and vassals.

◇◇◇◇◇◇◇◇◇◇◇◇◇

5. AMERICAN RELATIONS WITH FRANCE

(A) RELATIONS WITH THE VICHY GOVERNMENT [5]

IN RESPONSE to questions by the newspaper correspondents at a press conference held on November 8, the Secretary of State said that the people who have been concerned about the Vichy policy of the United States Government will now be able to see clearly and fully its entire content. He added that liberation of French Morocco by American military forces carries forward the various purposes and objectives of this Government in pursuing its policy toward Vichy. This policy, he said, has been directed toward the ultimate liberation of France from her German captors. The American, British, and Canadian Governments have whole-heartedly favored and supported this policy, he added.

The more important of those purposes, Secretary Hull pointed out, have been: (1) opportunity for the Government of the United States to get from week to week highly important information virtually from the inside of German-controlled territory and from North Africa regarding Axis subversive activities and other important phases of the international situation; (2) the maintenance of close relations with the French people and encouragement of leadership in opposition to Hitlerism wherever it exists; (3) the keeping alive of the basic concepts of freedom of the French people, looking toward ultimate restoration of free institutions for France as they existed before the German occupation; (4) the retention of the closest personal touch on the ground with all phases of the French and German situation under the armistice prevailing between Germany and France; resistance to increased German pressure on France to go beyond the armistice provisions and to collaborate with Germany; constant effort to prevent delivery of the French fleet or any part of it into German military hands or to give military support to German arms; that also includes French bases all along the Mediterranean and the Atlantic coast; and (5) last, but most important, paving the way and preparing the background, in the most effective manner possible, for the planning and sending of the military expedition into the western Mediterranean area, and assisting the movements supporting present British operations farther east.

The Secretary of State was asked, at his press conference on November 9, whether he would care to say whether he felt that the traditional friendship which had existed between the peoples of this country and France for so long would make it impossible for the Vichy Government to turn the French people against us in view of the developments in North Africa.

The Secretary permitted the press to quote him directly on the following statement:

---

[5] Remarks of Secretary Hull at Press Conferences, November 8 and 9, 1942. Department of State *Bulletin,* Vol. VII, pp. 903–4.

"The Vichy Government did all – reached its maximum stage by its plan and efforts to mislead the French people many months ago. The French people, I think, to the extent of not less than 95 per cent understand fully that the Laval government at Vichy has been a most willing puppet of Hitler and Hitler agencies, with the result that instead of being influenced in that Hitler direction by the Laval government, they – the French people – will, on the contrary, be most grateful for our having come to the relief of French Africa, which is the first and preliminary step in our plans, so far as I understand, to come to the relief of all enslaved peoples in Europe, including France proper. The French people will continue, I am sure, to be grateful to us for our policies and be wholly cooperative with us to the extent within their power."

(B) RELATIONS WITH ADMIRAL DARLAN [6]

I have accepted General Eisenhower's political arrangements made for the time being in Northern and Western Africa.

I thoroughly understand and approve the feeling in the United States and Great Britain and among all the other United Nations that in view of the history of the past two years no permanent arrangement should be made with Admiral Darlan. People in the United Nations likewise would never understand the recognition of a reconstituting of the Vichy Government in France or in any French territory.

We are opposed to Frenchmen who support Hitler and the Axis. No one in our Army has any authority to discuss the future Government of France and the French Empire.

The future French Government will be established, not by any individual in Metropolitan France or overseas but by the French people themselves after they have been set free by the victory of the United Nations.

The present temporary arrangement in North and West Africa is only a temporary expedient, justified solely by the stress of battle.

The present temporary arrangement has accomplished two military objectives. The first was to save American and British lives on the one hand, and French lives on the other hand.

The second was the vital factor of time. The temporary arrangement has made it possible to avoid a "mopping-up" period in Algiers and Morocco which might have taken a month or two to consummate. Such a period would have delayed the concentration for the attack from the west on Tunis, and we hope on Tripoli.

Every day of delay in the current operation would have enabled the Germans and Italians to build up a strong resistance, to dig in and make a huge operation on our part essential before we could win. Here again, many more lives will be saved under the present speedy offensive than if we had had to delay it for a month or more.

It will also be noted that French troops, under the command of General

6 Statement of President Roosevelt, November 17, 1942. Ibid., p. 935.

Giraud, have already been in action against the enemy in Tunisia, fighting by the side of American and British soldiers for the liberation of their country.

Admiral Darlan's proclamation assisted in making a "mopping up" period unnecessary. Temporary arrangements made with Admiral Darlan apply, without exception, to the current local situation only.

I have requested the liberation of all persons in Northern Africa who had been imprisoned because they opposed the efforts of the Nazis to dominate the world, and I have asked for the abrogation of all laws and decrees inspired by Nazi governments or Nazi ideologists. Reports indicate that the French of North Africa are subordinating all political questions to the formation of a common front against the common enemy.

6. RELATIONS WITH ITALY

[*The Italian Armistice*] [7]

Sicily, September 3rd, 1943

THE FOLLOWING conditions of an Armistice are presented by General *Dwight D. Eisenhower,* Commander-in-Chief of the Allied Forces, acting by authority of the Governments of the United States and Great Britain and in the interest of the United Nations, and are accepted by Marshal *Pietro Badoglio,* Head of the Italian Government.

1. Immediate cessation of all hostile activity by the Italian armed forces.
2. Italy will use its best endeavors to deny, to the Germans, facilities that might be used against the United Nations.
3. All prisoners or internees of the United Nations to be immediately turned over to the Allied Commander-in-Chief, and none of these may now or at any time be evacuated to Germany.
4. Immediate transfer of the Italian Fleet and Italian aircraft to such points as may be designated by the Allied Commander-in-Chief, with details of disarmament to be prescribed by him.
5. Italian merchant shipping may be requisitioned by the Allied Commander-in-Chief to meet the needs of his military-naval program.
6. Immediate surrender of Corsica and of all Italian territory, both islands and mainland, to the Allies, for such use as operational bases and other purposes as the Allies may see fit.
7. Immediate guarantee of the free use by the Allies of all airfields and naval ports in Italian territory, regardless of the rate of evacuation of the Italian territory by the German forces. These ports and fields to be protected by Italian armed forces until this function is taken over by the Allies.

[7] Department of State *Bulletin*, Vol. XIII, p. 748. The Armistice terms were released for publication on November 6, 1945.

8. Immediate withdrawal to Italy of Italian armed forces from all participation in the current war from whatever areas in which they may now be engaged.

9. Guarantee by the Italian Government that if necessary it will employ all its available armed forces to insure prompt and exact compliance with all the provisions of this armistice.

10. The Commander-in-Chief of the Allied Forces reserves to himself the right to take any measure which in his opinion may be necessary for the protection of the interests of the Allied Forces for the prosecution of the war, and the Italian Government binds itself to take such administrative or other action as the Commander-in-Chief may require, and in particular the Commander-in-Chief will establish Allied Military Government over such parts of Italian territory as he may deem necessary in the military interests of the Allied Nations.

11. The Commander-in-Chief of the Allied Forces will have a full right to impose measures of disarmament, demobilization and demilitarization.

12. Other conditions of a political, economic and financial nature with which Italy will be bound to comply will be transmitted at later date.

The conditions of the present Armistice will not be made public without prior approval of the Allied Commander-in-Chief. The English will be considered the official text.

[*The Status of Italy*][8]

. . . The Governments of Great Britain, the United States, and the Soviet Union acknowledge the position of the Royal Italian Government as stated by Marshall Badoglio and accept the active cooperation of the Italian nation and armed forces as a co-belligerent in the war against Germany. The military events since September eighth and the brutal maltreatment by the Germans of the Italian population, culminating in the Italian declaration of war against Germany have in fact made Italy a co-belligerent and the American, British and Soviet Governments will continue to work with the Italian Government on that basis. The three Governments acknowledge the Italian Government's pledge to submit to the will of the Italian people after the Germans have been driven from Italy, and it is understood that nothing can detract from the absolute and untrammelled right of the people of Italy by constitutional means to decide on the democratic form of government they will eventually have.

The relationship of co-belligerency between the Government of Italy and the United Nations governments cannot of itself affect the terms recently signed, which retain their full force and can only be adjusted by agreement between the allied governments in the light of the assistance which the Italian Government may be able to afford to the United Nations' cause.

[8] Joint statement issued October 13, 1943. Ibid., Vol. IX, p. 254.

◇◇◇◇◇◇◇◇◇◇◇◇◇◇

7. THE MOSCOW DECLARATIONS [9]

[*Declaration on General Security*]

. . . THE GOVERNMENTS of the United States of America, the United Kingdom, the Soviet Union and China: united in their determination, in accordance with the Declaration by the United Nations of January 1, 1942, and subsequent declarations, to continue hostilities against those Axis powers with which they respectively are at war until such powers have laid down their arms on the basis of unconditional surrender; conscious of their responsibility to secure the liberation of themselves and the peoples allied with them from the menace of aggression; recognizing the necessity of ensuring a rapid and orderly transition from war to peace and of establishing and maintaining international peace and security with the least diversion of the world's human and economic resources for armaments; jointly declare:

1. That their united action, pledged for the prosecution of the war against their respective enemies, will be continued for the organization and maintenance of peace and security.
2. That those of them at war with a common enemy will act together in all matters relating to the surrender and disarmament of that enemy.
3. That they will take all measures deemed by them to be necessary to provide against any violation of the terms imposed upon the enemy.
4. That they recognize the necessity of establishing at the earliest practicable date a general international organization, based on the principle of the sovereign equality of all peace-loving states, and open to membership by all such states, large and small, for the maintenance of international peace and security.
5. That for the purpose of maintaining international peace and security pending the reestablishment of law and order and the inauguration of a system of general security, they will consult with one another and as occasion requires with other members of the United Nations with a view to joint action on behalf of the community of nations.
6. That after the termination of hostilities they will not employ their military forces within the territories of other states except for the purposes envisaged in this declaration and after joint consultation.
7. That they will confer and co-operate with one another and with other members of the United Nations to bring about a practicable general agreement with respect to the regulation of armaments in the post-war period.

---

[9] Anglo-Soviet-American statement of October 30, 1943; released November 1, 1943. Ibid., pp. 307–11. The declaration on security was signed by representatives of the United States, the United Kingdom, the Soviet Union, and China. The declarations regarding Italy, Austria, and German atrocities were signed by representatives of the first three nations, but not by China.

[*Declaration Regarding Italy*]

The Foreign Secretaries of the United States of America, the United Kingdom and the Soviet Union have established that their three Governments are in complete agreement that Allied policy towards Italy must be based upon the fundamental principle that Fascism and all its evil influences and emanations shall be utterly destroyed and that the Italian people shall be given every opportunity to establish governmental and other institutions based upon democratic principles.

The Foreign Secretaries of the United States of America and the United Kingdom declare that the action of their Governments from the inception of the invasion of Italian territory, in so far as paramount military requirements have permitted, has been based upon this policy.

In the furtherance of this policy in the future the Foreign Secretaries of the three Governments are agreed that the following measures are important and should be put into effect:

1. It is essential that the Italian Government should be made more democratic by the introduction of representatives of those sections of the Italian people who have always opposed Fascism.
2. Freedom of speech, of religious worship, of political belief, of the press and of public meeting shall be restored in full measure to the Italian people, who shall also be entitled to form anti-Fascist political groups.
3. All institutions and organizations created by the Fascist regime shall be suppressed.
4. All Fascist or pro-Fascist elements shall be removed from the administration and from the institutions and organizations of a public character.
5. All political prisoners of the Fascist regime shall be released and accorded a full amnesty.
6. Democratic organs of local government shall be created.
7. Fascist chiefs and other persons known or suspected to be war criminals shall be arrested and handed over to justice.

In making this declaration the three Foreign Secretaries recognize that so long as active military operations continue in Italy the time at which it is possible to give full effect to the principles set out above will be determined by the Commander-in-Chief on the basis of instructions received through the Combined Chiefs of Staff. The three Governments parties to this declaration will at the request of any one of them consult on this matter.

It is further understood that nothing in this resolution is to operate against the right of the Italian people ultimately to choose their own form of government.

[*Declaration Regarding Austria*]

The Governments of the United Kingdom, the Soviet Union and the United States of America are agreed that Austria, the first free country to fall a victim to Hitlerite aggression, shall be liberated from German domination.

They regard the annexation imposed upon Austria by Germany on March 15, 1938, as null and void. They consider themselves as in no way bound by any changes effected in Austria since that date. They declare that they wish to see reestablished a free and independent Austria, and thereby to open the way for the Austrian people themselves, as well as those neighboring states which will be faced with similar problems, to find that political and economic security which is the only basis for lasting peace.

Austria is reminded, however, that she has a responsibility which she cannot evade for participation in the war on the side of Hitlerite Germany, and that in the final settlement account will inevitably be taken of her own contribution to her liberation.

[*Declaration Regarding German Atrocities*]

The United Kingdom, the United States and the Soviet Union have received from many quarters evidence of atrocities, massacres and cold-blooded mass executions which are being perpetrated by the Hitlerite forces in the many countries they have overrun and from which they are now being steadily expelled. The brutalities of Hitlerite domination are no new thing and all the peoples or territories in their grip have suffered from the worst form of government by terror. What is new is that many of these territories are now being redeemed by the advancing armies of the liberating Powers and that in their desperation, the recoiling Hitlerite Huns are redoubling their ruthless cruelties. This is now evidenced with particular clearness by monstrous crimes of the Hitlerites on the territory of the Soviet Union which is being liberated from the Hitlerites, and on French and Italian territory.

Accordingly, the aforesaid three allied Powers, speaking in the interests of the thirty-two [*thirty-three*] United Nations, hereby solemnly declare and give full warning of their declaration as follows:

At the time of the granting of any armistice to any government which may be set up in Germany, those German officers and men and members of the Nazi party who have been responsible for, or have taken a consenting part in the above atrocities, massacres and executions, will be sent back to the countries in which their abominable deeds were done in order that they may be judged and punished according to the laws of these liberated countries and of the free governments which will be created therein. Lists will be compiled in all possible detail from all these countries having regard especially to the invaded parts of the Soviet Union, to Poland and Czechoslovakia, to Yugoslavia and Greece, including Crete and other islands, to Norway, Denmark, the Netherlands, Belgium, Luxemburg, France and Italy.

Thus, the Germans who take part in wholesale shootings of Italian officers or in the execution of French, Dutch, Belgian or Norwegian hostages or of Cretan peasants, or who have shared in the slaughters inflicted on the people of Poland or in territories of the Soviet Union which are now being swept clear of the enemy, will know that they will be brought back to the scene of their crimes and judged on the spot by the peoples whom they have outraged. Let those who have hitherto not imbrued their hands with innocent blood beware lest they join the ranks of the guilty, for most assuredly the three allied Powers will pursue them to the uttermost ends of the earth and will deliver them to their accusers in order that justice may be done.

The above declaration is without prejudice to the case of the major criminals, whose offenses have no particular geographical localization and who will be punished by the joint decision of the Governments of the Allies.

◇◇◇◇◇◇◇◇◇◇◇◇◇

8. THE CAIRO CONFERENCE[10]

. . . THE SEVERAL military missions have agreed upon future military operations against Japan. The Three Great Allies expressed their resolve to bring unrelenting pressure against their brutal enemies by sea, land, and air. This pressure is already rising.

The Three Great Allies are fighting this war to restrain and punish the aggression of Japan. They covet no gain for themselves and have no thought of territorial expansion. It is their purpose that Japan shall be stripped of all the islands in the Pacific which she has seized or occupied since the beginning of the first World War in 1914, and that all the territories Japan has stolen from the Chinese, such as Manchuria, Formosa, and the Pescadores, shall be restored to the Republic of China. Japan will also be expelled from all other territories which she has taken by violence and greed. The aforesaid three great powers, mindful of the enslavement of the people of Korea, are determined that in due course Korea shall become free and independent.

With these objects in view the three Allies, in harmony with those of the United Nations at war with Japan, will continue to persevere in the serious and prolonged operations necessary to procure the unconditional surrender of Japan.

---

[10] Statement issued by President Roosevelt, Generalissimo Chiang Kai-shek, and Prime Minister Churchill, following the Cairo Conference of November 22–26, 1943. Ibid., Vol. IX, p. 393.

◇◇◇◇◇◇◇◇◇◇◇◇◇

9. THE TEHERAN CONFERENCE[11]

WE — The President of the United States, the Prime Minister of Great Britain, and the Premier of the Soviet Union, have met these four days past, in this, the Capital of our Ally, Iran, and have shaped and confirmed our common policy.

We express our determination that our nations shall work together in war and in the peace that will follow.

As to war — our military staffs have joined in our round table discussions, and we have concerted our plans for the destruction of the German forces. We have reached complete agreement as to the scope and timing of the operations to be undertaken from the east, west and south.

The common understanding which we have here reached guarantees that victory will be ours.

And as to peace — we are sure that our concord will win an enduring Peace. We recognize fully the supreme responsibility resting upon us and all the United Nations to make a peace which will command the goodwill of the overwhelming mass of the peoples of the world and banish the scourge and terror of war for many generations.

With our Diplomatic advisors we have surveyed the problems of the future. We shall seek the cooperation and active participation of all nations, large and small, whose peoples in heart and mind are dedicated, as are our own peoples, to the elimination of tyranny and slavery, oppression and intolerance. We will welcome them, as they may choose to come, into a world family of Democratic Nations.

No power on earth can prevent our destroying the German armies by land, their U Boats by sea, and their war plants from the air.

Our attack will be relentless and increasing.

Emerging from these cordial conferences we look with confidence to the day when all peoples of the world may live free lives, untouched by tyranny, and according to their varying desires and their own consciences.

We came here with hope and determination. We leave here, friends in fact, in spirit and in purpose.

---

11 Statement issued by President Roosevelt, Marshal Stalin, and Prime Minister Churchill, December 1, 1943. *Bulletin,* Vol. IX, p. 409. In addition to military decisions referred to in this statement, the three leaders agreed that their governments desired the "maintenance of the independence, sovereignty and territorial integrity of Iran," and agreed also to support the partisans of Yugoslavia and to urge Turkey to enter the war on the allied side. The text of the military conclusions were not released by the United States until March 24, 1947.

10. THE [YALTA] CRIMEA CONFERENCE[12]

. . . WE HAVE considered and determined the military plans of the three allied powers for the final defeat of the common enemy. The military staffs of the three allied nations have met in daily meetings throughout the Conference. These meetings have been most satisfactory from every point of view and have resulted in closer coordination of the military effort of the three allies than ever before. The fullest information has been interchanged. The timing, scope and coordination of new and even more powerful blows to be launched by our armies and airforces into the heart of Germany from the East, West, North and South have been fully agreed and planned in detail.

Our combined military plans will be made known only as we execute them, but we believe that the very close working partnership among the three staffs attained at this Conference will result in shortening the War. Meetings of the three staffs will be continued in the future whenever the need arises.

Nazi Germany is doomed. The German people will only make the cost of their defeat heavier to themselves by attempting to continue a hopeless resistance.

The Occupation and Control of Germany

We have agreed on common policies and plans for enforcing the unconditional surrender terms which we shall impose together on Nazi Germany after German armed resistance has been finally crushed. These terms will not be made known until the final defeat of Germany has been accomplished. Under the agreed plan, the forces of the three powers will each occupy a separate zone of Germany. Coordinated administration and control has been provided for under the plan through a central control commission consisting of the Supreme Commanders of the three powers with headquarters in Berlin. It has been agreed that France should be invited by the three powers, if she should so desire, to take over a zone of occupation, and to participate as a fourth member of the control commission. The limits of the French zone will be agreed by the four governments concerned through their representatives on the European Advisory Commission.

It is our inflexible purpose to destroy German militarism and Nazism and to ensure that Germany will never again be able to disturb the peace of the world. We are determined to disarm and disband all German armed

---

12 Statement issued by President Roosevelt, Marshal Stalin, and Prime Minister Churchill, at the end of the conference, February 11, 1945. Ibid., Vol. XII, pp. 213–16. The full text of the Yalta Agreements was not released by the Department of State until March 24, 1947. See the *New York Times*, March 25, 1947. Since the Agreements were published piecemeal, it seems desirable to present the important ones here in the order of their publication.

forces; break up for all time the German General Staff that has repeatedly contrived the resurgence of German militarism; remove or destroy all German military equipment; eliminate or control all German industry that could be used for military production; bring all war criminals to just and swift punishment and exact reparation in kind for the destruction wrought by the Germans; wipe out the Nazi Party, Nazi laws, organizations and institutions, remove all Nazi and militarist influences from public office and from cultural and economic life of the German people; and take in harmony such other measures in Germany as may be necessary to the future peace and safety of the world. It is not our purpose to destroy the people of Germany, but only when Nazism and militarism have been extirpated will there be hope for a decent life for Germans, and a place for them in the comity of nations.

Reparation by Germany

We have considered the question of the damage caused by Germany to the allied nations in this war and recognized it as just that Germany be obliged to make compensation for this damage in kind to the greatest extent possible. A commission for the compensation of damage will be established. The commission will be instructed to consider the question of the extent and methods for compensating damage caused by Germany to the allied countries. The commission will work in Moscow.

United Nations Conference

We are resolved upon the earliest possible establishment with our allies of a general international organization to maintain peace and security. We believe that this is essential, both to prevent aggression and to remove the political, economic and social causes of war through the close and continuing collaboration of all peace-loving peoples.

The foundations were laid at Dumbarton Oaks. On the important question of voting procedure, however, agreement was not there reached. The present Conference has been able to resolve this difficulty.

We have agreed that a conference of United Nations should be called to meet at San Francisco in the United States on April 25, 1945, to prepare the charter of such an organization, along the lines proposed in the informal conversations at Dumbarton Oaks.

The Government of China and the Provisional Government of France will be immediately consulted and invited to sponsor invitations to the conference jointly with the Governments of the United States, Great Britain and the Union of Soviet Socialist Republics. As soon as the consultation with China and France has been completed, the text of the proposals on voting procedure will be made public.

Declaration on Liberated Europe

The Premier of the Union of Soviet Socialist Republics, the Prime Minister of the United Kingdom, and the President of the United States of America have consulted with each other in the common interests of the peoples of their countries and those of liberated Europe. They jointly declare their mutual agreement to concert during the temporary period of instability in liberated Europe the policies of their three governments in assisting the peoples liberated from the domination of Nazi Germany and the peoples of the former Axis satellite states of Europe to solve by democratic means their pressing political and economic problems.

The establishment of order in Europe and the rebuilding of national economic life must be achieved by processes which will enable the liberated peoples to destroy the last vestiges of Nazism and Fascism and to create democratic institutions of their own choice. This is a principle of the Atlantic Charter — the right of all peoples to choose the form of government under which they will live — the restoration of sovereign rights and self-government to those peoples who have been forcibly deprived of them by the aggressor nations.

To foster the conditions in which the liberated peoples may exercise these rights, the three governments will jointly assist the people in any European liberated state or former Axis satellite state in Europe where in their judgment conditions require (A) to establish conditions of internal peace; (B) to carry out emergency measures for the relief of distressed peoples; (C) to form interim governmental authorities broadly representative of all democratic elements in the population and pledged to the earliest possible establishment through free elections of governments responsive to the will of the people; and (D) to facilitate where necessary the holding of such elections.

The three governments will consult the other United Nations and provisional authorities or other governments in Europe when matters of direct interest to them are under consideration.

When, in the opinion of the three governments, conditions in any European liberated state or any former Axis satellite state in Europe make such action necessary, they will immediately consult together on the measures necessary to discharge the joint responsibilities set forth in this declaration.

By this declaration we reaffirm our faith in the principles of the Atlantic Charter, our pledge in the declaration by the United Nations, and our determination to build in cooperation with other peace-loving nations world order under law, dedicated to peace, security, freedom and general well-being of all mankind.

In issuing this declaration, the three powers express the hope that the Provisional Government of the French Republic may be associated with them in the procedure suggested.

Poland

A new situation has been created in Poland as a result of her complete liberation by the Red Army. This calls for the establishment of a Polish provisional government which can be more broadly based than was possible before the recent liberation of Western Poland. The provisional government which is now functioning in Poland should therefore be reorganized on a broader democratic basis with the inclusion of democratic leaders from Poland itself and from Poles abroad. This new government should then be called the Polish Provisional Government of National Unity.

M. Molotov, Mr. Harriman and Sir A. Clark Kerr are authorized as a commission to consult in the first instance in Moscow with members of the present provisional government and with other Polish democratic leaders from within Poland and from abroad, with a view to the reorganization of the present government along the above lines. This Polish Provisional Government of National Unity shall be pledged to the holding of free and unfettered elections as soon as possible on the basis of universal suffrage and secret ballot. In these elections all democratic and anti-Nazi parties shall have the right to take part and to put forward candidates.

When a Polish Provisional Government of National Unity has been properly formed in conformity with the above, the government of the U.S.S.R., which now maintains diplomatic relations with the present provisional government of Poland, and the government of the United Kingdom and the government of the U.S.A. will establish diplomatic relations with the new Polish Provisional Government of National Unity, and will exchange ambassadors by whose reports the respective governments will be kept informed about the situation in Poland.

The three heads of government consider that the Eastern frontier of Poland should follow the Curzon line with digressions from it in some regions of five to eight kilometres in favour of Poland. They recognize that Poland must receive substantial accessions of territory in the North and West. They feel that the opinion of the new Polish Provisional Government of National Unity should be sought in due course on the extent of these accessions and that the final delineation of the western frontier of Poland should thereafter await the peace conference.

Yugoslavia

We have agreed to recommend to Marshal Tito and Dr. Subasic that the agreement between them should be put into effect immediately, and that a new government should be formed on the basis of that agreement.

We also recommend that as soon as the new government has been formed it should declare that:

(1) The anti-Fascist assembly of National Liberation (Avnoj) should be extended to include members of the last Yugoslav Parliament (Skupschina) who have not compromised themselves by collaboration with

the enemy, thus forming a body to be known as a temporary Parliament; and,

(2) Legislative acts passed by the anti-Fascist Assembly of National Liberation will be subject to subsequent ratification by a constituent assembly.

There was also a general review of other Balkan questions.

Meetings of Foreign Secretaries

Throughout the Conference, besides the daily meetings of the heads of governments and the Foreign Secretaries, separate meetings of the three Foreign Secretaries, and their advisors have also been held daily.

These meetings have proved of the utmost value and the Conference agreed that permanent machinery should be set up for regular consultation between the three Foreign Secretaries. They will, therefore, meet as often as may be necessary, probably about every three or four months. These meetings will be held in rotation in the three capitals, the first meeting being held in London, after the United Nations Conference on World Organization.

Unity for Peace as for War

Our meeting here in the Crimea has reaffirmed our common determination to maintain and strengthen in the peace to come that unity of purpose and of action which has made victory possible and certain for the United Nations in this war. We believe that this is a sacred obligation which our Governments owe to our peoples and to all the peoples of the world.

Only with the continuing and growing cooperation and understanding among our three countries and among all the peace-loving nations can the highest aspiration of humanity be realized – a secure and lasting peace which will, in the words of the Atlantic Charter, "afford assurance that all the men in all the lands may live out their lives in freedom from fear and want."

Victory in this war and establishment of the proposed international organization will provide the greatest opportunity in all history to create in the years to come the essential conditions of such a peace.

Yalta Agreement on World Organization [13]

1. THAT a United Nations conference on the proposed world organization should be summoned for Wednesday, 25 April, 1945, and should be held in the United States of America.

2. The nations to be invited to this conference should be:

(a) The United Nations as they existed on 8 Feb., 1945; and

(b) Such of the Associated Nations as have declared war on the com-

[13] The substance of this agreement was made known before or during the San Francisco Conference.

mon enemy by 1 March, 1945. (For this purpose, by the term "Associated Nations" was meant the eight associated Nations and Turkey.) When the conference on world organization is held, the delegates of the United Kingdom and United States of America will support a proposal to admit to original membership two Soviet Socialist Republics, i.e. the Ukraine and White Russia.

3. That the United States Government, on behalf of the three powers, should consult the Government of China and the French Provisional Government in regard to decisions taken at the present conference concerning the proposed world organization. . . .

Voting

1. Each member of the Security Council should have one vote.
2. Decisions of the Security Council on procedural matters should be made by an affirmative vote of seven members.
3. Decisions of the Security Council on all matters should be made by an affirmative vote of seven members, including the concurring votes of the permanent members; provided that, in decisions under Chapter VIII, Section A and under the second sentence of Paragraph 1 of Chapter VIII, Section C, a party to a dispute should abstain from voting. . . .

Territorial Trusteeship

It was agreed that the five nations which will have permanent seats on the Security Council should consult each other prior to the United Nations conference on the question of territorial trusteeship.

The acceptance of this recommendation is subject to its being made clear that territorial trusteeship will only apply to (a) existing mandates of the League of Nations; (b) territories detached from the enemy as a result of the present war; (c) any other territory which might voluntarily be placed under trusteeship; and (d) no discussion of actual territories is contemplated at the forthcoming United Nations conference or in the preliminary consultations, and it will be a matter for subsequent agreement which territories within the above categories will be placed under trusteeship.

Secret Yalta Agreement on the Kuriles [14]

The leaders of the three Great Powers – the Soviet Union, the United States of America and Great Britain – have agreed that in two or three months after Germany has surrendered and the war in Europe has terminated the Soviet Union shall enter into the war against Japan on the side of the Allies on condition that:

[14] Signed by President Roosevelt, Prime Minister Churchill, and Generalissimo Stalin, at Yalta on February 11, 1945, but not made public until February 11, 1946. The agreement was regarded by its signers as primarily military and was kept secret in order to avoid, if possible, a Japanese attack on Russia while the war continued on the western front. Department of State *Bulletin,* Vol. XIV, pp. 282–3.

1. The status quo in Outer-Mongolia (The Mongolian People's Republic) shall be preserved;

2. The former rights of Russia violated by the treacherous attack of Japan in 1940 shall be restored, viz:

(a) the southern part of Sakhalin as well as all the islands adjacent to it shall be returned to the Soviet Union,

(b) the commercial port of Dairen shall be internationalized, the preeminent interests of the Soviet Union in this port being safeguarded and the lease of Port Arthur as a naval base of the USSR restored,

(c) the Chinese-Eastern Railroad and the South-Manchurian Railroad which provides an outlet to Dairen shall be jointly operated by the establishment of a joint Soviet-Chinese Company it being understood that the preeminent interests of the Soviet Union shall be safeguarded and that China shall retain full sovereignty in Manchuria;

3. The Kuril islands shall be handed over to the Soviet Union.

It is understood, that the agreement concerning Outer-Mongolia and the ports and railroads referred to above will require concurrence of Generalissimo Chiang Kai-shek. The President will take measures in order to obtain this concurrence on advice from Marshal Stalin.

The Heads of the three Great Powers have agreed that these claims of the Soviet Union shall be unquestionably fulfilled after Japan has been defeated.

For its part the Soviet Union expresses its readiness to conclude with the National Government of China a pact of friendship and alliance between the USSR and China in order to render assistance to China with its armed forces for the purpose of liberating China from the Japanese yoke.

Secret Yalta Agreement Concerning Germany [15]

Dismemberment of Germany

It was agreed that Article 12 (a) of the Surrender Terms for Germany should be amended to read as follows:

The United Kingdom, the United States of America and the Union of Soviet Socialist Republics shall possess supreme authority with respect to Germany. In the exercise of such authority they will take such steps, including the complete disarmament, demilitarization and dismemberment of Germany as they deem requisite for future peace and security.

The study of the procedure of the dismemberment of Germany was referred to a committee consisting of Mr. [Anthony] Eden [their Foreign Secretary] (chairman), Mr. [John] Winant [of the United States] and Mr. [Fedor T.] Gusev. This body would consider the desirability of associating with it a French representative.

---

[15] The sections on dismemberment and occupation were published March 25, 1947. The section on reparation was published March 19, 1947.

Zone of Occupation for the French and Control Council for Germany

It was agreed that a zone in Germany, to be occupied by the French forces, should be allocated to France. This zone would be formed out of the British and American zones and its extent would be settled by the British and Americans in consultation with the French Provisional Government.

It was also agreed that the French Provisional Government should be invited to become a member of the Allied Control Council for Germany.

Reparation

The following protocol has been approved:

Protocol on the Talks between the Heads of Three Governments at the Crimean Conference on the German Reparations in Kind

1. Germany must pay in kind for the losses caused by her to the Allied nations in the course of the war. Reparations are to be received in the first instance by those countries which have borne the main burden of the war, have suffered the heaviest losses and have organized victory over the enemy.

2. Reparation in kind is to be exacted from Germany in three following forms:

(a) Removals within two years from the surrender of Germany or the cessation of organized resistance from the national wealth of Germany located on the territory of Germany herself as well as outside her territory (equipment, machine tools, ships, rolling stock, German investments abroad, shares of industrial, transport and other enterprises in Germany, etc.), these removals to be carried out chiefly for purpose of destroying the war potential of Germany.

(b) Annual deliveries of goods from current production for a period to be fixed.

(c) Use of German labor.

3. For the working out on the above principles of a detailed plan for exaction of reparation from Germany an Allied reparation commission will be set up in Moscow. It will consist of three representatives – one from the Union of Soviet Socialist Republics, one from the United Kingdom and one from the United States of America.

4. With regard to the fixing of the total sum of the reparation as well as the distribution of it among the countries which suffered from the German aggression, the Soviet and American delegations agreed as follows:

The Moscow reparation commission should take in its initial studies as a basis for discussion the suggestion of the Soviet Government that the total sum of the reparation in accordance with the points (a) and (b) of Paragraph 2 should be 20 billion dollars and that 50 per cent of it should go to the Union of Soviet Socialist Republics.

The British delegation was of the opinion that, pending consideration of the reparation question by the Moscow reparation commission, no figures of reparation should be mentioned.

The above Soviet-American proposal has been passed to the Moscow reparation commission as one of the proposals to be considered by the commission.

◇◇◇◇◇◇◇◇◇◇◇◇◇

11. THE POTSDAM DECLARATION [16]

(1) WE – the President of the United States, the President of the National Government of the Republic of China, and the Prime Minister of Great Britain, representing the hundreds of millions of our countrymen, have conferred and agree that Japan shall be given an opportunity to end this war.

(2) The prodigious land, sea and air forces of the United States, the British Empire and of China, many times reinforced by their armies and air fleets from the west, are poised to strike the final blows upon Japan. This military power is sustained and inspired by the determination of all the Allied Nations to prosecute the war against Japan until she ceases to resist.

(3) The result of the futile and senseless German resistance to the might of the aroused free peoples of the world stands forth in awful clarity as an example to the people of Japan. The might that now converges on Japan is immeasurably greater than that which, when applied to the resisting Nazis, necessarily laid waste to the lands, the industry and the method of life of the whole German people. The full application of our military power, backed by our resolve, *will* mean the inevitable and complete destruction of the Japanese armed forces and just as inevitably the utter devastation of the Japanese homeland.

(4) The time has come for Japan to decide whether she will continue to be controlled by those self-willed militaristic advisers whose unintelligent calculations have brought the Empire of Japan to the threshold of annihilation, or whether she will follow the path of reason.

(5) Following are our terms. We will not deviate from them. There are no alternatives. We shall brook no delay.

(6) There must be eliminated for all time the authority and influence of those who have deceived and misled the people of Japan into embarking on world conquest, for we insist that a new order of peace, security and justice will be impossible until irresponsible militarism is driven from the world.

(7) Until such a new order is established *and* until there is convincing

[16] Proclamation signed on July 26, 1945, at Potsdam by President Truman and Prime Minister Churchill, and concurred in by Generalissimo Chiang Kai-shek. Department of State *Bulletin,* Vol. XII, pp. 137–8.

proof that Japan's war-making power is destroyed, points in Japanese territory to be designated by the Allies shall be occupied to secure the achievement of the basic objectives we are here setting forth.

(8) The terms of the Cairo Declaration shall be carried out and Japanese sovereignty shall be limited to the islands of Honshu, Hokkaido, Kyushu, Shikoku and such minor islands as we determine.

(9) The Japanese military forces, after being completely disarmed, shall be permitted to return to their homes with the opportunity to lead peaceful and productive lives.

(10) We do not intend that the Japanese shall be enslaved as a race or destroyed as a nation, but stern justice shall be meted out to all war criminals, including those who have visited cruelties upon our prisoners. The Japanese Government shall remove all obstacles to the revival and strengthening of democratic tendencies among the Japanese people. Freedom of speech, of religion, and of thought, as well as respect for the fundamental human rights shall be established.

(11) Japan shall be permitted to maintain such industries as will sustain her economy and permit the exaction of just reparations in kind, but not those which would enable her to re-arm for war. To this end, access to, as distinguished from control of, raw materials shall be permitted. Eventual Japanese participation in world trade relations shall be permitted.

(12) The occupying forces of the Allies shall be withdrawn from Japan as soon as these objectives have been accomplished and there has been established in accordance with the freely expressed will of the Japanese people a peacefully inclined and responsible government.

(13) We call upon the government of Japan to proclaim now the unconditional surrender of all Japanese armed forces, and to provide proper and adequate assurances of their good faith in such action. The alternative for Japan is prompt and utter destruction.

CHAPTER XXXV

THE UNITED NATIONS

◇◇◇◇◇◇◇◇◇◇◇◇◇

IN THE Atlantic Charter of August 14, 1941, President Roosevelt and Prime Minister Churchill pledged themselves, and as far as they could, committed their countries to the establishment of a "permanent system of general security." The fourth point of the Joint Four-Nation Declaration of the Moscow Conference of October 1943, contained a similar promise. Advocates of such a policy in the United States endeavored to organize public opinion back of the idea and particularly to prevent the subject from becoming an issue of political partisanship. Resolutions sponsored by Congressman J. William Fulbright in the House of Representatives (1), and by Senator Tom Connally in the Senate (2), were passed by large bipartisan majorities, and appeared to insure the support of the United States for a new league of nations more powerful than the old League.

In May 1944 the United States invited Britain, Russia, and China to meet in Washington to prepare the ground work for the new international organization. This meeting, the Dumbarton Oaks Conference, was held August 21 to October 7, 1944, and drafted proposals which became the framework of the United Nations Charter, signed at San Francisco on June 26, 1945 (3).

The Senate gave its advice and consent to the ratification of the Charter almost without dissent. There was, it appeared, little ground on which dissent could rest. In a statement before the Committee of Foreign Relations of the Senate, John Foster Dulles, one of the chief official advisers to the United States delegation at the San Francisco Conference said this:

> Actually, the document before you charts a path which we can pursue joyfully and without fear. Under it we remain the masters of our own destiny. The Charter does not subordinate us to any supergovernment. There is no right on the part of the United Nations Organization to intervene in our domestic affairs. There can be no use of force without our consent. If the joint adventure fails, we can withdraw.

Obviously, if the Charter was powerless as against the United States it was equally powerless as against any other great power. Many people believed, therefore, that the Charter fell short of the promises for an international organization that could prevent aggression. The answer of the Department of State to this criticism was tacitly to admit that the Charter, unlike the Covenant, did not attempt to establish a security system, but relied, for world peace, upon the moral sanction of public opinion and the sense of responsibility along with the exercise of self restraint of the great powers (4).

Under the Charter all members of the United Nations became *ipso facto* parties to the Statute of the International Court of Justice. The Statute contained, however, a so-called optional clause which member states could accept or reject. The Senate accepted, with certain reservations, the compulsory jurisdiction of the Court as provided for in the clause (5).

The Charter was signed before the world at large knew about the powerful new weapon of destruction about to be used for the first time against Japan. Almost as soon, however, as the American people recovered from the first shock resulting from the knowledge of the atomic weapon, greater dissatisfaction arose with the impotence of the existing security system. The government responded to this sentiment and presented to the Atomic Energy Commission created by the General Assembly of the United Nations on January 24, 1946, a proposal for the control of atomic energy that indicated a basic change of theory from that underlying the Charter (6).

The American proposals were considered by the Atomic Energy Commission along with proposals submitted by Russia and suggestions advanced by other nations. The First Report of the Commission to the Security Council, December 31, 1946, approved, in the main, the American ideas but Russia and Poland abstained from agreeing to the Report. The contrast between the American and the Russian views was sharply drawn in a statement made to the Security Council by the Russian delegate Andrei A. Gromyko (7). Russia desired to outlaw the atomic bomb *before* measures were devised for the control of atomic energy, while the United States insisted upon security against the misuse of atomic energy before giving up its possession of atomic bombs. Russia desired also to place controls of atomic energy under the Security Council where the "big-power" veto obtained and to subject decisions regarding sanctions against a violator of control regulations to the same authority. The United States advocated the establishment of a separate authority under the United Nations in which the veto would not exist.

The basic agreements concerning postwar reconstruction on the part of the United States, the British Empire, and Russia, were reached at the Crimea Conference of February 4–11, 1945. The Berlin Conference of July 17–August 2, 1945 (8), effected means for accomplishing some of the aims agreed upon at the Crimea Conference, and established a Council of Foreign Ministers, of the five principal powers, to continue the preparatory work for the final peace settlement.

The Council of Foreign Ministers met at Moscow, December 6–26, 1945, at Paris, April 25–May 16, 1946, and at the same place June 15–July 12, 1946. A general peace conference of 21 nations assembled at Paris on July 29, 1946, where progress was made toward peace settlements, completed later, with Italy and the Axis satellite states. At these various conferences a cleavage developed between Russia and the western democracies, and the division was noted also in discussions in the Security Council, in the Atomic Energy Commission, and in events in central Europe, Korea, and China. The beginnings of a shift in American policy toward Germany, which reflected the growing rift between the United States and Russia, was shown in the Stuttgart address of Secretary Byrnes of September 6, 1946 (9). The fundamental principles of American foreign policy were stated by President Truman on October 27, 1945 (10).

◇◇◇◇◇◇◇◇◇◇◇◇

1. THE FULBRIGHT RESOLUTION [1]

RESOLVED by the House of Representatives (*the Senate concurring*), That the Congress hereby expresses itself as favoring the creation of appropriate international machinery with power adequate to establish and to maintain a just and lasting peace, among the nations of the world, and as favoring participation by the United States therein through its constitutional processes.

◇◇◇◇◇◇◇◇◇◇◇◇

2. THE CONNALLY RESOLUTION [2]

RESOLVED, That the war against all our enemies be waged until complete victory is achieved.

That the United States cooperate with its comrades-in-arms in securing a just and honorable peace.

That the United States, acting through its constitutional processes, join with free and sovereign nations in the establishment and maintenance of international authority with power to prevent aggression and to preserve the peace of the world.

---

1 House Concurrent Resolution No. 25, 78th Congress, 1st Session; sponsored by Congressman J. William Fulbright of Arkansas; passed by the House Sept. 21, 1943. *Cong. Record*, Vol. 89, p. 7729.

2 Senate Resolution No. 192, as amended, 78th Congress, 1st Session, Vol. 89, p. 9222, November 5, 1943.

That the Senate recognizes the necessity of there being established at the earliest practicable date a general international organization, based on the principle of the sovereign equality of all peace-loving states, and open to membership by all such states, large and small, for the maintenance of international peace and security.

That, pursuant to the Constitution of the United States, any treaty made to effect the purposes of this resolution, on behalf of the Government of the United States with any other nation or any association of nations, shall be made only by and with the advice and consent of the Senate of the United States, provided two-thirds of the Senators present concur.

◇◇◇◇◇◇◇◇◇◇◇◇

3. CHARTER OF THE UNITED NATIONS [3]

WE THE PEOPLES of the United Nations, determined to save succeeding generations from the scourge of war, which twice in our life-time has brought untold sorrow to mankind, and to reaffirm faith in fundamental human rights, in the dignity and worth of the human person, in the equal rights of men and women and of nations large and small, and to establish conditions under which justice and respect for the obligations arising from treaties and other sources of international law can be maintained, and to promote social progress and better standards of life in larger freedom, and for these ends to practice tolerance and live together in peace with one another as good neighbors, and to unite our strength to maintain international peace and security, and to ensure, by the acceptance of principles and the institution of methods, that armed force shall not be used, save in the common interest, and to employ international machinery for the promotion of the economic and social advancement of all peoples, have resolved to combine our efforts to accomplish these aims.

Accordingly, our respective Governments, through representatives assembled in the city of San Francisco, who have exhibited their full powers found to be in good and due form, have agreed to the present Charter of the United Nations and do hereby establish an international organization to be known as the United Nations.

Chapter I. *Purposes and Principles*

ARTICLE 1. The Purposes of the United Nations are:

1. To maintain international peace and security, and to that end: to take effective collective measures for the prevention and removal of threats to the peace, and for the suppression of acts of aggression or other breaches of the peace, and to bring about by peaceful means, and in conformity with the principles of justice and international law, adjustment

[3] Signed at San Francisco, June 26, 1945; ratification advised by the United States Senate, July 28, 1945. *Department of State,* Publication No. 2368, Conference Series 76.

or settlement of international disputes or situations which might lead to a breach of the peace;

2. To develop friendly relations among nations based on respect for the principle of equal rights and self-determination of peoples, and to take other appropriate measures to strengthen universal peace;

3. To achieve international cooperation in solving international problems of an economic, social, cultural, or humanitarian character, and in promoting and encouraging respect for human rights and for fundamental freedoms for all without distinction as to race, sex, language, or religion; and

4. To be a center for harmonizing the actions of nations in the attainment of these common ends.

Article 2. The Organization and its Members, in pursuit of the Purposes stated in Article 1, shall act in accordance with the following Principles.

1. The Organization is based on the principle of the sovereign equality of all its Members.

2. All Members, in order to ensure to all of them the rights and benefits resulting from membership, shall fulfil in good faith the obligations assumed by them in accordance with the present Charter.

3. All Members shall settle their international disputes by peaceful means in such a manner that international peace and security, and justice, are not endangered.

4. All Members shall refrain in their international relations from the threat or use of force against the territorial integrity or political independence of any state, or in any other manner inconsistent with the Purposes of the United Nations.

5. All Members shall give the United Nations every assistance in any action it takes in accordance with the present Charter, and shall refrain from giving assistance to any state against which the United Nations is taking preventive or enforcement action.

6. The Organization shall ensure that states which are not Members of the United Nations act in accordance with these Principles so far as may be necessary for the maintenance of international peace and security.

7. Nothing contained in the present Charter shall authorize the United Nations to intervene in matters which are essentially within the domestic jurisdiction of any state or shall require the Members to submit such matters to settlement under the present Charter; but this principle shall not prejudice the application of enforcement measures under Chapter VII.

CHAPTER II. *Membership*

Article 3. The original Members of the United Nations shall be the states which, having participated in the United Nations Conference on International Organization at San Francisco, or having previously signed the Declaration by United Nations of January 1, 1942, sign the present Charter and ratify it in accordance with Article 110.

Article 4. 1. Membership in the United Nations is open to all other peace-loving states which accept the obligations contained in the present

Charter and, in the judgment of the Organization, are able and willing to carry out these obligations.

2. The admission of any such state to membership in the United Nations will be effected by a decision of the General Assembly upon the recommendation of the Security Council.

Article 5. A Member of the United Nations against which preventive or enforcement action has been taken by the Security Council may be suspended from the exercise of the rights and privileges of membership by the General Assembly upon the recommendation of the Security Council. The exercise of these rights and privileges may be restored by the Security Council.

Article 6. A Member of the United Nations which has persistently violated the Principles contained in the present Charter may be expelled from the Organization by the General Assembly upon the recommendation of the Security Council.

CHAPTER III. *Organs*

Article 7. 1. There are established as the principal organs of the United Nations: a General Assembly, a Security Council, an Economic and Social Council, a Trusteeship Council, an International Court of Justice, and a Secretariat.

2. Such subsidiary organs as may be found necessary may be established in accordance with the present Charter.

Article 8. The United Nations shall place no restrictions on the eligibility of men and women to participate in any capacity and under conditions of equality in its principal and subsidiary organs.

CHAPTER IV. *The General Assembly*

COMPOSITION

Article 9. 1. The General Assembly shall consist of all the Members of the United Nations.

2. Each Member shall have not more than five representatives in the General Assembly.

FUNCTIONS AND POWERS

Article 10. The General Assembly may discuss any questions or any matters within the scope of the present Charter or relating to the powers and functions of any organs provided for in the present Charter, and, except as provided in Article 12, may make recommendations to the Members of the United Nations or to the Security Council or to both on any such questions or matters.

Article 11. 1. The General Assembly may consider the general principles of cooperation in the maintenance of international peace and security, including the principles governing disarmament and the regulation of armaments, and may make recommendations with regard to such principles to the Members or to the Security Council or to both.

2. The General Assembly may discuss any questions relating to the maintenance of international peace and security brought before it by any Member of the United Nations, or by the Security Council, or by a

state which is not a Member of the United Nations in accordance with Article 35, paragraph 2, and, except as provided in Article 12, may make recommendations with regard to any such questions to the state or states concerned or to the Security Council or to both. Any such question on which action is necessary shall be referred to the Security Council by the General Assembly either before or after discussion.

3. The General Assembly may call the attention of the Security Council to situations which are likely to endanger international peace and security.

4. The powers of the General Assembly set forth in this Article shall not limit the general scope of Article 10.

Article 12. 1. While the Security Council is exercising in respect of any dispute or situation the functions assigned to it in the present Charter, the General Assembly shall not make any recommendation with regard to that dispute or situation unless the Security Council so requests.

2. The Secretary-General, with the consent of the Security Council, shall notify the General Assembly at each session of any matters relative to the maintenance of international peace and security which are being dealt with by the Security Council and shall similarly notify the General Assembly, or the Members of the United Nations if the General Assembly is not in session, immediately the Security Council ceases to deal with such matters.

Article 13. 1. The General Assembly shall initiate studies and make recommendations for the purpose of:

a. promoting international cooperation in the political field and encouraging the progressive development of international law and its codification;

b. promoting international cooperation in the economic, social, cultural, educational, and health fields, and assisting in the realization of human rights and fundamental freedoms for all without distinction as to race, sex, language, or religion.

2. The further responsibilities, functions, and powers of the General Assembly with respect to matters mentioned in paragraph 1 (b) above are set forth in Chapters IX and X.

Article 14. Subject to the provisions of Article 12, the General Assembly may recommend measures for the peaceful adjustment of any situation, regardless of origin, which it deems likely to impair the general welfare or friendly relations among nations, including situations resulting from a violation of the provisions of the present Charter setting forth the Purposes and Principles of the United Nations.

Article 15. 1. The General Assembly shall receive and consider annual and special reports from the Security Council; these reports shall include an account of the measures that the Security Council has decided upon or taken to maintain international peace and security.

2. The General Assembly shall receive and consider reports from the other organs of the United Nations.

Article 16. The General Assembly shall perform such functions with respect to the international trusteeship system as are assigned to it under Chapters XII and XIII, including the approval of the trusteeship agreements for areas not designated as strategic.

Article 17. 1. The General Assembly shall consider and approve the budget of the Organization.

2. The expenses of the Organization shall be borne by the Members as apportioned by the General Assembly.

3. The General Assembly shall consider and approve any financial and budgetary arrangements with specialized agencies referred to in Article 57 and shall examine the administrative budgets of such specialized agencies with a view to making recommendations to the agencies concerned.

Voting

Article 18. 1. Each member of the General Assembly shall have one vote.

2. Decisions of the General Assembly on important questions shall be made by a two-thirds majority of the members present and voting. These questions shall include: recommendations with respect to the maintenance of international peace and security, the election of the non-permanent members of the Security Council, the election of the members of the Economic and Social Council, the election of members of the Trusteeship Council in accordance with paragraph 1(c) of Article 86, the admission of new Members to the United Nations, the suspension of the rights and privileges of membership, the expulsion of Members, questions relating to the operation of the trusteeship system, and budgetary questions.

3. Decisions on other questions, including the determination, of additional categories of questions to be decided by a two-thirds majority, shall be made by a majority of the members present and voting.

Article 19. A Member of the United Nations which is in arrears in the payment of its financial contributions to the Organization shall have no vote in the General Assembly if the amount of its arrears equals or exceeds the amount of the contributions due from it for the preceding two full years. The General Assembly may, nevertheless, permit such a Member to vote if it is satisfied that the failure to pay is due to conditions beyond the control of the Member.

Procedure

Article 20. The General Assembly shall meet in regular annual sessions and in such special sessions as occasion may require. Special sessions shall be convoked by the Secretary-General at the request of the Security Council or of a majority of the Members of the United Nations.

Article 21. The General Assembly shall adopt its own rules of procedure. It shall elect its President for each session.

Article 22. The General Assembly may establish such subsidiary organs as it deems necessary for the performance of its functions.

Chapter V. *The Security Council*

Composition

Article 23. 1. The Security Council shall consist of eleven Members of the United Nations. The Republic of China, France, the Union of Soviet

Socialist Republics, the United Kingdom of Great Britain and Northern Ireland, and the United States of America shall be permanent members of the Security Council. The General Assembly shall elect six other Members of the United Nations to be non-permanent members of the Security Council, due regard being specially paid, in the first instance to the contribution of Members of the United Nations to the maintenance of international peace and security and to the other purposes of the Organization, and also to equitable geographical distribution.

2. The non-permanent members of the Security Council shall be elected for a term of two years. In the first election of the non-permanent members, however, three shall be chosen for a term of one year. A retiring member shall not be eligible for immediate re-election.

3. Each member of the Security Council shall have one representative.

Functions and Powers

Article 24. 1. In order to ensure prompt and effective action by the United Nations, its Members confer on the Security Council primary responsibility for the maintenance of international peace and security, and agree that in carrying out its duties under this responsibility the Security Council acts on their behalf.

2. In discharging these duties the Security Council shall act in accordance with the Purposes and Principles of the United Nations. The specific powers granted to the Security Council for the discharge of these duties are laid down in Chapters VI, VII, VIII, and XII.

3. The Security Council shall submit annual and, when necessary, special reports to the General Assembly for its consideration.

Article 25. The Members of the United Nations agree to accept and carry out the decisions of the Security Council in accordance with the present Charter.

Article 26. In order to promote the establishment and maintenance of international peace and security with the least diversion for armaments of the world's human and economic resources, the Security Council shall be responsible for formulating, with the assistance of the Military Staff Committee referred to in Article 47, plans to be submitted to the Members of the United Nations for the establishment of a system for the regulation of armaments.

Voting

Article 27. 1. Each member of the Security Council shall have one vote.

2. Decisions of the Security Council on procedural matters shall be made by an affirmative vote of seven members.

3. Decisions of the Security Council on all other matters shall be made by an affirmative vote of seven members including the concurring votes of the permanent members; provided that, in decisions under Chapter VI, and under paragraph 3 of Article 52, a party to a dispute shall abstain from voting.

Procedure

Article 28. 1. The Security Council shall be so organized as to be able to function continuously. Each member of the Security Council shall for this purpose be represented at all times at the seat of the Organization.

2. The Security Council shall hold periodic meetings at which each of its members may, if it so desires, be represented by a member of the government or by some other specially designated representative.

3. The Security Council may hold meetings at such places other than the seat of the Organization as in its judgment will best facilitate its work.

Article 29. The Security Council may establish such subsidiary organs as it deems necessary for the performance of its functions.

Article 30. The Security Council shall adopt its own rules of procedure, including the method of selecting its President.

Article 31. Any Member of the United Nations which is not a member of the Security Council may participate, without vote, in the discussion of any question brought before the Security Council whenever the latter considers that the interests of that Member are specially affected.

Article 32. Any Member of the United Nations which is not a member of the Security Council or any state which is not a Member of the United Nations, if it is a party to a dispute under consideration by the Security Council, shall be invited to participate, without vote, in the discussion relating to the dispute. The Security Council shall lay down such conditions as it deems just for the participation of a state which is not a Member of the United Nations.

Chapter VI. *Pacific Settlement of Disputes*

Article 33. 1. The parties to any dispute, the continuance of which is likely to endanger the maintenance of international peace and security, shall, first of all, seek a solution by negotiation, enquiry, mediation, conciliation, arbitration, judicial settlement, resort to regional agencies or arrangements, or other peaceful means of their own choice.

2. The Security Council shall, when it deems necessary, call upon the parties to settle their dispute by such means.

Article 34. The Security Council may investigate any dispute, or any situation which might lead to international friction or give rise to a dispute, in order to determine whether the continuance of the dispute or situation is likely to endanger the maintenance of international peace and security.

Article 35. 1. Any Member of the United Nations may bring any dispute, or any situation of the nature referred to in Article 34, to the attention of the Security Council or of the General Assembly.

2. A state which is not a Member of the United Nations may bring to the attention of the Security Council or of the General Assembly any dispute to which it is a party if it accepts in advance, for the purposes of the dispute, the obligations of pacific settlement provided in the present Charter.

3. The proceedings of the General Assembly in respect of matters

brought to its attention under this Article will be subject to the provisions of Articles 11 and 12.

Article 36. 1. The Security Council may, at any stage of a dispute of the nature referred to in Article 33 or of a situation of like nature, recommend appropriate procedures or methods of adjustment.

2. The Security Council should take into consideration any procedures for the settlement of the dispute which have already been adopted by the parties.

3. In making recommendations under this Article the Security Council should also take into consideration that legal disputes should as a general rule be referred by the parties to the International Court of Justice in accordance with the provisions of the Statute of the Court.

Article 37. 1. Should the parties to a dispute of the nature referred to in Article 33 fail to settle it by the means indicated in that Article, they shall refer it to the Security Council.

2. If the Security Council deems that the continuance of the dispute is in fact likely to endanger the maintenance of international peace and security, it shall decide whether to take action under Article 36 or to recommend such terms of settlement as it may consider appropriate.

Article 38. Without prejudice to the provisions of Articles 33 to 37, the Security Council may, if all the parties to any dispute so request, make recommendations to the parties with a view to a pacific settlement of the dispute.

CHAPTER VII. *Action with Respect to Threats to the Peace, Breaches of the Peace, and Acts of Aggression*

Article 39. The Security Council shall determine the existence of any threat to the peace, breach of the peace, or act of aggression and shall make recommendations, or decide what measures shall be taken in accordance with Articles 41 and 42, to maintain or restore international peace and security.

Article 40. In order to prevent an aggravation of the situation, the Security Council may, before making the recommendations or deciding upon the measures provided for in Article 39, call upon the parties concerned to comply with such provisional measures as it deems necessary or desirable. Such provisional measures shall be without prejudice to the rights, claims, or position of the parties concerned. The Security Council shall duly take account of failure to comply with such provisional measures.

Article 41. The Security Council may decide what measures not involving the use of armed force are to be employed to give effect to its decisions, and it may call upon the Members of the United Nations to apply such measures. These may include complete or partial interruption of economic relations and of rail, sea, air, postal, telegraphic, radio, and other means of communication, and the severance of diplomatic relations.

Article 42. Should the Security Council consider that measures provided for in Article 41 would be inadequate or have proved to be inadequate, it may take such action by air, sea, or land forces as may be necessary to maintain or restore international peace and security. Such action may include demonstrations, blockade, and other operations by air, sea, or land forces of Members of the United Nations.

Article 43. 1. All Members of the United Nations, in order to contribute to the maintenance of international peace and security, undertake to make available to the Security Council, on its call and in accordance with a special agreement or agreements, armed forces, assistance, and facilities, including rights of passage, necessary for the purpose of maintaining international peace and security.

2. Such agreement or agreements shall govern the numbers and types of forces, their degree of readiness and general location, and the nature of the facilities and assistance to be provided.

3. The agreement or agreements shall be negotiated as soon as possible on the initiative of the Security Council. They shall be concluded between the Security Council and Members or between the Security Council and groups of Members and shall be subject to ratification by the signatory states in accordance with their respective constitutional processes.

Article 44. When the Security Council has decided to use force it shall, before calling upon a Member not represented on it to provide armed forces in fulfillment of the obligations assumed under Article 43, invite that Member, if the Member so desires, to participate in the decisions of the Security Council concerning the employment of contingents of that Member's armed forces.

Article 45. In order to enable the United Nations to take urgent military measures, Members shall hold immediately available national air-force contingents for combined international enforcement action. The strength and degree of readiness of these contingents and plans for their combined action shall be determined, within the limits laid down in the special agreement or agreements referred to in Article 43, by the Security Council with the assistance of the Military Staff Committee.

Article 46. Plans for the application of armed force shall be made by the Security Council with the assistance of the Military Staff Committee.

Article 47. 1. There shall be established a Military Staff Committee to advise and assist the Security Council on all questions relating to the Security Council's military requirements for the maintenance of international peace and security, the employment and command of forces placed at its disposal, the regulation of armaments, and possible disarmament.

2. The Military Staff Committee shall consist of the Chiefs of Staff of the permanent members of the Security Council or their representatives. Any Member of the United Nations not permanently represented on the Committee shall be invited by the Committee to be associated with it when the efficient discharge of the Committee's responsibilities requires the participation of that Member in its work.

3. The Military Staff Committee shall be responsible under the Security Council for the strategic direction of any armed forces placed at

the disposal of the Security Council. Questions relating to the command of such forces shall be worked out subsequently.

4. The Military Staff Committee, with the authorization of the Security Council and after consultation with appropriate regional agencies, may establish regional subcommittees.

Article 48. 1. The action required to carry out the decisions of the Security Council for the maintenance of international peace and security shall be taken by all the Members of the United Nations or by some of them, as the Security Council may determine.

2. Such decisions shall be carried out by the Members of the United Nations directly and through their action in the appropriate international agencies of which they are members.

Article 49. The Members of the United Nations shall join in affording mutual assistance in carrying out the measures decided upon by the Security Council.

Article 50. If preventive or enforcement measures against any state are taken by the Security Council, any other state, whether a Member of the United Nations or not, which finds itself confronted with special economic problems arising from the carrying out of those measures shall have the right to consult the Security Council with regard to a solution of those problems.

Article 51. Nothing in the present Charter shall impair the inherent right of individual or collective self-defense if an armed attack occurs against a member of the United Nations, until the Security Council has taken the measures necessary to maintain international peace and security. Measures taken by Members in the exercise of this right of self-defense shall be immediately reported to the Security Council and shall not in any way affect the authority and responsibility of the Security Council under the present Charter to take at any time such action as it deems necessary in order to maintain or restore international peace and security.

Chapter VIII. *Regional Arrangements*

Article 52. 1. Nothing in the present Charter precludes the existence of regional arrangements or agencies for dealing with such matters relating to the maintenance of international peace and security as are appropriate for regional action, provided that such arrangements or agencies and their activities are consistent with the Purposes and Principles of the United Nations.

2. The Members of the United Nations entering into such arrangements or constituting such agencies shall make every effort to achieve pacific settlement of local disputes through such regional arrangements or by such regional agencies before referring them to the Security Council.

3. The Security Council shall encourage the development of pacific settlement of local disputes through such regional arrangements or by such regional agencies either on the initiative of the states concerned or by reference from the Security Council.

4. This Article in no way impairs the application of Articles 34 and 35.

Article 53. 1. The Security Council shall, where appropriate, utilize such regional arrangements or agencies for enforcement action under its authority. But no enforcement action shall be taken under regional arrangements or by regional agencies without the authorization of the Security Council, with the exception of measures against any enemy state, as defined in paragraph 2 of this Article, provided for pursuant to Article 107 or in regional arrangements directed against renewal of aggressive policy on the part of any such state, until such time as the Organization may, on request of the Governments concerned, be charged with the responsibility for preventing further aggression by such a state.

2. The term enemy state as used in paragraph 1 of this Article applies to any state which during the Second World War has been an enemy of any signatory of the present Charter.

Article 54. The Security Council shall at all times be kept fully informed of activities undertaken or in contemplation under regional arrangements or by regional agencies for the maintenance of international peace and security.

CHAPTER IX. *International Economic and Social Cooperation*

Article 55. With a view to the creation of conditions of stability and well-being which are necessary for peaceful and friendly relations among nations based on respect for the principle of equal rights and self-determination of peoples, the United Nations shall promote:

a. higher standards of living, full employment, and conditions of economic and social progress and development;

b. solutions of international economic, social, health, and related problems; and international cultural and educational cooperation; and

c. universal respect for, and observance of, human rights and fundamental freedoms for all without distinction as to race, sex, language, or religion.

Article 56. All Members pledge themselves to take joint and separate action in cooperation with the Organization for the achievement of the purposes set forth in Article 55.

Article 57. 1. The various specialized agencies, established by intergovernmental agreement and having wide international responsibilities, as defined in their basic instruments, in economic, social, cultural, educational, health, and related fields, shall be brought into relationship with the United Nations in accordance with the provisions of Article 63.

2. Such agencies thus brought into relationship with the United Nations are hereinafter referred to as specialized agencies.

Article 58. The Organization shall make recommendations for the coordination of the policies and activities of the specialized agencies.

Article 59. The Organization shall, where appropriate, initiate negotiations among the states concerned for the creation of any new specialized agencies required for the accomplishment of the purposes set forth in Article 55.

Article 60. Responsibility for the discharge of the functions of the Organization set forth in this Chapter shall be vested in the General Assembly and, under the authority of the General Assembly, in the Economic and Social Council, which shall have for this purpose the powers set forth in Chapter X.

CHAPTER X. *The Economic and Social Council*

COMPOSITION

Article 61. 1. The Economic and Social Council shall consist of eighteen Members of the United Nations elected by the General Assembly.

2. Subject to the provisions of paragraph 3, six members of the Economic and Social Council shall be elected each year for a term of three years. A retiring member shall be eligible for immediate re-election.

3. At the first election, eighteen members of the Economic and Social Council shall be chosen. The terms of office of six members so chosen shall expire at the end of one year, and of six other members at the end of two years, in accordance with arrangements made by the General Assembly.

4. Each member of the Economic and Social Council shall have one representative.

FUNCTIONS AND POWERS

Article 62. 1. The Economic and Social Council may make or initiate studies and reports with respect to international economic, social, cultural, educational, health, and related matters and may make recommendations with respect to any such matters to the General Assembly, to the Members of the United Nations, and to the specialized agencies concerned.

2. It may make recommendations for the purpose of promoting respect for, and observance of, human rights and fundamental freedoms for all.

3. It may prepare draft conventions for submission to the General Assembly, with respect to matters falling within its competence.

4. It may call, in accordance with the rules prescribed by the United Nations, international conferences on matters falling within its competence.

Article 63. 1. The Economic and Social Council may enter into agreements with any of the agencies referred to in Article 57, defining the terms on which the agency concerned shall be brought into relationship with the United Nations. Such agreements shall be subject to approval by the General Assembly.

2. It may coordinate the activities of the specialized agencies through consultation with and recommendations to such agencies and through recommendations to the General Assembly and to the Members of the United Nations.

Article 64. 1. The Economic and Social Council may take appropriate steps to obtain regular reports from the specialized agencies. It may make arrangements with the Members of the United Nations and with the specialized agencies to obtain reports on the steps taken to give effect to its own recommendations and to recommendations on matters falling within its competence made by the General Assembly.

2. It may communicate its observations on these reports to the General Assembly.

Article 65. The Economic and Social Council may furnish information to the Security Council and shall assist the Security Council upon its request.

Article 66. 1. The Economic and Social Council shall perform such functions as fall within its competence in connection with the carrying out of the recommendations of the General Assembly.

2. It may, with the approval of the General Assembly, perform services at the request of Members of the United Nations and at the request of specialized agencies.

3. It shall perform such other functions as are specified elsewhere in the present Charter or as may be assigned to it by the General Assembly.

VOTING

Article 67. 1. Each member of the Economic and Social Council shall have one vote.

2. Decisions of the Economic and Social Council shall be made by a majority of the members present and voting.

PROCEDURE

Article 68. The Economic and Social Council shall set up commissions in economic and social fields and for the promotion of human rights, and such other commissions as may be required for the performance of its functions.

Article 69. The Economic and Social Council shall invite any Member of the United Nations to participate, without vote, in its deliberations on any matter of particular concern to that Member.

Article 70. The Economic and Social Council may make arrangements for representatives of the specialized agencies to participate, without vote, in its deliberations and in those of the commissions established by it, and for its representatives to participate in the deliberations of the specialized agencies.

Article 71. The Economic and Social Council may make suitable arrangements for consultation with non-governmental organizations which are concerned with matters within its competence. Such arrangements may be made with international organizations and, where appropriate, with national organizations after consultation with the Member of the United Nations concerned.

Article 72. 1. The Economic and Social Council shall adopt its own rules of procedure, including the method of selecting its President.

2. The Economic and Social Council shall meet as required in accordance with its rules, which shall include provision for the convening of meetings on the request of a majority of its members.

CHAPTER XI. *Declaration Regarding Non-Self-Governing Territories*

Article 73. Members of the United Nations which have or assume responsibilities for the administration of territories whose peoples have not yet attained a full measure of self-government recognize the principle that the interests of the inhabitants of these territories are paramount, and accept as a sacred trust the obligation to promote to the utmost, within the system of international peace and security established by the present Charter, the well-being of the inhabitants of these territories, and, to this end:

a. to ensure, with due respect for the culture of the peoples concerned, their political, economic, social, and educational advancement, their just treatment, and their protection against abuses;

b. to develop self-government, to take due account of the political aspirations of the peoples, and to assist them in the progressive development of their free political institutions, according to the particular circumstances of each territory and its peoples and their varying stages of advancement;

c. to further international peace and security;

d. to promote constructive measures of development, to encourage research, and to cooperate with one another and, when and where appropriate, with specialized international bodies with a view to the practical achievement of the social, economic, and scientific purposes set forth in this Article; and

e. to transmit regularly to the Secretary-General for information purposes, subject to such limitation as security and constitutional considerations may require, statistical and other information of a technical nature relating to economic, social, and educational conditions in the territories for which they are respectively responsible other than those territories to which Chapters XII and XIII apply.

Article 74. Members of the United Nations also agree that their policy in respect of the territories to which this Chapter applies, no less than in respect of their metropolitan areas, must be based on the general principle of good-neighborliness, due account being taken of the interests and well-being of the rest of the world, in social, economic, and commercial matters.

CHAPTER XII. *International Trusteeship System*

Article 75. The United Nations shall establish under its authority an international trusteeship system for the administration and supervision of such territories as may be placed thereunder by subsequent individual agreements. These territories are hereinafter referred to as trust territories.

Article 76. The basic objectives of the trusteeship system, in accordance with the Purposes of the United Nations laid down in Article 1 of the present Charter, shall be:

a. to further international peace and security;

b. to promote the political, economic, social, and educational advancement of the inhabitants of the trust territories, and their progressive development towards self-government or independence as may be appropriate to the particular circumstances of each territory and its peoples and the freely expressed wishes of the peoples concerned, and as may be provided by the terms of each trusteeship agreement;

c. to encourage respect for human rights and for fundamental freedoms for all without distinction as to race, sex, language, or religion, and to encourage recognition of the interdependence of the peoples of the world; and

d. to ensure equal treatment in social, economic, and commercial matters for all Members of the United Nations and their nationals, and also equal treatment for the latter in the administration of justice, without prejudice to the attainment of the foregoing objectives and subject to the provisions of Article 80.

Article 77. 1. The trusteeship system shall apply to such territories in the following categories as may be placed thereunder by means of trusteeship agreements:

a. territories now held under mandate;

b. territories which may be detached from enemy states as a result of the Second World War; and

c. territories voluntarily placed under the system by states responsible for their administration.

2. It will be a matter for subsequent agreement as to which territories in the foregoing categories will be brought under the trusteeship system and upon what terms.

Article 78. The trusteeship system shall not apply to territories which have become Members of the United Nations, relationship among which shall be based on respect for the principle of sovereign equality.

Article 79. The terms of trusteeship for each territory to be placed under the trusteeship system, including any alteration or amendment, shall be agreed upon by the states directly concerned, including the mandatory power in the case of territories held under mandate by a member of the United Nations, and shall be approved as provided for in Articles 83 and 85.

Article 80. 1. Except as may be agreed upon in individual trusteeship agreements, made under Articles 77, 79, and 81, placing each territory under the trusteeship system, and until such agreements have been concluded, nothing in this Chapter shall be construed in or of itself to alter in any manner the rights whatsoever of any states or any peoples or the terms of existing international instruments to which Members of the United Nations may respectively be parties.

2. Paragraph 1 of this Article shall not be interpreted as giving grounds for delay or postponement of the negotiation and conclusion of agreements for placing mandated and other territories under the trusteeship system as provided for in Article 77.

Article 81. The trusteeship agreement shall in each case include the terms under which the trust territory will be administered and designate the authority which will exercise the administration of the trust territory. Such authority, hereinafter called the administering authority, may be one or more states or the Organization itself.

Article 82. There may be designated, in any trusteeship agreement, a strategic area or areas which may include part or all of the trust territory to which the agreement applies, without prejudice to any special agreement or agreements made under Article 43.

Article 83. 1. All functions of the United Nations relating to strategic areas, including the approval of the terms of the trusteeship agreements and of their alteration or amendment, shall be exercised by the Security Council.

2. The basic objectives set forth in Article 76 shall be applicable to the people of each strategic area.

3. The Security Council shall, subject to the provisions of the trusteeship agreements and without prejudice to security considerations, avail itself of the assistance of the Trusteeship Council to perform those functions of the United Nations under the trusteeship system relating to political, economic, social, and educational matters in the strategic areas.

Article 84. It shall be the duty of the administering authority to ensure that the trust territory shall play its part in the maintenance of international peace and security. To this end the administering authority may make use of volunteer forces, facilities, and assistance from the trust territory in carrying out the obligations towards the Security Council undertaken in this regard by the administering authority, as well as for local defense and the maintenance of law and order within the trust territory.

Article 85. 1. The functions of the United Nations with regard to trusteeship agreements for all areas not designated as strategic, including the approval of the terms of the trusteeship agreements and of their alteration or amendment, shall be exercised by the General Assembly.

2. The Trusteeship Council, operating under the authority of the General Assembly, shall assist the General Assembly in carrying out these functions.

CHAPTER XIII. *The Trusteeship Council*

COMPOSITION

Article 86. 1. The Trusteeship Council shall consist of the following Members of the United Nations:

a. those Members administering trust territories;

b. such of those Members mentioned by name in Article 23 as are not administering trust territories; and

c. as many other Members elected for three-year terms by the General Assembly as may be necessary to ensure that the total number of members of the Trusteeship Council is equally divided between those Members of the United Nations which administer trust territories and those which do not.

2. Each member of the Trusteeship Council shall designate one specially qualified person to represent it therein.

FUNCTIONS AND POWERS

Article 87. The General Assembly and, under its authority, the Trusteeship Council, in carrying out their functions, may:

a. consider reports submitted by the administering authority;

b. accept petitions and examine them in consultation with the administering authority;

c. provide for periodic visits to the respective trust territories at times agreed upon with the administering authority; and

d. take these and other actions in conformity with the terms of the trusteeship agreements.

Article 88. The Trusteeship Council shall formulate a questionnaire on the politicial, economic, social, and educational advancement of the inhabitants of each trust territory, and the administering authority for each trust territory within the competence of the General Assembly shall make an annual report to the General Assembly upon the basis of such questionnaire.

Voting

Article 89. 1. Each member of the Trusteeship Council shall have one vote.

2. Decisions of the Trusteeship Council shall be made by a majority of the members present and voting.

Procedure

Article 90. 1. The Trusteeship Council shall adopt its own rules of procedure, including the method of selecting its President.

2. The Trusteeship Council shall meet as required in accordance with its rules, which shall include provision for the convening of meetings on the request of a majority of its members.

Article 91. The Trusteeship Council shall, when appropriate, avail itself of the assistance of the Economic and Social Council and of the specialized agencies in regard to matters with which they are respectively concerned.

Chapter XIV. *The International Court of Justice*

Article 92. The International Court of Justice shall be the principal judicial organ of the United Nations. It shall function in accordance with the annexed Statute, which is based upon the Statute of the Permanent Court of International Justice and forms an integral part of the present Charter.

Article 93. 1. All Members of the United Nations are *ipso facto* parties to the Statute of the International Court of Justice.

2. A state which is not a Member of the United Nations may become a party to the Statute of the International Court of Justice on conditions to be determined in each case by the General Assembly upon the recommendation of the Security Council.

Article 94. 1. Each Member of the United Nations undertakes to comply with the decision of the International Court of Justice in any case to which it is a party.

2. If any party to a case fails to perform the obligations incumbent upon it under a judgment rendered by the Court, the other party may have recourse to the Security Council, which may, if it deems necessary, make recommendations or decide upon measures to be taken to give effect to the judgment.

Article 95. Nothing in the present Charter shall prevent Members of the United Nations from entrusting the solution of their differences to other tribunals by virtue of agreements already in existence or which may be concluded in the future.

Article 96. 1. The General Assembly or the Security Council may request the International Court of Justice to give an advisory opinion on any legal question.

2. Other organs of the United Nations and specialized agencies, which may at any time be so authorized by the General Assembly, may also request advisory opinions of the Court on legal questions arising within the scope of their activities.

Chapter XV. *The Secretariat*

Article 97. The Secretariat shall comprise a Secretary-General and such staff as the Organization may require. The Secretary-General shall be appointed by the General Assembly upon the recommendation of the Security Council. He shall be the chief administrative officer of the organization.

Article 98. The Secretary-General shall act in that capacity in all meetings of the General Assembly, of the Security Council, of the Economic and Social Council, and the Trusteeship Council, and shall perform such other functions as are entrusted to him by these organs. The Secretary-General shall make an annual report to the General Assembly on the work of the Organization.

Article 99. The Secretary-General may bring to the attention of the Security Council any matter which in his opinion may threaten the maintenance of international peace and security.

Article 100. 1. In the performance of their duties the Secretary-General and the staff shall not seek or receive instructions from any government or from any other authority external to the Organization. They shall refrain from any action which might reflect on their position as international officials responsible only to the Organization.

2. Each Member of the United Nations undertakes to respect the exclusively international character of the responsibilities of the Secretary-General and the staff and not to seek to influence them in the discharge of their responsibilities.

Article 101. 1. The staff shall be appointed by the Secretary-General under regulations established by the General Assembly.

2. Appropriate staffs shall be permanently assigned to the Economic and Social Council, the Trusteeship Council, and, as required, to other organs of the United Nations. These staffs shall form a part of the Secretariat.

3. The paramount consideration in the employment of the staff and in the determination of the conditions of service shall be the necessity of securing the highest standards of efficiency, competence, and integrity. Due regard shall be paid to the importance of recruiting the staff on as wide a geographical basis as possible.

CHAPTER XVI. *Miscellaneous Provisions*

Article 102. 1. Every treaty and every international agreement entered into by any Member of the United Nations after the present Charter comes into force shall as soon as possible be registered with the Secretariat and published by it.

2. No party to any such treaty or international agreement which has not been registered in accordance with the provisions of paragraph 1 of this Article may invoke that treaty or agreement before any organ of the United Nations.

Article 103. In the event of a conflict between the obligations of the Members of the United Nations under the present Charter and their obligations under any other international agreement, their obligations under the present Charter shall prevail.

Article 104. The Organization shall enjoy in the territory of each of its Members such legal capacity as may be necessary for the exercise of its functions and the fulfillment of its purposes.

Article 105. 1. The Organization shall enjoy in the territory of each of its Members such privileges and immunities as are necessary for the fulfillment of its purposes.

2. Representatives of the Members of the United Nations and officials of the Organization shall similarly enjoy such privileges and immunities as are necessary for the independent exercise of their functions in connection with the Organization.

3. The General Assembly may make recommendations with a view to determining the details of the application of paragraphs 1 and 2 of this Article or may propose conventions to the Members of the United Nations for this purpose.

CHAPTER XVII. *Transitional Security Arrangements*

Article 106. Pending the coming into force of such special agreements referred to in Article 43 as in the opinion of the Security Council enable it to begin the exercise of its responsibilities under Article 42, the parties to the Four-Nation Declaration, signed at Moscow, October 30, 1943, and France, shall, in accordance with the provisions of paragraph 5 of that Declaration, consult with one another and as occasion requires with other Members of the United Nations with a view to such joint action on behalf of the Organization as may be necessary for the purpose of maintaining international peace and security.

Article 107. Nothing in the present Charter shall invalidate or preclude action, in relation to any state which during the Second World War has been an enemy of any signatory to the present Charter, taken or authorized as a result of that war by the Governments having responsibility for such action.

CHAPTER XVIII. *Amendments*

Article 108. Amendments to the present Charter shall come into force for all Members of the United Nations when they have been adopted by a vote of two-thirds of the members of the General Assembly and ratified in accordance with their respective constitutional processes by two-thirds of the members of the United Nations, including all the permanent members of the Security Council.

Article 109. 1. A General Conference of the Members of the United Nations for the purpose of reviewing the present Charter may be held at a date and place to be fixed by a two-thirds vote of the members of the General Assembly and by a vote of any seven members of the Security Council. Each Member of the United Nations shall have one vote in the conference.

2. Any alteration of the present Charter recommended by a two-thirds vote of the conference shall take effect when ratified in accordance with their respective constitutional processes by two-thirds of the Members of the United Nations including all the permanent members of the Security Council.

3. If such a conference has not been held before the tenth annual session of the General Assembly following the coming into force of the present Charter, the proposal to call such a conference shall be placed on the agenda of that session of the General Assembly, and the conference shall be held if so decided by a majority vote of the members of the General Assembly and by a vote of any seven members of the Security Council.

Chapter XIX. *Ratification and Signature*

Article 110. 1. The present Charter shall be ratified by the signatory states in accordance with their respective constitutional processes.

2. The ratifications shall be deposited with the Government of the United States of America, which shall notify all the signatory states of each deposit as well as the Secretary-General of the Organization when he has been appointed.

3. The present Charter shall come into force upon the deposit of ratifications by the Republic of China, France, the Union of Soviet Socialist Republics, the United Kingdom of Great Britain and Northern Ireland, and the United States of America, and by a majority of the other signatory states. A protocol of the ratifications deposited shall thereupon be drawn up by the Government of the United States of America which shall communicate copies thereof to all the signatory states.

4. The states signatory to the present Charter which ratify it after it has come into force will become original Members of the United Nations on the date of the deposit of their respective ratifications.

Article 111. The present Charter, of which the Chinese, French, Russian, English, and Spanish texts are equally authentic, shall remain deposited in the archives of the Government of the United States of America. Duly certified copies thereof shall be transmitted by that Government to the Governments of the other signatory states.

In Faith Whereof the representatives of the Governments of the United Nations have signed the present Charter.

Done at the city of San Francisco the twenty-sixth day of June, one thousand nine hundred and forty-five.

◇◇◇◇◇◇◇◇◇◇◇◇◇

4. DEFENSE OF THE GREAT POWER VETO[4]

. . . THE REQUIREMENT for unaniminity of the five great nations has been criticized because each of them can exercise a veto. I submit that these five nations, possessing most of the world's power to break or preserve peace, must agree and act together if peace is to be maintained, just as they have had to agree and act together in order to make possible a United Nations victory in this war.

The question is asked: What would happen if one of the five permanent members used the unanimity rule to veto enforcement action against itself? The answer is plain. If one of these nations ever embarked upon a course of aggression, a major war would result, no matter what the membership and voting provisions of the Security Council might be.

The Charter does not confer any power upon the great nations which they do not already possess in fact. Without the Charter the power of these nations to make or break the peace would still exist. What the Charter does is to place special and binding obligations upon the great nations to use – in unity together for peace, not separately for war – the power that is already in their hands. The unanimity rule is an expression of those special obligations and of their commensurate responsibilities.

With an important exception, the unanimity rule applies to peaceful settlement as well as to enforcement action, because any action toward settling a dispute peacefully may lead to the necessity for enforcement measures. Once the Council orders an investigation or takes similar action in a dispute, it must be prepared to follow through with whatever further measures, including the use of force, may ultimately be necessary. And this must be clear to the states involved in the dispute. If it were not, the authority and prestige which the Council needs in order to secure peaceful settlements of disputes might be fatally weakened. That is why the five permanent members are required to agree and vote together from the beginning of any dispute on which the Council takes action.

The power of veto does not, however, apply to consideration and discussion of a dispute by the Council before action is taken. Thus the right of any nation to bring a dispute before the Council and to obtain a hearing of its case cannot be blocked. Furthermore, no member of the Council – and this includes the permanent members – can vote in any decision involving peaceful settlement of a dispute to which it is a party. By this

[4] Statement of Edward R. Stettinius Jr., Secretary of State, to the Committee on Foreign Relations of the Senate. *Hearings on the Charter of the United Nations* (U. S. Government Printing Office, Washington, D.C., 1945), pp. 215–17.

provision the five permanent members must submit themselves to the same processes of peaceful adjustment and settlement that apply to any other member nation.

Additional checks are provided against abuse of their voting powers by the five permanent members. Any decision by the Council in either the peaceful settlement or enforcement stage requires at least seven votes. Thus at least two of the smaller nations on the Council must agree with the five permanent members before the Council can take action. The Charter also provides that the General Assembly, where the five major powers possess no special voting powers, may make recommendations to the Council on any questions relating to peace and security not being dealt with by the Council. It provides, further, that the Council must report at least once a year to the General Assembly on all measures it has taken to maintain peace. These provisions mean that the Council must act under the watchful eye of the whole organization, and its members can quickly be held accountable before the world opinion if they are derelict in their duty.

There is still another, and more compelling reason why the power of veto is not likely to be abused, or even to be exercised at all except in unusual circumstances. That is the compelling desire and need of the five great nations to work together for peace. Twice in 30 years they have been allies against aggression. Their common interest in preventing another war is fully as urgent as that of any other nation. Under this Charter they assume sacred obligations and heavy responsibilities for the maintenance of peace with justice. They do not assume these obligations and responsibilities lightly. They do so because it is in the vital national interest of each one of them to see that these obligations and responsibilities are fulfilled.

I believe that I speak for the entire United States delegation when I say that the requirement for unanimity among the five permanent members, with the safeguards that have been provided, is not only essential to the success of the United Nations Organization in the years immediately ahead, but that it recognizes and confirms a power which a majority of Americans believe the United States should have in view of the great responsibilities our country must inevitably assume for the maintenance of world peace.

The special position of the United States and the four other permanent members of the Security Council is also recognized in the provisions for ratification both of the Charter and of later amendments to the Charter.

The Charter itself will come into force when it has been ratified by the five permanent members of the Council and a majority of the other signatory states. Amendments will come into force when they have been adopted by a two-thirds vote of the General Assembly or of a special conference called for the purpose and have been ratified by two-thirds of the member states, including all the permanent members of the Security Council.

It should be noted that there is no power of veto over the adoption of amendments. The Security Council does not vote on amendments at all. The power of veto applies only to their ratification by the nations concerned.

In practice no important amendments to the Charter are likely to be adopted in the near future unless there is unanimous, or virtually unanimous, agreement upon them and ratification is regarded as assured. The General Assembly is not a legislative body. It is an international meeting of the representatives of sovereign nations. The act of voting on an important matter, therefore, is not likely to take place until all the means of adjustment usual in negotiations among nations have been brought to bear in order to reach a common viewpoint. It is interesting to note that at the San Francisco Conference there was no veto and the two-thirds rule applied. Yet the provisions of the Charter were adopted unanimously.

I feel that much of the criticism of the voting provisions of the Charter arises from failure to remember that the United Nations is neither a federal union nor a world state and that voting procedures among its sovereign member nations cannot necessarily be judged on the same basis as voting procedures in a State legislature or in the Congress.

As the peoples and governments gain experience and confidence in world organization in the years ahead I hope that they will learn to apply and adapt to international affairs many more of the principles and techniques of democracy. But I believe it would be fatal to this hope if we were to attempt now to go beyond what the nations are clearly ready to undertake today. The Charter affords full opportunity for later amendments whenever a sufficient majority of the people of the world is ready to go further.

◇◇◇◇◇◇◇◇◇◇◇◇◇

5. ACCEPTANCE BY THE UNITED STATES OF THE COMPULSORY JURISDICTION OF THE INTERNATIONAL COURT OF JUSTICE[5]

I, HARRY S. TRUMAN, President of the United States of America, declare on behalf of the United States of America, under Article 36, paragraph 2, of the Statute of the International Court of Justice, and in accordance with the Resolution of August 2, 1946, of the Senate of the United States of America (two-thirds of the Senators present concurring therein), that the United States of America recognizes as compulsory *ipso facto* and without special agreement, in relation to any other state accepting the same obligation, the jurisdiction of the International Court of Justice in all legal disputes hereafter arising concerning

a. the interpretation of a treaty;

[5] Department of State *Bulletin,* Vol. XV, pp. 452–3.

b. any question of international law;

c. the existence of any fact which, if established, would constitute a breach of an international obligation;

d. the nature or extent of the reparation to be made for the breach of an international obligation;

Provided, that this declaration shall not apply to

a. disputes the solution of which the parties shall entrust to other tribunals by virtue of agreements already in existence or which may be concluded in the future; or

b. disputes with regard to matters which are essentially within the domestic jurisdiction of the United States of America as determined by the United States of America; or

c. disputes arising under a multilateral treaty, unless (1) all parties to the treaty affected by the decision are also parties to the case before the Court, or (2) the United States of America specially agrees to jurisdiction; and

Provided further, that this declaration shall remain in force for a period of five years and thereafter until the expiration of six months after notice may be given to terminate this declaration.

Done at Washington this fourteenth day of August 1946.

◇◇◇◇◇◇◇◇◇◇◇◇◇

6. THE CONTROL OF ATOMIC ENERGY[6]

WE ARE HERE to make a choice between the quick and the dead.

That is our business.

Behind the black portent of the new atomic age lies a hope which, seized upon with faith, can work our salvation. If we fail, then we have damned every man to be the slave of Fear. Let us not deceive ourselves: We must elect World Peace or World Destruction.

Science has torn from nature a secret so vast in its potentialities that our minds cower from the terror it creates. Yet terror is not enough to inhibit the use of the atomic bomb. The terror created by weapons has never stopped man from employing them. For each new weapon a defense has been produced, in time. But now we face a condition in which adequate defense does not exist.

Science, which gave us this dread power, shows that it *can* be made a giant help to humanity, but science does *not* show us how to prevent its baleful use. So we have been appointed to obviate that peril by finding a meeting of the minds and the hearts of our peoples. Only in the will of mankind lies the answer. . . .

In this crisis, we represent not only our governments but, in a larger

[6] Address of Bernard M. Baruch before the United Nations Atomic Energy Commission, New York, June 14, 1946. Department of State *Bulletin,* Vol. 14, pp. 1057–62.

way, we represent the peoples of the world. We must remember that the peoples do not belong to the governments but that the governments belong to the peoples. We must answer their demands; we must answer the world's longing for peace and security.

In that desire the United States shares ardently and hopefully. The search of science for the absolute weapon has reached fruition in this country. But she stands ready to proscribe and destroy this instrument – to lift its use from death to life – if the world will join in a pact to that end. . . .

The United States proposes the creation of an International Atomic Development Authority, to which should be entrusted all phases of the development and use of atomic energy, starting with the raw material and including –

1. Managerial control or ownership of all atomic-energy activities potentially dangerous to world security.
2. Power to control, inspect, and license all other atomic activities.
3. The duty of fostering the beneficial uses of atomic energy.
4. Research and development responsibilities of an affirmative character intended to put the Authority in the forefront of atomic knowledge and thus to enable it to comprehend, and therefor to detect, misuse of atomic energy. To be effective, the Authority must itself be the world's leader in the field of atomic knowledge and development and thus supplement its legal authority with the great power inherent in possession of leadership in knowledge.

I offer this as a basis for beginning our discussion.

But I think the peoples we serve would not believe – and without faith nothing counts – that a treaty, merely outlawing possession or use of the atomic bomb, constitutes effective fulfilment of the instructions to this Commission. Previous failures have been recorded in trying the method of simple renunciation, unsupported by effective guaranties of security and armament limitation. No one would have faith in that approach alone.

Now, if ever, is the time to act for the common good. Public opinion supports a world movement toward security. If I read the signs aright, the peoples want a program not composed merely of pious thoughts but of enforceable sanctions – an international law with teeth in it.

We of this nation, desirous of helping to bring peace to the world and realizing the heavy obligations upon us arising from our possession of the means of producing the bomb and from the fact that it is part of our armament, are prepared to make our full contribution toward effective control of atomic energy.

When an adequate system for control of atomic energy, including the renunciation of the bomb as a weapon, has been agreed upon and put into effective operation and condign punishments set up for violations of the rules of control which are to be stigmatized as international crimes, we propose that –

1. Manufacture of atomic bombs shall stop;

2. Existing bombs shall be disposed of pursuant to the terms of the treaty; and

3. The Authority shall be in possession of full information as to the know-how for the production of atomic energy.

Let me repeat, so as to avoid misunderstanding: My country is ready to make its full contribution toward the end we seek, subject of course to our constitutional processes and to an adequate system of control becoming fully effective, as we finally work it out.

Now as to violations: In the agreement, penalties of as serious a nature as the nations may wish and as immediate and certain in their execution as possible should be fixed for—

1. Illegal possession or use of an atomic bomb;

2. Illegal possession, or separation, of atomic material suitable for use in an atomic bomb;

3. Seizure of any plant or other property belonging to or licensed by the Authority;

4. Willful interference with the activities of the Authority;

5. Creation or operation of dangerous projects in a manner contrary to, or in the absence of, a license granted by the international control body.

It would be a deception, to which I am unwilling to lend myself, were I not to say to you and to our peoples that the matter of punishment lies at the very heart of our present security system. It might as well be admitted, here and now, that the subject goes straight to the veto power contained in the Charter of the United Nations so far as it relates to the field of atomic energy. The Charter permits penalization only by concurrence of each of the five great powers—the Union of Soviet Socialist Republics, the United Kingdom, China, France, and the United States.

I want to make very plain that I am concerned here with the veto power only as it affects this particular problem. There must be no veto to protect those who violate their solemn agreements not to develop or use atomic energy for destructive purposes.

The bomb does not wait upon debate. To delay may be to die. The time between violation and preventive action or punishment would be all too short for extended discussion as to the course to be followed.

As matters now stand several years may be necessary for another country to produce a bomb, *de novo*. However, once the basic information is generally known, and the Authority has established producing plants for peaceful purposes in the several countries, an illegal seizure of such a plant might permit a malevolent nation to produce a bomb in 12 months, and if preceded by secret preparation and necessary facilities perhaps even in a much shorter time. The time required—the advance warning given of the possible use of a bomb—can only be generally estimated but obviously will depend upon many factors, including the success with which the Authority has been able to introduce elements of safety in the design of its plants and the degree to which illegal and secret preparation for the military use of atomic energy will have been eliminated. Presumably no nation would think of starting a war with only one bomb.

This shows how imperative speed is in detecting and penalizing violations.

The process of prevention and penalization – a problem of profound statecraft – is, as I read it, implicit in the Moscow statement, signed by the Union of Soviet Socialist Republics, the United States, and the United Kingdom a few months ago.

But before a country is ready to relinquish any winning weapons it must have more than words to reassure it. It must have a guarantee of safety, not only against the offenders in the atomic area but against the illegal users of other weapons – bacteriological, biological, gas – perhaps – why not? – against war itself.

In the elimination of war lies our solution, for only then will nations cease to compete with one another in the production and use of dread "secret" weapons which are evaluated solely by their capacity to kill. This devilish program takes us back not merely to the Dark Ages but from cosmos to chaos. If we succeed in finding a suitable way to control atomic weapons, it is reasonable to hope that we may also preclude the use of other weapons adaptable to mass destruction. When a man learns to say "A" he can, if he chooses, learn the rest of the alphabet too. . . .

I now submit the following measures as representing the fundamental features of a plan which would give effect to certain of the conclusions which I have epitomized.

1. *General.* The Authority should set up a thorough plan for control of the field of atomic energy, through various forms of ownership, dominion, licenses, operation, inspection, research, and management by competent personnel. After this is provided for, there should be as little interference as may be with the economic plans and the present private, corporate, and state relationships in the several countries involved.

2. *Raw Materials.* The Authority should have as one of its earliest purposes to obtain and maintain complete and accurate information on world supplies of uranium and thorium and to bring them under its dominion. The precise pattern of control for various types of deposits of such materials will have to depend upon the geological, mining, refining, and economic facts involved in different situations.

The Authority should conduct continuous surveys so that it will have the most complete knowledge of the world geology of uranium and thorium. Only after all current information on world sources of uranium and thorium is known to us all can equitable plans be made for their production, refining, and distribution.

3. *Primary Production Plants.* The Authority should exercise complete managerial control of the production of fissionable materials. This means that it should control and operate all plants producing fissionable materials in dangerous quantities and must own and control the product of these plants.

4. *Atomic Explosives.* The Authority should be given sole and exclusive

right to conduct research in the field of atomic explosives. Research activities in the field of atomic explosives are essential in order that the Authority may keep in the forefront of knowledge in the field of atomic energy and fulfill the objective of preventing illicit manufacture of bombs. Only by maintaining its position as the best-informed agency will the Authority be able to determine the line between intrinsically dangerous and non-dangerous activities.

5. *Strategic Distribution of Activities and Materials.* The activities entrusted exclusively to the Authority because they are intrinsically dangerous to security should be distributed throughout the world. Similarly, stockpiles of raw materials and fissionable materials should not be centralized.

6. *Non-Dangerous Activities.* A function of the Authority should be promotion of the peacetime benefits of atomic energy.

Atomic research (except in explosives), the use of research reactors, the production of radio-active tracers by means of non-dangerous reactors, the use of such tracers, and to some extent the production of power should be open to nations and their citizens under reasonable licensing arrangements from the Authority. Denatured materials, whose use we know also requires suitable safeguards, should be furnished for such purposes by the Authority under lease or other arrangement. Denaturing seems to have been overestimated by the public as a safety measure.

7. *Definition of Dangerous and Non-Dangerous Activities.* Although a reasonable dividing line can be drawn between dangerous and non-dangerous activities, it is not hard and fast. Provision should, therefore, be made to assure constant reexamination of the questions and to permit revision of the dividing line as changing conditions and new discoveries may require.

8. *Operations of Dangerous Activities.* Any plant dealing with uranium or thorium after it once reaches the potential of dangerous use must be not only subject to the most rigorous and competent inspection by the Authority, but its actual operation shall be under the management, supervision, and control of the Authority.

9. *Inspection.* By assigning intrinsically dangerous activities exclusively to the Authority, the difficulties of inspection are reduced. If the Authority is the only agency which may lawfully conduct dangerous activities, then visible operation by others than the Authority will constitute an unambiguous danger signal. Inspection will also occur in connection with the licensing functions of the Authority.

10. *Freedom of Access.* Adequate ingress and egress for all qualified representatives of the Authority must be assured. Many of the inspection activities of the Authority should grow out of, and be incidental to, its other functions. Important measures of inspection will be associated with the tight control of raw materials, for this is a keystone of the plan. The continuing activities of prospecting, survey, and research in relation to raw materials will be designed not only to serve the affirmative development

functions of the Authority but also to assure that no surreptitious operations are conducted in the raw-materials field by nations or their citizens.

11. *Personnel.* The personnel of the Authority should be recruited on a basis of proven competence but also so far as possible on an international basis.

12. *Progress by Stages.* A primary step in the creation of the system of control is the setting forth, in comprehensive terms, of the functions, responsibilities, powers, and limitations of the Authority. Once a charter for the Authority has been adopted, the Authority and the system of control for which it will be responsible will require time to become fully organized and effective. The plan of control will, therefore, have to come into effect in successive stages. These should be specifically fixed in the Charter or means should be otherwise set forth in the Charter for transitions from one stage to another, as contemplated in the resolution of the United Nations Assembly which created this Commission.

13. *Disclosures.* In the deliberations of the United Nations Commission on Atomic Energy, the United States is prepared to make available the information essential to a reasonable understanding of the proposals which it advocates. Further disclosures must be dependent, in the interests of all, upon the effective ratification of the treaty. When the Authority is actually created, the United States will join the other nations in making available the further information essential to that organization for the performance of its functions. As the successive stages of international control are reached, the United States will be prepared to yield, to the extent required by each stage, national control of activities in this field to the Authority.

14. *International Control.* There will be questions about the extent of control to be allowed to national bodies, when the Authority is established. Purely national authorities for control and development of atomic energy should to the extent necessary for the effective operation of the Authority be subordinate to it. This is neither an endorsement nor a disapproval of the creation of national authorities. The Commission should evolve a clear demarcation of the scope of duties and responsibilities of such national authorities. . . .

◇◇◇◇◇◇◇◇◇◇◇◇

7. THE REJECTION BY RUSSIA OF THE AMERICAN PROPOSAL FOR THE CONTROL OF ATOMIC ENERGY[7]

. . . IS IT possible to consider that the way outlined in the American proposals will lead us to a successful solution of the problem of atomic energy

[7] Speech of Andrei A. Gromyko in the Security Council of the United Nations, March 5, 1947. United Nations, S/P.V. 115.

control to ensure its use only for peaceful purposes? No, this cannot be said. Without the conclusion of a convention on the prohibition of atomic weapons one cannot speak seriously about rigid international control for the establishment of which the Soviet Union stood and is standing now. Without the conclusion of such a convention it will be difficult, if not impossible, to solve the problem of the establishment of such a rigid control. . . .

In my statement of February 14th of this year I already drew the attention of the Security Council to the fact that the conclusion of a convention on the prohibition of atomic weapons would not mean that the working out of other questions, including that of inspection, should not be continued. However, the consideration of all the questions related to the establishments of atomic energy control, will inevitably require some time, and in view of this, the postponement of the conclusion of a convention on the prohibition of atomic weapons cannot be justified.

The conclusion of such a convention, besides the fact that it should represent a concrete and practical step towards the fulfilment of the General Assembly decision of 14 December 1946, would create more favourable conditions for the solution of other questions following from the General Assembly Resolution, to say nothing of the fact that the conclusion of such a convention would contribute to the strengthening of the mutual confidence among the Member States of the United Nations and to the strengthening of the authority of our Organization. . . .

The position of the Soviet Union on the questions of the control of atomic energy and inspection is clear. Strict international control and inspection of atomic energy should be established. At the same time this strict international control and strict inspection should not develop into interference with those branches of industry which are not connected with the production of atomic energy. The international control of atomic energy should not deal with those questions which are not connected with atomic energy.

Logic tells us that any thought may be reduced to an absurdity. This applies even to good thoughts and ideas. The transformation of atomic energy control into an unlimited control would mean to reduce to an absurdity the very idea of control of atomic energy in order to prevent its use for military purposes. Unlimited control would mean an unlimited interference of the control and controlling organ – or organs – in the economic life of the countries on whose territories this control would be carried out, and interference in their internal affairs. . . .

The United States proposals on control proceed from the erroneous premise that the interests of other States should be removed to the background during the exercise by the control organ of its control and inspectorial functions. Only by proceeding from such fundamentally vicious premises, was it possible to come to the conclusion contained in the proposals submitted to the Atomic Energy Commission by the United States representative on the necessity of transferring atomic enterprises to the possession and ownership of the international organ which is to be charged with responsibility for the realization of control. A proposal of this sort shows that the authors of the so-called Baruch plan completely ignore national interests of other countries and proceed from the necessity of subordinating the interests of these countries to the interests actually of one country; that is, the United States of America. . . .

I have already pointed out that the proposal on granting to an international control organ the right to possess establishments for the production of atomic energy and unlimited power to carry out other important functions connected with the ownership and management of the establishments and with the disposition of their production would lead to interference by the control organ in the internal affairs and internal life of States and eventually would lead to arbitrary action by the control organ in the solution of such problems as fall completely within the domestic jurisdiction of a State. I deem it necessary to emphasize that granting broad rights and powers of such a kind to the control organ is incompatible with the State sovereignty. Therefore, such proposals are unacceptable and must be rejected as unfounded. Not only do they not facilitate the solution of the problem of establishing strict and effective international control, but, on the contrary, they complicate the solution of this problem. . . .

How does the Soviet Union conceive the carrying out by the control organ of practical day-by-day activities, and how shall this organ take decisions relating to such day-by-day activities?

The position of the Soviet Union on this question has already been stated more than once. If it is necessary, I am prepared to repeat that such an organ must have the right to take in appropriate cases, decisions by majority vote. Does this mean, however, that it is possible by using references to international control, to agree in reality to granting the right of interference in the economic life of a country even through the decision of the majority in the control organ? The Soviet Union does not wish and cannot allow such a situation. The Soviet Union is aware that there will be a majority in the control organs which may take one-sided decisions, a majority of whose benevolent attitude toward the Soviet Union the Soviet people cannot count. Therefore the Soviet Union, and probably not only the Soviet Union, cannot allow that the fate of its national economy be handed over to this organ. The correctness of such a conclusion is confirmed by historical experience including the brief but very instructive experience of the activities of the United Nations organs. The Soviet delegation does not doubt that all those who objectively appraise the situation will correctly understand the position of the Soviet Union on this question. . . .

In reality, to grant to the control organ unlimited rights and possession and management of the atomic establishments, cannot be looked upon as anything but an attempt by the United States to secure for itself world monopoly in the field of atomic energy. This tendency has found its expression in the proposals submitted by the representative of the United States on the Atomic Energy Commission and later laid down as the basis of the report of the Atomic Energy Commission. . . .

I have already had an opportunity to state the point of view of the Soviet Delegation on the question of the principle of unanimity of the Five Powers-permanent Members of the Security Council, in connection with the discussion of the questions of the atomic energy control. The Soviet Delegation considers that it will be impossible to reach an agreement on this question as long as the unacceptable proposal on the question of the so-called "veto" is defended, since such a proposal is in contradiction with the principles of the United Nations. I have already pointed out that there seems to be no difference of opinion among us on the question of the necessity of punishing violators, and there was not any on this subject. All agree that certain sanctions should be applied against violators, if their guilt is proved. There is a divergence of opinion as to who should take decisions on sanctions and how they should be taken. Should such decisions be taken in accordance with the basic principles of the United Nations or in violation of these principles? The Soviet Delegation considers that such decisions should be taken in strict conformity with the basic principles of our Organization and should be taken by the organ which is charged with the primary responsibility for the maintenance of peace, that is, by the Security Council. The principle of unanimity of the Five Powers as such is not an obstacle to the effective control of atomic energy, no matter how someone tries to prove the opposite. . . .

◇◇◇◇◇◇◇◇◇◇◇◇◇

8. THE BERLIN (POTSDAM) CONFERENCE[8]

I. *Establishment of a Council of Foreign Ministers.*

. . . 1. THERE SHALL BE established a Council composed of the foreign ministers of the United Kingdom, the Union of Soviet Socialist Republics, China, France and the United States. . . .

3. (i) As its immediate important task, the Council shall be authorized to draw up, with a view to their submission to the United Nations, treaties of peace with Italy, Rumania, Bulgaria, Hungary and Finland, and to

[8] President Truman, Prime Minister Churchill, and Generalissimo Stalin met in conference at the Cecilienhof near Potsdam on July 17, 1945. Mr. Clement R. Attlee of Great Britain, the foreign secretaries, the Chiefs of Staff, and other advisers of the three governments represented were in attendance. For two days, July 26–27, the conference was interrupted while the British general elections were being held. On July 28, Mr. Attlee returned as Prime Minister with the new Foreign Secretary, Mr. Ernest Bevin. The major part of the Protocol of Proceedings of the Conference was published in the Department of State *Bulletin,* Vol. XIII, No. 319, August 5, 1945. The full text of the Protocol was not released until March 24, 1947. The text here is taken from the *New York Times,* March 25, 1947.

propose settlements of territorial questions outstanding on the termination of the war in Europe. The Council shall be utilized for the preparation of a peace settlement for Germany to be accepted by the government of Germany when a government adequate for the purpose is established.

(ii) For the discharge of each of these tasks the Council will be composed of the members representing those states which were signatory to the terms of surrender imposed upon the enemy state concerned. For the purpose of the peace settlement for Italy, France shall be regarded as a signatory to the terms of surrender for Italy. Other members will be invited to participate when matters directly concerning them are under discussion.

(iii) Other matters may from time to time be referred to the Council by agreement between the member governments.

4. (i) Whenever the Council is considering a question of direct interest to a state not represented thereon, such state should be invited to send representatives to participate in the discussion and study of that question.

(ii) The Council may adapt its procedure to the particular problem under consideration. In some cases it may hold its own preliminary discussions prior to the participation of other interested states. In other cases, the Council may convoke a formal conference of the state chiefly interested in seeking a solution of the particular problem. . . .

II. *Germany*

. . . The Political and Economic Principles to Govern the Treatment of Germany in the Initial Control Period.

(A) POLITICAL PRINCIPLES

1. In accordance with the agreement on control machinery in Germany, supreme authority in Germany is exercised on instructions from their respective governments, by the Commanders-in-Chief of the armed forces of the United States of America, the United Kingdom, the Union of Soviet Socialist Republics, and the French Republic, each in his own zone of occupation, and also jointly, in matters affecting Germany as a whole, in their capacity as members of the Control Council.

2. So far as is practicable, there shall be uniformity of treatment of the German population throughout Germany.

3. The purposes of the occupation of Germany by which the Control Council shall be guided are:

(i) The complete disarmament and demilitarization of Germany and the elimination or control of all German industry that could be used for military production. To these ends:

(a) All German land, naval and air forces, the S.S., S.A., S.D., and Gestapo, with all their organizations, staffs and institutions, including the General Staff, the Officers' Corps, Reserve Corps, military schools, war veterans' organizations and all other military and quasi-military organizations, together with all clubs and associations which serve to keep alive the military tradition in Germany, shall be completely and finally abolished in such manner as permanently to prevent the revival or reorganization of German militarism and Nazism.

(b) All arms, ammunition and implements of war and all specialized facilities for their production shall be held at the disposal of the Allies or destroyed. The maintenance and production of all aircraft and all arms, ammunition and implements of war shall be prevented.

(ii) To convince the German people that they have suffered a total military defeat and that they cannot escape responsibility for what they have brought upon themselves, since their own ruthless warfare and the fanatical Nazi resistance have destroyed German economy and made chaos and suffering inevitable.

(iii) To destroy the National Socialist Party and its affiliated and supervised organizations, to dissolve all Nazi institutions, to ensure that they are not revived in any form, and to prevent all Nazi and militarist activity or propaganda.

(iv) To prepare for the eventual reconstruction of German political life on a democratic basis and for eventual peaceful cooperation in international life by Germany.

4. All Nazi laws which provided the basis of the Hitler regime or established discrimination on grounds of race, creed, or political opinion shall be abolished. No such discriminations, whether legal, administrative or otherwise, shall be tolerated.

5. War criminals and those who have participated in planning or carrying out Nazi enterprises involving or resulting in atrocities or war crimes shall be arrested and brought to judgment. Nazi leaders, influential Nazi supporters and high officials of Nazi organizations and institutions and any other persons dangerous to the occupation or its objectives shall be arrested and interned.

6. All members of the Nazi party who have been more than nominal participants in its activities and all other persons hostile to allied purposes shall be removed from public and semi-public office, and from positions of responsibility in important private undertakings. Such persons shall be replaced by persons who, by their political and moral qualities, are deemed capable of assisting in developing genuine democratic institutions in Germany.

7. German education shall be so controlled as completely to eliminate Nazi and militarist doctrines and to make possible the successful development of democratic ideas.

8. The judicial system will be reorganized in accordance with the principles of democracy, of justice under law, and of equal rights for all citizens without distinction of race, nationality or religion.

9. The administration of affairs in Germany should be directed towards the decentralization of the political structure and the development of local responsibility. To this end:

(i) Local self-government shall be restored throughout Germany on democratic principles and in particular through elective councils as rapidly as is consistent with military security and the purposes of military occupation;

(ii) All democratic political parties with rights of assembly and of public discussion shall be allowed and encouraged throughout Germany;

(iii) Representative and elective principles shall be introduced into regional, provincial and state (land) administration as rapidly as may be justified by the successful application of these principles in local self-government;

(iv) For the time being no central German government shall be established. Notwithstanding this, however, certain essential central German administrative departments, headed by state secretaries, shall be established, particularly in the fields of finance, transport, communications, foreign trade and industry. Such departments will act under the direction of the Control Council.

10. Subject to the necessity for maintaining military security, freedom of speech, press and religion shall be permitted, and religious institutions shall be respected. Subject likewise to the maintenance of military security, the formation of free trade unions shall be permitted.

(B) ECONOMIC PRINCIPLES

11. In order to eliminate Germany's war potential, the production of arms, ammunition and implements of war as well as all types of aircraft and sea-going ships shall be prohibited and prevented. Production of metals, chemicals, machinery and other items that are directly necessary to a war economy shall be rigidly controlled and restricted to Germany's approved post-war peacetime needs to meet the objectives stated in paragraph 15. Productive capacity not needed for permitted production shall be removed in accordance with the reparations plan recommended by the Allied Commission on reparations and approved by the governments concerned or if not removed shall be destroyed.

12. At the earliest practicable date, the German economy shall be decentralized for the purpose of eliminating the present excessive concentration of economic power as exemplified in particular by cartels, syndicates, trusts and other monopolistic arrangements.

13. In organizing the German economy, primary emphasis shall be given to the development of agriculture and peaceful domestic industries.

14. During the period of occupation Germany shall be treated as a single economic unit. To this end common policies shall be established in regard to:

(a) Mining and industrial production and allocations;
(b) Agriculture, forestry and fishing;
(c) Wages, prices and rationing;
(d) Import and export programs for Germany as a whole;
(e) Currency and banking, central taxation and customs;
(f) Reparation and removal of industrial war potential;
(g) Transportation and communications.

In applying these policies account shall be taken, where appropriate, of varying local conditions.

15. Allied controls shall be imposed upon the German economy but only to the extent necessary:

(a) To carry out programs of industrial disarmament and demilitarization, of reparations, and of approved exports and imports.

(b) to assure the production and maintenance of goods and services required to meet the needs of the occupying forces and displaced persons in Germany and essential to maintain in Germany average living standards not exceeding the average of the standards of living of European countries. (European countries means all European countries excluding the United Kingdom and the Union of Soviet Socialist Republics.)

(c) To ensure in the manner determined by the Control Council the equitable distribution of essential commodities between the several zones so as to produce a balanced economy throughout Germany and reduce the need for imports.

(d) To control German industry and all economic and financial international transactions, including exports and imports, with the aim of preventing Germany from developing a war potential and of achieving the other objectives named herein.

(e) To control all German public or private scientific bodies, research and experimental institutions, laboratories, et cetera, connected with economic activities.

16. In the imposition and maintenance of economic controls established by the Control Council, German administrative machinery shall be created and the German authorities shall be required to the fullest extent practicable to proclaim and assume administration of such controls. Thus it should be brought home to the German people that the responsibility for the administration of such controls and any breakdown in these controls will rest with themselves. Any German controls which may run counter to the objectives of occupation will be prohibited.

17. Measures shall be promptly taken:

(a) To effect essential repair of transport;

(b) To enlarge coal production;

(c) To maximize agricultural output; and

(d) To effect emergency repair of housing and essential utilities.

18. Appropriate steps shall be taken by the Control Council to exercise control and the power of disposition over German-owned external assets not already under the control of United Nations which have taken part in the war against Germany.

19. Payment of reparations should leave enough resources to enable the German people to subsist without external assistance. In working out the economic balance of Germany the necessary means must be provided to pay for imports approved by the Control Council in Germany. The proceeds of exports from current production and stocks shall be available in the first place for payment for such imports.

The above clause will not apply to the equipment and products referred to in paragraphs 4 (A) and 4 (B) of the Reparations Agreement.

III. *Reparations from Germany*

1. Reparation claims of the U.S.S.R. shall be met by removals from the zone of Germany occupied by the U.S.S.R. and from appropriate German external assets.

2. The U.S.S.R. undertakes to settle the reparation claims of Poland from its own share of reparations.

3. The reparation claims of the United States, the United Kingdom and other countries entitled to reparations shall be met from the western zones and from appropriate German external assets.

4. In addition to the reparations to be taken by the U.S.S.R. from its own zone of occupation, the U.S.S.R. shall receive additionally from the western zones:

(A) 15 per cent of such usable and complete industrial capital equipment, in the first place from the metallurgical, chemical and machine manufacturing industries, as is unnecessary for the German peace economy and should be removed from the western zones of Germany, in exchange for an equivalent value of food, coal, potash, zinc, timber, clay products, petroleum products, and such other commodities as may be agreed upon.

(B) 10 per cent of such industrial capital equipment as is unnecessary for the German peace economy and should be removed from the western zones, to be transferred to the Soviet Government on reparations account without payment or exchange of any kind in return.

Removals of equipment as provided in (A) and (B) above shall be made simultaneously.

5. The amount of equipment to be removed from the western zones on account of reparations must be determined within six months from now at the latest.

6. Removals of industrial capital equipment shall begin as soon as possible and shall be completed within two years from the determination specified in paragraph 5. The delivery of products covered by 4 (A) above shall begin as soon as possible and shall be made by the U.S.S.R. in agreed installments within five years of the date hereof. The determination of the amount and character of the industrial capital equipment unnecessary for the German peace economy and therefore available for reparations shall be made by the control council under policies fixed by the Allied Commission on Reparations, with the participation of France, subject to the final approval of the zone commander in the zone from which the equipment is to be removed.

7. Prior to the fixing of the total amount of equipment subject to removal, advance deliveries shall be made in respect of such equipment as will be determined to be eligible for delivery in accordance with the procedure set forth in the last sentence of Paragraph 6.

8. The Soviet Government renounces all claims in respect of reparations to shares of German enterprises which are located in the western zones

of occupation in Germany as well as to German foreign assets in all countries except those specified in Paragraph 9 below.

9. The Governments of the United Kingdom and the United States of America renounce their claims in respect of reparations to shares of German enterprises which are located in the eastern zone of occupation in Germany, as well as to German foreign assets in Bulgaria, Finland, Hungary, Rumania and Eastern Austria.

10. The Soviet Government makes no claims to gold captured by the Allied troops in Germany.

IV. *Disposal of the German Navy and Merchant Marine*

. . . 1. The total strength of the German surface navy . . . shall be divided equally among the U.S.S.R, U.K., and U.S.A. . . .

3. The larger part of the German submarine fleet shall be sunk. . . .

8. The German merchant marine surrendered to the three powers . . . shall be divided equally among the U.S.S.R., the U.K., and the U.S.A. . . .

V. *City of Koenigsberg and the Adjacent Area*

The conference examined a proposal by the Soviet Government that pending the final determination of territorial questions at the peace settlement the section of the western frontier of the Union of Soviet Socialist Republics which is adjacent to the Baltic Sea should pass from a point on the eastern shore of the Bay of Danzig to the east, north of Braunsberg-Goldap, to the meeting point of the frontiers of Lithuania, the Polish Republic and East Prussia.

The conference has agreed in principle to the proposal of the Soviet Government concerning the ultimate transfer to the Soviet Union of the City of Koenigsberg and the area adjacent to it as described above subject to expert examination of the actual frontier.

The President of the United States and the British Prime Minister have declared that they will support the proposal of the conference at the forthcoming peace settlement.

VI. *War Criminals*

The three governments have taken note of the discussions which have been proceeding in recent weeks in London between British, United States, Soviet and French representatives with a view to reaching agreement on the methods of trial of those major war criminals whose crimes under the Moscow Declaration of October 1943 have no particular geographical localization. The three governments reaffirm their intention to bring those criminals to swift and sure justice. They hope that the negotiations in London will result in speedy agreement being reached for this purpose, and they regard it as a matter of great importance that the trial of those major criminals should begin at the earliest possible date. The first list of defendants will be published before September first.

VII. *Austria*

The conference examined a proposal by the Soviet Government on the extension of the authority of the Austrian Provisional Government to all of Austria.

The three governments agreed that they were prepared to examine this question after the entry of the British and American forces into the City of Vienna.

It was agreed that reparations should not be exacted from Austria.

VIII. *Poland*

We have taken note with pleasure of the agreement reached among representative Poles from Poland and abroad which has made possible the formation, in accordance with the decisions reached at the Crimea Conference, of a Polish Provisional Government of National Unity recognized by the three powers. The establishment by the British and United States Governments of diplomatic relations with the Polish Provisional Government has resulted in the withdrawal of their recognition from the former Polish Government in London, which no longer exists.

The British and United States Governments have taken measures to protect the interest of the Polish Provisional Government as the recognized government of the Polish State in the property belonging to the Polish State located in their territories and under their control, whatever the form of this property may be. They have further taken measures to prevent alienation to third parties of such property. All proper facilities will be given to the Polish Provisional Government for the exercise of the ordinary legal remedies for the recovery of any property belonging to the Polish State which may have been wrongfully alienated.

The three powers are anxious to assist the Polish Provisional Government in facilitating the return to Poland as soon as practicable of all Poles abroad who wish to go, including members of the Polish armed forces and the Merchant Marine. They expect that those Poles who return home shall be accorded personal and property rights on the same basis as all Polish citizens.

The three powers note that the Polish Provisional Government in accordance with the decisions of the Crimea Conference has agreed to the holding of free and unfettered elections as soon as possible on the basis of universal suffrage and secret ballot in which all democratic and anti-Nazi parties shall have the right to take part and to put forward candidates, and that representatives of the Allied press shall enjoy full freedom to report to the world upon developments in Poland before and during the elections.

In conformity with the agreement on Poland reached at the Crimea Conference the three heads of government have sought the opinion of the Polish Provisional Government of National Unity in regard to the accession of territory in the north and west which Poland should receive. The President of the National Council of Poland and members of the Polish Provisional Government of National Unity have been received at the conference and have fully presented their views. The three heads of government reaffirm their opinion that the final delimitation of the western frontier of Poland should await the peace settlement.

The three heads of government agree that, pending the final determination of Poland's western frontier, the former German territories east of a line running from the Baltic Sea immediately west of Swinemunde, and thence along the Oder River to the confluence of the western Neisse River and along the western Neisse to the Czechoslovak frontier, including that portion of East Prussia not placed under the administration of the Union of Soviet Socialist Republics in accordance with the understanding reached at this conference and including the area of the former free City of Danzig, shall be under the administration of the Polish State and for such purposes should not be considered as parts of the Soviet zone of occupation in Germany.

IX. *Conclusion of Peace Treaties and Admission to the United Nations Organization*

The three governments consider it desirable that the present anomalous position of Italy, Bulgaria, Finland, Hungary and Rumania should be terminated by the conclusion of peace treaties. They trust that the other interested Allied governments will share these views.

For their part the three governments have included the preparation of a peace treaty for Italy as the first among the immediate important tasks to be undertaken by the new Council of Foreign Ministers. Italy was the first of the Axis powers to break with Germany, to whose defeat she had made a material contribution, and has now joined with the Allies in the struggle against Japan. Italy has freed herself from the Fascist regime and is making good progress toward the reestablishment of a democratic government and institutions. The conclusion of such a peace treaty with a recognized and democratic Italian government will make it possible for the three governments to fulfill their desire to support an application from Italy for membership of the United Nations.

The three governments have also charged the Council of Foreign Ministers with the task of preparing peace treaties for Bulgaria, Finland, Hungary and Rumania. The conclusion of peace treaties with recognized democratic governments in these states will also enable the three governments to support applications from them for membership of the United Nations. The three governments agree to examine each separately in the near future, in the light of the conditions then prevailing, the establishment of diplomatic relations with Finland, Rumania, Bulgaria, and Hungary to the extent possible prior to the conclusion of peace treaties with those countries.

The three governments have no doubt that in view of the changed conditions resulting from the termination of the war in Europe, representatives of the Allied press will enjoy full freedom to report to the world upon developments in Rumania, Bulgaria, Hungary and Finland.

As regards the admission of other states into the United Nations Organization, Article 4 of the Charter of the United Nations declares that:

"1. Membership in the United Nations is open to all other peace-loving states who accept the obligations contained in the present Charter and, in the judgment of the Organization, are able and willing to carry out these obligations;

"2. The admission of any such state to membership in the United Nations will be effected by a decision of the General Assembly upon the recommendation of the Security Council."

The three governments, so far as they are concerned, will support applications for membership from those states which have remained neutral during the war and which fulfill the qualifications set out above.

The three governments feel bound however to make it clear that they for their part would not favor any application for membership put forward by the present Spanish Government, which, having been founded with the support of the Axis powers, does not, in view of its origins, its nature, its record and its close association with the aggressor states, possess the qualifications necessary to justify such membership.

X. *Territorial Trusteeships*

The conference examined a proposal by the Soviet Government concerning trusteeship territories as defined in the decision of the Crimea Conference and in the Charter of the United Nations Organization.

After an exchange of views on this question it was decided that the disposition of any former Italian territories was one to be decided in connection with the preparation of a peace treaty for Italy and that the question of Italian territory would be considered by the September Council of Ministers of Foreign Affairs.

XI. *Revised Allied Control Commission Procedure in Rumania, Bulgaria, and Hungary*

The three governments took note that the Soviet representatives on the Allied Control Commissions in Rumania, Bulgaria and Hungary, have communicated to their United Kingdom and United States colleagues proposals for improving the work of the Control Commission, now that hostilities in Europe have ceased.

The three governments agreed that the revision of the procedures of the Allied Control Commissions in these countries would now be undertaken, taking into account the interests and responsibilities of the three Governments which together presented the terms of armistice to the respective countries. . . .

XII. *Orderly Transfers of German Populations*

The three governments having considered the question in all its aspects, recognize that the transfer to Germany of German populations, or elements thereof, remaining in Poland, Czechoslovakia and Hungary, will have to be undertaken. They agree that any transfers that take place should be effected in an orderly and humane manner.

Since the influx of a large number of Germans into Germany would increase the burden already resting on the occupying authorities, they consider that the Allied Control Council in Germany should in the first instance examine the problem with special regard to the question of the equitable distribution of these Germans among the several zones of occupation. They are accordingly instructing their respective representatives on the Control Council to report to their governments as soon as possible the extent to which such persons have already entered Germany from Poland, Czechoslovakia and Hungary, and to submit an estimate of the time and rate at which further transfers could be carried out, having regard to the present situation in Germany.

The Czechoslovak Government, the Polish Provisional Government and the Control Council in Hungary are at the same time being informed of the above, and are being requested meanwhile to suspend further expulsions pending the examination by the governments concerned of the report from their representatives on the Control Council.

9. AMERICAN POLICY CONCERNING GERMANY[9]

. . . I HAVE COME to Germany to learn at first hand the problems involved in the reconstruction of Germany and to discuss with our representatives the views of the United States Government as to some of the problems confronting us.

We in the United States have given considerable time and attention to these problems because upon their proper solution will depend not only the future well-being of Germany but the future well-being of Europe.

We have learned, whether we like it or not, that we live in one world, from which world we cannot isolate ourselves. We have learned that peace and well-being are indivisible and that our peace and well-being cannot be purchased at the price of the peace or the well-being of any other country.

I hope that the German people will never again make the mistake of believing that because the American people are peace-loving they will sit back hoping for peace if any nation uses force or the threat of force to acquire dominion over other peoples and other governments. . . .

In agreeing at Potsdam that Germany should be disarmed and demilitarized and in proposing that the four major powers should by treaty jointly undertake to see that Germany is kept disarmed and demilitarized for a generation, the United States was not unmindful of the responsibility resting upon it and its major Allies to maintain and enforce peace under the law. . . .

It is not in the interest of the German people or in the interest of world peace that Germany should become a pawn or a partner in a military struggle for power between the East and the West. . . .

The basis of the Potsdam Agreement was that, as part of a combined program of demilitarization and reparations, Germany's war potential

[9] Address of Secretary of State James F. Byrnes at Stuttgart, Germany, September 6, 1946, Department of State *Bulletin,* Vol. XV, pp. 496–501.

should be reduced by elimination and removal of her war industries and the reduction and removal of heavy industrial plants. It was contemplated this should be done to the point that Germany would be left with levels of industry capable of maintaining in Germany average European living standards without assistance from other countries. . . .

In fixing the levels of industry no allowance was made for reparations from current production. Reparations from current production would be wholly incompatible with the levels of industry now established under the Potsdam Agreement.

Obviously, higher levels of industry would have had to be fixed if reparations from current production were contemplated. The levels of industry fixed are only sufficient to enable the German people to become self-supporting and to maintain living standards approximating the average European living conditions.

That principle involves serious hardships for the German people, but it only requires them to share the hardships which Nazi aggression imposed on the average European.

The German people were not denied, however, the possibility of improving their lot by hard work over the years. Industrial growth and progress were not denied them. Being obliged to start again like the people of other devastated countries, with a peacetime economy not able to provide them more than the average European standard, the German people were not to be denied the right to use such savings as they might be able to accumulate by hard work and frugal living to build up their industries for peaceful purposes.

That was the principle of reparations to which President Truman agreed at Potsdam. And the United States will not agree to the taking from Germany of greater reparations than was provided by the Potsdam Agreement.

The carrying out of the Potsdam Agreement has, however, been obstructed by the failure of the Allied Control Council to take the necessary steps to enable the German economy to function as an economic unit. Essential central German administrative departments have not been established, although they are expressly required by the Potsdam Agreement. . . .

The United States is firmly of the belief that Germany should be administered as an economic unit and that zonal barriers should be completely obliterated so far as the economic life and activity in Germany are concerned. . . .

But just because suffering and distress in Germany are inevitable, the American Government is unwilling to accept responsibility for the needless aggravation of economic distress that is caused by the failure of the Allied Control Council to agree to give the German people a chance to solve some of their most urgent economic problems.

So far as many vital questions are concerned, the Control Council is neither governing Germany nor allowing Germany to govern itself. . . .

The principal purposes of the military occupation were and are to demilitarize and de-Nazify Germany but not to raise artificial barriers to the efforts of the German people to resume their peace-time economic life. . . .

From now on the thoughtful people of the world will judge Allied action in Germany not by Allied promises but by Allied performances. The American Government has supported and will continue to support the necessary measures to de-Nazify and demilitarize Germany, but it does not believe that large armies of foreign soldiers or alien bureaucrats, however well motivated and disciplined, are in the long run the most reliable guardians of another country's democracy. . . .

◇◇◇◇◇◇◇◇◇◇◇◇◇

10. THE FUNDAMENTALS OF AMERICAN FOREIGN POLICY [10]

. . . 1. WE SEEK no territorial expansion or selfish advantage. We have no plans for aggression against any other state, large or small. We have no objective which need clash with the peaceful aims of any other nation.

2. We believe in the eventual return of sovereign rights and self-government to all peoples who have been deprived of them by force.

3. We shall approve no territorial changes in any friendly part of the world unless they accord with the freely expressed wishes of the people concerned.

4. We believe that all peoples who are prepared for self-government should be permitted to choose their own form of government by their own freely expressed choice, without interference from any foreign source. That is true in Europe, in Asia, in Africa, as well as in the Western Hemisphere.

5. By the combined and cooperative action of our war Allies, we shall help the defeated enemy states establish peaceful, democratic governments of their own free choice. And we shall try to attain a world in which Nazism, Fascism, and military aggression cannot exist.

6. We shall refuse to recognize any government imposed upon any nation by the force of any foreign power. In some cases it may be impossible to prevent forceful imposition of such a government. But the United States will not recognize any such government.

7. We believe that all nations should have the freedom of the seas and equal rights to the navigation of boundary rivers and waterways and of rivers and waterways which pass through more than one country.

8. We believe that all states which are accepted in the society of nations should have access on equal terms to the trade and the raw materials of the world.

---

[10] Address of President Truman at New York, October 27, 1945. Department of State *Bulletin*, Vol. XIII, pp. 653–6.

9. We believe that the sovereign states of the Western Hemisphere, without interference from outside the Western Hemisphere, must work together as good neighbors in the solution of their common problems.

10. We believe that full economic collaboration between all nations, great and small, is essential to the improvement of living conditions all over the world, and to the establishment of freedom from fear and freedom from want.

11. We shall continue to strive to promote freedom of expression and freedom of religion throughout the peace-loving areas of the world.

12. We are convinced that the preservation of peace between nations requires a United Nations Organization composed of all the peace-loving nations of the world who are willing jointly to use force if necessary to insure peace. . . .

That is the foreign policy which guides the United States now. That is the foreign policy with which it confidently faces the future.

It may not be put into effect tomorrow or the next day. But none the less, it is our policy; and we shall seek to achieve it. It may take a long time, but it is worth waiting for, and it is worth striving to attain. . . .

Chapter XXXVI

THE DIPLOMACY OF SECURITY: EUROPE AND LATIN AMERICA

IN THE PERIOD immediately following the Second World War, American foreign policy was based on the primary assumption that a community of interests existed among the anti-Axis powers, and that these powers would collaborate to effect peace settlements in Europe and Asia and to solve world problems through the machinery and agencies of the United Nations. In harmony with this assumption the United States withdrew the bulk of its armed forces from Europe and from the Far East, urged the Government of China to cooperate with the Chinese Communist leaders, most of whom were trained in Russia, shared with Russia the control of Korea, and all but ignored the character of Russian policy toward the nations whose territories were within the perimeter of Russian wartime military advance. The weakness and the fallacy of this assumption were soon manifest in a growing list of unsolved issues including the civil war in China, the control of atomic energy, peace settlements in Germany and Austria, and stalemate in the United Nations. It is probably impossible to fix the exact moment when the United States realized the failure of its postwar policies. American diplomacy in this era was tortuous, singularly empty of distinction, and frequently contradictory. It was clear, however, that after 1946 American foreign policy gradually moved away from the basic postwar assumption. The shift in policy was foreshadowed by the proposals, noted in the preceding chapter, of the United States concerning the control of atomic energy – proposals that recognized the limitations of the United Nations – and by the Stuttgart speech of Secretary Byrnes. As far as Europe was concerned, the clean break with the postwar assumption came with the Truman Doctrine of 1947 (1).

The Vandenberg Resolution of June 11, 1942 (2) was a logical counterpart of the Truman Doctrine, and was comparable in its significance to the Connally Resolution of 1943. The attempt of the United States to revise the voting procedure in the Security Council (3), and the so-called "Uniting for Peace" resolutions of the General Assembly (4), reflected the belief of the United States that Russia had abused its legal rights as a permanent member of the Security Council, and that remedies could be found in new rules of procedure and in greater assertiveness on the part of the General Assembly over security matters. The Inter-American Treaty of Reciprocal Assistance, the Rio Pact (5), stemmed directly from the Act of Chapultepec, noted earlier, and not primarily from postwar events. It contained, however, the principle of collective security, and to that extent was a part of the new trend in American policy. It was incorporated into the Charter of the Organization of American States, signed on April 30, 1948, at Bogotá. The North Atlantic Treaty (6) extended the principle of collective security – sometimes called collective self-defense – to an area described in Article 6 of the Treaty. The interpretation of several important parts of the Treaty by the Senate is shown in the Report of the Committee on Foreign Relations (7). The Treaty was signed by Belgium, Canada, Denmark, France, Iceland, Italy, Luxembourg, the Netherlands, Norway, Portugal, Great Britain, and the United States. Greece and Turkey acceded to the Treaty under a protocol signed on September 15, 1951, and under a similar protocol the Treaty was extended to Western Germany (8).

The Economic Cooperation Act of 1948 (9) was the response of the United States to the continued dislocation of European economy and the consequent threat of European political disintegration. This Act implemented the Marshall Plan and established a basic policy which was extended, with minor adjustments, in subsequent economic cooperation acts. The "Point Four" program (10) was a special feature of the Economic Cooperation Act of 1950. These economic measures were in part humanitarian, but they were connected with American commitments under the North Atlantic Treaty, and with the program of arms aid to various nations, called the Mutual Defense Assistance Policy (11). Along with these efforts to achieve security and to extend the area of freedom the United States felt the need to have its objectives and the character of its society known abroad and to promote the interchange of knowledge and ideas. These ends were sought through the Information and Educational Exchange Act of 1948 (12).

As noted earlier, the shift in American policy toward Germany could be seen in the Stuttgart speech of Secretary Byrnes in 1946. The evolution of the new policy can be traced in the address of Secretary Acheson of April 28, 1949 (13), the Convention between Germany, Great Britain, France, and the United States of May 26, 1952 (14), and the Protocol – noted above (8) – to the North Atlantic Treaty. If any lingering doubt remained that American diplomacy was dominated by considerations of security, such doubt was dispelled by the signing, September 26, 1953, of a defense agreement between the United States and Spain, a nation whose government was motivated by none of the ideals characteristic of the Atlantic Charter (15).

◇◇◇◇◇◇◇◇◇◇◇◇◇

The Diplomacy of Security: Europe and Latin America

1. THE TRUMAN DOCTRINE [1]

THE GRAVITY of the situation which confronts the world today necessitates my appearance before a joint session of the Congress. The foreign policy and the national security of this country are involved.

One aspect of the present situation, which I wish to present to you at this time for your consideration and decision, concerns Greece and Turkey.

The United States has received from the Greek Government an urgent appeal for financial and economic assistance. Preliminary reports from the American Economic Mission now in Greece and reports from the American Ambassador in Greece corroborate the statement of the Greek Government that assistance is imperative if Greece is to survive as a free nation.

I do not believe that the American people and the Congress wish to turn a deaf ear to the appeal of the Greek Government.

Greece is not a rich country. Lack of sufficient natural resources has always forced the Greek people to work hard to make both ends meet. Since 1940, this industrious, peace loving country has suffered invasion, four years of cruel enemy occupation, and bitter internal strife.

When forces of liberation entered Greece they found that the retreating Germans had destroyed virtually all the railways, roads, port facilities, communications, and merchant marine. More than a thousand villages had been burned. Eighty-five per cent of the children were tubercular. Livestock, poultry, and draft animals had almost disappeared. Inflation had wiped out practically all savings.

As a result of these tragic conditions, a militant minority, exploiting human want and misery, was able to create political chaos which, until now, has made economic recovery impossible.

Greece is today without funds to finance the importation of those goods which are essential to bare subsistence. Under these circumstances the people of Greece cannot make progress in solving their problems of reconstruction. Greece is in desperate need of financial and economic assistance to enable it to resume purchases of food, clothing, fuel and seeds. These are indispensable for the subsistence of its people and are obtainable only from abroad. Greece must have help to import the goods necessary to restore internal order and security so essential for economic and political recovery.

The Greek Government has also asked for the assistance of experienced American administrators, economists and technicians to insure that the financial and other aid given to Greece shall be used effectively in creating a stable and self-sustaining economy and in improving its public administration.

1 Message of President Harry S. Truman to Congress on March 12, 1947. *New York Times,* March 13, 1947.

The very existence of the Greek state is today threatened by the terrorist activities of several thousand armed men, led by Communists, who defy the Government's authority at a number of points, particularly along the northern boundaries. A commission appointed by the United Nations Security Council is at present investigating disturbed conditions in Northern Greece and alleged border violations along the frontiers between Greece on the one hand and Albania, Bulgaria, and Yugoslavia on the other.

Meanwhile, the Greek Government is unable to cope with the situation. The Greek Army is small and poorly equipped. It needs supplies and equipment if it is to restore the authority to the Government throughout Greek territory.

Greece must have assistance if it is to become a self-supporting and self-respecting democracy. The United States must supply that assistance. We have already extended to Greece certain types of relief and economic aid but these are inadequate. There is no other country to which democratic Greece can turn. No other nation is willing and able to provide the necessary support for a democratic Greek Government.

The British Government, which has been helping Greece, can give no further financial or economic aid after March 31. Great Britain finds itself under the necessity of reducing or liquidating its commitments in several parts of the world, including Greece.

We have considered how the United Nations might assist in this crisis. But the situation is an urgent one requiring immediate action, and the United Nations and its related organizations are not in a position to extend help of the kind that is required.

It is important to note that the Greek Government has asked for our aid in utilizing effectively the financial and other assistance we may give to Greece, and in improving its public administration. It is of the utmost importance that we supervise the use of any funds made available to Greece, in such a manner that each dollar spent will count toward making Greece self-supporting, and will help to build an economy in which a healthy democracy can flourish.

No government is perfect. One of the chief virtues of a democracy, however, is that its defects are always visible and under democratic processes can be pointed out and corrected. The Government of Greece is not perfect. Nevertheless, it represents 85 per cent of the members of the Greek Parliament who were chosen in an election last year. Foreign observers, including 692 Americans, considered this election to be a fair expression of the views of the Greek people.

The Greek Government has been operating in an atmosphere of chaos and extremism. It has made mistakes. The extension of aid by this country does not mean that the United States condones everything that the Greek Government has done or will do. We have condemned in the past, and we condemn now, extremist measures of the right or the left. We have in the past advised tolerance, and we advise tolerance now.

Greece's neighbor, Turkey, also deserves our attention. The future of Turkey as an independent and economically sound state is clearly no less important to the freedom-loving peoples of the world than the future of Greece. The circumstances in which Turkey finds itself today are considerably different from those of Greece. Turkey has been spared the disasters that have beset Greece. And during the war, the United States and Great Britain furnished Turkey with material aid. Nevertheless, Turkey now needs our support.

Since the war Turkey has sought financial assistance from Great Britain and the United States for the purpose of effecting that modernization necessary for the maintenance of its national integrity. That integrity is essential to the preservation of order in the Middle East.

The British Government has informed us that, owing to its own difficulties, it can no longer extend financial or economic aid to Turkey. As in the case of Greece, if Turkey is to have the assistance it needs, the United States must supply it. We are the only country able to provide that help.

I am fully aware of the broad implications involved if the United States extends assistance to Greece and Turkey, and I shall discuss these implications with you at this time.

One of the primary objectives of the foreign policy of the United States is the creation of conditions in which we and other nations will be able to work out a way of life free from coercion. This was a fundamental issue in the war with Germany and Japan. Our victory was won over countries which sought to impose their will, and their way of life, upon other nations.

To ensure the peaceful development of nations, free from coercion, the United States has taken a leading part in establishing the United Nations. The United Nations is designed to make possible lasting freedom and independence for all its members. We shall not realize our objectives, however, unless we are willing to help free people to maintain their free institutions and their national integrity against aggressive movements that seek to impose upon them totalitarian regimes. This is no more than a frank recognition that totalitarian regimes imposed on free peoples, by direct or indirect aggression, undermine the foundations of international peace and hence the security of the United States.

The peoples of a number of countries of the world have recently had totalitarian regimes forced upon them against their will. The Government of the United States has made frequent protests against coercion and intimidation, in violation of the Yalta Agreement, in Poland, Rumania and Bulgaria. I must also state that in a number of other countries there have been similar developments.

At the present moment in world history nearly every nation must choose between alternative ways of life. The choice is too often not a free one.

One way of life is based upon the will of the majority, and is distinguished by free institutions, representative government, free elections, guarantees of individual liberty, freedom of speech and religion, and freedom from political oppression.

The second way of life is based upon the will of a minority forcibly imposed upon the majority. It relies upon terror and oppression, a controlled press and radio, fixed elections, and the suppression of personal freedoms.

I believe that it must be the policy of the United States to support free peoples who are resisting attempted subjugation by armed minorities or by outside pressures.

I believe that we must assist free peoples to work out their own destinies in their own way.

I believe that our help should be primarily through economic and financial aid which is essential to economic stability and orderly political processes.

The world is not static, and the status quo is not sacred. But we cannot allow changes in the status quo in violation of the Charter of the United Nations by such methods as coercion, or by such subterfuges as political infiltration. In helping free and independent nations to maintain their freedom, the United States will be giving effect to the principles of the Charter of the United Nations.

It is necessary only to glance at a map to realize that the survival and integrity of the Greek nation are of grave importance in a much wider situation. If Greece should fall under the control of an armed minority, the effect upon its neighbor, Turkey, would be immediate and serious. Confusion and disorder might well spread throughout the entire Middle East.

Moreover, the disappearance of Greece as an independent state would have a profound effect upon those countries in Europe whose peoples are struggling against great difficulties to maintain their freedoms and their independence while they repair the damages of war.

It would be an unspeakable tragedy if these countries, which have struggled so long against overwhelming odds, should lose that victory for which they sacrificed so much. Collapse of free institutions and loss of independence would be disastrous not only for them but for the world. Discouragement and possibly failure would quickly be the lot of neighboring peoples striving to maintain their freedom and independence.

Should we fail to aid Greece and Turkey in this fateful hour, the effect will be far reaching to the West as well as to the East. We must take immediate and resolute action.

I therefore ask the Congress to provide authority for assistance to Greece and Turkey in the amount of $400,000,000 for the period ending June 30, 1948. In requesting these funds, I have taken into consideration the maximum amount of relief assistance which would be furnished to Greece out of the $350,000,000 which I recently requested that the Congress authorize for the prevention of starvation and suffering in countries devastated by the war.

In addition to funds, I ask the Congress to authorize the detail of

American civilian and military personnel to Greece and Turkey, at the request of those countries, to assist in the tasks of reconstruction, and for the purpose of supervising the use of such financial and material assistance as may be furnished. I recommend that authority also be provided for the instruction and training of selected Greek and Turkish personnel.

Finally, I ask that the Congress provide authority which will permit the speediest and most effective use, in terms of needed commodities, supplies, and equipment, of such funds as may be authorized.

If further funds, or further authority, should be needed for purposes indicated in this message, I shall not hesitate to bring the situation before the Congress. On this subject the Executive and Legislative branches of the Government must work together.

This is a serious course upon which we embark. I would not recommend it except that the alternative is much more serious.

The United States contributed $341,000,000,000 toward winning World War II. This is an investment in world freedom and world peace.

The assistance that I am recommending for Greece and Turkey amounts to little more than 1 tenth of 1 per cent of this investment. It is only common sense that we should safeguard this investment and make sure that it was not in vain.

The seeds of totalitarian regimes are nurtured by misery and want. They spread and grow in the evil soil of poverty and strife. They reach their full growth when the hope of a people for a better life has died. We must keep that hope alive. The free peoples of the world look to us for support in maintaining their freedoms.

If we falter in our leadership, we may endanger the peace of the world – and we shall surely endanger the welfare of our own Nation.

Great responsibilities have been placed upon us by the swift movement of events. I am confident that the Congress will face these responsibilities squarely.

2. THE VANDENBERG RESOLUTION [2]

WHEREAS PEACE with justice and the defense of human rights and fundamental freedoms require international cooperation through more effective use of the United Nations: Therefore be it

Resolved, That the Senate reaffirm the policy of the United States to achieve international peace and security through the United Nations so that armed force shall not be used except in the common interest, and that the President be advised of the sense of the Senate that this Government, by constitutional process, should particularly pursue the following objectives within the United Nations Charter:

[2] Senate Resolution 239, 80th Congress, 2nd Session. Approved by the Senate on June 11, 1948.

(1) Voluntary agreement to remove the veto from all questions involving pacific settlements of international disputes and situations, and from the admission of new members.

(2) Progressive development of regional and other collective arrangements for individual and collective self-defense in accordance with the purposes, principles, and provisions of the Charter.

(3) Association of the United States, by constitutional process, with such regional and other collective arrangements as are based on continuous and effective self-help and mutual aid, and as affect its national security.

(4) Contributing to the maintenance of peace by making clear its determination to exercise the right of individual or collective self-defense under article 51 should any armed attack occur affecting its national security.

(5) Maximum efforts to obtain agreements to provide the United Nations with armed forces as provided by the Charter, and to obtain agreement among member nations upon universal regulation and reduction of armaments under adequate and dependable guaranty against violation.

(6) If necessary, after adequate effort toward strengthening the United Nations, review of the Charter at an appropriate time by a General Conference called under article 109 or by the General Assembly.

◇◇◇◇◇◇◇◇◇◇◇◇

3. AMERICAN POLICY ON THE VETO QUESTION [3]

. . . THE EXERCISE of the veto power on a number of occasions has seriously undermined the confidence of member states in the ability of the Security Council to maintain international peace and security. The chronic disagreement and deadlock in the United Nations is a matter of deepest concern to all those who wish to see this organization function as it was intended – as an effective instrument to safeguard our common interests in peace and security. The use of the veto and the threat of its use are symptoms of the prevailing disagreement. . . .

Looking now to the immediate problem of improving the functioning of the Security Council, we have before us a resolution which was jointly sponsored in the *Ad Hoc* Political Committee by four of the permanent members of the Security Council – all except the Soviet Union. The resolution incorporates the substance of the recommendations of the Interim Committee of the General Assembly. . . .

Even a superficial perusal of the resolution of the *Ad Hoc* Committee must disclose that it is not designed to alter fundamentally the unanimity principle as it is embodied in the Charter. A very great majority of the

[3] Statement of Warren R. Austin, United States Representative to the United Nations, before the General Assembly on April 13, 1949. Department of State *Bulletin*, Vol. XX, pp. 512–15.

members of the United Nations have expressed the view either explicitly or implicitly that the unanimity principle is and should remain a fundamental principle of the Charter. A majority of the members of the United Nations are opposed to any effort being made at this time to amend the Charter.

On the other hand, there is a large majority of the members of the United Nations who are making an anxious effort to design ways and means of giving life to the unanimity principle and making it work so that the Security Council can carry out its function effectively. . . . You will recall that efforts by the Assembly along similar lines in 1946 have resulted in a substantial improvement. I refer to the suggestions made by several members of the Assembly during the debates that abstention of a permanent member of the Security Council should not be considered a veto. That practice was adopted by common consent in the Security Council and has now become a well-accepted Security Council procedure. . . .

Let us now look at this resolution in more detail. The work of the Interim Committee on which the resolution is based revealed the great potentialities which can be progressively realized under the present Charter if there can be general agreement upon a moderate course. By adoption of this resolution, the Assembly would make an important decision to the effect that 34 specified and described decisions of the Security Council are procedural. . . .

The principal criteria for placing these 34 items in the category of decisions deemed procedural were –

(a) Decisions under procedure provisions of the Charter;
(b) Decisions relating to the internal procedure of the United Nations;
(c) Decisions relating to internal functioning of the Security Council;
(d) Decisions analogous to the foregoing;
(e) Decisions which implement procedural decisions.

In short, the Interim Committee, after a thorough study, concluded that these decisions are procedural in the light of the express language of the Charter, and of sound Charter interpretation. . . .

◇◇◇◇◇◇◇◇◇◇◇◇◇

4. RESOLUTIONS OF THE GENERAL ASSEMBLY ON UNITING FOR PEACE [4]

THE GENERAL Assembly . . .

1. Resolves that if the Security Council, because of lack of unanimity of the permanent members, fails to exercise its primary responsibility for the maintenance of international peace and security in any case where

[4] Approved by the General Assembly, November 3, 1950. U. N. General Assembly, *Official Records*, 5th Session, Supplement No. 20, p. 10.

there appears to be a threat to the peace, breach of the peace, or act of aggression, the General Assembly shall consider the matter immediately with a view to making appropriate recommendations to Members for collective measures, including in the case of a breach of the peace or act of aggression the use of armed force when necessary, to maintain or restore international peace and security. If not in session at the time, the General Assembly may meet in emergency special session within twenty-four hours of the request therefor. Such emergency special session shall be called if requested by the Security Council on the vote of any seven members, or by a majority of the Members of the United Nations;

2. Adopts for this purpose the amendments to its rules of procedure set forth in the annex to the present resolution;

3. Establishes a Peace Observation Commission . . . which could observe and report on the situation in any area where there exists international tension the continuance of which is likely to endanger the maintenance of international peace and security. . . .

8. Recommends to the States Members of the United Nations that each Member maintain within its national armed forces elements so trained, organized and equipped that they could promptly be made available, in accordance with its constitutional processes, for service as a United Nations unit or units, upon recommendation by the Security Council or the General Assembly, without prejudice to the use of such elements in exercise of the right of individual or collective self-defense recognized in Article 51 of the Charter; . . .

◇◇◇◇◇◇◇◇◇◇◇◇◇

5. INTER-AMERICAN TREATY OF RECIPROCAL ASSISTANCE (RIO PACT) [5]

. . . *ARTICLE 1.* The High Contracting Parties formally condemn war and undertake in their international relations not to resort to the threat or the use of force in any manner inconsistent with the provisions of the Charter of the United Nations or of this Treaty.

Article 2. As a consequence of the principle set forth in the preceding Article, the High Contracting Parties undertake to submit every controversy which may arise between them to methods of peaceful settlement and to endeavor to settle any such controversy among themselves by means of the procedures in force in the Inter-American System before referring it to the General Assembly or the Security Council of the United Nations.

Article 3.

1. The High Contracting Parties agree that an armed attack by any State against an American State shall be considered as an attack against

[5] Signed at Rio de Janeiro, September 2, 1947, and ratified by the United States on December 19, 1947. Senate document, *Executive II*, 80th Congress, 1st Session.

all the American States and, consequently, each one of the said Contracting Parties undertakes to assist in meeting the attack in the exercise of the inherent right of individual or collective self-defense recognized by Article 51 of the Charter of the United Nations.

2. On the request of the State or States directly attacked and until the decision of the Organ of Consultation of the Inter-American System, each one of the Contracting Parties may determine the immediate measures which it may individually take in fulfillment of the obligation contained in the preceding paragraph and in accordance with the principle of continental solidarity. The Organ of Consultation shall meet without delay for the purpose of examining those measures and agreeing upon the measures of a collective character that should be taken.

3. The provisions of this Article shall be applied in case of any armed attack which takes place within the region described in Article 4 or within the territory of an American State. When the attack takes place outside of the said areas, the provisions of Article 6 shall be applied.

4. Measures of self-defense provided for under this Article may be taken until the Security Council of the United Nations has taken the measures necessary to maintain international peace and security.

Article 4. The region to which this Treaty refers is bounded as follows: beginning at the North Pole; thence due South to a point 74 degrees north latitude, 10 degrees west longitude; thence by a rhumb line to a point 47 degrees 30 minutes north latitude, 50 degrees west longitude; thence by a rhumb line to a point 35 degrees north latitude, 60 degrees west longitude; thence due south to a point in 20 degrees north latitude; thence by a rhumb line to a point 5 degrees north latitude, 24 degrees west longitude; thence due south to the South Pole; thence due north to a point 30 degrees south latitude, 90 degrees west longitude; thence by a rhumb line to a point on the Equator at 97 degrees west longitude; thence by a rhumb line to a point 15 degrees north latitude, 120 degrees west longitude; thence by a rhumb line to a point 50 degrees north latitude, 170 degrees east longitude; thence due north to a point in 54 degrees north latitude; thence by a rhumb line to a point 65 degrees 30 minutes north latitude, 168 degrees 58 minutes 5 seconds west longitude: thence due north to the North Pole.

Article 5. The High Contracting Parties shall immediately send to the Security Council of the United Nations, in conformity with Articles 51 and 54 of the Charter of the United Nations, complete information concerning the activities undertaken or in contemplation in the exercise of the right of self-defense or for the purpose of maintaining inter-American peace and security.

Article 6. If the inviolability or the integrity of the territory or the sovereignty or political independence of any American State should be affected by an aggression which is not an armed attack or by an extra-continental or intra-continental conflict, or by any other fact or situation that might endanger the peace of America, the Organ of Consultation shall meet immediately in order to agree on the measures which must be taken in case of aggression to assist the victim of the aggression or, in any case, the measures which should be taken for the common defense and for the maintenance of the peace and security of the Continent.

Article 7. In the case of a conflict between two or more American States, without prejudice to the right of self-defense in conformity with Article 51 of the Charter of the United Nations, the High Contracting Parties, meeting in consultation shall call upon the contending States to suspend hostilities and restore matters to the *status quo ante bellum,* and shall take in addition all other necessary measures to reestablish or maintain inter-American peace and security and for the solution of the conflict by peaceful means. The rejection of the pacifying action will be considered in the determination of the aggressor and in the application of the measures which the consultative meeting may agree upon.

Article 8. For the purposes of this Treaty, the measures on which the Organ of Consultation may agree will comprise one or more of the following: recall of chiefs of diplomatic missions; breaking of diplomatic relations; breaking of consular relations or of rail, sea, air, postal, telegraphic, telephonic, and radiotelephonic or radiotelegraphic communications; and use of armed force.

Article 9. In addition to other acts which the Organ of Consultation may characterize as aggression, the following shall be considered as such:

a. Unprovoked armed attack by a State against the territory, the people, or the land, sea or air forces of another State;

b. Invasion, by the armed forces of a State, of the territory of an American State, through the trespassing of boundaries demarcated in accordance with a treaty, judicial decision, or arbitral award, or, in the absence of frontiers thus demarcated, invasion affecting a region which is under the effective jurisdiction of another State.

Article 10. None of the provisions of this Treaty shall be construed as impairing the rights and obligations of the High Contracting Parties under the Charter of the United Nations.

Article 11. The consultations to which this Treaty refers shall be carried out by means of the Meetings of Ministers of Foreign Affairs of the American Republics which have ratified the Treaty, or in the manner or by the organ which in the future may be agreed upon.

Article 12. The Governing Board of the Pan American Union may act provisionally as an organ of consultation until the meeting of the Organ of Consultation referred to in the preceding Article takes place.

Article 13. The consultations shall be initiated at the request addressed to the Governing Board of the Pan American Union by any of the Signatory States which has ratified the Treaty.

Article 14. In the voting referred to in this Treaty only the representatives of the Signatory States which have ratified the Treaty may take part.

Article 15. The Governing Board of the Pan American Union shall act in all matters concerning this Treaty as an organ of liaison among the

Signatory States which have ratified this Treaty and between these States and the United Nations.

Article 16. The decisions of the Governing Board of the Pan American Union referred to in Articles 13 and 15 above shall be taken by an absolute majority of the Members entitled to vote.

Article 17. The Organ of Consultation shall take its decisions by a vote of two-thirds of the Signatory States which have ratified the Treaty.

Article 18. In the case of a situation or dispute between American States, the parties directly interested shall be excluded from the voting referred to in the two preceding Articles.

Article 19. To constitute a quorum in all the meetings referred to in the previous Articles, it shall be necessary that the number of States represented shall be at least equal to the number of votes necessary for the taking of the decision.

Article 20. Decisions which require the application of the measures specified in Article 8 shall be binding upon all the Signatory States which have ratified this Treaty, with the sole exception that no State shall be required to use armed force without its consent. . . .

Article 25. This Treaty shall remain in force indefinitely, but may be denounced by any High Contracting Party by a notification in writing to the Pan American Union, which shall inform all the other High Contracting Parties of each notification of denunciation received. After the expiration of two years from the date of the receipt by the Pan American Union of a notification of denunciation by any High Contracting Party, the present Treaty shall cease to be in force with respect to such State, but shall remain in full force and effect with respect to all the other High Contracting Parties. . . .

◇◇◇◇◇◇◇◇◇◇◇◇◇

6. THE NORTH ATLANTIC TREATY [6]

. . . *ARTICLE 1.* The Parties undertake, as set forth in the Charter of the United Nations, to settle any international disputes in which they may be involved by peaceful means in such a manner that international peace and security, and justice, are not endangered, and to refrain in their international relations from the threat or use of force in any manner inconsistent with the purposes of the United Nations.

Article 2. The Parties will contribute toward the further development of peaceful and friendly international relations by strengthening their free institutions, by bringing about a better understanding of the principles upon which these institutions are founded, and by promoting conditions of stability and well-being. They will seek to eliminate conflict in

[6] Signed at Washington April 4, 1949, and ratified by the United States on July 25, 1949. Department of State *Bulletin*, Vol. XX, pp. 339–42.

their international economic policies and will encourage economic collaboration between any or all of them.

Article 3. In order more effectively to achieve the objectives of this Treaty, the Parties, separately and jointly, by means of continuous and effective self-help and mutual aid, will maintain and develop their individual and collective capacity to resist armed attack.

Article 4. The Parties will consult together whenever, in the opinion of any of them, the territorial integrity, political independence or security of any of the Parties is threatened.

Article 5. The Parties agree that an armed attack against one or more of them in Europe or North America shall be considered an attack against them all; and consequently they agree that, if such an armed attack occurs, each of them, in exercise of the right of individual or collective self-defense recognized by Article 51 of the Charter of the United Nations, will assist the Party or Parties so attacked by taking forthwith, individually and in concert with the other Parties, such action as it deems necessary, including the use of armed force, to restore and maintain the security of the North Atlantic area.

Any such armed attack and all measures taken as a result thereof shall immediately be reported to the Security Council. Such measures shall be terminated when the Security Council has taken the measures necessary to restore and maintain international peace and security.

Article 6. For the purpose of Article 5 an armed attack on one or more of the Parties is deemed to include an armed attack on the territory of any of the Parties in Europe or North America, on the Algerian departments of France, on the occupation forces of any Party in Europe, on the islands under the jurisdiction of any Party in the North Atlantic area north of the Tropic of Cancer or on the vessels or aircraft in this area of any of the Parties.

Article 7. This Treaty does not affect, and shall not be interpreted as affecting, in any way the rights and obligations under the Charter of the Parties which are members of the United Nations, or the primary responsibility of the Security Council for the maintenance of international peace and security.

Article 8. Each Party declares that none of the international engagements now in force between it and any other of the Parties or any third state is in conflict with the provisions of this Treaty, and undertakes not to enter into any international engagement in conflict with this Treaty.

Article 9. The Parties hereby establish a council, on which each of them shall be represented, to consider matters concerning the implementation of this Treaty. The council shall be so organized as to be able to meet promptly at any time. The council shall set up such subsidiary bodies as may be necessary; in particular it shall establish immediately a defense committee which shall recommend measures for the implementation of Article 3 and 5.

Article 10. The Parties may, by unanimous agreement, invite any other

European state in a position to further the principles of this Treaty and to contribute to the security of the North Atlantic area to accede to this Treaty. Any state so invited may become a party to the Treaty by depositing its instrument of accession with the Government of the United States of America. The Government of the United States of America will inform each of the Parties of the deposit of each such instrument of accession. . . .

Article 12. After the Treaty has been in force for ten years, or at any time thereafter, the Parties shall, if any of them so requests, consult together for the purpose of reviewing the Treaty, having regard for the factors then affecting peace and security in the North Atlantic area, including the development of universal as well as regional arrangements under the Charter of the United Nations for the maintenance of international peace and security.

Article 13. After the Treaty has been in force for twenty years, any Party may cease to be a party one year after its notice of denunciation has been given to the Government of the United States of America, which will inform the Governments of the other Parties of the deposit of each notice of denunciation. . . .

◇◇◇◇◇◇◇◇◇◇◇◇◇

7. INTERPRETATION OF THE NORTH ATLANTIC TREATY BY THE COMMITTEE ON FOREIGN RELATIONS OF THE SENATE [7]

. . . ARTICLE 4 carries no obligation other than that of consultation. Whether or not any action was taken following consultation, or what form such action might take, would be matters for each party to decide for itself. It should be emphasized, however, that in no event is collective enforcement action, such as that defined in articles 41 and 42 of the Charter, contemplated. . . .

Article 5 is the heart of the treaty. In it the parties establish the principle that an armed attack against one or more of them is to be considered an attack against them all. . . . The first question which would arise would be whether or not an armed attack had in fact occurred. If the circumstances were not clear, there would presumably be consultation but each party would have the responsibility of determining for itself the answer to this question of fact. . . .

The second problem is the nature and extent of the action contemplated as a result of armed attack. . . . In this connection, the committee calls particular attention to the phrase "such action as it deems necessary." These words were included in article 5 to make absolutely clear that each

[7] Report of the Committee on Foreign Relations, June 6, 1949. Senate Executive *Report,* No. 8, 81st Congress, 1st Session.

party remains free to exercise its honest judgment in deciding upon the measures it will take to help restore and maintain the security of the North Atlantic area. The freedom of decision as to what action each party shall take in no way reduces the importance of the commitment undertaken. Action short of the use of armed force might suffice, or total war with all our resources might be necessary. Obviously article 5 carries with it an important and far-reaching commitment for the United States; what we may do to carry out that commitment, however, will depend upon our own independent decision in each particular instance reached in accordance with our own constitutional processes.

During the hearings substantially the following questions were repeatedly asked: In view of the provision in article 5 that an attack against one shall be considered an attack against all, would the United States be obligated to react to an attack on Paris or Copenhagen in the same way it would react to an attack on New York City? In such an event does the treaty give the President the power to take any action, without specific congressional authorization, which he could not take in the absence of the treaty?

The answer to both these questions is "No." An armed attack upon any State of the United States by its very nature would require the immediate application of all force necessary to repel the attack. The Constitution itself recognizes the special significance of such a calamity by providing that the United States shall protect each State against invasion. . . .

Article 5 records what is a fact, namely, that an armed attack within the meaning of the treaty would in the present-day world constitute an attack upon the entire community comprising the parties to the treaty, including the United States. Accordingly, the President and the Congress, each within their sphere of assigned constitutional responsibilities, would be expected to take all action necessary and appropriate to protect the United States against the consequences and dangers of an armed attack committed against any party to the treaty. The committee does not believe it appropriate in this report to undertake to define the authority of the President to use the armed forces. Nothing in the treaty, however, including the provision that an attack against one shall be considered an attack against all, increases or decreases the constitutional powers of either the President or the Congress or changes the relationship between them. . . .

◇◇◇◇◇◇◇◇◇◇◇◇◇

8. PROTOCOL TO THE NORTH ATLANTIC TREATY [8]

THE PARTIES to the North Atlantic Treaty, signed at Washington on 4th April 1949,

[8] Signed at Paris, May 27, 1952 and approved by the Senate, July 1, 1952. *Congressional Record*, 82nd Congress, 2nd Session, Vol. XCVIII, Pt. 7, p. 8696.

Being satisfied that the creation of the European Defense Community set up under the Treaty signed at Paris on 27th May 1952 will strengthen the North Atlantic Community and the integrated defense of the North Atlantic area, and promote the closer association of the countries of Western Europe, and

Considering that the Parties to the Treaty setting up the European Defense Community have signed a Protocol, which will enter into force at the same time as the present Protocol, giving to the Parties to the North Atlantic Treaty guarantees equivalent to the guarantees contained in Article 5 of the North Atlantic Treaty;

Agree as follows:

Article I. An armed attack

(i) on the territory of any of the members of the European Defense Community in Europe or in the area described in Article 6 (i) of the North Atlantic Treaty or

(ii) on the forces, vessels or aircraft of the European Defense Community when in the area described in Article 6 (ii) of the said Treaty, shall be considered an attack against all the Parties to the North Atlantic Treaty, within the meaning of Article 5 of the said Treaty, and Article 5 shall apply accordingly.

The expression "member of the European Defense Community" in paragraph (i) of this Article means any of the following States which is a member of the Community, namely, Belgium, France, the German Federal Republic, Italy, Luxembourg, and the Netherlands.

Article II. The present Protocol shall enter into force as soon as each of the Parties has notified the Government of the United States of America of its acceptance and the Council of the European Defense Community has notified the North Atlantic Council of the entry into force of the Treaty setting up the European Defense Community. The Government of the United States of America shall inform all the Parties to the North Atlantic Treaty of the date of the receipt of each such notification and of the date of the entry into force of the present Protocol.

Article III. The present Protocol shall remain in force for so long as the North Atlantic Treaty and the Treaty setting up the European Defense Community remain in force and the Parties to the latter Treaty continue to give, in respect of themselves and the European Defense forces, guarantees to the Parties to the North Atlantic Treaty equivalent to the guarantees contained in the present Protocol.

Article IV. The present Protocol, of which the English and French texts are equally authentic, shall be deposited in the Archives of the Government of the United States of America. Duly certified copies thereof shall be transmitted by that Government to the Governments of all the Parties to the North Atlantic Treaty and of all the Parties to the Treaty setting up the European Defense Community. . . .

◇◇◇◇◇◇◇◇◇◇◇◇◇

9. THE ECONOMIC COOPERATION ACT OF 1948 [9]

. . . SEC. 102. (a) Recognizing the intimate economic and other relationships between the United States and the nations of Europe, and recognizing that disruption following in the wake of war is not contained by national frontiers, the Congress finds that the existing situation in Europe endangers the establishment of a lasting peace, the general welfare and national interest of the United States, and the attainment of the objectives of the United Nations. The restoration or maintenance in European countries of principles of individual liberty, free institutions, and genuine independence rests largely upon the establishment of sound economic conditions, stable international economic relationships, and the achievement by the countries of Europe of a healthy economy independent of extraordinary outside assistance. The accomplishment of these objectives calls for a plan of European recovery, open to all such nations which cooperate in such plan, based upon a strong production effort, the expansion of foreign trade, the creation and maintenance of internal financial stability, and the development of economic cooperation, including all possible steps to establish and maintain equitable rates of exchange and to bring about the progressive elimination of trade barriers. Mindful of the advantages which the United States has enjoyed through the existence of a large domestic market with no internal trade barriers, and believing that similar advantages can accrue to the countries of Europe, it is declared to be the policy of the people of the United States to encourage these countries through a joint organization to exert sustained common efforts as set forth in the report of the Committee of European Economic Cooperation signed at Paris on September 22, 1947, which will speedily achieve that economic cooperation in Europe which is essential for lasting peace and prosperity. It is further declared to be the policy of the people of the United States to sustain and strengthen principles of individual liberty, free institutions, and genuine independence in Europe through assistance to those countries of Europe which participate in a joint recovery program based upon self-help and mutual cooperation: *Provided,* That no assistance to the participating countries herein contemplated shall seriously impair the economic stability of the United States. It is further declared to be the policy of the United States that continuity of assistance provided by the United States should, at all times, be dependent upon continuity of cooperation among countries participating in the program.

PURPOSES OF TITLE

(b) It is the purpose of this title to effectuate the policy set forth in subsection (a) of this section by furnishing material and financial assist-

[9] Public Law 472, 80th Congress, 2nd Session. Approved by the President on April 3, 1948.

ance to the participating countries in such a manner as to aid them, through their own individual and concerted efforts, to become independent of extraordinary outside economic assistance within the period of operations under this title, by —

(1) promoting industrial and agricultural production in the participating countries;

(2) furthering the restoration or maintenance of the soundness of European currencies, budgets, and finances; and

(3) facilitating and stimulating the growth of international trade of participating countries with one another and with other countries by appropriate measures including reduction of barriers which may hamper such trade.

PARTICIPATING COUNTRIES

Sec. 103. (a) As used in this title, the term "participating country" means —

(1) any country, together with dependent areas under its administration, which signed the report of the Committee of European Economic Cooperation at Paris on September 22, 1947; and

(2) any other country (including any of the zones of occupation of Germany, any areas under international administration or control, and the Free Territory of Trieste or either of its zones) wholly or partly in Europe, together with dependent areas under its administration; provided such country adheres to, and for so long as it remains an adherent to, a joint program for European recovery designed to accomplish the purposes of this title. . . .

Sec. 114. (c) In order to carry out the provisions of this title . . . such funds shall be available as are hereafter authorized and appropriated to the President from time to time through June 30, 1952, . . . *Provided, however*, That for carrying out the provisions and accomplishing the purposes of this title for the period of one year following the date of enactment of this Act, there are hereby authorized to be so appropriated not to exceed $4,300,000,000. . . . Authorization in this title is limited to the period of twelve months in order that subsequent Congresses may pass on any subsequent authorizations. . . .

Sec. 115. (a) The secretary of State, after consultation with the Administrator, is authorized to conclude, with individual participating countries or any number of such countries or with an organization representing any such countries, agreements in furtherance of the purposes of this title. . . .

◇◇◇◇◇◇◇◇◇◇◇◇◇

10. THE "POINT FOUR" PROGRAM OF 1950[10]

TITLE IV

SEC. 401. This title may be cited as the "Act for International Development."

Sec. 402. The Congress hereby finds as follows:

(a) The peoples of the United States and other nations have a common interest in the freedom and in the economic and social progress of all peoples. Such progress can further the secure growth of democratic ways of life, the expansion of mutually beneficial commerce, the development of international understanding and good will, and the maintenance of world peace.

(b) The efforts of the peoples living in economically underdeveloped areas of the world to realize their full capabilities and to develop the resources of the lands in which they live can be furthered through the cooperative endeavor of all nations to exchange technical knowledge and skills and to encourage the flow of investment capital.

(c) Technical assistance and capital investment can make maximum contribution to economic development only where there is understanding of the mutual advantages of such assistance and investment and where there is confidence of fair and reasonable treatment and due respect for the legitimate interests of the peoples of the countries to which the assistance is given and in which the investment is made and of the countries from which the assistance and investments are derived. In the case of investment this involves confidence on the part of the people of the underdeveloped areas that investors will conserve as well as develop local resources, will bear a fair share of local taxes and observe local laws, and will provide adequate wages and working conditions for local labor. It involves confidence on the part of investors, through intergovernmental agreements or otherwise, that they will not be deprived of their property without prompt, adequate, and effective compensation; that they will be given reasonable opportunity to remit their earnings and withdraw their capital; that they will have reasonable freedom to manage, operate, and control their enterprises; that they will enjoy security in the protection of their persons and property, including industrial and intellectual property, and nondiscriminatory treatment in taxation and in the conduct of their business affairs.

Sec. 403. (a) It is declared to be the policy of the United States to aid the efforts of the peoples of economically underdeveloped areas to develop their resources and improve their working and living conditions

[10] Officially cited as the Act for International Development, and as Title IV of the Foreign Economic Assistance Act of 1950 (H.R. 7797), approved by Congress on May 25, 1950 and by the President on June 5, 1950. *Congressional Record,* 81st Congress, 2nd Session, Vol. 96, pp. 7313–17.

by encouraging the exchange of technical knowledge and skills and the flow of investment capital to countries which provide conditions under which such technical assistance and capital can effectively and constructively contribute to raising standards of living, creating new sources of wealth, increasing productivity and expanding purchasing power.

(b) It is further declared to be the policy of the United States that in order to achieve the most effective utilization of the resources of the United States, private and public, which are or may be available for aid in the development of economically underdeveloped areas, agencies of the United States Government, in reviewing requests of foreign governments for aid for such purposes, shall take into consideration (1) whether the assistance applied for is an appropriate part of a program reasonably designed to contribute to the balanced and integrated development of the country or area concerned; (2) whether any works or facilities which may be projected are actually needed in view of similar facilities existing in the area and are otherwise economically sound; and (3) with respect to projects for which capital is requested, whether private capital is available either in the country or elsewhere upon reasonable terms and in sufficient amounts to finance such projects. . . .

Sec. 405. The President is authorized to plan, undertake, administer, and execute bilateral technical cooperation programs carried on by any United States Government agency and, in so doing –

(a) To coordinate and direct existing and new technical cooperation programs.

(b) To assist other interested governments in the formulation of programs for the balanced and integrated development of the economic resources and productive capacities of economically underdeveloped areas. . . .

(e) To make and perform contracts or agreements in respect of technical cooperation programs on behalf of the United States Government with any person, corporation, or other body of persons however designated, whether within or without the United States, or with any foreign government or foreign government agency: *Provided,* That with respect to contracts or agreements which entail commitments for the expenditure of funds appropriated pursuant to the authority of this title, such contracts or agreements, within the limits of appropriations or contract authorizations hereafter made available may, subject to any future action of the Congress, run for not to exceed three years in any one case. . . .

(c) Assistance shall be made available only where the President determines that the country being assisted –

(1) Pays a fair share of the cost of the program.

(2) Provides all necessary information concerning such program and gives the program full publicity.

(3) Seeks to the maximum extent possible full coordination and integration of technical cooperation programs being carried on in that country.

(4) Endeavors to make effective use of the results of the program.

(5) Cooperates with other countries participating in the program in the mutual exchange of technical knowledge and skills. . . .

Sec. 416. (a) In order to carry out the provisions of this title, there shall be made available such funds as are hereafter authorized and appropriated from time to time for the purposes of this title: *Provided, however,* That for the purpose of carrying out the provisions of this title through June 30, 1951, there is hereby authorized to be appropriated a sum not to exceed $35,000,000, including any sums appropriated to carry on the activities of the Institute of Inter-American Affairs, and technical cooperation programs as defined in section 418 herein under the United States Information and Educational Exchange Act of 1948 (62 Stat. 6). . . .

Sec. 418. As used in this title—

(a) The term "technical cooperation programs" means programs for the international interchange of technical knowledge and skills designed to contribute to the balanced and integrated development of the economic resources and productive capacities of economically underdeveloped areas. Such activities may include, but need not be limited to, economic, engineering, medical, educational, agricultural, fishery, mineral, and fiscal surveys, demonstration, training, and similar projects that serve the purpose of promoting the development of economic resources and productive capacities of underdeveloped areas.

◇◇◇◇◇◇◇◇◇◇◇◇◇

11. MUTUAL DEFENSE ASSISTANCE POLICY [11]

I APPEAR here today to ask the support of these committees and the Congress for the continuation of military assistance to certain nations.

The Congress last year authorized and appropriated $1,314,010,000 for this purpose. For the coming fiscal year the President has recommended that $1,222,500,000 be appropriated. Of this amount, $1,000,000,000 would be used to go forward with our assistance to our North Atlantic Treaty partners. . . .

Before the end of January [1949], the North Atlantic Treaty organization had recommended, and the President had approved, a strategic concept for the integrated defense of the North Atlantic area. This accomplishment was only possible after a treaty organization had been established and was vigorously at work. It also required full agreement among twelve nations in an area where even in wartime agreement is not simple of achievement.

Before the end of January, bilateral agreements had been signed with

[11] Testimony of the Secretary of State, Dean Acheson, before the Senate Foreign Relations and Armed Services Committees, on June 2, 1950. The *New York Times,* June 3, 1950.

those North Atlantic countries which had requested assistance. The negotiation of these agreements was characterized by a healthy desire on the part of all countries concerned to explore all issues honestly and openly and by a refusal to cloak problems behind indecisive language.

By March, a detailed list of the specific equipment to be furnished had been fully developed. This list was consistent with, and in support of, the strategic concept. It was derived, in other words, not from traditional political desires to maintain large national forces in all three armed services, but, instead, from the recognized need to equip forces on the basis of the role to be played by each country in the coordinated defense of the North Atlantic area.

By early spring, a small organization had been established both here and abroad to administer the program. This organization is capable of assuring that the provisions of the legislation are carried out and is in a position to render the kind of technical assistance to recipient countries which will assure their most effective utilization of our equipment for the common defense. . . .

The efforts of the Europeans to increase the defensive capacity of the North Atlantic area, in compliance with Article III of the treaty, are encouraging. There is a new spirit in being which is characterized by the conviction that the defense of the Atlantic area is a real and attainable objective. . . .

The task, however, is far from completed. But the record of the past months is a forecast of what can be accomplished provided we and our partners are prepared to carry forward with full vigor the work which we have begun. . . .

No item of assistance is proposed in this program for nationalistic reasons. Each item is included because it is required for integrated defense of the North Atlantic area. In the aggregate, the program proposed, when joined with the planned programs of the other members of the treaty, represents another important step toward the eventual creation of an adequate common defense for the North Atlantic community. . . .

While the military assistance which is planned for the North Atlantic area accounts for a major portion of the President's recommendations, his proposals for aid to other areas where freedom is at stake are also essential to the security of our country. . . .

The success which has been achieved by the people of Greece is clear proof that the forces of aggression can be halted by invoking the proper measures at the proper time. For the first time since 1940, and as a result of American aid, the Government of Greece is now exercising full control over its territories and is in a position to concentrate its energies on the restoration of its civilian economy. . . .

The provision of further military assistance to Greece is essential to the success of this effort. It is required in order to insure a continuance of internal stability and to make certain that Greece will not again become an easy target for Communist guerrilla activities. . . .

Continued assistance to Turkey is also necessary. The record in Turkey is a good record and previous military assistance has been extremely effective. . . .

It is of the greatest importance to us that Turkey, within the limits of its economic ability, should develop the maximum capacity to resist aggression. We are well on the road toward this objective, and it is in our national interest to pursue this objective to the end. The program proposed for 1951 will bring us a long way toward this goal. For aid to Greece and Turkey the President has recommended the use of $120,000,000.

Iran is another Near Eastern country for which continued military assistance is recommended. The strategic position of Iran needs no elaboration, and the maintenance of its security is clearly of importance to the free world.

That security, in the face of constant Soviet pressure, is dependent upon modern, well-equipped forces. Unfortunately, Iran although she is devoting a very large share of her resources for this purpose, cannot, under present economic conditions, provide such forces without some outside aid. . . .

In spite of the initial successes achieved by communism in the Far East, there have also been favorable developments. The seeds of democracy have been well sown in Japan and a democratic government has been established in South Korea.

In the Philippines, although presently troubled by Communist-led and aided guerrillas, an independent government, based on democratic principles, has been established. The programs of military assistance to Korea and the Philippines authorized by the Congress last year have aided the peoples of those nations in their efforts to obtain security.

The continuation of such assistance is essential. . . .

In Southeast Asia, already torn by Communist guerrilla operations, the menace of Communist China threatens the peoples of Indo-China, Burma, Thailand, Malaya, and the newly created United States of Indonesia. . . .

We seek . . . to assure that the pattern of development [in this area] is one of steady evolution adjusted to the needs and capacities of the peoples. . . .

It is, of course, essential to this development that order be maintained and subversion dealt with effectively. The provision of funds by the Congress under the Mutual Defense Assistance Act of 1949 for the promotion of the purposes of the act in the general area of China has been of great value.

The Executive Branch has been enabled thereby to initiate measures designed to strengthen the non-Communist states in this area. Thus we have been able to announce our determination to support France and the states of the French Union in Indo-China – Vietnam, Laos and Cambodia – in their struggle to preserve the freedom and integrity of Indo-China from the Communist forces of Ho Chih Minh. . . .

The future course of events in Southeast Asia, in the Philippines, in Korea and in Japan as well as in China proper, are of great importance to the security of the United States. Our policy is and must be devoted to doing everything within our power to prevent the further spread of communism.

Military aid, when such aid can be effective, is an essential element of our course of action. The dynamic and complex nature of the situation, does not permit the same degree of precision in our policy as is possible elsewhere. Neither will it permit, however, any loss of time. The provision of $75,000,000 as requested by the President will enable the executive branch to take rapid action when and where the opportunity exists to advance our interests thereby.

The interests of the United States are global in character. A threat to the peace of the world anywhere is a threat to our security. Vigorous, intelligent and sustained action on our part is essential to the preservation of our liberty. . . .

◇◇◇◇◇◇◇◇◇◇◇◇◇

12. INFORMATION AND EDUCATIONAL EXCHANGE ACT OF 1948 [12]

SEC. 2. The Congress hereby declares that the objectives of this Act are to enable the Government of the United States to promote a better understanding of the United States in other countries, and to increase mutual understanding between the people of the United States and the people of other countries. . . .

Sec. 201. The Secretary is authorized to provide for interchanges on a reciprocal basis between the United States and other countries of students, trainees, teachers, guest instructors, professors, and leaders in fields of specialized knowledge or skill and shall wherever possible provide these interchanges by using the services of existing reputable agencies which are successfully engaged in such activity. The Secretary may provide for orientation courses and other appropriate services for such persons from other countries upon their arrival in the United States, and for such persons going to other countries from the United States. When any country fails or refuses to cooperate in such program on a basis of reciprocity the Secretary shall terminate or limit such program, with respect to such country, to the extent he deems to be advisable in the interests of the United States. . . .

Sec. 202. The Secretary is authorized to provide for interchanges between the United States and other countries of books and periodicals, including government publications, for the translation of such writings,

[12] Public Law 402, 80th Congress, 2nd Session. Approved by the President on January 27, 1948.

and for the preparation, distribution, and interchange of other educational materials.

Sec. 203. The Secretary is authorized to provide for assistance to schools, libraries, and community centers abroad, founded or sponsored by citizens of the United States, and serving as demonstration centers for methods and practices employed in the United States. In assisting any such schools, however, the Secretary shall exercise no control over their educational policies and shall in no case furnish assistance of any character which is not in keeping with the free democratic principles and the established foreign policy of the United States. . . .

Sec. 301. The Secretary is authorized, when the government of another country is desirous of obtaining the services of a person having special scientific or other technical or professional qualifications, from time to time to assign or authorize the assignment for service, to or in cooperation with such government, any citizen of the United States in the employ or service of the Government of the United States who has such qualifications, with the approval of the Government agency in which such person is employed or serving. No person shall be assigned for service to or in cooperation with the government of any country unless (1) the Secretary finds that such assignment is necessary in the national interest of the United States, or (2) such government agrees to reimburse the United States in an amount equal to the compensation, travel expenses, and allowances payable to such person during the period of such assignment in accordance with the provisions of section 302, or (3) such government shall have made an advance of funds, property, or services as provided in section 902. Nothing in this Act, however, shall authorize the assignment of such personnel for service relating to the organization, training, operation, development, or combat equipment of the armed forces of a foreign government. . . .

Sec. 501. The Secretary is authorized, when he finds it appropriate, to provide for the preparation, and dissemination abroad, of information about the United States, its people, and its policies, through press, publications, radio, motion pictures, and other information media, and through information centers and instructors abroad. Any such press release or radio script, on request, shall be available in the English language at the Department of State, at all reasonable times following its release as information abroad, for examination by representatives of United States press associations, newspapers, magazines, radio systems, and stations, and, on request, shall be made available to Members of Congress. . . .

Sec. 1005. In carrying out the provisions of this Act it shall be the duty of the Secretary to utilize, to the maximum extent practicable, the services and facilities of private agencies, including existing American press, publishing, radio, motion picture, and other agencies, through contractual arrangements or otherwise. It is the intent of Congress that the Secretary shall encourage participation in carrying out the purposes of this Act by the maximum number of different private agencies in each field consistent with the present or potential market for their services in each country. . . .

◇◇◇◇◇◇◇◇◇◇◇◇◇

13. AMERICAN POLICY TOWARD GERMANY – 1949 [13]

. . . EARLY THIS MONTH I met with the Foreign Ministers of France and the United Kingdom for talks on Germany, the outcome of which we all regarded as momentous. It was not by mere coincidence that these agreements were initialed during the week the North Atlantic Treaty was signed. That historic instrument marks a decisive step toward the creation of a community of democratic nations dedicated to the attainment of peace and determined to insure its preservation by all the material and moral means at their disposal.

The German problem cannot be disassociated from the general problem of assuring security for the free nations. No approach to German problems can be adequate which deals only with Germany itself and ignores the question of its relationship to the other nations of Europe. The objectives of United States policy toward the German people are interwoven with our interest in, and our policies toward, the other peoples of Europe. Here the basic considerations are the same whether they can extend to all of Germany or must be limited to Western Germany. . . .

The maintenance of restrictions and controls over the German economy and a German state, even for a protracted period, cannot alone guarantee the West against the possible revival of a German threat to the peace. In the long run, security can be insured only if there are set in motion in Germany those forces which will create a governmental system dedicated to upholding the basic human freedoms through democratic procedures. . . .

This Government made earnest efforts for two and a half years after the war to resolve the major issues arising from the defeat of Germany and to achieve a general settlement. During that period we participated in the four-power machinery for control of Germany established by international agreement in 1945.

By the end of 1947 it appeared that the Soviet Union was seeking to thwart any settlement which did not concede virtual Soviet control over German economic and political life. This was confirmed in two futile meetings of the Council of Foreign Ministers in Moscow and London. It was emphasized in the Allied Control Authority in Berlin, where the Soviet veto power was exercised three times as often as by the three Western Powers combined.

[13] Address of the Secretary of State, Dean Acheson, at New York on April 28, 1949. *Germany 1947–1949: The Story in Documents* (Department of State Publication 3556, Washington: U. S. Government Printing Office, 1950), pp. 16–21.

The resultant paralysis of interallied policy and control created an intolerable situation. Germany became divided into disconnected administrative areas and was rapidly being reduced to a state of economic chaos, distress, and despair. Disaster was averted primarily by American economic aid.

The German stalemate heightened the general European crisis. The European Recovery Program could not succeed without the raw materials and finished products which only a revived German economy could contribute.

By 1948 it became clear that the Western Powers could no longer tolerate an impasse which made it impossible for them to discharge their responsibilities for the organization of German administration and for the degree of German economic recovery that was essential for the welfare of Europe as a whole. These powers determined to concert their policies for the area of Germany under their control, which embraced about two thirds of the territory and three fourths of the population of occupied Germany.

These common policies were embodied in the London agreements, announced on June 1, 1948. This joint program, I wish to emphasize, is in no sense a repudiation of our international commitments on Germany, embodied in the Potsdam protocol and other agreements. It represents a sincere effort to deal with existing realities in the spirit of the original Allied covenants pertaining to Germany. . . .

The London agreements established a basic pattern for future action in the West. The bizonal area, formed by economic merger of the American and British zones in 1947, and the French zone were to be coordinated and eventually merged. The Western zones were to participate fully in the European Recovery Program. An International Authority for the Ruhr was to be created to regulate the allocation of coal, coke, and steel between home and foreign consumption, to insure equitable international access to Ruhr resources, and safeguard against remilitarization of Ruhr industry.

The Germans were authorized to establish a provisional government, democratic and federal in character, based upon a constitution of German inception. It would be subject, in accordance with an occupation statute, to minimum supervision by the occupation authorities in the interest of the general security and of broad Allied purposes for Germany. Coordinated three-power control was to be established, with the virtual abolition of the zonal boundaries.

Of exceptional importance were the guarantees of security against a German military revival, a point sometimes overlooked in present-day talk about the hazards inherent in rebuilding German economic and political life. The London agreements provide that there is to be consultation among the three occupying powers in the event of any threat of German military resurgence; that their armed forces are to remain in Germany until the peace of Europe is secure; that a joint Military Security Board should be created with powers of inspection to insure against both military and industrial rearrangement; that all agreed disarmament and demilitarization measures should be maintained in force; and that long-term demilitarization measures should be agreed upon prior to the end of the occupation. It should be observed that these far reaching safeguards are to accompany the more constructive aspects of the program and assure that the new powers and responsibilities assumed by the Germans may not be abused. . . .

A short time ago we all felt that we should have a fresh look at the German problem. This was done in Washington while Mr. Bevin and Mr. Schuman were there earlier this month. The genuine readiness of the participating governments to sacrifice special points of view to the common good has made it possible to reach a degree of accord far exceeding what could have been hoped for only a month or two ago.

There were three particularly important features about the agreements on German policy which resulted from these conversations. The first, was the striking harmony in essential outlook. The second, was the removal of the obstacles to the fulfillment of the constructive London program which had developed through diverse Allied disagreements. Thirdly, the three Governments acknowledged the need for the termination of Military Government and its replacement by a civilian Allied Commission at the time of the establishment of the German Federal Republic. This last is a great step forward toward peace, in my opinion. . . .

The agreement in Washington on the text of an occupation statute has removed one of the major obstacles to the establishment of the German Federal Republic. The Parliamentary Council met at Bonn on September 1, and has been working diligently to draft a basic law or provisional constitution for a Federal German Government. Since last December its leaders have requested the text of the occupation statute which had been promised to the Parliamentry Council before completion of its work. . . .

The establishment of a German Government does not, and cannot at this time, mean the end of the occupation of Germany. If democratic self-government is to be introduced in Germany it must be given a chance to live. It cannot thrive if its powers are in question, or if it is subject to arbitrary intervention. The occupation statute defines the powers to be retained by the occupying authorities upon the establishment of the German Federal Republic and sets forth the basic procedures for the operation of Allied supervision.

The reserved powers have been retained in such fields as disarmament and demilitarization; controls in regard to the Ruhr, reparations, and decartelization; foreign affairs; displaced persons; security of Allied forces and representatives; control over foreign trade. . . .

The Washington agreements envisage at the time of the establishment of the German Federal Republic the termination of Military Government and its replacement by an Allied High Commission of civilian character. Military functions will continue to be exercised by military commanders, but each of the Allied establishments in Germany, aside from occupation forces, will come under the direction of a High Commissioner. The functions of the Allied authorities are to become mainly supervisory. . . .

The people of Europe may rest assured that this Government will agree to no arrangements concerning Germany which do not protect the security interests of the European community.

The people of the United States may rest assured that in any discussions relating to the future of Germany, this Government will have foremost in mind their deep desire for a peaceful and orderly solution of these weighty problems which have been the heart of so many of our difficulties in the postwar period.

◇◇◇◇◇◇◇◇◇◇◇◇◇

14. CONVENTION BETWEEN GERMANY, GREAT BRITAIN, FRANCE, AND THE UNITED STATES [14]

THE UNITED STATES of America, the United Kingdom of Great Britain and Northern Ireland and the French Republic, of the one part, and the Federal Republic of Germany, of the other part: . . .

HAVE entered into the following Convention setting forth the basis for their new relationship:

Article 1

1. The Federal Republic shall have full authority over its internal and external affairs, except as provided in the present Convention.

2. The Three Powers will revoke the Occupation Statute and abolish the Allied High Commission and the Offices of the Land Commissioners upon the entry into force of the present Convention and the Conventions listed in Article 8 (hereinafter referred to as "the related Conventions").

3. The Three Powers will thenceforth conduct their relations with the Federal Republic through Ambassadors who will act jointly in matters the Three Powers consider of common concern under the present Convention and the related Conventions.

Article 2

1. The Three Powers retain, in view of the international situation, the rights, heretofore exercised or held by them, relating to (a) the station-

---

[14] Signed May 26, 1952, and approved by the Senate, July 1, 1952. *The Congressional Record*, 82nd Congress, 2nd Session, Vol. XCVIII, Pt. 7, pp. 8665–96. The United States Senate gave its advice and consent to the ratification of the convention with the following interpretation:

1. The constitutional procedures as referred to in this convention require that any military implementation of the provisions, other than the retained powers referred to in paragraph 1 of article 2, of this convention (including all other conventions, agreements, or understandings, which may become effective as a result of ratification of this convention) must have authorization by the Congress.

ing of armed forces in Germany and the protection of their security, (b) Berlin, and (c) Germany as a whole, including the unification of Germany and a peace settlement.

2. The Federal Republic, on its part, will refrain from any action prejudicial to these rights and will cooperate with the Three Powers to facilitate their exercise.

Article 3

. . . 2. The Federal Republic affirms its intention to associate itself fully with the community of free nations through membership in international organizations contributing to the common aims of the free world. The Three Powers will support applications for such membership by the Federal Republic at appropriate times. . . .

Article 4

. . . 4. The Federal Republic will participate in the European Defense Community in order to contribute to the common defense of the free world. . . .

◇◇◇◇◇◇◇◇◇◇◇◇◇

15. DEFENSE AGREEMENT BETWEEN THE UNITED STATES AND SPAIN [15]

. . . ARTICLE I. In consonance with the principles agreed upon in the Mutual Defense Assistance Agreement, the Governments of the United States and of Spain consider that the contingencies with which both countries may be faced indicate the advisability of developing their relations upon a basis of continued friendship, in support of the policy of strengthening the defense of the West. This policy shall include:

1. On the part of the United States, the support of Spanish defense efforts for agreed purposes by providing military and item assistance to Spain during a period of several years to contribute to the effective air defense of Spain and to improve the equipment of its military and naval forces, to the extent to be agreed upon in technical discussions in the light of the circumstances, and with the cooperation of the resources of Spanish industry to the extent possible. Such support will be conditioned as in the case of other friendly nations by the priorities and limitations due to the international commitments of the United States and the exigencies of the international situation and will be subject to Congressional appropriations.

2. In consequence of the above stated premises and for the same agreed purposes, the Government of Spain authorizes the Government of the

[15] Signed at Madrid, September 26, 1953. Department of State, *Bulletin*, Vol. XXIX, No. 745, p. 436.

United States, subject to terms and conditions to be agreed, to develop, maintain and utilize for military purposes, jointly with the Government of Spain, such areas and facilities in territory under Spanish jurisdiction as may be agreed upon by the competent authorities of both Governments as necessary for the purposes of this agreement.

3. In granting assistance to Spain within the policy outlined above, as the preparation of the agreed areas and facilities progresses, the Government of the United States will satisfy, subject to the provisions of paragraph one, the minimum requirements for equipment necessary for the defense of Spanish territory, to the end that should a moment requiring the wartime utilization of the areas and facilities arrive, from this moment, the requirements are covered to the extent possible as regards the air defense of the territory and the equipment of the naval units; and that the armament and equipment of the Army units be as far advanced as possible.

Article II. For the purposes of this agreement and in accordance with technical arrangements to be agreed upon between the competent authorities of both Governments, the Government of the United States is authorized to improve and fit agreed areas and facilities for military use, as well as to undertake necessary construction in this connection in cooperation with the Government of Spain, to station and house therein the necessary military and civilian personnel, and to provide for their security, discipline, and welfare; to store and maintain custody of provisions, supplies, equipment and materials; and to maintain and operate the facilities and equipment necessary in support of such areas and personnel.

Article III. The areas which, by virtue of this Agreement, are prepared for joint utilization will remain under Spanish flag and command, and Spain will assume the obligation of adopting the necessary measures for the external security. However, the United States may, in all cases, exercise the necessary supervision of United States personnel, facilities, and equipment.

The time and manner of wartime utilization of said areas and facilities will be as mutually agreed upon. . . .

Article V. The present Agreement will become effective upon signature and will be in force for a period of ten years, automatically extended for two successive periods of five years each unless the termination procedure hereafter outlined is followed.

At the termination of the first ten years or of either of the two extensions of five years, either of the two Governments may inform the other of its intention to cancel the Agreement, thus initiating a consultation period of six months. In the event concurrence is not reached on extension, this Agreement will terminate one year after the conclusion of the period of consultation. . . .

Chapter XXXVII

THE DIPLOMACY OF SECURITY: THE FAR EAST

◇◇◇◇◇◇◇◇◇◇◇◇◇

THE BASIC assumption concerning postwar cooperation among the wartime Allies, noted with reference to Europe in the introduction to Chapter XXXVI, was applied with equal force to American foreign policy in the Far East. It was assumed by the United States that the Allies, particularly China, Russia, Great Britain, and the United States would co-operate at the end of the war to strengthen and unify China under its Nationalist government, to establish a free and unified Korea, to promote self-government wherever practicable in eastern Asia, and to assist in the economic rehabilitation and advance of the entire area. Like Germany in Europe, Japan was regarded with suspicion, and it was thought that strong measures should be taken to prevent that nation from again becoming a menace to the peace of the world. These basic premises were evident in the wartime diplomacy of the United States regarding the Far East, notably in the Yalta agreement, and were clearly revealed in the directions given to the Allied Commander in Japan (1), and in the statement of President Truman on December 16, 1945, concerning China (2). The Trusteeship Agreement of the United States over the former Japanese mandated islands, of April 2, 1947 (3), recognized, in effect, the *status quo* of American possession.

During the period between 1946 and 1950, while the United States was slowly recognizing the failure in Europe of its postwar assumption concerning cooperation with Russia, and – in the latter part of the period – was building a new policy consonant with the Truman Doctrine, it clung tenaciously to the insistence that the Nationalist government of China should collaborate with the Chinese Communists. When the success of the Communist armies in China appeared to be imminent, the United States issued a "White Paper" placing the primary blame for the failure of the American policy on the Chinese Nationalist government, and later made it clear that the United States would not aid the Nationalist government to maintain itself on Formosa. One of the most important statements of American policy concerning the Far East at the end of this era was the address of Secretary of State, Dean Acheson, on January 12, 1950 (4).

After the outbreak of the Korean War, American policy in the Far East underwent a sudden and drastic change. The United States negotiated and virtually forced through a treaty of peace with Japan (5) and signed at the same time a Japanese-American security treaty (6). In order to relieve the anxiety of several Far Eastern states with regard to possible Russian or later Japanese aggression, treaties of mutual assistance were signed with the Philippine Republic (7), and with New Zealand and Australia (8).

After the armed attack of North Korean Communist forces on the Republic of Korea, the Security Council of the United Nations passed the Resolution of June 25, 1950 (9), finding that a breach of the peace had taken place, and the Resolution of June 27, 1950 (10), recommending that assistance be given the Republic of Korea. The United States, having sponsored both resolutions, complied as best it could and at the same time announced a new policy concerning Formosa (11). Early in July, the Security Council recommended that all members of the United Nations providing military aid to the Republic of Korea place their armed forces under a "unified command," and that the United States be requested to designate the commander of such forces. The United States designated General Douglas MacArthur. In October 1950 the General Assembly adopted a resolution (12) that was apparently intended and generally interpreted to authorize General MacArthur to enter North Korea for the purpose of defeating the North Korean forces and of establishing a unified Korea (13).

The entrance of Communist China into the war in support of the North Koreans initiated a new phase of the conflict and brought about a large debate over foreign policy within the United States and a controversy within the United Nations. The consequence was a shift in United Nations policy concerning the unification of Korea, as shown by the Resolutions of February 1, 1951 (14). Thereafter the policy was to achieve unification "by peaceful means," and although Communist China was named as an aggressor, it was clear that the United Nations was unwilling to deal with big aggression as it had with little aggression, and equally clear that the United States was unwilling to continue a war virtually alone. The removal of General MacArthur from command of the United Nations forces produced sharp criticism in the United States (15), particularly from leaders of the political party that subsequently came into control of the government and negotiated an armistice (16) embodying the policy so sharply denounced. The Report of the Unified Command to the United Nations on August 7, 1953 (17) containing a declaration of the sixteen nations that had participated in the war, and the Mutual Defense Treaty between the United States and Korea (18), were intended to provide a measure of security to the Republic of Korea, and perhaps a defense of the armistice policy.

The mutual security program of the United States (19) and the Mutual Defense Assistance Control Act of 1951 (20) were of general application and were integral parts of the diplomacy of security. But during the Korean War no member of the United Nations except the United States was willing to apply complete economic sanctions against Communist China (21).

◇◇◇◇◇◇◇◇◇◇◇◇◇

1. INITIAL POLICY OF THE UNITED STATES CONCERNING POSTWAR JAPAN [1]

THIS document is a statement of general initial policy relating to Japan after surrender. It has been approved by the President and distributed to the Supreme Commander for the Allied Powers and to appropriate United States departments and agencies for their guidance. . . .

Part I. Ultimate Objectives

The ultimate objectives of the United States in regard to Japan, to which policies in the initial period must conform are:

(a) To insure that Japan will not again become a menace to the United States or to the peace and security of the world.

(b) To bring about the eventual establishment of a peaceful and responsible government which will respect the rights of other states and will support the objectives of the United States as reflected in the ideals and principles of the Charter of the United Nations. The United States desires that this government should conform as closely as may be to principles of democratic self-government but it is not the responsibility of the Allied Powers to impose upon Japan any form of government not supported by the freely expressed will of the people.

These objectives will be achieved by the following principal means:

(a) Japan's sovereignty will be limited to the islands of Honshu, Hokkaido, Kyushu, Shikoku and such minor outlying islands as may be determined, in accordance with the Cairo Declaration and other agreements to which the United States is or may be a party.

(b) Japan will be completely disarmed and demilitarized. The authority of the militarists and the influence of militarism will be totally eliminated from her political, economic, and social life. Institutions expressive of the spirit of militarism and aggression will be vigorously suppressed.

(c) The Japanese people shall be encouraged to develop a desire for individual liberties and respect for fundamental human rights, particularly the freedoms of religion, assembly, speech, and the press. They shall also be encouraged to form democratic and representative organizations.

(d) The Japanese people shall be afforded opportunity to develop for themselves an economy which will permit the peacetime requirements of the population to be met. . . .

---

[1] The initial policy was prepared jointly by the Departments of State, War, and Navy, and was approved by the President on September 6, 1945. *A Decade of American Foreign Policy,* 1941–49, United States Senate, 81st Congress, 1st Session, Senate Document No. 123, pp. 627–33.

Part III. Political

1. Disarmament and Demilitarization

Disarmament and demilitarization are the primary tasks of the military occupation and shall be carried out promptly and with determination. Every effort shall be made to bring home to the Japanese people the part played by the military and naval leaders, and those who collaborated with them, in bringing about the existing and future distress of the people.

Japan is not to have an army, navy, air force, secret police organization, or any civil aviation. Japan's ground, air and naval forces shall be disarmed and disbanded and the Japanese Imperial General Headquarters, the General Staff and all secret police organizations shall be dissolved. Military and naval matériel, military and naval vessels and military and naval installations, and military, naval and civilian aircraft shall be surrendered and shall be disposed of as required by the Supreme Commander.

High officials of the Japanese Imperial General Headquarters, and General Staff, other high military and naval officials of the Japanese Government, leaders of ultra-nationalist and militarist organizations and other important exponents of militarism and aggression will be taken into custody and held for future disposition. Persons who have been active exponents of militarism and militant nationalism will be removed and excluded from public office and from any other position of public or substantial private responsibility. Ultra-nationalistic or militaristic social, political, professional and commercial societies and institutions will be dissolved and prohibited.

Militarism and ultra-nationalism, in doctrine and practice, including para-military training, shall be eliminated from the educational system. Former career military and naval officers, both commissioned and non-commissioned, and all other exponents of militarism and ultra-nationalism shall be excluded from supervisory and teaching positions. . . .

Part IV. Economic

1. Economic Demilitarization

The existing economic basis of Japanese military strength must be destroyed and not be permitted to revive.

Therefore, a program will be enforced containing the following elements, among others; the immediate cessation and future prohibition of production of all goods designed for the equipment, maintenance, or use of any military force or establishment; the imposition of a ban upon any specialized facilities for the production or repair of implements of war, including naval vessels and all forms of aircraft; the institution of a system of inspection and control over selected elements in Japanese economic activity to prevent concealed or disguised military preparation; the elimination in Japan of those selected industries or branches of production whose chief value to Japan is in preparing for war; the prohibition of specialized research and instruction directed to the development of war-making power; and the limitation of the size and character of Japan's heavy industries to its future peaceful requirements, and restriction of Japanese merchant shipping to the extent required to accomplish the objectives of demilitarization.

The eventual disposition of those existing production facilities within Japan which are to be eliminated in accord with this program, as between conversion to other uses, transfer abroad, and scrapping will be determined after inventory. Pending decision, facilities readily convertible for civilian production should not be destroyed, except in emergency situations. . . .

4. Reparations and Restitution

Reparations

Reparations for Japanese aggression shall be made:

(a) Through the transfer – as may be determined by the appropriate Allied authorities – of Japanese property located outside of the territories to be retained by Japan.

(b) Through the transfer of such goods or existing capital equipment and facilities as are not necessary for a peaceful Japanese economy or the supplying of the occupying forces. Exports other than those directed to be shipped on reparation account or as restitution may be made only to those recipients who agree to provide necessary imports in exchange or agree to pay for such exports in foreign exchange. No form of reparation shall be exacted which will interfere with or prejudice the program for Japan's demilitarization.

Restitution

Full and prompt restitution will be required of all identifiable looted property. . . .

◇◇◇◇◇◇◇◇◇◇◇◇◇

2. POLICY OF THE UNITED STATES CONCERNING POSTWAR CHINA [2]

. . . IT IS THE firm belief of this Government that a strong, united, and democratic China is of the utmost importance to the success of this United Nations Organization and for world peace. A China disorganized and divided either by foreign aggression, such as that undertaken by the Japanese, or by violent internal strife is an undermining influence to world stability and peace, now and in the future. The United States Government has long subscribed to the principle that the management of internal affairs is the responsibility of the peoples of the sovereign nations. Events of this century, however, would indicate that a breach of peace

[2] Statement of President Truman, December 16, 1945. *A Decade of American Foreign Policy,* 1941–49, United States Senate, 81st Congress, 1st Session, Senate Document No. 123, pp. 691–3.

anywhere in the world threatens the peace of the entire world. It is thus in the most vital interest of the United States and all the United Nations that the people of China overlook no opportunity to adjust their internal differences promptly by methods of peaceful negotiation.

The Government of the United States believes it essential:

(1) That a cessation of hostilities be arranged between the armies of the National Government and the Chinese Communists and other dissident Chinese armed forces for the purpose of completing the return of all China to effective Chinese control, including the immediate evacuation of the Japanese forces.

(2) That a national conference of representatives of major political elements be arranged to develop an early solution to the present internal strife – a solution which will bring about the unification of China.

The United States and the other United Nations have recognized the present National Government of the Republic of China as the only legal government in China. It is the proper instrument to achieve the objective of a unified China.

The United States and the United Kingdom by the Cairo Declaration in 1943 and the Union of Soviet Socialist Republics by adhering to the Potsdam Declaration of last July and by the Sino-Soviet treaty and agreements of August 1945 are all committed to the liberation of China, including the return of Manchuria to Chinese control. These agreements were made with the National Government of the Republic of China. . . .

The United States is cognizant that the present National Government of China is a "one-party government" and believes that peace, unity, and democratic reform in China will be furthered if the basis of this Government is broadened to include other political elements in the country. Hence, the United States strongly advocates that the national conference of representatives of major political elements in the country agree upon arrangements which would give those elements a fair and effective representation in the Chinese National Government. It is recognized that this would require modification of the one-party "political tutelage" established as an interim arrangement in the progress of the nation toward democracy by the father of the Chinese Republic, Dr. Sun Yat-sen.

The existence of autonomous armies such as that of the Communist army is inconsistent with, and actually makes impossible, political unity in China. With the institution of a broadly representative government, autonomous armies should be eliminated as such and all armed forces in China integrated effectively into the Chinese National Army.

In line with its often expressed views regarding self-determination, the United States Government considers that the detailed steps necessary to the achievement of political unity in China must be worked out by the Chinese themselves and that intervention by any foreign government in these matters would be inappropriate. The United States Government feels, however, that China has a clear responsibility to the other United Nations to eliminate armed conflict within its territory as constituting a threat to world stability and peace — a responsibility which is shared by the National Government and all Chinese political and military groups.

As China moves toward peace and unity along the lines described above, the United States would be prepared to assist the National Government in every reasonable way to rehabilitate the country, improve the agrarian and industrial economy, and establish a military organization capable of discharging China's national and international responsibilities for the maintenance of peace and order. In furtherance of such assistance, it would be prepared to give favorable consideration to Chinese requests for credits and loans under reasonable conditions for projects which would contribute toward the development of a healthy economy throughout China and healthy trade relations between China and the United States.

◇◇◇◇◇◇◇◇◇◇◇◇◇

3. TRUSTEESHIP AGREEMENT OF THE UNITED STATES OVER THE FORMER JAPANESE MANDATED ISLANDS [3]

. . . *ARTICLE 1.* The Territory of the Pacific Islands, consisting of the islands formerly held by Japan under mandate in accordance with Article 22 of the Covenant of the League of Nations, is hereby designated as a strategic area and placed under the trusteeship system established in the Charter of the United Nations. The Territory of the Pacific Islands is hereinafter referred to as the trust territory.

Article 2. The United States of America is designated as the administering authority of the trust territory.

Article 3. The administering authority shall have full powers of administration, legislation, and jurisdiction over the territory subject to the provisions of this agreement, and may apply to the trust territory, subject to any modifications which the administering authority may consider desirable, such of the laws of the United States as it may deem appropriate to local conditions and requirements. . . .

Article 5. . . . The administering authority shall be entitled:

1. to establish naval, military and air bases and to erect fortifications in the trust territory;

2. to station and employ armed forces in the territory; and

3. to make use of volunteer forces, facilities and assistance from the trust territory in carrying out the obligations towards the Security Council undertaken in this regard by the administering authority, as well as for the local defense and the maintenance of law and order within the trust territory.

---

[3] Resolution of the Security Council, April 2, 1947. The Security Council, *Official Records,* Second Year, No. 31, p. 680. The Senate and House of Representatives by Joint Resolution of July 18, 1947, authorized the President to approve the agreement.

Article 6. . . . The administering authority shall:

1. foster the development of such political institutions as are suited to the trust territory and shall promote the development of the inhabitants of the trust territory toward self-government or independence, as may be appropriate to the particular circumstances of the trust territory and its peoples and the freely expressed wishes of the peoples concerned; and to this end shall give to the inhabitants of the trust territory a progressively increasing share in the administrative services in the territory; shall develop their participation in government; shall give due recognition to the customs of the inhabitants in providing a system of law for the territory; and shall take other appropriate measures toward these ends;

2. promote the economic advancement and self-sufficiency of the inhabitants, and to this end shall regulate the use of natural resources; encourage the development of fisheries, agriculture, and industries; protect the inhabitants against the loss of their lands and resources; and improve the means of transportation and communication;

3. promote the social advancement of the inhabitants, and to this end shall protect the rights and fundamental freedoms of all elements of the population without discrimination; protect the health of the inhabitants; control the traffic in arms and ammunition, opium and other dangerous drugs, and alcohol and other spirituous beverages; and institute such other regulations as may be necessary to protect the inhabitants against social abuses; and

4. promote the educational advancement of the inhabitants, and to this end shall take steps toward the establishment of a general system of elementary education; facilitate the vocational and cultural advancement of the population; and shall encourage qualified students to pursue higher education, including training on the professional level.

Article 7. . . . The administering authority shall guarantee to the inhabitants of the trust territory freedom of conscience, and, subject only to the requirements of public order and security, freedom of speech, of the press, and of assembly; freedom of worship and of religious teaching; and freedom of migration and movement. . . .

Article 15. The terms of the present agreement shall not be altered, amended or terminated without the consent of the administering authority.

◇◇◇◇◇◇◇◇◇◇◇◇◇

4. AMERICAN POLICIES TOWARD ASIA PRIOR TO THE KOREAN WAR[4]

. . . I AM frequently asked: Has the State Department got an Asian policy? And it seems to me that that discloses such a depth of ignorance

[4] Statement of the Secretary of State, Dean Acheson, at Washington on January 12, 1950. Department of State *Bulletin,* Vol. XXII, pp. 111–19.

that it is very hard to begin to deal with it. The peoples of Asia are so incredibly diverse and their problems are so incredibly diverse that how could anyone, even the most utter charlatan believe that he had a uniform policy which would deal with all of them. On the other hand, there are very important similarities in ideas and in problems among the peoples of Asia and so what we come to . . . is the fact that there must be certain similarities of approach, and there must be very great dissimilarities in action. . . .

Let's come now to matters which Asia has in common. There is . . . a developing Asian consciousness . . . based upon two factors. . . .

One of these factors is a revulsion against the acceptance of misery and poverty as the normal condition of life. Throughout all of this vast area, you have that fundamental revolutionary aspect in mind and belief. The other common aspect that they have is the revulsion against foreign domination. Whether that foreign domination takes the form of colonialism or whether it takes the form of imperialism, they are through with it. . . .

Now let me come to another underlying and important factor which determines our relations and, in turn, our policy with the peoples of Asia. That is the attitude of the Soviet Union toward Asia, and particularly towards those parts of Asia which are contiguous to the Soviet Union. . . .

The attitude and interest of the Russians in North China, and in these other areas as well, long antedates communism. . . . But the Communist regime has added new methods, new skills, and new concepts to the thrust of Russian imperialism. This Communistic concept and techniques have armed Russian imperialism with a new and most insidious weapon of penetration. Armed with these new powers, what is happening in China is that the Soviet Union is detaching the northern provinces [areas] of China from China and is attaching them to the Soviet Union. This process is complete in outer Mongolia. It is nearly complete in Manchuria, and I am sure that in inner Mongolia and in Sinkiang there are very happy reports coming from Soviet agents to Moscow. This is what is going on. It is the detachment of these whole areas, vast areas – populated by Chinese – the detachment of these areas from China and their attachment to the Soviet Union.

I wish to state this and perhaps sin against my doctrine of nondogmatism, but I should like to suggest at any rate that this fact that the Soviet Union is taking the four northern provinces of China is the single most significant, most important fact, in the relation of any foreign power with Asia.

What does that mean for us? It means something very, very significant. It means that nothing that we do and nothing that we say must be allowed to obscure the reality of this fact. All the efforts of propaganda will not be able to obscure it. The only thing that can obscure it is the folly of ill-conceived adventures on our part which easily could do so, and I urge all who are thinking about these foolish adventures to remember that we must not seize the unenviable position which the Russians have carved out for themselves. We must not undertake to deflect from the Russians to ourselves the righteous anger, and the wrath, and the hatred of the Chinese people which must develop. It would be folly to deflect it to ourselves. We must take the position we have always taken – that anyone who violates the integrity of China is the enemy of China and is acting contrary to our own interest. That, I suggest to you this afternoon, is the first and the greatest rule in regard to the formulation of American policy toward Asia.

I suggest that the second rule is very like the first. That is to keep our own purposes perfectly straight, perfectly pure, and perfectly aboveboard and do not get them mixed-up with legal quibbles or the attempt to do one thing and really achieve another. . . .

What is the situation in regard to the military security of the Pacific area, and what is our policy in regard to it?

In the first place, the defeat and the disarmament of Japan has placed upon the United States the necessity of assuming the military defense of Japan so long as that is required, both in the interest of our security and in the interests of the security of the entire Pacific area and, in all honor, in the interest of Japanese security. We have American – and there are Australian – troops in Japan. I am not in a position to speak for the Australians, but I can assure you that there is no intention of any sort of abandoning or weakening the defenses of Japan and that whatever arrangements are to be made either through permanent settlement or otherwise, that defense must and shall be maintained.

This defensive perimeter runs along the Aleutians to Japan and then goes to the Ryukyus. We hold important defense positions in the Ryukyu Islands, and those we will continue to hold. In the interest of the population of the Ryukyu Islands, we will at an appropriate time offer to hold these islands under trusteeship of the United Nations. But they are essential parts of the defensive perimeter of the Pacific, and they must and will be held.

The defensive perimeter runs from the Ryukyus to the Philippine Islands. Our relations, our defensive relations with the Philippines are contained in agreements between us. Those agreements are being loyally carried out and will be loyally carried out. Both peoples have learned by bitter experience the vital connections between our mutual defense requirements. We are in no doubt about that, and it is hardly necessary for me to say an attack on the Philippines could not and would not be tolerated by the United States. But I hasten to add that no one perceives the imminence of any such attack.

So far as the military security of other areas in the Pacific is concerned, it must be clear that no person can guarantee these areas against military attack. But it must also be clear that such a guarantee is hardly sensible or necessary within the realm of practical relationship. . . .

Let's take the situation in Japan for a moment. There are three great factors to be faced. The security matter I have dealt with. Aside from that, there are the economic questions and the political questions. In the political field, General MacArthur has been very successful and the Japanese are hammering out with some effort, and with some backsliding, and regaining and backsliding again of progress, a political system which is based on nonmilitaristic institutions.

In the economic field, we have not been so successful. That is in very large part due to the inherent difficulty of the problem. The problem arises with the necessity of Japan being able to buy raw materials and sell goods. The former connections of Japan with the mainland and with some of the islands have been disrupted. That has produced difficulties. The willingness of other countries to receive Japanese goods has very much contracted since the war. . . .

In Korea, we have taken great steps which have ended our military occupation, and in cooperation with the United Nations, have established an independent and sovereign country recognized by nearly all the rest of the world. . . .

In the Philippines, we acted with vigor and speed to set up an independent sovereign nation which we have done. We have given the Philippines a billion dollars of direct economic aid since the war. We have spent another billion dollars in such matters as veterans' benefits and other payments in the Philippines. Much of that money has not been used as wisely as we wish it had been used, but here again, we come up against the matter of responsibility. It is the Philippine Government which is responsible. . . .

We are always ready to help and to advise. That is all we can and all we should do.

Elsewhere in southeast Asia, the limits of what we can do are to help where we are wanted. We are organizing the machinery through which we can make effective help possible. The western powers are all interested. We all know the techniques. We have all had expriences which can be useful to those governments which are newly starting out if they want it. It cannot be useful if they don't want it. . . .

So after this survey, what we conclude, I believe, is that there is a new day which has dawned in Asia. It is a day in which the Asian peoples are on their own, and know it, and intend to continue on their own. It is a day in which the old relationships between east and west are gone, relationships which at their worst were exploitation, and which at their best were paternalism. That relationship is over, and the relationship of east and west must now be in the Far East one of mutual respect and mutual helpfulness. We are their friends. Others are their friends. We and those others are willing to help, but we can help only where we are wanted and only where the conditions of help are really sensible and possible. So what we can see is that this new day in Asia, this new day which is dawning, may go on to a glorious noon or it may darken and it may drizzle out. But that decision lies within the countries of Asia and within the power of the Asian people. It is not a decision which a friend or even an enemy from the outside can decide for them.

◇◇◇◇◇◇◇◇◇◇◇◇

5. TREATY OF PEACE WITH JAPAN [5]

Article 1

. . . THE ALLIED POWERS recognize the full sovereignty of the Japanese people over Japan and its territorial waters.

Article 2

(a) Japan, recognizing the independence of Korea, renounces all right, title and claim to Korea, including the islands of Quelpart, Port Hamilton and Dagelet.

(b) Japan renounces all right, title and claim to Formosa and the Pescadores.

(c) Japan renounces all right, title and claim to the Kurile Islands, and to that portion of Sakhalin and the islands adjacent to it over which Japan acquired sovereignty as a consequence of the Treaty of Portsmouth of September 5, 1905.

(d) Japan renounces all right, title and claim in connection with the League of Nations Mandate System, and accepts the action of the United Nations Security Council of April 2, 1947, extending the trusteeship system to the Pacific Islands formerly under mandate to Japan.

(e) Japan renounces all claim to any right or title to or interest in connection with any part of the Antarctic area, whether deriving from the activities of Japanese nationals or otherwise.

(f) Japan renounces all right, title and claim to the Spratly Islands and to the Paracel Islands.

Article 3

Japan will concur in any proposal of the United States to the United Nations to place under its trusteeship system, with the United States as the sole administering authority, Nansei Shoto south of 29° north latitude (including the Ryukyu Islands and the Daito Islands), Nanpo Shoto south of Sofu Gan (including the Bonin Islands, Rosario Island and the Volcano Islands) and Parece Vela and Marcus Island. Pending the making of such a proposal and affirmative action thereon, the United States will have the right to exercise all and any powers of administration, legislation and jurisdiction over the territory and inhabitants of these islands, including their territorial waters. . . .

[5] Signed at San Francisco September 8, 1951, by the United States and 47 other countries at war with Japan. The Treaty was ratified by the United States on April 15, 1952, and became effective April 28, 1952. Department of State, *Treaties and Other International Acts Series 2490.*

Article 5

(a) Japan accepts the obligations set forth in Article 2 of the Charter of the United Nations. . . .

(c) The Allied Powers for their part recognize that Japan as a sovereign nation possesses the inherent right of individual or collective self-defense referred to in Article 51 of the Charter of the United Nations and that Japan may voluntarily enter into collective security arrangements.

Article 6

(a) All occupation forces of the Allied Powers shall be withdrawn from Japan as soon as possible after the coming into force of the present Treaty, and in any case not later than 90 days thereafter. Nothing in this provision shall, however, prevent the stationing or retention of foreign armed forces in Japanese territory under or in consequence of any bilateral or multilateral agreements which have been or may be made between one or more of the Allied Powers, on the one hand, and Japan on the other. . . .

Article 14

(a) It is recognized that Japan should pay reparations to the Allied Powers for the damage and suffering caused by it during the war. Nevertheless it is also recognized that the resources of Japan are not presently sufficient, if it is to maintain a viable economy, to make complete reparation for all such damage and suffering and at the same time meet its other obligations.

Therefore,

1. Japan will promptly enter into negotiations with Allied Powers so desiring, whose present territories were occupied by Japanese forces and damaged by Japan, with a view to assisting to compensate those countries for the cost of repairing the damage done, by making available the services of the Japanese people in production, salvaging and other work for the Allied Powers in question. Such arrangements shall avoid the imposition of additional liabilities on other Allied Powers, and, where the manufacturing of raw materials is called for, they shall be supplied by the Allied Powers in question, so as not to throw any foreign exchange burden upon Japan. . . .

◇◇◇◇◇◇◇◇◇◇◇◇◇

6. SECURITY TREATY BETWEEN THE UNITED STATES AND JAPAN[6]

. . . *ARTICLE I.* Japan grants, and the United States of America accepts, the right, upon the coming into force of the Treaty of Peace and of this

[6] Signed at San Francisco, September 8, 1951. Entered into force April 28, 1952. Department of State, *Treaties and Other International Acts Series 2491.*

Treaty, to dispose United States land, air and sea forces in and about Japan. Such forces may be utilized to contribute to the maintenance of international peace and security in the Far East and to the security of Japan against armed attack from without, including assistance given at the express request of the Japanese Government to put down large-scale internal riots and disturbances in Japan, caused through instigation or intervention by an outside power or powers.

Article II. During the exercise of the right referred to in Article I, Japan will not grant, without the prior consent of the United States of America, any bases or any rights, powers or authority whatsoever, in or relating to bases or the right of garrison or of maneuver, or transit of ground, air or naval forces to any third power.

Article III. The conditions which shall govern the disposition of armed forces of the United States of America in and about Japan shall be determined by administrative agreements between the two Governments.

Article IV. This Treaty shall expire whenever in the opinion of the Governments of the United States of America and Japan there shall have come into force such United Nations arrangements or such alternative individual or collective security dispositions as will satisfactorily provide for the maintenance by the United Nations or otherwise of international peace and security in the Japan Area. . . .

◇◇◇◇◇◇◇◇◇◇◇◇◇◇

7. MUTUAL DEFENSE TREATY BETWEEN THE UNITED STATES AND THE REPUBLIC OF THE PHILIPPINES [7]

. . . *ARTICLE II.* In order more effectively to achieve the objective of this Treaty, the Parties separately and jointly by self-help and mutual aid will maintain and develop their individual and collective capacity to resist armed attack.

Article III. The Parties, through their Foreign Ministers or their deputies, will consult together from time to time regarding the implementation of this Treaty and whenever in the opinion of either of them the territorial integrity, political independence or security of either of the Parties is threatened by external armed attack in the Pacific.

Article IV. Each Party recognizes that an armed attack in the Pacific Area on either of the Parties would be dangerous to its own peace and safety and declares that it would act to meet the common dangers in accordance with its constitutional processes.

Any such armed attack and all measures taken as a result thereof shall be immediately reported to the Security Council of the United Nations. Such measures shall be terminated when the Security Council has taken

[7] Signed August 30, 1951. Entered into force August 27, 1952. Department of State, *Treaties and Other International Acts Series* 2529.

the measures necessary to restore and maintain international peace and security.

Article V. For the purpose of Article IV, an armed attack on either of the Parties is deemed to include an armed attack on the metropolitan territory of either of the Parties, or on the island territories under its jurisdiction in the Pacific or on its armed forces, public vessels or aircraft in the Pacific. . . .

Article VIII. This Treaty shall remain in force indefinitely. Either Party may terminate it one year after notice has been given to the other Party. . . .

8. MUTUAL DEFENSE TREATY BETWEEN THE UNITED STATES, NEW ZEALAND, AND AUSTRALIA [8]

. . . *ARTICLE II.* In order more effectively to achieve the objective of this Treaty the Parties separately and jointly by means of continuous and effective self-help and mutual aid will maintain and develop their individual and collective capacity to resist armed attack.

Article III. The Parties will consult together whenever in the opinion of any of them the territorial integrity, political independence or security of any of the Parties is threatened in the Pacific.

Article IV. Each Party recognizes that an armed attack in the Pacific Area on any of the Parties would be dangerous to its own peace and safety and declares that it would act to meet the common danger in accordance with its constitutional processes. . . .

Article V. For the purpose of Article IV, an armed attack on any of the Parties is deemed to include an armed attack on the metropolitan territory of any of the Parties, or on the island territories under its jurisdiction in the Pacific or on its armed forces, public vessels or aircraft in the Pacific. . . .

Article VII. The Parties hereby establish a Council, consisting of their Foreign Ministers or their Deputies, to consider matters concerning the implementation of this Treaty. The Council should be so organized as to be able to meet at any time. . . .

Article X. This Treaty shall remain in force indefinitely. Any Party may cease to be a member of the Council established by Article VII one year after notice has been given to the Government of Australia, which will inform the Governments of the other Parties of the deposit of such notice. . . .

[8] Signed at San Francisco, September 1, 1951. Entered into force April 29, 1952. Department of State, *Treaties and Other International Acts Series 2493.*

9. KOREA: RESOLUTIONS OF THE SECURITY COUNCIL OF JUNE 25, 1950 [9]

THE SECURITY COUNCIL

Recalling the finding of the General Assembly in its resolution of 21 October 1949 that the Government of the Republic of Korea is a lawfully established government "having effective control and jurisdiction over that part of Korea where the United Nations Temporary Commission on Korea was able to observe and consult and in which the great majority of the people of Korea reside; and that this Government is based on elections which were a valid expression of the free will of the electorate of that part of Korea and which were observed by the Temporary Commission; and that this is the only such Government in Korea"; . . .

Noting with grave concern the armed attack upon the Republic of Korea by forces from North Korea,

Determines that this action constitutes a breach of the peace,

I. Calls for the immediate cessation of hostilities; and
Calls upon the authorities of North Korea to withdraw forthwith their armed forces to the thirty-eighth parallel;

II. Requests the United Nations Commission on Korea
(a) To communicate its fully considered recommendations on the situation with the least possible delay;
(b) To observe the withdrawal of the North Korean forces to the thirty-eighth parallel; and
(c) To keep the Security Council informed on the execution of this resolution;

III. Calls upon all Members to render every assistance to the United Nations in the execution of this resolution and to refrain from giving assistance to the North Korean authorities.

10. KOREA: RESOLUTIONS OF THE SECURITY COUNCIL OF JUNE 27, 1950 [10]

THE SECURITY COUNCIL,

Having determined that the armed attack upon the Republic of Korea by forces from North Korea constitutes a breach of the peace,

Having called for an immediate cessation of hostilities, and

Having called upon the authorities of North Korea to withdraw forthwith their armed forces to the 38th parallel, and

[9] United Nations Security Council, Document S/1501, June 25, 1950.
[10] United Nations Security Council, Document S/1511, June 27, 1950.

Having noted from the report of the United Nations Commission for Korea that the authorities in North Korea have neither ceased hostilities nor withdrawn their armed forces to the 38th parallel and that urgent military measures are required to restore international peace and security, and

Having noted the appeal from the Republic of Korea to the United Nations for immediate and effective steps to secure peace and security,

Recommends that the Members of the United Nations furnish such assistance to the Republic of Korea as may be necessary to repel the armed attack and to restore international peace and security in the area.

◇◇◇◇◇◇◇◇◇◇◇◇◇

11. STATEMENT OF PRESIDENT TRUMAN CONCERNING FORMOSA, JUNE 27, 1950 [11]

IN KOREA the Government forces, which were armed to prevent border raids and to preserve internal security, were attacked by invading forces from North Korea. The Security Council of the United Nations called upon the invading troops to cease hostilities and to withdraw to the 38th parallel. This they have not done, but on the contrary have pressed the attack. The Security Council called upon all members of the United Nations to render every assistance to the United Nations in the execution of this resolution. In these circumstances I have ordered United States air and sea forces to give the Korean Government troops cover and support.

The attack upon Korea makes it plain beyond all doubt that Communism has passed beyond the use of subversion to conquer independent nations and will now use armed invasion and war. It has defied the orders of the Security Council of the United Nations issued to preserve international peace and security. In these circumstances the occupation of Formosa by Communist forces would be a direct threat to the security of the Pacific area and to United States forces performing their lawful and necessary functions in that area.

Accordingly I have ordered the Seventh Fleet to prevent any attack on Formosa. As a corollary of this action I am calling upon the Chinese Government on Formosa to cease all air and sea operations against the mainland. The Seventh Fleet will see that this is done. The determination of the future status of Formosa must await the restoration of security in the Pacific, a peace settlement with Japan, or consideration by the United Nations.

I have also directed that United States Forces in the Philippines be strengthened and that military assistance to the Philippine Government be accelerated.

[11] State Department *Bulletin,* Vol. XIII, p. 5.

I have similarly directed acceleration in the furnishing of military assistance to the forces of France and the Associated States in Indo-China and the dispatch of a military mission to provide close working relations with those forces. . . .

◇◇◇◇◇◇◇◇◇◇◇◇◇◇

12. RESOLUTIONS OF THE GENERAL ASSEMBLY OF THE UNITED NATIONS ON THE UNIFICATION OF KOREA: OCTOBER 7, 1950 [12]

THE GENERAL ASSEMBLY,

Having regard to its resolutions of 14 November 1947, of 12 December 1948 and of 21 October 1949. . . .

Recalling the General Assembly declaration of 12 December 1948 that there has been established a lawful government (the Government of the Republic of Korea) having effective control and jurisdiction over that part of Korea where the United Nations Temporary Commission on Korea was able to observe and consult and in which the great majority of the people of Korea reside; that this government is based on elections which were a valid expression of the free will of the electorate of that part of Korea and which were observed by the Temporary Commission; and that this is the only such government in Korea,

Having in mind that United Nations armed forces are at present operating in Korea in accordance with the recommendations of the Security Council of 27 June 1950, subsequent to its resolution of 25 June 1950, that Members of the United Nations furnish such assistance to the Republic of Korea as may be necessary to repel the armed attack and to restore international peace and security in the area,

Recalling that the essential objective of the resolutions of the General Assembly referred to above was the establishment of a unified, independent and democratic Government of Korea,

1. Recommends that

(a) All appropriate steps be taken to ensure conditions of stability throughout Korea;

(b) All constituent acts be taken, including the holding of elections, under the auspices of the United Nations, for the establishment of a unified, independent and democratic government in the sovereign State of Korea;

(c) All sections and representative bodies of the population of Korea, South and North, be invited to cooperate with the organs of the United Nations in the restoration of peace, in the holding of elections and in the establishment of a unified government;

---

[12] United Nations, *Official Records,* Fifth Session, Supplement No. 20 (A/1775), pp. 9–10.

(d) United Nations forces should not remain in any part of Korea otherwise than so far as necessary for achieving the objectives specified in sub-paragraphs (a) and (b) above;

(e) All necessary measures be taken to accomplish the economic rehabilitation of Korea;

2. Resolves that

(a) A Commission . . . be established to (i) assume the functions hitherto exercised by the present United Nations Commission on Korea; (ii) represent the United Nations in bringing about the establishment of a unified, independent and democratic government of all Korea; (iii) exercise such responsibilities in connection with relief and rehabilitation in Korea as may be determined by the General Assembly after receiving the recommendations of the Economic and Social Council. The United Nations Commission for the Unification and Rehabilitation of Korea should proceed to Korea and begin to carry out its functions as soon as possible; . . .

◇◇◇◇◇◇◇◇◇◇◇◇◇◇

13. STATEMENTS MADE IN THE GENERAL ASSEMBLY ON THE MEANING OF THE ASSEMBLY RESOLUTION OF OCTOBER 7, 1950 [13]

GENERAL ROMULO (Philippines):

. . . The United Nations is not a belligerent, in the ordinary sense of the term, in Korea. Our forces are there at the request of the Security Council to put down aggression and to restore peace and security in the area. The only recommendation or order that can emanate from the United Nations at this stage is for the North Korean aggressor to lay down his arms. If he refuses to do so, then our forces must remain in Korea until the power of the aggressor is crushed. . . .

The goal is twofold: first, the establishment of a unified and democratic government of Korea and, secondly, the relief and economic rehabilitation of Korea.

The basic condition for the accomplishment of these two tasks is the restoration of peace and security throughout Korea. This means that the North Korean forces must lay down their arms. If they refuse to do so, then the United Nations forces must continue their campaign in Korea until all resistance is overcome, and remain there until the two goals are achieved. Direct responsibility for the accomplishment of these tasks is lodged in a United Nations commission for the unification and rehabilitation of Korea. In its task of unification, the commission will assume the functions hitherto exercised by the present United Nations Commission

[13] United Nations, *Official Records of the General Assembly,* A. PV. 292–293–294. October 6–7, 1950.

on Korea, including consultation with the Republic of Korea and with representative elements in North Korea, and supervision of all necessary constituent acts that may be taken, including the holding of free elections. In its task of relief and rehabilitation, the commission will exercise such responsibilities as may be determined by the General Assembly after receiving the recommendations of the Economic and Social Council. . . .

Mr. AUSTIN (United States of America):

We are about to take a major decision. That decision will have a profound effect on the future of the 30 million people in Korea. It will also have a profound effect upon the peoples of the world. It will openly prove whether we who are Members of this great Organization mean what we say in our pledges that Korea shall be independent and free to work out its own destiny in the way that the Korean people decide. . . .

The United States will cooperate in fulfilling the policy of this resolution that United Nations forces shall remain in Korea only as long as is necessary to achieve the essential objectives of the General Assembly—to wit, the establishment of a unified, independent and democratic government of Korea. After the end of the fighting, the quicker Korea is permitted to live its own life without foreign interference the better for the whole world and the better for us. . . .

In June and July of this year, the Security Council gave all the necessary military authority to the United Nations Commander to repel the aggressor army and restore peace in Korea. The United Nations forces have pursued that task with vigor and some success.

Two things appear necessary to be done now: first, to carry out the objectives of the United Nations in the northern area where United Nations observers have never yet had the opportunity to ascertain the political wishes of the people; secondly, to commence forthwith the task of rehabilitating the shattered Korean economy. . . .

The vote on this draft resolution is the culmination of all the work we have been doing over the years on behalf of Korea. With it the arch will be complete and strong. What the United Nations has worked for since 1947 is stability in Korea—a unified, independent and democratic government in a sovereign State. This has been our objective, and this is what we are voting for in approving this draft resolution. . . .

Mr. MONTEL (France):

. . . The Korean question can be solved only if Korea is regarded as an indivisible unit; it can be solved only if we conform to the principles which were defined in Moscow as early as 1945 by the United States, the United Kingdom and the Soviet Union, and which have since been repeated in the various recommendations of the General Assembly for the creation of a united democratic and independent Korea. . . .

In the present state of affairs, if the United Nations wishes Korea once more to become a unified, independent and democratic State, it cannot and must not merely stand by as a witness. It must inspire and guide the efforts of the entire Korean population towards the achievement of a stable and democratic regime. It can do so only by ensuring, first and foremost, the restoration of peace and security in the territory. That is its first and most pressing responsibility. To achieve this end, it is essential that strong armies should be present in all parts of the country for a time.

These aims are those of the eight-Power draft resolution and it is for that reason that the French delegation has given and will continue to give it its fullest support. . . .

Sir BENEGAL N. RAU (India):

. . . There is a great deal in the eight-Power draft resolution with which my delegation is in full agreement. Confining myself to its operative part, our main difference is with regard to sub-paragraph (d) at the beginning of the operative part, wherein the Assembly recommends: "That United Nations forces should not remain in any part of Korea otherwise than so far as necessary for achieving the objectives specified at (a) and (b) above."

Whatever may be the strict technical interpretation of this clause, it has been widely regarded as authorizing, if not positively, at least by implication, the United Nations forces to enter North Korea and to remain there until the unification of Korea has been completed and stability achieved. If such is the intention of the draft resolution – and there is a widespread impression that it is – then the draft resolution authorizes the United Nations forces not only to cross the 38th parallel but to remain in North Korea for a somewhat indefinite period of time, because no one knows how long unification may take.

My government fears that the result may be to prolong North Korean resistance, and even to extend the area of conflict. Our fears may turn out to be wrong, but each government has to judge the situation upon the best information at its disposal and to act accordingly. Thus we view with the gravest misgivings the particular recommendation that I have mentioned. . . .

◇◇◇◇◇◇◇◇◇◇◇◇◇

14. KOREA: RESOLUTIONS OF THE GENERAL ASSEMBLY OF FEBRUARY 1, 1951, REGARDING THE AGGRESSION OF COMMUNIST CHINA[14]

THE GENERAL ASSEMBLY, . . .

1. Finds that the Central People's Government of the People's Republic of China, by giving direct aid and assistance to those who were already committing aggression in Korea and by engaging in hostilities against United Nations forces there, has itself engaged in aggression in Korea;

2. Calls upon the Central People's Government of the People's Repub-

[14] United Nations General Assembly, Document A/1771, February 1, 1951.

lic of China to cause its forces and nationals in Korea to cease hostilities against the United Nations forces and to withdraw from Korea;

3. Affirms the determination of the United Nations to continue its action in Korea to meet the aggression;

4. Calls upon all States and authorities to continue to lend every assistance to the United Nations action in Korea;

5. Calls upon all States and authorities to refrain from giving any assistance to the aggressors in Korea;

6. Requests a Committee composed of the members of the Collective Measures Committee as a matter of urgency to consider additional measures to be employed to meet this aggression and to report thereon to the General Assembly, it being understood that the Committee is authorized to defer its report if the Good Offices Committee referred to in the following paragraph reports satisfactory progress in its efforts;

7. Affirms that it continues to be the policy of the United Nations to bring about a cessation of hostilities in Korea and the achievement of United Nations objectives in Korea by peaceful means, and requests the President of the General Assembly to designate forthwith two persons who would meet with him at any suitable opportunity to use their good offices to this end.

◇◇◇◇◇◇◇◇◇◇◇◇◇◇

15. CRITICISM OF AMERICAN FAR EASTERN POLICY [15]

. . . ONE of the most singular aspects of the administration's far-eastern policy is illustrated by its acknowledgment of the dynamic character of revolution. As Secretary Acheson has pointed out on so many occasions, international communism is a movement which plans to overthrow existing governments by force and violence if necessary. While holding this point of view our State Department has continually acted as though, if appeasement went far enough, the Russians and their satellites would consent to dwell peacefully side by side with the "free world."

It does not require prolonged reflection upon the disastrous results of the administration's far-eastern policy to draw some conclusions as to what the United States must do. Fear of Russia is no basis for a foreign policy; what we must have is a positive program based upon confidence in our abilities and resources. . . .

It has been extremely difficult to determine the full extent of the secret commitments which the administration has made. These commitments are the basis for a large part of our present foreign policy. The agreements

[15] Statement signed August 17, 1951, by eight Republican members of the Committee on Armed Services and the Committee on Foreign Relations of the United States Senate in connection with the inquiry into the removal of General Douglas MacArthur from his command in the Far East. United States Senate, 82nd Congress, 1st Session, *Hearings on the Military Situation in the Far East,* Part 5, pp. 3604–05.

made at Cairo, Teheran, Yalta, Quebec, Potsdam, and elsewhere were largely international executive arrangements drawn without consideration of the treaty-making power of the United States Senate.

In the past the confirmation and implementation of international commitments has required the advice and consent of the Senate. Treaties were public documents, open to the inspection of any citizen.

Ten years of secrecy changed all this. Negotiations were affected by the precarious health of some who represented us; decisions were made by irresponsible people. Practices of this character confused our people and left them in ignorance of what had been undertaken in their name. These hearings broke through this wall of secrecy. For the first time in years a congressional committee has been able to force out enough information to piece together a coherent picture of a foreign situation, discouraging though the picture was. . . .

Despite the legalistic administration arguments to the contrary, the fact remains that for the first time in the history of our Nation, the constitutional authority of Congress to declare war has been bypassed.

Recognizing the unique nature of the collective-security action of the United Nations, it is nevertheless our opinion that the Korean War should not be allowed to establish a precedent.

It is true that there was popular approval for the intervention of United States forces in Korea. It is also true, however, that this approval was, in measure, based upon the logical assumption that proper military plans and estimates were in existence. It was further assumed by most people that we were in a state of readiness to carry out whatever military objectives were assigned to our Armed Forces by our administration leaders.

Consultation after commitment, as was the case in the Korean intervention, is not in accordance with American constitutional procedures. . . .

If a truce is negotiated, based upon the restoration of the status quo at the thirty-eighth parallel, the Communists will remain in control of the northern half of the country, and the objectives of the United Nations will not have been fulfilled. We should be on our guard against any Munichlike respites which are only surrenders in disguise and make the ultimate reckoning infinitely more costly.

The aggressor, of course, has suffered grave losses, but for that matter, so has the victim of the attack. Indeed, all of Korea is the loser; the land and its people have suffered irreparable harm.

Any peace short of the liberation and unification of Korea is a delusion. Any settlement at the thirty-eighth parallel is a Chinese Communist victory.

General MacArthur had driven the North Koreans to the Yalu and had victory within his grasp when this new and formidable enemy entered the field. To make a settlement south of the Yalu therefore is to admit the success of the Chinese aggressors.

The United States will be confronted with a staggering bill for relief and rehabilitation in Korea; the taxpayer will be paying for generations for the cost of the conflict; and our troops will be pinned down in South Korea indefinitely.

On the other hand, the North Koreans will be able to resume their aggression on any flimsy pretext at any convenient opportunity, and the Russians having utilized the entire conflict as a proving ground similar to Finland and Spain can precipitate war somewhere else in the world.

STYLES BRIDGES.
ALEXANDER WILEY.
H. ALEXANDER SMITH.
BOURKE B. HICKENLOOPER.
WILLIAM F. KNOWLAND.
HARRY P. CAIN.
OWEN BREWSTER.
RALPH E. FLANDERS.

16. KOREA: THE ARMISTICE AGREEMENT [16]

. . . *ARTICLE I.* A military demarcation line shall be fixed and both sides shall withdraw two (2) kilometers from this line so as to establish a demilitarized zone between the opposing forces. A demilitarized zone shall be established as a buffer zone to prevent the occurrence of incidents which might lead to a resumption of hostilities. . . .

4. The military demarcation line shall be plainly marked as directed by the Military Armistice Commission hereinafter established. The Commanders of the opposing sides shall have suitable markers erected along the boundary between the demilitarized zone and their respective areas. The Military Armistice Commission shall supervise the erection of all markers placed along the military demarcation line and along the boundaries of the demilitarized zone. . . .

Article II

. . . 13. In order to insure the stability of the military armistice . . . the Commanders of the opposing sides shall:

(a) Within seventy-two (72) hours after this armistice agreement becomes effective, withdraw all of their military forces, supplies, and equipment from the demilitarized zone except as otherwise provided herein. . . .

(b) Within ten (10) days after this armistice agreement becomes ef-

[16] Signed at Panmunjom, July 27, 1953, and effective as of that time. Department of State Publication 5150, *Far Eastern Series* 61.

fective, withdraw all of their military forces, supplies, and equipment from the rear and the coastal islands and waters of Korea of the other side. . . .

(c) Cease the introduction into Korea of reinforcing military personnel; . . .

(d) Cease the introduction into Korea of reinforcing combat aircraft, armored vehicles, weapons, and ammunition; . . .

19. A military Armistice Commission is hereby established. . . .

24. The general mission of the Military Armistice Commission shall be to supervise the implementation of this armistice agreement and to settle through negotiations any violations of this armistice agreement. . . .

28. The Military Armistice Commission, or the senior member of either side thereof, is authorized to request the Neutral Nations Supervisory Commission to conduct special observations and inspections at places outside the demilitarized zone where violations of this armistice agreement have been reported to have occurred.

29. When the Military Armistice Commission determines that a violation of this armistice agreement has occurred, it shall immediately report such violation to the Commanders of the opposing sides. . . .

36. A Neutral Nations Supervisory Commission is hereby established.

37. The Neutral Nations Supervisory Commission shall be composed of four (4) senior officers, two (2) of whom shall be appointed by neutral nations nominated by the Commander-in-Chief, United Nations Command, namely, SWEDEN and SWITZERLAND, and two (2) of whom shall be appointed by neutral nations nominated jointly by the Supreme Commander of the Korean People's Army and the Commander of the Chinese People's Volunteers, namely, POLAND and CZECHOSLOVAKIA. . . .

41. The mission of the Neutral Nations Supervisory Commission shall be to carry out the functions of supervision, observation, inspection, and investigation, as stipulated in sub-paragraphs 13(c) and 13(d) and paragraph 28 hereof, and to report the results of such supervision, observation, inspection, and investigation to the Military Armistice Commission. . . .

Article III

51. . . . (a) Within sixty (60) days after this armistice agreement becomes effective each side shall, without offering any hindrance, directly repatriate and hand over in groups all those prisoners of war in its custody who insist on repatriation to the side to which they belonged at the time of capture. . . .

(b) Each side shall release all those remaining prisoners of war, who are not directly repatriated, from its military control and from its custody and hand them over to the Neutral Nations Repatriation Commission for disposition in accordance with the provisions in the annex hereto: "Terms of Reference for Neutral Nations Repatriation Commission." . . .

Article IV

60. In order to insure the peaceful settlement of the Korean question, the military commanders of both sides hereby recommend to the governments of the countries concerned on both sides that, within three (3) months after the armistice agreement is signed and becomes effective, a political conference of a higher level of both sides be held by representatives appointed respectively to settle through negotiation the questions of the withdrawal of all foreign forces from Korea, the peaceful settlement of the Korean question, etc. . . .

◇◇◇◇◇◇◇◇◇◇◇◇◇

17. REPORT OF THE UNITED STATES AND DECLARATION OF THE UNIFIED COMMAND ON THE KOREAN ARMISTICE [17]

THE GOVERNMENT of the United States, as the Unified Command, transmits herewith a special report on the United States action against aggression in Korea, together with a copy of the official text of the armistice agreement. . . .

In accordance with the terms of the armistice agreement, hostilities ceased at 2200 hours on 27 July, 1953, and the armistice agreement became effective at that time.

The armistice agreement is a military agreement between military commanders. It is intended to make possible a final peaceful settlement and assumes that this end will, in good faith, be pursued. The authority of the Unified Command under the resolutions of the Security Council of 27 June and 7 July, 1950, to conduct military operations in Korea against aggression included also the authority to negotiate a military armistice to end the fighting on a basis consistent with United Nations objectives and principles. The authority of the Unified Command to conclude an armistice and the desirability of an armistice generally along the lines finally incorporated in the armistice agreement of 27 July, 1953, were in effect affirmed by the General Assembly in its resolution of 3 December 1952.

The armistice agreement has brought about a cessation of hostilities in Korea after more than thirty-seven months of bloodshed and destruction resulting from the Communist aggression. The armistice was signed more than twenty-five months after the first indications that, due to the achievements of United Nations forces in Korea and the determination of the United Nations to bring an honorable end to the fighting in Korea, the Communist aggressors were prepared to consider ending hostilities. During these twenty-five months the representatives of the United Nations

[17] Report made to the Secretary General of the United Nations, August 7, 1953. The *New York Times*, August 8, 1953.

Command negotiated in good faith and made every effort to achieve an armistice. It was not until the spring of 1953 that the Communists appeared ready to settle the outstanding issues on an honorable basis. The intransigence of the aggressors was responsible for the continued loss of life and destruction, and for the long delay in bringing the armistice negotiations to a successful conclusion.

In negotiating this armistice agreement, the United Nations Command has been guided by the basic objectives of the United Nations military action in Korea – to repel the aggression against the Republic of Korea and to restore international peace and security in the area. The agreement leaves the forces of the Republic of Korea and of the United Nations in strong defensive position and contains provisions offering reasonable assurances against renewal of the aggression.

As safeguards against resumption of hostilities there are provisions for a demilitarized zone, with a Military Armistice Commission composed of representatives of both sides responsible for supervising the implementation of the armistice and for settling any violations of the agreement. . . .

The United Nations Command will do its utmost to ensure fulfillment of the terms of the armistice agreement. There can, of course, be no certain guarantee that the Communists will abide by its terms. The armistice, moreover, does not contain all the assurances against the renewal of aggression that might be desired. It became clear at the end of 1951 that it would not be possible to obtain all the arrangements behind enemy lines which the United Nations Command might have considered desirable. Moreover, while the safeguards achieved in the armistice are important, basically maximum assurance against the renewal of attack by the Communists lies in their knowledge that such unprovoked attack would meet with prompt reaction by the United Nations forces. The Unified Command, therefore, agreed to waive certain safeguards (e.g., in regard to the construction and rehabilitation of military airfields in North Korea) but asked that Governments with forces under the Command should make clear in a declaration to be issued after the signature of an armistice that if there was an unprovoked renewal of the armed attack by the Communists the sixteen Governments would again be united and prompt to resist. This arrangement was agreed upon in January, 1952, by the sixteen members of the United Nations whose armed forces were participating in the Korean action. The declaration signed by representatives of the sixteen participating nations in Washington on 27 July, 1953, shortly after the signature of the armistice agreement, provides:

"We, the United Nations members whose military forces are participating in the Korean action, support the decision of the Commander in Chief of the United Nations Command to conclude an armistice agreement. We hereby affirm our determination fully and faithfully to carry out the terms of that armistice. We expect that the other parties to the agreement will likewise scrupulously observe its terms.

"The task ahead is not an easy one. We will support the efforts of the

United Nations to bring about an equitable settlement in Korea based on the principles which have long been established by the United Nations, and which call for a united, independent and democratic Korea. We will support the United Nations in its efforts to assist the people of Korea in repairing the ravages of war.

"We declare again our faith in the principles and purposes of the United Nations, our consciousness of our continuing responsibilities in Korea, and our determination in good faith to seek a settlement of the Korean problem. We affirm, in the interests of world peace, that if there is a renewal of the armed attack, challenging again the principles of the United Nations, we should again be united and prompt to resist. The consequences of such a breach of the armistice would be so grave that, in all probability, it would not be possible to confine hostilities within the frontiers of Korea.

"Finally, we are of the opinion that the armistice must not result in jeopardizing the restoration or the safeguarding of peace in any other part of Asia."

The achievement in Korea is a collective achievement. The people of Korea and the people of the world are indebted to the men of many countries, namely, Australia, Belgium, Colombia, Canada, Ethiopia, France, Greece, Luxembourg, the Philippines, the Netherlands, New Zealand, Thailand, Turkey, Union of South Africa, the United Kingdom and the United States, who fought side by side with the forces of the Republic of Korea that aggression should not succeed. They were given assistance by the hospital units of Denmark, India, Italy, Norway and Sweden. Many other nations which made supporting contributions of other kinds also deserve the appreciation of the United Nations.

◇◇◇◇◇◇◇◇◇◇◇◇◇◇

18. MUTUAL DEFENSE TREATY BETWEEN THE UNITED STATES AND KOREA [18]

. . . *ARTICLE 2.* The parties will consult together whenever, in the opinion of either of them, the political independence or security of either of the parties is threatened by external armed attack. Separately and jointly, by self help and mutual aid, the parties will maintain and develop appropriate means to deter armed attack and will take suitable measures in consultation and agreement to implement this treaty and to further its purposes.

Article 3. Each party recognizes that an armed attack in the Pacific area on either of the parties in territories now under their respective control, or hereafter recognized by one of the parties as lawfully brought un-

[18] Text of a draft treaty signed by representatives of the United States and the Republic of Korea, August 7, 1953. The *New York Times,* August 8, 1953.

der the administrative control of the other, would be dangerous to its own peace and safety and declares that it would act to meet the common danger in accordance with its constitutional processes.

Article 4. The Republic of Korea grants, and the United States of America accepts, the right to dispose United States land, air and sea forces in and about the territory of the Republic of Korea as determined by mutual agreement. . . .

Article 6. This treaty shall remain in force indefinitely. Either party may terminate it one year after notice has been given to the other party.

◇◇◇◇◇◇◇◇◇◇◇◇

19. THE MUTUAL SECURITY PROGRAM OF THE UNITED STATES IN THE FAR EAST [19]

DURING the first half of 1953, 12 nations in the South Asian and Far Eastern area were participating in the Mutual Security Program. Four of these nations – India, Pakistan, Afghanistan, and Nepal – are in South Asia. Eight are in Southeast Asia and the Pacific region – the Republic of China on Formosa, the three Associated States of Indochina, the Philippines, Burma, Indonesia, and Thailand.

If Communist expansion is to be halted, it is essential that these countries of free Asia, with their wealth of human and material resources, continue to be aligned with the free world. In varying degree, they all face grave threats to their freedom and independence. The Communists have been waging open warfare in Korea and Indochina, while fostering militant subversion – armed and unarmed – in other parts of the area. In most of these countries, too, there is pervasive discontent, which can at any time flare up in violence and revolt. While free Asia thus offers fertile ground for Communist aggression, it also presents a challenge for effective action by the rest of the free world. The Mutual Security Program is the American response to that challenge. . . .

On the military side, in the first 6 months of 1953, matériel valued at $390 million was shipped from the United States to the nations in the Far East receiving military assistance. From the start of the military assistance program in this area in 1949 to the end of June 1953, a total of $1,626 million worth of aid had been programmed. By the end of June, $974 million worth had been shipped. In addition, offshore procurement contracts of nearly $38 million have been placed by the Department of Defense in Japan and Formosa for military matériel.

During the 6 months ended June 30, 1953, the total value of Mutual

[19] Report of President Eisenhower to Congress of August 17, 1953. *Report to Congress on the Mutual Security Program for the Six Months Ended June 30, 1953.* United States Government Printing Office, Washington, 1953.

Security Program expenditures for defense support, and economic and technical assistance in the Far East and South Asian area, was $130 million. Expenditures since the beginning of the program in June 1950, totaled $391 million.

Indochina. — . . . The defense of Indochina, an important gateway to the vast resources of Southeast Asia, is a matter of grave concern to the whole free world. Since France cannot fulfill her commitments both in Europe and Asia without outside assistance, the United States is providing needed weapons and equipment to the non-Communist forces in Indochina. . . .

Formosa. — It is in the interest of the United States to develop the military capabilities of the Republic of China on Formosa. The Mutual Security Program accordingly is furnishing military equipment and training assistance to the armed forces of the Chinese Government. This military aid program has materially helped to improve the combat efficiency of the Nationalist military establishment. . . .

Philippines. — Military commitments of the Philippines include those which pertain to preservation of its own internal security and those assumed under the United Nations and the mutual defense treaty with the United States. Military aid has made it possible for the armed forces of the Philippines to suppress in large measure the Huk insurrection which has been aided and, in part, led by Communists. The final elimination of armed dissidence, however, depends upon improved conditions in rural areas. . . .

Thailand. — The invasion of the state of Laos by the Communist-reinforced Viet Minh forces in April 1953 posed a potential threat to Thailand. High priority was given to the shipment of United States military equipment to combat this menace. Matériel delivered during the first 6 months of 1953 enabled Thailand to continue the process of modernizing its ground forces and training its small but efficient air arm.

The Royal Thai Air Force is a striking example of the utilization of military aid equipment. For example, from 1947 to 1950, the entire air force averaged 1,500 hours per year flying time, but in 1951 and 1952, it flew 48,000 hours per year or an increase of over 3,000 percent. Military assistance from the United States helped the Thai to maintain one battalion of troops in Korea under the United Nations Command. . . .

India. — The democratic way of life is today undergoing perhaps its most crucial test in India. Here we have . . . the largest self-governing nation in the free world engaged in a great effort to lift its millions onto a higher plane of social and economic life through the concept of democracy and the ways of freedom. . . .

Village improvement is a major phase of India's development plan, and United States technical cooperation is centered around this concept. For the fiscal years 1952 and 1953, a total of $11 million in United States funds and about $80 million in Indian rupees have been obligated for community development work. Out of 124 American technicians in India at the close of the fiscal year, over half were working directly with more than 1,000 Indian associates in village improvement projects. These projects are introducing more efficient agricultural tools and techniques, building schools, laying down farm-to-market roads, digging wells, installing sanitary sewage disposal systems, and opening new farm cooperatives. . . .

Pakistan. – The government of Pakistan is planning to improve the present critical agricultural situation and lay a foundation for future basic industrial development along lines suited to the country's requirements.

One method of achieving these purposes is through the establishment of agricultural-industrial development centers to train village-level workers in such fields as vocational agriculture, environmental sanitation, and village industry. . . .

Burma. – The government of the Union of Burma on March 17 notified this Government that it did not desire further United States aid after June 30, 1953. . . .

Japan. – Up to the present time, Japan has not participated directly in the Mutual Security Program. Yet the progress of all countries of the Far East is immeasurably influenced by the economic health and security of Japan. . . .

Although significant economic progress has been made since the end of World War II in rebuilding industries and restoring international trade, Japan's commercial exports during the first half of 1953 have been far below the level of a year ago. Sterling reserves are nearly exhausted. It has been possible to pay for increasing imports only on the basis of extraordinary dollar receipts. These receipts amounting to approximately $800 million a year are derived from procurement for United Nations forces in Korea, the support of American security forces in Japan, and the purchase of yen by those forces for their personal requirements.

As this temporary source of funds begins to dry up, Japan will be faced with crisis, unless in the meantime greatly augmented foreign trade with the free world, and particularly with the developing nations of the region, has been fostered. At present, the level of this trade is held down by various factors including high Japanese costs, import restrictions throughout the free world, reparations stalemates, and lingering distrust of the Japanese. . . .

The Security Treaty between the United States and Japan, signed at San Francisco on September 8, 1951, recognized Japan's inability at that time to provide adequately for its own defense and granted to the United States the right to station its forces in Japan. The treaty also expressed the expectation that Japan would "increasingly assume responsibility for its own defense." In its national safety forces, Japan is creating a means to maintain internal security and order. The United States is following a policy of assisting Japan in the development of these forces for its own defense by providing certain types of equipment which cannot be provided by the Japanese Government. In this connection, negotiations between the United States and Japan on a Mutual Defense Assistance Agreement under the mutual security legislation were commenced in Tokyo on July 15 [1953]. . . .

◇◇◇◇◇◇◇◇◇◇◇◇◇

20. MUTUAL DEFENSE ASSISTANCE CONTROL ACT OF 1951 [20]

. . . SEC. 101. The Congress of the United States, recognizing that in a world threatened by aggression the United States can best preserve and maintain peace by developing maximum national strength and by utilizing all of its resources in cooperation with other free nations, hereby declares it to be the policy of the United States to apply an embargo on the shipment of arms, ammunition, and implements of war, atomic energy materials, petroleum, transportation materials of strategic value, and items of primary strategic significance used in the production of arms, ammunition, and implements of war to any nation or combination of nations threatening the security of the United States, including the Union of Soviet Socialist Republics and all countries under its domination, in order to (1) increase the national strength of the United States and of the cooperating nations; (2) impede the ability of nations threatening the security of the United States to conduct military operations; and (3) to assist the people of the nations under the domination of foreign aggressors to reestablish their freedom.

It is further declared to be the policy of the United States that no military, economic, or financial assistance shall be supplied to any nation unless it applies an embargo on such shipments to any nation or combination of nations threatening the security of the United States, including the Union of Soviet Socialist Republics and all countries under its domination.

This Act shall be administered in such a way as to bring about the fullest support for any resolution of the General Assembly of the United Nations, supported by the United States, to prevent the shipment of certain commodities to areas under the control of governments engaged in hostilities in defiance of the United Nations.

Sec. 102. Responsibility for giving effect to the purposes of this Act shall be vested in the person . . . charged with principal responsibility for the administration of the provisions of the Mutual Defense Assistance Act of 1949. Such person is hereinafter referred to as the "Administrator."

Sec. 103. (a) The Administrator is hereby authorized and directed to determine . . . which items are, for the purpose of this Act, arms, ammunition, and implements of war, atomic energy materials, petroleum, trans-

[20] *Statutes at Large of the United States*, Vol. LXV, pp. 644–7. This Act was commonly referred to as the "Battle Act," named after Representative Laurie C. Battle of Alabama.

portation materials of strategic value, and those items of primary strategic significance used in the production of arms, ammunition, and implements of war which should be embargoed to effectuate the purposes of this Act. . . .

(b) All military, economic, or financial assistance to any nation shall, upon the recommendation of the Administrator, be terminated forthwith if such nation after sixty days from the date of a determination under section 103(a) knowingly permits the shipment to any nation or combination of nations threatening the security of the United States, including the Union of Soviet Socialist Republics and all countries under its domination, of any item which he has determined under section 103(a) . . . *Provided,* That the President after receiving the advice of the Administrator and after taking into account the contribution of such country to the mutual security of the free world . . . may direct the continuance of such assistance to a country which permits shipments of items other than arms, ammunition, implements of war, and atomic energy materials when unusual circumstances indicate that the cessation of aid would clearly be detrimental to the security of the United States. . . .

Sec. 105. For the purpose of this Act the term "assistance" does not include activities carried on for the purpose of facilitating the procurement of materials in which the United States is deficient.

Sec. 201. The Congress of the United States further declares it to be the policy of the United States to regulate the export of commodities other than those specified in title I of this Act to any nation or combination of nations threatening the security of the United States, including the Union of Soviet Socialist Republics and all countries under its domination, in order to strengthen the United States and other cooperating nations of the free world and to oppose and offset by nonmilitary action acts which threaten the security of the United States and the peace of the world. . . .

Sec. 203. All military, economic, and financial assistance shall be terminated when the President determines that the recipient country (1) is not effectively cooperating with the United States pursuant to this title, or (2) is failing to furnish to the United States information sufficient for the President to determine that the recipient country is effectively cooperating with the United States. . . .

◇◇◇◇◇◇◇◇◇◇◇◇◇

21. POLICY OF THE UNITED STATES CONCERNING TRADE WITH COMMUNIST CHINA [21]

. . . ONE OF THE CHIEF events in the development of . . . controls over shipments to Communist China had taken place on May 18, 1951.

[21] Third Report to Congress, September 27, 1953, of the Administrator of the Mutual Defense Control Act of 1951. *World Wide Enforcement of Strategic Trade Controls,* United States Government Printing Office, Washington, 1953, pp. 33 ff.

That was the day when the United Nations General Assembly recommended that all nations apply an embargo to Communist China and North Korea covering "arms, ammunition, and implements of war, atomic energy materials, petroleum, transportation materials of strategic value, and items useful in the production of arms, ammunition, and implements of war." . . .

The Congress provided that the Battle Act [Mutual Defense Assistance Control Act of 1951] shall be administered in such a way as to give the fullest support to the United Nations embargo of strategic shipments to Communist China, and this Government has indeed worked to extend that embargo throughout the free world and make it more effective. But this Government, in respect to its own exports, went even further.

United States exports to China had been $354 million in 1947, $273 million in 1948, $83 million in 1949, and $47 million in 1950. After the Chinese Communists entered the Korean fighting, the United States in December 1950 prohibited the export of all items, whether strategic or nonstrategic, to Communist China. In addition United States ships were forbidden to call at Communist Chinese ports. For a while, the United States continued to allow certain imports of Chinese origin. . . .

The reason for the United States prohibition against all exports to Communist China was not that every kind of merchandise was considered to be directly helpful on the battlefield. Rather the prohibition was based on a deep-felt conviction that an aggressor nation, engaged in fighting and killing the troops of the United States and other free countries, ought to be subjected to the maximum possible economic pressure, and that we ought not to supply its economy with any articles whatever, even civilian-type articles.

The United States also took into account the fact that the Chinese Communists, in addition to being aggressors, were trying to build a stronger war-potential base for their weak and primitive industry and needed outside help to do it; therefore many items were considered strategic to them which were not strategic to the rest of the Soviet bloc.

A policy of total embargo to Communist China has been the consistent position of the United States. And this Government suggested that other free nations take the same position.

Most of the major trading countries of Western Europe and Asia could not accept the position of the United States. These nations cooperated in the embargo of strategic items, but when it came to goods like cotton, fertilizer, textiles, textile machinery, dyes, and drugs, they were not willing to cut off their exports to China. One does not need to assume that these governments were any less sincere in their decisions than the United States, but only that they were in different circumstances and saw the problem through different eyes.

Many of these countries feel keenly their heavy dependence on foreign trade. They argued that they got economic benefits not only from selling nonstrategic exports to China but from the imports they received from

China in return, and from the shipping services they provided. They argued that this sort of trade was to the advantage of the free world, not of the Chinese military machine. It was contended, too, in some quarters, that it was wise to preserve a strong economic link between China and the West, in order to reduce China's dependence on Moscow and perhaps some day turn Mao into a Tito. The trading policies of some of these countries were also influenced by the fact that they, unlike the United States, had extended diplomatic recognition to the Chinese Communist Government.

So most of our allies kept on shipping what they considered to be nonstrategic items and obtaining Chinese goods in return. Exports from the free world to Communist China in 1952 were about $257 million. In 1951 they had been $433 million. The drop in 1952 was caused by a number of factors, including the free-world embargo of strategic items and the fact that in the first part of 1952, Communist China was outwardly cool toward trade with the West. In the latter part of 1951 and the early part of 1952 the Chinese were trying to orient their trade away from the free world and toward the Soviet Union. They reorganized and centralized their foreign trade machinery and carried on an "anti-five-vices" campaign, directed in part against "foreigners" and trade with the free world. The Chinese made an about-face in 1952, and by the fall of that year were actively seeking Western trade again. This campaign began to be reflected in the statistics in 1953. . . .

The difference between the China-trade policy of the United States and the policies of its major allies was one part of the many-sided Far Eastern problem that confronted the new administration [of President Eisenhower] when it took office in January.

With Chinese Communist soldiers fighting our troops in Korea, what was the best thing to do? Should we bomb Chinese territory and go all-out in the war against Communist China? Should we blockade the Chinese coast and attempt to stop all ships, whether belonging to the Soviet bloc or to our allies? Should we notify our allies that we would terminate or reduce our aid to them – or punish them in other ways – if they continue to trade with the Chinese Communists?

The policy chosen by the administration included building up South Korean strength in Korea, building up the Chinese Nationalist forces in Formosa, strengthening the forces fighting Communism in Indochina, and at the same time showing a willingness to reach a truce in Korea.

With respect to the China trade, the administration during the first half of 1953 followed a policy of concentrating on first things first. Our policy was to get our allies to exert economic pressure on Communist China, but we had no illusion as to the immediate feasibility of stopping trade in nonstrategic goods. We had to recognize that transactions in the China trade could be advantageous to the free world (the United States itself had imported strategic items from China in 1952). And we had to recognize that other sovereign countries were entitled to make judgments of their own with respect to their own trade, and that we could not stop their nonstrategic shipments without taking measures that in the long run would do the free world and the United States far more harm than the existing trade could possibly do.

Thus the United States Government, in the period under review, did not press other governments to cut off their nonstrategic trade with China.

Instead, this Government used its influence and its energies in a direction more likely to pay off in increased security for the United States and the free world – namely, toward the more effective control of *strategic* materials. . . .

The armistice in Korea was signed on July 27 [1953]. . . .

The United Nations resolution of May 18, 1951, did not go out of existence when the truce was signed.

The policy of the United States was to maintain its own strict controls over shipments to Communist China and to recommend that other countries maintain their controls also. . . .

SELECT BIBLIOGRAPHY

Bibliographical Aids

Bemis, Samuel Flagg, and Griffin, Grace Gardner: *Guide to the Diplomatic History of the United States, 1775–1921* (Washington: United States Government Printing Office, 1935).

Langer, William L., and Armstrong, Hamilton Fish: *Foreign Affairs Bibliography: A Selected and Annotated List of Books on International Relations, 1919–1932* (New York: Harper and Brothers, 1933).

Woolbert, Robert Gale: *Foreign Affairs Bibliography: A Selected and Annotated List of Books on International Relations, 1932–1942* (New York: Harper and Brothers, 1945).

Hasse, Adelaide R.: *Index to United States Documents relating to Foreign Affairs, 1828–1861* (Washington: The Carnegie Institution of Washington, 1914–24, 3 Vols.).

Catalogue of Public Documents of the Government of the United States (March 4, 1893–1946, 25 Vols.).

Diplomatic Correspondence

Wharton, Francis, Ed.: *The Revolutionary Diplomatic Correspondence of the United States* (Washington: United States Government Printing Office, 1889, 6 Vols.).

The Diplomatic Correspondence of the United States 1783 to 1789 (Washington: 1855, 3d Edition, 3 Vols.).

Lowrie, Walter, and Clark, Mathew St. Clair, Eds.: *American State Papers. Class I. Foreign Relations, 1789–1828* (Washington: 1832–1859, 6 Vols.).

Papers Relating to the Foreign Relations of the United States (Washington: Government Printing Office, 1862–1946).
(No volume in this series was issued for 1869. At present (October 22, 1946) one volume for 1931 has been released and two additional volumes for 1931 may be printed before the end of the year. Five volumes for the year 1932 are planned for publication in 1947.)

Savage, Carlton: *Policy of the United States Toward Maritime Commerce in War, 1774–1918* (Washington: Government Printing Office, 1934–36, 2 Vols.).

Manning, W. R., Ed.: *Diplomatic Correspondence of the United States Concerning the Independence of the Latin American Nations* (N. Y.: The Carnegie Endowment for International Peace, 1925, 3 Vols.).
Diplomatic Correspondence of the United States: Inter-American Affairs (Washington: Carnegie Endowment for International Peace, 1932–39, 12 Vols.).

Diplomatic Correspondence of the United States: Canadian Relations 1784–1860 (Washington: Carnegie Endowment for International Peace, 1943, 4 Vols.).

Treaties

Davenport, Frances Gardiner, Ed.: *European Treaties Bearing on the History of the United States and its Dependencies* (Washington: Carnegie Institution of Washington, 1917–1937). Volume IV was edited by Charles Oscar Paullin.

Miller, Hunter, Ed.: *Treaties and Other International Acts of the United States 1783–1855* (Washington: Government Printing Office, 1931–1942, 6 Vols.).

Treaties, Conventions, International Acts, Protocols, and Agreements between the United States of America and other Powers, 1776–1923 (Washington: Government Printing Office, Vol. I–II, 1910, Vol. III, 1923).

Treaties signed by the United States since 1908 may be found in the "Treaty Series" of the Department of State.

INDEX

Index

Index

Index

Index

Index